Rick Steves

EASTERN EUROPE

Rick Steves & Cameron Hewitt

CONTENTS

astern Europe Overview

The maps on the following pages show more detail.

LITHUANIA

Baltic Sea

KALININGRAD (RUSSIA)

Gdynia • Hel
Sopot • TRI-CITY
Gdańsk
■ Malbork

• Olsztyn

POMERANIA

• Białystok

Toruń • *Wisła*

Poznań •

Warsaw ★

Brest •

BELARUS

Berlin ★

GERMANY

WIELKOPOLSKA

MAZOVIA

Łódź •

POLAND

Lublin •

Elbe
ipzig

Dresden •

Wrocław •

MAŁOPOLSKA

Wisła

Lviv •

SILESIA

Częstochowa •

Katowice •

Kraków •

TEREZÍN

AUSCHWITZ ■

BOHEMIA

Labe
Bled

Prague ★

Kutná
Hora

Ostrava •

Zakopane •

SPIS

• Levoča

Plzeň •

Vltava

**CZECH
REPUBLIC**

• Olomouc

HIGH
TATRAMTNS.

Košice •

UKRAINE

Brno •

MORAVIA

Poprad •

Český
Krumlov

SLOVAKIA

Danube

Melk •

Bratislava ★

Eger •

Tokaj •

Vienna ★

Danube

DANUBE
BEND

Salzburg •

Győr •

Tisza

Debrecen •

AUSTRIA

Sopron •

Budapest ★

Szombathely •

PUSZTA

*Lake
Balaton*

HUNGARY

Graz •

Klagenfurt •

TRANSDANUBIA

Szeged •

Maribor •

OLOMITES

JULIAN
ALPS

Bled
Bohinj

Bled
Ljubljana ★

Pécs •

VOJVODINA

ROMANIA

lzano

Kobarid

Zagreb ★

Novi
Sad ★

Trieste •

KARST

SLOVENIA

SLAVONIA

Osijek •

Piran •

CROATIA

enice

Motovun

Rijeka •

Bihać •

Banja Luka •

Danube
★

ISTRIA

Plitvice
Lakes
National
Park

Belgrade

Rovinj
Pula

**BOSNIA -
HERZEGOVINA**

SERBIA

Zadar •

Sarajevo ★

ALY

DALMATIAN COAST

Trogir •

orence

Ancona •

Split

Mostar

MONTE-
NEGRO

ena

• Assisi

Hvar •

MEDUGORJE ■

Podgorica ★

KOSOVO

Korčula

Priština ★

Dubrovnik

Kotor •

Adriatic Sea

ALBANIA

Skopje ★
MACEDONIA

200 Kilometers

200 Miles

Czech Republic

LEGEND

- **A-4** Freeway/Autobahn
- Major Roads
- Major Rail Line
- ✈ Airport
- ■ Museum, Landmark, Other Point of Interest
- ▮ Castle, Monument, Palace

50 Kilometers

50 Miles

POLAND

GERMANY

SLOVAKIA

AUSTRIA

SILESIA

BOHEMIA

MORAVIA

CZECH REPUBLIC

Prague

Dresden
Freiberg
Chemnitz
Glauchau
Plauen
Hof
Pegnitz
Weiden
Regensburg
Oberstraubling
Plattling
Schwandorf
Bayerisch Eisenstein
Furth
Česká Kubice
Klatovy
Železná Ruda
Mariánské Lázně
Karlovy Vary
Loket
Cheb
Marktredwitz
Teplice
Chomutov
Ústí nad Labem
Litoměřice
TEREZÍN MEMORIAL
Děčín
Bad Schandau
Seiffen
Zittau
Liberec
Turnov
Jelenia Góra
Świdnica
Náchod
Hradec Králové
Kolín
Kutná Hora
Benešov
KONOPIŠTĚ
KARLŠTEJN
KŘIVOKLÁT
Karlová
Plzeň
Tábor
Jihlava
Telč
Slavonice
Třeboň
Veselí nad Lužnicí
České Velenice
Gmund
České Budějovice
HLUBOKÁ
Český Krumlov
Summerau
Krems
Sigmundsherberg
Retz
Znojmo
Moravský Krumlov
Třebíč
Brno
Mikulov
MIKULOV WINE REGION
VALTICE LEDNICE CASTLES
Pavlov
Hohenau
Stockerau
Břeclav
Kúty
Trnava
Hodonín
Nitra
Piešťany
Trenčín
Prievidza
Martin
Žilina
Čadca
Trojanovice
PUSTEVNY
WALLACHIAN OPEN-AIR MUSEUM
Rožnov pod Radhoštěm
Velké Karlovice
Petrovice
Ostrava
Štramberk
Opava
Krnov
Nysa
Brzeg
Opole
Šternberk
Lichkov
Letohrad
Ústí nad Orlicí
Zábřeh na Moravě
Olomouc
Přerov
Kroměříž
Zlín
Trebíč
Opava

To Berlin
To Görlitz
To Wroclaw
To Kraków
To Nürnberg & Munich
To Bratislava
To Vienna

Elbe R.
Vltava R.
Danube

ŠUMAVA MTS.
CARPATHIAN MTNS.
WALLACHIA

E-65, E-55, E-50, E-462, E-50, E-65

A-17, A-72, A-4, A-9, A-93, A-6, A-3, A-92, A-3

N

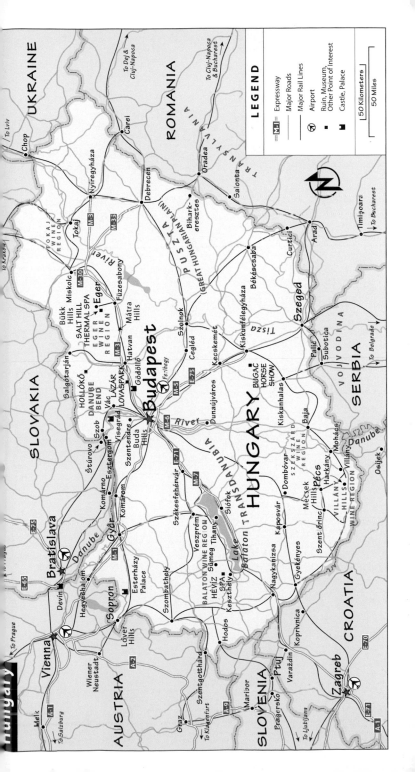

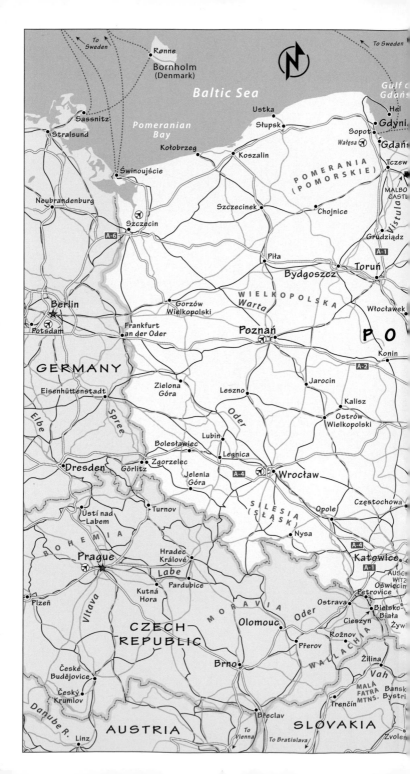

Croatia and Slovenia

HUNGARY

alaegerszeg · Keszthely · Lake Balaton · To Budapest

Kalocsa

M-7

agykanizsa · Kaposvár · Nagyatád · Komló · Szekszárd · Baja · Subotica

Letenye · Csurgó

Gyékényes · Szigetvár · Pécs · Mohács · Sombor

oprivnica

Bjelovar · Vicovitica · Barcs · Drava R. · Osijek · **SERBIA**

CROATIA

SLAVONIA · Našice · Vukovar · Novi Sad

Kutina · Đakovo · Vinkovci

E-70

Sisak · Požega · Nova Gradiška · Slavonski Brod · Novska · Županja · Šid · To Belgrade

Brčko

Novi Grad · Prijedor · Banja Luka · Doboj · Bijelina · **SERBIA**

Tuzla

BOSNIA-HERZEGOVINA · Zavidovići · Zvornik

Jajce

Drvar · Travnik · Zenica · Srebrenica

Visoko

DINARIC MTNS. · ★ Sarajevo

Knin · Livno · ▲ Ivan Planina · Goražde

Perković · Konjic · Srbinje

DIOCLETIAN'S PALACE · Jablanica

rogir · Split · Neretva R. · Mostar

Čiovo · Omiš · Makarska

Šolta · Brač · BOL · Drvenik · MEĐUGORJE · Buna · Nevesinje

Stari Grad · Vrgorac · Počitelj · Gacko · **MONTE-NEGRO**

Hvar · Hvar · Ploče · Stolac

Metković · Ljubinje

Vis · Orebić · Pelješac Peninsula · Neum · Bileća

miža · Vela Luka · Trebinje

Korčula · Korčula · Ston

Pomena · Elaphite Islands · Dubrovnik · Perast · Podgorica

Lastovo · Mljet · Sobra · Lokrum · Herceg Novi · Kotor · Cetinje

Čilipi · Cavtat · Bay of Kotor

To Bari, Italy · Budva · Sveti Stefan

DALMATIAN COAST

Prague

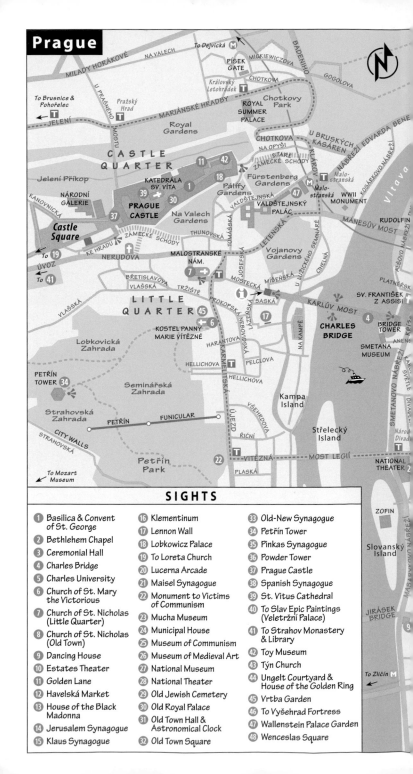

SIGHTS

1. Basilica & Convent of St. George
2. Bethlehem Chapel
3. Ceremonial Hall
4. Charles Bridge
5. Charles University
6. Church of St. Mary the Victorious
7. Church of St. Nicholas (Little Quarter)
8. Church of St. Nicholas (Old Town)
9. Dancing House
10. Estates Theater
11. Golden Lane
12. Havelská Market
13. House of the Black Madonna
14. Jerusalem Synagogue
15. Klaus Synagogue
16. Klementinum
17. Lennon Wall
18. Lobkowicz Palace
19. To Loreta Church
20. Lucerna Arcade
21. Maisel Synagogue
22. Monument to Victims of Communism
23. Mucha Museum
24. Municipal House
25. Museum of Communism
26. Museum of Medieval Art
27. National Museum
28. National Theater
29. Old Jewish Cemetery
30. Old Royal Palace
31. Old Town Hall & Astronomical Clock
32. Old Town Square
33. Old-New Synagogue
34. Petřín Tower
35. Pinkas Synagogue
36. Powder Tower
37. Prague Castle
38. Spanish Synagogue
39. St. Vitus Cathedral
40. To Slav Epic Paintings (Veletržní Palace)
41. To Strahov Monastery & Library
42. Toy Museum
43. Týn Church
44. Ungelt Courtyard & House of the Golden Ring
45. Vrtba Garden
46. To Vyšehrad Fortress
47. Wallenstein Palace Garden
48. Wenceslas Square

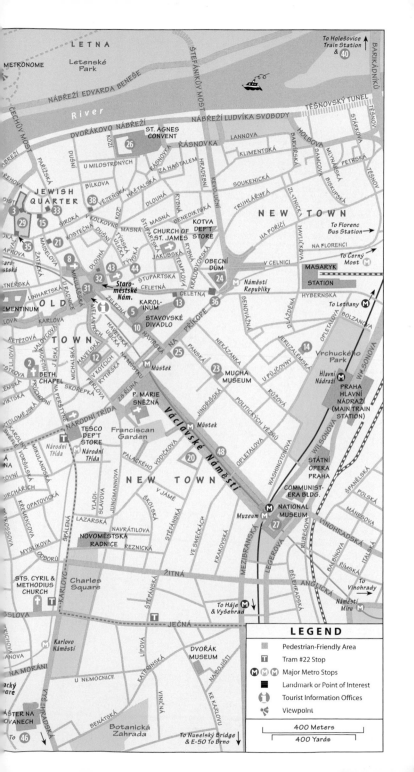

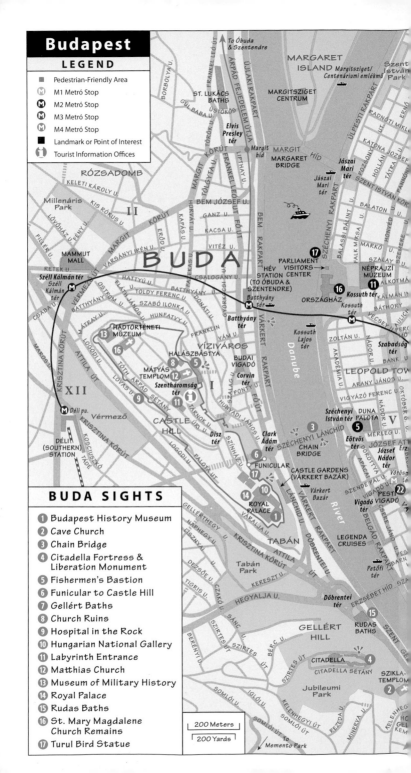

Budapest

LEGEND

- ■ Pedestrian-Friendly Area
- Ⓜ M1 Metró Stop
- Ⓜ M2 Metró Stop
- Ⓜ M3 Metró Stop
- Ⓜ M4 Metró Stop
- ■ Landmark or Point of Interest
- ⓘ Tourist Information Offices

BUDA SIGHTS

1. Budapest History Museum
2. Cave Church
3. Chain Bridge
4. Citadella Fortress & Liberation Monument
5. Fishermen's Bastion
6. Funicular to Castle Hill
7. Gellért Baths
8. Church Ruins
9. Hospital in the Rock
10. Hungarian National Gallery
11. Labyrinth Entrance
12. Matthias Church
13. Museum of Military History
14. Royal Palace
15. Rudas Baths
16. St. Mary Magdalene Church Remains
17. Turul Bird Statue

200 Meters
200 Yards

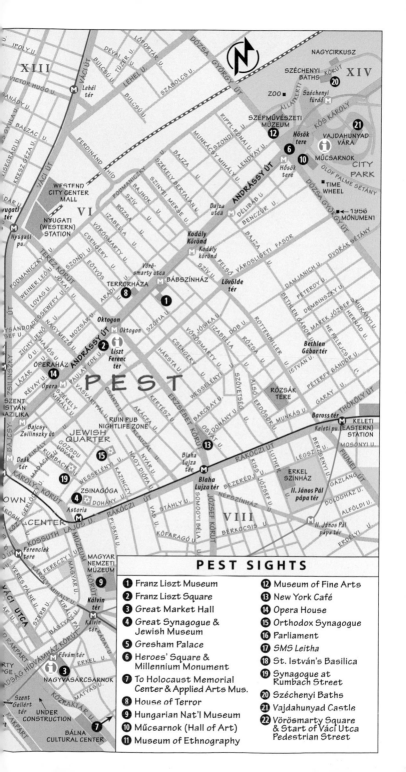

PEST SIGHTS

1. Franz Liszt Museum
2. Franz Liszt Square
3. Great Market Hall
4. Great Synagogue & Jewish Museum
5. Gresham Palace
6. Heroes' Square & Millennium Monument
7. To Holocaust Memorial Center & Applied Arts Mus.
8. House of Terror
9. Hungarian Nat'l Museum
10. Műcsarnok (Hall of Art)
11. Museum of Ethnography
12. Museum of Fine Arts
13. New York Café
14. Opera House
15. Orthodox Synagogue
16. Parliament
17. SMS Leitha
18. St. István's Basilica
19. Synagogue at Rumbach Street
20. Széchenyi Baths
21. Vajdahunyad Castle
22. Vörösmarty Square & Start of Váci Utca Pedestrian Street

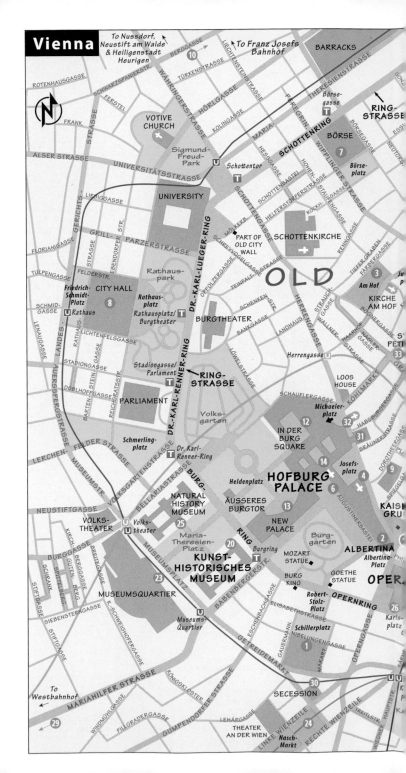

SIGHTS

1. Academy of Fine Arts
2. Albertina Museum
3. Am Hof Square
4. Augustinian Church & State Hall
5. To Belvedere Palace & Mus. of Military History
6. Butterfly House
7. Börse (Stock Exchange)
8. City Hall
9. Dorotheum Auction House
10. To Freud Museum
11. Haus der Musik
12. Hofburg Imperial Apartments
13. Hofburg New Palace Museums
14. Hofburg Treasury & Boys' Choir Chapel
15. Jewish Museum Dorotheergasse
16. Jewish Museum Judenplatz
17. Kaisergruft (Crypt)
18. To Karlskirche
19. To Kunst Haus Wien & Hundertwasserhaus
20. Kunsthistorisches Museum
21. Mozarthaus Vienna Museum
22. Museum of Applied Art (MAK)
23. MuseumsQuartier
24. Naschmarkt
25. Natural History Museum
26. Opera
27. Plague Column
28. To Prater Park
29. To Schönbrunn Palace & Imperial Furniture Collection
30. Secession Building
31. Spanish Riding School
32. St. Michael's Church Crypt
33. St. Peter's Church
34. St. Stephen's Cathedral
35. Wien Museum Karlsplatz
36. Wien Ticket Pavilion

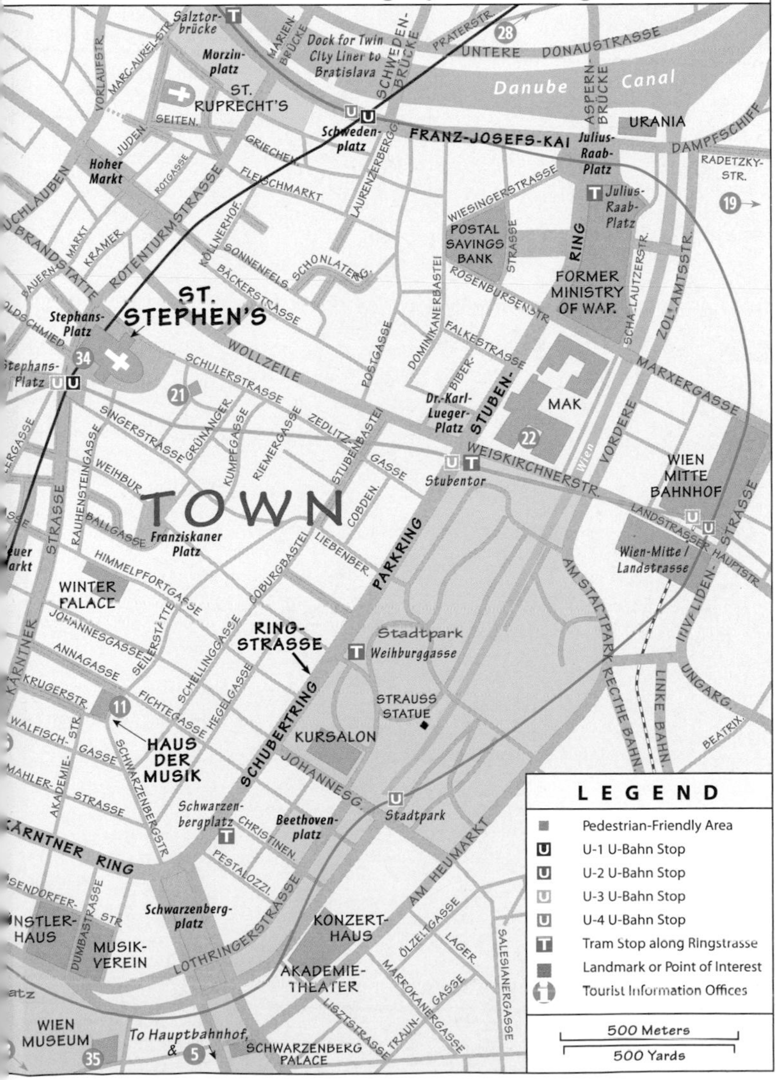
Salztor-brücke
Morzin-platz
ST. RUPRECHT'S
Dock for Twin City Liner to Bratislava
Schweden-platz
SCHWEDEN-BRÜCKE
PRATERSTR.
UNTERE DONAUSTRASSE
Danube Canal
ASPERN-BRÜCKE
URANIA
FRANZ-JOSEFS-KAI
Julius-Raab-Platz
DAMPFSCHIFF
RADETZKY-STR.
Hoher Markt
ROTENTURMSTRASSE
FLEISCHMARKT
GRIECHEN.
LAURENZERBERG
WIESINGERSTRASSE
POSTAL SAVINGS BANK
RING
FORMER MINISTRY OF WAR
ZOLLAMTSSTR.
ROSENBURSENSTR.
SONNENFELS.
SCHONLATERNG.
BÄCKERSTRASSE
ST. STEPHEN'S
Stephans-Platz
WOLLZEILE
SCHULERSTRASSE
FALKESTRASSE
MAK
MARXERGASSE
Dr.-Karl-Lueger-Platz
STUBEN-
WEISKIRCHNERSTR.
Stubentor
WIEN MITTE BAHNHOF
Wien-Mitte / Landstrasse
LANDSTRASSER HAUPTSTR.
SINGERSTRASSE
WEIHBURG
TOWN
Franziskaner Platz
PARKRING
HIMMELPFORTGASSE
WINTER PALACE
JOHANNESGASSE
ANNAGASSE
RING-STRASSE
Stadtpark
Weihburggasse
AM STADTPARK
STRAUSS STATUE
KURSALON
HAUS DER MUSIK
SCHUBERTRING
JOHANNESG.
Stadtpark
Schwarzen-bergplatz
Beethoven-platz
KÄRNTNER RING
AM HEUMARKT
UNGARG.
LINKE BAHN
Schwarzenberg-platz
KONZERT-HAUS
AKADEMIE-THEATER
LOTHRINGERSTRASSE
MUSIK-VEREIN
WIEN MUSEUM
To Hauptbahnhof, & 5
SCHWARZENBERG PALACE
SALESIANERGASSE
LEGEND
Pedestrian-Friendly Area
U-1 U-Bahn Stop
U-2 U-Bahn Stop
U-3 U-Bahn Stop
U-4 U-Bahn Stop
Tram Stop along Ringstrasse
Landmark or Point of Interest
Tourist Information Offices
500 Meters
500 Yards

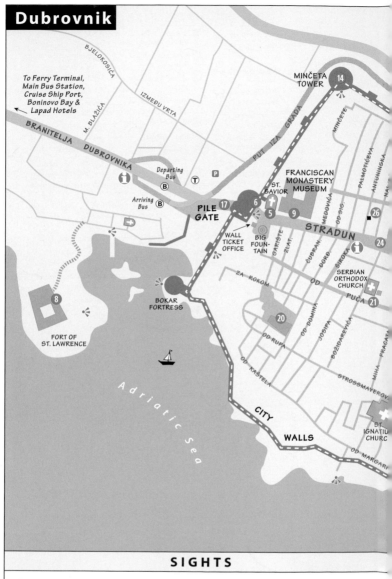

Dubrovnik

To Ferry Terminal,
Main Bus Station,
Cruise Ship Port,
Boninovo Bay &
Lapad Hotels

BJELOKOSIĆA

IZMEĐU VRTA

BRANITELJA DUBROVNIKA

M. BLAŽIĆA

PUT IZA GRADA

MINČETE

MINČETA TOWER

14

PALMOTIĆEVA

ANTUNINSKA

Departing Bus

P

B

T

Arriving Bus

B

PILE GATE

17

6

ST. SAVIOR

FRANCISCAN MONASTERY MUSEUM

5

9

26

STRADUN

GARIŠTE

ZLAT.

ŽUBRAN.

ĐORĐ.

MEDOVIĆA

ĐURĐ.

WALL TICKET OFFICE

BIG FOUNTAIN

ŠIROKA

24

SERBIAN ORTHODOX CHURCH

OD

PUČA

21

ZA ROKOM

BOKAR FORTRESS

8

FORT OF ST. LAWRENCE

20

OD DOMINA

JOSIPA

BOŽIDAREVIĆA

OD RUPA

OD KAŠTELA

STROSSMAYEROV.

MIHA

PRACATA

A d r i a t i c   S e a

CITY

WALLS

OD MARGARI

ST. IGNATI CHURC

SIGHTS

1. Bell Tower
2. Buža Gate
3. Cable Car
4. Cathedral
5. Church of St. Savior
6. City Wall Entrances (3)
7. Dominican Monastery Museum & Church
8. Fort of St. Lawrence
9. Franciscan Monastery Museum & Church
10. Jesuit St. Ignatius' Church
11. Lazareti (Old Quarantine Building)
12. Luža Square & Orlando's Column
13. Maritime Museum & Aquarium
14. Minčeta Tower
15. To Museum of Modern Art
16. Old Port
17. Pile Gate
18. Ploče Gate
19. Rector's Palace
20. Rupe Granary & Ethnographic Museum
21. Serbian Orthodox Church & Icon Museum
22. Sponza Palace & Memorial Room of Dubrovnik Defenders
23. St. Blaise's Church
24. Stradun (a.k.a. Placa)
25. Synagogue Museum
26. War Photo Limited

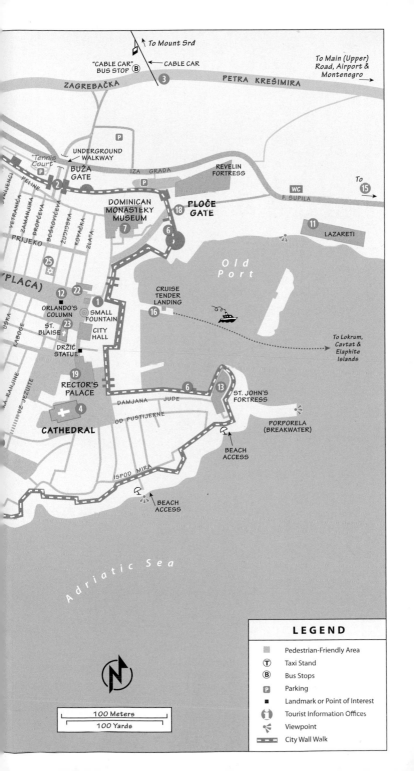

To Mount Srđ

"CABLE CAR"
BUS STOP Ⓑ —— CABLE CAR

To Main (Upper)
Road, Airport &
Montenegro →

ZAGREBAČKA ③ PETRA KREŠIMIRA

"Tennis
Court" Ⓟ
UNDERGROUND
WALKWAY Ⓟ

Ⓟ BUŽA
GATE IZA GRADA REVELIN
FORTRESS

② PEHNE To
⑮

VRIJENCI WC

VETRANIĆA DOMINICAN F. SUPILA
ZAMANJINA MONASTERY ⑱ PLOČE
ĐORĐIĆA MUSEUM GATE
ŽUDIOSKA ⑦ ⑪
BOŠKOVIĆEVA ⑥ LAZARETI
PRIJEKO KOVAČKA
ZLATA

⑤

Old
Port

(PLACA)

⑫ ㉒ CRUISE
ⓄRLANDO'S ① TENDER
COLUMN SMALL LANDING
FOUNTAIN ⑯
ST. ㉓
BLAISE CITY
HALL To Lokrum,
DRŽIĆ Cavtat &
STATUE Elaphite
Islands

⑲
RECTOR'S
PALACE ⑥ ⑬
DAMJANA JUDE ST. JOHN'S
FORTRESS
CATHEDRAL ④ OD PUSTIJERNE
PORPORELA
(BREAKWATER)
BEACH
ACCESS

ISPOD MIRA
BEACH
ACCESS

Adriatic Sea

N

100 Meters
100 Yards

LEGEND

▢	Pedestrian-Friendly Area
Ⓣ	Taxi Stand
Ⓑ	Bus Stops
Ⓟ	Parking
▪	Landmark or Point of Interest
⛨	Tourist Information Offices
⚐	Viewpoint
▬▬	City Wall Walk

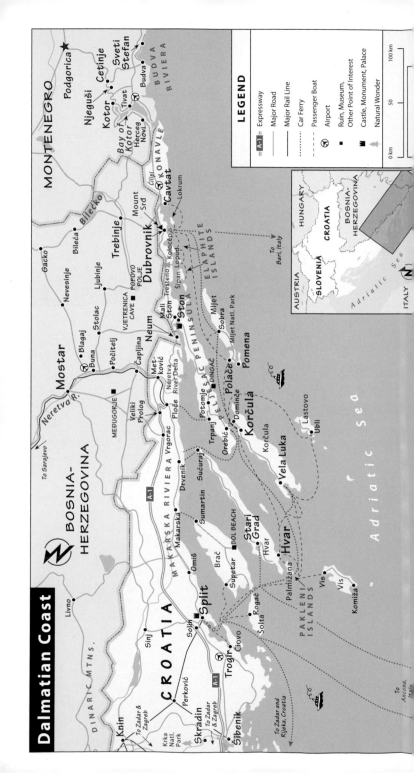

Rick Steves

EASTERN EUROPE

AVALON
TRAVEL

Top Destinations of Eastern Europe

GDAŃSK AND THE TRI-CITY

POMERANIA

WARSAW

AUSCHWITZ-BIRKENAU

KRAKÓW

PRAGUE

NEAR PRAGUE

ČESKÝ KRUMLOV

BRATISLAVA

EGER

VIENNA

BUDAPEST

LAKE BLED

JULIAN ALPS

LJUBLJANA

ZAGREB

ROVINJ & ISTRIA

PLITVICE LAKES

SPLIT

MOSTAR

DUBROVNIK

DCH

INTRODUCTION

Until 1989, Eastern Europe was a foreboding place—a dark and gloomy corner of the "Evil Empire." But the dismal grays and preachy reds of communism live on only in history books, museums, and kitschy theme restaurants. Today's Eastern Europe is a traveler's delight, with friendly locals, lively squares, breathtaking sights, fascinating history, reasonable prices, and a sense of pioneer excitement.

Wander among Prague's dreamy, fairy-tale spires, bask in the energy of Kraków's Main Market Square, and soak with chess players in a Budapest bath. Ponder Europe's most moving Holocaust memorial at Auschwitz. Enjoy nature as you stroll on boardwalks through the Plitvice Lakes' waterfall wonderland, or glide across Lake Bled to a church-topped island in the shadow of the Julian Alps. Taste a proud Hungarian vintner's wine and say, *"Egészségedre!"* (or stick with "Cheers!").

This book covers Eastern Europe's top big-city, small-town, and back-to-nature destinations—from the Hungarian metropolis of Budapest to the quaint Czech village of Český Krumlov to the pristine Julian Alps of Slovenia. It then gives you all the specifics and opinions necessary to wring the maximum value out of your limited time and money. If you're planning for a month or less in this region, this book is all you need.

Experiencing Europe's culture, people, and natural wonders economically and hassle-free has been my goal for several decades of traveling, tour guiding, and writing. With this book, I pass on to you all of the lessons I've learned.

I've been selective, including only the top destinations and sights. For example, Poland has dozens of medieval castles—but Malbork is a cut above the rest. The best is, of course, only my opinion. But after spending much of my life exploring and

Map Legend

↳	Viewpoint	✈	Airport	)⸺(	Tunnel
▲	Entrance	Ⓣ	Taxi Stand		Pedestrian Zone
⊕	Tourist Info	Ⓣ	Tram Stop	------	Railway
WC	Restroom	Ⓜ	Metro Stop	··········	Ferry/Boat Route
🏰	Castle	Ⓑ	Bus Stop	⊢─┼─┤	Tram
⛪	Church	Ⓟ	Parking	)/(	Mtn. Pass
✡	Synagogue		Park	· · · · ·	Walk/Tour Route
▪	Statue/Point of Interest		Cruise Ship Terminal	- - - - -	Trail
				O⊪⊪⊪⊪O	Funicular

Use this legend to help you navigate the maps in this book.

researching Europe, I've developed a sixth sense for what travelers enjoy. Just thinking about the places featured in this book makes me want to polka.

ABOUT THIS BOOK

Rick Steves Eastern Europe is a personal tour guide in your pocket. Better yet, it's actually two tour guides in your pocket: The co-author of this book is Cameron Hewitt. Cameron writes and edits guidebooks for my travel company, Rick Steves' Europe. Inspired by his Polish roots and by the enduring charm of the Eastern European people, Cameron has spent the last decade closely tracking the exciting changes in this part of the world. Together, Cameron and I keep this book up to date and accurate (though for simplicity we've shed our respective egos to become "I" in this book).

This book is organized by **destinations.** Each is a mini-vacation on its own, filled with exciting sights, strollable neighborhoods, affordable places to stay, and memorable places to eat. In the following chapters, you'll find these sections:

Planning Your Time suggests a schedule for how to best use your limited time.

Orientation includes specifics on public transportation, helpful hints, local tour options, easy-to-read maps, and tourist information.

Sights describes the top attractions and includes their cost and hours.

Self-Guided Walks take you through interesting neighborhoods, pointing out sights and fun stops.

Sleeping describes my favorite hotels, from good-value deals to cushy splurges.

Eating serves up a range of options, from inexpensive eateries to fancy restaurants.

Key to This Book

Updates
This book is updated regularly—but things change. For the latest, visit www.ricksteves.com/update.

Abbreviations and Times
I use the following symbols and abbreviations in this book:

Sights are rated:

▲▲▲ Don't miss

▲▲ Try hard to see

▲ Worthwhile if you can make it

No rating Worth knowing about

Tourist information offices are abbreviated as **TI,** and bathrooms are WCs. To categorize accommodations, I use a **Sleep Code** (described on page 1309).

Like Europe, this book uses the **24-hour clock.** It's the same through 12:00 noon, then keeps going: 13:00, 14:00, and so on. For anything over 12, subtract 12 and add p.m. (14:00 is 2:00 p.m.).

When giving **opening times,** I include both peak season and off-season hours if they differ. So, if a museum is listed as "May-Oct daily 9:00-16:00," it should be open from 9:00 a.m. until 4:00 p.m. from the first day of May until the last day of October (but expect exceptions).

For **transit** or **tour departures,** I first list the frequency, then the duration. So, a train connection listed as "2/hour, 1.5 hours" departs twice each hour, and the journey lasts an hour and a half.

Connections outlines your options for traveling to destinations by train, bus, and boat. For car-friendly regions, I've included route tips for drivers, with recommended roadside attractions along the way.

Country Introductions give you an overview of each country's culture, customs, money, history, current events, cuisine, language, and other useful practicalities.

Practicalities is a traveler's tool kit, with my best travel tips and advice about money, sightseeing, sleeping, eating, staying connected, and transportation (trains, buses, boats, car rentals, driving, and flights). There's also a list of recommended books and films.

The **appendix** has nuts-and-bolts information, including useful phone numbers and websites, a festival list, a climate chart, a handy packing checklist, and a guide to pronouncing Eastern European place names.

Browse through this book, choose your favorite destinations, and link them up. Then have a great trip! Traveling like a temporary local, you'll get the absolute most of every mile, minute, and

INTRODUCTION

What Is "Eastern Europe"?

"Eastern Europe" means different things to different people. To most Americans, Eastern Europe includes any place that was once behind the Iron Curtain, from the former East Germany to Moscow. But people who actually live in many of these countries consider themselves "Central Europeans." In fact, some even get a bit offended by the "Eastern" label. (To them, "Eastern Europe" is *really* eastern: Russia, Ukraine, Belarus, and Romania.)

In this book I use the term "Eastern Europe" the way most Americans do—to describe the **Czech Republic, Poland, Hungary, Slovenia,** and **Croatia.** I've also thrown in three cities in other countries worth a detour: **Vienna** (in Austria), **Mostar** (in Bosnia-Herzegovina), and **Bratislava** (in Slovakia). Vienna is a "gateway city" that feels more Western than Eastern, but it has important historical ties to the region. Nearby Bratislava is the impressively rejuvenated capital of Slovakia. And Mostar—a mostly Muslim city a short drive or bus trip from Croatia's Dalmatian Coast—provides an opportunity to splice in some diversity.

So what do my five core "Eastern European" countries have in common? All of these destinations fell under communist control during the last half of the 20th century. More importantly, for centuries leading up to World War I, they were all part of the Austrian Habsburg Empire. Before the Habsburgs, the kings and emperors of these countries also frequently governed their neighbors. And all of these countries (except Hungary) are populated by people of Slavic heritage.

I hope that natives, sticklers, and historians will understand the liberties I've taken with the title of this book. After all, would you buy a book called *Rick Steves Former Habsburg Empire*?

dollar. As you visit places I know and love, I'm happy that you'll be meeting some of my favorite Europeans.

Planning

This section will help you get started on planning your trip—with advice on trip costs, when to go, and what you should know before you take off.

TRAVEL SMART

Your trip to Europe is like a complex play—it's easier to follow and fully appreciate on a second viewing. While no one does the same trip twice to gain that advantage, reading this book before your trip accomplishes much the same thing.

Please Tear Up This Book!

There's no point in hauling around a big chapter on Vienna for a day in Dubrovnik. That's why I hope you'll rip this book apart. Before your trip, attack this book with a utility knife to create an army of pocket-sized mini-guidebooks—one for each area you visit.

I love the ritual of trimming down the size of guidebooks I'll be using: Fold the pages back until you break the spine, neatly slice apart the sections you want with a utility knife, then pull them out with the gummy edge intact. If you want, finish each one off with some clear, heavy-duty packing tape to smooth and reinforce the spine, or use a heavy-duty stapler along the edge to prevent the first and last pages from coming loose.

To make things even easier, I've created a line of laminated covers with slide-on binders. Every evening, you can make a ritual of swapping out today's pages for tomorrow's. (For more on these binders, see www.ricksteves.com.)

While you may be tempted to keep this book intact as a souvenir of your travels, you'll appreciate even more the foot-loose freedom of traveling light.

Design an itinerary that enables you to visit sights at the best possible times. Note festivals, holidays, specifics on sights, and days when sights are closed (all covered in this book). For example, most museums throughout Eastern Europe close on Mondays. Hotels in resort towns (such as those on the Croatian coast) are most crowded on Fridays and Saturdays, whereas weekdays are tight in convention cities (for instance, Budapest and Warsaw). Expect seasonal closures, especially in Croatia. To get between destinations smoothly, read the tips in Practicalities on taking trains and buses or renting a car and driving. A smart trip is a puzzle—a fun, doable, and worthwhile challenge.

When you're plotting your itinerary, strive for a mix of intense and relaxed stretches. To maximize rootedness, minimize one-night stands. It's worth taking a long drive after dinner (or a train/bus ride with a dinner picnic) to get settled in a town for two nights. Every trip—and every traveler—needs slack time (laundry, picnics, people-watching, and so on). Pace yourself. Assume you will return.

Reread this book as you travel, and visit local tourist information offices (abbreviated as TI in this book). Upon arrival in a new town, lay the groundwork for a smooth departure; get the schedule for the train, bus, or boat you'll take when you depart. Drivers can figure out the best route to their next destination.

Update your plans as you travel. You can carry a small mobile

Eastern Europe at a Glance

Czech Republic
▲▲▲**Prague** Romantic Czech capital with a remarkably well-preserved Old Town, sprawling hilltop castle, informative Jewish Quarter, and rollicking pubs.

▲**Near Prague** Kutná Hora's offbeat bone church and grand cathedral, Terezín's Nazi concentration camp memorial, and Franz Ferdinand's residence at Konopiště Castle.

▲▲**Český Krumlov** Picturesque town hugging a river bend under a castle.

Poland
▲▲▲**Kraków** Poland's cultural, intellectual, and historical capital, with a huge but cozy main square, easy-to-enjoy Old Town, thought-provoking Jewish quarter, and important castle.

▲▲▲**Auschwitz-Birkenau** The largest and most notorious Nazi concentration camp, now a compelling museum and memorial.

▲▲**Warsaw** Poland's modern capital, with an appealing urban tempo, a reconstructed Old Town, and good museums.

▲▲**Gdańsk and the Tri-City** Historic Hanseatic trading city, with a cancan of marvelous facades and the shipyard where the Solidarity trade union challenged the communists in 1980.

▲**Pomerania** The Teutonic Knights' gigantic, Gothic Malbork Castle and the red-brick, gingerbread-scented city of Toruń.

Hungary
▲▲▲**Budapest** Grand Danube-spanning cityscape peppered with opulent late-19th-century buildings, excellent restaurants, layers of epic history, and uniquely exhilarating thermal baths.

▲▲**Eger** Strollable town with a gaggle of gorgeous Baroque buildings and locally produced wines.

Slovenia
▲▲**Ljubljana** Slovenia's vibrant, relaxing capital, with fine architecture and an inviting riverside promenade and market.

▲▲▲**Lake Bled** Photogenic lake resort huddled in mountain foothills, with a church-topped island and cliff-hanging castle.

▲▲**The Julian Alps** Cut-glass peaks easily conquered by a twisty mountain road over the Vršič Pass, ending in the tranquil Soča River Valley, with the fine WWI museum in Kobarid.

Croatia
▲▲▲**Dubrovnik** The "Pearl of the Adriatic" and Croatia's best destination: a giant walled Old Town with a scenic wall walk, tons of crowds, an epic past, and an inspiring recent history.

▲▲**Split** Dalmatian transit hub, with a people-filled seaside promenade next to the remains of a massive Roman palace.

▲▲**Rovinj and Istria** Croatia's most enchanting small coastal town—with a romantic Venetian vibe—plus Roman ruins in the city of Pula and the hill town of Motovun.

▲**Zagreb** Croatia's underrated capital city, with interesting sight-seeing and a lively urban bustle.

▲▲▲**Plitvice Lakes National Park** Forested canyon filled with crystal-clear lakes and stunning waterfalls, all laced together by boardwalks and trails.

Other Destinations
▲▲▲**Mostar, Bosnia-Herzegovina** Fascinating town with a striking setting, vital Muslim culture, old Turkish architecture, evocative war damage, and an inspiring, rebuilt Old Bridge.

▲▲▲**Vienna, Austria** Glorious onetime Habsburg capital boasting stately palaces and world-class museums, convivial wine gardens, a rich musical heritage, and a genteel elegance that has long outlived the emperor's reign.

▲▲**Bratislava, Slovakia** The Slovak capital, with a rejuvenated Old Town and lots of new construction.

device (phone, tablet, laptop) to find out tourist information, learn the latest on sights (special events, tour schedules, etc.), book tickets and tours, make reservations, reconfirm hotels, research transportation connections, and keep in touch with your loved ones. If you don't want to bring a pricey device, you can use guest computers at hotels and make phone calls from landlines.

Enjoy the friendliness of the local people. Connect with the culture. Set up your own quest for the best bit of communist kitsch, mug of Czech beer, bowl of borscht, or scenic seafront perch. Slow down and be open to unexpected experiences. Ask questions—most locals are eager to point you in their idea of the right direction. Keep a notepad in your pocket for noting directions, organizing your thoughts, and confirming prices. Wear your money belt, learn the currency, and figure out how to estimate prices in dollars. Those who expect to travel smart, do.

TRIP COSTS

The countries in this book—while little more than two decades removed from communism—are no longer Europe's bargain basement. Although the global recession hit their economies along with everyone else's, the cost of living in most of Eastern Europe is approaching what it is in the West. But it can still be a good value to travel here. Things that natives buy—such as food and transportation—remain fairly inexpensive. Hotels can be pricey, but if you use my listings to find the best accommodations deals, a trip to these countries can be substantially cheaper than visiting, say, Italy, Germany, or France.

Five components make up your trip costs: airfare, surface transportation, room and board, sightseeing and entertainment, and shopping and miscellany. The prices I've listed below are more or less average for all of the destinations in this book. Prices are generally lower in Poland and Mostar and higher in Slovenia, Croatia, and Vienna; the Czech Republic and Hungary are in between. Of course, big cities (such as Prague and Budapest) are much more expensive than smaller towns (like Èeský Krumlov and Eger).

Airfare: A basic round-trip flight from the US to Prague can cost, on average, about $1,000-2,000 total, depending on where you fly from and when (cheaper in winter). Consider saving time and money in Europe by flying into one city and out of another; for instance, flying into Prague and out of Dubrovnik is almost certainly cheaper than the added expense (and wasted time) of an overland return trip to Prague. Overall, Kayak.com is the best place to start searching for flights on a combination of mainstream and budget carriers.

Surface Transportation: For a three-week whirlwind trip

Not Your Father's Eastern Europe

Americans sometimes approach Eastern Europe expecting grouchy service, crumbling communist infrastructure, and grimy, depressing landscapes. But those who visit are pleasantly surprised at the area's beauty and diversity, as well as how safe and easy it is.

Travel in Eastern Europe today is nearly as smooth as travel in the West. Most natives speak excellent English, and many pride themselves on impressing their guests. Service standards can sometimes be a bit lower than in other parts of Europe, but on the other hand, locals are generally less jaded and more excited to meet you than their counterparts in many big-name Western European destinations. Any rough edges add to the charm and carbonate the experience.

The East-West stuff still fascinates us, but to people here, the Soviet regime is old news, Cold War espionage is the stuff of movies, and oppressive monuments to Stalin are a distant memory (and those under age 25 have no firsthand memories of communism at all). More than 25 years after the fall of the Iron Curtain, Eastern Europeans (or, as they prefer to be called, *Central* Europeans) think about communism only when tourists bring it up. Freedom is a more than a generation old, and—for better or for worse—McDonald's, MTV, and mobile phones are every bit as entrenched here as anywhere else in Europe. All of the countries in this book (except Bosnia) belong to the European Union, and everyone seems to be looking forward to a bright future.

of my recommended destinations by public transportation, allow $300 per person. If you'll be renting a car, allow $300 per week, not including tolls, gas, and supplemental insurance. Car rentals are cheapest if arranged from the US. Train passes normally must be purchased outside Europe but aren't necessarily your best option—you may save money simply by buying tickets as you go. Don't hesitate to consider flying, as budget airlines can be cheaper than taking the train (check www.skyscanner.com for intra-European flights). For more on public transportation and car rental, see "Transportation" in Practicalities.

Room and Board: You can thrive in Eastern Europe on $100 a day per person for room and board. This allows $15 for lunch, $25 for dinner, and $60 for lodging (based on two people splitting the cost of a comfortable $120 double room that includes breakfast). Students and tightwads can enjoy Eastern Europe for as little as $50 a day ($30 per hostel bed, $20 for groceries and snacks).

Sightseeing and Entertainment: Sightseeing is cheap here. Figure $3-6 per major sight (with some more expensive sights at around $10), and $10-25 for splurge experiences (e.g., going to

INTRODUCTION

Eastern Europe: Best Three-Week Trip by Public Transportation

Few travelers have three weeks for this entire itinerary, and, in any event, this sprawling region is best split up into more manageable "zones" (for example, Vienna-Hungary-Czech Republic, Poland by itself, or Slovenia-Croatia-Bosnia). But if you want to squeeze as many highlights as possible into a three-week span, this is your best plan.

Day	Plan	Sleep in
1	Arrive in Kraków	Kraków
2	Kraków	Kraków
3	Side-trip to Auschwitz; night train or flight to Prague (or go by car—about 6 hours—with a stop at Auschwitz en route)	Night train (or possibly Kraków or Prague)
4	Prague	Prague
5	Prague	Prague
6	To Český Krumlov (by bus)	Český Krumlov
7	To Vienna (via shuttle bus)	Vienna
8	Vienna	Vienna
9	Train to Bratislava for lunch/sightseeing, then continue to Budapest	Budapest
10	Budapest	Budapest
11	Budapest	Budapest
12	To Ljubljana (direct 9-hour midday train)	Ljubljana
13	Ljubljana	Ljubljana
14	To Lake Bled	Lake Bled
15	Rent car for day trips around Julian Alps	Lake Bled
16	To Zagreb for sightseeing, then early-evening bus to Plitvice Lakes National Park	Plitvice
17	Plitvice hike in morning, then afternoon bus to Split	Split
18	Split	Split
19	Bus to Mostar	Mostar
20	Bus to Dubrovnik	Dubrovnik
21	Dubrovnik	Dubrovnik
22	Fly home	

This fast-paced, city-focused itinerary is ambitious—some would say foolishly so. Consider trimming the destinations that interest you less to carve out more time in the ones that interest you more. This itinerary is designed to work best by public transportation; except where noted, you'll take the train. Hiring your own private driver on certain journeys, while expensive,

can be a worthwhile splurge (for example, it enables you to visit Auschwitz on the way between Kraków and Prague).

If you have only **two weeks** and want to save Croatia, Slovenia, and Bosnia for another trip, end the itinerary in Budapest and spend any extra time squeezing in additional destinations (e.g., Eger, Warsaw, Prague day trips)—or simply slow down.

This itinerary isn't advisable **by car,** due to some long road days and potentially exorbitant international drop-off charges (see page 1335). I'd rather connect the longer distances by public transportation or budget flights, then rent cars for shorter periods where they're most useful.

INTRODUCTION

concerts, taking an Adriatic cruise, or soaking in a Budapest bath). You can hire your own private guide for four hours for about $100-150—a great value when divided among two or more people. An overall average of $20 a day works for most people. Don't skimp here. After all, this category is the driving force behind your trip—you came to sightsee, enjoy, and experience Eastern Europe.

Shopping and Miscellany: Figure $2 per postcard, coffee, beer, and ice-cream cone. Shopping can vary in cost from nearly nothing to a small fortune. Good budget travelers find that this category has little to do with assembling a trip full of lifelong and wonderful memories.

SIGHTSEEING PRIORITIES

So much to see, so little time. How to choose? Depending on the length of your trip, and taking geographic proximity into account, here are my recommended priorities.

3 days:	Prague
6 days, add:	Budapest
9 days, add:	Kraków, Auschwitz, Český Krumlov
12 days, add:	Ljubljana, Lake Bled
14 days, add:	Vienna
17 days, add:	Dubrovnik and Split
22 days, add:	Plitvice Lakes, Mostar

With more time or a special interest, choose among Gdańsk, Warsaw, Toruń, Bratislava, Eger, sights near Prague, Rovinj, and Zagreb.

This includes nearly everything on the map on page 11. If you don't have time to see it all, prioritize according to your interests. The "Eastern Europe a Glance" sidebar can help you decide where to go (page 6). The three-week itinerary (see sidebar) includes all of the stops in the first 22 days.

WHEN TO GO

The "tourist season" runs roughly from May through September. Summer has its advantages: the best weather, very long days (light until after 21:00), and the busiest schedule of tourist fun.

In spring and fall—May, June, September, and early October—travelers enjoy fewer crowds and milder weather. This is my favorite time to travel here. Cities are great at this time of year, but some small towns—especially resorts on the Croatian coast—get quieter and quieter the further off-season you get, and are downright deserted and disappointing in early May and late October.

Winter travelers find concert season in full swing, with absolutely no tourist crowds (except in always-packed Prague), but some accommodations and sights are either closed or run on a

Rick Steves Audio Europe

If you're bringing a mobile device, be sure to check out **Rick Steves Audio Europe,** where you can download free audio tours and hours of travel interviews (on the Rick Steves Audio Europe app, www.ricksteves.com/audioeurope, Google Play, or iTunes).

My self-guided **audio tours** are user-friendly, easy-to-follow, fun, and informative, covering sights and neighborhoods in Vienna (City Walk, Ringstrasse Tram Tour, St. Stephen's Cathedral) and Prague (City Walk). Compared to live tours, my audio tours are hard to beat: Nobody will stand you up, the quality is reliable, you can take the tour exactly when you like, and they're free.

Rick Steves Audio Europe also offers a far-reaching library of intriguing **travel interviews** with experts from around the globe. The interviews are organized by destination, including many of the places in this book.

limited schedule. Croatian coastal towns are completely shuttered in winter. Confirm your sightseeing plans locally, especially when traveling off-season. The weather can be cold and dreary, and night will draw the shades on your sightseeing before dinnertime. (For more information, see the climate chart in the appendix.)

KNOW BEFORE YOU GO

Your trip is more likely to go smoothly if you plan ahead. Check this list of things to arrange while you're still at home.

You need a **passport**—but no visa or shots—to travel in the countries covered in this book. You may be denied entry into certain European countries if your passport is due to expire within three months of your ticketed date of return. Get it renewed if you'll be cutting it close. It can take up to six weeks to get or renew a passport (for more on passports, see www.travel.state.gov). Pack a photocopy of your passport in your luggage in case the original is lost or stolen.

Book rooms well in advance if you'll be traveling during **peak season** (July and August in resort towns, September and October in convention cities), or over any major holidays or festivals (see list on page 1357).

Call your **debit- and credit-card companies** to let them know the countries you'll be visiting, to ask about fees, to request your PIN code (it will be mailed to you), and more (see page 1299 for details).

Do your homework if you want to buy **travel insurance.** Compare the cost of the insurance to the likelihood of your using it and your potential loss if something goes wrong. Also, check

How Was Your Trip?

Were your travels fun, smooth, and meaningful? If you'd like to share your tips, concerns, and discoveries, please fill out the survey at www.ricksteves.com/feedback. To check out readers' hotel and restaurant reviews—or leave one yourself—visit my travel forum at www.ricksteves.com/travel-forum. I value your feedback. Thanks in advance—it helps a lot.

whether your existing insurance (health, homeowners, or renters) covers you and your possessions overseas. For more tips, see www.ricksteves.com/insurance.

If you're taking an **overnight train** and need a couchette or sleeper—and you *must* leave on a certain day—consider booking it in advance through a US agent (such as www.ricksteves.com/rail), even though it may cost more than buying it in Europe. If you're planning on **renting a car** in Austria, Bosnia-Herzegovina, Hungary, Poland, or Slovenia, bring your driver's license and an International Driving Permit (see page 1332). Confirm pickup hours; many car-rental offices close Saturday afternoon and all day Sunday. Many countries require drivers to buy a toll sticker for driving on expressways; for details per country, see page 1338.

If you plan to visit the **Auschwitz-Birkenau Concentration Camp Memorial,** you're required to reserve ahead on their website (see page 353).

If you'd like to **tour the Hungarian Parliament in Budapest,** consider reserving online a few days ahead to ensure your choice of entrance time (see page 577).

If you plan on visiting **Schönbrunn Palace in Vienna** during the summer or on a weekend, make a reservation in advance (see page 1224).

If you plan to hire a local guide, reserve ahead by email. Popular guides can get booked up.

If you're bringing a **mobile device,** download any apps you might want to use on the road, such as translators, maps, and transit schedules. Check out **Rick Steves Audio Europe,** featuring audio tours of major sights, hours of travel interviews about Eastern Europe, and more (see page 13).

Check the **Rick Steves guidebook updates** page for any recent changes to this book (www.ricksteves.com/update).

Because **airline carry-on restrictions** are always changing, visit the Transportation Security Administration's website (www.tsa.gov) for a list of what you can bring on the plane and for the latest security measures (including screening of electronic devices, which you may be asked to power up).

Traveling as a Temporary Local

We travel all the way to Europe to enjoy differences—to become temporary locals. You'll experience frustrations. Certain truths

that we find "God-given" or "self-evident," such as cold beer, ice in drinks, bottomless cups of coffee, and bigger being better, are suddenly not so true. One of the benefits of travel is the eye-opening realization that there are logical, civil, and even better alternatives. A willingness to go local ensures that you'll enjoy a full dose of European hospitality.

Fortunately for you, hospitality is a local forte. The friendliness of the Eastern Europeans seems to have only been enhanced during the communist era: Tangible resources were in short supply, so an open door and a genial conversation were all that people had to offer. For many Eastern Europeans, the chance to chat with an American is still a delightful novelty. Even so, some people—hardened by decades of being spied on by neighbors and standing in long lines to buy food for their family—seem brusque at first. In my experience, all it takes is a smile and a little effort to befriend these residents of the former "Evil Empire."

Europeans generally like Americans. But if there is a negative aspect to the image of Americans, it's that we are loud, wasteful, ethnocentric, too informal (which can seem disrespectful), and a bit naive.

While Europeans look bemusedly at some of our Yankee excesses—and worriedly at others—they nearly always afford us individual travelers all the warmth we deserve.

Judging from all the happy feedback I receive from travelers who have used this book, it's safe to assume you'll enjoy a great, affordable vacation—with the finesse of an independent, experienced traveler.

Thanks, and happy travels!

Rick Steves

Back Door Travel Philosophy

From *Rick Steves Europe Through the Back Door*

Travel is intensified living—maximum thrills per minute and one of the last great sources of legal adventure. Travel is freedom. It's recess, and we need it.

Experiencing the real Europe requires catching it by surprise and going casual..."through the Back Door."

Affording travel is a matter of priorities. (Make do with the old car.) You can eat and sleep—simply, safely, and enjoyably—anywhere in Europe for $125 a day plus transportation costs. In many ways, spending more money only builds a thicker wall between you and what you traveled so far to see. Europe is a cultural carnival, and time after time, you'll find that its best acts are free and the best seats are the cheap ones.

A tight budget forces you to travel close to the ground, meeting and communicating with the people. Never sacrifice sleep, nutrition, safety, or cleanliness to save money. Simply enjoy the local-style alternatives to expensive hotels and restaurants.

Connecting with people carbonates your experience. Extroverts have more fun. If your trip is low on magic moments, kick yourself and make things happen. If you don't enjoy a place, maybe you don't know enough about it. Seek the truth. Recognize tourist traps. Give a culture the benefit of your open mind. See things as different, but not better or worse. Any culture has plenty to share.

Of course, travel, like the world, is a series of hills and valleys. Be fanatically positive and militantly optimistic. If something's not to your liking, change your liking.

Travel can make you a happier American, as well as a citizen of the world. Our Earth is home to seven billion equally precious people. It's humbling to travel and find that other people don't have the "American Dream"—they have their own dreams. Europeans like us, but with all due respect, they wouldn't trade passports.

Thoughtful travel engages us with the world. In tough economic times, it reminds us what is truly important. By broadening perspectives, travel teaches new ways to measure quality of life.

Globetrotting destroys ethnocentricity, helping us understand and appreciate other cultures. Rather than fear the diversity on this planet, celebrate it. Among your most prized souvenirs will be the strands of different cultures you choose to knit into your own character. The world is a cultural yarn shop, and Back Door travelers are weaving the ultimate tapestry. Join in!

THE CZECH REPUBLIC
Česká Republika

THE CZECH REPUBLIC

Česká Republika

The Czech Republic is geographically small. On a quick visit, you can enjoy a fine introduction while still packing in plenty of surprises. The country has a little of everything for the traveler. Quaint villages? Check. Beautiful landscapes? Check. World-class art? Czech, Czech, and Czech.

While the Czechs have long occupied the lands of the present-day Czech Republic, for most of their history they were second-class citizens, under the thumb of foreign rulers (generally from Germany or Austria). That the Czech nation exists as an independent state today is practically a Cinderella story. So let's get to know the underdog Czechs.

In Czech towns and villages, you'll find a simple joy of life—a holdover from the days of the Renaissance. The deep spirituality of the Baroque era still shapes the national character. The magic of Prague, the beauty of Český Krumlov, and the lyrical quality of the countryside relieve the heaviness caused by the turmoil that passed through here. Get beyond Prague and explore the country's medieval towns. These rugged woods and hilltop castles will make you feel as if you're walking through the garden of your childhood dreams.

Given their imaginative, sometimes fanciful culture, it's no surprise that the Czechs have produced some famously clever writers—from Franz Kafka (who wrote about a man waking up as a giant cockroach) to Karel Čapek (who wrote about artificially created beings he dubbed "roboti," or robots). The unique entertainment form of Black Light Theater—a combination of illusion, pantomime, puppetry, and modern dance—exemplifies Czech creativity (see page 127). And beloved Czech characters—such as the smiling Good Soldier Švejk, who befuddles his Austro-Hungarian army officers by cleverly playing dumb, and the ubiquitous little cartoon mole named Krtek—will quickly become familiar, as you'll see them all over the streets of Prague. (For more on Czech lit, see page 1342.)

Czechs refuse to dumb things down; if you want to visit one of the pretty countryside castles, they'll only let you do it on a

thoughtfully guided tour—as if to guarantee that every visitor will come away with a complete appreciation for the place. Education and intellect are important, and academics are honored in Czech society. At the end of communism, the nation elected a poet, playwright, and philosopher, Václav Havel, to serve two terms as president.

Beyond appreciating his intellect, voters no doubt also appreciated Havel's independent thinking and bold actions (he had been imprisoned by communist authorities for his activities promoting human rights). Perhaps because they've seen their national affairs bungled by centuries of foreign overlords, many Czechs have a healthy suspicion of authority and an admiration for those willing to flout it. Other Czechs with a rebellious spirit are national hero Jan Hus (who refused to recant his condemnation of Church corruption and was burned at the stake); contemporary artist David Černý (whose outrageous stunts are always a lightning rod for controversy); and, of course, the man voted by a wide margin to be the greatest Czech of all time, Jára Cimrman. A fictional character originally created in the 1960s by a pair of radio satirists, Cimrman has taken on a life of his own and today is something of a nationwide practical joke. (For more on Cimrman, see page 25.)

The Czechs' well-studied, sometimes subversive, often worldweary outlook can be perceived by outsiders as cynicism. Czechs have a sharp, dry, often sarcastic sense of humor, as well as a keen sense of irony. They don't suffer fools lightly...and watching a united nations of clueless tourists trample their capital city for the past generation hasn't done wonders for their patience. Cut the Czechs some slack, and show them respect: Be one of the very few visitors who bothers to learn a few pleasantries (hello, please, thank you) in their language. You'll notice the difference in how

Czech Republic Almanac

Official Name: It's the Česká Republika, born on January 1, 1993, along with Slovakia, when the nation of Czechoslovakia—formed after World War I and dominated by the USSR after World War II—split into two countries.

Population: 10.6 million people. About 64 percent are ethnic Czechs who speak Czech. Unlike some of their neighbors (including the very Catholic Poles and Slovaks), Czechs are inclined to be agnostic: One in 10 is Roman Catholic, but the majority (55 percent) list their religion as unaffiliated.

Latitude and Longitude: 50°N and 15°E (similar latitude to Vancouver, British Columbia).

Area: 31,000 square miles (similar to South Carolina or Maine).

Geography: The Czech Republic comprises three regions—Bohemia (Čechy), Moravia (Morava), and a small slice of Silesia (Slezsko). The climate is generally cool and partly cloudy.

Biggest Cities: Prague (the capital, 1.3 million), Brno (370,000), Ostrava (300,000), and Plzeň (168,000).

Economy: The gross domestic product equals about $286 billion (similar to Indiana). The GDP per capita is approximately $26,300 (just under half that of the average American). Major moneymakers for the country include machine parts, cars and trucks (VW subsidiary Škoda has become a highly respected automaker), and beer (leading brands are Pilsner Urquell and the original Budweiser, called "Czechvar" in the US). Industrial production

you're treated. (See "Czech Language," later.)

Of the Czech Republic's three main regions—Bohemia, Moravia, and small Silesia—the best-known is Bohemia. It has nothing to do with beatnik bohemians, but with the Celtic tribe of Bohemia that inhabited the land before the coming of the Slavs. A longtime home of the Czechs, Bohemia, with Prague as its capital, is circled by a naturally fortifying ring of mountains and cut down the middle by the Vltava River. The winegrowing region of Moravia (to the east) is more Slavic and colorful, and more about the land.

Tourists often conjure up images of Bohemia when they think of the Czech Republic. But the country consists of more than rollicking beer halls and gently rolling landscapes. It's also about dreamy wine cellars and fertile Moravian plains, with the rugged Carpathian Mountains on the horizon. Politically and geologically, Bohemia and Moravia are two distinct regions. The soils and climates in which the hops and wine grapes grow are very different...and so are the two regions' mentalities. The boisterousness of the Czech polka contrasts with the melancholy of the Moravian ballad; the political viewpoint of the Prague power broker is at declined during the recent economic crisis, but not beer consumption, which dropped only minimally (the vast majority of Czech beer is consumed domestically). More than a third of trade is with next-door-neighbor Germany; as a result, Germany's economic health one year generally predicts the Czech Republic's fortunes the next.

Currency: 20 Czech crowns (*koruna*, Kč) = about $1.

Government: From 1948 to 1989, Czechoslovakia was a communist state under Soviet control. Today, the Czech Republic is a member of the European Union (since 2004) and a vibrant democracy, with about a 60 percent turnout for elections. Its parliament is made up of 200 representatives elected every 4 years and 81 senators elected for 6 years. No single political party dominates; the current leadership is a coalition of three right-of-center parties united in their emphasis on fiscal responsibility. The president is selected every five years by popular vote. President Miloš Zeman, a populist elected in 2013, appears intent on remaking the country's parliamentary system in order to expand the power of his office.

Flag: The Czech flag is red (bottom), white (top), and blue (a triangle along the hoist side).

The Average Czech: The average Czech has 1.4 kids (slowly rising after the sharp decline that followed the end of communism), will live 78 years, and has one television in the house.

odds with the spirituality of the Moravian bard.

Only a tiny bit of Silesia—around the town of Opava—is part of the Czech Republic today; the rest of the region is in Poland and Germany. (The Habsburgs lost traditionally Czech Silesia to Prussia in the 1740s, and 200 years later, Germany in turn ceded most of it to Poland.) People in Silesia speak a wide variety of dialects that mix Czech, German, and Polish. Perhaps due to their diverse genes and cultural heritage, women from Silesia are famous for being intelligent and beautiful.

Ninety percent of the tourists who visit the Czech Republic see only Prague. But if you venture outside the capital, you'll enjoy traditional towns and villages, great prices, a friendly and gentle countryside dotted by nettles and wild poppies, and almost no international tourists. Since the time of the Habsburgs, fruit trees have lined the country roads for everyone to share. Take your pick.

HELPFUL HINTS

Telephone: In Prague, dial 112 for medical or other emergencies and 158 for police. To summon an ambulance, call 155. If a number starting with 0800 doesn't work, replace the 0800 with 822. For more details on dialing, see page 1318.

Tolls: If you're driving on highways in the Czech Republic, you're required to buy a toll sticker *(dálniční známka)* at the border, a post office, or a gas station (310 Kč/10 days, 440 Kč/1 month). Your rental car may already come with the necessary sticker—ask.

Rail Passes: The Czech Republic is covered by a Czech Republic pass, a Germany-Czech or an Austria-Czech rail pass, the four-country European East pass, the Global Pass, and the Select Pass. If your train travel will be limited to a handful of rides and/or short distances (for example, within the Czech Republic), you're probably better off without a pass—Czech tickets are cheap to buy as you go. But if you're combining Prague with international destinations, a rail pass could save you money. For more detailed advice on figuring out the smartest rail pass options for your train trip, visit the Trains & Rail Passes section of my website at www.ricksteves.com/rail.

CZECH HISTORY

The Czechs have always been at a crossroads of Europe—between the Slavic and Germanic worlds, between Catholicism and Protestantism, and between Cold War East and West. As if having foreseen all of this, the mythical founder of Prague—the beautiful princess Libuše—named her city "Praha" (meaning "threshold" in Czech). Despite these strong external influences, the Czechs have retained their distinct culture...and a dark, ironic sense of humor to keep them laughing through it all.

Charles IV and the Middle Ages (500s-1300s)

The pagan, Slavic tribes that arrived in this part of Europe in the sixth century A.D. were first united by the Prague-based Přemysl dynasty. The main figure of this era was Duke Václav I (A.D. 907-935)—later immortalized in a Christmas carol as "Good King Wenceslas"—who converted the Czechs to Christianity and founded a cathedral at Prague Castle, on a bluff overlooking the Vltava River.

In 1004, Bohemia was incorporated into the Holy Roman Empire (an alliance of mostly German-speaking kingdoms and dukedoms). Within 200 years—thanks to its strategic location and privileged status within the empire—Prague had become one of Europe's largest and most highly cultured cities.

The 14th century was Prague's Golden Age, when Holy Roman Emperor Charles

IV (1316-1378) ruled. Born to a Luxemburger nobleman and a Czech princess, Charles IV was a dynamic man on the cusp of the Renaissance. He lived and studied in several European lands, spoke five languages, and counted Petrarch as a friend —but always felt a deep connection to his mother's Czech roots. Selecting Prague as his seat of power, Charles imported French architects to make the city a grand capital, founded the first university north of the Alps, and invigorated the Czech national spirit. (He popularized the legend of Wenceslas to give his people a near-mythical, King Arthur-type cultural standard-bearer.) Much of Prague's history and architecture—including the famous Charles Bridge, Charles University, St. Vitus Cathedral, and Karlštejn Castle—can be traced to this man's rule. Under Charles IV, the Czech people gained esteem among Europeans.

Jan Hus and Religious Wars (1300s-1600s)

Jan Hus (c. 1369-1415) was a local preacher and professor who got in trouble with the Vatican a hundred years before Martin Luther. Like Luther, Hus preached in the people's language rather than in Latin. To add insult to injury, he complained about Church corruption. Tried for heresy and burned in 1415, Hus became both a religious and a national hero. While each age has defined Hus to its liking, the way he challenged authority while staying true to his beliefs has long inspired and rallied the Czech people. (For more on Hus, see page 58.)

Inspired by Hus' reformist ideas, the Czechs rebelled against both the Roman Catholic Church and German political control. This burst of independent thought led to a period of religious wars. Protestant Czech patriots—like the rough-and-rugged war hero Jan Žižka (often depicted in patriotic art with his trademark eye patch)—fought to maintain Czech autonomy. But ultimately, these rebels were overwhelmed by their Catholic opponents. The result of these wars was the loss of autonomy to Vienna.

Ruled by the Habsburgs of Austria, Prague stagnated—except during the rule of King Rudolf II (1552-1612), a Holy Roman Emperor. With Rudolf living in Prague, the city again emerged as a cultural and intellectual center. Astronomers Johannes Kepler and Tycho Brahe flourished, as did other scientists, and much of the inspiration for Prague's great art can be attributed to the king's patronage.

Not long after this period, Prague entered one of its darker spells. The Thirty Years' War (1618-1648) began in Prague when Czech Protestant nobles, wanting religious and political autonomy, tossed two Catholic Habsburg officials out the window of the castle. (This was one of Prague's many defenestrations—a uniquely Czech solution to political discord, in which offending politicians were literally thrown out the window.) The Czech Estates Uprising lasted two years, ending in a crushing defeat in the Battle of White Mountain (1620), which marked the end of Czech freedom. Twenty-seven leaders of the uprising were executed (today commemorated by crosses on Prague's Old Town Square), most of the old Czech nobility was dispossessed, and Protestants had to convert to Catholicism or leave the country.

Often called "the first world war" because it engulfed so many nations, the Thirty Years' War was particularly tough on Prague. During this period, its population dropped from 60,000 to 25,000. The result of this war was 300 years of Habsburg rule from afar, as Prague became a German-speaking backwater of Vienna.

Czech National Revival (1800s-1918)

The end of Prague as a German city came gradually. During the centuries that the Czech language and culture were suppressed, "Prag" and other cities were populated mainly by German-speaking urbanites, while "backward" peasants kept the old Czech ways alive in the countryside. But as the Industrial Revolution attracted Czech farmers and peasants to the cities, the demographics of the Czech population centers began to shift. Though it remained part of the Habsburg Empire, between 1800 and 1900 Prague went from being an essentially German town to a predominantly Czech one.

As in the rest of Europe, the 19th century was a time of great nationalism, when the age of divine kings and ruling families came to a fitful end. The Czech spirit was first stirred by the work of historian František Palacký, who dug deep into the Czech archives to forge a national narrative. During this time, Czechs were inspired by the completion of Prague's St. Vitus Cathedral, the symphonies of Antonín Dvořák, and the operas of Bedřich Smetana, which were performed in the new National Theater.

Alfons Mucha, a prodigiously talented Czech artist who made a name for himself in the high society of turn-of-the-century Paris, embodied this wave of nationalism. When he could have lived out his days in the lap of luxury in Paris or New York City, Mucha chose instead to return to his homeland and spend decades painting a magnum opus celebrating the historic journey of the Czechs and all Slavs—the *Slav Epic*.

After the Habsburgs' Austro-Hungarian Empire suffered defeat in World War I, their vast holdings broke apart and became independent countries. Among these was a union of Bohemia, Moravia, and Slovakia, the brainchild of a clever politician named Tomáš Garrigue Masaryk (see sidebar on page 104). The new nation, Czechoslovakia, was proclaimed in 1918, with Prague as its capital.

Jára Cimrman: The Greatest Czech?

"I am such a complete atheist that I am afraid God will punish me." Such is the pithy wisdom of Jára Cimrman, the man overwhelmingly voted the "Greatest Czech of All Time" in a 2005 national poll. Who is Jára Cimrman? A philosopher? An explorer? An inventor? He is all these things, yes, and much more.

Born in the mid-19th century, Cimrman studied in Vienna before journeying the world. He traversed the Atlantic in a steamboat he designed himself, taught drama to peasants in Peru, and drifted across the Arctic Sea on an iceberg. He invented the lightbulb, but Edison beat him to the patent office by five minutes. It was he who suggested to the Americans the idea for a Panama Canal, though, as usual, he was never credited. Indeed, Cimrman surreptitiously advised many of the world's greats: Eiffel on his tower, Einstein on his theories of relativity, Chekhov on his plays. ("You can't just have *two* sisters," Cimrman told the playwright. "How about three?") Long before the world knew of Sartre or Camus, Cimrman was writing tracts such as *The Essence of the Existence*, which would become the foundation for his philosophy of "Cimrmanism," also known as "nonexistentialism." (Its central premise: "Existence cannot not exist.")

Despite Jára Cimrman's genius, the "Greatest Czech" poll's sponsors had a single objection to his candidacy: He's not real, but the brainchild of Czech humorists Zdeněk Svěrák and Jiří Šebánek, who brought this patriotic Renaissance Man to life in 1967 in a satirical radio play.

How should we interpret the fact that the Czechs chose a fictional character as their greatest countryman over any of their flesh-and-blood national heroes—say, Charles IV (the 14th-century Holy Roman Emperor who established Prague as the cultural and intellectual capital of Europe), or Martina Navrátilová (someone who plays a sport with bright green balls)?

I like to think that the vote for Cimrman says something about the country's enthusiasm for blowing raspberries in the face of authority. From the times of the Czech kings who used crafty diplomacy to keep the German menace at bay, to the days of Jan Hus and his criticism of the Catholic Church, to the flashes of anticommunist revolt that at last sparked the Velvet Revolution in 1989—the Czechs have maintained a healthy disrespect for those who would tell them how to live their lives. Their vote for a fictional personage, says Cimrman's co-creator Svěrák, shows two things about the Czech nation: "That it is skeptical about those who are major figures and those who are supposedly the 'Greatest.' And that the only certainty that has saved the nation many times throughout history is its humor."

Troubles of the 20th Century (1918-1989)

Independence lasted only 20 years. In the notorious Munich Agreement of September 1938—much to the dismay of the Czechs and Slovaks—Great Britain and France peacefully ceded to Hitler the so-called Sudetenland (a fringe around the edge of Bohemia, populated mainly by people of German descent; see sidebar on page 200). It wasn't long before Hitler seized the rest of Czechoslovakia...and the Holocaust began. Under the Nazi puppet ruler Reinhard Heydrich, tens of thousands of Jews were sent first to the concentration camp at Terezín, and later to Auschwitz and other death camps. Even after Heydrich was assassinated by a pair of Czech paratroopers, the campaign of genocide continued. Out of the 55,000 Jews living in Prague before the war, more than 80 percent perished during the Holocaust; throughout the Czech lands, an estimated 260,000 Jews were murdered.

For centuries, Prague's cultural makeup had consisted of a rich mix of Czech, German, and Jewish people—historically, they were almost evenly divided. With the Jewish population decimated, part of that delicate tapestry was gone forever. And after World War II ended, the three million people of Germanic descent who lived in Czechoslovakia were pushed into Germany. Their forced resettlement—which led to the deaths of untold numbers of Germans (what we'd today call "ethnic cleansing")—was the initiative of Czechoslovak President Edvard Beneš, who had ruled from exile in London throughout the war (see page 200). Today's Czech Republic is largely homogenous—about 95 percent Czechs.

Although Prague escaped the bombs of World War II, it went directly from the Nazi frying pan into the communist fire. A local uprising freed the city from the Nazis on May 8, 1945, but the Soviets "liberated" them on May 9.

The early communist era (1948-1968) was a mixture of misguided zeal, Stalinist repressions, and attempts to wed socialism with democracy. The "Prague Spring" period of political reform—initiated by a young generation of progressive communists in 1968, led by the charismatic Slovak politician Alexander Dubček—came to an abrupt halt under the treads of Warsaw Pact tanks (for details, see page 84). Dubček was exiled (and made a backwoods forest ranger), and the years of "normalization" following the unsuccessful revolt were particularly disheartening. A wave of protests spread through the country in 1969, as furious young Czechs and Slovaks lit themselves on fire to decry communist oppression. But the status quo would hold strong for another 20 years.

In the late 1980s, the communists began constructing Prague's huge Žižkov TV tower (now the city's tallest structure)—not only to broadcast Czech TV transmissions, but also to jam Western signals. The Metro, built at about the same time, was intended for mass transit, but was also designed to be a giant fallout shelter for protection against capitalist bombs.

Every small town had its own set of loudspeakers for broadcasting propaganda. (If you look closely, you'll still see these as you pass through the countryside.) Locals remember growing up with these mouthpieces of government boasting of successes ("This year, despite many efforts of sabotage on the part of certain individuals in service of imperialist goals, we have surpassed the planned output of steel by 195 percent"); calling people to action ("There will be no school tomorrow as all will join the farmers in the fields for an abundant harvest"); or quelling disturbances ("Some citizens may have heard about alien forces in our society taking advantage of this week's anniversary to spread unrest. This is to reassure you that the situation is firmly under control and nothing is happening in Olomouc or in Prague. Nevertheless, for their own safety, we suggest all citizens stay home").

Eventually the Soviet empire crumbled, beginning with reforms in Hungary in the summer of 1989 and culminating in the fall of the Berlin Wall that October. A few weeks later, Czechoslovakia regained its freedom in the student- and artist-powered 1989 "Velvet Revolution," so called because there were no casualties...or even broken windows (for more information, see page 86). Václav Havel, a poet, playwright, and philosopher who had been imprisoned by the communist regime, became Czechoslovakia's first post-communist president.

"It's Not You, It's Me": The Velvet Divorce (1989-1993)

In the post-communist age of new possibility, the two peoples of Czechoslovakia began to wonder if, in fact, they belonged together.

Ever since they joined with the Czechs in 1918, the Slovaks felt overshadowed by Prague (unmistakably the political, economic, and cultural center of the country). And the Czechs resented the financial burden of carrying their poorer neighbors to the east. In this new world of flux and freedom, long-standing tensions came to a head.

The dissolution of Czechoslovakia began over a hyphen, as the Slovaks wanted to rename the country Czecho-Slovakia. Ideally, this symbolic move would come with a redistribution of powers: two capitals and two UN reps, but one national bank and a single currency. This idea was rejected, and in June of 1992, Slovak nationalist candidate Vladimír Mečiar fared surprisingly well in the elections, suggesting that the Slovaks were serious about secession. The politicians plowed ahead, getting serious about the split in September of 1992. The transition took only three months from start to finish.

The people of Czechoslovakia never actually voted on the separation; in fact, public opinion polls in both regions were two-thirds *against* the split. This makes Slovakia quite possibly the only country in history to gain independence even though its citizens didn't want it.

The Velvet Divorce became official on January 1, 1993, and each country ended up with its own capital, currency, and head of state. For most the divorce dissolved tensions, and a decade and a half later, Czechs and Slovaks still feel closer to each other than to any other nationality.

The Czech Republic Today (1990s to Present)

In recent times, the Czech Republic's most significant turning point occurred on May 1, 2004, when the country joined the European Union. Three and a half years later, it entered the Schengen Agreement, effectively erasing its borders for the purposes of travel.

After 14 years in office, a term-limited Václav Havel stepped down in 2003. He died in 2011. While he's fondly remembered by Czechs as a great thinker, writer, and fearless leader of the opposition movement during the communist days, many consider him to have been less successful as a president.

The next president, Václav Klaus, had been the pragmatic author of the economic reforms in the 1990s. Klaus' surprising win in the 2003 election symbolized a change from revolutionary times, when philosophers became kings, to modern humdrum politics, when offices are gained by bargaining with the opposition (Communist Party votes in the Parliament were the decisive factor in Klaus' election).

In 2008, Klaus' re-election campaign was blemished by revelations of widespread corruption in the privatizing business sector. The Greens and the Social Democrats had chosen as their candidate University of Michigan economics professor Jan Švejnar, the most outspoken critic of Klaus' reforms in the 1990s. And though public support was evenly divided between the two candidates, behind-the-scenes deals in Parliament allowed the ruling conservatives to maintain their majority and keep Klaus in power. Public outrage at Klaus' controversial re-election eventually led to a change in the country's constitution, which allowed for the first election of a president directly by the people (rather than by Parliament) in January of 2013.

The winner of this historic presidential election was Miloš Zeman, the other political heavyweight of the 1990s. President Zeman, a populist intent on increasing his share of power, quickly began dismantling an unpopular administration whose main goal was to introduce fiscal austerity measures to reduce the country's growing debt.

In the 2013 parliamentary elections, Czech voters—disillusioned with the perceived corruption of both the Social Democrats and the Conservatives—rejected the political status quo. Two newly emerged political entities, each formed around a successful businessman, gained almost a third of the votes. One of these new protest parties, ANO, eventually formed a ruling coalition with the Social and Christian Democrats, fueling hopes for more effective government and less corruption. (Cynics predict that corruption will shrink only because business interests will now have direct access to the government.)

But every country has its political wrangling and corruption scandals. What really matters to Czechs is sports. Like most Europeans, Czechs are obsessed with soccer. The Czech national team routinely finishes impressively in international tournaments. Domestically, the two oldest and most successful soccer clubs are the bitter Prague rivals, AC Sparta and AC Slavia. But Czechs are an even more impressive world power when it comes to hockey: the national team has won several world championships and Olympic medals. Currently, more than 40 Czech players take the ice in America's NHL—think of Jaromír Jágr, one of the NHL's all-time leading scorers, and Dominik "The Dominator" Hašek, a top goaltender.

Overall, the recent trajectory of Czech history is trending very positive. Both in the capital and in rural villages, the country feels more affluent than ever before, all while celebrating its inherent Czech-ness. And Prague is, quite justifiably, one of the most popular tourist destinations in Europe.

CZECH FOOD

The Czechs have one of Europe's most stick-to-your-ribs cuisines. Heavy on meat, potatoes, and cabbage, it's hearty and tasty—designed to keep peasants fueled through a day of hard work. Some people could eat this stuff forever, while others seek a frequent break in the form of ethnic restaurants (bigger towns such as Prague, Český Krumlov, and Kutná Hora have several options).

A Czech restaurant is a social place where people come to relax. Tables are not private. You can ask to join someone, and you will most likely make some new friends. After a sip of beer, ask for the *jídelní lístek* (menu).

Soups: *Polévka* (soup) is the most essential part of a meal. The saying goes: "The soup fills you up, the dish plugs it up." Some of the thick soups for a cold day are *zelná* or *zelňačka* (cabbage), *čočková* (lentil), *fazolová* (bean), and *dršťková* (tripe—delicious if

Czech Dumplings

Czech dumplings *(knedlíky)* resemble steamed white bread. They come in plain or potato *(bramborové)* varieties, are meant to be drowned in gravy (dumplings never accompany sauceless dishes), and are eaten with a knife and fork. Sweet dumplings, listed in the dessert section on a menu, are a tempting option during summer, when they are loaded with fresh strawberries, blueberries, apricots, or plums and garnished with custard and melted butter. Beware, though, that many restaurants like to cheat by filling the sticky dough with a smattering of jam or fruit preserve; before ordering, ask the waiter for details, or discreetly inspect that plate at your neighbor's table. Dumplings with frozen fruit lose some of the flavor, but are still worth trying.

fresh, chewy as gum if not). The lighter soups are *hovězí* or *slepičí vývar s nudlemi* (beef or chicken broth with noodles), *pórková* (leek), and *květáková* (cauliflower).

Bread: *Pečivo* (bread) is either delivered with the soup, or you need to ask for it; it's always charged separately depending on how many *rohlíky* (rolls) or slices of *chleba* (yeast bread) you eat.

Main Dishes: These can either be *hotová jídla* (quick, ready-to-serve standard dishes, in some places available only during lunch hours, generally 11:00-14:30) or the more specialized *jídla na objednávku* or *minutky* (plates prepared when you order).

The word *pečené* (roasted) shows up frequently on menus, whether it's *vepřová pečeně* (pork roast), *pečené kuře* (roasted chicken), or *pečená kachna* (roasted duck). Other popular meat dishes are *smažený řízek* (fried pork fillet, like Wiener schnitzel), *guláš* (a thick, meaty stew), and *svíčková na smetaně* (beef tenderloin in cream sauce). If you're spending the night out with friends, have a beer and feast on the huge *vepřové koleno* (pork knuckle), usually served with mustard *(hořčicí)*, horseradish sauce *(křenem)*, and yeast bread *(chleba)*.

In this landlocked country, fish options typically are limited to *kapr* (carp) and *pstruh* (trout), prepared in a variety of ways and served with potatoes or fries—although recently Czech perch and Norwegian salmon have cropped up on many local menus.

Vegetarians can go for the delicious *smažený sýr s bramborem* (fried cheese with potatoes) or default to *čočka s vejci* (lentils with fried egg).

Starches and Garnishes: *Hotová jídla* come with set garnishes, but if ordering à la carte *(jídla na objednávku)*, you'll typically need to order your garnishes separately (otherwise you'll get only the main dish). In either case, the most common sides are *knedlíky* (bread dumplings, described in the sidebar), *zelím* (cabbage), and *bramborem* (potatoes).

Salad: *Šopský salát,* like a Greek salad, is usually the best salad option (a mix of tomatoes, cucumbers, peppers, onion, and feta cheese with vinegar and olive oil). The waiter will bring it with the main dish, unless you specify that you want it before.

Dessert: For *moučník* (dessert), there are *palačinka* (crêpes served with fruit or jam), *lívance* (small pancakes with jam and curd), *zmrzlinový pohár* (ice-cream sundae), or fruit-filled dumplings. Many restaurants will offer different sorts of *koláče* (pastries) and *štrůdl* (apple strudel), but it's much better to get these directly from a bakery. A *větrník* is a super-decadent, glazed cream puff.

All over Prague's Old Town, you'll find kiosks selling a treat called *trdlo* or *trdelník.* This is a long ribbon of dough wrapped

around a stick, slowly cooked on a rotisserie, then rolled in cinnamon sugar or other toppings. While these aren't "traditional Czech" (they were imported recently from Hungary), they do offer a fresh, sweet treat. Try to get one that's still warm, rather than one wrapped in plastic—it makes a big difference.

Beverages: No Czech meal is complete without a cup of strong *turecká káva* (Turkish coffee—finely ground coffee that only partly dissolves, leaving "mud" on the bottom, highly caffeinated and drunk without milk). Although espressos and instant coffees have made headway in the past few years, some Czechs regard them as a threat to tradition.

Czech mineral waters (*minerálka)* have a high mineral content. They're naturally carbonated because they come from the springs in the many Czech spas (Mattoni, the most common brand, is from Carlsbad). If you want still water, ask for *voda bez bublinek* (water without bubbles). Tap water is generally not served. Water comes bottled and generally costs more than beer.

Bohemia is beer country, with Europe's best and cheapest brew (for all the details, see the sidebar). Moravians prefer wine and *slivovice* (SLEE-voh-veet-seh), a plum brandy so highly valued that it's the de facto currency of the Carpathian Mountains (often used for bartering with farmers and other mountain folk). *Medovina* ("honey wine") is mead.

THE CZECH REPUBLIC

Czech Beer

Czechs are among the world's most enthusiastic beer *(pivo)* drinkers—adults drink an average of 80 gallons a year. The pub is a place to have fun, complain, discuss art and politics, talk hockey, and chat with locals and visitors alike. Whether you're in a *restaurace* (restaurant), *hostinec* (pub), or *hospoda* (bar), a beer will land on your table upon the slightest hint to the waiter, and a new pint will automatically appear when the old glass is almost empty (until you tell the waiter to stop). Order beer from the tap (*točené* means "draft," *sudové pivo* means "keg beer"). A *pivo* is large (0.5 liter—17 oz); a *malé pivo* is small (0.3 liter—10 oz).

The Czechs invented Pilsner-style lager in nearby Plzeň and the result, Pilsner Urquell, is on tap in many local pubs. But the Czechs produce plenty of other good beers, including Krušovice, Gambrinus, Staropramen, and Kozel. Budvar, from the town of Budějovice ("Budweis" in German), is popular with Anheuser-Busch's attorneys. (The Czech and the American breweries for years disputed the "Budweiser" brand name. The solution: The Czech Budweiser is sold under its own name in Europe, China, and Africa, while in America it is marketed as Czechvar.)

The big degree symbol on bottles does not indicate alcohol content. Instead, it is a measurement used by brewers to track the density of certain ingredients. As a rough guide, 10 degrees is about 3.5 percent alcohol, 12 degrees is about 4.2 percent alcohol, and 11 and 15 degrees are dark beers. The most popular Czech beers are about as potent as German beers and only slightly stronger than typical American brews.

Each establishment has only one brand of beer on tap; to try a particular kind, look for its sign outside. A typical pub serves only one brand each of 10-degree, 12-degree, and dark beer. Czechs do not mix beer with anything, and they do not hop from pub to pub (in one night, it is said, you must stay loyal to one woman and to one beer). *Na zdraví* means "to your health" in Czech.

Microbrews are gaining in popularity. While the trend for much of the last 20 years has been for the biggest beer corporations to buy up or edge out the smaller companies, Czechs have been moving beyond "eurotaste" beers to creative microbrews. Now, more and more restaurants are making their own beer or serving beer only from independent breweries.

In bars and restaurants, you can go wild with memorable liqueurs, most of which cost about a dollar a shot. Experiment. *Fernet*, a bitter drink made from many herbs, is the leading Czech aperitif. Absinthe, made from wormwood and herbs, is a watered-down version of the hallucinogenic drink that's illegal in much of Europe. It's famous as the muse of many artists (including Henri de Toulouse-Lautrec in Paris more than a century ago). *Becherovka*, made of 13 herbs and 38 percent alcohol, was used to settle upset aristocratic tummies and as an aphrodisiac. This velvety drink remains popular today. *Becherovka* and tonic mixed together is nicknamed *beton* ("concrete"). If you drink three, you'll find out why.

CZECH LANGUAGE

Czech is a Slavic language closely related to its Polish and Slovak neighbors. These days, English is widely spoken, and you'll find the language barrier minimal. Among older people, German is a common second language.

Czech pronunciation can be tricky. The language has a dizzying array of diacritical marks (little doo-hickeys over some letters that affect pronunciation). Most notably, some letters can be topped with a *háček (č, š, ž, ň, ě)*. Here are some clues for Czech pronunciation:

- **j** sounds like "y" as in "yarn"
- **c** sounds like "ts" as in "cats"
- **č** sounds like "ch" as in "chicken"
- **š** sounds like "sh" as in "shrimp"
- **ž** sounds like "zh" as in "leisure"
- **ň** sounds like "ny" as in "canyon"
- **ě** sounds like "yeh" as in "yet"
- **ď** sounds like the "dj" sound in "ledge"

Czech has one sound that occurs in no other language: ř (as in "Dvořák"), which sounds like a cross between a rolled "r" and "zh." It takes a lot of practice, but if you can master this sound, you'll impress the Czechs.

An acute accent *(á, é, í, ó, ú, ý)* means you linger on that vowel; it does not indicate stress, which invariably falls on the first sylla-ble. For example, the word for "please" is *prosím*, with the emphasis on the first syllable but a long "i" sound at the end: PROH-zeeeem.

Prague is flooded with tourists, most of whom don't bother

to learn a single word of the local language. To ingratiate yourself to your hosts—not to mention be a sensitive traveler—take some time to learn the Czech essentials. You'll find Czech survival phrases on the following pages.

When navigating town, these words might be helpful: *město* (MYEHS-toh, town), *náměstí* (nah-myehs-tee, square), *ulica* (OO-leet-sah, street), *nábřeži* (NAH-bzheh-zhee, embankment road), and *most* (mohst, bridge).

Czech Survival Phrases

The emphasis in Czech words usually falls on the first syllable—though don't overdo it, as this stress is subtle. A vowel with an accent (á, é, í, ú, ý) is held longer. The combination ch sounds like the guttural "kh" sound in the Scottish word "loch." The uniquely Czech ř (as in Dvořák) sounds like a cross between a rolled "r" and "zh"; in the phonetics, it's "zh." Here are a few English words that all Czechs know: super, OK, pardon, stop, menu, problem, and no problem.

English	Czech	Pronunciation
Hello. (formal)	Dobrý den.	**doh**-bree dehn
Hi. / Bye. (informal)	Ahoj.	**ah**-hoy
Do you speak English?	Mluvíte anglicky?	**mloo**-vee-teh **ahn**-glits-kee
Yes. / No.	Ano. / Ne.	**ah**-noh / neh
I don't understand.	Nerozumím.	neh-roh-zoo-meem
Please. / You're welcome. / Can I help you?	Prosím.	**proh**-seem
Thank you.	Děkuji.	**dyeh**-kwee
Excuse me. / I'm sorry.	Promiňte.	**proh**-meen-teh
Good.	Dobře.	**dohb**-zheh
Goodbye.	Nashledanou.	**nah**-skleh-dah-noh
one / two / three	jeden / dva / tři	**yay**-dehn / dvah / tzhee
four / five / six	čtyři / pět / šest	**chtee**-zhee / pyeht / shehst
seven / eight	sedm / osm	**seh**-dum / **oh**-sum
nine / ten	devět / deset	**dehv**-yeht / **doh** ocht
hundred / thousand	sto / tisíc	stoh / **tee**-seets
How much?	Kolik?	**koh**-leek
local currency	koruna (Kč)	koh-**roo**-nah
Write it?	Napište to?	nah-**pish**-teh toh
Is it free?	Je to zadarmo?	yeh toh **zah**-dar-moh
Is it included?	Je to v ceně?	yeh tohf **tsay**-nyeh
Where can I find / buy...?	Kde mohu najít / koupit...?	guh-**deh** moh-hoo **nah**-yeet / **koh**-pit
I'd like... (said by a man)	Rád bych...	rahd bikh
I'd like... (said by a woman)	Ráda bych...	**rah**-dah bikh
We'd like...	Rádi bychom...	**rah**-dyee bee-khohm
...a room.	...pokoj.	**poh**-koy
...a ticket to ___. (destination)	...jízdenka do ___.	**yeez**-dehn-kah doh ___
Is it possible?	Je to možné?	yeh toh **mohzh**-neh
Where is...?	Kde je...?	guh-**deh** yeh
...the train station	...nádraží	**nah**-drah-zhee
...the bus station	...autobusové nádraží	**ow**-toh-boo-soh-veh **nah**-drah-zhee
...the tourist information office	...turistická informační kancelář	**too**-rih-stit-skah **een**-for-mahch-nee **kahn**-tseh-lahzh
...the toilet	...vécé	**veht**-seh
men / women	muži / ženy	**moo**-zhee / **zheh**-nee
left / right / straight	vlevo / vpravo / rovně	**vleh**-voh / **fprah**-voh / **rohv**-nyeh
At what time...?	V kolik...?	**fkoh**-leek
...does this open / close	...otevírají / zavírají	oh-teh-vee-rah-yee / **zah**-vee-rah-yee
Just a moment, please.	Moment, prosím.	**moh**-mehnt **proh**-seem
now / soon / later	teď / brzy / později	tedge / **bir**-zih / **pohz**-dyeh-yee
today / tomorrow	dnes / zítra	duh-**nehs** / **zee**-trah

THE CZECH REPUBLIC

In a Czech Restaurant

English	Czech	Pronunciation
I'd like to reserve... (said by a man)	Rád bych zarezervoval....	rahd bikh **zah**-reh-zehr-voh-vahl
I'd like to reserve... (said by a woman)	Ráda bych zarezervovala....	**rah**-dah bikh **zah**-reh-zehr-voh-vah-lah
...a table for one / two.	...stůl pro jednoho / dva.	stool proh **yehd**-noh-hoh / dvah
Non-smoking.	Nekuřácký.	neh-kuhzh-aht-skee
Is this table free?	Je tento stůl volný?	yeh **tehn**-toh stool **vohl**-nee
Can I help you?	Mohu vám pomoci?	**moh**-hoo vahm poh-**moht**-see
The menu (in English), please.	Jídelní lístek (v angličtině), prosím.	**yee**-dehl-nee **lee**-stehk (**fahn**-gleech-tee-nyeh) **proh**-eem
Service is / isn't included.	Spropitné je / není zahrnuto.	**sproh**-pit-neh yeh / **neh**-nee **zah**-har-noo-toh
"to go"	s sebou	**seh**-boh
with / and / or	s / a / nebo	suh / ah / **neh**-boh
ready-to-eat meal	hotová jídla	**hoh**-toh-vah **yeed**-lah
meal on request	minutky	**mih**-noot-kee
appetizers	předkrm	**pzhehd**-krim
bread	chléb	khlehb
cheese	sýr	seer
sandwich	sendvič	**sehnd**-vich
soup / salad	polévka / salát	poh-**lehv**-kah / **sah**-laht
meat	maso	**mah**-soh
poultry	drůbež	**droo**-behzh
fish	ryby	**rih**-bih
fruit / vegetables	ovoce / zelenina	**oh**-voht-seh / **zeh**-leh-nyee-nah
dessert	dezert	**deh**-zehrt
(tap) water	voda (z kohoutku)	**voh**-dah (**skoh**-hoht-koo)
mineral water	minerální voda	**mih**-neh-rahl-nyee **voh**-dah
carbonated / not carbonated (spoken)	s bublinkami / bez bublinek	**sboob**-leen-kah-mee / behz **boo**-blee-nehk
carbonated / not carbonated (printed)	perlivá / neperlivá	**pehr**-lee-vah / **neh**-pehr-lee-vah
milk	mléko	**mleh**-koh
(orange) juice	(pomerančový) džus	(**poh**-mehr-ahn-choh-vee) "juice"
coffee / tea	káva / čaj	**kah**-vah / chai
wine	víno	**vee**-noh
red / white	červené / bílé	**chehr**-veh-neh / **bee**-leh
sweet / dry	sladké / suché	**slahd**-keh / **soo**-kheh
glass / bottle	sklenka / lahev	**sklehn**-kah / **lah**-hehv
beer	pivo	**pee**-voh
light / dark	světlé / tmavé	**svyeht**-leh / **tmah**-veh
Cheers!	Na zdraví!	nah zdrah-**vee**
Enjoy your meal.	Dobrou chuť.	**doh**-broh khoot
More. / Another.	Více. / Další.	**veet**-seh / **dahl**-shee
The same.	To samé.	toh **sah**-meh
The bill.	Účet.	**oo**-cheht
I'll pay.	Zaplatím.	**zah**-plah-teem
tip	spropitné	**sproh**-pit-neh
Delicious!	Výborné!	**vee**-bohr-neh

PRAGUE

Praha

Few cities can match Prague's over-the-top romance, evocative Old World charm...and tourist crowds. Prague is equal parts historic and fun. No other place in Europe has become popular so quickly. And for good reason: Prague, the only Central European capital to escape the large-scale bombing of the last century's wars, is one of Europe's best-preserved cities. It's filled with sumptuous Art Nouveau facades, offers tons of cheap Mozart and Vivaldi concerts, and brews some of the best beer in Europe.

Prague is a photographer's delight. You'll wind through walkable neighborhoods, past statues of bishops and pastel facades adorned with gables, balconies, lanterns, and a zillion little architectural details. Prague itself seems a work of art. Besides its medieval and Baroque look, it's a world of willowy Art Nouveau paintings and architecture. You'll also see rich remnants of its strong Jewish heritage and stark reminders of the communist era. And you'll meet an entrepreneurial mix of locals and expats, all with their own brilliant schemes of how to make money in the tourist trade.

Escape the crowds into the back lanes and pretend you're strolling through the 18th century. Duck into pubs to enjoy the hearty food and good pilsner beer, and tour museums packed with fine art. Delve into one of Europe's top stops.

PLANNING YOUR TIME

A few days in Prague is plenty of time to get a solid feel for the city and enjoy some side-trips. If you're in a rush, you'll need a minimum of two full days (with three nights, or two nights and a night train) for a good introduction to the city. Keep in mind that Jewish Quarter sights close on Saturday and Jewish holidays. Some museums, mainly in the Old Town, are closed on Monday, as is Veletržní Palace (which houses the *Slav Epic*).

Prague in Two or More Days

Here's my suggested plan for fully experiencing Prague in two days. I've offered more suggestions should you have more time. Split your nights between beer halls, live music, and (if it interests you) Black Light Theater.

Day 1

9:00   Take my "Prague Old Town Walk" to get oriented to the city's core. Along the way, take time to enter some of the sights (including the Municipal House) and climb at least one of the old towers—at the Old Town Hall or at either end of the Charles Bridge—to enjoy the view.

13:00   Have lunch either in the Old Town or Little Quarter. Explore the Little Quarter (Kampa Island, Lennon Wall, Little Quarter Square).

15:00   Explore the Jewish Quarter.

Day 2

8:00   Get an early start from your hotel and zip up to the castle on the tram. Be at St. Vitus Cathedral when it opens at 9:00, then visit the rest of the castle sights.

11:00   As you leave the castle, tour the Lobkowicz Palace.

12:00   Have lunch in the Little Quarter, below the castle.

13:00   Ride the tram to Veletržní Palace to see Mucha's *Slav Epic*.

14:30   Tram back to town to see Wenceslas Square and tour the Mucha Museum to appreciate another facet of this talented artist (unless you're already Mucha-ed out).

16:30   Squeeze in one more museum—perhaps the Museum of Medieval Art or the Museum of Communism.

   Note: If you'd rather sleep in today, flip this plan—do Wenceslas Square, the Mucha Museum, and *Slav Epic* in the morning, then tram up to the castle in the early afternoon (by about 14:00), when the crowds are dispersing.

Day 3 and Beyond

If you have more time, fit in additional museums that interest you. If you have at least four days, Prague has a wide variety of worthwhile day trips at its doorstep. I'd prioritize Kutná Hora (delightful small town with gorgeous cathedral and famous bone church), the Terezín Memorial (for Holocaust history), and/or Konopiště Castle (with a lived-in Habsburg interior). Český Krumlov is

another wonderful destination, but it's a bit far for a side-trip from Prague—it's much better as an overnight.

Orientation to Prague

PRAGUE: A VERBAL MAP

Residents call their town "Praha" (PRAH-hah). It's big, with about 1.3 million people (swelling to 2 million in the metropolitan area). But during a quick visit, you'll focus on its relatively compact old center.

The Vltava River divides the city in two. East of the river are the Old Town and New Town, the Main Train Station, and most of the recommended hotels. To the west of the river is Prague Castle and, below that, the sleepy Little Quarter. Connecting the two halves are several bridges, including the landmark Charles Bridge.

Think of Prague as a collection of neighborhoods. In fact, until about 1800, Prague actually was four distinct towns with four town squares, all separated by fortified walls. Each town had a unique character, drawn from the personality of its first settlers. Today, much of Prague's charm survives in the distinct spirit of these towns.

Old Town (Staré Město): Nestled in the bend of the river, this is the historic core, where most tourists spend their time. It's

PRAGUE

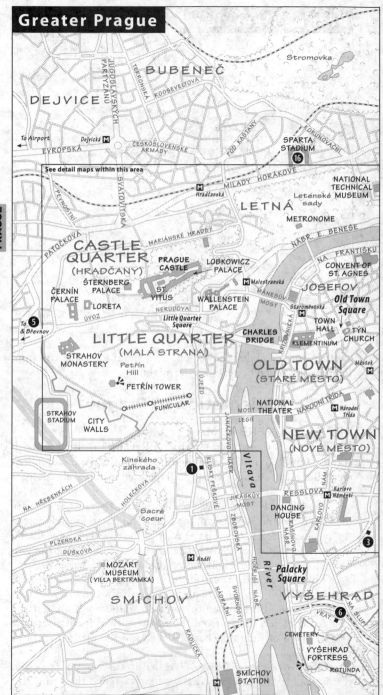

Greater Prague

Stromovka

BUBENEČ

DEJVICE

JUGOSLÁVSKÝCH PARTYZÁNŮ

TERRONSKÁ

ROOSEVELTOVA

To Airport

Dejvická Ⓜ

ČESKOSLOVENSKÉ ARMÁDY

EVROPSKÁ

POD KAŠTANY

KORUNOVAČNÍ

SPARTA STADIUM ⓰

See detail maps within this area

SVATOVÍTSKÁ

MILADY HORÁKOVÉ

Hradčanská Ⓜ

LETNÁ

Letenské sady

NATIONAL TECHNICAL MUSEUM

PEVNOSTNÍ

METRONOME

NÁBŘ. E. BENEŠE

PATOČKOVA

MARIÁNSKÉ HRADBY

NA FRANTIŠKU

CASTLE QUARTER (HRADČANY)

PRAGUE CASTLE

LOBKOWICZ PALACE

CONVENT OF ST. AGNES

Malostranská Ⓜ

JOSEFOV

ČERNÍN PALACE

ŠTERNBERG PALACE

ST. VITUS

MANESÚV MOST

Old Town Square

LORETA

WALLENSTEIN PALACE

Staroměstská Ⓜ

TOWN HALL

TÝN CHURCH

To Ⓢ & Břevnov

ÚVOZ

NERUDOVA

Little Quarter Square

CHARLES BRIDGE

KŘIŽOVNICKÁ

KLEMENTINUM

LITTLE QUARTER (MALÁ STRANA)

OLD TOWN (STARÉ MĚSTO)

Můstek Ⓜ

STRAHOV MONASTERY

Petřín Hill

PETŘÍN TOWER

FUNICULAR

STRAHOV STADIUM

CITY WALLS

ÚJEZD

MOST LEGII

NATIONAL THEATER

NÁRODNÍ TŘÍDA

NEW TOWN (NOVÉ MĚSTO)

Národní Třída Ⓜ

Kinského zahrada

Ⓞ

ELIŠKY PEŠKOVÉ

Vltava

NA HŘEBENKÁCH

HOLEČKOVA

JIRÁSKŮV MOST

ZBOROVSKÁ

RESSLOVA

KARLOVO NÁM.

Karlovo Náměstí Ⓜ

DANCING HOUSE

KARLOVO

RAŠÍNOVO NÁBŘ.

Ⓒ

PLZEŇSKÁ

DUŠKOVA

Sacré coeur

MOZART MUSEUM (VILLA BERTRAMKA)

Anděl Ⓜ

Palacky Square

RADLICKÁ

NÁDRAŽNÍ

SVORNOSTI

HOŘEJŠÍ NÁBŘ.

River

VYŠEHRAD

Ⓥ

VRAT

SMÍCHOV

CEMETERY

VYŠEHRAD FORTRESS

ROTUNDA

SMÍCHOV STATION

Ⓜ

NA SLUPI

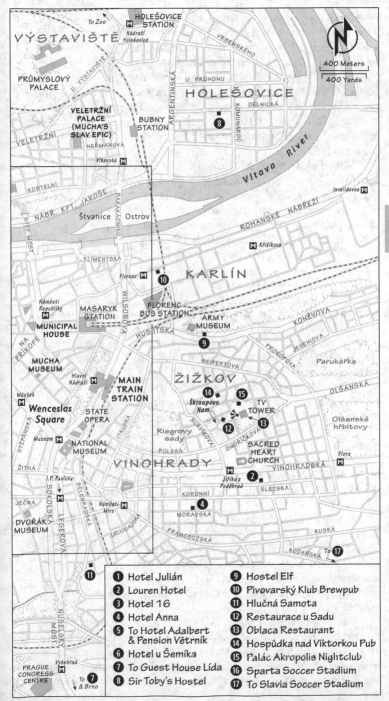

PRAGUE

1. Hotel Julián
2. Louren Hotel
3. Hotel 16
4. Hotel Anna
5. To Hotel Adalbert & Pension Větrník
6. Hotel u Šemíka
7. To Guest House Lída
8. Sir Toby's Hostel
9. Hostel Elf
10. Pivovarský Klub Brewpub
11. Hlučná Samota
12. Restaurace u Sadu
13. Oblaca Restaurant
14. Hospůdka nad Viktorkou Pub
15. Palác Akropolis Nightclub
16. Sparta Soccer Stadium
17. To Slavia Soccer Stadium

pedestrian-friendly, with small winding streets, old buildings, shops, and beer halls and cafés. In the center sits the charming Old Town Square. Slicing east-west through the Old Town is the main pedestrian axis, along Celetná and Karlova streets.

Within the Old Town, tucked closest to the river, is the **Jewish Quarter (Josefov),** a several-block area with a high concentration of old synagogues and sights from Prague's deep Jewish heritage. It also holds the city's glitziest shopping area (with big-name international designers filling gorgeously restored Art Nouveau buildings).

New Town (Nové Město): Stretching south from the Old Town is the long, broad expanse of Wenceslas Square, marking the center of the New Town. The New Town, shaped like a piece of elbow macaroni, hugs the edge of the Old Town—cutting a swath from riverbank to riverbank. As the name implies, it's relatively new ("only" 600 years old). It's the neighborhood for modern buildings, fancy department stores, and a few communist-era sights.

Castle Quarter (Hradčany): High atop a hill on the west side of the river stands the massive complex of Prague Castle, marked by the spires of St. Vitus Cathedral. For a thousand years, this has been the neighborhood of Czech rulers (including today's president and foreign minister). Consequently, the surrounding area is noble and leafy, with high art and grand buildings, little commerce, and few pubs.

Little Quarter (Malá Strana): Nestled at the foot of Castle Hill is this pleasant former town of fine palaces and gardens (and a few minor sights). This is Prague's diplomatic neighborhood, made to feel elegant by stately embassies, but lacking some of the funky personality of the Old Town.

Also on the castle side of the river, north of the riverbend, is the **Holešovice** district—with a secondary train station and the Veletržní Palace, which houses Prague's greatest art treasure: Alfons Mucha's *Slav Epic*.

Cutting through the towns—from the Powder Tower through the Old Town, crossing the Charles Bridge, and winding up to St. Vitus Cathedral—is the **Royal Way** (Královská Cesta), the ancient path of coronation processions. Today, this city spine (the modern streets of Celetná, Karlova, and Nerudova) is marred by tacky trinket shops and jammed by tour groups. Explore beyond it if you want to see the real Prague.

District System: Prague is administratively carved up into numerical districts (like Budapest, Vienna, and Paris). Almost everything of interest to tourists is in "Praha 1," in the old center on both sides of the river, but a few accommodations and attractions are in outlying districts. Addresses include the district number:

Prague's Best Views

Enjoy the "Golden City of a Hundred Spires" during the early evening, when the light is warm and the colors are rich. Good viewpoints include the following:

- The garden terrace in front of **Strahov Monastery,** above the castle (see page 115)
- The many balconies and spires at **Prague Castle**
- **Villa Richter** restaurants, overlooking the city from just below the castle past the Golden Lane
- The top of either tower on **Charles Bridge**
- The **Old Town Square clock tower** (with a handy elevator)
- **Hotel u Prince's** rooftop dining terrace overlooking the Old Town Square (also with an elevator)
- The steps of the **National Museum** overlooking Wenceslas Square
- The top of the **Žižkov TV tower,** offering spaceship views of the city, in the Žižkov/Vinohrady neighborhood east of the city center (150 Kč for elevator to observatory at 300 feet, free access to Oblaca restaurant at 200-foot-level for customers)

PRAGUE

For example, the Veletržní Palace (home of the *Slav Epic*) is in the seventh district, so its address is "Dukelských Hrdinů 47, Praha 7."

TOURIST INFORMATION

TIs are at several key locations, including on the **Old Town Square** (in the Old Town Hall, just to the left of the Astronomical Clock; Easter-Oct Mon-Fri 9:00-19:00, Sat-Sun 9:00-18:00; Nov-Easter Mon-Fri 9:00-18:00, Sat-Sun 9:00-17:00); on the castle side of **Charles Bridge** (Easter-Oct daily 10:00-18:00, closed Nov-Easter); and in the Old Town, around the corner from **Havelská Market** (at Rytířská 31, April-Oct Mon-Sat 9:00-19:00, closed Nov-March). For general tourist information in English, dial 221-714-444 (Mon-Fri 8:00-19:00), or check the useful TI website: www.praguewelcome.cz.

The TIs offer maps, a helpful transit guide, and information on guided walks and bus tours. They can book local guides, concerts, and, occasionally, hotel rooms.

Monthly event guides—all of them packed with ads—include the *Prague Guide* (29 Kč), *Prague This Month* (free), and *Heart of Europe* (free, summer only). The English-language weekly *Prague Post* newspaper is handy for entertainment listings and current events (60 Kč at newsstands, or read it online at www.praguepost.com).

Prague Card: This pricey sightseeing pass covers public

transit (including the airport bus); admission or discounts to a number of sights (including a few biggies, such as Prague Castle and Jewish Quarter sights); a free bus tour and river cruise; and discounts to other attractions, including some concerts and guided tours. For most travelers, it's not worth the steep cost (e.g., €48/2 days), but if you're planning to be very busy, check what's included and do the math (pick up a brochure at the TI , or go to www. praguecard.com and try their calculator feature).

ARRIVAL IN PRAGUE

Prague has multiple train stations, but most visitors arrive at the Main Train Station (Hlavní Nádraží), on the eastern edge of downtown—a 20-minute walk, short taxi ride, or bus ride to the Old Town Square and many of my recommended hotels. Prague's Václav Havel Airport—12 miles from downtown—is easily connected to the city center by public bus, airport bus, minibus shuttle, and taxis. For details on all of these options, see page 155.

HELPFUL HINTS

Rip-Offs: There's no particular risk of violent crime in Prague, but—as in any heavily touristed city—green, rich tourists can get taken by con artists. Most scams fall into the category of being charged a two-scoop price for one scoop of ice cream, having extra items appear on your restaurant bill, or not getting the correct change. Jaded salesclerks in the tourist zone know that the 20-to-1 exchange rate mystifies American visitors, and they may try to take advantage of your carelessness. Any time you pay for something, make a careful mental note of how much it costs, how much you're handing over, and how much you expect back. Count your change. Beware the "slow count," where clerks give back part of your change, then pause...hoping you'll think they're done and walk away. Wait until you get all the money you're due. Plainclothes policemen "looking for counterfeit money" are con artists—ask to see their badges and they'll shrink away.

Pickpockets: They're abundant in Prague. They can be little children or adults dressed as professionals—sometimes even as tourists. Many thieves drape jackets over their arms to disguise busy fingers. Thieves work the crowded and touristy places in teams—for example, they might create a commotion at the door to a Metro or tram car. Keep your wits about you, assume any big distraction is a smokescreen for theft, and wear a money belt. All of this can sound intimidating, but Prague is safe. Simply stay alert.

Medical Help: A 24-hour **pharmacy** is at Palackého 5 (a block from Wenceslas Square, tel. 224-946-982). For above-standard assistance in English (including dental service), consider the top-quality **Hospital Na Homolce** (less than 1,000 Kč for an appointment, 8:00-16:00 call 252-922-146, for after-hours emergencies call 257-211-111; bus #167 from Anděl Metro station, Roentgenova 2, Praha 5). The **Canadian Medical Care Center** is a small, private clinic with an English-speaking Czech staff at Veleslavínská 1 in Praha 6 (3,000 Kč for an appointment, 4,500 Kč for a house call, halfway between the city and the airport, tel. 235-360-133, after-hours emergency tel. 724-300-301).

Bookstores: Shakespeare and Sons is a friendly English-language bookstore with a wide selection of translations from Czech, the latest publications, and a reading space downstairs overlooking a river channel (daily 11:00-19:00, one block from Charles Bridge on Little Quarter side at U Lužického Semináře 10, tel. 257-531-894, www.shakes.cz). In the heart of the Jewish Quarter, the **Franz Kafka Society** has a lovely little bookstore with a thoughtfully curated shelf of Czech lit in English translation—from Kafka to Švejk to tales of the Little Mole (daily 10:00-18:00, Široká 14, tel. 224-227-452).

Maps: A good map of Prague is essential. For ease of navigation, look for one with trams and Metro lines marked, and tiny sketches of the sights drawn in (30-70 Kč, many different brands; sold at kiosks, exchange windows, and tobacco stands). The *Kartografie Praha* city map, which shows all the tram lines and major landmarks, also includes a castle diagram and a street index. It comes in two versions: 1:15,000 covers the city center (good enough for most visitors), and 1:25,000 includes the whole city (worthwhile if you're sleeping in the suburbs).

Also consider getting a mapping app for your smartphone, which uses GPS to pinpoint your location. To avoid data-roaming charges, look for an offline map that can be downloaded in its entirety before your trip. **City Maps 2Go** has a huge number of searchable offline maps, including a good Prague map ($2 pays for any/all of their maps).

Laundry: A **full-service laundry** near most of the recommended hotels is at Karolíny Světlé 11 (200 Kč/8-pound load, wash and dry in 3 hours, Mon-Fri 7:30-19:00, closed Sat-Sun, 200 yards from Charles Bridge on Old Town side, mobile 721-030-446); another laundry is at Rybná 27 (290 Kč/8-pound load, same-day pickup, Mon-Fri 8:00-18:00, Mon and Wed from 7:00, closed Sat-Sun, tel. 224-812-641). Or surf the Internet while your undies tumble dry at the **self-service launderette** at Korunní 14 (160 Kč/load wash and dry, Internet access-2 Kč/minute, daily 8:00-20:00, near Náměstí Míru Metro stop, Praha 2).

Bike Rental: Prague has improved its network of bike paths, making bicycles a feasible option for exploring the center of the town and beyond (see http://wgp.praha-mesto.cz for a map). Two bike-rental shops located near the Old Town Square are **Praha Bike** (daily 9:00-22:00, Dlouhá 24, mobile 732-388-880, www.prahabike.cz) and **City Bike** (daily 9:00-19:00, Králodvorská 5, mobile 776-180-284, www.citybike-prague.com). They rent bikes for about 300 Kč for two hours or 500 Kč per day (with a 1,500-Kč deposit) and also organize guided bike tours. Or try an **electric bike** (590 Kč/half-day, 890 Kč/day, April-Oct daily 9:00-19:00, tours available, just above American Embassy in Little Quarter at Vlašská 15, mobile 604-474-546, www.ilikeebike.com).

Car Rental: You won't want to drive within compact Prague, but a car can be handy for exploring the countryside. All of the biggies have offices in Prague (check each company's website, or ask at the TI). A locally operated alternative is **Prima Rent** (Mon-Fri 8:00-16:30, closed Sat-Sun, Kolbenova 40, Metro: Kolbenova, mobile 602-608-494, www.primarent.cz). The cheaper models are a great value (900 Kč/day with basic insurance and limited mileage, plus 250 Kč/day for full theft and damage insurance; 350 Kč for hotel or airport delivery).

Local Help: Magic Praha is a tiny travel service run by Lída Jánská. A Jill-of-all-trades, she can help with accommodations and transfers throughout the Czech Republic, as well as private tours and side-trips to historic towns (mobile 604-207-225, www.magicpraha.cz, magicpraha@magicpraha.cz).

Rowdy Stag Parties: Unfortunately, Prague, with its cheap beer and easy fun, has become a magnet for British "stag" and "hen" (bachelor and bachelorette) parties. Thanks to super-cheap flights, it can be more affordable to fly from London to Prague for a 48-hour bender than to spend an evening buying $8 pints in a London pub. While harmless, these revelers can be obnoxious; if you're in town on a weekend, don't be surprised if you hear English soccer songs echoing through the streets in the wee hours (wear earplugs).

Updates to This Book: For updates to this book, check www.ricksteves.com/update.

GETTING AROUND PRAGUE

You can walk nearly everywhere. Brown street signs (in Czech, but with helpful little icons) direct you to tourist landmarks. For a sense of scale, the walk from the Old Town Square to the Charles Bridge takes less than 10 minutes (depending on the crowds).

Still, it's worth figuring out the public transportation system, which helps you reach farther-flung sights (Prague Castle, Mucha's *Slav Epic,* and so on). The Metro is slick, the trams fun, and the taxis quick and easy. Prague's tram system is especially wonderful—trams rumble by frequently and take you just about anywhere. Be bold and you'll swing through Prague like Tarzan. For details, pick up the transit guide at the TI. City maps show the Metro, tram, and bus lines.

By Metro, Tram, and Bus

Excellent, affordable public transit is perhaps the best legacy of the communist era (locals ride all month for 550 Kč).

Tickets: The Metro, trams, and buses all use the same tickets:
- 30-minute **short-trip ticket** *(krátkodobá),* which allows as many transfers as you can make in a half hour—24 Kč
- 90-minute **standard ticket** *(základní)*—32 Kč
- **24-hour pass** *(jízdenka na 24 hodin)*—110 Kč
- **3-day pass** *(jízdenka na 3 dny)*—310 Kč

Buy tickets from your hotel, at Metro stops, newsstand kiosks, or from machines (select ticket price, then insert coins). To avoid wasting time looking for a ticket-seller when your tram is approaching, stock up on all the tickets that you think you'll need. Because Prague is a great walking town, most find that individual tickets work better than a pass.

Be sure to validate your ticket as you board the tram or bus, or as you enter the Metro station, by sticking it in the machine, which stamps a time on it—watch locals and imitate. Inspectors routinely ambush ticketless riders (including tourists) and fine them 700 Kč on the spot.

Schedules and Frequency: Trams run every 5-10 minutes in the daytime (a schedule is posted at each stop). The Metro closes at midnight, and the nighttime tram routes (identified with white numbers on blue backgrounds at tram stops) run all night at 30-minute intervals. You can find more information and a complete route planner in English at www.dpp.cz.

Trams: Navigate by signs that list the end stations. At the platform, a sign lists all the stops for each tram in order. Remember that trams going

PRAGUE

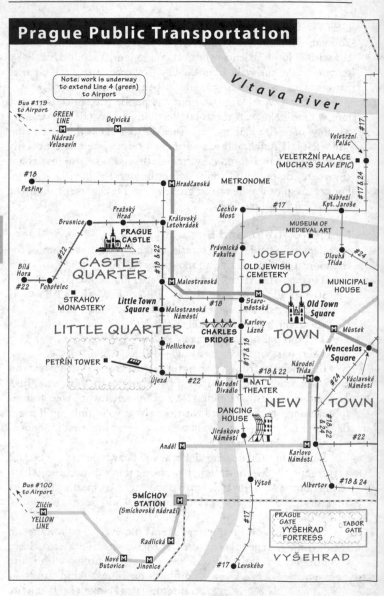

Prague Public Transportation

Note: work is underway to extend Line 4 (green) to Airport

Bus #119 to Airport

Vltava River

GREEN LINE

Nádraží Velasavín — Dejvická

#18 — Petřiny

Brusnice — Pražský Hrad — Královský Letohrádek — Hradčanská

METRONOME

Veletržní Palác

VELETRŽNÍ PALACE (MUCHA'S *SLAV EPIC*)

#17

Nábřeží Kpt. Jaroše

#17 & 24

Čechův Most

#17

MUSEUM OF MEDIEVAL ART

Bílá Hora

#22 — Pohořelec

PRAGUE CASTLE

CASTLE QUARTER

#18 & 22

Právnická Fakulta

JOSEFOV

OLD JEWISH CEMETERY

Dlouhá Třída

#24

MUNICIPAL HOUSE

STRAHOV MONASTERY

Malostranská

Little Town Square — Malostranská Náměstí

#18

Staroměstská

Old Town Square

OLD

TOWN

Můstek

LITTLE QUARTER

Hellichova

CHARLES BRIDGE

Karlovy Lázné

#17 & 18

Wenceslas Square

PETŘÍN TOWER

Újezd — #22

#18 & 22

Národní Divadlo — NAT'L THEATER

Národní Třída

#24

Václavské Náměstí

NEW

TOWN

DANCING HOUSE

Jiráskovo Náměstí

#18, 22 & 24

Anděl

Karlovo Náměstí

#22

Bus #100 to Airport

Zličín

YELLOW LINE

Výtoň

Albertov

#18 & 24

SMÍCHOV STATION (Smíchovské nádraží)

Radlická

#17

PRAGUE GATE   TABOR GATE

VYŠEHRAD FORTRESS

Nové Butovice — Jinonice

VYŠEHRAD

#17 — Levského

one direction leave from one platform, while the other direction might leave from a different platform nearby—maybe across the street or a half-block away. When the tram arrives, open the doors by pressing the green button. Once aboard, validate your ticket in the machine.

As you go, follow along carefully so you know when your stop comes up. Newer trams have electronic signs that show either

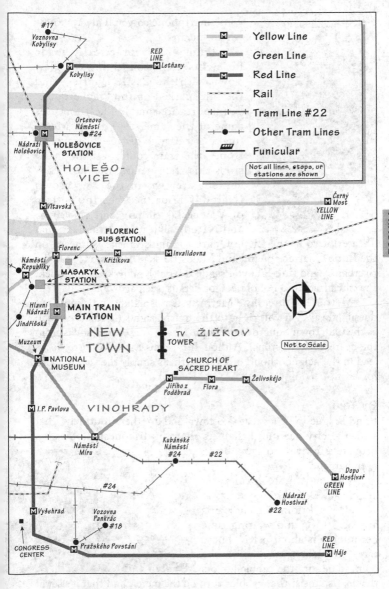

PRAGUE

the next stop *(příští)*, or a list of upcoming stops. Also, listen to the recorded announcements for the name of the stop you're currently at, followed by the name of the stop that's coming up next. (Confused tourists, thinking they've heard their stop, are notorious for rushing off the tram one stop too soon.) The surest way to know whether it's your stop is to check the platform for a sign that shows the name of the stop. Even better, use a mapping app on

your smartphone so you'll always know where you are.

Tram #22 is practically made for sightseeing, connecting the New Town with the Castle Quarter (find the line marked on the Prague Public Transportation map). The tram uses some of the same stops as the Metro (making it easy to get to—or travel on from—the tram route). Of the many stops this tram makes, the most convenient are two in the New Town (Národní Třída, between the bottom of Wenceslas Square and the river; and Národní Divadlo, at the National Theater), two in the Little Quarter (Malostranské Náměstí, on the Little Quarter Square; and Malostranská Metro stop, near the riverbank), and three above Prague Castle (Královský Letohrádek, Pražský Hrad, and Pohořelec; for details, see page 99).

Metro: The three-line Metro system is handy and simple but doesn't always get you right to the tourist sights (landmarks such as the Old Town Square and Prague Castle are several blocks from the nearest Metro stops). Although it seems that all Metro doors lead to the neighborhood of Výstup, that's simply the Czech word for "exit."

By Taxi

I find Prague to be a great taxi town and use them routinely. That said, the city has more than its share of dishonest cabbies, so here are a few tips to avoid being overcharged.

The legitimate local rates are cheap: Drop charge starts at 40 Kč; per-kilometer charge is around 30 Kč; and waiting time per minute is about 6 Kč. These rates are clearly marked on the door, so be sure the cabbie honors them. Also insist that cabbies turn on the meter, and that it's set at the right tariff, or "*sazba*" (usually but not always tariff #1). Unlike in many cities, there's no extra charge for calling a cab—the meter starts only after you get in. Tip by rounding up; locals never tip more than 5 percent.

Have a ballpark idea of what your ride will cost. Figure about 150-200 Kč for a ride between landmarks within the city center (for example, from the Main Train Station to the Old Town

Square, or from the Charles Bridge to the castle). Even the longest ride in the center should cost under 300 Kč.

To improve your odds of getting a fair metered rate, call for a cab (or ask someone at your hotel or restaurant to call one for you), rather than hailing one on the street. **AAA Taxi** (tel. 222-333-222) and **City Taxi** (tel. 257-257-257) are the most likely to have English-speaking staff and honest cabbies. I also find that hailing a passing taxi usually gets me a decent price, although at a slightly higher rate than when reserving by phone. Avoid cabs waiting at tourist attractions and train stations, who are far more likely to be crooked, waiting to prey on unwary tourists.

And what if the cabbie surprises you at the end with an astronomical fare? If you think you're being overcharged, challenge it. Point to the rates on the door. Get your hotel receptionist to back you up. Get out your phone and threaten to call the police. (Because of new legislation to curb dishonest cabbies, the police will stand up for you.) Or simply pay what you think the ride should cost—300 Kč should cover you for a long ride anywhere in the center—and walk away.

Tours in Prague

Walking Tours

A staggering number of small companies offer walking tours of the Old Town, the castle, and more (for the latest, pick up the walking tour fliers at the TI). Since guiding is a routine side-job for university students, you'll generally get hardworking young guides at good prices. While I'd rather go with my own local guide (described later), public walking tours are cheaper (about 450 Kč for a 4-hour tour), cover themes you might not otherwise consider, connect you with other English-speaking travelers, and allow for spontaneity. The quality depends on the guide rather than the company. Your best bet is to show up at the Astronomical Clock a couple of minutes before 8:00, 10:00, or 11:00, then chat with a few of the umbrella-holding guides there. Choose the one you click with. Guides also have fliers advertising additional walks.

"Free" Tours: As is the case all over Europe these days, you'll find "free" tours that are not really free; you're expected to tip your guide (with paper bills rather than coins) when finished. While these tours are fine for the backpacker and hostel crowd (for whom they're designed), the guides are really just expat students (generally from the US or Australia) who memorize a script and give an entertaining performance, with little respect for serious history as you walk through the Old Town. When it comes to guided tours, nothing is free (except for my self-guided audio tour; see page 13).

PRAGUE

Prague Pronunciations

English	Czech	Pronounced
Main Train Station	Hlavní Nádraží	*HLAV-nee NAH-drah-zhee*
Old Town	Staré Město	*STAR-eh MYEHS-toh*
Old Town Square	Staroměstské Náměstí	*STAR-oh-myehst-skeh NAH-myehs-tee*
New Town	Nové Město	*NOH-vay MYEHS-toh*
Little Quarter	Malá Strana	*MAH-lah STRAH-nah*
Jewish Quarter	Josefov	*YOO-zehf-fohf*
Castle Quarter	Hradčany	*HRAD-chah-nee*
Charles Bridge	Karlův Most	*KAR-loov most*
Wenceslas Square	Václavské Náměstí	*vaht-SLAHF-skeh NAH-myehs-tee*
Vltava River	Vltava	*VUL-tah-vah*

▲▲Local Guides

In Prague, hiring a guide is particularly smart. Guides meet you wherever you like and tailor the tour to your interests. Visit their websites in advance for details on various walks, airport transfers, countryside excursions, and other services offered, and then make arrangements by email. Because prices are usually per hour (not per person), small groups can hire an inexpensive guide for several days.

Small Companies: Personal Prague Guide Service's Šárka Kačabová uses her teaching background to help you understand Czech culture and has picked a team of personable and knowledgeable guides for her company (600 Kč/hour for 2-3 people, 800 Kč/hour for 4-8 people, fifth hour free, mobile 777-225-205, www.personalpragueguide.com, sarka@me.com).

PragueWalker is run by Katka Svobodová, a hardworking historian-guide who knows her stuff and manages a team of enthusiastic and friendly guides (600 Kč/hour for individuals, families, and small groups; mobile 603-181-300, www.praguewalker.com, katerina@praguewalker.com).

Individual Guides: These generally young guides (which is good, because they learned their trade post-communism) typically charge about 2,000-2,500 Kč for a half-day tour. **Jana Hronková** has a natural style—a welcome change from the more strict professionalism of some of the busier guides—and a penchant for the

Daily Reminder

Sunday: St. Vitus Cathedral at Prague Castle is closed Sunday morning for Mass. Some stores have shorter hours or are closed.

Monday: The Veletržní Palace, which houses Alfons Mucha's *Slav Epic*, and the Museum of Medieval Art are closed. Most of the other major sights—such as Prague Castle and the Jewish Quarter—are open, but a number of lesser sights, including Týn Church and Church of St. James, are closed.

   If you're day-tripping today, Terezín and Kutná Hora's Sedlec Bone Church and St. Barbara's Cathedral are open. Konopiště Castle is closed.

Tuesday-Friday: All sights are open.

Saturday: The Jewish Quarter sights are closed. In nearby Terezín, the Crematorium and Columbarium are closed.

Crowd-Beating Tips: Visit Prague Castle either first thing in the morning (be at St. Vitus Cathedral right at 9:00—except Sun morning, when it's closed for Mass) or midafternoon (closes at 17:00 in summer, 16:00 in winter). Hiring your own guide for a historic walk is relatively cheap and allows you to choose a time (evening or early morning) and route to avoid crowds.

Jewish Quarter (mobile 732-185-180, www.experience-prague.info, janahronkova@hotmail.com). **Zuzana Tlášková** speaks English as well as Hebrew (mobile 774-131-335, tlaskovaz@seznam.cz). **Martin Bělohradský,** who guides on the side when not doing his organic chemistry work, is particularly enthusiastic about fine arts and architecture (mobile 723-414-565, martinb5666@gmail.com). **Jana Krátká** especially enjoys sharing Prague's tumultuous 20th-century history with visitors (mobile 776-571-538, janapragueguide@gmail.com). **Kamil and Petra Vondrouš** design tours to fit your interests; they also guide/drive beyond Prague, as far as Vienna or Dresden (mobile 605-701-861, www.prague-extra.com, info@prague-extra.com).

   Specialty Tours: Taste Local Beer is run by Aaron John, an expat with a passion for local brews who's up to date on the evolving Prague microbrew scene (1,200 Kč/person, includes six beers at three pubs and a one-day transportation pass, www.tastelocalbeer.com). **Running Tours Prague** are guided by Radim Prahl, a local with an appetite for ultra-marathons; he'll run you past monuments, through parks, and down back alleys at your own pace (1,500 Kč for two people; mobile 777-288-862, www.runningtoursprague.com).

Jewish Quarter Tours

Jewish guides (of varying quality) meet small groups twice daily in season for three-hour English tours of the Jewish Quarter. **Wittmann Tours** charges a 880-Kč fee that includes entry to the Old-New Synagogue and the six other major Jewish Quarter sights (which cost 480 Kč total), so the tour actually costs only 400 Kč (May-Oct Sun-Fri at 10:30 and 14:00, Nov-Dec and mid-March-April Sun-Fri at 10:30 only, no tours Sat and Jan-mid-March, minimum 3 people). Tours meet in the little park (just beyond the café), directly in front of Hotel InterContinental at the end of Pařížská street. They also offer guided side-trip minibus tours to Terezín Memorial (tel. 603-168-427 or 603-426-564, www.wittmann-tours.com). Also note that several of the **private local guides** recommended earlier do good tours of the Jewish Quarter.

Tour Packages for Students

Andy Steves (Rick's son) runs **WSA Europe,** offering three-day (and longer) guided and unguided packages—including accommodations, sightseeing, and unique local experiences—for budget travelers across 11 top European cities, including Prague (from €99, see www.wsaeurope.com for details).

Tours Outside of Prague

To get beyond the sights listed in most guidebooks, call Tom and Marie Zahn from **P.A.T.H. Finders International.** Tom is American, Marie is Czech, and together they organize and lead family-friendly day excursions (in Prague and throughout the country). Their tours are creative and affordable, and they teach travelers how to find off-the-beaten-track destinations on their own. Their specialty is Personal Ancestral Tours & History (P.A.T.H.)—with sufficient notice, they can help Czech descendants find their ancestral homes, perhaps even a long-lost relative. Tom and Marie can also help with other parts of your Eastern European travel by linking you with associates in other countries, especially Germany, Hungary, Poland, Romania, Slovakia, and Ukraine (US tel. 360-450-5959, Czech tel. 257-940-113, www.pathfinders.cz, info@pathfinders.cz).

Reverend Jan Dus, an enthusiastic pastor who lived in the US for several years, now serves a small congregation about 100 miles east of Prague. Jan can design itineraries and likes to help travelers connect with locals in little towns, particularly in northeastern Bohemia and Moravia. He also has an outstanding track record in providing genealogical services (toll-free US tel. 800-807-1562, www.revjan.com, rev.jan.services@gmail.com).

Bus Tours

Because Prague's sightseeing core (Castle Quarter, Charles Bridge, and the Old Town) is not accessible by bus, I can't recommend any of the city's bus tour companies. (Most that you'll see advertised are basically walking tours that use buses for pickups and transfers.) Hiring a guide, many of whom can drive you around in their car, can be a much better value (described earlier, under "Local Guides").

Prague Old Town Walk

Nestled in the bend of the river is Prague's compact, pedestrian-friendly Old Town. A boomtown since the 10th century, the Old

Town has long been the busy commercial quarter, filled with merchants, guilds, and supporters of the Church reformer Jan Hus (who wanted a Czech-style Catholicism). Today it's Prague's tourism ground zero, jammed with tasteful landmarks and tacky amusements alike. This walk, which takes two to three hours, starts in the heart of the neighborhood, the Old Town Square (rated ▲▲▲), then dips into the New Town before winding back into the Old Town and ending at the Charles Bridge.

• *Begin with the square's centerpiece, the...*

❶ Memorial to Jan Hus

This monument is an enduring icon of the long struggle for Czech freedom. In the center, Jan Hus—the religious reformer who has

become a symbol of Czech nationalism—stands tall. Hus, born in 1369, was a Prague priest who stood up to both the Catholic Church and the Austrian Habsburg oppressors. His defiant stance—as depicted

so powerfully in this monument—galvanized the Czech people, who rallied to fight not just for their religious beliefs but for independence from foreign control.

But Hus was about a century ahead of his time. He was arrested, charged with heresy, excommunicated, and, in 1415, burned at the stake. His followers picked up the torch and fought on for two decades in the Hussite Wars, which killed tens of

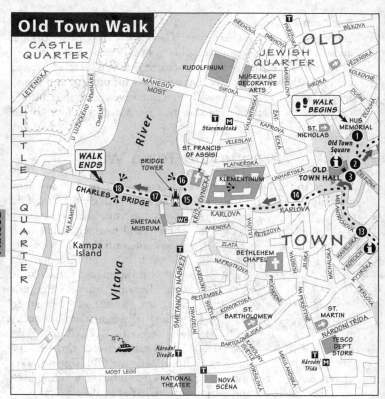

thousands and left Bohemia a virtual wasteland.

Surrounding Hus' statue are the Hussite followers who battled the Habsburgs. One patriot holds a cup, or chalice. This symbolizes one of the changes the Hussites were fighting for: the right of everyone (not just priests) to drink the wine at Communion. Look into the survivors' faces—it was a bitter fight. In 1620, their rebellious cause was brutally crushed by the Catholic Habsburgs at the pivotal Battle of White Mountain fought outside Prague—effectively ending Czech independence for three centuries.

Each subsequent age has interpreted Hus to its liking: For Protestants, Hus was the founder of the first Protestant church (though he was actually an ardent Catholic); for revolutionaries, this critic of the Church's power was a proponent of social equality; for nationalists, this Czech preacher was the defender of the language; and for communists, Hus was the first ideologue to preach the gospel of socialism. But regardless of who was in power, Hus' importance to the Czech people has never wavered.

• *Stepping away from the Hus Memorial, stand in the center of the Old Town Square and take a 360-degree...*

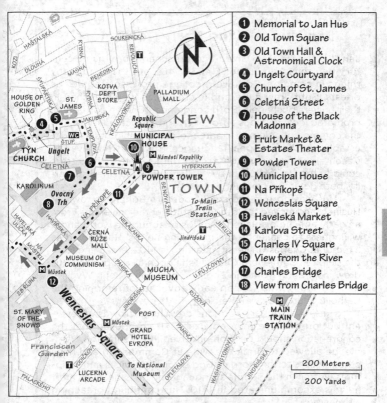

① Memorial to Jan Hus
② Old Town Square
③ Old Town Hall & Astronomical Clock
④ Ungelt Courtyard
⑤ Church of St. James
⑥ Celetná Street
⑦ House of the Black Madonna
⑧ Fruit Market & Estates Theater
⑨ Powder Tower
⑩ Municipal House
⑪ Na Příkopě
⑫ Wenceslas Square
⑬ Havelská Market
⑭ Karlova Street
⑮ Charles IV Square
⑯ View from the River
⑰ Charles Bridge
⑱ View from Charles Bridge

PRAGUE

❷ Old Town Square Orientation Spin-Tour

Whirl clockwise to get a look at Prague's diverse architectural styles: Gothic, Renaissance, Baroque, Rococo, and Art Nouveau. Remember, Prague was largely spared the devastating aerial bombardments of World War II that leveled so many European cities (such as Berlin, Warsaw, and Budapest). Few places can match the Old Town Square for Old World charm.

Start with the green domes of the Baroque **Church of St. Nicholas.** Originally Catholic, now Hussite, this church is a popular venue for concerts. The Jewish Quarter is a few blocks behind the church, down the uniquely tree-lined "Paris Street" (Pařížská), which also has the best lineup of Art Nouveau houses in Prague, and arguably in all of Europe.

Spin to the right. Behind the Hus Memorial is a fine yellow building that introduces us to Prague's wonderful world of Art Nouveau: pastel colors, fanciful stonework, wrought-iron balconies, colorful murals—and what are those statues on top doing? Prague's architecture is a wonderland of ornamental details.

Continue spinning a few doors to the right to the large,

Jan Hus and the Early Reformers

Jan Hus (c. 1369-1415) lived and preached more than a century before Martin Luther (1483-1546), but they had many things in common. Both were college professors as well as priests. Both drew huge public crowds as they preached in their university chapels. Both condemned Church corruption, promoted local religious autonomy, and advocated for letting the common people participate more in worship rituals. Both established their national languages. (It's Hus who gave the Czech alphabet its unique accent marks so that the letters could fit the sounds.) And, by challenging established authority, both got in big trouble.

Hus was born in the small southern Bohemian town of Husinec, and moved to Prague to study at the university. From an early age, he displayed a curiosity about the world and a willingness to challenge the prevailing norms. Hus served as a rector at Charles University starting in 1402. Preaching from the pulpit in Bethlehem Chapel (still open to the public), Hus drew inspiration from the English philosopher John Wycliffe (c. 1320-1384), who was an early advocate of reforming the Catholic Church to strip the clergy of its power.

Hus' revolutionary sermons drew huge crowds of reverent but progressive-minded Czechs. He proposed that the congregation should be more involved in worship (for example, be allowed to drink the wine at Communion) and have better access to the word of God through services and scriptures written in the people's language, not in Latin. Even after he was excommunicated in 1410, Hus continued preaching his message.

In 1414, the Roman Catholic Church convened the Council of Constance to grapple with the controversies of the day. First they posthumously excommunicated Wycliffe, proclaiming him a heretic and exhuming his corpse to symbolically burn at the stake. Then they called Hus to Constance, where on July 6, 1415, they declared him a heretic. After refusing to recant his beliefs and praying that God would forgive his enemies, Hus was tied to a stake and burned alive. But by this time, Hus' challenging ideas had been embraced by many Czechs, and his death sparked the bloodiest civil war in the country's history.

This early Catholic precursor to the Counter-Reformation kept things under control for generations. But in the 16th century, a German monk named Martin Luther found a more progressive climate for these same revolutionary ideas. Thanks to the new printing press, invented by Gutenberg, Luther was able to spread his message cheaply and effectively. While Hus loosened Rome's grip on Christianity, Luther orchestrated the Reformation that finally broke it. Today, both are honored as national heroes as well as religious reformers.

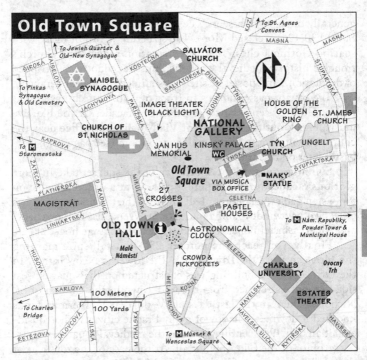

Old Town Square

To St. Agnes Convent

To Jewish Quarter & Old-New Synagogue

To Pinkas Synagogue & Old Cemetery

MAISEL SYNAGOGUE

SALVÁTOR CHURCH

KOŠTECNÁ

SALVÁTORSKÁ

DUŠNÍ

DLOUHÁ

TÝNSKÁ ULIČKA

MASNÁ

MASNÁ

KOZÍ

ŠIROKÁ

MAISELOVÁ

JÁCHYMOVA

PAŘÍŽSKÁ

ŠTUPARTSKÁ

IMAGE THEATER (BLACK LIGHT)

HOUSE OF THE GOLDEN RING

ST. JAMES CHURCH

CHURCH OF ST. NICHOLAS

NATIONAL GALLERY

KINSKÝ PALACE

WC

TÝN CHURCH

UNGELT

To M Staroměstská

KAPROVA

JAN HUS MEMORIAL

ZÁTECKÁ

TÝNSKÁ

ŠTUPARTSKÁ

Old Town Square

VIA MUSICA BOX OFFICE

MARY STATUE

PLATNÉŘSKÁ

U RADNICE

MIKULÁŠSKÁ

27 CROSSES

CELETNÁ

PASTEL HOUSES

To M Nám. Republiky, Powder Tower & Municipal House

MAGISTRÁT

LINHARTSKÁ

HUSOVA

OLD TOWN HALL

Malé Náměstí

ASTRONOMICAL CLOCK

ŽELEZNÁ

CHARLES UNIVERSITY

Ovocný Trh

CROWD & PICKPOCKETS

KARLOVA

100 Meters

100 Yards

MELANTRICHOVA

KOŽNÁ

HAVELSKÁ

ESTATES THEATER

HAVELSKÁ ULIČKA

KYTÍŘSKÁ

HAVÍŘSKÁ

To Charles Bridge

JALOVCOVA

JILSKÁ

M CHALSKÁ

ŘETĚZOVÁ

To M Můstek & Wenceslas Square

PRAGUE

red-and-tan Rococo **Kinský Palace,** which displays the National Gallery's Asian arts collection (and has a handy WC in the courtyard).

Farther to the right is the towering, Gothic **Týn Church** (pronounced "teen"), with its fanciful twin spires. It's been the Old Town's leading church in every era. In medieval times, it was Catholic. When the Hussites took power (c. 1420-1620), they made it the headquarters of their faith. After the Hussite defeat, the

Habsburgs returned it to Catholicism. The symbolism tells the story: Between the church's two towers, find a golden medallion of the Virgin Mary. Beneath that is a niche—now empty. But in Hussite times, a golden chalice stood there, symbolizing their cause. When the Catholics triumphed, they melted down the chalice and made it into this golden image of Mary. If you want to go inside, make your way through the cluster of buildings in front of it, entering at #14 (under the arcade that faces the square; 30-Kč requested donation, generally open to sightseers Tue-Sat 10:00-13:00 & 15:00-17:00, Sun 10:30-12:00, closed Mon). The structure is full of light, with soaring Gothic arches. The ornamentation reflects the church's troubled history: medieval Catholic; Hussite iconoclasm (stripped of decoration); and post-Hussite Habsburg (Baroque exuberance).

The row of pastel houses in front of Týn Church has a mixture of Gothic, Renaissance, and Baroque facades. If you like live music, check out the convenient **Via Musica box office** near the church's front door to find out all your options (see page 127); we'll pass it later on this walk.

Spinning right, to the south side of the square, take in more **glorious facades,** each a different color with a different gable on top—step gables, triangular, bell-shaped. The tan house at #16 has a steepled bay window and a mural of St. Wenceslas on horseback, and Albert Einstein once lectured at the light-orange house at #18.

Finally, you reach the pointed 250-foot-tall spire marking the 14th-century **Old Town Hall.** The tower is Neo-Gothic. In the 19th century, a building was constructed on the square's west side that once stretched from the Old Town to the Church of St. Nicholas. Then, in the last days of World War II, German tanks knocked it down...to the joy of many Prague citizens who considered it an ugly 19th-century stain on the medieval square.

Approach the Old Town Hall. At the base of the tower, near the corner of the tree-filled park, find **27 white crosses** inlaid in the pavement. These mark the spot where 27 Protestant nobles, merchants, and intellectuals were beheaded in 1621 after the Battle of White Mountain—still one of the grimmest chapters in the country's history.

• *Around the left side of the tower are two big, fancy, old clock faces, and they're being admired by many, many tourists.*

❸ Old Town Hall and Astronomical Clock

The Old Town Hall, with its distinctive trapezoidal tower, was built in the 1350s, during Prague's Golden Age. Check out the ornately carved Gothic entrance door to the left of the clock; a bit farther to the left is another door, leading to the TI, public pay WC, and ticket desk for riding the elevator up to the top of the clock tower, or touring the interior of the Old Town Hall (see "Sights Inside the Old Town Hall," later).

But for now, turn your attention to that famous **Astronomical Clock.** See if you can figure out how it works. Of the two giant dials on the tower, the top one tells the time on two rings: The outer one, with Roman numerals, is similar to present-day clocks, while the inner one, numbered 1 through 24 in a strange but readable Bohemian script, rotates to reset each day at sunset. Within the dial is yet another revolving disc, where today's zodiac sign is marked.

If all this seems complex to us, it must have been a marvel in the early 1400s, when the clock was installed. Remember that back then, everything revolved around the Earth (the fixed middle background—with Prague marking the center, of course). The clock was heavily damaged during World War II, and much of what you see today is a reconstruction.

The second dial, below the clock, was added in the 19th century. It shows the signs of the zodiac, scenes from the seasons of a rural peasant's life, and a ring of saints' names. There's one for each day of the year, and a marker on top indicates today's special saint. In the center is a castle, symbolizing Prague.

Four statues flank the upper clock. These politically incorrect symbols evoke a 15th-century outlook: The figure staring into a mirror stands for vanity, a Jewish moneylender holding a bag of coins is greed, and (on the right side) a Turk with a mandolin symbolizes hedonism. All these worldly goals are vain in the face of Death, whose hourglass reminds us that our time is unavoidably running out.

The clock strikes the top of the hour and puts on a little glockenspiel show daily from 9:00 to 21:00 (until 20:00 in winter). As

the hour approaches, keep your eye on Death. First, Death tips his hourglass and pulls the cord, ringing the bell, while the moneylender jingles his purse. Then the windows open and the 12 apostles shuffle past, acknowledging the gang of onlookers. Finally the rooster at the very top crows, and the hour is rung. The hour is often wrong because of Daylight Saving Time (completely senseless to 15th-century clockmakers). I find an alternative view just as interesting: As the cock crows, face the crowd and snap a photo of the mass of gaping tourists.

Sights Inside the Old Town Hall: Go through the door to the left of the Astronomical Clock, where the ticket desk shares a space with the TI. From here, continuing deeper into the building, you'll find pay WCs and a bank of elevators. Ride the elevator to Floor 3 to buy your ticket to ascend the **town hall's tower** (via another elevator—if it's busy, you may have to wait a few minutes). The tower offers ▲▲ views over Prague's prettiest square (110 Kč,

Tue-Sun 9:00-21:00, Mon 11:00-21:00; after 19:00 the entry is through the door immediately to the left of the clock rather than through the TI). On Floor 1, you can take a 45-minute **tour of the Old Town Hall,** which includes a Gothic chapel and a close-up look at the inner guts of the Astronomical Clock, plus its statues of the 12 apostles (100 Kč, or 160-Kč combo-ticket with tower, about 3 tours/day in English—see the schedule at the ticket desk).

• *Let's leave the Old Town Square. Our next stop is directly behind the Týn Church: Cross through the square and head down the street along the left side of the church (Týnska) for about 100 yards, passing the convenient **Via Musica box office**. A bit farther along, on the left, you'll pass the **House of the Golden Ring**, worth considering if you're curious about 20th-century Czech art.*

Continue straight through a sturdy gate, into a courtyard called...

❹ Ungelt

This pleasant, cobbled, quiet courtyard of upscale restaurants and shops is one of the Old Town's oldest places. During the Bohemian Golden Age (c. 1200-1400), it was a cosmopolitan center of international trade. Prague—located at the geographical center of Europe—attracted Germans selling furs, Italians selling fine art, Frenchmen selling cloth, and Arabs selling spices. They converged on this courtyard, where they could store their goods and pay their customs (which is what *Ungelt* means, in German). In return, the king granted them protection, housing, and a stable for their horses. By day, they'd sell their wares on the Old Town Square. At night, they'd return here to drink and exchange news from their native lands. Notice that, to protect the goods, there are only two entrances to the complex. After centuries of disuse, the Ungelt has been marvelously restored—a great place for dinner, and a reminder that Prague has been a cosmopolitan center for most of its history.

• *Exit the Ungelt at the far end. Just to your left, across the street, is the...*

❺ Church of St. James (Kostel Sv. Jakuba)

Perhaps the most beautiful church interior in the Old Town, the Church of St. James has been the home of the Minorite Order almost as long as merchants have occupied Ungelt. A medieval city was a complex phenomenon: Commerce, prostitution, and a life of contemplation existed side by side. (I guess it's not that much different from today.) Step

inside (free, Tue-Sun 9:30-12:00 & 14:00-16:00, closed Mon; if
it's locked, peek through the glass door). Artistically, St. James
is a stunning example of how simple medieval spaces could be
rebuilt into sumptuous feasts of Baroque decoration. The original interior was destroyed by fire in 1689; what's here now is an
early-18th-century remodel. The blue light in the altar highlights
one of Prague's most venerated treasures—the bejeweled Madonna
Pietatis. Above the *pietà*, as if held aloft by hummingbird-like
angels, is a painting of the martyrdom of St. James.

• *Exiting the church, do a U-turn to the left (heading up Jakubska
Street, along the side of the church, past some rough-looking bars). After
one block, turn right on Templova Street. Head two blocks down the
street (passing a nice view of the Týn Church's rear end, and some deluxe
toilets) and go through the arcaded passageway, where you emerge onto...*

⑥ Celetná Street

Since the 10th century, this street has been a corridor in the busy
commercial quarter—filled with merchants and guilds. These
days, it's still pretty commercial, and very touristy.

• *To your right is a striking, angular building called the...*

⑦ House of the Black Madonna
(Dům u Černé Matky Boží)

Back around the turn of the 20th century, Prague was a center
of avant-garde art, second only to Paris. Art Nouveau blossomed
here (as we'll soon see), as did
Cubism. The Cubist exterior is a
marvel of rectangular windows and
cornices—stand back and see how
masterfully it makes its statement
while mixing with its neighbors...
then get up close and study the
details. The interior houses a Cubist
café (the recommended Grand Café
Orient, one flight up the parabolic
spiral staircase)—complete with cube-shaped chairs and square-
shaped rolls. The Kubista gallery on the ground floor shows more
examples of this unique style.

• *The long, skinny square that begins just to the left of the House of the
Black Madonna is the...*

⑧ Fruit Market (Ovocný Trh) and the Estates Theater

This long, narrow square with a bulge in the middle is typical of
medieval Central European market towns. Market stalls would
pop up along the busy main drag right in the center of town—
making it easy to see how a town can swell as it grows. While no

fruit vendors still sell their wares here, this square has retained its traditional name.

The green-and-white building squatting in the middle of the square—right at the bulge—is the **Estates Theater** (Stavovské Divadlo). Built by a nobleman in the 1770s, this Classicist building was the prime opera venue in Prague at a time when an Austrian prodigy was changing the course of music. Wolfgang Amadeus Mozart premiered *Don Giovanni* in this building (with a bronze statue of Il Commendatore duly flanking the main entrance on the left), and he directed many of his works here. Today, the Estates Theater (part of the National Theater group) continues to produce *The Marriage of Figaro, Don Giovanni,* and occasionally *The Magic Flute.*

• *Backtrack a few steps to Celetná Street, turn right, and head about 50 yards to the...*

❾ Powder Tower

The big, black, 500-year-old Powder Tower was the main gate of the old town wall. It also housed the city's gunpowder—hence the name. This is the only surviving bit of the wall that was built to defend the city in the 1400s. (You can go inside, but it's not worth paying to tour the interior.)

• *Pass regally through the Powder Tower. In so doing, you're leaving the Old Town. You emerge into a big, busy intersection. To your left is the Municipal House, a cream-colored building topped with a green dome. Find a good spot where you can view the facade.*

❿ Municipal House (Obecní Dům)

The Municipal House, which celebrated its centennial birthday in 2011, is the "pearl of Czech Art Nouveau." Art Nouveau flourished during the same period as the Eiffel Tower and Europe's great Industrial Age train stations.

The same engineering prowess and technological advances that went into making those huge erector-set rigid buildings were used by artistic architects to create quite the opposite effect: curvy, organically flowing lines, inspired by vines

PRAGUE

Prague: The Queen of Art Nouveau

Prague is Europe's best city for Art Nouveau. That's the style of art and architecture that flourished throughout Europe around 1900. It was called "nouveau"—or new—because it was associated with all things modern: technology, social progress, and enlightened thinking. Art Nouveau was neo-nothing, but instead a fresh answer to all the revival styles of the late-19th century, and an organic response to the Eiffel Tower art of the Industrial Age.

By taking advantage of recent advances in engineering, Art Nouveau liberated the artist in each architect. Notice the curves and motifs expressing originality—every facade is unique. Artists such as Alfons Mucha believed that the style should apply to all facets of daily life. They designed everything from buildings and furniture to typefaces and cigarette packs.

Prague's three top Art Nouveau architects are Jan Koula, Josef Fanta, and Osvald Polivka (whose last name sounds like the Czech word for "soup"). Think "Cola, Fanta, and Soup"—easy to remember and a good way to impress your local friends.

Though Art Nouveau was born in Paris, it's in Prague where you'll find some of its greatest hits: the Municipal House and nearby buildings, Grand Hotel Evropa (on Wenceslas Square), the exuberant facades of the Jewish Quarter, the Jerusalem Synagogue, and—especially—the work of Prague's own Alfons Mucha. You can see his stained-glass window in St. Vitus Cathedral (at Prague Castle, page 106), the excellent Mucha Museum (near Wenceslas Square, page 88), and his masterpiece, *The Slav Epic* (on the city's outskirts, page 117).

PRAGUE

and curvaceous women. Art Nouveau was an adverse reaction to the sterility of modern-age construction. Look at the elaborate wrought-iron balcony—flanked by bronze Atlases hefting their lanterns—and the lovely stained glass (like in the entrance arcade).

Mosaics and sculptural knickknacks (see the faces above the windows) made the building's facade colorful and joyous. Study the bright mosaic above the balcony, called ***Homage to Prague***. A symbol of the city, the goddess Praha presides over a land of peace and high culture—an image that stoked cultural pride and nationalist sentiment. On the balcony is a medallion showing the three-tower castle that is the symbol of Prague.

The Municipal House was built in the early 1900s, when Czech nationalism was at a fever pitch. Having been ruled by the Austrian Habsburgs for the previous 300 years, the Czechs were demanding independence. This building was drenched in patriotic Czech themes. Within a few short years, in 1918, the nation of Czechoslovakia was formed—and the independence proclamation was announced to the people right here, from the balcony of the Municipal House.

The interior of the Municipal House has perhaps Europe's finest Art Nouveau decor. It's free to enter and wander the public areas. While to really appreciate the building you must attend a concert here or take one of the excellent tours offered throughout the day, any visit here gets a sweet dose of Art Nouveau (for a description of the interior, see page 90).

• *Now head west down Na Příkopě (to the left as you face the Powder Tower) toward the Metro station about 200 yards away. Enjoy the sights of...*

⓫ Na Příkopě, the Old City Wall

The street called Na Příkopě was where the old city wall once stood. More specifically, the name Na Příkopě means "On the Moat," and you're walking along what was once the moat outside the wall. To your right is the Old Town. To the left, the New. Look at your city map and conceptualize medieval Prague's smart design: The city was protected on two sides by its river, and on the other two sides by its walls (marked by the modern streets called Na Příkopě, Revoluční, and Národní Třída).The only river crossing back then was the fortified Charles Bridge.

• *Continue up Na Příkopě—passing the **Museum of Communism** (described on page 89)—to an intersection (and nearby Metro stop) called Můstek. To your left stretches the vast expanse of the wide boulevard called...*

⓬ Wenceslas Square

Wenceslas Square—with the National Museum and landmark statue of St. Wenceslas at the very top—is the centerpiece of Prague's New Town. This square was originally founded as a thriving horse market. Today it's a modern world of high-fashion stores, glitzy shopping malls, old facades (and some jarringly modern ones), fast-food restaurants, and sausage stands. (For a self-guided walk through Wenceslas Square, see page 81.)

• *Let's plunge back into the Old Town and return to the Old Town Square. Turn about face and head downhill (north) on the street called Na Můstku—"along the bridge" that crossed the moat (příkopě) we've been following until now.*

Walk down Na Můstku. After one touristy block, it jogs slightly to the left and becomes Melantrichova. A block farther along, on the left, is...

⓭ Havelská Market

This open-air market, offering crafts and produce, was first set up in the 13th century for the German trading community. Though

heavy on souvenirs these days (especially on weekends), the market—worth ▲—still feeds hungry locals and vagabonds. Lined with inviting benches, it's an ideal place to enjoy a healthy snack—and merchants are happy to sell a single vegetable or piece of fruit. The market is also a fun place to browse for crafts. It's a homegrown, homemade kind of place; you'll often be dealing with the actual artist or farmer. The many cafés and little eateries circling the market offer a relaxing vantage point from which to view the action.

• *Continue along Melantrichova street. Eventually, after passing increasingly tacky souvenir shops and a "museum of sex machines," Melantrichova curves right and spills out at the Old Town Square, right by the Astronomical Clock. At the clock, turn left down Karlova street. The rest of our walk follows Karlova (though the road twists and turns a bit) to the Charles Bridge, where our tour ends. Begin by heading along the top of the Small Market Square (Malé Náměstí, with lots of outdoor tables), then follow Karlova's twisting course—Karlova street signs keep you on track, and Karlův Most signs point to the bridge. Or just follow the crowds.*

⓮ Karlova Street

Although traffic-free, Karlova street is utterly jammed with tourists as it winds toward the Charles Bridge. But the route has plenty of historic charm if you're able to ignore the contemporary tourism. As you walk, look up. Notice historic symbols and signs of shops, which advertised who lived there or what they sold. Cornerstones, designed to protect buildings from careening carriages, also date from centuries past. The touristy feeding-frenzy of today's Prague is at its ugliest along this commercial gauntlet. Obviously, you'll find few good values on this drag.

Keep walking toward Charles Bridge. After the street jogs right to cross Husova, many of the buildings you'll see on your right are associated with Prague's **Charles University.** Behind the souvenir stalls lie venerable classrooms and lecture halls. For example, the **Klementinum** (which once housed the university's library) is the large building that borders Karlova Street on the right. Just past the intersection with Liliová, where the street opens into a little square, turn right through the archway (at #1) and into a tranquil courtyard that feels an eternity away from the touristy hubbub of Karlova. Locals enjoy using this courtyard as the key link of a less-crowded shortcut between Charles Bridge and the Old Town Square. You can also visit the Klementinum's impressive Baroque interior on a guided tour.

• *Karlova street leads directly to a tall medieval tower that marks the start of Charles Bridge. But before entering the bridge, stop on this side of the river. To the right of the tower is a little park with a great view of both the bridge and the rest of Prague across the river. Though it's officially called Křižovnické Náměstí, I think of it as...*

ⓕ Charles IV Square

Start with the statue of the bridge's namesake, **Charles IV** (1316-1378). Look familiar? He's the guy on the 100-koruna bill. Charles was the Holy Roman Emperor who ruled his vast empire from Prague in the 14th century—a high-water mark in the city's history. The statue shows one of Charles' many accomplishments: He holds a contract establishing Charles University, the first in central Europe. The women around the pedestal symbolize the school's four traditional subjects: theology, the arts, law, and medicine.

Charles was the pre-eminent figure in Europe in the Late Middle Ages and the father of the Prague we enjoy today. His domain encompassed the modern Czech Republic and parts of Germany, Austria, and the Low Countries.

Charles was cosmopolitan. Born in Prague, raised in Paris, crowned in Rome, and inspired by the luxury-loving pope in Avignon, Charles returned home bringing Europe's culture with him. Besides founding Charles University, he built Charles Bridge, Charles Square (where you're standing), much of Prague Castle and St. Vitus Cathedral, and the New Town (modeled on Paris). His Golden Bull of 1356 served as Europe's constitution for centuries. He expanded his empire through networking and shrewd marriages, not war. Charles traded ideas with the Italian poet Petrarch and imported artists from France, Italy, and Flanders (inspiring the art of the Museum of Medieval Art, described on page 81). Under Charles' rule, Prague became the most cultured city in Europe.

Now look up at the **bridge tower.** Built by Charles, it's one of the finest Gothic gates anywhere. The statuary shows the 14th-century hierarchy of society: people at street level, above them kings, and bishops above the kings. Speaking of hierarchy, check out Charles' statue from near the street. Some think that, from this angle, the emperor looks like he's peeing on the tourists. Which reminds me, public toilets are nearby.

• *Stroll to the riverside, belly up to the bannister, and take in the...*

⑯ View from the River

Before you are the Vltava River and Charles Bridge. Across the river, atop the hill, is Prague Castle topped by the prickly spires of St. Vitus Cathedral. **Prague Castle** has been the seat of power in this region for over a thousand years, since the time of Wenceslas. By some measures, it's the biggest castle on earth.

The **Vltava River** is better known by its German name, Moldau. It bubbles up from the Šumava Hills in southern Bohemia and runs 270 miles through a diverse landscape, like a thread connecting the Czech people. As we've learned, the Czechs have struggled heroically to carve out their identity while surrounded by mightier neighbors—Austrians, Germans, and Russians. The Vltava is their shared artery.

The **view of Charles Bridge** from here is photogenic to the max. The historic bridge is almost seven football fields long, lined with lanterns and 30 statues, and bookmarked at each end with medieval towers. This structure is not the first that has stood on this spot. In fact, the name "Prague" comes from the word "threshold," because the city was born at a convenient place to cross the wide river and enter a new place. But earlier wooden bridges were washed away by floods. Finally, following a massive flood in 1342, Charles IV commissioned a new stone span—Prague's only bridge for more than 400 years. It connects the Old Town with the district called the Little Quarter at the base of the castle across the river.

You can climb either of the **bridge towers.** The tower on the Old Town side of the river (Staroměstská Mostecká Věž) is the one looming above you. Climbing its 138 steps rewards you with some of Prague's best views: a stunning vista of the bridge itself, jammed with people heading for the castle and, 180 degrees away, a perfect panorama that reminds you why Prague is called the "Golden City of a Hundred Spires." Across the bridge on the Little Quarter side (Malostranská Mostecká Věž), you can huff up 146 steps for sweeping views of the bridge, the Little Quarter rooftops, and the castle. If you're trying to decide which to climb, consider that for snapping photos, the light is better if you climb the Old Town tower early in the day, and the Little Quarter tower late in the day (90 Kč to climb each tower, April-Sept daily 10:00-22:00, March and Oct until 20:00, Nov-Feb until 18:00).

PRAGUE

Prague at a Glance

Rather than a checklist of museums, Prague is a great place to wander around and just take in the fun atmosphere.

In the Old Town

▲▲▲**Old Town Square** Magical main square of Old World Prague, with dozens of colorful facades, the dramatic Jan Hus Memorial, looming Týn Church, and fanciful Astronomical Clock. **Hours:** Týn Church generally open to sightseers Tue-Sat 10:00-13:00 & 15:00-17:00, Sun 10:30-12:00, closed Mon; clock strikes on the hour daily 9:00-21:00, until 20:00 in winter; clock tower open Tue-Sun 9:00-21:00, Mon 11:00-21:00. See page 57.

▲▲▲**Charles Bridge** An atmospheric, statue-lined bridge that connects the Old Town to the Little Quarter and Prague Castle. **Hours:** Always open and crossable. See page 72.

▲▲▲**Jewish Quarter** The finest collection of Jewish sights in Europe, featuring various synagogues and an evocative cemetery. **Hours:** The quarter can be visited any time; museum sights open April-Oct Sun-Fri 9:00-18:00, Nov-March until 17:00, closed Sat and Jewish holidays; Old-New Synagogue open Sun-Thu 9:30-18:00, Fri until 17:00 or sunset, closed Sat and on Jewish holidays. See page 73.

▲▲**Museum of Medieval Art** The best Gothic art in the country, at the former Convent of St. Agnes. **Hours:** Tue-Sun 10:00-18:00, closed Mon, may close sporadically due to budget cuts. See page 81.

▲**Havelská Market** Colorful open-air market that sells crafts and produce. **Hours:** Daily 9:00-18:00. See page 67.

In the New Town

▲▲**Wenceslas Square** Lively boulevard at the heart of modern Prague. **Hours:** Always open. See page 81.

▲▲**Mucha Museum** Easy-to-appreciate collection of Art Nouveau works by Czech artist Alfons Mucha. **Hours:** Daily 10:00-18:00. See page 88.

▲▲**Municipal House** Pure Art Nouveau architecture, including Prague's largest concert hall and several eateries. **Hours:** Daily 10:00-18:00. See page 90.

▲**Museum of Communism** The rise and fall of the regime, from start to Velvet finish. **Hours:** Daily 9:00-21:00. See page 89.

▲**National Memorial to the Heroes of the Heydrich Terror** Tribute to members of the resistance, who assassinated a notorious Nazi architect of the Holocaust. **Hours:** Tue-Sun 9:00-17:00, closed Mon. See page 92.

In the Little Quarter
▲**Petřín Hill** Little Quarter hill with public art, a funicular, and a replica of the Eiffel Tower. **Hours:** Funicular—daily 8:00-22:00; tower—daily 10:00-22:00, shorter hours off-season. See page 98.

Church of St. Nicholas Jesuit centerpiece of Little Quarter Square, with ultimate High Baroque decor and a climbable bell tower. **Hours:** Church—daily 9:00-17:00, Nov-Feb until 16:00, opens at 8:30 for prayer; tower—daily April-Oct 10:00-22:00, shorter hours in winter. See page 95.

In the Castle Quarter
▲▲▲**St. Vitus Cathedral** The Czech Republic's most important church, featuring a climbable tower and a striking stained-glass window by Art Nouveau artist Alfons Mucha. **Hours:** Daily April-Oct 9:00-17:00, Nov-March 9:00-16:00, closed Sunday mornings year-round for Mass. See page 106.

▲▲**Prague Castle** Traditional seat of Czech rulers, with St. Vitus Cathedral (see above), Old Royal Palace, Basilica of St. George, shop-lined Golden Lane, and lots of crowds. **Hours:** Castle sights—daily April-Oct 9:00-17:00, Nov-March 9:00-16:00; castle grounds—daily 5:00-24:00. See page 101.

▲▲**Lobkowicz Palace** The most entertaining palace in town. **Hours:** Daily 10:00-18:00. See page 113.

▲**Strahov Monastery and Library** Baroque center of learning, with ornate reading rooms and old-fashioned science exhibits. **Hours:** Daily 9:00-11:45 & 13:00-17:00. See page 114.

Outside the Center
▲▲▲*The Slav Epic* Alfons Mucha's 20 enormous canvases at Veletržní Palace depicting momentous events of Slavic history. **Hours:** Tue-Sun 10:00-18:00, closed Mon. See page 117.

• Now wander onto the bridge. Make your way slowly across the bridge, checking out several of the statues, all on the right-hand side.

⑰ Charles Bridge

Among Prague's defining landmarks, this much-loved bridge offers one of the most pleasant and entertaining strolls in Europe and is worth ▲▲▲. Musicians, artisans, and a constant parade of people make it a festival every day. You can come back to this bridge and enjoy its charms differently at various times of day. Early and late, it can be enchantingly lonely. It's a photographer's delight during that "magic hour," when the sun is low in the sky. The statues on either side of the bridge depict saints, and all of them are impressively expressive.

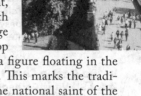

Partway along the bridge, on your right, find a small **brass relief** showing a cross with five stars embedded in the wall of the bridge (it's just below the little grate that sits on top of the stone bannister). The relief depicts a figure floating in the river, with a semicircle of stars above him. This marks the traditional spot where St. John of Nepomuk, the national saint of the Czech people, is believed to have been tossed off the bridge and into the river.

For the rest of that story, continue two more statue groups to the bronze Baroque statue of **St. John of Nepomuk,** with the

five golden stars encircling his head. This statue always draws a crowd. John was a 14th-century priest to whom the queen confessed all her sins. According to a 17th-century legend, the king wanted to know his wife's secrets, but Father John dutifully refused to tell. The shiny plaque at the base of the statue shows what happened next: John was tortured and eventually killed by being thrown off the bridge. The plaque shows the heave-ho. When he hit the water, five stars appeared, signifying his purity. Notice the date on the inscription: 1683. This oldest statue on the bridge was unveiled on the supposed 300th anniversary of the martyr's death. Traditionally, people believe that touching the St. John plaque will make a wish come true. But you get only one chance in life to make this wish, so think carefully before you commit.

• *A good way to end this walk is to enjoy the* ⓲ *city and river view from near the center of the bridge.*

From here, you can continue across the bridge to the Little Quarter (Kampa Island, on your left as you cross the bridge, is a tranquil spot to explore; for more on sights in this area, see page 94). Across the bridge and a 10-minute walk to the right is the Malostranská stop for the Metro or for the handy tram #22. You can also hike (or ride tram #22) up to the castle from here. Or retrace your steps across the bridge to enjoy more time in the Old Town.

Sights in the Old Town (Staré Město)

I've arranged Prague's sights by neighborhood for handy sightseeing. Remember that Prague started out as four towns—the Old Town and New Town on the east side of the river, and the Castle Quarter and Little Quarter on the west—and it's still helpful for sightseers to think of the city that way.

My "Prague Old Town Walk," earlier, covers the main sights in this area, including the **Old Town Square** and its many monuments—the **Týn Church** (see page 57) and the **Old Town Hall/ Astronomical Clock** (page 60)—along with the **Church of St. James** (page 62) and the **Charles Bridge** (page 72). It also points out key landmarks, including the **Ungelt** courtyard (page 62), **House of the Black Madonna** (page 63), and **Powder Tower** (page 64). Here are some additional sights in the Old Town.

▲▲▲JEWISH QUARTER (JOSEFOV)

The Jewish Quarter is Europe's most accessible sight for learning about an important culture and faith that's interwoven with the fabric of Central and Eastern Europe. Within a three-block radius, several original synagogues, cemeteries, and other landmarks survive, today collected into one big, well-presented museum—the Jewish Museum in Prague. It can get crowded here, so time your visit carefully (see "Avoiding Lines," below). For background on typical synagogue architecture, see the sidebar on page 304.

Jewish Museum in Prague (Židovské Muzeum v Praze)

The "museum" consists of four synagogues, a ceremonial hall, and a cemetery—each described here and covered by the same ticket.

Cost and Hours: 300 Kč, or 480-Kč "Jewish Town of Prague" combo-ticket with Old-New Synagogue; open April-Oct Sun-Fri 9:00-18:00; Nov-March Sun-Fri 9:00-17:00; closed year-round on Sat—the Jewish Sabbath—and on Jewish holidays; their website lists all of their closures; 300-Kč audioguide is overkill for most visitors; tel. 222-317-191, www.jewishmuseum.cz.

Getting There: The Jewish Quarter is an easy walk from Old Town Square, up delightful Pařížská street (next to the

PRAGUE

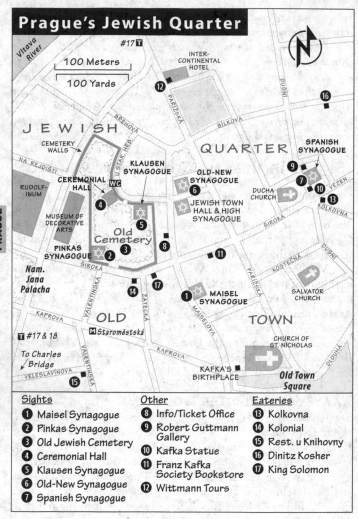

Prague's Jewish Quarter

Vltava River

#17

INTER-CONTINENTAL HOTEL

100 Meters

100 Yards

JEWISH

CEMETERY WALLS

NA REJDIŠTI

RUDOLF-INUM

CEREMONIAL HALL

MUSEUM OF DECORATIVE ARTS

PINKAS SYNAGOGUE

Nam. Jana Palacha

Old Cemetery

KLAUSEN SYNAGOGUE

WC

ŠIROKÁ

QUARTER

BÍLKOVA

BREHOVA

U STAR. HŘB.

PAŘÍŽSKA

OLD-NEW SYNAGOGUE

JEWISH TOWN HALL & HIGH SYNAGOGUE

DUSNI

SPANISH SYNAGOGUE

DUCHA CHURCH

VĚZEŇ

KOLKOVNA

ŠIROKÁ

DUSNI

KOSTECNÁ

PAŘÍŽSKA

SALVATOR CHURCH

MAISEL SYNAGOGUE

VALENTINSKÁ

ZÁTECKÁ

OLD

KAPROVA

#17 & 18

To Charles Bridge

VELESLAVÍNOVA

Staroměstská

MAISELOVA

TOWN

KAPROVA

KAFKA'S BIRTHPLACE

CHURCH OF ST. NICHOLAS

Old Town Square

DLOUHÁ

Sights
1. Maisel Synagogue
2. Pinkas Synagogue
3. Old Jewish Cemetery
4. Ceremonial Hall
5. Klausen Synagogue
6. Old-New Synagogue
7. Spanish Synagogue

Other
8. Info/Ticket Office
9. Robert Guttmann Gallery
10. Kafka Statue
11. Franz Kafka Society Bookstore
12. Wittmann Tours

Eateries
13. Kolkovna
14. Kolonial
15. Rest. u Knihovny
16. Dinitz Kosher
17. King Solomon

green-domed Church of St. Nicholas). The Staroměstská Metro stop is just a couple of blocks away.

Avoiding Lines: The Pinkas Synagogue can be packed, especially 9:30-12:00, so be there right as it opens or later in the day. To save time in line, buy your ticket at less-crowded locations, such as the Klaus or Spanish synagogues, instead of a more crowded one, such as the Pinkas Synagogue.

Dress Code: Men are expected to have their heads covered when entering a synagogue or cemetery. While you'll see many visitors ignoring this custom, it is respectful to borrow a museum-issued yarmulke.

Visiting the Museum: Your ticket comes with a map that locates the sights and lists admission appointments—the times you'll be let in if it's very busy. (Ignore the times unless it's extremely crowded.) You'll notice plenty of security, which can slow down entry. You can see the sights in any order. I recommend the order listed here, but you can rearrange it to avoid crowds at certain sights (most likely at Pinkas Synagogue).

Maisel Synagogue (Maiselova Synagóga): This Neo-Gothic synagogue, likely closed for renovation at least through the end of 2015, was built as a private place of worship for a wealthy family. It hosts a small but illuminating history exhibit about Jewish culture in the Czech lands. During Nazi occupation, this building became a warehouse for a vast collection of Judaica, which Hitler planned to turn into a "Museum of the Extinct Jewish Race"... perhaps explaining why these items, and the Jewish Quarter itself, managed to survive through those dark days.

Inside, the one-room exhibit shows a thousand years of Jewish history in Bohemia and Moravia. Well-explained in English, topics include the origin of the Star of David, Jewish mysticism, the history of discrimination, and the creation of Prague's ghetto. Notice the eastern wall, with the holy ark containing the scroll of the Torah. The central case shows the silver ornamental Torah crowns that capped the scroll.

Pinkas Synagogue (Pinkasova Synagóga): For many visitors, this house of worship—today used as a memorial to the victims of the Holocaust—is the most powerful of the Jewish Quarter sights.

Enter and go down the steps leading to the **main hall** of this small Gothic synagogue. Notice the old stone-and-wrought-iron bema in the middle, the niche for the ark at the far end, the crisscross vaulting overhead, and the Art Nouveau stained glass filling the place with light.

But the main focus of this synagogue is its walls, inscribed with the handwritten **names** of 77,297 Czech Jews sent to the gas chambers at Auschwitz and other camps. Czech Jews were especially hard hit by the Holocaust. More than 155,000 of them passed through the nearby Terezín camp alone. Most died with no grave marker, but they are remembered here. The names are carefully organized: Family names are in red, followed in black by the individual's first name, birthday, and date of death (if known) or date of deportation. You can tell by the dates that families often perished together. The names are gathered in groups by hometowns (listed in gold, as well as on placards at the base of the wall). As you ponder this sad sight, you'll hear the somber reading of the names alternating with a cantor singing the Psalms.

PRAGUE

Prague's Jewish Quarter

Jews are known to have been in Prague as long ago as the 10th century, when Jewish merchants traded in the city's markets. In the early days, Jews were free to live in any of Prague's districts. By the early 13th century, the Old Town had become the city's principal trading center, and the Jewish Quarter was established there (the area's main intersection—Maiselova and Široká streets—was the meeting point of two medieval trade routes).

The status of Prague's (and Europe's) Jews began to deteriorate after 1215 and the Lateran Council, when the pope declared that Jews must be separated from Christians. Jews could not own property or belong to guilds, and they were forced to wear identifying marks on their clothing. Over time, the Jewish Quarter became isolated from the Christian parts of Prague, eventually becoming an enclosed ghetto. In the 16th and 17th centuries, Prague had one of the biggest ghettos in Europe, with 11,000 inhabitants. Within its six gates, the Jewish Quarter was a gaggle of 200 wooden buildings.

Faced with institutionalized bigotry and harassment, Jews relied mainly on profits from moneylending (forbidden to Christians) and community solidarity to survive. While their money bought them protection (the kings taxed Jewish communities heavily), it was often also a curse. Throughout Europe, when times got tough and Christian debts to the Jewish community mounted, entire Jewish communities were evicted or killed. In the Prague pogrom of 1389, a Christian mob massacred the inhabitants of the Jewish Quarter and then set it ablaze.

In the 1780s, Emperor Josef II, motivated more by economic concerns than by religious freedom, eased much of the discrimination against Jews. In 1848, the Jewish Quarter's walls were torn down, and the neighborhood—named Josefov in honor of the emperor who provided this small measure of tolerance—was

On your way out, watch on the right for the easy-to-miss stairs up to the small **Terezín Children's Art Exhibit.** Well-described in English, these drawings were made by Jewish children imprisoned at Terezín, 40 miles northwest of Prague. This is where the Nazis shipped Prague's Jews for processing before transporting them east to death camps. Thirty-five thousand Jews died at Terezín, and many tens of thousands more died in other camps.

Of the 8,000 children transported from Terezín, only 240 survived until liberation. Their art looks like something from your typical elementary school—until you recall the tragic circumstances in which it was created. The collection is organized into poignant themes: dreams of returning to Prague; yearning for a fantasized Holy Land; sentimental memories of the simple times before imprisonment; biblical and folkloric tales focusing on the themes of good and evil; and scenes of everyday life at Terezín.

incorporated as a district of the Old Town. Wealthier Jews moved on to fashionable addresses elsewhere in the city. Although Jewish life continued to be centered here, the quarter declined into an overcrowded slum.

Beginning in 1897, ramshackle Josefov was razed and replaced by a new modern town. The medieval-era buildings (except the synagogues) came down, and the original 31 streets and 220 buildings became 10 streets and 83 buildings. This was perhaps Europe's finest Art Nouveau neighborhood, boasting stately facades with gables, turrets, elegant balconies, mosaics, statues, and all manner of architectural marvels.

By the 1930s, Prague's Jewish community was flourishing within the new Czechoslovakian state formed at the end of World War I. But everything quickly changed with Hitler's 1938 annexation of the Czech Sudetenland. Of the 55,000 Jews living in Prague in 1939 (many of whom were refugees from the Sudentenland and Austria), just 10,000 survived the Holocaust to see liberation in 1945. And in the communist era—when the atheistic regime was also anti-Semitic—recovery was slow.

Today there are only 3,000 "registered" Jews in the Czech Republic, and of these, only 1,700 are in Prague. (This number represents only active members of the Jewish community. There are undoubtedly more Jewish people here, but after their experiences with the Nazis and communists, it's understandable that many choose not to register.) Today, in spite of their tiny numbers, the legacy of Prague's Jewish community lives on. While today's modern grid plan has replaced the higgledy-piggledy medieval streets of old, Široká ("Wide Street") remains the main street. A few Jewish-themed shops and restaurants in the area add extra ambience to this (otherwise modern) neighborhood.

Perhaps saddest of all are the photographs of a few of these young artists. (Terezín makes an emotionally moving day trip from Prague; see page 176.)

Old Jewish Cemetery (Starý Židovský Hřbitov): Hiding behind a wall and sitting above the street level, this is where Prague's Jews buried their dead. A stroll through the crooked tomb-

stones is a poignant experience.

You enter one of the most wistful scenes in Europe. You meander along a path through 12,000 evocative tombstones. They're old, eroded, inscribed in Hebrew, and leaning this way and that. A few of the dead have larger ark-shaped tombs.

Most have a simple epitaph with the name, date, and a few of the deceased's virtues.

From 1439 until 1787, this was the only burial ground allowed for the Jews of Prague. Over time, the graves had to be piled on top of one another—layered seven or eight deep—so there are actually closer to 85,000 dead here. Graves were never relocated because of the Jewish belief that, once buried, a body should not be moved. Layer by layer, the cemetery grew into a small plateau. Tune into the noise of passing cars outside, and you realize that you're several feet above the modern street level, which is already high above the medieval level.

People place pebbles on honored tombstones. This custom, a sign of respect, shows that the dead have not been forgotten and

recalls the old days, when rocks were placed upon a sandy gravesite to keep the body covered. Others leave scraps of paper that contain prayers and wishes.

Ceremonial Hall (Obřadní Síň): This rustic stone tower (1911), sitting at the edge of the cemetery, was a mortuary house used to prepare the body and perform purification rituals before burial. The inside is painted in fanciful, flowery Neo-Romanesque style. It's filled with a worthwhile exhibition on Jewish medicine, death, and burial traditions.

Klausen Synagogue (Klauzová Synagóga): This 17th-century synagogue is devoted to Jewish religious practices. The ground-floor displays touch on Jewish holidays. Upstairs, exhibits illustrate the rituals of everyday Jewish life. It starts at birth. There are good-luck amulets to ensure a healthy baby, and a wooden cradle that announces, "This little one will become big." The baby is circumcised (see the knife) and grows to celebrate a coming-of-age Bar or Bat Mitzvah around age 12 or 13. Marriage takes place under a canopy, and the couple sets up their home—the exhibit ends with some typical furnishings.

Note that the Spanish Synagogue—described next—is a few blocks away from the core of the Jewish Quarter. Before heading over there, consider visiting the nearby **Old-New Synagogue** at this time (described at the end of this section).

Spanish Synagogue (Španělská Synagóga): Called "Spanish," though its design is Moorish (which was all the rage when this was built in the 19th century), this has the most opulently decorated interior of all of the synagogues. It marked a time of relative wealth and importance for Prague's Jews, who in this era were increasingly welcome in the greater community and (in many cases) chose to adopt a more reformed approach to worship. Exhibits explain the lives of Czech Jews in the 19th and early 20th centuries, when they believed to be living their best days yet... unaware that the Holocaust was looming.

Inside, the decor is exotic and awe-inspiring. Intricate inter-weaving designs (of stars and vines) cover every inch of the red-gold and green walls and ceiling. A rose window with a stylized Star of David graces the ark.

The new synagogue housed a new movement within Judaism: a Reform congregation, which worshipped in a more modern way. The bema has been moved to the front of the synagogue, so the officiant faces the congregation. There's also a prominent organ (upper right) to accompany the singing.

Displays of Jewish history bring us through the 18th, 19th, and tumultuous 20th centuries to today. In the 1800s, Jews were increasingly accepted and successful in the greater society. But tolerance brought a dilemma—was it better to assimilate within the dominant culture or to join the growing Zionist homeland movement? To reform the religion or to remain orthodox?

Upstairs, the **balcony exhibits** focus on Czech Jews in the 1900s. Start in the area near the organ, which explains the modern era of Jewish Prague, including the late 19th-century development of Josefov. Then work your way around the balcony, with exhibits on Jewish writers (Franz Kafka), philosophers (Edmund Husserl), and other notables (Freud). This intellectual renaissance came to an abrupt halt with World War II and the mass deportations to Terezín (see more sad displays on life there, including more children's art and a box full of tefillin prayer cases). The final displays bring it home: After 2,000 years of living away from their Holy Land roots, the Jewish people had a home-land—the modern nation of Israel.

Finish your visit across the landing in the **Winter Synagogue,** showing a trove of silver—Kiddush cups, Hanukkah lamps, Sabbath candlesticks, and Torah ornaments.

Old-New Synagogue (Staronová Synagóga)

The oldest surviving and most important building in the Jewish Quarter, the Old-New Synagogue goes back at least seven centuries. While the exterior seems simple compared with ornate neighboring townhouses, the interior is atmospherically 13th-century.

Cost and Hours: 200 Kč, or 480-Kč combo-ticket with Jewish Museum of Prague, Sun-Thu 9:30-18:00, Fri until 17:00 or sunset, closed Sat and on Jewish holidays, admission includes worthwhile 10-minute tour, tel. 222-317-191, www.synagogue.cz.

Visiting the Synagogue: Built in 1270, this is the oldest synagogue in Eastern Europe (and some say the oldest still-working synagogue in all of Europe). The name likely comes because it was "New" when built, but became "Old" when other, newer synagogues came on the scene. The exterior is simple, with a unique saw-tooth gable. Standing like a bomb-hardened bunker, it feels as though it has survived plenty of hard times.

As you enter, you descend a few steps below street level to 13th-century street level and the medieval world.

The **interior** is pure Gothic—thick pillars, soaring arches, and narrow lancet windows. If it looks like a church, well, the architects were Christians. The stonework is original, and the woodwork (the paneling and benches) is also old. This was one of the first Gothic buildings in Prague.

Seven centuries later, it's still a working synagogue. There's the stone bema in the middle where the Torah is read aloud, and the ark at the far end, where the sacred scrolls are kept. To the right of the ark, one chair is bigger, with a Star of David above it. This chair always remains empty out of respect for great rabbis of the past. Where's the women's gallery? Here, women worshipped in rooms that flanked the hall, watching the service through those horizontal windows in the walls.

Before leaving, check out the **lobby** (the long hall where you show your ticket). It has two fortified old lockers in which the most heavily taxed community in medieval Prague stored its money in anticipation of the taxman's arrival.

NORTH OF THE OLD TOWN SQUARE, NEAR THE RIVER

Stray just a couple of blocks north of the Old Town Square and you'll find a surprisingly tourist-free world of shops and cafés, pastel buildings with decorative balconies and ornamental statues, winding lanes, cobblestone streets, and mosaic sidewalks. It's also home to this underrated museum.

▲▲Museum of Medieval Art
(Středověké umění v Čechách a Střední Evropě)

Prague flourished in the 14th century, and the city has amassed an impressive collection of altarpieces and paintings from that age. Today this art is housed in the former Convent of St. Agnes, which was founded in the 13th century by a Czech princess-turned-nun as the first hospital in Prague. A visit here is a sightseeing twofer: Enjoy the well-presented art in a refreshingly uncrowded setting, and savor the tranquil corridors and cloisters.

PRAGUE

Cost and Hours: Museum-150 Kč, convent buildings are free, Tue-Sun 10:00-18:00, closed Mon, two blocks northeast of Spanish Synagogue, along the river at Anežská 12, tel. 224-810-628, www.ngprague.cz.

Sights in the New Town (Nové Město)

Enough of pretty, medieval Prague—let's leap into the modern era. The New Town, with Wenceslas Square as its focal point, is today's urban Prague. This part of the city offers bustling boulevards and interesting neighborhoods. Even today, the New Town is separated from the Old Town by a "moat" (the literal meaning of the street called Na Příkopě). As you cross bustling Na Příkopě, you leave the glass and souvenir shops behind and enter a town of malls and fancy shops that cater to locals and visitors alike. The New Town is one of the best places to view Prague's remarkable Art Nouveau art and architecture, and to learn more about its communist past.

WENCESLAS SQUARE AND NEARBY

These sights are on or within a few blocks of the elongated main square of the New Town.

▲▲Wenceslas Square (Václavské Náměstí)

More a broad boulevard than a square, this city landmark is named for St. Wenceslas, whose equestrian statue overlooks the square's top end. Wenceslas Square functions as a stage for modern Czech history: The creation of the Czechoslovak state was celebrated here in 1918; in 1968, the Soviets suppressed huge popular demonstrations (called the Prague Spring) at the square; and, in 1989, more than 300,000 Czechs and Slovaks converged here to demand their

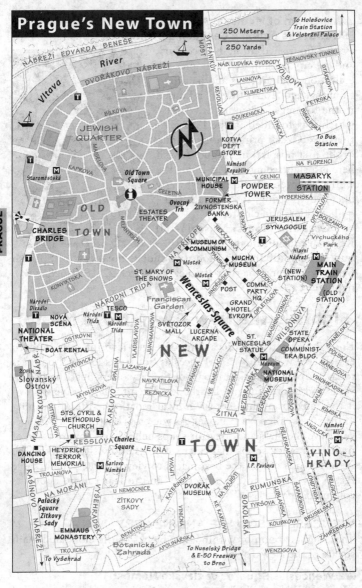

Prague's New Town

250 Meters
250 Yards

To Holešovice
Train Station
& Veletržní Palace

NÁBŘEŽÍ EDVARDA BENEŠE

River

Vltava

DVOŘÁKOVO NÁBŘEŽÍ

ŠTEFÁNIKŮV MOST

NÁB. LUDVÍKA SVOBODY

TĚŠNOVSKÝ TUNNEL

HOLBOVA

LANNOVA

KLIMENTSKÁ

REVOLUČNÍ

SOUKENICKÁ

ZLATNICKÁ

BÍLKOVA

JEWISH QUARTER

MASELNÁ

KAPROVA

Staroměstská

KOTVA
DEP'T
STORE

To Bus
Station

NA FLORENCI

Old Town
Square

Náměstí
Republiky

MASARYK
STATION

OLD

Ovocný
Trh

CELETNÁ

MUNICIPAL
HOUSE

POWDER
TOWER

V CELNICI

HYBERNSKÁ

OPLETALOVA

BOLZANOVA

TOWN

ESTATES
THEATER

FORMER
ŽIVNOSTENSKÁ
BANKA

JERUSALEM
SYNAGOGUE

Vrchuckého
Park

CHARLES
BRIDGE

MELANTRICH

NA PŘÍKOPĚ

NEKÁZANKA

SENOVÁŽNÁ

MUSEUM OF
COMMUNISM

Můstek

MUCHA
MUSEUM

RŮZOVÁ

Hlavní
Nádraží

MAIN
TRAIN
STATION

(NEW
STATION)

ST. MARY OF
THE SNOWS

KONVIKTSKÁ

NÁRODNÍ TŘÍDA

Franciscan
Garden

Můstek

JINDŘIŠSKÁ

POST

COMM.
PARTY
HQ

(OLD
STATION)

Národní
Divadlo

NOVÁ
SCÉNA

Národní
Třída

TESCO

Národní
Třída

JUNGMANNOVA

SVĚTOZOR
MALL

LUCERNA
ARCADE

GRAND
HOTEL
EVROPA

OPLETALOVA

WASHINGTONOVA

WILSONOVA

ŠPANĚLSKÁ

NATIONAL
THEATER

OSTROVNÍ

BOAT RENTAL

VLADISLAVOVA

Wenceslas Square

ST.
WENCESLAS
STATUE

STATE
OPERA

COMMUNIST-
ERA BLDG.

POLSKÁ

ŽOFÍN

Slovanský
Ostrov

MASARYKOVO NÁBŘ.

DITTRICHOVA

OPATOVICKÁ

SPÁLENÁ

LAZARSKÁ

ŠTĚPÁNSKÁ

NEW

Muzeum

NATIONAL
MUSEUM

MEZIBRANSKÁ

MANESOVA

VINOHRADSKÁ

MYSLÍKOVA

NAVRÁTILOVA

ŘEZNICKÁ

VE SMEČKÁCH

KRAKOVSKÁ

LEGEROVA

KUBELÍKOVA

BALBÍ

ŘÍMSKÁ

STS. CYRIL &
METHODIUS
CHURCH

KARLOVO

ŽITNÁ

TOWN

Náměstí
Míru

ANGLICKÁ

DANCING
HOUSE

RESSLOVA

Charles
Square

JEČNÁ

HÁLKOVA

LIPOVA

BĚLEHRADSKÁ

I.P. Pavlova

VINO-
HRADY

BELGICKÁ

RAŠÍNOVO

HEYDRICH
TERROR
MEMORIAL

Karlovo
Náměstí

RUMUNSKÁ

LUBLAŇSKÁ

SOKOLSKÁ

ŠAFAŘÍKOVA

LONDÝNSKÁ

TROJANOVA

NA MORÁNI

VYŠEHRADSKÁ

U NEMOCNICE

KATEŘINSKÁ

KE KARLOVU

TYRŠOVA

BRUSELSKÁ

Palacký
Square
Zítkovy
Sady

ZÍTKOVY
SADY

DVOŘÁK
MUSEUM

NA BOJIŠTI

KOUBKOVA

ZÁHŘEBSKÁ

NÁBŘ.

EMMAUS
MONASTERY

BENÁTSKÁ

APOLINÁŘSKÁ

WENZIGOVA

TROJICKÁ

Botanická
Zahrada

To Vyšehrad

To Nuselský Bridge
& E-50 Freeway
to Brno

freedom (in the Velvet Revolution). Today it's a busy thoroughfare of commerce.

○ **Self-Guided Walk:** For a taste of Prague's 20th-century history, take a stroll from the top of the square—with the big statue of Wenceslas—to the bottom. (To get here quickly, ride the Metro to the Muzeum stop.)

• *Begin at the big...*

Statue of Duke Wenceslas I: The "Good King" of Christmas-carol fame was actually a wise and benevolent 10th-century duke. Václav I (as he's called by locals) united the Czech people, back when this land was known as Bohemia. A rare example of a well-educated and literate ruler, Wenceslas Christianized and lifted the culture. He astutely allied the powerless Czechs with the Holy Roman Empire. And he began to fortify Prague's castle as a center of Czech government. After his murder in 929, Wenceslas was canonized as a saint. He became a symbol of

PRAGUE

Czech nationalism (and appears on the 20-Kč coin). Later kings knelt before his tomb to be crowned. And he remains an icon of Czech unity whenever the nation has to rally. Like King Arthur in England, Wenceslas is more legend than history, but he symbolizes the country's birth.

The statue is surrounded by the four other Czech patron saints. Notice the focus on books. A small nation without great military power, the Czechs have thinkers as national heroes, not warriors.

And this statue is a popular meeting point. Locals like to say, "I'll meet you under the horse's tail" (though they use a cruder term).

• *Circle behind the statue and stand below that tail, then turn your attention to the impressive building at the top of Wenceslas Square.*

National Museum: The building is grand and the interior is rich, though the collection itself is pretty dull. The build-

ing dates from the 19th century, back when there was no unified Czech nation—just Czech-speaking peasants and two-bit, wannabe-German aristocrats living under the auspices of Austria's Habsburg Empire. But throughout Europe, the mid-19th century was a time of national resurgence. Bold structures like this Neo-Renaissance building were a way to show the world that the Czech people had a distinct culture, a heritage of precious artifacts, and that they deserved their own nation.

Look closely at the columns on the building's facade. Those light-colored patches are covering holes where Soviet bullets hit

The Prague Spring and Its Fall

In January of 1968, Slovak politician Alexander Dubček replaced the aging apparatchiks at the helm of the Communist Party of Czechoslovakia. Handsome and relatively youthful, Dubček's brand was that of a smiling playboy; he appeared on magazine covers in his speedo, about to dive into a swimming pool. Young Czechs and Slovaks embraced Dubček as a potential hero of liberalization.

In April, Dubček introduced his "Action Program," designed to tiptoe away from strict and stifling Soviet communism and forge a more moderate Czechoslovak variation. Censorship eased, travel restrictions were relaxed, state companies began forming joint ventures with Western firms, money poured into the sciences, and a newspaper called "Tomorrow" (rather than "Today") became the most popular in the country. Plays put on at the Semafor Theater (in today's Světozor mall) lampooned Brezhnev and his ilk. During this so-called "Prague Spring," optimism soared.

But then, around midnight on August 20, 1968, the thundering sound of enormous airplanes ripped across the floodlit rooftops of Prague. The Soviets had dispatched over 200,000 Warsaw Pact troops to invade Czechoslovakia, airlifting tanks right into the capital city. Dubček and his team were arrested and taken to Moscow. Czechs and Slovaks—now living in a police state—were terrified as they took to the streets, boycotting and striking. Tanks rolled through Wenceslas Square, spraying protesters with bullets...some of which are still embedded in the National Museum's pillars. Over the course of the occupation, 72 Czechs and Slovaks were killed.

Dubček stepped down and went into internal exile, and his successor—the hardliner Gustáv Husák—immediately pursued a policy of "normalization." People who refused to sign a petition commending the "Russian Liberation" were fired from their jobs and forced to find worse ones. Some protesters—including Jan Palach—set themselves on fire to protest against the regime. Tens of thousands of Czechs and Slovaks reluctantly emigrated to the West, fearing what might come next.

While the ill-fated tale of the Prague Spring is pessimistic, it provides an insightful bookend to what happened 21 years later: The children of the generation that suffered Czechoslovakia's bitterest disappointment brought about its greatest success.

during the 1968 crackdown. The repair masons did an intentionally sloppy job, so that this dark moment could never be plastered over and forgotten.

• *To the left of the National Museum (as you face it), along the busy street, is a...*

Communist-Era Building: This ugly, modern structure once housed the rubber-stamp Czechoslovak Parliament back when it

voted in lock-step with Moscow. Between 1994 and 2008, this building was home to Radio Free Europe. After communism fell, RFE lost some of its funding and could no longer afford its Munich headquarters. In gratitude for its broadcasts—which had kept the people of Eastern Europe in touch with real news—the Czech government offered this building to RFE for 1 Kč a year.

PRAGUE

But as RFE energetically beamed its American message deep into the Muslim world from here, it drew attention—and threats—from Al-Qaeda. In 2009, RFE moved to a new fortress-like headquarters at an easier-to-defend locale farther from the center. Now this is an annex of the National Museum.

• *Start walking down Wenceslas Square. Pause about 30 yards along, at the little patch of bushes. In the ground on the downhill side of those bushes is a...*

Memorial to the Victims of 1969: After the Russian crackdown of 1968, a group of patriots wanted to stand up to the power-

ful Soviet occupation. One was a young philosophy student named Jan Palach. He decided that the best way to stoke the flame of independence was to set himself on fire. On January 16, 1969, Palach stood on the steps of the National Museum and ignited his body for the cause of Czech freedom. He died a few days later in a hospital ward. A month later, another student did the same thing, followed by another. Czechs are keen on anniversaries, and—20 years after Palach's brave and patriotic act, in 1989—Czechs gathered here for a huge demonstration. A sense of new possibility swept through the city, and 10 months later, the communists were history.

• *Continue down Wenceslas Square until you reach the median in front of Grand Hotel Evropa. It's the ornate, yellow building about 300 yards down Wenceslas Square, on the right.*

The Velvet Revolution of 1989

On the afternoon of November 17, 1989, 30,000 students gathered in Prague's New Town to commemorate the 50th anniversary of the suppression of student protests by the Nazis, which had led to the closing of Czech universities through the end of World War II. Remember, this was just a few weeks after the fall of the Berlin Wall, and the Czechs were feeling the winds of change blowing across Central Europe. The 1989 demonstration—initially planned by the Communist Youth as a celebration of the communist victory over fascism—spontaneously turned into a protest *against* the communist regime. "You are just like the Nazis!" shouted the students. The demonstration was supposed to end in the National Cemetery at Vyšehrad (the hill just south of the New Town). But when the planned events concluded in Vyšehrad, the students decided to march on toward Wenceslas Square... and make some history.

As they worked their way north along the Vltava River toward the New Town's main square, the students were careful to keep their demonstration peaceful. Any hint of violence, the demonstrators knew, would incite brutal police retaliation. Instead, as the evening went on, the absence of police became conspicuous. (In the 1980s, the police never missed a chance to participate in any demonstration...preferably outnumbering the demonstrators.) At about 20:00, as the students marched down Národní Třída toward Wenceslas Square, three rows of policemen suddenly blocked the demonstration at the corner of Národní and Spálená streets. A few minutes later, military vehicles with fences on their bumpers (having crossed the bridge by the National Theater) appeared behind the marching students. This new set of cops compressed the demonstrators into the stretch of Národní Třída between Voršilská and Spálená. The end of Mikulandská street was also blocked, and policemen were hiding inside every house entry. The students were trapped.

At 21:30, the "Red Berets" (a special anti-riot commando force known for its brutality) arrived. The Red Berets lined up on both sides of this corridor. To get out, the trapped students had to run through the passageway as they were beaten from the left and right. Police trucks ferried captured students around the corner to the police headquarters (on Bartolomějská) for interrogation.

The next day, university students throughout Czechoslovakia decided to strike. Actors from theaters in Prague and Bratislava joined the student protest. Two days later, the students' parents—shocked by the attacks on their children—marched into Wenceslas Square. Sparked by the events of November 17, 1989, the wave of peaceful demonstrations ended later that year on December 29, with the election of Václav Havel as the president of a free Czechoslovakia.

Architecture Along Wenceslas Square: As you walk, notice the architecture. Unlike the historic Old Town, nearly everything here is from the past two centuries. Wenceslas Square is a showcase of Prague's many architectural styles: You'll see Neo-Gothic, Neo-Renaissance, and Neo-Baroque from the 19th century. There's curvaceous Art Nouveau from around 1900. And there's the modernist response to Art Nouveau—Functionalism from the mid-20th century, where the watchword was "form follows function," and beauty took a back seat to practicality. You'll see what's nicknamed "Stalin Gothic" from the 1950s communist era; a good example of that is the Hotel Jalta building, halfway downhill on the right (the sandy facade with lots of balconies). And there are forgettable glass-and-steel buildings of the 1970s.

The Velvet Revolution: Opposite Grand Hotel Evropa (that is, on the left side of the square), find the Marks & Spencer building, which has a balcony on it (partly obscured by tree branches). Take a moment to picture the scene on this square on a cold November night in 1989. Czechoslovakia had been oppressed for the previous 40 years by communist Russia. But now the Soviet empire was beginning to crumble, jubilant Germans were dancing on top of the shattered Berlin Wall, and the Czechs were getting a whiff of freedom.

Czechoslovakia's revolution began with a bunch of teenagers, who—following a sanctioned gathering—decided to march on Wenceslas Square (see sidebar). After they were surrounded and beaten by the communist riot police, their enraged parents, friends, and other members of the community began to pour into this square to protest. Night after night, this huge square was filled with more than 300,000 ecstatic Czechs and Slovaks who believed freedom was at hand. Each night they would jangle their key chains in the air as if saying to their communist leaders, "It's time for you to go home now." Finally they gathered and found that their communist overlords had left—and freedom was theirs.

On that night, as thousands filled this square, a host of famous people appeared on that balcony to greet the crowd. There was a well-known priest and a rock star famous for his rebellion against authority. There was Alexander Dubček, the hero of the Prague Spring reforms of 1968. And there was Václav Havel, the charismatic playwright who had spent years in prison, becoming a symbol of resistance—a kind of Czech Nelson Mandela. Now he was free. Havel's voice boomed over the gathered masses. He proclaimed the resignation of the Politburo and the imminent freedom of the Republic of Czechoslovakia. He pulled out a ring of keys and jingled it. Thousands of keys jingled back in response. It was their symbolic way of saying: The communists have packed up and left, and now we're free to unlock our chains.

PRAGUE

In previous years, the communist authorities would have sent in tanks to crush the impudent masses. But by 1989, the Soviet empire was collapsing, and the Czech government was shaky. Locals think that Soviet head of state Mikhail Gorbachev (mindful of the Tiananmen Square massacre a few months before) might have made a phone call recommending a nonviolent response. Whatever happened, the communist regime was overthrown with hardly any blood being spilled. It was done through sheer people power—thanks to the masses of defiant Czechs who gathered here peacefully in Wenceslas Square, and Slovaks doing the same in Bratislava. They called it "The Velvet Revolution."

Franciscan Garden

Ahhh! This garden's white benches and spreading rosebushes are a universe away from the fast beat of the city, which throbs behind the buildings corralling this little oasis. The peacefulness reflects the purpose of its Franciscan origin. St. Francis, the founder of the order, thought God's presence could be found in nature. In the 1600s, Prague became an important center for a group of Franciscans from Ireland. Enjoy the herb garden, children's playground, and public WC. The park is a popular place for a discreet rendezvous; it's famous among locals for kicking off romances.

Cost and Hours: Free, open long hours daily.

Getting There: The garden is very central, but hidden—and worth seeking out if you want a break from the city. You can reach it by cutting through the Světozor Mall (a few steps from the middle of Wenceslas Square, just down Vodičkova street); or, a block from the bottom of Wenceslas Square, look for the gate tucked behind the Jungmann statue on Jungmannovo Náměstí.

▲▲Mucha Museum (Muchovo Museum)

This enjoyable little museum features a small selection of the insis-

tently likeable art of Alfons Mucha (MOO-khah, 1860-1939), a founding father of the Art Nouveau movement. It's all crammed into a tight space, some of the art is faded, and the admission price is steep, but there's no better place to gain an understanding of Mucha's talent, his career, and the influence he's had on the world art scene. And the museum, partly overseen by Mucha's grandson, gives you a peek at some of the posters that made Mucha famous. You'll learn how these popular patriotic banners, filled with Czech symbols and expressing his people's ideals and aspirations, aroused the national spirit. Enjoy decorative posters from his years in Paris, including his celebrated ads for the French actress Sarah Bernhardt. Check out the photographs of his models, which Mucha later re-created in pencil or paint, and be sure to see the 30-minute film on the artist's life. For more on Mucha, see "Background" on page 118.

Cost and Hours: 240 Kč, daily 10:00-18:00, good English descriptions, two blocks off of Wenceslas Square at Panská 7, tel. 224-233-355, www.mucha.cz. Peruse the well-stocked gift shop.

ALONG NA PŘÍKOPĚ

At the bottom of Wenceslas Square, the street running to the right is called Na Příkopě. As this street is a showcase of Art Nouveau, be sure to keep your eyes up as you stroll here. City tour buses leave from along this street, which also offers plenty of shopping temptations (see "Shopping in Prague," later).

▲Museum of Communism (Muzeum Komunismu)

Tucked away upstairs in a cramped and creaky old mansion, this humble but engaging museum traces the story of communism in Prague: the origin, dream, reality, and nightmare; the cult of personality; and, finally, the Velvet Revolution. Along the way, it gives a thought-provoking review of the Czech Republic's 40-year stint with Soviet economics, "in all its dreariness and puffed-up glory." You'll find propaganda posters and busts of communist All-Stars (Marx, Lenin, and others), and re-created slices of communist life. While dated and faded (like its subject), and lacking high-tech flair, the museum's clever displays and English descriptions evoke the time well—making this Prague's most accessible sight relating to its communist era.

Cost and Hours: 190 Kč, daily 9:00-21:00, Na Příkopě 10, tel. 224-212-966, www.muzeumkomunismu.cz.

Nearby: If you're curious to see communism outside of a museum, take a five-minute walk to the present-day **Headquarters of the Communist Party of Bohemia and Moravia (KSČM).** From the museum, hook around the corner (to the right) and head up Panská street a long block and a half—passing the Mucha Museum—to find Politických Vězňů 9 (on the left). The building, which sits on "Political Prisoners Street" (no joke), is painted an appropriately peachy shade of red, and protesters have spilled red paint on its threshold. Step inside (go ahead—the door's open) to pick up some propaganda brochures and see party leadership and candidate photos of today's midlevel apparatchiks in bad suits... who seem oblivious to the political (and fashion) changes since 1989. They've swapped the red star with a cheerier symbol—a pair of bright-red cherries, as if voting Communist is like playing a slot machine. Despite heavy public pressure to outlaw this artifact of a hated-by-most era, the Communist Party still commands between 10 and 15 percent of the national Czech vote—mostly from aging, nostalgic voters more concerned about predictability than freedom. Other, more pragmatic Czechs say they're glad the communists still have their own party—at least it keeps them marginalized, rather than being a vocal fringe that hijacks the agenda of a larger, more influential party.

▲▲Municipal House (Obecní Dům)

The cultural and artistic leaders who financed this Art Nouveau masterpiece (1905-1911) wanted a ceremonial palace to reinforce

self-awareness of the Czech nation. While the exterior is impressive (and described on page 64 of my "Prague Old Town Walk"), the highlight is the interior—and it's free. To extend your Art Nouveau bliss, take a guided tour or attend a concert here.

Cost and Hours: The entrance halls and public spaces are free to enter and explore, open daily 10:00-18:00. For an in-depth look at all the sumptuous halls and banquet rooms, take advantage of the daily one-hour English **tours** (290 Kč, usually 3/day, leaving between 11:00 and 17:00; limited to 35 people, so buy your ticket as soon as you can from the ground-floor shop where tours depart; pay 55 Kč extra to take photos; Náměstí Republiky 5, tel. 222-002-101, www.obecnidum.cz).

Concerts: Performances are held regularly in the lavish Smetana Hall (see schedule at www.obecnidum.cz/web/en/programme). Note that many concerts brag they are held in the Municipal House, but are performed in a smaller, less impressive hall in the same building.

Visiting the Municipal House: Don't be timid about poking around the interior, which is open to the public. Having lunch or a drink in one of the eateries is a great way to experience the decor, but you can also just glimpse them from the doorway (as you "check out the menu").

Enter under the green, wrought-iron arcade. In the **rotunda,** admire the mosaic floor, stained glass, the woodwork doorway and the lighting fixtures. To the left is the **café** *(kavárna)*—a harmony of woodwork, marble, metal, and glittering chandeliers (plus 150-Kč sandwiches, 250-Kč salads, and 200 Kč for coffee and apple strudel). Opposite the café is the equally stunning **restaurant.**

From the rotunda, step into the **lobby,** where you can look up the staircase that leads up to the main concert hall (no tourist access upstairs). Also in the lobby is the box office selling concert tickets and guided English tours of the building.

Facing the staircase, go right and head **downstairs**—yes, tourists are welcome there. Admire the colorful tiles in the stairwell and more colorful tiles in the downstairs main room. Look for the plaster model of this building and the adjacent Powder Tower, which shows how the angled facade conceals a surprisingly large performance space. Also check out the **American Bar** (salute the US flags above the bar) and the **Plzeňská Restaurant** (with its dark-wood booths and colorful tile scenes of happy peasants).

Finish your tour by going back upstairs and find the **Modernista shop** (tucked to the left as you face the main staircase)—full of fancy teacups and jewelry.

Also upstairs, you may find **temporary exhibits** (usually around 150 Kč), typically about Art Nouveau. This style was heavy on the applied arts (as opposed to fine arts such as painting), so you'll see elegant lamps, chairs, prints, and clothes. This period celebrated new technologies, which allowed high-quality objects to be mass-produced for the average Jan and Jana. They're functional and minimal in design, but always beautiful. To reach this space, you're allowed to ascend the main staircase, pass by the guard, and glimpse into the stylish Smetana Hall along the way.

SIGHTS NEAR THE VLTAVA RIVER

I've listed these sights from north to south, beginning at the grand, Neo-Renaissance National Theater, which is five blocks south of the Charles Bridge and stands along the riverbank at the end of Národní Třída.

National Theater (Národní Divadlo)

Opened in 1883 with Smetana's opera *Libuše,* this theater was the first truly Czech venue in Prague. From the very start, it was nicknamed the "Cradle of Czech Culture." The building is a key sym-

bol of the Czech National Revival that began in the late 18th century. In 1800, "Prag" was predominantly German. The Industrial Revolution brought Czechs from the countryside into the city, their new urban identity defined by patriotic teachers and priests. By 1883, most of the city spoke Czech, and the opening of this theater represented the birth of the modern Czech nation. It remains an important national icon: The state annually pours more subsidies into this theater than into all of Czech film production. It's the most beautiful venue in town for opera and ballet, often with world-class singers (for more details on performances, see page 129).

• A 10-minute walk (or one stop on tram #17) south from the National Theater, beyond the islands, is Jirásek Bridge (Jiráskův Most), where you'll find the...

Dancing House (Tančící Dům)

If ever a building could get your toes tapping, it would be this one, nicknamed "Fred and Ginger" by American architecture buffs.

This metallic samba is the work of Frank Gehry (who designed the equally striking Guggenheim Museum in Bilbao, Spain, and Seattle's Experience Music Project). Eight-legged Ginger's wispy dress and Fred's metal mesh head are easy to spot. Some Czechs prefer to think that the two "figures" represent the nation's greatest 20th-century heroes, Jozef Gabčík and Jan Kubiš (see the sidebar on the assassination of Heydrich). A contemporary art gallery occupies unused office space throughout the building (90 Kč, daily 11:00-19:00). The building's top-floor restaurant, **Céleste,** is a fine place for a fancy French meal. Whether you go up for lunch (reasonable, 12:00-14:30), a drink (16:00-18:00), or an expensive dinner, you'll be a louse in the Gehry haircut (tel. 221-984-160).

• Two blocks up Resslova street is the Sts. Cyril and Methodius Church, which contains in its crypt the...

▲National Memorial to the Heroes of the Heydrich Terror (Národní Památník Hrdinů Heydrichiády)

In 1942, WWII paratroopers Jozef Gabčík and Jan Kubiš assassinated the SS second-in-command Reinhard Heydrich, who con-

trolled the Nazi-occupied Czech lands and was one of the main architects of the Holocaust. In the weeks following his assassination, the two paratroopers hid, along with other freedom fighters, in the crypt of the Greek Orthodox Sts. Cyril and Methodius Church on Resslova street. Today, a modest exhibition in the church's crypt retells

The Assassination of Reinhard Heydrich

Visitors to the Sts. Cyril and Methodius Church are reminded of a fascinating slice of Nazi-era intrigue.

In September of 1941, Reinhard Heydrich—the SS second-in-command, Hitler's personal favorite, and one of the architects of the Holocaust—became the governor of the occupied Czech lands.

At the same time, the Czechoslovak government-in-exile was suffering a crisis of legitimacy in Britain's eyes. Following the British signing of the Munich Pact (an act of appeasement that would annex Czechoslovakia's Sudetenland area to the Nazis), thousands of Czechs and Slovaks went abroad to fight, and few of those left in the occupied lands were cut out for underground resistance.

It was under these circumstances that two paratroopers, Jozef Gabčík and Jan Kubiš, were chosen by British Special Operations and trained in Scotland for a secret and, as they were made to understand from the start, potentially suicidal mission to eliminate Heydrich.

On the morning of May 27, 1942, Heydrich was coming down Kobylisy hill on his daily commute. Just as the unaccompanied open car slowed down at a hairpin turn, Gabčík jumped in front of the car and pointed his Sten machine gun at Heydrich, and pulled the trigger. But the gun jammed. Heydrich, ordering his driver to stop, pulled out his revolver. At that moment, Kubiš, coming in from behind, threw a handmade grenade that missed and exploded outside the car. But the explosion was enough to wound Heydrich, who was transported to a nearby hospital, where he died a few days later. At his funeral—the Nazis' most elaborate funeral ceremony ever—Hitler appeared genuinely distressed, and Heydrich was eulogized as the model for all SS men.

The Nazi response in the Protectorate was brutal. Martial law was declared, two villages were summarily razed to the ground, and in the ensuing months, 5,000 individuals were executed. A reward was announced for tips leading to the capture of the assassins. Karel Čurda, a member of another paratrooper unit, betrayed his comrades. On June 18, at 4:15 in the morning, the Gestapo surrounded the Sts. Cyril and Methodius Church on Resslova street, where the two paratroopers were hiding. After a two-hour battle, Kubiš, on guard in the nave of the church, was killed along with two other defenders. Gabčík and three other paratroopers committed suicide in the crypt below.

Days after the assassination, the British government revoked its signature on the Munich Pact, recognizing Czechoslovakia's prewar boundaries; the French followed two months later. Heydrich—whose elimination was one of the most significant acts of resistance in occupied Europe—remains the highest-ranked Nazi official killed while in office.

PRAGUE

their story, along with the history of the Czech resistance movement. Outside, notice the small memorial, including bullet holes, plaque, and flowers on the street. Around the corner is the entry into the museum and the crypt.

Cost and Hours: 75 Kč, Tue-Sun 9:00-17:00, closed Mon, full history explained in small 25-Kč booklet, 2 blocks up from the Dancing House at Resslova 9A, tel. 224-916-100.

Prague's Embankment
Much of the city's Vltava-front embankment—especially the stretch between Palacký Square and Vyšehrad—has been gorgeously renovated in recent years, and has become a particularly nice (and untouristy) place to wander. Al fresco cafés and restaurant barges enliven the riverbank on sunny days, and a farmers' market bustles on Saturday morning (8:00-14:00).

Sights in the Little Quarter (Malá Strana)

Huddled under the castle on the west bank of the river, this neighborhood is pleasant, though low on blockbuster sights. The most enjoyable approach from the Old Town is across the Charles Bridge. From the end of the bridge (TI in tower), Mostecká street leads two blocks up to the Little Quarter Square (Malostranské Náměstí) and the huge Church of St. Nicholas. But before you head up there, consider a detour to Kampa Island.

BETWEEN CHARLES BRIDGE AND LITTLE QUARTER SQUARE

Kampa Island
One hundred yards from the castle end of the Charles Bridge, stairs on the left lead you down to the main square of Kampa Island (mostly created from the rubble of the Little Quarter, which was destroyed in a 1540 fire). The island features relaxing pubs, a breezy park, hippies, lovers, a fine contemporary art gallery, and river access. From the main square, Hroznová lane (on the right) winds around to a little bridge. The high-water mark at  the end of the bridge dates from 1890. The **old water wheel** is the last survivor of many mills that once lined the canal here. Each mill had its own protective water spirit *(vodník)*.

• *Fifty yards beyond the bridge (on the right, under the trees) is the...*

Lennon Wall (Lennonova Zeď)

While V. I. Lenin's ideas hung like a water-soaked trench coat upon the Czech people, rock singer John Lennon's ideas gave many

locals hope and a vision. When Lennon was killed in 1980, a large wall was spontaneously covered with memorial graffiti. Night after night, the police would paint over the "All You Need Is Love" and "Imagine" graffiti. And day after day, it would reappear. Until independence came in 1989, travelers, freedom lovers, and local hippies gathered here. Silly as it might seem, this wall is remembered as a place that gave hope to locals craving freedom. Even today, while the tension and danger associated with this wall are gone, people come here to imagine. *"John žije"* is Czech for "John lives."

• *From here, continue up to the Little Quarter Square.*

ON OR NEAR LITTLE QUARTER SQUARE

The focal point of this neighborhood, the Little Quarter Square (Malostranské Náměstí), is split into an upper and lower part by the domineering Church of St. Nicholas and its adjacent Jesuit college. A Baroque plague column oversees the upper square. Note that there's a handy Via Musica ticket office across from the plague column (on the uphill side).

Church of St. Nicholas (Kostel Sv. Mikuláše)

When the Jesuits came to Prague, they found the perfect piece of real estate for their church and its associated school—right on Little Quarter Square. The church (built 1703-1760) is the best example of High Baroque in town.

Cost and Hours: 70 Kč, daily 9:00-17:00, Nov-Feb until 16:00, opens at 8:30 for prayer.

Visiting the Church: The church's interior is giddy with curves and illusions. Stand directly under the tallest dome and look up. Spin slowly around, greeting four giant statues—the fathers of the Eastern Church. Pan up and see the earthly world merging with heaven above.

The **altar** features a lavish gold-plated Nicholas, flanked by the two top Jesuits: the founder, St. Ignatius Loyola, and his missionary follower, St. Francis Xavier.

Climb up the **gallery** through the staircase in the left transept for a close-up look at a collection of large canvases and illusionary frescoes by Karel Škréta, who is considered the greatest Czech Baroque painter. Notice that at first glance the canvases are utterly

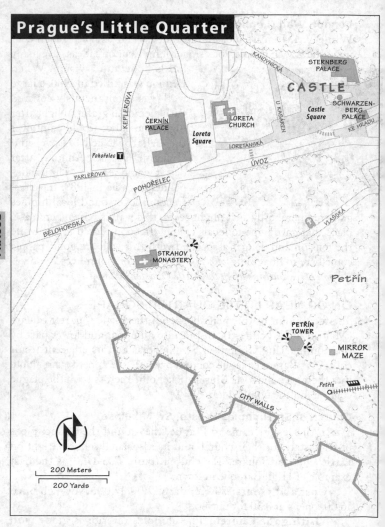

Prague's Little Quarter

dark, but as sunbeams shine through the window, various parts of the painting brighten up. Like a looking glass, the image reflects the light, creating a play of light and dark. This painting technique represents a central Baroque belief: The world is full of darkness, and the only hope that makes it come alive emanates from God. The church walls seem to nearly fuse with the sky, suggesting that happenings on earth are closely connected to heaven.

Tower Climb: For a good look at the city and the church's 250-foot dome, climb 215 steps up the bell tower. Closed to the public during the communist times, the deck was used by the

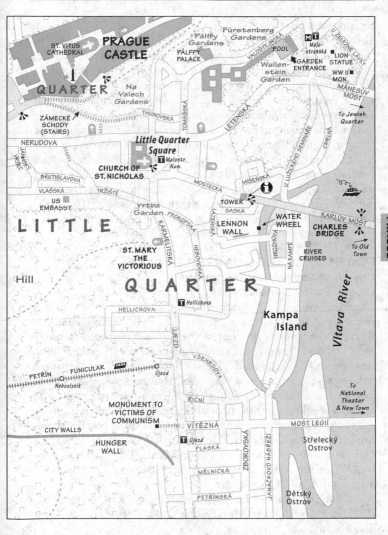

PRAGUE

secret police to spy on the activities at the nearby embassies of the US, Britain, and West Germany (90 Kč, daily April-Oct 10:00-22:00, shorter hours in winter, tower entrance is outside the right transept).

Concerts: The church is also an evening concert venue; tickets are usually on sale at the door (490 Kč, generally nightly at 18:00 except Tue, www.stnicholas.cz).

• *From here, you can hike 10 minutes uphill to the castle (and 5 more minutes to the Strahov Monastery). If you're walking up to the castle, consider going via...*

Nerudova Street

This steep, cobbled street, leading from Little Quarter Square to the castle, is named for Jan Neruda, a gifted 19th-century journalist (and somewhat less-talented fiction writer). It's lined with old buildings still sporting the characteristic doorway signs (such as the lion, three violinists, and house of the golden suns) that once served as street addresses. The surviving signs are carefully restored and protected by law. They represent the family name, the occupation, or the various passions of the people who once inhabited the houses. (If you were to replace your house number with a symbol, what would it be?) In the 1770s, in order to collect taxes more effectively, Habsburg empress Maria Theresa decreed that numbers be used instead of these quaint house names. This neighborhood is filled with old noble palaces, now generally used as foreign embassies and as offices of the Czech Parliament.

SOUTH OF LITTLE QUARTER SQUARE

Church of St. Mary the Victorious
(Kostel Panny Marie Vítězné)

This otherwise ordinary Carmelite church displays Prague's most worshipped treasure, the Infant of Prague (Pražské Jezulátko). Kneel at the banister in front of the tiny lost-in-gilded-Baroque altar, and find the prayer in your language (of the 13 in the folder). Brought to Czech lands during the Habsburg era by a Spanish noblewoman who came to marry a Czech nobleman, the Infant has become a focus of worship and miracle tales in Prague and Spanish-speaking countries. South Americans come on pilgrimage to Prague just to see this one statue. An exhibit upstairs shows tiny embroidered robes given to the Infant, including ones from Habsburg Empress Maria Theresa of Austria (1754) and the country of Vietnam (1958), as well as a video showing a nun lovingly dressing the doll-like sculpture.

Cost and Hours: Free, Mon-Sat 9:30-17:30, Sun 13:00-18:00, English-language Mass Sun at 12:00, Karmelitská 9, www.pragjesu.info.

▲Petřín Hill (Petřínské Sady)

This hill, topped by a replica of the Eiffel Tower, features several unusual sights. The sculptural figures of the poignant **Monument to Victims of Communism** (Pomník Obětem Komunismu), representing victims of the totalitarian regime, gradually atrophy as they range up the hillside steps. They do not die but slowly disappear, one limb at a time. The statistics inscribed on the steps say it all: From 1948 until 1989, in Czechoslovakia alone, 205,486 people were imprisoned, 248 were executed, 4,500 died in prison, 327 were shot attempting to cross the border, and 170,938 left the country.

To the left of the monument is the **Hunger Wall** (Hladová Zed'). This medieval defense wall was Charles IV's 14th-century equivalent of FDR's work-for-food projects. The poorest of the poor helped build this structure just to eke out a bit of income.

On the right (50 yards away) is the base of a handy **funicular**—hop on to reach Petřín Tower (uses tram/Metro ticket, runs daily every 10-15 minutes 8:00-22:00).

The summit of Petřín Hill is considered the best place in Prague to take your date for a romantic city view. Built for an

exhibition in 1891, the 200-foot-tall **Petřín Tower** is one-fifth the height of its Parisian big brother, which was built two years earlier. But, thanks to this hill, the top of the tower sits at the same elevation as the real Eiffel Tower. Climbing the 400 steps rewards you with amazing views of the city (105 Kč, daily 10:00-22:00, shorter hours off-season; the mirror maze next door is nothing special, but fun to wander through quickly since you're already here—75 Kč, daily 10:00-22:00, shorter hours off-season).

PRAGUE

Sights in the Castle Quarter (Hradčany)

Looming above Prague, dominating its skyline, is the Castle Quarter. Prague Castle and its surrounding sights are packed with Czech history, as well as with tourists. In addition to the castle, I enjoy visiting the nearby Strahov Monastery, which has a fascinating old library and beautiful views over all of Prague.

GETTING TO THE CASTLE QUARTER

You have three options: taxi, walk, or tram.

By **taxi,** take it to the top of Nerudova street, just below Castle Square. To **walk** up, figure 20 minutes uphill from Charles Bridge, along charming cobbled Nerudova street. After about 10 minutes, a steep lane on the right leads to Castle Square; or, if you continue straight, Nerudova becomes Úvoz and climbs to the Strahov Monastery.

For the **tram,** catch tram #22 at one of these three convenient stops: the Národní Třída stop (between Wenceslas Square and the National Theater in the New Town); in front of the National Theater (Národní Divadlo, on the riverbank in the New Town); and at Malostranská (the Metro stop in the Little Quarter). After rattling up the hill, tram #22 makes three stops near the castle (see map on page 102): **Královský Letohrádek** allows a scenic but slow approach through the Royal Gardens; **Pražský Hrad** offers the quickest commute to the castle—from the tram stop, simply walk along U Prašného Mostu and over the bridge, past the stone-faced-but-photo-op-friendly guards, and into the castle's Second Courtyard; and **Pohořelec** is best if you'd like to start with the Strahov Monastery, then hike down to the castle. After getting off at the Pohořelec tram stop, follow the tracks for 50 yards, take the pedestrian lane that rises up beside the tram tracks, and enter the fancy gate on the left near the tall red-brick wall. You'll see the twin spires of the monastery; the library entrance is on the little square with the monastery church.

AVOIDING CROWDS

Prague Castle is one of the city's most crowded sights. Huge throngs of tourists turn the grounds into a sea of people during peak times (9:30-12:30, especially May-Sept). The most cramped area is the free vestibule inside St. Vitus Cathedral; any sight that you pay to enter—including other parts of the cathedral—will be less jammed. The following plans are designed to minimize the effect of crowds and to maximize your enjoyment:

Early Bird Plan: If you prefer to visit the castle in the morning, leave your hotel no later than 8:00 (earlier is even better). Ride tram #22 up to the Pražský Hrad stop; leave yourself time to walk through the Royal Gardens on your way, then enter the complex's Second Courtyard and buy your tickets. See Castle Square, and most important, be sure that you're standing at the front door of St. Vitus Cathedral when it opens at the stroke of 9:00. For 10 minutes, you'll have the sacred space to yourself...then, on your way out, you'll pass a noisy human traffic jam of multinational tour groups clogging the entrance. Visit the rest of the castle sights at your leisure: the Old Royal Palace, the Basilica of St. George, and the Golden Lane. If you'd like to see the Strahov Monastery and/ or Loreta Church after your castle visit, you'll have to backtrack uphill to do it (either by foot, or by hopping back on tram #22 at a lower stop—near the castle, or even from the Malostranská stop near the river).

Afternoon Plan: Ride tram #22 to the Pohořelec stop. Tour the Strahov Monastery, then drop by Loreta Church on your way to Castle Square. By the time you hit the sights, the crowds should be thinning out (if St. Vitus is jammed, circle back later). The only risk here is running out of time to enter all the sights (which close at 17:00 in summer, or 16:00 in winter); in summer, I'd start at Strahov no later than 14:00.

Nighttime Visit: Least crowded of all is nighttime. True, the sights are closed, but the castle grounds are free, safe, peaceful, floodlit, and open late. For example, the tiny, normally jammed Golden Lane is empty and romantic at night—and no ticket is required.

OFFICIAL SIGHTS AT PRAGUE CASTLE (PRAŽSKÝ HRAD)

This vast, sprawling complex, worth ▲▲, has been the seat of Czech power for centuries. It collects a wide range of sights, including the country's top church, its former royal palace, a higgledy-piggledy lane, and an assortment of history and art museums. (These are listed here in order, from top to bottom, starting at the main gate.) While it's imposing and a bit intimidating to sightseers, the casual visitor finds that a quick and targeted visit is ideal. The sights listed here are part of the official castle complex and share opening hours and tickets. Which ticket you choose depends on which sights you want to enter, so familiarize yourself with the options before buying your ticket.

Ticket Options: While you can enter the grounds for free, most sights require tickets. For a quick visit, get the 250-Kč "Circuit B" ticket, which hits the highlights (St. Vitus Cathedral, Old Royal Palace, Basilica of St. George, Golden Lane). For a few bucks more, "Circuit A" (350 Kč) adds "The Story of Prague Castle" exhibit and some other sights that may be worthwhile for those with a healthy interest in history and art. You can buy tickets at three different ticket offices in the castle's second and third courtyards. Lines can be long at one and nonexistent at the next, so if it's crowded, check all three. Climbing St. Vitus Cathedral's Great South Tower requires a separate 150-Kč ticket.

Tours: Tours in English and an audioguide are available, but I'd skip both in favor of this book's self-guided tour (tours-100 Kč plus entry ticket, covers only the cathedral and Old Royal Palace; audioguide-350 Kč plus 500-Kč deposit).

Hours: Castle sights—daily April-Oct 9:00-17:00, Nov-March 9:00-16:00, last entry 15 minutes before closing; castle grounds—daily 5:00-24:00; castle gardens—10:00-21:00 in summer, shorter hours off-season. St. Vitus Cathedral is closed Sunday mornings for Mass and can be closed unexpectedly at other times. The Great South Tower of St. Vitus Cathedral is open daily 10:00-18:30, until 16:30 in winter, www.hrad.cz.

↻Self-Guided Tour

• *Begin your visit to the castle complex at its main entrance on...*

Castle Square (Hradčanské Náměstí)

You're standing at the tip of the medieval iceberg called Prague Castle. It's a 1,900-foot-long series of courtyards, churches, and

PRAGUE

PRAGUE

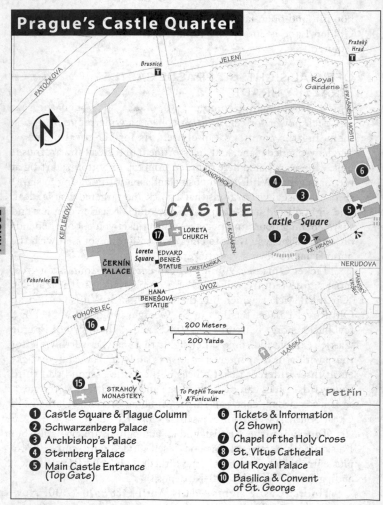

Prague's Castle Quarter

PATOČKOVA

Brusnice 🚇

JELENÍ

Pražský Hrad 🚇

Royal Gardens

U PRAŠNÉHO MOSTU

KANOVNICKÁ

C A S T L E

KEPLEROVA

4

3

6

U KAŠÁREN

Castle Square

1

2

5

LORETA CHURCH

17

Loreta Square

EDVARD BENEŠ STATUE

ČERNÍN PALACE

KE HRADU

NERUDOVA

Pohořelec 🚇

LORETÁNSKÁ

ÚVOZ

JÁNSKÝ VRŠEC

HANA BENEŠOVÁ STATUE

POHOŘELEC

16

200 Meters

200 Yards

VLAŠSKÁ

15

STRAHOV MONASTERY

To Petřín Tower & Funicular

Petřín

- **1** Castle Square & Plague Column
- **2** Schwarzenberg Palace
- **3** Archbishop's Palace
- **4** Sternberg Palace
- **5** Main Castle Entrance (Top Gate)
- **6** Tickets & Information (2 Shown)
- **7** Chapel of the Holy Cross
- **8** St. Vitus Cathedral
- **9** Old Royal Palace
- **10** Basilica & Convent of St. George

palaces, covering 750,000 square feet—by some measures, the largest castle on earth. In the center of the complex sits St. Vitus Cathedral (the two prickly steeples you see rising above the buildings).

You can't miss the **main entrance** to the castle: a gateway with a golden arch, guarded by two fighting-giant statues and two real-life soldiers in their blue-and-white guardhouses. The stoic guards make a great photo-op, as

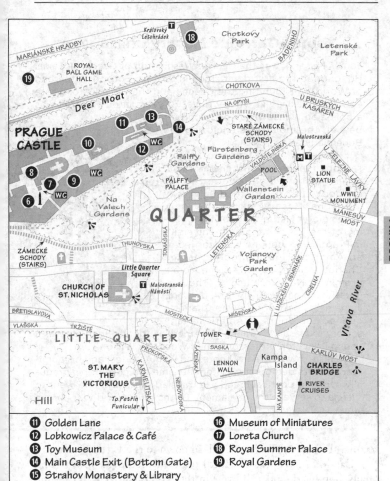

- ⑪ Golden Lane
- ⑫ Lobkowicz Palace & Café
- ⑬ Toy Museum
- ⑭ Main Castle Exit (Bottom Gate)
- ⑮ Strahov Monastery & Library
- ⑯ Museum of Miniatures
- ⑰ Loreta Church
- ⑱ Royal Summer Palace
- ⑲ Royal Gardens

PRAGUE

does the changing of the guard (on the hour from 5:00-23:00). In fact, there's a guard-changing ceremony at every gate: top, bottom, and side. The best ceremony and music occurs at noon, at the top gate.

Enjoy the awesome city view and the entertaining bands that play regularly at the gate. (If the Prague Castle Orchestra is playing, say hello to friendly, mustachioed Josef, and consider buying the group's CD—it's

Tomáš Garrigue Masaryk (1850-1937)

Tomáš Masaryk was the George Washington of Czechoslovakia. He founded the first democracy in Eastern Europe at the end of World War I, uniting the Czechs and the Slovaks to create Czechoslovakia. Like Václav Havel 70 years later, Masaryk was a politician whose vision extended far beyond the mountains enclosing the Bohemian basin.

Masaryk was born into a poor servant family in southern Moravia. After finishing high school, the village boy set off to attend university in Vienna. Masaryk earned his Ph.D. in sociology just in time for the opening of the Czech-language university in Prague. By then, he was married to an American music student named Charlotta Garrigue, who came from a prominent New York family. (The progressive Tomáš actually took her family name as part of his own.) Charlotta opened the doors of America's high society to Masaryk. Among the American friends he made was a young Princeton professor named Woodrow Wilson.

Masaryk was greatly impressed with America, and his admiration for its democratic system became the core of his gradually evolving political creed. He traveled the world and went to Vienna to serve in the parliament. By the time World War I broke

terrific.) From the square, stairs lead down to the Little Quarter.

Castle Square was the focal point of medieval power. The archbishop lived (and still lives) in the **Archbishop's Palace**—the ornate, white-and-yellow Rococo palace on the right. The portal on the left leads to the **Sternberg Palace** art museum, with European paintings.

On the left side of the square, the building with a step-gable roofline is **Schwarzenberg Palace,** where the aristocratic families of Český Krumlov "humbly" stayed when they were visiting from their country estates. Notice the envelope-shaped patterns stamped on the exterior. These Renaissance-era adornments etched into wet stucco—called sgraffito—decorate buildings throughout the castle, all over Prague, and across the Czech Republic. Today the castle is an art museum with a collection of Baroque-era Czech paintings and sculpture.

The black Baroque sculpture in the middle of the square is a **plague column.** Erected as a token of gratitude to Mary and the out, in 1914, Masaryk was 64 years old and—his friends thought—ready for retirement. But while most other Czech politicians stayed in Prague and supported the Habsburg Empire, Masaryk went abroad in protest and formed a highly original plan: to create an independent, democratic republic of Czechs and Slovaks. Masaryk and his supporters recruited an army of 100,000 Czech and Slovak soldiers who were willing to fight with the Allies against the Habsburgs, establishing a strong case to put on his friend Woodrow Wilson's Oval Office desk.

On the morning of October 28, 1918, news of the unofficial capitulation of the Habsburgs reached Prague. Local supporters of Masaryk's idea quickly took control of the city and proclaimed the free republic. As the people of Prague tore down double-headed eagles (a symbol of the Habsburgs), the country of Czechoslovakia was born.

On November 11, 1918, four years after he had left the country as a political unknown, Masaryk arrived in Prague as the greatest Czech hero since the revolutionary priest Jan Hus. The dignified old man rode through the masses of cheering Czechs on a white horse. He told the jubilant crowd, "Now go home—the work has only started." Throughout the 1920s and 1930s, Masaryk was Europe's most vocal defender of democratic ideals against the rising tide of totalitarian ideologies.

In 2001, the US government honored Masaryk's dedication to democracy by erecting a monument to him in Washington, D.C. He is one of only three foreign leaders (along with Gandhi and Churchill) to have a statue in the American capital.

saints for saving the population from epidemic disease, these columns are an integral part of the main squares of many Habsburg towns.

Closer to you, near the overlook, the statue of a man in a business suit (marked *TGM*) honors the father of modern Czechoslovakia: **Tomáš Garrigue Masaryk** (1850-1937). At the end of World War I, Masaryk—a former university prof and pal of Woodrow Wilson—united the Czechs and the Slovaks into one nation and became its first president (see the sidebar). He was the only 20th-century leader to actually live inside Prague Castle.

• *Let's enter the castle. Walk through the golden gate, into the so-called* **First Courtyard**. *Continue straight ahead, through the massive stone Matthias Gate (1614), where you'll emerge into the* **Second Courtyard**. *Two ticket offices (with information desks) are in this courtyard (to the left as you enter)—if the line isn't too long, buy your ticket now. Straight ahead as you enter is the...*

St. Vitus Treasury

Recently opened in the restored Chapel of the Holy Cross, this pricey-to-view collection shows off the accumulated wealth of the cathedral's ecclesiastical gear. The highlight, dating from Charles IV's reign (1360s), is a golden reliquary in the shape of a cross; used during coronation ceremonies, the cross contains what are supposedly the actual thorns, nails, sponge, rope, and fragments of the cross from Jesus' Crucifixion. You'll also see reliquary busts in the shape of saints (Vitus, Wenceslas, and Adalbert), monstrances slathered in diamonds and other precious stones, chalices, and icons. It's an impressive collection, but it's outrageously overpriced. Skip it unless you're a monstrance aficionado.

Cost and Hours: 300 Kč, includes torturously dull audioguide; buy ticket at entrance—not at castle ticket office, which sells only a combo-ticket that adds another museum; daily 10:00-18:00, last entry one hour before closing, tel. 224-372-432.

*• From the Second Courtyard, proceed into the **Third Courtyard**. You'll be face-to-face with...*

▲▲▲St. Vitus Cathedral (Katedrála Sv. Víta)

This towering house of worship—with its flying buttresses and spiny spires—is the top church of the Czech people. Many VIPs

from this nation's history—from saints to statesmen—are buried here. You can step into the very congested entry vestibule for a peek at the interior, but it's worth paying for a ticket that lets you go deeper, leave some of the crowds behind, and explore.

⊙Self-Guided Tour: Begin your cathedral tour out in front of the building.

Entrance Facade: The two soaring towers of this Gothic wonder rise 270 feet up. The ornate facade features pointed arches, elaborate tracery, Flamboyant pinnacles, a rose window, a dozen statues of saints, and gargoyles sticking their tongues out.

So what's up with the four guys in modern suits carved into the stone, as if supporting the big, round window on their shoulders? They're the architects and builders who finished the church six centuries after it was started. Even though church construction got underway in 1344, wars, plagues, and the reforms of Jan Hus conspired to stall its completion. Finally, fueled by a burst of Czech nationalism, Prague's top church was finished in 1929 for the 1,000th Jubilee anniversary of St. Wenceslas. The entrance facade and towers were the last parts to be finished.

• *Enter the cathedral. If it's not too crowded in the free entrance area, work your way to the middle of the church for a good...*

View Down the Nave: The church is huge—more than 400 feet long and 100 feet high—and flooded with light. Notice the intricate "net" vaulting on the ceiling, especially at the far end. It's the signature feature of the church's chief architect, Peter Parler (who also built the Charles Bridge).

• *Now make your way through the crowds and pass through the ticket turnstile (left of the roped-off area). The third window on the left wall is worth a close look.*

PRAGUE

Mucha Stained-Glass Window: This masterful 1931 Art Nouveau window was designed by Czech artist Alfons Mucha and executed by a stained-glass craftsman (if you like this, you'll love the Mucha Museum in the New Town—see page 88—and Mucha's masterpiece *Slav Epic*—described on page 117).

Mucha's window was created to celebrate the birth of the Czech nation and the life of Wenceslas. The main scene (in the four central panels) shows Wenceslas as an impressionable child kneeling at the feet of his Christian grandmother, St. Ludmila. She spreads her arms and teaches him to pray. Wenceslas would grow up to champion Christianity, uniting the Czech people.

Above Wenceslas are the two saints who first brought Christianity to the region: Cyril (the monk in black hood holding the Bible) and his older brother, Methodius (with beard and bishop's garb). They baptize a kneeling convert.

Follow their story in the side panels, starting in the upper left. Around A.D. 860 (back when Ludmila was just a girl), these two Greek missionary brothers arrive in Moravia to preach. The pagan Czechs have no written language to read the Bible, so (in the next scene below), Cyril bends at his desk to design the necessary alphabet (Glagolitic, which later developed into Cyrillic), while Methodius meditates. In the next three scenes, they travel to Rome and present their newly translated Bible to the pope. But Cyril falls ill, and Methodius has to watch his kid brother die.

Methodius carries on (in the upper right), becoming bishop of the Czech lands. Next, he's arrested for heresy for violating the pure Latin Bible. He's sent to a lonely prison. When he's finally set free, he retires to a monastery, where he dies mourned by the faithful.

But that's just the beginning of the story. At the bottom center are two beautiful (classic Mucha) maidens, representing the bright future of the Czech and Slovak peoples.

• *Continue circulating around the church, following the one-way, clockwise route.*

The Old Church: Notice that, just after the transept, there's a slight incline in the floor. That's because the church was actually constructed in two distinct stages. You're entering the older, 14th-century Gothic section. The front half (where you came in) is a Neo-Gothic extension that was finally completed in the 1920s (which is why much of the stained glass has a modern design). For 400 years—as the nave was being extended—a temporary wall kept the functional altar area protected from the construction zone.

• *In the choir area (on your right), soon after the transept, look for the big, white marble tomb surrounded by a black iron fence.*

Royal Mausoleum: This contains the remains of the first Habsburgs to rule Bohemia, including Ferdinand I, his wife Anne, and Maximilian II. The tomb dates from 1590, when Prague was a major Habsburg city.

• *Just after the choir, as you begin to circle around the back of the altar, watch on your right for the fascinating, carved-wood...*

Relief of Prague: This depicts the aftermath of the Battle of White Mountain, when the Protestant King Frederic escaped over the Charles Bridge (before it had any statues). Carved in 1630, the relief gives you a peek at old Prague. Find the Týn Church (far left) and St. Vitus Cathedral (far right), which was half-built at that time. Back then, the Týn Church was Hussite, so the centerpiece of its facade is not the Virgin Mary (more of a Catholic figure), but a chalice, a symbol of Jan Hus' ideals. The old city walls, now replaced by the main streets of the city, stand strong. The Jewish Quarter is the flood-prone zone along the riverside below the bridge on the left—land no one else wanted. The weir system on the river—the wooden barriers that help control its flow—survives to this day.

• *Circling around the high altar, you'll see various...*

Tombs in the Apse: Among the graves of medieval kings and bishops is that of **St. Vitus,** shown as a young man clutching a book and gazing up to heaven. Why is this huge cathedral dedicated to this rather obscure saint, who was martyred in Italy in A.D. 303 and never set foot in Bohemia? A piece of Vitus' arm bone (a holy relic) was supposedly acquired by Wenceslas I in 925. Wenceslas built a church to house the relic on this spot, attracting crowds of pilgrims. Vitus became quite popular throughout the Germanic and Slavic lands, and revelers danced on his feast day. (He's now the patron saint of dancers.) At the statue's feet is a rooster, because the saint was thrown into a boiling cauldron along with the bird (the Romans' secret sauce)...but he miraculously survived.

A few steps farther, the big silvery tomb with the angel-borne canopy honors **St. John of Nepomuk.** Locals claim it has more than a ton of silver (for more on St. John of Nepomuk and his halo of stars, see page 72). Just past the tomb, on the wall of the choir (on the right), is another finely carved, circa-1630 **wood relief** depicting an event that took place right here in St. Vitus: Protestant nobles trash the cathedral's Catholic icons after their (short-lived) victory.

Ahead on the left, look up at the **royal oratory,** a box supported by busy late-Gothic, vine-like ribs. This private box, connected to the king's apartment by a corridor, let the king attend Mass in his jammies. The underside of the balcony is morbidly decorated with dead vines and tree branches, suggesting the pessimism common in the late Gothic period, when religious wars and Ottoman invasions threatened the Czech lands.

• *From here, walk 25 paces and look left through the crowds and door to see the richly decorated chapel containing the tomb of St. Wenceslas. Two roped-off doorways give visitors a look inside. The best view is from the second one, around the corner and to the left, in the transept.*

Wenceslas Chapel: This fancy chapel is the historic heart of the church. It contains the tomb of St. Wenceslas, patron saint of the Czech nation, it's where Bohemia's kings were crowned, and it houses (but rarely displays) the Bohemian crown jewels. The chapel walls are paneled with big slabs of precious and semiprecious stones. The jewel-toned stained-glass windows (from the 1950s) admit a soft light. The chandelier is exceptional. The place feels medieval.

The tomb of St. Wenceslas is a colored-stone coffin topped with an ark. Above the chapel's altar is a statue of Wenceslas, bearing a lance and a double-eagle shield. He's flanked by (painted) angels and the four patron saints of the Czech people. Above Wenceslas are portraits of Charles IV (who built the current church) and his beautiful wife. On the wall to the

PRAGUE

left of the altar, frescoes depict the saint's life, including the episode where angels arrive with crosses to arm the holy warrior. (For more on Wenceslas, see page 83.) For centuries, Czech kings were crowned right here in front of Wenceslas' red-draped coffin.

• *Leave the cathedral, turn left (past the public WC), and survey the...*

Third Courtyard

The **obelisk** was erected in 1928—a single piece of granite celebrating the 10th anniversary of the establishment of Czechoslovakia

and commemorating the soldiers who fought for its independence. It was originally much taller, but broke in transit—an inauspicious start for a nation destined to last only 70 years.

From here, you get a great look at the sheer size of St. Vitus Cathedral and its fat green **tower** (325 feet tall). Up there is the Czech Republic's biggest **bell** (16.5 tons, from 1549), nicknamed "Zikmund." You can view the bell as you climb up the 287 steps of the tower to the observation deck at the top (buy 150-Kč ticket and enter near sculpture of St. George—a 1960s replica of the 13th-century original).

It's easy to find the church's **Golden Gate** (for centuries the cathedral's main entry)—look for the glittering 14th-century mosaic of the Last Judgment. The modern, cosmopolitan, and ahead-of-his-time Charles IV commissioned this monumental decoration, in 1370, in the Italian style. Jesus oversees the action, as some go to heaven and some go to hell. The Czech king and queen kneel directly beneath Jesus and six patron saints. On coronation day, royalty would walk under this arch, a reminder to them (and their subjects) that even those holding great power are not above God's judgment. See the grilled windows above this entryway? That's where the royal crown and national jewels are stashed.

Across from the Golden Gate, in the corner, notice the copper, scroll-like **awning** supported by bulls. This leads to a lovely garden just below the castle. The stairway, garden, and other features around the castle were designed by the Slovene architect Jože Plečnik (see page 762). Around the turn of the 20th century, Prague was considered the cultural standard-bearer of the entire Slavic world, making this a particularly prestigious assignment.

• *In the corner of the Third Courtyard, near the copper awning, is the entrance to the...*

▲Old Royal Palace (Starý Královský Palác)

The traditional seat of Czech power, this feels like a mostly empty historical shell. But its oversized Vladislav Hall—big enough for

horseback jousting competitions or bustling markets—is impressive. The smaller adjoining rooms called the "Czech Office" were the site of a famous defenestration—the Czech way of dealing with unwanted politicians: In 1618, angry Czech Protestant nobles poured into these rooms and threw the two Catholic governors out the window. An old print on the glass panel shows the second of Prague's many defenestrations. The two governors landed—fittingly—in a pile of horse manure. Even though they suffered only broken arms and bruised egos, this event kicked off the huge and lengthy Thirty Years' War. The palace also comes with a balcony offering fine views of the surrounding hillsides and assorted other royal portraits and bric-a-brac.

• *The next sight requires the "Circuit A" ticket; if you don't have one, skip down to the next stop.*

Otherwise, as you exit the Royal Palace, hook left around the side of the building and backtrack a few steps uphill to find stairs leading down to...

The Story of Prague Castle Exhibit (Příběh Pražského Hradu)

For those wanting to dig deeper into the history of Prague and its castle, this exhibit features well-described historical artifacts from the very first Czechs through the imported Habsburg monarchy of the 17th century. As this is the main addition to the pricier "Circuit A" ticket, visit here only if you have a bigger-than-average appetite for history.

▲Basilica and Convent of St. George (Bazilika Sv. Jiří)

The oldest-feeling place at the castle, this dimly lit, stripped-down Romanesque chapel offers

a subdued contrast to the big, bombastic spaces elsewhere. The church was founded by Wenceslas' dad around 920, and the present structure dates from the 12th century. (Its Baroque facade came later.) Inside, the place is beautiful in its simplicity. Notice the characteristic thick walls and rounded arches.

In those early years, building techniques were not yet advanced enough to use those arches for the ceiling—it's made of wood instead.

This was the royal burial place before St. Vitus was built, so the tombs here contain the remains of the earliest Czech kings. Climb the stairs that frame either side of the altar to study the area around the apse. St. Wenceslas' grandmother, Ludmila, was reburied here in 925. Her stone tomb is in the space just to the right of the altar. Inside the archway leading to her tomb, look for her portrait. Holding a branch and a book, she looks quite cultured for a 10th-century woman.

• *As you exit, notice the building across the lane from the basilica (with the columned and curved portico)—this was Maria Theresa's* **Institute for Noblewomen,** *created in the 1750s to empower and educate aristocratic but impoverished ladies.*

Now continue walking downhill on that lane. You'll see the basilica's Romanesque nave and towers—a strong contrast to the pretty Baroque facade. Farther down, to the left, were the residences of soldiers and craftsmen, and to the right, tucked together, were the palaces of Catholic nobility who wanted both to be close to power and able to band together should the Protestants grab the upper hand. The next street on the left leads up to the popular Golden Lane. As you pass through the entry turnstiles, the crowds turn right, but don't overlook the sights to your left (including a tiny café).

▲Golden Lane (Zlatá Ulička)

Named for the goldsmiths who likely worked here, this medieval merchant street retains its historic aura. When uncrowded, this atmospheric lane—lined with endearing little exhibits on the commerce and customs of a bygone era—is fun to explore. When busy, as it typically is, it's miserable.

Leaving the Castle Complex: Directly below the Golden Lane are two worthwhile sights that are not part of the castle complex—the **Toy Museum** and **Lobkowicz Palace,** both described later.

You'll exit the complex by squirting slowly through a fortified door at the bottom end of the castle. A scenic rampart just below the lower gate offers a commanding view of the city. From there you can head to the nearest Metro/tram station, Strahov Monastery, Little Quarter, or Castle Square.

To reach **Malostranská Station** for the Metro or tram, you can follow the 700-some steps down the steep lane called Staré

Zámecké Schody ("Old Castle Stairs") directly back to the river-bank. Alternatively, for a gentler descent, start heading down the steep lane. About 40 yards below the castle exit, a gate on the left leads you through a scenic vineyard and past the recommended Villa Richter restaurants (see page 152) to the station.

To reach the top of the **Little Quarter** or **Castle Square/Strahov Monastery,** as you leave the castle gate, take a hard right and stroll through the long, delightful park (free, April-Oct 10:00-18:00 or later, closed Nov-March). Along the way, notice the Modernist layout of the Na Valech Gardens, designed by the 1920s court architect, Jože Plečnik of Slovenia. Halfway through the long park is a viewpoint overlooking the terraced Pálffy Gardens (80 Kč, same hours as park). You can zigzag down through these gardens into the Little Quarter. Or, if you want to walk to Castle Square, continue uphill along the castle wall and through the garden to the square. You can hike up to the Strahov Monastery from here.

BELOW THE CASTLE

Extend your visit by dropping by a nobleman's palace and a toy museum with an entire floor devoted to the Barbie doll. These sights require separate admission tickets; they're not included in any castle tickets.

▲▲Lobkowicz Palace (Lobkowiczký Palác)

This palace, at the bottom of the castle complex, displays the private collection of a prominent Czech noble family, including paintings, ceramics, and musical scores. The Lobkowiczes' property was confiscated twice in the 20th century: first by the Nazis at the beginning of World War II, and then by the communists in 1948. In 1990, William Lobkowicz, then a Boston investment banker, returned to Czechoslovakia to fight a legal battle to reclaim his family's property and, eventually, to restore the castles and palaces to their former state. A conscientious host, William Lobkowicz himself narrates the delightful (and included) audioguide. While the National Gallery may seem a more logical choice for the art enthusiast, the obvious care that went into creating this museum, the collection's variety, and the personal insight that it opens into the past and present of Czech nobility make the Lobkowicz worth an hour of your time.

Cost and Hours: 275 Kč, includes audioguide, daily 10:00-18:00, last entry one hour before closing, tel. 233-312-925, www.lobkowicz.cz.

Eating: The Lobkowicz Palace Café, by the exit, has a creative, cosmopolitan menu and stunning panoramic views of the city (daily 10:00-18:00). The charming young man you may see selling ice cream out front is William's son, Will.

PRAGUE

Toy Museum (Muzeum Hraček)

Across the street from Lobkowicz Palace, a courtyard and a long wooden staircase lead to two entertaining floors of old toys and dolls, thoughtfully described in English. You'll see a century of teddy bears, some 19th-century model train sets, old Christmas decor, and an incredible Barbie collection. Find the buxom 1959 first edition, and you'll understand why these capitalistic sirens of material discontent weren't allowed here until 1989.

Cost and Hours: 70 Kč, 120-Kč family ticket, daily 9:30-17:30, WC next to entrance.

ABOVE THE CASTLE

The Strahov Monastery, with its landmark domes, sits above the castle. Remember: If you'd like to combine the monastery with your castle visit, it's easy to ride tram #22 up to the Pohořelec stop (beyond the castle), visit the monastery, enjoy the views, then walk 10 minutes down to Castle Square, passing Loreta Church on the way. (However, if you're rushing to beat the morning crowds at the castle, it's better to head straight for St. Vitus Cathedral in the castle complex, then backtrack to Strahov later.)

▲Strahov Monastery and Library (Strahovský Klášter a Knihovna)

Medieval monasteries were a mix of industry, agriculture, and education, as well as worship and theology. In its heyday, Strahov Monastery had a booming economy of its own, with vineyards, a brewery, and a sizeable beer hall—all open once again. You can explore the monastery complex, check out the beautiful old library, and even enjoy a brew (no longer monk-made, but still refreshing).

Cost and Hours: Grounds—free and always open; library—80 Kč, an extra 50 Kč to take photos—strictly enforced, daily 9:00-11:45 & 13:00-17:00, last entry 15 minutes earlier, www.strahovskyklaster.cz. (A pay WC is just to the right of the monastery entrance.)

Visiting the Monastery and Library: The monastery's **main church,** dedicated to the Assumption of St. Mary, is an originally Romanesque structure decorated by the monks in textbook Baroque (usually closed, but look through the gate inside the front door to see its interior). Notice the grand effect of the Baroque architecture—both rhythmic and theatric. Go ahead, inhale. That's the scent of Baroque.

Buy your ticket in the adjacent building, and head up the stairs to the **library,** offering a peek at how enlightened thinkers

in the 18th century influenced learning. The **display cases** in the library gift shop show off illuminated manuscripts, described in English. Some are in old Czech, but because the Enlightenment promoted the universality of knowledge (and Latin was the universal language of Europe's educated elite), there was little place for regional dialects—therefore, few books here are in the Czech language.

Two rooms (seen only from the doors) are filled with 10th- to 17th-century books, shelved under elaborately painted ceilings. The theme of the first and bigger hall is **philosophy,** with the history of Western man's pursuit of knowledge painted on the ceiling. The second hall—down a hallway lined with antique furniture—focuses on **theology.** As the Age of Enlightenment began to take hold in Europe at the end of the 18th century, monasteries still controlled the books. Notice the gilded, locked case containing the *libri prohibiti* (prohibited books) at the end of the room, above the mirror. Only the abbot had the key, and you had to have his blessing to read these books by writers such as Nicolas Copernicus, Jan Hus, Jean-Jacques Rousseau, and even the French encyclopedia.

The **hallway** connecting the two library rooms was filled with cases illustrating the new practical approach to natural sciences. In the crowded area near the philosophy hall, find the dried-up elephant trunks (flanking the narwhal or unicorn horn) and one of the earliest models of an electricity generator.

Nearby: That hoppy smell you're enjoying in front of the monastery is the recommended **Klášterní Pivovar,** where they brew beer just as monks have for centuries (in the little courtyard directly across from the library entrance; described on page 152).

Tucked in another courtyard across from the Strahov Monastery, the **Museum of Miniatures** (Muzeum Miniatur) displays 40 teeny exhibits—each under a microscope—crafted by an artist from a remote corner of Siberia. Yes, you could fit the entire museum in a carry-on-size suitcase, but good things sometimes come in very, very small packages—it's fascinating to see minutiae such as a padlock on the leg of an ant (100 Kč, kids-50 Kč, daily 9:00-17:00, Strahovské Nádvoří 11, tel. 233-352-371).

Just below the monastery, don't miss the **garden terrace** (look for the aptly named Bellavista Restaurant), with exquisite views over the domes and spires of Prague. The area just below the restaurant tables is free and open to visitors.

• *After enjoying the views, head through the small hole in the wall near the Museum of Miniatures, and go down the street to* **Loretánská street.** *Turning right, follow Loretánská to the castle, by way of Loreta Church (described next).*

Loreta Church

This church has been a hit with pilgrims for centuries, thanks to its dazzling bell tower, peaceful yet plush cloister, sparkling treasury, and much-venerated Holy House. Yes, in the middle of the cloister courtyard, you'll find what's considered by some pilgrims to be part of Mary's actual home in Nazareth. You'll also see one of Prague's most beautiful Baroque churches, a fine treasury collection (upstairs), and—in a tiny chapel in one corner—"St. Bearded Woman," the patron saint of unhappy marriages.

Cost and Hours: 130 Kč, daily April-Oct 9:00-12:15 & 13:00-17:00, Nov-March 9:30-12:15 & 13:00-16:00, audioguide-150 Kč, tel. 220-516-740, www.loreta.cz.

Nearby: The parking-lot square in front of the Loreta Church has a statue of **Edvard Beneš,** the second president of Czechoslovakia (in the 1930s and 1940s), who led the government-in-exile during the Nazi occupation. His forced relocation of Sudetenland Germans following World War II has left him with a controversial legacy; notice the slumping posture and look of worry on his face. (For more on Beneš, see the sidebar on page 200.)

Facing the church from across the square is the **Černín Palace,** a civic building that was the unfortunate site of a modern-day defenestration. In the spring of 1948, soon after the communists took over, an extremely popular Czechoslovak politician (Jan Masaryk, the son of the first president of Czechoslovakia) was found dead in this building's courtyard, below the bathroom window—an apparent suicide. When the official secret-police files were unsealed after 1989, they revealed that Masaryk had been assassinated by Russian agents.

ROYAL SUMMER PALACE AND ROYAL GARDENS

These minor sights, above Prague Castle, are worth visiting only if you get off tram #22 at Královský Letohrádek (the Royal Summer Palace is across the street from this stop, WC at gate).

Royal Summer Palace (Královský Letohrádek)

This gift of love is like a Czech Taj Mahal, presented by Emperor Ferdinand I to his beloved Queen Anne. It's the purest Renaissance building in town. You can't go inside, but the building's detailed reliefs are worth a close look.

• *From here, set your sights on the cathedral's lacy, black spires marking the castle's entrance. Stroll through the...*

Royal Gardens (Královská Zahrada)

Once the private grounds and residence (you'll see the building) of the communist presidents, these were opened to the public with the coming of freedom under Václav Havel. Walk through these gardens (with lovely views of St. Vitus Cathedral) to the gate, which leads you over the moat and into Castle Square, the entrance to the vast castle complex.

Cost and Hours: Free, April-Oct daily 10:00-18:00, closed Nov-March.

Sights Outside the Center

While the tourist's Prague is mostly contained to the Old Town, New Town, Little Quarter, and Castle Quarter, one of the city's most important sights sits just outside this core. The *Slav Epic*—Alfons Mucha's 20-canvas ode to his nation and its history—is a must-see while you're in Prague and is on display at Veletržní Palace, north of the New Town (across the river).

▲▲▲Alfons Mucha's *Slav Epic*

Alfons Mucha is the top Czech artist, who created a wide variety of Art Nouveau illustrations throughout his illustrious career. But his magnum opus hangs in Veletržní Palace, a modern art gallery just north of the river from the Old Town. This series of 20 thrilling, movie-screen-sized canvases tells the entire epic story of the Slavic people, from their humble beginnings in Ukrainian forests to the optimism of the post-WWI era, when Slavic nations (like the Czechs and Slovaks) created their own modern states (Czechoslovakia) for the first time. Each painting is a masterpiece in its own right, making the entire series special to behold. Upstairs in the same huge building is the National Gallery's extensive, fun-to-wander modern art collection, with pieces by artists both Czech and international (lesser-known works by Van Gogh, Picasso, Toulouse-Lautrec, Gauguin, and more).

Cost and Hours: 180 Kč, 240-Kč combo-ticket also includes modern art collection, Tue-Sun 10:00-18:00, closed Mon, buy the 10-Kč English guidebooklet, Dukelských Hrdinů 47 (Praha 7), tel. 224-301-122, www.ngprague.cz.

Getting There: You can reach Veletržní Palace by tram: Ride tram #17 from Národni Divadlo or Staroměstská, tram #24 from Náměstí Republiky, or tram #12 from Malostranská; in any case, get off at the Veletržní Pálac stop. You can also hire a taxi, or take the Metro to Vltavská, then walk a few minutes.

Background: Alfons Mucha (1860-1939) was born in the small Moravian town of Ivančice. Like most artists of his generation, he went to Paris to seek his fortune. After suffering as a starving artist, he was hired to design a poster for a play starring well-known French actress Sarah Bernhardt. Overnight, Mucha was famous. His florid style—featuring willowy maidens with flowing hair, amid flowery designs and backed with a halo-like circle—helped define what became known as Art Nouveau.

But even as he pursued a lucrative career in Paris and the US, Mucha was thinking about his native land. While preparing a piece for the Paris Exposition of 1900, he traveled widely through Slavic lands, soaking up culture, history, and proud traditions. He conceived a plan to immortalize great moments in Slavic history on an epic scale, and persuaded Chicago industrialist Charles Crane to sponsor his project.

At age 50, Mucha returned to Prague and started work. Using a rented castle as his studio, the artist cranked out his enormous canvases for the next 16-plus years. At the same time, he juggled fatherhood and the worries of World War I. When the war ended in 1918, the self-governing nation of Czechoslovakia was created. Mucha was immediately tapped by the new government to design the country's currency and stamps.

In 1928, on the 10th anniversary of modern Czechoslovakia, Mucha's lifework was finally unveiled. The response was lukewarm. In the experimental age of Picasso, Mucha's representational style was out of fashion. And with the rise of fascism in the 1930s, Mucha's overt Slavic nationalism came under attack.

In 1939, German tanks rumbled into Czechoslovakia. The Nazis considered Slavs an inferior race. They arrested the patriot Mucha—now 79 years old—and he was interrogated by the Gestapo. He died a few weeks later.

During World War II, Mucha's canvases were hidden from the Nazis but were damaged in the process. In 1963, after years of restoration, the paintings were put on display in the obscure Czech town of Moravský Krumlov, near Mucha's birthplace.

After Mucha's death, the city of Prague moved to reclaim the lost masterpiece. In 2011, after a decades-long legal battle, the *Slav Epic* was brought to Prague's Veletržní Palace.

Viewing the Paintings: In these 20 panels, Mucha traces the 1,500-year history of the Slavic people. The panels are roughly chronological, but Mucha isn't above veering from the facts to emphasize the people's spiritual journey. The canvases are mind-bogglingly big—some are 25 by 20 feet, and together they total 6,800 square feet, which is more than Michelangelo's Sistine ceiling. Mucha's magnum opus has been scorned by many Czech intellectuals for its style and overt patriotism. But the work goes beyond the style of the time, beyond Art Nouveau, and beyond Slavic nationalism.

Contemplate the *Slav Epic* on several levels. First, figure out what's being depicted, using my outline (buy the excellent pamphlet for details). With his ad-man expertise, Mucha sucks you right into the scene, using strong composition and a sense of color.

Next, read the symbolism: Red is the color of war, white is peace, blue is the past, and orange is the future. (Freemasons will find even more occult symbolism.) Study Mucha's painting technique. He employs egg-based tempera paint for the low-resolution background, then finishes with sharp-focus oil paint to make the details pop. Appreciate Mucha's unique ability to crystalize entire historical epochs into a single scene, expressed in the emotions of individuals and condensed into the expressions on their faces.

Finally, step back and consider the paintings as the works of an Impressionist or abstract artist. The fusion of colors stands far beyond any particular meaning. Like the tones of a 19th-century symphony, Mucha's visual concert has the power to stir the deepest emotions.

The Story: Moving from canvas to canvas, the epic tale of the Slavs unfolds. The first painting shows *The Slavs in Their Original Homeland*—humble, peace-loving farmers living in the wilds of today's Ukraine. Squeezed between Huns in the east and Germans in the west, and united by a common language, culture, and DNA—but with no culture to call their own—the Slavs (represented by the Adam and Eve figures cowering in the foreground) disperse throughout Eastern Europe.

The Slavs practice pagan harvest festivals *(The Celebration of Svantovit)* until they are converted to Christianity by Sts. Cyril and Methodius *(Introduction of the Slavonic Liturgy)*, ultimately finding success in various kingdoms throughout the region *(Tsar Simeon I of Bulgaria, King Přemysl Otakar II of Bohemia, and Coronation of Serbian Tsar Stefan Dušan)*.

The triptych tells the story of Jan Hus, the Czech reformer who boldly spoke out against Church corruption in Bethlehem Chapel (central panel), spurring centuries of bloody squabbles between Catholics and Protestants (which we can see brewing in the right panel, *The Meeting at Křížky*).

A series of battles ensues *(After the Battle of Grunwald, After the Battle of Vítkov Hill,* and *Petr Chelčický)*. Finally, *The Hussite*

King Jiří z Poděbrad signs—and attempts to enforce—a treaty with the pope (whose ambassador tries to weasel out of the deal). But the peace isn't to last, as the Slavs are soon forced to defend Eastern Europe from another threat: the Ottomans (from today's Turkey). At *The Defense of Szigetvár by Nikola Zrinski,* the Slavic, Hungarian, and Christian forces are overwhelmed by the Ottomans, who push deep into Central Europe...and stay for centuries.

The Czech lands, however, are far enough north to remain largely untouched by the Ottomans. And the next several canvases show the flourishing of a deeply rooted Slavic culture here: *The Brethren School in Ivančice*—Mucha's hometown (see his self-portrait at lower right, in white shirt, carrying a sheaf of papers)—translates the word of God from Latin into the local Slavic tongue. The Czech teacher *Jan Amos Komenský* basically invents textbooks and modern education. Slavs—including Mucha himself—make a pilgrimage to *The Holy Mount Athos,* the site of an important Orthodox monastery, and a reminder that Mucha saw Christianity as a unifying and enlightening element for the Slavic people. *The Oath of the Youth under the Slavic Linden Tree* is one small piece of the expansive cultural revival that swept Slavic countries through the 19th century. And *The Abolition of Serfdom in Russia* represents an important benchmark in nudging the Slavs into the modern, democratic world.

The grand-finale canvas, *Apotheosis "Slavs for Humanity!",* attempts to sum up the whole thing—the 1,500-year journey of the Slavic people, and where they're headed. Take a deep breath and dive in.

Start in the lower right. In blue, we see the huddled, oppressed people of the sixth century longing for a peaceful homeland. Poor Slavs. In the upper left (the band of red), it's the Middle Ages, and the Slavs rise to prominence under a series of strong kings (like the man on his throne to the right).

In the center (joyous yellow), it's 1918. World War I has ended, and gaily clad Slavs rejoice, waving flags of the victorious nations (including the Stars and Stripes) and olive branches to salute the troops. Emerging from the war is a new Slavic nation—Czechoslovakia—symbolized by the torso of a strong young man who rises up from the chaos, clutching the wreaths of freedom and Slavic unity. Behind him, Christ blesses the new nation, and a rainbow signals a new era of peace.

Today, the Slavic community is almost 400 million strong. They inhabit the Czech Republic, Slovakia, Poland, much of the Balkans, Ukraine, Belarus, Russia, and beyond (including 18 million Slavic Americans). Some are Catholic, some Orthodox; some write in Cyrillic script, some in Latin. But they share a common heritage, which Mucha has celebrated in the audacious artistic endeavor known as the *Slav Epic*.

While You're There: Upstairs from the *Slav Epic* is the National Gallery's modern art collection, with works by Monet, Van Gogh, Picasso, and Czech contemporaries such as František Kupka.

Shopping in Prague

Prague's entire Old Town seems designed to bring out the shopper in visitors. Puppets, glass, crystal, and garnets (deep-red gemstones) are traditional; these days, fashion and design (especially incorporating the city's rich Art Nouveau heritage) are also big business. Most shops are open on weekdays from 9:00 until 17:00 or 18:00—and often longer, especially for tourist-oriented shops. Some close on Saturday afternoons and/or all day Sunday.

SHOPPING STREETS IN THE CENTER

If you'd like to simply window-shop in the tourist zone, consider the following streets.

Ungelt, the courtyard tucked behind the Týn Church just off of the Old Town Square, is packed with touristy but decent-quality shops. Material has a nice selection of contemporary-style bead jewelry, and Botanicus is an excellent herbal cosmetics shop. Fajans Majolica has traditional blue-and-white Czech pottery. And two stores sell marionettes: V Ungeltu and Hračky, Loutky ("Toys, Puppets").

Michalská, a semi-hidden lane right in the thick of the tourist zone, has a variety of shops (from the Small Market Square/ Malé Náměstí near the Astronomical Clock, go through the big stone gateway marked *459*).

On **Havelská** street, you can browse the open-air Havelská Market, a touristy but enjoyable place to shop for inexpensive handicrafts and fresh produce (daily 9:00-18:00, two long blocks south of the Old Town Square; for details, see page 67).

Celetná, exiting the Old Town Square to the right of Týn Church, is lined with big stores selling all the traditional Czech goodies. Tourists wander endlessly here, mesmerized by the window displays. Good shops along here include Blue (contemporary glass, at #2), a store specializing in Turnov garnets (at #8), and Manufaktura (natural cosmetics and handmade souvenirs, at #12).

PRAGUE

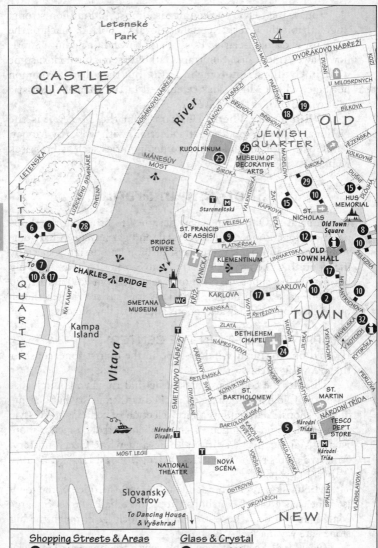

Shopping Streets & Areas
1. Ungelt Courtyard
2. Michalská
3. Celetná
4. Na Příkopě
5. Národní Třída

Puppets
6. Marionety Truhlář & Galerie Michael
7. To Loutky

Glass & Crystal
8. Moser (2)
9. Artěl Glass (3)
10. Blue (5)
11. More Crystal Shops
12. Galerie GOF+FA

Jewelry
13. Turnov Granát Co-op (3)
14. Studio Šperk
15. More Garnet Shops (3)
16. To Koralky

PRAGUE

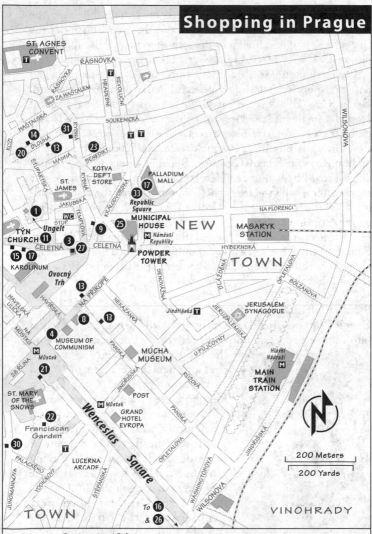

Shopping in Prague

Cosmetics/Gifts
- ⑰ Manufaktura (5)

Fashion/Design
- ⑱ Pařížská Street
- ⑲ Elišky Krásnohorské St.
- ⑳ Dlouhá Street
- ㉑ Baťa Shoes
- ㉒ Tribu
- ㉓ Benediktská Street
- ㉔ Futurista Universum

- ㉕ Modernista (3)
- ㉖ To Modernista Pavilon
- ㉗ Kubista

Books/Maps/Posters
- ㉘ Shakespeare & Sons
- ㉙ Franz Kafka Society
- ㉚ Kiwi Map Store
- ㉛ ProVás Posters

Outdoor Markets
- ㉜ Havelská Market
- ㉝ Republic Square Market

Na Příkopě, the mostly pedestrianized street following the former moat between the Old Town and the New Town, has the city center's handiest lineup of modern shopping malls. The best is Slovanský Dům ("Slavic House," at #22), where you'll wander past a 10-screen multiplex deep into a world of classy restaurants and designer shops surrounding a peaceful, park-like inner courtyard. Černá Růže ("Black Rose," at #12) has a great Japanese restaurant around a small garden; Moser's flagship crystal showroom is also here. The Galerie Myslbek, directly across the street, has fancy stores in a space built to Prague's scale. Na Příkopě street opens up into Republic Square (Náměstí Republiky)—boasting Prague's biggest mall, Palladium, hidden behind a pink Neo-Romanesque facade. Across the square is the communist-era brown steel-and-glass 1980s department store Kotva ("Anchor"), an obsolete beast on the verge of extinction.

Karlova, the tourist-clogged drag connecting the Old Town Square to the Charles Bridge, should be avoided entirely. Shops along here sell made-in-China trinkets at inflated prices to lazy and gullible tourists.

SOUVENIR IDEAS

Czech Puppets: It takes a rare artist to turn pieces of wood into nimble puppets, and prices for the real deal can reach into

the thousands of dollars. But given that puppets have a glorious past and vibrant present in the Czech Republic, even a simple jester, witch, or Pinocchio can make a thoughtful memento of your Czech adventure. You'll see cheap trinket puppets at souvenir stands across town. Buying a higher-quality keepsake is more expensive (starting in the $100 range). Shops I enjoy include **Marionety Truhlář** (near the Little Quarter end of Charles Bridge, U Lužického Semináře 5, www.marionety.com);

Galerie Michael, just a few doors down (U Lužického Semináře 7, www.marionettesmichael.cz); the no-name **loutky** ("Puppets") shop at the top of Nerudova (at #51, www.loutky.cz); and, closer to the Old Town Square in the Ungelt courtyard, **Hračky, Loutky.**

Glass and Crystal: Legally, to be called "crystal" (or "lead crystal"), it must contain at least 24 percent lead oxide, which lends the glass that special, prismatic sparkle. The lead also adds weight, makes the glass easier to cut, and produces a harmonious ringing when flicked. ("Crystal glass" has a smaller percentage of lead.) Well-respected sources for Czech glass and crystal include **Moser,** the most famous—and most expensive (flagship store at the Černá Růže shopping mall at Na Příkopě 12, plus another branch on the Old Town Square, www.moser-glass. com); **Artěl,** with a small but eye-pleasing selection of Art Nouveau- and Art Deco-inspired glassware (for locations, see listing later, under "Art Nouveau Design Shops"); and **Blue,** a chain specializing in sleek, modern designs—many of them in the namesake hue (several locations, including Malé Náměstí 13, Pařížská 3, Melantrichova 6, Celetná 2, Mostecká

24, and at the airport; www.bluepraha.cz). **Celetná street** is lined with touristy glass shops, some with a wide selection suitable for a surgical strike for a crystal souvenir.

Bohemian Garnets *(Granát):* These blood-colored gemstones have unique refractive—some claim even curative—properties. If you buy garnet jewelry, shop around, use a reputable dealer, and ask for a certificate of authenticity to avoid buying a glass imitation (these are common). Of the many garnet shops in Prague's shopping districts, **Turnov Granát Co-op** has the largest selection. It's refreshingly unpretentious, with a vaguely retro-communist vibe (shops at Dlouhá 28, Panská 1, and inside the Pánská Pasáž at Na Příkopě 23; www.granat.eu). **J. Drahoňovský's Studio Šperk** is a more upscale-feeling shop with more creative designs (Dlouhá 19, www.drahonovsky.cz). Additional shops specializing in Turnov garnets are at Dlouhá 1, Celetná 8, and Maiselova 3.

Costume Jewelry and Beads: You'll see *bižutérie* (costume jewelry) advertised all over town. Round, glass beads—sometimes called Druk beads—are popular and can range from large marble-sized beads to miniscule "seed beads." A handy spot to check out some stylish, modern pieces is **Material,** in the Ungelt courtyard behind Týn Church (www.i-material.com).

Organic Cosmetics and Handmade Gifts: Manufaktura is your classy, one-stop shop for good-quality Czech gifts, from organic cosmetics to handicrafts—all handmade in the Czech Republic. You'll find many branch locations in Prague, including several near the Old Town Square (at Melantrichova 17, Celetná 12, and Karlova 26); at Republic Square (in the Palladium mall); near the Little Quarter end of the Charles Bridge (Mostecká 17); in the Main Train Station; and even along Prague Castle's Golden Lane (www.manufaktura.cz). **Botanicus** is similar but smaller (in the Ungelt courtyard behind Týn Church, www.botanicus.cz).

Fashion and Design: Czechs have a unique sense of fashion. One popular trend is garments that are adorned with embroidery, leather, beads, hand-painted designs, or other flourishes—all handmade and therefore unique. Shops selling these come and go, and in many cases several small designers work together and share a boutique—look for an "atelier." Vintage clothes are also as popular among young Czech hipsters as they are with their American counterparts. The Jewish Quarter's **Pařížská street** has the highest concentration of big-name international designers, but for something more local, focus on some of the side-streets that run parallel to Pařížská. One block over, **Elišky Krásnohorské street** has the most engaging lineup of unpretentious local fashion. A block farther east, more boutiques line **Dušní street.** A short walk away, **Dlouhá street**, which exits the Old Town Square near the Jan Hus statue, offers more Czech designers.

Art Nouveau Design Shops: Prague is Europe's best Art Nouveau city—and several shops give you a chance to take home some of that eye-pleasing style, in the form of glasswear, home décor, linens, posters, and other items. **Artěl,** a chain owned by an American (Karen Feldman) who fell in love with Prague and its unique sense of style, is thoughtfully curated. There are three locations (one directly behind the Municipal House, at the corner of Rybná and Králodvorská, and shops near either end of the Charles Bridge—on the Old Town side at Platnéřská 7, and on the Little Quarter side at U Lužického Semináře 7; www.artelglass.com). Other good design shops include **Futurista Universum** (shares an entrance with the recommended Klub Architektů restaurant at Betlémské Náměstí 5a, www.futurista.cz), **Modernista** (downstairs inside the Municipal House, plus a flagship store in a sleek, gorgeously restored former train station in the Vinohrady neighborhood at Vinohradská 50, www.modernista.cz), and **Kubista,** in the House of the Black Madonna (Ovocný Trh 19, www.kubista.cz).

What Not to Buy: Many Prague souvenir shops sell very non-Czech (especially Russian) items to tourists who don't know better. Amber may be pretty, but—considering it's found along the Baltic Sea coast—obviously doesn't originate from this landlocked country. (The amber you'll see sold is mostly Russian and Polish.) Stacking dolls, fur hats, and vodka flasks also fall into this category.

Entertainment in Prague

Prague booms with live and inexpensive theater, classical music, jazz, and pop entertainment. Everything is listed in several monthly cultural events programs (free at TIs) and in the *Prague Post* newspaper (60 Kč at newsstands, or www.praguepost.com).

Buying Tickets: You'll be tempted to gather fliers as you wander through town. Don't bother. To really understand all your

options (the street Mozarts are pushing only their own concerts), drop by a **Via Musica** box office. There are two: One is next to Týn Church on the Old Town Square (daily 10:30-19:30, tel. 224-826-969), and the other is in the Little Quarter across from the Church of St. Nicholas (daily 10:30-18:00, tel. 257-535-568). The event schedule posted on the wall clearly shows everything that's playing today and tomorrow, including tourist concerts, Black Light Theater, and marionette shows, with photos of each venue and a map locating everything (www.viamusica.cz). If you don't see a posted list of today's events, just ask for it.

Ticketpro sells tickets for the serious concert venues and most music clubs (English-language reservations tel. 296-329-999, www.ticketpro.cz). Ticketpro has several outlets: at Rytířská 31 (daily 8:00-12:00 & 12:30-16:30, between Havelská Market and Estates Theater); in the Lucerna Arcade (daily 9:30-18:00, on Wenceslas Square, opposite Grand Hotel Evropa); and in the privately run Tourist Center at Rytířská 12 (Mon-Fri 11:00-19:00, closed Sat-Sun). As with most ticket box offices, you'll pay about 30 Kč extra per ticket.

Dress Code: Locals dress up for the more "serious" concerts, opera, and ballet, but many tourists wear casual clothes. As long as you don't show up in shorts, sneakers, or flip-flops, you'll be fine.

BLACK LIGHT THEATER

A kind of mime/modern dance variety show, Black Light Theater has no language barrier and is, for some, more entertaining than a classical concert. Unique to Prague, Black Light Theater originated in the 1960s as a playful and mystifying theater of the absurd. These days, aficionados and critical visitors lament that it's becoming a cheesy variety show, while others are uncomfortable with the sexual flavor of some acts. Still, it's an unusual theater experience that many enjoy. Shows last about an hour and a half. Avoid the first four rows, which get you so close that it ruins the illusion. Each of these four theaters has its own spin on what Black Light is supposed to be. (The other Black Light theaters advertised around town aren't as good.)

Ta Fantastika tries to be poetic, with haunting puppetry and a little artistic nudity, but it's less "fun" than some of the others. Of these choices, it takes itself perhaps the most seriously (680 Kč,

PRAGUE

Aspects of Alice nightly at 18:00 and 21:30, reserved seating, near east end of Charles Bridge at Karlova 8, tel. 222-221-366, www.tafantastika.cz).

Image Theater has more mime and elements of the absurd and tries to incorporate more dance along with the illusions. They offer the most diverse lineup of programs, including a "best of" and several short-term, themed shows—recent topics have been African safari and outer space. Some find Image's shows to be a bit too slapstick for their tastes (480 Kč, shows nightly at 20:00, open seating—arrive early to grab a good spot, just off Old Town Square at Pařížská 4, tel. 222-314-448, www.imagetheatre.cz).

Laterna Magika, in the big, glassy building next to the National Theater, mixes Black Light techniques with film projection, dance, and other elements into a multimedia performance that draws Czech audiences. Because the theater is used for other types of performances as well, this Black Light show is staged less frequently than some of the others—but if they have a performance while you're in town, they're well worth considering (680 Kč, *Wonderful Circus, Legends of Magic, Graffiti,* shows typically 3-4 nights a week at 20:00, tel. 224-931-482, www.laterna.cz).

Srnec Theater is an ensemble run by founder Jiří Srnec (credited with inventing the Black Light Theater concept in 1961) and his son. Fittingly, this is the most "back-to-basics" option—though narratively simplistic, it revels in the childlike, goofy wonder of the effects. Their primary show, *Anthology,* traces the development of the art over the past 50 years; they also plan additional shows in the future (380-680 Kč, generally one show weekly at 20:00, in the same courtyard as the Museum of Communism and the McDonald's at Na Příkopě 10, tel. 774-574-475, www.srnectheatre.com).

CLASSICAL CONCERTS

Each day, six to eight classical concerts designed for tourists fill delightful Old World halls and churches with music of the crowd-pleasing sort: Vivaldi, Best of Mozart, Most Famous Arias, and works by the famous Czech composer Antonín Dvořák. Concerts typically cost 400-1,000 Kč, start anywhere from 13:00 to 21:00, and last about an hour. Typical venues include two buildings on the Little Quarter Square (the Church of St. Nicholas and the Prague Academy of Music in Liechtenstein Palace), the Klementinum's Chapel of Mirrors, the Old Town Square (in a different Church of St. Nicholas), and the stunning Smetana Hall in the Municipal House. Musicians vary from excellent to amateurish.

To ensure a memorable venue and top-notch musicians, choose a concert in one of three places (Municipal House's Smetana Hall, Rudolfinum, or National Theater) featuring Prague's finest ensembles (such as the Prague Symphony Orchestra or Czech Philharmonic).

The **Prague Symphony Orchestra** plays in the gorgeous Art Nouveau Municipal House. Their ticket office is on the right side of the building, on U Obecního Domu street opposite Hotel Paris (Mon-Fri 10:00-18:00, tel. 222-002-336, www.fok.cz, pokladna@fok.cz). A smaller selection of tickets is sold in the information office inside the Municipal House.

The **Czech Philharmonic** performs in the classical Neo-Renaissance Rudolfinum in the Jewish Quarter. Their ticket office is on the right side of the Rudolfinum, under the stairs (250-1,000 Kč, open Mon-Fri 10:00-18:00, and until just before the show starts on concert days, on Palachovo Náměstí on the Old Town side of Mánes Bridge, tel. 227-059-352, www.ceskafilharmonie.cz, info@cfmail.cz).

Both orchestras perform in their home venues about five nights a month from September through June. Most other nights these spaces are rented to agencies that organize tourist concerts of varying quality for double the price. Check first whether your visit coincides with either ensemble's performance.

You'll find tickets for tourist concerts advertised and sold on the street in front of these buildings. An advantage of such a concert is that it allows you to experience music in one of Prague's best venues on the night of your choice. This is especially worth considering if you want to enjoy classical music in the Municipal House when the Symphony Orchestra isn't in town—but make sure your concert takes place in the building's Smetana Hall rather than in the much smaller Grégr Hall.

OPERA AND BALLET

A handy ticket office for all three of the following theaters is in the little square (Ovocný Trh) behind the Estates Theater, next to a pizzeria.

The **National Theater** (Národní Divadlo), on the New Town side of Legií Bridge, is best for opera and ballet. Enjoy its Neo-Renaissance interior (300-1,000 Kč, shows from 19:00, tel. 224-912-673, www.narodni-divadlo.cz).

The **Estates Theater** (Stavovské Divadlo) is where Mozart premiered and personally directed many of his most beloved works (see page 63). *Don Giovanni, The Marriage of Figaro,* and *The Magic Flute* are on the program a couple of times each month (800-1,400 Kč, shows from 20:00, between the Old Town Square and the New Town on a square called Ovocný Trh, tel. 224-214-339, www.narodni-divadlo.cz).

The **State Opera** (Státní Opera), formerly the German Theater, is not as architecturally rewarding as the National

Theater. Operas by non-Czech composers are typically performed here (400-1,200 Kč, shows at 19:00 or 20:00, 101 Wilsonova, on the busy street between the Main Train Station and Wenceslas Square, see map on page 82, tel. 224-227-693, www.narodni-divadlo.cz).

OTHER MUSIC

Young locals keep Prague's many music clubs in business. Most clubs—from rock to folk to jazz—are neighborhood institutions with decades of tradition, generally holding only 100-200 people. Check the website of each place below to see what's on while you're in town; most of these charge a cover for the music.

In the Old Town: Roxy, a few blocks from the Old Town Square, features live bands from outside the country twice a week—anything from Irish punk to Balkan brass—and experimental DJs other nights (Dlouhá 33, www.roxy.cz). **Agharta Jazz Club,** which showcases some of the best Czech and Eastern European jazz, is just steps off the Old Town Square in a cool Gothic cellar (Železná 16, www.agharta.cz).

In the New Town: Lucerna Music Bar is popular for its '80s and '90s video parties on Friday and Saturday nights (Vodičkova 36—in the basement inside the Lucerna Arcade midway down Wenceslas Square, www.musicbar.cz). The small **Reduta Jazz Club** launches you straight into the 1960s-era classic jazz scene (when jazz provided an escape for trapped freedom lovers in communist times). The top Czech jazzmen—Stivín and Koubková—regularly perform. President Bill Clinton once played the sax here (on Národní street next to Café Louvre, www.redutajazzclub.cz).

In the Little Quarter: Baráčnická Rychta, with a gymnasium-like hall, saw many great polka parties in the 1920s. Rock has long since replaced waltz, but the place still feels like a village dancehall (on Tržiště, tucked away in a small courtyard directly across from the American Embassy, see map on page 148, www.baracnickarychta.cz). **Malostranská Beseda**—with its tight, steamy, standing-room-only space—is the only club in the center with daily live performances (Malostranské Náměstí 21, see map on page 148, www.malostranska-beseda.cz).

In Žižkov: This hip neighborhood has Prague's highest concentration of cool pubs. **Palác Akropolis** is *the* home of Czech independent music. Originally a 1920s movie theater, in the 1990s it was turned into a chill-out lounge, a literary café, and two halls that offer a mix of concerts, disco, and theater (corner of Kubelíkova and Fibichova, under Žižkov TV tower, Metro: Jiřího z Poděbrad, see map on page 40, www.palacakropolis.cz).

Sleeping in Prague

Peak months for hotels in Prague are May, June, and September. Easter and New Year's are the most crowded times, when prices are jacked up a bit. I've listed peak-season prices—if you're traveling in July or August, you'll find rates generally 15 percent lower, and from November through March, about 30 percent lower.

OLD TOWN HOTELS AND PENSIONS

You'll pay higher prices to stay in the Old Town, but for many travelers, the convenience is worth the expense. These places are all within a 10-minute walk of the Old Town Square.

$$$ Hotel Metamorphis is a splurge, with solidly renovated rooms in Prague's former caravanserai (hostel for foreign merchants in the 12th century). Its breakfast room is in a spacious medieval cellar with modern artwork. Some of the street-facing rooms, located above two popular bars, are noisy at night (Db-3,800 Kč on average, check website for special rates and last-minute discounts, guest computer, Wi-Fi, Malá Štupartská 5, tel. 221-771-011, www.hotelmetamorphis.cz, hotel@metamorphis.cz).

$$ Hotel Maximilian is a sleek, mod, 71-room place with Art Deco black design; big, plush living rooms; and all the business services and comforts you'd expect in a four-star hotel. It faces a church on a perfect little square just a short walk from the action (Db-3,300 Kč, extra bed-1,200 Kč; online deal sometimes offered: stay 3 days and pay for 2; guest computer, Wi-Fi, Haštalská 14, tel. 225-303-111, www.maximilianhotel.com, reservation@maximilianhotel.com).

$$ Brewery Hotel u Medvídků ("By the Bear Cubs") has 43 comfortably renovated rooms in a big, rustic, medieval shell

---

Sleep Code

Abbreviations (20 Kč = about $1, country code: 420)
S = Single, **D** = Double/Twin, **T** = Triple, **Q** = Quad, **b** = bathroom, **s** = shower only.

Price Rankings

$$$ **Higher Priced**—Most rooms 3,500 Kč or more.

$$ **Moderately Priced**—Most rooms between 2,500-3,500 Kč.

$ **Lower Priced**—Most rooms 2,500 Kč or less.

Unless otherwise noted, credit cards are accepted, breakfast and tax are included, English is spoken, and Wi-Fi is generally free. Prices change; verify current rates online or by email. For the best prices, always book directly with the hotel.

PRAGUE

PRAGUE

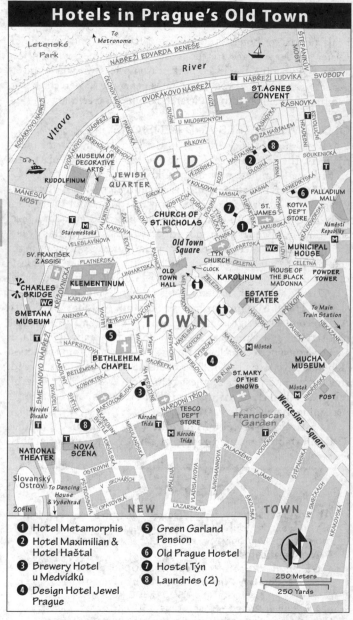

Hotels in Prague's Old Town

1. Hotel Metamorphis
2. Hotel Maximilian & Hotel Haštal
3. Brewery Hotel u Medvídků
4. Design Hotel Jewel Prague
5. Green Garland Pension
6. Old Prague Hostel
7. Hostel Týn
8. Laundries (2)

250 Meters
250 Yards

with dark wood furniture. Upstairs, you'll find lots of beams—or, if you're not careful, they'll find you (Sb-2,000 Kč, Db-3,000 Kč, "superior" Db with luxury bath-4,000 Kč, Tb-4,000 Kč, Qb-4,500 Kč, extra bed-500 Kč, "historical" rooms-10 percent more, apartment-20 percent more, manager Vladimír promises my readers a 10 percent discount with cash if you book directly with hotel, guest computer, Wi-Fi, Na Perštýně 7, tel. 224-211-916, www.umedvidku.cz, info@umedvidku.cz). The pension runs a popular beer-hall restaurant with live music most Fridays and Saturdays until 23:00—request an inside room for maximum peace.

$$ Design Hotel Jewel Prague (U Klenotníka), with 11 modern, comfortable rooms in a plain building, is three blocks off the Old Town Square (Sb-2,250 Kč, small double-bed Db-3,400 Kč, bigger double or twin-bed Db-3,800 Kč, Tb-4,050 Kč, 10 percent off when you book directly with the hotel and mention this book, no elevator, Wi-Fi, Rytířská 3, tel. 224-211-699, www.hoteljewelprague.com, info@jewelhotel.cz).

$ Green Garland Pension (U Zeleného Věnce), on a central cobbled lane, has a warm and personal feel rare for the Old Town. Located in a thick 14th-century building with open beams, it has a blond-hardwood charm decorated with a woman's touch. The nine clean and simply furnished rooms are two and three floors up, with no elevator (big Sb-2,300 Kč, Db-2,600 Kč, bigger Db-2,900 Kč, Tb-3,200 Kč, family suite, 5 percent cash discount, Wi-Fi, Řetězová 10, tel. 222-220-178, www.uzv.cz, pension@uzv.cz).

$ Hotel Haštal is next to Hotel Maximilian (listed earlier) on the same quiet, hidden square in the Old Town. A popular hotel even back in the 1920s, this family-run place has been renovated to complement the neighborhood's vibrant circa-1900 architecture. Its 31 rooms are comfortable and insulated against noise (Sb-1,800 Kč, Db-2,000 Kč, extra bed-500 Kč; manager Patrick promises my readers a 20 percent discount off their lowest online price, book by email to get the discount and avoid their online booking fee; free tea, coffee, and wine; air-con, Wi-Fi Haštalská 16, tel. 222-314-335, www.hastal.com, info@hastal.com).

UNDER THE CASTLE, IN THE LITTLE QUARTER

The first and third listings below are buried on quiet lanes deep in the Little Quarter, among cobbles, quaint restaurants, rummaging tourists, and embassy flags. Hotel Julián is a 10-minute walk up the river on a quiet and stately street, with none of the intense medieval cityscape of the others. For locations, see the map on page 148, unless otherwise noted.

$$$ Vintage Design Hotel Sax's 22 rooms are decorated in a retro, meet-the-Jetsons fashion. With a fruity atrium and a distinctly modern, stark feel, this is a stylish, no-nonsense place (Sb-4,100 Kč, Db-4,500 Kč, Db suite-5,000 Kč, extra bed-750 Kč, 10 percent off with this book—cannot be combined with other discounts, discount for 3-night stay, air-con, elevator, guest computer, Wi-Fi, free tea and pastries daily at 17:00, Jánský Vršek 3, tel. 257-531-268, www.sax.cz, hotel@sax.cz).

$$$ Hotel Julián is an oasis of professional, predictable decency in an untouristy neighborhood. Its 33 spacious, fresh, well-furnished rooms and big, homey public spaces hide behind a noble Neoclassical facade. The staff is friendly and helpful. Their official "rack rates" are ridiculous, but with the Rick Steves discount, you can generally get a double here for around 2,200 Kč (Sb-2,650 Kč, Db-2,900 Kč, Tb-3,500 Kč, suites and bigger rooms available, check website for discounts, 15 percent discount off website price when you book directly with the hotel and mention this book, air-con, elevator, guest computer, Wi-Fi, plush and inviting lobby, summer roof terrace, parking lot; Metro: Anděl, then take tram #6, #9, #12, or #20 to the left as you leave Metro station for two stops; Elišky Peškové 11, Praha 5, reservation tel. 257-311-150, www.hoteljulian.com, info@julian.cz). Free lockers and a shower are available for those needing a place to stay after checkout (while waiting for an overnight train, for example). For the location, see the map on page 40.

$$ Dům u Velké Boty ("House at the Big Boot"), on a quiet square in front of the German Embassy, is the rare quintessential family hotel in Prague: homey, comfy, and extremely friendly. Charlotta, Jan, and their two sons treat every guest as a (thirsty) friend, and the wellspring of their stories never runs dry. Each of their 12 rooms is uniquely decorated, most in a tasteful, 19th-century Biedermeier style (tiny Sb-2,100 Kč, D with shared bath-1,950 Kč, Db-2,900-3,750 Kč, family suite for 4-6 people-3,200-4,675 Kč, extra bed-725 Kč, 10 percent off with advance reservation and this book, prices can be soft when slow, cash only, children up to age 10 sleep free—toys provided, guest computer, Wi-Fi, Vlašská 30, tel. 257-532-088, www.bigboot.cz, info@dumuvelkeboty.cz). There's no hotel sign on the house—look for the splendid geraniums that Jan nurtures in the windows.

AWAY FROM THE CENTER

Sleeping just outside central Prague can save you money—and gets you away from other tourists and into more workaday residential neighborhoods. The following listings are great values compared with the downtown hotels listed previously, and are all within a short tram or Metro ride from the center. For locations, see the map on page 40, unless otherwise noted.

Beyond Wenceslas Square

These hotels are in urban neighborhoods on the outer fringe of the New Town, beyond Wenceslas Square. But they're still within several minutes' walk of the sightseeing zone and are well-served by trams.

$$ Louren Hotel, with 27 rooms, is a quality four-star, business-class hotel in an upscale, circa-1900 residential neighborhood (Vinohrady) that has recently become popular with Prague's expat community. They do a good job of being homey and welcoming (Sb-2,900 Kč, Db-3,200 Kč, extra bed-1,600 Kč, 5 percent off best online price when you book directly with the hotel and mention this book, Rick Steves readers receive free welcome drink, air-con, elevator, guest computer, Wi-Fi, 3-minute walk to Metro: Jiřího z Poděbrad, or tram #11, Slezská 55, Praha 3, tel. 224-250-025, www.louren.cz, reservations@louren.cz).

$$ Hotel 16 is a sleek and modern business-class place with an intriguing Art Nouveau facade, polished cherry-wood elegance, high ceilings, and 14 good rooms (Sb-2,300 Kč, Db-2,900 Kč, Tb-3,500 Kč, 10 percent discount when you book directly with the hotel and mention this book, check website for last-minute discounts, triple-paned windows, free tea, back rooms facing the garden are quieter, air-con, elevator, guest computer, Wi-Fi, limited free parking, 10-minute walk south of Wenceslas Square, Metro: I.P. Pavlova, Kateřinská 16, Praha 2, tel. 224-920-636, www.hotel16.cz, hotel16@hotel16.cz).

$ Hotel Anna offers 26 bright, simple, pastel rooms and basic service. It's a bit closer to the action—just 10 minutes by foot east of Wenceslas Square (Sb-1,600 Kč, Db-1,900 Kč, Tb-2,100 Kč, check website for discounts, elevator, Wi-Fi, Budečská 17, Praha 2, Metro: Náměstí Míru, tel. 222-513-111, www.hotelanna.cz, sales@hotelp1ro.cz).

The Best Values, Farther from the Center

These accommodations are a 10- to 20-minute tram ride from the center, but once you make the trip, you'll see it's no problem—and you'll feel pretty smug saving $50-100 a night per double by not sleeping in the Old Town. Hotel Adalbert is on the grounds of an ancient monastery, and Pension Větrník is adjacent, with two of Prague's best-preserved natural areas (Star Park and Šárka) just a short walk away. Hotel u Šemíka and Guest House Lída are within a stone's throw of peaceful Vyšehrad Park, with its legendary castle on a cliff overlooking the Vltava River.

$$ Hotel Adalbert occupies an 18th-century building in the Břevnov Monastery (one of the Czech Republic's oldest monastic institutions, founded in 993). Meticulously restored after the return of the Benedictine monks in the 1990s, the monastery complex is the ultimate retreat for those who come to Prague for soul-searching or just wanting a quiet place away from the bustle. Join the monks for morning (7:00) and evening (18:00) Mass in the St. Margaret Basilica, a large and elegant Baroque church decorated with unusual simplicity. You can help yourself in the monastery fruit orchard and eat in the atmospheric monastery pub (Klášterní Šenk). The hotel itself caters primarily to business clientele and takes ecology seriously: recycling, water conservation, and free tram tickets for guests. I prefer the first-floor rooms, as some of the attic rooms—room numbers in the 200s—feel a bit cramped (Sb-1,800 Kč, Db-2,600 Kč, extra bed-1,000 Kč, less on weekends, check website for special rates and last-minute discounts, Wi-Fi, free parking, halfway between city and airport at Markétská 1, Praha 6, tram #22 to Břevnovský Klášter; 5 minutes by tram beyond the castle, 20 minutes from Old and New Towns; tel. 220-406-170, www.hoteladalbert.cz, info@hoteladalbert.cz).

$$ Hotel u Šemíka, named for a heroic mythical horse, offers 18 rooms in a quiet residential neighborhood just below Vyšehrad Castle and the Slavín cemetery where Dvořák, Mucha, and Čapek are buried. It's a 10-minute tram ride south of the Old Town (Sb-1,540 Kč, Db-1,790 Kč, apartment-2,070 Kč for 2-4 people, extra bed-550 Kč, ask for the "direct booking" Rick Steves 10 percent discount when you reserve, guest computer, Wi-Fi; from the center, take tram #3, #17, or #21 to Výtoň, go under rail bridge, and walk 3 blocks uphill to Vratislavova 36; Praha 2, tel. 221-965-610, www.usemika.cz, usemika@usemika.cz).

$ Pension Větrník fills an attractive white-and-orange former 18th-century windmill in one of Prague's most popular residential areas, right next to the Břevnov Monastery and midway between the airport and the city. Talkative owner Miloš Opatrný is a retired prizewinning Czech chef. Although the elder Miloš no longer cooks, his namesake grandson has followed in his footsteps—on request, the younger Miloš will gladly prepare an unforgettable meal for you. The six rooms here are the pride of the Opatrný family, who live on the upper floors. The garden has a red-clay tennis court—rackets and balls are provided (Db-1,700 Kč, suite-2,000 Kč, extra bed-400 Kč, guest computer, U Větrníku 1, Praha 6; airport bus #179 stops near the house, tram #18 goes straight to Charles Bridge, both take 20 minutes; tel. 220-513-390, www.pensionvetrnik.cz, pension@vetrnik1722.cz).

$ Guest House Lída, with 12 homey and spacious rooms, fills a big house in a quiet residential area farther inland, a 15-minute tram ride from the center. Jan, Jitka, Jiří, and Jana Prouzas—who run the place—are a wealth of information and know how to make people feel at home (Sb-1,280 Kč, small Db-1,440 Kč, Db-1,760 Kč, Tb-2,100 Kč, Qb-2,530 Kč, cash only, family rooms, top-floor family suite with kitchenette, guest computer, Wi-Fi, parking garage-200 Kč/day, Metro: Pražského Povstání; exit Metro and turn left on Lomnického between the Metro station and big blue-glass ČSOB building, follow Lomnického for 500 yards, then turn left on Lopatecká, go uphill and ring bell at Lopatecká 26; Praha 4, tel. 261-214-766, www.lidabb.eu, lidabb@seznam.cz). The Prouzas brothers also rent two **apartments** across the river, an equal distance from the center (Db-1,400 Kč, Tb-1,700 Kč, Qb-2,000 Kč).

HOSTELS IN THE CENTER

It's tough to find a double for less than 2,500 Kč in the old center. But Prague has an abundance of fine hostels—each with a distinct personality, and each excellent in its own way for anyone wanting a 300-500-Kč dorm bed or an extremely simple twin-bedded room for about 1,300 Kč. With travelers seeking cheaper options these days, it's good to keep in mind that hostels are no longer the exclusive domain of backpackers. The first two hostels are centrally located, but lack care and character; the last two are found in workaday neighborhoods and have atmospheric interiors.

$ Old Prague Hostel is a small, well-worn place with 70 beds on the second and third floors of an apartment building on a back alley near the Powder Tower. The spacious rooms were once apartment bedrooms, so it feels less institutional than most hostels, but the staff can be indifferent and older travelers might feel a bit out of place. The TV lounge/breakfast room is a good hang-out (D-1,400 Kč, bunk in 4- to 8-person room-400-500 Kč; includes breakfast, sheets, towels, lockers, and Wi-Fi; in summer reserve 2 weeks ahead for doubles, a few days ahead for bunks; Benediktská 2, see map on page 132 for location, tel. 224-829-058, www.oldpraguehostel.com, info@oldpraguehostel.com).

$ Hostel Týn—quiet, mature, and sterile—is hidden in a silent courtyard two blocks from the Old Town Square. The management is very aware of its valuable location, so they don't have to bother being friendly (D-1,240 Kč, T-1,410 Kč, bunk in 4- to 8-bed co-ed room-420 Kč, lockers, guest computer, Wi-Fi, kitchen, reserve one week ahead, Týnská 19, see map on page 132 for location, tel. 224-808-301, www.hostelpraguetyn.com, info@hostelpraguetyn.com).

$ Sir Toby's is in a 1930s working-class neighborhood—a newly popular residential and dining-out area that's a 12-minute tram ride from the center. The owners have taken great pains to stamp the place with character: restored hardwood floors, a back garden with tables made out of sewing machines, and rooms filled with vintage 1930s furniture and photographs. Amenities include self- and full-service laundry, an on-site pub, and a friendly staff (130 beds, Sb-1,050 Kč, D-1,300 Kč, Db-1,580 Kč, Tb-1,800 Kč, bunk in 4- to 6-bed co-ed room-450 Kč, bunk in 8- to 10-bed co-ed room-350 Kč, guest computer, Wi-Fi; from the Main Train Station, take Metro line C to the Vltavska stop, then tram #1, #14, or #25 to Dělnická; at Dělnická 24, Praha 7, see map on page 40 for location, tel. 246-032-610, www.sirtobys.com, info@sirtobys.com). The owners also run two contemporary-design hostels in Vinohrady.

$ **Hostel Elf,** a 10-minute walk from the Main Train Station or one bus stop from the Florenc Metro station, is fun-loving, ramshackle, covered with noisy, self-inflicted graffiti, and the wildest of these hostels. They offer cheap, basic beds, a helpful staff, and lots of creative services—kitchen, free luggage room, free guest computer and Wi-Fi, laundry, no lockout, free tea and coffee, cheap beer, a terrace, and lockers (120 beds, D-1,100 Kč, bunk in 6- to 11-person room-320 Kč, includes sheets and breakfast, reserve 4 days ahead, Husitská 11, Praha 3, take bus #133 or #207 from Florenc Metro station for one stop to U Památníku, see map on page 40 for location, tel. 222-540-963, www.hostelelf.com, info@hostelelf.com).

Eating in Prague

A big part of Prague's charm is found in wandering aimlessly through the city's winding old quarters, marveling at the architecture, watching the people, and sniffing out fun restaurants. In addition to meat-and-potatoes Czech cuisine, you'll find trendy, student-oriented bars and lots of fine ethnic eateries. For ambience, the options include traditional, dark Czech beer halls; elegant Art Nouveau dining rooms; and hip, modern cafés.

Remember, there are two parallel worlds in Prague: the tourist town and the real city. Generally, if you walk two minutes away from the tourist flow, you'll find better value, atmosphere, and service. The more touristy a place is, the more likely you'll be paying too much—either in inflated prices or because waiters pad the bill. It's always smart to closely examine your itemized bill and understand each line. At touristy places, they may automatically tack on a 10 percent service charge; if you see this, there's no need to tip extra. If service is not included, locals tip by rounding up (usually 5 to 10 percent for good service, but never more). But stubborn tourists have trained local servers to expect American-size tips (15 percent or more) from their American customers. Not wanting to contribute to this overtipping epidemic, I still tip on the lower, local end of the scale. While many places accept credit cards, I usually pay for meals in cash—it seems to make waiters happier.

I've listed eating and drinking establishments by neighborhood. The most options—and highest prices—are in the Old

Town. For a light meal, consider one of Prague's many cafés (see page 153).

Unlike most European countries, the Czech Republic still permits smoking in restaurants and cafés. I've noted those that are either more or less smoky than the norm.

Fun, Touristy Neighborhoods: Several areas are pretty and well-situated for sightseeing, but lined only with touristy restaurants. While these places are not necessarily bad values, I've listed only a few of your many options—just survey the scene in these spots and choose whatever looks best. **Kampa Square,** just off the Charles Bridge, feels like a small-town square. **Havelská Market** is surrounded by colorful little eateries, any of which offer a nice perch for viewing the market scene while you munch. The massive **Old Town Square** is *the* place to nurse a drink or enjoy a meal while watching the tide of people, both tourists and locals, sweep back and forth. There's often some event on this main square, and its many restaurants provide tasty and relaxing vantage points.

Traditional Czech Places: With the inevitable closing of cheap student pubs (replaced by shops and hotels that make more money), it's getting difficult to find a truly Czech pub in the historic city center. Most Czechs no longer go to "traditional" eateries, preferring the cosmopolitan taste of the world to the mundane taste of sauerkraut. As a result, ancient institutions with "authentic" Czech ambience have become touristy—but they're still great fun, a good value, and respected by locals. Expect wonderfully rustic spaces, smoke, surly service, and reasonably good, inexpensive food. Understand every line on your bill. I've listed several of these characteristically Czech eateries.

Dining with a View: For great views, consider these options, all described in detail in the following pages: **Hotel u Prince's terrace** (rooftop dining above a fancy hotel, completely touristy but with awesome views); **Villa Richter** (next to Prague Castle, above Malostranská Metro stop); **Bellavista Restaurant** at the Strahov Monastery; **Petřínské Terasy** and **Nebozízek,** next to the funicular stop halfway up Petřín Hill; and **Čertovka** in the Little Quarter (superb views of the Charles Bridge).

Cheap-and-Cheery Sandwich Shops: All around town you'll find modern little sandwich shops (like the **Panería** chain) offering inexpensive fresh-made sandwiches (grilled if you like), pastries, salads, and drinks. You can get the food to go, or eat inside at simple tables.

Groceries and Farmers' Markets: Ask your hotelier for the location of the nearest grocery store; it'll probably be small, stocked with what you need, and close by. A popular supermarket chain is **Billa.**

Farmers' markets have become popular in the past few years,

PRAGUE

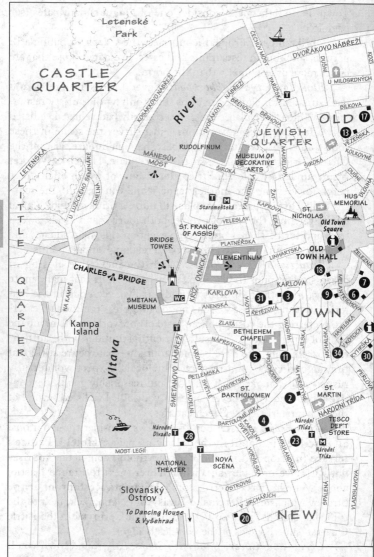

Letenské Park

CASTLE QUARTER

LITTLE QUARTER

River

KOŠÁŘKOVO NÁBŘEŽÍ

DVOŘÁKOVO NÁBŘEŽÍ

ČECHŮV MOST

DVOŘÁKOVO NÁBŘEŽÍ

KOZÍ

DUŠNÍ

U MILOSRDNÝCH

BŘEHOVA

BŘEHOVA

PAŘÍŽSKÁ

BÍLKOVA

OLD

17

VĚZEŇSKÁ

13

LETENSKÁ

U LUŽICKÉHO SEMINÁŘE

CHELNÁ

RUDOLFINUM

MÁNESŮV MOST

ŠIROKÁ

MUSEUM OF DECORATIVE ARTS

JEWISH QUARTER

MAISELOVA

ŠIROKÁ

KOLKOVNĚ

DUŠNÍ

DLOUHÁ

HUS MEMORIAL

ŽATECKÁ

TALENTINSKÁ

KAPROVA

Staroměstská

VELESLAV.

EČKA

ST. NICHOLAS

Old Town Square

ŽELEZNÁ

ST. FRANCIS OF ASSISI

PLATNÉŘSKÁ

LINHARTSKÁ

OLD TOWN HALL

18

7

BRIDGE TOWER

KLEMENTINUM

KARLOVA

9

6

MELANTRICHOVA

CHARLES BRIDGE

OVNICKÁ

KŘÍŽ

KARLOVA

31

3

TOWN

V KOTCÍCH

SMETANA MUSEUM

WC

ANENSKÁ

 RETĚZOVA

LILIOVÁ

JILSKÁ

MICHALSKÁ

HAVELSKÁ

RYTÍŘSKÁ

30

Kampa Island

Vltava

NA KAMPĚ

ZLATÁ

NÁPRSTKOVA

BETHLEHEM CHAPEL

HUSOVÁ

34

SMETANOVO NÁBŘEŽÍ

KAROLINY SVĚTLÉ

BETLÉMSKÁ

5

11

PROHODNÍ

PERLOVÁ

KONVIKTSKÁ

ST. BARTHOLOMEW

NA PERŠTÝNĚ

2

ST. MARTIN

NÁRODNÍ TŘÍDA

DIVADELNÍ

BARTOLOMĚJSKÁ

KAROLINY SVĚTLÉ

4

Národní Třída

TESCO DEP'T STORE

MIKULANDSKÁ

23

Národní Třída

Národní Divadlo

28

MOST LEGIÍ

NATIONAL THEATER

NOVÁ SCÉNA

KONVIKTSKÁ

OSTROVNÍ

V JIRCHÁŘÍCH

SPÁLENÁ

VLADISLAVOVA

Slovanský Ostrov

To Dancing House & Vyšehrad

20

NEW

Legend

1. Restaurace u Provaznice
2. U Medvídků Beer Hall
3. U Zlatého Tygra Pub
4. Jan Paukert Deli
5. Restaurace u Betlémské Kaple
6. Česká Kuchyně
7. Restaurace Mlejnice
8. Lokál Restaurant
9. Country Life Vegetarian Restaurant
10. Beas Cafeteria
11. Klub Architektů
12. Chez Marcel
13. Amici Miei Restaurant
14. Ariana Afghan Restaurant
15. Indian Jewel
16. James Joyce Irish Pub
17. La Casa Blů
18. Hotel/Restaurant u Prince Terasa

Prague Restaurants in Old & New Towns

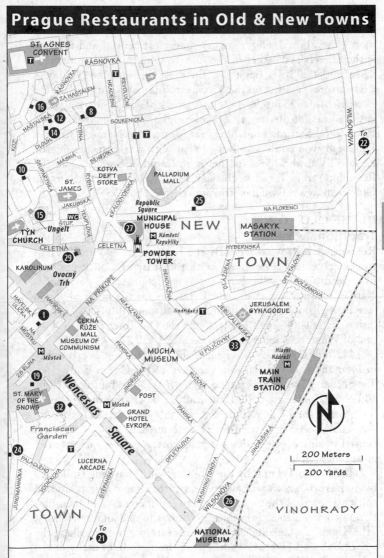

PRAGUE

19 Restaurace u Pinkasů
20 Hospoda u Nováka
21 To Pivovarský Dům
22 To Pivovarský Klub
23 Le Patio & Café Louvre
24 Pasha Kebab Turkish Restaurant
25 Brasserie La Gare
26 Kavárna Muzeum Café

27 Municipal House Eateries
28 Kavárna Slavia
29 Grand Café Orient
30 Café Café
31 Café Montmartre & Ebel Coffee House
32 Dobrá Čajovna Teahouse
33 Čajový Klub
34 Havelská Market

cropping up around the city and tantalizing picnickers. Apart from vegetables, you'll find quality cheeses, juices, cakes, coffee, and more (www.farmarsketrziste.cz). The most central and touristy is the **Havelská Market** in the Old Town (also has handicrafts, daily 9:00-18:00, see page 67). The most scenic is the **Náplavka** ("Riverbank") market on the Vltava embankment, just south of the Palacký Bridge (Sat 8:00-14:00). A smaller farmers' market enlivens the heart of the trendy **Žižkov** neighborhood on Wednesday, Friday, and Saturday mornings (at Metro stop Náměstí Jiřího z Poděbrad; you could combine a visit with a trip up the nearby Žižkov TV tower). And another is on **Republic Square** (Náměstí Republiky) from Tuesdays through Fridays, at the entrance to the Old Town (www.farmarsketrhyprahy1.cz).

IN THE OLD TOWN
Traditional Czech

Restaurace u Provaznice ("By the Ropemaker's Wife") has all the Czech classics, peppered with the story of a once-upon-a-time-faithful wife. (Check the menu for details of the gory story.) Natives congregate under bawdy frescoes for the famously good "pig leg" with horseradish and Czech mustard (100-300-Kč main dishes, daily 11:00-24:00, a block into the Old Town from the bottom of Wenceslas Square at Provaznická 3, tel. 224-232-528).

U Medvídků ("By the Bear Cubs") started out as a brewery in 1466 and is now a flagship beer hall of the Czech Budweiser. The one large room is bright, noisy, touristy, and a bit smoky (100-300-Kč main dishes, daily 11:30-23:00, a block toward Wenceslas Square from Bethlehem Square at Na Perštýně 7, tel. 224-211-916). The small beer bar next to the restaurant (daily 16:00 until late) is used by university students during emergencies—such as after most other pubs have closed.

U Zlatého Tygra ("By the Golden Tiger") has long embodied the proverbial Czech pub, where beer turns strangers into kindred spirits who cross the fuzzy line between memory and imagination as they tell their hilarious life stories to one another. Today, "The Tiger" is a buzzing shrine to one of its longtime regulars, the writer Bohumil Hrabal, whose fiction immortalizes many of the colorful characters that once warmed the wooden benches here. Only regulars have reserved tables. If you find a rare empty spot, you'll be treated as a surprise guest rather than as a customer—and likely will wait quite a while to land a beer (38-Kč pints of Pilsner, 50-Kč beer cheese, daily 15:00-23:00, just south of Karlova at Husova 17, tel. 222-221-111).

Jan Paukert is a traditional Czech deli that has been in business for a century, specializing in open-face sandwiches *(chlebíčky)*, cakes, and desserts. They also serve warm, ready-made meals in the seating area in back (30-Kč open-face sandwiches, 110-Kč main dishes, Mon-Fri 9:00-19:00, Sat 10:00-18:00, closed Sun, Národní 17, tel. 224-222-615).

Restaurace u Betlémské Kaple, behind Bethlehem Chapel, is not "ye olde" Czech. It has light wooden decor, cheap lunch deals, and fish specialties that attract natives and visitors in search of a good Czech bite for good Czech prices (100-200-Kč main dishes, daily 11:00-23:00, Betlémské Náměstí 2, tel. 222-221-639).

Česká Kuchyně ("Czech Kitchen") is a blue-collar cafeteria serving steamy old Czech cuisine. It's fast, practical, cheap, and traditional as can be. Pick up your tally sheet as you enter, grab a tray, point to whatever you'd like, and keep the paper to pay as you exit. It's extremely cheap...unless you lose your paper. As you enter, you'll come across serving stations in this order: salads, fruit dumplings and sweets, soups, main dishes, and finally, drinks (60-150-Kč main dishes, daily 9:00-20:00, very central, across from Havelská Market at Havelská 23, tel. 224-235-574).

Restaurace Mlejnice ("The Mill") is a fun little pub strewn with farm implements and happy eaters, located just out of the tourist crush two blocks from the Old Town Square. They serve hearty traditional and modern Czech plates for 150-180 Kč. Reservations are smart in the evening (150-300-Kč main dishes, daily 11:00-24:00, between Melantrichova and Železná at Kožná 14, tel. 224-228-635).

Lokál ("The Neighborhood Dump") is a hit with residents for its good-quality Czech classics at low prices. Filling a long, arched space, the restaurant plays on customers' nostalgia: The stark interior is a deliberate 1980s retro design, and the waiters have been instructed to be curt (but not impolite)—just as if they were serving in one of Prague's notorious train station "dumps." Reservations are smart (160-200-Kč main dishes, daily 11:00 until late, ask for English menu at the front by the tap, Dlouhá 33, tel. 222-316-265). The same group has a smaller branch, **Lokál u Bílé Kuželky,** in the Little Quarter (see listing later).

Vegetarian and Modern

These hip and trendy places have a fun, youthful vibe.

Country Life Vegetarian Restaurant is a bright, easy, non-smoking cafeteria with a well-displayed buffet of salads and hot veggie dishes. It's midway between the Old Town Square and the bottom of Wenceslas Square. They're serious about their vegetarianism, serving only plant-based, unprocessed, and unrefined food. Its quiet dining area is elegant for a cafeteria, with a few tables outside in the courtyard (pay by weight, expect 150-200 Kč per meal, Sun-Thu 9:00-20:30, Fri 9:00-17:00, closed Sat, through courtyard at Melantrichova 15/Michalská 18, tel. 224-213-366).

Beas Cafeteria, a little vegetarian restaurant, is ruled by a Punjabi chef. Diners grab a steel tray and scoop up whatever looks good, typically various choices of *dal* (lentils) and *sabji* (vegetables) with rice or *chapati* (pancakes). The food is sold by weight—you'll likely spend around 130 Kč for lunch. Tucked away in a courtyard behind the Týn Church, this place is popular with university students and young professionals (Mon-Fri 11:00-20:00, Sat 12:00-20:00, Sun 12:00-18:00, Týnská 19, mobile 608-035-727).

Klub Architektů, next to Bethlehem Chapel, is a modern hangout in a cave-like medieval cellar that also has straw-chair seating outside. The fun menu includes excellent original dishes, hearty salads, Moravian wines, and Slovak beer (150-300-Kč main dishes, daily 11:30-24:00, Betlémské Náměstí 169, tel. 224-248-878).

Beware that two popular Prague vegetarian restaurants, **Lehká Hlava** ("Clean Head") and **Maitrea** (a.k.a. "Buddha of the Future"), are owned by Antonín Koláček, a former manager of a state-controlled brown coal company (and more recently a Buddhist philanthropist) who was convicted in 2013 in a Swiss court as the mastermind behind a 1990s fraudulent privatization scheme that robbed the country of at least three billion crowns.

Ethnic Eateries and Bars

Dlouhá, the wide street leading away from the Old Town Square behind the Jan Hus Memorial, is lined with ethnic restaurants catering mostly to cosmopolitan locals. Within a couple of blocks, you can eat your way around the world. From Dlouhá, wander the Rámová/Haštalská/Vězeňská area to survey a United Nations of eateries: You'll find French (**Chez Marcel** at Haštalská 12); Italian (the expensive **Amici Miei** at Vězeňská 5, which prides itself on fresh *pesci* and *frutti di mare*); and Afghan (**Ariana** at Rámová 6).

These places deserve special consideration:

Indian: **Indian Jewel,** in the Ungelt courtyard behind the Týn Church, is the best place in Prague to find a full Indian menu that actually tastes Indian. Located in a pleasant, artfully restored courtyard, this is my choice for outdoor dining, with seriously executed sub-Continental classics and good-value lunch specials (110-Kč daily specials, 300-Kč main dishes, daily 11:00-23:00, Týn 6, tel. 222-310-156).

Irish: **James Joyce Irish Pub** may seem like a strange recommendation in Prague—home of some of the world's best beer—but it has the kind of ambience that locals (and few tourists) seek out. Expats have favored this pub (formerly known as Molly Malone's) for Guinness ever since the Velvet Revolution enabled the Celts to return to one of their homelands. Worn wooden floors, dingy walls, and the Irish manager transport you right into the heart of blue-collar Dublin, which was a popular place for young Czechs to seek jobs in the high-tech industry—before the recession hit (daily 11:00 until late, U Obecního Dvora 4, tel. 224-818-851).

Latin American: **La Casa Blů,** with cheap lunch specials, Mexican plates, Staropramen beer, and greenish mojitos, is your own little pueblo in Prague. It's one of the last student bastions in the Old Town. Painted in warm oranges and reds, energized by upbeat music, and guarded by creatures from Mayan mythology, La Casa Blů attracts a fiesta of happy eaters and drinkers (120-Kč specials, 170-Kč burritos and quesadillas, Mon-Sat 11:00-23:00, Sun 14:00-23:00, non-smoking, on the corner of Kozí and Bílkova, tel. 224-818-270).

In the Jewish Quarter

These eateries are well-located to break up a demanding tour of the Jewish Quarter—all within two blocks of one another on or near Široká (see map on page 74). Also consider the nearby ethnic eateries listed above.

Kolkovna, the flagship restaurant of a chain allied with Pilsner Urquell, is big and woody yet modern, serving a fun mix of Czech and international cuisine—ribs, salads, cheese plates, and beer. It feels a tad formulaic...but not in a bad way (a bit overpriced, 200-400-Kč main dishes, daily 11:00-24:00, across from Spanish Synagogue at V Kolkovně 8, tel. 224-819-701).

Kolonial ("Bicycle Place"), across the street from the Pinkas Synagogue, has a modern interior playing on the bicycle theme, six beers on tap, and an imaginative menu drawing from Czech, French, Italian, and Spanish cuisine (100-150-Kč daily specials, 150-400-Kč main dishes, daily 9:00-24:00, Široká 6, tel. 224-818-322).

Restaurace u Knihovny ("By the Library"), situated steps away from the City and National libraries as well as the Pinkas Synagogue, is a favorite lunch spot for locals who work nearby. The cheap daily lunch specials consist of seven variations on traditional Czech themes. The service is friendly, and the stylish red-brick interior is warm (80-150-Kč main dishes, daily 11:00-23:00, smoke-free at lunch, on the corner of Veleslavínova and Valentinská, mobile 732-835-876).

Dinitz Kosher Restaurant, around the corner from the Spanish Synagogue, is the most low-key and reasonably priced of the kosher restaurants in the Jewish Quarter (350-550-Kč main dishes, 800-Kč Shabbat meals by prepaid reservation only, Sun-Thu 11:30-22:30, Fri 11:30-14:30, Bílkova 12, tel. 222-244-000, www.dinitz.cz). For Shabbat meals, the fancier **King Solomon Restaurant** is a better value (Široká 8, tel. 224-818-752, www.kosher.cz).

Dining with an Old Town Square View

The **Hotel u Prince Terasa,** atop the five-star hotel facing the Astronomical Clock, is designed for foreign tourists. A sleek elevator takes you to the rooftop terrace, where every possible inch is used to serve good food (international with plenty of fish) from their open-air grill. The view is arguably the best in town—especially at sunset. The menu is a fun but overpriced mix, with photos that make ordering easy. Being in such a touristy spot, rude waiters are experts at nicking you with confusing menu charges; don't be afraid to confirm exact prices before ordering. This place is also great for a drink at sunset or late at night (240-300-Kč plates, fine salads, daily until 24:00, brusque staff, outdoor heaters when necessary, Staroměstské Náměstí 29, tel. 224-213-807, no reservations possible).

IN THE NEW TOWN
Traditional Czech

Restaurace u Pinkasů, founded in 1843, is known among locals as the first place to serve Pilsner beer. You can sit in its traditional interior, in front to watch the street action, or out back in a garden shaded by the Gothic buttresses of the St. Mary of the Snows Church. While the prices are straightforward, some of the waiters could win the rudest-service award (150-300-Kč main dishes, daily 9:00-24:00, 90-Kč lunch special, near the bottom of Wenceslas Square, between the Old Town and New Town, Jungmannovo Náměstí 16, tel. 221-111-150).

Hospoda u Nováka, behind the National Theater, is emphatically Czech, with few tourists. It takes good care of its regulars (you'll see the old monthly beer tabs in a rack just inside the door). Nostalgic communist-era signs are everywhere. During that time, pubs like this were close-knit communities where regulars escaped from the depression of daily life. Today the U Nováka is a bright and smoky hangout where you can still happily curse whatever regime you happen to live under. And though the English menu lists the well-executed Czech classics, it doesn't list the cheap daily specials (100-200-Kč main dishes, daily 10:00-23:00, V Jirchářích 2, tel. 224-930-639).

Pivovarský Dům ("The Brewhouse"), on the corner of Ječná and Lípová, is popular with locals for its rare variety of fresh beers (yeast, wheat, and fruit-flavored), fine classic Czech dishes, and an inviting interior that mixes traditional and modern (100-300-Kč main dishes, daily 11:00-23:00, reservations recommended in the evenings, variety of beer mugs sold; walk up Štěpánská street from Wenceslas Square for 10 minutes, or take tram #22 for two stops from Národní to Štěpánská; Lípová 15, tel. 296-216-666, www. pivovarskydum.com).

Modern and Ethnic

Pivovarský Klub ("The Brew Club," related to Pivovarský Dům, above) serves the widest selection of Czech microbrews in town in a modern, blond-wood restaurant. Every week different beers are featured on tap on the ground floor, while small breweries hold regular presentations in the basement (250-Kč main dishes, daily 11:30-23:30, evening reservations recommended; about 50 yards on the left along Křižíkova from Florenc Metro station, Křižíkova 17, see map on page 40 for location, tel. 222-315-7770, www. pivovarskyklub.com).

Le Patio, on the big and busy Národní Třída, has a hip, continental feel. But for a place that also sells furniture (head straight back and down the stairs), it definitely needs comfier dining chairs. Hanging lanterns and live music (Fri-Sat) contribute to the pleasant atmosphere. Dishes are from India, France, and points in between, and a serious vegetarian option is always available (200-350-Kč plates, daily 8:00-23:00, Národní 22, tel. 224-934-375).

Pasha Kebab Turkish Restaurant, near the bottom of Wenceslas Square, has American fast-food-chain ambience, good ingredients, and wonderful, authentic ready-to-eat Turkish dishes (120-Kč meals, daily 10:00-22:00, a block from Můstek Metro stop, just beyond Franciscan garden at Jungmannova 27, tel. 224-948-481).

Brasserie La Gare, just off Republic Square (Náměstí Republiky), opened with the mission to prove to Czechs that French food can be simple and inexpensive. The menu includes such classics as *escargots de Bourgogne* and coq au vin. The red-hued, modern interior also contains a French bakery and a deli (89-Kč lunch specials, 250-Kč entrées, daily 11:00-24:00, V Celnici 3, tel. 222-313-712).

Kavárna Muzeum, in the former communist parliament building (now part of the National Museum) at Wenceslas Square, offers daily menus, freshly roasted coffee, and sandwiches in a pleasant, kid-friendly setting (35-Kč soups, daily 10:00-19:00, Vinohradská 1, tel. 224-284-511).

Art Nouveau Splendor in the Municipal House

The Municipal House (Obecní Dům), the sumptuous Art

Nouveau concert hall, has three restaurants: a café, a French restaurant, and a beer cellar (all at Náměstí Republiky 5). The dressy café, **Kavárna Obecní Dům,** is drenched in chandeliered, Art Nouveau elegance and offers the best value and experience here. Light, pricey meals and drinks

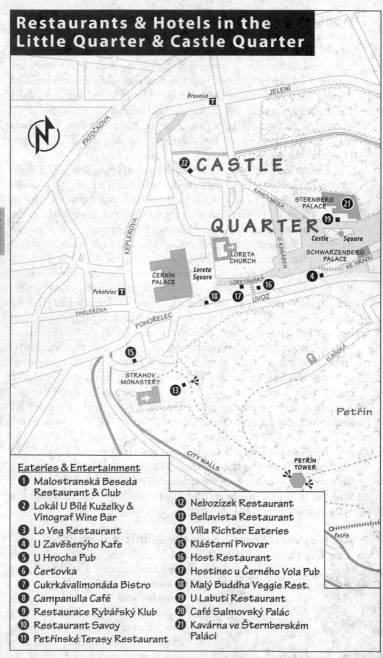

Restaurants & Hotels in the Little Quarter & Castle Quarter

Eateries & Entertainment

1. Malostranská Beseda Restaurant & Club
2. Lokál U Bílé Kuželky & Vinograf Wine Bar
3. Lo Veg Restaurant
4. U Zavěšeného Kafe
5. U Hrocha Pub
6. Čertovka
7. Cukrkávalimonáda Bistro
8. Campanulla Café
9. Restaurace Rybářský Klub
10. Restaurant Savoy
11. Petřínské Terasy Restaurant
12. Nebozízek Restaurant
13. Bellavista Restaurant
14. Villa Richter Eateries
15. Klášterní Pivovar
16. Host Restaurant
17. Hostinec u Černého Vola Pub
18. Malý Buddha Veggie Rest.
19. U Labutí Restaurant
20. Café Salmovský Palác
21. Kavárna ve Šternberském Paláci

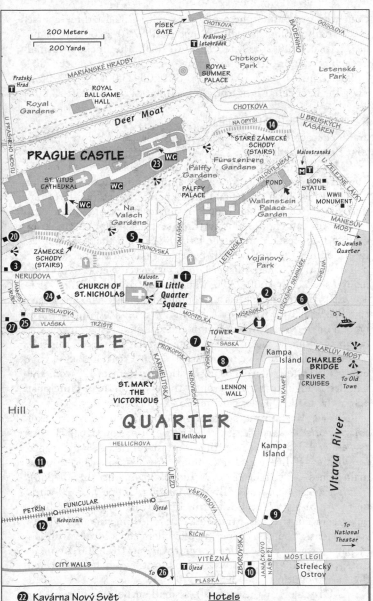

200 Meters
200 Yards

Pražský Hrad

PÍSEK GATE

CHOTKOVA

Královský Letohrádek

Chotkovy Park

Letenské Park

ROYAL SUMMER PALACE

MARIÁNSKÉ HRADBY

ROYAL BALL GAME HALL

Deer Moat

Royal Gardens

CHOTKOVA

NA OPYŠI

U BRUSKÝCH KASÁREN

STARÉ ZÁMECKÉ SCHODY (STAIRS)

14

PRAGUE CASTLE

23 WC

Pálffy Gardens

Fürstenberg Gardens

Malostranská

ST. VITUS CATHEDRAL

WC

WC

PÁLFFY PALACE

LION STATUE

WWII MONUMENT

MÁNESŮV MOST

WC

Na Valech Gardens

Wallenstein Palace Garden

POND

VALDŠTEJNSKÁ

LETENSKÁ

20

THUNOVSKÁ

TOMÁŠSKÁ

To Jewish Quarter

5

ZÁMECKÉ SCHODY (STAIRS)

3

NERUDOVA

Vojanovy Park

CHELNÁ

U LUŽICKÉHO SEMINÁŘE

6

CHURCH OF ST. NICHOLAS

Malostr. Nám. **Little Quarter Square**

1

2

MÍŠEŇSKÁ

24

JÁNSKÝ VRŠEK

BŘETISLAVOVA

VLAŠSKÁ

TRŽIŠTĚ

MOSTECKÁ

TOWER

LÁZEŇSKÁ

SASKÁ

Kampa Island

KARLŮV MOST

CHARLES BRIDGE

27

25

7

8

RIVER CRUISES

To Old Town

L I T T L E

PROKOPSKÁ

KARMELITSKÁ

NEBOVIDSKÁ

LENNON WALL

NA KAMPĚ

ST. MARY THE VICTORIOUS

Q U A R T E R

Kampa Island

Vltava River

Hill

Hellichova

HELLICHOVA

ÚJEZD

11

VŠEHRDOVA

PETŘÍN

FUNICULAR

Nebozízek

12

ŘÍČNÍ

9

To National Theater

CITY WALLS

To **26**

VITĚZNÁ

Újezd

PLASKÁ

ZBOROVSKÁ

JANÁČKOVO NÁBŘEŽÍ

MOST LEGII

10

Střelecký Ostrov

PRAGUE

22 Kavárna Nový Svět
23 Lobkowicz Palace Café
24 Baráčnická Rychta Concert Hall

Hotels
25 Vintage Design Hotel Sax
26 To Hotel Julián
27 Dům u Velké Boty

come with great atmosphere and bad service (280-Kč three-course special daily for lunch or dinner, open daily 7:30-23:00, live piano or jazz trio 16:00-20:00, tel. 222-002-763). The fine and formal **French restaurant** in the next wing oozes Mucha elegance (700-1,000-Kč meals, daily 12:00-16:00 & 18:00-23:00, tel. 222-002-777). The **beer cellar** is overpriced and touristy (daily 11:30-23:00).

IN THE LITTLE QUARTER

These characteristic eateries are handy for a bite before or after your Prague Castle visit.

Malostranská Beseda, in the impeccably restored former Town Hall, weaves together an imaginative menu of traditional Czech dishes (both classic and little known), vegetarian fare, and fresh fish. It feels a bit sterile and formulaic, but that follows a local trend. You can choose among three settings: the non-smoking ground-floor restaurant on the left; the café on the right (serves meals, but it's OK to have only coffee or cake); or the packed beer hall downstairs, where Pilsner Urquell is served well (150-300-Kč main dishes, daily 11:00-23:00, Malostranské Náměstí 21, tel. 257-409-112). The restaurant has a recommended music club upstairs.

Lokál u Bílé Kuželky ("By the White Bowling Pin"), a branch of the Old Town's recommended Lokál restaurant, is the best bet for quick, cheap, well-executed Czech classics on this side of the river (100-200-Kč main dishes, Mon-Fri 11:30-24:00, Sat-Sun 12:00-22:00, non-smoking section, Míšeňská 12; from the Charles Bridge, turn right around the U Tří Pštrosů Hotel just before the Little Quarter gate; tel. 257-212-014).

Lo Veg Restaurant, on the top two floors and a tiny terrace of a narrow medieval house, serves vegan variations on Czech classics as well as Asian fare. The setting is a tasteful mix of Renaissance roof beams, Balinese art, and some gorgeous vistas (150-200 Kč main dishes, daily 11:30-22:00, Nerudova 36, mobile 702-901-060).

U Zavěšenýho Kafe ("By the Hanging Coffee"), up 20 yards on the right after Nerudova turns into Úvoz, is a creative little pub/restaurant that has attracted a cult following among Prague's cognoscenti. You can "hang" a coffee here for a local vagabond by paying for an extra coffee on your way out (100-200-Kč main dishes, daily 11:00-24:00, Úvoz 6, look for the only house covered by vines, mobile 605-294-595).

U Hrocha ("By the Hippo"), a small authentic pub with tar dripping from its walls, is packed with beer drinkers. Expect simple, traditional meals—basically meat starters with bread. Just below the castle near Little Quarter Square (Malostranské Náměstí), it's actually the haunt of many members of Parliament, which is around the corner (40 Kč for a pint of Pilsner, 120 Kč for a chunk of meat, daily 12:00-23:00, chalkboard lists daily meals in

English, Thunovská 10, tel. 257-533-389).

Vinograf Wine Bar is a small, intimate place with just eight tables. It's run by Czech wine lover Karel, who speaks English and enjoys helping visitors appreciate his wines. Karel prepares a daily list of Czech wines available by the glass and serves meat-and-cheese plates for wine tasters who'd like a light meal (daily 16:00-24:00, a few steps off the end of Charles Bridge at Míšeňská 8, next to Lokál, tel. 603-116-085).

Čertovka, down an alley so narrow that it requires a signal to regulate foot traffic, offers outdoor seating on two small terraces right on the water, with some of the best views of the Charles Bridge. Given the location, the prices are reasonable (400-Kč meals, daily 11:30-23:30, off the little square at U Lužického Semináře 24, no reservations taken, arrive early to claim a spot, tel. 257-534-524).

Cukrkávalimonáda ("Sugar, Coffee, Lemonade") is part restaurant and part patisserie, serving big salads, ciabatta sandwiches, artful pastries, and freshly squeezed juice in a setting mixing old and new decor. The bistro—an oasis just a block away from the tourist crush—is 50 yards down the first street to the left after you exit the Charles Bridge (100-Kč sandwiches, 150 Kč salads, Mon-Sat 9:00-23:00, Sun 9:00-19:00, Lázeňská 7, tel. 257-225-396).

Campanulla Café, in the courtyard on the left side of the Lennon Wall, is a secluded spot serving fresh sandwiches, raspberry drinks, and Italian coffee next to a flower garden, an English lawn, and one of the oldest trees in Prague (170-Kč salads and pastas, daily 11:00-22:00, Velkopřevorské Náměstí 4, look for small gate at left end of Lennon Wall, entrance to indoor seating area is another 20 yards to the left, tel. 257-217-736).

Restaurace Rybářský Klub, just off the park on Kampa Island, is run by the Society of Czech Fishermen and serves a wide selection of local freshwater fish. Dine along the dock on fish-cream soup, pike, trout, carp, or catfish at a not-so-scenic part of the river—but still with a glimpse of the Charles Bridge (three-course meal about 500 Kč, daily 12:00-23:00, U Sovových Mlýnů 1, tel. 257-534-200).

Restaurant Savoy, at the foot of the Legií Bridge, is the closest you will get to Parisian food culture in Prague—with exquisite dishes, thoughtful service, and elegant Art Deco surroundings (500-Kč main dishes, 200-Kč lunch specials, Mon-Fri 8:00-22:30, Sat-Sun 9:00-22:30, Vítězná 5, tel. 257-311-562).

Near the Funicular, on Petřín Hill: These two places are near the funicular stop halfway up Petřín Hill, and offer great views over the city. **Petřínské Terasy** has woody seating indoors, or outside on the terrace (300-Kč main dishes, daily 12:00-23:00; Petřín 393, tel. 257-320-688), whereas **Nebozízek** is more modern, with glassed-in seating (600-Kč tasting menu, cash only, daily 11:00-23:00, Petřín 411, tel. 257-315-329).

IN THE CASTLE QUARTER

Bellavista Restaurant is in the garden of the Strahov Monastery, where the abbot himself would come to meditate in a peaceful garden setting. You'll pay for the amazing city views, but if the weather's nice, this is a good value, with traditional grilled meats, pasta, and salads (200-300-Kč main dishes, daily 11:00-24:00, tel. 220-517-274).

Villa Richter, at the end of the castle promontory (closest to the river) and surrounded by newly replanted vineyards, consists of three classy restaurants, each with killer Prague views. Forty yards below the lower castle gate, you'll see a gate leading to a vineyard. Stroll downhill through the vineyard and you'll come upon three distinct restaurants (all open daily 10:00-23:00, tel. 257-219-079). At **Panorama Pergola,** a string of outdoor tables lines a vineyard terrace overlooking the city (wine, sandwiches, cold plates, and hot views). **Piano Nobile** is more pretentious, with Italian and French dishes and romantic white-linen tables indoors and out—it's the perfect place to propose (1,000-Kč three-course meals). **Piano Terra** serves more affordable Czech dishes (200-300-Kč entrées).

Klášterní Pivovar ("Monastery Brewery"), founded by an abbot in 1628 and reopened in 2004, has two large rooms and a pleasant courtyard. This is the place to taste a range of unpasteurized beers brewed on the premises, including amber, wheat, and IPA. The wooden decor and circa-1900 newspaper clippings (including Habsburg Emperor Franz Josef's "Proclamation to My Nations," announcing the beginning of the First World War) evoke the era when Vienna was Europe's artistic capital, Prague was building its faux Eiffel Tower, and life moved much slower. To accompany the beer, try the strong beer-flavored cheese served on toasted black-yeast bread (150-300-Kč main dishes, daily 10:00-22:00, Strahovské Nádvoří 301, tel. 233-353-155). It's directly across from the entrance to the Strahov Library (don't confuse it with the enormous, tour group-oriented Klášterní Restaurace next door, to the right).

Host Restaurant is hidden in the middle of a staircase that connects Loretánská and Úvoz streets. This spot, which boasts super views of the Little Quarter and Petřín Hill, has a modern black-and-white design and an imaginative menu. Most entrées are priced around 350 Kč, but try asking for the "business lunch" menu (two courses for 145 Kč) advertised only in Czech (300-415-Kč main dishes, daily 11:30-22:00, as you go up Loretánská, watch for stairs leading down to the left at #15—just before the arcaded passageway, mobile 728-695-793).

Hostinec u Černého Vola ("By the Black Ox") is a smoky, dingy old-time pub—its survival in the midst of all the castle splendor and tourism is a marvel. It feels like a kegger on the banks of the river Styx, with classic bartenders serving up Kozel beer (traditional "Goat" brand with excellent darks) and beer-friendly gut-bomb snacks (fried cheese, local hot dogs). The pub is located on Loretánská (50 yards from Loreta Church, no sign outside, sniff for cigarette smoke and look for the only house on the block without an arcade, 35-Kč beers, 50-Kč sausages, daily 10:00-22:00, English menu on request, tel. 220-513-481).

Malý Buddha ("Little Buddha") serves delightful food—especially vegetarian—and takes its theme seriously. You'll step into a mellow, low-lit escape of bamboo and peace, where you'll be served by people with perfect complexions and almost no pulse to the rhythmless pulse of meditative music. Eating in their little back room is like being in a temple (100-200-Kč meals, Tue-Sun 12:00-22:30, closed Mon, non-smoking, between the castle and Strahov Monastery at Úvoz 46, tel. 220-513-894).

U Labutí ("By the Swans") offers Czech food for a good price in a tranquil courtyard, just across from the Plague Column on Castle Square (150-250-Kč main dishes, daily 10:00-22:00, Hradčanské Náměstí 11, tel. 220-511-191).

Café Salmovský Palác, just behind the Tomáš Masaryk statue on Castle Square, has a terrace with great city views and reasonably priced (given the location) soups, pasta, and coffee (daily 10:00-18:00, Hradčanské Náměstí 1, mobile 725-816-267).

Kavárna ve Šternberském Paláci ("Café in the Sternberg Palace") is the locals' getaway from the tourist scene on Castle Square. It's tucked behind the Archbishop's Palace (go through the gateway to the left of the palace, then pass through the ticket office). They serve soup or goulash with bread and drinks in a quiet courtyard at unbeatable prices. Check out the garden with some stunning sculptures that's through the door on the left corner of the courtyard (Tue-Sun 10:00-18:00, closed Mon, Hradčanské Náměstí 15, mobile 721-138-290).

Kavárna Nový Svět ("New World Café"), on a quiet lane down from the Loreta Church, offers a tasty break from the tourist crowds for cake and coffee (Mon-Sat 11:00-20:00, Sun 11:00-18:30, Nový Svět 2).

CAFÉS

Dripping with history, these places in the Old Town and New Town are as much about the ambience as they are about the coffee. Most cafés also serve sweets and light meals. For locations, see the map on page 141.

Kavárna Slavia, across from the National Theater (facing the

PRAGUE

Legií Bridge on Národní street), is a fixture in Prague, famous as a hangout for its literary elite. Today, it's tired and clearly past its prime, with an Art Deco interior, lousy piano entertainment, and celebrity photos on the wall. But its iconic status makes it a fun stop for a coffee—but skip the food (daily 8:00-23:00, sit as near the river as possible, Smetanovo Nábřeží 2, tel. 224-218-493). Notice the *Drinker of Absinthe* painting on the wall (and on the menu for 55 Kč)—with the iconic Czech writer struggling with reality.

Grand Café Orient is just one flight up off busy Celetná street, yet a world away from the crush of tourism below. Located in the Cubist House of the Black Madonna, the café is upstairs and fittingly decorated with a Cubist flair. With its stylish, circa-1910 decor toned to dark green, this space is full of air and light—and a good value as well. The café takes its Cubism seriously: Traditionally round desserts are served square (100-Kč sandwiches, 160-Kč salads, 40-Kč vanilla squares, other desserts about 100 Kč, great balcony seating, Mon-Fri 9:00-22:00, Sat-Sun 10:00-22:00, Ovocný Trh 19, at the corner of Celetná near the Powder Tower, tel. 224-224-240).

Café Café, just off to the right from the main drag connecting the Old Town and Wenceslas Square, serves salads, sandwiches, and cakes in a fancy setting (200-Kč salads, 100-Kč cakes, daily 9:00-23:00, Rytířská 10, tel. 224-210-597).

Café Montmartre, on a small street parallel to Karlova, combines Parisian ambience with unbeatable Czech prices for coffee (no food served). Dreamy Czech minds found their quiet asylum here after Kavárna Slavia (listed earlier) and other longtime favorites either closed down or became stuck in their past. The main room is perfect for discussing art and politics; the intimate room behind the courtyard is where you recite poetry to your partner (Mon-Fri 9:00-23:00, Sat-Sun 12:00-23:00, Řetězová 7, tel. 222-221-244).

Ebel Coffee House, adjacent to Café Montmartre, prides itself on its wide assortment of fresh brews from every coffee-bean-growing country in the world, inviting cakes, and colorful setting that delights the mind as much as the caffeine does (daily 9:00-22:00, Řetězová 3, tel. 224-895-788).

Café Louvre is a longtime elegant favorite (opened in 1902 and maintaining its classic atmosphere) that still draws an energetic young crowd that's crazy about their cheesecake and hot chocolate. From the big and busy Národní street, you walk upstairs into a venerable world of newspapers on sticks (including English) and waiters in vests and aprons. The back room has long been the place for billiard tables (100 Kč/hour). An English flier tells its history (200-Kč plates, 120-Kč two-course lunch offered 11:00-15:00, good gluten-free options, open daily 8:00-23:30, Národní 22, tel. 224-930-949).

TEAHOUSES

Many Czech people are bohemian philosophers at heart and prefer the mellow, smoke-free environs of a teahouse to the smoky, traditional beer hall. Young Czechs are much more interested in traveling to exotic destinations like Southeast Asia, Africa, or Peru than to Western Europe, so the Oriental teahouses set their minds in vacation mode. For locations, see the map on page 141.

While there are teahouses all over Prague, a fine example in a handy New Town locale is Prague's original one, established in 1991—just after freedom. **Dobrá Čajovna** ("Good Teahouse"), only a few steps off the bustle of Wenceslas Square, takes you into a very peaceful world that elevates tea to an almost religious ritual. You'll be given an English menu—which lovingly describes each tea—and a bell. The menu lists a world of tea (very fresh, prices by the small pot), "accompaniments" (such as Exotic Miscellany), and light meals "for hungry tea drinkers." When you're ready to order, ring your bell to beckon a tea monk—likely a member of the Lovers of Tea Society (80-200 Kč/teapot, Mon-Fri 10:00-21:30, Sat-Sun 14:00-21:30, near the base of Wenceslas Square, opposite McDonald's at Václavské Náměstí 14, tel. 224-231-480).

For a taste of tea from Prague's newly emerging Chinese middle class (rather than from some Czech's dreams of the Orient), head to **Čajový Klub** ("Tea Club"), just down the street from the Jerusalem Synagogue. Creatively run by a man from Beijing, here you'll find red cherrywood decor, expertly served tea, and the freshest green leaves in town (80-200 Kč/teapot, Mon-Sat 10:00-21:00, closed Sun, Jeruzalémská 10, tel. 222-721-072).

Prague Connections

BY TRAIN

Prague's Main Station (Hlavní Nádraží, or "Praha hl. n." on schedules) serves all international trains; most trains within the Czech Republic, including high-speed SC Pendolino trains; and buses to and from Nürnberg and Munich. Trains serving Berlin also stop at the secondary Holešovice Station (Nádraží Holešovice, located north of the river). Both stations have ATMs (best rates) and exchange bureaus (rotten rates). You'll find handy Czech train and bus schedules at www.idos.cz.

Main Train Station (Hlavní Nádraží)

The station is a busy hive of shops and services; posted maps help you find your way. Three parallel tunnels connect the tracks to the arrival hall. Taking any of these, you'll first reach a low-ceilinged corridor with several services: To the right are an exchange office with Internet booths, a variety of handy picnic-supply shops, and the "official" taxi stands (avoid these rip-off cabbies—explained later).

Continuing straight past this corridor, you'll reach the waste-of-space main hall, where you'll find four Metro entrances in the center (two for each direction; for more on the Metro, see "Getting from the Main Station to Your Hotel," later). One **ATM** is along the right wall; two more are in front of the ticketing area under the central stairs. **Lockers** are in the corner under the stairs on the right, and a **Billa supermarket** is in the corner under the stairs to the left.

The **Touristpoint** office—at the left end of the main hall (as you face the tracks)—offers a last-minute room-finding service; books car rentals; and sells maps, international phone cards, sight-seeing tours, and adrenaline experiences. Perhaps most importantly, they're willing to call you a taxi to avoid the "official" crooks out front: The driver will come to the desk to get you (Touristpoint open daily 8:00-22:00, tel. 224-946-010, www.touristpoint.cz, info@touristpoint.cz).

Buying Tickets: For most trains, head for the **Czech Railways (České Dráhy) ticket office**—marked *ČD Centrum*—in the middle of the main hall under the stairs. The regular ticket desks are faster if you already know your schedule and destination, but not all attendants speak good English. For more in-depth questions, look for the tiny **ČD Travel** office, on the left as you enter the main office, which sells both domestic and international tickets, and is more likely to provide English help (Mon-Fri 9:00-18:00, Sat 9:00-14:00, closed Sun, shorter hours in winter, tel. 972-241-861, www.cd.cz/en).

The **RegioJet travel office,** with desks at both sides of the main ticket office, sells international train tickets from the DB (Deutsche Bahn—German railways) system and offers various DB deals and discounts. RegioJet also runs its own trains to Olomouc (220 Kč) and Košice, Slovakia, and sells a variety of domestic (e.g., to Český Krumlov) and international (Vienna) bus tickets without a commission (Mon-Fri 5:00-19:45, Sat-Sun 6:45-19:45, tel. 539-000-511, www.regiojet.cz, jizdenky@regiojet.cz). Despite its name, RegioJet does not sell plane tickets.

The **Leo Express ticket office,** across the hall from the ČD Centrum, sells tickets for its new Swiss-made trains to Olomouc and Košice (www.le.cz).

Bus Stops: To reach the bus stops for the AE bus to the airport and the DB buses to Nürnberg and Munich, simply find your way up to the Art Nouveau Hall (explained later) and head outside.

Deciphering Schedules: Platforms are listed by number and, confusingly, sometimes also by letter. *S (sever)* means "south"—the corridor to the left as you face the tracks; *J (jih)* means "north"—the corridor to the right. But in practice, you can take any corridor and walk along the platform to your train. Also on schedules, *B1* means the bus platform (upstairs and out front), while *1B*—used by Leo Express trains—is the shorter track at the far-right end of platform 1.

A Bit of History: If you have time to kill waiting for a train, go exploring. First named for Emperor Franz Josef, the station was later renamed for President Woodrow Wilson (see the commemo-rative **plaque** in the main exit hall leading away from the tracks, and the large bronze **statue** in the park in front of the station). The Czechs appreciate Wilson's promotion of self-determination after World War I, which led to the creation of the free state of Czechoslovakia in 1918. Under the communists (who weren't big fans of Wilson), it was bluntly renamed Hlavní Nádraží—"Main Station." They enlarged the once-classy Art Nouveau station and painted it the compulsory dreary gray with reddish trim.

For a glimpse at the sta-tion's genteel pre-communist times, find your way up into its original **Art Nouveau Hall** (from the main con-course, look for up escalators with *Historical Building of the Station* signs). You'll emerge to stand under a grandly restored dome with elaborate decorations, providing an almost shocking contrast to the busi-nesslike aura of the rest of the station.

Getting from the Main Station to Your Hotel

Even though the Main Train Station is basically downtown, get-ting to your hotel can be a little tricky.

On Foot: Most hotels I list in the Old Town are within a 20-minute walk of the train station. Exit the station into a small park, walk through the park, and then cross the street on the other side. Head down Jeruzalémská street to the Jindřišská Tower and tram stop, walk under a small arch, then continue slightly to the right down Senovážná street. At the end of the street, you'll see the Powder Tower—the grand entry into the Old Town—to the left. Alternatively, Wenceslas Square in the New Town is a 10-minute walk—exit the station, cross the park, and walk to the left along Opletalova street.

By Metro: The Metro is easy. The entrance is right inside the station's main hall. Look for the red *M* with two directions: Háje or Letňany. To purchase tickets from the machine by the Metro entrance, you'll need Czech coins (get change at the change machine in the corner near the luggage lockers, or break a bill at a newsstand or grocery). Validate your ticket in the yellow machines *before* you go down the stairs to the tracks. To get to hotels in the Old Town, catch a Háje-bound train to the Muzeum stop, then transfer to the green line (direction: Dejvická) and get off at either Můstek or Staroměstská; these stops straddle the Old Town. The next stop, Malostranská, is handy for hotels in the Little Quarter. For more information on Prague's public transit, see page 47.

Taxi: The fair metered rate into the Old Town is about 200 Kč; if your hotel is farther out or across the river, it should be no more than 300 Kč. Avoid the "official" taxi stand that's marked inside the station: These thugs routinely overcharge arriving tourists (and refuse to take locals, who know the going rate and can't be fooled). Instead, to get an **honest cabbie,** exit the station's main hall through the big glass doors, then cross 50 yards through a park to Opletalova street. A few taxis are usually waiting there in front of Hotel Chopin, on the corner of Jeruzalémská street. Alternatively, the Touristpoint office, described earlier, can call a taxi for you (AAA Taxi—tel. 222-333-222; City Taxi—tel. 257-257-257). Before getting into a taxi, always confirm the maximum price to your destination, and make sure the driver turns on the meter. For more pointers on taking taxis, see page 50.

By Tram: The nearest tram stop is to the right as you exit the station (about 200 yards away). Tram #9 (headed away from railway tracks) takes you to the neighborhood near the National Theater and the Little Quarter, but isn't useful for most Old Town hotels.

Holešovice Train Station (Nádraží Holešovice)

This station, slightly farther from the center, is suburban mellow. The main hall has the same services as the Main Train Station, in a more compact area. On the left are international and local ticket windows (open 24 hours) and an information office. On the right is an uncrowded café with Internet access (1 Kč/minute, daily 8:00-19:30). Two ATMs are just outside the first glass doors, and the Metro is 50 yards to the right (follow signs toward *Vstup,* which means "entrance"; it's three stops to Hlavní Nádraží—the Main Station—or four stops to the city-center Muzeum stop). Taxis and trams are outside to the right (allow 300 Kč for a cab to the center).

Train Connections

Remember that all international trains pass through the Main Station (Hlavní Nádraží); some also stop at Holešovice Station

(Nádraží Holešovice). Direct overnight trains connect Prague to Vienna, Frankfurt, Cologne, Zurich, Budapest, Kraków, and Warsaw. For tips on rail travel, see the Practicalities chapter.

From Prague's Main Station to Domestic Destinations: Konopiště Castle (train to Benešov, 2/hour, 1 hour, then 1.5-mile walk to castle), **Kutná Hora** (11/day, 1 hour, more with change in Kolín; to reach Kutná Hora's town center or bone church, you'll need to transfer to a local train), **Terezín** (train to Bohušovice station, nearly hourly, 1-1.5 hours, then 5-minute taxi or bus ride—the direct bus from near Holešovice Station is better), **Český Krumlov** (8/day, 1/day direct, 4 hours—bus is faster, cheaper, and easier), **České Budějovice** (almost hourly, 2.5 hours), **Olomouc** (at least hourly, 2-3 hours), **Brno** (every 2 hours direct, 2.5 hours, more with changes).

From Prague's Main Station to International Destinations: Berlin (6/day direct, 5-5.5 hours), **Dresden** (every 2 hours, 2.5 hours), **Nürnberg** (1/day, 5 hours, bus is better—see below), **Munich** (2/day direct, 6 hours; bus is better—see below), **Frankfurt** (6/day, 6 hours, change to bus in Nürnberg; 1 night train, 9.5 hours), **Cologne** (bus to Nürnberg then hourly trains, 9 hours total; 1 night train, 12 hours); **Vienna**—Vídeň in Czech (6/day direct, 4.25 hours, more with 1 change, 5-6 hours; 1 night train, 6 hours), **Zürich** (1 night train, 15 hours), **Paris** (5/day, 12.5-18 hours; night train via Mannheim), **Budapest** (3/day, 7 hours; more with 2-3 changes, 8.5 hours; 1 night train, 8.5 hours), **Kraków** (4/day with 1-2 changes, 7-8.25 hours; 1 night train, 8.75 hours), **Warsaw** (2/day direct, including 1 night train, more with changes, 8.5-10.5 hours).

BY BUS

Prague's main bus station is at Florenc, east of the Old Town (Metro: Florenc). However, some connections use other stations, including Roztyly (Metro: Roztyly), Na Knížecí (Metro: Anděl), the Nádraží Holešovice train station (Metro: Nádraží Holešovice), Hradčanská (Metro: Hradčanská), or the Main Train Station (Metro: Hlavní Nádraží). Be sure to confirm which station your bus uses.

From Prague by Bus to: Terezín (hourly, 50 minutes, departs from Nádraží Holešovice train station), **Český Krumlov** (10/day, 3.5 hours, some leave from Florenc Station, others leave from Na Knížecí Station or Roztyly Station), **Brno** (2/hour from Florenc Station, 2.5 hours), **Nürnberg,** Germany (6/day via IC Bus, 3.75

hours, covered by rail passes, departs in front of Main Train Station), **Munich,** Germany (4/day via ExpressBus, 5 hours, covered by rail passes, also departs from Main Train Station), **Budapest** (1-4/day via Orange Ways, not covered by rail passes, 6.5-7.5 hours, www. orangeways.com).

BY PLANE
Václav Havel Airport
Prague's modern, tidy, user-friendly Václav Havel Airport (formerly Ruzyně Airport) is located 12 miles (about 30 minutes) west of the city center. Terminal 2 serves destinations within the EU except for Great Britain (no passport controls); Terminal 1 serves Great Britain and everywhere else. The airport has ATMs (avoid the change desks), desks promoting their transportation services (such as city transit and shuttle buses), kiosks selling city maps and phone cards, and a TI with few printed materials (airport code: PRG, airport tel. 220-113-314, operator tel. 220-111-111, www.prg. aero/en).

Getting from the Airport to Your Hotel
Getting between the airport and downtown is easy. Leaving either airport terminal, you have four options, listed from cheapest to priciest:

Dirt Cheap: Take bus #119 to the Nádraží Veleslavín stop, or #100 to the Zličín Metro station (20 minutes), then take the Metro into the center (32 Kč, buy tickets at info desk in airport arrival hall).

Budget: Take the airport express (AE) bus to the Main Train Station, or to the Masarykovo Nádraží Station near Republic Square—Náměstí Republiky (50 Kč, runs every half-hour daily 5:46-21:16, 40 minutes, look for the *AE* sign in front of the terminal and pay the driver, www.cd.cz/en). From either station, you can take the Metro, hire a taxi, or walk to your hotel. The Masarykovo Nádraží stop is slightly closer to downtown.

Moderate: Take the Čedaz minibus shuttle (from exit F at Terminal 1 or exit E at Terminal 2) to the Náměstí Republiky (Republic Square) Station, at the entrance to the Old Town. The shuttle stop is on V Celnici street, across the street from Hotel Marriott and near the recommended Brasserie La Gare (pay 130 Kč directly to driver, daily 7:30-19:00, 2/hour, info desk in arrival hall).

Expensive: Catch a taxi. Cabbies wait at the curb directly in front of the arrival hall. Or book a yellow AAA taxi through their office in the airport hall—you'll get a 50 percent discount coupon for the trip back (book your return trip by calling 222-333-222). AAA taxis wait in front of exit D at Terminal 1 and exit E at Terminal 2 (metered rate, generally 500-600 Kč to downtown).

BY PRIVATE CAR SERVICE

Mike's Chauffeur Service is a reliable, family-run company with fair and fixed rates around town and beyond. Friendly Mike's motto is, "We go the extra mile for you." If Mike is busy, he'll send one of his colleagues—all of whom speak English and are accommodating (round-trip fares, with waiting time included, guaranteed through 2016 with this book: Český Krumlov-3,800 Kč, Terezín-1,900 Kč, Karlštejn-1,700 Kč, Karlovy Vary and Pilsner Urquell brewery in Plzeň-3,800 Kč, 4 percent surcharge for credit-card payment; these prices for up to 4 people, minibus for up to 8 also available; tel. 241-768-231, mobile 602-224-893, www.mike-chauffeur.cz, mike.chauffeur@cmail.cz). On the way to Český Krumlov, Mike will stop at no extra charge at Hluboká Castle and/or České Budějovice, where the original Bud beer is made. Mike's service can also arrange a local guide for your time in many of these places. And for day trips from Prague, Mike can bring bicycles along and will pedal with you.

Mike also offers "Panoramic Transfers" to **Vienna** (7,000 Kč, depart Prague at 8:00, arrive Český Krumlov at 10:00, stay up to 5 hours, 1-hour scenic Czech riverside-and-village drive, then a 2-hour autobahn ride to your Vienna hotel, maximum 4 people), **Budapest** (9,500 Kč via Bratislava or Český Krumlov, 6 hours), and **Kraków** (9,300 Kč direct, or 9,800 Kč with a stop at Auschwitz; these prices include all road taxes). Mike can also pick you up in any of these cities, and bring you to Prague. Check Mike's website for special deals on last-minute transfers, including super-cheap "deadhead" rides when you travel in the opposite direction of a full-fare client.

NEAR PRAGUE

Kutná Hora • Terezín Memorial • Konopiště Castle

Prague has plenty to keep a traveler busy, but don't overlook the interesting day trips in the nearby Bohemian countryside. Within a short bus or train ride of Prague (in different directions), you'll find a variety of worthwhile stopovers.

Kutná Hora, once home to the world's largest silver mine, is a finely preserved yet still down-to-earth city. It's best known for two churches: an opulent cathedral, built with riches from the mining bonanza, and an evocative chapel decorated with human bones. The walled town of Terezín served as an internment camp for Jews during World War II, while an adjacent fortress was a notorious Gestapo prison; today, both house poignant memorials. And Konopiště Castle, the former residence of the Habsburg Archduke Franz Ferdinand and his Czech bride, has the most lived-in-feeling interior (and most interesting historical tour) of any Czech castle.

Kutná Hora

Kutná Hora (KOOT-nah HO-rah) is a refreshingly authentic, yet unmistakably gorgeous town that sits on top of what was once Europe's largest silver mine. In its heyday, the mine was so productive that Kutná Hora was Bohemia's "second city" after Prague. Much of Europe's standard coinage was minted here, and the king got a 12 percent cut of every penny. In addition to financing much of Prague's grand architecture, these precious deposits also paid for Kutná Hora's particularly beautiful cathedral. But by about 1700, the mining and minting petered out, and the city slumbered.

Once rich, then ignored, Kutná Hora is now appreciated by tourists looking for a handy side-trip from Prague. While most

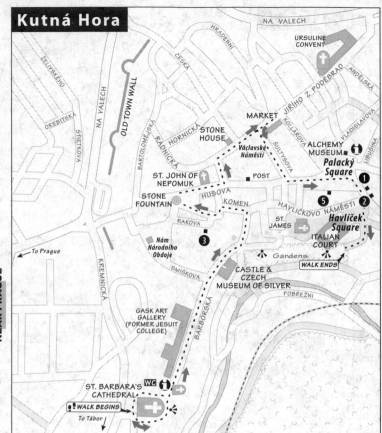

Kutná Hora

visitors come here primarily for the famous, offbeat Sedlec Bone Church, the delightful town itself trumps it—with one of the finest Czech churches outside of Prague (St. Barbara's Cathedral), a breathtaking promenade overlooking the valley, a fascinating silver mine, and a cute, cobbled town center with pretty pastel houses.

All in all, underrated Kutná Hora makes a strong case for the title of "best Czech stop outside of Prague." Unlike dolled-up Český Krumlov, Kutná Hora is a typical Czech town. The shops on the main square cater to locals, and the factory between the Sedlec Bone Church and the train station—since the 1930s, the biggest tobacco processor in the country—is now Philip Morris' headquarters for Central Europe. Kutná Hora is about as close to quintessential Czech life as you can get.

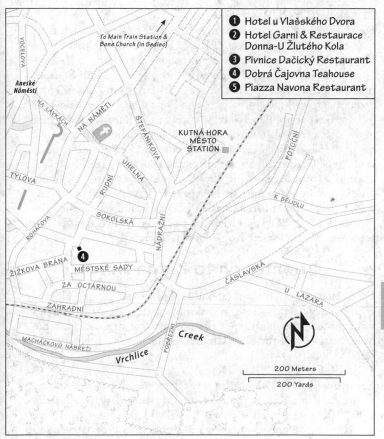

1. Hotel u Vlašského Dvora
2. Hotel Garni & Restaurace Donna-U Žlutého Kola
3. Pivnice Dačický Restaurant
4. Dobrá Čajovna Teahouse
5. Piazza Navona Restaurant

GETTING TO KUTNÁ HORA

The town is 45 miles east of Prague. Direct trains from Prague's Main Station stop at Kutná Hora's Main Station, two miles from the town center (11/day, 1 hour; other trains are slower and require transfer in Kolín). From the Kutná Hora Main Station, a local train shuttles visitors in just a few minutes to the Kutná Hora Sedlec Station (near the Sedlec Bone Church), then to the central Kutná Hora Město Station (near the rest of the sights). After getting off at the Main Station, follow the passage beneath the tracks to the cute little yellow local train. For train schedules, see www.jizdnirady.idnes.cz.

In Prague, make sure to buy a ticket to "Kutná Hora Město" rather than "Kutná Hora hl. n." (the Main Station)—the price is nearly the same, and this gives you the flexibility to get off and on at any of the three Kutná Hora stations.

PLANNING YOUR TIME

For the most efficient visit, head to the Sedlec Bone Church first, then explore the town center of Kutná Hora. Be aware that Kutná Hora is quiet on Sundays, when most shops are closed.

Here's my suggested plan: At Kutná Hora's Main Station, transfer to the local train. Get off at its first stop (Kutná Hora Sedlec), and walk five minutes to the Bone Church (see below for walking directions). After your visit, head to St. Barbara's Cathedral in the town center via tourist minivan, taxi, or public bus (for details, see page 168). After touring the cathedral, follow my self-guided walk to the Czech Museum of Silver and take an English-language mine tour (consider booking ahead online or by phone, or simply drop by in advance to sign up—see page 174). At the end of the day, walk to Kutná Hora Město Station (about 15 minutes) to catch the train back to Kutná Hora's Main Station, where you'll transfer to a train back to Prague (see "Kutná Hora Connections," later).

Orientation to Kutná Hora

For a relatively small town (about 20,000 people), Kutná Hora is tricky to navigate: It's long and skinny, with spaghetti-like lanes spilling across the summit of a promontory that stretches from the Main Station, past the Bone Church, to the historical center.

TOURIST INFORMATION

The main TI is on **Palacký Square** (Palackého Náměstí), housed in the same building as the Alchemy Museum (April-Sept daily 9:00-18:00; Oct-March Mon-Fri 9:00-17:00, Sat-Sun 9:00-16:00; tel. 327-512-378, www.kutnahora.cz). It offers Internet access and also rents bicycles (220 Kč/day, mobile 605-802-874).

A small TI kiosk, with handy WCs, is in front of the **cathedral;** you can also hire a local guide here. Reserve ahead if you can (500 Kč/hour Tue-Sun, no tours Mon, tel. 327-516-710, mobile 736-485-408, infocentrum@kh.cz).

ARRIVAL IN KUTNÁ HORA

The **Kutná Hora Sedlec Station** is a short walk from the Bone Church. From the station, head one block down the street perpendicular to the tracks, passing a large church on your right (a cathedral that predates the mine and the town). Cross the main street and find the small Bone Church in the middle of the cemetery directly ahead.

If you're skipping the Bone Church (or not visiting it first), stay on the train to the **Kutná Hora Město Station** in the valley. From there, hike up to St. Barbara's Cathedral (about 20 minutes) to find the start of my "Kutná Hora Walk."

Sights in Kutná Hora

The following sights are listed in order of sightseeing efficiency, starting with the Bone Church on the outskirts then moving on to the center of town (with the cathedral, silver mine/museum, and my self-guided walk).

▲▲SEDLEC BONE CHURCH (KOSTNICE V SEDLCI)

Located about a mile and a half outside of the historical center, the Sedlec Bone Church sits in a serene graveyard and looks unassum-

ing from the outside. But inside, it's filled with the bones of 40,000 people—stacked into neat, 20-foot-tall pyramids decorating the walls and ceilings. The 14th-century plagues and 15th-century wars provided all the raw material necessary for the monks who made these designs.

Cost and Hours: 90 Kč, daily April-Sept 8:00-18:00, March and Oct 9:00-17:00, Nov-Feb 9:00-16:00, good 40-Kč audioguide adds 15 minutes of commentary to make it more meaningful, tel. 327-561-143, www.kostnice.cz.

NEAR PRAGUE

Visiting the Church: Stand outside the church. This is a place of reflection. The cemetery here was "seeded" with holy earth brought from Jerusalem, which made this sacred ground. Demand was high, and corpses that could no longer pay the rent (i.e., those who lacked surviving relatives with enough disposable income for postmortem real estate) were "evicted." What to do with the bones? Recycle them as church decorations with a message.

The monks, who first placed these bones 400 years ago, were guided by the belief that in order to live well, one must constantly remember death (*memento mori*—"what we are now, someday you shall be"). They also wanted to remind viewers that the earthly church was a community of both the living and the dead, a countless multitude that would one day stand before God. Later bone stackers were more interested in design than theology...as evidenced by the many show-off flourishes you'll see around the church.

Approach the church. Ignore the dull upper chapel and head down below (look for the *kostinec* sign). Flanking the stairwell are two giant chalices made of bones (a symbol of Jan Hus' egalitarian approach to worship).

Downstairs, on either side are giant stacks of bones, reaching up to the top of the Gothic vaults (there are six such bone-pyramids in this small chapel). The skulls are neatly arranged on top, in the belief that this closeness to God would serve them well when Jesus returns to judge the living and the dead. Straight ahead dangles a chandelier, which supposedly includes at least one of every bone in the human body. In the glass case on the right (by the pillar), see the skulls with gnarly holes and other wounds. These belonged to soldiers who died fighting in the Hussite Wars—a boom time for this cemetery.

Finally, head into the left wing of the church, where you'll find a giant coat of arms of the aristocratic Schwarzenberg family—decorated with the skull of an Ottoman invader (a fearsome foe of the time), whose "eye" is being pecked out by a raven made of human bones.

Your visit is over. Go outside and head into town, thankful all of your limbs are intact.

Getting from the Church to Town: You have several options for getting to the center of Kutná Hora. The Bone Church runs a **tourist minivan** that can shuttle you from the church to sights in town (35 Kč/person, requires 3 passengers or pay the 105-Kč minimum fee, April-Sept 9:00-18:00, Oct-March 9:00-17:00, inquire at the desk, mobile 731-402-307). Ask the shuttle bus to drop you off at the park surrounding St. Barbara's Cathedral. If you prefer (or if the shuttle is on a break), church staff can call a **taxi,** which costs no more than 150 Kč to the cathedral. Another option is public **bus** #F01 (on weekdays) or #F07 (on weekends), which runs from near the Bone Church to a stop near the cathedral (12 Kč, buy ticket from driver, 2/hour Mon-Fri, 1/hour Sat-Sun, 20 minutes).

KUTNÁ HORA WALK

This self-guided walk connects virtually all of the sights in the historical center in a near-loop. Before you get too far into the walk, call or drop by the Czech Museum of Silver to book a spot on the 1.5-hour, claustrophobic mine tour. No stop on this walk is more than 10 minutes from the museum, so you can bail out and head for your tour at any point and easily resume the walk later.

• *Begin in the inviting park surrounding the cathedral.*

St. Barbara's Cathedral and Park: Rising like three pointy tents from a forest of buttresses, St. Barbara's strikes an exquisite Gothic profile. This culmination of Czech Gothic architecture was funded with a "spare no expense" attitude by a town riding the crest of a wave of mining wealth. Be sure to tour the **cathedral's interior** (see listing, later)—but also take the time to do a slow lap around the pristine park that surrounds it.

Behind the church's apse, belly up to the **viewpoint** for an orientation to the city. From left to right, visually trace the historical center that perches along the promontory's crest: The long former Jesuit College now houses a modern art museum. The big, gray building that plunges down the cliff is the town's "little castle" *(Hrádek),* with the Czech Museum of Silver. And the spire to the right of that bookends this walk. Surveying this scene, think about the history of a town made very, very rich by the glittering deposits it sits upon. Wealthy as it was, this was still an industrial town: The river below was so polluted they called it "Stink" in Czech. Notice the vineyards draping the hill. Kutná Hora is closer to Moravia (the eastern Czech Republic) than it is to Prague—here, you're beginning to see the transition from beer country in Bohemia to the wine country of Moravia.

• *After circling the church, walk along the grand...*

Terrace: Just before you head along the panoramic promenade, notice the handy TI in the little house on the left. Then stroll regally along the stately white building, which now houses the modern and contemporary **GASK** art collection (see listing, later). The statues of saints that line the terrace are a reminder of the building's Jesuit past. The Jesuits arrived here in 1626 with a mission: to make the Protestant population Catholic again. These chubby sandstone figures, just like those on the Charles Bridge in Prague, were initially commissioned as Counter-Reformation propaganda pieces.

Near the end of the terrace, continue following the broad cobbled footpath downhill...and keep an eye out for an army of white-jacketed, white-helmeted miners trudging up the hill for their daily shift. Or maybe they're tourists, about to explore the former silver mine at the **Czech Museum of Silver,** which occupies the big building on your right (see listing, later).

• *At the little park in front of the museum, take the left (level) fork, following* Stone Fountain *signs. When you hit the bigger street (with lots of parked cars), turn left (uphill, on Rejskova) and bear left around the big drab building. You'll emerge into a little square (Rejskovo Náměstí), with a big and impressive...*

Stone Fountain (Kamenná Kašna): The intensive mining under Kutná Hora released arsenic and other toxins, poisoning the water supply. This means that the city struggled with obtaining clean drinking water, which had to be brought to town by a sophisticated system of pipes, then stored in large tanks. At the end of the 15th century, the architect Rejsek built a 12-sided, richly decorated Gothic structure over one of these tanks. Although no longer functioning, the fountain survives unchanged—the only structure like it in Bohemia.

• *Facing the fountain, hook right around the corner and head down Husova street. On the left you'll pass the stately town library (Městská Knihovna), then the gorgeous late-Baroque/Rococo Church of St. John of Nepomuk (named for the ever-popular Czech patron saint). Turn left up the street after this church (Lierova). At the top of the street, turn right on Václavské Náměstí (Kutná Hora's own Wenceslas Square). On your left you'll spot the frilly decorations on the...*

Stone House (Kamenný Dům): Notice the meticulous detail in the grape leaves, branches, and animals on this house's facade and up in its gable. Talented Polish craftsmen delicately carved the brittle stone into what was considered a marvel of its time. Skip the boring museum of local arts and crafts inside.

• *Continue past the house as the street opens up into a leafy and inviting square. For a slice of authentic Czech life, continue straight when the street narrows again; a half-block down on your right, under the tržnice sign, is the town's humble...*

Market: This double row of stalls selling fake Nike shoes and cheap jeans is as much a part of Czech urban life today as farmers' markets were in the past. Many of the stalls are run by Vietnamese immigrants, the Czech Republic's third-largest minority (after Slovaks and Poles). Many came here in the 1970s as part of a communist solidarity program that sent Vietnamese workers to Czech textile factories. They learned the language, adapted to the environment, and, after 1989, set off on a road to entrepreneurial success that allowed them to bring over friends and relatives (Mon-Fri 7:30-16:45, shorter hours Sat, closed Sun).

• *Backtrack a few steps uphill, then turn left to walk down through the postcard-perfect Šultysova street, with a towering plague column at its center. Turn left at the street past the column, enjoying the pretty, colorful arcades. You'll emerge into the lively main square.*

Palacký Square (Palackého Náměstí): Beautiful but still somehow local, this square enjoys colorful facades, tempting al fresco restaurant tables, and generous public benches. Across the square on the left, notice the **TI;** inside the same building is the **Alchemy Museum** (described later).

• *Exit the square at the far-right corner, following the traffic-free street (in the gap between buildings, toward the green house). You'll enter...*

Havlíček Square (Havlíčkovo Náměstí): The monuments on this leafy, parklike square are a Who's Who of important Czech patriots.

Straight ahead, the stone statue with his arm outstretched is **Karel Havlíček** (1821-1856), the founder of Czech political journalism (and the square's namesake). From Kutná Hora, Havlíček ran an influential magazine highly critical of the Habsburg

government. In 1851, he was forced into exile and detained for five years in the Tirolean Alps under police surveillance. His integrity is reflected by the quote inscribed on the statue: "You can try to bribe me with favors, you can threaten me, you can torture me, yet I will never turn a traitor." His motto became an inspiration for generations of Czech intellectuals, most of whom faced a similar combination of threats and temptations. Havlíček (whose name means "little Havel") was much revered in the 1970s and 1980s, when the *other* Havel (Václav) was similarly imprisoned for his dissent.

Below and to the right, the bronze, walrus-mustachioed statue in front of the big building honors the founder of Czechoslovakia, **Tomáš Garrigue Masaryk** (1850-1937; see sidebar on page 104). Circle around behind the pedestal to see the brief inscription tracing the statue's up-and-down history, which parallels the country's troubled 20th-century history: erected by Kutná Hora townspeople on October 27, 1938 (the eve of Czechoslovakia's 20th birthday); torn down in 1942 (by occupying Nazis, who disliked Masaryk as a symbol of Czech independence); erected again on October 27, 1948 (by freedom-loving locals, a few months after the communist coup); torn down again in 1957 (by the communists, who considered Masaryk an enemy of the working class); and erected once again on October 27, 1991. Notice that the Czechs, ever practical, have left a blank space below the last entry.

Masaryk stands in front of the **Italian Court** (Vlašský Dvůr). Step inside its fine courtyard. This palace, located on the site where Czech currency was once made, became Europe's most important mint and the main residence of Czech kings in the 1400s. It's named for the Italian minters who came to Kutná Hora to teach the locals their trade. Most of the present-day building is a 19th-century reconstruction. Today, it hosts a moderately interesting museum on minting and local history. While the main Gothic hall (now a wedding chamber) and the Art Nouveau-decorated St. Wenceslas Chapel are interesting, you can visit them only with a 40-minute guided tour (rarely in English; Czech tour comes with English handout; April-Sept daily 9:00-18:00, shorter hours Oct-March).

Exiting the courtyard of the Italian Court, turn right and watch on the wall to your right for a small bronze tablet showing a hand flashing a peace sign, covered with barbed wire. This is an unassuming little **memorial** to the victims of the communist regime's misrule and torture.

Continue straight down the steps into a little park, and then turn right to reach a great **viewpoint.** It overlooks the distinctive roof of the cathedral and the scenic valley below.

• *Your walk is finished. If you're headed for your tour at the **Czech Museum of Silver,** take this scenic route: Walk back up to Havlíček Square, circle around the Italian Court, curl along the downhill side of St. James' Church, and enjoy the views. Eventually the view terrace dead-ends at a little lane that bends right and uphill, depositing you at the museum.*

*If you're headed back to Prague, it takes about 15 minutes to walk to the **Kutná Hora Město train station** from Havlíček Square: Head downhill past the park, which funnels you between two buildings. Take the first left on Roháčova, then the first right on Sokolská. When you reach the wide cross-street (Nádražní), turn left and follow the train tracks to the little pink station.*

SIGHTS IN THE CENTER

▲▲St. Barbara's Cathedral (Chrám Sv. Barbory)

The cathedral was founded in 1388 by miners, who dedicated it to their patron saint. The dazzling interior celebrates the town's sources of wealth, with frescoes featuring mining and minting. This church was a stunning feat of architecture by two Gothic geniuses of Prague, Matyáš Rejsek and Benedict Ried. And, like Prague's cathedral, it sat unfinished and sealed off for centuries, until it was finally completed in the early 20th century.

Cost and Hours: 60 Kč, daily 9:00-18:00, shorter hours Nov-March, audioguide-40 Kč, tel. 327-515-796, www.khfarnost.cz.

Visiting the Cathedral: Although this tour covers the highlights, you can ask to borrow slightly more detailed info sheets at the ticket desk or rent the more in-depth audioguide.

Head inside, walk to the middle of the main nave, and just take it all in. Intricate, lacy vaulting decorates an impossibly high ceiling that's also decorated with the coats of arms of local miners. This is the epitome of Gothic: a mind-bogglingly tall nave supported by flying buttresses that create space for not one, but two levels of big windows; pointed arches where the columns converge; and an overall sense of verticality and light.

Take in the gorgeous **high altar**— a Last Supper scene of carved and painted wood. Then circle clockwise around the apse, past Baroque altars. Tune into the fine **stained-glass windows** (throughout the church) by František Urban, a somewhat less talented contemporary of Alfons Mucha, who nevertheless employs a similarly eye-pleasing Art Nouveau flair to illustrate scenes from church history. (A tiny version of this church's distinctive triple-pointed roofline appears in the background of several windows.)

Continue around the apse. The second-to-last chapel, called the **Smíšek Chapel,** is an artistic highlight. The late-Gothic frescoes—*The Arrival of the Queen of Sheba, The Trial of Trajan,* and especially the fresco under the chapel's window depicting two men with candles—are the only remaining works of a Dutchtrained master in Gothic Bohemia. The final chapel, called the **St. Wenceslas Chapel,** has frescoes under the windows showing miners going about their daily labor.

Continue up the side nave. Midway along, look for the **miner statue** on a pillar on your right. He's wearing a typical white miner's coat. White fabric was the cheapest option (as it required no dyes) and was easier to see in the dark. The leather mat wrapped around his waist made it easier for him to slide down chutes inside the mine. Most miners were healthy, unattached men in their 20s. An average of five miners died each day—from cave-ins, collapsing scaffolding, built-up poisonous gases, fires, and so on. At the back wall of the long chapel on your left, notice the precious frescoes from 1463 showing two people minting coins.

Loop around the back of the church, coming back up the left nave. You'll pass finely carved wooden **choir benches** that blend in perfect Gothic harmony with the church's architecture.

Art Gallery of the Central Bohemian Region (GASK)

The huge, former Baroque Jesuit college, which stretches from the cathedral all the way to the castle, was recently restored and converted into an art museum. It boasts the second-biggest exhibition space in the country (after the National Gallery in Prague), filled with ever-changing temporary exhibits of 20th- and 21st-century art.

Cost and Hours: Combo-ticket for all exhibits-200 Kč, single exhibit-80 Kč, April-Dec Tue-Sun 10:00-18:00, March Tue-Sun 10:00-17:00, closed Mon year-round and Jan-Feb, Barborská 51-53, www.gask.cz.

▲Hrádek Castle and the Czech Museum of Silver (České Muzeum Stříbra)

Located in Kutná Hora's 15th-century Hrádek ("little castle"), the Czech Museum of Silver offers a fascinating look at the primary source of local wealth and pride. Over the centuries, this mine produced some 2,500 tons of silver, copper, and zinc. Today you can visit the facility only with a 1.5-hour tour, which lets you do some spelunking in the former miners' passages that run beneath the entire town center. Note that the tour involves some tight squeezes and may be overwhelming if you're claustrophobic. Also bring some warm clothing—mines are cold.

Cost and Tours: The English tour of the mine (Route II) costs 120 Kč; Route I, which includes only the aboveground museum, is pointless. You can book tours online only two or more days in advance. Better yet, try calling ahead (the day before or the morning of your visit) to ask when English tours are scheduled—wait through the Czech recording and ask to speak to someone in English. Without advance reservations, drop by the museum soon after you arrive in Kutná Hora to find out the schedule and reserve. Tel. 327-512-159, www.cms-kh.cz.

Hours: May-Sept Tue-Sun 10:00-18:00, April and Oct Tue-Sun 10:00-17:00, Nov Tue-Sun 10:00-16:00, closed Mon year-round and Dec-March.

Visiting the Museum and Mine: First, your guide takes you to see an intriguing horse-powered winch that once hoisted 2,000 pounds of rock at a time out of the mine. You'll learn the two methods miners used to extract the precious ore: Either by hammering with a chisel or pick, or by setting a fire next to a rock—heating it until it naturally cracked.

Then you'll don a miner's coat and helmet, grab a bulky communist-era flashlight, and walk like the Seven Dwarves through the town center to a secret doorway. It's time to climb deep into the mine for a wet, dark, and claustrophobic tour of the medieval shafts that honeycomb the rock beneath the town—walking down 167 steps, traversing 900 feet of underground passages (but it feels even longer), then walking back up 35 steps.

Along the way, you'll see white limestone deposits in the form of mini-stalagmites and stalactites, and peer down into a 26-foot-deep pool of crystal-clear water. Squeezing through very tight passages, you'll feel like (fill in your own childbirth joke here). The mine holds a steady, year-round temperature of 54 degrees Fahrenheit while fat drops of condensation fall continually from the ceiling thanks to the nearly 100 percent humidity. Prepare for the moment when all of the lights go out, plunging you into a darkness as total as you'll ever experience. You'll understand why miners relied on their other senses. For instance, when silver was struck, it made a telltale sound and smelled faintly like garlic.

Finally, ascending to ground level, your guide will explain safety mechanisms at the surface and walk you through the smelting and minting processes that turned those raw deposits into coins for an entire continent.

Alchemy Museum (Muzeum Alchymie)

The only one of its kind in the Czech Republic, situated in the surprisingly deep medieval cellars of this otherwise unassuming

---

Sleep Code

Abbreviations   (20 Kč = about $1, country code: 420)
S = Single, **D** = Double/Twin, **T** = Triple, **Q** = Quad, **b** = bathroom, **s** = shower only.

Price Rankings

 $$$ **Higher Priced**—Most rooms 1,500 Kč or more.

  $$ **Moderately Priced**—Most rooms between
                            1,000-1,500 Kč.

   $ **Lower Priced**—Most rooms 1,000 Kč or less.

Unless otherwise noted, credit cards are accepted, breakfast is included, and English is spoken. Prices can change without notice; verify the hotel's current rates online or by email. For the best prices, always book directly with the hotel.

---

house, this museum features a laboratory dedicated to the pursuit of *prima materia* (primal matter). The English descriptions do a good job explaining the goals and methods of alchemy and the fate of its failed practitioners. The rare Gothic tower in the rear of the house is set up as an alchemist's study (complete with ancient books), looking much as it did when a prince used this vaulted space in his quest to purify matter and spirit.

Cost and Hours: 60 Kč, daily April-Sept 9:00-18:00, Oct-March 9:00-17:00, on the main square in the same building as the TI, tel. 327-512-378.

Sleeping in Kutná Hora

Although one day is enough for Kutná Hora, staying overnight saves you money (hotels are much cheaper here than in Prague) and allows you to better savor the atmosphere of a small Czech town.

$$ Hotel u Vlašského Dvora and **Hotel Garni** are two renovated townhouses run by the same management. Furnished in a mix of 1930s and modern style, the hotels come with access to a fitness center and sauna. Hotel Garni is slightly nicer (Db-1,200 Kč, a few steps off main square at Havlíčkovo Náměstí 513, tel. 327-515-773, www.vlasskydvur.cz).

Eating in Kutná Hora

Pivnice Dačický has made a theme of its namesake, a popular 17th-century author who once lived in the house. Solid wooden tables rest under perky illustrations of medieval town life, and a once-local brew, also named after Dačický, flows from the tap. They serve standard Czech fare, as well as excellent game and fish.

While its regulars still come here for the cheap lunch specials, during tourist season the crowd is mostly international. Service can be slow when a group arrives (daily 11:00-23:00, Rakova 8, tel. 327-512-248, mobile 603-434-367, www.dacicky.com).

Dobrá Čajovna Teahouse also offers the chance to escape—not to medieval times, but to a Thai paradise. Filled with tea cases, water pipes, and character, this place is an ideal spot to dawdle away the time that this ageless town has reclaimed for you. On weekdays, they serve vegetarian lunch specials (Mon-Fri 11:00-22:00, Sat-Sun 14:00-22:00, Havlíčkovo Náměstí 84, mobile 777-028-481).

Restaurace Donna-U Žlutého Kola ("Yellow Wheels") serves the fastest, tastiest Czech dishes in town, attracting a local crowd. There's a long menu in English, but the lunch specials are only listed on a separate sheet in Czech. When the weather's nice, sit in the shady courtyard behind the restaurant (open daily, lunch specials until 15:00, on Havlíčkovo Náměstí, right above Hotel Garni, tel. 327-512-749).

Piazza Navona features irritating English-language advertising ("the only true Italian restaurant in town"), but it still draws loyal customers thanks to its decent food and superb location on the main square (open daily, Palackého Náměstí 90, tel. 327-512-588).

Kutná Hora Connections

To return to **Prague,** hop on a local train from Kutná Hora Město Station, near the historical center (or Kutná Hora Sedlec Station if you end your day at the Bone Church), and take it to the Kutná Hora Main Station for your train transfer to Prague. Note that the best Prague connection runs only about every two hours, so check schedules carefully; other options require an additional change and take much longer.

Terezín Memorial

Terezín (TEH-reh-zeen), an hour by bus from Prague, was originally a fortified town named after Habsburg Empress Maria Theresa (it's called "Theresienstadt" in German). It was built in the 1780s with state-of-the-art, star-shaped walls designed to keep out the Prussians. In 1941, the Nazis removed the town's 7,000 inhabitants and brought in 58,000 Jews, creating a horribly overcrowded ghetto. Ironically, the town's medieval walls, originally meant to keep Germans out, were later used by Germans to keep the Jews in. As the Nazis' model "Jewish town" for deceiving Red Cross inspectors, Terezín fostered the illusion that its Jewish inmates lived relatively normal lives—making the sinister truth all the more cruel.

Compared with other such sights in Eastern and Central Europe (such as Auschwitz or Mauthausen), Terezín, worth ▲▲,

feels different: First, it focuses less on the Nazis' ruthless and calculated methods, and instead celebrates the arts and culture that thrived here despite the conditions—imbuing the place with a tragic humanity. Second, the various museums, memorials, and points of interest are spread over a large area in two distinct parts: a still-thriving town and the original fortress (across the river, a short walk away). This means you're largely on your own to connect the dots and flesh out the story (use this chapter's self-guided tour to help).

GETTING TO TEREZÍN

The camp is about 40 miles northwest of Prague. It's most convenient to visit Terezín by **bus** (described next) or **tour bus** (various tour companies in Prague offer full-day tours to Terezín, including Wittman Tours, www.wittmann-tours.com; see page 54 for contact information).

Buses to Terezín leave about hourly from Prague's Holešovice train station (Nádraží Holešovice, on Metro line C). When you get off the Metro (coming from the city center), head toward the front of the train, go upstairs, turn right, and walk to the end of the corridor. You'll see bus stands directly ahead, outside the station. The Terezín bus departs from platform 7 (direction: Litoměřice, buy ticket from driver). You'll arrive in Terezín an hour later at the public bus stop on the main square, across from the TI and around the corner from the Museum of the Ghetto. Some buses also stop earlier, by the Small Fortress. The driver and fellow passengers may tell you to get off there, but my self-guided tour works best if you begin at the stop in town (after the bus passes a field of crosses on your right and travels across the river).

Two different companies (Busline and Kavka) run this route; for schedules that include both companies, see www.idos.cz—you want "Terezín LT" (be sure to check the return schedule, too; for details on getting back to Prague, see "Terezín Connections," later).

PLANNING YOUR TIME

Because the sights are scattered, plan on lots of walking, and give yourself plenty of time: Three hours is barely enough for a minimal visit (and requires skipping some sights); allow at least four hours to quickly see everything, and more like six to really delve in. Your understanding of Terezín becomes immeasurably deeper with the help of a local guide (for a list of Prague-based guides, see page 52).

With more time, stop in the nearby attractive town of Litoměřice (described later) for lunch before returning to Prague.

Orientation to Terezín

Cost: The 210-Kč combo-ticket includes all parts of the camp.

Hours: Most sights, including the Museum of the Ghetto, Magdeburg Barracks, and Hidden Synagogue, are open daily April-Oct 9:00-18:00, Nov-March 9:00-17:30. The Columbarium and Crematorium are closed Sat. The Crematorium opens at 10:00 year-round and closes at 16:00 Nov-March, and the Small Fortress opens at 8:00 year-round and closes at 16:30 Nov-March.

Tours: Guided tours in English are offered if enough people request them; call ahead to get the schedule and reserve a spot (included in entry).

Information: Terezín's town **TI,** in the corner of the town hall that faces the Prague bus stop, has staff that are helpful and speak English (Sun 9:00-15:00, Mon-Thu 8:00-17:00, Fri 8:00-13:30, closed Sat, Náměstí ČSA 179, tel. 416-782-616, www.terezin.cz). In their window, you'll find handy information (such as the Prague bus schedule and directions to town landmarks). Museum information—tel. 416-782-225, mobile 606-632-914, www.pamatnik-terezin.cz.

Eating: In Terezín town, the **Parkhotel Restaurant** is the most elegant place for lunch (daily 10:00-22:00, around the block from Museum of the Ghetto at Máchova 163, tel. 416-782-260, mobile 775-068-734). Avoid the stale sandwiches in the Museum of the Ghetto's dingy basement cafeteria, where most tour guides inexplicably bring their clients.

The **Small Fortress** has a cafeteria.

BACKGROUND

Terezín was the Nazis' model "Jewish town," a concentration camp dolled up for propaganda purposes. Here, in a supposedly "self-governed Jewish resettlement area," Jewish culture seemed to thrive, as "citizens" put on plays and concerts, published a magazine, and raised their families. But it was all a carefully planned deception, intended to convince Red Cross inspectors that Jews were being treated well. The Nazis even coached prisoners on how to answer the inspectors' anticipated questions.

The Nazi authorities also used Terezín as a place to relocate elderly and disabled Jews from throughout the Third Reich—so the ghetto was filled with prisoners not only from the Czech lands, but from all over Europe.

In the fall of 1944, the Nazis began transporting Jews from Terezín to even more severe death camps (especially Auschwitz) in large numbers. Virtually all of Terezín's Jews (155,000 over the course of the war) ultimately ended up dying—either here (35,000) or in extermination camps farther east.

One of the notable individuals held at Terezín was Viennese artist Friedl Dicker-Brandeis. This daring woman, a leader in the Bauhaus art movement, found her life's calling in teaching children freedom of expression. She taught the kids in the camp to distinguish between the central things—trees, flowers, lines—and peripheral things, such as the conditions of the camp. In 1944, Dicker-Brandeis volunteered to be sent to Auschwitz after her husband was transported there; she was killed a month later.

Of the 15,000 children who passed through Terezín from 1942 to 1944, fewer than 100 survived. The artwork they created at Terezín is a striking testimony to the cruel horror of the Holocaust. In 1994, Hana Volavková, a Terezín survivor and the director of the Jewish Museum in Prague, collected the children's artwork and poems in the book *I Never Saw Another Butterfly*. Selections of the Terezín drawings are also displayed and well-described in English in Prague's Pinkas Synagogue (described on page 75).

Of the cultural activities that took place at Terezín, the best known was the children's opera *Brundibár*. Written just before the war, the antifascist opera premiered secretly in Prague at a time when Jewish activities were no longer permitted. From 1943 to 1944, the play, performed in Czech, ran 55 times in the camp. After the war it was staged internationally, and was rewritten and published in the US in 2003 as a children's book by Tony Kushner and Maurice Sendak (whose version later appeared on Broadway).

Self-Guided Tour

The Terezín experience consists of two parts: the walled town of Terezín, which became a Jewish ghetto under Hitler; and (a half-mile walk east, across the river) the Small Fortress, which was a Gestapo prison camp for mostly political prisoners of all stripes (including non-Jewish Czechs). The complete tour involves about four miles of walking (including the walk from the town to the Small Fortress, then back again to catch your return bus to

NEAR PRAGUE

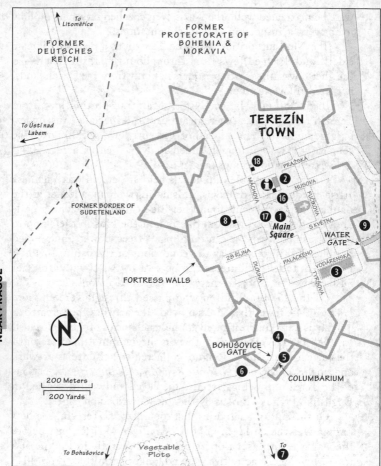

Prague). Pace yourself. If you want to cut it short, I've suggested sections that you could skip.

PART 1: TEREZÍN TOWN

• *The bus from Prague drops you off at Terezín town's spacious...*

Main Square (Náměstí Československé Armády): Today Terezín feels like a workaday, if unusually tidy, Czech town, with a tight grid plan hemmed in by its stout walls. And for much of its history, that's exactly what it was. But when Hitler annexed Czechoslovakia, he evicted the

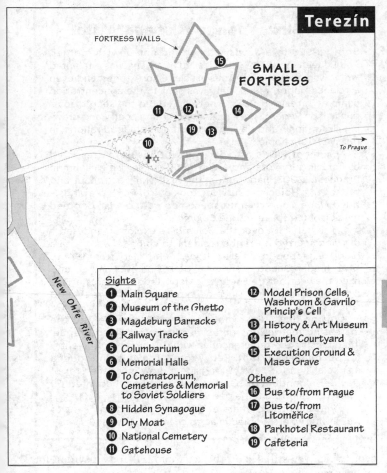

Terezín

FORTRESS WALLS

SMALL FORTRESS

To Prague

New Ohře River

NEAR PRAGUE

Sights
1. Main Square
2. Museum of the Ghetto
3. Magdeburg Barracks
4. Railway Tracks
5. Columbarium
6. Memorial Halls
7. To Crematorium, Cemeteries & Memorial to Soviet Soldiers
8. Hidden Synagogue
9. Dry Moat
10. National Cemetery
11. Gatehouse
12. Model Prison Cells, Washroom & Gavrilo Princip's Cell
13. History & Art Museum
14. Fourth Courtyard
15. Execution Ground & Mass Grave

Other
16. Bus to/from Prague
17. Bus to/from Litoměřice
18. Parkhotel Restaurant
19. Cafeteria

residents to create a ghetto for Jews forcibly transplanted here from Prague and elsewhere. Because it started out as a pretty town, rather than a gloomy prison or custom-built concentration camp, the Nazi authorities cultivated Terezín as a "model" to illustrate to the outside world how good the Jews had it here. (For more details, see "Background," earlier.)

Begin your tour by mentally filling the (now mostly empty) square with thousands of Jewish inmates, all wearing their yellow *Juden* Star of David patches. Picture the giant circus tent and barbed-wire fence that stood on this square for two years during the war. Inside, Jewish workers boxed special motors for German vehicles being used on the frigid Soviet front. As part of year-long preparations for the famous Red Cross visit (which lasted all of six hours on June 23, 1944), the tent and fence were replaced by flower

Petr Ginz, Young Artist and Writer

Born in 1928 to a Jewish father and non-Jewish mother, Prague teenager Petr Ginz excelled at art and was a talented writer who penned numerous articles, short stories, and even a science-fiction novel. Petr was sent to the concentration camp at Terezín in 1942, where he edited the secret boys' publication *Vedem (We Are Ahead)*, writing poetry and drawing illustrations, and paying contributors with food rations he received from home.

Some of Petr's artwork and writings were preserved by Terezín survivors and archived by the Jewish Museum in Prague. In 2003, Ilan Ramon, the first Israeli astronaut and the son of a Holocaust survivor, took one of Petr's drawings—titled *Moon Country*—into space aboard the final, doomed mission of the space shuttle *Columbia*.

The publicity over the *Columbia*'s explosion and Petr's drawing spurred a Prague resident to come forward with a diary he'd found in his attic. It was Petr's diary from 1941 to 1942, hidden decades earlier by Petr's parents and chronicling the year before the teen's deportation to Terezín. *The Diary of Petr Ginz* has since been published in more than 10 languages.

In the diary, Petr matter-of-factly documented the increasing restrictions on Jewish life in occupied Prague, interspersing the terse account with dry humor. In the entry for September 19, 1941, Petr wrote, "They just introduced a special sign for Jews" alongside a drawing of the Star of David. He continued, "On the way to school I counted 69 'sheriffs,'" referring to people wearing the star.

Petr spent two years at Terezín before being sent to Auschwitz, where he died in a gas chamber. He was 16.

beds (which you still see on the square today) and a pavilion for outdoor music performances.

• *The helpful little TI is across the street from the bus stop. Just around the corner, in the yellow former schoolhouse that faces the adjacent square, is the...*

Museum of the Ghetto: This modern, concise, well-presented museum, with artifacts and insightful English descriptions, sets the stage for your Terezín visit. You can buy the Terezín combo-ticket here (and ask about the day's film schedule—explained next). You'll find two floors of **exhibits** about the development of the Nazis' "Final Solution." The ground floor includes some evocative memorials (such as a stack of seized suitcases and a list of Terezín's victims). The exhibit upstairs illuminates life in the ghetto with historical documents (including underground publications and letters—inmates were allowed to mail one per month), items belonging to inmates, and video footage of survivors' testimonies. In the stairwell are large illustrations of ghetto life, drawn by people who lived here.

In the basement is a theater showing four excellent **films.** One film documents the history of the ghetto (31 minutes), offering a helpful, if dry, overview of the sights you'll see. Two others (14 and 20 minutes) focus on children's art in the camp, and the last is a 10-minute montage of clips from *Der Führer schenkt den Juden eine Stadt (The Führer Gives a City to the Jews),* by Kurt Gerron. Gerron, a Berlin Jew, was a 1920s movie star who appeared with Marlene Dietrich in *Blue Angel.* Deported to Terezín, Gerron in 1944 was asked by the Nazis to produce a propaganda film. The resulting film depicts healthy (i.e., recently arrived) "Jewish settlers" in Terezín happily viewing concerts, playing soccer, and sewing in their rooms—yet an unmistakable, deadly desperation radiates from their pallid faces. The only moment of genuine emotion comes toward the end, when a packed room of children applauds the final lines of the popular anti-Nazi opera *Brundibár:* "We did not let ourselves down, we chased the nasty Brundibár away. With a happy song, we won it all." Even the Nazis were not fooled: Gerron and his wife were shipped to Auschwitz, and the film was never shown in public.

• *To learn more about living conditions in the camp, return to the main square and continue straight past it, along Tyršova street. A few blocks down, just before the wall, on the left you'll find the...*

Magdeburg Barracks: Peek inside the large courtyard (you'll recognize it as the "soccer stadium" in Gerron's film), then con-

tinue upstairs and follow the one-way, counterclockwise loop. First you'll see a meticulously restored dormitory, complete with three-tiered beds, suitcases, eyeglasses, dolls, chessboards, sewing kits... and utterly no privacy. After Terezín's residents were evicted and Jews were imported in huge numbers, every available space was converted from single-family apartments to outrageously cramped slumber mills like this. Jaunty music lures you around the corner to the first of several rooms celebrating the arts here at Terezín. You'll see exhibits on composers, artists, and writers, who expressed their creativity even in these horrifying conditions. These include profiles of individuals (such as young Petr Ginz—see sidebar) and a wide variety of stirring art illustrating life in the ghetto. Near the end is a room reproducing the camp cabaret stage, where inmates entertained one another.

• *With limited time or energy, consider skipping the next several stops, which take a long, if poignant, detour outside the walls. Jump ahead to the moat (see "Dry Moat," later) by leaving the barracks, turning right, and walking 100 yards to a brick gate. (If you do decide to skip the following stops, you can easily fit in the Hidden Synagogue at the end, before hopping on your bus back to Prague, as it's one block from the main square.)*

To continue the full tour, exit the barracks, turn left, and walk until you dead-end at the city wall. Turn right and walk along the inside of the stout wall to the far corner. Slicing through the hole in the wall are the remnants of...

Railway Tracks: In the early years of the camp, Jews arrived at the train station in the nearby

town of Bohušovice and then had to walk the remaining 1.5 miles to Terezín. This was too public a display for the Nazis, who didn't want townspeople to observe the transports and become suspicious (or to try to interact with the inmates in any way). So the prisoners were forced to construct a railway line that led right to Terezín...and then back out again to Auschwitz.

• *Follow the tracks outside the wall.*

Columbarium and Memorial Halls: Exiting the wall, on the left is a Columbarium, where the Nazis deposited cardboard boxes containing the ashes of dead prisoners. The Germans originally promised that the remains would be properly buried after the war, but in 1945, to erase evidence, the ashes of Terezín victims were dumped into the Ohře River. Farther along, past the little pension/café and across the bridge, on the right you will find Jewish and Christian ceremonial halls and the main morgue.

• *When the main road swings right, take the left turn (marked* Krematorium*) and walk past bucolic vegetable plots and fruit gardens, and along a driveway lined with pointy poplar trees, to reach the...*

Crematorium and Cemeteries: The low-lying yellow building (to the left of the monumental menorah) is the **crematorium,** where Nazis would burn the bodies of those who died here. Step

inside to see a small exhibit on death and burial in the ghetto (explaining that, over time, single graves in coffins gave way to mass graves, then to simply burning bodies en masse and dumping the ashes in the river). Then head into the chilling main chamber, where four ovens were kept busy cremating bodies.

Outside, surrounding the crematorium, is a **Jewish cemetery** with the bodies of those who died before cremation became the norm. Farther to the right (as you face the crematorium) is a **Russian cemetery** and a **Memorial to Soviet Soldiers** (still proudly wearing its hammer and sickle, which you'll rarely see in the Czech Republic anymore). The Soviets liberated Terezín without a fight as the Nazis retreated, on May 8, 1945. But just days before, an epidemic of typhus had spread through the camp. In the weeks after the war ended, scores of Soviet soldiers and medical workers who tried to contain the epidemic died, along with hundreds of former prisoners.

• *Retrace your steps back through the wall, and continue straight ahead past the train tracks, up Dlouhá street. After three blocks, watch on the left for the low-profile green house at #17. Ring the bell to be admitted to the fascinating...*

Hidden Synagogue: Inside you'll find a courtyard; the bakery that used to be here hid the synagogue behind it. This is the only one of the camp's eight hidden synagogues that survived. The atmospheric space is still inscribed with two Hebrew captions, which are translated as "May my eyes behold, how You in compassion return to Sinai," and "If I forget Jerusalem, may my tongue rot and my right arm fall off." These words indicate that the prayer room belonged to a congregation of Zionists (advocates of a Jewish state), who, one would expect, were specifically targeted by the Nazis.

Upstairs, a few prisoners lived in a tight attic space. Even though the cramped rooms (reconstructed with period items) seem impossibly small, they were a far better accommodation than the mass housing in which most prisoners were interned. It's thought that a group of craftsmen who labored in a nearby workshop were "lucky" enough to live here.

• *Leaving the synagogue house, turn right, and at the corner, turn left to pop out at the main square. To proceed to the Small Fortress, head down Tyršova as if you're going to the Magdeburg Barracks. Before you get there, turn left along the park, then continue one block up Palackého to the brick gate. You'll cross a bridge over a...*

Dry Moat: Imagine this moat filled with plots of vegetables, grown by starving Jews for well-fed SS officers. Turn left and walk along the moat. The top of the fortification walls on the other side were once equipped with benches and pathways.

• *When you reach the main road, turn right across the New Ohře River (the original course of the river was diverted here when Terezín was built). After about five minutes, you'll come to a blocked-off, tree-lined driveway and the prison camp.*

PART 2: TEREZÍN PRISON CAMP

• On the right side of the driveway is the wedge-shaped...

National Cemetery: The remains of about 10,000 victims of Terezín (including 2,386 individual graves; the rest were moved here from mass graves elsewhere)

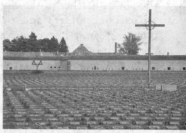

fill this cemetery, which was created after the war's end. The sea of headstones powerfully illustrates the scope of the crime that took place here. Notice that, in addition to the giant Star of David (closer to the fortress), a cross towers over the cemetery.

This is a reminder that we've left the Jewish ghetto and are about to enter a very different part of the Terezín complex. From 1940 to 1945, this fortress functioned as a Gestapo prison, through which 32,000 inmates passed (of whom nearly 10 percent died here)—chiefly members of the Czech resistance and communists. While the majority of the camp's victims weren't Jewish, the 1,500 Jews interned here were treated with particular severity.

• Now head under the black-and-white-striped gate.

The Gatehouse: Inside the gate, on the left, is a modest museum about the pre-WWII history of this fortress. If you

need a break before continuing, you could pause at the handy cafeteria. The wood-and-metal chandeliers inside were produced by Jewish workers for the SS officers who once dined in these two rooms.

• Continuing into the central part of the fortress, watch on the left for a turnstile into a long, skinny side courtyard. Go in and head to the end of the courtyard, under the notorious Arbeit Macht Frei *sign painted above an arched gate (a postwar replica of the viciously sarcastic "Work will set you free" sign*

that was displayed at all camps). Go under this gate to reach a courtyard ringed with...

Model Prison Cells: Step into some of the barracks on the right side of the courtyard to see tight, triple-decker bunks where prisoners were essentially stacked at bedtime. Halfway down the courtyard, under the *Block-A* sign, peek into the medical cell.

At the far end, the washroom in the right-hand corner (by #15) was built solely for the purpose of fooling Red Cross inspectors. Go ahead, turn the faucets: No pipes were ever installed to bring in water.

The shower room two doors to the left, on the other hand, was used to fool the Jews. Here they got used to the idea of communal bathing, so they wouldn't be suspicious when they were later taken to similar-looking installations at Auschwitz. (There were no gas chambers at Terezín—most of the deaths here were caused by malnutrition, disease, and, to a lesser extent, execution.)

Before the Nazis, the Austrian monarchy used the Small Fortress as a prison. In the little side courtyard next to the shower room, look for a ghostly doorway with a plaque that recalls the most famous prisoner from that time, Bosnian Serb **Gavrilo Princip,** whose assassination of Archduke Franz Ferdinand and his wife Žofie in 1914 sparked World War I (see sidebar on page 190). Princip died here in 1918 of tuberculosis; of the six Sarajevo conspirators imprisoned here, only two survived.

• *Return through the* Arbeit Macht Frei *gate, then back out into the fortress' central yard. Turn left and continue deeper into the complex. The large building on your right is marked by* Muzeum *signs.*

Museum: The ground floor of this building features an exhibit about the Nazi-era history of the Small Fortress. Photographs and brief descriptions identify many of the individuals who were imprisoned—and, in many cases, executed. Upstairs is a gallery of paintings by prominent Czech artists, mostly focusing on themes of camp life (and a few about the Spanish Civil War).

• *Back out in the main yard, continue straight ahead, through two gateways in a row. You'll emerge into the wide, eerie...*

Fourth Courtyard: Here you'll have more opportunities to step into former prison cells that flank the yard; some of these

house temporary exhibits. At the far end, you'll find a plaque in the ground listing the 17 countries whose citizens perished at Terezín.

• *Returning to the fortress' main yard once more, turn right and follow the long buildings. Turn right to find the...*

Execution Ground and Mass Grave: This is where firing squads executed somewhere between 200 and 300 of Hitler's enemies. Many of Terezín's victims were buried in mass graves along the fortress ramparts. After the war, these remains were moved to the National Cemetery we saw on the way into the fortress.

• *Our tour ends here. As you ponder Terezín, remember the message of all such memorials: Never again.*

Terezín Connections

The bus for **Prague** leaves from Terezín's main square (hourly, 1 hour). If the return bus doesn't fit your schedule, consider taking a taxi from Terezín to the Bohušovice station (5 minutes from Terezín, or walk about 1.5 miles; trains to Prague depart nearly hourly, 1-1.5 hours). There is no taxi service from Bohušovice to Terezín, making the train a good option only for the return journey. If you're continuing from Terezín to **Dresden,** Germany, take the train from Bohušovice to Ústí, then switch to the international express train. For bus and train schedules, see www.idos.cz.

Konopiště Castle

Konopiště (KOH-noh-peesh-tyeh) was the Neo-Gothic residence of the Archduke Franz Ferdinand d'Este—the heir to the Austro-Hungarian Empire, whose assassination sparked World War I. Located 30 miles south of Prague, it's workable either as a day trip or on the way to Český Krumlov. While it's the least visually arresting of the castles near Prague, its interior has some captivating stories to tell about its former inhabitants. Enjoyable for anyone, Konopiště is a must for Habsburg aficionados. It's rated ▲, but historians find it worth ▲▲▲.

Construction of the castle began in the 14th century, but today's exterior and furnishings date from about 1900, when Franz Ferdinand, renovated his new home. As one of the first castles in Europe to have an elevator, a WC, and running water, Konopiště shows "modern" living at the turn of the 20th century.

Those who lived at Konopiště played a role in one of the most important moments in European history: Franz Ferdinand's assassination in Sarajevo (chillingly illustrated by items displayed inside the castle). The shooting eventually meant the end of the age of hereditary, divine-right, multiethnic empires—and the dawn of a Europe of small, nationalistic, democratic nation-states. Historians get goose bumps at Konopiště, where if you listen closely, you can almost hear the last gasp of Europe's absolute monarchs.

The castle interior is only viewable by taking a guided tour.

There are several tour options, but the best is Route 3 (limited space, so call ahead to reserve; explained later, under "Orientation to Konopiště").

GETTING TO KONOPIŠTĚ

By Train: Trains from Prague's Main Station drop you in Benešov (2/hour, 1 hour, www.idos.cz); a well-marked trail goes from the station to the castle (1.5 miles). To walk to the castle, as you exit the Benešov train station, turn left and walk along the street parallel to the railroad tracks. Turn left at the first bridge you see crossing over the tracks. Along the way you'll see trail markers on trees, walls, and lampposts—one yellow stripe between two white stripes. Follow these markers. As you leave town, watch for a marker with an arrow pointing to a path in the woods. Take this path to bypass the castle's enormous parking lot, which is clogged with souvenir shops and bus fumes.

By Car: Konopiště is about a 45-minute drive from Prague and a two-minute detour off of the main route to Český Krumlov (head east toward Brno on the D-1 expressway; take exit #21 toward *Benešov/České Budějovice/Linz*; after about 15 kilometers, watch for the Konopiště turnoff on the right). Bypass the first, giant parking lot (ringed by restaurants); a bit farther along, on the left near the lake, is a smaller lot that's closer to the castle. From either lot, hike uphill about 10-15 minutes to Konopiště.

Orientation to Konopiště

Cost and Tours: The recommended Route 3 is 320 Kč (described later, under "Visiting the Castle"); Routes 1 and 2 are 220 Kč apiece; for all three it costs 690 Kč. Space on Route 3 is limited to eight people per hour. It's best to reserve a spot in advance by calling one day ahead or on the morning of your visit (worth the 20-Kč extra charge). All tickets are 30 percent cheaper if you join a Czech-speaking tour (but renting the English audioguide costs 50 Kč—effectively negating most of your savings). Tel. 317-721-366, www.zamek-konopiste.cz.

Hours: May-Aug Tue-Sun 9:00-12:30 & 13:00-17:00; Sept Tue-Fri 9:00-16:00, Sat-Sun 9:00-17:00; April and Oct Tue-Fri 9:00-15:00, Sat-Sun 9:00-16:00; closed Mon year-round and Nov-March.

Visiting the Castle

There are three different tour options, but **Route 3** is the most intimate and interesting. It takes you through the rooms where Franz Ferdinand, his Czech bride Žofie, and their three kids lived while

Archduke Franz Ferdinand (1863-1914)

Archduke Franz Ferdinand was born to the brother of the Habsburg emperor (Franz Josef) and a Neapolitan princess. After his cousin died under mysterious circumstances, Franz Ferdinand was thrust into the role of heir apparent to the throne of the Austro-Hungarian Empire—one of the biggest realms Europe has ever seen. But he had to be patient: His Uncle Franz Josef took the throne in 1848 and would hold onto it for nearly 70 years. In fact, he outlived his nephew.

While he waited, Franz Ferdinand kept himself busy by spending time at his bachelor pad in Konopiště. At a ball in Vienna, he met a gorgeous but low-ranking Czech countess, Žofie Chotková (also known by her German name, Sophie). The couple danced all night, and when morning came, Franz Ferdinand announced his intentions to make her his wife. His uncle was displeased—Žofie was "only" aristocratic, and the expected path for the heir apparent would be to marry a Western European princess. He insisted on a morganatic marriage so that Žofie could never be an empress and none of the children could inherit the throne. These family squabbles cemented Franz Ferdinand and Žofie's preference for living at Konopiště.

While waiting for a succession that would never arrive, Franz Ferdinand threw himself into his hobbies with an obsessive-compulsive zeal. He traveled around the world twice—partly for diplomatic reasons, but largely to pursue his passion

waiting for Uncle Franz Josef to expire. When the communists took over, they simply threw drop cloths over the furniture and let the place sit, untouched, for decades. Now everything has been meticulously restored (with the help of 1907 photographs)—launching you right into a turn-of-the-20th-century time capsule.

The tour takes you through halls upon halls of hunting trophies (each one marked with the place and date of the kill), paintings of royal relatives (including an entire wall of Italian kings—relations of Franz Ferdinand's Neapolitan mother), and photographs of the many places they traveled and the three kids as they grew up. The tour includes Franz Ferdinand's dressing room (with his actual uniform and his travel case all packed up and ready to go); his private study (which feels like he just stepped away from his desk for a cup of coffee); the living room (with 1,180 pairs of antlers on the walls); the private dining room (with the table set for an intimate family dinner for five); the master bedroom (with its huge bed); the children's bedrooms, for exotic hunting. Shooting at anything in sight—deer, bears, tigers, elephants, and crocodiles—he killed about 300,000 animals in all, a few thousand of whom stare morbidly at you from the walls at Konopiště. Franz Ferdinand and Žofie were also devoted parents, raising three children: young Žofie, Max, and Ernesto.

In the Kaiser's Pavilion on the grounds of Konopiště, Franz Ferdinand met with German Kaiser Wilhelm and tried to talk him out of plotting a war against Russia. Wilhelm argued that a war would work to the mutual benefit of Germany and Austria: Germans wanted colonies, and the Austro-Hungarian Empire—crippled by the aspirations of its many nationalities—could use a war to divert attention from its domestic problems. But Franz Ferdinand foresaw that war would be suicidal for Austria's over-stretched monarchy.

Soon after, Franz Ferdinand and Žofie went to Sarajevo, in the Habsburg-annexed territories of Bosnia and Herzegovina. On that trip, young Gavrilo Princip, a Bosnian Serb separatist, shot the Habsburg archduke who so loved shooting, as well as Žofie. Franz Ferdinand's assassination ironically gave the Germans (and their pro-war allies in the Austro-Hungarian administration) the pretext for starting the war against Serbia and its ally, Russia. World War I soon broke out. The event Franz Ferdinand had tried to prevent was, in fact, sparked by his death.

playrooms, and classroom (with their toys and books still on the shelves); three bathrooms with running water and flushing toilets; and in the final room, a glass display case containing the dress Žofie was wearing that fateful day in Sarajevo (including her still-blood-stained corset). Down the hall are the royal couple's death masks, Franz Ferdinand's bloody suspenders, and the actual bullet that ended Žofie's life.

Route 2, which covers the oldest wing of the castle, is also worth considering, and provides the most comprehensive look into the castle, its history, and celebrated collections. You'll see the oversized elevator (for a couch to make the family comfortable on the 45-second ride upstairs), the library, and the staggeringly large armory collection. **Route 1,** covering some other rooms, the hunting hall, and the balcony, is the least interesting.

Other Sights at the Castle: Your tour ticket includes two quirky additional sights that are worth poking into. **Franz Ferdinand's Shooting Range,** just off of the castle courtyard, offers a quick glimpse at the emperor-in-waiting's elaborate system of moving targets; a video demonstrates how the various targets would move around to keep his skills sharp. The **Museum of St. George,** tucked beneath the long terrace (around the side of the palace), displays Franz Ferdinand's collection of hundreds of sculptures and paintings of St. George slaying the dragon...taking a theme to an extreme.

While the stretch between the parking lot and the castle entrance is overrun by tour groups, the **gardens** and the **park** are surprisingly empty. In the summer, the flowers and goldfish in the rose garden are a big hit with visitors. The peaceful 30-minute walk through the woods around the lake (wooden bridge at the far end) offers fine castle views.

Tucked away in the bushes behind the pond is a pavilion coated with tree bark, a perfect picnic spot. This simple structure, nicknamed the **Kaiser's Pavilion,** was the site of a fateful meeting between the German Kaiser Wilhelm and the Archduke Franz Ferdinand (see the sidebar on page 190).

Eating at Konopiště Castle: Three touristy restaurants sit under the castle, and a café and restaurant are in the castle courtyard, but I'd rather bring picnic supplies from Prague (or buy them at the grocery store by the Benešov train station). While the crowds wait to pay too much for lousy food in the restaurants, you'll enjoy the peace and thought-provoking ambience of a **picnic** in the shaded Kaiser's Pavilion. Or eat cheaply on Benešov's main square (try **U Zlaté Hvězdy**—"The Golden Star").

ČESKÝ KRUMLOV

Lassoed by its river and dominated by its castle, this enchanting town feels lost in a time warp. When you see its awe-inspiring castle, delightful Old Town of shops and cobbled lanes, charming little restaurants, and easy canoeing options, you'll understand why having fun is a slam-dunk here. Romantics are floored by its spectacular setting; on a sunny day, you could spend all of your time doing aimless laps from one end of town to the other.

The sharp bend in the Vltava provides a natural moat, so it's no wonder Český Krumlov has been a choice spot for eons. Celtic tribes first settled here a century before Christ. Then came Germanic tribes. The Slavic tribes arrived in the ninth century. The Rožmberks—Bohemia's top noble family—ran the city from 1302 to 1602. You'll spot their rose symbol all over town.

The 16th century was the town's Golden Age, when Český Krumlov hosted artists, scientists, and alchemists from all over Europe. In 1588, the town became home to an important Jesuit college. In 1602, the Rožmberks ran out of money to fund their lavish lifestyles, so they sold their territory to the Habsburgs, who ushered in a more Germanic period. After that, as many as 75 percent of the town's people were German—until 1945, when most Germans were expelled (for more on this era and its repercussions, see the sidebar on page 200).

Český Krumlov's rich mix of Gothic, Renaissance, and Baroque buildings is easy to miss. As you wander, look up...notice the surviving details in the fine stonework and pretty gables. Step into shops. (Antiques are a hit in this antique burg.) Snoop into back lanes and tiny squares. Gothic buildings curve with the

From Ghost Town to Boom Town

The infamous 1938 Munich Agreement gave the largely Germanic Sudetenland region—including Český Krumlov—to Hitler. After the war, in retaliation, the Czechs emptied Český Krumlov of its predominantly German citizenry (see sidebar on page 200), turning the place into a ghost town.

In the new world order established after 1945, Český Krumlov fell under Soviet influence. Although the communist government established order, the period from 1945 to 1989 was a smelly interlude, as the town was infamously polluted. Its now-pristine river was foamy with effluent from the paper mill just upstream, while the hills around town were marred with prefab-concrete apartment blocks. The people who moved in never fully identified with the town—in Europe, a place without ancestors is a place without life. But the bleak years of communism paradoxically provided a cocoon to preserve the town. There was no money, so little changed, apart from a buildup of grime.

In the early 1990s, tourists discovered Český Krumlov, and the influx of money saved the buildings from ruin. Color returned to the facades, waiters again dressed in coarse linen shirts, and the main drag was flooded with souvenir shops.

With its new prosperity, the center of today's Český Krumlov looks like a fairy-tale town. With 1.5 million visits annually, it continues to be a major draw for tourists (second in the country only to Prague). While Americans once made up a sizeable chunk of the tourist trade, these days they've been eclipsed by a more international crowd.

winding streets. Many precious Gothic and Renaissance frescoes were whitewashed in Baroque times (when the colorful trimmings of earlier periods were way out of style). Today, these frescoes are being rediscovered and restored.

Český Krumlov is a huge tourist magnet, which makes things colorful and easy for travelers. At times it can feel like a medieval theme park—but not so much that it entirely tramples the place's charm. This town of 15,000 attracts a young bohemian crowd, drawn here for its simple beauty, cheap living, and fanciful bars.

PLANNING YOUR TIME

It's easy to enjoy strolling the town without ever paying to enter a sight. But it's worth considering the Baroque Theater at the castle, which can be seen only with a reserved tour. If you want to join an English tour, sign up first thing in the morning (call ahead or visit in person), and then build your day around your visit time. While you're at it, consider booking an English tour of the castle interior. Those who hate planning ahead on vacation can join a Czech tour of the theater or castle anytime (English information sheets provided).

A paddle down the river to Zlatá Koruna Abbey is a highlight (three hours), and a 20-minute walk up to the Křížový Vrch (Hill of the Cross) rewards you with a sweeping view of the town and its unforgettable riverside setting. Other sights are worthwhile only if you have a particular interest (Viennese artist Egon Schiele, brewery tour, puppets, and so on).

Many sights are closed on Monday, though the major attraction—the town itself—is always open. Evenings are for atmospheric dining and drinking.

Orientation to Český Krumlov

Český Krumlov (CHESS-key KROOM-loff) means, roughly, "Czech Bend in the River." Calling it "Český" for short sounds silly to Czech speakers (dozens of Czech town names begin with "Český")—rather, they call it "Krumlov."

Český Krumlov is extremely easy to navigate. The twisty Vltava River, which makes a perfect S through the town, ropes the Old Town into a tight peninsula. Above the Old Town is the Castle Town. Český Krumlov's one main street starts at the isthmus and winds through the peninsula, crossing a bridge before snaking through the Castle Town, the castle complex (a long series of courtyards), and the castle gardens high above. I've narrated this route on my self-guided walk. The main square, Náměstí Svornosti—with the TI, ATMs, and taxis—dominates the Old Town and marks the center of the peninsula. All recommended restaurants, hotels, and sights are within a few minutes' walk of this square.

TOURIST INFORMATION

The helpful TI is on the **main square** (daily 9:00-18:00, June-Aug until 19:00, shorter hours in winter, tel. 380-704-622, www.ckrumlov.info). Pick up the free city map. The 129-Kč *City Guide* book explains everything in Český Krumlov and includes a good town and castle map. The TI has a baggage-storage desk and can check train and bus schedules. Ask about concerts, city walking tours in English, and canoe trips on the river. They also rent an audioguide featuring a self-guided town walk (100 Kč/one hour). A second, less-crowded TI—actually a private business—is in the lowest courtyard of the **castle** (daily 9:00-18:00, tel. 380-725-110).

Český Krumlov Card: This 200-Kč card, sold at the TI and participating sights, covers entry to the Round Tower, Castle Museum (but not castle tours), Egon Schiele Art Center, Museum of Regional History, and Seidl Photographic Studio. Do the math to decide if it makes sense for you.

ARRIVAL IN ČESKÝ KRUMLOV

By Train: The train station is a 20-minute walk from town (turn right out of the station, then walk downhill onto a steep cobbled path leading to an overpass into the town center). Taxis are standing by to zip you to your hotel (about 100 Kč), or call 602-113-113 to summon one.

By Bus: The bus station is just three blocks away from the Old Town. To walk from the bus-station lot to the town center, follow the "walking man" signs out of the lot to *Centrum*, veer right and downhill on the small road, and cross the main road past the Co-op grocery. Figure on 60 Kč for a taxi from the station to your hotel.

By Car: Parking lots ring the town center, each one marked by a blue *P* sign. If your hotel is in the mostly traffic-free center, you'll be allowed to drive in (gingerly passing hordes of tourists) and park on the main square just long enough to drop off your bags and get directions to one of the outer lots. The flow of traffic is one-way: Enter at the east end of town, on Horní street, then exit across two bridges at the south end of town, on Linecká street (get additional details from your hotel before you arrive).

HELPFUL HINTS

Festivals: Locals drink oceans of beer and celebrate their medieval roots at big events such as the Celebration of the Rose (Slavnosti Růže), where blacksmiths mint ancient coins, jugglers swallow fire, mead flows generously, and pigs are roasted on open fires (late June, www.ckrumlov.info). The summer also brings a top-notch international music festival to town, performed in pubs, cafés, and the castle gardens (mid-July–mid-Aug, www.festivalkrumlov.cz). During the St. Wenceslas celebrations, the square becomes a medieval market and the streets come alive with theater and music (late Sept). Reserve a hotel well in advance if you'll be in town for these events.

Internet Access: Internet cafés are all over town, and many of my recommended accommodations offer Wi-Fi or Internet access. The TI on the main square has several fast, cheap, stand-up stations. Perhaps the best cybercafé is behind the TI by the castle (tel. 380-725-117).

Bookstore: **Shakespeare and Sons** is a good little English-
language bookstore (daily 11:00-19:00, a block below the main
square at Soukenická 44, tel. 380-711-203, www.shakes.cz).

Bike Rental: You can rent bikes at the **train station** (150 Kč/day
with train ticket, prices slightly higher otherwise, tel. 380-
715-000), **Vltava Sport Service** (see listing under "Canoeing
and Rafting the Vltava" on page 208), and the recommended
Hostel 99.

Tours in Český Krumlov

Walking Tours

Since the town itself, rather than its sights, is what it's all about
here, taking a guided walk is the key to a meaningful visit. The
TI sells tickets for several different guided walks. They are affordable, in English, and well worth your time. No reservations are
necessary—just meet in front of the TI on the main square and
pay the guide. Confirm times when you visit, as schedules can
change. The **Old Town Tour** offers the best general town introduction (300 Kč, daily at 12:30, 1.5 hours); in peak season, this tour
extends to include the castle exteriors (490 Kč, April-Oct daily at
14:30). There's also a nighttime version (departing between 19:30
and 20:30, depending on the season; get details from TI). For a
self-guided town walk, consider the TI audioguide (see "Tourist
Information," earlier).

Local Guides

Oldřiška Baloušková is a hardworking young guide who offers a
wonderful tour around her hometown (500 Kč/hour, mobile 737-
920-901, oldriskab@gmail.com). **Jiří (George) Václavíček,** a gentle and caring man who perfectly fits mellow Český Krumlov, is
a joy to share this town with (450 Kč/hour, mobile 603-927-995,
www.krumlovguide.com, jiri.vaclavicek@gmail.com). **Karolína
Kortušová** is an enthusiastic, experienced guide with great orga-
nizational skills. Her company, Krumlov Tours, can set you up
with a good local tour guide, palace and theater admissions, river
trips, and more (guides-500 Kč/hour, mobile 723-069-561, www.
krumlovtours.com, info@krumlovtours.com).

Český Krumlov Walk

The town's best sight is its cobbled cityscape, surrounded by a
babbling river and capped by a dramatic castle. Most of Český
Krumlov's modest sights are laced together in this charming
self-guided walk from the top of the Old Town, down its spine,
across the river, and up to the castle. The walk begins at a fine

viewpoint...and ends at an even better one. I've divided it into two parts: Downhill, through the Old Town to the river; then uphill, ascending through the castle complex on the other side. You can also do the two parts on different days. The second half of the walk makes a useful spine for organizing a visit to the castle quarter.

PART 1: THE OLD TOWN

• *Start at the bridge over the isthmus, which was once the fortified grand entry gate to the town (see map on page 199). For the best view, step down to the little terrace in front of the restaurant gate.*

Horní Bridge: From this "Upper Bridge," note the natural fortification provided by the tight bend in the river. Trace the river to your right, where it curves around the last building in town, with a smokestack. This is the Eggenberg Brewery, makers of Český Krumlov's very own hometown brew (with daily tours—see page 208). Behind that, on the horizon, is a pile of white apartment high-rises—built in the last decade of the communist era and considered the worst places in town to call home. Left of the brewery stands a huge monastery (with the pointy red steeple; not generally open to the public). Behind that, on Kleť Mountain—the highest hilltop—stands a TV tower that was built to jam Voice of America broadcasts.

Head back up to the middle of the bridge. Look down and left. Now look down and right. Notice how the Vltava wraps entirely around the town center. Rafters take about a half-hour to circle around the Old Town peninsula, beginning and ending under this bridge.

• *Head into town on...*

Horní Street: As you step off the bridge, Český Krumlov's aptly named "Upper Street" passes the **Museum of Regional History** on the right (see listing on page 207). Just past the museum, a little garden overlook affords a fine castle view.

Immediately across the street (on the left), notice the Renaissance facade of **Hotel Růže:** This former Jesuit college hides a beautiful courtyard. Pop inside to admire its decoration of faux sgraffito "bricks," made by scratching into an outer layer of one color of plaster to reveal a different color beneath. This style was all the rage during the town's boom time, and we'll be seeing several more examples on this walk.

• *Walk another block down the main drag, until you reach steps on the left leading to the...*

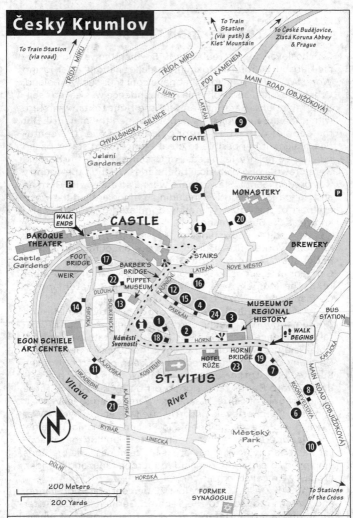

Český Krumlov

To Train Station (via road)

To Train Station (via path) & Klet' Mountain

To České Budějovice, Zlatá Koruna Abbey & Prague

TŘÍDA MÍRU

U LUNY

TŘÍDA MÍRU

POD KAMENEM

MAIN ROAD (OBJÍŽĎKOVÁ)

CHVALŠINSKÁ SILNICE

LATRÁN

CITY GATE

9

Jelení Gardens

PIVOVARSKÁ

MONASTERY

5

20

CASTLE

BAROQUE THEATER

BREWERY

Castle Gardens

FOOT BRIDGE

WEIR

WALK ENDS

17

STAIRS

LATRÁN

NOVE MĚSTO

BARBER'S BRIDGE

PUPPET MUSEUM

RADNIČNÍ

22

DLOUHÁ

13

12

16

SOUKENICKÁ

14

ŠIROKÁ

PARKÁN

15

4

24

3

MUSEUM OF REGIONAL HISTORY

BUS STATION

EGON SCHIELE ART CENTER

1

Náměstí Svornosti

18

2

HORNÍ

WALK BEGINS

KÁJOVSKÁ

11

HRADEBNÍ

KOSTELNÍ

HORNÍ BRIDGE

HOTEL RŮŽE

19

23

7

MAIN ROAD (OBJÍŽĎKOVÁ)

KAPLICKÁ

Vltava

ST. VITUS

River

RODENFELOVA

21

KÁJOVSKÁ

6

RYBÁŘ

Městský Park

LINECKÁ

10

DŮLNÍ

HORSKÁ

200 Meters

200 Yards

FORMER SYNAGOGUE

To Stations of the Cross

ČESKÝ KRUMLOV

1 Castle View Apartments
2 Hotel Konvice
3 Hotel Mlýn
4 Pension Olšakovský
5 Pension Danny
6 Little Pension Teddy
7 Hotel Garni Myší Díra & Maleček Boat Rental
8 Pension Anna
9 Hostel 99 & Hospoda 99 Rest.
10 Krumlov House Hostel
11 Na Louži Restaurant
12 Krčma u Dwau Maryí
13 Cikánská Jizba
14 Restaurace u Dobráka
15 Laibon Restaurant
16 Kolektiv
17 Rybářská Restaurace
18 Krčma v Šatlavské
19 Restaurace Barbakán
20 Dobrá Čajovna Teahouse
21 Vltava Sport Service
22 CK Shuttle Office
23 Start Quickie River Float
24 End Quickie River Float & Start Zlatá Koruna Float

The German Question

Czechoslovakia was created in 1918, when the vast, multiethnic Habsburg Empire broke into smaller nations after losing World War I. The principle that gave countries such as Poland, Czechoslovakia, and Romania independence was called "self-determination": Each nation had the right to its own state within the area in which its people formed the majority. But the peoples of Eastern Europe had mixed over the centuries, making it impossible to create functioning states based purely on ethnicity. In the case of Czechoslovakia, the borders were drawn along historical boundaries. Though the country was predominantly Slavic, there were also areas with German and Hungarian majorities, including a fringe around the western part of the country, mostly populated by Germans and known as the Sudetenland.

At first, the coexistence of Slavs and Germans in the new republic worked fine. But Hitler's rise encouraged German nationalism, even outside Germany. Soon 70 percent of Germans in Czechoslovakia voted for the Nazis. In September 1938, the Munich Agreement ceded the Sudetenland to Germany, and the Czech minority had to leave.

After the hard feelings produced by the Munich Agreement, most Czechs and Slovaks believed that peaceful coexistence with Germans in a single state was impossible. The postwar solution? Move the Sudeten Germans to Germany, much as the Czechs had been pushed out of the Sudetenland. Under a policy established by Czech president Edvard Beneš (and signed off on by the Allies), three million people of German ancestry were forced to leave their homes in Czechoslovakia shortly after the end of World War II. Millions of Germanic people in Poland, Romania, Ukraine, and elsewhere met with a similar fate. Many of these families had been living in these areas for centuries. The methods employed to expel them included murder, rape, and plunder. (Today, we'd call it "ethnic cleansing.")

In 1945, Český Krumlov lost 75 percent of its population, and Czechs moved into the vacated German homes. After 1989, displaced Sudeten Germans—the majority of whom now live in Bavaria—demanded that the Czechoslovak government apologize for the violent way in which the expulsion was carried out. Some challenged the legality of the decrees, and for a time the issue threatened otherwise good Czech-German relations.

The so-called Beneš Decrees remain divisive in Czech politics. In the former Sudetenland, where Czech landowners worry that Germans will try to reclaim their property, Beneš remains a hugely popular figure. The bridge behind the Old Town has been named for Beneš since the 1990s. The main square—the center of a thriving German community 70 years ago—is now, ironically, called "Square of Concord."

Church of St. Vitus: Český Krumlov's main church was built as a bastion of Catholicism in the 15th century, when the Roman Catholic Church was fighting the Hussites. The 17th-century Baroque high altar shows a totem of religious figures: the Virgin Mary (crowned in heaven); St. Vitus (above Mary); and, way up on top, St. Wenceslas, the patron saint of the Czech people—long considered their ambassador in heaven. The canopy in the back, though empty today, once supported a grand statue

of a Rožmberk atop a horse. The statue originally stood at the high altar. (Too egotistical for Jesuits, it was later moved to the rear of the nave, and then lost for good.) Notice the empty organ case. While the main organ is out for restoration, the cute little circa-1716 Baroque beauty is getting plenty of use (see photos of the restoration work on the far wall; church generally open daily 10:00-19:00—but don't count on it, Sunday Mass at 9:30, tel. 380-711-336).

• *Continuing on Horní street, you'll come to the...*

Main Square (Náměstí Svornosti): Lined with a mix of Renaissance and Baroque homes of burghers (all built on 12th-century Gothic foundations), the main square has a grand charm. Locals possessively guard this space. McDonald's tried three times to get a spot here but was turned away each time. The Town Hall (the crenellated white building, on the right) flies both the Czech flag and the town flag, which shows the rose symbol of the Rožmberk family, who ruled the town for 300 years.

Imagine the history that this square has seen: In the 1620s, the town was held by the (very Catholic) Habsburgs, just as Lutheran Protestantism was rising to threaten Catholic Europe. Krumlov was a seat of Jesuit power and learning, and the intellectuals of the Roman church allegedly burned books on this square.

Later, when there was a bad harvest, locals blamed witches—and burned them, too. Every so often, terrible plagues rolled through the countryside. In a nearby village, all but two residents were killed by a plague.

But the plague stopped before devastating the people of Český Krumlov, and in 1715—as thanks to God—they built the plague monument that stands on the square today (on the left). Much later, in 1938, Hitler stood right here before a backdrop of long Nazi banners to celebrate the annexation of the Sudetenland. And in 1968, Russian tanks spun their angry treads on these same cobblestones to intimidate locals who were demanding freedom. Today, thankfully, this square is part of an unprecedented time of peace and prosperity for the Czech people.

• *From the main square, walk down Radničí street (on the right, just past the Town Hall) and cross the...*

Barber's Bridge (Lazebnicky Most): This wooden bridge, decorated with two 19th-century statues, connects the Old Town and the Castle Town. On the right side stands a statue of St. John of Nepomuk, who's also depicted by a prominent statue on Prague's Charles Bridge (see page 72). Among other responsibilities, he's the protector against floods. In the great floods in August of 2002, the angry river submerged the bridge (but removable banisters minimized the damage). Stains just above the windows of the adjacent building show how high the water rose.

• *The second part of the walk involves lots of uphill hiking—but it's worth it to see the castle courtyards and dramatic views.*

PART 2: KRUMLOV CASTLE

Big and imposing, the town castle boasts several fine courtyards, spectacular viewpoints, and gorgeous gardens—all of which are open to the public, free to enter, and fun to roam (though some areas may be closed on Mon). This part of the walk focuses on those public spaces, leading you from Barber's Bridge, through the heart of the castle, and up to a picturesque viewpoint just before the gardens. The castle also has several individual sights (Round Tower, Castle Museum, Upper Castle, Baroque Theater) that can be laced into this walk but require paid admission and/or a reserved tour (for details, see their sight listings later).

• *Cross the bridge and head up shop-lined Latrán street, which bends to the right. Just after that bend, look for the stairs on your left (in front of the gray-and-white building). Head up, passing under a stone arch with the wood-carved rose symbol of the Rožmberk family. You'll emerge into the castle's...*

First (Lower) Courtyard: This is just the first of many courtyards that bunny-hop up through the castle complex. This was the site for workers and industry (stables, smithy, brewery, pharmacy, and so on)—convenient for aristocratic needs, but far enough away to keep noises and smells at bay.

Looking up, you can't miss the strikingly colorful **Round Tower** that marks the location of the first castle, built here to guard the medieval river crossing. With its 16th-century Renaissance paint job colorfully restored, it looks exotic, featuring fancy astrological decor, terra-cotta symbols of the zodiac, and a fine arcade.

• *Head up to the former drawbridge. Look over the sides of the bridge. Spot any bears?*

Bear Pits (Medvědí Příkop): These hold a family of European brown bears, as they have since the Rožmberks added bears to their coat of arms in the 16th century to demonstrate their (fake) blood relation to the distinguished Italian Orsini family (whose name means "bear-like"). Featured on countless coats of arms, bears have long been totemic animals for Europeans. Pronouncing the animal's real name was taboo in many cultures, and Czechs still refer to bears only indirectly. For example, in most Germanic languages the word "bear" is derived from "brown," while the Slavic *medvěd* literally means "honey eater."

Near the top of the bridge, notice the gently worded sign suggesting that—rather than toss down your junk-food leftovers—you add a few coins in the collection slot to finance "more varied meals and delicacies" for the bears.

• *Continue through the gateway into the...*

Second Courtyard: Here you'll spot more of the sgraffito (Renaissance faux features scraped into wet plaster) that decorates much of the castle. To your left, at the bottom of the courtyard, is the entrance to the **tower climb** and the **Castle Museum**. Farther up on the left is the **ticket office** for castle tours, including the Baroque Theater—stop in now (if you haven't already) to see about a tour.

• *From here, things get steep as we enter the...*

Heart of the Castle Complex: Head up the bridge, noticing the little view terrace on the left—the first of several along here. You'll emerge into the **Third Courtyard,** then (after a corridor) the **Fourth Courtyard.** Nicely preserved paintings enliven their blocky facades. Wrapped around these courtyards is the castle proper, a mighty Renaissance building sometimes called the Upper Castle (interiors open to visitors—notice the meeting points for various tour options). Continuing straight out through the end of the Fourth Courtyard, you'll cross the breathtaking **Cloak Bridge**—a triple-decker, statue-lined, covered bridge spanning a vast gorge and connecting the castle firmly with the gardens that sprawl behind it. Enjoy the views—but believe it or not, even better ones are coming up.

Notice the **Baroque Theater,** at the far end of the bridge, which still uses traditional methods for moving scenery and producing sound effects. Aspects of this back-in-the-day stage-craft still survive on Broadway today. This is one of only two such original theaters in Europe.

• *After the bridge, continue uphill through the...*

Fifth Courtyard: Really more of a pathway, this connects the castle to its gardens. Walk along the white wall—with peekaboo windows—until you are almost at the gate up top. High on the wall to the right, notice the **sundial.** Check the time: It's dead-on...except for Daylight Savings Time, which was unknown to medieval timekeepers. Notice that the sundial cuts into one of the faux windows, painted on the lower level of the building to create Renaissance symmetry.

Now step through the low-profile door directly across from the sundial. You'll emerge at a spectacular **viewpoint** that takes in the entire town, its curving river, and even the colorful tower and most of the castle complex you just came through. Jockey your way through the selfie-snapping crowd and drink it in. (Or literally drink, at the little adjacent bar.)

• *Our walk is finished. But if you still have stamina, you can consider exploring the **castle gardens**—they're just uphill, through the gate from the Fifth Courtyard.*

Sights in Český Krumlov

KRUMLOV CASTLE COMPLEX (KRUMLOVSKÝ ZÁMEK)

No Czech town is complete without a castle—and now that the nobles are gone, their mansions are open to us common folk.

Český Krumlov is no different. Its immense Krumlov Castle complex, one of the largest in Central Europe, perches on a rock promontory overlooking the Vltava River and the town. The original Gothic castle took shape here in the 13th century, and eventually the Rožmberk, Eggenberg, and

Schwarzenberg families each inherited it in turn. In successive waves of additions and renovations, they built it into the splendid Renaissance/Baroque property you see today.

The following sights are listed in the order you'll reach them as you climb up through the complex (ideally following my self-guided walk, earlier). The Round Tower and Castle Museum can be visited at your leisure, while other castle interiors—including the excellent Baroque Theater—can only be seen with a guided tour (see next). On a quick visit, the only sight I'd bother paying admission for is the theater.

Reservations for Baroque Theater and Upper Castle: It's worth the 10 Kč reservation fee to hold a slot on an English tour of the Upper Castle interior or the Baroque Theater (the theater is the castle attraction most likely to sell out). To book ahead, stop by the ticket office in person, or call 380-704-721 to check English tour times and reserve a space. No other castle sights require (or accept) reservations.

Information: Tel. 380-704-711, www.castle.ckrumlov.cz.

▲Round Tower (Zâmecká Věž) and Castle Museum (Hradní Muzeum)

These two sights share a ticket office at the bottom of the castle's middle courtyard. While neither is a must, both are worth con-

sidering if you want a peek inside the castle without committing to a guided tour. These are also the only castle sights open on Mondays (in peak season).

Colorfully impressive from the outside, the **tower** is also fun to climb. Twist up the 163 well-worn wood and stone steps to the top, where you'll be rewarded with grand, 360-degree views over the town, the rest of the castle complex, and happy boaters floating on the river.

The exhibits at the **Castle Museum** focus on key moments in the lives of the town's various ruling families: Rožmberks, Eggenbergs, and Schwarzenbergs. Be sure to pick up the good, included audioguide as you enter. You'll see a hall of aristocratic portraits; the offices, bedrooms, and dining rooms of the various inhabitants; and a modest religious treasury, armory, and musical instruments collection. At the end you can sit in old-timey cinema seats and watch archival footage of the castle's residents from the 1920s and 1930s.

Cost and Hours: Tower-50 Kč, museum-100 Kč, combo-ticket for both-130 Kč; both open daily 9:00-17:00, June-Aug until 18:00, closed Mon in Nov-March; last entry one hour before closing.

▲Upper Castle (Horní Hrad)

Though the Upper Castle grounds are free to explore, you'll need to take a tour to access the interiors. Two different tour routes give you a glimpse of the places where the Rožmberks, Eggenbergs, and Schwarzenbergs dined, studied, worked, prayed, entertained, and slept. (By European standards, the castle's not much, and the

ČESKÝ KRUMLOV

tours move slowly.) Imagine being an aristocratic guest here, riding the dukes' assembly line of fine living: You'd promenade through a long series of elegant spaces and dine in the sumptuous dining hall before enjoying a concert in the Hall of Mirrors, which leads you directly to the Baroque Theater

(described next). After the play, you'd go out into the château garden for a fireworks finale.

Cost and Hours: Choose from Tour I (Gothic and Renaissance rooms, of the most general interest) or Tour II (19th-century castle life). Tours run June-Aug Tue-Sun 9:00-12:00 & 13:00-18:00, spring and fall until 17:00, closed Mon and Nov-March. Tours in Czech cost 150 Kč, leave regularly, and include an adequate flier in English that contains about half the information imparted by the guide. English tours cost more (250 Kč), run less frequently, and are often booked solid. Pay to reserve a slot in advance; see "Reservations for Baroque Theater and Upper Castle," earlier, for details. You'll be issued a ticket with your tour time printed on it. Be in the correct courtyard at that time, or you'll be locked out.

▲▲Baroque Theater (Zámecké Divadlo)

Europe once had several hundred Baroque theaters. Using candles for light and fireworks for special effects, most burned down. Today, only two survive in good shape and are open to tourists: one at Stockholm's Drottningholm Palace; and one here, at Krumlov Castle. During the 45-minute tour, you'll sit on benches in the theater and then go under the stage to see the wood-and-rope contraptions that enabled scenes to be scooted in and out within seconds (while fireworks and smoke blinded the audience). It's a lovely little theater with an impressive 3-D effect that makes the stage look deeper than it really is, but don't bother with the tour unless you can snare a spot on an English one. The theater is used only once a year for an actual performance, attended by Baroque theater enthusiasts.

Cost and Hours: 300 Kč for English tour, 250 Kč for Czech tour, tours Tue-Sun May-Oct, no tours Mon and Nov-April; English departures at 10:00, 11:00, 13:00, 14:00, and 15:00. Due to the theater's fragility, groups are limited to 20 people, and English tours generally sell out in advance. It's advisable to reserve ahead—see "Reservations for Baroque Theater and Upper Castle," earlier.

ČESKÝ KRUMLOV

Castle Gardens (Zámecká Zahrada)

This lovely 2,300-foot-long garden crowns the castle complex. It was laid out in the 17th century, when the noble family would have it lit with 22,000 oil lamps, torches, and candles for special occasions. The lower part is geometrical and symmetrical—French garden-style. The upper part is wilder—English garden-style. Both are delightful.

Cost and Hours: Free, open May-Sept Tue-Sun 8:00-19:00, April and Oct until 17:00, closed Mon and Nov-March.

OTHER SIGHTS IN TOWN
Museum of Regional History
(Regionální Muzeum v Českém Krumlově)

This small museum gives you a quick look at regional costumes, tools, and traditions. When you pay, pick up the English translation of the displays (it also includes a lengthy history of Krumlov). Start on the top floor, where you'll see a Bronze Age exhibit, old paintings, a glimpse of noble life, and a look at how the locals rafted lumber from Krumlov all the way to Vienna (partly by canal). Don't miss the fun-to-study ceramic model of Český Krumlov in 1800 (note the extravagant gardens high above the town). The lower floor comes with fine folk costumes and domestic art.

Cost and Hours: 50 Kč, Tue-Sun 9:00-12:00 & 12:30-17:00, July-Aug until 18:00, closed Mon, Horní 152, tel. 380-711-674, www.muzeumck.cz.

Puppet Museum and Fairy Tale House
(Muzeum Loutek a Pohádkový Dům)

In three small rooms, you'll view fascinating displays of more than 200 movable creations (overwhelmingly of Czech origin, but also some from Burma and Rajasthan). At the model stage, children of any age can try their hand at pulling the strings on their favorite fairy tale.

Cost and Hours: 80 Kč, daily June-Aug 10:00-18:00, shorter hours off-season, tel. 380-711-175, Dlouhá 29, www.krumlovskainspirace.cz.

Egon Schiele Art Center (Egon Schiele Art Centrum)

This classy contemporary art gallery has temporary exhibits, generally featuring 20th-century Czech artists. The top-floor permanent collection celebrates the Viennese artist Egon Schiele (pronounced "Sheila"), who once spent a few weeks here during a secret love affair. A friend of Gustav Klimt and an important figure in the Secession movement in Vienna, Schiele lived a short life, from 1890 to 1918. His cutting-edge lifestyle and harsh art of graphic nudes didn't always fit the conservative, small-town style of Český Krumlov, but townsfolk are happy today to charge you to see this relatively paltry collection of his work. The Schiele collection in Vienna's Belvedere Palace is far better (see page 1215).

Cost and Hours: 140 Kč, Tue-Sun 10:00-18:00, closed Mon, café, Široká 71, tel. 380-704-011, www.schieleartcentrum.cz.

▲Eggenberg Brewery Tour

This may be one of the most intimate and accessible brewery tours in this land that so loves its beer. Tucked into a river bend on the edge of town, Eggenberg's spunky little brewery has an authenticity that can't be matched by the big, soulless corporate breweries (such as Pilsner Urquell, in Plzeň, or the Czech Budweiser, in nearby České Budějovice). This is your chance to learn about the beer-making process at a facility where

they're still using the same giant copper vats from 1915. While some of the facility has recently been modernized (and ongoing works may reroute the tour a bit), you'll still see lots of vintage equipment, including the original brew house (still in service), the fermentation vats, the cellars used for aging, and the bottling plant. Your tour ends with a visit to the pub, where you can sample some brews, including a "smoky" dark beer (Nakouřený Švihák) made with malt that tastes like salami, then aged for 100 days.

Cost and Hours: 100 Kč for the tour only, 130 Kč for tour and two tastes in the pub, 170 Kč for tour and four-pack of your choice of bottled beers to take away, 200 Kč includes everything; one-hour English tours daily at 11:00 year-round, also at 14:00 in May-Oct, tel. 380-711-426, www.eggenberg.cz.

Getting There: It's just a short stroll up Nové Město street from the main drag below the castle. During ongoing reconstruction, you may instead have to loop around town to the back entrance on Pivovarska—about a 10-minute walk.

ACTIVITIES

Český Krumlov lies in the middle of a valley popular for canoeing, rafting, hiking, and horseback riding. Boat-rental places are convenient to the Old Town, and several hiking paths start right in town.

▲▲▲Canoeing and Rafting the Vltava

Splash a little river fun into your visit by renting a rubber raft or fiberglass canoe for a quick 30-minute spin around Český Krumlov. Or go for a three-hour float and paddle through the Bohemian forests and villages of the nearby countryside. You'll end up at Zlatá

Koruna Abbey (described later), from where rafting companies will shuttle you back to town—or provide you with a bicycle to pedal back on your own along a bike path. This is a great hot-weather activity. Though the river is far from treacherous, be prepared to get wet.

You'll encounter plenty of inviting pubs and cafés for breaks along the way. There's a little whitewater, but the river is so shallow that if you tip, you can simply stand up and climb back in. (When that happens, pull the canoe up onto the bank to empty it, since you'll never manage to pour the water out while still in the river.)

Choose from a kayak, a canoe (faster, less work, more likely to tip), or an inflatable raft (harder rowing, slower, but very stable). Prices are per boat (2-6 people) and include a map, a waterproof container, and transportation to or from the start and end points. Here are your options:

Quickie Circle-the-Town Float: The easiest half-hour experience is to float around the city's peninsula, starting and ending on opposite sides of the tiny isthmus. Heck, you can do it twice (440 Kč for 2 people in a canoe or raft).

Three-Hour Float to Zlatá Koruna Abbey: This is your best basic trip, with pastoral scenery, a riverside pub about two hours down on the left, and a beautiful abbey as your destination (about 9 miles, 720 Kč for 2 people). From there you can bike back or catch a shuttle bus home—simply arrange a return plan with the rental company.

Longer and Faster Trips: If you start upriver from Krumlov (direction: Rožmberk), you'll go faster with more whitewater, but the river parallels a road, so it's a little less idyllic. Longer trips in either direction involve lots of paddling, even though you're going downstream. Rafting companies can review the many day-trip options with you.

Rental Companies: Several companies offer this lively activity. Perhaps the handiest are **Půjčovna Lodí Maleček Boat Rental** (open long hours daily April-Oct, closed Nov-March, at recommended Pension Myší Díra, Rooseveltova 28, tel. 380-712-508, www.malecek.cz, lode@malecek.cz) and **Vltava Sport Service** (daily April-Sept 9:00-17:00, closed Oct-March, Hradební 60, tel. 380-711-988, www.ckvltava.cz). Vltava also rents mountain bikes (320 Kč/day) and can bring a bike to the abbey for you to ride back.

Hiking

For an **easy 20-minute hike** to the Křížový Vrch (Hill of the

Cross), walk to the end of Rooseveltova street, cross at the traffic light, then head straight for the first (empty) chapel-like Station of the Cross. Turning right, it's easy to navigate along successive Stations of the Cross until you reach the white church on the hill (closed), set in the middle of wild meadows. Looking down into the valley at the medieval city nestled within the S-shaped river, framed by the rising hills, it's hard to imagine any town with a more powerful *genius loci* (spirit of the place). The view is best at sunset.

For **longer hikes,** start at the trailhead by the bear pits beneath the castle. Red-and-white trail markers guide you on an easy six-mile hike around the neighboring slopes and villages. The green-and-yellow stripes mark a five-mile hiking trail up Kleť Mountain—with an altitude gain of 1,800 feet. At the top, you'll find the Kleť Observatory, the oldest observatory in the country (and still a leading astronomical center). On clear days, you can see the Alps (observatory tours-50 Kč, hourly July-Aug Tue-Sun 10:30-15:30, closed Mon, April-June Sat-Sun only, closed Sept-March, www.hvezdarna.klet.cz).

Horseback Riding
Head about a mile out of town, beyond the Křížový Vrch (Hill of the Cross), for horseback rides and lessons at Slupenec Horseback Riding Club.

Cost and Hours: 300 Kč for one hour outdoors or in the ring, 2,200 Kč-all-day ride, Tue-Sun 10:00-15:00, closed Mon, helmets provided, Slupenec 1, worth a taxi trip, tel. 723 832 459, www.jk-slupenec.cz.

OUTSIDE OF ČESKÝ KRUMLOV
Zlatá Koruna Abbey (Klášter Zlatá Koruna)
This Cistercian abbey was founded in the 13th century by a Bohemian king to counter the growing influence of the Vítek family, the ancestors of the mighty Rožmberks. As you enter the grounds, notice the central linden tree, with its strange, cape-like leaves; it's said to have been used by the anti-Catholic Hussites when they hanged the monks. The short, guided abbey tour takes you through the rare two-storied Gothic Chapel of the Guardian Angel, the main church, and the cloister. After the order was dissolved in 1785, the abbey functioned briefly as a village school, before being turned into a factory during the Industrial Revolution. Damage from this period is visible on the cloister's crumbling arches. The abbey was restored in the 1990s and opened to the public only a few years ago.

Cost and Hours: 100 Kč for a tour in Czech—generally runs hourly, 180 Kč for an English tour, April-Oct Tue-Sun 9:00-16:00, until 17:00 June-Aug, closed Mon and Nov-March, call 380-743-126

Roma in Eastern Europe

Numbering 12 million, the Roma people constitute a bigger European nation than the Czechs, Hungarians, or the Dutch. (The term "Gypsies," which used to be the common name for this group, is now considered both derogatory and inaccurate.)

The Roma are thought to be descended from several low north-Indian castes (one of which may have given the Roma their name). A thousand years ago, the Roma began to migrate through Persia and Armenia into the Ottoman Empire, which later stretched across much of southeastern Europe. Known for their itinerant lifestyle, expertise in horse trading, skilled artisanship, and flexibility regarding private property, the Roma were both sought out and suspected in medieval Europe.

The Industrial Revolution removed the Roma's few traditional means of earning a livelihood, making their wandering lifestyle difficult to sustain. In the 1940s, Hitler sent hundreds of thousands of Roma to the gas chambers. After the war, communist governments in Eastern Europe implemented a policy of forced assimilation: Roma were required to speak the country's major language, settle in towns, and work in new industrial jobs. Rather than producing well-adjusted citizens, the policy eroded time-honored Roma values and shattered the cohesiveness of their traditional communities. It left the new Roma generation prone to sexual, alcohol, and drug abuse, and filled state-run orphanages with deprived Roma toddlers. When the obligation and right to work disappeared with the communist regimes in 1989, rampant unemployment and dependence on welfare joined the list of Roma afflictions.

As people all over Eastern Europe found it difficult to adjust to the new economic realities, they again turned on the Roma as scapegoats. Many Roma now live in segregated ghettos. Those who make it against the odds and succeed in mainstream society typically do so by turning their backs on their Roma heritage.

In this context, the Roma in Český Krumlov are a surprising success story. The well-integrated, proud Roma community here (numbering 1,000 strong, or 5 percent of the town's population) is considered a curious anomaly even by experts. Their success could be due to a number of factors: It could be the legacy of the multicultural Rožmberks, or the fact that almost everyone in Český Krumlov is a relative newcomer. Or maybe it's that local youngsters, regardless of skin color, tend to resolve their differences over a beer in the local "Gypsy Pub" (Cikánská Jizba), with a trendy Roma band setting the tune.

to arrange an English tour, www.klaster-zlatakoruna.eu.

Getting There: Drivers can reach the abbey in about 15 minutes from Český Krumlov (head north out of town and follow route #39). But it's more fun to get there by raft or canoe—the abbey is directly above the river at the end of a three-hour float (see "Canoeing and Rafting the Vltava," earlier).

Sleeping in Český Krumlov

Krumlov is filled with small, good, family-run pensions and hostels. Summer weekends and festivals (see "Helpful Hints," earlier) are busiest and most expensive; reserve ahead when possible. Hotels (not a Krumlov forte) have staff that speak some English and accept credit cards; pensions rarely have or do either. While you can find a room upon arrival here, it's better to book at least a few days ahead if you want to stay in the heart of town. Cars are not very safe overnight—locals advise paying for a garage.

IN THE OLD TOWN

$$$ Castle View Apartments, run by local guide Jiří Václavíček, rents seven apartments. These are the best-equipped rooms I found in town—the bathroom floors are heated, all come with kitchenettes, and everything's done just right. Their website describes each stylish apartment; the "view" ones really do come with eye-popping vistas (Db-1,800-3,400 Kč depending on size, view, and season; higher prices for more people, big 4,700-Kč apartment sleeps up to 6, reserve directly on their website with this book for 10 percent off online prices, non-smoking, breakfast in a nearby hotel, Wi-Fi, Šatlavská 140, mobile 731-108-677, www.castleview.cz, info@castleview.cz).

$$$ Hotel Konvice is run by a German couple and their

Sleep Code

Abbreviations   (20 Kč = about $1, country code: 420)

S = Single, **D** = Double/Twin, **T** = Triple, **Q** = Quad, **b** = bathroom, **s** = shower only

Price Rankings

$$$ Higher Priced—Most rooms 1,500 Kč or more.

$$ Moderately Priced—Most rooms between 1,000-1,500 Kč.

$ Lower Priced—Most rooms 1,000 Kč or less.

Unless otherwise noted, prices include breakfast and Wi-Fi is generally free. Prices change; verify current rates online or by email. For the best prices, always book directly with the hotel.

three children with a personal touch. Each room is uniquely decorated (Db-1,500-2,500 Kč, a block above the main square at Horní 144, tel. 380-711-611, www.boehmerwaldhotels.de, info@stadthotel-krummau.de).

BELOW THE MAIN SQUARE

Secluded Parkán street, which runs along the river below the square, has a hotel and a row of small pensions. These places have a family feel and views of the looming castle above.

$$$ Hotel Mlýn, at the end of Parkán, is a tastefully furnished hotel with more than 30 rooms and all the amenities (Sb-2,400 Kč, Db-3,000 Kč, elevator, Wi-Fi, pay parking, Parkán 120, tel. 380-731-133, www.hotelmlyn.eu, info@hotelmlyn.eu).

$$ Pension Olšakovský, which has a delightful breakfast area on a terrace next to the river, treats visitors as family guests (Db-1,120-1,620 Kč, includes parking, Parkán 114, mobile 604-430-181, www.olsakovsky.cz, info@olsakovsky.cz).

AT THE BASE OF THE CASTLE

A quiet, cobbled pedestrian street (Latrán) runs below the castle just over the bridge from the Old Town. Lined with cute shops, it's a 10-minute walk downhill from the train station.

$$ Pension Danny is a funky little place, with homey rooms and a tangled floor plan above a restaurant (Db-1,040 Kč, apartment Db-1,290 Kč, breakfast in room, Latrán 72, tel. 603-210-572, www.pensiondanny.cz, recepce@pensiondanny.cz).

BETWEEN THE BUS STATION AND THE OLD TOWN

Rooseveltova street, midway between the bus station and the Old Town (a four-minute walk from either), is lined with several lovely little places, each with easy free parking. The key here is tranquility—the noisy bars of the town center are out of carshot.

$$$ Hotel Garni Myší Díra ("Mouse Hole") hides 11 sleek, spacious, bright, and woody Bohemian contemporary rooms overlooking the Vltava River just outside the Old Town (Db-1,360-2,720 Kč, deluxe river-view Tb-3,277 Kč, prices include transfer to/from bus or train station, guest computer, Wi-Fi, Rooseveltova 28, tel. 380-712-853, www.malecek.cz). The no-nonsense reception, which closes at 20:00, runs the recommended boat rental company (Půjčovna Lodí Maleček, at the same address), along with a similar pension with comparable prices, **Villa Margarita,** farther along Rooseveltova.

$$ Little Pension Teddy offers three deluxe rooms that share a balcony overlooking the river and have original 18th-century furniture. Or stay in one of four modern-style rooms, some of which also face the river (Db-1,250 Kč, deluxe Db-1,400 Kč, cash only, staff may be unhelpful, guest computer, Wi-Fi, parking-200 Kč, Rooseveltova 38, tel. 777-713-277, mobile 724-003-981, www.pensionteddy.cz, info@pensionteddy.cz).

$$ Pension Anna is well-run, with two doubles, six apartments, and a restful little garden. Its apartments are spacious suites, with a living room and stairs leading to the double-bedded loft. The upstairs rooms can get stuffy during the summer (Db-1,250 Kč, Db apartment-1,550 Kč, extra bed-350 Kč, parking-100 Kč, Rooseveltova 41, tel. 380-711-692, www.pensionanna-ck.cz, pension.anna@quick.cz). If you book a standard Db and they bump you up to an apartment, don't pay more than the Db rate.

HOSTELS

Of the hostels in town, Hostel 99 (closest to the train station) is clearly the high-energy, youthful party place. Krumlov House (closer to the bus station) is more mellow. Both are well-managed, and each is a five-minute walk from the main square.

$ Hostel 99's picnic-table terrace looks out on the Old Town. While the gentle sound of the river gurgles outside your window late at night, you're more likely to hear a youthful international crowd having a great time. The hostel caters to its fun-loving young guests, offering a day-long river rafting and pub crawl, with a free keg of beer each Wednesday (65 beds in 4- to 10-bed coed rooms-300-350 Kč/bed, bunk in 16-bed rooms-250 Kč, D-700 Kč, Db-900-1,000 Kč, T-990 Kč, guest computer, Wi-Fi, laundry-200 Kč/load, use the lockers, no curfew or lockout, recommended Hospoda 99 restaurant, 10-minute downhill walk from train station or two bus stops to Spicak, Vezni 99, tel. 380-712-812, www.hostel99.cz, hostel99@hotmail.com).

$ Krumlov House Hostel is take-your-shoes-off-at-the-door, shiny, hardwood-with-throw-rugs mellow. Efficiently run by a Canadian/American couple, it has a hip, trusting vibe and feels welcoming to travelers of any age (24 beds, 6 beds in two dorms-300-350 Kč/bed, Db-800-900 Kč, 2-person apartment-900-1,000 Kč, family room with kitchenette-1,200-1,600 Kč, breakfast-150 Kč—July-Aug only, well-stocked guest kitchen, DVD library, Wi-Fi, laundry-200 Kč/load, Rooseveltova 68, tel. 380-711-935, www.krumlovhostel.com, info@krumlovhostel.com). The hostel sponsors "WriteAway," a literary retreat for traveling writers (www.writeaway.literarybohemian.com).

Eating in Český Krumlov

Krumlov, with a huge variety of creative little restaurants, is a fun place to eat. In peak times the good places fill fast, so make reservations or eat early.

Na Louži seems to be everyone's favorite Czech bistro, with 40 seats (many at shared tables) in one 1930s-style room decorated with funky old advertisements. They serve good, inexpensive, unpretentious local cuisine and hometown Eggenberg beer on tap (daily 10:00-23:00, Kájovská 66, tel. 380-711-280).

Krčma u Dwau Maryí ("Tavern of the Two Marys") is a characteristic old place with idyllic riverside picnic tables, serving ye olde Czech cuisine and drinks. The fascinating menu explains the history of the house and makes a good case that the food of the poor medieval Bohemians was tasty and varied. Buck up for buckwheat, millet, greasy meat, or the poor-man's porridge (daily 11:00-23:00, Parkán 104, tel. 380-717-228).

Cikánská Jizba ("Gypsy Pub") is a Roma tavern filling one den-like, barrel-vaulted room. The Roma staff serves Slovak-style food (most of the Czech Republic's Roma population came from Slovakia). Krumlov has a long Roma history (see sidebar on page 211). And though this rustic little restaurant, which packs its 10 tables under a mystic-feeling Gothic vault, won't win any culinary awards, you never know what festive and musical activities will erupt, particularly on Friday nights, when the owner's son's band, Cindži Renta (Wet Rag), performs here (Mon-Sat 15:00-24:00, closed Sun, 2 blocks toward castle from main square at Dlouhá 31, tel. 380-717-585).

Restaurace u Dobráka ("Good Man") is like eating in a medieval garage, with a giant poster of Karl Marx overseeing the action. Lojza, who's been tossing steaks and whole fish on his open fire for years, makes sure you'll eat well. Locals know it as the best place for grilled steak and fish. He charges too much for his beer in order to keep the noisy beer drinkers away (200-400-Kč grilled fish, 400-500-Kč steaks, open daily 17:30-24:00 from Easter until Lojza "has a shoebox full of money," Široká 74, tel. 380-717-776).

Laibon is the modern vegetarian answer to the carnivorous Middle Ages. Settle down inside or head out onto the idyllic river terrace, and lighten up your pork-loaded diet with soy goulash or Mútábúr soup (daily 11:00-23:00, Parkán 105).

Kolektiv tries to inject some modern sophistication into this ye olde town. Situated right along Latrán street across from the castle stairs, it has a sleek minimalist interior, a chalkboard menu, well-executed light café fare with some international flavors, a good cocktail selection, and stylish, if stuffy, service. It's a nice break from heavy Czech cuisine and offers good people-watching (50-Kč soups, 70-100-Kč sandwiches, 130-Kč salads, daily 8:00-20:00, Fri-Sat until 21:00, Latrán 13, tel. 776-626-644).

Rybářská Restaurace ("Fisherman's Restaurant") doesn't look particularly inviting from the outside, but don't be discouraged. This is *the* place in town to taste freshwater fish you've never heard of (and never will again). Try eel, perch, shad, carp, trout, and more. Choose between indoor tables under fishnets or riverside picnic benches outside (daily 11:00-22:00, on the island by the millwheel, mobile 723-829-089).

Krčma v Šatlavské is an old prison gone cozy, with an open fire, big wooden tables under a rustic old medieval vault, and tables outdoors on the pedestrian lane. It's great for a late drink or roasted game (cooked on an open spit). *Medovina* is hot honey wine (daily 12:00-24:00, on Šatlavská, follow lane leading to the side from TI on main square, mobile 608-973-797).

Restaurace Barbakán is built into the town fortifications, with a terrace hanging high over the river. It's a good spot for old-fashioned Czech cooking and beer, at the top of town and near the recommended Rooseveltova street accommodations (open long hours daily, reasonable prices, Horní 26, tel. 380-712-679).

Hospoda 99 Restaurace serves good, cheap soups, salads, and meals. It's the choice of hostelers and locals alike for its hamburgers, vegetarian food, Czech dishes, and cheap booze (meals served 10:00-22:00, bar open until 24:00, at Hostel 99, Vezni 99, tel. 380-712-812). This place is booming until late, when everything else is hibernating.

Dobrá Čajovna is a typical example of the quiet, exotic-feeling teahouses that flooded Czech towns in the 1990s as alternatives to smoky, raucous pubs. Though directly across from the castle entrance, it's a world away from the touristic hubbub. As is so often the case, if you want to surround yourself with locals, don't go to a traditional place...go ethnic. With its meditative karma inside and a peaceful terrace facing the monastery out back, it provides a relaxing break (daily 13:00-22:00, Latrán 54, mobile 777-654-744).

Český Krumlov Connections

BY PUBLIC TRANSPORTATION

Almost all trains and some buses to and from Český Krumlov require a transfer in the city of **České Budějovice,** a transit hub just to the north. Bus and train timetables are available at www.idos.cz.

In České Budějovice, the train and bus stations are next to each other: To transfer to a bus, exit the train station, turn left, and use the underpass to cross the street diagonally to the Mercury Centrum shopping center (the Autobusové Nádraží bus station is upstairs). Enter the shopping center and take the escalators to the third floor, following signs for *Bus*.

If you have time in České Budějovice between connections, consider a visit to the town's lovely main square, Náměstí Přemysla Otakara II (about a six-block walk from the stations). Store your bags in lockers at the train station, then exit the station to the right, cross the street at the crosswalk, and head straight down Lannova třida (which becomes Kanovnická street) to the square.

By Train
From Český Krumlov by Train to: České Budějovice (6/day, 1 hour), **Prague** (8/day, 1/day direct, 4 hours; bus is faster, cheaper, and easier—see below), **Vienna** (6/day with at least one change, 5-6 hours), **Budapest** (6/day with at least one change, 10-15 hours).

By Bus
The Český Krumlov bus station, a five-minute walk out of town, is just a big parking lot with numbered stalls for various buses (bus info tel. 380-711-190). The Student Agency bus company has

an online reservation and ticket system, the newest buses, and a free drink for passengers (www.studentagency.cz).

From Český Krumlov by Bus to: Prague (10/day, 3.5 hours; tickets can be bought at the Český Krumlov TI), **České Budějovice** (transit hub for other destinations; hourly, 40 minutes).

ČESKÝ KRUMLOV

BY SHUTTLE SERVICE
From Český Krumlov to Austria and Beyond: The town is very close to Austria, but train connections to places like Vienna, Salzburg, and Hallstatt are too complex to bother with. Several companies offer handy shuttle service. The best of the bunch is CK Shuttle, with free Wi-Fi on board and affordable fares: 800 Kč per person one-way to **Vienna** (4/day, 3.5 hours), **Salzburg** (4/day, 3 hours), **Hallstatt** (3/day, 3 hours), or **Prague** (3/day, 2.5 hours). They can also take you to Linz (where you can hop on the speedy east-west main rail line through Austria), Budapest, Munich, and other places. They offer door-to-door service to and from your hotel, and once you book on their website and receive a confirmation, your departure is guaranteed (office at Dlouhá 95, www.ckshuttle.cz). Another reliable option is Sebastian Tours (higher prices, mobile 607-100-234 or 608-357-581, www.sebastiancktours.com, sebastiantours@hotmail.com).

POLAND
Polska

POLAND

Polska

Americans who think of Poland as run-down—full of rusting factories, smoggy cities, and gloomy natives—are speechless when they step into Kraków's vibrant main square, Gdańsk's colorful Royal Way, or Warsaw's lively Old Town. While parts of the country are still cleaning up the industrial mess left by the Soviets, Poland also has some breathtaking medieval cities that show off its kindhearted people, dynamic history, and unique cultural fabric.

The Poles are a proud people—as moved by their spectacular failures as by their successes. Their quiet elegance has been tempered by generations of abuse by foreign powers. The Poles place a lot of importance on honor, and you'll find fewer scams and con artists here than in other Eastern European countries.

In a way, there are two Polands: lively, cosmopolitan urban centers, and countless tiny farm villages in the countryside. City-dwellers often talk about the "simple people" of Poland—those descended from generations of farmers, working the same plots for centuries and living an uncomplicated, agrarian lifestyle. This large contingent of salt-of-the-earth folks—who like things the way they are—is a major reason why Poland was hesitant to join the European Union and remains fiercely "Euroskeptic."

Poland is arguably Europe's most devoutly Catholic country. Catholicism has long defined these people, holding them together through times when they had little else. Squeezed between Protestant Germany (originally Prussia) and Eastern Orthodox Russia, Poland wasn't even a country for genera-  tions (1795-1918). Its Catholicism helped keep its spirit alive. In the last century, while "under communism" (as that age is referred to), Poles once again found their religion a source of strength as well as rebellion—they could express dissent against the atheistic regime

by going to church. Some of Poland's best sights are churches, usually filled with locals praying silently. While these church interiors are worth a visit, be careful to show the proper respect: Maintain silence, keep a low profile, and if you want to snap pictures, do so discreetly.

Visitors are sometimes surprised at how much of Poland's story is a Jewish story. Before World War II, 80 percent of Europe's Jews lived in Poland. Warsaw was the world's second-largest Jewish city (after New York), with 380,000 Jews (out of a total population of 1.2 million). Poland was a magnet for Jewish refugees because of its relatively welcoming policies. Still, Jews were forbidden from owning land; that's why they settled mostly in the cities. But the Holocaust (and a later Soviet policy of sending "troublemaking" Jews to Israel) decimated the Jewish population. This tragic chapter, combined with postwar border shifts and population movements, made Poland one of Europe's most ethnically homogeneous countries. Today, virtually everyone in the country is an ethnic Pole, and only a few thousand Polish Jews remain.

Poland has long been extremely pro-America. Of course, their big neighbors (Russia and Germany) have been their historic enemies. And when Hitler invaded in 1939, the Poles felt let down by their supposed European friends (France and Britain), who declared war on Germany but provided virtually no military support to the Polish resistance. America, meanwhile, has been regarded as the big ally from across the ocean—and the home of the largest population of Poles outside of Poland. In 1989, when Poland finally won its freedom, many Poles only half-joked that they should apply to become the 51st state of the US.

POLAND

Poland Almanac

Official Name: Rzeczpospolita Polska (Republic of Poland), or Polska for short.

Snapshot History: This thousand-year-old country has been dominated by foreigners for much of the past two centuries, finally achieving true independence (from the Soviet Union) in 1989.

Population: Nearly 38.5 million people, slightly more than California. About 97 percent are ethnic Poles who speak Polish (though English is also widely spoken). Three out of every four Poles are practicing Catholics. The population is younger than most European countries, with an average age of 39 (Germany's is 46).

Latitude and Longitude: 52°N and 20°E (similar latitude to Berlin, London, and Edmonton, Alberta).

Area: 121,000 square miles, the same as New Mexico (or Illinois and Iowa put together).

Geography: Because of its overall flatness, Poland has been a corridor for invading armies since its infancy. The Vistula River (650 miles) runs south-to-north up the middle of the country, passing through Kraków and Warsaw, and emptying into the Baltic Sea at Gdańsk. Poland's climate is generally cool and rainy—40,000 storks love it.

Biggest Cities: Warsaw (the capital, 1.7 million), Kraków (757,000), and Łódź (747,000).

Economy: The Gross Domestic Product is $814 billion, with a GDP per capita of $21,100. The 1990s saw an aggressive and success-ful transition from state-run socialism to privately owned capital-ism. Still, Poland's traditional potato-and-pig-farming society is behind the times, with 16 percent of the country's workers pro-ducing less than 3 percent of its GDP. About one in ten Poles is unemployed, and nearly one in five lives in poverty. And yet, per-haps because its economy is so primitive, Poland fared especially well through the recent economic downturn.

Currency: 1 złoty (zł, or PLN) = 100 groszy (gr) = about 30 cents; 3 zł = about $1.

On my first visit to Poland, I had a poor impression of Poles, who seemed brusque and often elbowed ahead of me in line. I've since learned that all it takes is a smile and a cheerful greeting—preferably in Polish—to break through the thick skin that helped these kind people survive the difficult communist times. With a friendly *Dzień dobry!*, you'll turn any grouch into an ally. It may help to know that, because of the distinct cadence of Polish, Poles speaking English sometimes sound more impatient, gruff, or irritated than they actually are. Part of the Poles' charm is that they're not as slick and self-assured as many Europeans: They're

Real Estate: A typical one-bedroom apartment in Warsaw (250 square feet) rents for roughly $600 a month.

Government: Poland's mostly figurehead president selects the prime minister and cabinet, with legislators' approval. They govern along with a two-house legislature (Sejm and Senat) of 560 seats. Since late 2014, the prime minister has been Ewa Kopacz, of the centrist Civic Platform. President Bronisław Komorowski, also of the Civic Platform, is up for re-election in 2015. (For more on Polish politics, see page 232.)

Flag: The upper half is white, and the lower half is red—the traditional colors of Poland. Poetic Poles claim the white represents honor, and the red represents the enormous amounts of blood spilled by the Poles to honor their nation. The flag sometimes includes a coat of arms with a crowned eagle (representing Polish sovereignty). Under Poland's many oppressors (including the Soviets), the crown was removed from the emblem, and its talons were trimmed. On regaining its independence, Poland coronated its eagle once more.

The Average Pole: In spite of its tumultuous history, Poland is a relatively upbeat nation: 74 percent of all Poles report they are "quite happy." Three-quarters use the Internet, and the average Pole will live to about age 77. The average Polish woman gets married at age 26 and will have 1.3 children.

Not-so-Average Poles: Poland's three big airports offer a run-down of just a few of the country's biggest names: St. John Paul II (in Kraków), Fryderyk Chopin (in Warsaw), and Lech Wałęsa (in Gdańsk). And, despite the many "Polack jokes" you've heard (and maybe repeated), you're already familiar with many other famous Polish intellectuals—you just don't realize they're Polish. The "Dumb Polack" Hall of Fame includes Mikołaj Kopernik **(Nicolas Copernicus),** scientist **Marie Curie** (née Skłodowska), writer Teodor Józef Korzeniowski (better known as **Joseph Conrad**, author of *Heart of Darkness*), filmmaker **Roman Polański** (*Chinatown, The Pianist*), **Daniel Libeskind** (the master architect for redeveloping the 9/11 site in New York City)...and one of this book's co-authors.

kind, soft-spoken, and quite shy. On a recent train trip in Poland, I offered my Polish seatmate a snack—and spent the rest of trip enjoying a delightful conversation with a new friend.

HELPFUL HINTS

Restroom Signage: To confuse tourists, the Poles have devised a secret way of marking their WCs. You'll see doors marked with *męska* (men) and *damska* (women)—but even more often, you'll simply see a triangle (for men) or a circle (for women). A sign with a triangle, a circle, and an arrow is directing you to

Top 10 Dates That Changed Poland

A.D. 966—The Polish king, Mieszko I, is baptized a Christian, symbolically uniting the Polish people and founding the nation.

1385—The Polish queen (called a "king" by sexist aristocrats of the time) marries a Lithuanian duke, starting the two-century reign of the Jagiełło family.

1410—Poland defeats the Teutonic Knights at the Battle of Grunwald, part of a Golden Age of territorial expansion and cultural achievement.

1572—The last Jagiellonian king dies, soon replaced by bickering nobles and foreign kings. Poland declines.

1795—In the last of three Partitions, the country is divvied up by its more-powerful neighbors: Russia, Prussia, and Austria.

1918—Following World War I, Poland gets back its land and sovereignty.

1939—The Free City of Gdańsk (then called Danzig) is invaded by Nazi Germany, starting World War II. At war's end, the country is "liberated" (i.e., occupied) by the Soviet Union.

1980—Lech Wałęsa leads a successful strike, demanding more freedom from the communist regime.

1989—Poland gains independence under its first president—Lech Wałęsa. Fifteen years later, Poland joins the European Union.

2010—President Lech Kaczyński and 95 other high-level government officials are killed in a plane crash in Russia.

the closest WCs.

Pay to Pee: Many Polish bathrooms charge a small fee (around 1 zł). You may even be charged at a restaurant where you're paying to dine.

Train Station Lingo: "PKP" is the abbreviation for Polish National Railways ("PKS" is for buses). In larger towns with several train stations, you'll normally use the one called Główny (meaning "Main"—except in Warsaw, where it's Centralna). *Dworzec główny* means "main train station." Most stations have several platforms *(peron)*, each of which has two tracks *(tor)*. Departures are generally listed by the *peron*, so keep your eye on both tracks for your train. Arrivals are *przyjazdy*, and departures are *odjazdy*. Left-luggage counters or lockers are marked *przechowalnia bagażu*. *Kasy* are ticket windows. These can be marked (sometimes only in Polish) for specific needs—domestic tickets, international tickets, and so on; ask fellow travelers to be sure you select the right line. The line you choose will invariably be the slowest one—leave plenty of time to buy your ticket before your train departs (or, if you're running out of time, buy it on board for 10 zł extra).

Larger stations have customer service centers where you may have to wait longer (take a number), but you're more likely to encounter English-speaking staff. For longer and/or express journeys, you'll likely be given two separate tickets: one for the trip itself, and the other for your seat assignment. On arriving at a station, to get into town, follow signs for *wyjście (sometimes followed by do centrum* or *do miasta)*. Ongoing construction to improve Poland's rail lines may make some of your train journeys take much longer than normal, and delays are common.

Museum Tips: Most museums in Poland are closed on Monday, and the ticket office typically closes a half-hour before the museum's closing time. Poland's museums tend to frequently tweak their opening times—try to confirm hours locally if you have your heart set on a particular place.

Polish Artists: Though Poland has produced world-renowned scientists, musicians, and writers, the country isn't known for its artists. Polish museums greet foreign visitors with fine artwork by unfamiliar names. If you're planning to visit any museums in Poland, two artists in particular are worth remembering: **Jan Matejko,** a 19th-century positivist who painted grand historical epics (see page 404), and one of his students, **Stanisław Wyspiański,** a painter and playwright who led the charge of the Młoda Polska movement—the Polish answer to Art Nouveau—in the early 1900s (see page 263).

Telephones: Remember these Polish prefixes: 800 is toll-free, and 70 is expensive (like phone sex). Many Poles use mobile phones (which come with the prefix 50, 51, 53, 60, 66, 69, 72, 78, 79, or 88). For details on how to dial, see page 1318.

POLISH HISTORY

Poland is flat. Take a look at a topographical map of Europe, and you'll immediately appreciate the Poles' historical dilemma: The path of least resistance from northern Europe to Russia leads right through Poland. Over the years, many invaders—from Genghis Khan to Napoleon to Hitler—have taken advantage of Poland's

strategic location. The country is nicknamed "God's playground" for the many wars that have rumbled through its territory. Poland has been invaded by Soviets, Nazis, French, Austrians, Russians, Prussians, Swedes, Teutonic Knights, Tatars, Bohemians, Magyars—and, about 1,300 years ago, Poles.

Medieval Greatness

The first Poles were the Polonians ("people of the plains"), a Slavic band that arrived here in the eighth century. In 966, Mieszko I, Duke of the Polonian tribe, adopted Christianity and founded the Piast dynasty (which would last for more than 400 years). Centuries before Germany, Italy, or Spain first united, Poland was born.

Poland struggled against two different invaders in the 13th century: the Tatars (Mongols who ravaged the south) and the Teutonic Knights (Germans who conquered the north—see page 502). But despite these challenges, Poland persevered. The last king of the Piast dynasty was also the greatest: Kazimierz the Great, who famously "found a Poland made of wood and left one made of brick and stone," bringing Poland (and its capital, Kraków) to international prominence (see page 261). The progressive Kazimierz also invited Europe's much-persecuted Jews to settle here, establishing Poland as a haven for the Jewish people, which it would remain until the Nazis arrived.

Kazimierz the Great died at the end of the 14th century without a male heir. His grand-niece, Princess Jadwiga, became "king" (the Poles weren't ready for a "queen") and married Lithuanian Prince Władysław Jagiełło, uniting their countries against a common enemy, the Teutonic Knights. Their marriage marked the beginning of the Jagiellonian dynasty and set the stage for Poland's Golden Age. During this time, Poland expanded its territory, the Polish nobility began to acquire more political might, Italy's Renaissance (and its architectural styles) became popular, and the Toruń-born astronomer Nicholas Copernicus shook up the scientific world with his bold new heliocentric theory. Up on the Baltic coast, the port city of Gdańsk took advantage of its Hanseatic League trading partnership to become one of Europe's most prosperous cities.

Foreign Kings and Partitions

When the Jagiellonians died out in 1572, political power shifted to the nobility. Poland became a republic of nobles governed by its wealthiest 10 percent—the *szlachta*, who elected a series of foreign kings. In the 16th and 17th centuries—with its territory spanning from the Baltic Sea to the Black Sea—the Polish-Lithuanian Commonwealth was the largest state in Europe.

But over time, many of the elected kings made poor diplomatic decisions and squandered the country's resources. To make matters worse, the nobles' parliament (Sejm) introduced the concept of *liberum veto* (literally "I freely forbid"), whereby any measure could be vetoed by a single member of parliament. This policy, which effectively demanded unanimous approval for any law to be passed, paralyzed the Sejm's waning power. Sensing the Commonwealth's weakness, in the mid-17th century forces from Sweden rampaged through Polish and Lithuanian lands in the devastating "Swedish Deluge." While Poland eventually reclaimed its territory, a third of its population was dead. The Commonwealth continued to import self-serving foreign kings, including Saxony's Augustus the Strong and his son, who drained Polish wealth to finance vanity projects in their hometown of Dresden.

By the late 18th century, Poland was floundering and surrounded by three land-hungry empires (Russia, Prussia, and Austria). The Poles were unaware that these neighbors had entered into an agreement now dubbed the "Alliance of the Three Black Eagles" (since all three of those countries, coincidentally, used that bird as their symbol); they began to circle Poland's white eagle like vultures. Stanisław August Poniatowski, elected king with Russian support in 1764, would prove to be Poland's last.

Over the course of less than 25 years, Russia, Prussia, and Austria divided Poland's territory among themselves in a series of three Partitions. In 1772 and again in 1790, Poland was forced into ceding large chunks of its territory to its neighbors. Desperate to reform their government, Poles enacted Europe's first democratic constitution (and the world's second, after the US Constitution) on May 3, 1791—still celebrated as a national holiday. This visionary document protected the peasants, dispensed with both *liberum veto* and the election of the king, and set up something resembling a modern nation. But the constitution alarmed Poland's neighbors, who swept in soon after with the third and final Partition in 1795. "Poland" disappeared from Europe's maps, not to return until 1918.

Even though Poland was gone, the Poles wouldn't go quietly. As the Partitions were taking place, Polish soldier Tadeusz Kościuszko (also a hero of the American Revolution) returned home to lead an unsuccessful military resistance against the Russians in 1794.

Napoleon offered a brief glimmer of hope to the Poles in the early 19th century, when he marched eastward through Europe and set up the semi-independent "Duchy of Warsaw" in Polish lands. But that fleeting taste of freedom lasted only eight years; with Napoleon's defeat, Polish hopes were dashed. The Congress of Vienna, which redistributed Polish territory to Prussia, Russia, and Austria, is sometimes called (by Poles) the "Fourth Partition." In a classic case of "my enemy's enemy is my friend," the Poles still have great affection for Napoleon for how fiercely he fought against their mutual foes.

The Napoleonic connection also established France as a safe haven for refugee Poles. After another failed uprising against

Russia in 1830, many of Poland's top artists and writers fled to Paris—including pianist Fryderyk Chopin and Romantic poet Adam Mickiewicz (whose statue adorns Kraków's main square and Warsaw's Royal Way). These Polish artists tried to preserve the nation's spirit with music and words; those who remained in Poland continued to fight with swords and fists. By the end of the 19th century, the image of the Pole as a tireless, idealistic insurgent emerged. During this time, some Romantics—with typically melodramatic flair—dubbed Poland "the Christ of nations" for the way it was misunderstood and persecuted by the world, despite its inherent nobility.

Poles didn't just flock to France during the Partitions. Untold numbers of Polish people uprooted their lives to pursue a better future in the New World. About 10 million Americans have Polish ancestry, and most of them came stateside from the mid-19th to early 20th centuries. Because the sophisticated and educated tended to remain in Poland, these new arrivals were mostly poor farmers who were (at first) unschooled and didn't speak English, placing them on a bottom rung of American society. It was during this time that the tradition of insulting "Polack jokes" emerged. Some claim these originated in Chicago, which was both a national trendsetter in humor and a magnet for Polish immigrants. Others suggest that German immigrants to America imported insulting stereotypes of their Polish neighbors from the Old World. Either way, the jokes only became more vicious through the 20th century, until the Polish government actually lobbied the US State Department to put a stop to them.

As the map of Europe was redrawn following World War I, Poland emerged as a reborn nation, under the war hero-turned-head of state, Marshal Józef Piłsudski. The newly reformed "Second Polish Republic," which patched together the bits and pieces of territory that had been under foreign rule for decades, enjoyed a diverse ethnic mix—including Germans, Russians, Ukrainians, Lithuanians, and an enormous Jewish minority. A third of Poland spoke no Polish. The historic Baltic port city of Gdańsk—which was bicultural (German and Polish)—was granted the special "Free City of Danzig" status to avoid dealing with the prickly issue of whether to assign it to Germany or Poland. But the peace was not to last.

World War II

On September 1, 1939, Adolf Hitler began World War II by attacking Danzig to bring it into the German fold. Before the month was out, Hitler's forces had overrun Poland, and the Soviets had taken over a swath of eastern Poland (today still part of Ukraine, Belarus, and Lithuania).

The Nazis considered the Poles *slawische Untermenschen,* "Slavic sub-humans" who were useful only for manual labor. Remember that Poland was also home to a huge population of another group the Nazis hated, Jews. Nazi Germany annexed Polish regions that it claimed historic ties to, while the rest (including "Warschau" and "Krakau") became a puppet state ruled by the *Generalgouvernement* and Hitler's handpicked governor, Hans Frank. The Nazis considered this area *Lebensraum*—"living space" that wasn't nice enough to actually incorporate into Germany, but served perfectly as extra territory for building things that Germans didn't want in their backyards...such as Auschwitz-Birkenau, the notorious death camp that functioned as a factory for the mass-production of murder.

The Poles anxiously awaited the promised military aid of France and Britain; when help failed to arrive, they took matters into their own hands, forming a ragtag "Polish Home Army" and staging incredibly courageous but lopsided battles against their powerful German overlords (such as the Warsaw Uprising—see page 418). Throughout the spring of 1945, as the Nazis retreated from their failed invasion of the Soviet Union, the Red Army gradually "liberated" Poland from Nazi oppression, guaranteeing it another four decades of oppression under another regime.

With six million deaths over six years—including both Polish Jews and ethnic Poles—Poland suffered the worst per-capita WWII losses of any nation. By the war's end, one out of every five Polish citizens was dead—and 90 percent of those killed were civilians. While the human and infrastructure loss of World War II was incalculable, that war's cultural losses were also devastating—some 60,000 paintings were lost.

At the war's end, the victorious Allies shifted Poland's borders significantly westward—folding historically German areas into Polish territory and appropriating previously Polish areas for the USSR. This prompted a massive movement of populations—which today we'd decry as "ethnic cleansing"—as Germans were forcibly removed from western Poland, and Poles from newly Soviet territory were transplanted to Poland proper. Entire cities were repopulated (such as the formerly German metropolis of Breslau, which was renamed Wrocław and filled with refugee Poles from Lwów, now Lviv, in Ukraine). After millions died in the war, millions more were displaced from their ancestral homes. When the dust settled, Poland was in rubble, and almost exclusively populated by Poles.

Saddle on a Cow: Poland Under Communism

Poland suffered horribly under the communists. A postwar intimidation regime was designed to frighten people "on board" and

The Heritage of Communism

Poland has been free, democratic, and capitalist since 1989, but some adults carry lots of psychological baggage from living under communism. While the vast majority of Poles much prefer the current system to the old one, even the gloomiest memories are tinged with nostalgia. A friend who was 13 in 1989 recalled those days this way:

"My childhood is filled with happy memories. Under communism, life was family-oriented. Careers didn't matter. There was no way to get rich, no reason to rush, so we had time. People always had time.

"But there were also shortages—many things were 'in deficit.' We stood in line not knowing what would be for sale. We'd buy whatever shoes were available and then trade. At grocery stores, vinegar and mustard were always on the shelf, along with plastic cheese to make it seem less empty. Milk and bread were very low quality—it wasn't unusual to find a cigarette butt in your loaf. We had to carry ration coupons, which we'd present when buying a staple that was in short supply. They'd snip a corner off the coupon after making the sale. We didn't necessarily buy what we needed—just anything that could be bartered on the black market. I remember my mother and father had to

coincided with government seizure of private property, rationing, and food shortages. The country enjoyed a relatively open society under Premier Władysław Gomułka in the 1960s, but the impractical, centrally planned economy began to unravel in the 1970s. Stores were marked by long lines stretching around the block.

The little absurdities of communist life—which today seem almost comical—made every day a struggle. For years, every elderly woman in Poland had hair the same strange magenta color. There was only one color of dye available, so if you had dyed hair, the choice was simple: Let your hair grow out (and look clownishly half red and half white), or line up and go red.

During these difficult times, the Poles often rose up—staging major protests in 1956, 1968, 1970, and 1976. Stalin famously noted that introducing communism to the Poles was like putting a saddle on a cow.

When an anti-communist Polish cardinal named Karol Wojtyła was elected pope in 1978, then visited his homeland in 1979, it was a sign to his countrymen that change was in the air. (For more on St. John Paul II, see page 268.) In 1980, Lech Wałęsa, 'organize' for special events...somehow find a good sausage and some Coca-Cola.

"Instead of a tidy roll of toilet paper, bathrooms came with a wad of old newspapers. Sometimes my uncle would bring us several toilet paper rolls, held together with a string—absolutely the best gift anyone could give.

"Boys in my neighborhood collected pop cans. Since drinks were very limited in Poland, cans from other countries represented a world of opportunities beyond our borders. Parents could buy their children these cans on the black market, and the few families who were allowed to travel returned home with a treasure trove of cans. One boy up the street from me went to Italy, and proudly brought home a Pepsi can. All of the boys in the neighborhood wanted to see it—it was a huge status symbol. But a month later, communism ended, you could buy whatever you wanted, and everyone's can collections were worthless.

"We had real chocolate only for Christmas. The rest of the year, for treats we got something called 'chocolate-like product,' which was sweet, dark, and smelled vaguely of chocolate. And we had oranges from Cuba for Christmas, too. Everybody was excited when the newspapers announced, 'The boat with the oranges from Cuba is just five days from Poland.' We waited with excitement all year for chocolate and those oranges. The smell of Christmas was so special. Now we have that smell every day. Still, my happiest Christmases were under communism."

an electrician at the shipyards in Gdańsk, became the leader of the Solidarity movement, the first workers' union in communist Eastern Europe. After an initial 18-day strike at the Gdańsk shipyards, the communist regime gave in, legalizing Solidarity (for more on Solidarity, see page 464).

But the union grew too powerful, and the communists felt their control slipping away. On Sunday, December 13, 1981, Poland's head of state, General Wojciech Jaruzelski, declared martial law in order to "forestall Soviet intervention." (Whether the Soviets actually would have intervened remains a hotly debated issue.) Tanks ominously rolled through the streets of Poland on that snowy December morning, and the Poles were terrified.

Martial law lasted until 1983. Each Pole has his or her own chilling memories of this frightening time. During riots, the people would flock into churches—the only place they could be safe from the ZOMO (riot police). People would go for their evening walks during the 19:30 government-sanctioned national news as a sign of protest. But Solidarity struggled on, going underground and becoming a united movement of all demographics, 10 million members strong (more than a quarter of the population).

In July of 1989, the ruling Communist Party agreed to hold open elections (reserving 65 percent of representatives for themselves). Their goal was to appease Solidarity, but the plan backfired: Communists didn't win a single contested seat. These elections helped spark the chain reaction across Eastern Europe that eventually tore down the Iron Curtain. Lech Wałęsa became Poland's first post-communist president. (For more on Lech Wałęsa, see page 466.)

Poland in the 21st Century

When 10 new countries joined the European Union in May 2004, Poland was the most ambivalent of the bunch. After centuries of being under other empires' authority, the Poles were hardly eager to relinquish some of their hard-fought autonomy to Brussels. Many Poles thought that EU membership would make things worse (higher prices, a loss of traditional lifestyles) before they got better. But most people agreed that their country had to join to survive in today's Europe. Today most Poles begrudgingly acknowledge that the benefits of EU membership have outweighed the drawbacks.

The most obvious initial impact of EU membership was the tremendous migration of young Poles seeking work in other EU countries (mostly Britain, Ireland, and Sweden, which were the first to waive visa requirements for Eastern European workers). Many found employment at hotels and restaurants. Visitors to London and Dublin noticed a surprising language barrier at hotel front desks, and Polish-language expat newspapers joined British gossip rags on newsstands. Those who remained in Poland were concerned about the "brain drain" of bright young people flocking out of their country. But with the recent global recession, quite a few Polish expats returned home. For more on this phenomenon, see "The Polish Plumber Syndrome" sidebar on page 1306.

Poland is by far the most populous of the recent EU members, with nearly 39 million people (about the same as Spain, or about half the size of Germany). This makes Poland the sixth-largest of the 27 EU member states—giving it serious political clout, which it has already asserted...sometimes to the dismay of the EU's more established powers.

On the American political spectrum, Poland may be the most "conservative" country in Europe. Poles are phobic when it comes to "big government"—likely because they've been subjugated and manipulated by so many foreign oppressors over the centuries. For most of the 2000s, the country's right wing was represented by a pair of twin brothers, Lech and Jarosław Kaczyński. (The Kaczyński brothers were child actors who appeared in several popular movies together.) Their conservative Law and Justice Party is

Polish Jokes

Through the dreary communist times, the Poles managed to keep their sense of humor. A popular target of jokes was the riot police, called the ZOMO. Here are just a few of the things Poles said about these unpopular cops:

- It's better to have a sister who's a whore than a brother in the ZOMO.
- ZOMO police are hired based on the 90-90 principle: They have to weigh at least 90 kilograms (200 pounds), and their I.Q. must be less than 90.
- ZOMO are dispatched in teams of three: one who can read, one who can write, and a third to protect those other two smart guys.
- A ZOMO policeman was sitting on the curb, crying. Someone came up to him and asked what was wrong. "I lost my dog!" he said. "No matter," the person replied. "He's a smart police dog. I'm sure he can find his way back to the station." "Yes," the ZOMO said. "But without him, I can't!"

The communists gave their people no options at elections: If you voted, you voted for the regime. Poles liked to joke that in some ways, this made communists like God—who created Eve, then said to Adam, "Now choose a wife." It was said that communists could run a pig as a candidate, and it would still win; a popular symbol of dissent became a pig painted with the words "Vote Red."

There were even jokes about jokes. Under communism, Poles noted that there was a government-sponsored prize for the funniest political joke: 15 years in prison.

pro-tax cuts, fiercely Euroskeptic (anti-EU), and very Catholic. In the 2005 presidential election, Lech Kaczyński emerged as the victor; several months later, he took the controversial step of appointing his identical twin brother Jarosław as Poland's prime minister.

The political pendulum swung back toward the center in October of 2007, when the Kaczyński brothers' main political rival, the pro-EU Donald Tusk, led his Civic Platform Party to victory in the parliamentary elections. The name Kaczyński loosely means "duck"—so the Poles quipped that they were led by "Donald and the Ducks."

Tragically, the levity wasn't to last. On April 10, 2010, a plane carrying President Lech Kaczyński crashed in a thick fog near the city of Smolensk, Russia. All 96 people on board—including top government, military, and business officials, high-ranking clergy, and others—were killed, plunging the nation into a period of stunned mourning. Poles wondered why, yet again, an

Bar Mleczny (Milk Bar)

When you see a "bar" in Poland, it doesn't mean alcohol—it means cheap grub. Eating at a *bar mleczny* (bar MLECH-neh) is an essential Polish sightsee-ing experience. These cafeterias, which you'll see all over the coun-try, are an incredibly cheap way to get a good meal...and, with the right attitude, a fun cultural experience.

In the communist era, the government subsidized the food at milk bars, allowing workers to enjoy a meal out. The tradi-tion continues today, as milk-bar prices remain astoundingly low: My bill for a filling meal usu-ally comes to about $5. And, while communist-era fare was gross, today's milk-bar cuisine is usually quite tasty.

Milk bars usually offer many of the traditional tastes listed in the "Polish Food" section. Common items are soups (like *żurek* and *barszcz*), a variety of cabbage-based salads, *kotlet* (fried pork chops), pierogi (like ravioli, with various fillings), and *naleśniki* (pancakes). You'll see glasses of juice and (of course) milk, but most milk bars also stock bottles of water and Coke.

There are two types of milk bars: updated, modern cafeterias that cater to tourists (English menus), add some modern twists to their traditional fare, and charge about 50 percent more; and time-machine dives that haven't changed for decades. At truly traditional milk bars, the service is aimed at locals, which means no English menu and a confusing ordering system.

Every milk bar is a little different, but here's the general procedure: Head to the counter, wait to be acknowledged, and point to what you want. Handy vocabulary: *to* (sounds like "toe") means "this"; *i* (pronounced "ee") means "and."

If the milk-bar lady asks you any questions, you have three options: nod stupidly until she just gives you something; repeat one of the things she just said (assuming she's asked you to choose between two options, like meat or cheese in your pierogi); or hope that a kindly English-speaking Pole in line will leap to your rescue. If nothing else, ordering at a milk bar is an adventure in gestures. Smiling seems to slightly extend the patience of milk-bar staffers.

Once your tray is all loaded up, pay the cashier, do a double-take when you realize how cheap your bill is, then find a table. After the meal, bus your own dishes to the little window.

unprecedented tragedy had befallen their nation. (Ironically, the group's trip was intended to put a painful chapter of Poland's history to rest: a commemoration of the Polish officers and enlisted men killed in the Soviet massacre at Katyń.)

The ensuing presidential election pitted the deceased president's brother, Jarosław Kaczyński, against Donald Tusk's Civic Platform compatriot, Bronisław Komorowski. Komorowski's victory—and Donald Tusk's re-election as prime minister in 2011 (the first re-election of a PM since the end of communism)—have given the centrist Civic Platform the reins of Poland for the foreseeable future.

Meanwhile, Poland's economy has kept chugging along, even as the rest of Europe and much of the world were bogged down by an economic downturn. More than a quarter of Poland's trade is with neighboring Germany—another of Europe's healthiest economies—and Poland was the only European Union country that didn't have a recession in 2009. When I asked some Polish friends about this, they replied—cynically, but not without a hint of truth—"Well, when you have a backwards, agrarian economy, you're pretty resistant to international market fluctuations." Poland is a big, self-sustaining, insular economy. In recent years, Poland's relatively weak currency ("cheaper" than the euro, yet also shielded from euro volatility) and robust economy are luring foreign investment, paradoxically threatening the very autonomy that has buffered it so far. As Europe struggles to deal with its debt crisis and flagging economic might, it will be interesting to see the role that Poland plays.

In 2014, in a move indicative of Poland's importance on the European stage, Donald Tusk left his post as prime minister to become the president of the European Council—the top job of the entire European Union. As Tusk moved to Brussels to assume his post, his successor (and fellow Civic Platform member), Ewa Kopacz, became prime minster—and, one would hope, will continue to spur Poland's evolution.

POLAND

POLISH FOOD

Polish food is hearty and tasty. Because Poland is north of the

Carpathian Mountains, its weather tends to be chilly, which limits the kinds of fruits and vegetables that flourish here. As in other northern European countries (such as Russia or Scandinavia), dominant staples include potatoes, dill, berries, beets, and rye. Much of what you might think of as "Jewish cuisine" turns up on Polish menus (gefilte fish, potato pancakes, chicken soup, and so forth)—which makes sense, given that Poles and Jews lived in the same area for centuries under the same climatic and culinary influences.

Polish soups are a highlight. The most typical are *żurek* and *barszcz*. *Żurek* (often translated as "sour soup" on menus) is a light-colored soup made from a sourdough base, usually containing a hard-boiled egg and pieces of *kiełbasa* (sausage). *Barszcz*, better known to Americans as borscht, is a savory beet soup that you'll see in several varieties: *Barszcz czerwony* (red borscht) is a thin, flavorful broth with a deep red color, sometimes containing dumplings or a hard-boiled egg. *Barszcz ukraiński* (Ukrainian borscht) is similar, but has vegetables mixed in (usually cabbage, beans, and carrots). In summer, try the "Polish gazpacho"—*chłodnik*, a cream soup with beets, onions, and radishes that's served cold. I never met a Polish soup I didn't like...until I was introduced to *flaki* (sometimes *flaczki*)—tripe soup.

Another familiar Polish dish is pierogi. These ravioli-like dumplings come with various fillings. The most traditional are minced meat, sauerkraut, mushroom, cheese, and blueberry; many restaurants also experiment with more exotic fillings. Pierogi are often served with specks of fatty bacon to add flavor. Pierogi are a budget traveler's dream: Restaurants serving them are everywhere, and they're generally cheap, tasty, and very filling.

Bigos is a rich and delicious sauerkraut stew cooked with meat, mushrooms, and whatever's in the pantry. *Gołąbki* is a dish of cabbage leaves stuffed with minced meat and rice in a tomato or mushroom sauce. *Kotlet schabowy* (fried pork chop)—once painfully scarce in communist Poland—remains a local favorite to this day. *Kaczka* (duck) is popular, as is freshwater fish: Look for *pstrąg* (trout), *karp* (carp, beware of bones), and *węgorz* (eel). On the Baltic Coast (such as in Gdańsk), you'll also see *łosoś* (salmon), *śledź* (herring), and *dorsz* (cod). Poles eat lots of potatoes, which are served with nearly every meal.

For a snack on the go, Poles love *zapiekanki* (singular *zapiekanek*): a toasted baguette with melted cheese, garlic, ketchup or other sauces, rubbery mushrooms from a can, and sometimes onions or other toppings. It's like the poor cousin of a French-bread pizza, and is a favorite late-night snack for bar-hopping young people. The bagel-like rings you'll see sold on the street, *obwarzanki* (singular *obwarzanek*), are also cheap, and usually fresh and tasty.

Poland has good pastries. A *piekarnia* is a bakery specializing in breads. But if you really want something special, look for a *cukiernia* (pastry shop). The classic Polish treat is *pączki*, glazed jelly doughnuts. They can have different fillings, but most typical is a wild-rose jam. *Szarlotka* is apple cake—sometimes made with chunks of apples (especially in season), sometimes with apple filling. *Sernik* is cheesecake, and *makowiec* is poppy-seed cake. *Winebreda* is an especially gooey Danish. *Babeczka* is like a cupcake filled with pudding. You may see *jabłko w cieście*—slices of apple cooked in dough, then glazed. *Napoleonka* is a French-style treat with layers of crispy wafers and custard.

Lody (ice cream) is popular. The tall, skinny cones of soft-serve ice cream are called *świderki*, sometimes translated as "American ice cream." The most beloved traditional candy is *ptasie mleczko* (birds' milk), which is like a semi-sour marshmallow covered with chocolate. E. Wedel is the country's top brand of chocolate, with outlets in all the big cities (see page 428).

Thirsty? *Woda* is water, *woda mineralna* is bottled water (*gazowana* is with gas, *niegazowana* is without), *kawa* is coffee, *herbata* is tea, *sok* is juice, and *mleko* is milk. Żywiec, Okocim, and Lech are the best-known brands of *piwo* (beer).

Wódka (vodka) is a Polish staple—the word means, roughly, "precious little water." Żubrówka, the most famous brand of vodka, comes with a blade of grass from the bison reserves in eastern Poland (look for the bottle with the bison). The bison "flavor" the grass...then the grass flavors the vodka. Poles often mix Żubrówka with apple juice, and call this cocktail *szarlotka* ("apple cake"); it also goes by the name *tatanka* (a Native American word for "bison"). For "Cheers!" say, "*Na zdrowie!*" (nah ZDROH-vyeh).

Unusual drinks to try if you have the chance are *kwas* (a cold, fizzy, Ukrainian-style nonalcoholic beverage made from day-old rye bread) and *kompot* (a hot drink made from stewed berries). Poles are unusually fond of carrot juice (often cut with fruit juice); Kubuś is the most popular brand.

"Bon appétit" *is* "*Smacznego*" (smatch-NEH-goh). To pay, ask for the *rachunek* (rah-KHOO-nehk).

POLISH LANGUAGE

Polish is closely related to its neighboring Slavic languages (Slovak and Czech), with the biggest difference being that Polish has lots of fricatives (hissing sounds—"sh" and "ch"—often in close proximity). Consider the opening line of Poland's most famous tongue-twisting nursery rhyme: *W Szczebrzeszynie chrząszcz brzmi w trzcinie* ("In Szczebrzeszyn, a beetle is heard in the reeds"—pronounced vuh shih-chehb-zheh-shee-nyeh khzhahshch bzh-mee vuh tzhuh-cheen-yeh...or something like that).

Polish intimidates Americans with long, difficult-to-pronounce words. But if you take your time and sound things out, you'll quickly develop an ear for it. One rule of thumb to help you out: The stress is always on the next-to-last syllable.

POLAND

Polish has some letters that don't appear in English, and some letters and combinations are pronounced differently than in English:

ć, ci, and **cz** all sound like "ch" as in "church"

ś, si, and **sz** all sound like "sh" as in "short"

ż, ź, zi, and **rz** all sound like "zh" as in "leisure"

dż and **dź** both sound like the "dj" sound in "jeans"

ń and **ni** sound like "ny" as in "canyon"

ę and **ą** are pronounced nasally, as in French: "en" and "an"

c sounds like "ts" as in "cats"

ch sounds like "kh" as in the Scottish "loch"

j sounds like "y" as in "yellow"

w sounds like "v" as in "Victor"

ł sounds like "w" as in "with"

So to Poles, "Lech Wałęsa" isn't pronounced "lehk wah-LEH-sah," as Americans tend to say—but "lehkh vah-WEHN-sah."

The Polish people you meet will be impressed and flattered if you take the time to learn a little of their language. To get started, check out the selection of Polish survival phrases on the following pages.

As you're tracking down addresses, these words will help: *miasto* (mee-AH-stoh, town), *plac* (plahts, square), *rynek* (REE-nehk, big market square), *ulica* (OO-leet-sah, road), *aleja* (ah-LAY-yah, avenue), and *most* (mohst, bridge).

Polish Survival Phrases

Keep in mind a few Polish pronunciation tips: **w** sounds like "v,"
ł sounds like "w," **ch** is a back-of-your-throat "kh" sound (as in the Scottish
"loch"), and **rz** sounds like the "zh" sound in "pleasure." The vowels with a
tail (**ą** and **ę**) have a slight nasal "n" sound at the end, similar to French.

English	Polish	Pronunciation
Hello. (formal)	*Dzień dobry.*	jehn **doh**-brih
Hi. / Bye. (informal)	*Cześć.*	cheshch
Do you speak English? (asked of a man)	*Czy Pan mówi po angielsku?*	chih pahn **moo**-vee poh ahn-**gyehl**-skoo
Do you speak English? (asked of a woman)	*Czy Pani mówi po angielsku?*	chih **pah**-nee **moo**-vee poh ahn-**gyehl**-skoo
Yes. / No.	*Tak. / Nie.*	tahk / nyeh
I (don't) understand.	*(Nie) rozumiem.*	(nyeh) roh-**zoo**-myehm
Please. / You're welcome. / Can I help you?	*Proszę.*	**proh**-sheh
Thank you (very much).	*Dziękuję (bardzo).*	jehn-**koo**-yeh (**bard**-zoh)
Excuse me. / I'm sorry.	*Przepraszam.*	psheh-**prah**-shahm
(No) problem.	*(Żaden) problem.*	(**zhah**-dehn) **proh**-blehm
Good.	*Dobrze.*	**dohb**-zheh
Goodbye.	*Do widzenia.*	doh veed-**zay**-nyah
one / two / three	*jeden / dwa / trzy*	**yeh**-dehn / dvah / tzhih
four / five / six	*cztery / pięć / sześć*	**chteh**-rih / pyench / sheshch
seven / eight	*siedem / osiem*	**shyeh**-dehm / **oh**-shehm
nine / ten	*dziewięć / dziesięć*	**jeh**-vyench / **jeh**-shench
hundred / thousand	*sto / tysiąc*	stoh / **tih**-shants
How much?	*Ile?*	**ee**-leh
local currency	*złoty (zł)*	**zwoh**-tih
Write it.	*Napisz to.*	**nah**-peesh toh
Is it free?	*Czy to jest za darmo?*	chih toh yehst zah **dar**-moh
Is it included?	*Czy jest to wliczone?*	chih yehst toh vlee-**choh**-neh
Where can I find / buy...?	*Gdzie mogę dostać / kupić...?*	guh-**dyeh** moh-geh doh-statch / **koo**-peech
I'd like... (said by a man)	*Chciałbym...*	**khchaw**-beem
I'd like... (said by a woman)	*Chciałabym...*	**khchah**-wah-beem
We'd like...	*Chcielibyśmy...*	**khchehl**-ee-bish-mih
...a room.	*...pokój.*	**poh**-kooy
...a ticket to ___.	*...bilet do ___.*	**bee**-leht doh
Is it possible?	*Czy jest to możliwe?*	chih yehst toh mohzh-**lee**-veh
Where is...?	*Gdzie jest...?*	guh-**dyeh** yehst
...the train station	*...dworzec kolejowy*	**dvoh**-zhehts koh-leh-**yoh**-vih
...the bus station	*...dworzec autobusowy*	**dvoh**-zhehts ow-toh-boos-**oh**-vih
...the tourist information office	*...informacja turystyczna*	een-for-**maht**-syah too-ris-**titch**-nah
...the toilet	*...toaleta*	toh-ah-**leh**-tah
men / women	*męska / damska*	**mehn**-skah / **dahm**-skah
left / right / straight	*lewo / prawo / prosto*	**leh**-voh / **prah**-voh / **proh**-stoh
At what time...?	*O której godzinie...?*	oh kuh-**too**-ray gohd-**zhee**-nyeh
...does this open / close	*...będzie otwarte / zamknięte*	**bend**-zheh oht-**vahr**-teh / zahm-**knyehn**-teh
Just a moment.	*Chwileczkę.*	khvee-**letch**-keh
now / soon / later	*teraz / niedługo / później*	**teh**-rahz / nyed-**woo**-goh / **poozh**-nyey
today / tomorrow	*dzisiaj / jutro*	**jee**-shigh / **yoo**-troh

In a Polish Restaurant

English	Polish	Pronunciation
I'd like to reserve... (said by a man)	Chciałbym zarezerwować...	**khchaw**-beem zah-reh-zehr-**voh**-vahch
I'd like to reserve... (said by a woman)	Chciałabym zarezerwować...	**khchah**-wah-beem zah-reh-zehr-**voh**-vahch
We'd like to reserve...	Chcielibyśmy zarezerwować...	**khchehl**-ee-bish-mih zah-reh-zehr-**voh**-vahch
...a table for one person / two people.	...stolik na jedną osobę / dwie osoby.	**stoh**-leek nah **yehd**-now oh-**soh**-beh / dvyeh oh-**soh**-bih
Is this table free?	Czy ten stolik jest wolny?	chih tehn **stoh**-leek yehst **vohl**-nih
Can I help you?	W czym mogę pomóc?	vchim **moh**-geh **poh**-moots
The menu (in English), please.	Menu (po angielsku), proszę.	**meh**-noo (poh ahn-**gyehl**-skoo) **proh**-sheh
service (not) included	usługa (nie) wliczona	oos-**woo**-gah (nyeh) **vlee**-choh-nah
cover charge	wstęp	vstenp
"to go"	na wynos	nah **vih**-nohs
with / without	z / bez	z / behz
and / or	i / lub	ee / loob
milk bar (cheap cafeteria)	bar mleczny	bar **mletch**-nih
fixed-price meal (of the day)	zestaw (dnia)	**zehs**-tahv (dih-**nyah**)
specialty of the house	specjalność zakładu	speht-**syahl**-nohshch zah-**kwah**-doo
half portion	pół porcji	poow **ports**-yee
daily special	danie dnia	**dah**-nyeh dih-**nyah**
appetizers	przystawki	pshih-**stahv**-kee
bread	chleb	khlehb
cheese	ser	sehr
sandwich	kanapka	kah-**nahp**-kah
soup	zupa	**zoo**-pah
salad	sałatka	sah-**waht**-kah
meat / poultry	mięso / drób	**myehn**-soh / droob
fish / seafood	ryba / owoce morza	**rih**-bah / oh-**voht**-seh **moh**-zhah
fruit / vegetables	owoce / warzywa	oh-**voht**-seh / vah-**zhih**-vah
dessert	deser	**deh**-sehr
(tap) water	woda (z kranu)	**voh**-dah (**skrah**-noo)
mineral water	woda mineralna	**voh**-dah mee-neh-**rahl**-nah
carbonated / not carbonated	gazowana / niegazowana	gah-zoh-**vah**-nah / **nyeh**-gah-zoh-vah-nah
milk	mleko	**mleh**-koh
(orange) juice	sok (pomarańczowy)	sohk (poh-mah-rayn-**choh**-vih)
coffee / tea	kawa / herbata	**kah**-vah / hehr-**bah**-tah
wine	wino	**vee**-noh
red / white	czerwone / białe	chehr-**voh**-neh / bee-**ah**-weh
sweet / dry / semi-dry	słodkie / wytrawne / półwytrawne	**swoht**-kyeh / vih-**trahv**-neh / poow-vih-**trahv**-neh
glass / bottle	szklanka / butelka	**shklahn**-kah / boo-**tehl**-kah
beer	piwo	**pee**-voh
vodka	wódka	**vood**-kah
Cheers!	Na zdrowie!	nah **zdroh**-vyeh
Enjoy your meal.	Smacznego.	smatch-**neh**-goh
More. / Another.	Więcej. / Inny.	**vyehnt**-say / ee-**nih**-nih
The same.	Taki sam.	**tah**-kee sahm
the bill	rachunek	rah-**khoo**-nehk
I'll pay.	Ja płacę.	yah **pwaht**-seh
tip	napiwek	nah-**pee**-vehk
Delicious!	Pyszne!	**pish**-neh

KRAKÓW

Kraków is easily Poland's best destination: a beautiful, old-fashioned city buzzing with history, enjoyable sights, tourists, and college students. Even though the country's capital moved from here to Warsaw 400 years ago, Kraków remains Poland's cultural and intellectual center. Of all of the Eastern European cities laying claim to the boast "the next Prague," Kraków is for real.

Kraków grew wealthy from trade in the late 10th and early 11th centuries. Traders who passed through were required to stop here for a few days and sell their wares at a reduced cost. Local merchants turned around and sold those goods with big price hikes...and Kraków thrived. In 1038, it became Poland's capital.

Tatars invaded in 1241, leaving the city in ruins. Krakovians took this opportunity to rebuild their streets in a near-perfect grid, a striking contrast to the narrow, mazelike lanes of most medieval towns. The destruction also paved the way for the spectacular Main Market Square—still Kraków's best attraction.

King Kazimierz the Great sparked Kraków's Golden Age in the 14th century (see page 261). In 1364, he established the university that still defines the city (and counts Copernicus and St. John Paul II among its alumni).

But Kraków's power waned as Poland's political center shifted to Warsaw. In 1596, the capital officially moved north. At the end of the 18th century, three neighboring powers—Russia, Prussia, and Austria—partitioned Poland, annexing all of its territory and dividing it among themselves. Warsaw ended up as a satellite of oppressive Moscow, and Kraków became a poor provincial backwater of Vienna. After Napoleon briefly reshuffled the map of

Kraków Essentials

English	Polish	Pronounced
Main Train Station	*Kraków Główny*	KROCK-oof GWOHV-nee
Old Town	*Stare Miasto*	STAH-reh mee-AH-stoh
Main Market Square	*Rynek Główny*	REE-nehk GWOHV-nee
Cloth Hall	*Sukiennice*	soo-kyeh-NEET-seh
Floriańska Street	*Ulica Floriańska*	OOH-leet-suh floh-ree-AHN-skah
Park around the Old Town	*Planty*	PLAHN-tee
Castle Hill	*Wawel*	VAH-vehl
Jewish Quarter	*Kazimierz*	kah-ZHEE-mehzh
Vistula River	*Wisła*	VEES-wah
Salt Mine	*Wieliczka*	vee-LEECH-kah
Planned Communist Suburb	*Nowa Huta*	NOH-vah HOO-tah

Europe in the early 19th century, Kraków was granted the status of a semi-independent city-state for about 30 years. The feisty Free City of Kraków, a tiny sliver wedged between three of Europe's mightiest empires, enjoyed an economic boom that saw the creation of the Planty park, the arrival of gas lighting and trams, and the construction of upscale suburbs outside the Old Town. Only after the unsuccessful Kraków Uprising of 1846 was Kraków forcefully brought back into the Austrian fold. But despite Kraków's reduced prominence, Austria's comparatively liberal climate allowed the city to become a haven for intellectuals and progressives (including a young revolutionary thinker from Russia named Vladimir Lenin).

The Nazis overran Poland in September of 1939, installing a ruling body called the *Generalgouvernement*, headed by former attorney Hans Frank. Germany wanted to quickly develop "Krakau" (as they called it) into the German capital of the nation. They renamed the Main Market Square "Adolf-Hitler-Platz," tore down statues of Polish figures (including the Adam Mickiewicz statue that dominates the Main Market Square today), and invested heavily in construction and industrialization (opening the door for Oskar Schindler to come and take over a factory from its

Jewish owners). The German overlords imposed a "New Order" that included seizing businesses, rationing, and a strict curfew for Poles and Jews alike. A special set of "Jewish laws" targeted, then decimated, Poland's huge Jewish population.

Kraków's cityscape—if not its people—emerged from World War II virtually unscathed. But when the communists took over, they decided to give intellectual (and potentially dissident) Kraków an injection of good Soviet values—in the form of heavy industry. They built Nowa Huta, an enormous steelworks and planned town for workers, on Kraków's outskirts, thereby dooming the city to decades of smog. Thankfully, Kraków is now much cleaner than it was 20 years ago.

St. John Paul II was born (as Karol Wojtyła) in nearby Wadowice and served as archbishop of Kraków before being called to Rome. Today, the hometown boy-turned-saint draws lots of pilgrims and is, for many, a big part of the city's attraction. Saintly ties aside, Kraków might be the most Catholic town in Europe's most Catholic country; be sure to visit a few of its many churches.

University life, small but thought-provoking museums, great restaurants, sprawling parks, and Jewish history round out the city's appeal. Over the last generation, Kraków has become the darling of Polish tourism. Today, with hundreds of creative places to eat and drink within its Old Town walls, and with more than its share of sights, it lures an estimated 7 million visitors a year.

PLANNING YOUR TIME

Don't skimp on your time in Kraków. It takes a minimum of two days to experience the city, and a third or fourth day lets you dig in and consider a world of fascinating side-trips. More than just good for sightseeing, Kraków is simply charming; more than any town in Europe, it seems made for aimless strolling.

Almost everyone coming to Kraków also visits the Auschwitz-Birkenau Concentration Camp Memorial—and should—which is about an hour and a half away. This demands the better part of a day to fully appreciate (either as a round-trip from Kraków, or en route to or from another destination), and also requires an online reservation. Auschwitz is covered in detail in the next chapter.

If you have only two full days (the "express plan"), start off with my self-guided walk through the Old Town and a quick stroll up to Wawel Castle, then wind down your day in Kazimierz (the Jewish and nightlife district). Your second day is for a side-trip to Auschwitz, and another evening in Kraków. This plan gives you an enticing once-over-lightly, but leaves almost no time for entering the sights.

More time buys you the chance to relax, enjoy, and linger: Tackle the Old Town and Wawel Castle on the first day,

Kraków's Old Town Sights

OLD MARKET

BAŁOKEGO

KARMELICKA

ASNYKA

ŁOBZOWSKA

DŁUGA

PADEREWSKIEGO

BASZTOWA

GARBARSKA

Planty

PIJARSKA

SŁAWKOWSKA

BARBICAN

FLORIAN GATE

CZARTORYSKI MUSEUM

DUNAJEWSKIEGO

SZCZEPAŃSKA

OLD

SW. MARKA

SW. JANA

FLORIAŃSKA

KRUPNICZA

SW. TOMASZA

SZOŁAYSKI HOUSE

STUDENSKA

PODWALE

SZEWSKA

SW. ANNY

Main Market Square

CLOTH HALL

5

ST. MARY'S

COLLEGIUM MAIUS

JAGIELLOŃSKA

4 3

MICKIEWICZ STATUE

Small Market Square

JABŁONOWSKICH

10

TOWN HALL TOWER

ST. ADALBERT'S

SIENNA

GOŁĘBIA

OLSZEWSKIEGO

PIŁSUDSKIEGO

PASAŻ 13 MALL

9

WIŚLNA

ARCH-BISHOP'S MANSION

BRACKA

GRODZKA

STOLARSKA

DOMINICAN CHURCH

DOMINIKAŃSKA

To Airport, Auschwitz & Kościuszko Mound

SMOLEŃSK

FRANCISZKAŃSKA

POST OFFICE

TOWN

FELICJANEK

6

ZWIERZYNIECKA

STRASZEWSKIEGO

ST. FRANCIS

WYSPIAŃSKI PAVILION

Planty

8

POSELSKA

MILK BAR

SENACKA

STS. PETER & PAUL

SAREGO

Mary Mag. Square

BISHOP ERAZM CIOŁEK PALACE

GRODZKA

ST. ANDREW'S

KANONICZA

ARCHDIOCESAN MUSEUM

JOHN PAUL II CENTER

POWIŚLE

PODZAMCZE

CATHEDRAL

SW. IDZIEGO

SW. GERTRUDY

1

INNER COURTYARD

Vistula River

WAWEL HILL

LOST WAWEL MUSEUM

2

DRAGON STATUE

ST. BERNARD'S

BERNARDYŃSKA

STRADOWSKA

KONOPNICKIEJ

KOLETEK

KRAKÓW

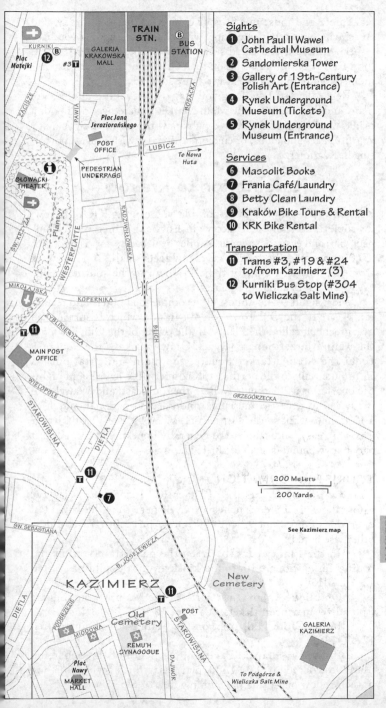

Sights

1. John Paul II Wawel Cathedral Museum
2. Sandomierska Tower
3. Gallery of 19th-Century Polish Art (Entrance)
4. Rynek Underground Museum (Tickets)
5. Rynek Underground Museum (Entrance)

Services

6. Massolit Books
7. Frania Café/Laundry
8. Betty Clean Laundry
9. Kraków Bike Tours & Rental
10. KRK Bike Rental

Transportation

11. Trams #3, #19 & #24 to/from Kazimierz (3)
12. Kurniki Bus Stop (#304 to Wieliczka Salt Mine)

Kazimierz and museums of your choice on the second day, and Auschwitz (and other side-trips) with additional days. If you have a special interest, you could side-trip to Wieliczka Salt Mine, St. John Paul II pilgrimage sites on the outskirts of town, or the communist architecture of the Nowa Huta suburb.

Regardless of how long you stay, your evening choices are many and varied: Savor the Main Market Square over dinner or a drink, take in a jazz show, do a pub crawl through the city's many youthful bars and clubs, or enjoy traditional Jewish music and cuisine in Kazimierz.

Orientation to Kraków

Kraków (Poles say KROCK-oof, but you can say KRACK-cow; it's sometimes spelled "Cracow" in English) is mercifully compact, flat, and easy to navigate. While the urban sprawl is big (with 757,000 people), the tourist's Kraków feels small. You can walk from the northern edge of the Old Town to the southern edge (Wawel Hill) in about 15 minutes.

Most sights—and almost all recommended hotels and restaurants—are in the Old Town (Stare Miasto), which is surrounded by a greenbelt called the Planty. In the center of the Old Town lies the Main Market Square (Rynek Główny, a.k.a. "the Square"). From the Main Market Square, the main train station is a 15-minute walk to the northeast; Kazimierz (the Jewish and nightlife quarter) is a 20-minute walk to the southeast; and Wawel Hill (with a historic castle, museums, and Poland's national church) is a 10-minute walk south. Just beyond Wawel is the Vistula River. Taxis are easy, and cabbies are generally honest; you can get just about anywhere in a snap for 10-15 zł.

TOURIST INFORMATION

Kraków has many helpful TIs, called InfoKraków (www. infokrakow.pl). Five branches are in or near the Old Town (all open daily May-Sept 9:00-19:00, Oct-April 9:00-17:00, unless otherwise noted):

• In the **Planty** park, between the main train station and Main Market Square (in round kiosk at ulica Szpitalna 25, tel. 12-432-0110)

• On **ulica Św. Jana,** just north of the Main Market Square (specializes in concert tickets, at #2, tel. 12-421-7787)

• In the **Cloth Hall** right on the Main Market Square (tel. 12-433-7310)

• In the **Wyspiański Pavilion,** just south of the Square on ulica Grodzka (daily 9:00-17:00, plac Wszystkich Świętych 3, not at the window but inside the building, tel. 12-616-1886)

• Just west of **Wawel Hill** (also covers the entire region, Powiśle 11, mobile 513-099-688)

Other TI branches are in **Kazimierz** (daily 9:00-17:00, ulica Józefa 7, tel. 12-422-0471) and the **airport** (daily 9:00-19:00, tel. 12-285-5341).

At any TI, ask what's new in fast-changing Kraków, browse the brochures, and pick up the free map and the *Kraków Tourist Information Compendium* booklet. The TIs also offer a free room-finding service and sell tickets for bus tours and walking tours (though only for one walking-tour company, See Kraków; for other options, see "Tours in Kraków," later).

Sightseeing Pass: The TI's **Kraków Tourist Card** isn't a good value for most visitors. It covers public transportation, includes admission to several city museums (basically everything except the Wawel Hill sights and Wieliczka Salt Mine), and offers discounts to outlying sights and tours—but Kraków's museums are already cheap, and public transportation is mostly unnecessary (75 zł/2 days, 95 zł/3 days).

Warning: Many private travel agencies, room-booking services, and tour operators masquerade as TIs, with deceptive blue-and-white *i* signs. If I haven't listed them in this section, they're not a real TI.

ARRIVAL IN KRAKÓW

By Train: Kraków's slick, new main train station (called "Kraków Główny"), just northeast of the Old Town, is very user-friendly. The main concourse has all of the amenities, and then some: ATMs, lockers (under the big schedule board between the ticket windows), WCs, takeaway coffee, a handy Biedronka mini-super-market, giant informational touchscreens, and a complete mini-shopping mall. The main concourse has a long row of numbered ticket windows (some for domestic tickets only, others for domestic and international—check signs before you line up). Consider booking your ticket at the Passenger Service Center (in the middle of the row of ticket windows, between #11 and #12)—it may have a longer wait, but they're more likely to speak English and can be helpful if you have a complicated request (no extra fee, daily 8:00-19:40). From the ticket area, numbered escalators lead directly up to the platforms above.

The halls of the train station flow into the vast, modern Galeria Krakowska shopping mall—a glittering gauntlet of con-sumerism. To find anything in this confusing complex, follow the English signs (*Station Hall* is for tickets). The mall and the station face a broad plaza (plac Dworcowy), across the ring road from the Planty park and Old Town.

Taxis from the station are cheap and easy: From the tracks, take the elevator or stairs to the rooftop above you, where you'll find a giant parking lot where taxis wait. Be sure to use a taxi clearly marked with a company name and telephone number. Additional taxis wait outside both ends of the station. The usual metered rate to downtown is a reasonable 10-15 zł.

Most hotels are within easy **walking** distance of the station. It's about a 15-minute stroll to the Main Market Square. Just follow *Exit to the City* and *Old Town* signs, and you'll be routed directly into, and through, the Galeria Krakowska mall. At the far end of the mall, you can either turn left and continue to follow signs for the Old Town; or, if you're headed to Kazimierz, go out the doors straight ahead to hop on tram #3. If you head to the Old Town, you'll pop out into plac Dworcowy; continue straight ahead to take the broad ramp down into a pedestrian underpass beneath the busy ring road. Emerging into the Planty on the other side, the Main Market Square is straight ahead (you'll see the twin spires of St. Mary's Church).

By Bus: The bus station is directly behind the main train station. When arriving by bus, it's easiest to get into town by first heading into the train station, then continuing through it, following the above directions.

To get *to* the bus station from the Old Town (such as to catch a bus to Auschwitz), first head to the main train station (go through the Planty park and use the underpass). Once in the station, head all the way through to the far end (past platform 5, exit marked for *bus station*). Exiting the train station, escalate up to the bus terminal (marked *MDA Dworzec Autobusowy*). Inside are the standard amenities (lockers and WCs), domestic and international ticket windows, and an electronic board showing the next several departures. Some bus departures, marked on the board with a green *G*, leave from the upper *(gorna)* stalls, which you can see out the window. Other bus departures, marked with a red *D*, leave from the lower *(dolna)* stalls; to find these, use the stairs or the elevator right in the middle of the bus terminal. Note that some minibuses, such as those to Auschwitz, also leave from, or near, this station (though the buses and minibuses that go to the Wieliczka Salt Mine leave from the opposite end of the station/mall complex—see page 320).

By Car: *Centrum* signs lead you into the Old Town—you'll know you're there when you hit the ring road that surrounds the Planty park. Parking garages surround the Old Town. Your hotelier can advise you on directions and parking.

By Plane: The small, modern **John Paul II Kraków-Balice Airport** is about 10 miles west of the center, with separate international and domestic terminals (airport code: KRK, airport info: tel. 12-295-5800, www.krakowairport.pl). To get to downtown

Kraków, you can take a speedy train, a slower public bus, or a taxi.

The handy train is the fastest choice (unless it's closed for maintenance)—it zips you from the terminal straight to the main train station's platform 1 (10 zł, buy ticket from machine or from conductor on train, 2/hour, 18 minutes; see train arrival instructions earlier).

To get from the airport to Kraków's main bus station by **public bus,** catch bus #208, #292, or (at night) #902 in front of the airport (4 zł, 50-minute trip depending on traffic, see bus arrival instructions earlier).

For door-to-door service, hop in a **cab** at the taxi stand in front of the terminal (ask about the fare up front—should be around 70-80 zł, more expensive at night, about 30 minutes). You can also arrange a taxi transfer in advance (such as with recommended driver Andrew Durman, listed later, under "Tours in Kraków"). Various shuttle services also operate for a slightly lower price; ask your hotelier.

Note that many budget flights—including those on Wizz Air and Ryanair—use the **International Airport Katowice in Pyrzowice** (Międzynarodowy Port Lotniczy Katowice w Pyrzowicach, airport code: KTW, www.katowice-airport.com). This airport is about 18 miles from the city of Katowice, which is about 50 miles west of Kraków. Direct buses run sporadically between Katowice Airport and Kraków's main train station (50 zł, trip takes 1.75 hours, generally scheduled to meet incoming flights). You can also take the bus from Katowice Airport to Katowice's train station (hourly, 50 minutes), then take the train to Kraków (hourly, 1.5 hours). Wizz Air's website is useful for figuring out your connection: www.wizzair.com.

HELPFUL HINTS

Sightseeing Schedules: Some sights are closed on Monday (including the Gallery of 19th-Century Polish Art, Szołayski House, and a few museums in Kazimierz), but many sights are open (including the churches and Jagiellonian University Museum, and in Kazimierz, all of the Jewish-themed sights). On Saturday, most of Kazimierz's Jewish-themed sights are closed. Before heading out, check the "Kraków at a Glance" sidebar on page 252. Also be aware of days that certain sights are free: On Sunday, the National Museum branches (including the Gallery of 19th-Century Polish Art in the Cloth Hall) are free, but some are open limited hours. And on Monday, Schindler's Factory Museum is free (and crowded), as well as two of the sights at Wawel Castle (but open only in the morning).

Post Office: The main post office (Poczta Główna) is at the intersection of Starowiślna and the Westerplatte ring road, a few

KRAKÓW

blocks east of the Main Market Square (Mon-Fri 7:30-20:30, Sat 8:00-14:00, closed Sun).

Bookstore: For an impressive selection of new and used English books, try **Massolit Books,** just west of the Old Town. They also have a café with drinks and light snacks, and a good children's section (Sun-Thu 10:00-20:00, Fri-Sat 10:00-21:00, ulica Felicjanek 4, tel. 12-432-4150, www.massolit.com).

Laundry: Frania Café is a dream come true for a traveler with dirty laundry. Halfway between the Old Town and Kazimierz, this inviting café/pub has ample washers and dryers, relaxing ambience, free Wi-Fi and a loaner laptop, a full bar serving up espresso drinks and laundry-themed hard drinks, very long hours, and a friendly staff. Those in search of a mellow hangout might want to come here even if they don't need to wash clothes (16 zł/load self-service, 26 zł for them to do it for you in 2 hours—consider dropping it off on your way to Kazimierz and picking it up on the way back, likely open daily 10:30-24:00, ulica Starowiślna 26, mobile 783-945-021, www.laundromat.pl).

    Betty Clean is a full-service laundry that's closer to the Old Town, but pricey (about 13 zł/shirt, 22 zł/pants, takes 24 hours, 50 percent more for express 3-hour service, Mon-Fri 7:30-19:30, Sat 8:00-15:30, closed Sun, just outside the Planty park at ulica Zwierzyniecka 6, tel. 12-423-0848).

GETTING AROUND KRAKÓW

Kraków's top sights and best hotels are easily accessible by foot. You'll need wheels only if you're going to the Kazimierz Jewish quarter or the Nowa Huta suburb.

    By Public Transit: Trams and buses zip around Kraków's urban sprawl. The same tickets work system-wide and can be purchased at most kiosks or at the machines (accepting coins and small bills) at most stops. You can also buy tickets on board—some trams have machines on board, which take only coins and cost the same; otherwise, you'll buy your ticket from the driver and pay a bit more.

    A *bilet jednoprzejazdowy,* which covers any single journey (including transfers) costs 3.80 zł. However, many journeys you're likely to take—such as between the Old Town and Kazimierz—are likely to be brief, so you'll save a bit by buying a 20-minute ticket *(20-minutowy)* for 2.80 zł. You can also get longer-term tickets for 24 hours (15 zł), 48 hours (24 zł), and 72 hours (36 zł)—though unless your accommodations are a tram ride away from the sights, you're unlikely to need these. These prices are for a "one-zone" ticket, which covers almost everything of interest in Kraków (including Nowa Huta, the St. John Paul II pilgrimage sites, and the Kościuszko Mound)—unless you're headed for the airport or Wieliczka Salt Mine, which are beyond the city limits and require a slightly more expensive *aglomeracyjny* ticket (4 zł for a single journey). Always validate your ticket when you board the bus or tram (24-, 48-, and 72-hour tickets must be validated only the first time you use them).

By Taxi: Just as in other Eastern European cities, only take cabs that are clearly marked with a company logo and telephone number. Kraków taxis start at 7 zł and charge about 3 zł per kilometer. Rides are usually very short and generally cost less than 20 zł; however, due to the Old Town's many traffic restrictions and pedestrian zones, a "short ride across town" may require looping all the way around the center. You're more likely to get the fair metered rate by calling or hailing a cab, rather than taking one waiting at tourist spots. To call a cab, try **Radio Taxi** (tel. 19191).

By Bike: The riverfront bike path is enticing on a nice day; the Planty park, while inviting, can be a bit crowded for biking. **Kraków Bike Tours** rents a wide variety of new, good-quality bikes (10 zł/first hour, cheaper per hour for longer rentals, 50 zł/day, 60 zł/24 hours, daily 9:30-19:00, just off the Square at Grodzka 2; see listing later, under "Tours in Kraków"). Nearby, **KRK Bike Rental** rents cheaper bikes (8 zł/hour, 45 zł/24 hours, April-Oct daily 9:00-21:00, less in bad weather, closed Nov-March, ulica Św. Anny 4, mobile 509-267-733, www.krkbikerental.pl).

Tours in Kraków

Local Guides

Hiring a guide in Kraków is fun and affordable, and makes a huge difference in your experience. I've enjoyed working with three in particular, any of whom can show you the sights in Kraków and also have cars for day-tripping into the countryside: **Marta Chmielowska** (350 zł/4 hours, 500 zł/day, same prices by foot or car, can be more for larger groups and for long-distance trips, mobile 603-668-008, martachm7@gmail.com); **Tomasz Klimek** (250 zł/half-day, 400 zł/day, slightly more with a car, mobile 605-231-923, www.krakow.tourism.pl, tomasz.klimek@interia.pl); and **Anna Bakowska** (same prices as Marta, mobile 604-151-293, www.leadertour.eu, leadertour@wp.pl). I wouldn't bother hiring a guide for the trip to Auschwitz (which generally costs 600-700 zł)—only official Auschwitz guides can legally give tours onsite, so you'll wind up joining one of the tours once there. While there's still a benefit to hiring a guide to take you to Auschwitz—door-to-door service and commentary en route—it's a better value to hire a driver (like Andrew, listed next).

Kraków at a Glance

▲▲▲**Main Market Square** Stunning heart of Kraków and a people magnet any time of day. **Hours:** Always open. See page 262.

▲▲▲**Schindler's Factory Museum** Historic building where Oskar Schindler saved more than 1,000 Jewish workers, now filled with engaging exhibit about Kraków's WWII experience. **Hours:** April-Oct Mon 10:00-16:00 (closes at 14:00 first Mon of month), Tue-Sun 10:00-20:00; Nov-March Mon 10:00-14:00, Tue-Sun 10:00-18:00. See page 308.

▲▲**Planty** Once a moat, now a scenic park encircling the city. **Hours:** Always open. See page 256.

▲▲**St. Mary's Church** Landmark church with extraordinary wood-carved Gothic altarpiece. **Hours:** Mon-Sat 11:45-17:45, Sun 14:00-17:45. See page 259.

▲▲**Cloth Hall** Fourteenth-century market hall with 21st-century souvenirs. **Hours:** Summer Mon-Fri 9:00-18:00, Sat-Sun 9:00-15:00, sometimes later; winter Mon-Fri 9:00-16:00, Sat-Sun 9:00-15:00. See page 264.

▲▲**St. Francis Basilica** Lovely Gothic church with some of Poland's best Art Nouveau. **Hours:** Daily 6:00-19:45. See page 266.

▲▲**Wawel Cathedral** Poland's splendid national church, with tons of tombs, a crypt, and a climbable tower. **Hours:** April-Sept Mon-Sat 9:00-17:00, Sun 12:30-17:00; Oct-March Mon-Sat 9:00-16:00, Sun 12:30-16:00. See page 273.

▲▲**Wawel Castle Grounds** Historic hilltop with views, castle, cathedral, courtyard with chakras, and a passel of museums. **Hours:** Grounds open daily 6:00 until dusk, but many of the museums closed Mon, and Sun in winter. See page 277.

▲▲**Gallery of 19th-Century Polish Art** Worthwhile collection of paintings by should-be-famous artists, upstairs in the Cloth Hall. **Hours:** Tue-Sun 10:00-18:00, closed Mon. See page 284.

▲▲**Rynek Underground Museum** Super-modern exhibit on medieval Kraków filling excavated cellars beneath the Main

Market Square. **Hours:** Mon 10:00-20:00, Tue 10:00-16:00 (closed first Tue of month), Wed-Sun 10:00-22:00, shorter hours in winter. See page 291.

▲▲**Old Jewish Cemetery** Poignant burial site in Kazimierz, with graves from 1552 to 1800. **Hours:** Sun-Fri 9:00-16:00, sometimes until 18:00 May-Sept, closes earlier in winter and by sundown on Fri, closed Sat. See page 300.

▲**Czartoryski Museum** Varied collection, with European paintings and Polish armor, handicrafts, and decorative arts. **Hours:** Likely closed for restoration, otherwise Tue-Sun 10:00-16:00, closed Mon. See page 289.

▲**Jagiellonian University Museum: Collegium Maius** Proud collection of historic university, surrounding a tranquil courtyard where medieval professors lived. **Hours:** Entry by guided tour; 30-minute version—Mon-Sat 10:00-15:00, until 18:00 Tue and Thu in April-Oct, no tours Sun; one-hour version in English—usually Mon-Fri at 13:00, no tours Sat-Sun. See page 292.

▲**New Jewish Cemetery** Graveyard with tombs from after 1800, partly restored after Nazi desecration. **Hours:** Sun-Fri 8:00-18:00, until 16:00 in winter, closed Sat. See page 302.

▲**Ethnographic Museum** Traditional rural Polish life on display. **Hours:** Tue-Sat 11:00-19:00, Thu until 21:00, Sun 11:00-15:00, closed Mon. See page 306.

▲**Pharmacy Under the Eagle** Small Podgórze exhibit about the Holocaust in Kraków, including three evocative historic films. **Hours:** April-Oct Mon 10:00-14:00, Tue-Sun 9:00-17:00; Nov-March Mon 10:00-14:00, Tue-Thu and Sat 9:00-17:00, Fri 10:00-17:00, closed Sun and the second Tue of each month. See page 307.

▲**Museum of Contemporary Art in Kraków** Today's thought-provoking art, displayed in renovated old warehouses behind Schindler's Factory Museum. **Hours:** Tue-Sun 11:00-19:00, closed Mon. See page 313.

KRAKÓW

Drivers

Since Kraków is such a useful home base for day trips, it can be handy to splurge on a private driver for door-to-door service. **Andrew (Andrzej) Durman,** a Pole who lived in Chicago and speaks fluent English, is a gregarious driver, translator, miracle worker, and all-around great guy. While not an officially licensed tour guide, Andrew is an eager conversationalist and loves to provide lively commentary while you roll. Although you can hire Andrew for a simple airport transfer or an Auschwitz day trip, he also enjoys tackling more ambitious itineraries, from helping you track down your Polish roots to taking you on multiple-day journeys around Poland and beyond (prices are for up to 4 people if you book direct: 400 zł to Auschwitz, 250 zł to Wieliczka Salt Mine, 80 zł for transfer from Kraków-Balice Airport, 500 zł for transfer from Katowice Airport, 600 zł for an all-day trip into the countryside—such as into the High Tatras or to track down your Polish roots near Kraków, more to cover gas costs for trips longer than 100 km one-way; long-distance transfers for up to 4 people to Prague, Budapest, Vienna, or Berlin for 1,800 zł; also available for multiday trips—price negotiable, all prices higher for bigger van, tel. 12-411-5630, mobile 602-243-306, www.tour-service.pl, andrew@tour-service.pl).

Local guide Marta Chmielowska's husband, **Czesław** (a.k.a. Chester), can also drive you to nearby locations (300 zł for all-day trip to Auschwitz for 1-2 people, 350 zł for 3-8 people; 220 zł to Wieliczka Salt Mine, including waiting time, or a very long day combining Wieliczka and Auschwitz for 550 zł; to book, see Marta's contact information, earlier).

Walking Tours

Various companies run daily city walking tours in English in summer. Most do a three-hour tour of the Old Town as well as a three-hour tour of Kazimierz, the Jewish district (most charge about 50 zł per tour, depending on company). Another option is to combine the Old Town and Kazimierz into a single, four-hour tour (130 zł). Because the scene is continually evolving, it's best to pick up local fliers (the TI works exclusively with one company, See Kraków, but hotel reception desks generally have more options), then choose the one that fits your interests and schedule. Three people can hire their own great local guide for about the same amount of money.

Crazy Guides

This irreverent company offers tours to the communist suburb of Nowa Huta and other outlying sights. For details, see page 321.

Bike and Segway Tours

Kraków Bike Tours is a well-established operation that runs daily three-hour bike tours in English in summer. The tours make 25 stops in the Old Town, Kazimierz, and Podgórze (90 zł, includes loaner bike, May-Sept daily at 10:00 and 15:00, spring and fall only 1/day at 12:00, confirm schedule and meet tour at their office down the passage at Grodzka 2—right at the bottom of the Square, tel. 12-430-2034, mobile 788-800-231, www.krakowbiketour.com, krakowbiketour@gmail.com). They also offer Segway tours (call to arrange, mobile 510-394-657).

Bus Tours

As Kraków is so easily seen on foot, taking a bus tour doesn't make much sense here. But they can be handy for reaching outlying sights. Various tour companies run bus-plus-walking itineraries (each of them around 100-130 zł), including Auschwitz (6 hours), Wieliczka Salt Mine (4 hours), and other regional side-trips. Look for fliers around town.

Buggy Tours

Romantic, horse-drawn buggies trot around Kraków from the Main Market Square. The going rate is a hefty 100 zł for a 30-minute tour.

Golf-Cart Tours

Several outfits around town (including on the Square) offer tours on a golf cart with recorded commentary. Given the limits on car traffic in the old center, this can be a handy way to connect the sights for those with limited mobility. Generally you'll pay about 160 zł for a 45-minute tour around the Old Town; add another 160 zł to extend the trip to Kazimierz, and another 160 zł if you want to continue all the way to the Podgórze former Jewish ghetto and Schindler's Factory Museum (this price is for the entire golf cart, up to 4 people; they also do point-to-point transfers within town for 50 zł).

Kraków's Royal Way Walk

Most of Kraków's major sights are conveniently connected by this self-guided walk. This route is known as the "Royal Way" because the king used to follow this same path when he returned to Kraków after a journey. After the capital moved to Warsaw, most kings still used Wawel Cathedral for important events. In fact, from 1320 to 1795, nearly every Polish king traversed Kraków's Royal Way at least twice: on the day he was crowned and on the day he was buried. You could sprint through this walk in about an hour and a half (less than a mile altogether), but it's much more fun if you take it like the kings did...slowly.

• *Begin just outside the main gate at the north end of the Old Town.*

▲Barbican (Barbakan) and City Walls

Tatars (mysterious and terrifying invaders from Central Asia) attacked Kraków three times in the 13th century. After the first attack destroyed the city in 1241, Krakovians built this wall. The original rampart had 47 watchtowers and eight gates. The big, round defensive fort standing outside the wall is a barbican—built to fortify the defenses after the Tatars had overrun Central and Eastern Europe. Structures like this provided extra fortification to weak sections—namely, the gates.

Imagine how it looked in 1500, when this barbican stood outside the town moat with a long bridge leading to the Florian Gate—the city's main entryway. Today you can pay to scramble along the passages and fortifications of the barbican, though there's little to see inside, other than a small but good exhibit giving you a sense of how the walls were designed. The same ticket also lets you climb up onto the surviving stretch of Old Town walls flanking the Florian Gate (entry from inside walls).

Cost and Hours: 8 zł, April-Oct daily 10:30-18:00, last entry 30 minutes before closing, closed Nov-March.

• *The greenbelt in which the Barbican sits is called the...*

▲▲Planty

By the 19th century, Kraków's no-longer-necessary city wall had fallen into disrepair. As Austrians were doing all over their

empire, they decided to tear down what remained, fill in the moat, and plant trees. (The name comes not from the English "plant," but from the Polish *plantovac,* or "flat"—because they flattened out this area to create it.) Today, the Planty is a beautiful park that stretches 2.5 miles around the entire perimeter of Kraków's Old Town. To give your Kraków visit an extra dimension, consider a quick bike ride around the Planty (best early in the morning, when it's less crowded) with a side-trip along the park-like riverbank near Wawel Castle; you'll see bike-rental places around the Old Town, including the two mentioned on page 251.

Circle around the left side of the Barbican. On your left, keep an eye out for a unique monument depicting an elderly, bearded man in the corner of a huge frame. This honors **Jan Matejko,** arguably Poland's most beloved painter, who specialized in giant-scale epic historical scenes that would easily fill this frame. We'll hear Matejko's name several more times on this walk.

As you continue around the Barbican, look down to see the much lower ground level around its base—making it easy to imagine that the Planty was once anything but flat.

• *Across the busy street from the Barbican, standing in the middle of the long park, is the...*

Grunwald Monument

This memorial honors one of the most important battles in the history of a nation that has seen more than its share: the Battle of Grunwald on July 15, 1410, when Polish and Lithuanian forces banded together to finally defeat the Teutonic Knights, who had been running roughshod over the lands along the Baltic. (For more on the battle and the knights, see page 502.) Lying dramatically slain at the base of this monument, like a toppled Goliath, is the defeated Grand Master of the Teutonic Knights—German crusaders who had originally been brought to Poland as mercenaries. It's easy to see this vanquished statue as a thinly veiled metaphor for one of Poland's powerful, often domineering, neighbors that the Poles stood up to—and defeated. When the Nazis took power here, this statue was one of the first things they tore down. When they left, it was one of the first things the Poles put back up.

• *If you'd like to see a slice of Krakovian life, side-trip one block to the left of the monument, to the local farmers market.*

The Old Market (Stary Kleparz)

The colorful Old Market offers a refreshing dash of today's Kraków that has nothing to do with history or tourism. It's just lots of hardscrabble people selling what they grow or knit, and lots of others buying. Wander around as if on a cultural scavenger hunt. Find the freshest doughnuts *(pączki)*, the most popular bakery, the villager selling slippers she knitted, and the old man with the smoked cheese.

Hours: Mon-Sat 7:00-18:00—but busiest and most interesting in the morning, closed Sun.

• *Now retrace your steps to the Barbican, and enter the Old Town by walking through the...*

Florian Gate (Brama Floriańska)

As you approach the gate, look up at the **white eagle**—representing courage and freedom—the historic symbol of the Polish people.

Inside the gate, notice the little chapel on the right with a replica of the famous **Black Madonna of Częstochowa,** probably the

most important religious symbol among Polish Catholics. The original, located in Częstochowa (70 miles north of Kraków), is an Eastern Orthodox-style icon of mysterious origin with several mystical legends attached to it. After the icon's believed role in protecting a monastery from Swedish invaders in the mid-17th century, it was named "Queen and Protector of Poland."

Once through the gate, look back at it. High above is **St. Florian,** patron of the fire brigade. As fire was a big concern for a wooden city of the 15th century, Florian gets a place of honor.

• *You're standing at the head of Kraków's historic (and now touristic) gamut...*

▲Floriańska Street (Ulica Floriańska)

Hanging on the inside of the city wall in both directions is a makeshift **art gallery,** where—traditionally—starving students hawk the works they've painted at the Academy of Fine Arts (across the busy street from the barbican). These days, the art is so kitschy, this stretch of the town's fortification is nicknamed "The Wailing Wall."

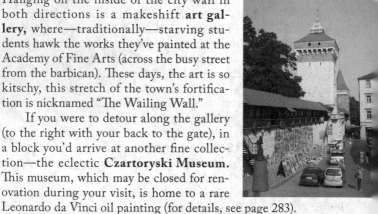

If you were to detour along the gallery (to the right with your back to the gate), in a block you'd arrive at another fine collection—the eclectic **Czartoryski Museum.** This museum, which may be closed for renovation during your visit, is home to a rare Leonardo da Vinci oil painting (for details, see page 283).

Standing at the top of Floriańska street, you can't miss two restaurant chains: **Coffee Heaven** (the local Starbucks) and **McDonald's.** When renovating the McDonald's building, a Gothic cellar was discovered—so it was excavated and seating was added. Today, you can super-size your ambience by dining on a Big Mac and fries under a medieval McVault.

About halfway down the long block, on the left (at #45, round green sign), look for **Jama Michalika** ("Michael's Cave"). This dark, atmospheric café, popular with locals for its coffee and pastries, began in 1895 as a simple bakery in a claustrophobic back room. Around the turn of the 20th century, this was a hangout of the Młoda Polska (Young Poland) movement—the Polish answer to Art Nouveau (explained on page 263). The walls are papered with sketches from poor artists—local bohemians who couldn't pay their tabs. In 1915, this was home to the first Polish cabaret. Today that stage is used by a folk troupe that performs traditional music and dance with dinner many evenings (pick up the flier, and see the description of **Jama Michalika** later, under "Entertainment in Kraków"). Poke around inside this circa-1900 time warp and appreciate this unique art gallery. Consider having coffee and dessert here, or a cigar in the charming smokers' bar in front (daily 9:00-22:00).

About a block farther down, at #20 (on the right), **Staropolskie Trunki** ("Old Polish Drinks") offers an education in vodka—with as much tasting as you'd like. It's a friendly little place with a long bar and countless local vodkas and liquors—all open and ready to be tasted. Best of all, there's a cheery local barista to talk you through the experience (five tastes for 10 zł with a fun explanation that amounts to a private tour, buy a bottle and the tastes are free, daily 10:00-24:00).

Continue strolling down Floriańska street. Notice that all over town, storefronts advertising themselves as "tourist information" offices are actually tourist sales agencies (legitimate TIs are listed on page 246). And money-exchange counters can be thieves with an address. (Do the arithmetic—the buying and selling rates should be within 6 percent or so, and there should be no fee.) Along with the fast-food joints, also notice some uniquely Polish snacks. The various pizza and kebab windows also sell *zapiekanki*—a toasted baguette with toppings, similar to a French bread pizza. Or, for an even quicker bite, buy an *obwarzanek* (ring-shaped, bagel-like roll, typically fresh) from a street vendor; many still use their old-fashioned blue carts.

Another block ahead on the left (at #3, 50 yards before the big church), you'll see **Jazz Club u Muniaka.** In the 1960s, Janusz Muniak was one of the first Polish jazzmen. Since 1994, he's run this place, and jams regularly here in a cool cellar surrounded by jazzy art. If you hang around the bar before the show, you might find yourself sitting next to Janusz himself as he smokes his pipe...and gets ready to smoke on the saxophone (for details, see "Entertainment in Kraków," later).

• *Continue into the Main Market Square, where you'll run into...*

▲▲St. Mary's Church (Kościół Mariacki)

A church has stood on this spot for 800 years. The original church was destroyed by the first Tatar invasion in 1241, but all subsequent versions—including the current one—have been built on the same foundation. You can look down the sides to see how the Main Market Square has risen about seven feet over the centuries.

How many church towers does St. Mary's have? Technically,

the answer is one. The shorter tower belongs to the church; the taller one is a municipal watchtower, from which you'll hear a bugler playing the hourly *hejnał* song. According to Kraków's favorite legend, during that first Tatar invasion, a town watchman saw the enemy approaching and sounded the alarm. Before he could finish the tune, an arrow pierced his throat—which is why, even today, the *hejnał* stops suddenly partway through. Today's buglers—12 in all—are firemen first, musicians second. Each one works a 24-hour shift up there, playing the *hejnał* on the hour, every hour (broadcast on national Polish radio at noon). Be sure to catch one of these tiny, hourly, broken performances.

To see one of the most finely crafted Gothic altarpieces anywhere, it's worth paying admission to enter the church. The front door is open 14 hours a day and is free to those who come to pray, but tourists use the door around the right side (buy your ticket across the little square from this door).

Cost and Hours: 10 zł, Mon-Sat 11:45-17:45, Sun 14:00-17:45 (these are last-entry times). The famous wooden altarpiece is open between noon and 18:00; try to be here by 11:50 for the ceremonial opening (Mon-Sat) or at 18:00 for the closing (except on Sat, when it's left open for the service on Sun).

Visiting the Church: Inside, you're struck by the lavish decor. This was the church of the everyday townspeople, built out of a spirit of competition with the royal high church at Wawel Castle. At the altar is one of the best medieval woodcarvings in existence—the exquisite, three-part **altarpiece** by German Veit Stoss (Wit Stwosz in Polish). Carved in 12 years and completed in 1489, it's packed with emotion rare in Gothic art. Get as close as you can and study the remarkable

details. Stoss used oak for the structural parts and linden trunks for the figures. When the altar doors are closed, you see scenes from the lives of Mary and Jesus. The open altar depicts the Dormition (death—or, if splitting theological hairs, heavenly sleep) of the Virgin. The artist catches the apostles around Mary, reacting in the seconds after she collapses. Mary is depicted in three stages:

Kazimierz the Great (1333-1370)

Out of the many centuries of Polish kings, only one earned the nickname "great," and he's the only one worth remembering: Kazimierz the Great.

K. the G., who ruled Poland from Kraków in the 14th century, was one of those larger-than-life medieval kings who left his mark on all fronts—from war to diplomacy, art patronage to womanizing. His scribes bragged that Kazimierz "found a Poland made of wood, and left one made of brick and stone." He put Kraków on the map as a major European capital. He founded many villages (some of which still bear his name) and replaced wooden structures with stone ones (such as Kraków's Cloth Hall). Kazimierz also established the Kraków Academy (today's Jagiellonian University), the second-oldest university in Central Europe. And to protect all these new building projects, he heavily fortified Poland by building a series of imposing forts and walls around its perimeter.

Most of all, Kazimierz is remembered as a progressive, tolerant king. In the 14th century, other nations were deporting—or even interning—their Jewish subjects, who were commonly scapegoated for anything that went wrong. But the enlightened Kazimierz created policies that granted Jews more opportunities (often related to banking and trade) and allowed them a chance for higher social standing—establishing the country as a safe haven for Jews in Europe.

Kazimierz the Great was the last of Poland's long-lived Piast dynasty. Although he left no male heir—at least, no legitimate one—Kazimierz's advances set the stage for Poland's Golden Age (14th-16th centuries). After his death, Poland united with Lithuania (against the common threat of the Teutonic Knights), the Jagiellonian dynasty was born, and Poland became one of Europe's mightiest medieval powers.

life leaving her earthly body, being escorted to heaven by Jesus, and (at the very top) being crowned in heaven. The six scenes on the sides are the Annunciation, birth of Jesus, visit by the Three Magi, Jesus' Resurrection, his Ascension, and Mary becoming the mother of the apostles at Pentecost.

There's more to St. Mary's than the altar. While you're admiring this church's art, notice the flowery Neo-Gothic painting covering the choir walls. Stare up into the starry, starry blue ceiling. As you wander around, consider that the church was renovated a century ago by three Polish geniuses from two very different artistic generations: the venerable positivist Jan Matejko and his Art Nouveau students, Stanisław Wyspiański and Józef Mehoffer (we'll learn more about these two later on our walk). The huge silver bird under the organ loft in back is a crowned white eagle, the symbol of Poland.

Tower Climb: In the summer, you may be able to climb up the 239 stairs to the top of the taller tower to visit the *hejnał* fireman. While it's a huff—with some claustrophobic stone stairs, followed by some steep, acrophobic wooden ones—the view up top is the best you'll find of the Square. However, in recent years the city and the church have been wrangling over whose job it is to renovate the rickety tower, so it may be closed during your visit. To see if it's open, look for the little door just to the left of the main entrance, which faces the Square.

• *Leaving the church, notice the neck clamps dangling from the exterior walls near the side door. If you were leaving Mass in centuries past, there would be locals chained here for public humiliation. You'd spit on them before turning right and stepping into one of the biggest market squares anywhere.*

▲▲▲Main Market Square (Rynek Główny), a.k.a. "The Square"

Kraków's marvelous Square, one of Europe's most gasp-worthy public spaces, bustles with street musicians, colorful flower stalls, cotton-candy vendors, loitering teenagers, breakdancing tweens, businesspeople commuting by foot, gawking tourists, and the lusty coos of pigeons. This Square is where Kraków lives. It's often filled with various special events, markets, and festivals. The biggest are the seasonal markets before Easter and Christmas, but you're also likely to stumble on something special going on here anytime between June and August.

The Square was established in the 13th century, when the city had to be rebuilt after being flattened by the Tatars. At the time, it was the biggest square in medieval Europe. It was illegal to sell anything on the street, so everything had to be sold here on the Main Market Square. It was divided into smaller markets, such as the butcher stalls, the ironworkers' tents, and the still-standing Cloth Hall (described later).

Notice the modern **fountain** with the glass pyramid at this end of the Square. A major excavation of the surrounding area created a museum of Kraków's medieval history that literally sprawls beneath the Square (for more on the recommended **Rynek Underground Museum,** see page 291).

The statue in the middle of the Square is a traditional meeting place for Krakovians. It depicts Romantic poet **Adam Mickiewicz** (1789-1855), who's considered the "Polish Shakespeare." His epic

The Młoda Polska (Young Poland) Art Movement

Polish art in the late 19th century was ruled by positivism, a school with a very literal, straightforward focus on Polish his-

tory (Jan Matejko led the charge; see page 404). But when the new generation of Kraków's artists came into their own in the early 1900s, they decided that the old school was exactly that. Though moved by the same spirit and goals as the previous generation—evoking Polish patriotism at a time when their country was being occupied—these new artists used very different methods. They were inspired by a renewed appreciation of folklore and peasant life. Rather than being earnest and literal (an 18th-century Polish war hero on horseback), the new art was playful and highly symbolic (the artist frolicking in a magical garden in the idyllic Polish countryside). This movement became known as Młoda Polska (Young Poland)—Art Nouveau with a Polish accent.

Stanisław Wyspiański (vees-PAYN-skee, 1869-1907) was the leader of Młoda Polska. He produced beautiful artwork, from simple drawings to the stirring stained-glass images in Kraków's St. Francis Basilica. Wyspiański was an expert at capturing human faces with realistic detail, emotion, and personality. The versatile Wyspiański was also an accomplished stage designer and writer. His patriotic play *The Wedding*—about the nuptials of a big-city artist and a peasant girl—is regarded as one of Poland's finest dramas. You'll find excellent examples of Wyspiański's art in Kraków's St. Francis Basilica and Szołayski House, and in Warsaw's National Museum.

Józef Mehoffer (may-HOH-fehr), Wyspiański's good friend and rival, was another great Młoda Polska artist. Mehoffer's style is more expressionistic and abstract than Wyspiański's, often creating an otherworldly effect. See Mehoffer's work in Kraków's St. Francis Basilica and at the artist's former residence (see the Józef Mehoffer House, page 291); and in Warsaw, at the National Museum.

Other names to look for include **Jacek Malczewski** (mahl-CHEHV-skee), who specialized in self-portraits, and **Olga Boznańska** (bohz-NAHN-skah), the movement's only prominent female artist. Both are featured in Warsaw's National Museum; Malczewski's works also appear in Kraków's Gallery of 19th-Century Polish Art.

KRAKÓW

masterpiece, *Pan Tadeusz,* is still regarded as one of the greatest works in Polish literature. A wistful, nostalgic tale of Polish-Lithuanian nobility, *Pan Tadeusz* stirred patriotism in a Poland that had been dismantled by surrounding empires. If you survey the Square from here, you'll notice that the Old Town was spared the bombs of World War II. The Nazis considered Kraków a city with Germanic roots and wanted it saved. But they were quick to destroy any symbols of Polish culture or pride. The statue of Adam Mickiewicz, for example, was pulled down immediately after occupation.

Near the end of the Square, you'll see the tiny, copper-domed **Church of St. Adalbert,** one of the oldest churches in Kraków (10th century). This Romanesque structure predates the Square. Like St. Mary's (described earlier), it seems to be at an angle because it's aligned east-west, as was the custom when it was built. (In other words, the churches aren't crooked—the Square is. Any other "crooked" building you see around town predates the 13th-century grid created during the rebuilding of Kraków.)

Drinks are reasonably priced at cafés on the Square (most around 10-15 zł). Find a spot where you like the view and the chairs, then sit and sip. Order a coffee, Polish *piwo* (beer, such as Żywiec, Okocim, or Lech), or a shot of *wódka* (Żubrówka is a good brand; for more on Polish drinks, see page 237). For a higher vantage point, the Cloth Hall's **Café Szał terrace,** overlooking the Square and St. Mary's Church, offers one of the nicest views in town (open daily until 24:00; terrace costs 2 zł to enter except free on Sun-Mon, after 20:00, and with art gallery ticket; 10-15-zł drinks, some light meals, enter through Gallery of 19th-Century Polish Art entrance).

As the Square buzzes around you, imagine this place before 1989. There were no outdoor cafés, no touristy souvenir stands, and no salesmen hawking cotton candy or neon-lit whirligigs. The communist government shut down all but a handful of the businesses. They didn't want people to congregate here—they should be at home, resting, because "a rested worker is a productive worker." The buildings were covered with soot from the nearby Lenin Steelworks in Nowa Huta. The communists denied the pollution, and when the student "Green Brigades" staged a demonstration in this Square to raise awareness in the 1970s, they were immediately arrested. How things have changed.

• *The huge, yellow building right in the middle of the Square is the...*

▲▲Cloth Hall (Sukiennice)

In the Middle Ages, this was the place where cloth-sellers had their market stalls. Kazimierz the Great turned the Cloth Hall into a permanent structure in the 14th century. In 1555, it burned

down and was replaced by the current building. The crowned letter *S* (at the top of the gable above the entryway) stands for King Sigismund the Old, who commissioned this version of the hall. As Sigismund fancied all things Italian (including women—he married an Italian princess), this structure is in the Italianate Renaissance style. Sigismund kicked off a nationwide trend, and you'll still see Renaissance-style buildings like this one all over the country, making the style as typically Polish as it is typically Italian. We'll see more works by Sigismund's imported Italian architects at Wawel Castle.

Recently restored and gleaming, the Cloth Hall is still a functioning market—selling mostly souvenirs, including wood carvings, chess sets, jewelry (especially amber), painted boxes, and trinkets (summer Mon-Fri 9:00-18:00, Sat-Sun 9:00-15:00, sometimes later; winter Mon-Fri 9:00-16:00, Sat-

Sun 9:00-15:00). Cloth Hall prices are slightly inflated, but still cheap by American standards. You're paying a little extra for the convenience and the atmosphere, but you'll see locals buying gifts here, too.

WCs are at each end of the Cloth Hall. The upstairs of the Cloth Hall is home to the excellent **Gallery of 19th-Century Polish Art** (enter behind the statue of Adam; for a self-guided tour, see page 284).

• *Browse through the Cloth Hall passageway. As you emerge into the other half of the Square, the big tower on your left is the...*

Town Hall Tower

This is all that remains of a town hall building from the 14th century—when Kraków was the powerful capital of Poland. After the 18th-century Partitions of Poland, Kraków's prominence took a nosedive. By the 19th century, Kraków was Nowheresville. As the town's importance crumbled, so did its town hall. It was cheaper to tear down the building than to repair it, and all that was left standing was this nearly 200-foot-tall tower. In summer, you can climb the tower, stopping along the way to poke around an exhibit on Kraków history, but the views from up top are disappointing.

Still you can step into the entryway to see a model of an earlier version of the church, with a fanciful, Prague-style, multispired tower.

Cost and Hours: 7 zł, April-Oct daily 10:30-18:00, last entry 30 minutes before closing, closed Nov-March.

Nearby: The **gigantic head** at the base of the Town Hall Tower is a sculpture by contemporary artist Igor Mitoraj, who studied here in Kraków. Typical of Mitoraj's works, the head is an empty shell that appears to be wrapped in cloth. While some locals enjoy having a work by their fellow Krakovian in such a prominent place, others disapprove of its sharp contrast with the Square's genteel Old World ambience. Tourists enjoy playing peek-a-boo with the head's eyes—a fun photo op.

• *When you're finished on the Square, we'll head toward Wawel Hill. But we'll take a one-block detour from the Royal Way to introduce you to one of Kraków's best churches. Leave on the street called ulica Bracka, in the middle of the bottom of the Square (next to the Deutsche Bank, straight ahead from the end of the Cloth Hall). Follow this one long block (and across the busy Franciszkańska street) directly to the low-key side door of a big red-brick church. Go ye.*

▲▲St. Francis Basilica (Bazylika Św. Franciszka)

This beautiful Gothic church, which was St. John Paul II's home church while he was archbishop of Kraków, features some of Poland's best Art Nouveau in situ (in the setting for which it was intended). After an 1850 fire, it was redecorated by the two leading members of the Młoda Polska (Young Poland) movement: Stanisław Wyspiański and Józef Mehoffer. These two talented and fiercely competitive Krakovians were friends who apprenticed together under Poland's greatest painter, Jan Matejko. The glorious decorations of this church are the result of their great rivalry run amok.

Cost and Hours: Free, daily 6:00-19:45—but frequent services, so be discreet.

❷ **Self-Guided Tour:** Before entering, notice the board to the right of the door displaying death announcements for community members.

Entering through this door, turn left into the altar area to enjoy the paintings and stained-glass windows by **Stanisław Wyspiański**. The windows flanking the high altar represent the Blessed Salomea (left, the church's founder, buried in a side chapel) and St. Francis (right, the church's namesake). Salomea was a medieval Polish woman who became queen of Hungary, but later returned to Poland and entered a convent after her husband's death. Notice she's dropping a crown—repudiating the earthly world and giving herself over to the simple, stop-and-smell-God's-roses lifestyle of St. Francis. Notice also the Mucha-like paintings by Wyspiański on

the pilasters between the windows.

As you face the back of the church, look at the window in the rear of the nave: *God the Father Let It Be,* Wyspiański's greatest masterpiece. The colors beneath the Creator change from yellows and oranges (fire) to soothing blues (water), depending on the light. Wyspiański was supposedly inspired by Michelangelo's vision of God in the Sistine Chapel, though he used a street beggar to model God's specific features. Wyspiański also painted the delightful floral designs decorating the walls of the nave—fitting for a church dedicated to a saint so famous for his spiritual connection to nature. (For more on Wyspiański, see page 263.)

Walk up the nave toward the door under that window. The chapel on the right side, after the transept, contains some evocative Stations of the Cross. This is **Józef Mehoffer**'s response to Wyspiański's work. The centerpiece of the room is a replica of the Shroud of Turin—which, since it touched the original shroud, is also considered a holy relic.

Back out in the nave, the modern painting (with an orange-and-blue background, midway up the nave on

Karol Wojtyła (1920-2005): The Greatest Pole

The man who became St. John Paul II began his life as Karol Wojtyła, born to a humble family in the town of Wadowice near Kraków on May 18, 1920. Karol's mother died when he was a young boy. When he was a teenager, he moved with his father to Kraków to study philosophy and drama at Jagiellonian University. Young Karol was gregarious and athletic—an avid skier, hiker, swimmer, and soccer goalie. During the Nazi occupation in World War II, he was forced to work in a quarry. In defiance of the Nazis, he secretly studied theology and appeared in illegal underground theatrical productions. When the war ended, he resumed his studies, now at the theology faculty.

After graduating in 1947, Wojtyła swiftly rose through the ranks of the Catholic Church hierarchy. By 1964, he was archbishop of Kraków, and just three years later, he became the youngest cardinal ever. Throughout the 1960s, he fought an ongoing battle with the regime when they refused to allow the construction of a church in the Kraków suburb of Nowa Huta. After years of saying Mass for huge crowds in open fields, Wojtyła finally convinced the communists to allow the construction of the Lord's Ark Church in 1977. A year later, Karol Wojtyła was called to the papacy—the first non-Italian pope in more than four centuries. In 1979, he paid a visit to his native Poland. In a series of cautiously provocative speeches, he demonstrated to his countrymen the potential for mass opposition to communism.

Imagine you're Polish in the 1970s. Your country was devastated by World War II and has struggled under an oppressive regime ever since. Food shortages are epidemic. Lines stretch around the block even to buy a measly scrap of bread. Life is bleak, oppressive, and hopeless. Then someone who speaks your language—someone you've admired your entire life, and one of the only people you've seen successfully stand up to the regime—becomes one of the world's most influential people. A Pole like you is the leader of a billion Catholics. He makes you believe that

KRAKÓW

the left) depicts **St. Maksymilian Kolbe,** the Catholic priest who sacrificed his own life to save a fellow inmate at Auschwitz in 1941 (notice the *16670*—his concentration camp number—etched into the background; read his story on page 361). Kolbe is particularly beloved here, as he actually served at this church.

Just before going out the back door (below Wyspiański's stained-glass window), find the **silver plate** labeled "Jan Paweł II" on the second pew from the last (on right); this was St. John Paul II's favorite place to pray when he lived in the Archbishop's Palace across the street.

• *Stepping outside (through the back door), look to the right. The light-yellow building across the street is the...*

the impossible can happen. He says to you again and again: "*Nie lękajcie się*"—"Have no fear." And you begin to believe it.

From his bully pulpit, the Pope had a knack for cleverly challenging the communists—just firmly enough to get his point across, but stopping short of jeopardizing the stature of the Church in Poland. Gentle but pointed wordplay was his specialty. The inspirational role he played in the lives of Lech Wałęsa and the other leaders of Solidarity emboldened them to rise up; it's no coincidence that the first successful trade-union strikes in the Soviet Bloc took place shortly after John Paul II became pope (for more on Solidarity, see page 464). Many people (including Mikhail Gorbachev) credit John Paul II for the collapse of Eastern European communism.

Even as John Paul II's easy charisma attracted new worshippers to the Church (especially young people), his conservatism on issues such as birth control, homosexuality, and female priests pushed away many Catholics. Under his watch, the Church struggled with pedophilia scandals. Many still fault him for turning a blind eye and not putting a stop to these abuses much earlier. By the end of his papacy, John Paul II's failing health and conservatism had caused him to lose stature in worldwide public opinion.

And yet, approval of the Pope never waned in Poland. His countrymen—even the relatively few atheists and agnostics—saw John Paul II both as the greatest hero of their people...and as a member of the family, like a kindly grandfather. When Pope John Paul II died on April 2, 2005, the mourning in his homeland was particularly deep and sustained. Musical performances of all kinds were canceled, and the irreverent MTV-style music channel simply went off the air out of respect.

A speedy nine years after his death, Karol Wojtyła became St. John Paul II in April of 2014. Out of 265 popes, only two have been given the title "great." There's already talk in Rome of increasing that number to three. Someday soon we may speak of this man as "St. John Paul the Great." His countrymen already do.

Archbishop's Palace

This building (specifically, the window over the stone entryway) was St. John Paul II's residence when he was the archbishop of Kraków. When he became Pope, it remained his home-away-from-Rome for visits to his hometown. After a long day of saying formal Mass during his visits to Kraków, he'd wind up here. Weary as he was, before going to bed he'd stand in the window for hours, chatting casually with the people assembled below—about religion, but also about sports, current events, and whatever was on their minds. In 2005, when the Pope's health deteriorated, this street filled with his supporters, even though he was in Rome. For days, somber locals focused their vigil on this same window, their eyes fixed on a black crucifix that had been placed here. At 21:37 on the night of April 2, 2005, the Pope passed away in Rome. Ten thousand Krakovians were on this street, under this window, listening to a Mass broadcast on loudspeakers from the church. When the priest announced the Pope's death, every single person simultaneously fell to their knees in silence. For the next several days, thousands of the faithful continued to stand on this street, staring intently at the window where they last saw the man they considered to be the greatest Pole.

• *Now turn right, walk along the side of the church, pass a few monuments and a tram stop, and turn right again down busy...*

Grodzka Street

Now you're back on the Royal Way proper. At the corner of Grodzka street stands the modern, copper-colored **Wyspiański Pavilion.** Step inside (daily 9:00-17:00), past the little TI, to see three new stained-glass windows based on designs Wyspiański once submitted for a contest to redecorate Wawel Cathedral. Although these designs were rejected back then, they were finally realized on the hundredth anniversary of his death (in 2007). Visible from inside the building during the day, and gloriously illuminated to be seen outside the building at night, they represent three Polish historical figures: the gaunt St. Stanisław (Poland's first saint), the skeletal Kazimierz the Great (in the middle), and the swooning King Henry the Pious.

Now continue down Grodzka street. This lively thoroughfare, connecting the Square with Wawel, is teeming with shops—and some of Kraków's best restaurants (see "Eating in Kraków," later). Survey your options now, and choose (and maybe reserve) your favorite for dinner tonight. This street is also characterized by its fine arcades over the sidewalks. While this might seem like a charming Renaissance feature, the arcades were actually added by the Nazis after they invaded in 1939; they wanted to convert Kraków into a city befitting its status as the capital of their Polish puppet state.

This is also a good street to find some of Kraków's **milk bars** (three are listed on page 346). The most traditional one is about two blocks down, on the right (at #45), with a simple *Bar Mleczny* sign. These government-subsidized cafeterias are the locals' choice for a quick, cheap, filling, lowbrow lunch. Prices are deliriously cheap (soup costs about a dollar), and the food isn't bad. For more on milk bars, see page 234.

• *One more block ahead, the small square on your right is...*

Mary Magdalene Square (Plac Św. Marii Magdaleny)

Back when Kraków was just a village, this was its main square. Today, it offers a great visual example of Kraków's deeply religious character. In the Middle Ages, Kraków was known as "Small Rome" for its many churches. Today, there are 142 churches and monasteries within the city limits (32 in the Old Town alone)—more per square mile than anywhere outside of Rome. You can see several of them from this spot: The nearest, with the picturesque white facade and row of saints out front, is the **Church of Saints Peter and Paul** (Poland's first Baroque church, and a popular tourist concert venue). The statues lining this church's facade are the 11 apostles (minus Judas), plus Mary Magdalene, the square's namesake. The next church to the right, with the twin towers, is the Romanesque **St. Andrew's** (now with a Baroque interior). This is the oldest church in town, from the 11th century, and was designed to double as a place of last refuge—notice the arrow slits around the impassable lower floor. According to legend, a spring inside this church provided water to citizens who holed up here during the Tatar invasions. The church was saved, but that didn't save the rest of Kraków from being overrun by marauding armies. Imagine this stone fortress of God being the only building standing amid a smoldering and flattened Kraków after the 13th-century destruction.

If you look farther down the street, you can see three more churches. And even the square next to you used to be a church, too—it burned in 1855, and only its footprint survives.

• *Go through the square and turn left down...*

Kanonicza Street (Ulica Kanonicza)

With so many churches around here, the clergy had to live somewhere. Many lived on this well-preserved street—supposedly the oldest street in Kraków. As you walk, look for the cardinal hats over three different doorways. The **Hotel Copernicus,** on the left at #16, is named for a famous guest who stayed here five centuries ago. Directly across the street at #17, the **Bishop Erazm Ciołek Palace** hosts a good exhibit of medieval art and Orthodox icons. Next door, the yellow house at #19 is where Karol Wojtyła lived for 10 years after World War II—long before he became St. John Paul II. Today this building houses the **Archdiocesan Museum,** which features a few sparse exhibits about Kraków's favorite son. Across the street is the **John Paul II Center,** which has another modest exhibit about the late pontiff and saint, and also provides information about the new Sanctuary of St. John Paul II on Kraków's outskirts (for more on this, see page 317). All three of these sights are described later, under "Sights in Kraków."

• *We're at the end of Kanonicza street, and our self-guided walk is finished. But there's still much more to see. Across the busy street, a ramp leads up to the most important piece of ground in all of Poland: Wawel.*

Sights in Kraków

WAWEL HILL: THE HEART AND SOUL OF POLAND

Wawel (VAH-vehl), a symbol of Polish royalty and independence, is sacred territory to every Polish person. A castle has stood here since the beginning of Poland's recorded history. Today, Wawel—awash in tourists—is the most visited sight in the country. Crowds and an overly complex admissions system for the hill's many historic sights can be exasperating. Thankfully, a stroll through the cathedral and around the castle grounds requires no tickets, and—with the help of the following commentary—is enough. I've described these sights in the order of a handy self-guided walk. The many museums on Wawel (all described in this section) are mildly interesting, but can be skipped (grounds open daily from 6:00 until dusk, inner courtyard closes 30 minutes earlier). In June, it's mobbed with students, as it's a required field trip for Polish school kids.

Wawel Sights: The sights you'll enter at Wawel are divided into two institutions: church and castle, each with separate tickets. Tickets for the castle sights are sold at two points (at the long line at the top of the ramp, or with no line at the top of the hill, across the central square). The most important church sight—the cathedral—is mostly free, but to enter the paid sights inside (or the museum), get a ticket at the office across from the cathedral entrance.

• *From Kanonicza street—where my self-guided walk ends—head up the long ramp to the castle entry.*

Entry Ramp

Huffing up this ramp, it's easy to imagine how this location—rising above the otherwise flat plains around Kraków—was both strategic and easy to defend. When Kraków was part of the Habsburg Empire in the 19th century, the Austrians turned this castle complex into a fortress, destroying much of its delicate beauty. When Poland regained its independence after World War I, the castle was returned to its former glory. The bricks you see on your left as you climb the ramp bear the names of Poles from around the world who donated to the cause.

The jaunty equestrian statue ahead is **Tadeusz Kościuszko** (1746-1817), a familiar name to many Americans. Kościuszko was a hero of the American Revolution and helped design West Point. When he returned to Poland, he fought bravely but unsuccessfully against the Russians (during the Partitions that would divide Poland's territory among three neighboring powers). Kościuszko also gave his name to several American towns, a county in Indiana, a brand of mustard from Illinois, and the tallest mountain in Australia.

• *Hiking through the Heraldic Gate next to Kościuszko, you pass the ticket office (if you'll be going into the museums, use the other ticket office, with shorter lines, on the top of the hill—see "Tickets and Reservations," later). As you crest the hill and pass through the stone gate, on your left is...*

▲▲Wawel Cathedral

Poland's national church is its Westminster Abbey. While the history buried here is pretty murky to most Americans, to Poles, this

church is *the* national mausoleum. It holds the tombs of nearly all of Poland's most important rulers and greatest historical figures.

Cost and Hours: It's usually free to walk around the main part of the church. You must buy a 12-zł ticket to climb up the tallest tower; visit the crypt, the royal tombs, and some of the lesser chapels; and tour the John Paul II Wawel Cathedral Museum. Buy this ticket at the house across from the cathedral entry, where you can also rent an audioguide (7 zł). The cathedral is open April-Sept Mon-Sat 9:00-17:00, Sun 12:30-17:00, closes one hour earlier Oct-March, last entry 30 minutes before closing (tel. 12-429-9516, www.katedra-wawelska.pl). Note that the cathedral's museum (described later) is closed on Sunday.

Cathedral Exterior

Go around to the far side of the cathedral to take in its profile. This uniquely eclectic church is the product of centuries of haphazard additions...yet somehow, it works. It began as a simple, stripped-down Romanesque church in the 12th century. (The white base of the nearest tower is original. Anything at Wawel that's made of white limestone like this was probably part of the earliest Romanesque structures.) Kazimierz the Great and his predecessors gradually surrounded the cathedral with some 20 chapels, which were further modified over the centuries, making this beautiful church a happy hodgepodge of styles. To give you a sense of the historical sweep, scan the chapels from left to right: 14th-century Gothic, 12th-century Romanesque (the base of the tower), 17th-century Baroque (the inside is Baroque, though the exterior is a copy of its Renaissance neighbor), 16th-century Renaissance, and 18th- and 19th-century Neoclassical. (This variety in styles is even more evident in the chapels' interiors, which we'll see soon.)

Pay attention to the two particularly interesting domed chapels to the right of the tall tower. The gold one is the Sigismund Chapel, housing memorials to the Jagiellonian kings—including Sigismund the Old, who was responsible for Kraków's Renaissance renovation in the 16th century. The Jagiellonian Dynasty was a high point in Polish history. During that golden 16th century, Poland was triple the size it is today, stretching all the way to the Ottoman Empire and the Black Sea. Poles consider the Sigismund Chapel, made with 80 pounds of gold, to be the finest Renaissance chapel north of the Alps. The copper-domed chapel next to it, home to the Swedish Waza dynasty, resembles its neighbor (but it's a copy built 150 years later, and without all that gold).

Go back around and face the church's **front entry** for more architectonic extravagance. The tallest tower, called the Sigismund Tower, has a clock with only an hour hand. Climbing a few steps into the entry, you see Gothic chapels (with pointy windows) flanking the door, a Renaissance ceiling, lavish Baroque decoration over the door, and some big bones (a simple whale rib, but thought to have been the bones of the mythic Wawel dragon in medieval times—and put here as an oddity to be viewed by the public). (Back then, there were no museums, so notable items like these were used to lure people to the church.) It's said that as long as the bones hang here, the cathedral will stand. The door is the original from the 14th century, with fine wrought-iron work. The *K* with the crown stands for Kazimierz the Great. The black marble frame is made of Kraków stone from nearby quarries.

Cathedral Interior

The cathedral interior is slathered in Baroque memorials and tombs, decorated with tapestries, and soaked in Polish history. The ensemble was designed to help keep Polish identity strong through the ages. It has...and it still does.

۞ Self-Guided Tour: After you step inside, you'll follow the one-way, clockwise route that leads you through the choir, then around the back of the apse, then back to the entry.

At the entry, look straight ahead to see the silver tomb under a **canopy,** inspired by the one in St. Peter's Basilica at the Vatican. It contains the remains of the first Polish saint, Stanisław (from the 11th century). In front of the canopy, look for a metallic reliquary that's shaped like a book with its pages being ruffled by the wind. The glass capsule in the reliquary holds a drop of St. John Paul II's blood. It takes this shape because of what believers consider a highly significant moment during his memorial service: Before a crowd of thousands on St. Peter's Square in Rome, a book was placed on John Paul II's simple wooden coffin. As the service processed, its pages were ruffled back and forth by the wind, until they were finally slammed shut...as if the Holy Spirit were "closing the book" on his life.

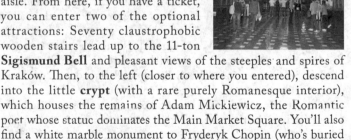

Go behind this canopy into the ornately carved **choir** area. For 200 years, the colorful chair to the right of the high altar has been the seat of Kraków's archbishops, including Karol Wojtyła, who served here for 14 years before becoming pope. It's here that coronations took place.

Now you'll continue into the left aisle. From here, if you have a ticket, you can enter two of the optional attractions: Seventy claustrophobic wooden stairs lead up to the 11-ton **Sigismund Bell** and pleasant views of the steeples and spires of Kraków. Then, to the left (closer to where you entered), descend into the little **crypt** (with a rare purely Romanesque interior), which houses the remains of Adam Mickiewicz, the Romantic poet whose statue dominates the Main Market Square. You'll also find a white marble monument to Fryderyk Chopin (who's buried in Paris), put here on the 200th anniversary of his birth in 2010.

Now continue around the apse (behind the main altar). After curving around to the right, look for the red-marble tomb (on

the right) of The Great One—**Kazimierz,** of course. Look for *Kazimierz Wielki*—at his feet you can see a little beaver. This is an allusion to a famous saying about Kazimierz, the nation-builder: He found a Poland made of wood, and left one made of brick and stone.

You may notice that there's one VIP (Very Important Pole) who's missing...Karol Wojtyła, a.k.a. John Paul II. Even so, a few more steps toward the entrance, on the left, is the **Chapel of St. John Paul II.** The late pontiff left no specific requests for his body, and the Vatican controversially (to Poles, at least) chose to entomb him in Vatican City, instead of sending him back home to Wawel. While Karol Wojtyła's remains are in St. Peter's Basilica, this chapel was recently converted to honor him—with a plaque in the floor and an altar with his picture. Someday, Poles hope, he may be moved here (but, the Vatican says, don't hold your breath).

Ten steps farther, on the right, is the white sarcophagus of **St. Jadwiga** (with a dog at her feet). This 14th-century "king" of Poland advanced the fortunes of her realm by partnering with the king of Lithuania. The resulting Jagiellonian dynasty fought off the Teutonic Knights, helped Christianize Lithuania, and oversaw a high-water mark in Polish history. (Despite the queen's many contributions, the sexism of the age meant that she was considered a "king" rather than a "queen.") All the flowers here demonstrate how popular she remains among Poles today; she was sainted by Pope John Paul II in 1997. Across from Jadwiga, peek into the gorgeous 16th-century **Sigismund Chapel,** with its silver altar (this is the gold-roofed chapel you just saw from outside). Locals consider this the "Pearl of the Polish Renaissance" and the finest Renaissance building outside Italy.

Just beyond is a door leading back outside. If you don't have a ticket, your tour is finished—head out here. But those with a ticket can keep circling around.

Next, look into the **Waza Chapel:** Remember that its exterior matches the restrained, Renaissance style of the Sigismund Chapel, but the interior is clearly Baroque, slathered with gold and silver—quite a contrast.

To the left of the main door, take a look at the Gothic **Holy Cross Chapel,** with its seemingly Orthodox-style 14th-century frescoes.

In the back corner of the church is the entrance to the **royal tombs** (you'll exit outside the church, so be sure you're done in here first). The first big room, an original Romanesque space called St. Leonard's Crypt, houses Poland's greatest war heroes: Kościuszko (of American Revolution fame), Jan III Sobieski (who successfully defended Vienna from the Ottomans; he's in the simple black coffin with the gold inscription *J III S*), Sikorski, Poniatowski, and so on. Poles consider this room highly significant as the place where St. John Paul II celebrated his first Mass after becoming a priest (in November of 1946). Then you'll wander through several rooms of second-tier Polish kings, queens, and their kids. Head down more stairs to find the plaque honoring the Polish victims of the

Katyń massacre in the USSR during World War II. Stepping into the next room, you'll see the cathedral's two newest tombs: President Lech Kaczyński and his wife Helena, who were among the 96 Polish politicians killed in a tragic 2010 plane crash—which was delivering those diplomats to a ceremony memorializing the Katyń massacre. Up a few stairs is the final grave, belonging to Marshal Józef Piłsudski, the WWI hero who seized power and ruled Poland from 1926 to 1935. His tomb was moved here so the rowdy soldiers who came to pay their respects wouldn't disturb the others.

• *Nearby (and covered by the same ticket as the tower and crypt) is the cathedral's museum.*

John Paul II Wawel Cathedral Museum

This small museum, up the little staircase across from the cathedral entry, was recently spiffed up and re-dedicated to Kraków's

favorite archbishop. It fills four rooms with artifacts relating to both the cathedral and St. John Paul II.

Downstairs is the Royal Room, with vestments, swords, regalia, holy robes, and items that were once buried with the kings, as well as early treasury items (from the 11th through 16th centuries). Upstairs are a later treasury collection (17th through 20th centuries) and a "Papal Room" with items from St. John Paul II's life: his armchair, vestments, and miter (pointy pope hat—notice how the golden decorations on this one incorporate the Black Madonna of Częstochowa), plus souvenirs from his travels.

Admission to this museum is included with your ticket to the cathedral's special options (Sigismund Bell tower, plus crypt and royal tombs), and its collection is worth a quick look, especially if you're interested in St. John Paul II (April-Sept Mon-Sat 9:00-17:00, Oct-March Mon-Sat 9:00-16:00, closed Sun year-round; pick up free brochure at entrance, tel. 12-429-3321).

• *When you're finished with the cathedral sights, stroll around the...*

▲▲Wawel Castle Grounds

In the rest of the castle, you'll uncover more fragments of Kraków's history and have the opportunity to visit several museums. I consider the museums skippable, but if you want to visit them, buy tickets before you enter the inner courtyard. Read the descriptions on page 280 to decide which museums appeal to you.

KRAKÓW

⊙ Self-Guided Walk: This tour, which doesn't enter any of the admission-charging attractions, is plenty for most visitors.

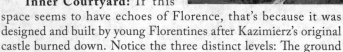

• *Behind the cathedral, a grand green-and-pink entryway leads into the palace's dramatically Renaissance-style...*

Inner Courtyard: If this space seems to have echoes of Florence, that's because it was designed and built by young Florentines after Kazimierz's original castle burned down. Notice the three distinct levels: The ground

floor housed the private apartments of the higher nobility (governors and castle administrators); the middle level held the private apartments of the king; and the top floor—much taller, to allow more light to fill its large spaces—were the public state rooms of the king. The ivy-covered wing to the right of where you entered is Fascist in style, built as the headquarters of the notorious Nazi governor of German-occupied Poland, Hans Frank. (He was tried and executed in Nürnberg after the war.) At the far end of the courtyard is a false wall, designed to create a pleasant Renaissance symmetry, and also to give the illusion that the castle is bigger than it is. Looking through the windows, notice that there's nothing but air on the other side. When foreign dignitaries visited, these windows could be covered to complete the illusion. The entrances to most Wawel museums are around this courtyard, and some believe that you'll find something even more special: chakra.

Adherents to the Hindu concept of **chakra** believe that a powerful energy field connects all living things. Some believe that, mirroring the seven chakra points on the body (from head to groin), there are seven points on the surface of the earth where this energy is most concentrated: Delhi, Delphi, Jerusalem, Mecca, Rome, Velehrad...and Wawel Hill—specifically over there in the corner (immediately to your left as you enter the courtyard—the stretches of wall flanking the door to the baggage-check room). Look for peaceful people (here or elsewhere on the castle grounds) with their eyes closed. One thing's for sure: They're not thinking of Kazimierz the Great. The smudge marks on the wall are from people pressing up against this corner, trying to absorb some good vibes from this chakra spot.

The Wawel administration seems creeped out by all this. They've done what they can to discourage this ritual (such as putting up information boards right where the power is supposedly most focused), but believers still gravitate from far and wide to hug the wall. Give it a try...and let the Force be with you. (Just for fun, ask a Wawel tour guide about the chakra, and watch her squirm—they're forbidden to talk about it.)

• *If you want to visit some of the **castle museums** (you can enter four of the five from this courtyard), you'll first need to buy tickets elsewhere. Stick with me for a little longer to finish our tour of the grounds, and we'll wind up near a ticket office.*

Head back out to the side of the cathedral to survey the...

Field of History: This hilltop has seen lots of changes over the years. Kazimierz the Great turned a small fortress into a mighty Gothic castle in the 14th century. Today, you'll see the cathedral and a castle complex, but little remains of Kazimierz's grand fortress (which burned to the ground in 1499) other than the white stones around the restaurant on the square. In the grassy field across from the cathedral, you'll see the **foundations** of two Gothic churches that were destroyed when the Austrians took over Wawel in the 19th century and needed a parade ground for their troops. (They built the red-brick hospital building beyond the field, now used by the Wawel administration.)

• *Head downhill through the square, across to the gap in the buildings beyond the field, to the...*

Viewpoint over the Vistula: Belly up to the wall and enjoy the panorama over the **Vistula River** and Kraków's outskirts. The "Polish Mississippi"—which runs its entire course in Polish lands—is the nation's artery for trade and cultural connection. It stretches 650 miles from the foothills of the Tatra Mountains in southern Poland, through most of the country's major cities (Kraków, Warsaw, Toruń), before emptying into the Baltic Sea in Gdańsk.

From this viewpoint, you can see some unusual landmarks, including the odd wavy-roofed building just across the river (which houses the Manggha Japanese art gallery) and the biggest conference center in Poland (opened in 2015, to the left of the wavy building). The ball to the left of that is the balloon that tourists ride for a vast view. To the right, the symmetrical little bulge that tops the highest hill on the horizon is the **Kościuszko Mound** (see page 323). And on a particularly crisp day, far in the distance (beyond the wavy building), you can see the Tatra Mountains marking the border of Slovakia.

Now look directly below you, along the riverbank, to find a fire-belching monument to the **dragon** that was instrumental in the founding of Kraków. Once upon a time, a prince named Krak founded a town on Wawel Hill. It was the perfect location—except for the fire-breathing dragon who lived in the caves under the hill and terrorized the town. Prince Krak had to feed the dragon all of the town's livestock to keep the monster from going after the townspeople. But Krak, with the help of a clever shoemaker, came up with a plan. They stuffed a sheep's skin with sulfur and left it outside the dragon's cave. The dragon swallowed it, and before long, developed a terrible case of heartburn. To put the fire out, the dragon started drinking water from the Vistula. He kept drinking and drinking until he finally exploded. The town was saved, and Kraków thrived. Today visitors enjoy watching the dragon blow fire into the air (about every four minutes, but can vary from a big plume to a tiny puff).

If you want to head down to see the Vistula and the dragon close up, take a shortcut through the nearby **Dragon's Den** (Smocza Jama, enter at the little copper-roofed brick building, at the far right of this viewpoint plaza). It's just a 135-step spiral staircase and a few underground caverns—worthwhile only as a quick way to get from the top of Wawel down to the banks of the Vistula 3 zł, pay at machine—coins only, April-Oct daily 10:00-17:00, July-Aug until 18:00, closed Nov-March).

If you'd like a higher viewpoint on the riverfront, you can pay 4 zł to climb 137 stairs to the top of **Sandomierska Tower** (at the far end of the hill, past the visitors center, no elevator). But I'd skip it—disappointingly, the view from up top is only through small windows (May-Sept daily 10:00-18:00, June-Aug until 19:00, Oct Sat-Sun only 10:00-17:00, closed Nov-April).

• *Our Wawel tour is finished. If you'd like to explore some of the museums, you can buy your tickets in the nearby visitors center (head back into the main Wawel complex—with the empty field—and turn right); here you'll also find WCs, a café, a gift shop, and other amenities. Or go down to the riverfront park: Walk downhill (through the Dragon's Den, or use the main ramp and simply circle around the base of the hill) to reach the park—one of the most delightful places in Kraków to simply relax, with beautiful views back on the castle complex.*

Wawel Castle Museums

There are five museums and exhibits in Wawel Castle (not including the cathedral and Cathedral Museum, the Dragon's Den, or Sandomierska Tower—all described above). A sixth exhibit, featuring Leonardo da Vinci's masterful painting *Lady with an*

Ermine, will likely be on display at least through 2015.

Remember: While the following sights are fascinating to Poles, casual visitors often find that the best visit is simply to enjoy the exteriors and the cathedral (following my self-guided tour, described earlier); the only ticket really worth considering is for the Leonardo. Each venue has its own admission and slightly different hours (tel. 12-422-5155, ext. 219, www.wawel.krakow.pl). English descriptions are posted, and you can rent an audioguide for 20 zł that covers some of the sights (State Rooms, Crown Treasury and Armory, and Oriental Art; get this at the ticket office on the courtyard). If you're visiting all of the sights, start with the Royal State Rooms and/or Royal Private Apartments (which share an entrance), then—on your way back down—see the Leonardo exhibit, the Oriental Art exhibit, and the Crown Treasury and Armory. Then head back out into the outer courtyard for the Lost Wawel exhibit.

Tickets and Reservations: Each sight has separate tickets (prices listed below), which you'll buy at one of two ticket windows. Most people line up at the top of the entry ramp, but it's faster to buy tickets at the visitors center at the far corner of the castle grounds (across the field from the cathedral, near the café). You generally can't buy tickets at the door of each sight (except for—sometimes—Lost Wawel), so decide in advance which ones you want to see and buy all your tickets at the start of your visit. A limited number of tickets are sold for each sight; boards count down the number of tickets available for each one on the day you're there. Tickets come with an assigned entry time (though you can usually sneak in before your scheduled appointment). In the summer, ticket lines can be long, and sights can sell out by midmorning. You can make a free reservation for some of the sights (tel. 12-422-1697, extra fee applies), but frankly, the sights aren't worth all the fuss—if they're sold out, you're not missing much.

Hours: Unless otherwise noted, the museums are open April-Oct Tue-Fri 9:30-17:00, Sat-Sun 11:00-17:00, closed Mon; Nov-March Tue-Sat 9:30-16:00, closed Sun-Mon; last entry one hour before closing.

Exceptions: In summer (April-Oct), Lost Wawel and the Crown Treasury and Armory are free and open on Mondays (9:30-13:00). Off-season (Nov-March), everything closes on Monday, but Lost Wawel, the Royal State Rooms, and the Leonardo exhibit (Jan-March only) remain open on Sunday.

Eating: Various light eateries circle the castle courtyard, but if you just want a drink, it's hard to beat the affordable self-service café next to the Lost Wawel entrance, with fine views across to the cathedral.

▲Royal State Rooms (Komnaty Królewskie)

While precious to Poles, these rooms are mediocre by European standards. Still, this is the best of the Wawel museums. First, climb up to the top floor and wander through some ho-hum halls with paintings and antique furniture. Along the way, you'll walk along the outdoor gallery (enjoying views down into the courtyard). Finally, you'll reach the Throne Room, with 30 carved heads in the ceiling. According to  legend, one of these heads got mouthy when the king was trying to pass judgment—so its mouth has been covered to keep it quiet. Continue into some of the palace's finest rooms, with 16th-century Brussels tapestries (140 of the original series of 300 survive), remarkably decorated wooden ceilings, and gorgeous leather-tooled walls. Wandering these halls (with their period furnishings), you get a feeling for the 16th- and 17th-century glory days of Poland, when it was a leading power in Eastern Europe. The Senate Room, with its throne and elaborate tapestries, is the climax.

Cost and Hours: 18 zł, see hours listed earlier, plus Nov-March also open—and free—Sun 10:00-16:00, enter through courtyard.

Royal Private Apartments (Prywatne Apartamenty Królewskie)

The rooms, which look similar to the State Rooms, can only be visited with a guided (and included) tour. As spaces are strictly limited, these tend to sell out the fastest (on busy days, they may already be booked up by around 10:00).

Cost and Hours: 25 zł, request English tour when buying your ticket—they depart 3/hour, see hours listed earlier, enter through courtyard.

Oriental Art (Sztuka Wschodu)

Though small, this exhibit displays swords, carpets, banners, vases, and other items dating from the 1683 Battle of Vienna, in which the Ottoman army attempted to capture the Austrian capital. These are trophies of Jan III Sobieski, the Polish king who led a pan-European army to victory in that battle.

Cost and Hours: 8 zł, see hours listed earlier, enter through courtyard; don't miss entry on your way back downstairs from Royal State Rooms.

Crown Treasury and Armory (Skarbiec i Zbrojownia)

This is a decent collection of swords, saddles, and shields; ornately decorated muskets, crossbows, and axes; and cannons in the basement. Off in a smaller side room are some of the most precious items. Look for the regalia given to Jan III Sobieski as thanks for his defeat of the Ottoman invaders in the Battle of Vienna: giant swords consecrated by the pope and the mantle (robe) of the Order of the Holy Ghost from France's King Louis XIV. Nearby is the 13th-century coronation sword of the Polish kings and some gorgeously inlaid rifles.

Cost and Hours: 18 zł, see hours listed earlier, plus April-Oct also open—and free—Mon 9:30-13:00, enter through courtyard.

▲▲Leonardo da Vinci's *Lady with an Ermine*

The single best and most famous painting in Kraków is normally displayed at the Czartoryski Museum. But while that space is closed for renovation (likely through 2015, and possibly longer), you'll most likely find the canvas at Wawel Castle. It's well worth the price of entry to view this rare, small (21 x 16 inches), but magnificently executed portrait of a teenage girl—a rare surviving work by one of history's greatest minds. (If you have your heart set on seeing this painting, make sure it's here before making the trip—it may be on loan or in storage.)

Cost and Hours: 10 zł, see hours listed earlier, plus Jan-March also open Sun 10:00-16:00, enter through courtyard.

Visiting the Museum: Spend some time lingering over the canvas (dating from 1489 or 1490). The girl is likely Cecilia Gallerani, the young mistress of Ludovico Sforza, the duke of Milan and Leonardo's employer. The ermine (white during winter) suggests chastity (thus bolstering Cecilia's questioned virtue), but is also a naughty reference to the duke's nickname, Ermellino—notice that his mistress is sensually, um, "stroking the ermine."

Painted before the *Mona Lisa*, the portrait was immediately recognized as revolutionary. Cecilia turns to look at someone, her gaze directed to the side. Leonardo catches this unguarded, informal moment, an unheard-of gesture in the days of the posed, front-facing formal portrait. Her simple body language and faraway gaze speak volumes about her inner thoughts and personality. Leonardo tweaks the generic Renaissance "pyramid" composition, turning it to a three-quarters angle, and softens it with curved lines that trace from Cecilia's eyes and down her cheek and sloping shoulders before doubling back across her folded arms. The background—once gray and blue—was painted black in the 19th century.

Lady with an Ermine is one of only three surviving oil paintings by Leonardo. It's better preserved than her famous cousin in

Paris *(Mona Lisa)*, and—many think—simply more beautiful. Can we be sure it's really by the enigmatic Leonardo? Yep—the master's fingerprints were found literally pressed into the paint (he was known to work areas of paint directly with his fingertips).

▲Lost Wawel (Wawel Zaginiony)

This exhibit traces the history of the hill and its various churches and castles. Begin by viewing the model of the entire castle complex in the 18th century (pre-Austrian razing). From here, the one-way route leads through scarcely explained excavations of a 10th-century church. The collection includes models of the cathedral at various historical stages (originally Romanesque—much simpler, before all the colorful, bulbous domes, chapels, and towers were added—then Gothic, and so on). Circling back to the entrance, find the display of fascinating decorative tiles from 16th-century stoves that once heated the place.

Cost and Hours: 10 zł, see hours listed earlier, plus April-Oct also open—and free—Mon 9:30-13:00; Nov-March also open—and free—Sun 9:30-13:00; enter near snack bar across from side of cathedral.

NATIONAL MUSEUM BRANCHES

Kraków's National Museum (Muzeum Narodowe) is made up of a series of small but interesting collections scattered throughout the city (www.muzeum.krakow.pl). I've listed the best of the National Museum's branches below. A 35-zł combo-ticket covers all of these museums (good for your entire stay), so consider that option if you'll be visiting more than three of them. National Museum branches are free to enter on Sunday (but some have reduced hours on that day, and only some exhibits at Szołayski House are free).

▲▲Gallery of 19th-Century Polish Art (Galeria Sztuki Polskiej XIX Wieku)

This small and surprisingly enjoyable collection of works by obscure Polish artists fills the upper level of the Cloth Hall. While you probably won't recognize any of the Polish names in here—and this collection isn't quite as impressive as Warsaw's National Gallery—many of these paintings are just plain delightful. It's worth a visit to see some Polish canvases in their native land, and to enjoy views over the Square from the hall's upper terraces.

Cost and Hours: 14 zł, free on Sun, Tue-Sun 10:00-18:00, closed Mon, last entry 30 minutes before closing, dry 7-zł audioguide, entrance on side of Cloth Hall facing Adam Mickiewicz statue, tel. 12-424-4600.

Background: Keep in mind that during the 19th century—when every piece of art in this museum was created—there was no "Poland." The country had been split up among its powerful neighbors in a series of three Partitions, and would not appear again on the map of Europe until after World War I. Meanwhile, the 19th century was a period of national revival throughout Europe, when various previously marginalized ethnic groups began to take pride in what made them different from their neighbors. So the artists you see represented here were grappling with trying to forge a national identity at a time when they didn't even have a nation. You'll sense a pessimism that comes from a country that feels abused by foreign powers, mingled with a resolute spirit of national pride.

⊘ Self-Guided Tour: The collection fills just four rooms: Two small rooms in the center and two big halls on either side. On a quick visit, focus on the highlights in the big halls I mention here.

Entering the Cloth Hall, buy your ticket and head up the stairs—pausing on the first floor to peek out onto the inviting

café terrace (your museum ticket gets you in) for a fine view of the Square and St. Mary's. Then continue up to the main exhibit, on the second floor.

The first two small rooms don't feature much of interest. You enter **Room I** (Bacciarelli Room), with works from the Enlightenment; straight ahead is **Room II** (Michałowski Room), featuring Romantic works from 1822 to 1863. The larger, twin halls on either side merit a linger.

Siemiradzki Room (Room III, on the right): This features art of the Academy—that is, "conformist" art embraced by the art critics of the day. Entering the room, turn right and survey the canvases counterclockwise. The space is dominated by the works of Jan Matejko, a remarkably productive painter who specialized in epic historical scenes that he presented in such a way as to comment on his own era (for more on Matejko, see page 404).

• *Circling the room, look for these paintings. The first two paintings you see are worth examining.*

1. Jan Matejko—*Wenyhora*: The first big canvas is Matejko's depiction of Wenyhora, a late-18th-century Ukrainian soothsayer who, according to legend, foretold Poland's hardships—the three Partitions, Poland's pact with Napoleon, and its difficulties regaining nationhood. Like many Poles of the era, Matejko was preoccupied with Poland's tragic fate, imbuing this scene with an air of inevitable tragedy.

2. Jacek Malczewski—*Death of Ellenai*: A similar gloominess is reflected in this canvas. The main characters in a Polish

Romantic poem, Ellenai and Anhelli, have been exiled to a remote cabin in Siberia (in Russia, one of the great powers occupying Poland). Just when they think things can't get worse, Ellenai dies. Anhelli sits immobilized by grief.

• *Dominating the right side of the hall is...*

3. Jan Matejko—*Tadeusz Kościuszko:* One of the heroes of the American Revolution, now back in his native Poland fight-

ing the Russians, doffs his hat after his unlikely victory at the battle at Racławice. In this battle (which ulti- mately had little bearing on Russia's drive to overtake Poland), a ragtag army of Polish peasants defeated the Russian forces. Kościuszko is clad in an American uniform, sym- bolizing Matejko's respect for the American ideals of democracy and self-determination.

• *Dominating the far wall is...*

4. Henryk Siemiradzki—*Nero's Torches:* On the left, Roman citizens eagerly gather to watch Christians being burned at the

stake. The symbolism is clear: The meek and down- trodden (whether Christians in the time of Rome, or Poles in the heyday of Russia and Austria) may be perse- cuted now, but we have faith that their noble ideals will ultimately prevail.

• *On the next wall, find...*

5. Pantaleon Szyndler—*Bathing Girl:* This piece evokes the orientalism popular in 19th-century Europe, when romanticized European notions of the Orient (such as harem slave girls) were popular artistic themes. Already voyeuristic, the painting was originally downright lewd until Szyndler painted over a man leer- ing at the woman from the left side of the canvas.

• *The huge canvas on this wall is...*

6. Jan Matejko—*The Prussian Homage:* The last Grand Master of the fearsome Teutonic Knights swears allegiance to the Polish king in 1525. This historic ceremony took place in the Main Market Square in Kraków, the capital at the time. Notice the Cloth Hall and the spires of St. Mary's Church in the background. Matejko has painted his own face on one of his favorite historical figures, the jester Stańczyk at the foot of the throne (for more on Stańczyk, see page 405).

• *Continue the rest of the way around the room. Keep an eye out for*

Tadeusz Ajdukiewicz's portrait of Helena Modrzejewska, a popular actress of the time, attending a party in this very building. Finally, backtrack through Room I and continue into the...

Chełmoński Room (Room IV): Featuring works of the late 19th century, this section includes Realism and the first inklings of Symbolism and Impressionism. Just as elsewhere in Europe (including Paris, where many of these artists trained), artists were beginning to throw off the conventions of the Academy and embrace their own muse.

• *As you proceed counterclockwise through the room, the first stretch of canvases features landscapes and genre paintings. Tune in to a couple of appealing nature scenes: Józef Chełmoński's small, misty Cranes, and...*

1. Wladyslaw Malecki—*A Gathering of Storks:* The majestic birds stand under big willows in front of the setting sun. Even seemingly innocent wildlife paintings have a political message: Storks are particularly numerous in Poland, making them a subtle patriotic symbol.

• *A few canvases down, find...*

2. Józef Brandt—*A Meeting on the Bridge:* This dramatic painting shows soldiers and aristocrats pushing a farmer into a ditch—a comment on the state of the Polish people at that time. Just to the right, see Brandt's *Fight for a Turkish Standard.* This artist specialized in battle scenes, frequently involving a foe from the East—as was often the reality here along Europe's buffer zone with Asia.

• *Just to the left of Brandt's works is...*

3. Samuel Hirszenberg—*School of Talmudists:* Young Jewish students pore over the Talmud. One of them, deeply lost in thought, may be pondering more than ancient Jewish law. This canvas suggests the inclusion of Jews in Poland's cultural tapestry during this age. While still subject to pervasive bigotry here, many Jewish refugees found Poland to be a relatively welcoming, tolerant place to settle on a typically hostile continent.

• *Dominating the end of the room is...*

4. Józef Chełmoński—*Four-in-Hand:* In this intersection of worlds, a Ukrainian horse-man gives a lift to a pipe-smoking nobleman. Feel the thrilling energy as the horses charge directly at you through splashing puddles.

• *Heading back toward the entrance, on the right wall, watch for...*

5. Witold Pruszkowski—*Water Nymphs:* Based on Slavic legends (and wearing traditional Ukrainian costumes), these mischievous, siren-like beings have just taken one victim (see his hand in the foreground) and are about to descend on another (seen faintly in the upper-right corner). Beyond this painting are some travel pictures from Italy and France (including some that are very Impressionistic, suggesting a Parisian influence).

• *Flanking the entrance/exit door are two of this room's best works. First, on the right, is...*

6. Władysław Podkowiński—*Frenzy:* This gripping painting's title *(Szał),* tellingly, has been translated as either *Ecstasy* or *Insanity.* A pale, sensuous woman—possibly based on a socialite for whom the artist fostered a desperate but unrequited love—clutches an all-fired-up black stallion, who's frothing at the mouth. This sexually charged painting caused a frenzy indeed at its 1894 unveiling, leading the unbalanced artist to attack his own creation with a knife (you can still see the slash marks in the canvas).

• *On the other side of the door is...*

7. Jacek Malczewski—*Introduction:* A young painter's apprentice on a bench contemplates his future. Surrounded by nature and with his painter's tools beside him, it's easy to imagine this as a self-portrait of the artist as a young man...wondering if he's choosing the correct path. Malczewski was an extremely talented Młoda Polska artist who tends to be overshadowed by his contemporary, Wyspiański. Viewing this canvas—and others by him—makes me feel grateful that he decided to stick with painting.

▲Szołayski House (Kamienica Szołayskich)

This restored mansion, just one block from the Main Market Square, features high-quality temporary exhibits, most often showcasing Art Nouveau works by the Młoda Polska movement (for more on this movement and its members, see page 263). If you're lucky, you may see the excellent "Forever Young! Poland and Its Art Around 1900" exhibit (likely on display at least through 2015), which offers a concise overview of this period of artistic flourishing. This exhibit collects the works of a variety of turn-of-the-20th-century artists around themes (scenery of Kraków—see Wyspiański's hauntingly beautiful *Planty Overlooking Wawel;* portraits; and some fine Art Nouveau posters and books). Whatever exhibits are on display, they typically feature some masterpieces by the movement's founder, Stanisław Wyspiański, though many of these are currently in restoration and/or storage (but you can still see his works inside St. Francis Basilica).

Cost and Hours: 11 zł, some exhibits free on Sun, open Tue-Sat 10:00-18:00, Sun 10:00-16:00, closed Mon, last entry 30 minutes before closing, 1 block northwest of the Square at plac Szczepański 9, tel. 12-292-8183.

Nearby: The charming, recently restored square that Szołayski House faces, **plac Szczepański,** is a hub for youthful, cutting-edge, artistic types. Tucked in a corner of the Old Town, just away from the Square, it's a strange and wonderful little oasis of urban sophistication holding out against the rising tide of tacky tourism. In addition to Szołayski House itself, the square has several bohemian cafés (including the recommended Charlotte). If you follow Szczepańska street one more block out to the Planty, then turn left, you'll find **Bunkier Sztuki,** an art gallery that fills an unfortunate communist-era building that really does feel like a bunker. But this conformist architecture is filled with quite the opposite: changing exhibitions of contemporary art (some exhibits free, others require a ticket, Tue-Sun 12:00-20:00, closed Mon, http://ha.art.pl). The gallery's fine café, under a delightfully airy canopy facing the Planty, has an almost Parisian ambience—a great place to escape the crowds (see "Eating in Kraków," later).

Bishop Erazm Ciołek Palace
(Pałac Biskupa Erazma Ciołka)

This branch of the National Museum features two separate art collections. Upstairs, the extensive "Art of Old Poland" section shows off works from the 12th through the 18th centuries, with room after room of altarpieces, sculptures, paintings, and more. The "Orthodox Art of the Old Polish Republic" section on the ground floor offers a taste of the remote Eastern reaches of Poland, with icons and other ecclesiastical art from the Orthodox faith. You'll see a sizeable section of the iconostasis (wall of icons) from the town of Lipovec. Both collections are covered by the same ticket and are very well-presented in a modern facility. Items are labeled in English, but there's not much description.

Cost and Hours: 12 zł, free on Sun, audioguide-5 zł, Tue-Sat 10:00-18:00, Sun 10:00-16:00, closed Mon, Kanonicza 17, tel. 12-424-9371.

▲Czartoryski Museum
(Muzeum Czartoryskich)

This eclectic collection, displaying armor, handicrafts, decorative arts, and paintings, is one of Kraków's best-known (and most overrated) museums. It's wrapping up a multi-year renovation; during your visit, some or all of its collection may already be open again. But the painting gallery—with its top pieces (a Leonardo and a Rembrandt)—may take longer to reopen. Likely through at least 2015, its undisputed highlight, Leonardo's *Lady with an Ermine,* will be displayed instead at Wawel Castle. Before visiting this museum, get the latest from a TI about how much is open.

Background: The museum's collection came about, in part, thanks to Poland's 1791 constitution (Europe's first), which inspired Princess Izabela Czartoryska to begin gathering bits of Polish history and culture. She fled with the collection to Paris after the 1830 insurrection, and 45 years later, her grandson returned it to its present Kraków location. When he ran out of space, he bought part of the monastery across the street, joining the buildings with a fancy passageway. The Nazis took the collection to Germany, and although most of it has been returned, some pieces are still missing.

The museum owns two undisputed masterpieces, which are in varying states of accessibility. Art lovers will want to ask around for the scoop on their latest locations. While the museum is closed, its top painting—**Leonardo da Vinci's** *Lady with an Ermine*—can likely be found at Kraków's Wawel Castle (described earlier). **Rembrandt van Rijn's** *Landscape with the Good Samaritan* (1638) may be on display in another city (or possibly in Kraków). The museum technically owns a third masterpiece, **Raphael's** *Portrait of a Young Man*, but its whereabouts are unknown. Arguably one of the most famous and most valuable stolen paintings of all time, it's quite likely a self-portrait (but possibly a portrait of Raphael by another artist), depicting a Renaissance dandy, clad in a fur coat, with a self-satisfied smirk. Painted (perhaps) by the Renaissance master in 1513 or 1514, and purchased by a Czartoryski prince around the turn of the 19th century, the work was seized by the occupying Nazis during World War II. Along with the paintings by Leonardo and Rembrandt, this Raphael decorated the Wawel Castle residence of Nazi governor Hans Frank. But when Frank and the Nazis fled the invading Red Army at the end of the war, many of their pilfered artworks were lost—including the Raphael. For decades, this canvas was synonymous with art theft—the (literal) poster boy for Nazi crimes against culture. Then, dramatically, a Polish news site announced in 2012 that the priceless painting had been found, safe and sound (in a bank vault in an undisclosed location). Unfortunately, this was a misinterpretation of remarks made by government officials. But authorities are still hopeful the painting "will surface sooner or later" and that the "Czartoryski Raphael," as it's called, will be returned to this museum.

Cost and Hours: If museum is open—around 12 zł, free on Sun, open Tue-Sun 10:00-16:00 or possibly until 18:00, closed

Mon, last entry 30 minutes before closing, 2 blocks north of the Main Market Square at ulica Św. Jana 19, tel. 12-422-5566, www. czartoryski.org.

Visiting the Museum: If the museum is open, you'll wander through rooms of ornate armor (including a ceremonial Turkish tent from the 1683 siege of Vienna, plus feathered Hussar armor), tapestries, treasury items, majolica pottery, and Meissen porcelain figures. Rounding out the exhibits are painting galleries (including Italian, French, and Dutch High Renaissance and Baroque, as well as Czartoryski family portraits) and ancient art (mostly sculptures and vases).

More National Museum Branches

While less interesting than the branches listed above, the National Museum's **Main Branch** (Gmach Główny) is worth a visit for museum completists. It features 20th-century Polish art and temporary exhibits (10 zł, west of the Main Market Square at aleja 3 Maja 1). The new **Europeum** collection, housed in a restored granary, features works by European masters, including Breughel and Veneziano, along with a range of lesser-known artists (just west of the Old Town at plac Sikorskiego 6). You can also check out the museum of Wyspiański's friend and rival, the **Józef Mehoffer House** (Dom Józefa Mehoffera, 6 zł, ulica Krupnicza 26, tel. 12-421-1143), and the former residence of their mentor, the **Jan Matejko House** (Dom Jana Matejki, 8 zł, ulica Floriańska 41, tel. 12-422-5926).

OTHER ATTRACTIONS

▲▲Rynek Underground Museum (Podziemia Rynku)

Recent work to renovate the Square's pavement unearthed a wealth of remains from previous structures. Now you can do some urban

spelunking with a visit to this high-tech medieval-history museum, which is literally underground—beneath all the photo-snapping tourists on the Square above.

Cost and Hours: 19 zł, free on Tue, open Mon 10:00-20:00, Tue 10:00-16:00 (but closed first Tue of each month), Wed-Sun 10:00-22:00, shorter hours in winter; last entry 1.25 hours before closing, enter at north end of Cloth Hall near the fountain, Rynek Główny 1, tel. 12-426-5060, www.podziemiarynku.com.

Visiting the Museum: You'll enter through a door near the north end of the Cloth Hall (close to the fountain, facing St.

KRAKÓW

Mary's). Climb down a flight of stairs, buy your ticket, then follow the numbered panels—1 to 70—through the exhibit (all in English). Cutting-edge museum technology illuminates life and times in medieval Kraków: Touchscreens let you delve into topics that intrigue you, 3-D virtual holograms resurrect old buildings, and video clips illustrate everyday life on unexpected surfaces (such as a curtain of fog).

All of this is wrapped around large chunks of early structures that still survive beneath the Square; several "witness columns" of rock and dirt are accompanied by diagrams helping you trace the layers of history. Interactive maps emphasize Kraków's Europe-wide importance as an intersection of major trade routes, and several models, maps, and digital reconstructions give you a good look at Kraków during the Middle Ages—when the Old Town looked barely different from today. You'll see a replica of a blacksmith's shop and learn how "vampire prevention burials" were used to ensure that the suspected undead wouldn't return from the grave. In the middle of the complex, look up through the glass of the Square's fountain to see the towers of St. Mary's above. Under the skylight is a model of medieval Kraków. While it looks much the same as today, notice a few key changes: the moat ringing the Old Town, where the Planty is today; and the several smaller market halls out on the Square.

Deeper in the exhibit, explore the long corridors of ruined buildings that once ran alongside the length of the Cloth Hall. There are many intriguing cases showing artifacts that shops would have sold (jewelry, tools, amber figurines, and so on). Also in this area, you'll find a corridor with images of the Square all torn up for the recent renovation, plus a series of five modern brick rooms, each showing a brief, excellent film outlining a different period of Kraków's history. These "Kraków Chronicles" provide a big-picture context to what otherwise seems like a loose collection of cool museum gizmos, and also help you better appreciate what you'll see outside the museum's doors.

▲Jagiellonian University Museum: Collegium Maius

Kraków had the second university in Central Europe (founded in 1364, after Prague's), boasting such illustrious grads over the centuries as Copernicus and St. John Paul II. With around 150,000 students (including 500 Norwegian med students), this city is still very much a university town, and Jagiellonian University proudly offers tours of its historic oldest building, the 15th-century Collegium Maius (one block west of the Main Market Square at ulica Jagiellońska 15). In the Middle Ages, professors were completely devoted to their scholarly pursuits. They were unmarried and lived, ate, and slept here in an almost monastic environment. They taught downstairs and lived upstairs. In many ways, this building feels more like a monastery than a university.

The university also comes with some chilling history. On November 6, 1939, the occupying Nazis called all professors together for a meeting. With 183 gathered unknowingly in a hall, they were suddenly loaded into trucks and sent to their deaths in concentration camps. You decapitate a culture when you kill its intelligentsia.

Tours: Student guides lead visitors through the musty and mildly interesting interior of the complex. You'll choose between two different guided tours: 30 minutes (very popular) or one hour. It's smart to call ahead to find out when the shorter tour is scheduled in English, and to reserve for either tour (tel. 12-663-1307 for advance reservations, or tel. 12-663-1521 for same day, www.maius. uj.edu.pl).

The **30-minute tour** covers the "main exhibition" route: the library, refectory (with a gorgeously carved Baroque staircase), treasury (including Polish filmmaker Andrzej Wajda's honorary Oscar), assembly hall, and some old scientific instruments (12 zł, a few tours per day in English, 20 people maximum, leaves every 20 minutes Mon-Sat 10:00-15:00, until 18:00 Tue and Thu in April-Oct, last tour departs 40 minutes before closing, no tours Sun). On Tuesday afternoons, the tour is free (runs 15:00-18:00, shorter hours in winter, last tour departs 40 minutes before closing). Be aware that these tours can book up—especially the free Tuesday afternoon departures.

The **one-hour tour** adds some more interiors, room after room of more old scientific instruments, medieval art (mostly church sculptures), a Rubens, a small landscape from the shop of Rembrandt, and Chopin's piano (16 zł, usually in English Mon-Fri at 13:00, no tours Sat-Sun).

Before you leave, enjoy a cup of hot chocolate at the chocolate shop (down the stairs near the entrance)—widely regarded as the best in town.

Dominican Church, a.k.a. Holy Trinity Church (Bazylika Trójcy Świętej)

Sitting in the middle of town, facing St. Francis Basilica from a couple of blocks away, this may not be Kraków's finest church, but it's still worth a peek. Inside, you'll find a Neo-Gothic space that was rebuilt after a devastating 1850 fire. You may be approached

and offered an audioguide to tour
the church, in exchange for a donation; it's a good little tour and
worth doing, if you have the time.
Or, for a quick visit, tune in to just
a few details: The unique metal
chandeliers are one of many modern flourishes added during the
late-19th-century restoration of
the church. Climb the staircase in
the left aisle to reach the chapel of

St. Hyacinth. Locally known as St. Jacek, this early Dominican
leader—called the "Apostle of the North"—is also the patron
saint of pierogi (stuffed dough, similar to ravioli). During a fam-
ine, St. Jacek supposedly invented pierogi and—in a loaves-and-
fishes-type miracle—produced plateful after plateful, feeding the
desperate locals. His image adorns Kraków's annual Pierogi Cup
contest, and to this day, when old-fashioned Poles are surprised,
they might exclaim, *"Święty Jacek z pierogami!"* ("St. Hyacinth and
his pierogi!"). Back down in the main part of the church, stroll
slowly past the gorgeously carved wooden seats of the choir area
(behind the altar); then, at the main altar, identify the three parts
of the trinity: Jesus (short beard), God (long beard), and Holy
Spirit (beardless dove).

Cost and Hours: Free but donation requested, daily 6:30-
13:00 & 16:00-20:00, facing plac Dominikański at Stolarska 12.

Archdiocesan Museum (Muzeum Archidiecezjalne)

This museum, in a building where St. John Paul II lived both as a
priest and as a bishop, consists of several parts: the underwhelming ground-floor collection of sacral art (with altars, paintings,
and vestments); various temporary exhibits; and the top-floor
museum devoted to St. John Paul II. Wandering past the scores
of paintings and photographs, the late pontiff's cult of personality
is almost palpable. Unfortunately, because the collection mostly
consists of elaborate gifts received by the Holy Father from around
the world, it offers little intimacy or insight into the man himself.
Still, admirers of St. John Paul II will appreciate it. This museum
shares a collection with the St. John Paul II Sanctuary (part of the
John Paul II Center) on the outskirts of town; visit here only if you
won't be going to the more interesting collection at the museum
there.

Cost and Hours: 5 zł, Tue-Fri 10:00-16:00, Sat-Sun 10:00-
15:00, closed Mon, Kanonicza 19-21, tel. 12-421-8963, www.
muzeumkra.diecezja.pl.

John Paul II Center Exhibition

This modest exhibition space, across the street from the Archdiocesan Museum, is the headquarters for the construction of the sprawling John Paul II Center (described later). If you can't make it out to the actual center, stop in here to learn more about it—with photographs, artifacts, and films relating to the late pontiff.

Cost and Hours: Free, daily 10:00-16:00, Kanonicza 18, tel. 12-429-6471, www.janpawel2.pl.

KAZIMIERZ (JEWISH QUARTER)

The neighborhood of Kazimierz (kah-ZHEE-mezh), 20 minutes by foot southeast of Kraków's Old Town, is the historic heart of Kraków's once-thriving Jewish community. After years of neglect, the district was rediscovered by Krakovians and tourists alike in the mid-2000s. Even so, visitors expecting a polished, touristy scene like Prague's Jewish Quarter will be surprised... and maybe disappointed. This is basically a local-feeling, slightly run-down neighborhood with a handful of Jewish cemeteries, synagogues, and restaurants, and often a few pensive Israeli tour groups wandering the streets. It's also the city's edgy, hipster culture center, jammed with colorful, creative bars and designer boutiques—sometimes oddly juxtaposed with a somber reverence for Judaism. But for many, this is where you'll find the true soul of the European Jewish experience. For more suggestions of what to do in Kazimierz, see page 330 of "Entertainment in Kraków," page 340 of "Sleeping in Kraków," and page 347 of "Eating in Kraków."

Try to visit any day except Saturday, when most Jewish-themed sights are closed (except the Old Synagogue, High Synagogue, and Galicia Jewish Museum). Monday comes with a few closures: the Ethnographic Museum, Museum of Contemporary Art in Kraków, and Museum of Municipal Engineering. On Monday, the Schindler's Factory Museum is free, but it's also open shorter hours and is more crowded than usual.

Note that it's respectful for men to cover their heads while visiting a Jewish cemetery or synagogue. While some of these sights offer loaner yarmulkes, it's easiest to bring your own hat.

Getting to Kazimierz: From the Old Town, it's about a 20-minute **walk,** which gets you out of the fairy-tale tourist zone and into the real, soot-stained, workaday Kraków (that's a good thing). From the Main Market Square, walk down ulica Sienna (near St. Mary's Church). At the fork, bear right through the Planty park. At the intersection with the busy Westerplatte ring road, you'll continue straight ahead (bear right at fork, then continue straight across the busy ring road) down Starowiślna for 15

KRAKÓW

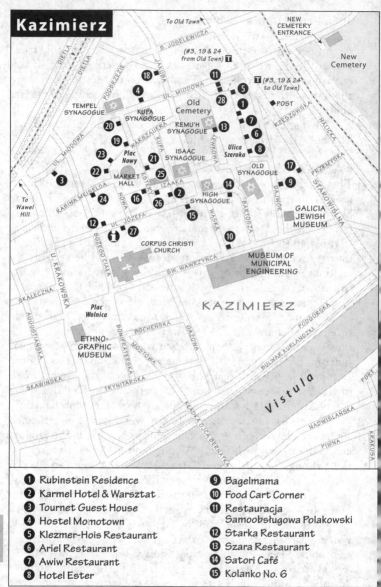

Kazimierz

1. Rubinstein Residence
2. Karmel Hotel & Warsztat
3. Tournet Guest House
4. Hostel Momotown
5. Klezmer-Hois Restaurant
6. Ariel Restaurant
7. Awiw Restaurant
8. Hotel Ester
9. Bagelmama
10. Food Cart Corner
11. Restauracja Samoobsługowa Polakowski
12. Starka Restaurant
13. Szara Restaurant
14. Satori Café
15. Kolanko No. 6

more minutes. To hop the **tram,** go to the stop on the left-hand side of ulica Sienna (at the intersection with Westerplatte, across the street from the Poczta Główna, or main post office). Catch tram #3, #19, or #24 and go two stops to Miodowa. Walking or by tram, at the intersection of Starowiślna and Miodowa, you'll see a small park across the street and to the right. To reach the heart of

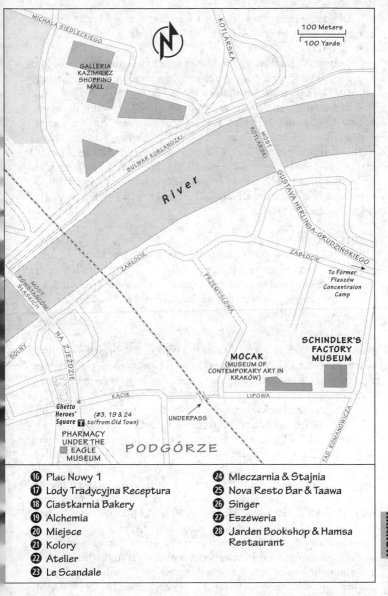

16 Plac Nowy 1
17 Lody Tradycyjna Receptura
18 Ciastkarnia Bakery
19 Alchemia
20 Miejsce
21 Kolory
22 Atelier
23 Le Scandale

24 Mleczarnia & Stajnia
25 Nova Resto Bar & Taawa
26 Singer
27 Eszeweria
28 Jarden Bookshop & Hamsa Restaurant

Kazimierz—ulica Szeroka—cut through this park. You can also take this tram from near the train station (see "Arrival in Kraków," earlier). To return to the Old Town, catch tram #3, #19, or #24 from the intersection of Starowiślna and Miodowa (kitty-corner from where you got off the tram), and go two stops back to the Poczta Główna stop.

Information: An official **TI** is just a few blocks off the bottom of ulica Szeroka, at ulica Józefa 7 (daily 9:00-17:00, tel. 12-422-0471).

Tours: As Kazimierz's sights are spread out and not presented in a unified way, it's a good place to hire a **local guide** (see listings on page 251). **Jarden Bookshop** (listed later) runs several tours (prices based on the number of people; I've listed the price per person for 2 people): Jewish Kazimierz overview (70 zł, 2 hours, walking tour), Kazimierz and the WWII ghetto (90 zł, 3 hours, walking, the best overview), *Schindler's List* sights (120 zł, 2 hours, by car), and Auschwitz-Birkenau (190 zł, 6-7 hours, by car). Call to reserve ahead, as tours are by appointment only. Pairs or singles may be able to join an already scheduled tour (which lowers the price for everybody).

Central Kazimierz

Ulica Szeroka is the core of Kazimierz; within a few blocks of here, you'll find two cemeteries (quite different and both worth a visit), six synagogues, and three museums, as well as the lively market square called plac Nowy. The various sights in this area operate independently and can be seen in any order.

Ulica Szeroka

Begin your visit by getting oriented on the neighborhood's hub, **ulica Szeroka ("Broad Street").** More of a long, parking-lot square than a street, this strip is surrounded by Jewish-themed restaurants, hotels, and synagogues.

The **Jarden Bookshop** at the top of the square is worth a stop. While there are many new bookstores in Kazimierz (mostly inside the various museums and synagogues), this is the original. It serves as an unofficial information point for the neighborhood and sells a wide variety of fairly priced books on Kazimierz and Jewish culture in the region, including a good 5-zł Kraków map of Jewish monuments and the well-illustrated 18-zł *Jewish Kraków* guidebook (Mon-Fri 9:00-18:00, Sat-Sun 10:00-18:00, ulica Szeroka 2, tel. 12-429-1374, www.jarden.pl, jarden@jarden.pl).

Circling around the left side of the building that houses Jarden and the recommended Hamsa restaurant, you'll find where a local entrepreneur has restored a row of rustic old Jewish **shop fronts,** as they would have appeared in Kazimierz's pre-Holocaust prime. This lane leads to **Miodowa street,** which you can follow left to reach two of Kazimierz's lesser-known synagogues (Tempel and Kupa, both described later). In the opposite direction, Miodowa crosses busy Starowiślna, then goes under a train tunnel to reach the New Cemetery (also described later).

Back on ulica Szeroka, circle around to the downhill side of the little **park** to find a low-profile monument honoring the "65 thousand Polish citizens of Jewish nationality from Kraków and its environs" who were murdered by the Nazis during the Holocaust. Tragically, this piece of Kraków's history was all but lost during the communist period. After 1989, interest in Kazimierz's unique Jewish history was faintly rekindled. But it was only when Steven Spielberg chose to film *Schindler's List* here in 1993 that the world took renewed interest in Kazimierz. (A local once winked to me, "They ought to build a statue to Spielberg on that square.")

Turn 180 degrees, facing the bottom end of ulica Szeroka, to get your bearings. On your left is a strip of hotels and restaurants, many of them offering live traditional Jewish **klezmer music** nightly in summer (for details on your various options, see page 347 in "Eating in Kraków," later). The Ester Hotel near the bottom of the square often has outdoor klezmer music in good weather—allowing you to get a taste of this unique musical form before committing to a full meal.

Halfway down this side of the square, the green house at #14 is where **Helena Rubinstein** was born in 1870. At age 31, she emigrated to Australia, where she parlayed her grandmother's traditional formula for hand cream into a cosmetics empire. Many cosmetics still used by people worldwide today were invented by Rubinstein, who died at age 92 in New York City as one of the most successful businesswomen of all time—just one of many illustrious Jewish residents of Kazimierz.

On the right side of the square, near the top, is the entrance to the **Rem'uh Synagogue and Old Cemetery.** Partway down this side, little Lewkowa lane zigzags through the heart of the district to **Isaac Synagogue** and the **plac Nowy market.** All of these are described later. Exploring these streets, you may see some dilapidated buildings that are typical of this district. Kazimierz is so ramshackle, in part, because many of the buildings are still under state control; during World War II, the Nazis seized Jewish-owned property, which was later nationalized by the communists, and therefore lacks clear ownership today.

Next, head down to the bottom end of ulica Szeroka, which dead-ends at the **Old Synagogue** (now a good museum, and perhaps Kazimierz's most worthwhile synagogue to enter—described later). The bit of white stone wall and rampart to the left of the Old Synagogue is a reconstruction of the original Kazimierz town wall from the 14th century.

Find the big **map of Kazimierz** directly in front of the synagogue, and use it for a historical orientation—reading the district's past into its current street plan. What are now Starowiślna and Dietla streets—which frame off Kazimierz in a triangle of land hemmed in by the riverbank—were once canals, meaning

KRAKÓW

that Kazimierz was built on an island. When King Kazimierz the Great—who reportedly didn't care much for Krakovians—founded this district in 1335, he envisioned it as a separate town to rival Kraków. (If you have a 50-zł note, take a look at it: That's Kazimierz the Great on the front, and on the back you'll see his capital, Cracovia, and the most important town he founded, Casmirus.) Examining the map, notice plac Wolnica, the big market square to rival Kraków's, and Corpus Christi Church, which was intentionally built to compete for attention with St. Mary's. After Jews began to settle here in the early 16th century, a wall along Jakuba street (directly behind the Old Cemetery) separated Jewish Kazimierz (where we are now) from Christian Kraków (around the market squares and big church, to the west). But by 1800, the dense Jewish population spilled over those boundaries and filled the entire district.

For much of Kazimierz's history, Jews and Christians lived in relative harmony, side-by-side. As an example of this, notice the intersection just west of plac Nowy, where ulica Bożego Ciała ("Corpus Christi Street") crosses ulica Meiselsa ("Rabbi Meisel Street"). Also notice the district called Podgórze, directly across the river from Kazimierz. This is where the Nazis ultimately forced Kazimierz's Jewish residents into a ghetto. It contains several powerful sights, including the **Pharmacy Under the Eagle** and the **Schindler's Factory Museum** (both described later).

While Kazimierz's Jewish story is powerful, don't miss its other, more recent claim to fame—its youthful counterculture. As you face the Old Synagogue, the street to the right, **ulica Józefa,** leads past the **High Synagogue,** then a stretch of engaging designer boutiques. This area—the best place in Kraków to spot up-and-coming fashion and design—is described on page 325 of "Shopping in Kraków."

▲▲Old Jewish Cemetery (Stary Cmentarz)

This small cemetery was used to bury members of the Jewish community from 1552 to 1800. With more than a hundred of the top Jewish intellectuals of that age buried here, this is considered one of the most important Jewish cemeteries in Europe. It has been renovated—so in a way, it actually feels newer than the New Cemetery. After the New Cemetery (described next) was opened in 1800, this one gradually fell into disrepair. What remained was further desecrated by the Nazis during World War II. In

Jewish Kraków

In the 14th century, King Kazimierz the Great created policies that encouraged Jews fleeing other kingdoms to settle in Poland. Kraków's Jewish community—which was originally concentrated in the university district—clashed with the students, and when a destructive fire broke out in 1495, the Jews were blamed. The king at the time forced all of Kraków's Jews to move to Kazimierz (which was then a separate town).

After several centuries as a town divided by a wall into Christian (west) and Jewish (east) neighborhoods, Kazimierz was integrated as part of Kraków around 1800, and the Jewish community flourished. Around that same time, Polish lands had the biggest Jewish population in the world (about 4 million)—and Kraków was a center of Jewish culture.

By the start of World War II, 65,000 Jews lived in Kraków (mostly in Kazimierz)—making up more than a quarter of the city's population. When the Nazis arrived, they immediately sent most of Kraków's Jews to the ghetto in the eastern Polish city of Lublin. Soon after, they forced Kraków's remaining 15,000 Jews into a walled ghetto at Podgórze, across the river. The Jews' cemeteries were defiled, their buildings ransacked and destroyed. In 1942, the Nazis began transporting Kraków's Jews to death camps (including Płaszów, just on Kraków's outskirts, and Auschwitz). Many others were worked to death in the Podgórze ghetto. Only a few thousand Kraków Jews survived the war. During World War II, occupied Poland had the strictest laws in the Nazi realm: This was the only place where, if you were caught trying to help Jews escape, your entire family could be executed. And yet, many Poles risked their lives to help escapees.

Today's Kraków has only about 200 Jewish residents. During the communist era, this waning population was ignored or mistreated. But in recent years, Kazimierz has enjoyed a renaissance of Jewish culture—thanks largely to the popularity of *Schindler's List* (which was partly filmed here). Look for handwritten letters from Steven Spielberg and the cast in local restaurants (such as Ariel) and hotels. While few Jews live here now, the spirit of the Jewish tradition lives on in the many synagogues, as well as in the soulful cemeteries.

the 1950s, it was discovered, excavated, and put back together as you see here. Shattered gravestones form a mosaic wall around the perimeter. As in all Jewish cemeteries, you'll see many small stones stacked on the graves. The tradition comes from placing stones—representing prayers—over desert graves to cover the body and prevent animals from disturbing it. Behind the little synagogue to the left, the tallest tombstone next to the tree belonged to Moses Isserles (a.k.a. Remu'h), an important 16th-century rabbi. He is believed to have been a miracle worker, and his grave was one of the only ones that remained standing after World War II. Notice the written prayers crammed into the cracks and crevices of the tombstone.

Cost and Hours: 5 zł, also includes entry to attached Remu'h Synagogue—described later; very sporadic hours according to demand—especially outside peak season—but generally open Sun-Fri 9:00-16:00, can be open until 18:00 May-Sept, closes earlier off-season and by sundown on Fri, always closed Sat, enter through Remu'h Synagogue at ulica Szeroka 40.

▲New Jewish Cemetery (Nowy Cmentarz)

This much larger site has graves of those who died after 1800. Nazis also vandalized this cemetery, selling many of its gravestones to stonecutters and using others as pavement in their concentration camps. Many of the gravestones have since been cemented back in their original positions. Other headstones could not be replaced and were used to create the moving mosaic wall and Holocaust monument (on the right as you enter). Most gravestones are in  one of four languages: Hebrew (generally the oldest, especially if there's no other language, though some are newer "retro" tombstones); Yiddish (sounds like a mix of German and Hebrew and uses the Hebrew alphabet); Polish (Jews who assimilated into the Polish community); and German (Jews who assimilated into the German community). The earliest graves are simple stones, while later ones imitate graves in Polish Catholic cemeteries—larger, more elaborate, and with a long stone jutting out to cover the body. Notice that some new-looking graves have old dates. These were most likely put here well after the Holocaust (or even after the communist era) by relatives of the dead.

Cost and Hours: Free, Sun-Fri 8:00-18:00, until 16:00 in winter, closed Sat. It's tricky to find: Go under the railway tunnel at the east end of ulica Miodowa, and jog left as you emerge. The cemetery is to your right (enter through gate with small *cmentarz żydowski* sign).

Synagogues

Six different synagogues in Kazimierz welcome visitors. Some synagogues have been converted into museums, while others are still used for services. The first two synagogues listed below are on Kazimierz's main square, ulica Szeroka; the next four are all within three blocks to the west (all are shown on the map on page 296).

Remu'h Synagogue, which is tight, cozy, and dates from 1553, has been carefully renovated and is fully active. Notice the original 16th-century frescoed walls and ceilings, and the money-box at the door (included in 5-zł entry fee for Old Cemetery, same unpredictable hours as Old Cemetery, ulica Szeroka 40).

The **Old Synagogue** (Stara Synagoga), the oldest surviving Jewish building in Poland, is now a good three-room museum on

local Jewish culture, with informative English descriptions. Most of the exhibits are displayed in the impressive main prayer hall. The synagogue is eight steps down from street level because Jewish buildings weren't allowed to be taller than Christian ones. In order to have the proper proportion for the building, the ground floor needed to be lower (9 zł, free on Mon; April-Oct Mon 10:00-14:00, Tue-Sun 9:00-17:00; Nov-March Mon 10:00-14:00, Tue-Wed and Sat-Sun 9:00-16:00, Fri 10:00-17:00; good 50-stop audioguide-10 zł; ulica Szeroka 24, tel. 12-422-0962).

The **High Synagogue**—so called because its prayer room is upstairs—displays changing exhibits, most of which focus on the people who lived here before the Holocaust (9 zł, daily 9:00-20:00, shorter hours in winter, just around the corner from the Old Synagogue at ulica Józefa 38, tel. 12-430-6889).

Isaac Synagogue (Synagoga Izaaka), one of Kraków's biggest, was built in the 17th century. On the walls in the prayer hall are giant paintings of prayers for worshippers who couldn't afford to buy books (with translations posted below). The synagogue also serves as the local center for the Hasidic Jewish group Chabad, with a kosher restaurant and a library (7 zł, 5 zł extra to borrow descriptions; April-Oct Sun-Thu 8:30-20:00, Fri 8:30-14:30, closed Sat; Nov-March Sun-Thu 8:30-18:00, Fri 8:30-13:30, closed Sat; a block west of ulica Szeroka at ulica Kupa 18, tel. 12-430-2222). In addition to its Sabbath services, this is Kraków's only synagogue

The Synagogue

A synagogue is a place of public worship, where Jews gather to pray, sing, and read from the Torah. Most synagogues have similar features, though they vary depending on the congregation.

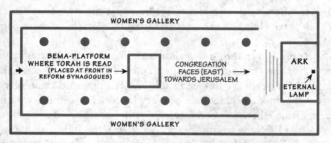

The synagogue generally faces toward Jerusalem (so in Kraków, worshippers face east). At the east end is an alcove called the **ark,** which holds the Torah. These scriptures (the first five books of the Old Testament) are written in Hebrew on scrolls wrapped in luxuriant cloth. The other main element of the synagogue is the **bema,** an elevated platform from which the Torah is read aloud (the equivalent of a pulpit in a Christian church). In traditional Orthodox synagogues, the bema is near the center of the hall, and the reader stands facing the same direction as the congregation. In other branches of Judaism, the bema is at the front, and the reader faces the worshippers. Orthodox synagogues have separate worship areas for men and women, usually with women in the balcony.

The synagogue walls might be decorated with elaborate patterns of vines or geometric designs, but never statues of people, as that might be seen as idol worship. A lamp above the ark is always kept lit, as it was in the ancient temple of Jerusalem, and candelabras called menorahs also recall the temple. Other common symbols are the two tablets of the Ten Commandments given to Moses, or a Star of David, representing the Jewish king's shield.

At a typical service, the congregation arrives at the start of Sabbath (Friday evening). As a sign of respect toward God, men don yarmulkes (small round caps). As the cantor leads songs and prayers, worshippers follow along in a book of weekly readings. At the heart of the service, everyone stands as the Torah is ceremoniously paraded, unwrapped, and placed on the bema. Someone—the rabbi, the cantor, or a congregant—reads the words aloud. The rabbi ("teacher") might give a commentary on the Torah passage.

that has daily prayers (at 8:30). They also host klezmer music concerts many evenings at 18:00 (60 zł).

Tempel Synagogue (Synagoga Templu) has the grandest interior—big and dark, with elaborately decorated, gilded ceilings and balconies—and the most lived-in feel of the bunch (5 zł, Sun-Fri 10:00-16:00, sometimes until 18:00, closed Sat, corner of ulica Miodowa and ulica Podbrzezie).

The smaller **Kupa Synagogue** (Synagoga Kupa), clean and brightly decorated, sometimes hosts temporary exhibits (5 zł, Sun-Fri 10:00-17:00, closed Sat, Miodowa 27).

▲Galicia Jewish Museum (Galicja Muzeum)

This museum focuses on the present rather than the past. With a series of photographs displayed around a restored Jewish furniture factory, the permanent "Traces of Memory" exhibit shows today's remnants of yesterday's Judaism in the area around Kraków (a region known as "Galicia"). From forgotten synagogues to old Jewish gravestones flipped over and used as doorsteps, these giant postcards of Jewish artifacts (with good English descriptions) ensure that an important part of this region's heritage won't be forgotten. Good temporary exhibits complement this permanent collection.

Cost and Hours: 15 zł, daily 10:00-18:00, 1 block east of ulica Szeroka at ulica Dajwór 18, tel. 12-421-6842, www.galicia jewishmuseum.org. The museum also serves as a sort of cultural center, with a good bookstore and café.

Kazimierz Market Square (Plac Nowy)

While tourists have overrun the historic buildings of the Jewish quarter, and throngs of young clubbers clog the Kazimierz streets after dark, the market square retains the gritty flavor of the district before tourism and gentrification. The circular brick building in the center is a slaughterhouse where the animals were properly killed—kosher-style—so Jewish butchers could sell the meat. It's surrounded by busy market stalls and grazing locals. This is a welcome real-world contrast to Kraków's touristy Main Market Square (stalls open Tue-Sun 6:00-14:00, a few also open later, closed Mon). Consider dropping by here for some shopping, people-watching, or a quick, cheap, and local lunch (see page 349). For dessert, buy some fruit from a vendor. There's a fun antique shop at #3. This square also has the highest concentration of nightlife in town, and several fun and funky spots are open during the day as stay-awhile cafés (see "Entertainment in Kraków," later). On Sunday mornings, the square is filled with flea-market stalls (see the stall numbers painted onto the pavement).

Museum of Municipal Engineering
(Muzeum Inżynierii Miejskiej)

This pleasant museum fills the immaculately restored red-brick buildings of an old tram depot in a quiet part of Kazimierz. Exhibits include a history of the town's public-transit system (including several antique trams), old Polish-made cars and motorcycles (among them the tiny commie-era Polski Fiat), typography and historical printing presses, and a hands-on area for kids called "Around the Circle."

Cost and Hours: 10 zł, family ticket-29 zł, includes English audioguide, free on Tue; open Tue-Sun 10:00-16:00, until 18:00 on Tue and Thu June-Sept, closed Mon, Św. Wawrzyńca 15, tel. 12-421-1242.

▲Ethnographic Museum (Muzeum Etnograficzne)

This clever, refreshingly good museum hides a few blocks west of the Jewish area of Kazimierz, in the former town hall. It sits on plac Wolnica, which was Kazimierz's primary market square and was once almost as big as Kraków's. On the ground floor, you'll find models of traditional rural Polish homes, as well as musty replicas of the interiors (like an open-air folk museum moved inside). The exhibit continues upstairs, where each in a long lineup of traditional Polish folk costumes is identified by specific region. You'll see exhibits on village lifestyles, rustic tools, and musical instruments (including a Polish bagpipe). A highlight is the explanation of traditional holiday celebrations—from elaborate crèche scenes at Christmas, to a wall of remarkably painted Easter eggs. Some items are labeled in English, but it's mostly in Polish. The top floor features temporary exhibits.

Cost and Hours: 13 zł, free on Sun, open Tue-Sat 11:00-19:00, Thu until 21:00, Sun 11:00-15:00, closed Mon, ulica Krakowska 46, tel. 12-430-6023, www.etnomuzeum.eu.

Nearby: From plac Wolnica, Mostowa street stretches two blocks south to the river and a newly built, modern, padlock-studded **pedestrian bridge** (called Kładka Ojca Bernatka) that crosses the Vistula to the Podgórze neighborhood described next. The bridge itself is a fun way to connect to Podgórze without hiking back to the main drag to catch a tram, and it comes with a nice look at the local side of Kazimierz: Mostowa street has become a popular place for trendy cafés and eateries, and the river embankment park near the bridge hosts some inviting cafés.

Near Kazimierz: Podgórze

The neighborhood called Podgórze (POD-goo-zheh), directly across the Vistula from Kazimierz, has one of Kraków's most famous sights: Schindler's Factory Museum.

Background: This is the neighborhood where the Nazis forced Kraków's Jews into a ghetto in early 1941. (*Schindler's List* and the films in the Pharmacy Under the Eagle museum depict the sad scene of the Jews loading their belongings onto carts and trudging over the bridge into Podgórze.) Non-Jews who had lived here were displaced to make way for the new arrivals. The ghetto was surrounded by a wall with a fringe along the top that resembled Jewish gravestones—a chilling premonition of what was to come. A short section of this wall still stands along Lwowska street. The tram continued to run through the middle of Podgórze, without stopping—giving Krakovians a chilling glimpse at the horrifying conditions inside the ghetto.

Getting There: To get to Ghetto Heroes' Square, continue through Kazimierz on tram #3, #19, or #24 (described earlier, under "Getting to Kazimierz") to the stop called plac Bohaterow Getta. You can also simply continue walking along Starowiślna, about 10 minutes past the other Kazimierz sights—it's just across the bridge. If you're coming from plac Wolnica (the big square with the Ethnographic Museum), be sure to take the recently opened, modern footbridge, which gives you a more interesting look at Kazimierz (see earlier).

Ghetto Heroes' Square (Plac Bohaterow Getta)

This unassuming square is the focal point of the visitor's Podgórze. Today the square is filled with a monument consisting of 68  empty metal chairs—representing the 68,000 people deported from here. This is intended to remind viewers that the Jews of Kazimierz were forced to carry all of their belongings—including furniture—to the ghetto on this side of the river. It was also here that many Jews waited to be sent to extermination camps. The small, gray building at the river end of Ghetto Heroes' Square feels like a train car inside, evocative of the wagons that carried people from here to certain death.

▲Pharmacy Under the Eagle (Apteka pod Orłem)

This small but newly modernized and excellent museum, on Ghetto Heroes' Square, tells the story of Tadeusz Pankiewicz, a Polish Catholic pharmacist who chose to remain in Podgórze when it became a Jewish ghetto. During this time, the pharmacy was an important meeting point for the ghetto residents, and Pankiewicz and his staff heroically aided and hid Jewish victims of the Nazis. (Pankiewicz survived the war and was later acknowledged by Israel as one of the "Righteous Among the Nations"—non-Jews who risked their lives to help the Nazis' victims during World War II. You'll see his medal on display in the white memorial room at the end of the museum.) Today the pharmacy hosts an exhibit about the Jewish ghetto. You'll enter into the re-created pharmacy, where the "windows" are actually screens that show footage from the era. Push buttons, pull out drawers, answer the phone—it's full of interactive opportunities to better understand what ghetto life was like. You'll learn about people who worked in the pharmacy (including riveting interviews with eyewitnesses—some in English, others subtitled) and hear Pankiewicz telling stories about that tense time. You'll also learn a bit about the pharmacy business from that period.

Cost and Hours: 10 zł; if you're also going to the Schindler's Factory Museum, buy the 23-zł combo-ticket, free on Mon; April-Oct Mon 10:00-14:00, Tue-Sun 9:00-17:00; Nov-March Mon 10:00-14:00, Tue-Thu and Sat 9:00-17:00, Fri 10:00-17:00; closed Sun and the second Tue of each month; plac Bohaterow Getta 18, tel. 12-656-5625, www.mhk.pl/branches/eagle-pharmacy.

▲▲▲Schindler's Factory Museum (Fabryka Emalia Oskara Schindlera)

One of Europe's best museums about the Nazi occupation fills some of the factory buildings where Oskar Schindler and his Jewish employees worked. While the museum tells the story of Schindler and his workers, it broadens its perspective to take in the full experience of all of Kraków during the painful era of Nazi rule—making it the top WWII museum in this country so profoundly affected by  that war. It's loaded with in-depth information (all in English), and touchscreens invite you to learn more and watch eyewitness interviews. Scattered randomly between the exhibits are replicas of everyday places from the age—a photographer's shop, a tram car, a hairdresser's salon—designed to give you a taste of 1940s Kraków. Throughout the museum are calendar pages outlining wartime events and giving a sense of chronology. Note that you'll see nothing of the actual factory or equipment, as the threat of the advancing Red Army forced Schindler to move his operation lock, stock, and barrel to Nazi-occupied Czechoslovakia in 1944.

Cost and Hours: 19 zł, 22-zł combo-ticket with next-door Museum of Contemporary Art, 23-zł "Memory Trail" combo-ticket with Pharmacy Under the Eagle; free on Mon; open April-Oct Mon 10:00-16:00 (except closes at 14:00 first Mon of month),

Tue-Sun 10:00-20:00; Nov-March Mon 10:00-14:00, Tue-Sun 10:00-18:00; last entry 1.5 hours before closing, tel. 12-257-1017, www.mhk.pl/branches/oskar-schindlers-factory. The museum limits the number of visitors, but it's rarely a problem except on particularly busy Mondays (when you might want to book ahead on their website).

Getting There: It's in a gloomy industrial area a five-minute walk from Ghetto Heroes' Square (plac Bohaterow Getta): Head up Kącik street (use the pedestrian underpass, then head to the left of the big, glass skyscraper), go under the railroad underpass marked *Kraków-Zabłocie*, and continue two blocks, past MOCAK (the Museum of Contemporary Art in Kraków, described later) to the second big building on the left (ulica Lipowa 4). Look for signs to *Emalia*.

Ⓞ Self-Guided Tour: You'll begin on the ground floor, where you'll buy your ticket and have the chance to tour the special exhibits. There's also a "film café" (interesting for fans of the movie) with refreshments. Then head upstairs to the first floor.

First Floor: The 35-minute **film**, called *Lipowa 4* (this building's address), sets the stage with interviews of both Jews

and non-Jews describing their wartime experience (find it just off of the museum's first, circular room; subtitled in English, it runs continuously 10:15-15:50). From here, the one-way route winds through the permanent exhibit, called "**Kraków Under Nazi Occupation 1939-1945.**" "Stereoscopic" (primitive 3-D) photos of prewar Kraków capture an idyllic age when culture flourished and the city's Jews (more than one-quarter of the population) blended more or less smoothly with their Catholic Pole neighbors. A video explains the Nazi invasion of Poland in early September of 1939: It took them only a few weeks to overrun the country (which desperately awaited the promised-for help of their British and French allies, who never arrived). Watch the film clip of SS soldiers marching through the Main Market Square—renamed "Adolf-Hitler-Platz"—and read stories about how the Nazis' *Generalgouvernement* attempted to reshape the life of its new capital, "Krakau." (Look for the decapitated head of the Grunwald monument—described on page 257—which had been a powerful symbol of a Polish military victory over German forces.) You'll see the story of a newly German-owned shop selling Nazi propaganda and learn how professors at Kraków's Jagiellonian University were arrested to prevent them from fomenting rebellion among their students. During this time,

Oskar Schindler (1908-1974) and His List

Steven Spielberg's instant-classic, Oscar-winning 1993 film, *Schindler's List*, brought the world's attention to the inspiring story of Oskar Schindler, the compassionate German business-man who did his creative best to save the lives of the Jewish workers at his factory in Kraków. Spielberg chose to film the story right here in Kazimierz, where the historical events actually unfolded. Today the Schindler's Factory Museum gives visitors the chance to learn not just about the man and his workers, but about the historical context of their story: the Nazi occupation of Poland.

Oskar Schindler was born in 1908 in the Sudetenland (cur-rently part of the Czech Republic, then predominantly German). Early on, he displayed an idiosyncratic interpretation of ethics that earned him both wealth and enemies. As Nazi aggressions escalated, Schindler (who was very much a Nazi) carried out espionage against Poland; when Germany invaded the coun-try in 1939, Schindler smelled a business opportunity. Early in the Nazi occupation of Poland, Schindler came to Kraków and lived in an apartment at ulica Straszewskiego 7 (a block from Wawel Castle, but unmarked and not available for tours). He took over the formerly Jewish-owned Emalia factory at ulica Lipowa 4, which produced metal pots and pans that were dipped into protective enamel; later the factory also began producing arma-ments for the Nazi war effort. The factory was staffed by about 1,000 Jews from the nearby Płaszów Concentration Camp, which was managed by the ruthless SS officer Amon Göth (depicted in *Schindler's List*—based on real events—shooting at camp inmates for sport from his balcony).

At a certain point, Schindler began to sympathize with his Jewish workers, and gradually did what he could to protect them and offer them better lives. Schindler fed them far better than most concentration-camp inmates and allowed them to sell some of the pots and pans they made on the black market to

Polish secondary schools were closed—effectively prohibiting learning among Poles, whom the Nazis considered inferior. But Polish students continued to meet clandestinely with their teach-ers. You'll also see images of Hans Frank—the hated puppet ruler of Poland—moving into the country's most important symbol of sovereignty, Wawel Castle. The exhibit also details how early Nazi policies targeted Jews, with roundups, torture, and execu-tion. (Down the staircase is an eerie simulation of a cellar prison.) As the Nazis ratcheted up their genocidal activities, troops swept through Kraków on March 3, 1941, forcing all the remaining Jews in town to squeeze into the newly created Podgórze ghetto. At the bottom of the stairs, look for the huge pile of plunder—Jewish wealth stolen by the Nazis.

make money. After he saw many of his employees and friends murdered during an SS raid in 1943, he ramped up these efforts. He would come up with bogus paperwork to classify those threatened with deportation as "essential" to the workings of the factory—even if they were unskilled. He sought and was granted permission to build a "concentration camp" barracks for his workers on the factory grounds, where they lived in far better conditions than those at Płaszów. These lucky few became known as *Schindlerjuden*—"Schindler's Jews."

As the Soviet army encroached on Kraków in October of 1944, word came that the factory would need to be relocated west, farther from the front line. While Schindler could easily have simply turned his workers over to the concentration-camp system and certain death—as most other industrialists did—he decided to bring them with him to his new factory at Brünnlitz (Brněnec, in today's Czech Republic). He assembled a list of 700 men and 300 women who worked with him, along with 200 other Jewish inmates, and at great personal expense, moved them to Brünnlitz. At the new factory, Schindler and the 1,200 people he had saved produced grenades and rocket parts—virtually all of them, the workers later claimed, mysteriously defective.

After the war, Schindler—who had spent much of his fortune protecting his Jewish workers—hopped around Germany and Argentina, repeatedly attempting but failing to break back into business (often with funding from Jewish donors). He died in poverty in 1974. In accordance with his final wishes, he was buried in Jerusalem, and today his grave is piled high with small stones left there by appreciative Jewish visitors. He has since been named one of the "Righteous Among the Nations" for his efforts to save Jews from the Holocaust. Thomas Keneally's 1982 book *Schindler's Ark* brought the industrialist's tale to a wide audience that included Steven Spielberg, who vaulted Schindler to the ranks of a pop-culture icon.

Second Floor: Climb upstairs using the long **staircase,** which was immortalized in a powerful scene in *Schindler's List*. At the top of the stairs on the right is a small room that served as "Schindler's office" for the film; more recently, it's been determined that his actual office was elsewhere (we'll see it soon).

You'll walk through a corridor lined by a replica of the wall that enclosed the **Podgórze ghetto** and see poignant exhibits about the horrific conditions there (including a replica of the cramped living quarters). The Nazis claimed that Jews had to be segregated here, away from the general population, because they "carried diseases."

Continue into the office of Schindler's secretary, with exhibits about Schindler's life and video touchscreens that play testimonial

KRAKÓW

footage of Schindler's grateful employees. Then proceed into the actual **Schindler's office.** The big map (with German names for cities) was uncovered only in recent years when the factory was being restored. Because Schindler's short tenure here was the only time in the factory's history that these Polish place names would appear in German, it's believed that this map was hung over his desk. Facing the map is a giant monument of enamel pots and pans, like those that were made in this factory. There are 1,200 pots—one for each Jewish worker that Schindler saved. Inside the monument, the walls are lined with the names on Schindler's famous list. The creaky floorboards are intentional: a reminder that the Nazis knew every step you took.

Proceeding through the exhibit, you'll learn more about everyday life—both for ghetto dwellers and for everyday non-Jewish Krakovians, including the Polish resistance (see the Home Army's underground print shop). More eyewitness accounts relate the terrifying days of March 13 and 14, 1943, when the Podgórze ghetto was liquidated, sending survivors to the nearby Płaszów

Concentration Camp. The replica of the Płaszów quarry, where inmates were forced to work in unimaginably difficult conditions, provides a poignant memorial for those who weren't fortunate enough to wind up on Schindler's list.

Now head all the way back down to the ground floor.

Ground Floor: Exhibits here capture the uncertain days near the end of the war in the summer of 1944, when Nazis arrested between 6,000 and 8,000 suspected saboteurs after the Warsaw Uprising, and sent them to Płaszów (see the replica of a basement hideout for 10 Jews who had escaped the ghetto); and later, when many Nazis had fled Kraków, leaving residents to await the Soviet Union's Red Army (see the replica air-raid shelters). The Red Army arrived here on January 18, 1945—at long last, the five years, four months, and twelve days of Nazi rule were over. The Soviets caused their own share of damage to the city before beginning a whole new occupation that would last for generations...but that's a different museum.

Finally, walk along the squishy floor—evoking how life for

anyone was unstable and unpredictable during the Nazi occupation—into the **Hall of Choices.** The six rotating pillars tell the stories of people who chose to act—or not to act—when they witnessed atrocities. Think about the ramifications of the choices they made...and what you would have done in their shoes. The final room holds two books: a white book listing those who tried to help, and a black book listing Nazi collaborators. Exiting the museum, notice the portraits of Oscar Schindler's workers who lived long and happy lives after the war.

Before heading back to downtown Kraków, consider paying a visit to the superb—and very different—museum that fills the buildings on the factory grounds, behind this main building.

▲Museum of Contemporary Art in Kraków (Muzeum Sztuki Współczesnej w Krakowie)

Called "MOCAK" for short, this museum exhibits a changing array of innovative and thought-provoking works by contemporary artists, often with heavy themes tied to the surrounding sites. With the slogan *Kunst macht frei* ("Art will set you free"—a pointed spin on the Nazis' *Arbeit macht frei* concentration-camp motto), the museum occupies warehouse buildings once filled by Schindler's workers. Now converted to wide-open, bright-white halls, the buildings house many temporary exhibits as well as two permanent ones (the MOCAK Collection in the basement, and the library in the smaller side building). Pick up the floor plan as you enter. It's all well-described in English, and engaging even for non-art lovers.

Cost and Hours: 10 zł, free on Tue, open Tue-Sun 11:00-19:00, closed Mon, Lipowa 4, tel. 12-263-4001, www.mocak.pl.

Sights Outside of Kraków

Along with the new St. John Paul II pilgrimage sights (best suited for believers), there are other interesting sights outside of town—an impressive salt mine, a purpose-built communist town, and an unusual earthwork. All require a bus or tram ride to reach.

ST. JOHN PAUL II AND PILGRIMAGE SITES

Pilgrims coming to Kraków eager to walk in the footsteps of St. John Paul II are sometimes disappointed by the lack of actual museums relating to the man in the city center (though the churches affiliated with him are dazzling). However, there are worthwhile sites outside the city: the John Paul II Center and Sanctuary on the outskirts of Kraków, and the John Paul II Family Home Museum in the town of Wadowice, an hour's drive away (and covered later).

The two biggest, most impressive JPII destinations are about four miles south of Kraków's Old Town. While the main attraction here for pilgrims is the John Paul II Center and Sanctuary, historically and geographically you'll come first to the Divine Mercy Sanctuary—so I've covered that first. As they're separated by a pensive 20-minute walk (on adjacent hilltops, so you'll hike down, then back up), it makes sense to combine them in a single visit unless your time is limited.

The sites aren't worth the trek for the merely curious, but they offer a glimpse of the powerful reverence and deep faith that characterizes the Polish character. If you're a pilgrim—or think you might be one—visiting these sites can be worthwhile; to make the most of your time, consider hiring a driver or a local guide with a car (see page 251).

Getting to the John Paul II Center and Sanctuaries: Public transportation from central Kraków is workable, but not ideal. The easiest public-transit route is to take **tram #8** (which loops around the Old Town, including stops next to St. Francis Basilica at plac Wszystkich Świętych, and near Wawel Castle) to the Divine Mercy Sanctuary (Sanktuarium Bożego Miłosierdzia stop)—about 30 minutes. From the tram stop, you'll huff uphill along the wall to find the entrance to the complex. After touring the Divine Mercy sights, you can walk to the St. John Paul II Sanctuary. (As the JPII Center approaches completion, better transportation connections may be added—ask at the TI before making the trip.) A **taxi** from downtown costs around 30-40 zł one-way and takes 20-30 minutes (or hire a local guide for an easy round-trip). Another option is to take the **Papa Bus,** a minibus that parks across the street from JPII's Kraków window, next to St. Francis Basilica. You can pay 10 zł one-way for the ride to the center, or (better) pay 20 zł round-trip for a loop that includes both the center and the Divine Mercy complex, with waiting time at both and a little commentary en route (though English may be limited...or nonexistent). They'll leave when enough people show up (2 people minimum, though they may prefer to hold out for more), so you may have to wait.

Divine Mercy Sanctuary
(Sanktuarium Bożego Miłosierdzia)
This complex, built around a humble red-brick convent, honors the important 20th-century St. Faustina. From an early age, Faustina Kowalska (1905-1938) felt a deep connection to the stories of Jesus

Christ. Despite her generally frail health, she became a nun at age 20. One cold and blustery evening in 1931, a young beggar rang the bell at the convent door and asked for some food. Faustina rustled around the kitchen, found some soup, and brought it to the man—who, upon eating it, revealed his true nature to Faustina: A figure of Jesus Christ clad in a white robe, with one hand raised in blessing, and the other touching his chest. Emanating from his chest were twin beams of light: red (representing blood, the life of souls) and white (water, which through baptism washes souls righteously clean). Transformed by her experience, Faustina worked with an artist to create a painted version of the image—called the Divine Mercy—which has been embraced by Polish Catholics as one of the most important symbols of their faith. She died at 33—the same age as Jesus. The story of Faustina deeply moved a young Karol Wojtyła, who came to study in Kraków the same year Faustina passed away. When he became pope, he dedicated the first Sunday after Easter as the day of Divine Mercy worldwide. In 2000, he made his fellow Krakovian the first Catholic saint of the third millennium. To properly revere the newly important St. Faustina, a bold, futuristic church and visitors center was built alongside her original convent.

Today, pilgrims from around the world come here to revere the relics both of Faustina and of John Paul II, and to learn more about her story from the convent's present-day sisters—many of whom speak English. While some pilgrimage sites can quickly be overtaken by tacky commercialism, the Divine Mercy complex retains a dignified and reverent air.

While strolling the campus, visitors can see three parts: the smaller original chapel; a replica of Faustina's cell; and the huge, modern church, with its soaring bell tower. All of them are free to enter, but donations are happily accepted; each one has slightly different hours.

Original Chapel: Entering the complex through the side gate, you'll come up a walkway with flags from around the world, and plaques translating the Divine Mercy's message—"Jesus, I trust in you"—in dozens of languages. Just before entering, look up and to the right—the window with the flowers marks the cell where Faustina died. Inside the chapel (daily 6:00-21:15), the altar to the left of the main altar displays an early copy of the famous painting of Faustina's Divine Mercy vision. Her relics are in the white case just below the painting; in the white kneeler just in front of the chapel, notice the little reliquary holding one of her bones (which worshippers can embrace as they pray).

Leaving the chapel, turn left and go to the far end of the accommodations building; enter the door on the right (follow signs for *Cela Św. Siostry Faustyny* and *Noclegi/Accommodations*) to find the...

Replica of Faustina's Cell: While this is a newer building, here they've re-created Faustina's convent cell, including many of her personal effects. Drop a coin in the slot for an evocative head-phone description of these items, and of the vision of Jesus that put her convent on the map (usually open daily 8:30-18:00).

Dominating the campus—and oddly juxtaposed with the old buildings—is the futuristic, glass-and-steel...

Main Church: Consecrated by Pope John Paul II on his final visit to Poland in 2002, this building has several parts (daily 7:00-20:00). The **lower level** has a vari-ety of small chapels, each one donated by Catholic worshippers in a different country (Germany, Hungary, Slovakia, and so on)—and each with a dramati-cally different style. The central chapel on this level has a mod-ern altar and another bone of St.

Faustina. Upstairs, the **main sanctuary** is a sleek cylindrical space with wooden sunbeams sharply radiating from the altar area. That altar—framed by the gnarled limbs of windblown trees, represent-ing the suffering of human existence—contains a replica of the Divine Mercy painting, flanked by the woman who saw the vision (Faustina, on the right) and the Polish pope who made it a world-wide phenomenon (John Paul II, on the left). Look back to the grand stained-glass window over the door—a sun sets low behind an illuminated cross, over the water.

Head back out to the terrace surrounding the church. The bold **tower**—as tall as St. Mary's on Main Market Square, and with a statue of John Paul II at the bottom—has an elevator that you can ride up to a glassed-in viewpoint offering panoramas over the Divine Mercy campus, the adjacent John Paul II Center, and—on the distant horizon—the spires of Wawel Cathedral and Kraków's Old Town. Near the base of the tower is a **canopy** where Mass is said on Divine Mercy Sunday each year, before a crowd of 100,000 who fill the fields below.

John Paul II Center (Centrum Jana Pawła II) and Sanctuary

This work-in-progress complex, funded entirely by private donors, celebrates the life and sainthood of Kraków's favorite son.

Construction is ongoing, but for now there are at least two sections of the complex worth visiting: the sanctuary (free, daily 7:30-19:00) and the museum (7 zł, Tue-Sun 10:00-16:00, closed Mon).

The **Sanctuary of St. John Paul II,** consecrated in 2013, is big and splendid. In the **downstairs** area, the central chapel features paintings of JPII's papal visits to various pilgrimage sites, both in Poland (Częstochowa) and abroad (Fátima, Lourdes). Most of the chapels ringing the outside have different depictions of the Virgin Mary. Find the chapel that's a replica of the St. Leonard's Crypt under Wawel Cathedral— the first place where John Paul II celebrated Mass as a young priestling—which contains JPII's actual papal tomb from the crypt beneath St. Peter's Basilica at the Vatican. (When he became a saint, his remains—which, controversially, are kept in Rome rather than his homeland—were moved up into the main part of the church, and this simple grave marker was donated to this church.) You'll also see a reliquary in the shape of a book with fluttering pages, holding a small amount of John Paul II's blood (for the story of the book, see page 275). This blood was kept in secret by JPII's personal secretary, only revealed after his death, when it was given to a select few churches. In another chapel, you'll find the tombs of a few recent cardinals; as they're running out of space below Wawel Cathedral, this chapel is poised to handle the overflow. And in yet another chapel, you'll see finely executed reliefs in rock salt, in the style of Wieliczka Salt Mine.

Head upstairs to the **main sanctuary,** with its sleek modern style. The concrete structure supports large white walls, which will

eventually be filled with dynamic mosaics of Bible stories (several of these are already in place). Above the main altar, in the middle, you'll see the Three Kings delivering their gifts to the Baby Jesus and the Virgin Mary—with St. John Paul II serenely overlooking the scene. In the back-left corner, a smaller chapel focuses on a painting of St. John Paul II; in the hazy background, you can see the dome of St. Peter's at the Vatican (left) and the twin spires of St. Mary's in Kraków (right)—driving home the point that although John Paul II belonged to the world, first and foremost he's considered a son of Kraków and of Poland.

The adjacent **St. John Paul II Museum** is filled with the many gifts bestowed on him (African carved masks and ivory tusks; Latin American tapestries; the key to the city of Long Branch, New Jersey; and a pair of glass doves of peace given to him—perhaps with a touch of irony—by US Vice President Dick Cheney); ornate worship aids (chalices, crosses, and so on); and modern art

KRAKÓW

that celebrates the modern pope and his life's work. There are also personal items, from his papal ski gear to the place settings from his Vatican dinner table to his stylish red leather shoes. You'll also see the throne from his last visit to Poland in 2002, and a replica of the humble room across the street from St. Francis Basilica where he stayed on visits back to his homeland.

John Paul II Sights in Wadowice

Karol Wojtyła was born and lived up until age 18 in Wadowice (VAH-doh-veet-seh), about 30 miles (a one-hour drive) southwest of Kraków. As it's roughly in the same direction as Auschwitz, a local guide or driver can help you connect both places for one busy day of contrasts. Visiting by public bus is possible; ask the TI for details.

The lovely town of Wadowice (about 20,000 people) has a quaint and beautifully restored main square with a pretty Baroque steeple. John Paul II pilgrims find it worth a visit to see the area's best museum on the man, which fills four floors of the tenement building where his family lived through his adolescence, right across the street from the town church. The **John Paul II Family Home Museum** offers visitors a multimedia overview of the life and times of one of the Catholic Church's newest saints. You'll see rooms of the family home, a collection of clothing and other articles that belonged to JPII, photographs and video clips of his life and of the tumultuous period in which he lived, and plenty of interactive displays to bring the entire story to life. Admission is limited, and you'll be accompanied the entire time. Ideally, time your visit to go with an English guide (typically 2/day, likely at 11:00 and 14:00—but confirm online or by phone); otherwise, you'll join the Polish tour. Either way, the tour can be a bit rushed, with less time to linger over the exhibits than you might like (18 zł with a Polish guide, or 25 zł with English guide, free and crowded on Tue; open daily May-Sept 9:00-19:00, April and Oct 9:00-18:00, Nov-March 9:00-16:00, closed the last Tue of each month, last entrance 1.5 hours before closing, ulica Kościelna 7, tel. 33-823-2662, www.domjp2.pl).

MORE SIGHTS OUTSIDE OF KRAKÓW

▲▲Wieliczka Salt Mine (Kopalnia Soli Wieliczka)

Wieliczka (veel-EECH-kah), a salt mine 10 miles southeast of Kraków, is beloved by Poles. Deep beneath the ground, the mine is filled with sculptures that miners have lovingly carved out of the salt. You'll explore this unique gallery—learning both about the art and about medieval mining techniques—on a required tour. Though the sight is a bit overrated, it's unique and practically obligatory if you're in Kraków for a few days. In my experience

with tour groups, about half the people love Wieliczka, while half feel it's
a waste of time—but it can be hard to
predict which half you're in. Read the
description here carefully before you
decide. And expect a lot of walking.

Cost and Hours: The standard "tourist route" costs 79 zł and
is by guided tour only. English tours
are offered daily year-round (June-
Sept every half-hour 8:30-18:00,
Oct-May every hour 9:00-17:00),
with the exception of a few holidays
when the mine is closed. If you miss the English-language tour
(or decide to just show up and take whatever's going next), you
can rent an audioguide for an extra 10 zł. They also have a more
in-depth, interactive "Miner's Route" where visitors wear cover-
alls and helmets and actually operate some of the old equipment
(details on website). The mine is in the town of Wieliczka at ulica
Daniłowicza 10 (tel. 12-278-7302, www.kopalnia.pl).

You'll pay an extra 10 zł for permission to use your camera—
but be warned that flash photos often don't turn out, thanks to the
irregular reflection of the salt crystals. Dress warmly—the mine is
a constant 57 degrees Fahrenheit.

Your ticket includes a dull **mine museum** at the end of the
tour. It adds an hour to the mine tour and is discouraged by locals
("1.5 miles more walking, colder, more of the same"). Make it clear
when you buy your ticket that you're not interested in the museum.

Getting There: The salt mine, 10 miles from Kraków, can
be reached a variety of ways: by **train** (take it to the Wieliczka
Rynek Kopalnia station, about a five-minute walk from the mine;
4 zł, about hourly, less Sat-Sun, departs from main train station); by **bus #304** (4-zł *aglomeracyjny* ticket, 3/hour, 40-minute
trip, catch bus at Kurniki stop across from church near Galeria
Krakowska mall, get off at stop called Wieliczka Kopalnia Soli);
by **minibus** (2.50 zł, 4/hour or with demand, *Wieliczka Soli* sign
in window, 30-40 minutes, generally departs from across Pawia
street from the Galeria Krakowska mall); or by **private driver**
(see page 254).

Background: Wieliczka Salt Mine has been producing
salt since at least the 13th century. Under Kazimierz the Great,
one-third of Poland's income came from these precious deposits.
Wieliczka miners spent much of their lives underground, leaving for work before daybreak and returning after sundown, rarely
emerging into daylight. To pass the time, and to immortalize their
national pride and religiosity in art, 19th-century miners began to

KRAKÓW

carve figures, chandeliers, and eventually even an elaborate chapel out of the salt. Until a few years ago, the mine still produced salt. Today's miners—about 400 of them—primarily work on maintaining the 200 miles of chambers. This entire network is supported by wooden beams (because metal would rust).

Visiting the Mine: From the lobby, your guide leads you 380 steps down a winding staircase. From this spot you begin a 1.5-mile stroll, generally downhill (more than 800 steps down altogether), past 20 of the mine's 2,000 chambers (with signs explaining when they were dug), finishing 443 feet below the surface. When you're done, an elevator beams you back up.

The tour shows how the miners lived and worked, using horses who spent their whole adult lives without ever seeing the light of day. It takes you through vast underground caverns, past subterranean lakes, and introduces you to some of the mine's many sculptures (including one of Copernicus—who actually visited here in the 15th century—as well as an army of salt elves, and this region's favorite son, St. John Paul II). Your jaw will drop as you enter the enormous **Chapel of St. Kinga,** carved over three decades in the early 20th century. Look for the salt-relief carving of the Last Supper (its 3-D details are astonishing, considering it's just six inches deep). You'll end your visit with a five-minute multimedia show.

While advertised as two hours, your tour finishes in a deep-down shopping zone 1.5 hours after you started (they hope you'll hang out and shop). Note when the next elevator departs (just 3/hour), and you can be outta there on the next lift. Zip through the shopping zone in two minutes, or step over the rope and be immediately in line for the great escape (you'll be escorted quite some distance to the elevator, into which you'll be packed like mine workers).

▲Nowa Huta

Nowa Huta (NOH-vah HOO-tah, "New Steel Works"), an enormous planned workers' town, offers a glimpse into the stark, grand-scale aesthetics of the communists. Because it's five miles east of central Kraków and a little tricky to see on your own, skip it unless you're determined. But architects and communist sympathizers may want to make a pilgrimage here.

Getting There: Tram #4 goes from near Kraków's Old Town (catch the tram on the ring road near Kraków's main train station, at the Basztowa stop) along Pope John Paul II Avenue (aleja Jana Pawła II) to Nowa Huta's main square, plac Centralny (about 30 minutes total), then continues a few minutes farther to the main gate of the Tadeusz Sendzimir Steelworks—the end of the line. From there it returns to plac Centralny and back to Kraków.

Lunch in Nowa Huta: Plan on munching a cheap, drab lunch in the no-name milk bar on Nowa Huta's plac Centralny (Mon-Sat 7:00-20:00, closed Sun, at #1 next to a grocery store under an arcade, about 100 yards from the tram stop for sector C).

Tours: True to its name, Mike Ostrowski's **Crazy Guides** is a loosely run operation that takes tourists to Nowa Huta in genuine communist-era vehicles (mostly Trabants and Polski Fiats). While the content is good, Mike and his comrades are laid back, very informal, and sometimes crude. If you're offended by a foul-mouthed hipster guide, or if you don't like the idea of careening down the streets of Kraków in a car that feels like a cardboard box with a lawnmower engine, skip this tour. For the rest of us, it's a fun and convenient way to experience Nowa Huta (139 zł/person for 2.5-hour "communism tour" of Nowa Huta; 179 zł/person for 4-hour "communism deluxe" tour that also includes lunch at a milk bar and a visit to their period-decorated communist apartment; 169 zł/person for 4-hour Real Kraków tour that covers the basic Nowa Huta trip plus outlying sights; other crazy experiences also available, cash only, reserve ahead and they'll pick you up at your hotel, mobile 500-091-200, www.crazyguides.com, info@crazyguides.com). If you're already hiring a **local guide** in Kraków, consider paying a little extra to add a couple of hours for a short side-trip by car to Nowa Huta.

Background: Nowa Huta was the communists' idea of paradise. It's one of only three towns outside the Soviet Union that were custom-built to show-case socialist ideals. (The others are Dunaújváros—once called Sztálin-város—south of Budapest, Hungary; and Eisenhüttenstadt—once called Stalinstadt—near Brandenburg, Germany.) Completed in just 10 years (1949-1959), Nowa Huta was built primarily because the Soviets felt that smart and sassy Kraków needed a taste of heavy industry. Farmers and villagers were imported to live and work in Nowa Huta. Many of the new residents, who weren't accustomed to city living, brought along their livestock (which grazed in the fields around unfinished buildings). For commies, it was downright idyllic: Dad would cheerily ride the tram into the steel factory, mom would dutifully keep house, and the kids could splash around at the man-made beach and learn how to cut perfect red stars out of construction paper. But Krakovians had the last laugh: Nowa Huta, along with Lech Wałęsa's shipyard in Gdańsk, was one of the home bases of the Solidarity strikes that eventually brought down the regime. Now, with the communists long gone, Nowa Huta remains a sooty suburb of Poland's cultural capital, with a whopping 200,000 residents.

Touring Nowa Huta: Nowa Huta's focal point used to be known simply as **Central Square** (plac Centralny), but in a fit of poetic justice, it was recently renamed for the anti-communist Ronald Reagan. This square is the heart of the planned town. A map of Nowa Huta looks like a clamshell: a semi-circular design radiating from Central/Reagan Square. Numbered streets fan out like spokes on a wheel, and trolleys zip workers directly to the immense factory.

Believe it or not, the inspiration for Nowa Huta was the Renaissance (which, thanks to the textbook Renaissance design of the Cloth Hall and other landmarks, Soviet architects considered typically Polish). Notice the elegantly predictable arches and galleries that would make Michelangelo proud. The settlement was loosely planned on the gardens of Versailles (comparing aerial views of those two very different sites—both with axes radiating from a central hub—this becomes clear). When first built (before it was layered with grime), Nowa Huta was delightfully orderly, primly painted, impeccably maintained, and downright beautiful... if a little boring. It was practical, too: Each of the huge apartment blocks is a self-contained unit, with its own grassy inner courtyard, school, and shops. Driveways (which appear to dead-end at underground garage doors) lead to vast fallout shelters.

Today's Nowa Huta is a far cry from its glory days. Wander around. Poke into the courtyards. Reflect on what it would be like to live here. It may not be as bad as you imagine. Ugly as they seem from the outside, these buildings are packed with happy little apartments filled with color, light, and warmth.

The wide boulevard running northeast of Central/Reagan Square, now called Solidarity Avenue (aleja Solidarności, lined with tracks for tram #4), leads to the **Tadeusz Sendzimir Steelworks.** Originally named for Lenin, this factory was supposedly built using plans stolen from a Pittsburgh plant. It was designed to be a cog in the communist machine—reliant on iron ore from Ukraine, and therefore worthless unless Poland remained in the Soviet Bloc. Down from as many as 40,000 workers at its peak, the steelworks now employs only about 10,000. Today there's little to see other than the big sign, stern administration buildings, and smokestacks in the distance. Examine the twin offices flanking the sign—topped with turrets and a decorative frieze inspired by Italian palazzos, these continue the Renaissance theme of the housing districts.

Another worthwhile sight in Nowa Huta is the **Lord's Ark Church** (Arka Pana, several blocks northwest of Central/Reagan Square on ulica Obrońców Krzyża). Back when he was archbishop of Kraków, Karol Wojtyła fought for years to build a church in this most communist of communist towns. When the regime refused, he insisted on conducting open-air Masses before crowds in fields—until the communists finally capitulated.

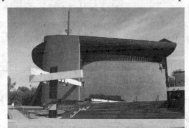

Consecrated on May 15, 1977, the Lord's Ark Church has a Le Corbusier–esque design that looks like a fat, exhausted Noah's Ark resting on Mount Ararat—encouraging Poles to persevere through the floods of communism. While architecturally interesting, the church is mostly significant as a symbol of an early victory of Catholicism over communism.

▲Kościuszko Mound (Kopiec Kościuszki)

On a sunny day, the parklands west of the Old Town are a fine place to get out of the city and commune with Krakovians at play. On the outskirts of town is the Kościuszko Mound, a nearly perfectly conical hill erected in 1823 to honor Polish and American military hero Tadeusz Kościuszko. The mound incorporates soil that was brought here from battlefields where the famous general fought, both in Poland and in the American Revolution. Later, under Habsburg rule, a citadel with a chapel was built around the mound, which provided a fine lookout over this otherwise flat terrain. And more recently, the hill was reinforced with steel and cement to prevent it from eroding away. You'll pay to enter the walls and walk to the top—up a curlicue path that makes the mound resemble a giant soft-serve cone—and inside you'll find a modest Kościuszko museum. While not too exciting, this is a pleasant place for an excursion on a nice day.

Cost and Hours: 12 zł, includes museum, mound open daily 9:00-dusk, until 23:00 Fri-Sun, museum open daily 9:30-16:30, café, tel. 12-425-1116, www.kopieckosciuszki.pl.

Getting There: Ride tram #1 or #6 (from in front of the Wyspiański Pavilion or the main post office) to the end of the line, called Salvator, then follow the well-marked path uphill for 20 minutes.

KRAKÓW

Shopping in Kraków

Two of the most popular Polish souvenirs—amber and pottery—come from areas far from Kraków. You won't find any great bargains on those items here, but several shops specializing in them are listed below. Somewhat more local are the many wood carvings you'll see.

The **Cloth Hall**, smack-dab in the center of the Main Market Square, is the most convenient place to pick up any Polish souvenirs. It has a great selection, respectable prices, and the city's highest concentration of pickpockets (summer Mon-Fri 9:00-18:00, Sat-Sun 9:00-15:00, sometimes later; winter Mon-Fri 9:00-16:00, Sat-Sun 9:00-15:00).

Here are some other souvenir ideas, and neighborhoods or streets that are particularly enjoyable for browsing.

JEWELRY

The popular **amber** *(bursztyn)* you'll see sold around town is found on northern Baltic shores; if you're also heading to Gdańsk, wait until you get there (for more on amber, see page 459). One unique alternative that's a bit more local is **"striped flint"** *(krzemień pasiasty)*, a stratified stone that's polished to a high shine. It's mined in a very specific subregion near Kraków, and has become popular recently among Hollywood celebrities. Each piece has its own unique wavy, sandy patterns.

Jewelry shops abound in the Old Town. For a good selection of striped flint, amber, and other jewelry, try the no-name shop on **plac Mariacki**, the little square facing the side entrance of St. Mary's Church; they also have a selection of Polish folk costumes in the basement (at #9). A few more jewelry and design shops cluster along Sławkowska street, which runs north from the Main Market Square. At #23, stop in at **Galeria Kreko**, with modern works mostly by Polish artists; the shop next door has more jewelry, plus hand-carved and painted wooden figures. **Galeria Skarbiec** ("Treasury"), two blocks south of the Main Market Square, is another good choice, with a more stylish, upscale vibe (Grodzka 35).

POLISH POTTERY

"Polish pottery," with distinctive blue-and-white designs, is made in the region of Silesia, west of Kraków (mostly in the town of Bolesławiec). But, assuming you won't be going there, you can browse one of the shops in Kraków. **Ceramika Bolesławiecka**, on a busy urban street between the Old Town and Kazimierz, has a tasteful selection of pottery that's oriented more for locals than tourists, with prices to match (closed Sun, Starowiślna 37). **Dekor**

Art, with slightly inflated prices but a convenient, central location, has a nice selection just a couple of blocks north of the Main Market Square (daily, Sławkowska 11).

FOODS, DRINKS, AND COSMETICS

Krakowski Kredens is a handy, well-curated shop for overpriced but good-quality traditional foods from Kraków and the surrounding region, Galicia. While the deli case in the back is a pricey place to shop for a picnic (head for a supermarket instead), this is a good chance to stock up on souvenir-quality Polish foods for the folks back home. They have several locations around Kraków—and elsewhere in Poland—but one handy branch is just steps south of the Main Market Square down Grodzka, at #7 (www.krakowskikredens.pl).

Szambelan, a block south of the Main Market Square, is a fun concept for vodka lovers: Peruse the giant casks of three dozen different flavored vodkas, buy an empty bottle, and they'll fill and seal it to take home (Gołębia 2 at the corner with Bracka).

Mydlarnia u Franciszka, with a few locations around Kraków (including a handy one just south of the Main Market Square at Gołębia 2), sells a variety of fragrant local soaps, lotions, shampoos, and other cosmetics, some produced locally.

STOLARSKA STREET

The relatively undiscovered, traffic-free Stolarska street—just a block off of the Main Market Square—is a fine place to stroll day or night, and to browse for gifts. (For more on this street, see page 343 in "Eating in Kraków.") Wander the street from north (Small Market Square) to south (Dominican Church) and window-shop. A few fun places are in the covered arcade on the left, after the Herring Embassy. One of the most interesting is **Galeria Plakatu Kraków,** a print, poster, and postcard shop with a wide variety of engaging images, from commie-retro to contemporary arts to unique Polish variations on American movie posters (closed Sun, Stolarska 8-10). Nearby are an antique bookstore and a pottery art gallery.

DESIGNER SHOPS ALONG ULICA JÓZEFA, IN KAZIMIERZ

As the epicenter of Kraków's low-rent, artsy, hipster scene, Kazimierz is the best place in town to browse one-off galleries—especially designer shops (both decor and fashion). Several good options line up along ulica Józefa, a borderline-drab urban street about a block south of ulica Szeroka and the plac Nowy market square. Begin near the High Synagogue and work your way west down the street; the highest concentration is on the two-block

KRAKÓW

Kraków's Old Town Shopping & Entertainment

N

OLD MARKET

DŁUGA

PADEREWSKIEGO

KARMELICKA

GARBARSKA

ŁOBZOWSKA

ASNYKA

BASZTOWA

DUNAJEWSKIEGO

Planty

PIJARSKA

BARBICAN

FLORIAN GATE

ŚŁAWKOWSKA

3

OLD

ŚW. MARKA

17

CZARTORYSKI MUSEUM

13

FLORIAŃSKA

ŚLEPSKA

KRUPNICZA

SZCZEPAŃSKA

P

SZOŁAYSKI HOUSE

ŚW. JANA

14

SW. TOMASZA

STUDENSKA

PODWALE

SZEWSKA

20

i

Main Market Square

15

ST. MARY'S

ŚW. ANNY

COLLEGIUM MAIUS

JAGIELLOŃSKA

16

CLOTH HALL

1

i

Mickiewicz Statue

Small Market Square

JABŁONOWSKICH

GOŁĘBIA

TOWN HALL TOWER

ST. ADALBERT'S

2

SIENNA

SIENNA

PIŁSUDSKIEGO

OLSZEWSKIEGO

7

WIŚLNA

BRACKA

19

18

12

GRODZKA

STOLARSKA

8

DOMINIKAŃSKA

To Airport, Auschwitz & Kościuszko Mound

SMOLEŃSK

ARCH- BISHOP'S MANSION

6

POST OFFICE

DOMINICAN CHURCH

Planty

FELICJANEK

ZWIERZYNIECKA

FRANCISZKAŃSKA

STRASZEWSKIEGO

Planty

ST. FRANCIS

WYSPIAŃSKI PAVILION

i

4

TOWN

MILK BAR

POSELSKA

SENACKA

STS. PETER & PAUL

SAREGO

Mary Mag. Square

BISHOP ERAZM CIOŁEK PALACE

ARCHDIOCESAN MUSEUM

JOHN PAUL II CENTER

KANONICZA

GRODZKA

ST. ANDREW'S

ŚW. GERTRUDY

POWIŚLE

PODZAMCZE

21

ŚW. IDZIEGO

KRAKÓW

i

CATHEDRAL

INNER COURTYARD

STRADOMSKA

Vistula River

WAWEL HILL

LOST WAWEL MUSEUM

ST. BERNARD'S

DRAGON STATUE

BERNARDYŃSKA

KONOPNICKIEJ

KOLETEK

Shopping

1. Cloth Hall
2. Plac Mariacki 9 Jewelry
3. Galeria Kreko & Dekor Art Pottery
4. Galeria Skarbiec
5. Ceramika Bolesławiecka
6. Krakowski Kredens Gift Store
7. Szambelan Vodkas & Mydlarnia u Franciszka Cosmetics
8. Galeria Plakatu Kraków
9. To Ulica Józefa Design Shops
10. Galeria Krakowska
11. Galeria Kazimierz
12. Pasaż 13 Mall

Entertainment

13. Jama Michalika (Folk Shows)
14. Staropolskie Trunki
15. Jazz Club u Muniaka
16. Harris Piano Jazz Bar
17. Stalowe Magnolie
18. Buddha Nightclub
19. Polonia House/Dom Polonii
20. Bonerowski Palace
21. St. Idziego/Giles Church

200 Meters
200 Yards

KRAKÓW

stretch between Estery and Bożego Ciała streets. This is an ever-changing lineup, but keep an eye out for these spots: **Blazko,** on the left at #11, has some modern, colorful jewelry, handmade right on the premises. A few doors down (also at #11), **Maly Styl** sells fashion for little kids, and **Galerie d'Art Naïf** features fascinating works by untrained artists. Next door, **Deccoria Galeria** feels like a junk shop, cluttered with handmade jewelry, art, accessories, and vintage clothes. After you pass another vintage shop, **Art Factory** (on the left, at #9) is worth a browse for colorful jewelry, accessories, and housewares by local designers. Across the street, **Mniejwięcej** ("Lessmore," on the right, at #18) highlights art by local designers. **Pracownia** ("Lab"), across the street at #9, sells handmade art, jewelry, and clothes. And more clothes by Polish designers are across the street at **Nuumi Boutique** (#14).

SHOPPING MALLS

Two enormous shopping malls lie just beyond the tourist zone. The gigantic **Galeria Krakowska,** with 270 shops, shares a square with the train station (Mon-Sat 9:00-22:00, Sun 10:00-21:00, has a kids' play area upstairs from the main entry). Only slightly smaller is **Galeria Kazimierz** (Mon-Sat 10:00-22:00, Sun 10:00-20:00, just a few blocks east of the Kazimierz sights, along the river at Podgórska 24). A small but swanky mall called **Pasaż 13** is a few steps off the southeast corner of the Main Market Square, where Grodzka street enters the Square. Enter the mall under the balcony marked *Pasaż 13.* You'll find a cool brick-industrial interior, with upscale international chains...and not much that's Polish (Mon-Sat 9:00-21:00, Sun 11:00-17:00).

Entertainment in Kraków

As a town full of both students and tourists, Kraków has plenty of fun options, especially at night.

IN THE OLD TOWN
Main Market Square

Intoxicating as the Square is by day, it's even better at night...pure enchantment. Have a meal or nurse a drink at an outdoor café, or just grab a bench and enjoy the scene. There's often live, al fresco music coming from somewhere (either at restaurants, at a temporary stage set up near the Town Hall Tower, or from talented buskers). You could spend hours doing slow laps around the Square after dark, and never run out of diversions.

Concerts

You'll find a wide range of musical events, from tourist-oriented Chopin concerts and classical "greatest hits" selections in quaint old ballrooms and churches, to folk-dancing shows, to serious philharmonic performances. While a variety of options exist, two companies typically offer competing shows, often on the same night; to compare both, see www.newculture.pl and www.cracowconcerts.com.

Popular Classical Concerts: Popular venues include churches (such as the churches of Sts. Peter and Paul on ulica Grodzka, St. Adalbert on the Square, or St. Idziego/Giles at the foot of Wawel Hill), various gardens around town (July-Aug only, as part of a festival), and fancy mansions on the Main Market Square (including the Polonia House/Dom Polonii at #14, near ulica Grodzka; and the Bonerowski Palace near the top of the Square at ulica Św. Jana 1; both of these typically offer Chopin concerts). Because Kraków's live-music scene is continually evolving, it's best to inquire locally about what's on during your visit. Hotel lobbies are stocked with fliers for upcoming concerts. But to get all of your options, visit any TI. The TI north of the Square on ulica Św. Jana, which specializes in cultural events, can book tickets for most concerts (no extra fee) and tell you how to get tickets for the others. The free, monthly *Karnet* cultural-events book lists everything (half in Polish and half in English, also online at www.karnet.krakow.pl).

Folk Music: Two different venues present dinner shows in the old center. At both, a small, hardworking ensemble of colorfully costumed Krakovian singers, dancers, and musicians put on a fun little folk show. While the food, the space, and the clientele are all a bit tired, it's a nice taste of Polish folk traditions—and the performers try hard to involve members of the audience in the polkas and circle dances. One option is in the historic **Jama Michalika,** with its dusty old Art Nouveau interior right along Floriańska street (85 zł includes dinner; Wed, Fri, and Sun at 19:00; Floriańska 45, mobile 604-093-570, www.cracowconcerts.com). A similar option is in the more modern **Tradycyja Restaurant,** right on the Main Market Square (next to the famous Wyzierniek Restaurant at #15; 60 zł for just the show, or 120 zł to add dinner; Wed, Fri, and Sat at 19:00; mobile 602-850-900, www.newculture.pl).

Jazz and Other Live Music

For something a little more edgy, delve into Kraków's thriving jazz scene. Several popular clubs hide on the streets surrounding the Main Market Square (open nightly, most shows start around 21:30).

The most famous and best for all-around jazz in a sophisticated

KRAKÓW

cellar environment is **Jazz Club u Muniaka** (10-20-zł cover, open nightly 19:00-1:00 in the morning, live music nightly from 21:30, best music when the owner Janusz plays on Thu-Sat, ulica Floriańska 3, tel. 12-423-1205; described earlier on my self-guided walk).

Harris Piano Jazz Bar, right on the Square (at #28), is more casual and offers a mix of traditional and updated "fusion" jazz, plus blues (free most nights, 15-25-zł cover for more serious shows—typically on Thu-Sat, music nightly from 21:30, tel. 12-421-5741, www.harris.krakow.pl).

Stalowe Magnolie—a former brothel still draped with red lights and waitresses dressing the part—is a bit more youthful, clubby-feeling, and snooty, with jazz about two nights a week and rock or pop the other nights (no cover on weeknights, on weekends 10-zł cover for men and free for women, music nightly from 22:00, 150 yards off Main Market Square at ulica Św. Jana 15, tel. 12-422-8472, www.stalowemagnolie.com).

Nightlife in the Old Town

The entire Old Town is crammed with nightclubs and discos pumping loud music on weekends. On a Saturday, the pedestrian streets can be more crowded at midnight than at noon. However, with the exception of the jazz clubs mentioned earlier, most of the nightspots in the Old Town are garden-variety dance clubs, completely lacking the personality and creativity of the Kazimierz nightspots described next. Worse, to save money, young locals stand out in front of nightclubs to drink their own booze (BYOB), rather than pay high prices for the drinks inside—making the streets that much more crowded and noisy. For low-key hanging out, people choose a café on the Square; otherwise, they head for Kazimierz.

In addition to the Harris Piano Jazz Bar, two places on the Square worth checking out are near the southeast corner. At #6, head into the passage to find the **Buddha** nightclub, with comfy lounge sofas under awnings in an immaculately restored old courtyard. For something funkier and even more local, go down the passage at #12, which runs a surprisingly long distance through the block. Soon you'll start to see tables for the **Herring Embassy;** you'll eventually emerge at **Stolarska street,** a still enjoyable but far less touristy scene (for more on the Herring Embassy and Stolarska, see page 343).

IN KAZIMIERZ

Aside from the Old Town's gorgeous Square, Kraków's best area to hang out after dark is Kazimierz, the former Jewish quarter. The Jewish Sabbath has nothing to do with the bar scene here.

Klezmer Music

Although there are only about 200 Jews still living in Kraków, you wouldn't know it from the lively klezmer scene. Several restaurants offer traditional Jewish klezmer music most evenings for a steep 25-zł cover charge (plus the cost of food); for details, see page 347. If you'd rather enjoy a concert separately from dinner, in summer you'll find concerts most evenings at 18:00 or 19:00 in various venues around town: Isaac Synagogue (arguably the most powerful space, in a giant old prayer hall); the Galicia Jewish Museum (a tasteful modern brick space); or at Astoria Hotel (least appealing). The price is typically 60-80 zł; look for posters and fliers around town. The music is evocative, but this is a fairly sedate scene. If you'd like to stay up a bit later, there's no better way to spend your time than exploring the bars of Kazimierz (described next).

Bars and Clubs

Squeezed between centuries-old synagogues and cemeteries are wonderful hangouts running the full gamut from sober and tasteful to wild and clubby. The classic recipe for a Kazimierz bar: Find a dilapidated old storefront, fill the interior with ramshackle furniture, turn the lights down low, and pipe in old-timey jazz music from the 1920s. Sprinkle with alcohol. Serves one to two dozen hipsters. After a few clubs of this type caught on, a more diverse cross-section of nightspots began to move in, including some loud dance clubs. The whole area is bursting with life—it's the kind of place where people just spontaneously start dancing—and locals still outnumber tourists. I've listed websites for places that feature periodic live music and other events.

On and near Plac Nowy: The highest concentration of bars ring the plac Nowy market square. While most of these are nondescript, a few stand out. **Alchemia,** one of the first—and still one of the best—bars in Kazimierz, is candlelit, cluttered, and claustrophobic, with cave-like rooms crowded with rickety old furniture, plus a cellar used for live performances (Estery 5, www.alchemia.com.pl). Just around the corner, Alchemia has a sleek, subway-tiled, side restaurant; this space has table service, but if you'd rather be in the creaky bar, you can order at the counter (20-40-zł meals). Hiding just a half-block down the street is **Miejsce** ("The Place"), which is brighter and more minimalist than the norm, with stripped-down walls and carefully chosen Scan-design old furniture—it's run by the owners of a design firm specializing in decor from the 50s, 60s, and 70s (Estery 1). Fronting the square, **Kolory** has a pleasant Parisian brasserie ambience (Estery 10), and **Atelier** has a relaxed, minimalist, art-gallery interior with cushy sofas and a hidden garden deep inside (plac Nowy 7 1/2). **Le Scandale** is all black leather and serves tapas, Italian fare, and

KRAKÓW

cocktails; don't miss the big garden in the back (plac Nowy 9).

Late at night, the little windows in the plac Nowy **market hall** do a big business selling *zapiekanki* (baguette with toppings) to hungry bar-hoppers.

On Rabina Meiselsa street, just a half-block off plac Nowy, two places share a long courtyard: **Mleczarnia,** a top-notch beer garden with rickety tables squeezed under the trees and its cozy old-fashioned pub across the street (at #20); and **Stajnia**, at the far end of the courtyard, where scenes from *Schindler's List* were filmed (see photos on wall at inner arch). Its interior feels like a Polish village drenched in red light and turned into a dance hall.

Near Isaac Synagogue: A block east of plac Nowy, a few more places cluster on the wide street in front of Isaac Synagogue. The huge **Nova Resto Bar** dominates the scene with a long covered terrace, a vast interior, and seating in their courtyard—all with a cool-color-scheme Las Vegas polka-dot style. This feels upscale and a bit pretentious compared to many of the others, but it's *the* place to be seen (25-40-zł meals, Estery 18). Upstairs is the similarly trendy music club **Taawa** (www.taawa.pl). Facing this double-decker wall of style are some smaller, more accessible options: **Singer** is classy and mellow, with most of its tables made of old namesake sewing machines (Estery 20), while **Warsztat** has an exploding-instruments-factory ambience (Izaaka 3; also recommended later, under "Eating in Kraków").

On Józefa Street: More good bars are just a short block south. Along Józefa, you'll find a pair of classic Kazimierz joints: **Eszeweria,** which wins the "best atmosphere" award, feels like a Polish speakeasy that's been in mothballs for the last 90 years—a low-key, unpretentious, and inviting hangout (Józefa 9). Their less enticing but still enjoyable sister café, **Esze,** is across the street. A block up, look for **Kolanko No. 6,** with a cozy bar up front, a pleasant beer garden in the inner courtyard, and a fun events hall in back (Józefa 17, www.kolanko.net; also recommended later, under "Eating in Kraków").

In Podgórze: If you run out of diversions in the heart of Kazimierz, head south. With the construction of a new pedestrian bridge over the river just south of this area, Kazimierz's nightlife scene is spreading to **Podgórze,** just across the river. Here in this fast-evolving zone, prices are a bit lower.

Sleeping in Kraków

Healthy competition—with new, cleverly run places cropping up all the time—keeps Kraków's accommodation prices reasonable and makes choosing a hotel fun rather than frustrating. Rates are soft; hoteliers don't need much of an excuse to offer you 10 to 20

Sleep Code

Abbreviations   (3 zł = about $1, country code: 48)
S = Single, **D** = Double/Twin, **T** = Triple, **Q** = Quad, **b** = bathroom, **s** = shower only.

Price Rankings

$$$ **Higher Priced**—Most rooms 400 zł or more.

$$ **Moderately Priced**—Most rooms between
300-400 zł.

$ **Lower Priced**—Most rooms 300 zł or less.

Unless otherwise noted, credit cards are accepted, breakfast is included, Wi-Fi is generally free, and English is spoken. Prices can change without notice; verify the hotel's current rates online or by email. For the best prices, always book directly with the hotel.

percent off, especially on weekends or off-season. I've focused my accommodations in two areas: in and near the Old Town; and in Kazimierz, a local-style, more affordable neighborhood that is home to both the old Jewish quarter and a thriving dining and nightlife zone.

The Old Town is jam-packed with discos that thump loud music on weekend nights to attract roving gangs of rowdy students, backpackers, and obnoxious "stag parties" of drunken louts from the UK in town for a weekend of carousing. The "quiet after 22:00" law is flagrantly ignored. Kazimierz is also home to various hip dance clubs. Because of all these clubs, virtually all of my accommodations come with some risk of noise; to help your odds, always ask for a quiet room when you reserve...and bring earplugs.

IN AND NEAR THE OLD TOWN

Most of my listings are inside (or within a block or two of) the Planty park that rings the Old Town. Sleeping inside the Old Town comes with pros (maximum atmosphere; handy location for sightseeing and dining) and cons (high prices; the potential for noise—especially on weekends—as noted earlier). I've also listed a few in this section that are just outside the Old Town, and are a bit quieter.

Guest Houses

These good-value pensions almost invariably come with lots of stairs (no elevators) and are run by smart, can-do, entrepreneurial owners. They're all located in the heart of the Old Town along busy pedestrian streets, and most don't have air-conditioning—so they can be noisy with the windows open in the summer, especially on weekends. These places book up fast, especially in

KRAKÓW

Kraków's Old Town Hotels & Restaurants

To 6

200 Meters
200 Yards

KRUPNICZA

KARMELICKA

GARBARSKA

LOBZOWSKA

ASNYKA

DLUGA

OLD MARKET

PADEREWSKIEGO

BASZTOWA

Planty

PIJARSKA

BARBICAN

FLORIAN GATE

SLAWKOWSKA

DUNAJEWSKIEGO

15

3

OLD

SW. MARKA

CZARTORYSKI MUSEUM

10

37

19

37

17

SZOLAYSKI HOUSE

SW. JANA

FLORIANSKA

SZCZEPANSKA

29

2

28

SZEWSKA

4

36

SW. TOMASZA

STUDENSKA

SW. ANNY

Main Market Square

SZPITALNA

COLLEGIUM MAIUS

25

CLOTH HALL

ST. MARY'S

1

JABLONOWSKICH

JAGIELLONSKA

GOLEBIA

Mickiewicz Statue

Small Market Square

32

7

PILSUDSKIEGO

OLSZEWSKIEGO

WISLNA

TOWN HALL TOWER

12

ST. ADALBERT'S

SIENNA

SMOLENSK

To Airport, Auschwitz & Kosciuszko Mound

5

ARCH-BISHOP'S MANSION

14

BRACKA

22

30

24

GRODZKA

21

POST OFFICE

18

35

STOLARSKA

DOMINICAN CHURCH

DOMINIKANSKA

FRANCISZKANSKA

ST. FRANCIS

41

39

TOWN

WYSPIANSKI PAVILION

23

20

13

FELICJANEK

ZWIERZYNIECKA

STRASZEWSKIEGO

Planty

POSELSKA

40

33

8

SENACKA

Mary Mag. Square

11

STS. PETER & PAUL

SAREGO

BISHOP ERAZM CIOLEK PALACE

GRODZKA

ST. ANDREW'S

ARCHDIOCESAN MUSEUM

KANONICZA

JOHN PAUL II CENTER

POWISLE

PODZAMCZE

CATHEDRAL

SW. IDZIEGO

27

SW. GERTRUDY

31

INNER COURTYARD

WAWEL HILL

LOST WAWEL MUSEUM

BERNARDYNSKA

ST. BERNARD'S

STRADOMSKA

Vistula River

34

DRAGON STATUE

KONOPNICKIEJ

KOLETEK

KRAKÓW

1. Tango House
2. Golden Lion Guest House
3. Globtroter Guest House
4. La Fontaine B&B #1
5. La Fontaine B&B #2
6. Cracowdays
7. Hotel Gródek
8. Hotel Maltański
9. Hotel Pugetów
10. Hotel Polski pod Białym Orłem
11. Hotel Senacki & Bar Grodzki
12. Wentzl Hotel, Wierzynek Restaurant & Słodki Wentzl
13. Hotel Wawel
14. Bracka 6
15. Hotel Amber
16. Hotel Wielopole
17. Kraków City Apts.
18. Grodzka Apt. House
19. Restauracja Farina
20. Miód Malina Restaurant
21. Marmolada
22. Wesele
23. Restauracja pod Aniołami
24. Aperitif Restaurant
25. Chimera Cafeteria
26. Restauracja Jarema
27. Pod Baranem
28. Charlotte Café
29. Café Bunkier
30. Ambasada Śledzia
31. Pod Wawelem Beer Hall
32. Cyklop Pizza & Jadłodajnia "U Stasi"
33. Pizzeria Trzy Papryczki
34. Pizza Garden
35. Lajkonik Sandwiches
36. Milkbar Tomasza
37. U Babci Maliny (2)
38. Academy of Music Café
39. Kwandras Lunch Bar
40. Bar Mleczny
41. Restauracja Samoobsługowa Polakowski

KRAKÓW

summer—reserve as far ahead as possible. Don't expect a 24-hour reception desk; it's always smart to tell them your arrival time, especially if it's late in the day.

$ Tango House, run by tango dance instructor Marcin Miszczak, is in a well-located building with an ancient-feeling stairwell decorated with faded Art Nouveau paintings. Its eight long, skinny, stylish rooms have parquet floors (tiny "economy" Sb/Db-260 zł, standard Sb/Db-300 zł, superior Sb/Db-340 zł, prices can be soft in slow times, cheaper Nov-March, Wi-Fi, ask for quieter courtyard room to avoid rowdy street noise on weekends, ulica Szpitalna 4, tel. 12-429-3114, www.tangohouse.pl, info@tangohouse.pl).

$ Golden Lion Guest House has 12 smallish, neat-but-slightly-dated rooms on a bustling pedestrian street a block off the Main Market Square (Sb-180 zł, Db-300 zł, 10 percent cheaper Nov-Feb, ask for quieter room in back, air-con in some rooms, guest computer, Wi-Fi, guest kitchen, no parking, ulica Szewska 19, mobile 501-066-958, tel. 12-422-9323, www.goldenlion.pl, reservation@goldenlion.pl, Łodziński family).

$ Globtroter Guest House offers 18 rustic-feeling rooms with high ceilings and big beams around a serene garden courtyard. Jacek (Jack), who really understands and respects travelers, conscientiously focuses on value—keeping prices as low as possible by not offering needless extras (April-Oct: Sb-180 zł, Db-300 zł; Nov-March: Sb-120 zł, Db-180 zł; ask for 10 percent discount with this book if you reserve direct, 2 people can cram into a single to save money—a little more than the Sb price, larger suites for up to five also available, no breakfast at hotel but you can buy 14-zł breakfast from nearby restaurant, guest computer, Wi-Fi, pay laundry service, fun 700-year-old brick cellar lounge down below, go down passageway at #7 at the square called plac Szczepański, tel. 12-422-4123, www.globtroter-krakow.com, globtroter@globtroter-krakow.com).

$ La Fontaine B&B, run by a French-Polish family, offers 14 rooms and 9 apartments in two different buildings just off the Main Market Square (one of them has lots of stairs and no elevator; the other does have an elevator). Tastefully decorated with French flair, it's cute as a poodle. Each room has a little lounge with a microwave and fridge—most in the hall, some inside the room (Sb-237 zł, Db-253 zł, extra bed-60 zł, apartment for up to four-420 zł, apartment for up to six-493 zł, gigantic apartment-677 zł, 30 percent cheaper Nov-Easter, air-con, low slanted ceilings in some rooms, Wi-Fi, guest kitchen, free self-service laundry machine—or pay them 25 zł to wash clothes for you, ulica Sławkowska 1, tel. 12-422-6564, www.bblafontaine.com, biuro@bblafontaine.com).

Outside of the Old Town: **$$ Cracowdays** is the farthest of my listings from the center of town, about a 15-minute walk away (a tram can cut a few minutes off the trek). But it's also a notch more refined than the guest houses listed previously. It sits in a pleasant residential neighborhood west of the Main Market Square, with six beautifully decorated and thoughtfully tended rooms, all sharing a central kitchen (Db-360 zł, superior Db-405 zł, stand-alone studio Db apartment in another building-425 zł, breakfast-25 zł extra, air-con, on the first floor with no elevator, 24-hour reception, Wi-Fi, Grabowskiego 7, mobile 666-971-478, www.cracowdays.com, reservation@cracowdays.com).

Hotels

For this section, I've listed the official, published "rack rates"—which are very soft. Most hotels discount their rates substantially, especially in slow times. Consider asking several hotels for their lowest price during your visit, and take the best deal.

$$$ Donimirski Boutique Hotels, with four different locations in or near Kraków's Old Town, set the bar for splurge hotels in Kraków (website for all: www.donimirski.com). All Donimirski hotels offer my readers a 15 percent discount (I've listed the rates below without the discount, during high season; the base price is cheaper Nov-March and at other slow times). You can expect any of these hotels to have some of the friendliest staff in Kraków and all of the classy little extras that add up to a memorable hotel experience. **Hotel Gródek**—the fanciest of the bunch—offers 23 rooms a three-minute walk behind St. Mary's Church on a quiet dead-end street overlooking the Planty park. This place is easily the best splurge in town, with a handy location, gorgeously decorated rooms, and a top-notch breakfast served in a room surrounded by a mini-museum of artifacts discovered during the recent renovation (Sb-650 zł, Db-850 zł, bigger "deluxe" Db-960 zł, suite-1,300 zł, guest computer, Wi-Fi, good cellar restaurant serves Polish cuisine, parking-50 zł/day, Na Gródku 4, tel. 12-431-9030, grodek@donimirski.com). **Hotel Maltański** has 16 rooms in the beautifully renovated former royal stables, just outside the Planty park and only two blocks from Wawel Castle (Sb-590 zł, Db-650 zł, 80 zł more for "deluxe" room with air-con, no elevator but only 2 floors, Wi-Fi, parking-50 zł/day, ulica Straszewskiego 14, tel. 12-431-0010, maltanski@donimirski.com). **Hotel Pugetów,** with seven small but plush and cozy rooms and a fun breakfast cellar, is on the other side of town, in a more workaday but convenient neighborhood between the Main Market Square and Kazimierz (Sb-390 zł, Db-680 zł, Db suite-950 zł, air-con, cable Internet, parking-50 zł/day, ulica Starowiślna 15A, tel. 12-432-4950, pugetow@donimirski.com). And the group recently took over

Hotel Polski pod Białym Orłem, just inside the north end of the Old Town, near the Florian Gate (rates and amenities may change with planned renovation, but likely Sb-390 zł, Db-590 zł, Tb-630 zł, apartment-850 zł, air-con in a few rooms, elevator, Wi-Fi, ulica Pijarska 17, tel. 12-422-1144, hotel.polski@donimirski.com).

$$$ Hotel Senacki is a business-class place renting 20 comfortable rooms between Wawel Castle and the Main Market Square. The location is handy, but it can be noisy on weekends—ask for a quieter back room. The staff is warm, professional, and conscientious. Top-floor "attic" rooms have low beams, skylight windows, and a flight of stairs after the elevator (prices change constantly with demand, but generally Sb-400 zł, Db-500 zł, deluxe Db-580 zł, extra bed-90 zł, better prices for longer stays, cheaper Nov-March, non-smoking, air-con, elevator—but doesn't go to "attic" rooms, Wi-Fi, ask about nearby parking for 80 zł/day, ulica Grodzka 51, tel. 12-422-7686, www.hotelsenacki.pl, senacki@hotelsenacki.pl).

$$$ Wentzl Hotel is your splurge-right-on-the-Square option, with 18 rooms. The decor is over-the-top-classy Old World with modern touches, like state-of-the-art TVs and bathrooms. When reserving, request a room with a view on the Square—which can be noisy, especially on weekends—or one of the three quieter back rooms (Sb-740 zł, Db-830 zł, bigger "deluxe" rooms cost 50 zł more, air-con, elevator, Wi-Fi, Rynek Główny 19, tel. 12-430-2664, www.wentzl.pl, hotel@wentzl.pl).

$$$ Hotel Wawel has 39 rooms on a well-located street that's quieter than the Old Town norm. It feels plush for the price, though its colorful decor verges on gaudy; above the swanky marble lobby are hallways creatively painted with the history of the building and images from around Kraków. Out back, a fountain gurgles in a cute little courtyard (Sb-340 zł, Db-480 zł, extra bed-100 zł/adult or 50 zł/child, rates are soft so ask for best price, 20 percent less Nov-March, non-smoking, air-con, elevator—but doesn't go to top floor, guest computer, Wi-Fi, ulica Poselska 22, tel. 12-424-1300, www.hotelwawel.pl, hotel@hotelwawel.pl).

$$$ Bracka 6, wonderfully located just one short block off the Main Market Square, is a sort of a hybrid between a hotel and an apartment house: The 16 stylish rooms—with sleek lines, lots of glass, and gentlemen's-hat chandeliers—each have a kitchen, so breakfast is 25 zł extra. It's on the second and third floors with no elevator, and the reception is open limited hours (daily 8:00-22:00 or so), but the lack of full hotel amenities keeps the prices very affordable for this level of modern elegance (standard Db-450 zł, bigger Db-500 zł, biggest Db-600 zł, air-con, Wi-Fi, Bracka 6, tel. 12-341-4011, www.bracka6.pl, info@bracka6.pl).

$$$ Hotel Amber sits on a dull but safe and quiet street just outside the Planty park, less than a 10-minute walk from the Square. The staff is proud of their attentive service (and circulates a handy little informative newsletter daily). The hotel has two parts: 18 perfectly fine, if smallish, rooms in the original building; and 20 slightly more upscale rooms in the newer "design" section. Both parts share a small gym, sauna, and garden in back. It's a good-value alternative to the places inside the Old Town (Sb-350 zł, standard Db-438 zł, bigger "superior" Db-479 zł, "deluxe" Db with fancier touches-499 zł; "design" rooms cost about 50 zł more; cheaper Nov-March, air-con, elevator, Wi-Fi, Garbarska 8-10, tel. 12-421-0606, www.hotel-amber.pl, office@hotel-amber.pl).

$$$ Hotel Wielopolc is conveniently located, a block outside of the Planty and on the way to the lively Kazimierz district. Its 35 tight rooms are tucked down a (relatively) quiet side street just past the main post office, facing a big Holiday Inn. Run by the same company as Hotel Amber (described above), it's a similarly good value, with an equally pleasant emphasis on welcoming service (Sb-360 zł, Db-450 zł, 40 zł more for "superior" rooms, 100 zł more for bigger and more ornate "deluxe" rooms, prices can be soft if you book direct, air-con, elevator, Wi-Fi, vegetarian restaurant in cellar, Wielopole 3, tel. 12-422-1475, www.wielopole.pl, office@wielopole.pl).

Apartments

You can save money by staying in your own apartment rather than a hotel. Apartments come with great locations, simple kitchens, and relatively low prices, but no big-hotel services (such as having your room cleaned daily)...in other words, you're on your own. Apartments aren't just for long stays—these places welcome even one-nighters. While the apartments themselves are neat and modern, most are in old buildings with dreary entryways and stairways. As reception times are limited, be sure to clearly communicate your arrival time. A wide variety of apartments are easy to find at online booking sites, but each of these two places has a reception desk that manages several units, making them a bit more hotelesque than the norm.

$ Kraków City Apartments, conscientiously run by Andrzej and Katarzyna, has 14 straightforward but modern and clean apartments tucked away in a quiet courtyard at the corner of the Old Town (small studio Db-240 zł, bigger deluxe Db-320 zł, 2-bedroom apartment-350 zł for 2 or 420 zł for 4, 2-bedroom apartment with view-420 zł for 2 or 650 zł for 4—can also sleep 6, 20 percent cheaper Oct-April, no breakfast but you can pay 30 zł for breakfast at a café on the Square, non-smoking, elevator to all rooms except studios, Wi-Fi, reception open daily 9:00-20:00, ulica Szpitalna

KRAKÓW

34, reception mobile 507-203-050, Andrzej's mobile 504-235-925, www.krakowapartments.info, info@krakowapartments.info).

$ Grodzka Apartment House offers 12 well-decorated apartments around a courtyard along one of Kraków's most happening streets, just a few steps off the Main Market Square. The studio apartments are as nice as a hotel room and a good value (studio-270 zł, 1-bedroom-360 zł, 2-bedroom-540 zł, prices soft, cheaper Nov-March, no breakfast but can buy 30-zł breakfast at nearby café, reception open daily 10:00-20:00, some apartments have street noise—light sleepers should ask for quieter courtyard room, lots of stairs with no elevator, Wi-Fi, go down the passage at Grodzka 4, tel. 12-421-4835, mobile 660-541-085, www.krakowforyou.com, info@krakowforyou.com, Mikołaj). They also have more apartments (though not quite as nice) in two other Old Town buildings.

IN KAZIMIERZ

Sleep in Kazimierz to be close to Kraków's Jewish heart—or simply to experience a cheaper, less touristy, more local-feeling neighborhood outside the Old Town. With the highest concentration of pubs and nightclubs in town, Kazimierz rivals the Old Town for nightlife—which means that all of these places can be subject to some noise, especially on weekends. Keep in mind that these accommodations put you a 20-minute walk or a 5-minute tram ride from the medieval ambience of Kraków's old center (for details on getting to Kazimierz from the Old Town, see page 295). Some of the klezmer music restaurants listed under "Eating in Kraków" also rent rooms, but they're generally an afterthought to the food and music, and not a good value. For locations, see the map on page 296.

$$$ Rubinstein Residence is your Kazimierz splurge, sitting right in the middle of ulica Szeroka—surrounded by klezmer restaurants and synagogues, in the heart of the neighborhood. It fills a painstakingly restored old townhouse (parts of it dating to the 15th century) with heavy wood beams and 28 swanky rooms—some of them palatial suites that incorporate old features like frescoes and pillars. The rooftop terrace—with views over Kazimierz and to the Old Town—sets this place above...literally (Db-500 zł, suites can be 1,000 zł or more, air-con, elevator, Wi-Fi, Szeroka 12, tel. 12-384-0000, www.rubinstein.pl, recepcja@rubinstein.pl).

$$$ Karmel Hotel, with 11 rooms on a pleasant side street near the heart of Kazimierz, offers elegance at a reasonable price (Sb-275 zł, tight twin Db-298 zł, more spacious "komfort plus" Db with one big bed and air-con-430 zł, pricier suites also available, extra bed-70 zł, about 20 percent less Nov-March, upstairs with no elevator, guest computer, Wi-Fi, some night noise on weekends, ulica Kupa 15, tel. 12-430-6697, www.karmel.com.pl, hotel@karmel.com.pl).

$ Tournet Guest House, well-run by friendly Piotr and Sylwia Działowy, is a great budget option offering 18 clean, colorful rooms near the edge of Kazimierz toward Wawel Hill. While all of the rooms are pretty basic, the ones they call "basic" lack TV sets (basic Sb-120 zł, standard Sb-150 zł, basic twin Db-160 zł, standard Db-200 zł, Tb-250 zł, extra bed-50 zł, 10 zł/person less Nov-March, elevator plus a few stairs, Wi-Fi, reception open 7:00-22:00, ulica Miodowa 7, tel. 12-292-0088, www.nocleg.krakow.pl, tournet@nocleg.krakow.pl).

Hostel: **$ Hostel Momotown** is a smidge more institutional and less party-oriented than your average hostel, but it's still loose and friendly. Run by Paweł Momot, it has 52 dorm beds and a fun garden for hanging out (bunk in 4-bed dorm-60 zł, in 6-bed dorm-55 zł, in 8-bed dorm-55 zł, in 10-bed dorm-45 zł, includes breakfast and sheets, towels-2.50 zł, guest computer, Wi-Fi, kitchen, laundry, lockers, ulica Miodowa 28, tel. 12-429-6929, www.momotownhostel.com, info@momotownhostel.com). Two blocks away, they also rent 14 basic but cheap private rooms that share a kitchenette, overlooking Kazimierz's main square, ulica Szeroka (Sb-140 zł, Db-180 zł).

Eating in Kraków

Kraków has a wide array of great restaurants—for every one I've listed, there are two or three nearly as good. (The downside is a lack of variation; little distinguishes one place from another.) Polish food is rivaled by Italian in popularity. As the restaurant scene changes constantly, I've chosen places that are well-established and have a proven track record for reliably good food.

IN THE OLD TOWN

Kraków's Old Town is loaded with dining options. Prices are reasonable even on the Main Market Square. And a half-block away, they get even better. All of these eateries (except the milk bars) are likely to be booked up on weekends—always reserve ahead.

Restauracja Farina, with a fish-and-bottles theme, features a welcoming atmosphere and Polish and Mediterranean cuisine with an emphasis on fresh fish (30-35-zł pastas, 30-60-zł main dishes). Part of their menu consists of seasonal offerings, and they serve some special seafood dishes (60-100 zł) only on the days that they get their fresh delivery (about twice weekly; open daily 12:00-23:00, 2 blocks north of the Square at ulica Św. Marka 16, at intersection with ulica Św. Jana, tel. 12-422-1680, www.farina.com.pl).

Miód Malina ("Honey Raspberry") is a delightful Polish-Italian fusion restaurant filled with the comforting aroma of its wood-fired oven. The menu is half Polish and half Italian—yet, remarkably, they do both cuisines equally well. For example, you can start with borscht and follow it with lasagna Bolognese. Sit in the cozy, warmly painted interior, or out in the courtyard (19-zł pierogi, 25-30-zł pastas, 40-70-zł main dishes, reservations smart, daily 12:00-23:00, ulica Grodzka 40, tel. 12-430-0411, www.miodmalina.pl). The same people run two other restaurants a bit closer to the Square, with similar atmosphere and equally good food, but are more focused on Polish fare: **Marmolada** (Grodzka 5) and **Wesele** (on the Square at #10).

Restauracja pod Aniołami ("Under Angels") offers a dressy, candlelit atmosphere on a wonderful covered patio, or in a deep, steep, romantic cellar with rough wood and medieval vaults. Peruse the elaborately described menu of medieval noblemen's dishes. The cuisine is traditional Polish, with an emphasis on grilled meats and trout (on a wood-fired grill). Every meal begins with *smalec* (spread made with lard, fried onion, bacon, and apple). Don't go here if you're in a hurry—only if you want to really slow down and enjoy your dinner. Reservations are smart (20-30-zł starters, 45-70-zł main dishes, daily 13:00-24:00, ulica Grodzka 35, tel. 12-421-3999, www.podaniolami.pl).

Aperitif is a cheery, colorful bistro serving tasty international cuisine with Mediterranean flair on the appealing Small Market Square (Mały Rynek) behind St. Mary's Church. It's classy but casual, with a cozy interior and a pleasant garden in back. Their 19- or 25-zł lunch specials are a great deal (30-40-zł pastas, 40-60-zł main dishes, daily 10:00-23:00, ulica Sienna 9, tel. 12-432-3333, www.aperitif.com.pl).

Chimera Cafeteria, just off the Main Market Square, is a handy spot for a quick lunch in the center. It serves fast traditional meals to a steady stream of students. You'll order at the counter—choose a big plate (6 items, 17 zł) or medium plate (4 items, 13 zł), and select from an array of salads and main dishes by pointing to what looks good. Then eat outside on their quiet courtyard (good for vegetarians, daily 9:00-22:00, near university at ulica Św. Anny 3). I'd skip their expensive full-service restaurant (in the basement), which shares an entryway.

Restauracja Jarema (yah-RAY-mah) offers a tasty reminder that Kraków used to rule a large swath of Ukraine and Lithuania. They serve eastern Polish/Ukrainian cuisine (with well-described specialties) amid 19th-century aristocratic elegance—you'll feel like you're dining in an old mansion. It's very sedate and feels a bit tired, but the food satisfies (30-55-zł main dishes, several good vegetarian options, daily 12:00-22:00, usually live music from 19:00, reservations wise, across the street from barbican at plac Matejki 5—facing the Grunwald monument, tel. 12-429-3669, www.jarema.pl).

Pod Baranem ("Under the Ram") is a popular local recommendation for traditional Polish food done very well. It sits just outside of the tourist chaos, quietly facing the Planty near Wawel Castle—keeping the prices reasonable and the passing tourist trade at bay. Several cozy rooms—tasteful but not stuffy—sprawl through an old building (25-30-zł light meals until 19:00, otherwise 25-45-zł main courses, Św. Gertrudy 21, tel. 12-429-4022, www.podbaranem.com).

Youthful Style at Plac Szczepański: While seemingly every corner of the Old Town is jammed with tourists (and businesses catering to them), the pleasant square called plac Szczepański—huddled at the northwest corner of the Old Town—feels like a carefully protected bastion of the local upscale art culture. Come here if you'd like to browse a small array of cafés and galleries that feel more Warsaw-urbane than ye olde Kraków. **Charlotte** is a winner—it's a classy, French-feeling bakery/café/wine bar. They make their own breads and pastries in the basement (with lots of seating—you can watch the bakers work if you come early enough in the morning), cultivate a stay-awhile coffee house ambience upstairs, and throw in a few square-facing sidewalk tables to boot. And it's affordable, serving up 10-20-zł sandwiches, pastries, and salads. While the food is light café fare rather than a filling dinner, after 18:00 they redecorate the borderline-hipster space to give it a more sophisticated flair (Mon-Fri 7:00-24:00, Sat 9:00-24:00, Sun 9:00-22:00, plac Szczepański 2, tel. 12-431-5610). Just around the corner, facing the Planty park, is the delightful **Café Bunkier.** It belongs to the hulking Bunker Sztuki contemporary art gallery, but—in contrast to that building's concrete vibe—the café sits under a delightful glass canopy that faces the lush greenbelt, with well-worn wooden tables and an almost Parisian ambience. While it's not the place for a filling meal, it's worth coming here for some light food and drinks while enjoying Kraków's greenbelt in any weather (light 20-30-zł meals, daily 9:00-24:00, plac Szczepański 3a, tel. 12-431-0585).

On Stolarska Street: Stolarska street, a neatly pedestrianized, oddly untrammeled "embassy row" just a block away from the Main Market Square, is worth exploring for a meal or a drink. Stolarska has a fun variety of more locals-oriented bars and cafés. Begin at the Small Market Square (Mały Rynek) behind St. Mary's Church and head south. On the left, look for the ridiculously long sign that perfectly identifies the business: Pierwszy Lokal Na Stolarskiej Po Lewej Stronie Idąc Od Małego Rynku ("The first pub on the left side of Stolarska coming from the Small Market Square"). Notice that this once-sleepy street is lined with embassies and consulates—it's easy to spot the flags of Germany, the US, and France. On the left, in the stretch of cafés under canopies, you'll see the

Ambasada Śledzia ("Herring Embassy"), with a divey, youthful atmosphere and a "Polish tapas" approach: 10 different types of 8-zł herring, plus a variety of vodka to wash it down, are posted on the menu. You'll order at the bar (there can be a language barrier, but try asking for translation help), then find a table, or take it to go (open long hours daily, Stolarska 8). Across the street, the Pasaż Bielaka (an easy-to-miss passage—look for the low-profile stone doorway and *Rynek Główny* sign at #5) runs through the middle of the block all the way out to the Main Market Square (emerging at Rynek Główny #12); partway along is another sprawling branch of the Herring Embassy.

Beer Hall: Pod Wawelem ("Under Wawel") is a rollicking Austrian-style beer hall right on the Planty park near Wawel Castle. It's packed with locals seeking big, sloppy, greasy portions of meaty fare, with giant mugs of various beers on tap (including Polish and Bavarian). Choose between the bustling interior or the outdoor terrace right on the Planty (20-35-zł main dishes, different specials every day—such as giant schnitzel, pork ribs, or roasted chicken; daily 12:00-24:00, ulica Św. Gertrudy 26-29, tel. 12-421-2336).

Pizza: Two well-established places in the Old Town are reliable choices. **Cyklop,** with 10 tables wrapped around the cook and his busy oven, has good wood-fired pizzas and a cozy, charming ambience (15-25-zł one-person pizzas, 18-30-zł two-person pizzas, daily 11:00-23:00, near St. Mary's Church at Mikołajska 16, tel. 12-421-6603). **Pizzeria Trzy Papryczki** ("Three Peppers"), whose wood-fired pizzas aren't quite as good as Cyklop's, also has inviting ambience, either in the country-cozy interior or out in the welcoming garden (17-25-zł one-person pizzas, 20-29-zł two-person pizzas, daily 11:00-23:00, ulica Poselska 17, tel. 12-292-5532). But the best pizza in town is at **Pizza Garden,** run by Stanisław, who worked at a respected New York City pizzeria for a decade and has brought the art of brick-oven pizza back home. The catch is that his place is well outside the Old Town, about a 10-minute walk across the river from Wawel Hill (the walk is mostly along the pretty riverside parkland and across Dębnicki Bridge, with great views back on the castle). This makes it a good post-Wawel lunch or dinner spot (16-30-zł 1-person pizzas, 20-25-zł 2-person pizzas, Mon-Wed 13:00-22:00, Thu-Sun 13:00-23:00; cross Dębnicki Bridge, then look right to find M. Konopnickiej 11/1; tel. 12-266-7309, www.pizzagarden.pl).

Quick Sandwich: If you need a break from milk bars (described next), but want to grab a sandwich on the go, stop by **Lajkonik,** a modern bakery/coffee shop *(piekarnia i kawiarnia)* that sells fresh 7-10-zł takeout sandwiches (Mon-Fri 7:00-19:00, Sat 8:00-20:00, Sun 8:00-22:00, handy location right in front of the Dominican Church at Dominikański 2, others are just outside of the Old Town).

Milk Bars

Kraków is a good place to try the cheap cafeterias called "milk bars." For pointers on eating at a milk bar, review the sidebar on page 234. I've listed them by neighborhoods: north or south of the Main Market Square.

North of the Main Market Square

These options, easy to squeeze in to a busy day of sightseeing, are good for a quick, cheap bite:

Milkbar Tomasza is an updated, upgraded milk bar, popular with local students. Modern and relatively untouristy, it has a hipster ambience and serves big, splittable portions of high-quality food—often with some international flourishes—plus breakfast dishes all day (2-course 18-zł meals, 12-20-zł main dishes, great big salads, daily 8:00-22:00, ulica Tomasza 24, tel. 12-422-1706).

Jadłodajnia "U Stasi" is a throwback that makes you feel like you're in on Kraków's best-kept secret. Its hidden location—tucked at the far end of the passage that leads to, then beyond, the recommended Cyklop pizzeria—attracts a wide range of loyal local clientele, from homeless people to politicians, artists, and actors. They're all here for well-executed, unpretentious, home-style Polish lunch grub. There can be a bit of a language barrier, so go with the flow: Pick up the English menu as you enter, find a table, wait for them to take your order, enjoy your meal, then pay as you leave. This is an excellent value and a real, untouristy Polish experience. The short menu changes every day—and when they're out, they're out (10-15-zł main dishes, Mon-Fri 12:00-17:00, closed Sat-Sun, Mikołajskiej 16).

U Babci Maliny ("Granny Raspberry"), with a grinning Granny on the sign, is another well-established and popular milk bar (9-23-zł main dishes). One location, frequented almost entirely by Krakovians, is designed for university students and staff and is tucked into an inner courtyard of the Science Academy. Find the door at Sławkowska 17, then follow signs through the stuffy complex to find a rustic cellar where it looks like a kitschy cottage bomb went off (Mon-Fri 11:00-21:00, Sat-Sun 12:00-21:00). Another location is across the street from the National Theater building at Szpitalna 38 (daily 11:00-23:00; self-service upstairs, table service in basement). Both locations have walls of photos of the owner posing with bodybuilders and ultimate fighters...entertaining, if not quite in keeping with the country theme.

The **Academy of Music Café** (a.k.a. Restauracja U Romana) is a no-frills student cafeteria that enjoys a restful, top-floor perch with views over the back of St. Mary's Church and the rooftops of Kraków. It has a short, basic menu of food and drinks; come here not for high cuisine, but for high-up cuisine. You'll enter the Academy of Music at Św. Tomasza 43—using the heavy metal door opposite Hotel Campanile—then angle left inside to find the elevator in the stairwell and ride it to floor 6. Order at the counter, get your food, then head out to the tranquil terrace (12-15-zł grub, Mon-Fri 9:00-18:00, Sat 9:00-16:00, closed Sun).

On Grodzka Street, South of the Main Market Square

Ulica Grodzka, the busy street that cuts south from the Main Market Square, has a convenient little pocket of three milk bars within a few steps of each other (all are open daily for lunch and dinner, but only until 19:00 or 20:00, sometimes later in summer). Survey all three options before you dive in. If they look full, just wait—there's a lot of turnover, so a table should free up soon.

Approaching from the Square, the first one you'll come to (just after the modern copper-colored Wyspiański Pavilion, on the left) is the most modern and trendy of the three, more popular with students than with their grandparents: **Kwandras Lunch Bar** ("Quarter"—as in, you can eat here in a quarter-hour; pierogi and other dishes for 9-12 zł, full dinner for 14 zł—plus soup for 1 zł more, ulica Grodzka 32, tel. 12-294-2222).

Two blocks down the street and on the right (at the corner with Senacka) is the most basic and traditional milk bar, with a sign reading simply **Bar Mleczny** ("Milk Bar"; a low-profile sign over the door gives the eatery's name, *Restauracja "pod Temidą"*). The next best thing to a time machine to the communist era, this place has grumpy monolingual service, a mostly local clientele, and cheap but good food (12-16-zł main dishes).

A few more steps down, also on the right (just before the two churches), is **Bar Grodzki,** a single tight little room with shared

tables. In addition to the standard milk-bar fare, Bar Grodzki specializes in tasty potato pancake dishes *(placki ziemniaczane)*. Order high on the menu and try the rich and hearty "Hunter's Delight"— potato pancake with sausage, beef, melted cheese, and spicy sauce for 23 zł. The English menu posted by the counter makes ordering easy. Order, sit, and wait to be called to fetch your food (most main dishes 11-23 zł).

Nearby: **Restauracja Samoobsługowa Polakowski** is a glorified milk bar with country-kitchen decor and cheap, tasty

Polish fare. The tongue-twisting *samoobsługowa* simply means "self-service"—as at other milk bars, you'll order at the counter and bus your dishes when done. Curt service...cute hats (10-13-zł main dishes, daily 9:00-22:00, facing St. Francis Basilica at plac Wszystkich Świętych 10).

Splurging on the Main Market Square

You'll find plenty of relatively expensive, tourist-oriented restaurants on the Square. Though all of these places have rich interiors, there's not much point in paying a premium to dine here unless you're sitting outside on the Square. While tourists go for ye olde places, natives hang out at pizza joints (like Sphinx, part of a wildly popular Poland-wide chain). Poles generally afford this zone on their meager incomes by just having a drink on the Square after eating at home.

If any place here is a cut above, it's probably **Wierzynek,** with an elegant upstairs and prime on-the-Square seating. It's famous for the greatest feast in Polish history: In 1364, a royal wedding was celebrated here with 20 days and 20 nights of dining (it's named for the caterer, Nicolas Wierzynek). They pride themselves on their beautifully presented, traditional Polish cuisine (30-40-zł starters, 60-90-zł main dishes, daily 13:00-23:00, consider reserving a window seat upstairs, on corner of Grodzka and Main Market Square—at #15, tel. 12-424-9600, www.wierzynek.com.pl).

And for Dessert: **Słodki Wentzl** ("Sweets") is a local favorite for enjoying dessert on the Square. Consider dining more cheaply elsewhere, then finishing up with coffee, ice cream, or cake here (12-20-zł desserts, daily 11:00-23:00, at #19).

IN KAZIMIERZ

The entire district is bursting with lively cafés and bars—it's a happening night scene. Jewish food is the specialty here, but in general the neighborhood offers more diversity than the Old Town. The non-Jewish places I've listed are fast, cheap, and convenient. For locations, see the map on page 296.

Klezmer Concerts and Jewish Food

Kazimierz is a hub of Jewish restaurants, featuring cuisine and music that honors the neighborhood's Jewish heritage (and caters to its Jewish visitors). On a balmy summer night, the air is filled with the sound of klezmer music—traditional Jewish music from 19th-century Poland, generally with violin, string bass, clarinet, and accordion. Skilled klezmer musicians can make their instruments weep or laugh like human voices. Several places on ulica Szeroka (Kazimierz's main square) offer klezmer concerts. All of these have several rooms, which the musicians move between

KRAKÓW

as the evening goes on. While most places claim to do concerts nightly year-round, in reality they can be canceled anytime it's slow (especially off-season). For this reason—and because these places fill up—it's important to reserve ahead. (If you're in Kazimierz for some daytime sightseeing, visit several places, pick your favorite, and reserve dinner.) Don't expect great cuisine—you're here for the music.

With a Cover Charge: Several well-established, old-fashioned restaurants offer klezmer concerts most nights at around 20:00; you'll pay a cover charge of about 25-30 zł per person. These restaurants have similar menus, with main dishes for 25-60 zł. Sometimes you'll need to order sides and starches separately. At **Klezmer-Hois,** which fills a venerable former Jewish ritual bath-house, you'll feel like you're dining in a rich grandparent's home. This is probably your best option for the traditional klezmer-concert-during-Jewish-dinner experience (daily 8:00-22:00, at #6, tel. 12-411-1245, www.klezmer.pl). **Ariel,** which dominates the square, was once quite popular but has faded.

No-Cover Alternatives: Two competitive options on the square work great for those wanting only a taste of klezmer music (rather than the full-blown dinner concert). Both of these places generally put their performers outside, facing the square (rather than tucked away inside)—so you can also hear it just fine sitting at other restaurants and bars facing the square, or even just from a bench. **Awiw** is the poor man's option for live klezmer music. Each evening from 18:00 to 23:00, they have live music outside on their patio on ulica Szeroka with no cover charge (Polish and Jewish food, 30-70-zł main dishes, daily 10:00-23:00, Szeroka 13, tel. 12-341-4279). **Hotel Ester**—at the end of the square closest to the Old Synagogue—has outdoor music every day in good weather, generally from about 13:00 to 17:00, and again from 18:00 until 22:00. You can sit and enjoy the music even if you just buy a drink, or stay for a full meal (30-40-zł main dishes, open daily, Szeroka 20, tel. 12-429-1188).

Fast and Cheap

Bagelmama, run by an American named Nava (who has worked as a private chef for US tennis star John McEnroe), is a casual bagel shop that's understandably popular with expats. This place was a Kazimierz pioneer—one of the first innovative eateries to plant its flag in the neighborhood. And today, Nava and his staff still serve up a wide range of sandwiches, soups, salads, burritos, desserts, and good espresso drinks. The bagels come dressed with a wide variety of spreads, from simple cream cheese or peanut butter to lox, tuna, or curried chicken. You can eat in or get it to go (most items 10-17 zł, selection of "bagel tapas" with various toppings for

20 zł/person for 2 people, daily 9:00-18:30, possibly later in summer, ulica Dajwór 10, tel. 12-346-1646).

Polish Fast Food on Plac Nowy: The **plac Nowy market,** around the circular brick slaughterhouse, offers a fully authentic, very cheap, blue-collar Polish experience—join the workers on their lunch break at the little food windows on Kazimierz's market square. This area is particularly known for its *zapiekanki*—the uniquely Polish fast food of a toasted baguette with cheese, ketchup, and other toppings. These are enormous—basically a foot-long baguette sliced lengthwise—splittable, and cheap (7-10 zł, depending on toppings). More recently, a wide range of trendy restaurants and bars has sprung up around the square. Survey your options and choose your favorite.

Food Carts: While food carts haven't quite caught on in Poland, an undiscovered corner of Kazimierz has an inviting little pocket of hipster foodie-mobiles. The parking lot at the corner of Św. Wawrzyńca and Wąska, facing the Museum of Municipal Engineering, is usually filled with a fun little cluster of creative pop-up eateries under dramatic graffiti murals. Although the lineup is always changing, the Big Red Bustaurant (fish-and-chips sold from a double-decker London bus) is a fixture here, along with burgers, Belgian-style fries, milkshakes, and fusion cuisine.

Milk Bar: **Restauracja Samoobsługowa Polakowski,** the good-quality milk bar described on page 346, has a handy location in Kazimierz—just behind the top of ulica Szeroka at ulica Miodowa 39.

Dining in Kazimierz

For a good-quality sit-down meal, consider these options.

Hamsa, with a prime location at the top of ulica Szeroka, offers "hummus and happiness," with an updated take on Israeli food (that's Middle Eastern, not traditional Jewish fare). Don't come here for matzo balls and klezmer music, but for an enticing menu of 15-20-zł *mezes* (small plates, like hummus and various dips) and 35-60-zł grilled meat dishes in a modern, hip atmosphere (daily 9:00-24:00, ulica Szeorka 2, mobile 515-150-145).

Starka has romantic, dark-red decor and walls hung with sketches from a circa-1910 Berlin cartoonist. In addition to good Polish cuisine, they have 16 types of their own homemade flavored vodkas (25-30-zł starters, 30-45-zł main dishes, daily 12:00-23:00, Józefa 14, tel. 12-430-6538).

Szara is a well-respected Kraków institution (with another location near the Main Market Square). This popular spot—a bit more upscale and dressy than the tired klezmer joints—provides refined food at reasonable prices (20-30-zł starters, 40-70-zł main dishes, 30-zł lunch special includes soup and a main dish, daily

KRAKÓW

11:00-23:00, Szeroka 39, tel. 12-429-1219, www.szarakazimierz.pl).

Satori is a relaxing eddy of a café/bistro, just outside of the Kazimierz tourist chaos. With an artfully mismatched-furniture atmosphere that encourages lingering, this is a good choice either for a coffee or a full meal (15-25-zł homemade pastas and salads, daily 11:00-22:00, Sun until 21:00, Józefa 25, mobile 660-508-840).

Kazimierz Bars with Food

Three of my favorite atmospheric Kazimierz bars also serve food. It's not high cuisine—the food is an afterthought to the busy bar.

Kolanko No. 6 has a classic Kazimierz atmosphere. The bar up front is filled with old secondhand furniture. Walking toward the back, you discover an inviting garden with tables and, beyond that, a hall where they host events. They serve light meals, specializing in crêpes, toasted sandwiches, and salads (15-20 zł, 25-30-zł main dishes, daily 10:00-24:00, Józefa 17, tel. 12-292-0320).

Warsztat ("Workshop") is littered with musical instruments: The bar is a piano, and the tight interior is crammed with other instruments and rakishly crooked lampshades. The menu is an odd hybrid of Italian, Middle Eastern, and Polish cuisine, and the portions are big (15-25-zł salads, pizzas, and pastas, 30-45-zł meat dishes, daily 9:00-24:00, Izaaka 3, tel. 12-430-1451). They also have two other locations: a small one (focusing on Polish dishes) by the front door of the Tempel Synagogue, and a bigger one on Bożego Ciała street.

Plac Nowy 1 specializes in Polish microbrews, served either at the outdoor tables facing the plac Nowy market square, or in the industrial mod, split-level brick interior. The service can be spotty, and the food is an afterthought, but this is a nice setting to sample a local Polish craft beer (25-40-zł pastas, salads, pizzas, and burgers, 35-60-zł main dishes, open long hours daily, plac Nowy 1, tel. 12-442-7711).

Kazimierz Desserts

Ice Cream: **Lody Tradycyjna Receptura** has, true to its name, some of the best "ice cream from a traditional recipe" in Kraków—if not in Poland. The straightforward, seasonal flavors—just a few varieties—are made fresh each morning and sold until they run out. Locals line up here—and if you have a sweet tooth, you should, too (daily 9:00-19:00, Starowiślna 83).

Cakes: **Ciastkarnia** ("Confectionery") is a cute little bakery selling top-quality but still affordable cakes from traditional recipes (daily 9:00-20:00, shorter hours off-season, Brzozowa 13, mobile 602-790-988).

Kraków Connections

For getting between Kraków and **Auschwitz,** see page 369 in the next chapter. To confirm rail journeys, check specific times online (www.rozklad-pkp.pl) or at the main train station.

From Kraków by Train to: Warsaw (hourly, about 2.5 hours, requires seat reservation), **Gdańsk** (6/day direct, 5.5 hours, 1 more with change in Warsaw; plus night train, 11 hours), **Toruń** (1/day direct, 6.5 hours; better to transfer at Warsaw's Zachodnia station: 8/day, 5.5-6 hours), **Prague** (4/day with 1-2 changes, 7-8.25 hours; 1 night train, 8.75 hours), **Berlin** (3/day, 8.25-9.25 hours, transfer in Warsaw; plus 1 direct Deutsche Bahn bus, 8 hours, www.bahn.com), **Budapest** (2/day, 9.5-11 hours, transfer in Katowice, Poland, and Břeclav, Czech Republic; plus 1 night train, 10.5 hours; faster by infrequent Orange Ways bus: 5/week, 7 hours, www.orangeways.com), and **Vienna** (2/day, 6.5 hours, transfer in Katowice; 1 night train, 8 hours).

By Bus: Though train connections are typically faster, buses can be less expensive and make sense for some trips. Polski Bus prides itself on offering buses with Wi-Fi and electrical outlets (www.polskibus.com). However, some of my readers have reported hot, crowded, uncomfortable rides on these buses—you get what you pay for.

KRAKÓW

AUSCHWITZ-BIRKENAU

The unassuming regional capital of Oświęcim (ohsh-VEENCH-im) was the site of one of humanity's most unspeakably horrifying tragedies: the systematic murder of at least 1.1 million innocent people. From 1941 until 1945, Oświęcim was the home of Auschwitz, the biggest, most notorious concentration camp in the Nazi system. Today, Auschwitz is the most poignant memorial anywhere to the victims of the Holocaust.

A visit here is obligatory for Polish 14-year-olds; students usually come again during their last year of school, as well. You may see Israeli high school groups walking through the grounds wearing Star of David emblems. Many visitors leave flowers and messages. One of the messages—from a German visitor—reads, "Nations who forget their own history are sentenced to live it again."

Orientation to Auschwitz

"Auschwitz" (OWSH-vits) actually refers to a series of several camps in Poland—most importantly Auschwitz I, in the village of Oświęcim (50 miles, or a 1.25-hour drive, west of Kraków), and Auschwitz II, a.k.a. Birkenau (about 2 miles west of Oświęcim). Those visiting Auschwitz generally see both parts, starting with **Auschwitz I**, where public transportation from Kraków arrives. Auschwitz I has the main museum building, the *Arbeit Macht Frei* gate, and indoor museum exhibits in former prison buildings. A brief shuttle-bus ride takes visitors to **Birkenau** (BEER-keh-now)—on a much bigger scale and mostly outdoors, with the infamous guard tower (and another bookshop and more WCs), a

vast field with ruins of barracks, a few tourable rough barracks, the notorious "dividing platform," a giant monument flanked by remains of destroyed crematoria, and a prisoner processing facility called "the Sauna."

Begin at Auschwitz I. The museum's main building has ticket booths (to pay for a tour or to make a donation), bookshops (consider the good 5-zł *Guide-Book* brochure or the bigger laminated map), exchange offices, baggage storage (large bags aren't allowed on site), WCs, and basic eateries. You'll also find maps of the camp (posted on the walls) and a theater that shows a powerful film. A helpful **information desk**—where you can ask questions, buy tickets for the tour (see "Tours at Auschwitz," later), and find out about bus schedules for the return trip to Kraków—is halfway down the main entrance hall on the right, in the back corner.

Cost: Entrance to the grounds is free (though donations are gladly accepted). However, during busy times (April-Oct 10:00-15:00), you'll need to pay 40 zł at Auschwitz I to join a required organized tour, plus 5 zł per person for headphones to hear the guide's commentary (hiring a private guide is another option). At other times, you're allowed to visit Auschwitz I on your own, though the tour is still well worth considering. Any time of year, the grounds at Birkenau can be toured without a guide, though you'll likely need to be accompanied by a guide if you want to climb the guard tower.

Mandatory Reservations: With more than one million visitors each year, Auschwitz struggles with crowd control. Reservations are required, whether visiting on your own or with a tour. Reserving is free and easy at http://visit.auschwitz.org. Select

Why Visit Auschwitz?

Why visit a notorious concentration camp on your vacation? Auschwitz-Birkenau is one of the most moving sights in Europe, and certainly the most important of all the Holocaust memorials. Seeing the camp can be difficult: Many visitors are overwhelmed by a combination of sadness and anger over the tragedy, as well as inspiration at the remarkable stories of survival. Auschwitz survivors and victims' families want tourists to come here and experience the scale  and the monstrosity of the place. In their minds, a steady flow of visitors will ensure that the Holocaust is always remembered—so nothing like it will ever happen again.

Auschwitz isn't for everyone. But I've never met anyone who toured Auschwitz and regretted it. For many, it's a profoundly life-altering experience—at the very least, it will forever affect the way you think about the Holocaust.

"Visit for individuals," then select a date, and finally choose between "General Tour 3,5 h" (for the 40-zł, 3.5-hour guided tour—be sure to select one in English) or "Tour for individuals without an educator" (to visit on your own, for free). After you fill out the form, you'll be emailed an eticket. Print this out and bring it along when you visit the memorial.

Hours: The museum opens every day at 8:00, and closes June-Aug at 19:00, May and Sept at 18:00, April and Oct at 17:00, March and Nov at 16:00, and Dec-Feb at 15:00. These are technically "last entry" times; the grounds at Auschwitz I stay open one hour later (though many buildings—including the national memorials—close promptly at these times). The grounds at Birkenau, where many groups end their visits, may stay open even later. Information: Tel. 33-844-8100, www.auschwitz.org.

Getting There: For details on getting between Kraków and Auschwitz, see "Auschwitz Connections," at the end of this chapter.

Getting from Auschwitz I to Birkenau: Buses shuttle visitors two miles between the camps (free, about 4/hour in peak season, less off-season, times posted at the bus stop outside the main building of each site, timed to correspond with tours). Taxis are also standing by (about 15 zł). Many visitors, rather than wait for the next bus, decide to walk the 20 minutes between the camps, offering a much-needed chance for reflection. Along the way, you'll pass the Judenrampe, an old train car like the ones used to transport prisoners, explained by an informational sign.

Film: The 17-minute movie (too graphic for children) was shot by Ukrainian troops days after the Red Army liberated the camp (4 zł, buy ticket on arrival; schedule for showings in English varies—ask when you arrive).

Photography: Because the philosophy of the camp is to spread the story of Auschwitz, taking photographs of anything outdoors is encouraged. However, to ease the movement of visitors, photography is not allowed inside certain museum buildings (when it *is* allowed, don't use a flash or tripod).

Eating: A café and decent cafeteria (Bar Smak) are at the main Auschwitz building. More options are in the commercial complex across the street.

Etiquette: The camp encourages visitors to remember that Auschwitz is the place where more than a million people lost their lives. Behave and dress here as you would at a cemetery.

Tours at Auschwitz

Visiting Auschwitz on your own works well, given the abundance of English descriptions (and this chapter's self-guided tour). However, due to crowd-control issues, from May through October individual visitors are not allowed to enter the Auschwitz I part of the complex on their own between the peak times of 10:00 and 15:00. Instead, you're required to either join one of the museum's organized tours or reserve your own private museum guide (both options are explained next). Note that even during these busy times, individuals may enter the Auschwitz II/Birkenau part of the complex without a guide.

Organized Museum Tours

The Auschwitz Museum's excellent guides are serious and frank, and they feel a strong sense of responsibility about sharing the story of the camp. Appropriately, these well-trained guides are more historians than entertainers. The regularly scheduled 3.5-hour English tour covers Auschwitz, Birkenau, and the film (40 zł, plus 5 zł to rent headphones to hear the guide). Remember: These tours must be prebooked online at http://visit.auschwitz.org. Most of the year, there are generally at least four English tours scheduled each day. You'll watch the film first; the actual tour begins 30 minutes later (the film usually begins at the top of the hour, while English tours start at :30 past each hour from 9:30-15:30; in winter, tours generally begin at 10:30, 11:30, 12:30, and 13:20).

Auschwitz Renovation

The International Auschwitz Council is planning to renovate the site over the next several years. The museum at Auschwitz I, widely considered the oldest Holocaust exhibit in the world, has remained largely unchanged in the more than 50 years since it opened. Now the museum displays will be modernized and better organized to accommodate the growing number of visitors. The key elements described in this chapter (such as the displays of human hair, eyeglasses, and suitcases) will still be part of the exhibit, but will likely be spread into more buildings (mostly on the ground floor, to avoid congestion on stairways). At Birkenau, restorers will build retaining walls to prevent the remains of the huge crematoria—key evidence of Nazi crimes—from slowly sinking into the ground.

Because of the renovation, be aware that the information in this chapter (especially the locations of exhibits on the self-guided tour) is subject to change. Ask about recent developments when you arrive at the camp.

Private Official Museum Guides

If you have a special interest, a small group, or just want a more personalized visit, it's affordable and worthwhile to hire one of the museum's guides for a private tour. Choose between the basic 3.5-hour tour of the camp (250 zł), or a longer "study tour" (320 zł/4 hours only at Auschwitz I, 400 zł/6 hours at both Auschwitz I and Birkenau in one day, 500 zł/8 hours at Auschwitz I and Birkenau spread over 2 days). For groups larger than 10 people, you'll pay an additional 5 zł per person for headphones to hear the guide's commentary. Because English-speaking guides are limited, try to reserve at least two months in advance (fill out the online form at http://visit.auschwitz.org, or call 33-844-8099 or 33-844-8100). At busy times, individuals might not be able to reserve a private guide between 10:00 and 14:00, when they're needed for bigger groups.

Tours from Kraków

Various Kraków-based companies sell round-trip tours from Kraków to Auschwitz (generally around 130 zł; see "Tours in Kraków" on page 251). While these take care of transportation for you and include a guided tour, you'll pay triple and have to adhere to a strict schedule, and the tours tend to be impersonal.

Local Guides and Drivers from Kraków

For hassle-free transportation to the camp, you can hire a Kraków-based guide or driver to bring you to Auschwitz; I've listed my favorites on page 251. However, since these people are not officially registered museum guides, they technically aren't allowed to show you around the site. Instead, they will most likely arrange a private museum guide to join you, or time your visit so you can join an organized English tour (both options described earlier). While it's pricey, some travelers consider hiring a driver/guide to be a worthwhile splurge, since you'll have door-to-door service to the camp and three hours in the car with a local expert.

Auschwitz Tour

AUSCHWITZ I

• *From the entrance building, step out and look over the grassy field to get oriented.*

Before World War II, this camp was a base for the Polish army. When Hitler occupied Poland, he took over these barracks and

turned it into a concentration camp for his Polish political enemies. The location was ideal, with a nearby rail junction and rivers providing natural protective boundaries. An average of 14,000 prisoners were kept at this camp at one time. (Birkenau could hold up to 100,000.) In 1942, Auschwitz became a death camp for the extermination of European Jews and others whom Hitler considered "undesirable." By the time the camp was liberated in 1945, at least 1.1 million people had been murdered here—approximately 960,000 of them Jewish.

• *Go closer to the camp entrance, approaching the notorious...*

"Arbeit Macht Frei" Gate

Although this gate imparts the message "Work Sets You Free," the only way out of the camp for the prisoners was through the crematorium chimneys. Note that the "B" was welded on upside down by belligerent inmates, who were forced to make this sign (and much of the camp). This is actually a replica; the original was stolen one night in December of 2009, then recovered two days later, cut up into several pieces. The original is now safely in the museum's possession, but no longer displayed in public.

Just inside the gate and to the right, the camp orchestra (made up of prisoners) used to play marches; having the prisoners march made them easier to count.

• *From the gate, proceed straight up the "main street" of the camp.*

You'll pass two rows of barracks. The first one holds a variety of national memorials. We'll circle back here later, if you'd like to enter some of them. But these are of less general interest than the second row of barracks, which hold the main museum exhibitions.

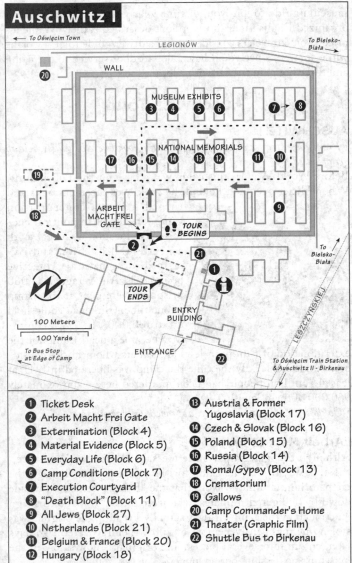

Auschwitz I

1. Ticket Desk
2. Arbeit Macht Frei Gate
3. Extermination (Block 4)
4. Material Evidence (Block 5)
5. Everyday Life (Block 6)
6. Camp Conditions (Block 7)
7. Execution Courtyard
8. "Death Block" (Block 11)
9. All Jews (Block 27)
10. Netherlands (Block 21)
11. Belgium & France (Block 20)
12. Hungary (Block 18)
13. Austria & Former Yugoslavia (Block 17)
14. Czech & Slovak (Block 16)
15. Poland (Block 15)
16. Russia (Block 14)
17. Roma/Gypsy (Block 13)
18. Crematorium
19. Gallows
20. Camp Commander's Home
21. Theater (Graphic Film)
22. Shuttle Bus to Birkenau

AUSCHWITZ-BIRKENAU

Blocks 4 and 5 focus on how Auschwitz prisoners were killed. Blocks 6, 7, and 11 explore the conditions for prisoners who survived here a little longer than most. In each block, arrows send you on a one-way route from numbered room to numbered room; in many cases, there are also exhibits downstairs and upstairs—don't miss these.

• *Start with...*

Block 4: Extermination

In Room 1, a map identifies the countries from which Auschwitz prisoners were brought—as far away as the Norwegian fjords and the Greek Islands. In an alcove along the side of the room is an urn filled with ashes, a symbolic memorial to all of the camp's victims.

Room 2 shows photographs of Jewish ghettos from all over Europe being "liquidated"—that is, its residents assembled and deported to various concentration camps. Thanks to its massive occupancy, Auschwitz was a common destination for many.

Room 3 displays rare photos of scenes inside the camp, taken by arrogant SS men. To prevent a riot, the Nazis claimed at first that this was only a transition camp for resettlement in Eastern Europe. At the far end of Room 3, a helpful orientation map for visitors shows the town of Oświęcim, Auschwitz I, Auschwitz II (Birkenau), and other parts of the camp network.

Upstairs in Room 4 is a model of a Birkenau crematorium. People entered on the left, then got undressed in the underground rooms (hanging their belongings on numbered hooks and encouraged to remember their numbers to retrieve their clothes later). They then moved into the "showers" and were killed by Zyklon-B gas (hydrogen cyanide), a German-produced cleaning agent that is lethal in high doses. This efficient factory of murder took about 20 minutes to kill 8,000 people in four gas chambers. Elevators brought the bodies up to the crematorium. Members of the *Sonderkommand*—Jewish inmates who were kept isolated and forced by the Nazis to work here—removed the corpses' gold teeth and shaved off their hair (to be sold) before putting the bodies in the ovens. It wasn't unusual for a *Sonderkommand* worker to discover a wife, child, or parent among the dead. A few of these workers committed suicide by throwing themselves at electric fences; those who didn't were systematically executed by the Nazis after a two-month shift. Across from the model of the crematorium are canisters of Zyklon-B.

Across the hall in the dimly lit Room 5 is one of the camp's most powerful exhibits: a wall of actual victims' hair—4,400 pounds of it. Also displayed is cloth made of the hair, used to make Nazi uniforms. The Nazis were nothing if not efficient...nothing, not even human body parts, could be wasted.

Back downstairs in Room 6 is an exhibit on the plunder of victims' personal belongings. People being transported here were encouraged to bring luggage—and some victims had even paid in advance for houses in their new homeland. After they were killed, everything of value was sorted and stored in warehouses that prisoners named "Canada" (after a country they associated with great wealth). Although the Canada warehouses were destroyed, you can see a few of these items in the next building.
• *Head next door.*

Block 5: Material Evidence of the Nazis' Crimes

The exhibits in this block consist mostly of piles of the victims' goods, a tiny fraction of everything the Nazis stole. As you wander through the rooms, you'll see eyeglasses; fine Jewish prayer shawls; crutches and prosthetic limbs (the first people the Nazis exterminated were mentally and physically ill German citizens); and a pile of pots and pans. Then, upstairs, you'll witness a seemingly endless mountain of shoes; children's clothing; and suitcases with names of victims—many marked *Kind,* or "child." Visitors often wonder if the suitcase with the name "Frank" belonged to Anne, one of the Holocaust's most famous victims. After being discovered in Amsterdam by the Nazis, the Frank family was transported here to Auschwitz, where they were split up. Still, it's unlikely this suitcase was theirs. Anne Frank and her sister Margot were sent to the Bergen-Belsen camp in northern Germany, where they died of typhus shortly before the war ended. Their father, Otto Frank, survived Auschwitz and was found barely alive by the Russians, who liberated the camp in January of 1945.
• *Proceed to the next block.*

St. Maksymilian Kolbe (1894-1941)

Among the many inspirational stories of Auschwitz is that of a Polish priest named Maksymilian Kolbe. Before the war, Kolbe traveled as a missionary to Japan, then worked in Poland for a Catholic newspaper. While he was highly regarded for his devotion to the Church, some of his writings had an unsettling anti-Semitic sentiment. But during the Nazi occupation, Kolbe briefly ran an institution that cared for refugees—including Jews.

In 1941, Kolbe was arrested and interned at Auschwitz. When a prisoner from Kolbe's block escaped in July of that year, the Nazis punished the remaining inmates by selecting 10 of them to be put in the Starvation Cell until they died—based on the Nazi "doctrine of collective responsibility." After the selection had been made, Kolbe offered to replace a man who expressed concern about who would care for his family. The Nazis agreed. (The man Kolbe saved is said to have survived the Holocaust.)

All 10 of the men—including Kolbe—were put into Starvation Cell 18. Two weeks later, when the door was opened, only Kolbe had survived. The story spread throughout the camp, and Kolbe became an inspiration to the inmates. To squelch the hope he had given the others, Kolbe was executed by lethal injection.

In 1982, Kolbe was canonized by the Catholic Church. Some critics—mindful of his earlier anti-Semitic rhetoric—still consider Kolbe's sainthood controversial. But most Poles feel he redeemed himself for his earlier missteps through this noble act at the end of his life.

Block 6: Everyday Life

Although the purpose of Auschwitz was to murder its inmates, not all of them were killed immediately. After an initial evaluation, some prisoners were registered and forced to work. (This did not mean they were chosen to live—just to die later.) This block shows various aspects of daily existence at the camp.

The halls are lined with photographs of victims, each one identified with a name, birthdate, occupation, date of arrival at Auschwitz, date of death, and camp registration number. Examining these dates, it's clear that those registered survived here an average of two to three months. (Flowers are poignant reminders that

19472
DĄBROWSKI JAN
ur. 8.1.1920 r., robotnik
przybył 30.7.1941, zginął wrzesień 1942.

these victims are survived by loved ones.) Similar photographs hang in several other museum buildings, as well; as with the plundered items in the last block, keep in mind that these represent only a tiny fraction of the masses of people murdered at Auschwitz.

Room 1 (on the left as you enter the front door) displays drawings of the arrival process. After the initial selection, those chosen to work were showered, shaved, and photographed. After a while, photographing each prisoner got to be too expensive, so prisoners were tattooed instead (see photographs): on the chest, on the arm, or—for children—on the leg. A display shows the symbols that prisoners had to wear to show their reason for internment—Jew, Roma (Gypsy), homosexual, political prisoner, and so on. At the end of the room, a display case holds actual camp uniforms.

Across the hall, Room 4 shows the starvation that took place here. The 7,500 survivors that the Red Army found when the camp was liberated were essentially living skeletons (the "healthier" inmates had been forced to march to Germany). Of those liberated, 20 percent died soon after of disease and starvation.

In Room 5, you can see scenes from the prisoner's workday (sketched by survivors after liberation). Prisoners worked as long as the sun shone—eight hours in winter, up to twelve hours in summer—mostly on farms or in factories.

Room 6 is about Auschwitz's child inmates, 20 percent of the camp's victims. Blond, blue-eyed children were either "Germanized" in special schools or, if younger, adopted by German families. Dr. Josef Mengele conducted gruesome experiments here on children, especially twins and triplets, ostensibly to find ways to increase fertility for German mothers. Also in this room, look for a display of the prisoners' daily ration (in the glass case): a pan of tea or coffee in the morning; thin vegetable soup in the afternoon; and a piece of bread (often made with sawdust or chestnuts) for dinner. This makes it clear that Auschwitz was never intended to be a "work camp," where people were kept alive, healthy, and efficient to do work. Rather, people were meant to die here—if not in the gas chambers, then through malnutrition and overwork.

• *Block 7 shows living and sanitary conditions at the camp, which you'll see in more detail later at Birkenau. Blocks 8–10 are vacant (medical experiments were carried out in Block 10). And Block 11 was the most notorious of all.*

Block 11: The Death Block

Step into the walled-in **courtyard** between Blocks 10 and 11. The wall at the far end is where the Nazis shot several thousand political prisoners, leaders of camp resistance, and religious leaders. Notice that the windows are covered, so that nobody could

witness the executions. Also take a close look at the memorial—the back of it is made of a material designed by Nazis to catch the bullets without a ricochet. Inmates were shot at short range—about three feet. The pebbles represent prayers from Jewish visitors.

Now head into the **"Death Block"** (#11), from which nobody ever left alive. Death here required a "trial"—but it was never a fair trial. Room 2 (on the left as you enter) is where these sham trials were held, lasting about two minutes each. In Room 5, you can see how prisoners lived in these barracks—three-level bunks, with three prisoners sleeping in each bed (they had to sleep on their sides so they could fit). In Room 6, people undressed before they were executed.

In the **basement,** you'll see several different types of cells. The Starvation Cell (#18) held prisoners selected to starve to death when a fellow prisoner escaped; Maksymilian Kolbe spent two weeks here to save another man's life (see sidebar on Kolbe). In the Dark Cell (#20), which held up to 30, people had only a small window for ventilation—and if it became covered with snow, the prisoners suffocated. In the Standing Cells (#22), four people would be forced to stand together for hours at a time (the bricks went all the way to the ceiling then).

Upstairs, you'll find gallows and a bench used for administering lashes. Filling this floor are exhibits on various forms of punishment, mostly focusing on resistance within the camp, escapees, and local Poles who were executed—either for trying to assist the prisoners, or for fighting with Nazi officers.

• *Leaving Block 11, proceed straight ahead, between the buildings, to the other row of barracks. Several of these blocks house...*

National Memorials

These exhibits were created not by museum authorities, but by representatives of the home countries of the camps' victims. As these memorials overlap with the general exhibits, and are designed for Europeans to learn more about the victims from their own home countries, most visitors skip this part of the site. On the other hand, while the main museum exhibits await renovation and modernization, the displays in these national memorials tend to be slicker and better-presented than the ones we just saw. (Some of these may be works in progress, as old exhibits are routinely upgraded.) As you walk along this street toward our next stop (the crematorium), consider stepping into the ones that interest you.

The first one you see is the memorial to **Jewish** victims (Block 27). It's compelling and thoughtfully presented, relying heavily on video clips, evocative music, and sound effects.

Most of the other national memorials are on the right side of the street. Across from the Jewish memorial, Block 21 honors **Dutch Jews;** it begins with a quote by perhaps the most famous Dutch victim of the concentration camps, Anne Frank (whose story is also told—among many others'—throughout the exhibit).

Block 20, a former hospital block, is shared by **Belgium** and **France.** A room near the entrance explains how some prisoners were killed by lethal injection, with portraits and biographical sketches of victims. Upstairs is the powerful Belgium exhibit, with a room featuring victims' portraits. Block 18 holds a very modern, conceptual exhibit about **Hungary**'s victims, with an eerie heart-beat sound pervading the space. Block 17, which is likely a work in progress, is intended to memorialize victims from **Austria** and the **former Yugoslavia.** Across from this block, notice the long gallows used for mass hangings. Block 16 contains a new and well-presented exhibit about **Czech** and **Slovak** victims.

Block 15 honors victims from **Poland,** focusing on the 1939 Nazi invasion of the country, which resulted in the immediate internment of Polish political prisoners. Exhibits explain the process of "Germanization"—such as renaming Polish streets with German names—and (upstairs) the underground resistance that fought to re-assert some control over Poland.

Block 14 is the **Russian** national memorial. However, this one's a bit controversial: While Russia claims to have lost "Russian" Jews to the Holocaust, virtually all of them were technically Polish Jews who had been living within Russia. (They spoke Polish, not Russian.) To sidestep the hot topic of how to identify these victims, this memorial focuses not on victims, but on the Russian liberation of the camp.

Block 13 houses the **Roma (Gypsy)** exhibit. You'll learn that the Roma, along with the Jews, were considered no better than "rats, bedbugs, and fleas," and explore elements of the so-called *Zigeunerfrage*—the "Gypsy question" about what to do with this "troublesome" population.

• *At the end of this row of barracks, you reach a guard tower and a barbed-wire fence. Jog a few steps to the right, through the hole in the fence, then angle left toward the earthen mound with the giant, ominous brick chimney. The entrance is at the far end of the building.*

Crematorium

Up to 700 people at a time could be gassed here. People undressed outside, or just inside the door. As you enter, bear right and find your way into the big "shower room." Look for the vents in the ceiling—this is where the SS men dropped the Zyklon-B. In the adjacent room is a replica of the furnace. This facility could burn 340 bodies a day—so it took two days to burn all of the bodies from one round of executions. (The Nazis didn't like this inefficiency, so they built four more huge crematoria at Birkenau.)

• *Turning left as you exit the crematorium takes you back to the entrance building. But first, circle around to the opposite side of the crematorium for the closest thing this story has to a happy ending.*

Shortly after the war, camp commander Rudolf Höss was tried, convicted, and sentenced to death. Survivors requested that he be executed at Auschwitz, and in 1947, he was hanged here. The **gallows** are preserved behind the crematorium (about a hundred yards from his home where his wife—who loved her years here— read stories to their children, very likely by the light of a human-skin lampshade).

• *Take your time with Auschwitz I. When you're ready, continue to the second stage of the camp—Birkenau (see "Getting from Auschwitz I to Birkenau" on page 354).*

AUSCHWITZ II—BIRKENAU

In 1941, realizing that the original Auschwitz camp was too small

to meet their needs, the Nazis began a second camp in some nearby farm fields. The original plan was for a camp that could hold 200,000 people, but at its peak, Birkenau (Brzezinka) held only about 100,000. They were still adding onto it when the camp was liberated in 1945.

• *Train tracks lead past the main building and into the camp. The first sight that greeted prisoners was the...*

Guard Tower

If you've seen *Schindler's List*, the sight of this icon of the Holocaust—shown in stirring scenes from the movie—may make you queasy.

Climb to the top of the entry building (also houses WCs and bookstore) for an overview of the massive camp. As you look over the camp, you'll see a vast field of chimneys and a few intact wooden and brick barracks. Some of the barracks were destroyed by Germans. Most were dismantled to be used for fuel and building materials shortly after the war. But the first row has been reconstructed (using components from the original structures). The train tracks lead straight back to the dividing platform, and

Auschwitz II – Birkenau

MONUMENT

Creek

CREMATORIA

FORMER RAIL LINE

FORMER

BARRACKS

GUARD TOWER

TOUR ENDS

CREMATORIA

P

MIESZKAŃCÓW / NARODOW

TOUR BEGINS

To Auschwitz I & Oświęcim Town

200 Meters
200 Yards

☐ Foundations
▬ Existing Buildings

❶ Guard Tower, Viewpoint, WC & Bookstore
❷ Latrine & Restored Barracks
❸ Dividing Platform
❹ Brick Barracks
❺ Crematoria Ruins (4)

❻ Monument
❼ "The Sauna"
❽ "Canada" Foundations
❾ Shuttle Bus to Auschwitz I

then dead-end at the ruins of the crematorium and camp monument at the far side.

• *Descend the tower, enter the camp, turn right, and walk through the barbed-wire fence to reach the...*

Wooden Barracks

The first of these barrack buildings was the **latrine:** The front half of the building contained washrooms, and the back was a row of toilets. There was no running water, and prisoners were in charge of keeping the latrine clean. Because of the resulting unsanitary conditions and risk of disease, the Nazis were afraid to come in here—so

the latrine became the heart of the black market and the inmates' resistance movement.

The third barrack was a **bunkhouse.** Each inmate had a personal number, a barrack number, and a bed number. Inside,

you can see the beds (angled so that more could fit). An average of 400 prisoners—but up to 1,000—would be housed in each of these buildings. These wooden structures, designed as stables by a German company (look for the horse-tying rings on the wall), came in prefab pieces that made them cheap and convenient. Two chimneys connected by a brick duct provided a little heat. The bricks were smoothed by inmates who sat here to catch a bit of warmth.

• *Return to the train tracks, and follow them toward the monument about a half-mile away, at the back end of Birkenau. At the intersection of these tracks and the perpendicular gravel road (halfway to the monument)—now marked by a lonely train car—was the gravel pitch known as the...*

Dividing Platform

A Nazi doctor would stand facing the guard tower and evaluate each prisoner. If he pointed to the right, the prisoner was sentenced to death, and trudged—unknowingly—to the gas chamber. If he pointed to the left, the person would be registered and live a little longer. It was here that families from all over Europe were torn apart forever.

• *Photographs near the wooden building—on the left-hand side as you face the back of the camp complex—show the sad scene. Just beyond that building is a field with some...*

Brick Barracks

Enter one of these buildings. The supervisors lived in the two smaller rooms near the door. Farther in, most barracks still have the wooden bunks that held about 700 people per building. Four or five people slept on each bunk, including the floor—reserved for new arrivals. There were chamber pots at either end of the building. After a Nazi doctor died of typhus, sanitation improved, and these barracks got running water.

Now head back to the train tracks. As you walk along the camp's only road, which leads along the tracks to the crematorium, imagine the horror of this place—no grass, only mud, and all the barracks packed with people, with smoke blowing in from the busy crematoria. This was an even worse place to die than Auschwitz I.

• *The train tracks lead to the camp memorial and crematorium. At the end of the tracks, go 50 yards to the left and climb the three concrete steps to view the ruin of the...*

Crematorium

This is one of four crematoria here at Birkenau, each with a capacity to cremate more than 4,400 people per day. At the far-right end of the ruins, see the stairs where people entered the rooms to undress. They were given numbered lockers, conning them into thinking they were coming back. (The Nazis didn't want a panic.) Then they piled into the "shower room"—the underground passage branching away from the memorial—and were killed. Their bodies were burned in the crematorium (on the left), giving off a scent of sweet almonds (from the Zyklon-B). Beyond the remains of the crematorium is a hole—once a gray lake where tons of ashes were dumped. This efficient factory of death was destroyed by the Nazis as the Red Army approached, leaving the haunting ruins you see today.

When the Soviets arrived on January 27, 1945, the nightmare of Auschwitz-Birkenau was over. The Polish parliament voted to turn these grounds into a museum, so that the world would understand, and never forget, the horror of what happened here.

• *At the back of the camp stands the...*

Monument

Built in 1967 by the communist government in its heavy "Socialist Realism" style, this monument represents gravestones and the chimney of a crematorium. The plaques, written in each of the languages spoken by camp victims (including English, far right), explain that the memorial is "a cry of despair and a warning to humanity."

• *With more time, you could continue deeper into...*

The Rest of the Camp

There's much more to see for those who are interested—Birkenau sprawls for a frightening distance. One place worth seeing is the reception and disinfection building that prisoners called **"the Sauna"** (the long building with four tall chimneys). It was here that prisoners would be forced to strip and be deloused; their belongings were seized and taken to the "Canada" warehouses (described earlier) to be sorted.

Walking through here (on glass floors designed to protect the original structure below), you'll see artifacts of the grim efficiency with which prisoners were "processed"—their heads were shaved, they were tattooed with a serial number, and they were assigned uniforms and wooden clogs to wear. Portraits at the end of the building humanize those who passed through here. Look for the cart, which was used to dispose of ashes. In front of the Sauna is a field of foundations of the **"Canada" warehouses.** Nearby are the other two destroyed **crematoria.**

Auschwitz Connections

The Auschwitz Museum is in the town of Oświęcim, about 50 miles west of Kraków. By bus, minibus, or train, the journey takes around an hour and 45 minutes each way; driving shaves off about 10-20 minutes.

FROM KRAKÓW TO AUSCHWITZ

The easiest way to reach Auschwitz is with a **package tour** (figure around 130 zł per person) or **private guide or driver** (300-500 zł for the carload); both of these options are described on page 251. While the package tours are more convenient than going on your own, three people can hire their own driver for less and have a more intimate experience.

If you're using public transportation, here are your choices:

The most comfortable public-transit option is to take one of the frequent **buses,** mostly run by PKS Oświęcim (14 zł, at least hourly, 1.75 hours, get the most recent schedule at any Kraków TI, buses depart from Kraków's main bus station behind the train station). Buy a one-way ticket from the bus-station ticket office or from the driver to leave your options open for getting home. Look for buses to "Oświęcim" (not necessarily "Auschwitz"). Note that these buses can be full, and because most come from other towns, there's no way to reserve a seat—so line up early (generally about 15 minutes ahead). If you don't get on a bus, you'll have to wait for the next one (or, if there's a minibus leaving sooner, you can take one of those—described next). Once in the town of Oświęcim, buses from Kraków stop first at the train station, then continue on to one of two stops near the museum: About half of the buses go directly into the parking lot at the museum itself, while the rest use a low-profile bus stop on the edge of the Auschwitz camp grounds (you'll see a small *Muzeum Auschwitz* sign on the right just before the stop, and a blue *Oświęcim Muzeum PKS* sign at the stop itself). From this bus stop, follow the sign down the road and into the parking lot; the main museum building is across the lot on your left. Note that since some buses don't actually go into the

On the Way to Auschwitz: The Polish Countryside

You'll spend about an hour gazing out the window as you drive or ride to Auschwitz. This may be your only real look at the Polish countryside. Ponder these thoughts about what you're passing...

The small houses you see are traditionally inhabited by three generations at the same time. Nineteenth-century houses (the few that survive) often sport blue stripes. Back then, parents announced that their daughters were now eligible by getting out the blue paint. Once they saw these blue lines, local boys were welcome to come a-courtin'.

Big churches mark small villages. Like in the US, tiny roadside memorials and crosses indicate places where fatal accidents have occurred.

Polish farmers traditionally had small lots that were notorious for not being very productive. These farmers somewhat miraculously survived the communist era without having to merge their farms. For years, they were Poland's sacred cows: producing little, paying almost no tax, and draining government resources. But since Poland joined the European Union in 2004, they're being forced to get up to snuff...and, in many cases, collectivize their farms after all.

Since most people don't own cars, bikes are common and public transit is excellent. There are lots of bus stops, as well as minibuses that you can flag down anywhere for a 2-zł ride. The bad roads are a legacy of communist construction, exacerbated by heavy truck use and brutal winters.

Poland has more than 2,000 counties, or districts, each with its own coat of arms; you'll pass several along the way. The forests are state-owned, and locals enjoy the right to pick berries in the summer and mushrooms in the autumn (you may see people—often young kids—selling their day's harvest by the side of the road). The mushrooms are dried and then boiled to make tasty soups in the winter.

museum's parking lot, the Auschwitz stop can be easy to miss—don't be shy about letting your driver know where you want to go: "*Muzeum?*"

Several **minibuses** from Kraków head for Auschwitz (10 zł, sporadic departures—generally 1-2/hour, 1.75 hours). Like the buses, some go directly to the museum, while others use the bus stop at the edge of camp. These generally depart from the lower platform of the main bus station (but confirm the departure point at the TI). Some of my readers report that the minibuses are a bit more cramped than the buses and, while intended for local commuters, can be crammed with tourists. But they work fine in a pinch.

You could ride the **train** to Oświęcim, but it's less convenient than the bus because it leaves you at the train station, farther from the museum (15/day, less Sat-Sun, 1.5 hours, 14 zł). If you do wind up at the Oświęcim train station, it's about a 20-minute walk to the camp (turn right out of station, go straight, then turn left at roundabout, camp is several blocks ahead on left). Or you can take a taxi (around 15 zł).

RETURNING FROM AUSCHWITZ TO KRAKÓW

Upon arrival at Auschwitz I, plan your departure by visiting the information window inside the main building (halfway down the main entry hall, on the right, in the back corner behind the tables). They can give you a schedule of departures and explain where the bus or minibus leaves from. (If you'll be staying late into the afternoon, make a point of figuring out the last possible bus or train back to Kraków, and plan accordingly.) Remember to allow enough time to make it from Birkenau back to Auschwitz I to catch your bus.

Although most minibuses and a few buses back to Kraków leave from the camp parking lot itself, if you're taking the bus, you'll most likely catch it from the stop on the edge of the Auschwitz I grounds. To reach this bus stop, leave the Auschwitz I building through the main entry and walk straight along the parking lot, then turn right on the road near the end of the lot. At the T-intersection, cross the street to the little bus stop with the blue *Oświęcim Muzeum PKS* sign. Don't be distracted by the ads for a nearby travel agency—you can buy tickets on board. There's no public transportation back to Kraków from Birkenau, where most people end their tours; you'll have to take the shuttle bus back to Auschwitz I first.

WARSAW

Warszawa

Warsaw (Warszawa, vah-SHAH-vah in Polish) is Poland's capital and biggest city. It's huge, famous, and important...but not particularly romantic. If you're looking for Old World quaintness, head for Kraków. If you're tickled by spires and domes, get to Prague. But if you want to experience a truly 21st-century city, Warsaw's your place.

Stroll down revitalized boulevards that evoke the city's glory days, pausing at an outdoor café to sip coffee and nibble at a *pączek* (the classic Polish jelly doughnut). Stroll through a leafy park to an al fresco Chopin concert, packed with pensive Poles. Commune with the soul of Poland through its artists (at the National Museum), its favorite composer (at the Chopin Museum), its dramatic history (at the Warsaw Historical Museum and Warsaw Uprising Museum), its dedication to the sciences (at the Copernicus Science Center), and its Jewish story (at the Museum of the History of Polish Jews). And ponder the wide range of Warsaw's postwar urban architecture, from dreary communist monstrosities to innovative skyscrapers designed by *the* top names in global architecture.

Varsovians are embracing their role as the capital city of a newly influential nation. The European Union has two universities aimed at educating future political leaders (or "Eurocrats"). One is in Bruges, Belgium, just down the road from the EU capital of Brussels. The other one is right here. You can almost feel Warsaw peeling back the layers of communist grime as it replaces potholed highways with pedestrian-friendly parks. Today's Warsaw has gleaming new office towers and street signs, stylishly dressed locals, cutting-edge shopping malls, swarms of international businesspeople, hipster culture as vivid as anything in Brooklyn, and a gourmet coffee shop on every corner.

Warsaw has good reason to be a city of the future: The past hasn't been very kind. Since becoming Poland's capital in 1596, Warsaw has seen wave after wave of foreign rulers and invasions—especially during the last hundred years. But in this horrific crucible, the enduring spirit of the Polish people was forged. As one proud Varsovian told me, "Warsaw is ugly because its history is so beautiful."

The city's darkest days came during the Nazi occupation of World War II. First, its Jewish residents were forced into a tiny ghetto. They rose up...and were slaughtered. Then, its Polish residents rose up...and were slaughtered. Hitler sent word to systematically demolish this troublesome city. At the war's end, Warsaw was devastated. An estimated 800,000 residents were dead—nearly two out of every three Varsovians.

The Poles almost gave up on what was then a pile of rubble to build a brand-new capital city elsewhere. But ultimately they decided to rebuild, creating a city of contrasts: painstakingly restored medieval lanes, retrofitted communist apartment blocks (*bloki* in Polish), and sleek skyscrapers. Between the buildings you'll find fragments of a complex, sometimes tragic, and often inspiring history.

A product of its complicated past, sprinkled with the big-city style and sophistication of its present, Warsaw remains quintessentially Polish. It is a place worth grappling with to understand the Poland of today...and the Europe of tomorrow. Many tourists here make the mistake of focusing on Warsaw's Old Town. It's pleasant enough, but that's simply not the point of coming to Warsaw. Rather, focus on the urban cityscape, edgy neighborhoods, and high-tech, top-quality museums; it's in these arenas that Warsaw trumps other Polish destinations.

PLANNING YOUR TIME

Warsaw can easily fill two or three days, but if you're pressed for time, one full day is enough. Get your bearings by taking a stroll through Polish history on the Royal Way, using my self-guided walk. Then visit other sights according to your interests: Polish artists, Jewish history, the Warsaw Uprising, royalty, hands-on science gizmos, hipster hangouts, or Chopin. To slow down and take a break from the city, relax in Łazienki Park.

WARSAW

Orientation to Warsaw

Warsaw sprawls with 1.7 million residents. Everything is on a big scale—it seems to take forever to walk just a few "short" blocks. Get comfortable with public transportation and plan your sightseeing wisely to avoid backtracking.

Virtually everything of interest to travelers is on a mild hill on the west bank of the Vistula River. The city's central train station (Warszawa Centralna) is in the shadow of its biggest landmark: the can't-miss-it, skyscraping Palace of Culture and Science. From here, Jerusalem Avenue (aleja Jerozolimskie) runs east toward the river, past the National Museum. It crosses the "Royal Way" boulevard, which connects the sights in the north (Old Town and New Town) with those in the south (Łazienki Park, and at the outskirts of town, Wilanów Palace). Most major sights and recommended hotels and restaurants are along or near these two thoroughfares (Jerusalem Avenue and the Royal Way).

Another tip: You'll hear about two distinct uprisings against the Nazis during World War II. They're easy to confuse, but try to keep them straight: the **Ghetto Uprising** was staged by Warsaw's dwindling Jewish population in the spring of 1943 (see page 412); the **Warsaw Uprising,** a year later, was led by the (mostly non-Jewish) Polish Home Army (see page 418).

TOURIST INFORMATION

Warsaw's helpful, youthful TI has three branches: on the **Old Town Market Square** (daily May-Sept 9:00-20:00, Oct-April 9:00-18:00), at the **Palace of Culture and Science** (enter on the side facing the train station, on Emilii Plater; daily May-Sept 8:00-20:00, Oct-April 8:00-18:00), and at **Chopin Airport** (daily May-Sept 8:00-20:00, Oct-April 8:00-18:00). The general information number for all TIs is 19431 from inside Warsaw, or 22-19431 from outside Warsaw. All branches offer piles of free, useful materials: a city map and a wide variety of brochures on sights and activities ("city breaks," Jewish heritage, Chopin, mer-maids, St. John Paul II, and so on); everything is also available online (www.warsawtour.pl). The TI also has a free room-booking service and can give you advice about live music in town. I'd skip the Warsaw Pass, which covers public transportation and admis-sion to some major sights, and discounts to others; because the shortest pass is good for 72 hours, you'd have to sightsee like mad for three straight days to get your money's worth.

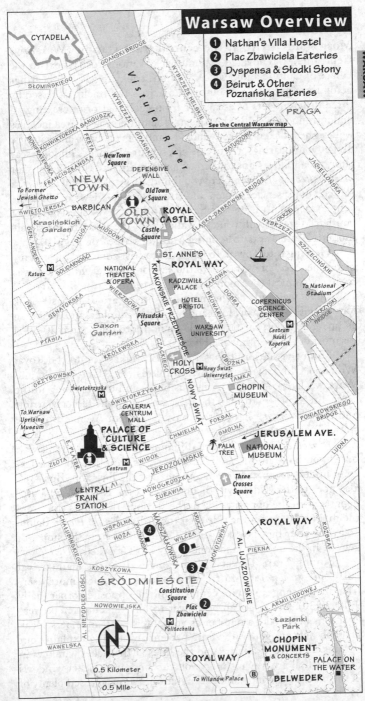

Warsaw Overview

1. Nathan's Villa Hostel
2. Plac Zbawiciela Eateries
3. Dyspensa & Słodki Słony
4. Beirut & Other Poznańska Eateries

ARRIVAL IN WARSAW
By Train

Most trains arrive at the **central train station** (Warszawa Centralna), a renovated communist-era monstrosity next to the Palace of Culture and Science. It can be tricky to get your bearings here: Three parallel concourses run across the tracks, accessed by three different sets of escalators from each platform, creating an underground maze. But be patient: The underground area includes well-signed lockers, ticket windows, and lots of shops and eateries. To get your bearings, try to ride up on your platform's middle escalator, then follow signs to the vast, open **main hall** (follow signs for *main hall/hala główna*). Here you'll find a row of ticket windows, a rail customer service center, and (from outside) views of the adjacent Palace of Culture and Science and Złota 44 skyscrapers. If you have time to kill, you can walk across the street to the supermodern **Złote Tarasy Shopping Mall** (described on page 411).

Getting into Town: To reach the tourist zone and most of my recommended hotels, taxis are the easiest choice, while the bus is more economical (but more challenging to find).

Taxis wait outside the main hall (many are dishonest—look for one with a company logo and telephone number, and ask for an estimate up front; the fare should be no more than about 20-30 zł for most of my recommended hotels).

From the station, **bus #175** or **#128** takes you to the Royal Way and Old Town in about 10 minutes (see "Getting Around Warsaw," later). You can catch this bus—and others going in the same direction—in front of the skyscraper with the Hotel Marriott and big *Bridgestone* sign (across busy Jerusalem Avenue from the station). From the corridors under the main hall, carefully track *Aleje Jerozolimskie* signs. Several different exits are marked this way, but if you hone in on *Hotel Marriott* signs, you'll reach a pedestrian underpass that pops you out next to the bus stop. **Bus #160** also goes to the Old Town (though not via the Royal Way), but it departs from the opposite side of the station: To find its stop from the main hall, go out the side door toward *ul. Emilii Plater*. Before boarding your bus, buy a ticket at the machine near the stop—or get one in the underground zone at any kiosk marked *RUCH*.

Buying Train Tickets: Lining one wall of the main arrival hall *(hala główna)* are 16 **ticket windows.** A much more userfriendly **passenger service center** is in the opposite corner (daily 9:00-20:30). While it can be slower to buy tickets or make reservations here (take a number as you enter), staff members speak English and are generally more patient in helping explain your options. If you're in a hurry and the lines at the ticket windows in the main hall are way too long, you can find more ticket windows in the maze of corridors under the station. Allow yourself plenty of

WARSAW

Warsaw Essentials

English	Polish	Pronounced
Warsaw	*Warszawa*	vah-SHAH-vah
Central Train Station	*Warszawa Centralna*	vah-SHAH-vah tsehn-TRAHL-nah
Palace of Culture and Science	*Pałac Kultury i Nauki (or simply "Pałac")*	PAH-wahts kool-TOO-ree ee nah-OO-kee
New Town	*Nowe Miasto*	NOH-vay mee-AH-stoh
Old Town	*Stare Miasto*	STAH-reh mee-AH-stoh
Old Town Market Square	*Rynek Starego Miasta*	REE-nehk stah-RAY-goh mee-AH-stah
Royal Way	*Szłak Królewski*	shwock kroh-LEHV-skee
Popular restaurant street on Royal Way	*Nowy Świat*	NOH-vee SHVEE-aht
Attraction-lined street on Royal Way	*Krakowskie Przedmieście*	krah-KOHV-skyeh pzhehd-MYESH-cheh
Royal Castle	*Zamek Królewski*	ZAH-mehk kroh-LEHV-skee
Castle Square	*Plac Zamkowy*	plahts zahm-KOH-vee
Piłsudski Square	*Plac Marszałka Józefa Piłsudskiego*	plahts mar-SHAW-kah yoh-ZEH-fah pew-sood-SKYAY-goh
Łazienki Park	*Park Łazienkowski*	park wah-zhehn KOV-skee
Vistula River	*Wisła*	VEES-wah

time to wait in line to buy tickets. Some locals bypass these lines altogether and buy their tickets on the train for an extra charge (10 zł extra; find the conductor before he finds you).

Note that even if you have a rail pass, a reservation is still required on certain trains (including express trains to Kraków). If you're not sure, it's worth asking at the service center.

To get to your train, first find your way to the right platform

WARSAW

Warsaw at a Glance

▲▲**Royal Castle** Warsaw's best palace, rebuilt after World War II, but retaining its former opulence and many original furnishings. **Hours:** May-Sept Mon-Sat 10:00-18:00, Thu until 20:00, Sun 11:00-18:00; Oct-April Tue-Sat 10:00-16:00, Sun 11:00-16:00, closed Mon. See page 395.

▲▲**Old Town Market Square** Re-creation of Warsaw's glory days, with lots of colorful architecture. **Hours:** Always open. See page 400.

▲▲**National Museum** Collection of mostly Polish art, with unknown but worth-discovering works by Jan Matejko and the Młoda Polska (Art Nouveau) crew. **Hours:** Tue-Sun 10:00-18:00, Thu until 21:00, closed Mon. See page 403.

▲▲**Museum of the History of Polish Jews** High-tech exhibit on the full Jewish experience through Polish history, displayed in a purpose-built facility. **Hours:** Wed-Mon 10:00-18:00, Sat until 20:00, closed Tue. See page 414

▲▲**Warsaw Uprising Museum** State-of-the-art space tracing the history of the Uprising and celebrating its heroes. **Hours:** July-Aug Wed-Mon 10:00-18:00, Thu until 20:00; Sept-June Mon and Wed-Fri 8:00-18:00, Thu until 20:00, Sat-Sun 10:00-18:00, closed Tue year-round. See page 417.

▲▲**Copernicus Science Center** Spiffy new science museum with well-explained, hands-on exhibits in English; Warsaw's best family activity. **Hours:** Tue-Fri 9:00-18:00, Sat-Sun 10:00-19:00, closed Mon. See page 408.

(*peron*, as noted on schedules), then keep an eye on both tracks *(tor)* for your train. Train info: Tel. 19436 (22-19436 from outside Warsaw), www.rozklad-pkp.pl.

By Plane

Warsaw's **Fryderyk Chopin International Airport** (Port Lotniczy im. Fryderyk Chopina, airport code: WAW) is about six miles southwest of the center. The airport has just one terminal (Terminal A), which is divided into five check-in areas split between two zones: the southern hall (areas A and B) and the northern hall (areas C, D, E). The airport is small and manageable; outside of the arrivals area, you'll find a TI, ATMs, car-rental offices, and exchange desks *(kantor)*. Airport info: tel. 22-650-4220, www.lotnisko-chopina.pl.

You have two options to get into town, both of which cost the

▲**Castle Square** Colorful spot with whiffs of old Warsaw—Royal Castle, monuments, and a chunk of the city wall—and cafés just off the square. **Hours:** Always open. See page 394.

▲**Łazienki Park** Lovely, sprawling green space with Chopin statue, peacocks, and Neoclassical buildings. **Hours:** Always open; wonderful outdoor Chopin concerts mid-May-late Sept Sun at 12:00 and 16:00. See page 420.

Chopin Museum Elegant old mansion featuring slick exhibits but not much substance about Chopin; occasional piano concerts worthwhile. **Hours:** Tue-Sun 11:00-20:00, closed Mon. See page 407.

Warsaw Museum Glimpse of the city before and after World War II, with excellent movie in English. **Hours:** Museum—Tue-Sun 10:00-20:00, off-season until 18:00, closed Mon year-round; Movie—Tue-Fri at 10:00 and 12:00; Sat-Sun at 12:00 and 14:00. See page 401.

Palace of Culture and Science Huge "Stalin Gothic" skyscraper with a more impressive exterior than interior, housing theaters, multiplex cinema, observation deck, and more. **Hours:** Observation deck—June-Aug daily 9:00-20:00, Fri-Sat until 24:00; Sept-May daily 9:00-18:00. See page 410.

Jewish Ghetto: Path of Remembrance Pilgrimage from Ghetto Heroes Square to the infamous Nazi "transfer spot" where Jews were sent to death camps. **Hours:** Always open. See page 415.

same (a standard 4.40-zł transit ticket, which also covers transfers for up to 75 minutes). The train is faster, while the bus makes more stops in the city center and may get you closer to your hotel. From the arrivals area, just follow signs to either option, and buy your ticket at the red machine before you board.

The **train** departs about every 15 minutes and takes 20-30 minutes. The route is operated by two different companies (SKM and KM)—just take the one that's departing first. Be ready for your stop: Half of the trains make fewer stops and take you to Centralna Station; the others make a few more stops and use the Warszawa Śródmieście station—which feeds into the same underground passages as Centralna (these trains also continue one more stop to the Warszawa Powiśle station, which is a bit closer to Nowy Świat and can be more convenient to some hotels than Śródmieście). Whether arriving at Centralna Station or Warszawa

Śródmieście, see the "By Train" arrival instructions, earlier.

Bus #175 departs every 15-20 minutes and runs into the city center (Centralna Station, the Royal Way, and Old Town, 30-45 minutes depending on traffic).

Only certain **taxi** companies are authorized to pick up arriving travelers at the airport; go to the official taxi stand and avoid random hucksters offering you a ride out front (these creeps are notorious for overcharging). The 30-minute taxi ride to the center shouldn't cost you more than 50 zł. The trip into town can take much longer during rush hour.

Modlin Airport (airport code: WMI), about 21 miles northwest of the city center, primarily serves budget airlines (especially Ryanair). The most direct option for getting to downtown Warsaw is **ModlinBus,** whose shuttle bus goes from the airport terminal to near the Palace of Culture and Science (price depends on how far ahead you buy ticket—can be 10-30 zł, 8-9/day, 1 hour, smart to book well ahead at www.modlinbus.com). A more frequent, well-coordinated **bus-plus-train connection** is operated by Koleje Mazowieckie (KM). You'll take a shuttle bus to Modlin's main train station, then hop on a train to Warsaw's Centralna Station (15 zł, 2-3/hour, 1-1.5 hours total, www.mazowieckie.com.pl). If you want to ride a **taxi** all the way into Warsaw, the maximum legitimate fare is 200 zł (or 250 zł at night). Airport info: www.modlinairport.pl.

GETTING AROUND WARSAW

By Public Transit: In this big city, it's essential to get a handle on public transportation. You'll rely mostly on buses and trams, but the new Metro line can be useful for reaching a few sights (the Warsaw Uprising Museum and the Copernicus Science Center). Everything is covered by the same tickets. A single ticket costs 4.40 zł (called *bilet jednorazowy,* good for one trip up to 75 minutes). But most trips you'll be taking should last no longer than 20 minutes, so you can save a zloty by buying a 3.40-zł "20-minute city travelcard" (*bilet 20-minutowy;* also available in 40- and 60-minute versions). A 24-hour travelcard *(bilet dobowy)*—which pays for itself if you take at least five trips—costs 15 zł. Ticket machines at most major stops and on board some trams are easy to use (English instructions, coins and small bills accepted). Or you can buy tickets at any kiosk with a *RUCH* sign. Be sure to validate your ticket as you board by inserting it in the little yellow box. Transit info: www.ztm.waw.pl.

Most of the city's major attractions line up on a single axis, the Royal Way, which is served by several different buses (but no trams). **Bus #175,** particularly useful on arrival, links Chopin Airport, the central train station, the Royal Way, and Old Town.

Once you're in town, the designed-for-tourists **bus #180** conveniently connects virtually all of the significant sights and neighborhoods: the former Jewish Ghetto, Castle Square/Old Town, the Royal Way, Łazienki Park, and Wilanów Palace (south of the center). This particularly user-friendly bus lists sights in English on the posted schedule inside (other buses don't). Those two buses, as well as buses **#116, #128, #195,** and **#222,** go along the most interesting stretch of the Royal Way (between Jerusalem Avenue and Castle Square in the Old Town). **Bus #178** conveniently connects Castle Square to the Warsaw Uprising Museum. Bus routes beginning with "E" (marked in red on schedules) are express, so they go long distances without stopping; these operate only off-season (Oct-May).

Note that on Saturdays and Sundays in summer (June-Sept), the Nowy Świat section of the Royal Way is closed to traffic, so the above routes detour along a parallel street.

Warsaw's two-line **Metro** system is handy for commuters, but less so for visitors. Still, it can be useful for some trips. Line 1 runs roughly parallel to the Royal Way, several blocks to the west; the most useful stops for tourists are Centrum (near the Palace of Culture and Science) and Świętokrzyska (where it crosses line 2). The new line 2 (which runs deep under the Vistula River) cuts through the city from west to east, making stops near some points of interest: near the Warsaw Uprising Museum (Rondo Daszyńskiego stop); at Świętokrzyska (a transfer station between the two lines); on Nowy Świat (near the Copernicus Monument, Nowy Świat-Uniwersytet stop); near the Copernicus Science Center, by the river (Centrum Nauki Kopernik stop); and at the National Stadium (Stadion Narodowy stop).

By Taxi: As in most big Eastern European cities, it's wise to use only cabs that are clearly marked with a company logo and telephone number (or call your own: Locals like City Taxi, tel. 19459; MPT Radio Taxi, tel. 19191; or Ele taxi, tel. 22-811-1111). All official taxis have similar rates: 8 zł to start, then 3 zł per kilometer (4.50 zł after 22:00 or in the suburbs). The drop fee may be higher if you catch the cab in front of a fancy hotel.

By Bike: The city is trying to be bike-friendly. Because there are few actual bike paths, bikes share the sidewalks with pedestrians. Considering how the city is both level and spread out, biking can be a joy. The TI can direct you to bike-rental offices, and some hotels have loaner bikes.

Tours in Warsaw

Walking Tours

Each year, new companies crop up offering **walking tours** in Warsaw. These tend to have one of two approaches: A "free" tour of the main sights (with generous tipping expected); or communism-themed tours, often with a ride to a gloomy apartment-block area for a taste of the Red old days. None of these companies are firmly established, so survey the latest options, do some homework (check online reviews), and pick one that suits your interests. The TI and most hotels have brochures.

Private Guides

Having a talented local historian as your guide in this city, with such a complex and powerful story to tell, greatly enhances your experience. I've worked with two excellent young guides: the smart and charming **Monika Oleśko** (180 zł/3 hours, 350 zł/6 hours, mobile 784-832-718, warsawteller.wordpress.com, olesko.monika@gmail.com) and the professorial **Hubert Pawlik** (500 zł or €125 for 5 hours on foot or with his car, mobile 502-298-105, www.warsaw-guide.waw.pl). Hubert's big, comfy SUV can fit a small group. Both Monica and Hubert can do theme tours or tailor the time to your interests.

Bus Tours

Two competing companies offer hop-on, hop-off bus tours around Warsaw (60 zł/24 hours, 80 zł/48 hours): CitySightseeing (with red buses) and City-Tour (with yellow buses). While Warsaw's spread-out landscape makes it a natural for a hop-on, hop-off bus, both of these companies have limited frequency (about one bus each hour, and much less than that outside of summer), making them less enticing.

Warsaw's Royal Way Walk

The Royal Way (Szlak Królewski) is the six-mile route that the kings of Poland used to travel from their main residence (at Castle Square in the Old Town) to their summer home (at Wilanów Palace, south of the center and not worth visiting). This self-guided walk covers a one-mile section of the Royal Way in the heart of the city—from the Palm Tree Circle to the castle. This is a busy, mostly pedestrian boulevard with two different names: At the south end, hip and vibrant **Nowy Świat** offers lots of shops and restaurants and a good glimpse of urban Warsaw; to the north, and ending at the Old Town, **Krakowskie Przedmieście** is lined with historic landmarks and is better for sightseeing.

Since this spine connects most of my recommended hotels, restaurants, and sights, you'll almost certainly use it—on foot or by bus—sometime during your trip (key buses are noted earlier, under "Getting Around Warsaw"). This walk should make your commute more interesting. Not counting sightseeing stops, figure about 15 minutes to walk along Nowy Świat ("Part 1"), then another 30 minutes along Krakowskie Przedmieście to the Old Town ("Part 2").

PART 1: PALM TREE CIRCLE AND NOWY ŚWIAT

• *Start this walk at the traffic circle officially named for Charles de Gaulle, but colloquially known as...*

Palm Tree Circle

This is one of the city's main intersections, marked by the quirky and now iconic palm tree. Stand near the communist-era monument under the spruce trees, on the curb opposite (kitty-corner) the biggest building.

You're standing at the intersection of two major boulevards: Nowy Świat (where we're heading next) and **Jerusalem Avenue (aleja Jerozolimskie,** which leads from the central train station across the river). This street once led to a Jewish settlement called New Jerusalem. Like so much else in Warsaw, it's changed names many times. Between the World Wars, it became "May 3rd Avenue," celebrating Poland's 1791 constitution (Europe's first). But this was too nationalistic for the occupying Nazis, who called it simply Bahnhofstrasse ("Train Station Street"). Then the communists switched it back to "Jerusalem," strangely disregarding the religious connotations of that name. (Come on, guys—what about a good, old-fashioned "Stalin Avenue"?)

The strikingly wide boulevards are part the city's post-WWII Soviet rebuilding. Communist urban planners felt that eight-to twelve-lane roads were ideal for worker pageantry like big May Day parades...and, when the workers aren't happy, for Soviet tanks to thunder around, maintaining order.

You can't miss the giant, out-of-place **palm tree** in the middle of Jerusalem Avenue. When a local artist went to the real Jerusalem, she was struck at how many palm trees she saw there. She decided it was only appropriate that one should grace Warsaw's own little stretch of "Jerusalem." This artificial palm tree went up years ago as a temporary installation. It was highly controversial, dividing the neighborhood. One snowy winter day, the pro-palm tree faction—who appreciated the way the tree spiced up this otherwise predictable metropolis—camped out here in bikinis and beachwear to show their support. They prevailed, and the tree still continues to bring a little sunshine to gray Warsaw.

The big, blocky building across the street (behind statue of de Gaulle) was the **headquarters of the Communist Party,** built in 1948. *Nowy Świat* translates as "New World," leading to a popular communist-era joke: What do you see when you turn your back on the Communist Party? A "New World." Ironically, when the economy was privatized in 1991, this building became home to Poland's stock exchange. To make matters even worse, the country's only dealership for Ferraris—certainly not an automobile for the proletariat—moved in downstairs.

On the corner, in front of the former Communist Party HQ, a statue of **Charles de Gaulle** strides confidently up the street. A gift from the government of France, this celebrates the military tactician who came to Warsaw's rescue when the Red Army invaded from the USSR after World War I.

To the left of the Communist Party building is the vast **National Museum**—a good place for a Polish art lesson (more interesting than it sounds—see the self-guided tour later, under "Sights in Warsaw").

Before walking down Nowy Świat, notice the small but powerful **monument** 20 yards behind you. In 1956, this was dedicated to the "Poles who fought for People's Poland"—with a strong communist connotation. In a classic example of Socialist Realism, the communists appropriated a religious theme that Poles were inclined to embrace (this *pietà* composition)...and politicized it. But in 2014, the statue was rededicated to the "*partyzantom* who fought for free Poland in World War II." "Partisan" was a bad word in the 1950s, when it was used to describe the soldiers of the Polish Home Army—which fought against both the Nazis and the Soviets.

The little **park** stretching right from the monument is meaningful to older locals who remember when it first opened in 1955. That was a celebratory year as, 10 years after the city's destruction, Warsaw was reawakening and small gestures like this park were making life more livable for its residents.

• *From here, turn your back to the Communist Party building and head into a new world—down Nowy Świat—to the first intersection. As you stroll, notice how massive and intense Warsaw suddenly becomes more intimate and charming.*

Nowy Świat

This charming shopping boulevard is lined with boutiques, cafés, and restaurants—it's the most upscale, elegant-feeling part of the

city. Before World War II, Nowy Świat was Warsaw's most popular neighborhood. And today, once again, rents are higher here than anywhere else in town. While most tourists flock into the Old Town, Varsovians and visiting businesspeople prefer this zone. The city has worked hard to revitalize this strip with broader, pedestrian-friendly sidewalks, flower boxes, and old-time lampposts.

Look down the street and notice the consistent architecture. In the 1920s, this was anything but cohesive: an eclectic and decadent strip of Art Deco facades, full of individualism. Rather than rebuild in that "trouble-causing" style, the communists used an idealized, more conservative (less capitalistic), Neoclassical style, which feels more linked with the 1820s than the 1920s.

Ulica Chmielna, the first street to the left, is an appealing pedestrian boutique street leading to Emil Wedel's chocolate heaven (a five-minute walk away; described later, under "Eating in Warsaw"). Between here and the Palace of Culture and Science stretches one of Warsaw's trendiest shopping neighborhoods (culminating at the Galleria Centrum mall, just across from the Palace).

Across the street from Chmielna (on the right) is the street called **Foksal,** one of Warsaw's most pleasant and trendy dining zones. On a balmy summer evening, this street is filled with chatty al fresco diners, sipping drinks and nibbling at plates of cutting-edge international cuisine.

A few steps farther down Nowy Świat, on the left, don't miss the recommended **A. Blikle** pastry shop and café—*the* place in Poland to buy sweets, especially *pączki* (rose-flavored jelly doughnuts; see page 236). Step inside for dose of the 1920s: good-life Art Deco decor and historic photos. Or, if you're homesick for Starbucks, drop in to one of the many gourmet coffee shops that line this stretch of Nowy Świat—with American-style lattes "to go" (one of many customs that the Poles have adopted from American culture, which they adore).

A half-block down the street (on the left, at #39) is a rare surviving bit of pre-glitz Nowy Świat: Bar Mleczny Familijny, a classic **milk bar**—a government-subsidized cafeteria filled with locals seeking a cheap meal (an interesting cultural artifact, but not recommended for a meal; for more about milk bars, see page 234).

WARSAW

Central Warsaw

Rondo Babka

Z. SŁOMIŃSKIEGO

PARKING LOT WITH FORMER GHETTO WALL

STAWKI

MIĘDZYPARKOWA

KONWIKTORSKA SANGUSZKI

10

UMSCHLAGPLATZ MONUMENT

MURANÓW
(Former Jewish Ghetto)

FRANCISZKAŃSKA

OKOPOWA

AL. JANA PAWŁA II

STAWKI

FORMER SS HQ

NISKA

DUBOIS

BUNKER

MUSEUM OF THE HISTORY OF POLISH JEWS

MIŁA

ZAMENHOFA

Plac Krasińskich

GHETTO HEROES SQUARE

Muranów

LEWARTOWSKIEGO

M. ANIELEWICZA

Nalewki

Krasińskich Garden

KARMELICKA

Ratusz

Plac Bankowy

SOLIDARNOŚCI

ELEKTORALNA

PTASIA

PL. MIROWSKI

AL. JANA PAWŁA II

GRZYBOWSKA

Plac Grzybowski

WALICÓW

CIEPŁA

TWARDA

ŚWIĘTOKRZYSKA

Accommodations
❶ Hotel Le Régina
❷ Novotel
❸ Chopin Boutique B&B
❹ Duval Apartments
❺ Castle Inn
❻ Between Us B&B
❼ Royal Route Residence & Old Town Apts. Office
❽ Hotel Harenda
❾ Zgoda Apartment Hotel
❿ Ibis Warszawa Stare Miasto
⓫ Oki Doki Hostel
⓬ Szkolne Schronisko Hostel

Eateries
⓭ Papaya Restaurant
⓮ Kamanda Lwowska
⓯ Wiking Milk Bar
⓰ Mleczarnia Jerozolimska
⓱ Borpince, Krokiecik & Restauracja Zgoda
⓲ A. Blikle Bakery
⓳ E. Wedel Pijalnia Czekolady (Chocolate Shop)
⓴ Butchery & Wine
㉑ Warszawa Powiśle Café

GRZYBOWSKA

TOWAROWA

Muzeum Powstania Warszawskiego

ŁUCKA

PROSTA

ŻELAZNA

PRZYOKOPOWA

WARSAW UPRISING MUSEUM

Rondo Daszyńskiego

WRONIA

PAŃSKA

SIENNA

ZŁOTA

ZŁOTE TARASY MALL

Dworzec Centralny Bus #160

CENTRAL TRAIN STATION

Rondo Daszyńskiego

PROSTA

MIEDZIANA

ZŁOTA

CHMIELNA

Dw. Centralny

Dworzec Centralny Bus #175

400 Meters

400 Yards

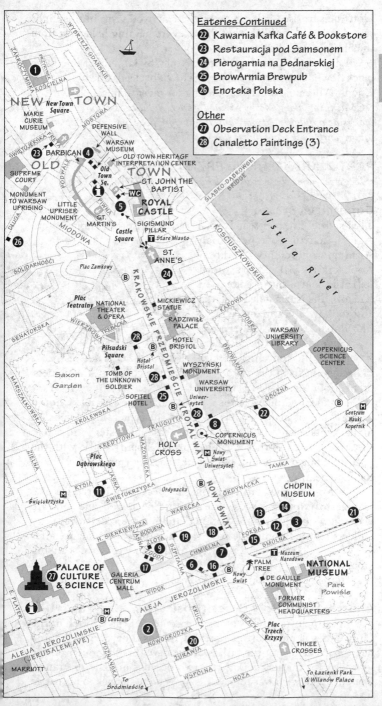

Eateries Continued
22 Kawarnia Kafka Café & Bookstore
23 Restauracja pod Samsonem
24 Pierogarnia na Bednarskiej
25 BrowArmia Brewpub
26 Enoteka Polska

Other
27 Observation Deck Entrance
28 Canaletto Paintings (3)

Don't be surprised if it's gone by the time you visit; in this high-rent district, it's unlikely that these few remaining holdovers from the old days will survive for much longer.

Eat and shop your way along Nowy Świat. About one more block down, **Ordynacka street** (on the right) leads downhill to the Chopin Museum, worth considering for musical pilgrims.

• *Continuing along Nowy Świat through a duller stretch, you'll walk alongside a hulking, gloomy building before popping out in a pleasant square with a big Copernicus statue.*

PART 2: KRAKOWSKIE PRZEDMIEŚCIE
• *The street name changes to Krakowskie Przedmieście at the big...*

Copernicus Statue
This statue, by the great Danish sculptor Bertel Thorvaldsen, stands in front of the Polish Academy of Science. Mikołaj Kopernik (1473-1543) was born in Toruń and went to college in Kraków. The Nazis stole his statue and took it to Germany (which, like Poland, claims Copernicus as its own). Now it's back where it belongs. The concentric circles radiating out from the statue represent the course of the planets' orbits, from Mercury to Saturn.

Just to Copernicus' left is a low-profile, black-marble **Chopin bench**—one of many scattered around the center. These benches mark points related to his life (in this case, his sister lived across the street). Each of these benches plays Chopin's music with the push of a button (though because of passing traffic, this one is tough to hear).

In front of the statue, in the glass case, find a replica of a **Canaletto painting** of this same street scene in 1778, and compare it to today's reality. As the national archives were destroyed, city builders referred to historic paintings like these for guidance after WWII. You'll see other Canaletto replicas like this one scattered around the city.

• *Across from Copernicus, the Church of the Holy Cross is worth a look.*

Church of the Holy Cross (Kościół Św. Krzyża)
We'll pass many churches along this route, but the **Church of the Holy Cross** is unique (free entry). Composer Fryderyk Chopin's heart is inside one of the pillars of the nave (first big pillar on the left, look for the marker). After two decades of exile in France, Chopin's final wish was to have his heart brought back to his native

Poland after his death. During World War II, the heart was hidden away in the countryside for safety. Check out the bright gold chapel, located on the left as you face the altar, near the front of the church. It's dedicated to a saint whom Polish Catholics believe helps them with "desperate and hopeless causes." People praying here are likely dealing with some tough issues. The beads draped from the altarpieces help power their prayers, and the many little brass plaques are messages of thanks for prayers answered.

In the back-left corner (as you face the altar) is a chapel dedicated to Poland's favorite son, St. John Paul II. His ghostly image appears out of the wall; beneath him is a rock inscribed with the words *Tu es Petrus* (Latin for "You are Peter"—what Jesus said when he made St. Peter the first-ever pope), embedded with a capsule containing JPII's actual blood. Just opposite, in the back-right corner, behind the giant barbed wire, is a memorial to the 22,000 Polish POWs—mostly officers and prominent civilians—massacred by Soviet soldiers in 1940 near Katyń, a village in today's Russia. Stalin was determined to decapitate Poland's military intelligentsia in a ruthless mass killing, which Poles have never forgotten.

• *Leaving the church, imagine how locals would relate to the 19th-century, bronze-and-granite...*

Statue of Christ Bearing the Cross

In front, a placard reads, "Lift up your hearts." Even as Warsaw bore the burden of Russian occupation, this statue inspired them to be strong and not lose hope. It was one of many crosses they bore: a Catholic nation pinched between Orthodox Russians and Protestant Germans.

• *Cross the street (appreciating how pedestrian-friendly it's become in recent years—this used to be a game of Frogger) and continue left.*

Warsaw University

A long block up the street on the right, you'll see the gates (marked *Uniwersytet*) to the main campus of **Warsaw University,** founded in 1816. This lively student district has plenty of bookstores and cafeterias. Venture in, and you'll find cheap food and English-speaking students who'd love to talk.

The 18th century was a time of great political decline for Poland, as a series of incompetent foreign kings mishandled crises

WARSAW

and squandered funds. But ironically, it was also Warsaw's biggest economic boom time. Along this boulevard, aristocratic families of the period built **mansions**—most of them destroyed during World War II and rebuilt since. Some have curious flourishes (just past the university on the right, look for the doorway supported by four bearded brutes admiring their overly defined abs). Over time, many of these families donated their mansions to the university. (Across the street on the corner, look for the recommended BrowArmia brewpub, with some of the best people-watching al fresco tables on the Royal Way.)

• *The bright-yellow church a block up from the university, on the right, is the...*

Church of the Nuns of the Visitation (Kośicół Sióstr Wizytek)

This Rococo confection from 1761 is the only church on this walk that survived World War II, and is notable because Chopin was the organist here in 1825-26.

The monument in front of the church commemorates **Cardinal Stefan Wyszyński,** who was the Polish primate (the head of the Polish Catholic Church) from 1948 to 1981. He took this post soon after the arrival of the communists, who opposed the Church, but also realized it would be risky for them to shut down the churches in such an ardently religious country. The Communist Party and the Catholic Church coexisted tensely in Poland, and when Wyszyński protested a Stalinist crackdown in 1953, he was arrested and imprisoned. Three years later, in a major victory for the Church, Wyszyński was released. He continued to fight the communists, becoming a great hero of the Polish people in their struggle against the regime. Across the street is another then-and-now Canaletto illustration.

• *Farther up (on the right, past the park) is the elegant, venerable...*

Hotel Bristol

A striking building with a round turret on its corner, the Hotel Bristol was used by the Nazis as a VIP hotel and bordello, and survived World War II. If you wander through any fancy Warsaw lobby...make it this one. Step in like you're staying here and explore its fine public spaces, with fresh Art Deco and Art Nouveau flourishes. The café in front retains its Viennese atmosphere, but the *pièce de résistance* is the stunning Column Bar deeper in,

past the dramatically chandeliered lounge.

• *Leave the Royal Way briefly here to reach Piłsudski Square (a block away on the left, up the street opposite Hotel Bristol).*

Piłsudski Square
(plac Marszałka Józefa Piłsudskiego)

The vast, empty-feeling **Piłsudski Square** has been important Warsaw real estate for centuries, constantly changing with the times. In the 1890s, the Russians who controlled this part of Poland began construction of a huge and magnificent Orthodox cathedral on this spot. But soon after it was completed, Poland regained its independence, and anti-Russian sentiments ran hot. So in the 1920s, just over a decade after the cathedral went up, it was torn down. During the Nazi occupation, this square took the name "Adolf-Hitler-Platz." Under the communists, it was Zwycięstwa, meaning "Victory" (of the Soviets over Hitler's fascism). When the regime imposed martial law in 1981, the people of Warsaw silently protested by filling the square with a giant cross made of flowers. The huge **plaque** in the ground near the road (usually marked by flowers) commemorates two monumental communist-era Catholic events on this square: John Paul II's first visit as pope to his homeland on June 2, 1979, and the May 31, 1981 funeral of Cardinal Stefan Wyszyński, whom we met across the street. The cross nearby also honors the 1979 papal visit, with one of his most famous and inspiring quotes to his countrymen: "Let thy spirit descend, let thy spirit descend, and renew the face of the earth—of *this* earth" (meaning Poland, in a just-barely-subtle-enough dig against the communist regime that was tolerating his visit). More recently, on April 17, 2010, more than 100,000 Poles convened on this square for a more solemn occasion: a memorial service for President Lech Kaczyński, who had died in a tragic plane crash in Russia.

Stand in the center, near the giant plaque, with the Royal Way at your back, for this quick spin-tour orientation: Ahead are the Tomb of the Unknown Soldier and Saxon Garden (explained later); 90 degrees to the right is the old National Theater, eclipsed by a modern business center/parking garage; another 90 degrees to the right is a statue of Piłsudski (which you passed to get here—described later); and 90 more degrees to the right is the Sofitel—formerly the Victoria Hotel, the ultimate plush, top-of-the-top hotel where all communist-era VIPs stayed. To the right of the hotel, on the horizon, you can see Warsaw's newly emerging skyline. The imposing Palace of Culture and Science, which once stood alone over the city, is now joined by a cluster of brand-new skyscrapers, giving Warsaw a Berlin-esque vibe befitting its important role as a business center of the "New Europe."

Walk to the fragment of colonnade by the park that marks the **Tomb of the Unknown Soldier** (Grób Nieznanego Żołnierza). The colonnade was once part of a much larger palace built by the Saxon prince electors (Dresden's Augustus the Strong and his son), who became kings of Poland in the 18th century. After the palace was destroyed in World War II, this fragment was kept to memorialize Polish soldiers. The names of key battles over 1,000 years are etched into the columns, the urns contain dirt from major Polish battlefields, and the two soldiers are pretty stiff. Every hour on the hour, they do a crisp Changing of the Guard—which, poignantly, honors those who have perished in this country, so shaped by wars against foreign invaders.

Just behind the Tomb is the stately **Saxon Garden** (Ogród Saski), inhabited by genteel statues, gorgeous flowers, and a spurting fountain. This park was also built by the Saxon kings of Poland. Like most foreign kings, Augustus the Strong and his son cared little for their Polish territory, building gardens like these for themselves instead of investing in more pressing needs. Poles say that foreign kings such as

Augustus did nothing but "eat, drink, and loosen their belts" (it rhymes in Polish). According to Poles, these selfish absentee kings were the culprits in Poland's eventual decline. But they do appreciate having such a fine venue for a Sunday stroll.

Walk back out toward the Royal Way, stopping at the statue you passed earlier. In 1995, the square was again renamed—this

time for **Józef Piłsudski** (1867-1935), the guy with the big walrus moustache. With the help of a French captain named Charles de Gaulle (whom we met earlier), Piłsudski forced the Russian Bolsheviks out of Poland in 1920 in the so-called Miracle on the Vistula. Piłsudski is credited with creating a once-again-independent Poland after more than a century of foreign oppression, and he essentially ran Poland as a virtual dictator after World War I. Of course, under the communists, Piłsudski was swept under the rug. But since 1989, he has enjoyed a renaissance as many Poles' favorite prototype anti-communist hero (his name adorns streets, squares, and bushy-mustachioed monuments all over the country).

• *Return to Hotel Bristol, turn left, and continue your Royal Way walk.*

Radziwiłł Palace

Next door to the hotel, you'll see the huge **Radziwiłł Palace.** The Warsaw Pact was signed here in 1955, officially uniting the Soviet satellite states in a military alliance against NATO. This building has also, from time to time, served as the Polish "White House."

• *Beyond Radziwiłł Palace, on the right, you'll reach a park with a...*

Statue of Adam Mickiewicz

Poland's national poet, Adam Mickiewicz spearheaded Poland's cultural survival during more than a century when the country disappeared from maps—absorbed by Austria, Prussia, and Russia. This was an age when underdog nations (and peoples without nations) all over Europe had their own national revival movements. The statue was erected in 1898 with permission from the Russian czar, as long as the people paid for it themselves. It's still an important part of community life: Polish high school students have a big formal ball (like a prom) 100 days before graduation. After the ball, if students come here and hop around the statue on one leg, it's supposed to bring them good luck on their finals. Mickiewicz, for his part, looks like he's suffering from a heart attack—perhaps in response to the impressively ugly National Theater and Opera a block in front of him.

• *Continue to the end of the Royal Way, marked by the big pink palace. Just before the castle, on your right, is...*

St. Anne's Church

This church is Rococo, with playful capitals inside and out and a fine pulpit shaped like the prow of a ship—complete with a big anchor. The richly ornamented apse, behind the altar, survived World War II. This church offers organ concerts nearly daily in summer (see "Entertainment in Warsaw," later).

For a scenic finale to your Royal Way stroll, climb the 150 steps of the **view tower** by the church (5 zł, generally open daily 10:00-18:00, in summer until 22:00, closed in bad winter weather). You'll be rewarded with

WARSAW

excellent views—particularly of Castle Square and the Old Town. From up top, visually retrace your steps along the Royal Way, and notice the emerging skyline surrounding the Palace of Culture and Science. The tower also affords a good look at the Praga district across the river, where the Red Army waited for the Nazis to level Warsaw during the uprising. Help was so close at hand...but stayed right where it was.

• *Just across from the view tower entrance, look for another Chopin bench. From St. Anne's Church, it's just another block—past inviting art galleries and restaurants—to Castle Square, the TI, and the start of the Old Town.*

Sights in Warsaw

THE OLD TOWN

In 1945, not a building remained standing in Warsaw's "Old" Town (Stare Miasto). Everything you see is rebuilt, mostly finished by 1956. Some think the Old Town seems artificial and phony, in a Disney World kind of way. For others, the painstaking postwar reconstruction feels just right, with Old World squares and lanes charming enough to give Kraków a run for its money. Before 1989, stifled by communist repression and choking on smog, the Old Town was an empty husk of its historic self. But now, the outdoor restaurants and market stalls have returned, and Varsovians and tourists are out strolling.

These sights are listed in order from south to north, and linked with walking directions, beginning at Castle Square and ending at the entrance to the New Town. For the best route from the "downtown" at Jerusalem Avenue to the Old Town, see "Warsaw's Royal Way Walk," earlier.

▲Castle Square (Plac Zamkowy)

This lively square is dominated by the big, pink Royal Castle that is the historic heart of Warsaw's political power.

After the second great Polish dynasty—the Jagiellonians—died out in 1572, it was replaced by the Republic of Nobles (about 10 percent of the population), which elected various foreign kings to their throne. The guy on the 72-foot-tall **pillar** is Sigismund III, the first Polish king from the Swedish Waza family. In 1596, he relocated the capital from Kraków to Warsaw. This move made sense, since Warsaw was closer to the center of 16th-century Poland (which had expanded to the east), and because the city had gained political importance over the past 30 years as the meeting point of the Sejm, or parliament of nobles. Along the right side of the castle, notice the two previous versions of this pillar lying on a lawn. The first one, from 1644, was falling apart and had to be replaced in 1887 by a new one made of granite. In 1944, a Nazi tank broke this second pillar—a symbolic piece of Polish heritage—into the four pieces (still pockmarked with bullet holes) that you see here today. As Poland rebuilt, its citizens put Sigismund III back on his pillar. Past the pillars are great views of Warsaw's brand-new, red-and-white National Stadium across the river.

Across the square from the castle, you'll see the partially reconstructed **defensive wall.** This rampart once enclosed the entire Old Town. Like all of Poland, Warsaw has seen invasion from all sides.

Explore the café-lined lanes that branch off Castle Square. Street signs indicate the year that each lane was originally built.

The first street is **ulica Piwna** ("Beer Street"), where you'll find **St. Martin's Church** (Kościół Św. Martina, on the left). Run by Franciscan nuns, this church has a simple, modern interior. Walk up the aisle and find the second pillar on the right. Notice the partly destroyed crucifix—it's the only church artifact that survived World War II. Across the street and closer to Castle Square, admire the carefully carved doorway of the house called *pod Gołębiami* ("Under Doves")—dedicated to the memory of an old woman who fed birds amidst the Old Town rubble after World War II.

Back on Castle Square, find the white **plaque** on the wall (at plac Zamkowy 15/19). It explains that 50 Poles were executed by Nazis on this spot on September 2, 1944. You'll see plaques like this all over the Old Town, each one commemorating victims or opponents of the Nazis. The brick planter under the plaque is often filled with fresh flowers to honor the victims.

• *Turn your attention to the...*

▲▲Royal Castle (Zamek Królewski)

A castle has stood here since the Mazovian dukes built a wooden version in the 14th century. It has grown through the ages, being

rebuilt and remodeled by many different kings. When Warsaw became the capital in 1596, this massive building served a dual purpose: It was both the king's residence and the meeting place of the parliament (Sejm). It reached its peak under Stanisław August Poniatowski—the final Polish king—who imported artists and architects to spiff up the interior, leaving his mark all over the place. Luftwaffe bombs destroyed it in World War II (only one wall remained standing). Rebuilding stalled because Stalin considered it a palace for the high-class elites. It was finally rebuilt in the more moderate 1970s, funded by local donations.

Warsaw's Royal Castle has a gorgeous interior—the most opulent I've seen in Poland. Many of the furnishings are original (hidden away when it became clear the city would be demolished in World War II). A visit to the castle is like perusing a great Polish history textbook. In fact, you'll likely see grade-school classes sitting cross-legged on the floors. Watching the teachers quizzing eager young history buffs, try to imagine what it's like to be a young Pole, with such a tumultuous history.

Cost and Hours: 22 zł, free on Sun; open May-Sept Mon-Sat 10:00-18:00, Thu until 20:00, Sun 11:00-18:00; Oct-April Tue-Sat 10:00-16:00, Sun 11:00-16:00, closed Mon; last entry one hour before closing; plac Zamkowy 4, tel. 22-355-5170, www.zamek-krolewski.pl. A public WC is on the courtyard just around the corner of the castle.

Tours: The castle has a well-produced audioguide (17 zł, worth the extra cost) and good English information posted throughout. For the basics, use my commentary to follow the one-way route through the castle.

◗ Self-Guided Tour: Because the castle visit procedure is always changing, it's possible you won't see these rooms in this exact order; if that happens, match the labels in each room to the corresponding text below.

Entering the courtyard, go to the right to buy tickets, then cross to the opposite side to tour the interior. (If you want an audioguide, go downstairs to rent it first.) Head up the stairs and follow *Castle Route* signs.

Start in the Oval Gallery, then head into the **Council Chamber,** where a "Permanent Council" consisting of the king, 18 senators, and 18 representatives met to chart Poland's course. Next is the **Great Assembly Hall,** heavy with marble and chandeliers. The statues of Apollo and Minerva flanking the main door are modeled after King Stanisław August Poniatowski and Catherine the Great of Russia, respectively. (The king enjoyed a youthful romantic dalliance with Catherine on a trip to Russia, and never quite seemed to get over her...much to his wife's consternation, I'm sure.)

The **Knights' Hall** features the Polish Hall of Fame, with paintings of great events and busts and portraits of VIPs—Very Important Poles. The statue of Chronos—god of time, with the globe on his shoulders—is actually a functioning clock, though now it's stopped at 11:15 to commemorate the exact time in 1944 when the Nazis bombed this palace to bits. Just off this hall is the **Marble Room,** with more portraits of Polish greats ringing the top of the room. Above the fireplace is a portrait of Stanisław August Poniatowski.

Continuing through the Knights' Hall, you'll wind up in the remarkable **Throne Room.** Notice the crowned white eagles, the

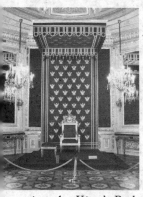

symbol of Poland, decorating the banner behind the throne. The Soviets didn't allow anything royal or aristocratic, so postwar restorations came with crown-less eagles. Only after 1989 were these eagles crowned again. Peek into the **Conference Room,** with portraits of other major European monarchs—Russia's Catherine the Great, England's George III, and France's Louis XVI—in whose esteemed royal league Stanisław August Poniatowski liked to consider himself.

After four more grand rooms (including the King's Bedroom, with a gorgeous silk canopy over the bed), you'll enter the **Canaletto Room,** filled with canvases of late-18th-century Warsaw painted in exquisite detail by this talented artist. (This Canaletto, also known for his panoramas of Dresden, was the nephew of another more famous artist with the same nickname, known for painting Venice's canals.) Paintings like these helped post-WWII restorers resurrect the city from its rubble. To the left, on the lower wall, the biggest canvas features the view of Warsaw from the Praga district across the river; pick out the few landmarks that are still standing (or, more precisely, have been resurrected). The castle you're standing in dominates the center of the painting, overlooking the river. Notice the artist's self-portrait in the lower-left. Opposite, on the right side of the room, is Canaletto's depiction of the election of Stanisław August Poniatowski as king, in a field outside Warsaw (notice the empty throne in the middle of the group). Among the assembled crowd, each flag represents a different Polish province.

From here, head left of the big "view of Warsaw" painting into the **side chapel,** reserved for the king. In the box to the left of the altar is the heart of Tadeusz Kościuszko, a hero of both the American Revolution and the Polish struggle against the Partitions (for more about the Partitions, see page 226).

As you cross over to the other part of the castle, you'll pass through the **Four Seasons Gallery** (with some fine but faded Gobelin tapestries) before entering a few rooms occupied by the houses of parliament—a reminder that this "castle" wasn't just the king's house, but also the meeting place of the legislature. In the

Parliamentary Chambers, notice the maps showing Poland's constantly in-flux borders—a handy visual aid for the many school groups who visit here.

After several rooms, you'll reach the grand **Senators' Chamber,** with the king's throne, surrounded by different coats of arms. Each one represents a region that was part of Poland during its Golden Age, back when it was united with Lithuania and its territory stretched from the Baltic to the Black Sea (see the map on the wall). In this room, Poland adopted its 1791 constitution (notice the replica in the  display case to the left of the throne). It was the first in Europe, written soon after America's and just months before France's. And, like the Constitution of the United States, it was very progressive, based on the ideals of the Enlightenment. But when the final Partitions followed in 1793 and 1795, Poland was divided between neighboring powers and ceased to exist as a country until 1918—so the constitution was never fully put into action.

Next, the **Crown Princes Room** features paintings by Jan Matejko that capture the excitement surrounding the adoption of this ill-fated constitution (for more on Matejko, see page 404). The next room has another Matejko painting: King Stefan Batory negotiating with Ivan the Terrible's envoys to break their siege of a Russian town. Notice the hussars—fearsome Polish soldiers wearing winged armor. Finally, you'll wind through more rooms with yet more paintings of great historical events and portraits of famous Poles.

Other Castle Sights: Sharing an entrance lobby with the main castle interiors, the **Gallery of Paintings, Sculpture, and**  **Decorative Arts** isn't worth the 20-zł extra admission fee for most visitors; save your time and money for the National Museum instead. But art lovers may be interested to see the 36 paintings of the Landkrońoski Collection. These originally belonged to Stanisław August Poniatowski, who sold them to an aristocratic family that eventually presented them to Poland as a gift. The prize of this collection—and this entire gallery—are two canvases by Rembrandt (both from 1641). *Girl in a Picture Frame* is exactly that—except that she's "breaking the frame" by resting her hands on a faux frame that Rembrandt has painted inside the real one...shattering the fourth wall in a way that was unusual for the time. The other, *A Scholar at His Writing Table*, shows the hirsute academic glancing up from his notes. Circle around behind the canvases to see X-rays of the paintings, which have helped experts better understand the master's techniques. The rest of the gallery consists of roomfuls of portraits and a fine cabinet of silver and crystal.

Consider a detour to the **Kubicki Arcades** (Arkady Kubiciego), the impressively excavated arcades deep beneath the castle. From the entrance lobby, head downstairs to the area with the cloakroom, bathrooms, and bookshop, then find the long escalator that takes you down to the arcades. It's free to wander the long, cavernous, and newly clean and gleaming space, made elegant by grand drapes.

The castle has a vast collection, which it organizes into various exhibitions—some permanent (well, as permanent as anything around here) and some temporary. The extensive **oriental carpet collection** in the "Tin-Roofed Palace" (Pałac pod Blachą) is sparsely described and skippable for most; the same building also features seven unimpressive apartments of Prince Józef Poniatowski, the king's brother (14 zł for both, free on Sun, same hours as castle, around the right side of the castle as you face it—past the two fallen columns, buy ticket at main ticket desk). When you're buying your castle ticket, keep an eye out for **temporary exhibits** of interest.

• *After you finish touring the castle and are ready to resume exploring the Old Town, turn left at the end of the square onto...*

St. John's Street (Świętojańska)
On the plaque under the street name sign, you can guess what the dates mean, even if you don't know Polish: This building was constructed from 1433 to 1478, destroyed in 1944, and rebuilt from 1950 to 1953.

• *Partway down the street on the right, you'll come to the big brick...*

Cathedral of St. John the Baptist (Katedra Św. Jana Chrzciciela)
This cathedral-basilica is the oldest (1339) and most important church in Warsaw. Superficially unimpressive, the church's own archbishop admitted that it was "modest and poor"—but "the historical events that took place here make it magnificent." Poland's constitution was consecrated here on May 3, 1791. Much later, this church became the final

battleground of the 1944 Warsaw Uprising—when a Nazi "tracked mine" (a huge bomb on tank tracks—this one appropriately named *Goliath*) drove into the church and exploded, massacring the rebels. You can still see part of that tank's tread hanging on the outside wall of the church (through the passage on the right side, near the end of the church).

Cost and Hours: Free, crypt-2 zł, good guidebook-5 zł, open to tourists daily 10:00-13:00 & 15:00-17:30, closed during services and organ concerts. The cathedral hosts organ concerts in summer (see "Entertainment in Warsaw," later).

Visiting the Cathedral: Head inside. Typical of brick churches, it has a "hall church" design, with three naves of equal height. Look for the crucifix ornamented with real human hair (chapel left of high altar). The high altar holds a copy of the Black Madonna—proclaimed "everlasting queen of Poland" after a victory over the Swedes in the 17th century. The original Black Madonna is in Częstochowa (125 miles south of Warsaw)—a mecca for Slavic Catholics, who visit in droves in hopes of a miracle. In the back-left corner, find the chapel with the tomb of Cardinal Stefan Wyszyński—the great Polish leader who, as Warsaw's archbishop, morally steered the country through much of the Cold War. (Notice the request to pray for his beatification, as Poles would love to see him become a saint.) The crypt holds graves of several important Poles, including Stanisław August Poniatowski (the last Polish king) and Nobel Prize-winning author Henryk Sienkiewicz.

• *Continue up the street and enter Warsaw's grand...*

▲▲Old Town Market Square (Rynek Starego Miasta)

For two centuries, this was a gritty market square. Sixty-five years ago, it was a pile of bombed-out rubble. And today, like a phoenix from the ashes, it's risen to remind residents and tourists alike of the prewar glory of the Polish capital.

Head to the **mermaid fountain** in the middle of the square. The mermaid is an important symbol in Warsaw—you'll see her everywhere. Legend has it that a mermaid *(syrenka)* lived in the Vistula River and protected the townspeople. While this siren supposedly serenaded the town, Varsovians like her more for her strength (hence the sword). This square seems to declare that life goes on in Warsaw, as it always has. I've often seen children frolicking here, oblivious to the turmoil their forebears withstood. When the fountain gurgles, the kids giggle.

Each of the square's four sides is named for a prominent 18th-century Varsovian: Kołłątaj, Dekert, Barss, and Zakrzewski. These men served as "Presidents" of Warsaw (mayors, more or less), and Kołłątaj was also a framer of Poland's 1791 constitution. Take some time to explore the square. Enjoy the colorful architecture. Notice that many of the buildings were intentionally built to lean out into the square—to simulate the higgledy-piggledy wear and tear of the original buildings.

If you're curious to learn more about the history and restoration of the Old Town, look around behind the buildings on the river side of the square (behind the mermaid's back), and find the **Old Town Heritage Interpretation Center**—a fine little visitors center with lots of before-and-after photos and videos, glass floors looking down onto original fragments, and thoughtful English explanations (2 zł, daily 10:00-20:00, Nov-April until 18:00, ulica Brzozowa 11/13, www.mhw.pl).

• *On the Dekert (north) side of the square is the...*

Warsaw Museum (Muzeum Warszawy)

When this museum's lengthy restoration is complete, it should provide an insightful look at the history of this city—particularly the Old Town. For now, you can enter the museum to see the network of cellars underneath, and to watch an interesting film.

Cost and Hours: 10 zł, free on Thu, open Tue-Sun 10:00-20:00, off-season until 18:00, closed Mon year-round, last entry 45 minutes before closing, Rynek Starego Miasta 28/42, tel. 22-635-1625, muzeumwarszawy.pl.

Film: Unless you're fascinated by Warsaw's history, skip the museum collection and just buy the separate 10-zł ticket to watch the excellent 20-minute film in English, worth ▲▲; unfortunately, it runs only twice daily (Tue-Fri at 10:00 and 12:00; Sat-Sun at 12:00 and 14:00). With somber narration and black-and-white scenes from before, during, and after the wartime devastation, this film is best appreciated after you've had a chance to see some of today's Warsaw (especially along the Royal Way). The movie ends with, "They say that there are no miracles. Then what is this city on the Vistula?" Emotionally drained, you can only respond, "Amen."

• *Leave the square on Nowomiejska (at the mermaid's 2 o'clock, by the second-story niche sculpture of St. Anne). After a block, you'll reach the...*

Barbican (Barbakan)

This defensive gate of the Old Town, similar to Kraków's, protected the medieval city from invaders.

• *Once you've crossed through the barbican, you're officially in Warsaw's...*

New Town (Nowe Miasto)

This 15th-century neighborhood is "new" in name only: It was the first part of Warsaw to spring up outside of the city walls (and therefore slightly newer than the Old Town). The New Town is a fun place to wander: Only a little less charming than the Old Town, but with a more real-life feel—people live and work here. Its centerpiece is the **New Town Square** (Rynek Nowego Miasta), watched over by the distinctive green dome of St. Kazimierz Church.

Scientists might want to pay homage at the museum (and birthplace) of Warsaw native **Marie Skłodowska-Curie,** a.k.a. Madame Curie (1867-1934); it's along the street between the New Town Square and the Barbican. This Nobel Prize winner was the world's first radiologist—discovering both radium and polonium (named for her native land) with her husband, Pierre Curie. Since she lived at a time when Warsaw was controlled by oppressive Russia, she conducted her studies in France. The museum—with photos, furniture, artifacts, and a paucity of English information—is a bit of a snoozer, best left to true fans (overpriced at 11 zł, Tue-Fri 9:30-16:00, Sat 10:00-16:00, Sun 10:00-15:00, closed Mon, ulica Freta 16, tel. 22-831-8092, http://muzeum-msc.pl).

From the New Town to Castle Square

You can backtrack the way you came, or, to get a look at the Old Town's back streets, consider this route from the big, round barbican gate (where the New Town meets the Old): Go back through the barbican and over the little bridge, turn right, and walk along the houses that line the inside of the wall. You'll pass a leafy garden courtyard on the left—a reminder that people actually live in the tourist zone within the Old Town walls. Just beyond the garden on the right, look for the carpet-beating rack, used to clean rugs (these are common fixtures in people's backyards). Go left into the square called Szeroki Dunaj ("Wide Danube") and look for another mermaid (over the Thai restaurant). Continue through the square and turn right at Wąski Dunaj ("Narrow Danube"). After about 100 yards, you'll pass the city wall. Just to the right (outside the wall), you'll see the monument to the **Little Upriser** of 1944, a child wearing a grown-up's helmet and too-big boots, and carrying a machine gun. Children—especially Scouts (Harcerze)—played a key role in the resistance against the Nazis. Their job was mainly carrying messages and propaganda.

Now continue around the wall (the upper, inner part is more

pleasant). Admire more public art as you head back to Castle Square.

BETWEEN NOWY ŚWIAT AND THE RIVER
▲▲National Museum (Muzeum Narodowe)

While short on big-name pieces, this museum interests art lovers and offers a good, accessible introduction to some talented Polish artists who are largely unknown outside their home country. A modern, state-of-the-art exhibition space allows these unsung canvases to really belt it out. Polish and other European artists are displayed side-by-side, as if to assert Poland's worthiness on the world artistic stage. After seeing a few of the masterpieces here, you won't disagree.

Cost and Hours: 15 zł, more for temporary exhibits, permanent collection free on Tue; open Tue-Sun 10:00-18:00, Thu until 21:00, closed Mon, last entry 45 minutes before closing; one block east of Nowy Świat at aleja Jerozolimskie 3, tel. 22-629-3093, www.mnw.art.pl.

❿ Self-Guided Tour: The collection fills several separate galleries. The museum's strongest point—and the bulk of this tour—is the 19th-century Polish art. But before diving in, consider some of the other collections.

Overview: To get your bearings, pick up a floor plan as you enter. On the ground floor are Ancient Art (from Greek pieces to artifacts left by early Polish tribes); Gallery Faras (highlighting the museum's fine collection of archaeological findings from that ancient Egyptian city); and a good collection of Medieval Art, which gathers altarpieces from churches around Poland—organized both chronologically and geographically—and displays some of the most graphic crucifixes and pietàs I've seen.

Upstairs is the excellent Gallery of 19th-Century Art (described next), which flows into the Old Polish and European Portrait Gallery (as interesting as somebody else's yearbook). Nearby, through the gift shop, is the worthwhile 20th- and 21st-Century Art collection, with an impressive array of Modern and Postmodern Polish artists, including photography and film. The underwhelming Old European Painting collection—pre-19th-century canvases arranged by theme and juxtaposed to highlight the differences between southern and northern European art—is split up among all three floors.

To cut to the chase, focus on the **Gallery of 19th-Century Art.** We'll start with the granddaddy of Polish art, Jan Matejko.

• *From the entrance lobby, head up the left staircase, then do a U-turn left across the mezzanine and enter the collection. Matejko is hiding at the far end of this wing: Entering the collection, angle right, then head all the way to the room at the far end, which is dominated by a gigantic*

Jan Matejko (1838-1893)

Jan Matejko (yawn mah-TAY-koh) is Poland's most important painter, period. In the mid- to late-19th century, the nation of Poland had been dissolved by foreign powers, and Polish artists struggled to make sense of their people's place in the world. Rabble-rousing Romanticism seemed to have failed (inspiring many brutally suppressed uprisings), so Polish artists and writers turned their attention to educating the people about their history, with the goal of keeping their traditions alive.

Matejko was at the forefront of this so-called "positivist" movement. Matejko saw what the tides of history had done to Poland, and was determined to make sure his countrymen learned from it. He painted two types of works: huge, grand-scale epics depicting monumental events in Polish history; and small, intimate portraits of prominent Poles. Polish schoolchildren study history from books with paintings of virtually every single Polish king—all painted by the incredibly prolific Matejko.

Matejko is admired not for his technical mastery (he's an unexceptional painter) or for the literal truth of his works—he was notorious for fudging historical details in order to give his canvases a bit more propagandistic punch. But he is revered for the emotion behind—and inspired by—his works. His paintings are utilitarian, straightforward, and dramatic enough to stir the patriot in any Pole. The intense focus on history by Matejko and other positivists is one big reason why today's Poles are still so in touch with their heritage.

You'll see Matejko's works in Warsaw's National Museum and Royal Castle, as well as in Kraków's Gallery of 19th-Century Polish Art (above the Cloth Hall). You can also visit his former residence in Kraków.

canvas. (*If you get lost, ask the attendants, "mah-TAY-koh?"*)

Jan Matejko: While not the most talented of artists—he's a fairly conventional painter, lacking a distinctive, recognizable style—Matejko more than made up for it with vision and productivity. His works—often on oversized canvases—are steeped in proud Polish history. Matejko's biggest work here—in fact, the biggest canvas in the whole building—is the enormous ***Battle of Grunwald***. This epic painting commemorates one of Poland's highwater marks: the dramatic victory of a Polish-Lithuanian army over the Teutonic Knights, who had been terrorizing northern Poland for decades (for more on the Teutonic Knights, see page 502). On July 15, 1410, some 40,000 Poles and Lithuanians (led by the sword-waving Lithuanian in red, Grand Duke Vytautas) faced off against 27,000 Teutonic Knights (under their Grand Master, in white) in one of the medieval world's bloodiest battles. Matejko plops us right in the thick of the battle's chaos, painting life-size figures and framing off a 32-foot-long slice of the actual two-mile battle line.

In the center of the painting, the Teutonic Grand Master is about to become a shish kebab. Duke Vytautas, in red, leads the final charge. And waaaay up on a hill (in the upper-right corner, on horseback, wearing a silver knight's suit) is Władysław Jagiełło, the first king of the Jagiellonian dynasty...ensuring his bloodline will survive another 150 years.

Matejko spent three years covering this 450-square-foot canvas in paint. The canvas was specially made in a single seamless piece. This was such a popular work that almost as many fans turned out for its unveiling as there are figures in the painting. The TV nearby shows how the vast painting was recently restored.

From Poland's high point in the *Battle of Grunwald*, look on the right wall for another, much smaller Matejko canvas, **Stańczyk After the Loss of Smolensk**, to see how Poland's fortunes shifted drastically a century later. This more intimate portrait depicts a popular Polish figure: the court jester Stańczyk, who's smarter than the king, but not allowed to say so. This complex character, representing the national conscience, is a favorite symbol of Matejko's. Stańczyk slumps in gloom. He's just read the news (on the table beside him) that the city of Smolensk has fallen to the Russians after a three-year siege (1512-1514). The jester had tried to warn the king to send more troops, but the king was too busy partying (behind the curtain). The painter Matejko—who may have used his own features for Stańczyk's face—also blamed the nobles of his own day for fiddling while Poland was partitioned.

More Matejkos fill this room. Just to the right of Stańczyk is a self-portrait of the gray-bearded artist (compare their features), then a painting of the hoisting of the Sigismund Bell to the cathedral tower in Kraków (it's still there). Farther right, you'll see his portraits of his children and his wife.

On the final wall is a smaller but very dramatic scene, **The Sermon of Skarga**. In the upper-right corner, a charismatic, early-17th-century Jesuit priest, Piotr Skarga, waves his arms to punctuate his message: Poland's political system is broken. He's addressing fat-cat nobles and the portly King Sigismund II Wasa (seated and wearing a ruffled collar), who were acting in their own self-interests instead of prioritizing what was best for Poland. Notice that Skarga's audience isn't hearing his ravings—they seem bored, or bugged, or both. The king is even taking a nap. They should have listened: Poland's eventual decline is often considered the fault of its unworkable political system. After the Partitions, the ahead-of-his-time Skarga was rehabilitated as a visionary who should have been heeded. Notice that, like Stańczyk, Skarga is a self-portrait of Matejko.

• *Leaving Matejko, we'll pass through several more rooms of lesser-known Polish painters to the opposite wing, where we'll meet several of the great artists' students—each of whom developed his own style and left his mark on the Polish art world. But on the way, I'll point out a few canvases that may be worth pausing at.*

Other Polish Painters: First, head back down the long corridor the way you came (passing some Matejko copycats), cutting through a corner of the Portrait Gallery. When you reach the door you came in, bear right to stay inside the gallery. At the end of that first, large room, you'll find some battle scenes by **Józef Brandt**—the only painter who rivaled Matejko in capturing epic warfare on canvas. Many of Brandt's scenes focus on confronting an enemy from the east, which was Poland's lot for much of its history. His biggest work here, *Rescue of Tatar Captives,* is typical of his scenes.

Continue straight into the next room, with some fine landscape scenes. This room (the partition in the middle) also has works by the talented **Józef Chełmoński:** *Indian Summer* and (around back) *Storks*—a young boy and his grandfather look to the sky, as a formation of storks flies overhead.

Turn right and go through one more long room (watching, on the right wall, for **Aleksander Gierymski's** small, evocative *Jewish Woman Selling Oranges*).

• *You'll emerge into a big room that kicks off the collection of...*

Młoda Polska: Matejko's pupils took what he taught them, and incorporated the Art Nouveau styles that were emerging around Europe, to create a new movement called "Young Poland" (see page 263). This room features works by two of the movement's big names. On the left wall are paintings by **Jacek Malczewski,** some of them depicting the goateed, close-cropped artist in a semi-surrealistic, Polish countryside context. Malczewski painted more or less realistically, but enjoyed incorporating one or two subtle, symbolic elements evocative of Polish folkloric tradition—like magical realism on canvas. *The Death of Ellenai* (1907) shows the pivotal scene in Juliusz Słowacki's epic 1838 poem, *Anhelli*, in which a young nobleman exiled from Poland during the Partitions is forced to make his way through the wastelands of Siberia. When his young and idealistic travel companion, Ellenai, perishes, Anhelli kisses her feet and abandons all hope.

Most of the works on the opposite wall are by **Józef Mehoffer,** who paints with brighter colors in a more stylized form, with more abstraction. This creates more dreamlike scenes that are, consequently, somehow less poignant than Malczewski's. Mehoffer's hypnotic *Strange Garden* is a bucolic vision of blue-clad Mary Poppinses, nude cherubs, lots of flowers...and a gigantic, hovering, golden dragonfly that places the otherwise plausible scene in the realm of pure fantasy. In the middle of the room, the small version of Auguste Rodin's *The Kiss* reminds us how this emotion-conveying style, called Symbolism, was also finding expression elsewhere in Europe.

The next room, at the end of the hall, features some lesser-known painters from the age. Among these, **Olga Boznańska**'s works are worth lingering over: gauzy, almost Impressionistic portraits that skillfully capture the humanity of each subject.

Head back into the Malczewski/Mehoffer room and find the small, darkened adjoining rooms. The first one features additional Malczewski paintings; the second is a treasure trove of works by the founder and biggest talent of Młoda Polska, **Stanisław Wyspiański.** The specific items in this room are subject to change—as Kraków, which owns the best collection of hometown boy Wyspiański, is shuffling its works in and out of special exhibitions—but you'll likely see both paintings and pastel works by this Art Nouveau juggernaut. Wyspiański also designed stage sets and redecorated some important churches; some of the large pastel-on-paper works you may see here were used as studies for those projects. And you'll likely see some self-portraits and portraits of his wife and children. Pondering the works here—and throughout the museum—think about how such a talented artist from a small country can be left out of textbooks across the ocean.

Chopin Museum (Muzeum Fryderyka Chopina)

The reconstructed Ostrogski Castle houses this museum honoring Poland's most famous composer. The museum was overhauled

for the "Year of Chopin" in 2010, when all of Poland celebrated the composer's 200th birthday. You'll see manuscripts, letters, and original handwritten compositions by the composer. Unfortunately, the museum's slick and high-tech gadgetry does more to distract from this rich collection of historic artifacts than to bring it to life. While Chopin devotees may find it riveting, those with only a passing familiarity with the composer may leave feeling like they still don't know much about this Polish cultural giant.

Cost and Hours: 22 zł, free on Sun, open Tue-Sun 11:00-20:00, closed Mon, 3 blocks east of Nowy Świat at ulica Okólnik 1, tel. 22-441-6251, www.chopin.museum. Because the museum is highly interactive, only 70 visitors are allowed per hour. But, except for rare occasions, just dropping in should be no problem.

Visiting the Museum: Buy your ticket at the adjacent building, then enter the mansion that houses the exhibit. You'll be given an electronic card; tap it against glowing red dots to access additional information. You'll proceed more or less chronologically through the composer's life, with various opportunities to hear his compositions. You'll see a replica of Chopin's drawing room in Paris, and his last piano, which he used for composing during the final two years of his life (1848-1849). Exhibits here trace themes of the composer's life, such as the women he knew (including his older sister Ludwika, his mother, and George Sand—the French author who took a male pseudonym in order to be published, and who was romantically linked with Chopin). The exhibit ends in the basement, where you can nurture your appreciation of Chopin by listening to his music.

Concerts: Under the palace is a new **concert hall,** which hosts performances by students (call museum to ask for concert schedule; usually Oct-July Thu at 18:00, and typically free).

Other Chopin Sight: The composer's tourable **birth house** is in a park in Żelazowa Wola, 34 miles from Warsaw. While interesting to Chopin devotees, it's not worth the trek for most. On summer weekends, the Chopin Museum sometimes runs a handy bus to the house—ask at the museum (departs from Marszałkowska street, 30 minutes each way; 7 zł for the bus, 7 zł for the park, 23 zł for the park and birth house, 39 zł also includes museum in Warsaw; birth house open Tue-Sun 9:00-19:00, Oct-March until 17:00, closed Mon year-round, tel. 46-863-3300).

▲▲Copernicus Science Center (Centrum Nauki Kopernik)

This facility, a wonderland of completely hands-on scientific doodads that thrill kids and adults alike, is a futuristic romper room. Filling two floors of an industrial-mod, purpose-built space, this is Warsaw's best family activity. Exhibits are grouped more or less thematically and described in both Polish and English.

Cost and Hours: 25 zł, 16 zł for kids 19 and under, 66-zł family ticket for up to 4 people; open Tue-Fri 9:00-18:00, Sat-Sun 10:00-19:00, closed Mon, last entry one hour before closing; Wybrzeże Kościuszkowskie 20, tel. 22-596-4100, www.kopernik. org.pl.

Crowd-Beating Tips: As a relatively new attraction, the center can get crowded—especially on weekends and school holidays, when the line can be long. On weekdays, it's generally no problem to walk right in.

Getting There: It's an easy downhill walk from Warsaw's Royal Way, but the hike back up is fairly steep. The nearest bus stop, called Pomnik Syreny, is on a nearby corner, next to the modern bridge; from here, bus #102 goes to Nowy Świat, then up the Royal Way (Uniwersytet and Zachęta stops) before heading south to the central train station. The new Metro line 2 connects the science center to the National Stadium, the Royal Way, and the Warsaw Uprising Museum.

Visiting the Center: Your ticket is a plastic "log-in card" that you can insert into certain interactive exhibits. On the ground floor, the **"Roots of Civilization"** features working models of various tools and machines, demonstrating how humanity has mastered the mechanics of physics. By playing with a model piston, I grasped for the first time how that

technology works. Other exhibits let you play archaeologist in a sandbox, listen to *Ode to Joy* while tuning into different instruments (depending on where you sit), and see a small "fire tornado" (every bit as cool as it sounds). A playroom for toddlers, called **"Buzzz!,"** has a nature theme. Meanwhile, **"RE: Generation"** targets teens and adults with computer touchscreens that investigate the biological underpinnings of emotion—from what makes you laugh to what grosses you out—and examines how cultures around the world are both similar and different.

The **"Heavens of Copernicus" planetarium** requires a separate ticket (18 zł, 13 zł for kids 19 and under, in Polish with English headset, open later than main center, show starts at the top of each hour, ask for schedule at ticket desk).

The fun continues upstairs, where **"Humans and the Environment"** illuminates the human body (find out just how long your intestines are, identify and place the organs, and see how various joints work like hinges). One area focuses on exercise, including the engaging arena, where you can compete with various virtual animals (can you jump as high as a kangaroo or hang like a chimp?). The **"Lightzone"** illustrates how light travels in waves, lets you try out an old-fashioned but still impressive camera obscura, and use prisms and lenses to play a game of "light billiards." **"On the Move"** features fascinating hands-on physics demos, including an earthquake simulator, an air cannon, and a tube that lets you harness sound waves to make water vibrate.

Nearby: The **Discovery Park** surrounding the museum was created when the busy riverfront highway was rerouted into an underground tunnel, creating this delightful people zone. From here you have good views of the modern Holy Cross Bridge (Most Świętokrzyski, from 2000) and the National Stadium, built to host matches for the 2012 Euro Cup and proudly wrapped in the patriotic red and white of the Polish flag.

Two short blocks inland from the science center is the

architecturally innovative **Warsaw University Library** (Biblioteka Uniwersytecka w Warszawie, or BUW), with its distinctive oxidized-copper-colored facade decorated with open books from various cultures. The facade is fun to ogle, and the rooftop holds a huge and inviting garden.

NEAR THE CENTRAL TRAIN STATION

These sights are near Nowy Świat, within a few blocks of the central train station.

Palace of Culture and Science (Pałac Kultury i Nauki, or PKiN)

This massive skyscraper, dating from the early 1950s, is the tallest building between Frankfurt and Moscow (760 feet with the spire,

though several new buildings are threatening to eclipse that peak). While you can ride the lift to its top for a commanding view, the highlight is simply viewing it up close from ground level.

Viewing the Skyscraper: This building was a "gift" from Stalin that the people of Warsaw couldn't refuse. Varsovians call it "Stalin's Penis"... using cruder terminology than that. (There are seven such "Stalin Gothic" erections in Moscow.) If it feels like an Art Deco Chicago skyscraper, that's because the architect was inspired by the years he spent studying and working in Chicago in the 1930s. Because it was to be "Soviet in substance, Polish in style," Soviet architects toured Poland to absorb local culture before starting the project. Notice the frilly decorative friezes that top each level—evocative of Poland's many Renaissance buildings (such as Kraków's Cloth Hall). The clock was added in 1999 as part of the millennium celebrations. Since the end of communism, the younger generation doesn't mind the structure so much—and some even admit to liking it for the way it enlivens the new, predictable glass-and-steel skyline springing up around it.

Everything about the Pałac is big. Approach it from the east side (facing the busy Marszałkowska street and the slick Galeria Centrum shopping mall). Stand in front of the granite tribune where communist VIPs surveyed massive May Day parades and pageantry on the once-imposing square, which today is a sloppy parking lot. From there, size up the skyscraper—its grand entry flanked by massive statues of Copernicus on the right (science) and the great poet Mickiewicz on the left (culture). It's designed to show off the strong, grand-scale Soviet aesthetic and architectural skill. The Pałac contains various theaters (the culture), museums of evolution and technology (the science), a congress hall, a multiplex (showing current movies), an observation deck, and lots of office space. With all of this Culture and Science under one Roof, it's a shame that only the ground-floor lobby (which feels like stepping into 1950s Moscow and is free to enter) and the 30th-floor observatory deck are open to the public.

Observation Deck: You can zip up to the observation deck (billed as "XXX Floor") in 20 seconds on the retrofitted Soviet elevators—but it's overpriced and the view's a letdown. While you'll get a nice overview of Warsaw's forest of new skyscrapers, you can hardly see the Old Town, and Warsaw's most prominent big building—the Pałac itself—is missing (18 zł, includes Polish-oriented special exhibitions; deck open daily June-Aug 9:00-20:00, Fri-Sat until 24:00; Sept-May 9:00-18:00, enter through main door on east side of Pałac—opposite from central train station, tel. 22-656-7600, www.pkin.pl).

Złote Tarasy Shopping Mall

Tucked behind the central train station, "Golden Terraces" is a super-modern shopping mall with a funky, undulating glass-and-steel roof. Even though you didn't come all the way to Poland to visit a shopping mall, it's worth detouring here to get a taste of Poland's race into the future. In many ways, this—and not humble farmers munching pierogi—is the face of today's Poland.

Hours: Mon-Sat 10:00-22:00, Sun 10:00-20:00, lots of designer shops, good food court on top level, www.zlotetarasy.pl.

Złota 44

This skyscraper, with its dramatic swooping lines rising high from the Złote Tarasy shopping mall, was designed by world-renowned architect Daniel Libeskind (who is also redeveloping the 9/11 site in New York City). Born in Poland, at a very young age Libeskind emigrated with his family to the US, returning only recently to embark on this project. Its shape evokes an eagle (a common symbol for Poland) just beginning to take flight. Of all the shiny new towers popping up in Warsaw's skyline, this is the most architecturally interesting—and offers a striking counterpoint to the Stalinist Palace of Culture and Science nearby. (For more on the building, visit www.zlota44tower.com.)

WARSAW

Warsaw's Jews and the Ghetto Uprising

From the Middle Ages until World War II, Poland was a relatively safe haven for Europe's Jews. While other kings were imprisoning and deporting Jews in the 14th century, the progressive king Kazimierz the Great welcomed Jews into Poland, even granting them special privileges (see page 261).

By the 1930s, there were more than 380,000 Jews in Warsaw—nearly a third of the population (and the largest concentration of Jews in any European city). The Nazis arrived in 1939. Within a year, they had pushed all of Warsaw's Jews into one neighborhood and surrounded it with a wall, creating a miserably overcrowded ghetto (crammed full of half a million people, including many from nearby towns). Over the next year, the Nazis brought in more Jews from throughout Poland, and the number grew by a million.

By the summer of 1942, more than a quarter of the Jews in the ghetto had either died of disease, committed suicide, or been murdered. The Nazis started moving Warsaw's Jews (at the rate of 5,000 a day) into what they claimed were "resettlement camps." Most of these people were actually murdered at Treblinka or Auschwitz. After hundreds of thousands of Jews had been taken away, the waning population—now about 60,000—began to get word from concentration camp escapees about what was actually going on there. Spurred by this knowledge, Warsaw's surviving Jews staged a dramatic uprising.

JEWISH WARSAW

In the early 1600s, an estimated 80 percent of all Jews lived in Poland (which at that time included Lithuania and was the largest country in Europe). But after centuries of dwelling in relative peace in tolerant and pragmatic Poland, Warsaw's Jews suffered terribly at the hands of the Nazis. Several sights in Warsaw commemorate those who were murdered, and those who fought back. Because the Nazis leveled the ghetto, there is literally nothing left except the street plan, some monuments, and the heroic spirit of its former residents. However, the brand-new Museum of the History of Polish Jews is rejuvenating the area, making it even more of a magnet for those interested in this chapter of Polish history.

Getting There: To reach Ghetto Heroes Square and the museum from the Old Town, you can hop a **taxi** (10 zł) or take a **bus** (to the Nalewki-Muzeum stop; bus #180 is particularly useful; bus #111 reaches this stop from farther south—Piłsudski Square, the university, and the National Museum). You can also **walk** there in about 15 minutes: Go through the barbican gate two blocks into the New Town, turn left on Świętojerska, and walk straight 10 minutes—passing the new green-glass Supreme Court building—until you reach a grassy park on Zamenhofa Street. At the corner

On April 19, 1943, the Jews attacked Nazi strongholds and had some initial success. The overwhelming Nazi war machine—which had rolled over much of Europe—imagined they'd be able to put down the rebellion easily. Instead, they struggled for a month to finally crush the Ghetto Uprising. The ghetto's residents and structures were "liquidated." About 300 of Warsaw's Jews survived, thanks in part to a sort of "underground railroad" of courageous Varsovians.

Warsaw's Jewish sights are emotionally moving, but even more so if you know some of their stories. You may have heard of **Władysław Szpilman,** a Jewish concert pianist who survived the war with the help of Jews, Poles, and even a Nazi officer. Szpilman's life story was turned into the highly acclaimed, Oscar-winning 2002 film *The Pianist*, which powerfully depicts events in Warsaw during World War II.

Less familiar to non-Poles—but equally affecting—is the story of Henryk Goldszmit, better known by his pen name, **Janusz Korczak.** Korczak wrote imaginative children's books that are still enormously popular among Poles. He worked at an orphanage in the Warsaw ghetto. When his orphans were sent off to concentration camps, the Nazis offered the famous author a chance at freedom. Korczak turned them down, choosing to die at Treblinka with his children.

of Świętojerska and Nowiniarska, look for the pattern of bricks in the sidewalk, marking *Ghetto Wall 1940-1943*.

▲Ghetto Heroes Square (Plac Bohaterow Getta)

The square is in the heart of what was the Jewish ghetto—now surrounded by bland Soviet-style apartment blocks. After the uprising, the entire ghetto was reduced to dust by the Nazis, leaving the communists to rebuild to their own specifications. The district is called Muranów ("Rebuilt") today.

The **monument** in the middle of the square commemorates those who fought and died "for the dignity and freedom of the Jewish Nation, for a free Poland, and for the liberation of human-kind." The statue features heroic Jewish men who knew that an inglorious death at the hands of the Nazis awaited them. Flames in the background show Nazis burning the ghetto. The opposite side features a sad procession of Jews trudging to concentration

camps, with subtle Nazi bayonets and helmets moving things along.

As you face the monument, look through the trees to the right to see a seated statue. **Jan Karski** (1914-2000) was a Catholic Pole and resistance fighter who traveled extensively through Poland during the Nazi occupation, collected evidence, and then reported on the Warsaw Ghetto and the Holocaust to the leaders of the Western Allies (including a personal meeting with FDR). In 1944, while the Holocaust was still going on, Karski published his eyewitness account, *The Story of a Secret State* (which you can see on this statue's armrest), to spread the story of what was happening in Poland. After the war he became a US citizen, and in 2012 President Barack Obama awarded him a posthumous Presidential Medal of Freedom.

• *The huge, glassy building facing the monument from across the square is the...*

▲▲Museum of the History of Polish Jews (Muzeum Historii Żydów Polskich, a.k.a. POLIN)

Opened in 2014, this powerful, long-overdue museum traces the epic, nearly millennium-long story of Jews in Poland. This is not a "Holocaust museum," but a celebration of the full and very rich Polish Jewish experience across the centuries. The striking building, designed by Finnish architect Rainer Mahlamäki, is pierced by a dramatically asymmetrical hole (visible from the outside). The building also hosts cultural events and temporary exhibits.

Cost and Hours: Core exhibition-25 zł, more for temporary exhibits, includes audioguide, Wed-Mon 10:00-18:00, Sat until 20:00, closed Tue, 6 Anielewicza, tel. 22-471-0300, www.jewishmuseum.org.pl. It's a modern facility with a cafeteria and children's area.

Visiting the Museum: In the "Core Exhibition," high-tech, interactive exhibits in eight galleries mingle with actual artifacts to bring history to life. You'll pass through a simulated forest—evocative of legends about the Jews' arrival in Poland—to reach the **"First Encounters"** exhibit, focusing on early Jewish settlers during the Middle Ages. You'll learn about Ibrahim ibn Jakub—a Sephardic Jew who penned early travelogues about Europe—and see a prayer book from 1272, with the oldest-known sentence written in Yiddish. Then, **"Paradisus Iudaeorum"** explains the ways Jewish culture flourished in tolerant Poland in the 15th and

16th centuries. An interactive model lets you explore the city of Kraków—and its Jewish quarter, Kazimierz—as it was during the golden age of Polish Jews. But with the Khmelnytsky Uprising in the mid-17th century came pogroms, anti-Semitism, and a more difficult life. **"Into the Country"** traces the spread of Jews throughout the Eastern European countryside, where they forged a unique type of settlement called a *shtetl*. The replica of a roof of a wooden synagogue from the village of Gwoździec illustrates the architecture of the time.

"Encounters with Modernity" examines how, after the Partitions (when Polish territory was divided among neighboring powers at the end of the 18th century), Jews struggled to integrate with the respective societies of their new overlords. This was also the time of the Industrial Revolution, when Jewish businessmen were making their mark on the society. As Poland—and its Jewish population—accelerated into the modern age, it brought about changes to Jewish tradition...and saw the emergence of a hateful and aggressive new breed of anti-Semitism.

"The Street" re-creates an early 20th-century shopping street from a Jewish community, demonstrating how Jewish culture thrived in the vibrant urban life of Poland between the World Wars. The **Holocaust** section explains the horrific events that claimed the lives of some 9 out of every 10 Polish Jews. This exhibit focuses on the Warsaw ghetto and its residents, whose daily lives and shocking fate are chronicled in a set of contemporaneous diaries and documents remarkably preserved in an underground archive.

Finally, **"The Postwar Years"** follows Holocaust survivors as they navigate an unfriendly, anti-Semitic communist regime. In 1968, the communists launched an "anti-Zionist" campaign; eventually around 15,000 Polish Jews lost their citizenship and left for Israel, Western Europe, and the US. Those who remained had to wait for the fall of communism to finally enter a world of new possibilities.

Ghetto Walking Tour

To see more faint echoes of the ghetto, take this brief, lightly guided walk for a few blocks. Facing the monument with the museum behind you, head left (with the park on your left) and walk along Zamenhofa—which, like many streets in this neighborhood, is named for a hero of the Ghetto Uprising. From the monument, you'll follow a series of three-foot-tall black stone memorials to uprising heroes—the **Path of Remembrance.** Like Stations of the Cross, each recounts an event of the uprising. Every April 19th (the day the uprising began), huge crowds follow this path. In a block, just beyond the corner of Miła (partly obscured by some bushes), you'll find a **bunker** where about 100 organizers of the uprising hid (and where they committed suicide when the Nazis discovered them on May 8, 1943).

Continue following the black stone monuments up Zamenhofa (which becomes Dubois), then turn left at the corner, onto broad and busy Stawki. The ugly gray building on your left (a half-block down at #5/7, near the tram stop) was the **headquarters of the SS** within the ghetto. This is where the transportation of Warsaw's Jews to concentration camps was organized.

Using the crosswalk at the tram stop, cross Stawki and proceed straight ahead into the gap between the two buildings. At the back of this parking lot is a surviving part of the red-brick **ghetto wall,** with a few remaining scraps of 1940s barbed wire.

Farther up Stawki street, on the right, you can stop at the **Umschlagplatz** monument—shaped like a cattle car. That's German for "transfer place," and it marks the spot where the Nazis brought Jewish families to prepare them to be loaded onto trains bound for Treblinka or Auschwitz. This was the actual site of the touching scene in the film *The Pianist* where the grandfather shares bits of chocolate with his family before being forever separated. In the walls of the monument are inscribed the first names of some of the victims.

WARSAW UPRISING SIGHTS

While the 1944 Warsaw Uprising is a recurring theme in virtually all Warsaw sightseeing, two sights in particular—one a monument, the other a museum—are worth a visit for anyone with a special interest. Neither is right on the main tourist trail; the monument is closer to the sightseeing action, while the museum is a subway, tram, or taxi ride away.

Warsaw Uprising Monument

The most central sight relating to the Warsaw Uprising is the monument at plac Krasińskich (intersection of ulica Długa and Miodowa, one long block and about a five-minute walk northwest of the New Town). Larger-than-life soldiers and civilians race for the sewers in a desperate attempt to flee the Nazis. Just behind the monument is the oxidized-copper facade of Poland's Supreme Court.

▲▲Warsaw Uprising Museum
(Muzeum Powstania Warszawskiego)

Thorough, modern, and packed with Polish field-trip groups, the museum celebrates the heroes of the uprising. It's a bit cramped, and finding your way through the exhibits can be confusing, but it helps illuminate this complicated chapter of Warsaw's history. The location is inconvenient (a 10-minute tram or bus ride west of central train station) and, because it eats up several hours to visit, may not be worth the trek for those with a casual interest. But history buffs find it worthwhile.

Cost and Hours: 14 zł, free on Sun (but you'll pay 2 zł for the good *City of Ruins* movie—buy ticket at cashier before entering museum); July-Aug Wed-Mon 10:00-18:00, Thu until 20:00; Sept-June Mon and Wed-Fri 8:00-18:00, Thu until 20:00, Sat-Sun 10:00-18:00, closed Tue year-round; last entry 30 minutes before closing, tel. 22-539-7947, www.1944.pl.

Audioguide: The informative, two-hour audioguide is ideal if you really want to delve into the whole story (10 zł, rent it in the gift shop). But the museum is so well-described, you can just wander aimlessly and be immersed in the hellish events.

Eating: The museum's café is oddly pleasant, serving drinks and light snacks amidst genteel ambience from prewar Warsaw. In summer you can dine on a peaceful terrace.

Getting There: It's on the western edge of downtown—a long, dull walk through urban gloom—at ulica Przyokopowa 28. While it's easiest to reach by taxi (figure about 20 zł from the Royal Way), you can also ride a tram or bus: Tram #22 and #24 come here from near the central train station (from the underground passageways, follow signs for *Ochota* to find the tram tracks) and near the corner of Nowy Świat and Jerusalem Avenue (in the middle of the street in front of the National Museum). You can also get to the museum on bus #109 (departs in front of the central train station—from the main hall, go out the door with the bus icon). From Castle Square in the Old Town, bus #178 goes to the museum. On the Royal Way, catch bus #105 from the Uniwersytet stop (next to the university building) or the Nowy Świat stop. All of these options take you to the Muzeum Powstania Warszawskiego stop. From this stop, cross the tracks and the busy street, walk straight one short block up Grzybowska, and take a left on Przyokopowa. The museum is the big, red-brick building on the left.

If traveling on Metro line 2, you can ride it (from Nowy Świat, among other stops) to Rondo Daszyńskiego—a bit farther away, but still within a few short blocks south of the museum.

❸ Self-Guided Tour: Buy your ticket at the little house on the left (marked *kasa*), then head into the main hall. The high-tech **main exhibit** sprawls across three floors. It chronologically tells

The Warsaw Uprising

By the summer of 1944, it was becoming clear that the Nazis' days in Warsaw were numbered. The Red Army drew near, and by late July, Soviet tanks were within 25 miles of downtown Warsaw.

The Varsovians could simply have waited for the Soviets to cross the river and force the Nazis out. But they knew that Soviet "liberation" would also mean an end to Polish independence. The Polish Home Army numbered 400,000—30,000 of them in Warsaw alone—and was the biggest underground army in military history. The uprisers wanted Poland to control its own fate, and they took matters into their own hands. The resistance's symbol was an anchor made up of a *P* atop a *W* (which stands for *Polska Walcząca*, or "Poland Fighting"—you'll see this icon all around town). Over time, the Home Army had established an extensive network of underground tunnels and sewers, which allowed them to deliver messages and move around the city without drawing the Nazis' attention. These tunnels gave the Home Army the element of surprise.

On August 1, 30,000 Polish resistance fighters launched an attack on their Nazi oppressors. They poured out of the sewers and caught the Nazis off guard. The ferocity of the Polish fighters stunned the Nazis, who thought they'd put down the uprising within hours. But the Nazis regrouped, and within a few days, they had retaken several areas of the city—murdering tens of thousands of innocent civilians as they went. In one notorious incident, some 5,500 Polish soldiers and 6,000 civilians who were surrounded by Nazis in the Old Town were forced to flee through the sewers; many drowned or were shot. (This scene is depicted in the Warsaw Uprising Monument on plac Krasińskich.)

Two months after it had started, the Warsaw Uprising was over. The Home Army called a cease-fire. About 18,000 Polish uprisers had been killed, along with nearly 200,000 innocent civilians. An infuriated Hitler ordered that the city be destroyed—which it was, systematically, block by block, until virtually nothing remained.

Through all of this, the Soviets stood still, watched, and waited. When the smoke cleared and the Nazis left, the Red Army marched in and claimed the wasteland that was once called Warsaw. After the war, General Dwight D. Eisenhower said that the scale of destruction here was the worst he'd ever seen. The communists later tracked down the surviving Home Army leaders, killing or imprisoning them.

Depending on whom you talk to, the desperate uprising of Warsaw was incredibly brave, stupid, or both. As for the Poles, they remain fiercely proud of their struggle for freedom. The city of Warsaw has recently commemorated this act of bravery with the new Warsaw Uprising Museum.

the story of the uprising, with a keen focus on military history. The exhibit covers several topics, but doesn't provide a big-picture narrative; to fully understand the context of what you're seeing, read the sidebar before your visit.

The **ground floor** sets the stage with Germany's invasion and occupation of Poland. The children's area (to the right as you enter) reminds visitors that Varsovian kids played a role in the Warsaw Uprising, too. The Generalgouvernement (Nazi puppet government of occupied Poland, ruled by Hans Frank in Kraków) wasted no time in asserting its control over the Poles; you'll learn how they imprisoned and executed priests, professors, and students. You'll also hear the story of the earlier, smaller uprisings that preceded the Warsaw Uprising, including the Poland-wide Operation Tempest (Burza) in 1943. During those earliest rebellions, Warsaw was intentionally left out of the fray...but the Varsovians' time would come.

To keep with the chronological flow, skip the middle floor for now, and ride the elevator to the **top floor** (#2), which covers the main part of the uprising. You'll meet some of the uprising's heroes and learn about their uniforms, weapons, and methods. The "Kino Palladium" movie screen shows fascinating Home Army newsreel footage from the period (with English subtitles). To the right of the screen, you'll walk through a simulated sewer, reminiscent of the one that many Home Army soldiers and civilians used to evade the Germans. Imagine terrified troops quietly traversing a more than mile-long sewer line like this one (but with lower ceilings)—and doing it while knee-deep in liquid sewage. At the end of the "sewer," stairs lead down to the middle floor.

The **middle floor** focuses on the grueling aftermath of the uprising. The later days of the uprising are outlined, battle by battle. A chilling section describes how Warsaw became a "city of graves," with burial mounds and makeshift crosses scattered everywhere. As you learn about the uprising's aftermath, consider that the Nazis tried to destroy Warsaw four separate times during World War II (at the outbreak of war, to put down the Ghetto Uprising, to put down the Warsaw Uprising, and finally just to be mean). One room honors the Field Postal Service, which, at great personal risk, continued mail delivery of both military communiqués and civilian correspondences. Many of these brave "mailmen" were actually Scouts who were too young to fight. Nearby, another room re-creates a clandestine radio broadcast station set up in a living room.

If you need a break, look for the red corridor leading through the USSR section to the **café** and WC.

End your visit by walking down the stairs into the **main hall**, which is dominated by two large-scale exhibits: a replica of an RAF Liberator B-24 J, used for airborne surveillance of wartime Warsaw; and a giant movie screen showing more fascinating newsreels assembled by the Home Army's own propaganda unit during the uprising. Under the screen, behind the black curtains, an exhibit tells the story of Germans in Warsaw, along

with another, more claustrophobic walk-through sewer. Also in the main hall, look for the entrance to the seven-minute 3-D film *City of Ruins*, with aerial footage of the postwar devastation. This gives you a look at the reality of the thousand people (nicknamed "Robinson Crusoes") who lived in bombed-out Warsaw immediately after the war. It's worth waiting in line to see this powerful film.

The **park** surrounding the building features several thought-provoking sights. A Chevy truck armored by the Home Army is both a people's tank and an example of how outgunned they were. Along the back is the Wall of Memory, a Vietnam War Memorial-type monument to soldiers of the Polish Home Army who were killed in action. You'll see their rank and name, followed by their code name, in quotes. The Home Army observed a strict policy of anonymity, forbidding members from calling each other by anything but their code names. The bell in the middle is dedicated to the commander of the uprising, Antoni Chruściel (code name "Monter").

SOUTH OF THE CENTER
▲Łazienki Park (Park Łazienkowski)
This huge, idyllic park is where Varsovians go to play. The park is sprinkled with fun Neoclassical buildings, strutting peacocks, and young Poles in love. It was built by Poland's very last king (before the final Partition), Stanisław August Poniatowski, to serve as his summer residence and provide a place for his citizens to relax.

On the edge of the park (along Belwederska) is a **monument to Fryderyk Chopin.** The

monument, in a rose garden, is flanked by platforms, where free summer piano **concerts** of Chopin's music are given weekly (mid-May-late Sept only, generally Sun at 12:00 and 16:00—confirm at TI). The statue shows Chopin sitting under a wind-blown willow tree. Although he spent his last 20 years and wrote most of his best-known music in France, his inspiration came from wind blowing through the willow trees of his native land, Poland. The Nazis were quick to destroy this statue, which symbolizes Polish culture. They melted the original (from 1926) down for its metal. Today's copy was recast after World War II. Savor this spot; it's great in summer, with roses wildly in bloom, and in autumn, when the trees provide a golden backdrop for the black, romantic statue.

Venture down into the ravine and to the center of the park, where (after a 10-minute hike) you'll find King Poniatowski's striking **Palace on the Water** (Pałac na Wodzie)—literally built in the middle of a river. Nearby, you'll spot a clever amphitheater with seating on the riverbank and the stage on an island. The king was a real man of the Enlightenment, hosting weekly Thursday dinners here for artists and intellectuals. But Poland's kings are long gone, and proud peacocks now rule this roost.

Łazienki Park is also slated to be the future home of the state-of-the-art **Museum of Polish History,** which is being built along the Łazienkowska highway (near Ujazdów Castle, at the northeastern edge of the park). While it likely won't open until at least 2018, this museum will be yet another big draw for visitors (to check on the progress, see www.en.muzhp.pl).

Getting There: The park is just south of the city center on the Royal Way. Buses #116, #180, and #195 run from Castle Square in the Old Town along the Royal Way directly to the park (get off at the stop called Łazienki Królewskie, by Belweder Palace—you'll see Chopin squinting through the trees on your left). Maps at park entrances locate the Chopin monument, Palace on the Water, and other park attractions.

Entertainment in Warsaw

Warsaw fills the summer with live music options. In addition to more serious options (opera, symphony, etc.), consider these crowd-pleasing choices.

CHOPIN

My favorite Warsaw music option is to enjoy a Chopin performance. There's nothing like hearing Chopin's compositions passionately played by a teary-eyed Pole who really feels the music. The best option is the outdoor concert in front of the big Chopin statue in **Łazienki Park,** but it is held only one day a week in summer (free, mid-May-late-Sept Sun at 12:00 and 16:00, www.lazienki-krolewskie.pl; for more on this option see the Łazienki Park listing on page 420).

If you're not in town on a Sunday, the next best thing is the **Chopin Salon.** Jarek Chołodecki, who runs the recommended Chopin Boutique B&B, hosts an intimate piano concert in his delightful salon nightly at 19:30. The performance can cover a range of musical styles and composers—but generally there are piano pieces featuring Chopin. The concert lasts from 45 minutes to more than an hour and is followed by wine, homemade cakes, and social time. A small group of locals and travelers gathers around Jarek's big shiny Steinway grand to hear great music by talented young artists in a great city (50 zł, ulica Smolna 14/6, reservations required, tel. 22-829-4801, www.bedandbreakfast.pl).

The **Chopin Museum** has a concert series where music academy students recommended by their professors perform an hourlong concert. These are free and typically take place October through July each Thursday at 18:00—but they can be cancelled, so it's smart to confirm (tel. 22-441-6100, http://en.chopin.nifc.pl; no concerts Aug-Sept).

OTHER MUSIC

Two big, opulent churches in and near the Old Town put on 30-minute **organ concerts** most days through the summer. Choose between the Cathedral of St. John the Baptist, with lots of history and a pretty plain brick interior, right in the heart of the Old Town (10 zł, Aug-late Oct Mon-Sat at 14:00, no concerts Sun); or the frilly, Rococo St. Anne's Church, with a more sumptuous interior, just outside of the Old Town (10 zł, May-early Oct Mon-Sat at 12:00, no concerts Sun). Both are run by the same company (mobile 501-158-477, www.kapitula.org).

Free outdoor **jazz concerts** take place each Saturday in summer right on the Old Town Square (July-Aug at 19:00).

Sleeping in Warsaw

Most accommodations in central Warsaw are either overpriced business-class hotels (whose rates can drop dramatically when demand is low—especially on weekends and in summer), or gloomy, impersonal communist-holdover hotels. Thankfully, there are a few happy exceptions—such as the Chopin Boutique B&B and the Duval Apartments, easily the best options in Warsaw. While pricing in most Polish cities is pretty straightforward, most Warsaw hotels employ dynamic pricing, which fluctuates wildly—even from day to day—depending on demand. For comparison's

Sleep Code

Abbreviations
(3 zł = about $1, country code: 48)

S = Single, **D** = Double/Twin, **T** = Triple, **Q** = Quad, **b** = bathroom, **s** = shower only.

Price Rankings

$$$ **Higher Priced**—Most rooms 400 zł or more.

$$ **Moderately Priced**—Most rooms between 300-400 zł.

$ **Lower Priced**—Most rooms 300 zł or less.

Unless otherwise noted, credit cards are accepted, breakfast is included, Wi-Fi is generally free, and English is spoken. Prices can change without notice; verify current rates online or by email. For the best prices, always book directly with the hotel.

sake, I've listed the average high-season price for a standard double room. For locations, see the map on page 386.

$$$ Hotel Le Régina is a tempting splurge buried in the quiet and charming New Town (just beyond the Old Town). From its elegant public spaces to its 61 top-notch rooms, everything here is done with class. Choose between plenty nice "standard" and "classic" rooms, or pay an extra 200 zł for bigger "superior" rooms, with hand-painted frescoes over each bed. While the official rates are ridiculously high, you'll often find amazingly lower promotional prices on their website (for a standard room in summer figure Db-550 zł on weekdays, as low as 350 zł on weekends, prices change constantly—check online for latest deals, more expensive during winter convention season, prices don't include the 110-zł breakfast—skip this very overpriced option, pricier suites, elevator, non-smoking floor, guest computer, Wi-Fi, exercise room, pool, Kościelna 12, tel. 22-531-6000, www.leregina.com, reception. leregina@mamaison.com).

$$$ Novotel, a chain hotel with 733 uninspired cookie-cutter rooms across the street from the Palace of Culture and Science, overlooks Poland's busiest intersection. Recently renovated inside and out, this is a good option for a big, business-class, downtown hotel that's handy to the central train station (rates change daily, in slow times—especially weekends—you might pay 250-450 zł, best deals online, optional breakfast-65 zł, non-smoking rooms, elevator, guest computer, Wi-Fi, Marszałkowska 94/98, tel. 22-596-0000, www.novotel.com, h3383@accor.com).

$$ Chopin Boutique B&B offers more comfort and class than a hotel twice its price, in a beautifully renovated and well-located old building near the National Museum. Jarek Chołodecki, who lived near Chicago for many years, returned to Warsaw and converted apartments into this wonderful bed-and-breakfast with 24 rooms. It's a friendly, casual, stylish place, creatively decorated and impeccably maintained. You'll feel like you're staying with your Warsaw sophisticate cousin—quirky, charismatic Jarek loves to chat with his guests, many of whom return and become  his good friends. Each morning, conversation percolates at the big, family-style breakfast table over a morning meal made mostly from organic and locally sourced foods. The drawing room plays host to nightly music concerts—see "Entertainment in Warsaw," earlier (Sb-270 zł, standard Db-320 zł, junior suite-360 zł, big suite-500 zł, these special rates for Rick Steves readers who book directly with hotel, elevator, guest computer, Wi-Fi, ulica Smolna 14/6, tel. 22-829-4801, www.bedandbreakfast.pl, office@bedandbreakfast.pl).

$$ Duval Apartments, named for a French woman who supposedly had an affair with the Polish king in this building, offers four beautifully appointed rooms above a restaurant (called Same Fusy) a few steps off the square in the Old Town. Each room has a different theme: traditional Polish, Japanese, glass, or retro (Sb-280 zł, Db-320 zł, Tb-400 zł, includes breakfast, lots of stairs with no elevator, some restaurant noise—light sleepers should request a quiet room, Wi-Fi, Nowomiejska 10, mobile 608-679-346, www.duval.net.pl, duval@duval.net.pl). There's no reception, and the rooms aren't officially affiliated with the restaurant, so arrange a meeting time with Agnieszka (or, if she's busy, Marcin) when you reserve. On arrival, go up the stairs and ring doorbell #5; the restaurant closes at 23:00.

$$ Castle Inn, sitting right on Castle Square at the entrance to the Old Town, is the next rung up the ladder for youth hostelers who've outgrown the grungy backpacker scene. Run by the owners of Oki Doki Hostel (described later), it has 22 creative and colorful rooms, each with completely different but equally artsy decor. Its location in the heart of the tourist zone is handy, but does come with some noise (very slushy rates depending on demand, generally Sb-300 zł, Db-350 zł, "delux" Db-500 zł, 35 zł extra for continental breakfast—have it delivered to your room for the same price, lots of stairs and no elevator, guest computer, Wi-Fi, Świętojańska 2, tel. 22-425-0100, www.castleinn.pl, castleinn@castleinn.pl).

$$ Between Us B&B is an ideal home-away-from-home for hipsters in Warsaw. Beata rents three trendy rooms above a youthful café centrally located in downtown Warsaw. As this place books up early, reserve far ahead (Db-300-525 zł depending on

size and length of stay, on second floor, no elevator, Wi-Fi, check in at Miedzy Nami café downstairs, Bracka 20, tel. 22-828-5417, mobile 603-096-701, www.between-us.eu, info@between-us.eu).

$$ Old Town Apartments offers 17 studio, one-bedroom, and two-bedroom apartments inside Warsaw's Old Town. Don't expect romantic Old World ambience—the apartments are modern, practical, and IKEA-furnished. The prices are good and the location is excellent, but you're pretty much on your own (no real reception, no breakfast but all have kitchens). View the apartments on their website, pick the one that looks best, and set up a meeting to get the keys at their Nowy Świat office (prices flex with demand, but figure studio-300 zł, 1-bedroom-350 zł, 2-bedroom-450 zł, some more expensive "featured" apartments on the square also available, slightly cheaper Oct-April and last-minute, Wi-Fi, tel. 22-887-9800, www.apartmentsapart.com, warsaw@bookaa.net). They also rent 15 pricey apartments on Nowy Świat, called **Royal Route Residence** (similar rates, breakfast-25 zł, corner of Nowy Świat and Chmielna). For either place, you'll check in at the office at Nowy Świat 27 (Mon-Fri 10:00-20:00, Sat-Sun 9:00-17:00, at other times arrange a meeting to get the keys). After checking in here, they'll send you in a taxi to your Old Town apartment.

$$ Hotel Harenda, a reliable old standby, has 43 rooms with leather-bound doors on the second and third floors of an office building right in the middle of the Royal Way, by the Copernicus monument. The tired, communist-era rooms are crying out for a renovation, but the location is ideal, and the ground-floor pub is a popular hangout (May-June and Sept-Oct: Sb-340 zł, Db-380 zł; July-Aug and Nov-April: Sb-310 zł, Db-340 zł; breakfast-30 zł, second night is free Fri-Sun, some rowdy street noise—especially on weekends—so request a quiet room, lots of stairs with no elevator, guest computer, Wi-Fi, Krakowskie Przedmieście 4/6, tel. 22-826-0071, www.hotelharenda.com.pl, rezerwacja@hotelharenda.com.pl).

$ Zgoda Apartment Hotel is conveniently located on an urban street between the Palace of Culture and Science and the Royal Way. With 51 classy-feeling apartments designed for business travelers, it's a comfortable—if impersonal—home base in the city center (small Sb/Db-200 zł, studio Sb/Db-250 zł, bigger "comfort" Sb/Db-300 zł, "superior" Sb/Db-400 zł, fancier rooms also available, rates are soft—especially for longer stays, extra bed-50 zł, breakfast-40 zł or use the kitchenette, air-con, elevator, Wi-Fi, Zgoda 6, tel. 22-553-6200, www.desilva.pl, zgoda@desilva.pl).

$ Ibis Warszawa Stare Miasto, with 333 cookie-cutter rooms, is the place for predictable comfort with zero personality. This hotel, part of the popular European chain, overlooks a WWII memorial in a nondescript, businessy-feeling neighborhood a

10-minute walk north of the Old Town (Sb/Db-289 zł, or 219 zł Fri-Sun, can be higher during conventions, sometimes better deals online, breakfast-33 zł, air-con, non-smoking rooms, elevator, Muranowska 2, tel. 22-310-1000, www.ibishotel.com, h3714@ accor.com).

HOSTELS

$ Nathan's Villa Hostel has 13 dorm rooms (with 95 beds) and 6 private rooms overlooking a cozy courtyard, and plenty of opportunities for backpacker bonding. It's near the Śródmieście dining zone, requiring a 15-minute walk or easy bus ride south of the central train station area (dorm bed in 4-bed room-72 zł, in 6-bed room-60 zł, in 12-bed room-50 zł, D-184 zł, Db-194 zł, all rates about 10 zł/person less on off-season weeknights, includes sheets, lockers, guest computer, Wi-Fi, pay laundry service, guest kitchen, hiding behind a modern glass office building at ulica Piękna 24/26—the nearby square called plac Konstytucji has easy bus connections, for location see map on page 375, tel. 22-622-2946, www.nathansvillahostel.com).

$ Oki Doki Hostel, on a pleasant square a few blocks in front of the Palace of Culture and Science, is colorful, creative, and easygoing. Each of its 37 rooms was designed by a different artist with a special theme—such as Van Gogh, Celtic spirals, heads of state, or Lenin. It's run by Ernest—a Pole whose parents loved Hemingway—and his wife Łucja, with help from their sometimes-jaded staff (complicated pricing structure flexes with demand, approximate high-season prices: dorm bed in 4-bed room-70 zł, in 5- to 6-bed room-60 zł, in 8-bed room-55 zł; S-160 zł, D-180 zł, Db-220 zł, T-220 zł; prices include breakfast except for dorm-dwellers—who pay 15 zł, guest computer, Wi-Fi, laundry service-15 zł, kitchen, lots of stairs with no elevator, plac Dąbrowskiego 3, tel. 22-826-5112, 22-828-0122, www.okidoki.pl, okidoki@okidoki.pl).

$ Szkolne Schronisko, the IYHF hostel, with 110 beds and lots of school groups, is institutional, well-run, bright, and clean. The downside: It's five floors up, with no elevator (nonmembers welcome, all prices per person: dorm beds-40 zł, S-80 zł, twin D-70 zł, T-60 zł, Q-55 zł, towel-3 zł, no breakfast but members' kitchen, 10 percent cheaper for hostel members, all rates 5-10 zł more expensive for guests over age 26, closed 10:00-16:00, curfew at 24:00; email ahead to reserve limited S, D, and T rooms; good location across the street from National Museum at ulica Smolna 30, tel. 22-827-8952, www.hostelsmolna30.pl, info@ hostelsmolna30.pl).

Eating in Warsaw

Tourists are drawn to the Old Town, where you can find decent (if generally overpriced) traditional Polish food. But the best eating options in this city are elsewhere: on or near Nowy Świat or—for a younger take—the emerging Śródmieście zone, to the south. In these neighborhoods, you'll find some traditional (or updated) Polish cuisine mixed in with some more interesting, international options. Wherever you dine, most restaurants are open until the "last guest," which usually means about 23:00 (sometimes later in summer).

ON OR NEAR NOWY ŚWIAT

While most Old Town eateries are traditional and cater to tourists, locals flock to the Nowy Świat neighborhood (near the National Museum and central train station) for a fun night on the town.

Fancy Eateries on Foksal Street: Foksal—the first cross street as you go down Nowy Świat from Jerusalem Avenue—has a thriving assortment of about a half-dozen cafés and restaurants: Mexican, Italian, Asian, international, and more. Most have inviting outdoor seating that's ideal on a balmy summer evening. The clientele is young and sophisticated, and there's not a pierogi in sight. Find the place with the cuisine and ambience you like best. **Papaya** has tasty pan-Asian fare and a trendy, minimalist, black-and-white interior (30-60-zł main dishes plus pricier splurges, daily 12:00-24:00, at #16, tel. 22-826-1199). A block beyond this area is a far more traditional option, **Kamanda Lwowska,** named for the former Polish city that's now in Ukraine. It has a few outdoor seats and a charming, cluttered old cellar; the friendly and fun staff serves up Polish classics (40-55-zł main dishes, daily 10:00-24:00, Foksal 10, tel. 22-828-1031).

Cheap Milk Bars: **Wiking Bar,** a colorful milk bar, serves up Polish grub right on Nowy Świat, with inviting sidewalk seating (10-15-zł main dishes, Mon-Fri 7:30-22:00, Sat 12:00-23:00, Sun 12:00-20:00, Nowy Świat 28). **Mleczarnia Jerozolimska,** just around the corner on busy Jerusalem Avenue, is a more classic milk-bar experience (4-7-zł soups, 9-14-zł main dishes, Mon-Fri 10:00-20:00, Sat-Sun 11:00-19:00, aleja Jerozolimskie 32). For more on milk bars, see page 234.

Hungarian and Polish Cuisine on Zgoda Street: **Borpince** ("Wine Cellar") is a cozy cellar serving up very authentic

Hungarian fare a long block off of Nowy Świat (toward the Palace of Culture and Science). As you dive into spicy goulash and *paprikás,* you'll see just how different the cuisine can be on the other side of the Carpathians. If you won't be visiting Hungary on your trip, this is the next best way to sample Hungarian favorites. The restaurant also has a long list of Hungarian wines (40-50-zł main dishes, daily 12:00-23:00, closes earlier when it's slow, ulica Zgoda 1, tel. 22-828-2244). For Magyar flavors at lower prices, try **Krokiecik** ("Croquette"), the simpler self-service restaurant located next door, at street level. Choose from Polish or Hungarian food, order at the counter, then take a seat (10-15-zł main dishes, daily 9:00-21:00, ulica Zgoda 1, tel. 22-827-3037). **Restauracja Zgoda,** across the street and owned by the same people, has affordable, reliable Polish cuisine in an Old World setting; it's popular among traditionalists dining out (9-15-zł soups, 20-zł salads, 20-35-zł fish and meat dishes, Mon-Sat 9:00-23:00, Sun 12:00-23:00, Zgoda 4, tel. 22-827-9934).

Uniquely Polish Treats

These two places are on or close to the busy Nowy Świat boulevard.

A. Blikle, Poland's most famous pastry shop, serves a wide variety of delicious treats. This is where locals shop for cakes when they're having someone special over for coffee. The specialty: *pączki* (PONCH-kee), the quintessential Polish doughnut, filled with rose-flavored jam. You can get your goodies "to go" in the shop (3-zł *pączki,* daily 9:00-21:00), or pay double to enjoy them with coffee in the swanky, classic café with indoor or outdoor seating (7-zł *pączki,* Mon-Sat 9:00-22:00, Sun 10:00-22:00; both at Nowy Świat 35, tel. 22-828-6601). They also have a sit-down restaurant (30-50-zł main dishes), but I come here only for the *pączki.*

E. Wedel Pijalnia Czekolady thrills chocoholics. Emil Wedel made Poland's favorite chocolate, and today, his former residence houses this chocolate shop and genteel café. This is the spot for delicious pastries and a *real* hot chocolate—*czekolada do picia* ("drinking chocolate"), a cup of actual melted chocolate, not just hot chocolate milk (12 zł). The staff describes it as, "True Wedel ecstasy for your mouth that will take you to a world of dreams and desires." Or, if you fancy chocolate mousse, try *pokusa* ("Wedel Temptation"). Wedel's was *the* Christmas treat for locals under communism. Cadbury bought the company when Poland privatized, but they kept the E. Wedel name, which is close to all Poles' hearts...and taste buds (Mon-Fri 8:00-22:00, Sat 10:00-22:00, Sun 10:00-21:00, between Palace of Culture and Science and Nowy Świat at ulica Szpitalna 8, tel. 22-827-2916, www.wedelpijalnie.pl/en).

IN THE ŚRÓDMIEŚCIE DISTRICT

Warsaw's Śródmieście ("Downtown") district, south of Jerusalem Avenue, is emerging as the epicenter of Polish hipster/foodie culture. While this is a bit farther from the main tourist/sightseeing zone, that's sort of the point. And while the Old Town/New Town are for tourists, and the Nowy Świat area is for yuppies and business travelers, in the Śródmieście you'll find young Varsovian foodies digging into affordable dishes at the trendiest new places. This area is a 15-minute walk south of Jerusalem Avenue, and also well-served by public transportation (for example, trams #4, #15, #18, and #35 run frequently along the main north-south Marszałkowska corridor to plac Zbawiciela; of these, tram #4 stops in the middle of the road below Palace Square, where the Royal Way meets the Old Town). Listed next are a few different restaurant-hunting zones, with some specific recommendations for each one. I'd just hop a tram to plac Zbawiciela and explore from there...within a few steps, you'll find more temptations than in the rest of the city combined.

Plac Zbawiciela: Named "Holiest Savior Square" for the looming church, this is a dizzying six-way intersection with a big traffic circle ringed by elegant old colonnades. To get a quick taste of the emerging Śródmieście scene, come here first and just do a slow loop around the circle, surveying your options. Starting to the right of the steeple and moving clockwise, here are a few options you'll see: **Izumi Sushi** and **Karma** coffee shop have their fans, but **Tuk Tuk**—serving quick and delicious Thai street food (order you choice of 20-30-zł dishes at the counter, then take a seat)—is a popular choice. Across the street, **Rumburak** is an inviting café with an impressive menu of 30-40-zł international dishes and atmospheric seating under the colonnade. Just down Mokotowska from the circle, look for the line of people at **Lody Naturalne,** an unpretentious hole-in-the-wall serving all-natural, homemade ice cream. In the next section, **Charlotte** designer bakery and wine bar is another popular choice, with homemade treats and tables spilling out all over the square. Up above, **Plan B** is a hipster dive bar with drinks, snacks, and views down over the square (find the graffiti-slathered staircase up, just past Charlotte). In the unlikely event that you don't find something to your liking around this square, head up Mokotowska (past the ice-cream place, described next).

Mokotowska: This street, stretching north from plac Zbawiciela, has fewer choices—but they're good ones. **Dyspensa** may be the best option in the Śródmieście for a serious sit-down meal in a dressy but not stuffy environment. They serve a thoughtfully selected menu of updated Polish cuisine, plus a few international options, as well as a handwritten list of daily specials.

Reservations are smart (60-85-zł main courses, daily 12:00-23:00, Mokotowska 39, tel. 22-629-9989, www.dyspensa.pl). A half-block up the street is the mellower **Słodki Słony** ("Sweet Salty"), at the casual end of the scale of Polish celebrity chef Magda Gessler's restaurant empire. Up front is a big, tempting display case bursting with over-the-top decadent desserts (10-20 zł); farther in is a cozy dining area where you can dig into 20-35-zł sandwiches, salads, and other light fare (daily 11:00-24:00, Mokotowska 45, tel. 22-622-4934, www.slodkislony.pl).

Poznańska: A few short blocks to the west, this street is also lined with trendy and youthful eateries (particularly between Wilcza and Żurawia). Strolling this strip, you'll find **Kaskrut** (a pun on *casse-croûte,* with 20-25-zł sandwiches); **Leniviec** café and cocktails; **Dwie 3,** offering Mediterranean fusion in a modern and spacious setting; and **Tel Aviv,** with gluten-free and vegan Middle Eastern food. But the foodie anchor in this neighborhood is **Beirut,** a gregariously crowded bar serving up excellent Middle Eastern food. The hummus bar, on the left, has a wide variety of *mezes* (small plates) and grilled meats, while the "Kraken Rum Bar" on the right has fish dishes (15-30 zł dishes on both sides; portions are modest, so plan to share a few). At either side, line up at the bar, ask for the English menu, place your order, try to find a table, then wait for your number to be called. It can be a bit chaotic, but it's delicious and fun (daily 12:00-late, Poznańska 12).

Classy Steakhouse: **Butchery & Wine,** in an unassuming location on a drab urban street, is a pocket of chic international cuisine in the heart of Warsaw. The waiters, smartly dressed in pinstripe aprons, serve upscale comfort food (specializing in steaks) to a small, lively room of business travelers. The wine list is extensive, and reservations are smart (55-85-zł steaks, Mon-Sat 12:00-22:00, closed Sun, across aleja Jerozolimskie from Nowy Świat at Żurawia 22, tel. 22-502-3118, www.butcheryandwine.pl).

HANGOUT CAFÉS NEAR THE RIVER

If you just want to grab a drink (and possibly a light meal) and watch the world go by, Warsaw has two inviting cafés downhill, near the river, that are worth the short trip from the main tourist zone. The first one serves mostly drinks and is a hip hangout by day and by night; the second has a wider menu of food and is open only during the day.

Warszawa Powiśle occupies the old, communist-style ticket office for the suburban train station of the same name. Now it's

been taken over by hipsters and converted into one of the most happening hangouts in town. Tucked along a picturesque bike lane beneath the towering legs of a bridge, its sidewalk is jammed with cool Varsovians and in-the-know visitors living well. The building itself has some indoor seating, but it's quite small—making this a better good-weather option (light sandwiches, daily 9:00 until late, Kruczkowskiego 3B, tel. 22-474-4084). The most direct way to get here from the palm tree at the head of Nowy Świat is to walk down Jerusalem Avenue toward the bridge, enter the rail station, go down the stairs, walk all the way along *peron* (platform) 1 to the end, then go down the stairs at the far end: You'll pop out right at the bar. Alternatively, you can walk partway across the bridge at Jerusalem Avenue, then go down the stairs at the first tower.

Kawarnia Kafka combines a used bookstore (with books sold by weight) with a hip, creative café. You'll find comfy chairs, stay-awhile tables, and checkerboard tiles inside, while outside on the lawn across from the café, guests lounge in slingback chairs (8-18-zł sandwiches and crêpes, 15-25-zł pastas and salads, Wi-Fi, Mon-Fri 9:00-22:00, Sat-Sun 10:00-22:00, Oboźna 3, tel. 22-826-0822).

IN OR NEAR THE OLD TOWN

The restaurants in the Old Town and surrounding streets are 100 percent for tourists. I'd much rather dine at one of the more characteristic areas noted earlier, but if you need to grab a meal near here, the following places are worth considering. Rather than spending too much to eat on the Old Town Market Square, I prefer to venture a few blocks to find a place with good food and much lower prices. For locations, see the map on page 386.

Restauracja pod Samsonem ("Under Samson") is a touristy standby for dining on affordable Jewish and Polish comfort food. The ambience is pleasant—with enjoyable outdoor seating in good weather—the service is playfully opinionated, and the low prices make up for the fact that you have to pay to check your coat and use the bathroom (25-35-zł main courses, daily 10:00-23:00, ulica Freta 3/5, tel. 22-831-1788).

Pierogarnia na Bednarskiej brags, "only our grandmothers make better pierogi." In addition to the classic Polish dumplings, the menu includes soups and a fun variety of drinks (from unusual fruit juices to *kvas*, the nonalcoholic, rye-flavored dark beer). Order at the counter and take a seat—they'll call you when your food's ready. With mellow country decor, wooden menus, and a loyal crowd, this is a handy spot for a quick, cheap meal along the Royal Way (15-zł plates of pierogi, 18-zł combo-plate includes soup and salad, daily 12:00-20:00, hiding down a quiet street behind the statue of Adam Mickiewicz at ulica Bednarska

28/30, tel. 22-828-0392).

BrowArmia is a hit with beer lovers. This sprawling brew-pub makes four different types of beer (plus special seasonal beers) and serves decent pub grub. The dark, mod, long interior fills two levels (including a fun cellar), but in good weather I'd stake out a spot on the terrace—ideal for people-watching along the Royal Way. The food is overpriced, but you're paying for the beer and the location (40-70-zł main dishes, daily 12:00-24:00, live music or DJ in cellar on weekends, right on Krakowskie Przedmieście near Piłsudski Square at ulica Królewska 1, tel. 22-826-5455).

Italian: **Enoteka Polska** is a dressy wine cellar serving Italian food at rustic tables squeezed between crates of wine bottles. Although the location is in the middle of nowhere (about a 10-minute walk through drab sprawl from the Old Town), the decor is nicely modern, and there's a pleasant garden in the summer. Reservations are smart (30-40-zł pastas, 40-60-zł main dishes, daily 12:00-24:00, Sun 13:00-21:00, Długa 23/25, tel. 22-635-5510, www.enotekapolska.pl).

Warsaw Connections

Almost all trains into and out of Warsaw go through the hulking central train station (described earlier, under "Arrival in Warsaw"; pay special attention to the "Buying Train Tickets" section). If you're heading to Gdańsk, note that the red-brick Gothic city of Toruń and the impressive Malbork Castle are on the way (though on separate train lines, so you can't do both en route; see the Gdańsk and Pomerania chapters). Also be aware that express trains to many destinations—including Kraków and Gdańsk—require seat reservations, even if you have a rail pass.

To confirm rail journeys, check specific times online (www.rozklad-pkp.pl) or at the central train station.

From Warsaw's Central Station by Train to: Kraków (hourly, about 2.5 hours, requires seat reservation), **Gdańsk** (hourly, 3 hours), **Toruń** (9/day, 3 hours direct, more with transfer in Kutno or Iława), **Malbork** (hourly, 2.5 hours), **Prague** (2/day direct, including 1 night train, more with changes, 8.5-10.5 hours), **Berlin** (4/day direct, 5.5 hours), **Budapest** (2/day with transfer in Břeclav, Czech Republic, 9.75 hours; 1 direct night train, 11 hours), **Vienna** (2/day direct, 7 hours; plus 1 night train, 8.75 hours).

By Bus: PolskiBus runs bus routes throughout Poland (www.polskibus.com).

GDAŃSK & THE TRI-CITY

Gdańsk (guh-DAYNSK) is a true find on the Baltic Coast of Poland. You may associate Gdańsk with dreary images of striking dockworkers from the nightly news in the 1980s—but there's so much more to this city than shipyards, Solidarity, and smog. It's surprisingly easy to look past the urban sprawl to find one of northern Europe's most historic and picturesque cities. Gdańsk is second only to Kraków as Poland's most appealing destination.

Exploring Gdańsk is a delight. The gem of a Main Town boasts block after block of red-brick churches and narrow, colorful, ornately decorated Hanseatic burghers' mansions. The riverfront embankment, with its trademark medieval crane, oozes salty maritime charm. Gdańsk's history is also fascinating—from its 17th-century Golden Age to the headlines of our own generation, big things happen here. You might even see portly old Lech Wałęsa still wandering the streets. And yet Gdańsk is also looking to its future, steadily repairing some of its WWII damage after a long communist hibernation. Over the past decade, whole swaths of the city have been remade with a bold new modernity...but always with a respect for the past.

Gdańsk and two nearby towns (Sopot and Gdynia) together form an area known as the "Tri-City," offering several day-trip opportunities north along the coast (see page 489). The once-faded, now-revitalized elegance of the seaside resort of Sopot beckons to tourists, while the modern burg of Gdynia sets the pace for today's Poland. Beyond the Tri-City, the sandy Hel Peninsula is a popular spot for summer sunbathing.

PLANNING YOUR TIME

This region merits two days to make the trip here worthwhile. Gdańsk's major sights can be seen in a day, but a second day allows you to see everything in town at a more relaxing pace, and take your pick from among several possible side-trips.

Gdańsk sightseeing has two major components: the Royal Way (historic main drag with good museums) and the modern shipyard where Solidarity was born (with a fascinating museum). With just one day, do one of these activities in the morning, and the other in the afternoon. With two days, do one each day, and round out your time with other attractions: Art lovers enjoy the National Museum (with a stunning altar painting by Hans Memling), history buffs make the pilgrimage to Westerplatte (where World War II began), and church and pipe organ fans might visit Oliwa Cathedral in Gdańsk's northern suburbs (on the way to Sopot).

If you have more time, consider the wide variety of side-trips. The most popular option is the half-day round-trip to Malbork Castle (30-45 minutes each way by train, plus two or three hours to tour the castle—see next chapter). Closer to Gdańsk, it only takes a quick visit to get a feel for the resort town of Sopot (25 minutes each way by train), but the town's beaches may tempt you to laze around longer. Consider a sprint through Gdynia to round out your take on the Tri-City. If you have a full day and great weather, and you don't mind fighting the crowds for a patch of sandy beach, go to Hel.

Gdańsk gets busy in late June, when school holidays begin, and it's downright crowded with mostly German tourists from July to mid-September—especially during St. Dominic's Fair (Jarmark Św. Dominika, three weeks from late July to mid-Aug), with market stalls, concerts, and other celebrations.

Orientation to Gdańsk

With 460,000 residents, Gdańsk is part of the larger urban area known as the Tri-City (Trójmiasto, total population of 1 million). But the tourist's Gdańsk is compact, welcoming, and walkable—virtually anything you'll want to see is within a 20-minute stroll of everything else.

Focus on the Main Town (Główne Miasto), home to most of the sights described, including the spectacular Royal Way main drag, ulica Długa. The Old Town (Stare Miasto) has a handful of old brick buildings and faded, tall, skinny houses—but the area is mostly drab and residential, and not worth much time. Just beyond the northern end of the Old Town (about a 20-minute walk from the heart of the Main Town) is the entrance to the Gdańsk Shipyard, with the excellent European Solidarity Center and its top-notch museum. From here, shipyards sprawl for miles.

The second language in this part of Poland is German, not English. As this was a predominantly German city until the end of World War II, German tourists flock here in droves. But you'll win no Polish friends if you call the city by its more familiar German name, Danzig. You'll also find that Gdańsk is becoming an increasingly popular cruise destination, with about 100 ships calling here each year (most dock at the nearby city of Gdynia, and passengers take a bus or train in). During summer daytime hours, the town is filled with little tour groups.

TOURIST INFORMATION

Confusingly, Gdańsk has three different TI organizations. The regional TI occupies the **Upland Gate,** facing the busy road that hems in the Main Town, at the start of my self-guided walk (May-Sept Mon-Fri 9:00-20:00, Sat-Sun 9:00-18:00; Oct-April daily 9:00-18:00; tel. 58-732-7041). The city TI has three branches—one conveniently located at the bottom (river) end of the main drag, at **Długi Targ 28** (just to the left as you face the gate; July-Aug daily 9:00-19:00; Sept-June Mon-Sat 9:00-17:00, Sun 9:00-16:00; tel. 58-301-4355, www.gdansk4u.pl). Satellites TIs are at the **main train station** (in the underpass, same hours, tel. 58-721-3277) and at the **airport** (open 24/7, tel. 58-348-1368). Skip the other TI, which is prominently located (in the red, high-gabled building across ulica Długa from the Town Hall) but sloppily run by the national government.

Sightseeing Card: Busy sightseers should consider the **Tourist Card,** which includes entry to 24 sights in Gdańsk, Gdynia, and Sopot, and discounts at others (such as 20 percent off admission to Malbork Castle). Check the list of what's covered (most of the biggies in town are free with the card, while the European Solidarity Center is 50 percent off), and do the arithmetic. If you'll be seeing several included museums, this card could save you some money (sightseeing-only card: 38 zł/24 hours, 48 zł/72 hours; "max" card also includes local public transit: 58 zł/24 hours, 88 zł/72 hours; sold only at TIs).

ARRIVAL IN GDAŃSK

By Train: Gdańsk's main train station (Gdańsk Główny) is a pretty brick palace on the western edge of the old center. (To save money, architects in Colmar, France, copied this exact design to build their city's station.) Trains to other parts of Poland (marked *PKP*) use platforms 1-3; regional trains with connections to the Tri-City (marked *SKM*) use the shorter platforms 3-5 (for instructions on riding these regional SKM trains, see page 489).

Inside the terminal building, you'll find lockers, ATMs, and ticket windows. Outside, the pedestrian underpass by the McDonald's has a TI and leads you beneath the busy road (first set of exits: tram stop; end of corridor: shopping mall at the edge of the Old Town).

The easiest choice for reaching your hotel is to hop in a **taxi** (which shouldn't cost more than 15 zł to any of my recommended hotels). Alternatively, to reach the heart of the Main Town, you can **walk** 15 minutes: Go through underpass, exit to the right, circle around the right side of Cinema City, and follow the busy road until you reach LOT airlines office, then head left toward all the brick towers. Riding the **tram** can shave a few minutes off this walk (buy tickets—*bilety*—at the *RUCH* kiosk by track 4 or at any window marked *Bilety ZKM* in pedestrian underpass; access tram stop via underpass, then board tram #2, #3, #6, #8, or #11 going to the right with your back to the station; go just one stop to Brama Wyżynna, in front of the LOT airlines office).

By Plane: Gdańsk's newly expanded airport, named for Lech Wałęsa, is about five miles west of the city center (airport code: GDN, tel. 58-348-1163, www.airport.gdansk.pl). In the arrivals area, you'll find a helpful TI and ATMs. You have several ways to get downtown: bus, shuttle, taxi, or (possibly) airport train. Public **bus** #210 connects the airport with downtown, stopping near the main train station and at Brama Wyżynna, near the heart of the Main Town (take it in the direction of Orunia; 3 zł, buy ticket at machine at stop—takes coins, small bills, and credit cards—or buy on board for a bit more; 2/hour on weekdays, 1/hour on weekends, 40 minutes, exit terminal and turn left to find bus stop). The **Airportbus shuttle** zips you directly to various points downtown, though the schedule is sporadic and it must be booked in advance (9-12 zł depending on where you go, various companies including www.mpapoland.pl). The 25-minute **taxi** ride into town will cost you about 50-60 zł. A new **airport train** is expected to start running (likely in late 2015 or early 2016); you'll ride this "metropolitan line" from the terminal to the end of the line at Gdańsk Wrzeszcz; from there you can easily transfer to the regional SKM train line that takes you the rest of the way to the main train station or Gdańsk Śródmieście station (about 30 minutes total; ask for details at the TI in the arrivals area).

HELPFUL HINTS

Blue Monday: Off-season, most of Gdańsk's museums are closed Monday. In the busy summertime, the Gdańsk Historical Museum branches are open—and free—for limited hours on Monday. If museums are closed, Monday is a good day to visit churches or take a side-trip to Sopot (but not to Malbork Castle, which is also closed Mon).

Internet Access: You'll find several free Wi-Fi hotspots in major tourist zones around central Gdańsk.

St. Dominic's Fair: Each summer for three weeks around St. Dominic's Day (last week in July through first half of August), Gdańsk is packed with visitors for its venerable St. Dominic's Fair. You'll find otherwise stately streets jammed with stalls selling crafts and edibles, concert stages (there's a lot of free music), and people from all over Poland milling about. While this is a huge draw, as long as you have a hotel booked (well in advance), the fair has surprisingly little impact on sights or restaurants.

GETTING AROUND GDAŃSK

Everything is within easy walking distance of my recommended hotels. Public transportation is generally unnecessary for sightseers on a short visit, but it's useful for reaching outlying sights such as Oliwa Cathedral, Westerplatte, Sopot, Gdynia, and Hel (specific transportation options for these places are described in each listing).

By Public Transportation: Gdańsk's trams and buses work on the same tickets: Choose between a single-ride ticket (3 zł), one-hour ticket (3.60 zł), and 24-hour ticket (12 zł). Major stops have handy ticket machines, which take coins, small bills, and credit cards. Otherwise, buy tickets *(bilety)* at kiosks marked *RUCH* or *Bilety ZKM,* or pay a little more to buy tickets on board. In the city center, the stops worth knowing about are Plac Solidarności (near the shipyards and European Solidarity Center), Gdańsk Główny (in front of the main train station), and Brama Wyżynna (near the Upland Gate and the new Gdańsk Śródmieście commuter train station). When buying tickets, don't confuse *ZKM* (the company that runs Gdańsk city transit) with *SKM* (the company that runs commuter trains to outlying destinations).

One public bus worth knowing about is Gdańsk's **bus #100.** Every 20 minutes, this made-for-tourists minibus (designed to navigate the twisty streets of the town center) makes a loop through the Old Town and Main Town, with strategic stops near Mariacka street, just south of the Royal Way, at the main train station, and near Solidarity Square. As this is a new service, confirm that it's running and get details at the TI (covered by regular

Gdańsk at a Gdlance

▲▲▲**Royal Way/Ulica Długa Walk** Gdańsk's colorful show-piece main drag, cutting a picturesque swath through the heart of the wealthy burghers' neighborhood. **Hours:** Always open. See page 442.

▲▲▲**Solidarity Sights and Gdańsk Shipyard** Home to the beginning of the end of Eastern European communism, housing a towering monument and an excellent museum. **Hours:** Memorial and shipyard gate—always open. European Solidarity Center exhibit—daily May-Sept 10:00-20:00, Oct-April 10:00-18:00. See page 469.

▲▲**Main Town Hall** Ornately decorated meeting rooms, town artifacts, and climbable tower with sweeping views. **Hours:** Mid-June-mid-Sept Mon-Thu 9:00-16:00, Fri-Sat 10:00-18:00, Sun 10:00-16:00; mid-Sept-mid-June Tue 10:00-13:00, Wed-Sat 10:00-16:00, Thu until 18:00, Sun 11:00-16:00, closed Mon. See page 460.

▲▲**Artus Court** Grand meeting hall for guilds of Golden Age Gdańsk, boasting an over-the-top tiled stove. **Hours:** Same as Main Town Hall. See page 461.

▲▲**St. Mary's Church** Giant red-brick church crammed full of Gdańsk history. **Hours:** June-Sept Mon-Sat 9:00-18:30, Sun 13:00-18:30; closes progressively earlier off-season. See page 451.

▲**Amber Museum** High-tech exhibit of valuable golden globs of petrified tree sap. **Hours:** Same as Main Town Hall, above. See page 458.

▲**Uphagen House** Tourable 18th-century interior, typical of the pretty houses that line ulica Długa. **Hours:** Same as Main Town Hall. See page 459.

transit ticket, may run in summer only).

By Taxi: Taxis cost about 8 zł to start, then 2-3 zł per kilometer (a bit more at night). Find a taxi stand, or call a cab (try Neptun, tel. 19686; or Dejan, tel. 58-19628).

Tours in Gdańsk

Private Guides

Hiring a local guide is an exceptional value. **Agnieszka Syroka**—youthful, bubbly, and personable—is a wonderful guide. She has a big SUV for tours of Malbork Castle and the region, too (400

▲**National Maritime Museum** Sprawling exhibit on all aspects of the nautical life, housed in several venues (including the landmark medieval Crane and a permanently moored steamship) connected by a ferry boat. **Hours:** July-Aug daily 10:00-18:00; Sept-Oct and March-June Tue-Sun 10:00-16:00, closed Mon; Nov-Feb Tue-Sun 10:00-15:00, closed Mon. See page 463.

Historical Zone of the Free City of Gdańsk Tiny museum examining Gdańsk's unique status as a "Free City" between the World Wars. **Hours:** Tue-Sun 12:00-17:00, until 18:00 May-Aug, closed Mon year-round. See page 462.

Archaeological Museum Decent collection of artifacts from this region's past. **Hours:** July-Aug Tue-Fri 9:00-17:00, Sat-Sun 10:00-17:00; Sept-June Tue and Thu-Fri 8:00-16:00, Wed 9:00-17:00, Sat-Sun 10:00-16:00; closed Mon year-round. See page 462.

National Museum in Gdańsk Ho-hum art collection with a single blockbuster highlight: Hans Memling's remarkable *Last Judgment* altarpiece. **Hours:** June-Aug Tue-Wed and Fri-Sun 10:00-17:00, Thu 12:00-19:00; May and Sept Tue-Sun 10:00-17:00; Oct-April Tue-Fri 9:00-16:00, Sat-Sun 10:00-17:00, closed Mon year-round. See page 475.

"Blue Lion" Archaeological Education Center Kid-friendly exhibit about medieval Gdańsk. **Hours:** May-Aug Tue-Sun 10:00-18:00, Sept-April Tue-Sun 9:00-17:00, closed Mon year-round. See page 477.

Oliwa Cathedral Suburban church with long, skinny nave and playful organ. **Hours:** Church open long hours daily; frequent organ concerts in summer. See page 477.

zł for up to 4 hours, more for all day, mobile 502-554-584, www. tourguidegdansk.com, asyroka@interia.pl or syroka.agnieszka@ gmail.com). **Jacek "Jake" Podhorski,** who teaches economics at the local university, guides in the summer. He's been around long enough to have fascinating personal memories of the communist days (400 zł/3 hours, 100 zł extra with his car, mobile 603-170-761, ekojpp@univ.gda.pl).

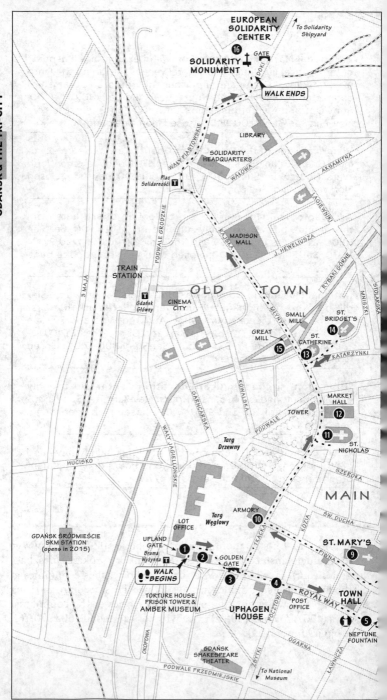

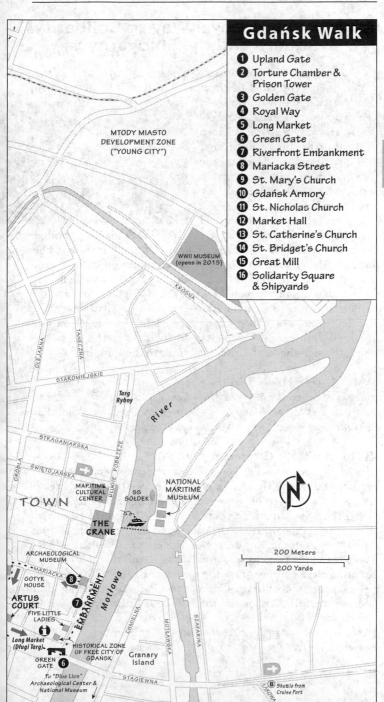

Gdańsk Walk

1. Upland Gate
2. Torture Chamber & Prison Tower
3. Golden Gate
4. Royal Way
5. Long Market
6. Green Gate
7. Riverfront Embankment
8. Mariacka Street
9. St. Mary's Church
10. Gdańsk Armory
11. St. Nicholas Church
12. Market Hall
13. St. Catherine's Church
14. St. Bridget's Church
15. Great Mill
16. Solidarity Square & Shipyards

MŁODY MIASTO DEVELOPMENT ZONE ("YOUNG CITY")

WWII MUSEUM (opens in 2015)

KROSNA

STAROMIEJSKIE

Targ Rybny

River

STRAGANIARSKA

TANECZNA

OLEJARNA

ŚWIĘTOJAŃSKA

GROBLA

MARITIME CULTURAL CENTER

SS SOŁDEK

DŁUGIE POBRZEŻE

NATIONAL MARITIME MUSEUM

TOWN

THE CRANE

ARCHAEOLOGICAL MUSEUM

MARIACKA

GOTYK HOUSE

ARTUS COURT

FIVE LITTLE LADIES

Long Market (Długi Targ)

GREEN GATE

To "Dług Lwów" Archaeological Center & National Museum

EMBANKMENT

Motława

HISTORICAL ZONE OF FREE CITY OF GDAŃSK

CHMIELNA

Granary Island

STAGIEWNA

MOTŁAWSKA

SZAFARNIA

200 Meters

200 Yards

Shuttle from Cruise Port

SKOWA

Gdańsk Walk: Royal Way to Solidarity Square and the Shipyards

In the 16th and 17th centuries, Gdańsk was Poland's wealthiest city, with gorgeous architecture (much of it in the Flemish Mannerist style) rivaling that in the two historic capitals, Kraków and Warsaw. During this Golden Age, Polish kings would visit this city of well-to-do Hanseatic League merchants and gawk along the same route trod by tourists today.

The following self-guided walk (rated ▲▲▲) introduces you to the best of Gdańsk. It bridges the two historic centers (the Main Town and the Old Town), dips into St. Mary's Church (the city's most important church), and ends at the famous shipyards and Solidarity Square (where Poland began what ultimately brought down the USSR). I've divided the walk into two parts (making it easier to split up, if you like): The first half focuses on a loop through the Main Town (with most of the high-profile sights), while the second part carries on northward, through the less touristy Old Town to the shipyards.

PART 1: THE MAIN TOWN

• *Begin at the west end of the Main Town, just beyond the last gate at the edge of the busy road (at a road sign that says* Sztokholm...*a reminder that the car ferry to Sweden leaves from near here).*

❶ Upland Gate (Brama Wyżynna)

The Main Town's fortifications were expanded with a Renaissance wall bound by the Upland Gate (built in 1588). "Upland" refers to the hills you see beyond—considered high country in this flat region. Standing with your back to the busy arterial (which traces the old moat), study the gate. Find its three coats of arms (the black eagle for Royal Prussia, the crowned white eagle for Poland, and the two crosses for Gdańsk). Recall that this city has, for almost the entirety of its history before the mid-20th century, been (at least) bicultural—German and Polish, coexisting more or less peacefully. Also notice the little wheels that once hoisted a drawbridge.

• *It's a straight line from here to the river. Walk through the arch (which houses a TI) to the next arch, just a few steps ahead.*

❷ Torture Chamber (Katownia) and Prison Tower (Wieża Więzienna)

The tall, Gothic brick gate before you was part of an earlier protective wall made useless after the Renaissance walls were built in 1588. While today these structures house the Amber Museum (described later), it's free to walk through the evocative passage (except on Mon, when the passage is closed). Inside, find gargoyles (on the left, a town specialty) and the shackles from which prisoners were hung (on the right). Look up at the inside of the high gable to the headless man, identifying this as the torture chamber. This old jail—with its 15-foot-thick walls—was used as a prison even in modern times, under Nazi occupation.

As you leave the Torture Chamber and Prison Tower, look to your left (100 yards away) to see a long, brick building with four fancy, uniform gables. This is the **Armory** (Zbrojownia), one of the finest examples of Dutch Renaissance architecture anywhere. Though this part of the building appears to have the facades of four separate houses, it's a kind of urban camouflage to hide its real purpose from potential attackers. But there's at least one clue to what the building is really for: Notice the exploding cannonballs at the tops of the turrets. (We'll get a better look at the Armory from the other side, later in this walk.)

The round, pointy-topped tower next to the Armory is the **Straw Tower** (Baszta Słomiana). Gunpowder was stored here, and the roof was straw—so if it exploded, it would blow its top without destroying the walls.

• Straight ahead, the final and fanciest gate between you and the Main Town is the...

❸ Golden Gate (Złota Brama)

While the other gates were defensive, this one's purely ornamental. The four women up top represent virtues that the people of Gdańsk should exhibit toward outsiders (left to right): Peace, Freedom,

Prosperity, and Fame. The gold-lettered inscription, a psalm in medieval German, compares Gdańsk to Jerusalem: famous and important. Directly above the arch is the Gdańsk coat of arms: two white crosses under a crown on a red shield. We'll see this symbol all over town. Photographers love the view of the Main Town framed in this arch. Inside the arch, study the old photos showing the 1945 bomb damage. On the left is the glorious view you just enjoyed...ravaged by war. And on the right is a heartbreaking aerial view of the city in

1945, when 80 percent of its buildings were in ruins.

• *Passing through the Golden Gate, you reach the Main Town's main drag.*

❹ The Royal Way

Before you stretches ulica Długa (cleverly called the "Long Street"), the main promenade of what, 600 years ago, was the biggest and richest city in Poland (thanks to its profitable ties to the Hanseatic League of merchant cities). This promenade is nicknamed the "Royal Way" because (just as in Warsaw and Kraków) the king would follow this route when visiting town.

Walk half a block, and then look back at the Golden Gate. The women on top of this side represent virtues the people of Gdańsk should cultivate in themselves (left to right): Wisdom, Piety, Justice, and Concord (if an arrow's broken, let's take it out of the quiver and fix it). The inscription—sharing a bit of wisdom as apropos today as it was in 1612—reads, "Concord makes small countries develop, and discord makes big countries fall." Gdańsk was cosmopolitan and exceptionally tolerant in the Middle Ages, attracting a wide range of people, including many who were persecuted elsewhere: Jews, Scots, Dutch, Flemish, Italians, Germans, and more. Members of each group brought with them strands of their culture, which they wove into the tapestry of this city—demonstrated by the eclectic homes along this street. Each facade and each gable were different, as nobles and aristocrats wanted to display their wealth. On my last visit, a traveler seeing this street for the first time gasped to me, "It's like stepping into a Fabergé egg."

During Gdańsk's Golden Age, these houses were taxed based on frontage (like the homes lining Amsterdam's canals)—so they were built skinny and deep. The widest houses belonged to the super-elite. Different as they are from the outside, every house had the same general plan inside. Each had three parts, starting with the front and moving back: First was a fancy drawing room, to show off for visitors. Then came a narrow corridor to the back rooms—often along the side of an inner courtyard. Because the houses had only a few windows facing the outer street, this courtyard provided much-needed sunlight to the rest of the house. The residential quarters were in the back, where the family actually lived: bedroom, kitchen, office. To see the interior of one of these homes, pay a visit to the interesting **Uphagen House** (at #12, on the right, a block and a half in front of the Golden Gate; described later).

This lovely street wasn't always so lively and carefree. At the end of World War II, the Royal Way was in ruins. That epic war actually began here, in what was then the "Free City of Danzig." Following World War I, nobody could decide what to do with this influential and multiethnic city, so rather than assign it to Germany or Poland, it was set apart as its own little autonomous statelet. In 1939, Danzig was 80 percent German-speaking—enough for Hitler to consider it his. And so, on September 1 of that year, the Nazis seized it in one day with relatively minor damage (though the attack on the Polish military garrison on the city's Westerplatte peninsula lasted a week).

But six years later, when the Soviets arrived (March 30, 1945), the city was left devastated. This was the first major, traditionally German city that the Red Army took on their march toward Berlin. And, while it was easy for the Soviets to seize the almost empty city, the commander then insisted that it be leveled, building by building—in retaliation for all the pain the Nazis had caused in Russia. (Soviets didn't destroy nearby Gdynia, which they considered Polish, not German.) Soviet officers turned a blind eye as their soldiers raped and brutalized residents. An entire order of horrified nuns committed suicide by throwing themselves into the river.

It was only thanks to detailed drawings and photographs that these buildings could be so carefully reconstructed. Notice the cheap plaster facades done in the 1950s—rough times under communism, in the decade after World War II. (Most of the town's medieval brick was shipped to Warsaw for a communist-sponsored "rebuild the capital first" campaign.) While the fine facades were restored, the buildings behind the facades were completely rebuilt to modern standards.

Just beyond Uphagen House, the **Cukiernia Sowa** ("The Owl," on the right at #13) is *the* place for cakes and coffee. Directly across the street, **Grycan** (at #73) has been a favorite for ice cream here for generations.

Just a few doors down, on the left, are some of the most strik-ing **facades** along the Royal Way. The blue-and-white house with the three giant heads is from the 19th century, when the hot style was eclecticism—borrowing bits and pieces from various architectural eras. This was one of the few houses on the street that survived World War II.

At the next corner on the right is the huge, blocky, red **post office,** which doesn't quite fit with the skinny facades lining the rest of the street. Step inside. With doves fluttering under an airy glass atrium, the interior's a class act. Directly across the street, the candy shop **(Ciuciu Cukier Artist)** is often filled with children clamoring to see

Gdańsk History

Visitors to Gdańsk are surprised at how "un-Polish" the city's history is. In this cultural melting pot of German, Dutch, and Flemish merchants (with a smattering of Italians and Scots), Poles were only a small part of the picture until the city became exclusively Polish after World War II. However, in Gdańsk, cultural backgrounds traditionally took a back seat to the bottom line. Wealthy Gdańsk was always known for its economic pragmatism—no matter who was in charge, merchants here made money.

Gdańsk is Poland's gateway to the waters of Europe, where its main river (the Vistula) meets the Baltic Sea. The town was first mentioned in the 10th century, and was seized in 1308 by the Teutonic Knights (who called it "Danzig"; for more on the Teutonic Knights, see page 502). The Knights encouraged other Germans to settle on the Baltic coast, and gradually turned Gdańsk into a wealthy city. In 1361, Gdańsk joined the Hanseatic League, a trade federation of mostly Germanic merchant towns that provided mutual security. By the 15th century, Gdańsk was a leading member of this mighty network, which virtually dominated trade in northern Europe (and also included Toruń, Kraków, Lübeck, Hamburg, Bremen, Bruges, Bergen, Tallinn, Novgorod, and nearly a hundred other cities).

In 1454, the people of Gdańsk rose up against the Teutonic Knights, burning down their castle and forcing them out of the city. Three years later, the Polish king borrowed money from wealthy Gdańsk families to hire Czech mercenaries to take the Teutonic Knights' main castle, Malbork (described in the next chapter). In exchange, the Gdańsk merchants were granted special privileges, including exclusive export rights. Gdańsk now acted as a middleman for much of the trade passing through Polish lands, and paid only a modest annual tribute to the Polish king.

The 16th and 17th centuries were Gdańsk's Golden Age. Now a part of the Polish kingdom, the city had access to an enormous hinterland of natural resources to export—yet it maintained a privileged, semi-independent status. Like Amsterdam, Gdańsk became a progressive and booming merchant city. Its mostly Germanic and Dutch burghers imported Dutch, Flemish, and Italian architects to give their homes an appropriately Hanseatic flourish. At a time of religious upheaval in the rest of Europe, Gdańsk became known for its tolerance—a place that opened

lollipop-making demos. Step in and inhale a universal whiff of childhood.

A few doors farther down, on the left at #62, pop into the **Millennium Gallery** amber shop (which would love to give you an educational amber polishing demo) to see the fascinating collection of old-timey photos, letting you directly compare Gdańsk's cityscape before and after the WWII destruction.

its doors to all visitors (many Mennonites and Scottish religious refugees emigrated here). It was also a haven for great thinkers, including philosopher Arthur Schopenhauer and scientist Daniel Fahrenheit (who invented the mercury thermometer).

Gdańsk declined, along with the rest of Poland, in the late 18th century, and became a part of Prussia (today's northern Germany) during the Partitions. But the people of Gdańsk—even those of German heritage—had taken pride in their independence and weren't enthusiastic about being ruled from Berlin. After World War I, in a unique compromise to appease its complex ethnic makeup, Gdańsk did not fall under German or Polish control, but once again became an independent city-state: the Free City of Danzig (populated by 400,000 ethnic Germans and 15,000 Poles). The city, along with the so-called Polish Corridor connecting it to Polish lands, effectively cut off Germany from its northeastern territory. On September 1, 1939, Adolf Hitler started World War II when he invaded Gdańsk in order to bring it back into the German fold. Later, nearly 80 percent of the city was destroyed when the Soviets "liberated" it from Nazi control.

After World War II, Gdańsk officially became part of Poland, and was painstakingly reconstructed (mostly replicating the buildings of its Golden Age). In 1970, and again in 1980, the shipyard of Gdańsk witnessed strikes and demonstrations that would lead to the fall of European communism. Poland's great anti-communist hero and first post-communist president, Lech Wałęsa, is Gdańsk's most famous resident, and still lives here. When he flies around the world to give talks, he leaves from Gdańsk's "Lech Wałęsa Airport."

A city with a recent past that's both tragic and uplifting, Gdańsk celebrated its 1,000th birthday in 1997. Very roughly, the city has spent about 700 years as an independent entity, and about 300 years under Germanic overlords (the Teutonic Knights, Prussia, and the Nazis). But today, Gdańsk is decidedly its own city. And, as if eager to prove it, Gdańsk is making big improvements at a stunning pace: new museums (the European Solidarity Center), cultural facilities (the Shakespeare Theater), sports venues (a stadium that resembles a blob of amber, built for the 2012 Euro Cup tournament), and an ongoing surge of renovation and refurbishment that has the gables of the atmospheric Hanseatic quarter gleaming once again.

Above the next door, notice the colorful **scenes.** These are slices of life from 17th-century Gdańsk: drinking, talking, buying, playing music. The ship is a *koga*, a typical symbol of Hanseatic ports like Gdańsk.

A couple of doors down—still on the left—is **Neptun Cinema** (marked *KINO*). In the 1980s, this was the only movie theater in the city, and locals lined up for blocks to get in. Old-timers remember coming here with their grandparents to see a full day of cartoons. Now, as with traditional main-street cinemas in the US, this theater is threatened by the rising popularity of multiplexes outside the town center.

Across the street from the theater are the fancy facades of three houses belonging to the very influential medieval **Ferber family,** which produced many burghers, mayors, and even a bishop. On the house with the little dog over the door (#29), look for the heads in the circular medallions. These are Caesars of Rome. At the top of the building is Mr. Ferber's answer to the constant question, "Why build such an elaborate house?"—*PRO INVIDIA,* "For the sake of envy."

A few doors down, on the right, is Gdańsk's most scenically situated milk bar, the recommended **Bar Mleczny Neptun.** Back in communist times, these humble cafeterias were subsidized to give workers an affordable place to eat out. To this day, they offer simple and very cheap grub.

Next door (at #35) is the **Russian Culture Center,** with Russian movies and art exhibits. With the dark past and the Polish support for Ukraine in the recent escalations of tensions there, this is a poignant address.

Before you stands the **Main Town Hall** (Ratusz Głównego Miasta) with its mighty brick clock tower. Consider climbing its observation tower and visiting its superb interior, which features ornately decorated meeting rooms for the city council (described later).

• *Just beyond the Main Town Hall, ulica Długa widens and becomes...*

➎ The Long Market (Długi Targ)

Step from the Long Street into the Long Market, and do a slow, 360-degree spin to appreciate the amazing array of proud architecture here in a city center that rivals the magnificent Grand Place in Brussels. The centerpiece of this square is one of Gdańsk's

most important landmarks, the statue of **Neptune**—god of the sea. He's a fitting symbol for a city that dominates the maritime life of Poland. Behind him is another worthwhile museum, the **Artus Court.** Step up to the magnificent door and study the golden relief just above, celebrating the Vistula River (in so many ways the lifeblood of the Polish nation): Lady Vistula is exhausted after her heroic journey, and is finally carried by Neptune to her ultimate destination, the Baltic Sea. (This is just a preview of the ornate art that fills the interior of this fine building—described later.)

Midway down the Long Market (on the right, across from the Hard Rock Café) is a glass case with the **thermometer and barometer of Daniel Fahrenheit.** Although that scientist was born here, he did his groundbreaking work in Amsterdam.

• *At the end of the Long Market is the...*

❻ Green Gate (Zielona Brama)

This huge gate (named for the Green Bridge just beyond) was actually built as a residence for visiting kings...who usually preferred to stay back by Neptune instead (maybe because the river, just on the other side of this gate, stank). It might not have been good enough for kings and queens, but it's plenty fine for a former president: Lech Wałęsa's office is upstairs (see the plaque on the left side, *Biuro Lecha Wałęsy*). His windows, up in the gable, overlook the Long Market. A few steps down the skinny lane to the left is the endearing little **Historical Zone of the Free City of Gdańsk** museum, which explains the interwar period when "Danzig" was an independent and bicultural city-state (described later).

• *Now go through the gate, walk out onto the Green Bridge, anchor yourself in a niche on the left, and look downstream.*

❼ Riverfront Embankment

The Motława River—a side channel of the mighty Vistula—flows into the nearby Baltic Sea. This port was the source of Gdańsk's phenomenal Golden Age wealth. This embankment was jam-packed in its heyday, the 14th and 15th centuries. It was so crowded with boats that you hardly would have been able to see the water, and boats had to pay a time-based moorage fee for tying up to a post.

Look back at the Green Gate and notice that these bricks are much smaller than the locally made ones we saw earlier on this walk. These bricks are Dutch: Boats from Holland would come here empty of cargo, but with a load of bricks for ballast. Traders filled their ships with goods for the return trip, leaving the bricks behind.

The old-fashioned **galleons** and other tour boats moored nearby depart hourly for a fun cruise to Westerplatte (where on September 1, 1939, Germans fired the first shots of World War II) and back. Though kitschy, the galleons are a fun way to get out on the water (details on page 478).

Across the river is **Granary Island** (Spichrze), where grain was stored until it could be taken away by ships. Before World War II, there were some 400 granaries here. Today, much of the island is still in ruins while developers make their plans. Recently, the city ringed the island with an inviting boardwalk, which offers a restful escape from the city and fine views across the narrow river to the embankment. In the summer, sometimes they erect a big Ferris wheel here. And someday there will be several more rebuilt granaries in this area (likely mixed with modern buildings) to match the ones you already see on either side of the bridge. The three rebuilt granaries downstream, in the distance on the next island, house exhibits for the National Maritime Museum (described later).

From your perch on the bridge, look down the embankment (about 500 yards, on the left) and find the huge wooden **Crane (Żuraw)** bulging over the water. This monstrous 15th-century crane—a rare example of medieval port technology—was once used for loading and repairing ships...beginning a shipbuilding tradition that continued to the days of Lech Wałęsa. The crane mechanism was operated by several workers scrambling around in giant hamster wheels. Treading away to engage the gears and pulleys, they could lift 4 tons up 30 feet, or 2 tons up 90 feet.

• *Walk along the embankment about halfway to the Crane, passing the lower embankment, with excursion boats heading to the Westerplatte monument. Pause when you reach the big brick building with green window frames and a tower. This red-brick fort houses the **Archaeological Museum** (described later). Its collection includes the five ancient stones in a small garden just outside its door (on the left). These are the **Prussian Hags**—mysterious sculptures from the second century A.D. (each described in posted plaques).*

Turn left through the gate in the middle of the brick building. You'll find yourself on the most charming lane in town...

❽ Mariacka Street

The calm, atmospheric "Mary's Street" leads from the embankment to St. Mary's Church. Stroll the length of it, enjoying the most romantic lane in Gdańsk. The **porches** extending out into the street, with access to cellars underneath, were a common feature in Gdańsk's Golden Age. For practical reasons, these were only restored on this street after the war. Notice how the porches are bordered with fine stone relief panels and gargoyles attached to storm drains. If you get stuck there in a hard rainstorm, you'll understand why in Polish these are called "pukers." Enjoy a little amber comparison-shopping. As you stroll up to the towering brick St. Mary's Church, imagine the entire city like this cobbled lane of proud merchants' homes, with street music, delightful facades, and brick church towers high above.

Look up at the church tower viewpoint—filled with people who hiked 409 steps for the view. Our next stop is the church, which you'll enter on the far side under the tower. Walk around the left side of the church, appreciating the handmade 14th-century bricks on the right and the plain post-WWII facades on the left. (Reconstructing the Royal Way was better funded. Here, the priority was simply getting people housed again.) In the distance is the fancy facade of the Armory (where you'll head after visiting the church).

• But first, go inside...

❾ St. Mary's Church (Kościół Mariacki)

Of Gdańsk's 13 medieval red-brick churches, St. Mary's (rated ▲▲) is the one you must visit. It's the largest brick church in the world—with a footprint bigger than a football field (350 feet long and 210 feet wide), it can accommodate 20,000 standing worshippers.

Cost and Hours: 4 zł, June-Sept Mon-Sat 9:00-18:30, Sun 13:00-18:30, closes progressively earlier off-season.

Visiting the Church: Inside, sit directly under the fine carved and painted 17th-century Protestant pulpit, midway down the nave, to get oriented.

Overview: Built from 1343 to 1502 by the Teutonic Knights (who wanted a suitable centerpiece for their newly captured main city), St. Mary's remains an important symbol of Gdańsk. The church started out Catholic, became Lutheran in the mid-1500s, and then became Catholic again after World War II. (Remember, Gdańsk was a Germanic city before World War II and part of the big postwar demographic shove, when Germans were sent west, and Poles from the east relocated here. Desperate, cold, and homeless, the new Polish residents moved into what was left of the German homes.) While the church was originally frescoed from top to bottom, the Lutherans whitewashed the entire place. Today, some of the 16th-century whitewash has been peeled back (behind the high altar—we'll see this area soon), revealing a bit of the original frescoes. The floor is paved with 500 gravestones

of merchant families. Many of these were cracked when bombing sent the brick roof crashing down in 1945.

Most Gothic stone churches are built of stone in the basilica style—with a high nave in the middle, shorter aisles on the side, and flying buttresses to support the weight. (Think of Paris' Notre-Dame.) But with no handy source of stone available locally, most Polish churches are built of brick, which won't work with the basilica design. So, like all Gdańsk churches, St. Mary's is a "hall church"—with three naves the same height and no exterior buttresses.

Also like other Gdańsk churches, St. Mary's gave refuge to the Polish people after the communist government declared martial law in 1981. When a riot broke out and violence seemed imminent, people flooded into churches, knowing that the ZOMO riot police wouldn't follow them inside.

Most of the church decorations are original. A few days before the Soviets arrived to "liberate" the city in 1945, locals—knowing what was in store—hid precious items in the countryside. Take some time now to see a few of the highlights.

• *From this seat, you can see most of what we'll visit in the church: As you face the altar, the astronomical clock is at 10 o'clock, the Ferber family medallion is at 1 o'clock, the Priests' Chapel is at 3 o'clock (under a tall colorful window), and the magnificent 17th-century organ is directly behind you (it's played at each Mass and during free concerts on Fri in summer).*

Pulpit: For Protestants, the pulpit is important. Designed as an impressive place from which to share the Word of God in the people's language, it's located mid-nave, so all can hear.

• *Opposite the pulpit is the moving...*

Priests' Chapel: The 1965 statue of Christ weeping commemorates 2,779 Polish chaplains executed by the Nazis because they were priests. See the grainy black-and-white photo of one about to be shot, above on the right.

• *Head up the nave to the...*

High Altar: The main altar, beautifully carved in 1517, is a triptych showing the coronation of Mary. She is surrounded by the Trinity: flanked by God and Jesus, with the dove representing the Holy Spirit overhead. The church's medieval stained glass was destroyed in 1945. Poland's biggest stained-glass window, behind the altar, is from 1980.

• *Start circling around the right side of the altar. Look right to find (high on a pillar) the big, opulent family marker.*

Ferber Family Medallion: The falling baby (under the crown) is Constantine Ferber. As a precocious child, li'l Constantine leaned out his window on the Royal Way to see the king's processional come through town. He slipped and fell, but landed in a salesman's barrel of fish. Constantine grew up to become the mayor of Gdańsk.

• *As you continue around behind the altar, search high above you, on the walls to your right, to spot those restored pre-Reformation frescoes. Directly behind the altar, under the big window, is the...*

Empty Glass Case: This case was designed to hold Hans Memling's *Last Judgment* painting, which used to be in this church, but is currently being held hostage by the National Museum. To counter the museum's claim that the church wasn't a good environment for such a precious work, the priest had this display case built—but that still wasn't enough to convince the museum to give the painting back. (You'll see a small replica of the painting in the rear of this church, but the real thing is in the National Museum.)

• *Now circle back the way you came to the area in front of the main altar, and proceed straight ahead into the transept. High on the wall to your right, look for the...*

Astronomical Clock: This 42-foot-tall clock is supposedly the biggest wooden clock in the world. Below it is an elaborate circular calendar that, like a medieval computer, calculates on which day each saint's festival day falls in different years (see the little guy on the left, with the pointer). Above are zodiac signs and the time (back then, the big hand was all you needed). Way up on top, Adam and Eve are naked and ready to ring the bell. Adam's been swinging his clapper at the top of the hour since 1473...but sadly, the clock is broken.

• *A few steps in front of the clock is a modern chapel with the...*

Memorial to the Polish Victims of the 2010 Plane Crash: The gold-shrouded Black Madonna honors the 96 victims of an air disaster that the killed much of Poland's government—including the president and first lady—during a terrible storm over Russia. The main tomb is for Maciej Płażyński, from Gdańsk, who was leader of the parliament. On the left, the jagged statue has bits of the wreckage and lists each victim by name.

• *In a small chapel in the rear corner of the church—on the far right with your back to the high altar—you'll find the...*

***Pietà* and Memling Replica:** The *pietà,* carved of limestone and painted in 1410, is by the Master of Gdańsk. In the same room is a musty old copy of Memling's *Last Judgment*—the exquisite original once graced this very chapel. If you're not planning to go see it at the National Museum, you could read the description on page 476 now.

• *Next door are stairs leading to the...*

Church Tower: You can climb 409 steps to burn off some pierogi and earn a grand city view (5 zł, Mon-Sat 9:00-17:00, Sun 13:00-17:30). It's a long hike (and you'll know it—every 10th step is numbered). But because the viewpoint is surrounded by a roof, the views are distant and may not be worth the effort. The first third is up a tight, medieval spiral staircase. Then you'll walk through the eerie, cavernous area between the roof and the ceiling, before huffing up steep concrete steps that surround the square tower (as you spiral up, up, up around the bells). Finally you'll climb a little metal ladder and pop out at the viewpoint.

• *Leaving the church, angle left and continue straight up ulica Piwna ("Beer Street") toward the sprightly facade of the Armory.*

⓾ The Gdańsk Armory (Zbrojownia)

The 1605 **Armory,** which we saw from a distance at the start of this walk, is one of the best examples of Dutch Renaissance architecture in Europe. Athena, the goddess of war and wisdom, stands in the center, amid motifs of war and ornamental pukers.

• *If you want to make your walk a loop, you're just a block away from where we started (to the left). But there's much more to see. Facing the Armory, turn right and start the second half of this walk.*

PART 2: THROUGH THE OLD TOWN TO THE SHIPYARDS

• *From here we'll work our way out of the Main Town and head into the Old Town, toward Solidarity Square and the shipyards. We'll be walking along this street (which changes names a couple of times) nearly all the way. Keep in mind that this part of the walk ends at the European Solidary Center's fine museum. You'll want plenty of time to tour the museum and linger over its exhibits, so if you're already pooped or it's getting late in the day, consider finishing this walk another time.*

From the Armory, head down Kołodziejska, which quickly becomes Węglarska. After two blocks (that is, one block before the big market hall), detour to the right down Świętojańska and use the side door to enter the brick church.

⓫ St. Nicholas Church (Kościół Św. Mikołaja)

Near the end of World War II, when the Soviet army reached Gdańsk on its march westward, they were given the order to burn all the churches. Only this one survived—because it happened to be dedicated to Russia's patron saint. As the best-preserved church in town, it has a more impressive interior than the others, with lavish black-and-gold Baroque altars.

• *Backtrack out to the main street and continue to the right, passing a row of seniors selling their grown and foraged edibles. Immediately after the church is Gdańsk's...*

⓬ Market Hall

Built in 1896 and renovated in 2005, Gdańsk's market hall is fun to explore. Appreciate the delicate steel-and-glass canopy overhead. This is a totally untouristy scene: You'll see everything from skintight *Polska* T-shirts, to wedding gowns, to maternity wear. The meat is downstairs, and the veggies are outside on the adjacent square. As this was once the center of a monastic community, the basement has the graves of medieval Dominican monks, which were exposed when the building was refurbished: Peer over the glass railing, and you'll see some of those scant remains.

Across the street from the Market Hall, a round, red-brick **tower,** part of the city's protective wall back in 1400, marks the

end of the Main Town and the beginning of the Old Town.
• *Another block up the street, on the right, is the huge...*

ⓑ St. Catherine's Church (Kościół Św. Katarzyny)

"Katy," as locals call it, is the oldest church in Gdańsk. In May of 2006, a carelessly discarded cigarette caused the church roof to burst into flames. Local people ran into the church and pulled everything outside, so nothing valuable was damaged; even the carillon bells were saved. However, the roof and wooden frame were totally destroyed. The people of Gdańsk were determined to rebuild this important symbol of the city. Within days of the fire, fundraising concerts were held to scrape together most of the money needed to raise the roof once more. Step inside. On the left side of the gate leading to the nave, photos show bomb damage. Farther in, on the left, are vivid photos of the more recent conflagration. The interior is evocative, with still-bare-brick walls that almost seem intentional—as if they're trying for an industrial-mod look.

• *The church hiding a block behind Katy—named for Catherine's daughter Bridget—has important ties to Solidarity and is worth a visit. Go around the right side of Katy and skirt the parking lot to find the entrance.*

ⓒ St. Bridget's Church (Kościół Św. Brygidy)

This was the home church of Lech Wałęsa during the tense days of the 1980s. The church and its priest, Henryk Jankowski, were particularly aggressive in supporting the ideals of Solidarity. Jankowski became a mouthpiece for the movement. In gratitude for the church's support, Wałęsa named his youngest daughter Brygida.

Cost and Hours: 2 zł, daily 10:00-18:00.

Visiting the Church: Head inside. For your visit, start at the high altar, then circle clockwise back to the entry.

The enormous, unfinished **high altar** is made entirely of amber—more than a thousand square feet of it. Features that are already in place include the Black Madonna of Częstochowa, a royal Polish eagle, and the Solidarity symbol (tucked below the Black Madonna). The structure, like a scaffold, holds pieces as they are completed and added to the ensemble. The video you may see playing overhead gives you a close-up look at the amber elements.

The wrought-iron gate of the adjacent **Chapel of Fatima** (right of main altar) recalls great battles and events in Polish history from 966 to 1939, with important dates boldly sparkling in gold. Some say the Polish Church is too political. But it was only through a politically engaged Church that this culture survived the Partitions of Poland over a century and a half, plus the brutal anti-religious policies of the communist period. The national soul of the Polish people—whether religious or not—is tied up in the Catholic faith.

Henryk Jankowski's tomb—a white marble box with red trim—is a bit farther to the right. Jankowski was a key hero during

Solidarity times; the tomb proclaims him *Kapelan Solidarności* ("Solidarity Chaplain"). But his public standing took a nosedive near the end of his life—thanks to ego-driven projects like his amber altar, as well as accusations of anti-Semitism and corruption. Forced to retire in 2007, Jankowski died in 2010. (An offering box is next to his tomb, if you'd like to donate to the amber altar project.)

In the rear corner, where a figure lies lifeless on the floor under a wall full of wooden crosses, is the tomb of Solidarity martyr **Jerzy Popiełuszko.** A courageous and famously outspoken Warsaw priest, in 1984 Popiełuszko was kidnapped, beaten, and murdered by the communist secret police. Notice that the figure's hands and feet are bound—as his body was found. The crosses are historic—each one was carried at various strikes against the communist regime. The communists believed they could break the spirit of the Poles with brutality—like the murder of Popiełuszko. But it only made the rebels stronger and more resolved to ultimately win their freedom. (Near the exit, on a monitor, a fascinating 12-minute video shows great moments of this church, with commentary by Lech Wałęsa himself.)

• *Return to the main street, turn right, and continue on. The big brick building ahead on the left, with the many windows, is the Great Mill. Walk past that and look down at the canal that once powered it.*

⓯ The Great Mill

This huge brick building dates from the 14th century. Look at the waterfalls and imagine standing here in 1400—with the mill's 18 wheels spinning 24/7, powering grindstones that produced 20 tons of flour a day. Like so much else here, the mill survived until 1945. Today the rebuilt structure houses a modern shopping mall.

The **park** just beyond the mill is worth a look. In the distance is the Old City Town Hall (Dutch Renaissance style, from 1595). The monument in the middle honors the 17th-century astronomer Jan Haweliusz. He's looking up at a giant, rust-colored wall with a map of the heavens. Haweliusz built the biggest telescopes of his era to better appreciate and understand the cosmos. Behind the mill stands the miller's home—its opulence indicates that, back

in the Middle Ages, there was a lot of money in grinding. Just steps into the family-friendly park is a fountain that brings shrieks of joy to children on hot summer days. Watching families enjoy this park, I'm struck that these are good times for Poland—stability, one of the EU's healthiest economies, and freedom. But next we walk through a stretch that, if you take away the colors, advertising, and smiles, reminds me of the dark days before 1989. And beyond that are the shipyards, where freedom from communism was born.

• *To get to the shipyards, keep heading straight up Rajska. You'll pass the modern Madison shopping mall. After another long block, jog right, passing to the right of the big, ugly, and green 1970s-era skyscraper. On your right, marked by the famous red sign on the roof, is today's* **Solidarity headquarters** *(which remains the strongest trade union in Poland, with 700,000 members, and is also active in many other countries). Just in front of the Solidarity building, you may see two big chunks of* **wall:** *a piece of the Berlin Wall and a stretch of the shipyard wall that Lech Wałęsa scaled to get inside and lead the strike. The message: What happened behind one wall eventually led to the fall of the other Wall.*

From here, hike on (about 100 yards) to the finale of this walk.

⑯ Solidarity Square and the Shipyards

Three tall crosses mark Solidarity Square and the rust-colored European Solidarity Center (with an excellent museum). For the exciting story of how Polish shipbuilders set in motion events that led to the end of the USSR, turn to page 464.

Sights in Gdańsk

MAIN TOWN (GŁÓWNE MIASTO)

The following sights are all in the Main Town, listed roughly in the order you'll see them on the self-guided walk of the Royal Way.

Gdańsk Historical Museum

The Gdańsk Historical Museum has four excellent branches: the Amber Museum, Uphagen House, Main Town Hall, and Artus Court. Along with St. Mary's Church (described on page 451), these are the four most important interiors in the Main Town. All have the same hours, but you must buy a separate ticket for each.

Cost and Hours: 10 zł apiece—except Main Town Hall, which is 12 zł; hours fluctuate, but typically open mid-June-mid-Sept Mon-Thu 9:00-16:00, Fri-Sat 10:00-18:00, Sun 10:00-16:00; mid-Sept-mid-June Tue 10:00-13:00, Wed-Sat 10:00-16:00, Thu until 18:00, Sun 11:00-16:00, closed Mon; last entry 30 minutes before closing.

Information: The museums share a phone number and website (central tel. 58-767-9100, www.mhmg.gda.pl).

▲Amber Museum (Muzeum Bursztynu)

Housed in a pair of connected brick towers (the former Prison Tower and Torture Chamber) just outside the Main Town's

Golden Gate, this museum has two oddly contradictory parts. One shows off Gdańsk's favorite local resource, amber, while the other focuses on implements of torture (cost and hours above, overpriced 1.5-hour audioguide—25 zł). You'll follow the one-way route through four exhibits on amber (with lots of stairs), and then walk the rampart to the other tower for a little torture. Exhibits are explained in English. For a primer before you visit, read the "All About Amber" sidebar.

Visiting the Museum: The exhibit has four parts: First, head up to the **second floor** for a scientific look at amber. View inclusions (organic items trapped in resin) through a magnifying glass and microscope, and see dozens of samples showing the full rainbow of amber shades. Interactive video screens explain the creation of amber. The **third-floor** exhibit explains the "Amber Route" (the ancient Celtic trade road connecting Gdańsk to Italy) and medicinal uses of the stuff, and displays a wide range of functional items made from amber—clocks, pipe stems, candlesticks, chandeliers, jewelry boxes, and much more. Take a whiff—what's that smell? It's a cathedral. Amber is an ingredient in incense. The **fourth floor** shows off more artistic items made of amber—sculptures, candelabras, beer steins, chessboards, and a model ship with delicate sails made of amber. At the **top floor,** you'll find a modern gallery showing more recent amber craftsmanship and displays about amber's role in fashion today.

Then, walking along the upper rampart level of the courtyard, you'll enter an exhibit about the building itself and the town's fortifications. This leads to the **Prison Tower** and the torture exhibit—with sound effects, scant artifacts, and mannequins helpfully demonstrating the grisly equipment.

All About Amber

Poland's Baltic seaside is known as the Amber Coast. You can see amber (*bursztyn*) in Gdańsk's Amber Museum, in the collection at Malbork Castle (see the Pomerania chapter), and in shop windows everywhere. This fossilized tree resin originated here on the north coast of Poland 40 million years ago. It comes in as many different colors as Eskimos have words for snow: 300 distinct shades, from yellowish white to yellowish black, from opaque to transparent. (I didn't believe it either, until I toured Gdańsk's museum.) Darker-colored amber is generally mixed with ash and sand—making it more fragile, and generally less desirable. Lighter amber is mixed with gasses and air bubbles.

Amber has been popular since long before there were souvenir stands. Archaeologists have found Roman citizens (and their coins) buried with crosses made of amber. Almost 75 percent of the world's amber is mined in northern Poland, and it often simply washes up on the beaches after a winter storm. Some of the elaborate amber sculptures displayed at the museum are joined with "amber glue"—melted-down amber mixed with an adhesive agent. More recently, amber craftsmen are combining amber with silver to create artwork—a method dubbed the "Polish School."

In addition to being good for the economy, some Poles believe amber is good for their health. A traditional cure for arthritis pain is to pour strong vodka over amber, let it set, and then rub it on sore joints. Other remedies call for mixing amber dust with honey or rose oil. It sounds superstitious, but users claim that it works.

▲Uphagen House (Dom Uphagena)

This interesting place, at ulica Długa 12, is your chance to glimpse what's behind the colorful facades lining this street (see cost and hours above). It's the only grand Gdańsk mansion rebuilt as it was before 1945. The model near the entry shows the three parts: dolled-up visitors' rooms in front, a corridor along the courtyard, and private rooms in the back. The finely decorated salon was used to show off for guests. Most of this furniture is original (saved from WWII bombs by locals who hid it in the countryside). Passing into the dining room, note the knee-high paintings of hunting and celebrations. Along the passage to the back, each room has a theme: butterflies in the smoking room, then flowers in the next room, then birds in the music room. In the private rooms at the back, the decor is simpler. Downstairs, you'll pass through the kitchen, the pantry, and a room with photos of the house before the war, which were used to reconstruct what you see today.

▲▲Main Town Hall (Ratusz Głównego Miasta)

This landmark building contains remarkable decorations from Gdańsk's Golden Age (see cost and hours earlier). You can also climb 293 concrete steps to the top of the **tower** for commanding views (5 zł extra, mid-June-mid-Sept only).

Visiting the Main Town Hall: In the entry room, examine the photos showing this building at the end of World War II and ogle the finely crafted spiral staircase. The ornately carved wooden **door,** which we'll pass through in a minute, is all original, from the 1600s. Above the door are two crosses under a crown. This seal of Gdańsk is being held—as it's often depicted—by a pair of lions. The felines are stubborn and independent, just like the citizens of Gdańsk. The surface of the door is carved with images of crops. Around the frame of the door are mermen, reminding us that this agricultural bounty, like so many of Poland's resources, is transported on the Vistula and out through Gdańsk.

Go through the door into the **Red Hall,** where the Gdańsk city council met in the summertime. (The lavish fireplace, with another pair of lions holding the coat of arms of Gdańsk, was just for show. There's no chimney.) City council members would sit in the seats around the room, debating city policy. Marvel at the 17th-century inlaid wood panels (just above eye level) showing slices of local life. Paintings on the wall above represent the seven virtues that the burghers meeting in this room should possess. And the exquisite ceiling—with 25 paintings in total—is all about theology. Including both Christian and pagan themes, the ceiling was meant to inspire the decision-makers in this room to make good choices. Study the oval painting in the middle (from 1607)—the museum's highlight. It shows the special place Gdańsk occupies between God, Poland, and the rest of the world. In the foreground, the citizens of Gdańsk go about their daily lives. Above them, high atop the arch, God's hand reaches down (from within clouds of Hebrew characters) and grasps the Main Town Hall's steeple. The rainbow arching above also symbolizes God's connection to Gdańsk. Mirroring that is the Vistula River, which begins in the mountains of southern Poland (on the right), runs through the country, and exits at the sea in Gdańsk (on the left, where the rainbow ends).

Continue into the less impressive **Winter Hall,** with another fireplace (this one actually hooked up to a chimney) and another coat of arms held by lions. Keep going through the next room, into a room with photos of **WWII damage.** The twist of wood is all that's left of the main support for the spiral staircase (today reconstructed in the room where you entered). Ponder the inspiring ability of a city to be reborn after the tragedy of war.

Upstairs are some temporary exhibits and several examples of **Gdańsk-style furniture.** These pieces are characterized by three big, round feet along the front, lots of ornamentation, and usually a virtually impossible-to-find lock (sometimes hidden behind a movable decoration). You can also see a coin collection, from the days when Gdańsk had the elite privilege of minting its own currency.

Then head upstairs, to a fascinating exhibit about Gdańsk's time as a **"free city"** between the World Wars—when, because of its delicate ethnic mix of Poles and Germans, it was too precarious to assign it to either country. You'll see border checkpoints, uniforms, signs in German (the predominant language of "Danzig"), and reconstructed rooms (homes and shops) from the era. Near the end of this room, you have the option to climb up to the top of the tower. Otherwise, you'll take stairs down—with huge photos at each landing showing the city in ruins after World War II, then triumphantly being rebuilt—and into the cellars, where you'll wander through some pointless subterranean chambers before emerging back into the courtyard where you started.

▲▲Artus Court (Dwór Artusa)

In the Middle Ages, Gdańsk was home to many brotherhoods and guilds (like businessmen's clubs). For their meetings, the city provided this elaborately decorated hall, named for King Arthur—a medieval symbol for prestige and power. Just as in King Arthur's Court, this was a place where powerful and important people came together. Of many such halls in Baltic Europe, this is the only original one that survives (cost and hours on page 458, dry and too-thorough audioguide-3 zł extra; in tall, white, triple-arched building behind Neptune statue at Długi Targ 43).

Visiting the Artus Court: In the grand hall, various **cupboards** line the walls. Each organization that met here had a place to keep its important documents and office supplies. Suspended

from the ceiling are seven giant **model ships** that depict Baltic vessels, symbolic of the city's connection to the sea.

In the far-back corner is the museum's highlight: a gigantic **stove** decorated with 520 colorful tiles featuring the faces of kings, queens, nobles, mayors, and burghers—a mix of Protestants and Catholics, as a reminder of Gdańsk's religious tolerance. Almost all of the tiles are original, having survived WWII bombs.

Notice the huge **paintings** on the walls above, with 3-D animals emerging from flat frames. Hunting is a popular theme in local artwork. Like minting coins, hunting was a privilege usually reserved for royalty, but extended in special circumstances to the burghers of special towns...like Gdańsk. These "paintings" are new, digitally generated reproductions of the originals, which were damaged in World War II.

The next room—actually in the next building—is a typical **front room** of the burghers' homes lining ulica Długa. Ogle the gorgeously carved wooden staircase. Upstairs is a hall of knights—once again evoking Arthurian legend. If you've rented an audioguide, take it back up front to return it; otherwise, you can exit through the back.

Other Museums in the Main Town
Historical Zone of the Free City of Gdańsk (Strefa Historyczna Wolne Miasto Gdańsk)

In a city so obsessed with its Golden Age and Solidarity history, this charming little collection illuminates a unique but often-overlooked chapter in the story of Gdańsk: The years between World Wars I and II, when—in an effort to find a workable compromise in this ethnically mixed city—Gdańsk was not part of Germany or Poland, but a self-governing "free city" *(wolne miasto)*. Like a holdover from medieval fiefdoms in modern times, the city-state of Gdańsk even issued its own currency and stamps. This modest museum earnestly shows off artifacts from the time—photos, stamps, maps, flags, promotional tourist leaflets, and other items from the free city, all marked with the Gdańsk symbol of two white crosses under a crown on a red shield. The brochure explains that four out of five people living in the free city identified themselves not as German or Poles, but as "Danzigers." While some might find the subject obscure, this endearing collection is a treat for WWII history buffs. Be sure to borrow the English translations at the entrance.

Cost and Hours: 8 zł, Tue-Sun 12:00-17:00, until 18:00 May-Aug, closed Mon year-round, down the little alley just in front of the Green Gate at Warzywnicza 10A, tel. 58-320-2828, www.tpg.info.pl.

Archaeological Museum (Muzeum Archeologiczne)

This simple museum is worth a quick peek for those interested in archaeology. The ground floor has exhibits on excavated finds from Sudan, where the museum has a branch program. Upstairs, look for the distinctive urns with cute faces, which date from the Hallstatt Period and were discovered in slate graves around Gdańsk. Also upstairs are some Bronze and Iron Age tools; before-and-after photos of WWII Gdańsk; and a reconstructed 12th-century Viking-like Slavonic longboat. You can also climb the building's tower, with good views up Mariacka street toward St. Mary's Church.

Cost and Hours: Museum-8 zł (free on Sat), tower-5 zł; July-Aug Tue-Fri 9:00-17:00, Sat-Sun 10:00-17:00; Sept-June Tue and Thu-Fri 8:00-16:00, Wed 9:00-17:00, Sat-Sun 10:00-16:00; closed Mon year-round; ulica Mariacka 25, tel. 58-322-2100, www. archeologia.pl.

▲National Maritime Museum (Narodowe Muzeum Morskie)

Gdańsk's history and livelihood are tied to the sea. This collection, spread among several buildings on either side of the river, examines all aspects of this connection. Nautical types may get a thrill out of the creaky, sprawling museum, but most visitors find it little more than a convenient way to pass some time and enjoy a cruise across the river. The museum's lack of English information is frustrating; fortunately, some exhibits have descriptions you can borrow.

Cost and Hours: Each part of the museum has its own admission (6-8 zł). The Maritime Cultural Center is worth neither the time nor the money for grown-ups; I'd consider the 18-zł "karnet" combo-ticket that combines the other, better parts. It's open July-Aug daily 10:00-18:00; Sept-Oct and March-June Tue-Sun 10:00-16:00, closed Mon; Nov-Feb Tue-Sun 10:00-15:00, closed Mon; ulica Ołowianka 9, tel. 58-301-8611, www.cmm.pl.

Visiting the Museum: The exhibit has four parts. The first two parts—the Crane and Maritime Cultural Center—are on the Main Town side of the river. The landmark medieval **Crane** (Żuraw), Gdańsk's most important symbol, houses a humble exhibit on living in the city during its Golden Age (16th-17th centuries). For more on the Crane itself, see page 450.

The **Maritime Cultural Center,** a modern exhibit right next door to the Crane, is not worth the exercise unless you are leading a school group. For adults, the most interesting areas are on the third floor ("Working Boats," with examples of vessels from around the world and English explanations) and the fourth floor (temporary exhibits).

The rest of the museum—the Old Granaries and the *Sołdek* steamship—is across the river on Ołowianka Island, which you can reach via the little **ferry** (named the *Motława*, like the river; 1.50 zł one-way). The ferry runs about every 15 minutes in peak season (during museum hours only) and much less in the off-season.

Once on the island, visit the three rebuilt **Old Granaries** (Spichlerze). These make up the heart of the exhibit, tracing the history of Gdańsk—particularly as it relates to the sea—from prehistoric days to the present.

Models of the town and region help put things into perspective. Other exhibits cover underwater exploration, navigational aids, artifacts of the Polish seafaring tradition, peekaboo cross-sections of multilevel ships, and models of the modern-day shipyard where Solidarity was born. This place is home to more miniature ships than you ever thought you'd see, and the Nautical Gallery upstairs features endless rooms with paintings of boats.

Finally, crawl through the holds and scramble across the deck of a decommissioned steamship docked permanently across from the Crane, called the *Sołdek* (ship generally closed in winter). This was the first postwar vessel built at the Gdańsk shipyard. Below decks, you can see where they shoveled the coal; wander through a maze of pipes, gears, valves, gauges, and ladders; and visit the rooms where the sailors lived, slept, and ate. You can even play captain on the bridge.

SOLIDARITY (SOLIDARNOŚĆ) AND THE GDAŃSK SHIPYARD (STOCZNIA GDAŃSKA)

Gdańsk's single most memorable experience is exploring the shipyard that witnessed the beginning of the end of communism's stranglehold on Eastern Europe. Taken together, the sights in this area are worth ▲▲▲. Here in the former industrial wasteland that Lech Wałęsa called the "cradle of freedom," this evocative site tells the story of the brave Polish shipyard workers who took on—and ultimately defeated—an Evil Empire. A visit to the Solidarity sights has two main parts: Solidarity Square (with the memorial and gate out in front of the shipyard), and the outstanding museum inside the European Solidarity Center.

Getting to the Shipyard: These sights cluster around Solidarity Square (Plac Solidarności), at the north end of the Old Town, about a 20-minute walk from the Royal Way. For the most interesting approach, follow "Part 2" of my self-guided walk (earlier), which ends here.

Background: After the communists took over Eastern Europe at the end of World War II, oppressed peoples throughout the Soviet Bloc rose up in different ways. The most dramatic uprisings—Hungary's 1956 Uprising (see page 582) and Czechoslovakia's 1968 "Prague Spring" (see page 84)—were brutally crushed under the treads of Soviet tanks. The formula for freedom that finally succeeded was a patient, nearly decade-long series of strikes and protests spearheaded by Lech Wałęsa and his trade union, called Solidarność—"Solidarity." (The movement also benefited from good timing, as it coincided with the *perestroika* and *glasnost* policies of Soviet premier Mikhail Gorbachev.) While some American politicians might like to take credit for defeating communism, Wałęsa and his fellow workers were the ones fighting on the front lines, armed with nothing more than guts.

Solidarity Square (Plac Solidarności) and the Monument of the Fallen Shipyard Workers

The seeds of August 1980 were sown a decade before. Since becoming part of the Soviet Bloc, the Poles staged frequent strikes, protests, and uprisings to secure their rights, all of which were put down by the regime. But the bloodiest of these took place in December of 1970—a tragic event memorialized by the **three-crosses monument** that towers over what's now called Solidarity Square.

The 1970 strike was prompted by price hikes. The communist government set the prices for all products. As Poland endured drastic food shortages in the 1960s and 1970s, the regime frequently announced what it called "regulation of prices." Invariably, this meant an increase in the cost of essential foodstuffs. (To be able to claim "regulation" rather than "increase," the regime would symbolically lower prices for a few select items—but these were always nonessential luxuries, such as elevators and TV sets, which nobody could afford anyway.) The regime was usually smart enough to raise prices on January 1, when the people were fat and happy after Christmas, and too hung over to complain. But on December 12, 1970, bolstered by an ego-stoking visit by West German Chancellor Willy Brandt, Polish premier Władysław Gomułka increased prices. The people of Poland—who cared more about the price of Christmas dinner than relations with Germany—struck back.

A wave of strikes and sit-ins spread along the heavily industrialized north coast of Poland, most notably in Gdańsk, Gdynia, and Szczecin. Thousands of angry demonstrators poured through the gate of this shipyard, marched into town, and set fire to the Communist Party Committee building. In an attempt to quell the riots, the government-run radio implored the people to go back to work. On the morning of December 17, workers showed up at shipyard gates across northern Poland, and were greeted by the

Lech Wałęsa

In 1980, the world was turned on its ear by a walrus-mustachioed shipyard electrician. Within three years, this seemingly run-of-the-mill Pole had precipitated the collapse of communism, led a massive 10-million-member trade union with enormous political impact, been named *Time* magazine's Man of the Year, and won a Nobel Peace Prize.

Lech Wałęsa was born in Popowo, Poland, in 1943. After working as a car mechanic and serving two years in the army, he became an electrician at the Gdańsk Shipyard in 1967. Like many Poles, Wałęsa felt stifled by the communist government, and was infuriated that a system that was supposed to be for the workers clearly wasn't serving them.

When the shipyard massacre took place in December of 1970 (see description on page 465), Wałęsa was at the forefront of the protests. He was marked as a dissident, and in 1976, he was fired. Wałęsa hopped from job to job and was occasionally unemployed—under communism, a rock-bottom status reserved for only the most despicable derelicts. But he soldiered on, fighting for the creation of a trade union and building up quite a file with the secret police.

In August of 1980, Wałęsa heard news of the beginnings of the Gdańsk strike and raced to the shipyard. In an act that has since become the stuff of legend, Wałęsa scaled the shipyard wall to get inside.

Before long, Wałęsa's dynamic personality won him the unofficial role of the workers' leader and spokesman. He negotiated with the regime to hash out the August Agreements, becoming a rock star-type hero during the so-called 16 Months of Hope...until martial law came crashing down in December of 1981. Wałęsa was arrested and interned for 11 months in a country

army and police. Without provocation, the Polish army opened fire on the workers. While the official death toll for the massacre stands at 44, others say the true number is much higher. The monument, with a trio of 140-foot-tall crosses, honors those lost to the regime that December.

Go to the middle of the **wall** behind the crosses, to the monument of the worker wearing a flimsy plastic work helmet, attempting to shield himself from bullets. Behind him is a list—pockmarked with symbolic bullet holes—of workers murdered on that day. *Lat* means "years old"—many teenagers were among the dead. The quote at the top of the wall is from St. John Paul house. After being released, he continued to struggle underground, becoming a symbol of anti-communist sentiment.

Finally, the dedication of Wałęsa and Solidarity paid off, and Polish communism dissolved—with Wałęsa rising from the ashes as the country's first post-communist president. But the skills that made Wałęsa a rousing success at leading an uprising didn't translate well to the president's office. Wałęsa proved to be a stubborn, headstrong politician, frequently clashing with the parliament. He squabbled with his own party, declaring a "war at the top" of Solidarity and rotating higher-ups to prevent corruption and keep the party fresh. He also didn't choose his advisors well, enlisting several staffers who wound up immersed in scandal. His overconfidence was his Achilles' heel, and his governing style verged on authoritarian.

Unrefined and none too interested in scripted speeches, Wałęsa was a simple man who preferred playing ping-pong with his buddies to attending formal state functions. Though lacking a formal education, Wałęsa had unsurpassed drive and charisma... but that's not enough to lead a country—especially during an impossibly complicated, fast-changing time.

Wałęsa was defeated at the polls, by the Poles, in 1995, and when he ran again in 2000, he received a humiliating 1 percent of the vote. Since leaving office, Wałęsa has kept a lower profile, but still delivers speeches worldwide. Many poor Poles grumble that Lech, who started life simple like them, has forgotten the little people. But his fans point out that he gives much of his income to charity. And on his lapel, he still always wears a pin featuring the Black Madonna of Częstochowa—the most important symbol of Polish Catholicism.

Poles say there are at least two Lech Wałęsas: the young, bombastic, working-class idealist Lech, at the forefront of the Solidarity strikes, who will always have a special place in their hearts; and the failed President Wałęsa, who got in over his head and tarnished his legacy.

II, who was elected pope eight years after this tragedy. The pope was known for his clever way with words, and this very carefully phrased quote—which served as an inspiration to the Poles during their darkest hours—skewers the regime in a way subtle enough to still be tolerated: "Let thy spirit descend, and renew the face of the earth—of *this* earth." (that is, Poland). Below that is the dedication: "They gave their lives so you can live decently."

Stretching to the left of this center wall are plaques representing labor unions from around Poland—and around the world (look for the Chinese characters)—expressing solidarity with these workers. To the right is an enormous Bible verse: "May the Lord give strength to his people. May the Lord bless his people with the gift of peace" (Psalms 29:11).

Inspired by the brave sacrifice of their true comrades, shipyard workers rose up here in August of 1980, formulating the "21 Points" of a new union called Solidarity. Their demands included the right to strike and form unions, the freeing of political prisoners, and an increase in wages. The 21 Points are listed in Polish on the panel at the far end of the right wall, marked *21 X TAK* ("21 times yes"). An unwritten precondition to any agreement was the right for the workers of 1980 to build a memorial to their comrades slain in 1970. The government agreed, marking the first time a communist regime ever allowed a monument to be built to honor its own victims. Wałęsa called it a harpoon in the heart of the communists. The towering monument, with three crucified anchors on top, was designed, engineered, and built by shipyard workers. The monument was finished just four months after the historic agreement was signed.

• *Now continue to the gate and peer through into the birthplace of Eastern European freedom.*

Gdańsk Shipyard (Stocznia Gdańska) Gate #2

When a Pole named Karol Wojtyła was elected pope in 1978—and visited his homeland in 1979—he inspired his 40 million coun-

trymen to believe that impossible dreams can come true. Prices continued to go up, and the workers continued to rise up. By the summer of 1980, it was clear that the dam was about to break.

In August, Anna Walentynowicz—a Gdańsk crane operator and known dissident—was fired unceremoniously just short of her retirement. This sparked a strike in the Gdańsk Shipyard (then called the Lenin Shipyard) on August 14, 1980. An electrician named Lech Wałęsa had been fired as an agitator years before and wasn't allowed into the yard. But on hearing news of the strike, Wałęsa went to the shipyard and climbed over the wall to get inside. The strike now had a leader.

These were not soldiers, nor were they idealistic flower children. The strike participants were gritty, salt-of-the-earth manual laborers: forklift operators, welders, electricians, machinists. Imagine being one of the 16,000 workers who stayed here for 18 days during the strike—hungry, cold, sleeping on sheets of Styrofoam, inspired by the new Polish pope, excited about finally standing up to the regime...and terrified that at any moment you might be gunned down, like your friends had been a decade before. Workers, afraid to leave the shipyard, communicated with the outside world through this gate—wives and brothers showed up here and asked for a loved one, and those inside spread the word until the striker came forward. Occasionally, a truck pulled up inside the gate, with Lech Wałęsa standing atop its cab with a megaphone. Facing the thousands of people assembled outside the gate, Wałęsa gave progress reports on the negotiations and pleaded for supplies. The people of Gdańsk responded, bringing armfuls of bread and other food to keep the workers going. Solidarity.

During the strike, two items hung on the fence. One of them (which still hangs there today) was a picture of Pope John Paul II—a reminder to believe in your dreams and have faith in God (for more on the Pope and his role in Solidarity, see page 268). The other item was a makeshift list of the strikers' 21 Points—demands scrawled in red paint and black pencil on pieces of plywood.

• *Walk around the right end of the gate and enter the former shipyard.*

The shipyard churned out over a thousand ships from 1948 to 1990, employing 16,000 workers. About 60 percent of these ships were exported to the USSR—and so, when the Soviet Bloc broke apart in the 1990s, they lost a huge market. Today the facilities employ closer to 1,200 workers...who now make windmills.

Before entering the museum, take a look around. Let me guess: lots of construction? This part of the shipyard, long abandoned, is being redeveloped into a **"Young City"** (Młode Miasto)—envisioned as a new city center for Gdańsk, with shopping, restaurants, offices, and homes. Rusting shipbuilding equipment has been torn down, and old brick buildings are being converted into gentrified flats. The nearby boulevard called Nowa Wałowa will be the spine connecting this area to the rest of the city. Farther east, the harborfront will also be rejuvenated, creating a glitzy marina and extending the city's delightful waterfront people zone to the north (see www.ycgdansk.com). Fortunately, the shipyard gate, monument, and other important sites from the Solidarity strikes—now considered historical monuments—will remain.

• *The massive, rust-colored European Solidarity Center, which faces Solidarity Square, houses the museum where we'll learn the rest of the story.*

▲▲▲European Solidarity Center (Europejskie Centrum Solidarności)

Europe's single best sight about the end of communism is made even more powerful by its location: in the very heart of the place where those events occurred. Filling just one small corner of a huge, purpose-built educational facility, the permanent exhibition uses larger-than-life photographs, archival footage, actual artifacts,

interactive touchscreens, and a state-of-the-art audioguide to eloquently tell the story of the end of Eastern European communism.

Cost and Hours: 17 zł, includes audioguide, daily May-Sept 10:00-20:00, Oct-April 10:00-18:00, last entry one hour before closing, Plac Solidarności 1, tel. 506-195-673, www.ecs.gda.pl.

◆ **Self-Guided Tour:** First, appreciate the architecture of the **building** itself. From the outside, it's designed to resemble the rusted hull of a giant ship—seemingly gloomy and depressing. But step inside to find an interior flooded with light, which cultivates a surprising variety of life—in the form of lush gardens that make the place feel like a very expensive greenhouse. You can interpret this symbolism a number of ways: Something that seems dull and dreary from the outside (the Soviet Bloc, the shipyards themselves, what have you) can be full of brightness, life, and optimism inside.

In the lobby, buy your ticket and pick up the essential, included audioguide. The exhibit has much to see, and some of it is arranged in a conceptual way that can be tricky to understand without a full grasp of the history. I've outlined the basics in this self-guided tour, but the audioguide can illuminate more details—including translations of films and eyewitness testimony from participants in the history.

• *The permanent exhibit fills seven lettered rooms—each with its own theme—on two floors. From the lush lobby, head up the escalator and into...*

The Birth of Solidarity (Room A): This room picks up right in the middle of the dynamic story we just learned out on the square. It's August of 1980, and the shipyard workers are rising up. You step straight into a busy shipyard: punch clocks, workers' lockers, and—up on the ceiling—hundreds of plastic helmets. A big **map** in the middle of the room shows the extent of the shipyard in 1980. Inside the cab of the **crane,** you can watch an interview with spunky Anna Walentynowicz, whose firing led to the first round of strikes. Nearby stands a **truck;** Lech Wałęsa would stand on top of the cab of a truck like this one to address the nervous locals who had amassed outside the shipyard gate, awaiting further news.

In the middle of the room, carefully protected under glass, are those original **plywood panels** onto which the strikers scrawled their 21 demands, then lashed to the gate. Just beyond that, a giant wall of photos and a map illustrate how the strikes that began here spread like a virus across Poland. At the far end of the room, behind the partition, stand **two tables** that were used during the talks to end the strikes (each one with several actual items from that era, under glass).

After 18 days of protests, the communist authorities finally agreed to negotiate. On the afternoon of August 31, 1980, the Governmental Commission and the Inter-Factory Strike Committee (MKS) came together and signed the August Agreements, which legalized Solidarity—the first time any communist government permitted a workers' union. As Lech Wałęsa sat at a big table and signed the agreement, other union reps tape-recorded the proceedings and played them later at their own factories to prove that the unthinkable had happened. Take a moment to linger over the rousing **film** that plays on the far wall, which begins with the strike, carries through with the tense negotiations that a brash young Lech Wałęsa held with the authorities, and ends with the triumphant acceptance of the strikers' demands. Lech Wałęsa rides on the shoulders of well-wishers out to the gate to spread the good news.

• Back by the original 21 demands, enter the next exhibit...

The Power of the Powerless (Room B): This section traces the roots of the 1980 strikes, which were preceded by several far less successful protests. It all begins with a kiss: a giant photograph of Russian premier Leonid Brezhnev mouth-kissing the Polish premier Edward Gierek, with the caption **"Brotherly Friendship."** Soviet premiers and their satellite leaders really did greet each other "in the French manner," as a symbolic gesture of their communist brotherhood.

Working your way through the exhibit, you'll see the door to a **prison cell**—a reminder of the intimidation tactics used by the Soviets in the 1940s and 50s to deal with their opponents as they exerted their rule over the lands they had liberated from the Nazis.

The typical **communist-era apartment** is painfully humble. After the war, much of Poland had been destroyed, and population shifts led to housing shortages. People had to make do with tiny space and ramshackle furnishings. Communist propaganda blares from both the radio and the TV.

A map shows **"red Europe"** (the USSR plus the satellites of Poland, Czechoslovakia, Hungary, and East Germany), and a **timeline** traces some of the smaller Soviet Bloc protests that led up to Solidarity: in East Germany in 1953, in Budapest and Poznań in 1956, the "Prague Spring" of 1968, and other 1968 protests in Poland.

In the wake of these uprisings, the communist authorities cracked down even harder. Peek into the **interrogation room,** with a wall of file cabinets and a lowly stool illuminated by a bright spotlight. (Notice that the white Polish eagle on the seal above the desk is missing its golden crown—during communism, the Poles were allowed to keep the eagle, but its crown was removed.)

The next exhibit presents a day-by-day rundown of the **1970 strikes,** from December 14 to 22, which resulted in the massacre of the workers who are honored by the monument in front of this building. A wall of mug shots gives way to exhibits chronicling the steady rise of dissent groups through the 1970s, culminating in the June 1976 protests in the city of Radom (prompted, like so many other uprisings, by unilateral price hikes).

• *Loop back through Room A, and proceed straight ahead into...*

Solidarity and Hope (Room C): While the government didn't take the August Agreements very seriously, the Poles did...and before long, 10 million of them—one out of every four, or effectively half of the nation's workforce—joined Solidarity. So began what's often called the **"16 Months of Hope."** Newly legal, Solidarity continued to stage strikes and make its opposition known. Slick Solidarity posters and children's art convey the childlike enthusiasm with which the Poles seized their hard-won kernels of freedom. The communist authorities' hold on the Polish people began to slip. Support and aid from the outside world poured in, but the rest of the Soviet Bloc looked on nervously, and the Warsaw Pact army assembled at the Polish border and glared at the uprisers. The threat of invasion hung heavy in the air.

• *Exiting this room, head up the staircase and into...*

At War with Society (Room D): You're greeted by a wall of TV screens delivering a stern message. On Sunday morning, December 13, 1981, the Polish head of state, **General Wojciech Jaruzelski**—wearing his trademark dark glasses—appeared on national TV and announced the introduction of **martial law.** Solidarity was outlawed, and its leaders were arrested. Frightened Poles heard the announcement and looked out their windows to see Polish Army tanks rumbling through the snowy streets. (On the opposite wall, see footage of tanks and heavily armed soldiers intimidating their countrymen into compliance.) Jaruzelski claimed that he imposed martial law to prevent the Soviets from invading. Today, many historians question whether martial law was really necessary, though Jaruzelski remained unremorseful through his death in 2014.

Continuing deeper into the exhibit, you come to a **prisoner transport.** Climb up inside to watch chilling scenes of riots, demonstrations, and crackdowns by the ZOMO riot police. In one gruesome scene, a demonstrator is quite intentionally—and practically in slow motion—run over by a truck. From here, pass through a gauntlet of *milicja* riot-gear shields to see the truck crashing through a gate. Overhead are the uniforms of miners from the **Wujek mine** who were massacred on December 16, 1981 (their names are projected on the pile of coal below).

Martial law was a tragic, terrifying, and bleak time for the Polish people. It didn't, however, kill the Solidarity movement, which continued its fight after going underground. Passing prison cells, you'll see a wall plastered with handmade, underground posters and graffiti. Notice how in this era, **Solidarity propaganda** is much more primitive; circle around the other side of the wall to see several presses that were actually used in clandestine Solidarity print shops during this time. The outside world sent messages of support as well as supplies—represented by the big wall of cardboard boxes. This approval also came in the form of a Nobel Peace Prize for Lech Wałęsa in 1983; you'll see video clips of his wife accepting the award on his behalf (Wałęsa feared that if he traveled abroad to claim it, he would not be allowed back into the country).

• *But even in these darkest days, there were glimmers of hope. Enter...*

The Road to Democracy (Room E): By the time the Pope visited his homeland again in 1983, martial law had finally been lifted, and Solidarity—still technically illegal—was gaining momentum, gradually pecking away at the communists. Step into the small inner room with footage of the **Pope's third pilgrimage** to his homeland in 1987, by which time (thanks in no small part to his inspirational role in the ongoing revolution) the tide was turning.

Step into the room with the big, white **roundtable.** With the moral support of the pope and the entire Western world, the brave Poles were the first European country to throw off the shackles of communism when, in the spring of 1989, the "Roundtable Talks" led to the opening up of elections. (If you look through the viewfinders of the TV cameras in the corners, you'll see footage of those meetings.) The government arrogantly called for parliamentary elections, reserving 65 percent of seats for themselves.

In the next room, you can see Solidarity's strategy in those **elections:** On the right wall are posters showing Lech Wałęsa with each candidate. Another popular "get out the vote" measure was the huge poster of Gary Cooper—an icon of America, which the Poles deeply respect and viewed as their friendly cousin across the Atlantic—except that, instead of a pistol, he's packing a ballot. Rousing reminders like this inspired huge voter turnout. The communists' plan backfired, as virtually every open seat went to Solidarity. It was the first time ever that opposition candidates had taken office in the Soviet Bloc. On the wall straight ahead, flashing a V-for-*wiktoria* sign, is a huge photo of Tadeusz Mazowiecki—an early leader of Solidarity, who became prime minister on June 4, 1989.

• *For the glorious aftermath, head into the final room.*

The Triumph of Freedom (Room F): This room is dominated by a gigantic **map of Eastern Europe.** A countdown clock on the right ticks off the departure of each country from communist clutches, as the Soviet Bloc "decomposes." You'll see how the success of Solidarity in Poland—and the ragtag determination of a scruffy band of shipyard workers right here in Gdańsk—inspired people all over Eastern Europe. By the winter of 1989, the Hungarians had opened their borders, the Berlin Wall had crumbled, and the Czechs and Slovaks had staged their Velvet Revolution. (Small viewing stations that circle the room reveal the detailed story for each country's own road to freedom.) Lech Wałęsa—the shipyard electrician who started it all by jumping over a wall—became the first president of post-communist Poland. And a year later, in Poland's first true elections since World War II, 29 different parties won seats in the parliament. It was a free-election free-for-all.

In the middle of the room stands a white wall with **inspirational quotes** from St. John Paul II and Václav Havel—the Czech poet-turned-protester-turned-prisoner-turned-president—which are repeated in several languages. On the huge wall, the **Solidarity "graffiti"** is actually made up of thousands of little notes left behind by visitors to the museum. Feel free to grab a piece of paper and a pen and record your own reflections.

• *Finally, head downstairs and find the...*

John Paul II Room (Room G): Many visitors find that touring this museum—with vivid reminders of a dramatic and pivotal moment in history that took place in our own lifetimes, which was brought about not by armies or presidents, but by everyday people—puts them in an emotional state of mind. Designed for silent reflection, this room overlooks the monument to those workers who were gunned down in 1970.

• *For an epilogue, if you're not already pooped, continue deeper into the former shipyard to see one more important landmark from 1980. The path leads to a low-profile, red-brick building, the...*

Sala BHP

This is the building where the communists sat down across the table from Lech Wałęsa and his team and worked out a compromise (as seen in the videos inside the European Solidarity Center). Entering, turn left to walk through a series of photos—all described in English—that illustrate Solidarity history; these are all the more poignant because they lack the bombastic presentation of the glitzy museum. The images speak for themselves. The other side of the building (right from the entrance) is the actual hall where those fateful meetings took place, with a long table set up on the stage.

Cost and Hours: Free, daily May-Sept 10:00-18:00, Oct-April 10:00-16:00, www.salabhp.pl.

NORTH OF THE MAIN TOWN
World War II Museum
Gdańsk is building this large, state-of-the-art museum just east of the Solidarity shipyard, along the river. When open, it promises high-tech interactive exhibits about Gdańsk's experience during the war that began on its doorstep. It could be open as early as 2015; ask the TI for the latest details (or check www.muzeum 1939.pl).

SOUTH OF THE MAIN TOWN
A 10- to 15-minute walk south of the Main Town, these sights round out your Gdańsk experience. They're most worthwhile to those with a special interest in each one's subject matter: art, theater, and kids who love archaeology.

National Museum in Gdańsk
(Muzeum Narodowe w Gdańsku)
This art collection, housed in what was a 15th-century Franciscan monastery, is worth ▲▲ to art lovers for one reason: Hans Memling's glorious *Last Judgment* triptych altarpiece, one of the two most important pieces of art to be seen in Poland (the other is Leonardo da Vinci's *Lady with an Ermine,* usually in Kraków's Czartoryski Museum). If you're not a purist, you can settle for seeing the much smaller replica in St. Mary's Church. But if medieval art is your bag, make the 10-minute walk here from the Main Town.

Cost and Hours: 10 zł; June-Aug Tue-Wed and Fri-Sun 10:00-17:00, Thu 12:00-19:00; May and Sept Tue-Sun 10:00-17:00; Oct-April Tue-Fri 9:00-16:00, Sat-Sun 10:00-17:00; closed Mon year-round; last entry 45 minutes before closing; walk 10 minutes due south from ulica Długa's Golden Gate, after passing the Shakespeare Theater take the pedestrian underpass beneath the big cross street, then continue down the busy street until you see signs for the museum; ulica Toruńska 1, tel. 58-301-7061, www.muzeum.narodowe.gda.pl.

Visiting the Museum: From the entry, the altarpiece by Hans Memling (c. 1440-1494) is at the top of the stairs and to the right. The history of the painting is as interesting as the work itself. It was commissioned in the mid-15th century by the Medicis' banker in Florence, Angelo di Jacopo Tani. The ship delivering the painting from Belgium to Florence was hijacked by a Gdańsk pirate, who brought the altarpiece to his hometown to be displayed in St. Mary's Church. For centuries, kings, emperors, and czars

GDAŃSK & THE TRI-CITY

admired it from afar, until Napoleon seized it in the early 19th century and took it to Paris to hang in the Louvre. Gdańsk finally got the painting back, only to have it exiled again—this time into St. Petersburg's Hermitage Museum—after World War II. On its return to Gdańsk in 1956, this museum claimed it—though St. Mary's wants it back.

Have a close look at Memling's well-traveled work. It's the end of the world, and Christ rides in on a rainbow to judge humankind. Angels blow reveille, waking the dead, who rise from their graves. The winged archangel Michael—dressed for battle and wielding the cross like a weapon—weighs the grace in each person, sending them either to the fires of hell (right panel) or up the sparkling-crystal stairway to heaven (left).

It takes all 70 square feet of paneling to contain this awesome scene. Jam-packed with dozens of bodies, a Bible's worth of symbolism, and executed with astonishing detail, the painting can keep even a non-art lover occupied. Notice the serene, happy expressions of the righteous, as they're greeted by St. Peter (with his giant key) and clothed by angels. And pity the condemned, their faces filled with terror and sorrow as they're tortured by grotesque devils more horrifying than anything Hollywood could devise.

Tune in to the exquisite details: the angels' robes, the devils' genetic-mutant features, the portrait of the man in the scale (a Medici banker), Michael's peacock wings. Get as close as you can to the globe at Christ's feet and Michael's shining breastplate: You can just make out the whole scene in mirror reflection. Then back up and take it all in—three panels connected by a necklace of bodies that curves downward through hell, crosses the earth, then rises up to the towers of the New Jerusalem. On the back side of the triptych are reverent portraits of the painting's patron, Angelo Tani, and his new bride, Catarina.

Beyond the Memling, the remainder of the collection isn't too thrilling. The rest of the upstairs has more Flemish and Dutch art, as well as paintings from Gdańsk's Golden Age and various works by Polish artists. The ground floor features a cavernous, all-white cloister filled with Gothic altarpiece sculptures, gold and silver wares, majolica and Delft porcelain, and characteristic Gdańsk-style furniture.

Gdańsk Shakespeare Theater (Teatr Szekspirowski)

Gdańsk has a long and proud tradition of staging plays by Shakespeare. As early as the 17th century, theater troupes from England were coming to this cosmopolitan trading city to perform. In 1993, local actors revived the tradition with an annual Gdańsk Shakespeare Festival. And in 2014, the city built the state-of-the-art Gdańsk Shakespeare Theater to honor its connection to the Bard.

The building's minimalist, black-brick, blocky architecture—with a few symbolic faux-buttresses to echo the gables of the surrounding buildings—was criticized for not blending in very well with its surroundings. But the celebration of theater that takes place inside is welcomed by all. The main theater can be modified to create three different types of performance spaces (proscenium, thrust stage, and theater in the round)—and even has a retractable roof to wash the actors with direct sunlight. There's not much to see—unless you're attending a play, you can only get as far as the box office. But if you want to take a peek, the building is on ulica Zbytki—just follow Pcztowa street south from the middle of ulica Długa.

Shakespeare contributes only a tiny piece of the theater's full lineup—it plays host to a wide variety of performances and festivals throughout the year. You're most likely to find Shakespeare performed in English during the annual Shakespeare Festival, which is typically in late summer or early fall (www.shakespearefestival.pl). For details on all upcoming performances, see www.teatrszekspirowski.pl (box office open daily 13:00-18:00).

"Blue Lion" Archaeological Education Center (Centrum Edukacji Archeologicznej "Błękitny Lew")

Hiding far from the Main Town on Granary Island, this kid-friendly exhibit re-creates the atmosphere of medieval Gdańsk. Occupying a rebuilt granary called the "Blue Lion," its highlight is a full-scale replica of an atmospheric medieval street, populated by mannequins whose features are based on actual human remains. Also telling the tale are artifacts from the period, a selection of films (subtitled in English), and touchscreens that provide some background. Though information is a bit sparse (especially along the medieval street), the collection tries hard not to be just another fuddy-duddy, dusty old museum, making it popular with kids on field trips.

Cost and Hours: 10 zł, May-Aug Tue-Sun 10:00-18:00, Sept-April Tue-Sun 9:00-17:00, closed Mon year-round, ulica Chmielna 53, tel. 58-320-3188, www.archeologia.pl.

OUTER GDAŃSK

These two sights—worthwhile only to those with a particular interest in them—are each within the city limits of Gdańsk, but they take some serious time to see round-trip.

Oliwa Cathedral (Katedra Oliwska)

The suburb of Oliwa, at the northern edge of Gdańsk, is home to this visually striking church. The quirky, elongated facade hides a surprisingly long and skinny nave. The ornately decorated 18th-century organ over the main entrance features angels and stars that move around when the organ is played. While locals are proud of this place, it's hard to justify the effort it takes to get out here. Skip it unless you just love Polish churches or you're going to a concert.

Concerts: The animated organ performs its 20-minute show frequently, especially in summer (concerts at the top of each hour: July-Aug Mon-Fri 10:00-13:00 & 15:00-17:00, Sat 10:00-15:00, Sun 15:00-17:00; June Mon-Sat 10:00-13:00, Sun 15:00-17:00; May and Sept Mon-Sat 10:00-13:00, Sun at 15:00 and 16:00; 1-2/day off-season, www.archikatedraoliwa.pl). Confirm the schedule at the TI before making the trip. Note that on Sundays and holidays, there are no concerts before 15:00.

Getting There: Oliwa is about six miles northwest of central Gdańsk, on the way to Sopot and Gdynia. To get to Oliwa, you have two options: The tram is slower (30 minutes) but gets you closer, while the SKM commuter train is faster (15 minutes) but requires a longer walk. **Tram** #6 or #12 from Gdańsk's main train station lets you off right at the entrance to Oliwski Park. Go straight through to the back of the park; near the end, you can see the copper roof and two skinny, pointy spires of the cathedral on your right. Exit through the back of the park, bear right, and go one block to find the entrance to the church. **SKM commuter trains** from Gdańsk's main train station zip to the "Gdańsk Oliwa" stop in 15 minutes (see "Getting Around the Tri-City" on page 489). From the Oliwa train station, it's a 15-minute walk or 10-zł taxi ride to the cathedral. Walk straight ahead out of the station and turn right when you get to the busy road. Cross the road at the light and enter the tree-filled Park Oliwski at the corner, then follow the directions above.

Westerplatte

World War II began on September 1, 1939, when Adolf Hitler sent the warship *Schleswig-Holstein* to attack this Polish munitions depot, which was guarding Gdańsk's harbor. Though it may interest serious WWII history buffs, most visitors will find little to see here aside from a modest museum, a towering monument, and some old bunkers. As it's surrounded by shipyard sprawl, it's not a particularly scenic trip, either.

Getting There: The most enjoyable approach is on a cruise—either on a modern boat, or on the fun old-fashioned galleons (45-50 minutes each way; see page 478). You can also take **bus** #138 from the main train station (about 30 minutes).

Shopping in Gdańsk

The big story in Gdańsk is amber *(bursztyn)*, a fossil resin available in all shades, shapes, and sizes (see the "All About Amber" sidebar, earlier). While you'll see amber sold all over town, the best place to browse and buy is along the atmospheric ulica Mariacka (between the Motława River and St. Mary's Church). This pretty street, with old-fashioned balconies and dozens of display cases, is fun to wander even if you're not a shopper. Other good places to buy amber are along the riverfront embankment and on ulica Długa. To avoid rip-offs—such as amber that's been melted and reshaped—always buy it from a shop, not from someone standing on the street. (But note that most shops also have a display case and salesperson out front, which are perfectly legit.) Prices everywhere are about the same, so rather than seeking out a specific place, just window-shop until you see what you want. Styles range from gaudy necklaces with huge globs of amber, to tasteful smaller pendants in silver settings, to cheap trinkets. All shades of amber—from near-white to dark brown—cost about the same, but you'll pay more for inclusions (bugs or other objects stuck in the amber).

Gdańsk also has several modern shopping malls, most of them in the Old Town or near the main train station. The walk between the Main Town and the Solidarity shipyard goes past some of the best malls (see page 457).

Sleeping in Gdańsk

I've listed rates here for the high season, generally May through September; at all of these places, you'll pay a bit less in the off-season (Oct-April). Many hotels are booked up (mostly with German tourists) in peak season (mid-June-mid-Sept)—reserve ahead.

ACROSS THE RIVER

These hotels are across the river from the Main Town. That puts you a bit farther from the sightseeing action, but it's a relatively short walk (no more than 10 minutes from any of these), and the rooms are a better value.

$$$ Hotel Podewils is the top choice for a friendly splurge. Filling a storybook-cute house from 1728, overlooking the marina and across the river from a fine panorama of the Gdańsk embankment, it's classy. The public spaces and 10 rooms have all the modern amenities, but with plush, almost Baroque, decor (Db-600-800 zł depending on size of room—each one is different—and demand, air-con, Wi-Fi, Szafarnia 2, tel. 58-300-9560, www.podewils.pl, gdansk@podewils.pl).

Sleep Code

Abbreviations   (3 zł = about $1, country code: 48)
S = Single, **D** = Double/Twin, **T** = Triple, **Q** = Quad, **b** = bathroom, **s** = shower only.

Price Rankings

$$$ Higher Priced—Most rooms 400 zł or more.

 $$ Moderately Priced—Most rooms between 300-400 zł.

   $ Lower Priced—Most rooms 300 zł or less.

Unless otherwise noted, breakfast is included, credit cards are accepted, Wi-Fi is generally free, and English is spoken. Prices can change without notice; verify the hotel's current rates online or by email. For the best prices, always book directly with the hotel.

$$$ Hotel Królewski, a classy hotel in a beautifully renovated red-brick granary, offers 30 stylish rooms sitting right along the river, facing classic Gdańsk embankment views. It's just beyond the three granaries of the National Maritime Museum, across the river from the Crane. The Polish Baltic Philharmonic is right next door, so you may be serenaded by a rehearsal or performance (Sb-400 zł, Db-450 zł, fancier suite-like Db "plus"-500 zł, pricier apartments, lower rates mid-Oct-April, 50 zł to reserve a view room—or try asking for one when you check in for no extra charge, non-smoking rooms, elevator, Wi-Fi, good restaurant, ulica Ołowianka 1, tel. 58-326-1111, www.hotelkrolewski.pl, office@hotelkrolewski.pl). You can commute to your sightseeing by ferry (take the 1.50-zł boat trip across the river offered by the Maritime Museum). But the ferry runs only during the museum's opening hours and is sporadic off-season. If the ferry isn't running, it's a scenic 15-minute walk along the river, past the marina, and over the bridge into the Main Town.

$$ Willa Litarion, run by the eager Owsikowski family, sits on the back side of a charmingly restored row of colorful houses on the island just across the river from the main drag. It's tall and skinny, with no elevator, and faces a gloomy parking lot, but it's a handy location at a decent price. Each of the 13 small rooms has a totally different design, but all are artsy and mod (Sb-255 zł, Db-330 zł, bigger "deluxe" Db-360 zł, 20-25 percent cheaper Oct-April, extra bed-60 zł, Wi-Fi, parking garage-30 zł/day, ulica Spichrzowa 18, tel. 58-320-2553, www.litarion.pl, recepcja@litarion.pl). Several other, similar (but less appealing) "villas" line this same street—if you're in a pinch for a room, this is a handy place to go ringing doorbells.

At the Academy of Music: **$$ Dom Muzyka** rents 87 simple, tidy rooms in a nondescript residential neighborhood. The catch:

It's very difficult to find, hiding in the back of the big Academy of Music building (Akademia Muzyczna). But the prices are worth the hunt, and once you're set up, it's an easy 10-minute walk to the sights. Their "deluxe" rooms, mostly twins, are bigger and overlook the quiet courtyard; most of the standard rooms face a busy street but have good windows and air-conditioning (Sb-250 zł, standard Db-340 zł, deluxe Db-360 zł, apartment-500 zł, extra bed-100 zł, cheaper Oct-April, elevator, guest computer, Wi-Fi, popular with tour groups, good restaurant, free and easy parking, ulica Łąkowa 1, tel. 58-326-0600, www.dommuzyka.pl, biuro@dommuzyka.pl).

In the same complex, **$ Dom Sonata** is a tempting budget option. Its 60 rooms—nearly as nice as the Dom Muzyka's, but with fewer hotelesque amenities—house students for most of the year, but are rented out to tourists from July through September. Given the good quality of the rooms, the price is right (Db-150 zł, breakfast-19 zł extra, air-con, elevator, Wi-Fi, ulica Łąkowa 1, tel. 58-300-9260, www.domsonata.com.pl, domsonata@amuz.gda.pl). From the Main Town's Green Gate, cross the two bridges, then walk a long block along the modern commercial building and turn right just before the park (on Łąkowa, across from the big brick church). Walk to the end of this block; before the busy road, go through the gate just before the big yellow-brick building on the right. Once inside the gate checkpoint, the hotel is around the back of the yellow building, the farthest door down. If you get lost, just ask people, "Hotel?"

IN THE MAIN TOWN

With a recent increase in midrange accommodations inside the Main Town, this prime location has become more affordable. However, the Main Town can come with more nighttime noise, particularly in summer, when loud bars and discos keep things lively. Request a quiet room...and pack earplugs.

$$$ Hotel Wolne Miasto ("Free City") offers rich, wood-carved public spaces with photos of old Gdańsk and 68 elegant rooms on the edge of the Main Town, just two blocks from the main drag. It's above a popular disco that gets noisy on weekends (Thu-Sat nights), so it's especially important to request a quieter room when you reserve (Sb-390 zł, Db-470 zł, bigger "deluxe" Db-570 zł, all rooms 20 zł less Fri-Sun, even cheaper Oct-March, elevator, guest computer, Wi-Fi, ulica Świętego Ducha 2, tel. 58-322-2442, www.hotelwm.pl, rezerwacja@hotelwm.pl).

$$$ Hotel Admirał is simply practical: a big, impersonal, business-class place with 44 nicely decorated rooms tucked in a quiet residential alley at the north end of the embankment, just a few steps off the old fish market. This is especially worth

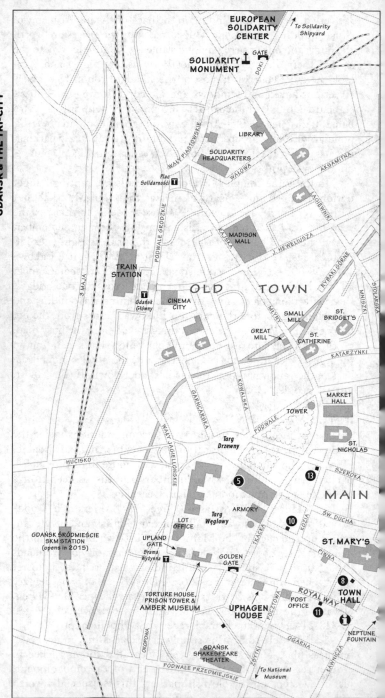

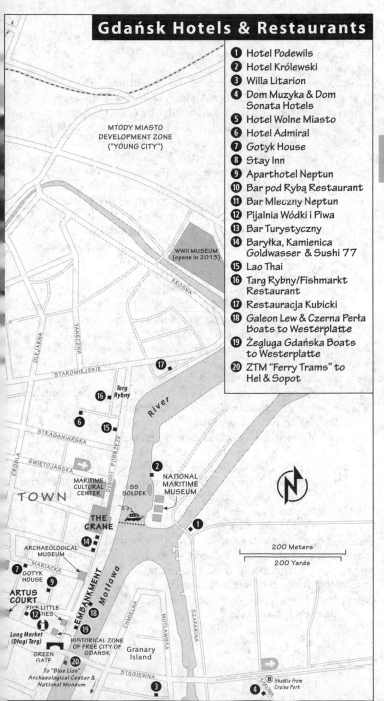

Gdańsk Hotels & Restaurants

1. Hotel Podewils
2. Hotel Królewski
3. Willa Litarion
4. Dom Muzyka & Dom Sonata Hotels
5. Hotel Wolne Miasto
6. Hotel Admiral
7. Gotyk House
8. Stay Inn
9. Aparthotel Neptun
10. Bar pod Rybą Restaurant
11. Bar Mleczny Neptun
12. Pijalnia Wódki i Piwa
13. Bar Turystyczny
14. Baryłka, Kamienica Goldwasser & Sushi 77
15. Lao Thai
16. Targ Rybny/Fishmarkt Restaurant
17. Restauracja Kubicki
18. Galeon Lew & Czerna Perła Boats to Westerplatte
19. Żegluga Gdańska Boats to Westerplatte
20. ZTM "Ferry Trams" to Hel & Sopot

considering if you can get a good deal (rates fluctuate but generally around Db-400 zł in high season, air-con, elevator, Wi-Fi, Tobiasza 9, tel. 58-320-0320, www.admiralhotel.pl, recepcja@admiralhotel.pl).

$$ Gotyk House, a good value, is run with warmth and pride by the Rybicki family. Owner Andrzej is an energetic armchair historian who works hard to make his little hotel comfortable while still respecting the sanctity of what's supposedly Gdańsk's oldest house. The chimes from St. Mary's Church, next door, provide a pleasant soundtrack. The cellar houses a minuscule gingerbread museum and small shrine to Copernicus (whose longtime lover may have lived here). The seven straightforward rooms share a tiny breakfast room, so you'll have to tell them what time you'd like to eat (Sb-280 zł, Db-310 zł, cheaper Oct-April, Wi-Fi in most rooms, tight public spaces, ulica Mariacka 1, tel. 58-301-8567, mobile 516-141-133, www.gotykhouse.eu, reservation@gotykhouse. eu).

$-$$ Stay Inn, a self-declared "hostel with vibe," is fresh and young, but still feels practical. The location couldn't be more central—facing the side of St. Mary's Church, right in the heart of the Main Town—and, while the street it's on is quieter than most, a downstairs pub can be noisy on weekends. It combines 29 beds in small 5- to 8-bed dorms with 10 private rooms that are as hotel-like as any in this price range. The dorm dwellers and fancier folks alike share the same kitchen/lounge/breakfast room. Everything feels tidy and well-designed; as it lacks the grungy party personality of some hostels, it's well worth considering even for non-hostelers (dorm bed-60 zł, tiny Db with cozy platform double bed-300 zł, more spacious twin Db-350 zł, includes breakfast, elevator, guest computer, Wi-Fi, bike rental, Piwna 28, tel. 58-354-1543, www.stayinngdansk.com, booking@stayinngdansk.com).

$$ Aparthotel Neptun lacks personality, but owns a great location—on a slightly dreary side-street between delightful Mariacka and bustling Długi Targ ("Long Square"). While it's just a few steps to most of the town's big sights, it's just far enough away to avoid the crowds and the weekend noise. The 30 rooms and apartments are modern, efficient, well-equipped, and forgettable...but well-priced for the central location (Db-350 zł, apartments start at 450 zł, breakfast-25 zł extra, elevator, Wi-Fi, Grzaska 1, mobile 604-466-466, www.aparthotelgdansk.com, info@aparthotelgdansk.com).

Eating in Gdańsk

In addition to traditional Polish fare, Gdańsk has some excellent Baltic seafood. Herring *(śledź)* is popular here, as is cod *(dorsz)*. Natives brag that their salmon *(łosoś)* is better than Norway's. For a stiff drink, sample *Goldwasser* (similar to Goldschlager). This sweet and strong liqueur, flecked with actual gold, was supposedly invented here in Gdańsk. The following options are all in the Main Town, within three blocks of the Royal Way.

BUDGET RESTAURANTS IN THE CITY CENTER

These places are affordable, tasty, quick, and wonderfully convenient—on or very near the Royal Way (ulica Długa). They're worth considering even if you're not on a tight budget.

Bar pod Rybą ("Under the Fish") is nirvana for fans of baked potatoes *(pieczony ziemniak)*. They offer more than 20 varieties, piled high with a wide variety of toppings and sauces, from Mexican beef to herring to Polish cheeses. They also serve fish dishes with salad and potatoes, making this a cheap place to sample local seafood. The tasteful decor—walls lined with old bottles, antique wooden hangers, and old street signs—is squeezed into a single cozy room packed with happy eaters. In the summer, order inside, and they'll bring your food to you at an outdoor table (potatoes and fish dishes are each about 20-30 zł, daily 10:00-22:00, ulica Piwna 61, tel. 58-305-1307).

Bar Mleczny Neptun is your handiest milk-bar option in the Main Town. A hearty meal, including a drink, runs about 15-20 zł. This popular place has more charm than your typical institutional milk bar, including outdoor seating along the most scenic stretch of the main drag, and an upstairs dining room overlooking it all. The items on the counter are for display—point to what you want and they'll dish it up fresh (Mon-Fri 7:30-19:30, Sat-Sun 10:00-19:00, may have shorter hours off-season, free Wi-Fi, ulica Długa 33, tel. 58-301-4988). For more on milk bars, see page 234.

Pijalnia Wódki i Piwa, part of a popular Polish chain, hides half a block behind the Hard Rock Café (on Kuśnierska). This little vodka-and-herring bar takes you back to the 1970s. Pop in to study the retro decor—ads from the 1970s and photos of the lines people routinely endured. The place is literally wallpapered with pages from the "Tribune of the Masses" newspaper infamous for its propaganda that passed for news. They play pop hits from the last years of communism. The menu is fun, accessible, and simple: 4 zł for vodka or other drinks, and 8 zł for herring or other bar nibbles (open daily 9:00-late).

Bar Turystyczny is misnamed—while it seems to harbor the illusion that it's for tourists, it has become beloved by locals as the central area's favorite milk bar. Easy to miss on the way between the Main Town and the Solidarity sights, it's always jammed (9-13-zł main dishes, Mon-Fri 8:00-18:00, Sat-Sun 9:00-17:00, Szeroka 8, tel. 58/301-6013).

ON THE RIVERFRONT EMBANKMENT

Perhaps the most appealing dining zone in Gdańsk stretches along the riverfront embankment near the Crane. On a balmy summer evening, the outdoor tables here are enticing. As it's a popular area, consider scouting a table during your sightseeing, and reserve your choice for dinner later that night. While these places are mostly interchangeable, I've listed a few to consider, in the order you'll reach them as you walk north along the embankment.

Baryłka ("Barrel") is a simpler, more affordable alternative to some of the pricier places along here. While the outdoor seating is enticing, the elegant upstairs dining room, with windows overlooking the river, is also appealing (35-45-zł main dishes, daily 9:00-24:00, Długie Pobrzeże 24, tel. 58-301-4938).

Kamienica Goldwasser offers high-quality Polish and international cuisine. Choose between cozy, romantic indoor seating on several levels, or scenic outdoor seating (most main dishes 60-75 zł, daily 10:00-24:00, occasional live music, Długie Pobrzeże 22, tel. 58-301-8878).

Sushi 77, serving up a wide selection of surprisingly good sushi right next to the Crane, is a refreshing break from ye olde Polish food. Choose between the outdoor tables bathed in red light, or the mod interior (30-50-zł sushi sets, daily 12:00-23:00, Długie Pobrzeże 30, tel. 58-682-1823).

Past the Crane

About 100 yards past the Crane, near the old fish market (Targ Rybny), cluster several more options.

Lao Thai is a modern space right along the embankment selling surprisingly high-quality, yet still affordable, Thai cuisine (35-50-zł dishes, daily 12:00-22:00, ulica Targ Rybny 11, tel. 58/305-2525).

Targ Rybny/Fishmarkt ("The Fish Market") has less appealing outdoor seating that overlooks a park and parking lot. But the warm, mellow-yellow nautical ambience inside is pleasant, making this a good bad-weather option. It features classy but not stuffy service, and an emphasis on fish (most main dishes 40-55 zł, plus pricier seafood splurges, daily 10:00-23:00, ulica Targ Rybny 6C, tel. 58-320-9011).

Restauracja Kubicki, along the water just past the Hilton, has a long history (since 1918), but a recent remodel has kept the atmosphere—and its food—feeling fresh. This is a good choice for high-quality Polish and international food in a fun, sophisticated-but-not-stuffy interior that's a clever mix of old and new elements (30-55-zł main dishes, daily 12:00-23:00, Wartka 5, tel. 58-301-0050).

Gdańsk Connections

BY TRAIN

Gdańsk is well-connected to the Tri-City via the commuter SKM trains (explained later, under "Getting Around the Tri-City"). It's also connected to Warsaw and Kraków by the new, high-speed EIC line (which requires reservations). Given the distance between Gdańsk and other Polish destinations, also consider domestic flights; Eurolot often has easy flights between Gdańsk and Kraków for about the same price as a train ticket, while LOT and others connect Gdańsk to Warsaw.

From Gdańsk by Train to: Hel (town on Hel Peninsula, 3/day direct July-Aug only, 2-3 hours; otherwise about hourly with transfer in Gdynia), **Malbork** (2/hour, about half are express EIC trains that take 30 minutes, the rest are slower regional trains that take around 45 minutes), **Toruń** (5/day, about 3 hours; more with a transfer in Bydgoszcz, 3.5 hours), **Warsaw** (hourly, 3 hours), **Kraków** (6/day direct, 5.5 hours, 1 more with change in Warsaw; plus 11-hour night train), **Berlin** (1/day direct, 5.75 hours; 2/day, 6-8 hours, transfer in Poznań).

BY BOAT

Various boats depart from Gdańsk's embankment to nearby destinations, including **Westerplatte** (the monument marking where World War II started) and **Hel** (the beachy peninsula, described below). While boats also run sporadically to Sopot and Gdynia, the train is better for those trips (described under "Getting Around the Tri-City," later). As these boat schedules tend to change from year to year, confirm your plans carefully at the TI. All boat trips are weather permitting, especially the faster hydrofoils. In shoulder season (April-June and Sept-Oct), even though most boats stop running from Gdańsk, several routes still run between Sopot, Gdynia, and Hel. Boats generally don't run in winter (Nov-March).

To Westerplatte: To travel by boat to the monument at Westerplatte, you have three options. The most enjoyable one is to ride the replica **17th-century galleons,** either the *Galeon Lew* ("Lion Galleon") or the *Czarna Perła* ("Black Pearl"). These over-the-top, touristy boats depart hourly from the embankment just outside the Green Gate for a lazy 1.5-hour round-trip cruise to Westerplatte and back. (You can choose to get off at Westerplatte

after 45 minutes and take a later boat back.) Both of them have English commentary on the way there and live nautical music on the return trip (if you've ever wanted to hear "What Shall We Do with a Drunken Sailor?" in Polish, here's your chance). It's not exactly pretty—you'll see more industry than scenery—but it's a fun excuse to set sail, even if you don't care about Westerplatte (40 zł round-trip, 30 zł one-way, the two boats take turns departing at the top of each hour 10:00-19:00 in July-Aug, fewer departures May-June and Sept, from the embankment near the Crane, mobile 601-629-191, www.galeony.pl). Two other, duller alternatives leave from right nearby: big, modern **Żegluga Gdańska** boats (40 zł round-trip, 30 zł one-way, 50 minutes each way, daily April-Oct, 3-6/day in each direction, www.zegluga.pl); or much cheaper but less frequent city-run **ZTM "ferry trams"** *(tramwaj wodny),* which depart from the embankment on the south side of the bridge (10 zł each way, line #F5, 3/day).

To Hel: Various boats zip out to Hel in two hours during the summer. Though the specifics change from year to year, this route is most likely run by Żegluga Gdańska (May-June weekends only, July-Aug 3/day, 35 zł each way, www.zegluga.pl).

BY CRUISE SHIP

While many cruises advertise a stop in "Gdańsk," most actually dock in the nearby town of Gdynia. For details on this town—and what to do if you arrive there—see page 493.

The Tri-City (Trójmiasto)

Gdańsk is the anchor of the three-part metropolitan region known as the Tri-City (Trójmiasto). The other two parts are as different as night and day: Sopot, a once-swanky resort town; and Gdynia, a practical, nose-to-the-grindstone business center. The Tri-City as a whole is home to bustling industry and a sprawling university, with several campuses and plenty of well-dressed, English-speaking students. Beyond the Tri-City, the long, skinny Hel Peninsula—a sparsely populated strip of fishing villages and fun-loving beaches—arches dramatically into the Baltic Sea.

Sopot—boasting sandy beaches, tons of tourists, and a certain elegance—is clearly the most appealing day-trip option. Gdynia offers a glimpse into workaday Poland, but leaves most visitors cold. Hel, which requires the better part of a day to visit, is worthwhile only if you've got perfect summer weather and a desire to lie on the beach.

GETTING AROUND THE TRI-CITY

Gdańsk, Sopot, and Gdynia are connected by regional commuter trains (*kolejka*, operated by SKM) as well as by trains of Poland's

national railway (operated by PKP). Tickets for one system can't be used on the other. While trains for the two systems chug along the same tracks, they use different (but nearby) platforms/stations. For example, at Gdańsk's main train station, national PKP trains use platforms 1-3, while regional SKM trains use platforms 3-5. And in Sopot, the SKM station is a few hundred feet before the PKP station. Regional SKM trains are much more frequent than long-distance PKP trains—they go in each direction about every 10-15 minutes (less frequently after 19:30).

Traditionally, the easiest place to catch the SKM trains is at Gdańsk's main train station. However, the new Gdańsk's Śródmieście station (which may open in late 2015) is a bit closer to the tourist zone, just across the street from the Upland Gate. At either place, buy tickets at the machine marked *SKM Bilety* (English instructions). Some likely trip durations and prices: 3.80 zł and 15 minutes to Oliwa, 3.80 zł and 25 minutes to Sopot, or 5.70 zł and 35 minutes to Gdynia. Tickets purchased from a machine come already validated. But if you buy one from a kiosk, you'll need to stamp it in the easy-to-miss yellow slots under the boards with SKM information.

Each city has multiple stops. In Gdańsk, use "Gdańsk Główny" (the main station) or—if it's open—"Gdańsk Śródmieście" (closer to the Main Town); for Sopot, use the stop called simply "Sopot"; and for Gdynia, it's "Gdynia Główna" (the main station).

The bigger PKP trains are faster, but less frequent—unless you notice one that happens to be leaving at a convenient time, I'd skip them and stick with the easy SKM trains. But note that trains to Hel are always operated by PKP.

For a more romantic—and much slower—approach, consider the boat (see "Gdańsk Connections," earlier).

Sopot

Sopot (SOH-poht), dubbed the "Nice of the North," was a celebrated haunt of beautiful people during the 1920s and 1930s, and remains a popular beach getaway to this day.

Sopot was created in the early 19th century by Napoleon's doctor, Jean Georges Haffner, who believed Baltic Sea water to be therapeutic. By the 1890s, it had become a fashionable seaside resort. This gambling center boasted enough high-roller casinos to garner comparisons to Monte Carlo.

The casinos are gone, but the health resorts remain, and you'll still see more well-dressed people here per capita than just about anywhere else in the country. While it's not quite Cannes, Sopot feels relatively high class, which is unusual in otherwise unpretentious Poland. But even so, a childlike spirit of summer-vacation fun pervades this St-Tropez-on-the-Baltic, making it an all-around enjoyable place.

PLANNING YOUR TIME
You can get the gist of Sopot in just a couple of hours. Zip in on the train, follow the main drag to the sea, wander the pier, get your feet wet at the beach, then head back to Gdańsk. Why not come here in the late afternoon, enjoy those last few rays of sunshine, stay for dinner, then take a twilight stroll on the pier?

Orientation to Sopot

The main pedestrian drag, Monte Cassino Heroes street (ulica Bohaterów Monte Cassino), leads to the Molo, the longest pleasure pier in Europe. From the Molo, a broad, sandy beach stretches in each direction. Running parallel to the surf is a tree-lined, people-filled path made for strolling.

TOURIST INFORMATION
Sopot's helpful TI is near the base of the Molo at Plac Zdrojowy 2 (look for blue *it* sign). Pick up the free map, info booklet, and events schedule. They also offer a free room-booking service (daily June-mid-Sept 9:00-20:00, mid-Sept-May 10:00-18:00, ulica Dworcowa 4, tel. 58-550-3783, www.sopot.pl).

ARRIVAL IN SOPOT
From the SKM station, exit to the left and walk down the street. After a block, you'll see the PKP train station on your left. Continue on to the can't-miss-it main drag, ulica Bohaterów Monte Cassino (marked by the big red-brick church steeple). Follow it to the right, down to the seaside.

Sights in Sopot

▲Monte Cassino Heroes Street
(Ulica Bohaterów Monte Cassino)
Nicknamed "Monciak" (MOHN-chak) by locals, this in-love-with-life promenade may well be Poland's most manicured street (and is named in honor of the Polish soldiers who helped the

Allies pry Italy's Monte Cassino monastery from Nazi forces during World War II). Especially after all the suburban and industrial dreck you passed through to get here, it's easy to be charmed by this pretty drag. The street is lined with happy tourists, trendy cafés, al fresco restaurants, movie theaters, and late-19th-century facades (known for their wooden balconies).

The most popular building along here (on the left, about half-way down) is the so-called **Crooked House** (Krzywy Domek), a trippy, Gaudí-inspired building that looks like it's melting. Hard-partying Poles prefer to call it the "Drunken House," and say that when it looks straight, it's time to stop drinking.

Molo (Pier)

At more than 1,600 feet long, this is Europe's longest wooden entertainment pier. While you won't find any amusement-park rides, you will be surrounded by vendors, artists, and Poles having the time of their lives. Buy a *gofry* (Belgian waffle topped with whipped cream and fruit) or an oversized cloud of *wata cukrowa* (cotton candy), grab your partner's hand, and stroll with gusto (7.50 zł, free Oct-April, open long hours daily, www.molo.sopot.pl).

Climb to the top of the Art Nouveau lighthouse for a waterfront panorama. Scan the horizon for sailboats and tankers. Any pirate ships? For a jarring reality check, look over to Gdańsk. Barely visible from the Molo are two of the most important sites in 20th-century history: the towering monument at Westerplatte, where World War II started, and the cranes rising up from the Gdańsk Shipyard, where Solidarity was born and European communism began its long goodbye.

In spring and fall, the Molo is a favorite venue for pole vaulting—or is that Pole vaulting?

The Beach

Yes, Poland has beaches. Nice ones. When I heard Sopot compared to places like Nice, I'll admit that I scoffed. But when I saw those stretches of inviting sand as far as the eye can see, I wished I'd packed my swim trunks. (You could walk from Gdańsk to Gdynia on beaches like this.) The sand is finer than anything I've seen in Croatia...though the water's not exactly crystal-clear. Most of the beach is public, except for a small private stretch in front of the Grand Hotel Sopot. Year-round, it's crammed with locals. At these northern latitudes, the season for bathing is brief and crowded.

Overlooking the beach next to the Molo is the **Grand Hotel Sopot.** It was renovated to top-class status just recently, but its history goes way back. They could charge admission for room #226, a multiroom suite that has hosted the likes of Adolf Hitler,

Marlene Dietrich, and Fidel Castro (but not all at the same time). With all the trappings of Sopot's belle époque—dark wood, plush upholstery, antique furniture—this room had me imagining Hitler sitting at the desk, looking out to sea, and plotting the course of World War II.

Gdynia

Compared to its flashier sister cities, straightforward Gdynia (guh-DIN-yah) has retained a more working-class vibe, still in touch with its salty, fishing-village roots. Gdynia is less historic than Gdańsk or Sopot, as it was mostly built in the 1920s to be Poland's main harbor after Gdańsk became a free city. Although nowhere as attractive as Gdańsk or Sopot, Gdynia has an authentic feel and a lovely waterfront promenade (www.gdynia.pl).

Gdynia is a major business center, and—thanks to its youthful, progressive city government—has edged ahead of the rest of Poland in transitioning from communism. It enjoys one of the highest income levels in the country. Many of the crumbling downtown buildings have been renovated, and Gdynia is becoming known for its top-tier shopping—all the big designers have boutiques here. If a local woman has been shopping on Świętojańska street in Gdynia, it means that she's got some serious złoty.

Because Gdańsk's port is relatively shallow, the biggest cruise ships must put in at Gdynia...leaving confused tourists to poke around town looking for some medieval quaintness, before coming to their senses and heading for Gdańsk. Gdynia is also home to a major military harbor and an important NATO base.

To get a taste of Gdynia, take the SKM train to the "Gdynia Główna" station, follow signs to *wyjście do miasta,* cross the busy street, and walk 15 minutes down Starowiejska. When you come to the intersection with the broad Świętojańska street, turn right (in the direction the big statue is looking) and walk two blocks to the tree-lined park on the left. Head through the park to the Southern Pier (Molo Południowe). This concrete slab—nowhere near as charming as Sopot's wooden-boardwalk version—features a modern shopping mall and a smattering of sights, including an aquarium and a pair of permanently moored museum boats.

Plans are afoot to convert the big warehouse at the Nabrzeże Francuskie pier into an emigration museum, possibly as early as mid-2015; when this opens, it will offer a handy sightseeing opportunity for cruisers arriving here (for the latest, see www.muzeumemigracji.pl).

ARRIVING BY CRUISE IN GDYNIA

Many Northern European cruises include a stop at "Gdańsk"; most of these actually put in at Gdynia's sprawling port. And, while Gydnia's town center is relatively manicured and pleasant, its port area is the opposite—like a Soviet Bloc bodybuilder, it's muscular and hairy. Cruise ships are shuffled among hardworking industrial piers that make the area feel uninviting. Three of the port's many piers are used for cruises: **Nabrzeże Francuskie** (French Quay), where most large ships dock; **Nabrzeże Stanów Zjednoczonych** (United States Quay), farther out, a secondary option for large ships; and convenient **Nabrzeże Pomorskie** (Pomeranian Quay, part of the Southern Pier), used by small ships and located alongside Gdynia's one "fun" pier, with museums and pleasure craft (from here, it's easy to simply walk into downtown Gdynia). Port information: www.port.gdynia.pl.

Unfortunately, there are no **ATMs** or money-exchange options at or near the cruise-ship berths; but cash machines are plentiful in downtown Gdynia.

To get from your cruise ship to Gdańsk, the best option is a **shuttle bus-plus-train connection.** First, ride your cruise line's shuttle bus into downtown Gdynia (5-minute trip; price depends on the cruise line). The shuttle drops you off at Skwer Kościuski; from here, it's a 10-minute walk (gradually uphill) to the train station. Start by walking away from the water on the broad, parklike boulevard. After the street becomes ulica 10 Lutego (you'll pass the TI on your right), it curves to the right; once you're around the corner, use the crosswalk to reach the train station (marked *Dworzec Podmiejski*). From here you can ride the handy *kolejka* commuter train into Gdańsk (runs every 10-15 minutes, 35 minutes; for details on this train, see "Getting Around the Tri-City," earlier). Arriving at the Gdańsk train station ("Gdańsk Główny" stop), turn to "Arrival in Gdańsk—By Train," on page 435, and follow the instructions into the town center. If the new "Gdańsk Śródmieście" stop—one stop beyond Gdańsk Główny—is open, get off there instead, and simply cross the busy street to the Upland Gate and the start of my self-guided walk. Returning on the train, you want the "Gdynia Główna" stop.

Taxi drivers line up to meet arriving cruise ships. Cabbies here tend to overcharge, but if they use the meter, these are the legitimate rates: 20 zł to Gdynia's train station (*Dworzec*, DVOH-zhets); 125 zł to Gdańsk's Main Town; and 60-80 zł to Sopot. Taxi drivers generally take euros, though their off-the-cuff exchange rate may not be favorable.

For more details on Gdynia's port—and several others on the Baltic, North Sea, and beyond—pick up the *Rick Steves Northern European Cruise Ports* guidebook.

Hel Peninsula (Mierzeja Helska)

Out on the edge of things, this slender peninsula juts 20 miles into the ocean, providing a sunny retreat from the big cities—even as it shelters them from Baltic winds. Trees line the peninsula, and the northern edge is one long, sandy, ever-shifting beach.

On hot summer days, Hel is a great place to frolic in the sun with Poles. Sunbathing and windsurfing are practically religions here. Small resort villages line Hel Peninsula: Władysławowo (at the base), Chałupy, Kuźnica, Jastarnia, Jurata, and—at the tip—a town also called Hel. Beaches right near the towns can be crowded in peak season, but you're never more than a short walk away from your own stretch of sand. There are few permanent residents, and the waterfront is shared by budget campgrounds, hotels hosting middle-class families, and mansions of Poland's rich and famous (former president Aleksander Kwaśniewski has a summer home here).

The easiest way to go to Hel—aside from coveting thy neighbor's wife—is by boat (see "Gdańsk Connections," earlier). Trains from Gdańsk also reach Hel (summer only), and from Gdynia, you can take a train, bus, or minibus. But overland transit is crowded and slow—especially in summer, when Hel is notorious for its hellish traffic jams.

POMERANIA

Malbork Castle • Toruń

The northwestern part of Poland—known as Pomerania (Pomorze)—has nothing to do with excitable little dogs, but it does offer two attractions worth singling out, both conveniently located between Gdańsk and Warsaw. Malbork, the biggest Gothic castle in Europe, is one of the most interesting castles in Eastern Europe. Farther south, the Gothic town of Toruń—the birthplace of Copernicus, and a favorite spot of every proud Pole—holds hundreds of red-brick buildings...and, it seems, even more varieties of tasty gingerbread.

PLANNING YOUR TIME

Malbork works well as a side-trip from Gdańsk (frequent trains, 30-45 minutes each way), and it's also on the main train line from

Gdańsk to Warsaw. While Toruń doesn't merit a long detour, it's worth a stroll or an overnight if you want to sample a smaller Polish city. Unfortunately, Toruń is on a different train line than Malbork—if you visit both in one day, it'll be a very long one. Ideally, if traveling round-trip from Warsaw, see one of these destinations coming to Gdańsk, and visit the other on the way back. Or do Malbork as a side-trip from Gdańsk, then visit Toruń on the way to or from Warsaw.

Malbork Castle

Malbork Castle is soaked in history. The biggest brick castle in the world, the largest castle of the Gothic period, and one of Europe's most imposing fortresses, it sits smugly on a marshy plain at the edge of the town of Malbork, 35 miles southeast of Gdańsk. This was the headquarters of the notorious Teutonic Knights, a Germanic band of ex-Crusaders who dominated northern Poland in the Middle Ages.

GETTING THERE

Malbork is on the train line between Gdańsk and Warsaw. Coming by train from Gdańsk, you'll enjoy views of the castle on your right as you cross the Nogat River. Store your luggage at the station's lockers and head into town.

POMERANIA

To get from the station to the castle, consider taking a **taxi** (shouldn't cost more than 10 zł, though many corrupt cabbies charge twice that—keep asking until someone agrees to 10 zł). Or you can **walk** 15 minutes to the castle: Leave the station to the right, walk straight, and go through the pedestrian underpass beneath the busy road (by the red staircase). When you emerge on the other side, follow the busy road (noticing peek-a-boo views on your right of the castle's main tower) and take your first right turn (onto Kościuszki, the main shopping street). On Kościuszki, you'll pass the fancy pink building housing the TI on the right. Near the bottom of Kościuszki, at the fountain and the McDonald's, jog right, then bear left over two moats to find the ticket office (marked *kasa*).

Orientation to Malbork Castle

Cost and Hours: Mid-April-mid-Sept—40 zł, open Tue-Sun 9:00-19:00; mid-Sept-mid-April—30 zł, open Tue-Sun 10:00-15:00; closed Mon year-round; grounds stay open an hour later than the castle, ticket office opens 30 minutes before the castle; tel. 55-647-0978, www.zamek.malbork.pl.

Tours: You are technically required to enter the castle with a three-hour **guided tour** or an audioguide, but this is rarely enforced—you can usually just walk in. (If they do enforce this rule, simply enter with a Polish group—tours leave from the ticket booth every 15 minutes—and split off on your own once inside.) My self-guided tour covers the basics.

Your ticket includes a good **audioguide,** but supply is limited—they're generally available only before 11:00 and after 15:00. Ideally, try to get an audioguide, which lets you wander aimlessly through this fascinating place, keying in *audio-tour stop* numbers as you explore.

In July and August, **English tours** run three times a day (likely at 11:00, 14:00, and 15:30; 8 zł extra). Otherwise, year-round, you can pay 210 zł for a private English tour (English guides are easy to arrange in summer—even on short notice—but more difficult in winter). Ideally, contact the castle a few days ahead to reserve a guide (tel. 55-647-0978, kasa@zamek.malbork.pl), or hire your own guide in Gdańsk (such as Agnieszka Syroka—see page 438).

If you show up and there's no scheduled English tour, ask whether an English-speaking guide is available. Then take the initiative, play "tour organizer," and get together a group of frustrated English speakers by the cashier. On a recent visit, it took me only a few minutes to gather a dozen strangers eager for some English information—bringing the per-person cost of the private tour down to less than 20 zł.

Best Views: The views of mas-sive Malbork are stunning—especially at sunset, when its red brick glows. Be sure to walk out across the bridge over the Nogat River. The most scenic part of the castle is probably the twin-turreted, riverside Bridge Gate, which used to be connected by a bridge to the opposite bank.

BACKGROUND

When the Teutonic Knights were invited to Polish lands to con-vert neighboring pagans in the 13th century, they found the per-fect site for their new capital here, on the bank of the Nogat River. Construction began in 1274. After the Teutonic Knights con-quered Gdańsk in 1308, the order moved its official headquarters from Venice to Malbork, where they remained for nearly 150 years. They called the castle Marienburg, the "Castle of Mary," in honor of the order's patron saint.

At its peak in the early 1400s, Malbork was both the imposing home of a seemingly unstoppable army and Europe's final bastion of chivalric ideals. Surrounded by swamplands, with only one gate in need of defense, it was a tough nut to crack. Malbork Castle was never taken by force in the Middle Ages, though it had to withstand various sieges by the Poles during the Thirteen Years' War (1454-1466)—including a campaign that lasted over three years. Finally, in 1457, the Polish king gained control of Malbork by buying off Czech mercenaries guarding the castle. Malbork became a Polish royal residence for 300 years. But when Poland was partitioned in the late 18th century, this region went back into German hands. The castle became a barracks, windows were sealed up, delicate vaulting was damaged, bricks were quarried for new buildings, and Malbork deteriorated.

In the late 19th century, Romantic German artists and poets rediscovered the place. An architect named Konrad Steinbrecht devoted 40 years of his life to Malbork, painstakingly restoring the palace to its medieval splendor. A half-century later, the Nazis used the castle to house POWs. Hitler—who, like many Germans, had a soft spot for Malbork's history—gave the order to defend it to the last man. About half of it was destroyed by the Soviet army, who saw it as a symbol of long-standing German domination. But it was restored once again, and today Malbork has been returned to its Teutonic glory.

Malbork Castle Tour

The official tour of Malbork lasts about three hours. And, while there's plenty to see, this self-guided tour allows you to see the highlights at your own pace. Use the map on the next page to navigate and jump around as needed. The castle complex is a bit of a maze, with various entrances and exits for each room, often behind closed (but unlocked) doors. Don't be shy about grabbing a medieval doorknob and letting yourself in.

LOWER CASTLE AND ENTRANCE GATE

Just past the ticket taker, step through the front gate and stand on the castle's drawbridge. Look up at one of Europe's most intimidating fortresses—home to the Grand Master, monks, and knights of the Teutonic Order.

Above the door to the brick gate is a sculpture of the Virgin Mary with Baby Jesus...next to a shield and helmet. The two messages to visitors: This castle is protected by Mary, and the Teutonic Knights are here to convert pagans—by force, if necessary.

From the drawbridge, look right to observe the formidable fortifications. The rooster-capped tower (which contains a toilet) is connected by a sky bridge to the fancy Gothic 14th-century facade of the brick infirmary—kept at a distance for disease control.

Pass through the gate, into the entry area. Imagine the gate behind you closing. Look up to see wooden chutes where archers are preparing to rain arrows down on you. Your last thought: Maybe we should have left the Teutonic Knights alone, after all.

Before you're pierced by arrows, read the castle's history in its walls: The foundation is made of huge stones brought from

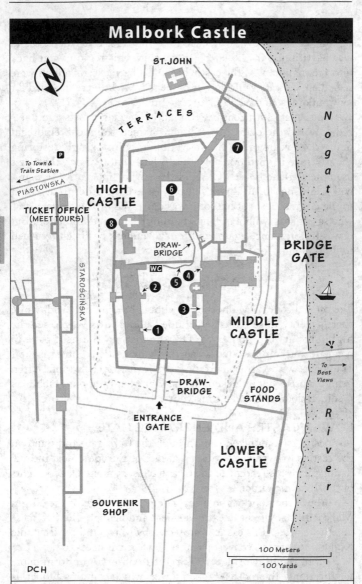

Malbork Castle

ST. JOHN

TERRACES

Nogat

To Town &
Train Station

P

PIASTOWSKA

HIGH CASTLE

6

7

TICKET OFFICE
(MEET TOURS)

8

BRIDGE GATE

DRAW-BRIDGE

WC

4

STAROŚCIŃSKA

2

5

3

MIDDLE CASTLE

1

To Best Views

DRAW-BRIDGE

FOOD STANDS

River

ENTRANCE GATE

LOWER CASTLE

SOUVENIR SHOP

100 Meters

100 Yards

DCH

POMERANIA

1 Amber Collection (downstairs)
2 Armory (upstairs) & Gothic Café (downstairs)
3 "Boiler Room" (downstairs) & Grand Refectory (upstairs)
4 Grand Master's Palace

5 Grand Master Statues
6 Well
7 Dansker Tower
8 St. Mary's Church (temp. closed)

Sweden, which are rare in these marshy lands. But most of the castle, like so many other buildings in northern Poland, was built with handmade red brick. Throughout the castle, the darker-colored, rougher brick is original, and the lighter-colored, smoother brick was used during later restorations (in the 19th century, and again after World War II). Marvel at the ironclad doors and the heavy portcullis.

Venture through two more enclosed spaces, watching for the holes in the wall (for more guards and soldiers). The Teutonic Knights connected nearby lakes to create a system of canals, forming a moat around the castle that could be crossed only by this drawbridge. Ponder the fact that you have to go through five separate, well-defended gates to reach the...

MIDDLE CASTLE (ZAMEK ŚREDNI)

This part of Malbork, built at an uphill incline to make it even more imposing, was designed to impress. Knights and monks lived here.

Let's get oriented: To your left is the east wing, where visiting monks would sleep. Today this houses the Amber Collection

(ground floor) and the armory (upstairs). To the right (west) as you enter the main courtyard is the Grand Refectory (closer to the entrance) and the Grand Master's Palace (the taller, squarer building at the far end).

• *Before we move on, this is a good time to read up on the history of the Teutonic Knights (see sidebar). When you're ready to continue, enter the ground floor of the building on the left (at audiotour stop #15; remember, don't be shy about opening closed doors), and visit the...*

Amber Collection

This exhibit will make jewelry shoppers salivate. For a primer, read the "All About Amber" sidebar on page 459. You'll start 42 million years ago and follow the story of amber. Begin at the huge chunks of raw amber and the illuminated display of inclusions (bugs and other organic objects stuck in the amber, à la *Jurassic Park*). Some of the ancient amber artifacts displayed here are up to 3,000 years old. These were found in graves, put there by people who thought amber would help the deceased enter a better world. Wandering the hall, you'll see all manner of amber creations: boxes, brooches, necklaces, chess sets, pipes, miniature ships, wine glasses, and belts for skinny-waisted, fashion-conscious women. Look for

POMERANIA

The Teutonic Knights

Historically, Germans in Poland have had a volatile track record. And that goes all the way back (at least) to the arrival of the Teutonic Knights in the northern Polish lands in the 13th century.

The Order of the Teutonic Knights began in the Holy Land in 1191, during the Third Crusade. These German militarized monks, who took vows of poverty, chastity, and obedience, built hospitals, and cared for injured knights. When the Crusades ended in the 12th century, the order returned to Europe and reorganized as a chivalric order of Christian mercenaries—pagan-killers for hire.

In 1226, a northern Polish duke was struggling to subdue a tribe of pagans who had been attacking his lands, so he called in the Teutonic Knights. Clad in their white cloaks with skinny black crosses, and claiming to be "missionaries," the Teutonic Knights spent 60 years "saving" the pagans by turning them into serfs or brutally massacring them.

Job done, the Teutonic Knights decided they enjoyed northern Poland—and stuck around. With the support of the pope and the Holy Roman Emperor (who were swayed by their religious zeal), the Knights built one of Europe's biggest and most imposing fortresses: Malbork. In 1308, they seized large parts of northern Poland, including Gdańsk—cutting off Polish access to the Baltic Sea. Other Germans flocked to join the Knights, further developing a Germanic city-state—the Teutonic Grand Master's own mini-empire. The Knights grew rich from Hanseatic trade, specializing in amber, grain, and timber. By the late 14th century, the Teutonic Knights had conquered Estonia and Latvia,

two truly exquisite pieces: a small casket and an altar. Many of the finely decorated jewelry boxes and chests have ivory, silver, or shell inlays—better for contrast than gold. The portable religious shrines and altars allowed travelers to remain reverent on the road and still pack light. Find the amber crucifix. This is a small replica of a six-foot-tall amber and silver cross, presented to St. John Paul II by the people of Gdańsk. Another exhibit case contains necklaces displaying the full range of amber colors, from opaque white at the top, to transparent yellow in the middle, to virtually black at the bottom.

• *Go back outside and turn left, to the wooden staircase above the recommended Gothic Café (described later). Go up that staircase, and several more inside, to the top-floor...*

creating Europe's largest-ever monastic state, and were threatening Poles' pagan neighbor to the east, Lithuania.

Inspired by a mutual desire to fight back against the Teutonic Knights, the Poles and the Lithuanians merged their two realms. In 1386, Polish Princess Jadwiga married Lithuanian Prince Władysław Jagiełło (who converted to Christianity for the occasion), uniting Poland and Lithuania and kick-starting a grand new dynasty, the Jagiellonians.

Just as every American knows the date July 4, 1776, every Pole knows the date July 15, 1410—the Battle of Grunwald. King Władysław Jagiełło and Lithuanian Grand Duke Vytautas the Great led a ragtag army of some 40,000 soldiers—Lithuanians, Poles, other Slavs, and even speedy Tatar horsemen—against 27,000 Teutonic Knights. At the end of the day, some 18,000 Poles and Lithuanians were dead—but so were half of the Teutonic Knights, and the other half had been captured. Poland and Lithuania were victorious.

The Battle of Grunwald marked a turning point. The Teutonic Knights' political power waned, they pulled out of Lithuania, and they once again allowed free trade on the Vistula. A generation later, the Thirteen Years' War (1454-1466) finally put an end to the Teutonic Knights' domination of northern Poland. The order officially dissolved in 1575, when they converted to Protestantism (though some conspiracy theorists claim the Teutonic Knights are still very much active). Much of their land eventually became part of Prussia.

The 19th-century Romantics who fanned the flames of Polish patriotism reimagined the Teutonic Knights as a symbol of Germanic oppression, which resonated among Poles throughout the troubled 20th century. Even today, Poles—and all Slavs—think of the Teutonic Knights as murderous invaders whereas Germans see them as a mere footnote in their history.

Armory

This is a small armory for such a massive castle. In its two rooms you'll see an impressive array of swords, armor, and other armaments (English descriptions). Look for the 600-year-old "hand-and-a-half" swords—too big to be held in one hand. At the end, in the display of cannons, pikes, and spears, find the giant shield. These shields could be lined up to form a portable "wall" to protect the knights. Downstairs, the suit of armor from the Hussars—Polish horseback knights—came with wings, which created a terrifying sound when galloping.

• *Head back outside (noticing the handy and rare WC straight ahead). Cross the main courtyard going downhill and enter the smaller courtyard through the passage next to the stubby, dark-wood-topped tower. Find the dark, steep, and unlabeled steps down into the...*

"Boiler Room"

The Teutonic Knights had a surprisingly sophisticated method for heating this huge complex. You see a furnace down below and a holding area for hot rocks above. The radiant heat given off by the rocks spread through the vents without also filling them with smoke (illustrated by a chart on the wall). This is one of 11 such "boiler rooms" in the castle complex. As you tour the rest of the castle, keep an eye out for little saucer-sized heating vents in the floor.

• *Climb back up the stairs, take an immediate left through a tiny arch, and then go left again, up through the door labeled #5 (not down, which takes you out of castle). This leads into the...*

Grand Master's Palace

This was one of the grandest royal residences in medieval Europe, used in later times by Polish kings and German Kaisers. (Today it's sometimes used for special exhibitions.)

• *Walk through the kitchen into the big and bright...*

Grand Refectory: With remarkable palm vaulting and grand frescoes, this dining hall hosted feasts for up to 400 people to celebrate a military victory or to impress visiting dignitaries. Notice the 36 heating vents—which are directly above the boiler room you just visited—designed to keep the VIPs warm.

• *From here, climb the stairs into the...*

Private Rooms of the Grand Master: Though the Teutonic Order dictated that the monks sleep in dormitories, the Grand Master made an exception for himself—with a suite of private rooms that came with his own toilet (with a river view) and his own chapel, dedicated to St. Catherine. Exploring the Top Knight's residence, appreciate the show-off decor (including some 15th-century original frescoes of wine leaves and grapes). His private bedroom was decorated with frescoes of four virgins—female martyrs. The passage outside the private rooms came with a washbasin, as anyone wanting an audience with the Grand Master had to wash both his hands and his feet.

Next, enter the private dining room, the **Winter Refectory,** with fewer windows (better insulation) and little manhole-like openings in the floor where the "central heating" entered the room. The adjacent **Summer Refectory** had big stained-glass windows. With all the delicate vaulting supported by a single pillar in the middle, this room was clearly not designed with defense in mind. In fact, medieval Polish armies focused their attacks on this room. On one legendary occasion, the attackers—tipped off by a spy—knew that an important meeting was going on here and fired a cannonball into the room. It just missed the pillar. (You can see where the cannonball hit the wall, just above the fireplace.) The ceiling eventually did collapse during World War II.

• *Back out in the courtyard, look for the four...*

Grand Master Statues

Though this was a religious order, these powerful guys look more like kings than monks. From left to right, shake hands with Hermann von Salza (who was Grand Master when the Teutonic Knights came to Poland); Siegfried von Feuchtwangen (who actually moved the T. K. capital from Venice to Malbork, and who conquered Gdańsk for the Knights—oops, can't shake his hand, which was supposedly chopped off by Soviet troops); Winrich von Kniprode (who oversaw Malbork's Golden Age and turned it into a castle fit for a king); and Markgraf Albrecht von Hohenzollern (the last Grand Master before the order dissolved and converted to Protestantism).

• *To the right of the statues, continue into the High Castle by passing over the...*

Drawbridge

As you cross, notice the extensive system of fortifications and moats protecting the innermost part of the castle just ahead. Check out the cracks in the walls (on right)—an increasing threat to this ever-settling castle set on marshy, unstable terrain. On the left is a collection of stone catapult balls that were actually fired at this castle when it was under siege. (Look high above to see the dents such stones can make.) The passage ahead is lined with holes (for surveillance) and with chutes up above (to pour scalding water or pitch on unwanted visitors). It's not quite straight—so a cannon fired here would hit the side wall of the passage, rather than entering the High Castle and its central courtyard. Which is what you're about to do now.

HIGH CASTLE (ZAMEK WYSOKI)

This is the heart of the castle, and its oldest section. From this spot, the Teutonic Knights governed their vast realm—the largest monk-ruled territory in European history. As much a monastery as a fortress, the High Castle was off-limits to all but 60 monks of the Teutonic Order and their servants. (The knights stayed in the Middle Castle.) Here you'll find the monks' dormitories, chapels, church, and refectory. As this was the nerve center of the Teutonic Knights—the T. K. HQ—it was also their last line of defense. They stored enormous amounts of food here in case of a siege.

In the middle of the High Castle courtyard is a **well**—an

POMERANIA

essential part of any inner castle, especially one as prone to sieges as Malbork. At the top is a sculpture of a pelican. Because this noble bird was believed to kill itself to feed its young (notice that it's piercing its own chest with its beak), it was often used in the Middle Ages as a symbol for the self-sacrifice of Jesus.

• *Take some time to explore the...*

High Castle—Ground Floor

Work clockwise around the courtyard from where you entered. A door leads to the prison (with small "solitary confinement" cells near the entrance). Along the next wall of the cloister is a post-WWII photo of bombed-out Malbork. Just adjacent, hiding in the far corner, is an exhibit on stained-glass windows from the castle church. Somewhere around here, you should see a demonstration of how medieval money was made. The Teutonic Knights minted their own coins—and you can buy your very own freshly minted replica today.

• *Continuing around the courtyard, you'll find the...*

Kitchen: This exhibit—with a long table piled with typical ingredients from that time—really gives you a feel for medieval monastery life. The monks who lived here ate three meals a day, along with lots of beer (made here) and wine (imported from France, Italy, and Hungary). A cellar under the kitchen was used as a primitive refrigerator—big chunks of ice were cut from the frozen river in winter, stored in the basement, and used to keep food cool in summer. Behind the long table, see the big dumbwaiter (with five shelves for hot dishes), which connects this kitchen with the refectory upstairs. Step into the giant stove and look up the biggest chimney in the castle.

• *Now go back out into the courtyard and climb up the stairs near where you first entered.*

High Castle—Middle Floor

• *From the top of the stairs, the first door on the left (with the colorfully painted arch) leads to the most important room of the High Castle, the...*

Chapter Room: Monks gathered here after Mass, and it was also the site for meetings of Teutonic Knights from around the countryside. If a Grand Master was killed in battle, the new one would be elected here. Carvings above each chair indicated the status of the man who sat there. The big chair belonged to the Grand Master. Notice the little windows above his chair, connecting this room to the church next door. Ecclesiastical music would filter in through these windows; imagine the voices of 60 monks bouncing around with these acoustics.

While monks are usually thought to pursue simple lives, the elegant vaulting in this room is anything but plain. The

14th-century frescoes (restored in the 19th century) depict Grand Masters. In the floor are more vents for the central heating.

• *Leave the Chapter House and walk straight ahead, imagining the monk-filled corridors of Teutonic times. The first door on the right is the...*

Treasury: As you explore the five rooms of the tax collector and the house administrator, notice the wide variety of safes and other lock boxes. Documents, amber, and coins were kept behind heavily armored and well-locked doors.

• *Continue around the cloister. At the end of the corridor, spot the little devil at the bottom of the vaulting (on the right, about eye level). He's pulling his beard and crossing his legs— pointing you down the long corridor leading about 50 yards away from the cloister to the...*

Dansker Tower: From the devil's grimace, you might have guessed that this tower houses the latrine. Four wooden toilet stalls filled this big room. Where one is missing, you can look down to see how the "toilets" simply dropped the waste into the moat. For obvious sanitary (and olfactory) reasons, this potty tower is set apart from the main part of the castle. The bins above the toilets were filled with cabbage leaves, to be used by the T. K. as TP (and as an organic form of Preparation H). This tower could also serve as a final measure of defense—it's easier to defend than the entire castle. Food was stored above, just in case. More info on this grand castle WC is on the wall.

• *Return down the long corridor. Before the end, on the right-hand side of the long passage, a door leads into the...*

Church Exhibition: Once dormitories for the monks, these three rooms today display a wide range of relics from the church (with English descriptions). In the last room, on the far wall, is the artistic highlight of the castle: a finely carved and painted three-panel altarpiece from about 1500 featuring the coronation of Mary. Mary's face is mesmerizing. Characteristic of the late Gothic period, the robes seem to fly unrealistically (as if they were bent metal).

• *Back out in the main cloister, turn right, and continue to the end, arriving at the...*

Golden Gate: This elaborate doorway—covered in protective glass—marks the entrance to St. Mary's Church (which is closed for a multi-year renovation). This is a rare original door in the castle. Ringed with detailed carvings from the Old Testament, and symbolic messages about how monks of the Teutonic Order should live their lives, it's a marvelous example of late-13th-century art. At the bottom-left end of the arch, find the five wise virgins who, having filled their lamps with oil and conserved it wisely, are headed to heaven. On

the right, the five foolish virgins who overslept and used up all their oil are damned, much to their dismay.

• *Go through the narrow door next to the Golden Gate (on the right) and hike up the tight spiral staircase to the final set of exhibits.*

High Castle—Top Floor

Walk through an exhibit about the illustrious guests of the castle. At the end, descend into the monks' common room (left at the bot-

tom of the stairs). Over the fireplace is a relief depicting the Teutonic Knights fighting the pagans. To the left and above (see the stone windows) is a balcony where musicians entertained the monks after a meal. The next, very long room, with

seven pillars, is the refectory, where the monks ate in silence. Along the right-hand wall are lockable storage boxes for tableware. At the end of this room, just beyond another ornate fireplace, notice the grated hole in the wall. This is where the dumbwaiter comes up from the kitchen (which we saw below). Beyond this room is an exhibit about the architectural renovation of the castle.

• *Your Malbork tour ends here. You leave the way you came. En route, you can walk around terraces lining the inner moat, between the castle walls (stairs lead down off of the drawbridge, by the catapult balls). It's hardly a must-see, but it's pleasant enough, with the Grand Master's garden, a cemetery for monks, and the remains of the small St. Anne's Chapel (with Grand Master tombs).*

Eating at Malbork Castle

Several cheap food stands cluster outside the castle (by the river). For a meal inside the castle complex, the **Gothic Café,** under the stairs to the armory in the Middle Castle, is good. Dishing up traditional Polish food inspired by old dishes once served here, it's handy for its 39-zł lunch deal that includes a main dish and soup.

You can eat in the busy cellar or out in the garden (30-50-zł main dishes, open same hours as castle, tel. 55-647-0889, www.gothic.com.pl, Chef Bogdan is passionate and welcoming).

Malbork Connections

From Malbork by Train to: Gdańsk (2/hour, about half are express EIC trains that take 30 minutes, the rest are slower regional trains that take around 45 minutes), **Toruń** (about every 2 hours, 3 hours, transfer in Tczew or Iława), **Warsaw** (hourly, 2.5 hours on express EIC train).

Toruń

Toruń (TOH-roon) is a pretty, lazy Gothic town conveniently located about halfway between Warsaw and Gdańsk. It's worth a

couple of hours to stroll the lively streets, ogle the huge red-brick buildings, and savor the flavor of perhaps Poland's most livable city.

With about 210,000 residents and 30,000 students (at Copernicus University), Toruń is a thriving burg. Like Kraków (and unlike most other Polish cities), Toruń escaped destruction

during World War II and remains well-preserved today. Locals brag that their city is a "mini-Kraków." But that sells both cities short. Toruń lacks Kraków's over-the-top romanticism, and its sights are quickly exhausted. On the other hand, Toruń may well be Poland's most user-friendly city: tidy streets with a sensible grid plan (and English signposts to keep you on track), wide pedestrian boulevards crammed with locals who greet each other like they're long-lost friends, and an easygoing ambience that seems to say, "Hey—relax." And, while it has its share of tourists, Toruń feels more off-the-beaten-path than the other Polish destinations in this book.

Toruń clings fiercely to its two claims to fame: It's the proud birthplace of the astronomer Copernicus (Mikołaj Kopernik), and home to a dizzying variety of gingerbread treats (*piernika;* pyer-NEE-kah).

Orientation to Toruń

Everything in Toruń worth seeing is in the walled Old Town, climbing up a gentle hill from the Vistula River. The broad, traffic-free main drag, ulica Szeroka (called Różana at the entrance of town) bisects the Old Town, running parallel to the river.

ARRIVAL IN TORUŃ

Toruń's main train station (called Toruń Główny) is across the river from the Old Town, about a mile away. The main hall has ticket windows, an ATM, and lockers.

To reach the Old Town, you have two options: If you go out the door from the main hall, you'll spot **taxis** waiting to take you into town (the trip costs around 15-20 zł). To take the **bus,** buy a 2.80-zł ticket from the *RUCH* kiosk overlooking the tracks near the main hall. Then follow the pedestrian underpass beneath track 4 (entrance to underpass marked with low-profile *wyjście do miasta* sign and bus icon, outside main hall and to the left). When you emerge on the other side, the bus stop for bus #22, #25, or #27 into the center is ahead and on your right. Take the bus to Plac Rapackiego, the first stop after the long bridge. To return to the station, catch bus #22, #25, or #27 across the busy road from where you got off.

TOURIST INFORMATION

The TI is on the main square, behind the Old Town Hall. Pick up the free map and get information about hotels in town and city tours (Tue-Fri 9:00-18:00, Mon and Sat 9:00-16:00; closed Sun except May-Sept, when it's open 9:00-16:00; Rynek Staromiejski 25, tel. 56-621-0930, www.it.torun.pl).

Toruń Walk

This brief self-guided walk takes you through the heart of Toruń. With no stops, you could do it in 20 minutes.

• *From the Plac Rapackiego bus stop, head into town through the passageways under the colorful buildings. Within a block, you're at the bustling...*

Old Town Market Square (Rynek Staromiejski): This square is surrounded by huge brick buildings and outdoor restaurants buzzing with lively locals. The **Old Town Hall** (Ratusz Staromiejski) fills the middle of the square, as was often the case in medieval Hanseatic towns. Its fine museum and climbable tower are Toruń's main sights worth visiting (described later, under "Sights in Toruń"). The building with the pointy spires on the right (across from the Old Town Hall) is the **Artus Court,** where

Toruń

ETHNOGRAPHIC PARK

To Main Bus Station

LEONA SZUMANA

WYSOKA

DOMINISKA

PROSTA

N

100 Meters
100 Yards

WAŁY GEN. WŁADYSŁAWA SIKORSKIEGO

PODMURNA

CHEŁMIŃSKA

SZEWSKA

O L D

New Market Square

FRANCISZKAŃSKA

CHURCH OF VIRGIN MARY

T O W N

KRÓL. JADWIGI

PANNY MARII

Old Town Market Square

TOWN HALL
MUSEUM & TOWER

WIELKE GARBARY

CHURCH OF HOLY SPIRIT

ULIKA SZEROKA

COPERNICUS STATUE

PRZEDZAMCZE

Plac Rapackiego

RÓŻANA

PIERNIKI GINGERBREAD SHOP

U. MOSTOWA

PODMURNA

CASTLE RUINS

B
#22, 25 & 27

WALK BEGINS

PIEKARY

MIKOŁAJA KOPERNIKA

ŻEGLARSKA

CIASNA

TOWN WALLS

GINGERBREAD MUSEUM

CATHEDRAL OF TWO ST. JOHNS

TOILET TOWER

ALEJA JANA PAWŁA II

ŁABIAŃSKA

COPERNICUS HOUSE

❶

BANKOWA

❷

MOSTOWA GATE

KLASZTORNA GATE

ŻEGLARSKA GATE

BULWAR FILADELFIJSKI

RIVERSIDE PROMENADE

River

P

PIŁSUDSKIEGO BRIDGE

To Main Train Station (Toruń Głowny)

Vistula

❶ Hotel Karczma "Spichrz"
❷ Hotel Retman

POMERANIA

the medieval town council and merchants' guilds met. While the town was founded in 1231, the current building is Neo-Gothic, dating from the 19th century.

The guy playing his violin in front of the Old Town Hall is a **rafter** *(retman)*—one of the medieval lumberjacks who lashed tree trunks together and floated them down the Vistula to Gdańsk. This particular rafter came to Toruń when the town was infested with frogs. He wooed them with his violin and marched them out of town. (Hmm...sounds like a certain pied piper....)

The bigger statue, at the other end of the Old Town Hall, depicts **Mikołaj Kopernik,** better known as Nicholas Copernicus (1473-1543). This Toruń-born son of aristocrats turned the world on its ear when he suggested that the sun, not the earth, is the center of the universe (the "heliocentric theory"). Toruń is serious about this local boy done good—he's the town mascot, as well as the namesake of the local university. Among its fields of study, Copernicus U. has a healthy astronomy program. There's a planetarium in the Old Town (just past the far corner of the square) and a giant radio telescope on the town outskirts. Despite all the local fuss over Copernicus, there's some dispute about his ethnicity; he was born in Toruń, all right, but at a time when it was the predominantly German town of "Thorn." So is he Polish or German? (For more on Copernicus, visit his birth house—now a modest museum on the astronomer—just two blocks away and described later, under "Sights in Toruń").

Copernicus faces a shiny donkey at the corner of **Szeroka** and Żeglarska streets. We'll venture down Żeglarska first, and then return to walk down Szeroka. By the way, that shiny donkey with a sharp ridge on his back, while happy today, recalls a humiliating punishment. Centuries ago, delinquents and petty criminals needing to be set straight would be forced to straddle this donkey— after townspeople had tied heavy stones to their feet, weighing them down painfully.

• *But you're on vacation and, rather than humiliation, you get ginger-bread. Head down Żeglarska to #25 (on the right).*

Pierniki (Gingerbread) Shop: For Poles, Toruń is synonymous with **gingerbread** *(piernika)*—you'll smell its sweet scent all over town. This Toruń treat can be topped with different kinds of jams or glazes, and/or dipped in chocolate. This shop has a fun system: All of the varieties cost the same, so you can create just the mix you like by pointing. *Róża* is rose, *malina* is raspberry, *czarna porzeczka* is black currant, *morela* is apricot, and—of course—*cze-kolada* is chocolate.

• *A few steps down and across the street is the...*

Cathedral of Two Saint Johns (Katedra Św. Jana Chrz-ciciela i Jana Ewangelisty): Dedicated in the 12th century to John the Baptist and John the Evangelist, this is the parish church of the Old Town. From the street, notice the architectural heaviness: This marshy land lacked big stones, so instead of flying buttresses, they designed a bulky and sturdy brick structure so they could build big. Stepping inside, you find pure Gothic architecture (free, open daily until last Mass at 18:00). The gravestones of big shots pave the floor. Each trade guild had its own chapel. To the left of the altar, notice the finely restored 13th-century *Last Judgment*. In the rear of the church (on the right) is the baptismal font where, in 1473, Copernicus was baptized.

• *Having satisfied your ginger tooth and seen the town's most important church, head back to the square and that painful donkey, turn right, and join the human stream down the appropriately named...*

Ulica Szeroka ("Wide Street"): This enjoyable pedestrian promenade leads through the heart of town. Embedded in the paving bricks are the coats of arms of Toruń's medieval trading partners. And on each side of the street is an eclectic commotion of fun facades.

About 30 yards before the road forks at the stately, white Empik building, look down narrow Przedzamcze street to the right to see fragments of the town wall. This marks the border between the Old Town and the New Town (chartered only about 30 years later—both in the 13th century). While these areas are both collectively known today as the unified "Old Town," they were quite different in the Middle Ages—each with its own market square, and separated by a wall. (If you're curious to see the New Town Square and Town Hall, take the left fork at the Empik building and walk two blocks up ulica Królowej Jadwigi.)

• *Turn right down Przedzamcze, bear left at the parking lot, and continue under the stubby, stand-alone brick gate to the...*

Toruń Castle Ruins: This castle, built by the Teutonic Knights who were so influential in northern Poland in the Middle Ages (see page 502), was destroyed in the 15th century by the locals—who, aside from a heap of bricks, left only the tower that housed the Teutonic toilets. The ruins have nothing much to offer, but what survives is one of the better toilet towers in Europe— which was connected to the castle by an elevated walkway and located far enough away to keep things hygienic. The old mill next to the toilet is now a hotel named 1231, for the date the Teutonic Order arrived here.

• *Our walk is over. You can backtrack the way you came and explore more of the city (including the sights listed next). Or you can take a quick riverside stroll: Go under the toilet tower and down to the Vistula River, turn right, and stroll along the castle and 14th-century city walls back to your starting point. The road is called Bulwar Filadelfijski—for Toruń's sister city in Pennsylvania.*

Sights in Toruń

Toruń is more about strolling than it is about sightseeing—the town's museums are underwhelming. Aside from its half-dozen red-brick churches (any of which are worth dropping into), the following attractions are worth considering on a rainy day.

▲City Hall Museum and Tower

Like Kraków's Cloth Hall, this building, dominating the town square, was a general market. It served as the heart of the city. Today it offers the only chance to see historic artifacts in town, all well-described in English. It gives a good history of the Teutonic Knights, who first came to Toruń in 1231. You'll see intimate bits and pieces of history, from pewter tankards to old gingerbread molds, that show the richness of this traders' city. Another wing of the ground floor is filled with medieval church art saved from the region's churches. Much of it is pre-Reformation Catholic art, with lots of Marys (as she was the patron of the Teutonic Order) and a close-up look at some 14th-century stained glass. The royal halls upstairs feature portraits and fine 17th-century inlaid wooden doors. The 130-foot-tall tower can be climbed (on narrow wooden steps) for great views over the city center.

Cost and Hours: 11 zł apiece for museum and tower, 17-zł combo-ticket for both; May-Sept Tue-Sun 10:00-18:00, Oct-April Tue-Sun 10:00-16:00, tower may be open later, closed Mon year-round; Rynek Staromiejski 1, tel. 56-660-5612, www.muzeum. torun.pl.

Gingerbread Museum (Muzeum Piernika)

This fun attraction—by far Toruń's liveliest—is an actual working gingerbread bakery of yore. Barefoot, costumed medieval bakers walk you through the traditional process of rolling, cutting out, baking, and tasting your own batch of gingerbread cookies (30-40 minutes, start to finish). After aging for 12 weeks to achieve the proper consistency, the dough bakes for only 12 minutes—or, according to the medieval bakers, about 50 Hail Marys.

Cost and Hours: 12 zł, daily 10:00-18:00, Polish tours start at the top of each hour, English demonstrations most likely at 13:00 and 16:00, can be crowded in peak times—call ahead to confirm schedule and reserve a spot, 2 blocks toward the river from Old Town Market Square at Rabiańska 9, tel. 56-663-6617, www. muzeumpiernika.pl.

Copernicus House (Dom Kopernika)

Filling a pair of beautiful, gabled brick buildings, this dull, over-priced little museum celebrates the hero of Toruń. As much about medieval Toruń as about the famous astronomer, and sprawling over several floors in the two buildings, the exhibits loosely explain Nicolaus Copernicus' life and achievements. The displays are copies of important documents and paintings, and models of his instruments—all with English descriptions. The second part of the exhibit is an 18-minute slideshow with recorded commentary about medieval Toruń, with a model of the city that lights up dramatically at appropriate moments (plays on the half-hour, in English by request).

Cost and Hours: Museum only-11 zł, model/slideshow only-20 zł, 22-zł combo-ticket for both; May-Sept Tue-Sun 10:00-18:00, Oct-April Tue-Sun 10:00-16:00, closed Mon year-round; Kopernika 15, tel. 56-662-7038, www.muzeum.torun.pl. To get to the museum, head down Żeglarska and take the first right—on Kopernika, of course.

Ethnographic Park (Park Etnograficzny)

This open-air folk museum, while not ranking with Europe's best, is at least your most convenient opportunity to stroll through some traditional buildings from the region. It's in the middle of a pleasant park just outside the Old Town. Even if you're not interested in the museum, the park is a fine place to pass some time.

Cost and Hours: 14 zł; mid-April-June Tue and Thu 9:00-17:00, Wed and Fri 9:00-16:00, Sat-Sun 10:00-18:00; July-Sept Tue, Thu, and Sat-Sun 10:00-18:00, Wed and Fri 9:00-16:00; shorter hours off-season; closed Mon year-round; Wały Gen. Sikorskiego 19, www.etnomuzeum.pl. To get there from the Old Town Market Square, walk up Chełmińska with the river at your back and the Old Town Hall on your left. Cross the busy road, and you're in the park.

Sleeping in Toruń

Toruń's Old Town has more than its share of good value hotels. The TI has a brochure listing the options and can help you find a room for no extra charge.

$$ Hotel Karczma "Spichrz" ("Granary") is a fresh, atmospheric hotel in a renovated old granary. Its 23 rooms and public spaces are a fun blend of old and new—with huge wooden beams around every corner and the scent of the restaurant's wood-fired grill wafting through the halls. It's comfortable, central, well-priced, and a little kitschy (Sb-230 zł, Db-290 zł, 10-20 percent cheaper on weekends, tall people may not appreciate low ceilings and beams, elevator, a block off the main drag toward the river at ulica Mostowa 1, tel. 56-657-1140, www.spichrz.pl, hotel@spichrz.pl). The restaurant is also good (30-55-zł grilled meat dishes, daily 12:00-23:00).

$ Hotel Retman ("Rafter") has 29 older but nicely appointed rooms over a restaurant just down the street from the Gingerbread Museum (Sb-190 zł, Db-250 zł; Fri-Sun prices drop to Sb-160 zł, Db-200 zł; ulica Rabiańska 15, tel. 56-657-4460, www.hotel-retman.pl, recepcja@hotelretman.pl).

Sleep Code

Abbreviations   (3 zł = about $1, country code: 48)
S = Single, **D** = Double/Twin, **T** = Triple, **Q** = Quad, **b** = bathroom, **s** = shower only.

Price Rankings
   $$ Higher Priced—Most rooms more than 250 zł.
   $ Lower Priced—Most rooms 250 zł or less.

Unless otherwise noted, credit cards are accepted, breakfast is included, Wi-Fi is generally free, and English is spoken. Prices change; verify current rates online or by email. For the best prices, always book directly with the hotel.

Toruń Connections

Toruń is a handy stopover on the way between Warsaw and Gdańsk. It's on a different train line than Malbork—so visiting both Toruń and the mighty Teutonic castle in the same day is surprisingly time-consuming.

From Toruń by Train to: Warsaw (9/day, 3 hours direct, longer with a transfer in Kutno or Iława), **Gdańsk** (5/day, about 3 hours; additional options with a transfer in Bydgoszcz, 3.5 hours), **Malbork** (about every 2 hours, 3 hours, transfer in Tczew or Iława), **Kraków** (1/day direct, 6.5 hours; better to transfer at Warsaw's Zachodnia station: 8/day, 5.5-6 hours), **Berlin** (4/day, 5.75-6 hours, transfer in Poznań).

POMERANIA

HUNGARY
Magyarország

HUNGARY

Magyarország

Hungary is an island of Asian-descended Magyars in a sea of Slavs. Even though the Hungarians have thoroughly integrated with their Slavic and German neighbors in the millennium-plus since they arrived, there's still something about the place that's distinctly Magyar (MUD-jar). Here in quirky, idiosyncratic Hungary, everything's a little different from the rest of Europe—in terms of history, language, culture, customs, and cuisine—but it's hard to put your finger on exactly how.

Just a century ago, this country controlled half of one of Europe's grandest realms: the Austro-Hungarian Empire. Today, perhaps clinging to their former greatness, many Hungarians remain old-fashioned and nostalgic. With their dusty museums and bushy moustaches, they love to remember the good old days. Buildings all over the country are marked with plaques boasting *MŰEMLÉK* ("historical monument").

Thanks to this focus on tradition, the Hungarians you'll encounter are generally polite, formal, and professional. Hungarians have class. Everything here is done with a proud flourish. People in the service industry seem to wear their uniforms as a badge of honor rather than a burden. When a waiter comes to your table in a restaurant, he'll say, *"Tessék parancsolni"*—literally, "Please command, sir." The standard greeting, *"Jó napot kívánok,"* means "I wish you a good day." Women sometimes hear the even more formal greeting, *"Kezét csókolom"*—"I kiss your hand." And when your train or bus makes a stop, you won't be alerted by a mindless, blaring beep—but instead, by peppy music. (You'll be humming these contagious little ditties all day.) Perhaps thanks to this artful blending of elegance and formality, Hungarians have a cultural affinity for the French.

Hungarians are also orderly and tidy...in their own sometimes unexpected ways. Yes, Hungary has its share of litter, graffiti, and crumbling buildings, but you'll find great reason within the chaos. The Hungarian railroad has a long list of discounted fares—for seniors, kids, dogs...and monkeys. (It could happen.) My favorite town name in Hungary: Hatvan. This means "Sixty"

in Hungarian...and it's exactly 60 kilometers from Budapest. You can't argue with that kind of logic.

This tradition of left-brained thinking hasn't produced many great Hungarian painters or poets who are known outside their homeland. But the Hungarians, who are renowned for their ingenuity, have made tremendous contributions to science, technology, business, and industry. Hungarians of note include Edward Teller (instrumental in creating the A-bomb), John von Neumann (a pioneer of computer science), András Gróf (who, as Andy Grove, emigrated to the US and founded Intel), and George Soros (the billionaire investor famous—or notorious—for supporting left-wing causes). A popular local joke claims that Hungarians are so clever that they can enter a revolving door behind you and exit in front of you.

Perhaps the most famous Hungarian "scientist" invented something you probably have in a box in your basement: Ernő Rubik, creator of the famous cube. Hungarians' enjoyment of a good mind-bending puzzle is also evident in their fascination with chess, which you'll see played in cafés, parks, and baths.

Like their Viennese neighbors, Hungarians know how to enjoy the good life. Favorite activities include splashing and soaking in their many thermal baths (see page 632). "Taking the waters," Hungarian-style, deserves to be your top priority while you're here. Though public baths can sound intimidating, they're a delight. In the following chapters I recommend my three favorite baths in Budapest, a fine bath in Eger, and two more just outside of Eger. For each, I've included careful instructions to help you

Hungary Almanac

Official Name: Magyarország (Hungary).

Snapshot History: Settled by the Central Asian Magyars in A.D. 896, Hungary became Catholic in the year 1000 and went on to become Christian Europe's front line in fighting against the Ottomans (Muslims from today's Turkey) in the 16th-17th centuries. After serving as co-capital of the vast Austro-Hungarian Empire and losing World Wars I and II, Hungary became a Soviet satellite until achieving independence in 1989.

Population: Hungary's 10 million people (similar to Michigan) are 92 percent ethnic Hungarians who speak Hungarian. One in 50 is Roma (Gypsy). About 40 percent of the populace is Catholic, with nearly 15 percent Protestant and around 30 percent listed as "other" or unaffiliated. Of the world's approximately 12 million ethnic Hungarians, one in six lives outside Hungary (mostly in areas of Romania, Slovakia, Serbia, and Croatia that were once part of Hungary).

Latitude and Longitude: 47°N and 20°E; similar latitude to Seattle, Paris, and Vienna.

Area: 36,000 square miles, similar to Indiana or Maine.

Geography: Hungary is situated in the Carpathian Basin, bound on the north by the Carpathian Mountains and on the south by the Dinaric Mountains. Though it's surrounded by mountains, Hungary itself is relatively flat, with some gently rolling hills. The Great Hungarian Plain, which begins on the east bank of the Danube in Budapest, stretches all the way to Asia. Hungary's two main rivers—the Danube and Tisza—run north-south through the country, neatly dividing it into three regions.

Biggest Cities: Budapest (the capital on the Danube, nearly 2 million), Debrecen (in the east, 206,000), and Miskolc (in the north, 170,000).

enjoy the warm-water fun like a pro. (To allay your first fear: Yes, you can wear your swimsuit.)

Hungarians have also revived an elegant, Vienna-style café culture that was dismantled by the communists. Whiling away the afternoon at a genteel coffeehouse, as you nurse a drink or a delicate dessert, is a favorite pastime. (For the best options in Budapest, see "Budapest's Café Culture" on page 681.)

Classical music is revered in Hungary, perhaps as nowhere else outside Austria. Aside from scientists and businessmen, the best-known Hungarians are composers: Béla Bartók, Zoltán Kodály, and Franz Liszt.

While one in five Hungarians lives in Budapest, the countryside plays an important role in Hungary's economy—this has always been a highly agricultural region. The sprawling Great

Economy: The Gross Domestic Product is $197 billion (a quarter of Poland's), but the GDP per capita is $19,800 (only slightly less than Poland's). Thanks to its progressive "goulash communism," Hungary had a head start on many other former Soviet Bloc countries and is now thriving, privatized...and largely foreign-owned. In the 1990s, many communist-era workers (especially women) lost their jobs. Today, the workforce is small (only 57 percent of eligible workers) but highly skilled. Grains, metals, machinery, and automobiles are major exports, and about one-quarter of trade is with Germany.

Currency: 225 forints (Ft, or HUF) = about $1 (though the exchange rate can fluctuate significantly).

Government: The single-house National Assembly (199 seats) is the only ruling branch directly elected by popular vote. The legislators in turn select the figurehead president (currently János Áder) and the ruling prime minister (Viktor Orbán); both belong to the right-of-center Fidesz party.

Flag: Three horizontal bands, top to bottom: red (representing strength), white (faithfulness), and green (hope). It's identical to the Italian flag, but flipped 90 degrees counterclockwise. It often includes the Hungarian coat of arms: horizontal red-and-white stripes (on the left); the patriarchal, or double-barred, cross (on the right); and the Hungarian crown (on top).

The Average János: The typical Hungarian eats a pound of lard a week (they cook with it). The average family has three members and spends almost three-fourths of its income on housing. According to a recent condom-company survey, the average Hungarian has sex 131 times a year (behind only France and Greece), making them Europe's third-greatest liars.

Hungarian Plain (Puszta) that makes up a vast swath of Hungary is the country's breadbasket. You'll pass through fields of wheat and corn, but the grains are secondary to Hungarians' (and tourists') true love: wine. Hungarian winemaking standards plummeted under the communists, but many vintner families are now reclaiming their land, returning to their precise traditional methods, and making wines worth being proud of once more. (For details, see the "Hungarian Wines" sidebar, later.)

Somehow Hungary, at the crossroads of Europe, has managed to become cosmopolitan while remaining perfectly Hungarian. The Hungarians—like Hungary itself—are a cross-section of Central European cultures: Magyars, Germans, Czechs, Slovaks, Poles, Serbs, Jews, Ottomans, Romanians, Roma (Gypsies), and many others. Still, no matter how many generations removed they are from Magyar stock, there's something different about Hungarians—and not just the language. Look a Hungarian in the eye, and you'll see a glimmer of the marauding Magyar, stomping in from the Central Asian plains a thousand years ago.

HELPFUL HINTS

First Name Last: Hungarians list a person's family name first, and the given name is last—just as in many other Eastern cultures (think of Kim Jong Il). So the composer known as "Franz Liszt" in German is "Liszt Ferenc" in his homeland. (To help reduce confusion, many Hungarian business cards list the surname in capital letters.)

Hello Goodbye: Hungarians have a charming habit of using the English word "hello" for both "hi" and "bye," just like the Italians use "ciao." You might overhear a Hungarian end a telephone conversation with a cheery "Hello!"

Telephones: Like many things in Hungary, the telephone system is uniquely confusing. You must dial different codes whether you're calling locally, long distance within the country, or internationally to Hungary.

    Dialing Fixed Lines: To dial a number in the same city, simply dial direct, with no area code.

    To dial long-distance within Hungary, add the prefix 06, followed by the area code (e.g., Budapest's area code is 1, so you dial 06-1, then the rest of the number).

    To make an international call to Hungary, dial the international access code (00 if calling from Europe, 011 from the United States or Canada), then Hungary's country code (36), then the area code (but not the 06) and number.

    To make an international call from Hungary, dial 00, the country code of the country you're calling (see chart in Practicalities), the area code if applicable (may need to drop initial zero), and the local number.

    Dialing Mobile Phones and Other Unusual Numbers: Certain Hungarian phone numbers are particularly confusing to dial. Numbers beginning with 0620, 0630, or 0670 are mobile phones; those beginning with 0680 are toll-free; and 0681 and 0691 are expensive toll lines.

    To call these numbers from a fixed line within Hungary, simply dial the number direct, as it appears in this book.

    To dial these numbers from a fixed line outside Hungary, you need to replace the initial 06 with 011-36 (from the US) or 00-36 (from Europe). Then dial the rest of the number. So, to call my favorite Budapest guide from a fixed line inside Hungary, you'd dial 0620-926-0557; from North America, you'd dial 011-36-20-926-0557; and from another European country, you'd dial 00-36-20-926-0557.

To dial them from a mobile phone (whether inside or outside of Hungary), replace the initial 06 with +36, then dial the rest of the number.

Toll Sticker: Driving on Hungarian expressways requires a toll sticker (*autópálya matrica*, also called a "vignette," 2,975 Ft/week, 4,780 Ft/month, www.motorway.hu). Ask about this when you rent your car (if it's not already included, you'll have to buy one).

HUNGARIAN HISTORY

The Hungarian story—essentially the tale of a people finding their home—is as epic as any in Europe. Over the course of a millennium, a troublesome nomadic tribe that was the scourge of Europe gradually assimilated with its neighbors and—through a combination of tenacity and diplomacy—found itself controlling a vast swath of Central and Eastern Europe. Locals toss around the names of great historical figures such as Kossuth, Széchenyi, and Nagy as if they're talking about old friends. Take this crash course so you can keep up.

The story begins long, long ago and far, far away...

Welcome to Europe

The land we call Hungary today has long been considered the place—culturally and geographically—where the West (Europe) meets the East (Asia). The Roman province of Pannonia extended to the final foothills of the Alps that constitute the Buda Hills, on the west side of the Danube. Across the river, Rome ended and the barbarian wilds began. From here the Great Hungarian Plain stretches in a long, flat expanse all the way to Asia—hemmed in to the north by the Carpathian Mountains. (Geologists consider this prairie-like plain to be the westernmost steppe in Europe—resembling the terrain that covers much of Central Asia.) After Rome collapsed and Europe fell into the Dark Ages, Hungary became the territory of Celts, Vandals, Huns, and Avars...until some out-of-towners moved into the neighborhood.

The seven Magyar tribes, led by the mighty Árpád (and,  according to legend, guided by the mythical Turul bird), thundered into the Carpathian Basin in A.D. 896. They were a rough-and-tumble nomadic people from Central Asia who didn't like to settle down in one place. And yet, after their long and winding westward odyssey, the Great

Hungarian Plain felt comfortingly like home to the Magyars—reminiscent of the Asian steppes of their ancestors.

The Magyars would camp out in today's Hungary in the winters, and in the summers, they'd go on raids throughout Europe. They were notorious as incredibly swift horsemen, whose use of stirrups (an eastern innovation largely unknown in Europe at the time) allowed them to easily outmaneuver foes and victims. Italy, France, Germany's Rhine, the Spanish Pyrenees, all the way to Constantinople (modern-day Istanbul)—the Magyars had the run of the Continent.

For half a century, the Magyars ranked with the Vikings as the most feared people in Europe. To Europeans, this must have struck a chord of queasy familiarity: a mysterious and dangerous eastern tribe running roughshod over Europe, speaking a gibberish language, and employing strange, terrifying, relentless battle techniques. No wonder they called the new arrivals "Hun-garians."

Now planted in the center of Europe, the Magyars effectively drove a wedge in the middle of the sprawling Slavic populations of the Great Moravian Kingdom (basically today's "Eastern Europe"). The Slavs were split into two splinter groups, north and south—a division that persists today: Czechs, Slovaks, and Poles to the north; and Croats, Slovenes, Serbs, Bosniaks, and Bulgarians to the south. (You can still hear the division caused by the Magyars in the language: While Czechs and Russians call a castle *hrad,* Croats and Serbs call it *grad.*)

After decades of terrorizing Europe, the Magyars were finally defeated by a German and Czech army at the Battle of Augsburg in 955. The Magyars' King Géza—realizing that if they were to survive, his people had to put down roots and get along with their neighbors—made a fateful decision that would forever shape Hungary's future: He adopted Christianity; baptized his son, Vajk; and married him to a Bavarian princess at a young age.

On Christmas Day in the year 1000, Vajk changed his name to István (Stephen) and was symbolically crowned by the pope (for more on István, see page 621). A Venetian missionary, Gellért, came to Buda to attempt to convert the Hungarians—and was martyred (and later sainted) for his efforts. The domestication of the nomadic Magyars was difficult, thanks largely to the resistance of István's uncles, but was ultimately successful. Hungary became a legitimate Christian kingdom, welcomed by its neighbors. Under kings such as László I, Kálmán "the Book Lover," and András II, Hungary entered a period of prosperity.

The Tatars, the Ottomans, and Other Outsiders (A.D. 1000-1686)

One of Hungary's earliest challenges came at the hands of fellow invaders from Central Asia. Through the first half of the 13th century, the Tatars—initially led by Genghis Khan—swept into Eastern Europe from Mongolia. In the summer of 1241, Genghis Khan's son and successor, Ögedei Khan, broke into Hungarian territory. The Tatars sacked and plundered Hungarian towns, laying waste to the kingdom. It was only Ögedei Khan's death in early 1242—and the ensuing dispute about succession—that saved the Hungarians, as Tatar armies rushed home and the Mongolian Empire contracted. The Hungarian king at the time, Béla IV, was left to rebuild his ruined kingdom from the rubble—creating the first of many stout hilltop castles that still line the Danube.

Each of Béla's successors left his own mark on Hungary, as the Magyar kingdom flourished. They barely skipped a beat when the original Árpád dynasty died out in 1301, as they imported French kings (from the Naples-based Anjou, or Angevin, dynasty) to continue building their young realm. King Károly Róbert (Charles Robert) won over the Magyars, and his son Nagy Lajos (Louis the Great) expanded Hungarian holdings.

This was a period of flux for all of Central and Eastern Europe, as the nearby Czech and Polish kingdoms also saw their longstanding dynasties expire. For a time, royal intermarriages juggled the crowns of the region between various ruling families. Most notably, for 50 years (1387-1437) Hungary was ruled by Holy Roman Emperor Sigismund of Luxembourg, whose holdings also included the Czech lands, parts of Italy, much of Croatia, and more.

For more than 150 years, Hungary did not have a Hungarian-blooded king. This changed in the late 15th century, when a shortage

of foreign kings led to the ascension to the throne of the enlightened King Mátyás (Matthias) Corvinus. The son of popular military hero János Hunyadi, King Matthias fostered the arts, sparked a mini-Renaissance, and successfully balanced foreign threats to Hungarian sovereignty (the Habsburgs to the north and west, and the Ottomans to the south and east). Under Matthias, Hungarian culture and political power reached a peak. (For more on this great Hungarian king, see page 616.)

But even before the reign of "good king Mátyás," the Ottomans (from today's Turkey) had already begun slicing their way through the Balkan Peninsula toward Central Europe. (It's ironic that the two greatest threats to the Magyar kingdom came in the form of fellow Asian invaders: Tatars and Turks. Or maybe it's not surprising, as these groups all found the steppes of Hungary so familiar and inviting.) In 1526, the Ottomans entered Hungary when Sultan Süleyman the Magnificent killed Hungary's King Lajos II at the Battle of Mohács. By 1541, they took Buda. The Ottomans would dominate Hungarian life (and history) until the 1680s—nearly a century and a half.

The Ottoman invasion divided Hungary into thirds: Ottoman-occupied "Lower Hungary" (more or less today's Hungary); rump "Upper Hungary" (basically today's Slovakia), with its capital at Bratislava (which they called "Pozsony"); and the loosely independent territories of Transylvania (in today's Romania), ruled by Hungarian dukes. During this era, the Ottomans built some of the thermal baths that you'll still find throughout Hungary.

Ottoman-occupied Hungary became severely depopulated, and many of its towns and cities fell into ruins. While it

was advantageous for a Hungarian subject to adopt Islam (for lower taxes and other privileges), the Ottomans rarely forced conversions—unlike the arguably more oppressive Catholics who controlled other parts of Europe at the time (such as the monarchs of Spain, who expelled the Jews and conducted the Spanish Inquisition). Ottoman rule meant that Hungary took a different course than other parts of Europe during this time. The nation fully enjoyed the Renaissance, but missed out on other major European historical events—both good (the Age of Discovery and Age of Reason) and bad (the devastating Catholic-versus-Protestant wars that plagued much of the rest of Europe).

Crippled by the Ottomans and lacking power and options, Hungarian nobles desperately offered their crown to the Austrian Habsburg Empire, in exchange for salvation from the invasion. The Habsburgs instead used Hungary as a kind of "buffer zone" between the Ottoman advance and Vienna. And that was only the beginning of a very troubled relationship between the Hungarians and the Austrians.

Habsburg Rule, Hungarian National Revival, and Revolution (1686-1867)

In the late 17th century, the Habsburg army, starting from Vienna, began a sustained campaign to push the Ottomans out of Hungary in about 15 years. They finally wrested Buda and Pest from the Ottomans in 1686. The Habsburgs repopulated Buda and Pest with Germans, while Magyars reclaimed the countryside.

The Habsburgs governed the country as an outpost of Austria. The Hungarians—who'd had enough of foreign rule—fought them tooth and nail. Countless streets, squares, and buildings throughout the country are named for the "big three" Hungarian patriots who resisted the Habsburgs during this time: Ferenc Rákóczi (who led the unsuccessful War of Independence in 1703-1711), István Széchenyi (a wealthy count who funded grand structures to give his Magyar countrymen something to take pride in), and Lajos Kossuth (who led the Revolution of 1848).

The early 19th century saw a thawing of Habsburg oppression. Here as throughout Europe, "backward" country traditions began to trickle into the cities, gaining more respect and prominence. It was during this time of reforms that Hungarian (rather than German) became the official language. It also coincided with a Romantic Age of poets and writers (such as Mihály Vörösmarty and Sándor Petőfi) who began to use the Hungarian tongue to create literature for the first time. By around 1825, the Hungarian National Revival was underway, as the people began to embrace the culture and traditions of their Magyar ancestors. Like people across Europe—from Ireland to Italy, and from Prague to Scandinavia—the Hungarians were rediscovering what made them a unique people.

In March of 1848, a wave of Enlightenment-fueled nationalism that began in Paris spread like wildfire across Europe, igniting a revolutionary spirit in cities such as Budapest. On March 15, the Revolution of 1848 began on the steps of the National Museum in Pest.

In the spring of 1849, the Hungarians mounted a bloody but successful offensive to take over a wide swath of territory, including Buda and Pest. But in June, Franz Josef enlisted the aid of his fellow divine monarch, the Russian czar, who did not want the Magyars to provide an example for his own independence-minded subjects. Some 200,000 Russian reinforcements flooded into Hungary, crushing the revolution by August. After the final battle, the Habsburgs executed 13 Hungarian generals, then celebrated by clinking mugs of beer. To this very day, clinking beer mugs is, for many traditional Hungarians, just bad style.

For a while, the Habsburgs cracked down on their unruly Hungarian subjects. After an important military loss to Bismarck's

Prussia in 1866, Austria began to agree that it couldn't control its rebellious Slavic holdings all by itself. And so, just 18 years after crushing the Hungarians in a war, the Habsburgs handed them the reins. With the Compromise *(Ausgleich)* of 1867, Austria granted Budapest the authority over the eastern half of their lands, creating the so-called Dual Monarchy of the Austro-Hungarian Empire. Hungary was granted their much-prized "home rule," where most matters (except finance, foreign policy, and the military) were administered from Budapest rather than Vienna. The Habsburg emperor, Franz Josef, agreed to a unique "king and emperor" *(König und Kaiser)* arrangement, where he was emperor of Austria, but only king of Hungary. In 1867, he was crowned as Hungarian king in both Buda (at Matthias Church) and Pest (on today's March 15 Square). The insignia "K+K" *(König und Kaiser)*—which you'll still see everywhere—evokes these grand days of Franz Josef's reign.

Budapest's Golden Age (1867-1918)

The *Ausgleich* marked a precipitous turning point for the Hungarians, who once again governed their traditional holdings: large parts of today's Slovakia, Serbia, and Transylvania (northwest Romania); and smaller parts of today's Croatia, Slovenia, Ukraine, and Austria. To better govern their sprawling realm, in 1873, the cities of Buda, Pest, and Óbuda merged into one mega-metropolis: Budapest.

Serendipitously, Budapest's new prominence coincided with the 1,000th anniversary of the Hungarians' ancestors, the Magyars, arriving in Europe...one more excuse to dress things up. Budapest's long-standing rivalry with Vienna only spurred them to build bigger and better. The year 1896 saw an over-the-top millennial celebration, for which many of today's greatest structures were created (see page 561).

This was clearly Budapest's Golden Age. No European city grew faster in the second half of the 19th century than Budapest; in the last quarter of the 19th century alone, Budapest doubled in size, building on the foundation laid by Széchenyi and other patriots. By 1900, the city was larger than Rome, Madrid, or Amsterdam. But before long, the Hungarians began to make the same mistakes the Habsburgs had—trampling on the rights of their minorities and enforcing a policy of "Magyarization" that compelled subjects from all ethnic backgrounds to adopt the Hungarian language and culture. Soon the Golden Age came crashing to an end, and Hungary plunged into its darkest period.

The Crisis of Trianon (1918-1939)

World War I marked the end of the age of divine monarchs, as

Pre-Trianon Hungary

- Pre-Trianon Hungary (1920)
- Current Hungarian Border

200 Kilometers
200 Miles

POLAND
UKRAINE
CZECH. REP.
Danube R.
SLOVAKIA
MOLDOVA
Vienna
AUSTRIA
Budapest
TRANSYLVANIA
SLOVENIA
ROMANIA
ITALY
CROATIA
VOJVODINA
Danube R.
Black Sea
Adriatic Sea
BOSNIA-HERZ.
SERBIA
BULGARIA

HUNGARY

the Romanovs of Russia, the Ottomans of Asia Minor, and, yes, the Habsburgs of Austria-Hungary saw their empires break apart. Hungary, which had been riding the Habsburgs' coattails to power and prominence for the past half-century, now paid the price. As retribution for their role on the losing side of World War I, the 1920 Treaty of Trianon (named for the palace on the grounds of Versailles where it was signed) reassigned two-thirds of Hungary's former territory and half of its population to Romania, Ukraine, Czechoslovakia, and Yugoslavia (parts of today's Slovenia, Croatia, and Serbia).

It is impossible to overstate the impact of the Treaty of Trianon on the Hungarian psyche—and on Hungarian history. Not unlike the overnight construction of the Berlin Wall, towns along the new Hungarian borders were suddenly divided down the middle. Many Hungarians found themselves unable to visit relatives or commute to jobs that were in the same country the day before. This sent hundreds of thousands of Hungarian refugees—now "foreigners" in their own towns—into Budapest, sparking an enormous but bittersweet boom in the capital.

To this day, the Treaty of Trianon is regarded as one of the greatest tragedies of Hungarian history. Like the Basques and the Serbs, the Hungarians feel separated from one another by circumstances outside their control. Today, more than two million ethnic Hungarians live outside Hungary (mostly in Romania)—and many Hungarians claim that these lands still belong to the Magyars. The sizeable Magyar minorities in neighboring countries have often been mistreated—particularly in Romania (under Ceaușescu), Yugoslavia (under Milošević), and Slovakia (under Mečiar). You'll see maps, posters, and bumper stickers with the

distinctive shape of a much larger, pre-WWI Hungary...patrioti-
cally displayed by Magyars who feel as strongly about Trianon as
if it happened yesterday. Some Hungarians see the enlargement of
the European Union as a happy ending in the big-picture sense:
They have finally been reunited with Slovakia, Romania, and
Croatia.

After Trianon, the newly shrunken Kingdom of Hungary had
to reinvent itself. The Hungarian crown sat unworn in the Royal
Palace, as if waiting for someone worthy to claim it. WWI hero
Admiral Miklós Horthy had won many battles with the Austro-
Hungarian navy. Though the new Hungary had no sea and no
navy, Horthy retained his rank and ruled the country as a regent.
A popular joke points out that during this time, Hungary was a
"kingdom without a king" and a landlocked country ruled by a sea
admiral. This sense of compounded deficiency pretty much sums
up the morose attitude Hungarians have about those gloomy post-
Trianon days.

A mounting financial crisis, and lingering resentment about
the strict post-WWI reparations, made Hungary fertile ground
for some bold new fascist ideas.

World War II and the Arrow Cross
(1939-1945)

As Adolf Hitler rose to power in Germany, some other countries
that had felt mistreated in the aftermath of World War I—including Hungary—saw Nazi Germany as a vehicle to greater independence. Admiral Horthy joined forces with the Nazis with the
hope that they might help Hungary regain the crippling territorial losses of Trianon. In 1941, Hungary (somewhat reluctantly)
declared war on the Soviet Union in June—and against the US
and Britain in December.

Being an ally to the Nazis, rather than an occupied state, also
allowed Hungary a certain degree of self-determination through
the war. And, while Hungary had its own set of anti-Semitic laws,
the vast majority of its sizeable Jewish population was spared from
immediate deportation to Nazi concentration camps. Winning
back chunks of Slovakia, Transylvania, and Croatia in the early
days of World War II also bolstered the Nazis' acceptance in
Hungary.

As Nazism took hold in Germany, the Hungarian fascist movement—spearheaded by the Arrow Cross Party
(Nyilaskeresztes Párt)—gained popularity within Hungary.
Germany increased its demands for Hungarian soldiers and food,
and Admiral Horthy resisted...until Hitler's patience wore thin. In
March of 1944, the Nazis invaded and installed the Arrow Cross
in power. The Arrow Cross made up for lost time, immediately

beginning a savage campaign of executing Hungary's Jews—not only sending them to death camps, but butchering them in the streets. As the end of the war neared, Hungarian Nazi collaborators resorted to desperate measures, such as lining up Jews along the Danube and shooting them into the river. To save bullets, they'd sometimes tie several victims together, shoot one, and throw him into the freezing Danube—dragging the others in with him. Hungary lost nearly 600,000 Jews to the Holocaust.

The Soviet Army eventually "liberated" Hungary, but at the expense of Budapest: A months-long siege, from Christmas of 1944 to mid-February of 1945, reduced the proud city to rubble. One in 10 Hungarian citizens perished in the war.

Communism...with a Pinch of Paprika (1945-1989)

After World War II, Hungary was gradually compelled to adopt Moscow's system of government. The Soviet-puppet hardliner premier, Mátyás Rákosi, ruled Hungary with an iron fist. Everyday people were terrorized by the KGB-style secret police, called the ÁVO and ÁVH, and intimidated into accepting the new regime. Non-Hungarians were deported, potential and actual dissidents disappeared into the horrifying gulag system of Siberia (and similar forced-work camps in Hungary), food shortages were epidemic, people were compelled to spy on their friends and families, and countless lives were ruined.

Beginning on October 23, 1956, the Hungarians courageously staged a monumental uprising, led by Communist Party reformer Imre Nagy. Initially, it appeared that one of the cells on the Soviet Bloc might win itself the right to semi-autonomy. But Moscow couldn't let that happen. In a Tiananmen Square-style crackdown, the Soviets sent in tanks to brutally put down the uprising and occupy the city. When the dust settled, 2,500 Hungarians were dead, and 200,000 fled to the West. (If you know any Hungarian Americans, their families more than likely fled in 1956.) Nagy was arrested, given a sham trial, and executed in 1958. For more on these events, see the "1956" sidebar on page 582.

After the uprising, the USSR installed János Kádár—a colleague of Nagy's who was also loyal to Moscow—to lead Hungary. For a few years, things were bleak, as the secret police ratcheted up their efforts against potential dissidents. But in the 1960s, Kádár's reformist tendencies began to cautiously emerge. Seeking to gain the support of his subjects (and avoid further uprisings), Kádár adopted the optimistic motto, "If you are not against us, you are with us." While still mostly cooperating with Moscow, Kádár gradually allowed the people of Hungary more freedom than citizens of neighboring countries had—a system dubbed "goulash communism." The "New Economic Mechanism" of 1968 partly opened Hungary to foreign trade. People from other Warsaw Pact countries—Czechs, Slovaks, and Poles—flocked to Budapest's Váci utca to experience "Western evils" unavailable to them back home, such as Adidas sneakers and Big Macs. People half-joked that Hungary was the happiest barrack in the communist camp.

In the late 1980s, the Eastern Bloc began to thaw. And Hungary, which was always skeptical of the Soviets (or any foreign rule), was one of the first satellite states that implemented real change. In February of 1989, the Hungarian communist parliament, with little fanfare, essentially voted to put an expiration date on their own regime. There were three benchmarks in that fateful year: May 2, when Hungary was the first Soviet Bloc country to effectively open its borders to the West (by removing its border fence with Austria); June 16, when communist reformer Imre Nagy and his comrades were given a proper, ceremonial reburial on Heroes' Square; and August 19, when, in the first tentative steps toward the reunification of Europe, Hungarians and Austrians came together in a field near the town of Sopron for the so-called "Pan-European Picnic." (Some 900 East Germans seized this opportunity to make a run for the border...and slipped into the West when Hungarian border guards refused their orders to shoot defectors.) On October 23—the anniversary of the 1956 Uprising—the truly democratic Republic of Hungary triumphantly replaced the People's Republic of Hungary.

Hungary Today (1989-Present)

The transition from communism to capitalism has been rocky in Hungary. Although many Hungarians were eager for the freedom to travel and pursue the interests that democracy allowed them, many others struggled to cope with the sudden reduction of government-provided services. In 2004, Hungary took the monumental step of joining the European Union (along with nine other, mostly former-communist nations). Many of the new members demonstrated great ambivalence about joining the EU, fearing that they would lose their hard-fought autonomy. And EU membership has come with its share of heavy-handed regulation and convoluted bureaucracy. The question of whether Hungary is better off with or without the EU continues, as the ruling Fidesz regime is sternly Euroskeptic.

Hungary has been in the international news many times over the last several years, as its fitful transition to democracy has taken some attention-grabbing turns. The Hungarian Socialist

Party (MSzP), which took control of parliament in 2002, stubbornly maintained and even extended some social programs, despite worries that mounting public debt would bankrupt the country. Rampant inflation continued to wrack the country. In late 2008, with Prime Minister Ferenc Gyurcsány warning of "state bankruptcy" and a currency collapse, Hungary received a $25 billion bailout package from the EU, International Monetary Fund, and World Bank. Gyurcsány finally resigned in early 2009, acknowledging that he was getting in the way of Hungary's economic recovery.

Viktor Orbán, of the nationalistic, right-of-center Fidesz Party, became prime minister in a landslide in May of 2010. Fidesz—a strange hybrid of populist and authoritarian—stands for traditional Christian and Hungarian values, economic interventionism, and a healthy skepticism toward European Union membership. Orbán has said his goal for Hungary is an "illiberal democracy."

Orbán seized on his two-thirds majority to adopt a new, Fidesz-favorable constitution that stripped away checks and balances and entrenched party leaders in institutions that had previously been considered apolitical. Almost immediately, international observers—including the EU and US—grew concerned.

In early 2011, Orbán's party created a new FCC-like media authority with broad latitude for suppressing material that it considers inappropriate. Fidesz also extended Hungarian citizenship to people of Hungarian descent living in neighboring countries. This stoked century-old Hungarian resentment about the post-World War I Treaty of Trianon territorial losses. Orbán also insists on flying the flag of Transylvania (a part of Hungary that was lost in Trianon)—and not the EU flag—above the Hungarian Parliament.

Fidesz has a penchant for reinterpreting Hungarian history—rehabilitating some figures (such as Miklós Horthy, who led Hungary between the two World Wars—and forged an alliance with Hitler's Nazi Germany), while brushing other, less Fidesz-friendly figures under the rug. The party went on a renaming binge—rechristening more than two dozen streets, squares, and other features of Budapest—and have been aggressive about tearing down old monuments and erecting new ones.

On a positive note, Fidesz has also been proactive about funneling European Union funds into public-works projects, and

Budapest has made stunning progress in renovating formerly dreary streets and squares. But this always seems to come with a Fidesz-approved aesthetic that evokes the party's values. Some critics have described these new spaces—vast and bombastic, as if designed to trumpet historical greatness and host military parades—as "fascistic."

Other Orbán and Fidesz policies have also been controversial—from nationalizing the school system (the same Fidesz-approved textbooks are now used in every school in Hungary) to proposing a per-use Internet tax. (That last one resulted in enormous public protests in the fall of 2014, and Orbán quickly backpedaled.) In 2014, Orbán spoke favorably about Vladimir Putin, whose authoritarian ruling style has been compared with Orbán's.

Outrageous as Fidesz seems to younger, EU-supporting, highly educated Hungarians, the party pleased its base enough to easily retain its power in the 2014 parliamentary elections. (Fidesz's control of the media didn't hurt its chances either.) Many international observers worry that Fidesz's success could be the death knell for true democracy in Hungary. Whether Orbán can continue to ride his wave of popularity remains to be seen.

Fortunately, tourists visiting today's Hungary are scarcely aware of its economic and political woes. The Hungarian people—relieved to be free of oppression and allowed to pursue their lovably quirky customs with a renewed vigor—enthusiastically welcome and charm visitors. It's been a long road for the Hungarians from those distant, windblown steppes of Central Asia...but today they seem to be doing better than ever.

HUNGARIAN FOOD

Hungarian cuisine is the undisputed best in Central Europe. It delicately blends Magyar peasant cooking (with rich spices), refined by the elegance of French preparation, with a delightful smattering of flavors from the vast, multiethnic Austro-Hungarian Empire (including Germanic, Balkan, Jewish, and Carpathian). Everything is heavily seasoned with paprika, tomatoes, and peppers of every shape, color, size, and flavor.

An *étterem* ("eatery") is a nice sit-down restaurant, while a *vendéglő* is usually more casual (similar to a tavern or an inn). A *söröző* ("beer place") is a pub that sells beer and food, ranging from a small selection of snacks to a full menu. A *kávéház* ("coffeehouse"), or café, is where Hungarians gather to meet friends, get a caffeine fix...

and sometimes to have a great meal. Other cafés serve only light food, or sometimes only desserts. But if you want a wide choice of cakes, look for a *cukrászda* (pastry shop—*cukr* means "sugar").

When foreigners think of Hungarian cuisine, what comes to mind is goulash. But tourists are often disappointed when "real Hungarian goulash" isn't the thick stew that they were expecting. The word "goulash" comes from the Hungarian *gulyás leves,* or "shepherd's soup"—a tasty, rustic, nourishing dish originally eaten by cowboys and shepherds on the Great Hungarian Plain. Here in its homeland, it's a clear, spicy broth with chunks of meat, potatoes, and other vegetables. Elsewhere (such as in the Germanic and Slavic countries that are Hungary's neighbors), the word "goulash" does describe a thick stew. The hearty Hungarian stew called *pörkölt* is probably closer to what most people think of as goulash.

Aside from the obligatory *gulyás,* make a point of trying another unusual Hungarian specialty: cold fruit soup *(hideg gyümölcs leves).* This sweet, cream-based treat—generally eaten before the meal, even though it tastes more like a dessert—is usually made with *meggy* (sour cherries), but you'll also see versions with *alma* (apples) or *körte* (pears). Other Hungarian soups *(levesek)* include *bableves* (bean soup), *zöldségleves* (vegetable soup), *gombaleves* (mushroom soup), *halászlé* (fish broth with paprika), and *húsleves* (meat or chicken soup). The ultimate staple of traditional Hungarian home-cooking, but rarely served in restaurants, is *főzelék*—a simple but tasty wheat flour-thickened stew that can be supplemented with various vegetables and meats.

Hungarians adore all kinds of meat. *Hús* or *marhahús* is beef, *csirke* is chicken, *borjú* is veal, *kacsa* is duck, *liba* is goose, *sertés* is

pork, *sonka* is ham, *kolbász* is sausage, *szelet* is schnitzel (*Bécsi szelet* means Wiener schnitzel)—and the list goes on. One trendy ingredient you'll see on menus is *mangalica.* This uniquely Hungarian, free-range, wooly pig (basically a domesticated boar) is high in unsaturated fat—which fits perfectly with the current foodie culture that elevates the mighty pig. *Libamáj* is goose liver, which shows up everywhere (anything prepared "Budapest style" is topped with goose liver). Lard is used extensively in cooking, making Hungarian cuisine very rich and filling.

Meat is often covered with delicious sauces or garnishes, from rich cream sauces to spicy pastes to fruit jam. For classic Hungarian flavors, you can't beat chicken or veal *paprikás* (described in the "Paprika Primer" sidebar).

Paprika Primer

The quintessential ingredient in Hungarian cuisine is paprika. In Hungarian, the word *paprika* can mean both peppers (red or green) and the spice that's made from them. Peppers can be stewed, stuffed, sautéed, baked, grilled, or pickled. For seasoning, red shakers of dried paprika join the salt and pepper on tables.

Locals say paprika is best from the sunny south of Hungary. There are more than 40 varieties of paprika spice, with two main types: hot (*csípős* or *erős*) and sweet (*édesnemes* or simply *édes*, often comes in a white can; sometimes also called *csemege*—"delicate"). Hungarians typically cook with sweet paprika to add flavor and color. Then, at the table, they put out hot paprika so each diner can adjust the heat to his or her preferred taste. A can or bag of paprika is a handy and tasty souvenir of your trip.

On menus, anything cooked *paprikás* (PAW-pree-kash) comes smothered in a spicy, creamy red stew. Most often you'll see this option with *csirke* (chicken) or *borjú* (veal), and it's generally served with dumpling-like boiled egg noodles called *nokedli* (similar to German *Spätzle*). This dish is *the* Hungarian staple—if you sample just one dish in Hungary, make it chicken or veal *paprikás*.

To add even more kick to your food, ask for a jar of the bright-red paste called *Erős Pista* (EH-rewsh PEESH-taw). Literally "Spicy Steve," this Hungarian answer to Tabasco is best used sparingly. Or try *Édes Anna* (AY-desh AW-naw, "Sweet Anna"), a variation that's more sweet than spicy.

Vegetarians have a tricky time in traditional Hungarian restaurants, many of which offer only a plate of deep-fried vegetables. A traditional Hungarian "salad" is composed mostly or entirely of pickled vegetables (pickles, cabbage, peppers, and others); even many modern restaurants haven't quite figured out how to do a good, healthy, leafy salad. Fortunately, the more modern, trendy eateries in the capital often offer excellent vegetarian options.

Starches *(köretek)*—which you'll sometimes order separate from the meat course—can include *nokedli* (small potato dumplings, a.k.a. *Spätzle*), *galuska* (noodles), *burgonya* (potatoes), *krumpli* (French fries), *krokett* (croquettes), or *rizs* (rice). *Kenyér* (bread) often comes with the meal. A popular snack—especially to accompany a wine-tasting—is a *pogácsa*, a deep-fried savory doughnut.

Sometimes your main dish will come with steamed, grilled, or deep-fried vegetables. A common side dish is *káposzta* (cabbage, often prepared like sauerkraut). You may also see *töltött káposzta* (cabbage stuffed with meat) or *töltött paprika* (stuffed peppers). *Lescó* (LEH-chew) is the Hungarian answer to ratatouille: a richly flavorful stew of tomatoes, peppers, and other vegetables.

Thin, crêpe-like pancakes *(palacsinta)* are sometimes served as a main dish. A delicious traditional Hungarian dish is *Hortobágyi palacsinta* (Hortobágy pancakes, named for the Hungarian Great Plain where the dish originates). This is a savory crêpe wrapped around a tasty meat filling and drenched with creamy paprika sauce.

Pancakes also appear as desserts, stuffed and/or covered with fruit, jam, chocolate sauce, walnuts, poppy seeds, or whipped cream. Most famous is the *Gundel palacsinta,* named for *the* top-of-the-line Budapest restaurant—stuffed with walnuts and raisins in a rum sauce, topped with chocolate sauce, and flambéed.

Pastries are a big deal in Hungary. In the late 19th century, pastry-making caught on here in an attempt to keep up with the

renowned desserts of rival Vienna. Today Hungary's streets are still lined with *cukrászda* (pastry shops) where you can simply point to whichever treat you'd like. Try the *Dobos torta* (a many-layered chocolate-and-caramel cream cake), *somlói galuska* (a dumpling with vanilla, nuts, and chocolate), anything with *gesztenye* (chestnuts), and *rétes* (strudel with various fillings, including *túrós,* curds). And many *cukrászda* also serve *fagylalt* (ice cream, *fagyi* for short), sold by the *gomboc* (ball).

When the server comes to take your order, he might say *"Tessék"* (TEHSH-shayk), or maybe the more formal *"Tessék parancsolni"* (TEHSH-shayk PAW-rawn-chohl-nee)—"Please command, sir." When they bring the food, they will probably say, *"Jó étvágyat!"* (yoh AYT-vah-yawt)—"Bon appétit." When you're ready for the bill, you can simply say, *"Fizetek"* (FEE-zeh-tehk)—"I'll pay."

DRINKS

Kávé (KAH-vay) and *tea* (TEH-aw) are coffee and tea. (Confusingly, *tej* is not tea—it's milk.) As for water (*víz,* veez) it comes as *szódavíz* (soda water, sometimes just carbonated tap water) or *ásványvíz* (spring water, more expensive).

Hungary is first and foremost a wine country. For the

Hungarian Wines

Wine *(bor)* is an essential part of Hungarian cuisine. Whites *(fehér)* can be sweet *(édes)*, half-dry *(félszáraz)*, or dry *(száraz)*. Whites include the standards (riesling, chardonnay), as well as some wines made from more typically Hungarian grapes: *leányka* ("little girl"), a half-dry, fairly heavy, white table wine; *cserszegi fűszeres,* a spicy, light white that can be fruity; the half-dry, full-bodied *hárslevelű* ("linden leaf"); and the dry *furmint* and *kéknyelű* ("blue stalk").

Reds *(vörös)* include the familiar varieties (cabernet sauvignon, cabernet franc, merlot, pinot noir) and some that are less familiar. *Kekporto* is better known as *blauer Portugieser* in

German-speaking countries. In Eger, don't miss **Bull's Blood,** a.k.a. Egri Bikavér, a distinctive blend of reds that comes with a fun local legend (described on page 703). The spicy, medium-body *kékfrankos* ("blue Frankish") supposedly got its name because when Napoleonic soldiers were here, they could pay either with valuable blue-colored bank

complete rundown on Hungarian wines, see the sidebar.

Hungary isn't particularly well-known for its beer *(sör,* pronounced "shewr"), but Dreher and Borsodi are two of the better brands. *Villagos* is lager; if you prefer something darker, look for *barna* (brown).

Hungary is almost as proud of its spirits as its wines. The local firewater, *pálinka,* is a powerful schnapps made from various fruits (most often plum, *szilva;* or apricots, *barack*). Also look for the pear-flavored Vilmos brandy.

Unicum is a unique and beloved Hungarian bitter liquor made of 40 different herbs and aged in oak casks. Look for the round bottle with the red cross on the label. The flavor is powerfully unforgettable—like Jägermeister, but harsher. Unicum started out as a medicine and remains a popular digestif for easing an upset stomach (especially if you've eaten too much rich food—not an uncommon problem in Hungary). Purists claim it's better to drink it at room temperature (so you can fully appreciate its bouquet), but novices find it easier to slug back when chilled. If the original notes or unstable white ones...and local vintners wanted the blue francs. (Like most wine origin legends, this story is untrue—*kék-frankos* wasn't cultivated here until after Napoleon's time.)

Probably the most famous Hungarian wine is **Tokaji Aszú,** a sweet, late-harvest, honey-colored dessert wine made primarily from *furmint* grapes. Known as the "wine of kings, and the king of wines," Tokaji Aszú is a D.O.C. product, meaning that to have that name, it must be grown in a particular region. Tokaj is a town in northeastern Hungary, while *aszú* is a "noble rot" grape. The wine's unique, concentrated flavor is made possible by a fungus *(Botrytis cinerea)* that thrives on the grapes in the late fall. The grapes are left on the vine, where they burst and wither like raisins before they are harvested in late October and November. This sucks the water out of the grape, leaving behind very high sugar content and a deep golden color. Tokaji Aszú wines are numbered, from three to six, indicating how many eight-gallon tubs *(puttony)* of these "noble rot" grapes were added to the base wine—the higher the number, the sweeter the wine. Other variations on Tokaji can be less sweet. (This might sound like another bizarre Hungarian custom, but the French Sauterne and German Beerenauslese wines are also made from "noble rot" grapes. The similarly named French Tokay wine—which derives from the same word—is a different story altogether.)

Finally, note that, except for Bull's Blood and Tokaji Aszú, Hungarian wines are not widely available in the US. Packing home a bottle or two (in your checked luggage) makes for a unique souvenir.

Unicum overwhelms your palate, try one of the newer variations: Unicum Next, with more of a citrus flavor, and Unicum Szilva (with a golden plum on the label), which is aged in plums that cut some of the bitterness with a rich sweetness (www.zwack.hu).

If you're drinking with some new Magyar friends, impress them with the standard toast: *Egészségedre* (EH-gehs-shay-gehdreh; "to your health").

HUNGARIAN LANGUAGE

Even though Hungary is surrounded by Slavs, Hungarian is not at all related to Slavic languages (such as Polish, Czech, or Croatian). In fact, Hungarian isn't related to *any* European language, except for very distant relatives Finnish and Estonian. It isn't even an Indo-European language—meaning that English is more closely related to Hindi, Russian, and French than it is to Hungarian.

Hungarian is agglutinative: To create meaning, you start with a simple root word and then start tacking on suffixes—sometimes resulting in a pileup of extra sounds. The emphasis always goes on the first syllable, and the following syllables are droned in a kind of a monotone—giving the language a distinctive cadence that Hungary's neighbors love to tease about.

While the language can be overwhelming for tourists, one easy word is *"Szia"* (SEE-yaw), which means both hello and good-bye (like "ciao" or "aloha"). Confusingly, sometimes Hungarians simply say the English word "hello" to mean either "hi" or "bye." Another handy word that Hungarians (and people throughout Central Europe) will understand is *Servus* (SEHR-voos, spelled *Szervusz* in Hungarian)—the old-fashioned greeting from the days of the Austro-Hungarian Empire. If you draw a blank on how to say hello, just offer a cheery, *"Servus!"*

Hungarian pronunciation is straightforward, once you remember a few key rules. The trickiest: *s* alone is pronounced "sh," while *sz* is pronounced "s." This explains why you'll hear in-the-know travelers pronouncing Budapest as "BOO-daw-pesht." You might catch the *busz* up to Castle Hill—pronounced "boose." And "Franz Liszt" is easier to pronounce than it looks: It sounds just like "list." To review:

s sounds like "sh" as in "shirt"

sz sounds like "s" as in "saint"

Hungarian has a set of unusual palatal sounds that don't quite have a counterpart in English. To make these sounds, gently press the thick part of your tongue to the roof or your mouth (instead of using the tip of your tongue behind your teeth, as we do in English):

gy sounds like "dg" as in "hedge"

ny sounds like "ny" as in "canyon" (not "nee")

ty sounds like "tch" as in "itch"

cs sounds like "ch" as in "church"

As for vowels: The letter *a* almost sounds like o (aw, as in "hot"); but with an accent *(á)*, it brightens up to the more standard "ah." Likewise, while *e* sounds like "eh," *é* sounds like "ay." An accent *(á, é, í, ó, ú)* indicates that you linger on that vowel, but not necessarily that you stress that syllable. Like German, Hungarian has umlauts *(ö, ü)*, meaning you purse your lips when you say that vowel: roughly, *ö* sounds like "ur" and *ü* sounds like "ew." A long umlaut *(ő, ű)* is the same sound, but you hold it a little longer. Words ending in *k* are often plural.

Here are a few other letters that sound different in Hungarian than in English:

c and **cz** both sound like "ts" as in "cats"

zs sounds like "zh" as in "leisure"

j and **ly** both sound like "y" as in "yellow"

OK, maybe it's not *so* simple. But you'll get the hang of it... and Hungarians will appreciate your efforts.

For a complete list of Hungarian survival phrases, see the following pages.

As you navigate, remember these key Hungarian terms: *tér* (pronounced "tehr," square), *utca* (OOT-zaw, street), *út* (oot, boulevard), *körút* (KUR-root, ring road), *híd* (heed, bridge), and *város* (VAH-rohsh, town). To better match what you'll see locally, in the following chapters I've mostly used these Hungarian terms (instead of the English equivalents).

Hungarian Survival Phrases

Remember, the letter *a* is pronounced "aw," while *á* is a brighter "ah." In the phonetics, *dj* is pronounced like the *j* in "jeans."

English	Hungarian	Pronunciation
Hello. (formal)	Jó napot kívánok.	yoh **nah**-poht **kee**-vah-nohk
Hi. / Bye. (informal)	Szia. / Hello.	**see**-yaw / "Hello"
Do you speak English?	Beszél angolul?	beh-sayl **awn**-goh-lool
Yes. / No.	Igen. / Nem.	**ee**-gehn / nehm
I (don't) understand.	(Nem) értem.	(nehm) **ayr**-tehm
Please.	Kérem.	**kay**-rehm
You're welcome.	Szívesen.	**see**-veh-shehn
Thank you (very much).	Köszönöm (szépen).	**kur**-sur-nurm (**say**-pchn)
Excuse me. / I'm sorry.	Bocsánat.	**boh**-chah-nawt
No problem.	Semmi gond	**sheh**-mee gohnd
Good.	Jól.	yohl
Goodbye.	Viszontlátásra.	**vee**-sohnt-lah-tahsh-raw
one / two / three	egy / kettő / három	edj / **keh**-tur / **hah**-rohm
four / five / six / seven	négy / öt / hat / hét	naydj / urt / hawt / hayt
eight / nine / ten	nyolc / kilenc / tíz	nyolts / **kee**-lehnts / teez
hundred / thousand	száz / ezer	sahz / **eh**-zehr
How much?	Mennyi?	**mehn**-yee
local currency	forint (Ft)	**foh**-reent
Where is it?	Hol van?	hohl vawn
Is it free (no charge)?	Ingyen van?	**een**-**john** vawn
Where can I find / buy...?	Hol találok / vehetek...?	hohl **taw**-lah-lohk / **veh**-heh-tehk
I'd like / We'd like...	Kérnék / Kérnénk...	**kayr**-nayk / **kayr**-naynk
...a room.	...egy szobát.	edj **soh**-baht
...a ticket (to ___).	...egy jegyet (___-ig).	edj **yehdj**-eht (___-ig)
Is it possible?	Lehet?	leh-**heht**
Where is the ___?	Hol van a ___?	hohl vawn aw ___
big train station (in Budapest)	pályaudvar	**pah**-yood-vawr
small train station (elsewhere)	vasútállomás	**vaw**-shoot-ah-loh-mahsh
bus station	buszpályaudvar	**boos**-pah-yood-vawr
tourist information office	turista információ	**too**-reesh taw **een**-for-maht-see-yoh
toilet	toalet / WC	**toh**-aw-leht / **vayt**-say
men / women	férfi / női	**fayr**-fee / **nur**-ee
left / right	bal / jobb	bawl / yohb
straight	egyenesen	**edj**-eh-neh-shehn
At what time...?	Mikor...?	**mee**-kor
...does this open / close	...nyit / zár	nyit / zahr
Just a moment.	Egy pillanat.	edj **pee**-law-nawt
now / soon / later	most / hamarosan / később	mohsht / **haw**-maw-roh-shawn / **kay**-shurb
today / tomorrow	ma / holnap	maw / **hohl**-nawp

In a Hungarian Restaurant

English	Hungarian	Pronunciation
I'd like to reserve a table for one / two people.	Szeretnék foglalni egy asztalt egy / két fő részére.	**seh**-reht-nayk **fog**-lawl-nee edj **aws**-tawlt edj / kayt few **ray**-say-reh
Is this table free?	Ez az asztal szabad?	ehz oz **aws**-tawl saw-**bawd**
Can I help you?	Tessék?	**tehsh**-shayk
The menu (in English), please.	Kérem az (angol), étlapot.	**kay**-rehm oz (**awn**-gohl) **ayt**-law-poht
service (not) included	a számla a felszolgálási díjat (nem) tartalmazza	aw **sahm**-law aw **fehl**-sohl-gah-lah-shee **dee**-yawt (nehm) **tawr**-tawl-maw-zaw
"to go"	elvitelre	**ehl**-vee-tehl-reh
with / without	___-val / nélkül	___-vawl / **nayl**-kewl
and / or	és / vagy	aysh / **vawdj**
fixed-price meal (of the day)	(napi) menü	(**naw**-pee) **meh**-new
daily special	napi ajánlat	**naw**-pee aw-**yahn**-lawt
main courses	főételek	**fur**-ay-teh-lehk
appetizers	előételek	**eh**-lur-ay-teh-lehk
bread / cheese	kenyér / sajt	**kehn**-yayr / **shayt**
sandwich	szendvics	**send**-veech
soup / salad	leves / saláta	**leh**-vehsh / **shaw**-lah-taw
meat / poultry	hús / szárnyasok	**hoosh** / **sahr**-nyaw-shohk
fish	halak	**haw**-lawk
seafood	tengeri halak	**tehn**-geh-ree **haw**-lawk
fruit / vegetables	gyümölcs / zöldség	**jewm**-urlch / **zulrd**-shayg
dessert	desszert	**deh**-sehrt
vegetarian	vegetáriánus	**veh**-geh-tah-ree-ah-noosh
(tap) water	(csap) víz	(**chawp**) veez
mineral water	ásványvíz	**ash**-vawn-veez
milk / (orange) juice	tej / (narancs) lé	**tay**ee / (**naw**-rawnch) lay
coffee / tea	kávé / tea	**kah**-vay / **teh**-aw
beer / wine	sör / bor	**shohr** / **bohr**
red / white	vörös / fehér	**vur**-rursh / **feh**-hayr
sweet / dry / semi-dry	édes / száraz / félszáraz	**ay**-dehsh / **sah**-rawz / **fayl**-sah-rawz
glass / bottle	pohár / üveg	**poh**-hahr / **ew**-vehg
Cheers!	Egészségedre!	**eh**-gehs-sheh-geh-dreh
More. / Another.	Még. / Máskikat.	mayg / **mah**-shee-kawt
The same.	Ugyanazt.	**oodj**-aw-nawst
Bill, please. (literally, "I'll pay.")	Fizetek.	**fee**-zeh-tehk
tip	borravaló	**boh**-raw-vaw-loh
Bon appétit!	Jó étvágyat!	yoh **ayt**-vah-yawt
Delicious!	Finom!	**fee**-nohm

BUDAPEST

Budapest (locals say "BOO-daw-pesht") is a unique metropolis at the heart of a unique nation. Here you'll find experiences like nothing else in Europe: Feel your stress ebb away as you soak in hundred-degree water, surrounded by opulent Baroque domes...and by Speedo- and bikini-clad Hungarians. Ogle some of Europe's most richly decorated interiors, which echo a proud little nation's bygone glory days. Perk up your ears with a first-rate performance at one of the world's top opera houses—at bargain prices. Ponder the region's once-bleak communist era as you stroll amid giant Soviet-style statues designed to evoke fear and obedience. Try to wrap your head around Hungary's colorful history...and your tongue around its notoriously difficult language. Dive into a bowl of goulash, the famous paprika-flavored peasant soup with a kick. Go for an after-dinner stroll along the Danube, immersed in a grand city that's bathed in floodlights.

Europe's most underrated big city, Budapest can be as challenging as it is enchanting. The sprawling Hungarian capital on the banks of the Danube is, in so many ways, the capital of Eastern Europe. It's a city of nuance and paradox—cosmopolitan, complicated, and tricky for the first-timer to get a handle on. Like a full-bodied Hungarian wine, Budapest can overwhelm visitors...even as it intoxicates them with delights.

Think of Budapest as that favorite Hungarian pastime, chess: It's simple to learn...but takes a lifetime to master. This chapter is your first lesson. Then it's your move.

Budapest Essentials

English	Hungarian	Pronounced
Budapest	*Budapest*	BOO-daw-pesht
Pest Town Center	*Belváros*	BEHL-vah-rohsh
Pest's Leopold Town	*Lipótváros*	LEE-poht-vah-rohsh
Pest Town Center's Main Pedestrian Street	*Váci utca*	VAHT-see OOT-zaw
Pest Town Center's Main Square	*Vörösmarty tér*	VEW-rewsh-mar-tee tehr
Pest's Grand Boulevard	*Andrássy út*	AWN-drah-shee oot
Heroes' Square	*Hősök Tere*	HEW-shewk TEH-reh
City Park	*Városliget*	VAH-rohsh-lee-geht
(Buda) Castle	*(Budai) Vár*	BOO-die vahr
Castle Hill	*Várhegy*	VAHR-hayj
Buda's "Water Town"	*Víziváros*	VEE-zee-vah-rohsh
Chain Bridge	*Széchenyi Lánchíd*	SAY-chehn-yee LAHNTS-heed
Liberty Bridge (green, a.k.a. Franz Josef Bridge)	*Szabadság Híd*	SAW-bawd-shahg heed
Elisabeth Bridge (white, modern)	*Erzsébet híd*	EHR-zay-beht heed
Margaret Bridge (crosses Margaret Island)	*Margit híd*	MAWR-geet heed
Danube River	*Duna*	DOO-naw
Eastern Train Station	*Keleti pályaudvar*	KEH-leh-tee PAH-yuh-uhd-vawr
Western Train Station	*Nyugati pályaudvar*	NYOO-gaw-tee PAH-yuh-uhd-vawr
Southern Train Station	*Déli pályaudvar*	DAY-lee PAH-yuh-uhd-vawr
Suburban Train System	*HÉV*	hayv

PLANNING YOUR TIME

Visitors attempting to "do" Budapest in just one day leave dazed, exhausted...and yearning for more. Two days are the bare minimum, and force you to tackle the city at a breakneck pace (and you still won't see everything). Three days work, but assume you'll go fast and/or skip some things. Four days are ideal, and a fifth day (or even sixth) gives you time for various day-trip options.

Budapest is quite decentralized: Plan your day ahead to minimize backtracking, and refer to your map frequently. Just about everything is walkable, but distances are far, and public transit can save you valuable time.

When divvying your time between Buda and Pest, keep in mind that (aside from the Gellért and Rudas Baths) Buda's sightseeing is mostly concentrated on Castle Hill, and can easily be seen in less than a day, while Pest deserves as much time as you're willing to give it. Start by getting your bearings in Pest (where you'll likely spend most of your time), then head for relatively laid-back Buda when you need a break from the big city.

Listed next are some possible plans, depending on the length of your trip. Note that these very ambitious itineraries assume you want to sightsee at a speedy pace. In the **evening,** you have a wide range of options (many of which are outlined under "Entertainment in Budapest" on page 647, and "Nightlife in Budapest" on page 650): enjoying good restaurants, taking in an opera or concert, snuggling on a romantic floodlit river cruise, relaxing in a thermal bath, exploring the city's unique ruin pubs, or simply strolling the Danube embankments and bridges.

Budapest in Two Days

Your time will be full but memorable. Spend Day 1 in Pest. Begin at the Parliament and stroll through Leopold Town, then walk through the Pest Town Center to the Great Market Hall. From there, circle around the Small Boulevard to Deák tér; if you're not wiped out yet, walk up Andrássy út to Heroes' Square and City Park. Or, if you're exhausted already, just take the M1/yellow Metró line to Hősök tere, ogle the Heroes' Square statues and Vajdahunyad Castle, and reward yourself with a soak at Széchenyi Baths. (Note that this schedule leaves virtually no time for entering any museums—though you might be able to fit in one or two big sights, such as the Parliament—for which you should book tickets online, as well as for the Opera House, Great Synagogue, or House of Terror.)

On the morning of Day 2, tackle any Pest sights you didn't have time for yesterday (or take the bus out to Memento Park). After lunch, ride bus #16 from Deák tér to Buda's Castle Hill. Head back to Pest for some final sightseeing and dinner.

Budapest in Three or Four Days

Your first day is for getting your bearings in Pest. Choose between touring the Parliament or the Opera House; for the Parliament, book your tickets online. Then stroll through Leopold Town and up Andrássy út to Heroes' Square and City Park, ending with a soak at the Széchenyi Baths.

On Day 2, delve deeper into Pest, starting with a stroll through the Town Center. After visiting the Great Market Hall, you can cross the river to Buda for a soak at the Gellért or Rudas Baths (if you want more spa time), or circle around the Small Boulevard to see the National Museum and/or Great Synagogue.

On Day 3, use the morning to see any remaining sights, then ride from Deák tér out to Memento Park on the park's 11:00 direct bus. On returning, grab a quick lunch and take bus #16 from Deák tér to Castle Hill.

With a fourth day, spread the Day 1 activities over more time, and circle back to any sights you've missed so far.

Orientation to Budapest

Budapest is huge, with nearly two million people. Like Vienna, the city was built as the head of a much larger empire than it currently governs—which can make it feel a bit too grandiose for the capital of a small country. But the city is surprisingly easy to manage once you get the lay of the land and learn the excellent public transportation network. Those who are comfortable with the Metró, trams, and buses have the city by the tail (see "Getting Around Budapest" on page 564).

The city is split down the center by the Danube River. On the east side of the Danube is flat **Pest** (pronounced "pesht"), and on the west is hilly **Buda.** A third part of the city, **Óbuda,** sits to the north of Buda.

Buda: Buda is dominated by **Castle Hill** (packed with tourists by day, dead at night). The pleasant **Víziváros** ("Water Town"; VEE-zee-vah-rohsh) neighborhood is between the castle and the river; nearby is the square called Batthyány tér (a handy hub for the Metró—M2/red line—plus tram lines and the HÉV suburban

Budapest Neighborhoods

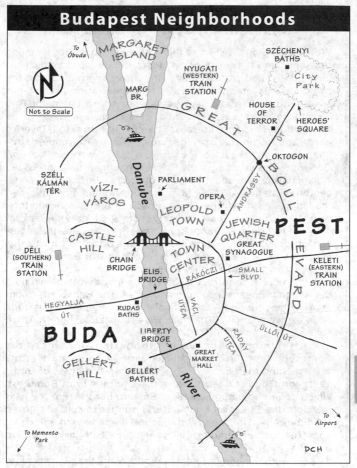

Not to Scale

To Óbuda

MARGARET ISLAND

MARG BR.

SZÉCHENYI BATHS

City Park

NYUGATI (WESTERN) TRAIN STATION

HOUSE OF TERROR

HEROES' SQUARE

GREAT

BOUL

ÚT

OKTOGON

SZÉLL KÁLMÁN TÉR

VÍZI-VÁROS

Danube

PARLIAMENT

OPERA

ANDRÁSSY

EVARD

LEOPOLD TOWN

JEWISH QUARTER

PEST

CASTLE HILL

GREAT SYNAGOGUE

CHAIN BRIDGE

TOWN CENTER

DÉLI (SOUTHERN) TRAIN STATION

ELIS. BRIDGE

RÁKÓCZI

SMALL BLVD.

KELETI (EASTERN) TRAIN STATION

HEGYALJA ÚT

RUDAS BATHS

VÁCI UTCA

BUDA

LIBERTY BRIDGE

RADAY UTCA

ÜLLŐI ÚT

GELLÉRT HILL

GELLÉRT BATHS

GREAT MARKET HALL

River

To Memento Park

To Airport

DCH

BUDAPEST

railway). To the south is the taller, wooded **Gellért Hill,** capped by the Liberation Monument, with a pair of thermal baths, Gellért and Rudas, at its base.

Pest: Just across the river from Castle Hill, **"Downtown" Pest** is divided into two sections. The more polished northern half, called **Leopold Town** (Lipótváros), surrounds the giant Parliament building. This is the governmental, business, and banking district (sleepy after hours). The southern half, the grittier and more urban-feeling **Town Center** (Belváros, literally "Inner Town"), is a thriving shopping, dining, nightlife, and residential zone that bustles day and night. Major landmarks here include the vast Great Market Hall and the famous (and overrated) Váci utca shopping street.

Additional key sights lie along the **Small Boulevard** ring

BUDAPEST

Snapshot History of Budapest

When describing the story of this grand metropolis, it's tempting to fall back on the trusty onion metaphor: Budapest, which has been adored and destroyed by many different groups across the centuries, is layered with history...sometimes stinky, sometimes sweet. You could spend days, years, or an entire lifetime peeling back those layers. But here's the quick version:

Budapest is hot—literally. The city sits on a thin layer of earth above thermal springs, which power its many baths. Even the word "Pest" comes from a Slavic word for "oven." Two thousand years ago, the Romans had a settlement (called Aquincum) on the northern edge of today's Budapest. Several centuries later, in A.D. 896, a mysterious nomadic group called the Magyars arrived from the steppes of Central Asia and took over the Carpathian Basin (roughly today's Hungary). After running roughshod over Europe for a time, the Magyars—the ancestors of today's Hungarians—settled down, adopted Christianity, and became fully European. The twin towns of Buda and Pest emerged as the leading cities of Hungary.

In the 16th century, the Ottomans invaded and occupied the region for nearly a century and a half. The Habsburgs (monarchs of neighboring Austria) finally forced them out, but Buda and Pest were in ruins. The cities were rebuilt in a more Austrian style.

After many decades of Hungarian uprisings, the Compromise of 1867 granted Hungary an equal stake in the Austro-Hungarian Empire. Six years later, the cities of Buda, Pest, and Óbuda united to form the capital city of Budapest, which governed a huge chunk of Eastern Europe. For the next few decades, Budapest boomed, and Hungarian culture enjoyed a Golden Age. The expansion reached its peak with a flurry of construction surrounding the year 1896—Hungary's 1,000th birthday.

But with Hungary's defeat in World War I, the city's fortunes

road (connected by trams #47 and #49), including—from north to south—the Great Synagogue (marking the start of the **Jewish Quarter,** which feels a bit run-down but features several Jewish sights as well as a hopping nightlife zone with cool "ruin pubs"), the National Museum, and the Great Market Hall. Even more points of interest are spread far and wide along the **Great Boulevard** ring road (circled by trams #4 and #6), including Margaret Island (the city's playground, in the middle of the Danube), the Nyugati/Western train station, the prominent Oktogon intersection (where it crosses Andrássy út), the opulent New York Café (with the Keleti/Eastern train station just up the street), and the intersection with Üllői út, near the Holocaust Memorial Center and Applied Arts Museum.

reversed. World War II left Budapest in ruins...and in the hands of the Soviets. A bold uprising in 1956 was brutally dealt with, but before long a milder "goulash communism" emerged in Hungary. Budapest, though still oppressed, was a place where other Eastern Europeans could come to experiment with "Western evils," from Big Macs to Nikes.

Since communism's graceful exit in 1989, Budapest has once again reinvented itself. During this time of transition, the city has struggled with whether to cling to its past glory days, or to leave all that behind and create something new. Budapest has a rich architectural heritage that rivals any European city—but many of those buildings were in a state of horrible disrepair. Now many have been fixed up to their prewar, pre-communist peak, while others have been melded with modern elements.

The latest chapter in Budapest's history has been written by its current prime minister, Viktor Orbán, and his party, Fidesz. Highly controversial both at home and abroad, but also beloved by the majority of Hungarians, Orbán has boldly set about reshaping Budapest and Hungary: restructuring its government, reinterpreting its history, and rebuilding much of the city. Orbán's rule has come with the renaming of squares to honor formerly obscure Hungarian historical-footnote figures, but has also seen an unprecedented burst of urban renewal. Ten years ago, many of Budapest's squares, streets, and parks were miserable, smoggy no-go zones. Today, they are gleaming and filled with happy locals.

Through it all, Budapest—atmospherically shot through with the crumbling elegance of former greatness—remains the heart and soul of Eastern Europe. It's a rich cultural stew made up of Hungarians, Germans, Slavs, and Jews, with a dash of Turkish paprika—simmered for centuries in a thermal bath. Each group has left its mark, but through it all, something has remained that is distinctly...Budapest.

Roads: The Town Center is hemmed in by the first of Pest's four concentric **ring roads** *(körút)*. The innermost ring is called the Kiskörút, or "Small Boulevard." The next ring, several blocks farther out, is called the Nagykörút, or "Great Boulevard." These ring roads change names every few blocks, but they are always called *körút*. Arterial **boulevards,** called *út,* stretch from central Pest into the suburbs like spokes on a wheel. One of these boulevards, **Andrássy út,** begins near Deák tér in central Pest and heads out to Heroes' Square and City Park; along the way it passes some of the city's best eateries, hotels, and sights (Opera House, House of Terror).

Bridges: Buda and Pest are connected by a series of characteristic bridges. From north to south, there's the low-profile

BUDAPEST

N

1/2 Kilometer

1/2 Mile

To Óbuda &
Danube Bend

Margaret
Island

ST.
ISTVÁN PARK

XIII

II

Elvis
Presley
tér

MARGARET BRIDGE

SZENT ISTVÁN

Széll
Kálmán
tér

B U D A

MARGIT KÖRÚT

MUSEUM OF
MILITARY
HISTORY

VIENNA
GATE

Batthyány
tér

Kossuth
tér

MUSEUM OF
ETHNOGRAPHY

PARLIAMENT

CASTLE
HILL

VÍZI-
VÁROS

Szabadság
tér

LEOPOLD
TOWN

XII

HILTON
HOTEL

FISHERMEN'S
BASTION

ST.
ISTVÁN'S
BASILICA

"HOSPITAL
IN THE
ROCK"

MATTHIAS
CHURCH

I

CHAIN
BRIDGE

V

DÉLI
(SOUTHERN)
STATION

GRESHAM
PALACE

FUNICULAR

HUNGARIAN
NATIONAL
GALLERY

Vörösmarty
tér

Deák
tér

TOWN
CENTER

ROYAL
PALACE

KÖRÚT ALKOTÁS UTCA

BUDAPEST
HISTORY
MUSEUM

VÁCI UTCA

TABÁN

HEGYALJA ÚT

ELISABETH
BRIDGE

D a n u b e

RUDAS
BATHS

Gellért
Hill

CITADELLA

CAVE
CHURCH

LIBERTY
BRIDGE

VILLÁNYI ÚT

GELLÉRT HOTEL
& BATHS

See
Buda Sights
detail map

To M-1& M-7 Freeways
& Lake Balaton

KARINTHY FRIGYES

To Memento
Park

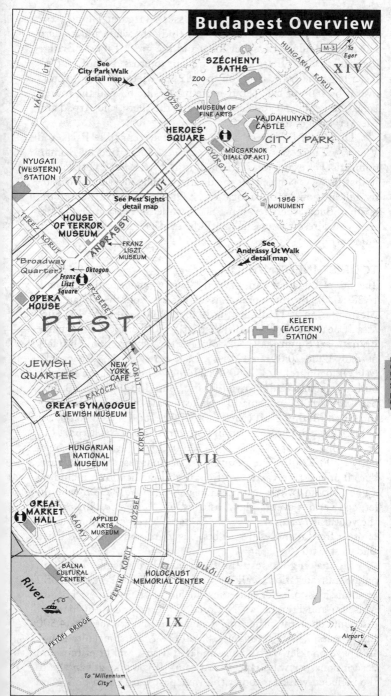

Budapest Overview

VÁCI ÚT

See
City Park Walk
detail map ►

SZÉCHENYI
BATHS

ZOO

MUSEUM OF
FINE ARTS

HEROES'
SQUARE

HUNGARIA KÖRÚT

M-3

To
Eger

XIV

VAJDAHUNYAD
CASTLE

DÓZSA

MŰCSARNOK
(HALL OF ART)

GYÖRGY

CITY PARK

NYUGATI
(WESTERN)
STATION

VI

ANDRÁSSY ÚT

See Pest Sights
detail map

1956
MONUMENT

ÚT

TERÉZ KÖRÚT

HOUSE
OF TERROR
MUSEUM

FRANZ
LISZT
MUSEUM

See Andrássy Út Walk
detail map ◄

"Broadway
Quarter" ← Oktogon

Franz
Liszt
Square

ERZSÉBET

OPERA
HOUSE

P E S T

KELETI
(EASTERN)
STATION

JEWISH
QUARTER

NEW
YORK
CAFÉ

RÁKÓCZI

KÖRÚT

ÚT

GREAT SYNAGOGUE
& JEWISH MUSEUM

HUNGARIAN
NATIONAL
MUSEUM

JÓZSEF

VIII

GREAT
MARKET
HALL

APPLIED
ARTS
MUSEUM

RÁDAY

BÁLNA
CULTURAL
CENTER

FERENC KÖRÚT

HOLOCAUST
MEMORIAL CENTER

ÜLLŐI ÚT

River

PETŐFI BRIDGE

IX

To
Airport

To "Millennium
City" ▼

BUDAPEST

Margaret Bridge (Margit híd, crosses Margaret Island), the famous **Chain Bridge** (Széchenyi lánchíd), the white and modern **Elisabeth Bridge** (Erzsébet híd), and the green **Liberty Bridge** (Szabadság híd). These bridges are fun to cross on foot, but it's faster to go under the river (on the M2/red Metró line), or to cross over it by tram or bus. (Four more bridges lie beyond the tourist zone: the Petőfi and Rákóczi bridges to the south, and Árpád and Megyeri bridges to the north.)

Districts: Budapest uses a district system (like Paris and Vienna). There are 23 districts *(kerület),* identified by Roman numerals. For example, Castle Hill is in district I and City Park is in district XIV. Notice that the district number does not necessarily indicate how central a location is: Districts II and III are to the north of Buda, where few tourists go, while the heart of Pest is district V. Addresses often start with the district number (as a Roman numeral).

TOURIST INFORMATION

The city of Budapest runs several TIs (www.budapestinfo.hu, tel. 1/438-8080). The main branch is a few steps from the M2 and M3 Metró station at **Deák tér** (daily 8:00-20:00, free Wi-Fi, Sütő utca 2, near the McDonald's, district V). Other locations include **Franz Liszt Square,** a block south of the Oktogon on Andrássy út (daily 12:00-20:00, free Wi-Fi, Liszt Ferenc tér 11, district VII, M1: Oktogon, tel. 1/322-4098), **Heroes' Square** (in the ice rink building facing Vajdahunyad Castle, Sun-Thu 10:00-18:00, Fri-Sat 10:00-20:00), in a small kiosk just inside the main entrance of the **Great Market Hall** (Mon 6:00-17:00, Tue-Fri 6:00-18:00, Sat 6:00-15:00, closed Sun), and in both terminals at the **airport** (TI at Terminal 2A open daily 8:00-22:00; TI at Terminal 2B open daily 10:00-22:00). The helpfulness of Budapest's TIs can vary, but all offer a nice variety of free, useful publications, including a good city map, the information-packed *Budapest Guide* booklet, and various events planners: *Budapest Panorama, Servus,* and the youthful *Budapest Funzine.* At any TI, you can collect a pile of other free brochures (for sights, bus tours, and more) and buy a Budapest Card.

Sightseeing Passes: The **Budapest Card** includes use of all public transportation, walking tours of Buda and Pest, a handful of admissions to lesser museums (including the Budapest History Museum and Hungarian National Gallery), and 10-50 percent discounts on many other major museums and attractions (4,500 Ft/24 hours, 7,500 Ft/48 hours, 8,900 Ft/72 hours; includes handy 100-page booklet with maps, updated hours, and brief museum descriptions; www.budapest-card.com). If you take advantage of the included walking tours, the Budapest Card could be a good value for a very busy sightseer—do the arithmetic.

TourInform: The Hungarian National Tourist Office operates a small TI on Castle Hill. It's in the circular, white building in the park across from Matthias Church (daily 9:00-19:00, or 10:00-18:00 in winter).

Discover Budapest: Ben Frieday, an American in love with Budapest (and one of its women), runs this agency, which specializes in answering questions Americans have about Budapest and Hungary. It's conveniently located near Andrássy út, behind the Opera House at Lázár utca 16 (district VI, M1: Opera). At their office, you can get online (150 Ft/15 minutes at a terminal, free Wi-Fi) or rent a bike (open daily 9:00-20:00, until 19:00 Nov-March, tel. 1/269-3843, mobile 0620-929-7506, www. discoverbudapest.com). This location is also the meeting point for Ben's various tours: Absolute Walking Tours and Yellow Zebra bike and Segway tours (all described later, under "Tours in Budapest").

ARRIVAL IN BUDAPEST
By Train

Budapest has three major train stations (*pályaudvar,* abbreviated *pu.*): Keleti ("Eastern") Station, Nyugati ("Western") Station, and Déli ("Southern") Station. Before departing from Budapest, it's essential to carefully confirm which station your train leaves from.

The Keleti/Eastern train station and the Nyugati/Western train station are both cavernous, slightly run-down, late-19th-century Erector-set masterpieces in Pest. The Déli/Southern train station—behind Castle Hill in Buda—mingles its dinginess with modern, concrete flair.

All three stations are seedy and overdue for renovation. This makes them a bit intimidating—not the most pleasant first taste of Budapest. But once you get your bearings, they're easy to navigate. A few key words: *pénztár* or *jegypénztár* is ticket window, *vágány* is track, *induló vonatok* is departures, and *érkező vonatok* is arrivals. At all stations, access to the tracks is monitored: You might have to show your ticket to reach the platforms (though this is very loosely enforced).

The taxi stands in front of each train station are notorious for ripping off tourists; it's better to call for a taxi (or, better yet, stick to public transit). For tips on this—and on using the Metró system to connect into downtown Budapest—see "Getting Around Budapest" on page 564.

Keleti/Eastern Station

Keleti train station (Keleti pu.) is just south of City Park, east of central Pest. The station faces a pretty, split-level, newly renovated

BUDAPEST

plaza called Baross tér, with stops for two different Metró lines (M2/red and M4/green).

On arrival, go to the front of long tracks 6-9 to reach the exits and services. Several travel agencies masquerading as TIs cluster near the head of the tracks. A handy **ATM** is just to the left of the main door (and two more ATMs are inside banks that face the square out front). There's no official TI at the station, but the railroad runs a customer service office with train advice and basic city info (near the front of track 9, in the left corner, near the ATM).

Along track 6, from back to front, you'll see a side door (leading to a beautifully restored arrivals hall and an exit to a taxi stand), Interchange exchange booth (with bad rates—use the ATM instead), international ticket windows (*nemzetközi jegypénztár*), grubby gyros stands, and the classy Baross Restaurant. Pay WCs are down the hall past the gyros places.

Across the main hall, more services run **along track 9,** including domestic ("inland") ticket windows and lockers. The big staircase at the head of the tracks leads down to more domestic ticket windows, WCs, telephones, and more lockers.

To get **into the city center,** the easiest option is to take the Metró: Heading down the main stairs where the tracks dead-end, you'll pass through a grubby ticket area, and then (on your right) a public transit ticket and information office (a handy place to pick up a transit ticket, if you need one). Just beyond that, the underpass opens up: Turn left to reach the M2/red Metró line, or right to reach the M4/green Metró line.

I'd avoid taxis—the ones waiting alongside the station (through the exit by track 6) are likely to be dishonest, but you can try asking for a rough estimate: the fair rate to downtown should be no more than 2,000 Ft. If you must take a taxi, it's far more reliable to phone for one (call 211-1111 or 266-6666, tell the English-speaking dispatcher where you are, and go outside to meet your taxi).

Nyugati/Western Station

Nyugati train station (Nyugati pu.) is the most central of Budapest's stations, facing the Great Boulevard on the northeast edge of downtown Pest. The square in front of Nyugati Station is slated for a complete renovation over the next few years. Expect the station area to be torn up, and many of the services or tram

stops mentioned here may be temporarily relocated. Look for signs or ask officials for help.

Most international arrivals use tracks 1-9, which are set back from the main entrance. From the head of these tracks, use the stairs or escalator just inside the doors to reach an underpass and the Metró (M3/blue line), or exit straight ahead into a parking lot with buses and taxis. Note that the taxi drivers here are often crooked—it's far better to call for your own cab (see instructions and taxi phone numbers described previously for Keleti Station).

Ticket windows are through an easy-to-miss door across the tracks by platform 13 (marked *cassa* and *információ;* once you enter the ticket hall, international windows are in a second room at the far end—look for *nemzetközi jegypénztár,* daily 7:30-19:00). Lockers are down the hall next to the international ticket office, on the left. An **ATM** is just inside the main door, on the right.

From the head of tracks 10-13, exit straight ahead and you'll be on Teréz körút, the very busy Great Boulevard—and, quite likely, a chaotic, torn-up construction zone. In front of the building should be the stop for handy trams #4 and #6 (which zip around Pest's Great Boulevard ring road); to the right are stairs leading to an underpass (use it to avoid crossing this busy intersection, or to reach the Metró's M3/blue line); and to the left is the classiest Art Nouveau McDonald's on the planet, filling the station's former waiting room. (Seriously. Take a look inside.)

Déli/Southern Station

In the late 19th century, local newlyweds caught the train at Déli train station (Déli pu.) for their honeymoon in Venice. Renovated by the heavy-handed communists, today the station—tucked behind Castle Hill on the Buda side—is dreary, dark-stone, smaller, and more modern-feeling than the other train stations. From the tracks, go straight ahead into the vast, empty-feeling main hall, with well-marked domestic and international ticket windows at opposite ends. A left-luggage desk is outside beyond track 1. Downstairs you'll find several shops and eateries, and access to the very convenient M2/red Metró line, which takes you to several key points in town: Batthyány tér (on the Buda embankment, at the north end of the Víziváros neighborhood), Deák tér (the heart of Pest, with connections to two other Metró lines), and Keleti train station (where you can transfer to the M4/green Metró line).

By Plane

Budapest's **Liszt Ferenc Airport** is 10 miles southeast of the center (airport code: BUD, tel. 1/296-7000, www.bud.hu). Many Hungarians still call the airport by its former name, "Ferihegy." The airport's lone passenger terminal is, perhaps optimistically, called "Terminal 2" ("Terminal 1" closed in 2012). The terminal has two adjacent parts, which you can easily walk between in just a few minutes: the smaller Terminal 2A is for flights from EU/Schengen countries (no passport control required), while Terminal 2B is for flights from other countries. Both sections have ATMs and TI desks (open daily 8:00-23:00 in 2A, and daily 10:00-22:00 in 2B). Car rental desks are in the arrivals area for 2B.

From the Airport to Budapest: The fastest door-to-door option is to take a **taxi**. Főtaxi has a monopoly at the taxi stand out front; figure about 6,000-7,000 Ft to downtown, depending on traffic.

The **airport shuttle** minibus is cheaper for solo travelers, but two people will pay only a few dollars more to share a taxi (3,200 Ft/1 person, 4,790 Ft/2 people; minibus ride to any hotel in the city center takes about 30-60 minutes depending on hotel location, plus waiting time; tel. 1/296-8555, www.airportshuttle.hu; if arranging a minibus transfer *to* the airport, call at least 24 hours in advance). To save time, you can book your transfer at their handy desk inside the baggage claim area, or wait until you're out in the arrivals lobby. Because they prefer to take several people at once, you may have to wait awhile at the airport for a quorum to show up (about 20 minutes in busy times, up to an hour when it's slow—they can give you an estimate).

Finally, there's the cheap but slow **public bus #200E.** This stops at both Terminals 2A and 2B and runs in about 25 minutes to the Kőbánya-Kispest station on the M3/blue Metró line; from there, take the Metró the rest of the way into town (entire journey covered by basic 350-Ft transit ticket, allow about an hour total for the trip to the center).

To Eger: Eger makes an enjoyable small-town entry point in Hungary for getting over your jet lag. Unfortunately, there is no direct connection there from Budapest's airport. The easiest plan is to ride the airport shuttle minibus to Budapest's Keleti/Eastern train station, then catch the Eger-bound train from there. Or, to save a little money, you could take public bus #200E to Kőbánya-Kispest, ride the M3/blue Metró line to Deák tér, and transfer to the M2/red Metró line, which stops at both Keleti Station (for the train to Eger) and Stadionok (for the bus to Eger).

By Car

Avoid driving in Budapest if you can—roads are narrow, and

fellow drivers, bikes, and pedestrians make the roads feel like an obstacle course. Especially during rush hour (7:00-9:00 and 16:00-18:00), congestion is maddening, and since there's no complete expressway bypass, much of the traffic going through the city has to go *through* the city—sharing the downtown streets with local commuters. The recent wave of roadwork and other construction around Budapest only complicates matters. Signage can be confusing. Don't drive down roads marked with a red circle, or in lanes marked for buses; these can be monitored by automatic traffic cameras, and you could be mailed a ticket.

There are four concentric ring roads, all of them slow: the Small Boulevard (Kiskörút), Great Boulevard (Nagykörút), and outermost Hungária körút, from which highways and expressways spin off to other destinations. Farther out, the M-0 expressway makes a not-quite-complete circle around the city center, helping to divert some traffic.

Parking: While in Budapest, unless you're heading to an out-of-town sight (such as Memento Park), park the car at or near your hotel and take public transportation. Public street parking costs 175-525 Ft per hour (pay in advance at machine and put ticket on dashboard—watch locals and imitate). Within the Great Boulevard, it's generally free to park from 20:00 until 8:00 the next morning (farther out, it's free after 18:00). But in some heavily touristed areas, you may have to pay around the clock—in any event, check signs carefully, and confirm with a local (such as your hotelier) that you've parked appropriately. Also, be sure to park within the lines—otherwise, your car is likely to get "booted" (I've seen more than one confused tourist puzzling over the giant red brace on his wheel). A guarded parking lot is safer, but more expensive (figure 3,000-4,000 Ft/day, ask your hotel or look for the blue *P*s on maps). Rental-car theft can be a problem, so ask at your hotel for advice.

HELPFUL HINTS

Rip-Offs: Budapest feels—and is—safe, especially for a city of its size. While there's little risk of violent crime, and I've rarely had someone try to rip me off here, you might run into a petty crook or two (such as con artists or pickpockets). As in any big city, it's especially important to secure your valuables and wear a money belt in crowded and touristy places, particularly on the Metró and in trams. Keep your wits about you and refuse to be bullied or distracted.

Restaurants on the Váci utca shopping street are notorious for overcharging tourists. Here or anywhere in Budapest, don't eat at a restaurant that doesn't list prices on the menu, and always check your bill carefully. Increasingly, restaurants are adding a (legitimate) service charge of 10 to 12 percent to your bill; if you don't notice this, you might accidentally double-tip (for more on tipping, see page 1302).

If you're a male in a touristy area and a gorgeous local girl takes a liking to you, avoid her. She's a *konzumlány* ("consumption girl"), and the foreplay going on here will climax in your grand rip-off. You'll wind up at her "favorite bar," with astronomical prices enforced by a burly bouncer.

Budapest's biggest crooks? Unscrupulous cabbies. For tips on outsmarting them, see "Getting Around Budapest— By Taxi" on page 570. Bottom line: Locals *always* call for a cab, rather than hail one on the street or at a taxi stand. If you're not comfortable making the call yourself, ask your hotel or restaurant to call for you.

Sightseeing Tips: Budapest boomed in the late 19th century, after it became the co-capital of the vast Habsburg Empire. Most of its finest buildings (and top sights) date from this age. To appreciate an opulent interior—a Budapest experience worth ▲▲▲—I strongly recommend touring either the Parliament or the Opera House, depending on your interests. The Opera tour is more crowd-pleasing, whereas the Parliament tour is a bit drier (with a focus on history and parliamentary process)—but the spaces are even grander. Seeing both is also a fine option. "Honorable mentions" go to the interiors of St. István's Basilica, the Great Synagogue, New York Café, and both the Széchenyi and the Gellért Baths. The early 21st century has also been a boom time in Budapest. Many formerly dreary squares, parks, and streets have been refurbished, as have many museums. The latest plan is to create an ambitious "Museum Quarter" in City Park, which will be the new home to the National Gallery and museums of contemporary art (Ludwig collection), ethnography, photography, architecture, and music. However, this is unlikely to happen before 2018 (though construction may be under way when you visit—see www.ligetbudapest.org for details).

Medical Help: Near Buda's Széll Kálmán tér, **FirstMed Centers** is a private, pricey, English-speaking clinic (by appointment or urgent care, call first, Hattyú utca 14, 5th floor, district I, M2: Széll Kálmán tér, tel. 1/224-9090, www.firstmedcenters. com).

Pharmacies: The helpful **Dorottya Gyógyszertár** pharmacy is dead-center in Pest, between Vörösmarty and Széchenyi squares. Because they cater to clientele from nearby international hotels, they have a useful directory that lists the Hungarian equivalent of US prescription medicines (Mon-Fri 8:00-20:00, closed Sat-Sun, Dorottya utca 13, district V, M1:

Tonight We're Gonna Party Like It's 1896

Visitors to Budapest need only remember one date: 1896. For the millennial celebration of their ancestors' arrival in Europe,  Hungarians threw a huge blowout party. In the thousand years between 896 and 1896, the Magyars had gone from being a nomadic Central Asian tribe that terrorized the Continent to sharing the throne of one of the most successful empires Europe had ever seen.

Budapest used its millennial celebration as an excuse to build monuments and buildings appropriate for the co-capital of a huge empire, including these landmarks:

- Heroes' Square and the Millennium Monument
- Vajdahunyad Castle (in City Park)
- The riverside Parliament building (96 meters tall, with 96 steps at the main entry)
- St. István's Basilica (also 96 meters tall)
- The M1/yellow Metró line, a.k.a. Földalatti ("Underground")—the first subway on the Continent
- The Great Market Hall (and four other market halls)
- Andrássy út and most of the fine buildings lining it
- The Opera House
- A complete rebuilding of Matthias Church (on Castle Hill)
- The Fishermen's Bastion decorative terrace (by Matthias Church)
- The green Liberty Bridge (then called Franz Josef Bridge, in honor of the ruling Habsburg emperor)

Ninety-six is the key number in Hungary—even the national anthem (when sung at the proper tempo) takes 96 seconds. But after all this fuss, it's too bad that the date was wrong: A commission—convened to establish the exact year of the Magyars' debut—determined it happened in 895. But city leaders knew they'd never make an 1895 deadline, so they requested the finding be changed to 896.

Vörösmarty tér, for location see map on page 663, tel. 1/317-2374). Each district has one 24-hour pharmacy (these should be noted outside the entrance to any pharmacy).

Calling Mobile Numbers: In Hungary, mobile numbers (generally beginning with 0620, 0630, or 0670) are dialed differently, depending on where you're calling from. I've listed them as you'd dial them from a fixed line within Hungary. From another country, or from a mobile phone in Hungary, omit the initial 06, and replace it with the international access code (011 from the US, 00 from Europe, or + on a mobile phone), then 36, then the number. For more tips on calling, see page 1318.

Monday Closures: Most of Budapest's museums are closed on Mondays. But you can still take advantage of plenty of other sights and activities: all three major baths, Memento Park, Great Synagogue and Jewish Quarter, Matthias Church on Castle Hill, St. István's Basilica, Parliament tour, Great Market Hall, Opera House tour, City Park (and Zoo), Danube cruises, concerts, and bus, walking, and bike tours.

Train Tickets: Ticket-buying lines can be long at train stations, particularly for long-distance international trains. If you want to buy your ticket in advance, **MÁV** (Hungarian Railways) has a very convenient ticket office right in the heart of downtown Pest. They generally speak English and sell tickets for no additional fee (Mon-Fri 9:00-18:00, closed Sat-Sun, just up from the Chain Bridge and across from Erzsébet tér at József Attila utca 16, district V, M1: Vörösmarty tér, for location see map on page 663).

Internet Access: Most hotels offer Wi-Fi or cable Internet (usually free, sometimes for a fee). Internet cafés are common—just look for signs or ask your hotel. In Pest, I like **Discover Budapest,** with fast access and good prices (free Wi-Fi, Internet terminals-150 Ft/15 minutes; see "Discover Budapest" listing on page 555).

Post Offices: These are marked with a smart green *posta* logo (usually open Mon-Fri 8:00-18:00, Sat 8:00-12:00, closed Sun).

Laundry: The handiest option for full service is **Laundromat-Mosómata,** just behind the Opera House (2,400 Ft to wash and dry a big load, generally takes 3-5 hours, Mon-Fri 10:00-18:00, Sat 10:00-14:00, closed Sun; walk straight behind the Opera House and turn right on Ó utca, then look left for signs at #24—you'll go up the main stairs and turn left to find it in the arcade; district VI, M1: Opera, for location see map on page 659, mobile 0670-340-0478). Two self-service launderettes are in the Jewish Quarter/nightlife zone (both charge 800 Ft to wash, 800 Ft to dry): **Laundry Budapest,** a humble but functional option with lots of machines tucked behind an Internet café, sits at the far end of this area, near the Blaha Lujza tér Metró stop. If you ask nicely and tip them, they may be willing to put it in the dryer and fold it for you (daily 9:00-24:00, last wash at 22:00, Dohány utca 37, tel. 1/781-0098, www.laundrybudapest.hu). **Bazar Hostel,** closer to the Great Synagogue, has just a few machines downstairs from their reception (open daily 24 hours, free Wi-Fi, Dohány utca 22).

English Bookstores: The **Central European University**

Bookshop offers the best selection anywhere of scholarly books about this region (and beyond). They also sell guidebooks, literary fiction, and some popular American magazines—all in English (Mon-Fri 10:00-19:00, Sat 11:00-15:00, closed Sun, just down the street in front of St. István's Basilica at Zrínyi utca 12, district V, for location see map on page 663, tel. 1/327-3096).

Bestsellers has a fine selection of new books, mostly in English; it's just around the corner from CEU Bookshop, near St. István's Basilica (Mon-Fri 9:00-18:30, Sat 10:00-17:00, Sun 10:00-16:00, Október 6 utca 11, tel. 1/312-1295).

The **Discover Budapest** office sells a wide range of secondhand books at its location just behind the Opera House at Lázár utca 16 (daily 9:00-20:00, until 19:00 Nov-March, see listing on page 555).

Bike Rental: Budapest, whose streets are congested with traffic, isn't the easiest city for bicycling—though things are improving, with more and more bike lanes being included in renovated urban zones. Those comfortable with urban cycling may find that it helps them zip around the city more smoothly. You can rent a bike at **Yellow Zebra,** part of Discover Budapest (2,000-3,000 Ft/all day, 3,000-4,500 Ft/24 hours, price depends on type of bike; see "Discover Budapest" listing on page 555).

Budapest also has a subsidized borrow-a-bike system called **Bubi** (for "**Bu**dapest **Bi**kes"). Bike stations are scattered throughout the Town Center and adjoining areas; you can pick a bike up at any station and drop it off at any other—making this handy for one-way trips. It's free to use a bike for 30 minutes or less, then costs 500 Ft for each 30 additional minutes. But it requires either a membership card (9,450 Ft for a year) or a short-term "ticket" (500 Ft/24 hours, 1,000 Ft/72 hours, 2,000 Ft/week, plus a 25,000-Ft deposit on your credit card for the duration of the ticket; you can buy a ticket at www.bkk.hu/bubi or at many docking stations; your PIN is sent to your mobile phone). If you'll be using a bike for short rides several times throughout your visit, this system is worth considering. You can get all of the details at www.bkk.hu/bubi, or ask at the TI.

Drivers: Friendly, English-speaking **Gábor Balázs** can drive you around the city or into the surrounding countryside (4,000 Ft/hour, 3-hour minimum in city, 4-hour minimum in countryside—good for a Danube Bend excursion, mobile 0620-936-4317, bgabor.e@gmail.com). **Zsolt Gál** is also available for transfers and side-trips, and specializes in helping people track down Jewish sites in the surrounding areas (mobile

0670-452-4900, forma111562@gmail.com). Note that these are drivers, not tour guides. For tour guides who can drive you to outlying sights, see "Tours in Budapest," later.

Best Views: Budapest is a city of marvelous vistas. Some of the best are from the Citadella fortress (high on Gellért Hill), the promenade in front of the Royal Palace and the Fishermen's Bastion on top of Castle Hill, and the embankments or many bridges spanning the Danube (especially the Chain Bridge). Don't forget the view from the tour boats on the Danube—particularly lovely at night.

Updates to This Book: For updates to this book, check www.ricksteves.com/update.

GETTING AROUND BUDAPEST

Budapest sprawls. Connecting your sightseeing on foot is tedious and unnecessary. It's crucial to get comfortable with the public transportation system—Metró lines, trams, buses, trolley buses, and boats that can take you virtually anywhere you want to go. Budapest's well-planned cityscape and thoughtfully coordinated transit network combine to make it one of the easiest big European cities to zip around. Budapest's transit system website, www.bkk.hu, offers a useful route-planner and a downloadable app for on-the-go transit info.

Tickets: The same tickets work for the entire system. Buy them at kiosks, Metró ticket windows, or machines (with English instructions). As it can be frustrating to find a ticket machine (especially when you see your tram or bus approaching), I generally invest in a multiday ticket to have the freedom of hopping on at will.

Your options are as follows:

• **Single ticket** (*vonaljegy,* for a ride of up to an hour on any means of transit; transfers allowed only within the Metró system)—350 Ft (or 450 Ft if bought from the driver)

• **Short single Metró ride** (*Metrószakaszjegy,* 3 stops or fewer on the Metró)—300 Ft

• **Transfer ticket** (*átszállójegy*—allowing up to 90 minutes, including one transfer between Metró and bus)—530 Ft

• **Pack of 10 single tickets** (*10 darabos gyűjtőjegy*), which can be shared—3,000 Ft (that's 300 Ft per ticket, saving you 50 Ft per ticket; note that these must stay together as a single pack—they can't be sold separately)

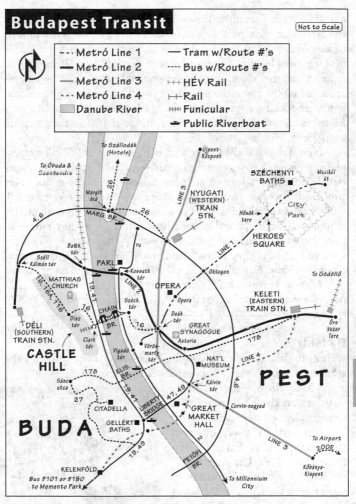

Budapest Transit

Not to Scale

--- Metró Line 1
— Metró Line 2
— Metró Line 3
--- Metró Line 4
▨ Danube River

— Tram w/Route #'s
--- Bus w/Route #'s
+++ HÉV Rail
+—+ Rail
+++ Funicular
⚓ Public Riverboat

To Szállodák (Hotels)

To Óbuda & Szentendre

Újpest-Központ

SZÉCHENYI BATHS

Mexikói út

Margit híd

MARG. BR.

LINE 3

NYUGATI (WESTERN) TRAIN STN.

City Park

Hősök tere

HEROES' SQUARE

4, 6

Batth. tér

LINE 1

Oktogon

Széll Kálmán tér

PARL.

Kossuth tér

Opera

KELETI (EASTERN) TRAIN STN.

To Gödöllő

MATTHIAS CHURCH

LINE 2

OPERA

16, 16A, 116

Sz, 19, 41

Széch. tér

Deák tér

Örs Vezér Tere

DÉLI (SOUTHERN) TRAIN STN.

Disz tér

CHAIN BR.

16

Astoria

GREAT SYNAGOGUE

178

CASTLE HILL

Clark tér

Vigadó tér

Vörösmarty tér

NAT'L MUSEUM

LINE 4

PEST

Sánc utca

ELIS. BR.

Kálvin tér

4, 6

27

19, 41

LIBERTY BRIDGE

47, 49

Corvin-negyed

To Airport

CITADELLA

GREAT MARKET HALL

LINE 3

200E

BUDA

GELLÉRT BATHS

19, 49

PETŐFI BR.

Kőbánya-Kispest

KELENFÖLD

Bus #101 or #150 to Memento Park

To Millennium City

BUDAPEST

• Unlimited multiday travel cards for Metró, bus, and tram, including a **24-hour travelcard** (*24 órás jegy,* 1,650 Ft), **72-hour travelcard** (*72 órás jegy,* 4,150 Ft/72 hours), and **seven-day travelcard** (*hetijegy,* 4,950 Ft/7 days)

• **24-hour group travel card** (*csoportos 24 órás jegy,* 3,300 Ft), covering up to five adults—a great deal for groups of three to five people

• The **Budapest Card,** which combines a multiday ticket with sightseeing discounts (but it's generally a bad value—see page 554)

Always validate single-ride tickets as you enter the bus, tram, or Metró station (stick it in the elbow-high box). On older buses and trams that have little red validation boxes, stick your ticket in the black slot, then pull the slot toward you to punch holes in your ticket. Multiday tickets need be validated only once. The stern-looking people with blue-and-green armbands waiting as you enter or exit the Metró want to see your validated ticket. Cheaters are fined 6,000 Ft on the spot, and you'll be surprised how often you're checked—they seem to be stationed at just about every Metró escalator. All public transit runs from 4:30 in the morning until 23:10.

New Transit Cards: Likely starting in 2016 or 2017, Budapest plans to phase in pay-as-you-go cards, which will replace the paper tickets described above. As is now common in many major cities worldwide (from London's Oyster card to New York's Metrocard), public transit passengers will buy a card and load it up with credit, which will be deducted according to how long they ride—so they'll need to "touch in" and "touch out" as they enter and exit the system. For short-time tourists, individual electronic "smart paper" tickets will also be available. See www.bkk.hu for the latest.

Handy Terms: *Á* ____ *felé* means "in the direction of ____." *Megálló* means "stop" or "station," and *Végállomás* means "end of the line."

By Metró

Riding Budapest's Metró, you really feel like you're down in the efficient guts of the city. There are four working lines:

• **M1/yellow**—The first subway line on the Continent, this line runs just 20 steps below street level under Andrássy út from the center to City Park. Dating from 1896, "the Underground" *(Földalatti)* is so shallow that you must follow the signs on the street (listing end points—*ua Mexikói út felé* takes you toward City Park) to gauge the right direction, because there's no underpass for switching platforms. Though recently renovated, the M1 line retains its 1896 atmosphere, with fun black-and-white photos of the age.

• **M2/red**—Built during the communist days, it's 115 feet deep and designed to double as a bomb shelter. This line has undergone a thorough renovation, leaving its stations new and shiny. Going under the Danube to Buda, the M2 connects the Déli/Southern train station, Széll Kálmán tér (where you catch bus #16, #16A, or #116 to the top of Castle Hill), Batthyány tér (Víziváros and the HÉV suburban railway), Kossuth tér (behind the Parliament), Astoria (near the Great Synagogue on the Small Boulevard), and the Keleti/Eastern train station (where it crosses the M4/green line).

• **M3/blue**—This line makes a broad, boomerang-shaped swoop north to south on the Pest side. It's noticeably older but slated for renovation soon. Key stops include the Nyugati/Western train station, Ferenciek tere (in the heart of Pest's Town Center), Kálvin tér (near the Great Market Hall and many recommended hotels; this is also where it crosses the M4/green line), and Corvin-negyed (near the Holocaust Memorial Center).

• **M4/green**—The newest line (opened in 2014) runs from southern Buda to the Gellért Baths, under the Danube to Fővám tér (behind the Great Market Hall) and Kálvin tér (where it crosses the M3/blue line), then up to Rákóczi tér (on the Grand Boulevard) and the Keleti/Eastern train station (where it crosses the M2/red line). Many of its stations boast boldly modern, waste-of-space concrete architecture that's eye-opening to simply stroll through; the one at Gellért tér has a thermal spring-fed waterfall coursing past the main staircase.

The three original lines—M1, M2, and M3—cross only once: at the **Deák tér** stop (often signed as *Deák Ferenc tér*) in the heart of Pest, near where Andrássy út begins.

Aside from the historic M1 line, most Metró stations are at intersections of ring roads and other major thoroughfares. You'll usually exit the Metró into a confusing underpass packed with kiosks, fast-food stands, and makeshift markets. Directional signs (listing which streets, addresses, and tram or bus stops are near each exit) help you find the right exit. Or do the prairie-dog routine: Surface to get your bearings, then head back underground to find the correct stairs up to your destination.

Metró stops themselves are usually very well-marked, with a list of upcoming stops on the wall behind the tracks. Digital clocks either count down to the next train's arrival, or count up from the previous train's departure; either way, you'll rarely wait more than five minutes during peak times.

By HÉV

Budapest's suburban rail system, or HÉV (pronounced "hayv," stands for Helyiérdekű Vasút, literally "Railway of Local Interest"), branches off to the outskirts and beyond. On a short visit, it's unlikely that you'll need to use it, unless you're heading to the Óbuda neighborhood (for its museums), the charming Danube Bend town of Szentendre, or the royal palace at Gödöllő.

The HÉV line that begins at Batthyány tér in Buda's Víziváros neighborhood heads through Óbuda to Szentendre; from the station at Örs vezér tere, a different line runs east to Gödöllő. The HÉV is covered by standard transit tickets and passes for rides within the city of Budapest (such as to Óbuda). But if going beyond—such as to Szentendre or Gödöllő—you'll have to pay more. Tell the ticket-seller (or punch into the machine) where you're going, and you'll be issued the proper ticket.

By Tram

Budapest's trams are handy and frequent, taking you virtually anywhere the Metró doesn't. Here are some trams you might use (note that all of these run in both directions):

Tram **#2:** Follows Pest's Danube embankment, parallel to Váci utca. From north to south, it begins at the Great Boulevard (near Margaret Bridge) and stops on either side of the Parliament (north side near the visitors center/Országház stop, as well as south side near the Kossuth tér Metró stop), Széchenyi István tér and the Chain Bridge, Vigadó tér, and the Great Market Hall.

Trams **#19** and **#41:** Run along Buda's Danube embankment from Batthyány tér (with an M2/red Metró station, and HÉV trains to Óbuda and Szentendre). From Batthyány tér, these trams run (north to south) through Víziváros to Clark Ádám tér (the bottom of the Castle Hill funicular, near the stop for bus #16 up to Castle Hill; get off here and walk a few minutes to take the Várkert Bazár grand staircase up to the Royal Palace), then under Elisabeth Bridge (get off at Döbrentei tér stop for the Rudas Baths) and around the base of Gellért Hill to the Gellért Hotel and Baths (Gellért tér stop).

Trams **#4** and **#6:** Zip around Pest's Great Boulevard ring road (Nagykörút), connecting Nyugati/Western train station and the Oktogon with the southern tip of Margaret Island and Buda's Széll Kálmán tér (with M2/red Metró station).

Trams **#47** and **#49:** Connect the Gellért Baths in Buda with Pest's Small Boulevard ring road (Kiskörút), with stops at the Great Market Hall, the National Museum, the Great Synagogue (Astoria stop), and Deák tér (end of the line).

By Bus and Trolley Bus

I use the Metró and trams for most of my Budapest commuting. But some buses are useful for shortcuts within the city, or for reaching outlying sights. Note that the transit company draws a distinction between gas-powered

"buses" and electric "trolley buses" (which are powered by over-head cables). Unless otherwise noted, you can assume the following are standard buses:

Buses **#16, #16A,** and **#116:** All head up to the top of Castle Hill (get off at Dísz tér, in the middle of the hill—the closest stop to the Royal Palace). You can catch any of these three at Széll Kálmán tér (M2/red Metró line). When coming from the other direction, bus #16 makes several handy stops in Pest (Deák tér, Széchenyi István tér), then crosses the Chain Bridge for more stops in Buda (including Clark Ádám tér, at Buda end of Chain Bridge on its way up to the castle).

Trolley buses **#70** and **#78:** Zip from near the Opera House (intersection of Andrássy út and Nagymező utca) to the Parliament (Kossuth tér).

Bus **#178:** Goes from Keleti/Eastern train station to central Pest (Astoria and Ferenciek tere Metró stops), then over the Elisabeth Bridge to Buda.

Bus **#26:** Begins at Nyugati/Western train station and heads around the Great Boulevard to Margaret Island, making several stops along the island.

Bus **#27:** Runs from either side of Gellért Hill to just below the Citadella fortress at the hill's peak (Búsuló Juhász stop).

Bus **#200E:** Connects Liszt Ferenc Airport to the Kőbánya-Kispest M3/blue Metró station.

Buses **#101** and **#150:** Run from Keletenföld (the end of the line for the M4/green Metró line) to Memento Park.

By Boat

Budapest's public transit authority operates a system of Danube riverboats *(hajójárat)* that connect strategic locations throughout the city. The riverboat system has drawbacks: Frequency is sparse (1-2/hour on weekdays, hourly on weekends; off-season weekdays only, hourly), and it's typically slower than hopping on the Metró or a tram. But it's also a romantic, cheap alternative to pricey riverboat cruises, and can be a handy way to connect some sightseeing points.

A 750-Ft ticket covers any trip; on weekdays, it's also covered by a 24-hour, 72-hour, or 7-day travelcards (but not by the Budapest Card; on weekends, you have to buy a ticket regardless of your pass).

Lines **#D11** (on weekdays) and **#D13** (on weekends) run in both directions through the city, including these stops within downtown Budapest:

• **Margitsziget/Szállodák** and **Margitsziget/Centenáriumi emlékmű**, at the northern and southern ends of Margaret Island (respectively)

- **Jászai Mari tér,** at the Pest end of Margaret Bridge
- **Batthyány tér,** on the Buda embankment in Víziváros
- **Kossuth Lajos tér,** near the Parliament on the Pest side
- **Várkert Bazár,** at the base of the grand entrance staircase to Buda Castle
- **Petőfi tér,** on the Pest embankment next to the Danube Legenda riverboats (dock 8)
- **Szent Gellért tér,** at the Buda end of Liberty Bridge, next to the Gellért Baths

Some stops may be closed if the river level gets very low; as this is a relatively new service, expect changes. For details, see www.bkk.hu.

By Taxi

Budapest's public transportation is good enough that you probably won't need to take many taxis. But if you do, you may run into a dishonest driver. Arm yourself with knowledge: Budapest has recently introduced stringent new regulations. Official taxis must be painted yellow and black and must charge identical rates, regardless of company: a drop rate of 450 Ft, and then 280 Ft/kilometer, plus 70 Ft/minute for wait time. (The prices go up at night, between 22:00 and 6:00 in the morning.) Prices are per ride, not per passenger. A 10 percent tip is expected. A typical ride within central Budapest shouldn't run more than 2,000 Ft. Despite what some slimy cabbies may tell you, there's no legitimate extra charge for crossing the river.

Instead of hailing a taxi on the street, do as the locals do and call a cab from a reputable company—it's cheaper, and you're more likely to get an honest driver. Try **City Taxi** (tel. 1/211-1111), **Taxi 6x6** (tel. 1/266-6666), or **Főtaxi** (tel. 1/222-2222). Most dispatchers speak English, but if you're uncomfortable calling, you can ask your hotel or restaurant to call for you.

Many "cabs" you'd hail on the streets are there only to prey on rich, green tourists. Avoid unmarked taxis (nicknamed "hyenas" by locals), as well as any cabs that wait at tourist spots and train stations. If you do wave down a cab on the street, choose one that's yellow and black, and marked with an official company logo and telephone number (otherwise, it's not official). Ask for a rough estimate before you get in—if it doesn't sound reasonable, walk away. If you wind up being dramatically overcharged for a ride, simply pay what you think is fair and go inside. If the driver follows you (unlikely), your hotel receptionist will defend you.

Tours in Budapest

BY FOOT
▲▲▲Local Guides

Budapest has an abundance of enthusiastic, hardworking young guides who speak perfect English and enjoy showing off their city.

Given the reasonable fees and efficient use of your time, hiring your own personal expert is an excellent value. While they might be available last-minute, it's better to reserve in advance by email.

I have three favorites, any of whom can do half-day or full-day tours, and can also drive you into the countryside (€90/4 hours, €150/8 hours): **Péter Pölczman** is an exceptional guide who really puts you in touch with the Budapest you came to see (mobile 0620-926-0557, www.budapestyourself.com, polczman@freestart.hu, or peter@budapestyourself.com). **Andrea Makkay** has professional polish and a smart understanding of what visitors really want to experience (mobile 0620-962-9363, www.privateguidebudapest.com, andrea.makkay@gmail.com—arrange details by email; if Andrea is busy, she can arrange to send you with another guide). And **George Farkas** is particularly well-attuned to the hip, stylish side of this fast-changing metropolis (mobile 0670-335-8030, georgefarkas@gmail.com).

Elemér Boreczky, a semi-retired university professor, leads walking tours with a soft-spoken, scholarly approach, emphasizing Budapest's rich tapestry of architecture as "frozen music." Elemér is ideal if you want a walking graduate-level seminar about the easy-to-miss nuances of this grand city (€25/hour, tel. 1/386-0885, mobile 0630-491-1389, www.culturaltours.mlap.hu, borcczky.elemer@gmail.com).

Péter, Andrea, George, and Elemér have all been indispensable help to me in writing and updating this book.

Walking Tours

Budapest has several backpacker-oriented walking-tour companies. Although most travelers can get by with the self-guided walks and tours in this book—and I highly recommend hiring one of the excellent local guides listed above—these outfits are handy for those who want a live guide without paying for a private tour.

Budapest's best-established outfit is **Absolute Walking Tours,** run by Oregonian Ben Frieday and offering tours that are informal but informative. Travelers with this book get a 500-Ft discount on any tour booked in person; or, if you book online,

BUDAPEST

you get a discount (5-30 percent off the full price, depending on tour; enter coupon code "RICK"). The Absolute Walk gives you a good overview of Budapest (4,500 Ft, daily at 10:00, 3.5 hours). The Hammer & Sickle Tour begins at a mini-museum of communist artifacts, then takes you out into the streets to see sites related to the 1956 Uprising (4,500 Ft, 2-3/week, 3.5 hours). The Hungro Gastro Food and Wine Tasting Tour gives you information on traditional recipes and ingredients, and a chance to taste several specialties at the Great Market Hall and nearby specialty shops (21,000 Ft, 6/week, 3.5 hours, reservations required). In the evening, consider the Night Stroll, which includes a one-hour cruise on the Danube (11,000 Ft, 4/week March-Oct, 2/week Nov-Feb, 3 hours). They also offer nightlife tours, pub crawls, a Christmas Market tour (Dec only), and an "Alternative Budapest" tour that visits artsy, edgy, off-the-beaten path parts of town (for details, see www.absolutetours.com or contact the Discover Budapest office at tel. 1/269-3843, mobile 0620-929-7506). Most tours depart from the Discover Budapest office behind the Opera House (see the "Discover Budapest" listing on page 555); however, the food-and-wine tour meets at the Great Market Hall, and the "Alternative" tour departs from the blocky, green-domed Lutheran church at Deák tér, near the Metró station. Note: These prices are for 2015 and may be slightly higher in 2016.

You'll also see various companies advertising **"free" walking tours.** While there is no set fee to take these tours, guides are paid only if you tip (they're hoping for 2,000 Ft/person). They offer a basic 2.5-hour introduction to the city (departing daily at 10:30, and again at 14:00 or 14:30), as well as itineraries focusing on the communist era and the Jewish Quarter. Because they're working for tips, the generally good-quality, certified guides are highly motivated to impress their customers. But because the "free" tag attracts very large groups, these tours tend to be less intimate than paid tours, and (especially the introductory tours) take a once-over-lightly "infotainment" approach. Still, these tours get rave reviews from travelers and offer an inexpensive introduction to the city. As this scene is continually evolving, look for local fliers to learn about the options and meeting points.

BY BOAT
▲▲Danube Boat Tours

Though touristy, cruising the Danube is a fun and convenient way to get a feel for the city's grand layout. The most established company, **Danube Legenda,** is a class act that runs well-maintained, glassed-in panoramic boats day and night. All cruises include a free drink and romantic headphone commentary. By night, TV monitors show the interiors of the great buildings as you float by.

I've negotiated a special discount with Legenda for my readers (but you must book directly in person and ask for the Rick Steves price). By **day,** the one-hour "Duna Bella" cruise costs 3,120 Ft for Rick Steves readers; if you want, you can hop off at Margaret Island to explore on your own, then return after 1.5 hours on a later cruise (6/day May-Aug, 5/day April and Sept, 4/day March and Oct, 1/day Nov-Feb—but no Margaret Island stop in winter). By **night,** the one-hour "Danube Legend" cruise (with no Margaret Island visit) costs 4,400 Ft for Rick Steves readers (4/day March-Oct, 1/day Nov-Feb). On weekends, it's smart to call ahead and reserve a spot for the evening cruises. Note: These special prices are for 2015 and may be slightly higher in 2016.

The Legenda dock is in front of the Marriott on the Pest embankment (find pedestrian access under tram tracks at downriver end of Vigadó tér, district V, M1: Vörösmarty tér, tel. 1/317-2203, www.legenda.hu). Competing river-cruise companies are nearby, but given the discount, Legenda offers the best value.

ON WHEELS
Bike and Segway Tours

Various companies offer **bike tours** around the city; as the most interesting part of town (Pest) is flat and spread out, this is a good way to see the place. The best-established option is Yellow Zebra, a sister company of Absolute Walking Tours (8,000 Ft, 3.5 hours; April-Oct daily at 11:00; additional shorter tour June-Aug daily at 17:00 for 6,500 Ft; Nov and March only Fri-Sun at 11:00—cancelled in below-freezing temperatures; no tours Dec-Feb).

The same company also offers tours of the city by **Segway** (a stand-up electric scooter). Although expensive, it's a unique way to see Budapest while trying out a Segway. Each tour begins with a 30-minute training; my readers get a 15 percent discount when booking online, or 500 Ft off if booking in person (18,000 Ft/2.5 hours, daily at 9:30 and 15:00, also an evening tour April-Oct daily at 18:00). You can reserve and prepay online (www.yellowzebratours.com, enter coupon code "RICK").

The bike and Segway tours both meet at the Discover Budapest office behind the Opera House (see page 555; tel. 1/269-3843, mobile 0620-929-7506, www.yellowzebratours.com).

Bus Tours

Various companies run hop-on, hop-off bus tours, which make 12 to 16 stops as they cruise around town on a two-hour loop with headphone commentary (generally 5,000/24 hours, 6,000 Ft/48 hours). Most companies also offer a wide variety of other tours, including dinner boat cruises and trips to the Danube Bend. Pick up fliers about all these tours at the TI or in your hotel lobby.

Budapest at a Glance

In Pest

▲▲▲Széchenyi Baths Budapest's steamy soaking scene in City Park—the city's single best attraction. **Hours:** Swimming pool—daily 6:00-22:00, thermal bath—daily 6:00-19:00. See page 610.

▲▲Hungarian Parliament Vast riverside government center with remarkable interior. **Hours:** English tours usually daily at 10:00, 12:00, 13:00, 14:00, and 15:00. See page 576.

▲▲Great Market Hall Colorful Old World mall with produce, eateries, souvenirs, and great people-watching. **Hours:** Mon 6:00-17:00, Tue-Fri 6:00-18:00, Sat 6:00-15:00, closed Sun. See page 592.

▲▲Great Synagogue The world's second-largest, with fancy interior, good museum, and memorial garden. **Hours:** March-Oct Sun-Thu 10:00-18:00, Fri 10:00-16:30—until 15:30 in March; Nov-Feb Sun-Fri 10:00-16:00; always closed Sat and Jewish holidays. See page 595.

▲▲Hungarian State Opera House Neo-Renaissance splendor and affordable opera. **Hours:** Lobby/box office open Mon-Sat from 11:00 until show time—generally 19:00; Sun open 3 hours before performance—generally 16:00-19:00, or 10:00-13:00 if there's a matinee; English tours nearly daily at 15:00 and 16:00, and maybe at 14:00 June-Oct. See page 600.

▲▲House of Terror Harrowing remembrance of Nazis and communist secret police in former headquarters/torture site. **Hours:** Tue-Sun 10:00-18:00, closed Mon. See page 602.

▲▲Heroes' Square Mammoth tribute to Hungary's historic figures, fronted by art museums. **Hours:** Square always open. See page 607.

▲▲City Park Budapest's backyard, with Art Nouveau zoo, Transylvanian Vajdahunyad Castle replica, amusement park, and Széchenyi Baths. **Hours:** Park always open. See page 608.

▲▲Vajdahunyad Castle Epcot-like replica of a Transylvanian castle and other historical buildings. **Hours:** Always viewable. See page 609.

▲▲**Holocaust Memorial Center** Excellent memorial and museum honoring Hungarian victims of the Holocaust. **Hours:** Tue-Sun 10:00-18:00, closed Mon. See page 611.

▲**St. István's Basilica** Budapest's largest church, with a saint's withered fist and great city views. **Hours:** Mon 9:00-16:30, Tue-Fri 9:00-17:00, Sat 9:00-13:00, Sun 13:00-17:00; panorama terrace daily June-Sept 10:00-18:30, March-May and Oct 10:00-17:30, Nov-Feb 10:00-16:30. See page 587.

▲**Hungarian National Museum** Expansive collection of fragments from Hungary's history. **Hours:** Tue-Sun 10:00-18:00, closed Mon. See page 594.

▲**Margaret Island** Budapest's traffic-free urban playground, with spas, ruins, gardens, a game farm, and fountains, set in the middle of the Danube. **Hours:** Park always open. See page 589.

In Buda

▲▲**Matthias Church** Landmark Neo-Gothic church with gilded history-book interior and revered 16th-century statue of Mary and Jesus. **Hours:** Mon-Fri 9:00-17:00—possibly also 19:00-20:00 in summer, Sat 9:00-13:00, Sun 13:00-17:00. See page 619.

▲▲**Gellért Baths** Touristy baths in historic Buda hotel. **Hours:** Daily 6:00-20:00. See page 624.

▲▲**Rudas Baths** Half-millennium-old Turkish dome over a series of hot-water pools. **Hours:** Daily 6:00-20:00. See page 624.

▲▲**Memento Park** Larger-than-life communist statues collected in one park, on the outskirts of town. **Hours:** Daily 10:00-sunset. See page 625.

▲**Hungarian National Gallery** Top works by Hungarian artists, housed in the Royal Palace. **Hours:** Tue-Sun 10:00-18:00, closed Mon. See page 615.

▲**Hospital in the Rock** Fascinating underground network of hospital and bomb-shelter corridors from WWII and the Cold War. **Hours:** Daily 10:00-20:00. See page 622.

RiverRide

This company offers a bus tour with a twist: Its amphibious bus can actually float on the Danube River, effectively making this a combination bus-and-boat tour. The live guide imparts dry English commentary as you roll (and float). While it's a fun gimmick, the entry ramp into the river (facing the north end of Margaret Island) is far from the most scenic stretch, and the river portion is slow-paced—showing you the same Margaret Island scenery twice, plus a circle in front of the Parliament. The Danube Legenda boat tours, described earlier, give you more scenic bang for your buck (7,500 Ft, 2 hours, 4/day April-Oct, 3/day Nov-March, departs from Széchenyi tér near Gresham Palace, tel. 1/332-2555, www.riverride.com).

Sights in Pest

Most of Pest's top sights cluster in four neighborhoods: **Leopold Town** and the **Town Center** (together forming the city's "downtown," along the Danube), along **Andrássy út,** and at **Heroes' Square and City Park.** Several other excellent sights are not contained in these areas: along the **Small Boulevard** (Kiskörút), in the **Jewish Quarter,** along the **Great Boulevard** (Nagykörút), and along the boulevard called **Üllői út.**

Remember, most sights in town offer a discount if you buy a Budapest Card (described on page 554). If you have a Budapest Card, always ask about discounts when you buy your ticket.

LEOPOLD TOWN (LIPÓTVÁROS)

The Parliament building, which dominates Pest's skyline, is the centerpiece of the city's banking and business district. Called Lipótváros ("Leopold Town"), this snazzy "uptown" quarter features some of the best of Budapest's many monuments. Below, I've linked up the top sights in Leopold Town as a self-guided walk, starting at the grandiose Parliament building and ending at the Chain Bridge.

▲▲Hungarian Parliament (Országház)

With an impressive facade and an even more extravagant interior, the oversized Hungarian Parliament dominates the Danube riverbank. A hulking Neo-Gothic base topped by a soaring Neo-Renaissance dome, it's one of the city's top landmarks. Touring the building

offers the chance to stroll through one of Budapest's best interiors. While the guides can be hit-or-miss, the dazzling building speaks for itself.

Cost and Hours: 5,200 Ft, half-price for EU citizens if you show your passport; English tours usually daily at 10:00, 12:00, 13:00, 14:00, and 15:00—but there can be more tours with demand and fewer for no apparent reason, so confirm in advance; on Mon when parliament is in session—generally Sept-May—the only English tour is generally at 10:00 (and likely to sell out).

Getting There: Ride tram #2 to the Országház stop, which is next to the visitors center entrance (Kossuth tér 1, district V, M2: Kossuth tér).

Getting Tickets: Tickets come with an appointed tour time and often sell out. To ensure getting a space, it's worth paying an extra 200 Ft per ticket to **book online** a day or two in advance at www.jegymester.hu. Select "Parliament Visit," then a date and time of an English tour, and be sure to specify "full price" (unless you have an EU passport). You'll have to create an account, but it's no problem to use a US address, telephone number, and credit card. Print out your eticket and show up at the parliament visitors center at the appointed time (if you can't print it, show up early enough to have them print it out for you at the ticket desk—which can have long lines, especially in the morning).

If you didn't prebook a ticket, go to the **visitors center**—a modern, underground space at the northern end of the long parliament building (look for the statue of a lion on a pillar)—and ask what the next available tour time is. The first English tour of the day is almost always sold out with online tickets, but later tours (especially in the afternoon) may have space. The visitors center and ticket desk are open Mon-Fri 8:00-18:00 (or until 16:00 Nov-March), Sat-Sun 8:00-16:00, and only sell tickets for the same day—if booking in advance, you need to use the website.

Information: Tel. 1/441-4904, www.parlament.hu.

Background: The Parliament was built from 1885 to 1902 to celebrate the Hungarian millennium year of 1896 (see sidebar on page 561). Its elegant, frilly spires and riverside location were inspired by its counterpart in London (where the architect studied). When completed, the Parliament was a striking and cutting-edge example of the mix-and-match Historicist style of the day—just as Frank Gehry's undulating buildings are examples of today's bold new aesthetic. Like the Hungarian people, this building is at once grandly ambitious and a somewhat motley hodgepodge of various influences—a Neo-Gothic palace topped with a Neo-Renaissance dome, which once had a huge, red communist star on top of the tallest spire. Fittingly, it's the city's top icon. The best views of the Parliament are from across the Danube—especially in

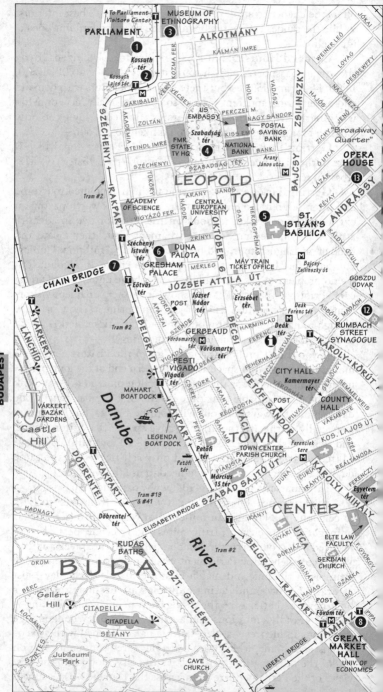

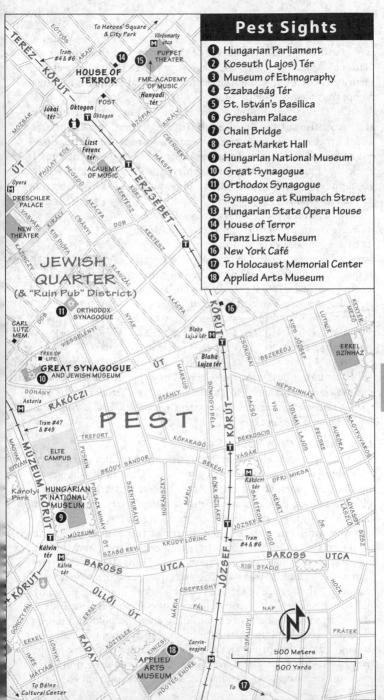

Pest Sights

1. Hungarian Parliament
2. Kossuth (Lajos) Tér
3. Museum of Ethnography
4. Szabadság Tér
5. St. István's Basilica
6. Gresham Palace
7. Chain Bridge
8. Great Market Hall
9. Hungarian National Museum
10. Great Synagogue
11. Orthodox Synagogue
12. Synagogue at Rumbach Street
13. Hungarian State Opera House
14. House of Terror
15. Franz Liszt Museum
16. New York Café
17. To Holocaust Memorial Center
18. Applied Arts Museum

BUDAPEST

the late-afternoon sunlight.

Visiting the Parliament: The visitors center has WCs, a café, a gift shop, and a Museum of the History of the Hungarian National Assembly. Once you have your ticket in hand, be at the security checkpoint inside the visitors center at least five minutes before your tour departure time.

On the 45-minute tour, your guide will explain the history and symbolism of the building's intricate decorations and offer a lesson in the Hungarian parliamentary system. You'll see dozens of bushy-mustachioed statues illustrating the occupations of workaday Hungarians through history, and find out why a really good speech was nicknamed a "Havana" by cigar-aficionado parliamentarians.

To begin the tour, you'll climb a 133-step staircase (with an elevator for those who need it) to see the building's monumental entryway and 96-step grand staircase—slathered in gold foil and frescoes, and bathed in shimmering stained-glass light. Then you'll gape up under the ornate gilded dome for a peek at the heavily guarded Hungarian crown, which is overlooked by statues of 16 great Hungarian monarchs, from St. István to Habsburg Empress Maria Theresa. Finally, you'll walk through a cushy lounge—across one of Europe's largest carpets—to see the legislative chamber.

• *The vast square behind the Parliament is studded with attractions. Stay where you are for a quick...*

▲Kossuth Tér Spin-Tour

This square is sprinkled with interesting monuments and packed with Hungarian history. But it's gone through a lot of changes in the past few years, at the hands of architects and urban planners under the steady guidance of the ruling Fidesz party, led by Viktor Orbán. A highly nationalistic, right-wing party, which swept to power after Hungarians grew weary of the bumblings of the poorly organized, shortsighted left-wing opposition party, Fidesz has exerted its influence over every walk of Hungarian life...beginning with the look of this building and square and the monuments around it. The square itself used to be a more higgledy-piggledy mix of ragged asphalt, parks, monuments, and trees. But Fidesz wanted the mighty Parliament building to stand bold and unobstructed. Several ragtag older monuments (including, ironically, an "eternal" flame honoring victims of the communists) were swept away. Trees were cut down overnight, before would-be protesters could make a peep. And today the square has a scrubbed-clean look that some critics consider almost fascist.

Look to the right end of the Parliament. Poking up is a **pillar** topped by a lion being strangled and bitten by a giant snake (a typically heavy-handed Fidesz monument). This pillar marks the entrance to the Parliament visitors center; if you want to check on availability of tours today, now's a good time (see details earlier).

Looking a bit farther to the right, at the end of the park you'll see another stony tribute, this one to the square's namesake, **Lajos Kossuth,** who led the 1848 Revolution against the Habsburgs. The street that leaves this square behind Kossuth's right shoulder is Falk Miksa utca, Budapest's **"antique row"**—a great place to browse for nostalgic souvenirs.

Panning right from the Kossuth statue, across the tram tracks you'll see the stately home of the **Museum of Ethnography.** While its collection of Hungarian folk artifacts is good (closed Mon), the building is even more notable. The design was the first runner-up for the Parliament building, so it was built here, where it originally housed the Supreme Court.

To the right, the **Ministry of Agriculture** was the second runner-up for the Parliament. Today it features a very low-profile, but poignant, monument to the victims of the 1956 Uprising against Soviet rule (see the "1956" sidebar): At the right end of the protruding arcade, notice that the walls are pockmarked with little metal dollops (you may have to walk closer to see these clearly). Two days into the uprising, on October 25, the ÁVH (communist police) and Soviet troops on the rooftop above opened fire on demonstrators gathered in this square—massacring many and leaving no doubt that Moscow would not tolerate dissent. In the monument, each of the little metal knobs represents a bullet.

Spin farther to the right, where a dramatic equestrian statue of **Ferenc Rákóczi** stands in the park. Rákóczi valiantly—but unsuccessfully—led the Hungarians in their War of Independence (1703-1711) against the Habsburgs. Although they lived more than a century apart, Rákóczi and Kossuth—who now face each other across this square—were aligned in their rebellion against the Habsburgs.

Complete your 360 and face the Parliament again. Every so often, costumed soldiers appear on the front steps for a brief "changing of the guard" ceremony set to recorded music...another very new, very patriotic custom, compliments of Fidesz.

Along the two grassy parks that flank the dome, look for low-profile black walls marked *1956,* which enclose staircases down under the square. These lead to a new museum to the 1956 Uprising (which may be open during your visit).

• *Now let's take a quick...*

1956

The year 1956 is etched into the Hungarian psyche. In that year, the people of Budapest staged the first major uprising against the communist regime. It also marked the first time that the Soviets implicitly acknowledged, in brutally putting down the uprising, that the people of Eastern Europe were not "communist by choice."

The seeds of revolution were sown with the death of a tyrant: Josef Stalin passed away on March 5, 1953. Suddenly the choke-hold that Moscow had held on its satellite states loosened. During this time of "de-Stalinization," Hungarian premier Imre Nagy presided over two years of mild reform, before his political opponents (and Moscow) became nervous and demoted him. (For more on Nagy, see page 585.)

In 1955, Austria declared its neutrality in the Cold War. This thrust Hungary to the front line of the Iron Curtain, and raised the stakes both for Hungarians who wanted freedom and for Soviets who wanted to preserve their buffer zone. When Stalin's successor, Nikita Khrushchev, condemned Stalin's crimes in a "secret speech" to communist leaders in February of 1956, it emboldened the Soviet Bloc's dissidents. A workers' strike in Poznań, Poland, in October inspired Hungarians to follow their example.

On October 23, 1956, the Hungarian uprising began. A student union group gathered in Budapest at 15:00 to articulate a list of 16 demands against the communist regime. Then they marched toward Parliament, their numbers gradually swelling. One protester defiantly cut the Soviet-style insignia out of the center of the Hungarian flag, which would become the uprising's symbol.

By nightfall, some 200,000 protesters filled Kossuth tér behind Parliament, calling for Imre Nagy, the one communist leader they believed could bring change. Nagy finally appeared around 21:00. Ever the pragmatic politician, he implored patience. Following the speech, a large band of protesters took matters into their own hands, marched to City Park, and tore down the hated Stalin statue that stood there (see page 608).

Another group went to the National Radio building to read their demands on the air. The ÁVH (communist police) refused to let them do it, and eventually opened fire on the protesters. The peaceful protests evolved into an armed insurrection, as frightened civilians gathered weapons and supplies.

Overnight, Moscow decided to intervene. Budapesters awoke on October 24 to find Red Army troops occupying their city. That morning, Imre Nagy—who had just been promoted again to prime minister—promised reforms and tried to keep a lid on the simmering discontent.

The next day, October 25, a huge crowd gathered on Kossuth tér behind the Parliament to hear from Nagy. In the hubbub, shots rang out as Hungarian and Soviet soldiers opened fire on the (mostly unarmed) crowd. At least 70 protesters were killed and more than 100 injured.

The Hungarians fought back with an improvised guerilla resistance. They made use of any guns they could get their hands on, as well as Molotov cocktails, to strike against the Soviet occupiers. Many adolescents (the celebrated "Pest Youth") participated. The fighting tore apart the city, and some of the fallen were buried in impromptu graves in city parks.

Political infighting in Moscow paralyzed the Soviet response, and an uneasy ceasefire fell over Budapest. For 10 tense days, it appeared that the Soviets might allow Nagy to push through some reforms. Nagy, a firmly entrenched communist, had always envisioned a less repressive regime...but within limits. While he was at first reluctant to take on the mantle of the uprising's leadership, he gradually began to echo what he was hearing on the streets. He called for free elections, the abolishment of the ÁVH, the withdrawal of Soviet troops, and Hungary's secession from the Warsaw Pact.

But when the uprisers attacked and killed ÁVH officers and communist leaders in Budapest, it bolstered the case of the Moscow hardliners. On November 4, the Red Army launched a brutal counterattack in Budapest that left the rebels reeling. At 5:20 that morning, Imre Nagy's voice came over the radio to beg the world for assistance. Later that morning, he sought asylum at the Yugoslav Embassy across the street from City Park. He was never seen alive in public again.

János Kádár—an ally of Nagy's who was palatable to the uprisers, yet firmly loyal to Moscow—was installed as prime minister. The fighting dragged on for about another week, but the uprising was eventually crushed. By the end, 2,500 Hungarians and more than 700 Soviets were dead, and 20,000 Hungarians were injured. Communist authorities arrested more than 15,000 people, of whom at least 200 were executed (including Imre Nagy). Anyone who had participated in the uprising was blacklisted; fearing this and other forms of retribution, some 200,000 Hungarians fled to the West.

Though the 1956 Uprising met a tragic end, within a few years Kádár did succeed in softening the regime, and the milder, so-called "goulash communism" emerged. And today, even though the communists are long gone, the legacy of 1956 pervades the Hungarian consciousness. Some Budapest buildings are still pockmarked with bullet holes from '56, and many Hungarians who fled the country in that year still have not returned. October 23 remains Hungary's most cherished holiday.

BUDAPEST

Monuments Stroll

Budapest is a city of great monuments, and some of the most vivid are on or near this square.

• *Circle around the left side of the giant Parliament building, passing another statue on a pillar, and walk all the way to the bannister overlooking a spectacular view of Buda. Walk along the banister to the left until you come upon a statue of a young man, lost deep in thought, gazing into the Danube.*

Attila József (1905-1937): This beloved modern poet lived a tumultuous, productive, and short life before he killed himself at age 32 by jumping in front of a train. József's poems of life, love, and death—mostly written in the 1920s and 1930s—are considered the high point of Hungarian literature. His birthday (April 11) is celebrated as National Hungarian Poetry Day. Here József re-enacts a scene from one of his best poems, "At the Danube." It's a hot day—his jacket lies in a heap next to him, his shirtsleeves are rolled up, and he cradles his hat loosely in his left hand. "As I sat on the bank of the Danube, I watched a watermelon float by," he begins. "As if flowing out of my heart, murky, wise, and great was the Danube." In the poem, József uses the Danube as a metaphor for life—for the way it has interconnected cities and also times— as he reflects that his ancestors likely pondered the Danube from this same spot. Looking into his profound eyes, you can sense the depth of an artist's tortured inner life.

• *Walk down the steps next to József and stand at the railing just above the busy road. If you visually trace the Pest riverbank to the left about 100 yards, just before the tree-filled, riverfront park, you can just barely see several low-profile dots lining the embankment. This is a...*

Holocaust Monument: Consisting of 50 pairs of bronze shoes, this monument commemorates the Jews who were killed when the Nazis' puppet government, the Arrow Cross, came to power in Hungary in 1944. While many Jews were sent to concentration camps, the Arrow Cross massacred some of them right here, shooting them and letting their bodies fall into the Danube.

• *If you'd like a closer look at the shoes, use the crosswalk (50 yards to your right) to cross the busy embankment road and follow the waterline. When you're ready to move on, turn your back to the Danube and walk inland, along the ugly building (with an entrance to the Metró), up to the back corner of Kossuth tér. Cross the street in a little park (at Vértanúk tere), where you'll see a monument to...*

Imre Nagy (1896-1958): The Hungarian politician Imre Nagy (EEM-ray nodge), now thought of as an anti-communist hero, was actually a lifelong communist. When the 1956 Uprising broke out on October 23, Imre Nagy was drafted (reluctantly, some say) to become the head of the movement to soften the severity of the communist regime. Because he was an insider, it briefly seemed that Nagy might hold the key to finding a middle path (represented by the bridge he's standing on) between the suffocating totalitarian model of Moscow and the freedom of the West. But the optimism was short-lived. The Soviets violently put down the uprising, arrested

and sham-tried Nagy, executed him, and buried him disgracefully, face-down in an unmarked grave. The regime forced Hungary to forget about Nagy. Later, when communism was in its death throes in 1989, the Hungarian people rediscovered Nagy as a hero. His body was located, exhumed, and given a ceremonial funeral at Heroes' Square. And today, thanks to this monument, Nagy keeps a watchful eye on today's lawmakers in the Parliament across the way.

• *Go up the short, diagonal street behind Nagy, called Vécsey utca. After just one block, you emerge into...*

▲Szabadság Tér ("Liberty Square")

One of Budapest's most genteel squares, this space is marked by a controversial monument to the Soviet soldiers who liberated

Hungary at the end of World War II, and ringed by both fancy old apartment blocks and important buildings (such as the former Hungarian State Television headquarters, the heavily fortified US Embassy, and the National Bank of Hungary). A fine café, fun-filled playgrounds, statues of prominent Americans (Ronald Reagan and Harry Hill Bandholtz), and yet another provocative monument (to the Hungarian victims of the Nazis) round out the square's many attractions. Take a moment to tune in to two of the more recent (and more divisive) monuments on the square.

• *The first person you'll see as you enter the square, striding confidently and charismatically away from the Parliament, is an actor-turned-politician you may recognize...*

Ronald Reagan: When Fidesz took power in 2010, the government quickly began rolling back previous democratic reforms and placing alarming constraints on the media. Many international observers—including the US government—spoke out against what they considered an infringement on freedom of the press. In an effort to appease American concerns, Prime Minister Viktor Orbán erected this statue on one of his capital's main squares—and then, perhaps not quite grasping the subtleties of American political divisions, invited Secretary of State Hillary Clinton to the unveiling. It's fun to watch the steady stream of passersby (both Hungarians and tourists) do a double-take, chuckle, then snap a photo with The Gipper.

• *Now enjoy a slow stroll to the opposite end of the square, where you'll find the...*

Monument to the Hungarian Victims of the Nazis: This recent addition to the square—another heavy-handed Fidesz

production—commemorates the German invasion of Hungary on March 19, 1944. Standing in the middle of a broken colonnade, an immaculate angel holds a sphere with a double cross (part of the crown jewels and a symbol of Hungarian sovereignty). Overhead, a mechanical-looking black eagle (a traditional symbol of Germany) screeches in, its talons poised to strike. Although offensive enough for its lack of artistry, this monument was instantly controversial for the way it whitewashes Hungarian history. Viewing this, you might imagine that Hungary was a peaceful land that was unwittingly caught up in the Nazi war machine. In fact, the Hungarian government was an ally of Nazi Germany for more than three years before this invasion. And there's no question that, after the invasion, many Hungarians enthusiastically collaborated with their new Nazi overlords. Mindful of the old adage about people who forget their own history, locals have created a makeshift memorial to the victims of the World War II-era Hungarians (not just Germans) in front of this official monument.

On a lighter note, the **fountain** that faces the monument is particularly entertaining. Sensors can tell when you're about to walk through the wall of water...and the curtain of water automatically parts long enough for you to pass. Try it.

• *From the monument, continue two blocks straight ahead, up Hercegprímás utca. You'll emerge into a broad plaza in front of...*

▲St. István's Basilica (Szent István Bazilika)

Budapest's biggest church is one of its top landmarks. The grand interior celebrates St. István, Hungary's first Christian king. You

can see his withered, blackened, millennium-old fist in a gilded reliquary in the side chapel. Or you can zip up on an elevator (or climb up stairs partway) to a panorama terrace with views over the rooftops of Pest. The skippable treasury has ecclesiastical items, historical exhibits, and artwork (reached by elevator, to the right as you face the church). The church also hosts regular organ concerts (advertised near the entry).

Cost and Hours: Interior—free but 200-Ft donation strongly suggested, open to tourists Mon 9:00-16:30, Tue-Fri 9:00-17:00, Sat 9:00-13:00, Sun 13:00-17:00, open slightly later for worshippers; panorama terrace—500 Ft, daily June-Sept 10:00-18:30, March-May and Oct 10:00-17:30, Nov-Feb 10:00-16:30; treasury-400 Ft, same hours as terrace; Szent István tér, district V, M1: Bajcsy-Zsilinszky út or M3: Arany János utca.

Visiting the Church: The church is only about 100 years old—like most Budapest landmarks, it was built around the millennial celebrations of 1896. Head up the grand stairs to get oriented. To the right is the ticket desk, the elevator to the **treasury,** and the entrance to the church. To the left is the elevator to the **panoramic tower.**

The church's **interior** is dimly lit but gorgeously restored; all the gilded decorations glitter in the low light. You'll see not Jesus, but St. István (Stephen), Hungary's first Christian king, glowing above the high altar.

The church's main claim to fame is the **"holy right hand" of St. István.** The sacred fist—a somewhat grotesque, 1,000-year-old withered stump—is in a jeweled box in the chapel to the left of the main altar (follow signs for *Szent Jobb Kápolna,* chapel often closed). Pop in a 200-Ft coin for two minutes of light. Posted information describes the hand's unlikely journey to this spot (chapel open April-Sept Mon-Sat 9:00-16:30, Sun 13:00-16:30; Oct-March Mon-Sat 10:00-16:00, Sun 13:00-16:30).

On your way out, in the exit foyer, you'll find a small **exhibit** about the building's history.

• *From here, you're very close to the boulevard called **Andrássy út**, which leads to the Opera House, House of Terror, and City Park (all described starting on page 598). To get there, walk around the right side of the basilica and turn right on busy Bajcsy–Zsilinszky út; Andrássy út begins across the street, on your left.*

*But for now, we'll head to the Danube for a good look at the mighty Chain Bridge. Walk straight ahead from St. István's main staircase down **Zrínyi Utca**. This recently pedestrianized people zone passes (on the right) **Central European University**, a graduate school largely funded by Hungarian-American George Soros, and its good bookshop. Later, after crossing Nádor utca, on the left you'll see **Duna Palota**, a venue and ticket office for Hungária Koncert's popular tourist shows (described on page 648).*

*Zrínyi utca dead-ends at the big traffic circle called **Roosevelt tér**. Turn left and walk a half-block to the entrance (on the left) of the...*

▲Gresham Palace

This was Budapest's first building in the popular Historicist style, and also incorporates elements of Art Nouveau. Budapest boomed in an era when architectural eclecticism—mashing together bits and pieces of different styles—was in vogue. But because much of the city's construction was compressed into a short window of time, even these disparate styles enjoy an unusual harmony. Damaged in World War II, the building was an eyesore for decades. (Reportedly, an aging local actress refused to move out, so developers had to wait for her to, ahem, vacate before they could reclaim the building.) In 1999, the Gresham Palace was meticulously restored to its former glory and converted to a luxury hotel. Even if you can't afford to stay here (see page 665), saunter into the lobby and absorb the gorgeous details (lobby open 24 hours daily, Széchenyi tér 5, district V, M1: Vörösmarty tér or M2: Kossuth tér).

• *Grandly spanning the Danube from this spot is Budapest's best bridge...*

▲Chain Bridge (Széchenyi Lánchíd)

One of the world's great bridges connects Pest's Széchenyi tér and Buda's Clark Ádám tér. This historic, iconic bridge, guarded by lions (symbolizing power), is Budapest's most enjoyable and convenient bridge to cross on foot.

Until the mid-19th century, only pontoon barges spanned

the Danube between Buda and Pest. In the winter, the pontoons had to be pulled in, leaving locals to rely on ferries (in good weather) or a frozen river. People often walked across the frozen Danube, only to get stuck on the other side during a thaw, with nothing to do but wait for another cold snap.

Count István Széchenyi was stranded for a week trying to get to his father's funeral. After missing it, Széchenyi commissioned Budapest's first permanent bridge—which was also a major symbolic step toward another of Széchenyi's pet causes, the unification of Buda and Pest. The Chain Bridge was built by Scotsman Adam Clark between 1842 and 1849, and it immediately became an important symbol of Budapest. Széchenyi—a man of the Enlightenment— charged both commoners and nobles a toll for crossing his bridge, making it an emblem of equality in those tense times. Like all of the city's bridges, the Chain Bridge was destroyed by the Nazis at the end of World War II, but was quickly rebuilt.

• *As you look out to the Danube from here, to the right you can see the tip of...*

▲Margaret Island (Margitsziget)

In the Middle Ages, this island in the Danube (just north of the Parliament) was known as the "Isle of Hares." In the 13th century, a desperate King Béla IV swore that if God were to deliver Hungary from the invading Tatars, he would dedicate his youngest daughter Margaret to the Church. Hungary was spared...and Margaret was shipped to a nunnery here. But, the story goes, Margaret embraced her new life as a castaway nun and later refused her father's efforts to force her into a politically expedient marriage with a Bohemian king. She became St. Margaret of Hungary, and this island was named for her.

Today, Margaret Island remains Budapest's playground. Although the island officially has no permanent residents, urbanites flock to relax in this huge, leafy park...in the midst of the busy city, yet so far away (no cars are allowed on the island—just public buses). The island rivals City Park as the best spot in town for strolling, jogging, biking (you can rent a bike at Bringóhintó, with branches at both ends of the island), and people-watching. Rounding out the island's attractions are an iconic old water tower, the remains of Margaret's convent, a rose garden, a game farm, and a "musical fountain" that performs to the strains of Hungarian folk tunes.

BUDAPEST

Getting There: Bus #26 begins at Nyugati/Western train station, crosses the Margaret Bridge, then drives up through the middle of the island—allowing visitors to easily get from one end to the other (3-6/hour). **Trams** #4 and #6, which circulate around the Great Boulevard, cross the Margaret Bridge and stop at the southern tip of the island, a short walk from some of the attractions. You can also reach the island by **boat;** the public riverboats have two stops on the island (see page 569), or you can catch a Mahart shuttle boat from Vigadó tér (see page 1262). It's also a long but scenic **walk** between Margaret Island and other points in the city.

• *If you'd like to head for the heart of Pest, Vörösmarty tér (and the sights listed next), it's just two long blocks away: Turn left out of the Gresham Palace, and walk straight on Dorottya utca.*

PEST TOWN CENTER (BELVÁROS)

Pest's Belváros ("Inner Town") is its gritty urban heart—simultaneously its most beautiful and ugliest district. You'll see fancy facades, some of Pest's best views from the Danube embankment, richly decorated old coffee houses that offer a whiff of the city's Golden Age, and a cavernous, colorful market hall filled with Hungarian goodies. But you'll also experience crowds, grime, and pungent smells like nowhere else in Budapest. Remember: This is a city in transition. Local authorities plan to ban traffic from more and more Town Center streets in the coming years. If construction and torn-up pavement (common around here) impede your progress, be thankful that things will be nicer for your next visit. Within a decade, all of those rough edges will be sanded off...and tourists like you will be nostalgic for the "authentic" old days.

Below, I've linked the main landmarks in the Town Center with a self-guided walk, starting at the square called Vörösmarty tér and ending at the Great Market Hall.

▲Vörösmarty Tér

The central square of the Town Center, dominated by a giant statue of the revered Romantic poet Mihály Vörösmarty and the venerable Gerbeaud coffee shop, is the hub of Pest sightseeing.

At the north end of the square is the landmark **Gerbeaud café** and pastry shop. Between the World Wars, the well-to-do ladies of Budapest would meet here after shopping their way up Váci utca. Today it's still *the* meeting point in Budapest...for tourists, at least. Consider stepping

inside to appreciate the elegant old decor, or for a cup of coffee and a slice of cake (but meals here are overpriced). Better yet, hold off for now—even more appealing cafés are nearby (and listed under "Budapest's Café Culture" on page 681).

The yellow **M1 Metró stop** in front of Gerbeaud is the entrance to the shallow *Földalatti*, or "underground"—the first subway on the Continent (built for the Hungarian millennial celebration in 1896). Today, it still carries passengers to Andrássy út sights, running under that boulevard all the way to City Park.

Walk to the far end of the square, and look up the street that's to your left. This traffic-free street (Deák utca)—also known as **"Fashion Street,"** with top-end shops—is the easiest and most pleasant way to walk to Deák tér and, beyond it, through Erzsébet tér to Andrássy út.

• *Extending straight ahead from Vörösmarty tér is a broad, bustling, pedestrianized shopping street. Look—but do not walk—down...*

Váci Utca

Dating from 1810 to 1850, **Váci utca** (VAHT-see OOT-zah) is one of the oldest streets of Pest. Váci utca means "street to Vác"—a town 25 miles to the north. This has long been the street where the elite of Pest would go shopping, then strut their stuff for their neighbors on an evening promenade. Today, the tourists do the strutting here—and the Hungarians go to American-style shopping malls.

This boulevard—Budapest's tourism artery—was a dreamland for Eastern Bloc residents back in the 1980s. It was here that they fantasized about what it might be like to be free, while drooling over Nikes, Adidas, and Big Macs before any of these "Western evils" were introduced elsewhere in the Warsaw Pact region. In fact, partway down the street (on the right, at Régi Posta utca) is the **first McDonald's behind the Iron Curtain,** where people from all over the Eastern Bloc flocked to dine. Since you had to wait in a long line—stretching around the block—to get a burger, it wasn't "fast food"...but at least it was "West food."

Ironically, this street—once prized by Hungarians and other Eastern Europeans because it felt so Western—is what many Western tourists today mistakenly think is the "real Budapest." Visitors mesmerized by this people-friendly stretch of souvenir stands, tourist-gouging eateries, and upscale boutiques are likely to miss some more interesting and authentic areas just a block or two away. Don't fall for this trap. You could have a fun and fulfilling trip to this city without setting foot on Váci utca.

• *For a more appealing people zone than Váci utca, detour from Vörösmarty tér a block toward the river, to the inviting...*

Danube Promenade (Dunakorzó)

Some of the best views in Budapest are from this walkway facing Castle Hill—especially this stretch, between the white Elisabeth Bridge (left) and the iconic Chain Bridge (right). This is a favorite place to promenade *(korzó)*, strolling aimlessly and greeting friends.

Dominating this part of the promenade is the Neo-Romantic-style **Pesti Vigadó**—built in the 1880s, and recently restored. Charmingly, the word *vigadó*—used to describe a concert hall—literally means "joyous place." In front, the playful statue of **the girl with her dog** captures the fun-loving spirit along this drag. At the gap in the railing, notice the platform to catch **tram #2**, which goes frequently in each direction along the promenade—a handy and scenic way to connect riverside sights in Pest. (You can ride it to the right, to the Parliament; or to the left, to the Great Market Hall.)

About 30 more yards toward the Chain Bridge, find the little statue wearing a jester's hat. She's playing on the railing, with the castle behind her. The *Little Princess* is one of Budapest's symbols and a favorite photo-op for tourists. Many of the city's monuments have interesting back-stories, but

more recent statues (like this one) are simply whimsical and fun.

Now walk down the promenade to the left (toward the white bridge). Directly in front of the corner of the Marriott Hotel, watch for the easy-to-miss stairs leading down under the tram tracks, to a crosswalk that leads you safely across the busy road to the riverbank. From the top of these stairs, look along the river.

Lining the **embankment** are several long boats: Some are excursion boats for sightseeing trips up and down the Danube (especially pleasant at night), while others are overpriced (but scenic) restaurants. Kiosks along here dispense info and sell tickets for the various boat companies—look for Danube Legenda (their dock is just downstream from here—go down the stairs, cross the road, then walk 100 yards left; for details, see page 572).

• *From here, both the promenade and Váci utca cut south through the Town Center. At the end of this zone is one of Budapest's top attractions.*

▲▲Great Market Hall (Nagyvásárcsarnok)

"Great" indeed is this gigantic marketplace. The Great Market Hall has somehow succeeded in keeping local shoppers happy, even as it's evolved into one of the city's top tourist attractions.

Goose liver, embroidered tablecloths, golden Tokaji Aszú wine, pickled peppers, communist-kitsch T-shirts, savory *lángos* pastries, patriotic green-white-and-red flags, kid-pleasing local candy bars, and paprika of every degree of spiciness...if it's Hungarian, you'll find it here. Come to shop for souvenirs, to buy a picnic, or just to rattle around inside this vast, picturesque, Industrial Age hall.

Hours and Location: Mon 6:00-17:00, Tue-Fri 6:00-18:00, Sat 6:00-15:00, closed Sun, Fővám körút 1, district IX, M4: Fővám tér or M3: Kálvin tér.

Visiting the Market Hall: Step inside the market and get your bearings: The cavernous interior features three levels. The

ground floor has produce stands, bakeries, butcher stalls, heaps of paprika, goose liver, and salamis. Upstairs are stand-up eateries and souvenirs. And in the basement are a supermarket, a fish market, and piles of pickles.

Stroll along the market's "main drag" (straight ahead from the entry), enjoying the commotion of produce stands and vendors selling authentic Hungarian products. About halfway along, you'll see paprika on both sides. To sample before you buy, turn left before entering this block, go down the street, then turn right at the next corner. The **Csárdi és Csárdi** stall (on the right) lets you sample both types of paprika: sweet (*édes*, used for flavor) and hot (*csípós*, used sparingly to add some kick). Note the difference, choose your favorite, and buy some to take home.

After you've worked your way to the far end of the hall, take the escalator to the upper level. You're immersed in a world of Hungarian **souvenirs** (for tips, see "Shopping in Budapest," page 654). If you're in the mood for some shopping, this is a convenient place to look—with a great selection of souvenirs both traditional (embroidery) and not-so-traditional (commie-kitsch T-shirts). While there are no real bargains here, the prices are a bit better than out along Váci utca. The left wall (as you face the front) is lined with fun, cheap, stand-up, Hungarian-style fast-food joints and six-stool pubs. About two-thirds of the way along the hall (after the second bridge), the **Lángos** stand is the best eatery in the market, serving up the deep-fried snack called *lángos*—similar to elephant ears, but savory rather than sweet. The most typical version is *sajtos tejfölös*—with sour cream and cheese. You also add garlic *(fokhagyma)*. The **Fakanál Étterem** cafeteria above the main entrance is handy but pricey.

For a less glamorous look at the market, head down the

escalators near the front of the market (below the restaurant) to the basement. It's pungent with tanks of still-swimming carp, catfish, and perch, and piles of pickles (along the left side of the supermarket). Stop at one of the pickle stands and take a look. Hungarians pickle just about anything: peppers and cukes, of course, but also cauliflower, cabbage, beets, tomatoes, garlic, and so on.

Nearby: Along the river behind the Great Market Hall is the sleek, glass-roofed **Bálna Cultural Center,** a super-modern cultural complex (with an extension of the Great Market Hall's vendors, an art gallery, and inviting public spaces). Completed in 2013, the complex was created by bridging a pair of circa-1881 brick warehouses with a swooping glass canopy that earns its name, "The Whale" (the meaning of *bálna;* free to enter, Sun-Thu 10:00-20:00, Fri-Sat 10:00-22:00, www.balnabudapest.hu).

ALONG THE SMALL BOULEVARD (KISKÖRÚT)

These two major sights are along the Small Boulevard, between the Liberty Bridge/Great Market Hall and Deák tér. (Note that the Great Market Hall, listed earlier, is also technically along the Small Boulevard.) The former Jewish Quarter, which sprawls behind the Great Synagogue, is also one of Budapest's most happening nightlife zones, with a fun selection of "ruin pubs" (for details, see "Nightlife in Budapest," later).

▲Hungarian National Museum (Magyar Nemzeti Múzeum)

One of Budapest's biggest museums features all manner of Hungarian historic bric-a-brac, from the Paleolithic age to a more recent infestation of dinosaurs (the communists). Artifacts are explained with good, if dry, English descriptions. The museum adds substance to your understanding of Hungary's story—but it helps to have a pretty firm foundation first (read "Hungarian History" on page 523). The most engaging part is Room 20, with an exhibit on the  communist era, featuring both pro- and anti-Party propaganda. The exhibit ends with video footage of the 1989 end of communism—demonstrations, monumental parliament votes, and a final farewell to the last Soviet troops leaving Hungarian soil. Another uprising—the 1848 Revolution against Habsburg rule—was declared from the steps of this impressive Neoclassical building.

Cost and Hours: 1,600 Ft—but can change depending on temporary exhibits, audioguide available, Tue-Sun 10:00-18:00, closed Mon, last entry 30 minutes before closing, near Great Market Hall at Múzeum körút 14, district VIII, M3: Kálvin tér, tel. 1/327-7773, www.hnm.hu.

▲▲Great Synagogue (Nagy Zsinagóga)

Also called the Dohány Street Synagogue, Budapest's gorgeous synagogue is the second biggest in the world (after the Temple Emanu-El of New York). A visit here has three parts: touring its ornately decorated interior; exploring the attached museum, which offers a concise lesson in the Jewish faith; and lingering in the evocative memorial garden, with its weeping-willow *Tree of Life* sculpture and other poignant monuments.

Cost and Hours: 2,500 Ft for Great Synagogue, Hungarian Jewish Museum, and Memorial Garden (or pay 500 Ft for just the garden), 500 Ft extra to take photos; March-Oct Sun-Thu 10:00-18:00, Fri 10.00-16:30—until 15:30 in March; Nov-Feb Sun-Fri 10:00-16:00; always closed Sat and Jewish holidays, last entry 30 minutes before closing; Dohány utca 2, district VII, near M2: Astoria or the Astoria stop on trams #47 and #49, tel. 1/344-5131, www.dohanyutcaizsinagoga.hu.

Tours: Aviv Travel, with a kiosk just outside the Great Synagogue entrance, leads tours of the synagogue, museum, and related sights. You have three options: A quick 45-minute tour combines the Great Synagogue and Memorial Garden (2,850 Ft). A longer 80-minute tour covers the above, plus a guided visit to the Hungarian Jewish Museum (3,200 Ft). The 90-minute version includes the Great Synagogue, Memorial Garden, and the nearby synagogue on Rumbach Street, plus free time in the museum (5,650 Ft). Since these tours include admission, you're paying only a small price for the guiding—making this an affordable way to really understand the place (shorter tours leave every 30 minutes during the Great Synagogue's open hours, other tours depart less frequently, last tour departs one hour before closing).

❸ Self-Guided Tour: While the tours described above are worthwhile, the following commentary covers the basics.

Great Synagogue: Before going inside, check out the synagogue's striking **facade,** which captures the rich history of the building and the people it represents: The synagogue was built in 1859 just outside what was then the city limits. Although

Budapest's Jews held fast to their own faith, they also wished to demonstrate their worth and how well-integrated they were with the greater community.

The two tall towers (which are not typical of traditional synagogues) and the rosette (rose window) helped the synagogue resemble Christian churches of the time. In fact, when it was built, the synagogue was dubbed by one observer as "the most beautiful Catholic synagogue in the world."

Now step inside. Notice that the synagogue interior really feels like a church with the symbols switched—with a basilica

floor plan, three naves, two pulpits, and even a pipe organ. The organ, which Franz Liszt played for the building's inauguration, is a clue that this synagogue belonged to the most progressive of the three branches of Judaism here at the time. (Orthodox Jews would never be able to do the "work" of playing an organ on the Sabbath.) The Moorish-flavored decor—which looks almost Oriental—is a sign of the Historicist style of the time, which borrowed eclectic elements from past styles. Specifically, it evokes the Sephardic Jewish culture that flourished in Iberia; many Hungarian Jews are descended from that group, who fled here after being expelled from Spain in 1492.

In the ark, behind the white curtain, 25 surviving Torah scrolls are kept. Catholic priests hid these scrolls during World War II (burying them temporarily in a cemetery). The two-tiered balconies on the sides of the nave were originally for women, who worshipped separately from the men.

Ponder this building's recent history: Although it survived World War II, the Great Synagogue sat neglected for 40 years. But since the thawing of communism, Hungarian Jews have taken a renewed interest in preserving their heritage. In 1990, the Great Synagogue was painstakingly rebuilt. As you tour the place, think of all the famous and influential people of Hungarian-Jewish descent: Harry Houdini (born Erich Weisz), Elie Wiesel, Joseph Pulitzer, Tony Curtis (and his daughter Jamie Lee), Goldie Hawn, Peter Lorre, and Eva and Zsa Zsa Gabor.

• *When you're finished inside, exit through the main doors, turn right, and go to the opposite end of the front courtyard. Here you'll find the entrance to the...*

Hungarian Jewish Museum (Magyar Zsidó Múzeum): This small but informative museum illuminates the Jewish faith, with artifacts and succinct but engaging English explanations.

Pick up the audioguide as you enter (included with ticket). In the long hall you'll find descriptions of **rituals and holidays,** from Rosh Hashanah and Yom Kippur to Passover and Chanukah. The exhibit also explains the symbolism of **objects** such as prayer shawls, the mezuzah, and so on.

The next room focuses on **family life,** tracing the Jewish lifeline from birth to marriage to death. The final room holds a small, powerful exhibit about the **Holocaust.** Follow the exhibit chronologically as it wraps clockwise around the room. In another is a bar of soap made of human fat—a grotesquely "efficient" use of "resources" from the Nazi concentration-camp system. In the same case is a menorah made by a resourceful inmate out of scraps of bread. In the middle of the room is an exhibit honoring non-Jews who risked everything to rescue Jews during this dark time. Stairs lead down to a small Holocaust memorial. (For more about this tragic chapter of the Hungarian Jewish experience, don't miss the outstanding Holocaust Memorial Center—see page 611.)

• *Exiting back into the front courtyard, go down the passageway between the synagogue and the museum (straight ahead from the security checkpoint, past the gift shop).*

Tree of Life and **Memorial Garden:** As you walk alongside the Great Synagogue, notice the small **park** on your left. During

the Soviet siege that ended the Nazi occupation of Budapest in the winter of 1944-1945, many Jews in the ghetto here died of exposure, starvation, and disease. Soon after the Soviets liberated the city, a mass grave was dug here for an estimated 2,281 Jews. The trees and headstones (donated by survivors) were added later. The pillars you'll pass have historical photos of the synagogue and Jewish Quarter.

In the garden behind the synagogue is the *Tree of Life*, created by renowned artist Imre Varga. This weeping willow, cast in steel, was erected in 1990, soon after the fall of communism made it possible to acknowledge the Holocaust. The willow makes an upside-down menorah, and each of the 4,000 metal leaves is etched with the name of a Holocaust victim. New leaves are added all the time, donated by families of the victims.

In the center of the garden is a symbolic grave of **Raoul Wallenberg** (1912-1947). An improbable hero, this ne'er-do-well Swedish playboy from a prominent family was sent as a diplomat to Hungary because nobody else wanted the post. He was empowered by the Swedish government to do whatever he could—bribe, threaten, lie, or blackmail—to save as many Jews as possible from the Nazis. He surpassed everyone's low expectations by dedicating (and ultimately sacrificing) his life to the cause. By giving Swedish passports to Jews and admitting them to safe houses, he succeeded in rescuing tens of thousands of people from certain death. Shortly after the Soviets arrived, Wallenberg was arrested, accused of being a US spy, sent to a gulag...and never seen alive again. Russian authorities recently acknowledged he was executed, but have not revealed the details.

The grave is also etched with the names of other "righteous Gentiles" who went above and beyond to save Jews. According to the Talmud, "Whoever saves one life, saves the world entire."

Other Jewish Quarter Sights

In the area around the Great Synagogue are several other sights. The building just behind the memorial garden houses the Hungarian Jewish Archives. Its **Family Research Center** has birth, marriage, and death records for Jews from Budapest and much of Hungary. For 1,000 Ft, you're welcome to use their archives (ideally, let them know you're coming in advance—www.milev.hu, family@milev.hu). Upstairs is a small **virtual exhibition** about the Jewish Quarter.

The **Orthodox Synagogue** is located on a nondescript urban street two blocks from the Great Synagogue. Built in the Vienna-inspired Secession style in 1912, damaged and deserted for decades after World War II, and now renovated, today this temple invites visitors to see its colorful, sumptuously decorated interior (completed in 2006).

The **Synagogue at Rumbach Street** has a colorful but faded Moorish-style interior that survives from the Golden Age of Jewish culture in Budapest. The building may be closed during your visit for a much-needed restoration.

ANDRÁSSY ÚT

Connecting downtown Pest to City Park, Andrássy út is Budapest's main boulevard, lined with plane trees, shops, theaters, cafés, and locals living very well. Budapesters like to think of Andrássy út as the Champs-Elysées and Broadway rolled into one. While that's a stretch, it is a good place to stroll, get a feel for today's urban Pest, and visit a few top attractions (most notably the Opera House and the House of Terror) on the way to Heroes' Square and City Park.

I've arranged these sights in the order you'll reach them if you walk up the boulevard from where it begins, near Deák tér. The handy M1/yellow Metró line runs every couple of minutes just under the street, making it easy to skip several blocks ahead, or to backtrack (stops marked by yellow signs).

• *Three blocks up Andrássy út on the left is the...*

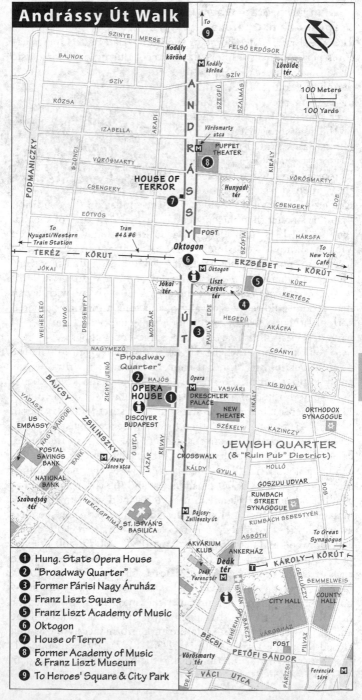

Andrássy Út Walk

BUDAPEST

1. Hung. State Opera House
2. "Broadway Quarter"
3. Former Párisi Nagy Áruház
4. Franz Liszt Square
5. Franz Liszt Academy of Music
6. Oktogon
7. House of Terror
8. Former Academy of Music & Franz Liszt Museum
9. To Heroes' Square & City Park

▲▲Hungarian State Opera House (Magyar Állami Operaház)

The Neo-Renaissance home of the Hungarian State Opera features performances (almost daily except during outdoor music season, late June-early Sept) and delightful tours. The building dates from the 1890s, not long after Budapest became co-capital of the Habsburg Empire. The Hungarians wanted to put their city on the map as a legitimate European capital, and that meant they needed an opera house.

Emperor Franz Josef provided half the funds...on the condition that it be smaller than the opera house in his hometown of Vienna. And so, Miklós Ybl designed a building that would exceed Vienna's famous Staatsoper in opulence, if not in size. (Franz Josef was reportedly displeased.) It was built using almost entirely Hungarian materials. After being damaged in World War II, it was painstakingly restored in the early 1980s. Today, with lavish marble-and-gold-leaf decor, a gorgeous gilded interior slathered with paintings of Greek myths, and high-quality performances at bargain prices, this is one of Europe's finest opera houses.

You can drop in whenever the box office is open to ogle the ostentatious **lobby** (Mon-Sat from 11:00 until showtime—generally 19:00, or until 17:00 if there's no performance; Sun open 3 hours before the performance—generally 16:00-19:00, or 10:00-13:00 if there's a matinee; Andrássy út 22, district VI, M1: Opera).

The 45-minute **tours** of the Opera House are a must for music lovers, and enjoyable for anyone, though the quality of the guides can be erratic: Most spout plenty of fun, if silly, legends, but others can be quite dry. You'll see the main entryway, the snooty lounge area, some of the cozy but plush boxes, and the lavish auditorium. You'll find out why clandestine lovers would meet in the cigar lounge, how the Opera House is designed to keep the big spenders away from the nosebleed-seats rabble, and how to tell the difference between real marble and fake marble (2,900 Ft, 500 Ft extra to take photos, 600 Ft extra for 5-minute mini-concert of two arias after the tour; English tours nearly daily at 15:00 and 16:00, June-Oct maybe also at 14:00; tickets are easy to get—just show up 10 minutes before the tour; buy ticket in opera shop—enter the main lobby and go left, shop open daily 11:00-18:00—or until the end of the second intermission during performances, Oct-March closed for lunch 13:30-14:00; tel. 1/332-8197). The real appeal is the chance to see the interior, so skip the tour if you're going to an opera performance.

To experience the Opera House in action, take in an excellent and affordable **performance** (see "Entertainment in Budapest" on page 647).

• *The Opera House marks the beginning of an emerging dining-and-nightlife neighborhood dubbed the...*

"Broadway Quarter"

The next major cross-street, **Nagymező utca,** features a chic cluster of restaurants, bars, and theaters (especially on the left side of Andrássy). This is an enjoyable place to stroll on a summer evening. Many of my recommended restaurants described under "Eating in Budapest," later, are in this neighborhood.

A half-block down Andrássy út on the right (at #39) is a grand old early 20th-century building marked **Párisi Nagy Áruház** (Paris Department Store), with a recommended café inside. Go in and head up the escalator. One of the city's first department stores, this was a popular shopping stop for years, even through communism. But as was common in Budapest, the store closed down and sat deserted and glum for years until investors came along to rescue it. The new owners, the Alexandra bookstore chain, turned the main area into a great bookshop, created office space above, and—inside, up the escalator at the back—fully restored the sumptuous Lotz Hall to create an excellent café with tinkling-piano ambience and reasonable prices (free entry, daily 10:00-22:00; for more details, see page 683). Upstairs is an art gallery and antiques shop.

• *Just after the end of the block is a popular outdoor-dining area.*

Franz Liszt Square (Liszt Ferenc Tér)

This leafy square is surrounded by hip, expensive cafés and restaurants. (The best is the recommended, kitschy, communist-themed restaurant **Menza.**)

Strangely, neither the statue on this square nor the one facing it, across Andrássy út, is of Franz Liszt. But deeper in the park, you'll find a modern statue of Liszt energetically playing an imaginary piano. And at the far end of the square is the **Franz Liszt Academy of Music,** founded by and named for this half-Hungarian, half-Austrian composer who had a Hungarian name and passport. Liszt loved his family's Magyar heritage (though he didn't speak Hungarian) and spent his final six years in Budapest. His Academy of Music has been stunningly restored inside and out—step into the sumptuous lobby. This space, though smaller, gives the Opera House a run for its money...and speaking of

BUDAPEST

money, the concerts here are much more affordable even than at the already reasonably priced Opera (for details, see page 647).

• *One block up from Franz Liszt Square is the gigantic crossroads known as the...*

Oktogon

This vast intersection with its corners snipped off—where Andrássy út meets the Great Boulevard ring road (Nagykörút)—was called Mussolini tér during World War II, then November 7 tér in honor of the Bolshevik Revolution. Today kids have nicknamed it American tér for the fast-food joints littering the square and streets nearby.

From here, if you have time to delve into workaday Budapest, hop on tram #4 or #6, which trundle in both directions around the ring road. If you've got time for a short detour to the most opulent coffee break of your life, head for the recommended **New York Café** (see page 681): Just hop on a tram to the right (tram #6 toward Móricz Zsigmond körtér or tram #4 toward Fehérvári út), and get off at the Wesselényi utca stop.

• *There's one more major sight between here and Heroes' Square. Walk two more blocks up Andrássy út to reach the...*

▲▲House of Terror (Terror Háza)

The building at Andrássy út 60 was home to the vilest parts of two destructive regimes: first the Arrow Cross (the Gestapo-like

enforcers of Nazi-occupied Hungary), then the ÁVO and ÁVH secret police (the insidious KGB-type wing of the Soviet satellite government). Now re-envisioned as the "House of Terror," this building uses high-tech, highly conceptual, bombastic exhibits to document (if not proselytize about) the ugliest moments in Hungary's difficult 20th century. Enlightening and well-presented, it rivals Memento Park as Budapest's best attraction about the communist age.

Cost and Hours: 2,000 Ft, possibly more for special exhibits, audioguide-1,500 Ft, Tue-Sun 10:00-18:00, closed Mon, last entry 30 minutes before closing, Andrássy út 60, district VI, M1: Vörösmarty utca—*not* the Vörösmarty tér stop, tel. 1/374-2600, www.terrorhaza.hu.

Audioguide and Information: The English audioguide is good but almost too thorough, and can be difficult to hear over the din of Hungarian soundtracks in each room. You can't fast-forward through the dense and sometimes long-winded commentary. As an alternative, my self-guided tour covers the key points. A silver plaque in each room provides the basics (in English), and each room is stocked with free English fliers providing more in-depth information (very similar to what's covered by the audioguide). Tel. 1/374-2600, www.terrorhaza.hu.

Background: In the lead-up to World War II, Hungary initially allied with Hitler—both to retain a degree of self-determination and to try to regain its huge territorial losses after World War I's devastating Treaty of Trianon (see page 528). But in March of 1944, the Nazi-affiliated Arrow Cross Party was forcibly installed as Hungary's new government. The Nazi surrogates deported nearly 440,000 Jewish people to Auschwitz, murdered thousands more on the streets of Budapest, and executed hundreds in the basement of this building. When the communists moved into Hungary after the war, they took over the same building as headquarters for their secret police (the ÁVO, later renamed ÁVH). To keep dissent to a minimum, the secret police terrorized, tried, deported, or executed anyone suspected of being an enemy of the state.

❍ Self-Guided Tour: Buy your ticket (and rent an audioguide, if you wish) and head into the museum.

The **atrium** features a Soviet T-54 tank and a vast wall covered with 3,200 portraits of people who were murdered by the Nazis

or the communists in this very building. The one-way exhibit begins two floors up, then spirals down to the cellar—just follow signs for *Kiállítás/Exhibition*. To begin, you can either take the elevator (to floor 2), or walk up the red stairwell nearby, decorated with old Socialist Realist sculptures from the communist days.

Once upstairs, the first room gives you an overview of the **Double Occupation**. The video by the entrance sets the stage for Hungary's 20th century: its territorial losses after World War I; its alliance with, then invasion by, the Nazis; and its "liberation," then occupation, by the USSR.

After passing through a room displaying uniforms and other gear belonging to Hungarian Nazis, you'll reach the room devoted to the **Gulag.** The word "gulag" refers to a network of secret Soviet prison camps, mostly

in Siberia. These were hard-labor camps where potential and actual dissidents were sent in order to punish them, remove their dangerous influence from society, and make an example of those who would dare to defy the regime. On the carpet, a giant map of the USSR shows the locations of some of these camps, where an estimated 600,000 to 700,000 Hungarian civilians and prisoners of war were sent...about half of whom never returned.

The **Changing Clothes** room—with rotating figures dressed alternately in Arrow Cross and communist uniforms—satirizes the readiness of many Hungarians to align with whoever was in power.

The room on **The Fifties** examines the gradual insinuation of the communist regime into the fabric of Hungary. Their methods ranged from pre-marked ballots to glossy propaganda—such as the paintings celebrating the peasants of the "people's revolution" and romanticized depictions of communist leaders (look for Lenin as the brave sailor). Behind the distorted stage is the dark underbelly of the regime: the constant surveillance that bred paranoia among the people. The **Resistance** room—empty aside from three very different kitchen tables—symbolizes the way that resistance to the regime emerged in every walk of life.

The exhibition continues downstairs, where the **Resettlement and Deportation** section explains the ethnic cleansing—or, in the more pleasant parlance of the time, "mutual population exchange"—that took place throughout Central and Eastern Europe in the years following World War II. In Hungary alone, 230,000 Germans were uprooted and deported. Meanwhile, Hungarians who had become ethnically "stranded" in other nations after the Treaty of Trianon were sent to Hungary (100,000 from Slovakia, 140,000 from Romania, and 70,000 from Yugoslavia). Most have still not returned to their ancestral homes.

In **Surrender of Property and Land,** we learn that under communism, the Hungarian people had to survive on increasingly sparse rations. Enter the labyrinth of pork-fat bricks, which remind old-timers of the harsh conditions of the 1950s (lard on bread for dinner). Look for the ration coupons, which people had to present before being allowed to buy even these measly staples.

The next room examines the ÁVO, the communist secret police who intimidated the common people of Hungary—equivalent to the KGB in the Soviet Union. Before they were finished, the ÁVO imprisoned, abused, or murdered one person from every third Hungarian family. Their power came from enlisting untold numbers of civilians as informants.

After passing through the office of Gábor Péter (the first director of the ÁVO), you'll reach the **"Justice"** exhibit, which explores the concept of "show trials"—high-profile, loudly publicized, and completely choreographed trials of people who had supposedly subverted the regime. The burden of proof was on the accused, not on the accuser, and coerced confessions were fair game. From 1945 until the 1956 Uprising, more than 71,000 Hungarians were accused of political crimes, and 485 were executed.

Next you'll encounter another, more upbeat method for con-

trolling the people: bright, cheery communist **Propaganda.** The poster about the Amerikai Bogár warns of the threat of the "American Beetle" (from Kolorádó), which threatened Hungarian crops. The communists collectivized traditional family farm plots, removing the trees and hedgerows that separated them—thereby removing birds that had kept pest populations in check. When a potato beetle epidemic hit, rather than acknowledging their own fault, the communists blamed an American conspiracy.

Rounding out this floor are sections on **"Hungarian Silver"** (actually aluminum—lampooning the lowbrow aesthetic of that era) and **Religion** (those who were publicly faithful were discriminated against, closely supervised by the secret police, and often arrested). Then you'll board an **elevator** that gradually lowers into the cellar. As it descends, you'll watch a three-minute video of a guard explaining the grotesque execution process. When the door opens, you're in the **Prison Cellar**. Wander through **former cells** used for different purposes. In the large room after the cells, you'll see a stool with a lamp; nearby are the **torture** devices: hot pads and electrical appliances. The bucket and hose were used to revive torture victims who had blacked out. After the torture room, a small room on the right contains a **gallows** that was used for executions (described earlier on your journey, in the elevator video).

The room commemorating the **1956 Uprising** features a symbol of that uprising—a Hungarian flag

BUDAPEST

with a hole cut out of the middle (a hastily removed Soviet emblem) and the slogan *Ruszkik Haza!* ("Russkies go home!"). For more on '56, see page 582.

After a sobering room that displays six symbolic gallows, the **Emigration** room features a wall of postcards. More than 200,000 Hungarians simply fled the country after the uprising. The **Hall of Tears** memorial commemorates all of the victims of the communists from 1945 to 1967 (when the final prisoners were released from this building). The **Room of Farewell** shows several color video clips that provide a (relatively) happy ending: the festive and exhilarating days in 1991 when the Soviets departed, making way for freedom; the reburial of the Hungarian hero, Imre Nagy, at Heroes' Square; and the dedication of this museum.

The chilling finale: walls of photographs of the **Victimizers**— members and supporters of the Arrow Cross and ÁVO, many of whom are still living and who were never brought to justice. The Hungarians have a long way to go to reconcile everything they lived through in the 20th century. For many of them, this museum is an important first step.

• *Across the street and a few steps up Andrássy út is the...*

Franz Liszt Museum

In this surprisingly modest apartment where the composer once resided, you'll find a humble but appealing collection of artifacts. A pilgrimage site for Liszt fans, it's housed in the former Academy of Music, which also hosts Saturday-morning concerts (see page 649).

Cost and Hours: 1,300 Ft; dry English audioguide with a few snippets of music-700 Ft, otherwise scarce English information— borrow the information sheet as you enter; Mon-Fri 10:00-18:00, Sat 9:00-17:00, closed Sun, Vörösmarty utca 35, district VI, M1: Vörösmarty utca—*not* Vörösmarty tér stop, tel. 1/322-9804, www.lisztmuseum.hu.

• *While you can walk from here to Heroes' Square (visible in the distance, about a 15-minute walk), there's less to see along the rest of Andrássy út. If you prefer, hop on the Metró here and ride it three stops to Hősök tere.*

HEROES' SQUARE AND CITY PARK

The grand finale of Andrássy út, at the edge of the city center, is also one of Budapest's most entertaining quarters. Here you'll find the grand Heroes' Square, dripping with history (both monumental and recent); the vast tree-filled expanse of City Park, dressed up with fanciful buildings that include a replica Transylvanian castle and an Art Nouveau zoo; and, tucked in the middle of it all, Budapest's finest thermal spa and single best experience, the Széchenyi Baths. If the sightseeing grind gets you down, take a mini-vacation from your busy vacation and relax the way Budapesters do: Escape to City Park.

▲▲Heroes' Square (Hősök Tere)

Built in 1896 to celebrate the 1,000th anniversary of the Magyars' arrival in Hungary, this vast square culminates at a bold **Millennium Monument.**

Standing stoically in its colonnades are 14 Hungarian leaders who represent the whole span of this nation's colorful and illustrious history. In front, at the base of a high pillar, are the seven original Magyar chieftains, the Hungarian War Memorial, and young Hungarian skateboarders of the 21st century. Look for names you may recognize: István, Béla IV, Mátyás Corvinus. The sculptures on the top corners of the two colonnades represent, from left to right: Work and Welfare, War, Peace, and the Importance of Packing Light. The square is also flanked by a pair of museums.

Museums on Heroes' Square: The **Museum of Fine Arts** (Szépművészeti Múzeum) is Budapest's best chance to appreciate some European masters. It's likely closed for renovation through 2017. If it's open, you'll see mostly Germanic, Dutch, Belgian, and Spanish, rather than Hungarian art, plus lesser works by the likes of Dürer, the Bruegels, Murillo, Velázquez, El Greco, Goya, and more (likely 1,800 Ft, may be more for special exhibits, audioguide-500 Ft, WC and coat check downstairs, Tue-Sun 10:00-17:30, closed Mon, last entry 30 minutes before closing, Dózsa György út 41, tel. 1/469-7100, www.szepmuveszeti.hu). Facing the Museum of Fine Arts from across Heroes' Square, the **Műcsarnok** ("Hall of Art") shows temporary exhibits by contemporary artists—of interest only to art lovers (price varies depending on the exhibits; Tue-Wed and Fri-Sun 10:00-18:00, Thu 12:00-20:00, closed Mon, Dózsa György út 37, tel. 1/460-7000, www.mucsarnok.hu).

• *The area along the busy street beyond the Műcsarnok was once used for communist parades. While the original communist monuments are long gone, a new one has taken their place...*

BUDAPEST

1956 Monument

This monument, which sits just beyond the parking lot behind the Műcsarnok, celebrates the historic uprising against the communists (see page 582). During the

early days of the Soviet regime, this was the site of a giant monument to Josef Stalin that towered 80 feet high (Stalin himself was more than 25 feet tall). While dignitaries stood on a platform at Stalin's feet, military parades would march past. From the inauguration of the monument in 1951, the Hungarians saw it as a hated symbol of an unwanted regime. When the 1956 Uprising broke out, the removal of the monument was high on the protesters' list of 16 demands. On the night the uprising began, October 23, some rebels decided to check this item off early. They came here, cut off Stalin just below the knees, and toppled him from his platform. The current monument was erected in 2006 to commemorate the 50th anniversary of the uprising. Symbolizing the way Hungarians came together to attempt the impossible, it begins with scattered individuals at the back (rusty and humble), gradually coming together and gaining strength and unity near the front—culminating in a silver ship's prow boldly plying the ground.

▲▲City Park (Városliget)

Budapest's not-so-central "Central Park," which sprawls beyond Heroes' Square, was the site of the overblown 1896 Millennial

Exhibition, celebrating Hungary's 1,000th birthday. This particularly enjoyable corner of Budapest is endlessly entertaining. Explore the fantasy castle of Vajdahunyad (described next). Visit the animals and ogle the playful Art Nouveau buildings inside the city's zoo, ride a roller coaster at the amusement park, or enjoy a circus under the big top. Go for a stroll, rent a rowboat, eat some cotton candy, or challenge a local Bobby Fischer to a game of chess. Or, best of all, take a dip in Budapest's ultimate thermal spa, the Széchenyi Baths (described later). This is a great place to just be on vacation.

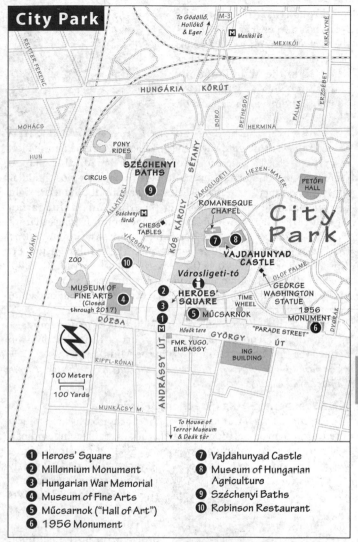

City Park

To Gödöllő, Hollókő & Eger — M-3 — M Mexikói út

MEXIKÓI

REITTER FERENC — KIRÁLYNÉ — ERZSÉBET

HUNGÁRIA KÖRÚT

MOHÁCS

HUN

BORÓ — BETHESDA — HERMINA — PÁLMA

PONY RIDES

SZÉCHENYI BATHS

CIRCUS

⑨

ÁLLATKERTI

Széchenyi fürdő — M

CHESS TABLES

VÁROSLIGETI — SÉTÁNY — LIEZEN-MAYER

PETŐFI HALL

ROMANESQUE CHAPEL

City Park

VÁGÁNY

KÓS KÁROLY

VÁSONY

ZOO

⑩

⑦ ⑧

VAJDAHUNYAD CASTLE

OLOF PÁLME

Városligeti-tó ℹ

MUSEUM OF FINE ARTS (Closed through 2017)

④

② HEROES' SQUARE

③

① M

GEORGE WASHINGTON STATUE

TIME WHEEL

⑤ MŰCSARNOK

1956 MONUMENT ⑥

DÓZSA

Hősök tere

GYÖRGY

"PARADE STREET"

DVORÁK

FMR. YUGO. EMBASSY

ING BUILDING

ÚT

RIPPL-RÓNAI

ANDRÁSSY ÚT

100 Meters
100 Yards

MUNKÁCSY M.

To House of Terror Museum & Deák tér

BUDAPEST

① Heroes' Square
② Millennium Monument
③ Hungarian War Memorial
④ Museum of Fine Arts
⑤ Műcsarnok ("Hall of Art")
⑥ 1956 Monument

⑦ Vajdahunyad Castle
⑧ Museum of Hungarian Agriculture
⑨ Széchenyi Baths
⑩ Robinson Restaurant

▲▲Vajdahunyad Castle (Vajdahunyad Vára)

Many of the buildings for Hungary's Millennial Exhibition were
erected with temporary materials, to be torn down at the end of
the festival—as was the case for most world fairs at the time. But
locals so loved Vajdahunyad Castle that they insisted it stay, so it
was rebuilt in brick and stone. The complex actually has four parts,
each representing a high point in Hungarian architectural style:
Romanesque chapel, Gothic gate, Renaissance castle, and Baroque
palace (free and always open to walk around the grounds).

From this direction, the **Renaissance castle** dominates the view. It's a replica of a famous castle in Transylvania that once belonged to the Hunyadi family (János and Mátyás Corvinus—both of whom we met back on Heroes' Square).

Cross over the bridge and through the **Gothic gateway.** Once inside the complex, on the left is a replica of a 13th-century Romanesque **Benedictine chapel.** Consecrated as an actual church, this is Budapest's most popular spot for weddings on summer weekends. Farther ahead on the right is a big Baroque mansion housing the **Museum of Hungarian Agriculture** (Magyar Mezőgazdasági Múzeum). It brags that it's Europe's biggest agriculture museum, but most visitors will find the lavish interior more interesting than the exhibits (1,100 Ft; April-Oct Tue-Sun 10:00-17:00; Nov-March Tue-Fri 10:00-16:00, Sat-Sun 10:00-17:00; closed Mon year-round, last entry 30 minutes before closing, tel. 1/363-1117, www.mezogazdasagimuzeum. hu).

Facing the museum entry is a monument to **Anonymous**—specifically, the Anonymous from the court of King Béla IV who penned the first Hungarian history in the Middle Ages.

• *The park's highlight is the big yellow building across the street from Vajdahunyad Castle...*

▲▲▲Széchenyi Baths (Széchenyi Fürdő)

My favorite activity in Budapest, the Széchenyi Baths are an ideal way to reward yourself for the hard work of sightseeing and call it a culturally enlightening experience. Soak in hundred-degree

water, surrounded by portly Hungarians squeezed into tiny swimsuits, while jets and cascades pound away your tension. Go for a vigorous swim in the lap pool, giggle and bump your way around the whirlpool, submerge yourself to the nostrils in water green with minerals, feel the bubbles from an underwater jet gradually caress their way up your leg, or challenge the locals to a game of Speedo-clad chess. And it's all surrounded by an opulent yellow palace with shiny copper domes. The bright blue-and-white of the sky, the yellow of the buildings, the pale pink of the skin, the turquoise of the water...Budapest simply doesn't get any better (for all the details, see "Experiences in Budapest," later).

NEAR ÜLLŐI ÚT

This museum is near the city center, on the boulevard called Üllői út. You could stroll there in about 10 minutes from the Small Boulevard ring road (walking the length of the Ráday utca café street gets you very close), or hop on the M3/blue Metró line to Corvin-negyed (just one stop beyond Kálvin tér).

▲▲Holocaust Memorial Center (Holokauszt Emlékközpont)

This sight honors the nearly 600,000 Hungarian victims of the Nazis...one out of every ten Holocaust victims. The impressive modern complex (with a beautifully restored 1920s synagogue as its centerpiece) is a museum of the Hungarian Holocaust, a monument to its victims, a space for temporary exhibits, and a research and documentation center of Nazi atrocities. Interesting to anybody, but essential to those interested in the Holocaust, this is Budapest's—and one of Europe's—best sights about that dark time.

Cost and Hours: 1,400 Ft, Tue-Sun 10:00-18:00, closed Mon, Páva utca 39, district IX, M3: Corvin-negyed, tel. 1/455-3333, www.hdke.hu.

Getting There: From the Corvin-negyed Metró stop, use the exit marked *Holokauszt Emlékközpont* and take the left fork at the exit. Walk straight ahead two long blocks, then turn right down Páva utca.

Visiting the Center: You'll pass through a security checkpoint to reach the courtyard. Once inside, a black marble wall is etched with the names of victims. Head downstairs to buy your ticket. The excellent permanent exhibit, called "From Deprivation of Rights to Genocide," traces in English the gradual process of disenfranchisement, marginalization, exploitation, dehumanization, and eventually extermination that befell Hungary's Jews as World War II wore on. The finale is the interior of the synagogue, now a touching memorial filled with glass seats, each one etched with the image of a Jewish worshipper who once filled it. Up on the mezzanine level you'll find temporary exhibits and an information center that helps teary-eyed descendants of Hungarian Jews track down the fate of their relatives.

Nearby: A few blocks away (at Üllői út 33) is the fanciful, late-19th-century **Applied Arts Museum**—a green-roofed castle that's worth a quick look (from the outside, at least) for architecture fans.

Sights in Buda

Nearly all of Buda's top sights are concentrated on or near its two riverside hills: Castle Hill and Gellért Hill.

CASTLE HILL (VÁRHEGY)

Once the seat of Hungarian royalty, and now the city's highest-profile tourist zone, Castle Hill is a historic spit of land looming above the Buda bank of the Danube. Scenic from afar, but (frankly) a bit soulless from up close, it's best seen quickly. This walk gives you the lay of the land and leads you to the hill's most worthwhile attractions and museums, including Matthias Church, the Fishermen's Bastion, the Hungarian National Gallery, and the WWII-era Hospital in the Rock. You'll also appreciate the bird's-eye views that a visit to Castle Hill offers across the Danube to Pest. I've listed these sights in order from south to north, and linked them together with a self-guided walk.

When to Visit: Castle Hill is packed with tour groups in the morning, but it's much less crowded in the afternoon. Because restaurants up here are touristy and a bad value, Castle Hill is an ideal after-lunch activity.

Getting There: The Metró and trams won't take you to the top of Castle Hill. Instead, you can hike, taxi, catch a bus, or ride the funicular. For most visitors, the easiest bet is to hop on bus **#16,** with handy stops in both Pest (at the Deák tér Metró hub—on Harmincad utca alongside Erzsébet tér, use exit "E" from the station underpass; and at Széchenyi tér at the Pest end of the Chain Bridge) and Buda (at Clark Ádám tér at the Buda end of the Chain Bridge—across the street from the lower funicular station, and much cheaper than the funicular). Or you can go via Széll Kálmán tér (on the M2/red Metró line or by taking tram #4 or #6 around Pest's Great Boulevard); from here, bus **#16,** as well as buses **#16A** and **#116,** head up the hill (at Széll Kálmán tér, catch the bus just uphill from the Metró station—in front of the red-brick, castle-looking building). All buses stop at Dísz tér, at the crest of the hill, about halfway along its length (most people on the bus will be getting off there, too). From Dísz tér, cross the street and walk five minutes along the row of flagpoles toward the green dome, then bear left to find the big Turul bird statue at the start of this walk.

The **funicular** (*sikló,* SHEE-kloh) lifts visitors from the Chain Bridge to the top of Castle Hill (1,200 Ft one-way, 1,800 Ft

round-trip, not covered by transit pass, daily 7:30-22:00, departs every 5-10 minutes, closed for maintenance every other Mon). It leaves you right at the Turul bird statue, where this walk begins.

If you'd like to **hike** up, the most interesting approach is through the castle gardens called Várkert Bazár. From the monumental gateway facing the Danube embankment (just below the Royal Palace, between the Clark Ádám tér and Döbrentei tér stops for trams #19 and #41), head up the stairs into a fine Renaissance garden, then walk (or ride the long escalator) about two-thirds of the way up the hill. From there, a series of two elevators takes you directly up to the palace promenade with minimal climbing—or you can take the scenic route, walking up the delightful switchback ramparts. Either way, you'll wind up at the Royal Palace.

To **leave the hilltop,** most visitors find it easiest just to walk down after their visit (see the end of this tour). But if you'll be taking the bus down, it's smart to buy tickets for the return trip before you ascend Castle Hill—the only place to buy them up top is the post office near Dísz tér (Mon-Fri until 16:00, closed Sat-Sun).

• *Begin the walk at the big statue of the...*

Turul Bird

This mythical bird of Magyar folktales supposedly led the Hungarian migrations from the steppes of Central Asia in the ninth century. He dropped his sword in the Carpathian Basin, indicating that this was to be the permanent home of the Magyar people. While the Hungarians have long since integrated into Europe, the Turul remains a symbol of Magyar pride. During a surge of nationalism in the 1920s, a movement named after this bird helped revive traditional Hungarian culture. And today, the bird is invoked by right-wing nationalist politicians.

• *We'll circle back this way later. But for now, go through the monumental gateway by the Turul and climb down the stairs, then walk along the broad terrace in front of the...*

Royal Palace (Királyi Palota)

The imposing palace on Castle Hill barely hints at the colorful story of this hill since the day that the legendary Turul dropped

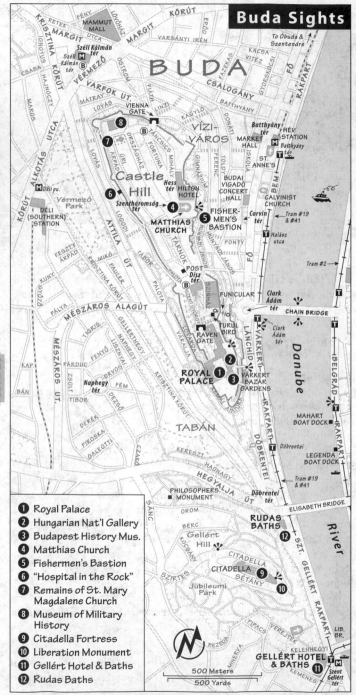

Buda Sights

BUDA

VÍZIVÁROS

Castle Hill

1. Royal Palace
2. Hungarian Nat'l Gallery
3. Budapest History Mus.
4. Matthias Church
5. Fishermen's Bastion
6. "Hospital in the Rock"
7. Remains of St. Mary Magdalene Church
8. Museum of Military History
9. Citadella Fortress
10. Liberation Monument
11. Gellért Hotel & Baths
12. Rudas Baths

500 Meters
500 Yards

his sword. It was once the top Renaissance palace in Europe...but that was several centuries and several versions ago. In the early 15th century, the Renaissance king Mátyás (Matthias) Corvinus—who we'll learn more about soon— converted a humble medieval palace on this site into one of Europe's most extravagant residences, putting Buda and Hungary on the map. Just a few decades later, invading Ottomans occupied Buda and turned the palace into a military garrison. When the Habsburgs laid siege to the hill for 77 days in 1686, gunpowder stored in the cellar exploded, destroying the palace. The Habsburgs took the hill, but Buda was deserted and in ruins. The palace was rebuilt, then damaged again during the 1848 Revolution, then repaired again. As World War II drew to a close, Budapest became the front line between the Nazis and the approaching Soviets. The Red Army laid siege to the hill for 100 days. They eventually succeeded in taking Budapest...but the city—and the hill—were devastated.

The current palace—a historically inaccurate, post-WWII reconstruction—is a loose rebuilding of previous versions. It's big but soulless. The most prominent feature of today's palace—the green dome—didn't even exist in earlier versions. Fortunately, the palace does house some worthwhile museums and boasts the fine terrace you're strolling on, with some of Budapest's best views.

• *Behind the big equestrian statue is the main entrance to the...*

▲Hungarian National Gallery (Magyar Nemzeti Galéria)

The best place in Hungary to appreciate the works of home-grown artists, this art museum offers a peek into the often-morose Hungarian worldview. The collection includes a remarkable group of 15th-century, wood-carved altars from Slovakia (then "Upper Hungary"); piles of gloomy canvases dating from the dark days after the failed 1848 Revolution; several works by two great Hungarian Realist painters, Mihály Munkácsy and László Paál; and paintings by the troubled, enigmatic, and recently in-vogue Post-Impressionist Tivadar Csontváry Kosztka (considered by some to be Hungary's greatest painter). While not quite a must-see, the collection's highlights can be viewed quickly.

Cost and Hours: 1,400 Ft, may cost more for special exhibits, audioguide-800 Ft, 500 Ft extra to take photos, Tue-Sun 10:00-18:00, closed Mon, required bag check for large bags, café, in the Royal Palace—enter from terrace by Eugene of Savoy statue, district I, mobile 0620-439-7325, www.mng.hu.

BUDAPEST

Mátyás (Matthias) Corvinus: The Last Hungarian King

The Árpád dynasty—descendants of the original Magyar tribes—died out in 1301. For more than 600 years, Hungary would be ruled by foreigners...with one exception.

In the mid-15th century, two of Hungary's foreign kings died unexpectedly within seven years. Meanwhile, homegrown military general János Hunyadi was enjoying great success on the battlefield against the Ottomans. When five-year-old László V was elected king, Hunyadi was appointed regent and essentially ruled the country.

Hunyadi defeated the Ottomans in the crucial 1456 Battle of Belgrade, which kept them out of Hungary (at least for another 70 years) and made him an even greater hero to the Hungarian people. But soon afterward, Hunyadi died from the plague. When the young king also died (at age 16), the nobles looked for a new leader. At first they settled on Hunyadi's eldest son, László. But the Habsburgs—who were trying to project their influence from afar—had László killed.

At this dark moment, the Hungarians turned to the younger Hunyadi son, Mátyás (or Matthias in English). At the time, Matthias was at court in Prague (his first wife was a Czech princess). According to legend, Matthias' mother sent for him with a raven with a ring in its beak. The raven supposedly flew nonstop from Transylvania to Prague. The raven-with-ring motif became part of the family crest, as well as the family name: Corvinus (Latin for "raven").

Matthias Corvinus returned to Buda, becoming the first Hungarian-descended king in more than 150 years. Progressive and well-educated in the Humanist tradition, Matthias Corvinus (r. 1458-1490) was the quintessential Renaissance king. A lover of

*• Head back outside and face the palace. Go through the passage to the right of the National Gallery entrance (next to the café). You'll emerge into a courtyard decorated with a gorgeous **fountain** dedicated to King Matthias Corvinus (see sidebar). Go around the right side of the fountain and through the passage, into the palace courtyard. At the far end of this too-big space is the entrance to the...*

Budapest History Museum (Budapesti Történeti Múzeum)

This earnest but dusty collection strains to bring the history of this city to life. If Budapest really intrigues you, this is a fine place to explore its history. Otherwise, skip it. The dimly lit fragments of 14th-century seulptures, depicting early Magyars, allow you to see how Asian those original Hungarians truly looked. The "Budapest: Light and Shadow" exhibit deliberately but effectively traces the union between Buda and Pest. Rounding out the collection are exhibits on prehistoric residents and a sprawling cellar that unveils

the Italian Renaissance, he patronized the arts and built palaces legendary for their beauty. As a benefactor of the poor, he dressed as a commoner and ventured into the streets to see firsthand how the nobles of his realm treated his people.

A strong, savvy leader, Matthias created Central Europe's first standing army—30,000 mercenaries known as the Black Army. No longer reliant on the nobility for military support, Good King Matthias was able to drain power from the nobles and make taxation of his subjects more equitable—earning him the nickname the "people's king."

Matthias was also a shrewd military tactician. Realizing that squabbling with the Ottomans would squander his resources, he made peace with the Ottoman sultan to stabilize Hungary's southern border. Then he swept north, invading Moravia, Bohemia, and even Austria. By 1485, Matthias moved into his new palace in Vienna, and Hungary was enjoying a Golden Age.

Five years later, Matthias died mysteriously at the age of 47, and his empire disintegrated. It is said that when Matthias died, justice died with him. To this day, Hungarians rank him the greatest of all kings, and they sing of his siege of Vienna in their national anthem. They're proud that for a few decades in the middle of half a millennium of foreign oppression, they had a truly Hungarian king—and a great one at that.

fragments from the oh-so-many buildings that have perched on this hill over the centuries.

Cost and Hours: 1,800 Ft, audioguide-1,200 Ft, some good English descriptions posted; March-Oct Tue-Sun 10:00-18:00, Nov-Feb Tue-Sun 10:00-16:00, closed Mon year-round; last entry 30 minutes before closing, district I, tel. 1/487-8800, www.btm.hu.

• *From the palace courtyard, it's time to...*

Walk to Matthias Church

Leaving the palace courtyard, walk straight up the slight incline. In good weather, you might see an opportunity to try your hand at shooting an old-fashioned bow and arrow. Then you'll pass under a gate with a raven holding a ring in its mouth (a symbol of King Matthias).

As you continue along the line of flagpoles, the big white building on your right (near the funicular station) is the **Sándor**

Palace, the Hungarian president's office. This is where you can see the relatively low-key changing of the guard each hour on the hour, with a special show at noon. After Sándor Palace is the yellow former **Court Theater** (Várszínház), which has seen

many great performances over the centuries—including a visit from Beethoven in 1800. Until recently, this housed the National Dance Theater. But current Hungarian Prime Minister Viktor Orbán (not known for humble gestures) grew jealous of the president's swanky digs, kicked out the dancers, and renovated this building as the prime minister's residence. In the field in the middle of this terrace, you'll notice the **ruins** of a medieval monastery and church. Along the left side (past the flagpoles) is the ongoing excavation of the medieval Jewish quarter—more reminders that most of what you see on today's Castle Hill has been destroyed and rebuilt many times over.

At the end of the field, passing the hulking former **Ministry of War** building, you'll reach **Dísz tér** (Parade Square). Here you'll see convenient bus stops for connecting to other parts of Budapest (bus #16, #16A, or #116 to Széll Kálmán tér; or bus #16 to the Pest side of the Chain Bridge).

On the left is a handy post office (bus tickets sold here Mon-Fri before 16:00, closed Sat-Sun). On the right, behind the yellow wall, is a courtyard with an open-air Hungarian **folk-art market.** While it's fun to browse, prices here are high (haggle away). The Great Market Hall has a better selection and generally lower prices (see page 592).

Continue straight uphill on **Tárnok utca** (noticing, on the left, the recommended Vár Bistro—a handy lunch cafeteria). This area often disappoints visitors. After being destroyed by Ottomans, it was rebuilt in sensible Baroque, lacking the romantic time-capsule charm of a medieval old town. But if you poke your head into some courtyards, you'll almost always see some original Gothic arches and other medieval features.

As you continue along, ponder the fact that there are miles of **caves** burrowed under Castle Hill—carved out by water, expanded by the Ottomans, and used by locals during the siege of Buda at the end of World War II. If you'd like to spelunk under Castle Hill and learn about how the caves were used during the 20th century, it's worth going on the lengthy Hospital in the Rock tour (described later). A block to your left is the entrance to the less interesting and skippable Labyrinth of Buda Castle.

Finally, you'll come to a little park. The white, circular

building in the park, marked *TourInform*, is a **TI** that can answer questions and has a handy pictorial map of the castle area (daily 10:00-18:00).

Across the street from the park (on the left), the **CBA grocery store** sells reasonably priced cold drinks, and has a coffee shop upstairs (open daily). A good spot for dessert is just around the corner: **Rétesbár,** selling strudel *(rétes)* with various fillings for 300 Ft each (just down the little lane—Balta köz—next to the grocery store, daily 8:00-19:30).

Just beyond the park, a warty plague column from 1713 marks **Szentháromság tér** (Holy Trinity Square), the main square of old Buda.

• *Dominating the square is...*

▲▲Matthias Church (Mátyás-Templom)

Arguably Budapest's finest church inside and out, this historic house of worship—with a frilly Neo-Gothic spire and gilded Hungarian historical motifs slathered on every interior wall—is Castle Hill's best sight. From the humble Loreto Chapel (with a tranquil statue of the Virgin that helped defeat the Ottomans), to altars devoted to top Hungarian kings, to a replica of the crown of Hungary, every inch of the church oozes history.

Cost and Hours: 1,200 Ft, includes Museum of Ecclesiastical Art (unless closed for renovation), audioguide may be available, Mon-Fri 9:00-17:00—possibly also open 19:00-20:00 in summer, Sat 9:00-13:00, Sun 13:00-17:00, Szentháromság tér 2, district I, tel. 1/488-7716, www.matyas templom.hu.

Background: Budapest's best church has been destroyed and rebuilt several times in the 800 years since it was founded by King Béla IV. Today's version—renovated at great expense in the late 19th century and restored after World War II—is an ornately decorated lesson in Hungarian history. The church's actual name is the Church of Our Lady or the Coronation Church (because its unofficial namesake, Matthias Corvinus, isn't a saint, it can't be formally named for him). But everyone calls it Matthias Church, for the popular Renaissance king who got married here—twice.

➋ Self-Guided Tour: Examine the **exterior**. While the nucleus of the church is Gothic, most of what you see outside—including the frilly, flamboyant steeple—was added for the 1896 celebrations. At the top of the stone corner tower facing the river, notice the raven—the ever-present symbol of King Matthias Corvinus.

Buy your ticket across the square from the church's side door, at the ticket windows embedded in the wall. Then enter the church. The good English descriptions posted throughout will amplify this tour.

The sumptuous **interior** is wallpapered with gilded pages from a Hungarian history textbook. Different eras are represented by symbolic motifs. Entering the side door, turn left and go to the back end of the church. The wall straight ahead represents the Renaissance, with a giant coat of arms of beloved King Matthias Corvinus. (The tough guys in armor on either side are members of his mercenary Black Army, the source of his power.) Notice another raven, with a ring in its beak.

Work your way clockwise around the church. The first chapel (in the back corner, to the left as you face the closed main doors)—

the **Loreto Chapel**—holds the church's prize possession: a 1515 statue of Mary and Jesus. Anticipating Ottoman plundering, locals walled over its niche. The occupying Ottomans used the church as their primary mosque—oblivious to the precious statue hidden behind the plaster. Then, a century and a half later, during the siege of Buda in 1686, gunpowder stored in the castle up the street detonated, and the wall crumbled. Mary's triumphant face showed through, terrifying the Ottomans. Supposedly this was the only part of town taken from the Ottomans without a fight.

Facing the doors, look to the top of the stout pillar on the right to see a **carved capital** showing two men gesturing excitedly at a book. Dating from 1260, these carvings are some of the earliest surviving features in this church, which has changed much over the centuries.

As you look down the **nave,** notice the banners. They've hung here since the Mass that celebrated Habsburg monarch Franz Josef's coronation at this church on June 8, 1867. In a sly political compromise to curry favor in the Hungarian part of his territory, Franz Josef was "emperor" *(Kaiser)* of Austria, but only "king" *(König)* of Hungary. (If you see the old German phrase "K+K"—still used today as a boast of royal quality—it refers to this *"König und Kaiser"* arrangement.) So, after F. J. was crowned emperor in Vienna, he came down the Danube and said to the Hungarians, "King me."

Now stand at the modern altar in the middle of the church, and look down the nave to the **main altar.** Mary floats above it all, and hovering over her is a full-scale replica of the Hungarian crown, which was blessed by St. John Paul II. More than a millennium after István, Mary still officially wears this nation's crown.

Climb the circular stone staircase (in the corner, near the chapel of László) up to the **gallery.** Walk along the royal oratory to a small room that overlooks the altar area. Here, squeezed in the corner between luxurious vestments, is another replica of the Hungarian crown (the original is under the Parliament's dome, and described on page 580). Then you'll huff up another staircase for more views down over the nave, and an exhibit on the church's recent restoration, displaying original statues and architectural features. You'll exit back down into the nave.

• *Back outside, at the end of the square next to Matthias Church, is the...*

Fishermen's Bastion (Halászbástya)

Seven pointy domes and a double-decker rampart run along the cliff in front of Matthias Church. Evoking the original seven Magyar tribes, and built for the millennial celebration of their arrival, the Fishermen's Bastion is one of Budapest's top landmarks. This fanciful structure adorns Castle Hill like a decorative frieze or wedding-cake flowers. While some suckers pay for the views from here, parts of the rampart are free and always open. Or you can enjoy virtually the same view through the windows next to the bastion café for free. Note that the grand staircase leading down from the bastion offers a handy shortcut to the Víziváros neighborhood.

Cost and Hours: 700 Ft, buy ticket at ticket office along the park wall across the square from Matthias Church, daily mid-March–mid-Oct 9:00-19:30; after closing time and off-season, no tickets are sold, but bastion is open and free to enter; Szentháromság tér 5, district I.

• *Between the bastion and the church stands a statue of...*

St. István (c. 967-1038)

Hungary's first Christian king tamed the nomadic, pagan Magyars and established strict laws and the concept of private property. In

the late 900s, King Géza of Hungary lost a major battle against the forces of Christian Europe—and realized that he must raise his son Vajk (c. 967-1038) as a Catholic and convert his people, or they would be forcefully driven out of Europe. Vajk took the Christian name István (EESHT-vahn, "Stephen") and was baptized in the year 1000. The reliefs on this statue show the commissioners of the pope crowning St. István, bringing Hungary into the fold of Christendom. This put Hungary on the map as a fully European kingdom, forging alliances that would endure for centuries. Without this pivotal event, Hungarians believe that the Magyar nation would have been lost.

• *Head down the charming street (named* **Szentháromság utca**) *that leads away from Matthias Church. Halfway down this street on the right, look for the venerable, recommended* **Ruszwurm** *café—the oldest in Budapest. Then continue out to the terrace and appreciate views of the* **Buda Hills**—*the "Beverly Hills" of Budapest, draped with orchards, vineyards, and the homes of the wealthiest Budapesters.*

If you go down the stairs here, then turn right up the street, you'll reach the entrance of the...

BUDAPEST

▲Hospital in the Rock and Nuclear Bunker (Sziklakórház és Atombunker)

Sprawling beneath Castle Hill is a 25,000-square-foot labyrinthine network of hospital and fallout-shelter corridors built during the mid-20th century. After decades in mothballs, the complex opened its doors to tourists a few years ago. Though pricey, this visit is a must for doctors, nurses, and World War II buffs. I enjoy this as a lively interactive experience to balance out an otherwise sedate Castle Hill visit.

Cost and Hours: 3,600 Ft for required one-hour tour, 10 percent discount with Matthias Church ticket, additional discount if you're in the medical profession and can show your ID, daily 10:00-20:00, English tours at the top of each hour, last tour departs at 19:00, gift shop like an army-surplus store, Lovas utca 4C, district I, mobile 0670-701-0101, www.sziklakorhaz.eu/en.

Getting There: To find the hospital, stand with your back to Matthias Church and the Fishermen's Bastion. Walk straight past the plague column and down the little street (Szentháromság utca), then go down the covered steps at the wall. At the bottom of the stairs, turn right on Lovas utca and walk 50 yards to the well-marked bunker entrance.

Visiting the Hospital and Bunker: First you'll watch a 10-minute movie (with English subtitles) about the history of the place. Then, on the tour, your guide leads you through the tunnels to see room after room of perfectly preserved WWII and 1960s-era medical supplies and equipment, most still in working order. More than 200 wax figures engagingly bring the various hospital rooms to life: giant sick ward, operating room, and so on. On your way to the fallout shelter, you'll pass the decontamination showers, and see primitive radiation detectors and communist propaganda directing comrades how to save themselves in case of capitalist bombs or gas attacks. In the bunker, you'll also tour the various mechanical rooms that ventilated and provided water to this sprawling underground city.

• *Our Castle Hill walk is finished. If you're ready to head back down to the river (and the Víziváros neighborhood), you can make a graceful exit down the big staircase below the Fishermen's Bastion.*

*If you'd like to spend more time exploring Castle Hill, poke around the northern part of the hill, where you'll find several interesting sights. Next door to Matthias Church, the modern **Hilton Hotel** is built around the fragments of a 13th-century Dominican church (to see them, go inside, find the lounge, and look out the window toward Pest). A few blocks farther north stand the remains of **St. Mary Magdalene Church**, destroyed during the Ottoman occupation but whose bell tower has been rebuilt. Around the corner is the dusty **Museum of Military History**. And along the tree-shaded terrace at the northern tip of the hilltop, look for the **Turkish grave** of a pasha (Ottoman ruler).*

From the northern end of the hill, you can head out through the Vienna Gate and follow the road downhill to bustling Széll Kálmán tér and its handy Metró stop (M2/red line).

GELLÉRT HILL (GELLÉRTHEGY) AND NEARBY

The hill rising from the Danube just downriver from the castle is Gellért Hill. When King István converted Hungary to Christianity

in the year 1000, he brought in Bishop Gellért, a monk from Venice, to tutor his son. But some rebellious Magyars had other ideas. They put the bishop in a barrel, drove long nails in from the outside, and rolled him down this hill...tenderizing him to death. Gellért became the patron saint of Budapest and gave his name to the hill that killed him. Today the hill is a fine place to commune with nature on a hike or jog, followed by a restorative splash in its namesake baths.

BUDAPEST

Citadella

This strategic, hill-capping fortress was built by the Habsburgs after the 1848 Revolution to keep an eye on their Hungarian subjects. There's not much to do up here (no museum or exhibits), but it's a good destination for an uphill hike, and provides the best panoramic view over all of Budapest.

The hill is crowned by the **Liberation Monument,** featuring a woman holding aloft a palm branch. Locals call it "the lady with the big fish" or "the great bottle opener." A heroic Soviet soldier, who once inspired the workers with a huge red star from the base of the monument, is now in Memento Park.

Getting There: It's a steep hike up from the river to the Citadella. Bus #27 cuts some time off the trip, taking you up to the Búsuló Juhász stop (from which it's still an uphill hike to the fortress). You can catch bus #27 from either side of Gellért Hill. From the southern edge of the hill, catch this bus at the Móricz Zsigmond körtér stop (easy to reach: ride trams #19 or #41 south from anywhere along Buda's Danube embankment, or trams #47 or #49 from Pest's Small Boulevard ring road; you can also catch any of these trams at Gellért tér, in front of the Gellért Hotel).

▲▲Gellért Baths

Located at the famous and once-exclusive Gellért Hotel, right at the Buda end of the Liberty Bridge, this elegant bath complex has long been the city's top choice for a swanky, hedonistic soak. It's also awash in tourists, and the Széchenyi Baths beat it out for pure fun...but the Gellért Baths' mysterious thermal spa rooms, and its giddy outdoor wave pool, make it an enticing thermal bath option. For details, see "Experiences in Budapest," later.

Nearby: Burrowed into the cliff across the street from the Gellért Baths is the unique, tourable Cave Church.

▲▲Rudas Baths

Along the Danube toward Castle Hill from Gellért Baths, Rudas (ROO-dawsh) offers Budapest's most old-fashioned, Turkish-style bathing experience. The historic main pool of the thermal bath section sits under a 500-year-old Ottoman dome. Bathers move from pool to pool to tweak their body temperature. On weekdays, it's a nude, gender-segregated experience, while it becomes more accessible (and mixed) on weekends, when men and women put on swimsuits and mingle beneath that historic dome. For details, see "Experiences in Budapest," later.

Day Trips from Budapest

On a visit of a few days, Budapest will keep even the most avid sightseer busy. And after Budapest, Eger, covered in a chapter of its own, is one of the best Hungarian towns. But for a longer stay, a few outlying sights are worth knowing about. I've listed them here roughly in order of proximity to downtown Budapest.

▲▲Memento Park (a.k.a. Statue Park)

When regimes fall, so do their monuments...literally. Just think of all those statues of Stalin and Lenin that crashed to the ground

in late 1989, when people throughout Eastern Europe couldn't wait to get rid of these reminders of their oppressors. But some clever entrepreneur hoarded Budapest's, collecting them in a park in the countryside just southwest of the city—where tourists flock to get a taste of the communist era. Though it can be time-consuming to visit, this collection is worth ▲▲▲ for those fascinated by Hungary's commie past. You'll see the great figures of the Soviet Bloc, both international (Lenin, Marx, and Engels) and Hungarian (local bigwig Béla Kun) as well as gigantic, stoic figures representing Soviet ideals. This stiff dose of Socialist Realist art is rewarding for those curious for a taste of history that most Hungarians would rather forget.

Cost and Hours: 1,500 Ft, daily 10:00-sunset, tel. 1/424-7500, www.mementopark.hu.

Getting There: It's in the countryside, six miles southwest of city center, at the corner of Balatoni út and Szabadka út, in district XXII. The park runs a handy **direct bus** from Deák tér in downtown Pest to the park (April-Oct daily at 11:00, Nov-March Sat-Mon at 11:00—no bus Tue-Fri, round-trip takes 2.5 hours total, including a 1.5-hour visit to the park, 4,900-Ft round-trip includes park entry, book online for discount: www.mementopark.hu).

The **public transport** option requires a transfer: Ride the Metró's M4/green line to the end of the line at Kelenföld. Head up to street level and catch bus #101, which takes you to Memento Park in about 15 minutes (second stop, runs every 10 minutes—but only on weekdays). On weekends, when bus #101 doesn't run, take bus #150, which takes longer (2/hour, about 25 minutes). On either bus, be sure the driver knows where you want to get off.

Tours and Information: My self-guided tour gives you all the information you need. Alternatively, 50-minute English tours

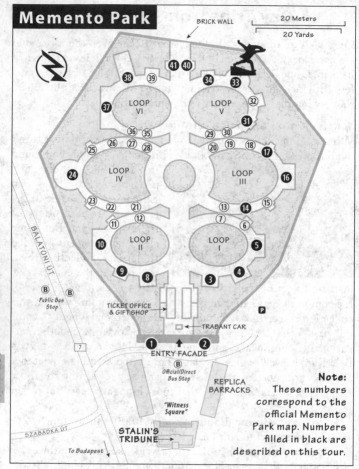

Memento Park

BRICK WALL

20 Meters
20 Yards

LOOP VI

LOOP V

LOOP IV

LOOP III

LOOP II

LOOP I

TICKET OFFICE & GIFT SHOP

TRABANT CAR

Public Bus Stop

P

ENTRY FACADE

Official/Direct Bus Stop

"Witness Square"

REPLICA BARRACKS

STALIN'S TRIBUNE

To Budapest

BALATONI UT

SZABADKA UT

BUDAPEST

Note: These numbers correspond to the official Memento Park map. Numbers filled in black are described on this tour.

depart from the entrance (1,200 Ft, 33 percent discount if you prebook online; April-Oct daily at 11:45, May-Sept also generally daily at 13:00 and 14:00; Nov-March Sat-Mon at 11:45—no tours Tue-Fri off-season). The 1,500-Ft English guidebook, *In the Shadow of Stalin's Boots,* is very informative. Tel. 1/424-7500, www. mementopark.hu.

Background: The communists discouraged creativity. The primary purpose of art was to further the goals of the state, with creative expression only an afterthought. This **Socialist Realist** art served two purposes: It was Realistic, breaking with the "decadent" bourgeois art that came before it (Impressionism, Post-Impressionism, and other modern -isms); and Socialistic, encouraging complicity with the brave new world the communists were forging. From 1949 until 1956, Socialist Realism was legally enforced as the sole artistic style of the Soviet Bloc.

As propaganda was an essential weapon in the Soviet arsenal, the regime made ample use of Socialist Realist art. Aside from a few important figureheads, individuals didn't matter. Everyone was a cog in the machine—strong, stoic, doing their job well and proudly for the good of the people. Individual characteristics and distinguishing features were unimportant; people were represented as automatons serving their nation. Artistic merit was virtually ignored. Most figures are trapped in stiff, unnatural poses that ignore the 3,000 years of artistic evolution since the Egyptians. Sculptures and buildings alike from this era were designed to evoke feelings of power and permanence.

❍ **Self-Guided Tour:** The numbers in the following tour match the statue labels in the park, the official park map, and the map in this chapter.

As you approach the park, you encounter the imposing red-brick Entry Facade featuring three of the Communist All-Stars: ❶ **Vladimir Lenin,** a leader of Russia's Bolshevik Revolution; and ❷ **Karl Marx** and **Friedrich Engels,** the German philosophers whose *Communist Manifesto* first articulated the principles behind communism in 1848. (These three figures weren't offensive enough to be destroyed, but very few statues survive anywhere of the biggest "star" of all, the hated Josef Stalin.) Like the rest of the park, this gate's design is highly conceptual: It looks impressive and monumental...but, like the rotted-out pomp of communism, there's nothing behind it. It's a glossy stage-set with no substance. If you try to go through the main, central part of the gate, you'll run into an always-locked door. Instead, as with the communist system, you have to find another way around (in this case, the side gate to the left).

Inside the gate, buy your ticket and head into the park. Surveying the layout, notice that the main road takes you confidently toward...a dead end (the brick wall). Once again, as with life under the communists, you'll have to deviate from this main axis to actually accomplish anything. Even so, notice that the six walkways branching off the main road all loop you right back to where you started—representing the endless futility of communism.

• *Work your way counterclockwise around the park.*

Liberation Monuments (Loop I): Dominating this loop is a ❸ **giant soldier** holding the Soviet flag. This statue once stood at the base of the Liberation Monument that still overlooks the Danube from Gellért Hill (see page 623). Typical of Socialist Realist art, the soldier has a clenched fist (symbolizing strength) and a face that is inspired by his egalitarian ideology.

To the left of this soldier, see the ❹ **two comrades** stiffly shaking hands: the Hungarian worker thrilled to meet the

BUDAPEST

Soviet soldier—protector of the proletariat.

Beyond them is a ❺ **long wall,** with a triumphant worker breaking through the left end—too busy doing his job to be very excited. Just another brick in the wall.

• *Cross "main street" to a group of statues commemorating the key communist holiday of...*

April 4, 1945 (Loop II): On this date, the Soviets forced the final Nazi soldier out of Hungary. The tall panel nearest the entrance shows a Hungarian woman and a Soviet woman setting free the ❽ **doves of peace.** According to the inscription, "Our freedom and peace is founded upon the enduring Hungarian-Soviet friendship." (With friends like these....)

The ❾ **woman holding the palm leaf** is reminiscent of the Liberation Monument back on the Danube—which, after all, celebrates the same glorious day. Check out the size of that palm leaf: Seems like she's overcompensating...

At the back of the loop, the ❿ **Hungarian worker and Soviet soldier** (who appear to be doing calisthenics) are absurdly rigid even though they're trying to be dynamic. (Even the statues couldn't muster genuine enthusiasm for communist ideals.)

• *Cross over and head up to the next loop to pay homage to...*

Heroes of the Workers' Movement (Loop III): Look for the ⓮ bust of the Bulgarian communist leader **Georgi Dimitrov** (ruled 1946-1949)—one of communist Hungary's many Soviet

Bloc comrades. At the back of this loop are ⓰ three blocky portraits. The middle figure is the granddaddy of Hungarian communism, **Béla Kun.**

To the left is one of the park's best-loved, most-photographed, and most artistic statues: ⓱ **Vladimir Lenin,** in his famous "hailing a cab" pose.

• *Cross over—passing the giant red star made of flowers—to meet...*

More Communist Heroes (Loop IV): This group is dominated by a ㉔ dramatic, unusually emotive sculpture by a genuine artist, **Imre Varga.** Designed to commemorate the 100th anniversary of Béla Kun's birth, this clever statue accomplishes seemingly contradictory feats. On the one hand, it reinforces the communist message: Under the able leadership of Béla Kun (safely overlooking the fray from

above), the crusty, bourgeois old regime of the Habsburg Empire (on the left, with the umbrellas and fancy clothes) was converted into the workers' fighting force of the Red Army (on the right, with the bayonets). And yet, those silvery civilians in back seem more appealing than the lunging soldiers in front. And notice the lamppost next to Kun: In Hungarian literature, a lamppost is a metaphor for the gallows. This reminds viewers that Kun—in spite of his groundbreaking and heroic work for the communist movement in Hungary—was ultimately executed by the communists during Stalin's purges of the late 1930s.

• *Zig and head up again, for a lesson in...*

Communist Concepts (Loop V): Look for a rusty pair of ❸ **workers' hands** holding a sphere (which was once adorned with a red star). This represented the hard-won ideals of communism, carefully protected by the hands—but also held out for others to appreciate. Dominating this group is a ❸ **communist worker** charging into the future, clutching the Soviet flag. Budapesters of the time had a different interpretation: a thermal bath attendant running after a customer who'd forgotten his towel. This is a favorite spot for goofy posed photos. To the

left is a monument to the communist version of the Boy Scouts: the elementary-school-age ❸ **Little Drummers** and the older **Pioneers.** Although these organizations existed before the communists, they were slowly infiltrated and turned into propaganda machines by the regime. These kids—with their jaunty red-and-blue neckerchiefs—were sent to camp to be properly raised as good little communists; today, many of them have forgotten the brainwashing but still have fond memories of the socializing.

• *Now zag once more to learn about...*

More Communist Concepts (Loop VI): The ❸ long, **white wall** at the back of this section tells quite a story (from left to right): The bullet holes lead up to a jumbled, frightful clutter (reminiscent of Pablo Picasso's *Guernica*) representing World War II. Then comes the bright light of the Soviet system, and by the end everyone's properly regimented—striking *Charlie's Angels* poses—and looking boldly to the future (and enjoying a bountiful crop, to boot).

Next is a ❸ **fallen hero** with arm outstretched, about to collapse to the ground—mortally wounded, yet victorious. This monument to "the Martyrs of the Counter-Revolution" also commemorates those who died attempting to put down the 1956 Uprising.

• *Now continue down the main drag to, um, a...*

Dead End: The main path dead-ends at the wall, symbolizing life's frustrations under communism. Here stand statues of two Soviet officers who negotiated with the Nazis to end the WWII siege of Budapest. ❹ **Captain Miklós Steinmetz** (on the right) was killed by a Nazi land mine;

❹ **Ilja Ostapenko** (on the left) was shot under mysterious circumstances as he returned from the successful summit. Both became heroes for the communist cause. Were they killed by wayward Nazi soldiers, as the Soviets explained—or by their own Red Army, to create a pair of convenient martyrs?

Heading back out to the entry gate, peruse the fun parade of communist kitsch at the **gift shop.** The stirring music may just move you to pick up the CD of *Communism's Greatest Hits*, and maybe a model of a Trabant (the classic two-stroke commie-mobile). A real **Trabant** is often parked just inside the gate.

• *Now head out across the parking lot to find...*

Stalin's Tribune: This section of the complex is a re-creation of the giant grandstand that once stood along Parade Street (the boulevard next to City Park; the original site is described on page 608). Hungarian and Soviet leaders stood here, at the feet of a giant Stalin statue, to survey military and civilian processions. But during the 1956 Uprising, protesters cut Stalin off at the knees... leaving only the boots. If you circle around behind the tribune, you'll find stairs up top for a view over the park.

• *Flanking the lot in front of the tribune are replica...*

Barracks: These are reminiscent of the ramshackle barracks where political prisoners lived in communist-era work camps (sometimes called gulags, described on page 603). These hold special exhibits, often including a good explanation of "Stalin's Boots" (with a plaster replica and photos of the original tribune) and the events of 1956. Sit down for the creepy film, *The Life of an Agent*—a loop of four training films (10-15 minutes each) that were actually used to teach novice spies about secret-police methods and policies.

BUDAPEST

• *Our tour is over. Now, inspired by the bold propaganda of your Hungarian comrades, march proudly into the dawn of a new day.*

Óbuda

"Old Buda," just north of Buda, is the oldest part of Budapest, with roots going back to Celtic and Roman times. It has various sights that cluster around the Szentlélek tér stop of the HÉV suburban train line (catch the HÉV from the Batthyány tér Metró stop in Buda). The most interesting museum displays works by Hungarian sculptor **Imre Varga,** who worked from the 1950s through the 1990s and created many popular sculptures in Budapest and throughout Hungary. You'll also find a museum filled with eye-popping, colorful paintings by **Victor Vasarely,** the founder of Op Art. If you ride the HÉV farther north to the Aquincum stop, you'll reach an archaeological museum at the remains of the 2,000-year-old Roman town of **Aquincum** and its amphitheater. All of these sights are closed on Mondays.

Gödöllő Royal Palace

Holding court in an unassuming town on the outskirts of Budapest, this pink Baroque palace was once the residence of Habsburg Emperor Franz Josef and his wife, Empress Elisabeth—better known to her beloved Hungarian subjects as Sisi (see pages 1192 and 1194). While the Habsburg sights in Vienna and near Prague are better, this is the best place in Hungary to learn about its former monarchs.

Cost and Hours: 2,200 Ft; April-Oct daily 10:00-18:00, last entry one hour before closing; Nov-March open only by guided tour at :30 past each hour Mon-Fri 10:30-14:30 (palace closes at 16:00), Sat-Sun 10:00-17:00; tel. 28/410-124, www.kiralyikastely.hu.

Getting There: Take the M2/red Metró line to Örs vezér tere, then catch the HÉV suburban train from to Gödöllő—figure about one hour each way from downtown Budapest.

The Danube Bend

This string of three river towns north of Budapest offers a convenient day-trip getaway for urbanites who want to commune with nature. I find "the Bend" less than thrilling, but it's undeniably convenient to reach from the capital by train or boat. These destinations make for handy stopovers if you're driving between Budapest and Bratislava or Vienna.

Szentendre is a colorful, Balkan-feeling artist colony. With a tidy main square, a few engaging art galleries, and several Orthodox churches built by the Serbs and Greeks who settled the town, it offers a relaxing escape from the city. This is the easiest pleasant small town to reach from Budapest, which means it's also deluged by tourists. To reach Szentendre, hop on the HÉV suburban train at Budapest's Batthyány tér Metró (the same one that goes to Óbuda, described above).

Visegrád offers a small riverside museum at the scant remains of a Renaissance palace built by King Mátyás Corvinus and a dramatic hilltop castle with lovely views over the Bend. While you can get here by boat or by train (to the Nagymaros-Visegrád station, then boat across the river), it's not worth the trip unless you're driving.

Esztergom Basilica is Hungary's biggest and most important church, built on the site where István, Hungary's first Christian king, was crowned in A.D. 1000. Packed with history, it looms grandly above the Danube (free, daily April-Oct 8:00-18:00, Nov-March 8:00-16:00, www.bazilika-esztergom.hu). The easiest way to reach it is by bus from Budapest's Újpest-Városkapu bus station (at the Metró stop of the same name); trains and other buses from Budapest take you to the far end of town, an inconvenient 45-minute walk to the basilica.

Experiences in Budapest

THERMAL BATHS (FÜRDŐ)

Splashing and relaxing in Budapest's thermal baths is the city's top attraction. Though it might sound daunting, bathing with

the Magyars is far more accessible than you'd think. The first two thermal baths I've described (Széchenyi and Gellért) are basically like your hometown swimming pool—except the water is 100 degrees, there are plenty of jets and bubbles to massage away your stress, and you're surrounded by scantily clad Hungarians. If you want a more "authentic" and naked experience, I've also described one of those (Rudas, which also has a more modern "wellness" area).

All this fun goes way back. Hungary's Carpathian Basin is essentially a thin crust covering a vast reservoir of hot water. The Romans named their settlement near present-day Budapest Aquincum—"abundant waters"—and took advantage of those waters by building many baths. Centuries later, the occupying Ottomans revived the custom. And today, thermal baths are as Hungarian as can be.

Locals brag that if you poke a hole in the ground anywhere in Hungary, you'll find a hot-water spring. Judging from Budapest, they could be right: The city has 123 natural springs and some two dozen thermal baths *(fürdő)*. The baths, which are all operated by the same government agency, are actually a part of the health-care system. Doctors regularly prescribe treatments that include massage, soaking in baths of various heat and mineral compositions, and swimming laps. For these patients (who you might see carrying a blue ticket), a visit to the bath is subsidized.

But increasingly, there's a new angle on Hungary's hot water: entertainment. Adventure water parks are springing up all over the country, and even the staid old baths have some enjoyable jets and currents. Overcome your jitters, follow my instructions, and dive in...or miss out on *the* quintessential Budapest experience.

Taking the Waters

American tourists often feel squeamish at the thought of bathing with Speedo-clad, pot-bellied Hungarians. Relax! It's less intimidating than it sounds—and the fun you'll have far outweighs the jitters. I was nervous on my first visit, too. But now I feel like a trip to Hungary just isn't complete without a splish-splash in the bath.

While Budapest has several mostly nude, gender-segregated Turkish baths (such as Rudas), my favorites—Széchenyi and Gellért—are less intimidating: Men and women are usually together, and you can keep your swimsuit on the entire time. (Even at mixed baths, there generally are a few clothing-optional, gender-segregated areas, where locals are likely to be nude—or wearing a *kötény*, a loose-fitting loincloth.)

Bring along these items, if you have them: swimsuit, towel, flip-flops, bottle of water, soap and shampoo for a shower afterward, comb or brush, swim or shower cap (required—see below), plastic shopping bag or sealable baggie (for your wet swimsuit), and maybe sunscreen and leisure reading. Hotels typically frown on guests taking their room towels to the baths. Try asking nicely if they have some loaner towels just for this purpose (they'll probably tell you to rent one there...but what they don't know won't hurt them). At Budapest's baths, you can usually rent a towel or swimsuit (for men, Speedos are always available, trunks sometimes)— bring enough cash for the deposit, which will be refunded when you leave. A swim cap is required in lap pools at each bath. You can rent or buy a flimsy one there, but if you know you'll be swimming laps, see if you can grab a shower cap from your hotel—it will work fine.

Each bath complex has multiple pools, used for different purposes. Big pools with cooler water are for serious swimming, while the smaller, hotter thermal baths *(gyógyfürdő*, or simply *gőz)* are for relaxing, enjoying the jets and current pools, and playing chess. The water bubbles up from hot springs at 77° Celsius (170°

BUDAPEST

Fahrenheit), then is mixed with cooler water to achieve the desired temperatures. Most pools are marked with the water temperature in Celsius (cooler pools are about 30°C/86°F; warmer pools are closer to 36°C/97°F or 38°C/100°F, about like the hot tub back home; and the hottest are 42°C/108°F...yowtch!). Locals hit the cooler pools first, then work their way up to the top temps.

While the lap pools are chlorinated, most of the thermal baths are only lightly chlorinated, or not at all. Unlike swimming pools in the US—where the water is recycled back into the pool—water here is slowly drained out and replaced with fresh water from the hot springs. Locals figure this continuous natural flushing makes chemicals unnecessary. Still, total germophobes may not be entirely comfortable at the baths; either convince yourself to go with the flow, or skip the trip.

You'll also usually find a dry sauna, a wet steam room, a cold plunge pool (for a pleasurable jolt when you're feeling overheated), and sunbathing areas (which may be segregated and clothing-optional). Some baths have fun flourishes: bubbles, whirlpools, massage jets, wave pools, and so on.

The most challenging part of visiting a Hungarian bath is the complicated entrance procedure. Things have gotten much easier in recent years, but you'll still be confronted with a complex payment scheme, lengthy menus of massages and other treatments, and occasionally monolingual staff. It seems confusing at first, but it's more logical than you might think—and, thankfully, English translations of your ticket options and directions to various parts of the complex are posted. Although I've carefully outlined the specifics for each bath, they can change from year to year.

Advance tickets for the baths are sold in hotel lobbies and other sales outlets all over town. But as there's rarely a line to buy a bath ticket, prebooking makes little sense—just buy your tickets when you arrive at the bath.

Budapest's baths recently upgraded to a system that uses a plastic, watch-like wristband as your ticket. When you enter, touch the wristband to the entry turnstile, then again to be assigned a changing cabin or to access a locker, then again each time you want to unlock your cabin or locker. When you're done, drop the wristband into a slot as you exit the turnstile.

You can leave your clothing and other belongings in your locked cabin or locker while enjoying the baths. Although I've found these to be safe, and bath employees assure me that thefts are rare (a cabin is safer than a locker), it's at your own risk. Another option is to leave valuables in a safe (generally costs 600 Ft, ask when you buy ticket). Many locals bring plastic shopping bags to hold their essentials: towels, leisure reading, and sunscreen.

Be aware that the jets, bubbles, waves, waterfalls, and

whirlpools sometimes take turns running. For example, a current pool runs for 10 minutes, then a series of jets starts up and the current pool stops for 10 minutes, then the current pool starts up again, and so on. If a particularly fun feature of the pool doesn't seem to be working, just give it a few minutes.

While many treatments require a doctor's prescription, anyone can enjoy a massage. Typically you'll book this when you buy your ticket, and arrange a time; on busy days (especially Mon, Fri, and Sat), you may have to wait an hour or two—if you don't want to spend all day at the baths, ask when the soonest available time is before you book. On other days, you may be able to get your massage immediately (or whenever you want).

You'll be offered a choice of different kinds of massage. Remember that the spas are medical facilities, so the massage may be more functional and less serene than what you're used to back home. There are three basic kinds: A **"relax massage"** or **"aroma massage"** is a restful rubdown, typically using oil (often scented). This is what's sometimes called a Swedish-style massage. The other option is a **"scrub massage"** or **"skin-firming massage."** Similar to a Turkish-style massage, this is (for some) less restful, as it's intended to exfoliate your skin and involves some very hard scrubbing. Yet another choice is a **Thai massage:** You'll lie on a mat for more of a full-body stretching-and-cracking massage, using feet, knees, and elbows.

Here are some useful phrases:

English	Hungarian	Pronounced
Bath	*Fürdő*	FEWR-dur
Men	*Férfi*	FAYR-fee
Women	*Női*	NUR-ee
Changing Cabin	*Kabin*	KAH-been
Locker	*Szekrény*	SEHK-rayn
Ticket Office	*Pénztár*	PAYNZ-tar
Thermal Bath	*Gyógyfürdő, Gőz*	JODGE-fewr-dur, gorz

Please trust me, and take the plunge. My readers almost unanimously report that the thermal baths were their top Hungarian experience. If you go into it with an easygoing attitude and a sense of humor, I promise you'll have a blast.

The Baths

The three baths listed here are the best-known, most representative, and most convenient for first-timers: The Széchenyi Baths are more casual and popular with locals; the Gellért Baths are touristy, famous, and genteel; and the Rudas Baths are old-school Turkish, with more nudity and less "fun" (unless you find public nudity fun...but that's a whole other book). Rudas also has a modern "wellness" section, offering an interesting contrast under one roof. To me, Széchenyi is second to none, but some travelers prefer the Gellért or Rudas experience. As they're all quite different, doing more than one is an excellent option. For more information on all of Budapest's baths, see www.budapestgyogyfurdoi.hu or www.spasbudapest.com.

▲▲▲Széchenyi Baths (Széchenyi Fürdő)

To soak with the locals, head for this bath complex—the big, yellow, copper-domed building in the middle of City Park. Széchenyi

(SAY-chehn-yee) is the best of Budapest's many bath experiences. Relax and enjoy some Hungarian good living. Magyars of all shapes and sizes stuff themselves into tiny swimsuits and strut their stuff. Housewives float blissfully in the warm water. Intellectuals and roly-poly elder statesmen stand in chest-high water around chessboards and ponder their next moves. This is Budapest at its best.

Cost: 4,500 Ft for locker (in gender-segregated locker room), 500 Ft more for personal changing cabin, 200 Ft more on weekends, cheaper if you arrive after 19:00. The price includes the outdoor swimming pool area and the indoor thermal bath and sauna (but note that the indoor sections close earlier—see below). Couples can share a changing cabin: One person pays the cabin rate, the other pays the locker rate, but both use the same cabin. As the cabins are tight, you may need to take turns...or get very cozy.

Hours: Swimming pool (the best part, outdoors) open daily 6:00-22:00, indoor thermal bath and sauna open daily 6:00-19:00, last entry one hour before closing. On some summer weekends, the baths may be open later (see "Night Bathing," later).

Location and Entrances: In City Park at Állatkerti körút 11, district XIV, M1: Széchenyi fürdő. The huge bath complex has three entrances. The busiest one—technically the **"thermal bath entrance"**—is the grand main entry, facing south (roughly toward

Vajdahunyad Castle). I avoid this entrance—there's often a line during peak times, and it's a bit more confusing to find your way once inside. Instead, I prefer the **"swimming pool entrance,"** facing the zoo on the other side of the

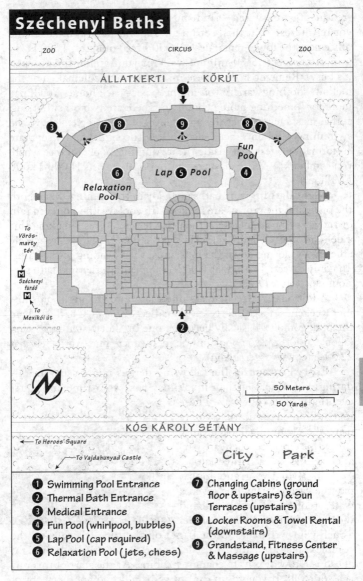

Széchenyi Baths

ZOO   CIRCUS   ZOO

ÁLLATKERTI   KÖRÚT

Fun Pool

Lap Pool

Relaxation Pool

To Vörösmarty tér

Ⓜ Széchenyi fürdő

Ⓜ

To Mexikói út

KÓS KÁROLY SÉTÁNY

← To Heroes' Square

To Vajdahunyad Castle

City Park

50 Meters

50 Yards

① Swimming Pool Entrance
② Thermal Bath Entrance
③ Medical Entrance
④ Fun Pool (whirlpool, bubbles)
⑤ Lap Pool (cap required)
⑥ Relaxation Pool (jets, chess)

⑦ Changing Cabins (ground floor & upstairs) & Sun Terraces (upstairs)
⑧ Locker Rooms & Towel Rental (downstairs)
⑨ Grandstand, Fitness Center & Massage (upstairs)

BUDAPEST

complex—it's more user-friendly, has shorter lines, and is open later. A third, smaller **"medical entrance,"** to the right as you face the zoo entry (near the Metró station), provides access to either the thermal bath changing rooms or the swimming pool changing rooms, but can also have long lines (tel. 1/363-3210, www. szechenyibath.hu).

Massage: A wide array of massages and other special

treatments are offered—find the English menu in the lobby. If you're interested in this, set up an appointment and pay at the office near the towel-rental desk (3,300 Ft/20 minutes, 4,500 Ft/30 minutes, expect 15-30-minute wait for your appointment when it's busy). Remember that these massages are medicinal—not the mellow, soothing variety you might expect back home. You'll pay more for something more hedonistic. There are two other options: a Thai massage parlor at the upper level of the complex (above the swimming pool entrance—just follow the signs) and a separate "information" desk just inside the swimming-pool entrance where you can book a "V.I.P. massage" (either option costs 11,000-14,000 Ft/1 hour).

Night Bathing: The baths are a joy in the evening, when both the price and the crowds are reduced. In cool weather, or even rain or snow, the pools maintain their hot temperatures—making this a delightful after-hours activity. Busy sightseers can be extremely efficient by closing down the museums, then heading to the baths. The only caveat: The indoor (and less appealing) thermal bath sections close after 19:00.

Additionally, Széchenyi is open late into the night on summer weekends, for a "sparty" event called *Szecska* ("Chaff"), where the bath complex basically becomes one big hot-water dance club (about 7,000 Ft if you book online in advance, mid-April-Sept Sat 22:30-late, www.szecska.hu).

Entry Procedure: The following details might seem intimidating, but it's easier than it sounds. Take your time and you'll eventually find your way. These instructions assume that you're using the swimming pool entrance (from this entrance, there are parallel facilities in each direction).

First, in the grand lobby, pay the cashier. You'll be given a waterproof, watch-like wristband with an electronic chip inside. Touch your wristband to the panel on the turnstile to enter the complex. Just after the turnstile, pause to get oriented: Straight ahead is a row of private changing cabins. At the start of this row is a stairwell. If you go **up the stairs,** you'll find another floor of changing cabins (as well as the Thai massage area, gender-segregated "solarium" sun terraces, and a fun grandstand overlooking the main pool—these are ideal vantage points to snap some photos before you change). If you go **down the stairs,** you'll find a long hallway lined with hairdryers and mirrors; the locker rooms are at each end (remember, men are *férfi* and women are *női*). Also downstairs, you'll find the counter where you can rent a towel or swimsuit (do this before you change, as you'll need money: towel-700 Ft plus refundable 1,500-Ft deposit; swimsuit-1,100 Ft plus refundable 4,400-Ft deposit). Renting a small safe for your valuables costs 500 Ft.

Report to the area that you paid for (private cabin or locker room). If you paid for a **cabin,** look for an electronic panel on the wall and hold your wristband against this panel for a few seconds—you'll automatically be assigned a number for a cabin. Go find your cabin. When you touch your wristband to the lock, the light turns blue and the door unlocks. The door should lock automatically when you close it (but test it to be sure). You can reopen your cabin as often as you like. If you forget the number of your cabin, just touch your wristband to the panel in the hall, and it'll remind you.

If you paid for a **locker,** you can head for the locker room and choose any open one. Once you hold your wristband against it to lock it, it can only be unlocked by that same wristband.

If you get confused, the attendants (who usually speak a few words of English) can help you find your way.

Phew. Now that you've changed into your swimsuit and stored your belongings, let's have some fun.

Taking the Waters: The bath complex has two parts, outside and inside.

For most visitors, the best part is the swimming pool area **outside.** Orient yourself to the three pools (facing the main, domed building): The pool to the left is for fun (cooler water—30°C/86°F, warmer in winter, lots of jets and bubbles, lively and often crowded, includes circular current pool); the pool on the right is for relaxation (warmer water—38°C/100°F, mellow atmosphere, a few massage jets, chess); and the main pool in the center is all business (cooler water—28°C/82°F in summer, 26°C/79°F in winter, people doing laps, swim cap required). You get extra credit for joining the gang in a chess match. Stairs to saunas (with cold plunge pools, cold showers, and even an ice maker) are below the doors to the indoor thermal bath complex.

There's a basic **snack bar** right in the middle of the complex, but you're also allowed to bring in your own food if you munch discreetly.

For good **views**—or to use the well-equipped **fitness center**—climb up the stairs near the front of the changing-cabin hallways. There you'll find the grandstand area overlooking the main pool, with the fitness center just above it.

If you're feeling waterlogged and need a break from the baths, it's fun just to explore the sprawling complex. It's a bit of a maze, but don't be afraid to poke around (keep in mind that several areas—such as the solarium sun terraces up top—are clothing-optional; again, men are *férfi* and women are *nõi*). Go for a photo safari, and don't miss the grandstand.

Inside the main building is the thermal bath section, a series of indoor pools; each of these is designed for a specific medical treatment. You'll notice each one is labeled with the temperature (ranging from 28°C/82°F to 36°C/97°F to 38°C/100°F; you'll also find steam rooms with a 18°C/64°F cold plunge pool nearby). The pools also have varying types and amounts of healthy minerals—some of which can make the water quite green and/or stinky. Hungarians who use Széchenyi Baths medicinally have worked out a specific regimen for moving from pool to pool. But if all of this smelly water is lost on you (as it is on many foreigners), it's totally fine to focus on the fun outdoor pools. (I've had many great visits to Széchenyi Baths without ever going inside the thermal bath complex.)

Exit Procedure: When you leave, be sure to leave your locker open. If you rented a towel or swimsuit, return it to the desk where you got it to reclaim your deposit. Then, as you exit the complex, insert your wristband into the little slot at the turnstile to exit. Then continue your sightseeing...soggy, but relaxed.

If you're heading to the **Metró,** the station is very close but easy to miss: It's basically a pair of nondescript stairwells in the middle of the park, roughly toward Heroes' Square from the thermal bath entrance (look for the low-profile, yellow *Földalatti* sign; to head for downtown, take the stairwell marked *a Vörösmarty tér felé*).

▲▲Gellért Baths (Gellért Fürdő)

Using the baths at Gellért (GEH-layrt) Hotel costs a bit more than the Széchenyi Baths, and you won't run into nearly as many locals; this is definitely a more upscale, touristy, spa-like scene. While its thermal areas are smaller, they're arguably even more atmospheric—with exquisite porcelain details and an air of mystery. If you want a soothing, luxurious bath experience in an elegant setting, this is the place. And if it's fun you're looking for, the Gellért Baths have something that Széchenyi doesn't: a huge, deliriously enjoyable wave

pool that'll toss you around like a queasy surfer (summer only).

Cost: 4,900 Ft for a locker, 400 Ft more for a personal changing cabin, cheaper if you arrive after 17:00.

Hours: Daily 6:00-20:00, last entry one hour before closing.

Location: It's on the Buda side of the green Liberty Bridge (M4: Szent Gellért tér; or take trams #47 and #49 from Deák tér in Pest, or trams #19 and #41 along the Buda embankment from Víziváros below the castle, Gellért tér stop). The entrance to the baths is under the stone dome opposite the bridge, around the right side of the hotel (Kelenhegyi út 4, district XI, tel. 1/466 6166, ext. 165, www.gellertbath.com).

Entry Procedure: The grand entry hall is fully open to visitors, so feel free to poke around to get the lay of the land before buying your ticket (good views from the gallery up above). The entrance doors are flanked by ticket windows; just past those, on the right, is an information booth that usually has English-speaking staff.

In the summer, they sell two different tickets based on which changing area you'll use (same price for either ticket, and both options allow you to move freely between the thermal baths and swimming pool areas once you're inside). With a **thermal bath ticket,** you'll change in a large, gender-segregated area with wooden stalls separated by curtains. With a **swimming pool ticket,** you'll go to a mixed area where opposite-sex couples can share a cabin (this area also has gender-segregated locker rooms). I prefer the swimming pool section, which has more secure lockers. Couples who want to share a cabin should ask for "swimming pool ticket, one cabin, one locker." As the cabins can be tight, you may have to take turns changing.

A dizzying array of **massages** and other treatment options are also sold at the ticket windows. Most are available only with a doctor's note, but some massages are for anyone (generally 3,500 Ft/20 minutes, 4,700 Ft/30 minutes, 5,700 Ft/40 minutes; arrange a time when you buy your ticket). You can also book a Thai massage upstairs.

Buy your ticket (and, if you like, pay for a massage), and you'll be issued a plastic wristband that acts as your ticket. Then glide through the swanky lobby. The indoor swimming pool is on your right, about halfway down the main hall; look for Gate II. Looking through the window to the pool, visualize the perfectly symmetrical bath complex: The men's thermal bath, changing cabins, and lockers are on the left, while the identical women's facilities are on the right. The two sections meet at this shared pool in the center.

If you bought a swimming pool ticket, you'll touch your wristband to the turnstile and enter here: Men/*férfi* go down the stairs on the left, and women/*nöi* on the right (either way, you'll head down a long hallway, then up stairs to the changing areas—a mixed-gender area for cabins down below, with a segregated locker area up above). If you have a thermal bath ticket, the entrances are a bit farther away: women to the right, closer to the entrance (Gate I); and men to the left, at the end of the hall (Gate III).

If you want to rent a towel (700 Ft) or swimsuit (1,000 Ft; both with a 4,000-Ft deposit, cash only), look for the desk near the entrance to the changing cabin area.

Once inside the changing area, if you bought a cabin ticket, hold your wristband against the electronic panel to be assigned a changing cabin number. Once you track it down, touch your wristband to the cabin to open it. The door locks automatically behind you (but test it just to be sure). If you bought a locker ticket, you can choose any open locker, then lock it with your wristband. It can only be unlocked using that same wristband.

Taking the Waters: Once you've changed, you can spend your time either indoors or out. From the locker room, look for signs *to the effervescent bath-pool* (for the indoor section) or *to the swimming-pool with artificial waves* (for the outdoor section).

Inside, the central, genteel-feeling hall is home to a cool-water swimming pool (swim cap required—you can buy a cheap one for 700 Ft) and a crowded hot-water pool (36°C/97°F). On sunny days, they crank open the retractable roof; for nice views down onto the pool, find the stairs up near the locker rooms. Back toward the main hall are doors to the thermal baths (easy to miss—

walk to far end of pool and look for signs). The doors may still be marked for men's and women's sections, but both sides are now open to both genders. These grand old halls are probably the most atmospheric part of the bath—slathered with colorful porcelain decorations (especially the men's side). There are big pools at either end: 36°C (97°F) and 38°C (100°F) in the men's section, and slightly cooler in the women's section. Notice that these temperatures perfectly flank the normal temperature of the human body, allowing you to toggle your temp at will. At the far end of the bath are a steam room (45-50°C/113-122°F) and a cold plunge pool (18°C/64°F). Back out near the changing cabins is a dry sauna (a.k.a. "dry sweating rooms," 50-70°C/122-158°F). If you paid for a massage, report to the massage room in this section at your appointed time—or just show up and see if they can take you.

Outside, you'll find several sunbathing areas and a warm thermal pool, along with an atmospheric woody sauna and a big barrel-shaped plunge pool with cold water (all hiding up the stairs on the right). But the main attraction is the big, unheated wave pool in the center (generally closed Oct-April, weather-dependent). Not for the squeamish, this pool thrashes fun-loving swimmers around like driftwood. The swells in the deeper area are fun and easy to float on, but the crashing waves at the shallow end are vigorous, if not dangerous. If there are no waves, just wait around for a while (you'll hear a garbled message on the loudspeaker five minutes before the tide comes in).

Exit Procedure: When you're finished, return your towel and swimsuit to reclaim your deposit, then insert your wristband into the slot at the exit turnstile.

▲▲Rudas Baths (Rudas Fürdő)

To get to the Turkish roots of Budapest's obsession with thermal baths, head for Rudas (ROO-dawsh). It's the most historic, local,

and potentially intimidating of the three baths I list—but it may also be the most rewarding, as it offers the most variety. Rudas has three sections (covered by separate tickets): the Turkish-style thermal bath zone; the swimming pool area; and the wellness section. While the swimming pool is nothing special, the other two are strikingly different—and equally worthwhile. Read these quick descriptions before your visit, to decide which area(s) you want to experience.

Rudas' **thermal section** feels more like the classic Turkish baths of yore: On most days, the main thermal bath section is men-only, and those men wander around nude or in flimsy loincloths under a 500-year-old dome first built by the Ottoman Turks. These baths are not about splashy fun—there are no jets, bubbles, or whirlpools. Instead, Rudas is about history, and about serious temperature modulation—stepping your body temperature up and down between very hot and very cold. Not for the skittish, Rudas offers adventurous travelers and bath connoisseurs another facet of the Budapest baths experience. Be aware that all of Budapest's single-sex, nude baths are (to varying degrees) a popular meeting point for the local gay community—though Rudas is less so than some others (such as Király Baths). Rudas becomes far more widely accessible to all visitors on weekends (Sat-Sun), when men and women mingle together in swimsuits under the fine old dome; then, at nighttime (Fri-Sat only), this old chamber becomes a modern nightclub until the wee hours.

The newly opened **wellness area**—with a handful of relaxing jet pools—is the modern, accessible yin to the thermal baths' antique yang. The main reason to visit this section is the rooftop terrace, where you can sunbathe or soak while looking out over sweeping views of the Budapest skyline. Imagine: You're up to your earlobes in hot water, looking out over commuters slogging across the city's clogged bridges...and feeling pretty happy to be on vacation.

Finally, Rudas' **swimming pool** is similar to, but far less elegant than, Gellért's, and is only worthwhile for those who want to swim laps.

Cost: The various parts are covered by separate tickets. The historic thermal bath alone costs 3,000 Ft, the wellness center alone costs 2,900 Ft, and the swimming pool can be added to either ticket for a few hundred extra forints. But I'd spring for the 4,500-Ft combo-ticket that covers everything—thermal, wellness, and swimming pool—to enjoy the full scope of what Rudas offers. The combo-ticket costs 5,500 Ft on weekends.

Hours: Daily 6:00-20:00, last entry one hour before closing. While the wellness area is mixed-gender every day, the thermal baths are open only to men Mon and Wed-Fri, only to women Tue, and to both men and women Sat-Sun. The night bathing (described later) is also mixed-gender.

Location: It's in a low-profile building at the foot of Gellért Hill, just south of the white Elisabeth Bridge (Döbrentei tér 9, district I, tel. 1/375-8373, www.rudasbaths.com). From the Döbrentei tér stop on trams #19 and #41 (along the Buda riverfront, between the Gellért Baths and Batthyány tér), walk under the off-ramps for the big white bridge, pass the statue of Elisabeth, and go through the tunnel. The baths are straight ahead. Tram #18 from Szent Gellért tér drops you off right in front. From Pest you can ride bus #7 or #107 from Astoria or Ferenciek tere to the Rudas Gyógyfürdő stop; in the other direction, these buses also reach Rudas from Szent Gellért tér.

Night Bathing: The baths are open—to both men and women, in swimsuits—with a dance hall ambience Fri-Sat 22:00-late (4,400 Ft).

Entry Procedure: Buy your ticket (see options above), and if you want, rent a towel (400 Ft for a "bath sheet," plus 1,000-Ft refundable deposit) or a swimsuit (1,200 Ft plus 4,000-Ft deposit), or book a massage—either a relaxing "aroma relax massage," or a rougher, exfoliating "water massage with soap" in a noisy, busy room (either costs 3,100 Ft/20 minutes, 4,100 Ft/30 minutes, 5,000 Ft/40 minutes).

You'll be issued a plastic wristband, which you'll use to go through the turnstile into the changing area (two floors of private cabins—there are no lockers in the thermal bath section). If you paid to rent a towel or swimsuit, give your receipt to the attendant to claim it now. Hold your wristband against the electronic panel on the wall for a few seconds to be assigned a cabin number, then find that cabin and touch your wristband to the lock in order to open it. After you change and are ready to explore the complex, lock the cabin door (unlike the other baths in town, it doesn't lock automatically)...then go have fun.

In the wellness and swimming pool areas, you'll wear your swimsuit everywhere, every day. For the thermal bath area, if you're here on a mixed day (Sat-Sun), the dress code is swimsuits. On other days, bathers can go nude, and many of the men wear a flimsy loincloth called a *kötény* (issued as you enter). If you're a self-conscious, gawky tourist (it happens to the best of us), you can wear your swimsuit...although you might get some funny looks.

Taking the Waters: This historic complex was thoroughly renovated a few years ago, making the outer section feel almost institutional. But the innermost section transports you half a millennium back in time.

Rudas' **thermal bath** area is all about modulating your body temperature—pushing your body to its limit with heat, then dousing off quickly with a bucket of cold water, then heating up again, and so on. The different temperatures are designed to let you do this as gradually or quickly as you like.

The central chamber, under an original 35-foot-high Turkish dome supported by eight pillars, is the historic core of the baths. The main, octagonal pool in the center is surrounded by four smaller pools, each in its own corner. Working clockwise from the right as you enter, the four corner pools get progressively hotter: 28°C (82°F), 30°C (86°F), 33°C (91°F), and 42°C (108°F). And though the hottest pool feels almost scalding at first, you can ease your way into it, the same way you would into cold water. Conveniently, the largest, central pool—at 36°C (97°F)—is not too hot, not too cold...juuuust right.

Along one wall are entrances to the wet sauna (*nedves gőzkamra*, to the left), with 50°C (122°F) scented steam; and the dry sauna (*hőlégkamra*, to the right), with three progressively hotter rooms ranging from 45°C (113° F) to 72°C (161°F). Near the entrance to each one is a shower or—if you don't want to beat around the bush—a bucket of frigid water (pull the rope for immediate relief if you're feeling overheated).

Surrounding this central chamber are hallways with other areas: resting rooms, tanning beds (*szolarium*, costs extra), massage rooms, a cold plunge pool, and a scale to see how much sweat you've lost.

Float on your back for a while in the main octagonal pool, pondering the faintly glittering translucent tiles embedded in the old Turkish dome. You'll notice that the voices echoing around that dome are mostly Hungarians—there are very few tourists here. You might see people stretching, moving from pool to pool very purposefully, or even doing chin-ups from the metal supports; some are athletes, training for their next event.

When you're ready for a change of pace, head back through the lobby to the other half of the building. First you'll walk along the **swimming pool** (for laps), then enter the turnstile for the **wellness area.** The first room, with a huge window looking out over the busy embankment road, has three small pools of different temperatures (32°C/90°F, 36°C/97°F, and a sweltering 42°C/108°F), all with powerful massage jets. In the cold plunge (12-14°C/54-57°F), notice the ice maker that continually drops in a cube or two, every few seconds. Thirsty? Get a drink at the stately ram's-head tiled fountains that line the walls.

But the real highlight of the wellness area is upstairs: At the end of the room, find the staircase and head on up, passing the inviting restaurant (with loaner bathrobes and fine views across the Danube) on your way to the rooftop terrace. While other Budapest baths envelop you in opulent architecture, this is the only one that envelops you in Budapest itself. Whether soaking in rays on the sun deck, or taking a dip in the 36°C/97°F thermal pool, you're surrounded by the bustle of the city. Scanning the horizon, you'll see a workaday burg going about its business...oblivious to the swimsuit-clad barnacle clinging onto the base of Gellért Hill. Your solace is broken only by the periodic rumble of trams trundling past on the road beneath you.

Exit Procedure: After changing, return your rental towel and swimsuit to the attendant and get your receipt; present this at the front desk (along with your original towel receipt) to get your deposit back. Then drop your wristband through the little slot at the turnstile, head out the door, and stumble along the Danube... as relaxed as you'll ever be.

Aaaaahhh.

Entertainment in Budapest

Budapest is a great place to catch a good—and inexpensive—musical performance. In fact, music lovers from Vienna often make the three-hour trip here just to take in a fine opera in a luxurious setting at a bargain price. Options range from a performance at one of the world's great opera houses to light, touristy Hungarian folk concerts. The tourist concerts are the simplest option—you'll see the fliers everywhere—but you owe it to yourself to do a little homework and find something that really appeals to you.

For **event schedules,** pick up the free monthly *Budapest Panorama,* which makes things easy—listing performances with dates, venues, performers, and contact information for getting tickets (get it at the TI, or visit www.budapestpanorama.com). The TI also hands out two other helpful guides with a more youthful slant: *Servus* and *Budapest Funzine* (www.funzine.hu). Other helpful websites include www.wherebudapest.hu (general), www.welovebudapest.com (general), www.xpatloop.com (expat news), and www.muzsikalendarium.hu (classical).

To buy **tickets,** I've given strategies for the top options (Opera House and Hungária Koncert). Resources such as *Budapest Panorama* usually explain how you can get tickets for specific performances. You can search for information about—and buy tickets for—many Budapest events at www.jegymester.hu and www.kulturinfo.hu.

What's on can vary by **season.** Some of the best nightclubs and bars are partly or entirely outdoors, so they're far more enjoyable in the summer. Meanwhile, the Hungarian State Opera and other indoor cultural events tend to take a summer break from late June into early September (though that's prime time for outdoor music and Hungária Koncert's touristy shows).

While locals dress up for the more "serious" concerts and opera, many tourists dress casually—just don't show up in shorts, sneakers, or flip-flops.

A Night at the Opera

Take in an opera by one of the best companies in Europe, in one of

Europe's loveliest opera houses, for bargain prices. The Hungarian State Opera performs almost nightly, both at the main Opera House (Andrássy út 22, district VI, M1: Opera, see page 600) and in the Erkel Színház theater (not nearly as impressive). If you want classical opulence, be careful to get a performance in the Opera

House—not the Erkel Színház. Note that there are generally no performances from late June into early September. Most performances are in the original language with Hungarian and English supertitles.

Ticket prices range from 1,200 to 20,000 Ft, but the best music deal in Europe may be the 500-Ft, obstructed-view tickets (easy to get, as they rarely run out—even when other tickets are sold out). If you buy one of these $2.25 opera tickets, you'll get a seat in one of two places: If you're sitting at the back of one of the boxes along the side of the theater, you can either sit comfortably and see nothing; or stand and crane your neck to see about half the stage. If you sit on the top of the side balcony, you can stand near the door for a view of the stage. If the seats in front of you don't fill up, scooting up to an empty seat when the show starts is less than a capital offense. Either way, you'll hear every note along with the big spenders.

To get tickets, book online (www.opera.hu or www. jegymester.hu), print your eticket, and waltz right in. Or you can book by phone with a credit card (tel. 1/332-7914, phone answered Mon-Fri 10:00-17:00), then pick up your ticket at the Opera House before the performance. Maybe best of all, just drop by in person and see what's available during your visit. There are often a few tickets for sale at the door, even if it's supposedly "sold out" (box office open Mon-Sat from 11:00 until show time—generally 19:00, or until 17:00 if there's no performance; Sun open 3 hours before the performance—generally 16:00-19:00, or 10:00-13:00 if there's a matinee). If you're desperate to attend a specific performance and it looks sold out online, don't give up: Try calling or stopping by the Opera House, or ask your hotelier. There's almost always a way to get a ticket.

Tourist Concerts by Hungária Koncert

Hungária Koncert offers a wide range of made-for-tourists performances of traditional music. These take place in one of two historic venues: the **Budai Vigadó** ("Buda Concert Hall," on Corvin tér in Víziváros, between Castle Hill and the Danube, district I, M2: Batthyány tér—for location, see map on page 668), or in the former Budapest Ritz, now called the **Duna Palota**

("Danube Palace," 3 long blocks north of Vörösmarty tér in Pest, behind Széchenyi tér and the Gresham Palace at Zrínyi utca 5, district V, M1: Vörösmarty tér).

Highbrow classical music buffs will want a more serious concert, but these shows are crowd-pleasers. The most popular options are **Hungarian folk music-and-dance shows** by various interchangeable troupes (3,900-6,500 Ft, June-Oct Sun-Fri at 20:00, can be at either theater) and **classical "greatest hits"** by the Danube Symphony Orchestra (with some traditional Hungarian instruments as well; 6,700-9,200 Ft, June-Oct Sat at 20:00, always at Duna Palota). Or you can take in an **organ concert** (usually mixing Bach and Mozart with Liszt or Bartók) in the impressive St. István's Basilica (4,800-8,100 Ft, May-Oct Thu at 20:00; see page 587).

If you book direct, you'll get a 10 percent Rick Steves discount on anything they offer (must book in person, by phone, or by email; on their website, you can book the "student rate"; discount may not be honored if you buy your tickets through your hotel). The main office is in the Duna Palota at Zrínyi utca 5 (daily April-Dec 8:00-21:00, Jan-March 8:00-18:00, open later during concerts, tel. 1/317-2754 or 1/317-1377, www.ticket.info.hu, hunkonc@ticket. info.hu). Hungária Koncert also offers lunch and dinner cruises on the Danube, in-depth tours of the Jewish Quarter, and (pointless) advance tickets for the baths.

Other Venues
Budapest has many other grand spaces for enjoying a performance. You can find details for each of these on their websites.

The most appealing is the **Franz Liszt Academy of Music** (Liszt Ferenc Zeneművészeti Egyetem, a.k.a. Zeneakadémia), on Franz Liszt Square, which hosts high-quality professional concerts every night. Recently restored to its stunning late-19th-century splendor, this venue rivals even the Opera House for opulence. If attending a concert, try to make sure it's in the Grand Hall, or Nagyterem (just off of Andrássy út at Liszt Ferenc tér 8, M1: Oktogon, www.zeneakademia.hu). The **Former Academy of Music** (Régi Zeneakadémia)—just up Andrássy út near the House of Terror—houses the Franz Liszt Museum and hosts performances on Saturday mornings at 11:00 (Vörösmarty utca 35, www. lfze.hu).

The **Pesti Vigadó** ("Pest Concert Hall"), gorgeously restored and sitting proudly on the Pest embankment, is another great place for a concert in elegant surroundings (Vigadó tér 1, www.vigado. hu).

The **National Dance Theater** (Nemzeti Táncszínház) puts on performances ranging from ballet to folk to contemporary at various venues around town, including the Palace of Arts (at the Millennium City Center—see below), the MOM Cultural Center (near the Great Synagogue, at Csörsz utca 18), and the Royal

Garden Pavilion in the Várkert Bázár complex, along the Buda riverbank just below the Royal Palace (www.dancetheatre.hu).

The **"Millennium City Center"** complex, sitting on the Pest riverbank near the Rákóczi Bridge south of downtown (district IX, ride tram #2 south along the Pest embankment to the Millenniumi Kulturális Központ stop), is a state-of-the-art facility with multiple venues. The **Palace of Arts** (Művészetek Palotája) features art installations as well as musical performances in two venues: the 1,700-seat Béla Bartók National Concert Hall and the 460-seat Festival Theater (www.mupa.hu). The **National Theater** (Nemzeti Színház) presents mostly Hungarian-language drama and lectures (www.nemzetiszinhaz.hu).

Nightlife in Budapest

In addition to strolling the floodlit promenades, and taking a dip at a thermal bath (Széchenyi and Rudas are both partly open late—see "Experiences in Budapest," earlier), here are some ideas for after-hours fun.

YUPPIE DRINKING ZONES

The plaza in front of **St. István's Basilica** has recently become Budapest's most fashionable locale for a glass of wine. Of the many upscale restaurants and bars in this area, DiVino—a bar with contemporary decor and a wide range of Hungarian wines by the glass—is a good choice (see page 674).

Young locals also meet up for happy hour after work at the many trendy bars on **Franz Liszt Square** (Liszt Ferenc tér, on page 601). **Ráday utca** (described on page 673) has a similar scene, but has become touristy in recent years. Many of these places also serve food.

For something a bit more genteel—evocative of this city's late-19th-century Golden Age—locals pass their evenings sipping wine or nibbling dessert at a **café** (see "Budapest's Café Culture" on page 681).

RUIN PUBS

If you're looking for memorable, lively, smoke-filled, trendy pubs crammed with twentysomething Budapesters and backpackers, explore the dingy streets of the Jewish Quarter, behind the Great Synagogue. (This area is between the Small and Great Boulevards, south of Király utca and north of

Rákóczi út.) Damaged in World War II (like most of the city), this neighborhood sat, dilapidated and forgotten, for decades—and remained neglected even when other parts of town were rejuvenated in the 1990s and early 2000s. Now it's finally getting some attention from innovative young people—though it retains a certain endearing scruffiness, still lacking the spit and polish of central neighborhoods just across the Small Boulevard. This unusual combination of a very central location and low rents has attracted a funky new breed of bars, dubbed "ruin pubs" *(romkocsma)*; some also bill themselves as *kert* (garden), *mulató* (club), or *kávézó* (coffeehouse). The low profile entryways look abandoned, but once you walk back through a maze of hallways, you'll emerge into large halls and open-air courtyards filled with people huddled around ramshackle tables...rickety-chic.

Most of the clientele are in their 20s or 30s, but hip oldsters feel welcome; there's a wide variety of ruin pubs, ranging from rollicking to mellow, so survey several to find your favorite. Though dingy and gloomy, this neighborhood is generally considered safe by locals. And at night, the streets can be jammed with bar-hoppers. But it's always smart to be prudent—stick to well-lit streets. Note that most ruin pubs have vast outdoor zones, but small interiors—so they're better in good weather. In addition to the places noted below, you can find a partial listing at www. ruinpubs.com.

Ruin Pub Crawl in the Jewish Quarter

I've connected several of Budapest's most interesting ruin pubs on this pub crawl through the core of Budapest's Jewish Quarter. This area can be very lively any night of the week (especially in good weather), but it's best Thursday through Saturday.

Start on **Király utca,** which runs parallel to Andrássy út, two blocks south (for this tour, it's handiest to ride the M1 Metró line to the Opera stop, then walk south). From Király, at the park with the huge graffiti mural, head down **Kazinczy utca.** After one short block, poke down the unnamed alley on the right (after Piritós). This strip is lined with several enticing places, including **Négyszáz** ("400") and **My Way,** with an older clientele. Continuing straight ahead to the end of the lane, you can enter right into the middle of the long series of courtyards called **Gozsdu Udvar,** which is jammed with lively bars and cafés—and is worth exploring in its own right.

Head back out to Kazinczy and turn right. Watch for **Mika Tivadar Mulató** (at #47), **Mika Kert** (their next-door garden), **Ellátó Kert** ("Supplier," at #48), and **Kőleves** ("Stone Soup," at #41—also a recommended restaurant). Just after Kőleves, Kazinczy utca crosses Dob street. Turn right onto Dob, which is lined with

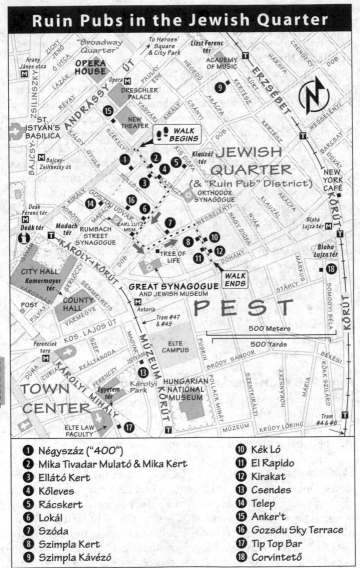

Ruin Pubs in the Jewish Quarter

1 Négyszáz ("400")
2 Mika Tivadar Mulató & Mika Kert
3 Ellátó Kert
4 Kőleves
5 Rácskert
6 Lokál
7 Szóda
8 Szimpla Kert
9 Szimpla Kávézó
10 Kék Ló
11 El Rapido
12 Kirakat
13 Csendes
14 Telep
15 Anker't
16 Gozsdu Sky Terrace
17 Tip Top Bar
18 Corvintető

more ruin pubs, including **Lokál** (at #18, facing the intersection with Síp street) and another entrance to the **Gozsdu Udvar** passageway.

Continuing past Gozsdu Udvar on Dob utca, turn left when you reach Rumbach utca, walk one short block to the side gate of the Great Synagogue, then turn left up **Wesselényi utca.** Stroll here for a few blocks, passing **Szóda** (at #18), then turn right on

Kazinczy utca. This next block is the home of the first and still the best of the ruin pubs, **Szimpla Kert** ("Simple Garden," on the right at #14) sprawls through an old building that ought to be condemned, and spills out into an equally shoddy courtyard. Surrounding the garden is a warren of tiny rooms—each one different. This space also hosts a farmers market on Sunday mornings.

Other copycat places have sprung up around Szimpla in recent years, including **Kék Ló** ("Blue Horse," across the street at #10, combines a fashion boutique with a low-key bar); **El Rapido** (at #11, a small ruin pub-slash-taquería with a bodega upstairs and a junk-crammed cellar); and **Kirakat** ("Shop Window," at #3, with a minimalist-graffiti interior).

Elsewhere in Budapest: Within a few blocks of this route are some other good options. **Csendes** ("Silent") is a mellower, more grown-up-feeling place tucked behind Károlyi Park, right in the heart of the Town Center, with pleasant, wine-bar sidewalk tables at the gate to the park (Ferenczy István utca 7). **Instant**—closer to the Opera House and the "Little Broadway" quarter—fills three floors and a warren of dozens of rooms and alcoves (Nagymező utca 38). **Telep** ("Site") is a tumble-down secondhand bar incongruously located in a residential and office-block neighborhood just around the corner from the heart of the ruin-pub scene (Madách Imre utca 8, just off Rumbach utca). And **Anker't** has a minimalist charm (across the street from the Opera House at Paulay Ede utca 33).

Summer Terraces (Tető)

In addition to *kert* ("garden"), a key term for enjoying Budapest in the summer is *tető* ("roof"). Rooftop terraces—offering laid-back scenery high above the congested city—are the newest wave of hangouts. Most roof terraces are open only in good weather, start serving drinks and light food around mid-afternoon, and are open only in the summer (typically May-Sept; check websites to confirm they're open). Several offer live music. While this is an emerging scene, here are a few worth checking out: **360 Bar** on the roof of the old Párisi Nagy Áruház department-store building, enter next door to Alexandra bookshop, Andrássy út 39, www.360bar.hu). **Gozsdu Sky Terrace** is high above the Gozsdu Udvar gallery in

Escape Room Games

If you enjoy haunted houses at Halloween, you'll love the latest trend in Budapest: "escape room games." Taking root in the fertile soil of the ruin-pub scene, dozens of local tour operators are setting up this fun (for some) and terrifying (for others) experience: Your small group is locked in a room in a spooky, derelict building. To escape, you'll have to solve a series of clues and puzzles (in English) within the allotted time. Various hazards and hurdles pop up as you go, and you'll need to work together to achieve the goal. The escape room game concept—popular for team-building outings, but accessible to curious tourists—has taken off in a big way, and Hungary is now exporting the games to other European cities. Companies come and go, but well-established options include www.claustrophilia.hu, www.trap.hu, www.exitpoint-games.hu, and www.parapark.hu. As the lineup is constantly changing and each outfit has its own personality, read some online reviews to find the one that suits your interests. Then book ahead, have fun...and good luck.

the heart of the Jewish Quarter (find the easy-to-miss entrance near the vintage car collection inside Gozsdu Udvar, www.gozsduudvar.hu). **Tip Top Bar** is in the Town Center, overlooking University Square (Egyetem tér; at Kecskeméti utca 3/Királyi Pál utca 4). **Raqpart** owns a stunning setting, on the Pest side of the Chain Bridge, overlooking the beautiful Buda panorama (in front of the Hotel InterContinental on Jane Haining rakpart, www.raqpart.hu). **Corvintető** ("Corvin Roof"), one of the original rooftop bars, feels a bit dingier (on top of the old Corvin department store, across from New York Café at Blaha Lujza tér 1, enter on Somogyi Béla utca, www.corvinteto.hu).

Shopping in Budapest

While it's not quite a shopper's mecca, Budapest does offer some enjoyable opportunities to hunt for that perfect Hungarian souvenir.

For a look at local life and a chance to buy some mementos, Budapest's single best shopping venue is the **Great Market Hall** (described on page 592). In addition to all the colorful produce downstairs, the upstairs gallery is full of fiercely competitive souvenir vendors. There's also a **folk-art market on Castle Hill** (near the bus stop at Dísz tér), but it's generally more touristy and a little more expensive. And, while **Váci utca** has been Budapest's main shopping thoroughfare for generations, today it features the city's highest prices and worst values.

For something a bit less touristy—but still evolving—drop by the **Bálna ("Whale") Cultural Center,** which sits along the Danube just behind the Great Market Hall (described on page 594). This modern space is a combined cultural center and shopping mall, but has yet to figure out its commercial identity. You'll see some souvenir stands similar to what's upstairs in the Great Market Hall, but you'll also find unique, one-off designers who are still just establishing their reputation. It may be potluck for shoppers, but it's worth exploring—and the architecture is interesting.

As a big, cosmopolitan capital, Budapest has its share of international fashion boutiques. Most of these are along or near **Deák utca** (called "Fashion Street," connecting Vörösmarty tér and Deák tér), or along the first stretch of **Andrássy út.** A few more big-ticket shops are along and near **Váci utca,** with an intriguing cluster along the cross-street **Irányi utca** (just south of Ferenciek tere, near the river in the Town Center). A block over, at Nyáry Pál utca 7, **Eventuell Gallery** displays and sells the works of local designers (www.eventuell.hu).

To see how Hungarian urbanites renovate their crumbling concrete flats, don't miss the home-improvement shops that line **Király utca,** which runs parallel to Andrássy út (two short blocks south). For a taste of the good old days—which somehow just feels right, here in nostalgic Budapest—wander up the city's **"antique row,"** Falk Miksa utca, just north of the Parliament.

Budapesters do most of their shopping in big, American-style **shopping malls**—three of which are downtown (most shops generally open Mon-Sat 10:00-21:00, Sun 10:00-18:00):

• **WestEnd City Center,** next door to Nyugati/Western train station (Váci út 1, district VI, M3: Nyugati pu., tel. 1/374-6573, www.westend.hu)

• **Mammut** ("Mammoth"), two separate malls a few steps from Buda's Széll Kálmán tér (Lövőház utca 2, district II, M2: Széll Kálmán tér, tel. 1/345-8020, www.mammut.hu)

• **Arena Plaza,** near Keleti/Eastern train station (Kerepesi út 9, district XIV, M2: Keleti pu., tel. 1/880-7000, www.arenaplaza.hu)

SOUVENIR IDEAS

The most popular souvenir is that quintessential Hungarian spice, **paprika.** Sold in metal cans, linen bags, or porcelain vases—and often accompanied by a tiny wooden scoop—it's a nice way to spice up your cooking with memories of your trip. (But remember that only sealed containers will make it through customs on your way back home.) For details, see the "Paprika Primer" on page 536.

Special drinks are a fun souvenir, though they're tricky to bring home (you'll have to wrap them very carefully and put them

BUDAPEST

in your checked luggage—not permitted in carry-on; for customs regulations, see page 1304). Good choices include the unique Hungarian spirit **Unicum,** or a bottle of Hungarian **wine** (both described on page 538).

Another popular local item is a hand-embroidered **linen tablecloth.** The colors are often red and green—the national colors of Hungary—but white-on-white designs are also available (and classy). If the thread is thick and the stitching is very even, it was probably done by machine, and obviously is less valuable.

Other handicrafts to look for include **chess sets** (most from Transylvania) and **nesting dolls.** While these dolls have more to do with Russia than with Hungary, you'll see just about every modern combination available: from classic girl dolls, to Russian heads of state, to infamous terrorists, to American presidents. Tacky...but fun.

Fans of **communist kitsch** can look for ironic T-shirts that poke fun at that bygone era. But remember that the best selection is at the Memento Park gift shop, which also sells communist memorabilia and CDs of commie anthems (see page 625).

Music lovers can shop for a CD of **Hungarian music** at the Opera House gift shop (see page 600).

For a wearable souvenir, **Tisza shoes** (Tisza Cipő) are retro and newly hip. They make both athletic and work shoes, as well as bags, shirts, and accessories. You'll find Tisza products sold around the country; however, their flagship store is along the Small Boulevard near the Great Synagogue (at Károly körút 1, www.tiszacipo.hu).

HIPSTER DESIGN AND VINTAGE

Budapest is becoming a hipster mecca, and that means fun and idiosyncratic design, home decor, and vintage shops are popping up all around town. The fast-evolving scene makes it tricky to recommend a specific shop, but many intriguing boutiques have emerged in the **Jewish Quarter/"Ruin Pub" zone.** Scout Király (with an emphasis on home decor), Dob, Rumbach, Dohány, Wesselényi, Kazinczy, and neighboring streets. **Printa,** a print shop and coffeehouse, is one reliable place to get a taste of the neighborhood's vendors; they may sell a map directing you to what's hot in the area right now (Rumbach 10, www.printa.hu). **Kék Ló** ("Blue Horse"), a recommended ruin pub, also has a fine gallery of affordable clothes designed by the owner (Kazinczy utca 10, www.keklo.hu). Just across the street, **Szimpla**—the original ruin pub—hosts a colorful farmers market each Sunday (9:00-14:00, Kazinczy utca 14, www.szimpla.hu). Nearby, just across Andrássy út from the Jewish Quarter, is a smattering of intriguing shops along **Hajós utca,** behind the Opera House.

Check to see if you're in town for the **Wamp Design Fair.** One or two Sundays each month, dozens of local artists and designers gather to show off their products (free entry, 11:00-19:00, schedule at www.wamp.hu). In summer, this takes place in the city-center Elisabeth Square; off-season it moves to Millenáris Park (on the Buda side, near M2: Széll Kálmán tér).

Sleeping in Budapest

Book your accommodations well in advance, especially if you'll be traveling during busy times. September is extremely tight (because of conventions), with October close behind. The Formula 1 races (one weekend in late July or early Aug) send rates through the roof. Most rates drop 10-25 percent in the off-season (generally Nov-March). For tips on making reservations, see page 1312.

The majority of hotels don't include the 4 percent tourist tax in their rates. Be warned that some big chains also don't include the whopping 22 percent sales tax, which can make your hotel cost nearly a quarter more than you expected. (Independent hotel rates typically do include sales tax.)

In Budapest, most hotels quote their rates in euros (for the convenience of international guests), and I've followed suit. (Outside of the capital, hotels more often quote rates in forints.) However, most places prefer to be paid in forints (figured at the exchange rate on the day of payment). Credit cards are accepted—though smaller places always prefer cash.

Since my €100 listings are substantially nicer than my €85 listings, I'd spring for the extra expense to have a comfortable home base.

If you're on a tight budget, don't overlook the good-value **Belle-vue B&B** (page 669) and **Mária and István**'s place (page 666).

Sleep Code

Abbreviations
(€1 = $1.40, 225 Ft = about $1, country code: 36, area code: 1)
S = Single, **D** = Double/Twin, **T** = Triple, **Q** = Quad, **b** = bathroom, **s** = shower only.

Price Rankings
$$$ **Higher Priced**—Most rooms €100 or more.
$$ **Moderately Priced**—Most rooms between €70-100.
$ **Lower Priced**—Most rooms €70 or less.

Unless otherwise noted, breakfast is included, English is spoken, Wi-Fi is available, and credit cards are accepted. Prices can change without notice; verify current rates online or by email. For the best prices, always book directly with the hotel.

Most hotels listed here include a buffet breakfast. Some smaller budget places serve no breakfast at all, while larger chain hotels charge (too much) extra for it; in these cases, I've noted it in the listing. Consider having breakfast instead at one of two good cafés I've recommended in "Eating in Budapest," later: Gerlóczy Café or Callas.

IN PEST

Most travelers find staying in Pest more convenient than sleeping in Buda. Most sights worth seeing are in Pest, which also has a much higher concentration of Metró and tram stops, making it a snap to get around. Pest feels more lively and local than stodgy, touristy Buda, but it's also much more urban (if you don't enjoy big cities, sleep in Buda instead). I've arranged my listings by neighborhood, clustered around the most important sightseeing sectors.

Near Andrássy Út

Andrássy Boulevard is handy, local-feeling, and fun. With its ample restaurants, upscale-residential vibe, and easy connection to downtown (via the M1/yellow line), it's the neighborhood where I prefer to sleep. Most of the hotels listed here are within a two-block walk of this main artery. For locations, see the map on page 659.

$$$ K+K Hotel Opera is wonderfully situated beside the Opera House in the fun "Broadway Quarter"—my favorite home-base location in Budapest. It's a regal splurge, with 200 classy rooms and helpful, professional service. The published rates are sky-high (Sb-€215, Db-€265), but most of the time you can score a better deal (often Sb-€110, Db-€125 in summer and on weekends; €25 more for bigger and fancier "executive" rooms, non-smoking floors, air-con, elevator, guest computer, Wi-Fi, parking garage-€16/day, Révay utca 24, district VI, M1: Opera, tel. 1/269-0222, www.kkhotels.com, hotel.opera@kkhotels.hu).

$$$ Kapital Inn is an upscale boutique B&B tucked behind the House of Terror. Its six rooms are pricey but perfectly stylish—there's not a pillow out of place. Albert, who lived in Boston, gives his B&B a sense of real hospitality. You'll enjoy the public spaces, from the restful, momentum-killing terrace to the giant kitchen, where Albert serves breakfast at a huge shared counter (D-€89—a particularly good value, Db-€125, bigger Db-€149, 2-bedroom suite-€199, cheaper Nov-March, air-con, guest computer, Wi-Fi, free communal minibar, up several flights of stairs with no elevator, Aradi utca 30, district VI, M1: Vörösmarty utca, mobile 0630-915-2029, www.kapitalinn.com, kapitalinn@kapitalinn.com).

$$$ Casati Budapest Hotel is a solid value, and is conveniently located a block off Andrássy út (across the boulevard from

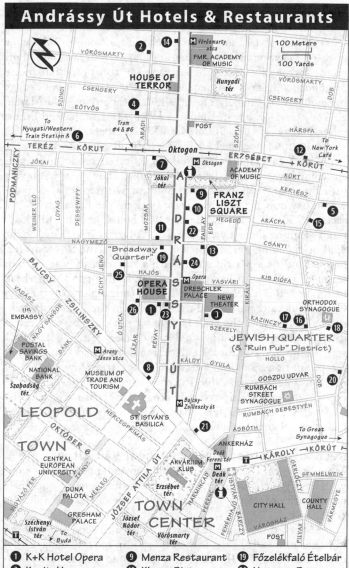

Andrássy Út Hotels & Restaurants

1. K+K Hotel Opera
2. Kapital Inn
3. Casati Budapest Hotel
4. easyHotel
5. Hotel Queen Mary
6. To Aventura Boutique Hostel
7. Home Made Hostel
8. Belvárosi Lugas Étterem
9. Menza Restaurant
10. Klassz Bistro
11. Pesti Diszno
12. Bock Bisztró
13. Két Szerecsen
14. Millennium da Pippo
15. Shalimar Rest.
16. Macesz Huszár
17. Kőleves
18. Soul Food
19. Főzelékfaló Ételbár
20. Hummus Bar
21. Duran Szendvics
22. Alexandra Bookstore Café
23. Callas Café
24. Müvész Kávéház
25. Laundry
26. Discover Budapest

BUDAPEST

the Opera House, then down a side street—just steps from the edge of the ruin-pub zone). This classy, Swiss-run hotel has 25 rooms in four different styles, ranging from "classic" to "cool" (all the same price—review your options online and choose your favorite). Many rooms surround a peaceful courtyard—in this potentially noisy neighborhood, it's worth requesting one of these (prices change constantly, but generally Db-€110-130, cheaper Nov-mid-March, air-con, elevator, guest computer, Wi-Fi, free sauna and fitness room, Paulay Ede utca 31, district VI, M1: Opera, tel. 1/343-1198, www.casatibudapesthotel.hu, info@casatibudapesthotel.hu).

The **$ easyHotel** chain follows a similar model to its parent company, the no-frills easyJet airline: They charge you very little up front, then nickel-and-dime you with optional extras—so you pay only for what you want (pick up the list at entry: TV access-€7.50/24 hours; hairdryer-€1/24 hours; laundry-€10/load; room-cleaning during your stay-€10; €10 extra if arriving before 8:00 or checking out after 14:00, and so on). The 59 rooms feel popped out of a plastic mold, with a nauseating orange color scheme, sterile quasi-linoleum floors, and tiny prefab ship's-head bathrooms. But it's conveniently located (just a block off the busy Great Boulevard and around the corner from the Oktogon), well-run by Zoltán, and the price is right...if you can resist the extras (Sb/Db-€19-69 depending on demand, average rate is €31 for a small room and €35 for a standard room, no breakfast, 24-hour reception, non-smoking, air-con, elevator, free slow Wi-Fi—or pay for faster access, cable Internet access-€2/hour or €10/24 hours, two wheelchair-accessible rooms, Eötvös utca 25A, district VI, M1: Oktogon, tel. 1/411-1982, www.easyhotel.com, info@budapestoktogon.easyhotel.com).

Pest Town Center (Belváros), near Váci Utca

Most hotels on the very central and convenient Váci utca come with overly inflated prices. But these less expensive options—just a block or two off Váci utca—offer some of the best values in Budapest.

$$$ Gerlóczy Café & Rooms, which also serves good meals in its recommended café, is the best spot in central Budapest for affordable elegance. The 19 rooms, set around a classy old spiral-staircase atrium with a stained-glass ceiling, are thoughtfully and stylishly appointed. This gem is an exceptional value (cozy low-beamed attic Db-€104, standard Db-€119, Sb for €12 less, rates include great à la carte breakfast in café, some restaurant noise on lower floors until 23:00, air-con, elevator, Wi-Fi, free mini-bar, 2 blocks from Váci utca, just off Városház utca at Gerlóczy utca 1, district V, M3: Ferenciek tere or M2: Astoria or M1/M2/

M3: Deák tér, tel. 1/501-4000, www.gerloczy.com, info@gerloczy.com).

$$ Butterfly Home, run with care by András (OHN-drash) and Timea, is a B&B with seven spacious, contemporary-style rooms overlooking a quiet pedestrianized lane a block from the happening University Square (Egyetem tér). You'll enjoy the (included) à la carte breakfast in the neighboring restaurant. András really hustles to help you fully appreciate Budapest (Sb-€72-82, Db-€99-112, price depends on size, top-floor "economy" room with bathroom down a half-flight of stairs-Sb-€62/Db-€79, 25 percent cheaper Nov-March, book directly with hotel for the best rates, air-con, guest computer, Wi-Fi, Képíró utca 3, district V, M3/M4: Kálvin tér, mobile 0630-964-7287, www.butterflyhome.hu, info@butterflyhome.hu).

$$ Peregrinus Hotel, just a block off Váci utca, has 25 high-ceilinged, spacious, old-fashioned, parquet-floored rooms (most of which lack air-conditioning—in summer, request a third-floor room with air-con for the same price). Because it's owned by the big ELTE university, many of its guests are visiting professors and lecturers (Sb-€60, Db-€85, Tb-€95, cheaper June-Aug and Nov-March, rates very soft—email to ask about deals, elevator, guest computer, Wi-Fi, free loaner bikes, Szerb utca 3, district V, M4: Fővám tér, tel. 1/266-4911, www.peregrinushotel.hu, peregrinushotel@elte.hu).

$$ Kálvin-Ház, a long block up from the Great Market Hall, has quirky management, a nice classic feel, and 36 big rooms with old-fashioned furnishings and squeaky parquet floors. The newer top-floor rooms have a bit less classic character, but are air-conditioned and tidier than the older rooms (all rooms cost the same, slippery rates vary with demand—generally around Sb-€59, Db-€79, extra bed-€20, elevator, guest computer, Wi-Fi, Gönczy Pál utca 6, district IX, M4: Fővám tér, tel. 1/216-4365, www.kalvinhouse.hu, info@kalvinhouse.hu).

$$ Loft V65 is a peaceful oasis of an apartment right on Váci utca, rented by the family that also runs the recommended Butterfly Home (described earlier). The large, well-appointed apartment has two double bedrooms, one-and-a-half baths, and a kitchen. You can rent just one bedroom (for 2 people, €85 mid-March-mid-Oct, €60-75 off-season) or both bedrooms (for up to 4 people, €95 mid-March-mid-Oct, €75-85 off-season). After you reserve, Gábor and András will arrange a meeting time to give you the keys (non-smoking, air-con, elevator, Wi-Fi, Váci utca 65, district V, M4: Fővám tér or M3: Ferenciek tere, in the mornings call András at mobile 0630-964-7287, in the afternoons call Gábor at US tel. 917-880-3656, www.LoftV65.com, LoftV65@gmail.com).

To Parliament & 15

CENTRAL EUROPEAN UNIVERSITY 27 33 22

ACADEMY OF SCI. 23

To 32

RÉVAY

To Heroes' Square & City Park

LEOPOLD

32

SAS

ST. ISTVÁN'S BASILICA

BAJCSY - ZSILINSZKY

26

ANDRÁSSY ÚT

KÁLDY

SZÉKELY

Bajcsy-Zsilinszkyút

GYULA

HOLLÓ

GOSZDU UDVAR

RUMBACH STREET SYNAGOGUE 8

RUMBACH SEBESTYÉN

LASBÓTH

Széchenyi István tér

ZRÍNYI

DUNA PALOTA 40

OKTÓBER 6

41

24

VIGYÁZÓ FER

11

GRESHAM PALACE

13

MÉRLEG

TOWN

25

39

12

CHAIN BRIDGE

JÓZSEF ATTILA ÚT

BÉCSI

33

AKVÁRIUM KLUB

ANKERHÁZ

Eötvös tér

To Buda & Castle Hill

Tram #2

APÁCZAI

BELGRÁD RAKPART

DOROTTYA

SZENDE

38

POST

József Nádor tér

Erzsébet tér

HARMINCAD

Deák Ferenc tér

Deák tér

KÁROLY KÖRÚT

GERBEAUD CAFÉ

FERENC

Vörösmarty tér

M

Vörösmarty tér

FEHÉRHAJÓ ISTVÁN

BÁRCZY

VÁROSHÁZ

CITY HALL

Pesti Vigadó

VIGADÓ

DEÁK

Vigadó tér

CSERE

TÜRR I.

ARANY

PETŐFI SÁNDOR

Kamermayer tér

1

SEMMELWEIS

COUNTY HALL

MAHART BOAT DOCK

Historic McDonald's

JÁNOSS

RÉGIPOSTI

POST

PILVAX

FORMER PILVAX CAFÉ

VÁRMEGYE

LEGENDA BOAT DOCK

"SORRARAS" HISTORICISM BLDG. (#15)

JUGENDSTIL BLDG. (#18)

TOWN

KOSSUTH LAJOS UTCA

SZER

REÁLTANODA

Petőfi tér

PIARISTA UTCA

KIGYÓ

36

Ferenciek tere

31

FRANCISCAN CHURCH

Petőfi tér

PIARISTA KÖZ

KLOTILD PALACES

KÁROLYI MIHÁLY

FERENCZY

Károlyi Park

Tram #19 & #41

SZABAD SAJTÓ ÚT

35

CENTER

Egyetem

Döbrentei tér

ELISABETH BRIDGE

Március 15 tér

IRÁNYI

18

PAPNÖV.

32

ELTE LAW FACULTY

KIR. PÁL

17

RUDAS BATHS

Tram #2

VÁCI UTCA

NYÁRI PÁL

VERES PÁLNÉ

SZERB

F. GYÖRGY

BELGRÁD RAKPART

SORHÁZ

SERBIAN CHURCH

3

BÁSTYA

Gellért Hill

CITADELLA

CITADELLA

21

5

MOLNÁR

16

HAVAS

SZARKA

SÓ

POST

Fővám tér

M

VÁMHÁZ KÖRÚT

PIPA

19

GREAT MARKET HALL

SÓHÁZ

SÉTÁNY

SZT. GELLÉRT RAKPART

Danube

UNIV. OF ECONOMICS

BUDA

CAVE CHURCH

VEREJTÉK

River

KELENHEGYI

LIBERTY BRIDGE

N

200 Meters

200 Yards

GELLÉRT HOTEL & BATHS

Szent Gellért tér

M

Szent Gellért tér

KEMENES

Pest Town Center Hotels & Restaurants

1. Gerlóczy Café & Rooms
2. Butterfly Home
3. Peregrinus Hotel
4. Kálvin-Ház Hotel
5. Loft V65
6. Brody House
7. Budapest Rooms
8. ROOMbach Hotel Budapest Center
9. Danube Guest House
10. BudaBaB
11. Four Seasons Gresham Palace
12. Hotel Central Basilica
13. Starlight Suiten
14. Mária & István Rooms
15. To GuestBed Budapest
16. Halkakas Halbisztró
17. Borssó Bistro
18. BorLabor Restaurant
19. Great Market Hall
20. Café Intenzo
21. Trattoria Toscana & Taverna Dionysos
22. Café Kör
23. Mák Bistro
24. DiVino Wine Bar
25. Borkonyha Wine Bar
26. Belvárosi Lugas Étterem
27. Első Pesti Rétesház
28. Macesz Huszár
29. Kőleves
30. Soul Food
31. Főzelékfaló Ételbár
32. Hummus Bar (4)
33. Duran Szendvics (2)
34. To Laundry Budapest & New York Café
35. Centrál Kávéház
36. Jégbüfé Café
37. Bazar Hostel (Laundry)
38. Dorottya G. Pharmacy
39. MÁV Train Ticket Office
40. CEU Bookshop
41. Bestsellers Bookstore

JEWISH QUARTER
(& "Ruin Pub" District)

ORTHODOX SYNAGOGUE

GREAT SYNAGOGUE AND JEWISH MUSEUM

PEST

ELTE CAMPUS

HUNGARIAN NATIONAL MUSEUM

Kálvin tér

APPLIED ARTS MUSEUM

BÁLNA CULTURAL CENTER

HOLOCAUST MEMORIAL CENTER

BUDAPEST

Near the National Museum

These two places are within a block or two of the National Museum, just across the Small Boulevard from the Town Center, near M3/M4: Kálvin tér (district VIII).

$$ Brody House comes from artistic DNA—it began as an art gallery that provided a place for its guests to crash, and has evolved into a comfortable, full-service B&B. It fills three spacious floors of a townhouse with eight rooms and three apartments that all ooze a funky, idiosyncratic style. The sprawling public spaces may tempt you to just hang out. Each room is named for an artist who once used it as a studio; they're wildly different and thoughtfully described on their website (Db-€70-120 depending on size, 2-room apartment with kitchenette-€100-130, continental breakfast-€8, air-con in most of the rooms, 2 stories up with no elevator, Wi-Fi, Bródy Sándor utca 10, tel. 1/266-1211, www.brodyhouse. com, reception@brodyhouse.com).

$ Budapest Rooms is a great budget option, where the Boda family rents five simple but surprisingly stylish, nicely appointed rooms in a dreary residential zone (Sb-€48, Db-€62, Tb-€74, Qb-€84, all have en-suite bathrooms except one room with private bathroom across the hall, includes continental breakfast, Wi-Fi, Szentkirályi 15, tel. 1/630-4743, mobile 0620-569-9513, www. budapestrooms.eu, info@budapestrooms.eu).

In the Jewish Quarter

District VII—the city's Jewish Quarter—has emerged as one of Budapest's most happening nightlife zones, with ramshackle "ruin pubs" popping up all over. These three options offer proximity to the fun, which means they also come with some noise.

$$ ROOMbach Hotel Budapest Center, tucked down a gloomy but central street facing the Rumbach Street Synagogue, has 51 sleek, basic, smallish rooms with a stylish industrial-mod design. Part of a good-value chain, it feels fresh and modern, and the triple-glazed windows work hard to keep out the ruin pub noise (Db-€85-95 in high season, can be as low as €75 off-season, air-con, elevator, Wi-Fi, parking-€12, Rumbach Sebestyén utca 14, tel. 1/413-0253, www.roombachhotel.com, info@roombach.com).

$ Danube Guest House's six basic, tidy, gaudily decorated rooms can be noisy for light sleepers (more so in warm weather, as open windows are the only "air-conditioning" here—ask for a quieter courtyard room). But if you want proximity to one of the city's liveliest nightlife areas, this place is a great value (Sb-€45, small Db-€49, bigger Db-€59, guest computer, Wi-Fi, Dohány utca 16, district VII, M2/red: Astoria, tel. 1/788-2891, mobile 0620-419-3986, www.danubeguesthouse.com, danube.guesthouse@upcmail. hu).

BUDAPEST

$ At **BudaBaB,** thoughtful Americans Ryan and Ron rent two rooms in their apartment. You'll feel like you're a houseguest, as everybody shares the bathrooms and the comfy living room; they appreciate conscientious guests (smaller room: S-€30, D-€45, T-€55; larger room: S-€40, D-€55, T-€70, Q-€85; cash or pre-pay with PayPal for 3 percent surcharge, Akácfa utca 18, district VII, M2: Blaha Lujza tér, or tram #4 or #6 to Wesselényi stop, tel. 1/267-5240, www.budabab.com, info@budabab.com).

In Leopold Town, near the Chain Bridge

The first listing is the city's most prestigious address; the next two are business-class options that are nicely located and worth booking if you can get a discounted rate. All of these are a short stroll from the delightful St. István tér/Zrínyi utca restaurant zone.

$$$ Four Seasons Gresham Palace is Budapest's top hotel—and one of its most expensive. Stay here only if money is truly no object. You'll sleep in what is arguably Budapest's finest Art Nouveau building. Damaged in World War II, the Gresham Palace sat in disrepair for decades. Today it's sparkling from a recent head-to-toe renovation, and every detail in its lavish public spaces and 179 rooms is perfectly in place. Even if you're not sleeping here, dip into the lobby and café to soak in the elegance (non-view Db-€420-510, Danube-view Db-€630, prices don't include 22 percent tax—not a typo, breakfast-€30-35, non-smoking rooms, air-con, elevator, guest computer, Wi-Fi, top-floor spa, Széchenyi tér 5, district V, between M1: Vörösmarty tér and M2: Kossuth tér, tel. 1/268-6000, www.fourseasons.com/budapest, budapest.reservations@fourseasons.com). For more on the building's history, see page 588.

$$ Hotel Central Basilica has 47 forgettable business-class rooms in the heart of the tidy and sane Leopold Town, near St. István's Basilica and the surrounding yuppie dining and nightlife zone. The location makes it worth considering if you can score a good price (Sb-€99, Db-€109, superior Db-€139, but prices very soft—usually more like Db-€89, even cheaper Nov-March, air-con, elevator, pay Wi-Fi, Hercegprímás utca 8, district V, M1: Bajcsy-Zsilinszky út, tel. 1/328-5010, www.hotelcentral-basilica.hu, info@hotelcentral-basilica.hu).

$$ Starlight Suiten has 54 spacious suites—each with a living room, bedroom, and kitchenette—on a quiet but dull street directly behind the Gresham Palace (listed earlier). While rates can range widely (€80-130), suites often go for €90—at that price, this place is a great deal (includes small breakfast—or pay for a bigger one, air-con, elevator, guest computer, pay Wi-Fi, free fitness room and sauna, Mérleg utca 6, district V, M1: Vörösmarty tér, tel. 1/484-3700, www.starlighthotels.com, manager.merleg@starlighthotels.com).

BUDAPEST

On or near the Great Boulevard

All of these places are on or near Budapest's Great Boulevard (Nagykörút) ring road—though they are spread far and wide. Trams #4 and #6 travel around the Great Boulevard, connecting all of these, and most are also near a Metró stop.

Friendly Budget Beds near Üllői Út: **$ Mária and István,** your chatty Hungarian aunt and uncle, are saving a room for you in

their Old World apartment. For warmth and hospitality at youth-hostel prices, you can bunk in one of their two simple, old-fashioned rooms, which share a bathroom. The smaller room is cheaper and quieter; the bigger room gets some street noise on weekends

(S-€20-22, D-€30-34, T-€39-42, price depends on size of room and length of stay—longer is cheaper, no breakfast but guests' kitchen, cash only, elevator plus a few stairs, Ferenc körút 39, district IX, M3 or tram #4/#6: Corvin-negyed, tel. 1/216-0768, www. mariaistvan.hu, mariaistvan@upcmail.hu). From the Corvin-negyed Metró stop, follow signs for exit *"E,"* bear right up the stairs, and walk straight about a block and a half, looking for #39 (on the left; dial 19 at the door and ride the elevator to floor 4).

Near Margaret Bridge: **$ GuestBed Budapest** has five apartments—two in a mellow residential zone near the Margaret Bridge and the Great Boulevard, north of downtown Pest, and three more in the Andrássy út area (one in the Jewish Quarter, another near the Nyugati/Western train station, and another near St. István's Basilica—all well-described on their website). The straightforward apartments, all with full kitchens, are not luxurious—they're an old-fashioned mix of parquet floors and Ikea furniture. But this place is distinguished by its welcoming and conscientious owners, János and József. When you book, arrange a time to meet to check in and get oriented. They also rent a "B&B" room in their own apartment (sharing their bathroom)—you'll really feel like you're staying with local friends (B&B room-€45, apartment-€60, 2-bedroom apartment-€65, for best rates book directly with hotel, Wi-Fi, airport pick-up service, János also offers bike and walking tours, Katona József utca 39, district XIII, tram #4/#6: Jászai Mari tér, mobile 03670-258-5194, www.guestbudapestapartment.com, budapestrentapartment@gmail.com).

Near the Oktogon: **$ Hotel Queen Mary** (named not for the British monarch, but for the owner's wife) is mysteriously cheap and often empty, with impersonal service and 26 unimaginative rooms. The neighborhood is dingy and gloomy (two blocks beyond the end of the happening Franz Liszt Square), but the place is affordable for those on a tight budget and also likely to have rooms when other hotels are full (Sb-€50, Db-€60, Tb-€70, prices vary with demand, 20 percent cheaper Nov-March, air-con, elevator, Wi-Fi, Kertész utca 34—for location see map on page 659, district VII, between M1: Oktogon and M2: Blaha Lujza tér, closer to tram #4/#6: Király utca, tel. 1/413-3510, www.hotelqueenmary.hu, info@hotelqueenmary.hu).

Hostels

Budapest has seemingly dozens of apartments that have been taken over by young entrepreneurs, offering basic, rough-around-the-edges hostel charm. You'll buzz in at the door and climb up a creaky, dank, and smelly staircase to a funky little enclave of fellow backpackers. Most of these places have just three rooms (one double and two small dorms) and feel more like communes than the finely tuned, high-capacity youth-hostel machines common in many other cities. As each of these fills a niche (party, artsy, communist-themed, etc.), it's hard to recommend just one—read reviews on a hostel site (such as www.hostels.com) and find one that suits your hosteling philosophy. For hostel locations, see the map on page 659.

$ Aventura Boutique Hostel is a low-key, colorful, and stylish place in a dreary urban neighborhood near the Nyugati/Western train station. Well-run by friendly Ágnes, it's both homey and tastefully mod, with clean, imaginatively decorated rooms (4 rooms, bed in 4- to 8-bed dorm-€20, D-€42, price can be much less off-season and if you book in advance, breakfast-€2-5, includes sheets, towel rental-450 Ft, guest computer, Wi-Fi, kitchen, laundry service, massage available, across the busy Great Boulevard ring road and a very long block from Nyugati train station at 12 Visegrádi utca, district XIII, M3: Nyugati pu., tel. 1/239-0782, www.aventurahostel.com, info@aventurahostel.com). They also rent several apartments—two nearby, the other near St. István's Basilica (all Db-€84).

$ Home Made Hostel is a fun-and-funky slumbermill artfully littered with secondhand furniture. It's run and decorated with a sense of humor. With 20 beds in four rooms located near the Oktogon, it's another good option (bunk in 8-bed dorm-€14, in 4-bed dorm-€16, D-€39, apartment Db-€42, includes sheets and towels, no breakfast, guest computer, Wi-Fi, kitchen, laundry service, Teréz körút 22, district VI, M1: Oktogon, tel. 1/302-2103, www.homemadehostel.com, info@homemadehostel.com).

BUDAPEST

Buda Hotels & Restaurants

1. Hotel Victoria
2. art'otel
3. Bellevue B&B
4. St. George Residence
5. Hotel Castle Garden
6. Burg Hotel
7. Vár Bistro
8. Ruszwurm Café
9. 21 Magyar Vendéglő
10. Baltazár
11. Batthyány tér Eateries
12. To Csalogány 26
13. CBA Grocery

BUDAPEST

Széll Kálmán tér
Széll Kálmán tér
Bus #16, #16A & #116
MARGIT
VÉRMEZŐ
VÁRFOK UTCA
KRISZTINA KÖRÚT
HAJNÓCZY
MÁTRAY
OSTROM
CSALOGÁNY
HATTYÚ
BATTHYÁNY
TOLDY FERENC
LOVAS
MUS. OF MILITARY HIST.
TURKISH GRAVE
FIÁTH
LINZI
HUNFALVY
ST. MARY MAGDALENE
VIENNA GATE
Bus #16, #16A & #116
ORSZÁGHÁZ
TÁNCSICS
LOVAS ÚRI
ÁRPÁD
DÁRDA
FORTUNA
MIHÁLY
SZABÓ ILONKA
DONÁTI
FRANKLIN
ISKOLA

B U D A
Castle Hill
"HOSPITAL IN THE ROCK"
Hess tér
Szenth. tér
ATTILA UTCA
LOGODI
TÁBOR
BZENT
MATTHIAS CHURCH
LABYRINTH ENTRANCE
FISHERMEN'S BASTION
Bus #16
HUNYADI JÁNOS
GIMNÁZIUM
VÍZI-VÁROS
MARKET HALL
Batthyány tér
HÉV STATION
ST. ANNE'S
Batthyány tér
BUDAI VIGADÓ CONCERT HALL
CALVINIST CHURCH
Corvin tér
IBEM RAKPART
To Óbuda & Szentendre

Bus #16, #16A & #116
Dísz tér
POST
Vár Bistro
TÁRNOK
PALOTA
SZALAG
PONTY
JÉGVEREM
KAPUCINUS
FŐ
HAL
Halász utca
100 Meters
100 Yards
River
Tram #2

FMR. MIN. OF WAR
NAT. DANCE THEATER
SZÍNHÁZ
SZENT GYÖRGY
SÁNDOR PALACE
Bus #16
Tram #19 & #41
CLARK ÁDÁM
Clark Ádám tér
Clark Ádám tér
CHAIN BRIDGE
ACADEMY OF SCIENCES
Bus #16
Széchenyi István tér
GRESHAM PALACE
DUNA PALOTA

RAVEN GATE
TURUL BIRD
ROYAL PALACE
NAT. GALLERY
BUD. HIST. MUSEUM
VÁRALJA
LOVARDA
Eötvös tér
To Deák tér

Danube
KRISZTINA KÖRÚT
SZML. ATTÜRK
DÖBRENTEI
VÁRKERT
LÁNCHÍD RAKPART
To Rudas & Gellért Baths
Döbrentei

P E S T

To Csalogány 26

IN BUDA
Víziváros

The Víziváros neighborhood—or "Water Town"—is the lively part of Buda squeezed between Castle Hill and the Danube, where fishermen and tanners used to live. Víziváros is the most pleasant central area to stay on the Buda side of the Danube, with sweeping views across the river toward the Parliament building and bustling Pest. It's expensive and a little less convenient than Pest, but feels less urban.

The following hotels are in district I, between the Chain Bridge and Buda's busy Margit körút ring road. Trams #19 and #41 zip along the embankment in either direction. Batthyány tér, a few minutes' walk away, is a handy center with lots of restaurants (see page 678), a Metró stop (M2/red line), and the HÉV train to Óbuda and Szentendre. All of these places come with professional, helpful staff.

$$$ Hotel Victoria, with 27 stylish, business-class rooms—each with a grand river view and attention to detail—is a class act. This tall, narrow place (three rooms on each of nine floors) is run with pride and attention to detail by on-the-ball manager Zoltán and his friendly staff (Sb-€129, Db-€134, extra bed-€30, 20 percent cheaper Nov-March, air-con, elevator, guest computer, Wi-Fi, cheap international phone calls, free sauna, free afternoon tea for guests 16:00-17:00, reserve ahead for €16/day parking garage or park free on street, Bem rakpart 11, tel. 1/457-8080, www.victoria.hu, victoria@victoria.hu). The painstakingly restored 19th-century Hubay Palace behind the hotel (entrance next to reception) is used for concerts and other events. It feels like a museum, with inlaid floors, stained-glass windows, and stuccoed walls and ceilings—even if you're not staying at Hotel Victoria, drop in and ask to see it.

$$$ art'otel impresses New York City sophisticates. Every detail—from the breakfast dishes to the carpets to the good-luck blackbird perched in each room—was designed by American artist Donald Sultan. This stylish, fun hotel has 165 rooms spread between two attached buildings: the new section fronting the Danube and a restored older house just behind it (high rack rates, but usually Sb/Db-€99-165 depending on season, figure Sb/Db-€129 in summer, Danube view-€20 more, bigger "art rooms plus"-€35 more, deluxe "art suites"-€60 more, breakfast-€14, non-smoking rooms, air-con, elevator, guest computer, Wi-Fi, free sauna and mini-exercise room, bike rental, Bem rakpart 16, tel. 1/487-9487, www.artotels.com, budapest@artotels.com).

$ Bellevue B&B is one of Budapest's best deals. It hides in a quiet residential area on the Víziváros hillside just below the Fishermen's Bastion staircase. This gem is run by retired economists Judit (YOO-deet) and Lajos (LIE-yosh) Szuhay, who lived in Canada for four years and speak flawless English. The breakfast room and some of the six straightforward, comfortable rooms have views across the Danube to the Parliament and Pest. Judit and Lajos love to chat, and pride themselves on offering genuine hospitality and a warm welcome (let them know what time you're arriving). As this B&B is understandably popular, book ahead (Sb-€50-65, Db-€60-75; price depends on room size, view, and length of stay; 20-30 percent cheaper Nov-March, cash only, non-smoking, air-con, Wi-Fi; M2: Batthyány tér plus a 10-minute uphill walk, or bus #16 from Deák, Széchenyi, or Adam Clark squares to Dónati utca plus a 2-minute walk uphill, then downhill—they'll email you detailed directions; Szabó Ilonka utca 15/B, mobile 0630-370-8678 or 0630-951-5494, www.bellevuebudapest. com, judit@bellevuebudapest.com).

Castle Hill

Romantics may enjoy calling Castle Hill home (district I). These places couldn't be closer to the Castle Hill sights, but they're in a tourist zone—dead at night, and less convenient to Pest than other listings.

$$$ St. George Residence, just a couple of short blocks from Matthias Church, rents 24 elegant rooms around a restful garden courtyard. Each room is different and comes with a kitchenette (Db-€129, more for bigger rooms, air-con, Wi-Fi, Fortuna utca 4, tel. 1/393-5700, www.stgeorgehotel.hu, info@stgeorgehotel.hu).

$$ Hotel Castle Garden huddles above an Italian restaurant in a tranquil, park-like neighborhood just outside the castle's Vienna Gate (north end). As it's roughly on the way between the castle and Széll Kálmán tér, it's relatively handy, though still less convenient than the Víziváros listings. But its 39 tastefully appointed, contemporary rooms are a good value for the quality (Sb-€79, Db-€89, maybe less June-Aug and Nov-April, "superior" room with terrace for €20 more, air-con, elevator, guest computer, Wi-Fi, parking garage-€10, Lovas út 41, M2: Széll Kálmán tér; exit the castle through the Vienna Gate and turn left along the wall, or hike up from Széll Kálmán tér and turn right along the castle wall; tel. 1/224-7420, www.castlegarden.hu, hotel@castlegarden.hu).

$$ Burg Hotel, with 26 overpriced rooms on Holy Trinity Square (Szentháromság tér), is simply efficient: concrete, spacious, and comfy, if a bit worn, with a professional staff. You'll find more conveniently located hotels for less money elsewhere, but if you simply *must* stay in a modern hotel across the street from Matthias Church, this is it (official rates: Sb-€105, Db-€115, Db apartment-€134, but rates very soft—usually more like €85-99, extra bed-€15, 10 percent discount off their official online rate if you book direct and mention this book—unless they're very busy, 20 percent cheaper Nov-March, request view room for no extra charge, entirely non-smoking, no elevator, air-con, top-floor rooms are extremely long, family rooms, guest computer, Wi-Fi, Szentháromság tér 7, tel. 1/212-0269, www.burghotelbudapest. com, hotel.burg@mail.datanet.hu).

Eating in Budapest

Thanks to Budapest's ever-evolving culinary scene, there's no shortage of places to dine. I can barely keep track of what's new—and scouting new restaurants is the highlight of my research chores. The broad range of options and healthy sense of one-upmanship among local chefs keep prices reasonable and quality high. The foodie scene here is boom-and-bust: A place quickly acquires a huge and enthusiastic following but soon falls from grace when an even more enticing competitor opens up shop.

While you'll find the standard Hungarian fare, most big-city restaurants like to dabble in international cuisine. Many of my listings feature an international menu with some Hungarian flourishes. (If you want truly traditional Hungarian fare, you'll actually do better in smaller towns.) The good news: Most Hungarian chefs are so skilled that any cuisine is well-executed here.

Most Hungarians dine between 19:00 and 21:00, peaking around 20:00; trendy zones such as St. István Square and Franz Liszt Square, which attract an after-work crowd, are lively earlier in the evening.

Check Your Bill: Though most Hungarian restaurateurs are honest, rip-off joints abound in downtown Budapest's tourist zone—especially along the main walking street, Váci utca. (Frankly, I'd never eat on Váci utca, which practically guarantees bad food and service for high prices.) Avoid any place with a menu that doesn't list prices, and tune in to the fine print. For example, many Budapest restaurants automatically tack on a 10 to 12 percent service charge. Check for it as a line-item at the end of bill: Look for "service," "tip," *felszolgálási díj*, or *szervízdíj*. If you see this charge, an additional tip is not necessary for adequate service. For more on tipping, see page 1302.

Lunch Specials: Many Budapest restaurants offer lunch specials, called *napimenü*, on weekdays. As these are designed for local office workers on their lunch breaks rather than for tourists, they're often not advertised in English—but if you see the magic word *napimenü*, ask about it. Even at trendy, otherwise pricey eateries, you'll generally pay around 1,000 Ft for a fixed menu (soup and main dish or main dish and dessert; no choices—take it or leave it).

IN PEST

I've listed these options by neighborhood, for easy reference with your sightseeing.

In Pest's Town Center (Belváros), near Váci Utca

When you ask natives about good places to eat on Váci utca, they just roll their eyes. But wander a few blocks off the tourist route, and you'll discover alternatives with fair prices and better food. For locations, see the map on page 663.

Gerlóczy Café is tucked on a peaceful little square next to the giant City Hall. This classy café features French, Hungarian, and

international cuisine with several seating options (out on the square, in the coffee-house interior, or upstairs). There's a good permanent menu, plus changing specials (Friday is fish day). The clientele is a mix of tourists and upscale-urban Budapesters, including local politicians and actors from several nearby theaters. With a take-your-time ambience that's argu-ably more Parisian than Hungarian—and with live harp or piano music inside from 19:00 to 23:00—this is a particularly inviting spot (3,000-5,000-Ft main dishes, 1,900-Ft two-course or 2,500-Ft three-course lunch specials available Mon-Thu, good break-fasts, fresh-baked pastries and bread, daily 7:00-23:00, 2 blocks from Váci utca, just off Városház utca at Gerlóczy utca 1, district V, M3: Ferenciek tere, tel. 1/501-4000). They rent good rooms, too (see page 660).

Halkakas Halbisztró ("Fishrooster Fish Bistro") is a tight, tidy, cheery, colorful French-style bistro serving up mostly Hungarian fish with a variety of sauces. In this landlocked coun-try, that means freshwater fish (catfish, pikeperch, trout, and so on)—better than it sounds, and very local (1,600-2,000-Ft main dishes, Mon-Sat 12:00-22:00, closed Sun, Veres Pálné utca 33, mobile 0630-226-0638).

Borssó Bistro, in the newly spiffed-up area near University Square (Egyetem tér), is a trendy eatery offering small por-tions of delicately assembled modern French cuisine with a bit of Hungarian flair. The cozy two-story interior's ambience, like the cuisine, is an elegant yet accessible blend of old and new. They also have outdoor tables and occasional live music. Reservations are important at this pricey, popular place (3,600-5,000-Ft main dishes, Tue 18:00-23:00, Wed-Sun 12:00-23:00, closed Mon, Király Pál utca 14, district V, M3/M4: Kálvin tér, tel. 1/789-0975, mobile 0620-807-7087).

BorLabor ("Wine Lab") features traditional, regional, updated Hungarian specialties at reasonable prices in a warm, mod, romantic wine-cellar atmosphere. It's not as trendy as many other Budapest eateries...but that's the point (2,500-3,000-Ft main dishes, daily 12:00-24:00, a block north of Váci utca at Veres Pálné utca 7, district V, M3: Ferenciek tere, tel. 1/328-0382).

Great Market Hall: At the far south end of Váci utca, you can eat a quick lunch on the upper floor of the Great Market Hall

(Nagyvásárcsarnok). **Fakanál Étterem**—the glassed-in, sit-down cafeteria above the main entrance—is touristy, but offers good seating (2,000-3,200-Ft main dishes, Mon-Fri 10:00-17:00, Sat 10:00-14:00, closed Sun; live music most days 12:00-15:00). The sloppy, stand-up stalls along the right side of the building are cheaper, but quality can vary (grab a bar stool or you'll stand while you munch). Locals love the **Lángos** stand for deep-fried bread slathered with sour cream and cheese (add garlic for some kick).

Or you can assemble a **picnic**—produce and butcher stands line the main floor, and an Aldi supermarket is in the basement (the end nearest Váci utca; market hall open Mon 6:00-17:00, Tue-Fri 6:00-18:00, Sat 6:00-15:00, closed Sun; supermarket open longer hours, Fővám körút 1, district IX, M4: Fővám tér).

Ráday Utca: This mostly pedestrianized street is lined with a variety of cafés and restaurants, mostly catering to tourists and specializing in big portions of listlessly executed traditional Hungarian fare. But while its trendy heyday has largely passed, Ráday utca is still a marginally better alternative to the tourist traps along nearby Váci utca. To reach Ráday utca, take the M3/blue or M4/green Metró line to Kálvin tér—a five-minute walk from the Great Market Hall—and head south (district IX). For something a bit better than the rest, stop by **Café Intenzo,** hiding around the corner from the start of Ráday utca, where it meets the busy ring road. Low-key and with a loyal local following, they serve Hungarian and international cuisine, either in a non-descript interior or out in a pleasant courtyard garden (1,400-Ft sandwiches, 1,700-2,000-Ft pastas, 2,000-4,000-Ft main dishes, Mon-Fri 11:00-24:00, Sat-Sun 12:00-23:00, Kálvin tér 9, tel. 1/219-5243).

Danube Promenade

The riverbank facing the castle is lined with hotel restaurants and permanently moored restaurant boats. You'll find bad service, mediocre food, mostly tourists, and sky-high prices...but the atmosphere and people-watching are enticing.

For a more affordable and more local experience, head a bit farther south, near the green Liberty Bridge. Along the embankment road called Belgrád Rakpart is a cluster of fun and lively ethnic restaurants (including good Italian at **Trattoria Toscana,** #13, and a mini-Santorini with Greek fare at **Taverna Dionysos,** #16).

Various companies run **dinner cruises** along the Danube, including Legenda (see page 572) and Hungária Koncert (see page 648), both of which offer a discount to Rick Steves readers. And though these can be romantic, Budapest's real restaurants are too tempting to pass up. Instead, dine at your choice of eateries, then take the Legenda nighttime cruise.

Near St. István's Basilica

The streets in front of St. István's Basilica are jammed with upscale, dressy, yuppie-oriented eateries. You could simply browse the options along Zrínyi utca (which stretches straight down to the Danube from the basilica's front door) and its cross streets. But the following choices are worth seeking out. For locations, see the map on page 663.

Café Kör ("Circle") has long been a mainstay in this fast-emerging zone. This stylish but unsnooty eatery serves up mostly Hungarian and some Mediterranean fare in a tasteful, tight one-room interior and at a few sidewalk tables. It prides itself on being friendly and providing a good value. Because it's beloved by local foodies, reservations are smart any time—and essential on weekends (2,000-4,000-Ft main dishes, small portions for 30 percent less, good salads, daily specials, cash only, Mon-Sat 10:00-22:00, closed Sun, Sas utca 17, district V, between M3: Arany János utca and M1: Bajcsy-Zsilinszky út, tel. 1/311-0053).

Mák Bistro is a pricey but unpretentious with a loyal local following (reservations are smart, especially on weekends). It feels like a well-kept secret, tucked down a forgotten side street parallel to the bustling Zrínyi utca main drag. Inside it has a lively brasserie ambience under white-painted brick vaults. The short, carefully selected seasonal menu is based on what's fresh (5,500-7,500-Ft main courses, Tue-Sat 12:00-15:00 & 18:00-23:00, closed Sun-Mon, Vigyázó Ferenc 4, mobile 0630-723-9383, www.mak.hu).

Wine-Focused Eateries: Two wine bars—one casual, the other upscale—have helped turn this neighborhood into a happening nightspot. **DiVino** is all about the wine, serving 130 different types of exclusively Hungarian wines, listed by region on the chalkboard—all of them available either by the glass or by the bottle. The well-versed staff can help introduce you to Hungary's underrated wines—just tell them what you like and let them guide you to something to try. While DiVino doesn't do flights or "tastings," per se, couples are invited to share glasses to try several varieties. The interior has a hip black-chalkboard atmosphere, and there's also very inviting seating out on the square (many glasses affordable at around 600-1,000 Ft, also 1,300-2,500-Ft meals, daily 16:00-24:00, later on weekends, St. István tér 3, mobile 0670-935-3980; they also have another, bigger location in the Gozsdu Udvar passage in the Jewish Quarter). Just around the corner, **Borkonyha** ("Winekitchen") focuses both on its list of high-quality (and pricey) Hungarian wines, and on its modern Hungarian cuisine ("Hungarian dishes—but less paprika, less fat"). Because they're enthusiastic about their wines, they sell even pricey bottles by the glass (about 45 types—700-3,000 Ft per glass). The menu—especially the adventurous chalkboard specials—ventures into "nose-to-tail" cooking, using ingredients you won't find everywhere. The decor is sophisticated black, white, and gold—it's a dressy place where wine snobs feel at home. As this place has received a lot of international press, reservations are smart (3,800-4,200-Ft main dishes, Mon-Sat 12:00-24:00, closed Sun, Sas utca 3, tel. 1/266-0835, www.borkonyha.hu).

Behind St. István's Basilica: **Belvárosi Lugas Étterem** is your cheap-and-charming, no-frills option. *Lugas* is a Hungarian word for a welcoming garden strewn with grape vines, and the cozy dining room—with a dozen tables of happy eaters under overhanging vines—captures that spirit. Or sit at one of their sidewalk tables outside on busy Bajcsy-Zsilinszky. The food is simply good Hungarian (1,500-3,200-Ft main dishes, order starches separately, daily 12:00-23:30, directly behind and across the street from St. István's Basilica at Bajcsy-Zsilinszky út 15, district VI, M1: Bajcsy-Zsilinszky út, tel. 1/302-5393).

Homemade Strudel: **Első Pesti Rétesház** is a favorite among fans of *rétes* (strudel). Step inside to watch them roll out the long, paper-thin sheets of dough, then wrap them around a variety of fillings. Get a 300-Ft piece to go at the takeaway counter, or sit and enjoy your *rétes* with a cup of coffee (also has a full food menu, daily 9:00-23:00, Október 6 utca 22, tel. 1/428-0134).

Near Andrássy Út and the Oktogon

Some of Budapest's best eateries are in this area—a hotbed for capable chefs and restaurateurs. For locations, see the map on page 659.

Franz Liszt Square (Liszt Ferenc Tér): Franz Liszt Square, a leafy park on the most interesting stretch of Andrássy út, boasts a stylish cluster of pricey, pretentious, yuppie restaurants, many with outdoor seating (lively on a summer evening; most places have main dishes around 3,000-5,000 Ft). My favorite Liszt Square eatery, **Menza** (the old communist word for "School Cafeteria"),

BUDAPEST

wins the "Best Design" award. Recycling 1970s-era furniture and an orange-brown-gray color scheme, it's a postmodern parody of an old communist café—half kitschy-retro, half contemporary-stylish. When old-timers come in here, they can only chuckle and say, "Yep. This is how it was."

With tasty and well-priced updated Hungarian and international cuisine, embroidered leather-bound menus, brisk but efficient service, breezy jazz on the soundtrack, and indoor or outdoor seating, it's a memorable spot (2,300-3,500-Ft main dishes, daily 10:00-24:00, halfway up Andrássy út at Liszt Ferenc tér 2, district VII, tel. 1/413-1482, www.menza.co.hu). If you like the Franz Liszt Square scene, you'll find a similar energy on Kertész utca beyond the end of the square, and in the "Broadway Quarter" near the Opera House (on Hajós utca and Nagymező utca).

Right on Andrássy út: **Klassz** is a trendy bistro with a similarly postmodern "eclectic-mod" aesthetic, both in its decor and its food. Serving surprisingly affordable international/nouvelle cuisine with Hungarian flair, it's a favorite among Budapest's value-seeking foodies (1,900-4,600-Ft main dishes, daily 11:30-22:30, Andrássy út 41, district VI, between M1: Opera and M1: Oktogon, no reservations possible).

In the "Broadway Quarter": **Pesti Disznó** ("Pest Pig"), set right along the liveliest stretch of theaters in town, is dedicated to serving delicious and surprisingly affordable food that celebrates Hungarian pork: the prized hairy pig called *mangalica*. The menu ranges from well-executed Hungarian classics to international fare to creative fusion dishes—like a *mangalica* hamburger. While the interior, with tall tables surrounding the open kitchen, is fine, I'd rather sit out under the red-and-white striped awnings facing the bright lights of Budapest's theater scene (2,000-3,500-Ft main dishes, daily 11:00-24:00, Nagymező 19, tel. 1/951-4061).

On the Great Boulevard: **Bock Bisztró,** run by a prominent Hungarian vintner from Villány, offers traditional Hungarian staples presented with modern flourish—almost "deconstructed" but still recognizable. The ambience is that of an unpretentious wine bar, with cork-filled tables. Pricey and well-regarded, with 250 different wines on the menu (including 60 by the glass), it's a good opportunity to sample food and wine from around the country. The service can be a bit stuffy, but the food lives up to its reputation. Reservations are essential (3,700-4,700-Ft main dishes, Mon-Sat 12:00-24:00, closed Sun, in the Corinthia Grand Royal Hotel, a couple of blocks west of the Oktogon on the Great Boulevard,

Erzsébet körút 43, district VII, M1: Oktogon, right by Király utca stop on trams #4 and #6, tel. 1/321-0340, http://bockbisztropest. hu).

On Nagymező utca: **Két Szerecsen** ("Two Saracens"), named for a historic coffee shop at this location a century ago that a trader filled with exotic goods, features eclectic and well-executed international cuisine—including Mediterranean and Asian. With good indoor and outdoor seating, reasonable prices, and relatively small portions, it's a reliable choice (1,600-2,000-Ft pastas and salads, 2,200-3,800-Ft main dishes, daily 9:00-24:00, a block off Andrássy út at Nagymező utca 14, district VI, M1: Opera, tel. 1/343-1984).

Italian: **Millennium da Pippo,** run by a Sicilian who speaks only Italian, greets you with a robust *"Buona sera!"* A neighborhood favorite for pasta and pizza, it's a handy choice near the House of Terror (1,900-2,800-Ft pizza and pastas, daily 12:00-24:00, Andrássy út 76, district VI, M1: Vörösmarty utca, tel. 1/374-0880).

Indian: Hungarians seem to have an affinity for Indian cuisines, which, like Hungarian cuisine, smooth together powerful spices. **Shalimar**'s high-ceilinged, nondescript dining room hides in a dreary neighborhood two blocks beyond the end of Franz Liszt Square. Everything about this place is unexceptional...except the food, which is my favorite for a break from pork and kraut. I can never resist the *murg makhani*...and I'm never disappointed (1,600-3,000-Ft main dishes, half-portions 40 percent less, daily 11:30-16:00 & 18:00-23:00, Dob utca 33, district VII, between M1: Oktogon and M2: Blaha Lujza tér, tel. 1/352-0305).

In the Jewish Quarter and "Ruin Pub" Nightlife Zone

Along with the rise of "ruin pubs" (see page 650), Budapest's Jewish Quarter has seen the arrival of several good restaurants in recent years. Some of these feature Jewish food (either kosher or updated); others are more eclectic, catering to a younger clientele. As this is a fast-emerging scene, you could just explore here. The following are some reliably good options. For locations, see the map on page 663.

Macesz Huszár is a grandma's-dining-room-cozy corner restaurant serving traditional Jewish recipes with modern attention to ingredients and technique. It's a good value and has quickly gained a loyal following, so reserve ahead (2,300-3,500-Ft main courses, daily 11:30-24:00, Dob utca 26, tel. 1/787-6164, www. maceszhuszar.hu).

Kőleves ("Stone Soup") runs a ruin pub garden, but their restaurant feels upscale and put-together without being stuffy. The eclectic, international menu includes several Jewish (though not kosher) dishes. This is a good place to try if Macesz Huszár (listed above) is full (2,000-3,600-Ft main dishes, daily 12:00-24:00, Kazinczy utca 41, mobile 0620-213-5999).

Soul Food is a casual Cajun and creole-inspired eatery run by Attila, who's a well-traveled singer by profession and chef by passion. It feels like a creative college dive: Create your own rice or noodle bowl, or order a sandwich or burger (1,300-1,800-Ft meals, daily 12:00-23:00, later on weekends, takeaway also available, Kazinczy utca 32, mobile 0670-313-8804).

In City Park

I wouldn't go out of my way to eat in City Park, but if you're enjoying a day here and would like a scenic meal, Robinson is a good option. For the location, see the map on page 609.

Robinson, stranded on an island in City Park's lake, is a hip, playful, mellow theme restaurant. With island-castaway ambience and more outdoor seating than indoor, it's made to order for lazing away a sunny afternoon at the park. The terrace and elegant, glassed-in dining room feature pricey international and Hungarian cuisine, and upstairs is a swanky steak house. In good weather, I'd come here for the terrace, to just sip a coffee or have a slice of cake (3,500-Ft pastas, 4,000-5,000-Ft main dishes, daily 11:00-17:00 & 18:00-23:00, reserve ahead and ask for lakefront seating, Városligeti tó, district XIV, M1: Hősök tere, tel. 1/422-0222).

For something quicker and more casual, closer to the end of the lake, look for the **BRGR** burger stand.

IN BUDA

Eateries on Castle Hill are generally overpriced and touristy—as with Váci utca, locals never eat here. The Víziváros ("Water Town") neighborhood, between the castle and the river, is a bit better. Even if sleeping in Buda, try to dine in Pest—that's where you'll find the city's best restaurants. All of the restaurants listed here (except Szent Jupát) are in district I. For locations, see the map on page 668.

Castle Hill

If you must eat atop Castle Hill, and just want a quick bite, visit the handy, affordable **CBA** grocery store (Mon-Fri 7:00-20:00, Sat 8:00-20:00, Sun 9:00-18:00).

For coffee and cakes, try the historic **Ruszwurm** (described later, under "Budapest's Café Culture"). If you'd rather have a meal—and don't want to head down to Víziváros—try the following choices:

Vár Bistro is a convenient, affordable cafeteria that makes for an easy and quick way to grab a meal between sightseeing; best of all, it has delightful outdoor seating overlooking a pretty park (1,000-2,500-Ft main dishes, 1,300-Ft "tourist menu" main dish and soup combo available at lunch, open daily 8:00-20:00, Dísz tér 8, mobile 0630-237-0039).

21 Magyar Vendéglő ("21 Hungarian Kitchen") features traditional Hungarian fare that's updated for the 21st century (hence the name). While the mod interior is pleasant, it's also fun to sit out on pretty Fortuna utca (near the north end of the hill). Most restaurants on Castle Hill are overpriced, and this is no exception—but the quality is also good. This is a rare castle-zone eatery that really takes pride in its food rather than being a crank-'em-out tourism machine (2,300-3,800-Ft light meals, 3,500-5,400-Ft bigger meals, chalkboard specials, daily 11:00-24:00, Fortuna utca 21, tel. 1/202-2113).

Baltazár, near the ruins of St. Mary Magdalene Church (a few short blocks from the main sights), is singlehandedly trying to inject some youthful liveliness into the staid, sleepy north end of Castle Hill. It's a fun choice, with bright, brash decor, pleasant outdoor seating, and a wood-fired charcoal grill that churns out smoky dishes. They also have an inviting beer garden just up the street, under the church tower (2,700-3,800-Ft main dishes, daily 7:30-24:00, Országház utca 31, tel. 1/300-7050).

Batthyány Tér and Nearby

This bustling square—the transportation hub for Víziváros—is overlooked by a recently renovated, late-19th-century market hall (today housing a big Spar supermarket and various shops). Several worthwhile, affordable eateries—nothing fancy, just practical—cluster around this square. Survey your options before settling in.

Nagyi Palacsintázója ("Granny's Pancakes")—just to the right of the market hall entrance—serves up cheap and tasty crêpes *(palacsinta)* to a local crowd (200-400-Ft sweet or savory small crêpes—order more than one for a filling meal, ask for English menu, open 24 hours daily, Batthyány tér 5).

As you face the market hall, go up the street that runs along its left side (Markovits Iván utca) to reach more good eateries: At the end of the block on the right is **Édeni Végan,** a self-service, point-and-shoot vegetarian cafeteria (main dishes less than 1,000 Ft, daily 8:00-20:00, tel. 1/375-7575). And tucked behind the market hall is **Bratwursthäusle/Kolbászda,** a fun little beer hall/beer garden with Bavarian specialties and blue-and-white checkerboard decor to match. Sit outside, or in the woody interior (900-1,200-Ft sausages, daily 11:00-23:00, Gyorskocsi utca 6, tel. 1/225-3674).

Fine Dining near Batthyány Tér: **Csalogány 26** is a stylish, upscale bistro a few short blocks from Batthyány tér in an otherwise dull urban neighborhood. Its modern international cuisine, served in a classy contemporary dining room, has earned it raves as one of the best eateries in this part of town. You can order à la carte (2,600-5,000-Ft main dishes), or go for one of their fixed-price *menus:* 9,000 Ft/four courses, 13,000 Ft/eight courses (Tue-Sat 12:00-15:00 & 19:00-22:00, closed Sun-Mon, Csalogány utca 26, tel. 1/201-7892, www.csalogany26.hu).

SNACKS AND LIGHT MEALS

A popular snack is *lángos*—a savory deep-fried doughnut (similar to an elephant ear or Native American fry bread). Sold at stands on the street, the most typical versions are spread with cheese and sour cream, and sometimes topped with garlic. Some restaurants serve a fancier version (often with meat) as an entrée. The Lángos stand upstairs in the Great Market Hall is a local favorite (see page 672).

For quick, inexpensive, and very local grub, head for the chain called **Főzelékfaló Ételbár** (roughly, "Soup Slurper Eating Bar"). This self-service cafeteria dishes up simple fare to businesspeople on their lunch break. *Főzelék,* a simple soup that's thickened with roux (wheat flour mixed into lard or butter) and can be supplemented with various vegetables, is a staple of Hungarian home cooking. Go to the counter, choose your *főzelék* soup (various flavors, 400 Ft), then choose from a variety of basic meat dishes (chicken, pork, meatballs, and more for 500-1,000 Ft apiece; some English spoken, but pointing also works). A filling meal here typically runs 1,000-2,000 Ft. Because of the limited seating, most people get their grub to go (though the location near Andrássy út has fine outdoor tables). There are two locations in central Pest: One is just off Andrássy út in the "Broadway Quarter" (Mon-Fri 9:00-21:00, Sat 10:00-21:00, Sun 11:00-18:00, Nagymező utca 22, a block north of the Opera House, district VI, M1: Opera); the other is in a big building along the busy highway at Ferenciek tere (Mon-Fri 10:00-21:30, Sat 12:00-20:00, closed Sun, Kossuth Lajos utca 2A, district V, M3: Ferenciek tere).

Hummus Bar, while not authentically Hungarian, is a popular expat-run chain that offers cheap Middle Eastern vegetarian meals to grateful backpackers and young locals. Their falafel is tasty (800-1,300 Ft for a pita-wrapped sandwich, combination plates for 1,000-1,900 Ft). You can either eat in or get it to go. They have several locations: in the Town Center on Egyetem tér at Kecskeméti utca 1, district V, M3/M4: Kálvin tér; in Leopold Town at Alkotmány utca 20, district V, M2: Kossuth tér; between Liberty Square and St. István Square at Október 6 utca 19; and in the ruin pub district at the corner of Síp and Wesselényi. All are open roughly the same hours (Mon-Fri 10:00-22:00, Sat-Sun 12:00-22:00).

All around town, you'll see cheery **open-face sandwich**

shops, each displaying a dozen or so tempting little treats in its front window—thin slices of bread piled with egg salad, veggies, cold cuts, cream spreads, cheese, salmon, affordable caviar, or other toppings for 180-300 Ft apiece. There's no English menu—just point at what looks good. Two sandwiches and a drink make a quick and healthy meal for about $5 (they'll also box things to go for a classy picnic). The selection wanes as the day goes on, making these a better option for lunch or a light, early dinner. Of the various chains, **Duran Szendvics** is the dominant operation, with a convenient location near the start of Andrássy út (Mon-Fri 8:00-19:00, Sat 8:00-15:00, Sun 8:00-12:00, Bajcsy-Zsilinszky út 7, district VII, M1: Bajcsy-Zsilinszky út, tel. 1/267-9624) and another branch in Leopold Town (Mon-Fri 8:00-17:00, Sat 9:00-13:00, closed Sun, Október 6 utca 15, district V, M3: Arany János utca).

For a fast snack, you'll see **Fornetti** stands everywhere (on street corners and Metró underpasses). This Hungary-based chain, which is becoming wildly popular across Central and Eastern Europe, sells small, tasty, freshly baked phyllo dough-based pastries by weight. They have both sweet and savory varieties. For a bite on the go, just point to what you want and hold your fingers up for how many you'd like of each type (around 30 Ft apiece). If you smell something heavenly in the Metró passages...it's probably a Fornetti.

BUDAPEST'S CAFÉ CULTURE

In the late 19th century, a vibrant café culture boomed here, just as it did in Vienna and Paris. The *kávéház* ("coffeehouse") was a local institution. By 1900, Budapest had more than 600 cafés. In this crowded and fast-growing cityscape, a neighborhood café allowed urbanites to escape their tiny flats (or get a jolt of caffeine to power them through a 12-hour workday). Local people (many who'd moved to the city from the countryside) didn't want to pay to heat their homes during the day. So instead, for the price of a cup of coffee, they could come to a café to enjoy warmth, companionship, and loaner newspapers.

Realizing that these neighborhood living rooms were breeding grounds for dissidents, the communists closed the cafés or converted them into *eszpresszó*s (with uncomfortable stools instead of easy chairs) or *bisztró*s (stand-up fast-food joints with no chairs at all). Today, nostalgia is bringing back the *kávéház* culture—both as a place to get coffee and food, and as a social institution. While some serve only coffee and cakes, most serve light meals, and some serve full meals (as noted below).

On the Great Boulevard: **New York Café** makes the others listed here look like Starbucks. Originally built in 1894 as part of the "New York Palace" (and it really is palatial), this fanciful,

BUDAPEST

over-the-top explosion of Neo-
Baroque and Neo-Renaissance
epitomizes the "mix and match,
but plenty of everything" Historicist style of the day. In the
early 20th century, artists, writers, and musicians came here to
sip overpriced coffee and bask
in opulence. After decades of

neglect, Italian investors completely restored it in 2006, and now
it once again welcomes guests. You'll be met at the door and asked
if you want a table; they'll typically let you gape at the inside for
a few minutes if you ask nicely, but only paying customers may
take photos. The food is drastically overpriced and disappointing—don't bother eating a meal here, but do consider coffee and
cake. If you're up for a coffee break, this place might actually be
worth an $8 cup of coffee. Be sure to read the fun history in the
menu (4,000-6,500-Ft main dishes, 1,000-1,500-Ft coffee and hot
chocolate drinks, 1,800-2,300-Ft desserts). While it's a few blocks
beyond the tourist zone, it's worth the trip out here for the ultimate in turn-of-the-20th-century Budapest elegance (daily 9:00-
24:00, inside the Boscolo Hotel at Erzsébet körút 9, district VII,
tel. 1/886-6167). Take the M2/red Metró line to Blaha Lujza tér,
and exit toward *Erzsébet körút* and walk a block. You can also take
tram #4 or #6 from the Oktogon (at Andrássy út) around the Great
Boulevard to the Wesselényi utca stop. For location, see the color
map at the front of this book.

Two blocks up from Váci utca: **Gerlóczy Café**, listed as a restaurant on page 672, nicely recaptures Budapest's early-1900s
ambience, with loaner newspapers on racks and a management
that encourages loitering. Nearby, another good choice for coffee and cakes is the similarly old-fashioned **Centrál Kávéház**.
While the food here is pricey and hit-or-miss (don't bother having
a meal), it has an enjoyable and atmospheric two-story interior and
a handy central location (daily 8:00-23:00, Károlyi Mihály utca 9,
district V, M3: Ferenciek tere, tel. 1/266-2110). For location, see
the map on page 663.

Near Ferenciek tere: **Jégbüfé** is where Pest urbanites get their
quick, cheap, stand-at-a-counter fix of coffee and cakes. And for
those feeling nostalgic for the communist days, little has changed
at this typical *bisztró*. First, choose what you want at the counter.
Then explain it to the cashier across the aisle. Finally, take your
receipt back to the appropriate part of the counter (figure out the
four different zones: coffee, soft drinks, ice cream, cakes), trade
your receipt for your goodie, go to the bar, and enjoy it standing up (cakes for under 400 Ft, Mon-Sat 7:00-21:30, Wed until

20:30, Sun 8:00-21:30, Ferenciek tere 10, district V, M3: Ferenciek tere—for location, see the map on page 663). Not sure what to get? Here are some traditional Hungarian favorites: *krémes* (KRAY-mesh) is custard sandwiched between delicate wafers. *Rákóczi turós* (RAH-koht-see TOO-rohsh) is a cake of sweet cottage cheese (a Hungarian dessert staple) with jam on top. *Dobos torta* (DOH-bohsh TOR-taw) has alternating layers of chocolate and vanilla cake topped with caramelized sugar. *Somlói galuska* (SHOM-lowee GAW-losh-kaw) is made of pieces of moist sponge cake soaked in rum and drizzled with chocolate. And *flódni* (FLOHD-nee)—in the pie section (in this area, you can pay directly at the counter)—has layers of nut paste and poppy seeds...another Hungarian dessert staple. For a simpler procedure, get in line at the waffle *(gofry)* window facing the street, where you can pay cash for a steaming-hot Belgian waffle with toppings (window open daily 10:00-18:00).

On Andrássy út, near the Opera House: Three fine and very different cafés are within a block of the Opera (for locations, see

the map on page 659). The **Alexandra** book-store—in the Lotz Hall of the newly refurbished Párisi Nagy Áruház (Paris Department Store)—hides a spectacular gilded café that immerses you in turn-of-the-century splendor (walk straight in and go up the escalator). Because this prominent local chain encourages loitering, the service here is no-pressure, and the drinks and desserts are bargain-priced (600-1,000-Ft coffee drinks and cakes). Rounding out this café's appeal are the occasional live piano music, periodic evening concerts, and mirrors at either end that make the hall seem to go on forever (daily 10:00-22:00, can close unexpectedly for private events, Andrássy út 39, district VI, M1: Opera, tel. 1/461-5835). **Callas** features ideal outdoor seating facing the Opera House and one of the finest Art Nouveau interiors in town, with gorgeous *Jugendstil* chandeliers. While their full meals are pricey (4,000-5,000 Ft), this is a wonderful spot on Andrássy út for a coffee break, a tasty dessert, or breakfast (ham and eggs plus coffee for around 2,000 Ft, 800-Ft pastries; daily 10:00-24:00, Andrássy út 20, district VI, M1: Opera, tel. 1/354-0954). Across the street and a block toward the Oktogon, **Művész Kávéház** ("Artists Coffee House") is a classic café with 19th-century elegance, a hoity-toity high-ceilinged interior, snobby staff, and fine outdoor seating on Andrássy út. True to its name, this institution in the "Broadway Quarter" is a favorite after-rehearsal haunt of famous (to Hungarians) actors and musicians (700-900 Ft cakes, 1,500-Ft sandwiches, 3,400-Ft main dishes, 900-1,600-Ft breakfasts,

Mon-Sat 9:00-22:00, Sun 10:00-22:00, Andrássy út 29, district VI, M1: Opera, tel. 1/333-2116).

In Buda, atop Castle Hill: **Ruszwurm** lays claim to being Budapest's oldest café (since 1827). Tiny but classy, with old-style Biedermeier furnishings and fine sidewalk seating, it carries on its venerable reputation with pride. Its dead-central location—a block in front of Matthias Church in the heart of the castle district—means that it has become a popular tourist spot (though it remains dear to locals' hearts). Look for gussied-up locals chatting here after the 10:00 Sunday-morning Mass at the church (700-Ft coffees, 400-600-Ft desserts, daily 10:00-19:00, Szentháromság utca 7, district I, for location see map on page 668, tel. 1/375-5284).

Budapest Connections

BY TRAIN

Hungary's train network is run by MÁV (Magyar Államvasutak). From centrally located Budapest, train lines branch out across Hungary. Most connections between outlying cities aren't direct—you often end up having to go back through Budapest. While Hungary's trains are generally good, many are old and fairly slow; major routes (especially those connecting to international destinations such as Bratislava or Vienna) use faster, newer, and slightly more expensive InterCity trains (marked with an "IC" or a boxed "R" on schedules). To ride an InterCity train, you must pay extra for a required reservation (which is printed on a separate ticket). Warning: Trains can be very crowded on weekends, when it's smart to book a reservation for any train trip.

For timetables, the first place to check is Germany's excellent all-Europe site, www.bahn.com. You can also check Hungary's timetable website at http://elvira.mav-start.hu. For general rail information in Hungary, call 0640-494-949 (from outside Hungary, dial +36-1-444-4499).

It's best to buy your ticket in advance at the MÁV ticket office in downtown Pest (see page 562). Be aware that ticket lines can be very long at the train stations; if you're buying a ticket there, it's smart to arrive with plenty of time to spare.

Remember that Budapest has three major train stations (*pályaudvar,* abbreviated *pu.*): Keleti ("Eastern") Station, Nyugati ("Western") Station, and Déli ("Southern") Station. The station used by a particular train can change from year to year. Before departing from Budapest, it's essential to carefully confirm which station your train leaves from.

From Budapest by Train to: Eger (every 2 hours direct, 2 hours, more with transfer in Füzesabony, usually from Budapest's Keleti/Eastern Station), **Pécs** (every 2 hours direct,

3 hours; a few more connections possible with transfer at suburban Budapest-Kelenföld station), **Sopron** (6/day direct, 3 hours, more with transfer in Győr), **Visegrád** (trains arrive at Nagymaros-Visegrád station, across the river—take shuttle boat to Visegrád; hourly, 50 minutes, usually from Budapest's Nyugati/Western Station), **Esztergom** (hourly, 1.5 hours, usually from Budapest's Nyugati/Western Station, may be discontinued due to construction—if so, take the bus, described on page 709), **Kecskemét** (hourly, 1.5 hours), **Szeged** (hourly, 2.5 hours), **Bratislava** (that's **Pozsony** in Hungarian, 7/day direct, 2.75 hours; more with transfers), **Vienna** (that's **Bécs** in Hungarian, every 2 hours direct on express Railjet, 3 hours; more with transfers), **Prague** (3/day direct, 7 hours, more with transfers in Győr and/or Vienna; plus 1 night train/day, 8 hours), **Kraków** (2/day, 9.5-11 hours, transfer in Katowice, Poland, and Břeclav, Czech Republic; plus 1 night train, 10.5 hours; faster by infrequent Orange Ways bus: 5/week, 7 hours, www.orangeways.com), **Zagreb** (2/day direct, 6-7 hours), **Ljubljana** (1/day direct, 9 hours; additional options with transfers, 8-10 hours, no convenient night train), **Munich** (5/day by express Railjet, 7.5 hours, additional options with transfers; 1 direct night train/day, 9 hours), and **Berlin** (1/day direct, 12 hours; 1 night train/day, 13 hours).

BY BUS

Buses can be relatively inexpensive, but are typically slower and less convenient than trains. The only bus you you're likely to take is the one to **Eger** (2/hour, 2 hours), which leaves from the Stadionok bus station (at the M2/Métró red line stop of the same name). You can search bus schedules at the (Hungarian-only) website www.menetrendek.hu (click on "VOLÁN Menetrend").

BY PLANE

For information about Budapest's Liszt Ferenc Airport, see "Arrival in Budapest—By Plane" on page 558.

ROUTE TIPS FOR DRIVERS

For pointers on driving into (and parking in) Budapest, see "Arrival in Budapest—By Car" on page 558. Remember, to use Hungary's expressways, you'll need to buy a toll sticker (see page 1338). To get out of town, here are some pointers.

To Eger and Other Points East: Head out of the city center on Andrássy út, circling behind Heroes' Square to access Kós Károly sétány through the middle of City Park. You'll pass Széchenyi Baths on the left, then (exiting the park) go over the Hungária körút ring road, before getting on M-3. This expressway zips you conveniently to Eger (exit #114 for Füzesabony; go north on road 33, then follow road 3, then road 25 into Eger).

To Bratislava, Vienna, and Other Points West: From central Pest, head over the Danube on the white, modern Elisabeth Bridge (Erzsébet híd). Once in Buda, the road becomes Hegyalja út; simply follow *Wien* signs to get on M-1.

BY BOAT

In the summer, Mahart runs high-speed hydrofoils up the Danube to **Vienna.** It's not particularly scenic, and it's slower than the train, but it's a fun alternative for nautical types. The boat leaves Budapest at 9:00 and arrives in Vienna at 15:30; on the return trip, a boat leaves from Vienna at 9:00 and reaches Budapest at 14:30 (May-late Sept only, departs from Budapest Tue, Thu, and Sat; from Vienna Wed, Fri, and Sun). The trip costs €99 one-way between Budapest and Vienna (or €109 the other direction). To confirm times and prices, and to buy tickets, contact Mahart in Budapest (tel. 1/484-4010, www.mahartpassnave.hu) or DDSG Blue Danube in Vienna (Austrian tel. 01/58880, www.ddsg-blue-danube.at).

BUDAPEST

EGER

Eger (EH-gehr) is a county-seat town in northern Hungary, with about 60,000 people and a thriving teacher-training college. While you've probably never heard of Eger, the town has various claims to fame among Hungarians. Its powerful bishops have graced it with gorgeous churches. It has some of the best and most beloved spas in this hot-water-crazy country (including the excellent Salt Hill Thermal Spa in the nearby countryside). And, perhaps most of all, Eger makes Hungarians proud as the town that, against all odds, successfully held off the Ottoman advance into Europe in 1552. This stirring history makes Eger the mecca of Hungarian school field trips. If the town is known internationally for anything, it's for the surrounding wine region (its best-known red wine is Bull's Blood, or Egri Bikavér).

And yet, refreshingly, enchanting Eger remains mostly off the

tourist trail. Egerites go about their daily routines amidst lovely Baroque buildings, watched over by one of Hungary's most important castles. Everything in Eger is painted with vibrant colors, and even the communist apartment blocks seem quaint. The sights are few but fun, the ambience is great, and strolling is a must. It all comes together to make Eger an ideal introduction to small-town Hungary.

PLANNING YOUR TIME

Mellow Eger is a great side-trip from Budapest. It's doable round-trip in a single day (about two hours by train or bus each way), but it's much more satisfying and relaxing to spend the night.

A perfect day in Eger begins with a browse through the very local-feeling market and a low-key ramble on the castle ramparts. Then head to the college building called the Lyceum to visit the library and astronomy museum, and climb up to the thrillingly low-tech camera obscura. Take in the midday organ concert in the cathedral across the street from the Lyceum (mid-May-mid-Oct only). In the afternoon, unwind on the square or, better yet, at a thermal bath (in Eger, or at the Salt Hill Thermal Spa in nearby Egerszalók). If you need more to do, consider a drive into the countryside (including visits to local vintners—get details at TI). Round out your day with dinner on Little Dobó Square, or a visit to Eger's touristy wine caves in the Sirens' Valley.

In July and August (when Hungarians prefer to go to Lake Balaton), Eger is busy with international visitors; in September and October, around the wine harvest, most of the tourists are Hungarians.

Orientation to Eger

Eger Castle sits at the top of the town, hovering over Dobó Square (Dobó István tér). This main square is divided in half by Eger Creek, which bisects the town. Two blocks west of Dobó Square is the main pedestrian drag, Széchenyi utca, where you'll find the Lyceum and the cathedral. A few blocks due south from the castle (along Eger Creek) is Eger's thermal baths complex.

TOURIST INFORMATION

Eger's TI (TourInform) offers a town map, as well as piles of brochures about the city and region. They can help you find a room and are eager to answer your questions (mid-June-Aug Mon-Fri 9:00-18:00, Sat-Sun 9:00-13:00; Sept-mid-June Mon-Fri 8:00-16:00, closed Sat-Sun—except open Sat 8:00-16:00 in Sept-Oct; Bajcsy-Zsilinszky utca 9, tel. 36/517-715, www.eger.hu).

ARRIVAL IN EGER

By Train: Eger's tiny train station is a 20-minute walk south of the center. The baggage-deposit desk is out along the platform by track 1, between the WCs (daily 7:00-19:00, attendant often waits in the adjacent *büfé*). For those in need of Hungarian cash, the closest ATM is at the Spar grocery store just up the street (turn left out of station, walk about 100 yards, and look for red-and-white supermarket on your right; the ATM is next to the main door, around front).

Eger ↑
To Firefighters Museum

- ❶ Imola Udvarház Rooms
- ❷ Senator Ház Hotel & Rest.
- ❸ Offi Ház Hotel
- ❹ Szent János Hotel
- ❺ Dobó Vendégház Rooms
- ❻ Imola Hostel
- ❼ HBH Restaurant
- ❽ Palacsintavár Rest.
- ❾ Szantofer Vendéglő Rest.
- ❿ Elefanto
- ⓫ Dobós Cukrászda Pastries
- ⓬ Sárvári Cukrászda Pastries
- ⓭ Kürtőskalács Window
- ⓮ Bikavér Borház Wine Shop
- ⓯ Kopcsik Marzipan Museum
- ⓰ Hist. Exhibition of Weapons
- ⓱ Palóc Folklore Museum
- ⓲ Town Under the Town
- ⓳ Castle Entrance

EGER

Taxis generally wait out front to take new arrivals into town (1,000-1,200 Ft). Even in little Eger, it's always best to take a taxi marked with a company name and number.

To catch the **bus** toward the center, go a block straight out of the station. Buses #11, #12, and #14 cut about 10 minutes off the walk into town (tickets are 300 Ft from driver or 240 Ft at train station newsstand facing track 1—ask for *helyijárat buszjegy*). Get off the bus when you reach the big, yellow cathedral.

To **walk** all the way, leave the station straight ahead, walk one block, take the hard right turn with the road, and then continue straight (on busy Deák Ferenc utca) about 10 minutes until you run into the cathedral. With your back to the cathedral entry, the main square is two blocks ahead of you, then a block to the left.

By Car: In this small town, most hotels will provide parking or help you find a lot. For a short visit, the most central lots are behind the department store on Dobó Square, or in the square surrounding the Lyceum.

GETTING AROUND EGER

Everything of interest in Eger is within walking distance. But a taxi can be helpful to reach outlying sights, including the Sirens' Valley wine caves and the Salt Hill Thermal Spa in Egerszalók (taxi meter starts at 310 Ft, then around 250 Ft/km; try City Taxi, tel. 36/555-555, toll-free tel. 0680-622-622).

HELPFUL HINTS

Blue Monday: Note that the castle museums and the Kepes Institute are closed on Mondays, and the Lyceum is open on Monday only from May to August. But even on Mondays you can visit the cathedral (and enjoy its organ concert), swim in the thermal bath, explore the market, see the castle grounds, and enjoy the local wine.

Organ Concert: Daily from mid-May to mid-October, Hungary's second-biggest organ booms out a glorious 30-minute concert in the cathedral (800 Ft, Mon-Sat at 11:30, Sun at 12:30).

Local Guide: The TI can arrange a private guide to give you a tour of town (8,000 Ft/hour, tel. 36/517-715, eger@tourinform.hu).

Tourist Train: A variety of hokey little tourist trains leave the main square regularly (at least at the top of each hour, and often other times when it's busy). These trains do a circuit around town, then head out to the Sirens' Valley wine caves (800 Ft, 50-minute trip).

Sights in Eger

DOBÓ SQUARE AND DOBÓ UTCA
▲▲Dobó Square (Dobó István Tér)

Dobó Square is the heart of Eger. In most towns this striking, the main square is packed with postcard stalls and other tourist traps. Refreshingly, Eger's square seems mostly packed with Egerites. Ringed by pretty Baroque buildings and watched over by Eger's historic castle, this square is one of the most pleasant spots in Hungary.

István Dobó and the Siege of Eger

In the 16th century, Ottoman invaders swept into Hungary. They easily defeated a Hungarian army—in just two hours—at the Battle of Mohács in 1526. When Buda and Pest fell to the Ottomans in 1541, all of Europe looked to Eger as the last line of defense. István Dobó and his second-in-command, István Mekcsey, were put in charge of Eger's forces. They prepared the castle (which still overlooks the square) for a siege and waited.

On September 11, 1552—after a summer spent conquering more than 30 other Hungarian fortresses on their march northward—40,000 Ottomans arrived in Eger. Only about 2,000 Egerites (soldiers, their wives, and their children) remained to protect their town. The Ottomans expected an easy victory, but the siege dragged on for 39 days. Eger's soldiers fought valiantly, and the women of Eger also joined the fray, pouring hot tar down on the Ottomans...everyone pitched in. A Hungarian officer named Gergely Bornemissza, sent to reinforce the people of Eger, startled the Ottomans with all manner of clever and deadly explosives. One of his brilliant inventions was a "fire wheel"—a barrel of gunpowder studded with smaller jars of explosives, which they'd light and send rolling downhill to wreak havoc until the final, deadly explosion. Ultimately, the Ottomans left in shame, Eger was saved, and Dobó was a national hero.

The unfortunate epilogue: The Ottomans came back in 1596 and, this time, succeeded in conquering an Eger Castle guarded by unmotivated mercenaries. The Ottomans sacked the town and then controlled the region for close to a century.

In 1897, a castle archaeologist named Géza Gárdonyi moved from Budapest to Eger, where tales of the siege captured his imagination. Gárdonyi wrote a book about István Dobó and the 1552 Siege of Eger called *Egri Csillagok* ("Stars of Eger," translated into English as *Eclipse of the Crescent Moon*, available at local bookstores and souvenir stands). The book—a favorite of many Hungarians—is taught in schools, keeping the legend of Eger's heroes alive today.

The statue in the middle is **István Dobó** (EESHT-vahn DOH-boh), the square's namesake and Eger's greatest hero, who defended the city—and all of Hungary—from an Ottoman invasion in 1552 (see his story in the sidebar). Next to Dobó is his co-commander, István Mekcsey. And right at their side is one of the brave women of Eger—depicted here throwing a pot down onto the attackers.

Dominating the square is the exquisitely photogenic **Minorite Church**—often said to be the most beautiful Baroque church in Hungary. The shabby interior is less interesting, but has some appealing details (free entry, daily 9:30-17:30). Notice that each of the hand-carved wooden pews has a different motif. Pay close attention to the side altars that flank the nave: The first set (left and right) are 3-D illustrations, painted to replicate the wood altars that burned in a fire; the next set are real. And, looking up at the faded ceiling frescoes, you'll see (in the second one from the entrance) the church's patron: St.

Anthony of Padua, who's preaching God's word to the fishes after the townspeople refused to hear him. The green, arcaded building to the right of the Minorite Church is the Town Hall, next to an old-fashioned pharmacy.

Use the square to orient yourself to the town. Behind the statue of Dobó is a bridge over the stream that bisects the city. Just before you reach that bridge, look to the left and you'll see the northernmost Ottoman **minaret** in Europe—once part of a mosque, it's now a tourist attraction. Across the bridge is the charming **Little Dobó Square** (Kis-Dobó tér), home to the town's best hotels, its outdoor dining zone, and a handy and atmospheric opportunity to sample local wines at the Bikavér Borház wine shop (see page 703). Hovering above Little Dobó Square is Eger Castle; to get there, hang a right at the Senator Ház Hotel and go up Dobó utca. (All of these places are described later in more detail.)

Now face the opposite direction, with the castle at your back. On your right is a handy supermarket (with an ATM by the door). At the bottom end of this square, various pedestrian shopping lanes lead straight ahead two short blocks to Eger's main "walking

EGER

street," Széchenyi utca (with the cathedral and the Lyceum at its left end).

▲Dobó Utca

This street, which leads from Little Dobó Square to the entrance of the castle, is lined with colorful shops and attractions. You'll encounter these sights in the following order from the main square (begin by heading up the street to the right of Senator Ház Hotel):

The **antique shop** (Régiségbolt, at #24) is worth a peek. If musty old things from the communist era—a painting of Lenin or a classic old radio—are cluttering your attic, you can sell them here.

The **wine-tasting courtyard** (#18) features a different local winery each week from May through October. Pop in to the brightly lit, vaulted tasting room in the back to try a glass (200-600 Ft/glass).

A few steps down Fazola Henrik (on the right), the **Historical Exhibition of Weapons** (Törteni Tárház) features centuries of Eger armaments: clubs, rifles, and everything in between (400 Ft, Tue-Sun 10:00-18:00, closed Mon, 300-Ft English book gives a full weapon-by-weapon tour).

The **Palóc Folklore Museum** (#12) displays a handful of traditional tools, textiles, ceramics, costumes, and pieces of furniture (200 Ft; open sporadically—likely May-Sept Tue-Sun 10:15-16:15, closed Oct-April and Mon year-round; no English information).

▲Eger Castle (Egri Vár)

The great St. István—Hungary's first Christian king—founded a church on this hill a thousand years ago. The church was destroyed

by Tatars in the 13th century, and this fortress was built to repel another attack. Most importantly, this castle is Hungary's Alamo, where István Dobó defended Eger from the Ottomans in 1552—as depicted in the relief just outside the entry gate. These days, it's usually crawling with field-tripping schoolchildren from all over the country. (Every Hungarian sixth grader reads *Eclipse of the Crescent Moon,* which thrillingly recounts the heroic siege of Eger.) For those of us who didn't grow up hearing the legend of István Dobó, the complex is hard to appreciate, and English information is sparse. Most visitors find that the most rewarding plan is simply to stroll up, wander the grounds, play "king of the castle" along the ramparts, and enjoy the sweeping views over Eger's rooftops.

Cost and Hours: A 700-Ft "walking ticket" gets you into

the castle grounds only; the 1,100-Ft ticket includes the big castle sights (history museum, art gallery, casements tour). The castle grounds are open daily (April-Aug 8:00-20:00, Sept until 19:00, March and Oct until 18:00, Nov-Feb until 17:00). The castle museums have shorter hours (April-Oct Tue-Sun 10:00-17:00, Nov-March Tue-Sun 10:00-16:00, closed Mon year-round).

Casements Tours: The underground casements and Heroes' Hall are only accessible by a one-hour tour in Hungarian (included in ticket price, tours depart frequently in summer, sporadically off-season).

Information: Tel. 36/312-744, www.egrivar.hu.

Getting There: To reach the castle from Dobó Square, cross the bridge toward Senator Ház Hotel, then jog right around the hotel, turning right onto Dobó utca (with its own set of attractions, described earlier). Take this street a few blocks until it swings down to the right; the ramp up to the castle is on your left.

Visiting the Castle: Buy your ticket at the lower gate, then hike up the entry ramp and through the inner gate into the main courtyard—with grassy fields, souvenir stands, and easy access to the ramparts. Straight ahead—through the corridor with the little information window—is a pink, Gothic-style courtyard, which contains two small museums. The **history museum** (in the top floor of the main building) is the best of its kind in town, with lots of artifacts and good English descriptions. The **picture gallery** (top floor of building to the left as you enter the courtyard) is worth a few minutes, with paintings giving you a look at traditional life in Hungary.

Exploring the **grounds,** you'll see the remains of a once-grand cathedral and a smaller rotunda dating from the days of St. István (10th or 11th century; at the far-right corner as you enter). The underground **casements** (tunnels through the castle walls, which include the Heroes' Hall with the symbolic grave of István Dobó) are accessible only by guided tour, but you can dip into the **dungeon** any time with the museum ticket (to the left as you enter).

Other Castle Sights: The castle hosts a few privately run exhibits (with sporadic hours and prices).

The **waxworks,** or "Panoptikum" (500 Ft, daily April-Oct 9:00-17:00, shorter hours off-season; at far-left corner as you enter), while kind of silly, is fun for kids or those who never really grew up. Think of it as a very low-tech, walk-through *Ottomans of the Caribbean.* You'll see a handful of eerily realistic heroes and villains from the siege of Eger (including István Dobó himself and the leader of the Ottomans sitting in his colorful tent). Notice the exaggerated Central Asian features of the Egerites—a reminder that the Magyars were more Asian than European. A visit to the waxworks lets you scramble through a segment of the tunnels that run inside the castle walls (a plus since it's not really worth it to wait around through the similar, Hungarian-language casements tour).

The *Eger 1552* **3-D movie** offers a fun little lesson in the town's history. Appropriately low-budget for this small town, the film's graphics are closer to a retro video game than a blockbuster, but it does a fine job of re-creating the medieval townscape. A second 3-D movie features a baby Tyrannosaurus rex (400 Ft for one movie, 600 Ft for both, 10 minutes each, English subtitles).

Additional sights include an **archery** exhibit (in summer, look for archers just to the right of the Gothic courtyard, and pay them for the chance to shoot old-fashioned bows and crossbows) and **temporary exhibits** in the ground floor of the Gothic courtyard. The castle also has a **café** and a **1552 Restaurant**.

ON SZÉCHENYI UTCA
▲▲Lyceum (Líceum)

In the mid-18th century, Bishop Károly Eszterházy wanted a university in Eger, but Habsburg Emperor Josef II refused to allow

it. Instead, Eszterházy built the most impressive teacher-training college on the planet and stocked it with the best books and astronomical equipment that money could buy. The Lyceum still trains local teachers (enrollment: about 2,000). The halls of the Lyceum are also roamed by tourists who have come to visit its classic old library and its astronomy museum, with a fascinating camera obscura. The library and museum are tucked away in the big, confusing building.

Cost and Hours: Library-800 Ft, museum-1,000 Ft; both open May-Aug daily 9:30-17:30; mid-March-April and Sept-Oct Tue-Sun 9:30-15:30, closed Mon; Nov-mid-March Tue-Sun 9:30-13:30, closed Mon; Eszterházy tér 1, at south end of Széchenyi utca at intersection with Kossuth utca, enter through main door across from cathedral and buy tickets just inside and to the left.

Visiting the Lyceum: First, visit the old-fashioned **library** one floor up (from the main entry hall, cut through the middle of the courtyard, go up the stairs to the next floor, and look for Room 223, marked *Bibliothek*—it's on the right side of the complex as you face it from the entrance). This library houses 60,000 books (here and in the two adjoining rooms, with several stacked two deep). Dr. Erzsébet Löffler and her staff have spent the last decade cataloging these books. This is no easy task, as they're in over 30 languages—from Thai to Tagalog—and are shelved according to size, rather than topic. Only one percent of the books are in Hungarian—but half of them are in Latin. The ticket-taker can give you an English information sheet highlighting the collection's most prized pieces. The shelves are adorned with golden seals depicting some

of the great minds of science, philosophy, and religion. Marvel at the gorgeous ceiling fresco, dating from 1778. To thank the patron of this museum, say *köszönöm* to the guy in the second row up, to the right of the podium (above the entry door, second from left, not wearing a hat)—that's Bishop Károly Eszterházy.

Turn right as you leave the library to find the staircase that leads up the **Astronomical Tower** (*Varázstorony*, follow signs several flights up) to the **Astronomical Museum.** Some dusty old stargazing instruments occupy one room, as well as a meridian line in the floor (a dot of sunlight dances along this line each day around noon). Across the hall is a fun, interactive **magic room,** where you can try out scientific experiments—such as using air pressure to make a ball levitate or sending a mini "hot-air balloon" up to the ceiling.

A few more flights up is the Lyceum's treasured **camera obscura**—one of just two originals surviving in Europe (the other is in Edinburgh). You'll enter a dark room around a big, bowl-like canvas, and the guide will fly you around the streets of Eger (presentations about 2/hour, maybe more when busy). Fun as it is today, this camera must have astonished viewers when it was built in 1776—well before anyone had seen "moving pictures." It's a bit of a huff to get up here (9 flights of stairs, 302 steps)—but the camera obscura, and the actual view of Eger from the outdoor terrace just outside, are worth it.

▲▲Eger Cathedral

Eger's 19th-century bishops peppered the city with beautiful buildings, including the second-biggest church in Hungary (after Esztergom's—see page 632). With a quirky, sumptuous, Baroque-feeling interior, Eger's cathedral is well worth a visit.

Cost and Hours: 300-Ft donation requested (but you must buy ticket if visiting before an organ concert, 11:00-12:00), open Mon-Sat 8:30-18:00, Sun 13:00-18:00. The cathedral is the big, can't-miss-it yellow building at Pyrker János tér 1, facing the start of Széchenyi utca.

Visiting the Cathedral: Eger Cathedral was built in the 1830s by an Austrian archbishop who had previously served in

Venice, and who thought Eger could use a little more class. The colonnaded Neoclassical **facade,** painted a pretty Habsburg yellow, boasts some fine Italian sculpture. As you walk up the main stairs, you'll pass saints István and László—Hungary's first two Christian kings—and then the apostles Peter and Paul.

Enter the cathedral and walk to the first collection box, near the start of the nave. Then, turning back to face the door, look up at the ornate **ceiling fresco:** On the left, it shows Hungarians in traditional dress; and on the right, the country's most important historical figures. At the bottom, you see this cathedral, celestially connected with St. Peter's in Rome (opposite). This symbol of devotion to the Vatican was a brave state-

ment when it was painted in 1950. The communists were closing churches in other small Hungarian towns, but the Eger archbishop had enough clout to keep this one open.

Continue to the transept, stopping directly underneath the main dome. The **stained-glass windows** decorating the north and south transepts were donated to the cathedral by a rich Austrian couple to commemorate the 1,000th anniversary of Hungary's conversion to Christianity—notice the dates 1000 (when St. István converted the Magyars to Christianity) and 2000.

As you leave, notice the enormous **organ**—Hungary's second-largest—above the door. In the summer, try to catch one of the cathedral's daily half-hour organ concerts (800 Ft, mid-May–mid-Oct Mon-Sat at 11:30, Sun at 12:30, no concerts off-season).

Near the back-right corner, look for the statue of **Szent Rita,** a local favorite; the votive plaques that say *köszönöm* and *hálából* are offering "thanks" and "gratitude" for prayers answered.

Nearby: If you walk up Széchenyi utca from here, you'll see the fancy **Archbishop's Palace** on your left—still home to Eger's archbishop.

Just to the right of the steps leading up to the cathedral is the entrance to the **Town Under the Town** (Város a Város Alatt), a 45-minute guided tour of the archbishop's former wine-cellar network (950 Ft, generally departs at the top of each hour—schedule posted at door, 5-person minimum, you'll get a little English sprinkled in with the Hungarian, daily in summer 10:00-17:00, shorter hours off-season, last tour departs one hour before closing, tel. 20/961-4019, www.varosavarosalatt.hu).

NORTH OF DOBÓ SQUARE
▲Market Hall (Piaccsarnok)
Wandering Eger's big indoor market will give you a taste of local life—and maybe some samples of local food, too. This ramshackle hall is a totally untouristy scene, with ugly plastic tubs piled high with an abundance of fresh, local produce. Tomatoes and peppers of all colors and sizes are plentiful—magic ingredients that give Hungarian food its kick.

Hours: Opens daily at 6:00; while open weekday afternoons, it's best in the mornings.

Minaret

Once part of a mosque, this slender, 130-foot-tall minaret represents the century of Ottoman rule that left its mark on Eger and all of Hungary. The little cross at the top symbolizes the eventual Christian victory over Hungary's Ottoman invaders. You can climb the minaret's 97 steps for fine views of Eger, but it's not for those scared of heights or enclosed spaces. Because the staircase was designed for one man to climb to call the community to prayer, it's very tight. To avoid human traffic jams, groups of visitors are allowed in about twice an hour.

Cost and Hours: 300 Ft, daily April-Sept 10:00-18:00, Oct 10:00-17:00, closed Nov-March; if it's locked, ask around for the key.

Experiences in Eger

AQUA EGER
Swimming and water sports are as important to Egerites as good wine. They're proud that many of Hungary's Olympic medalists in aquatic events have come from the surrounding county. The men's

water polo team took the gold for Hungary at three Olympiads in a row (2000-2008), and speed swimmer László Cseh might have been a multiple gold medal-winner at Beijing in 2008 if he hadn't been swimming next to Michael Phelps. The town's Bitskey Aladár swimming pool—arguably the most striking building in this part of Hungary—is practically a temple to water sports.

Eger also has several appealing thermal bath complexes: one right in town, and two more a few miles away (near the village of Egerszalók). Budapest offers classier bath experiences, but the Eger options are more modern and a bit more accessible, and allow you to save your Budapest time for big-city sights. Before you go, be sure to read the "Taking the Waters" section in the Budapest chapter.

Baths and Pools in Eger

Note that you can't rent a swimsuit or a towel at either of these places; bring both with you, along with shower sandals for the locker room (if you've got them).

Bitskey Aladár Pool

This striking swimming pool was designed by Imre Makovecz, the father of Hungary's Organic architectural style. Some Eger

taxpayers resented the pool's big price tag, but it left the city with a truly distinctive building befitting its love of water sports. You don't need to be an architecture student to know that the pool is special. It's worth the five-minute walk from Dobó Square just to take a look. Oh, and you can swim in it, too.

Cost and Hours: 1,050 Ft, Mon-Fri 6:00-21:30, Sat-Sun 7:30-18:00, follow Eger Creek south from Dobó Square to Frank Tivadar utca, tel. 36/511-810, www.egertermal.hu.

▲Eger Thermal Bath (Eger Thermálfürdő)

For a refreshing break from the sight-seeing grind, consider a splash at the spa. This is a great opportunity to try a Hungarian bath: relatively accessible (men and women are clothed and together most of the time), but frequented mostly by locals.

Cost and Hours: 1,900 Ft (cheaper Sun-Wed after 16:00), 1,300 Ft extra gives you access to sauna and Turkish

EGER

Hungary's Organic Architecture

Hungary's post-communist generation has embraced a unique, eye-catching style of architecture called Organic, which was developed and championed by Imre Makovecz (1935-2011).

As a young architect, Makovecz pursued a flowing style that was intentionally at odds with the rigid right angles of communist architecture. He was inspired by the Hungarian Art Nouveau of a bygone and "decadent" Golden Age, and by pioneering Organic architects from other countries (including American Frank Lloyd Wright, who had a more angular style but a similar aesthetic of making sure his works fit their surroundings).

After being blacklisted by the regime for his stubborn adherence to his architectural vision—and for his nationalistic politics—Makovecz ramped up his pursuit of something new. Because the authorities denied him access to modern building supplies, Makovecz made do with sticks, rocks, and other foraged building materials. He was also inspired by Transylvanian village architecture: whitewashed walls with large, overhanging mansard roofs to maximize attic space (resembling a big mushroom).

After the fall of the regime, Makovecz swiftly became Hungary's premier architect, but he still kept things simple. He believed that a building should be a product of its environment, rather than a cookie-cutter copy. Organic buildings use indigenous materials (especially wood) and take on unusual forms—often inspired by animals or plants—that blend in with the landscape. Organic buildings look like they're rising up out of the ground, rather than plopped down on top of it. You generally won't find this back-to-nature style in big cities like Budapest; Makovecz preferred to work in small communities such as Eger (see Bitskey Aladár Pool photo on page 699) instead of working for large corporations. Makovecz wanted his creations—from churches, thermal baths, and campgrounds to cultural centers, restaurants, and bus stations—to represent the civic pride of the local community. For more on Makovecz, visit www.makovecz.hu.

bath for two hours; June-Aug Mon-Wed 8:30-19:00, Thu-Fri 8:30-21:00, Sat 8:00-21:00, Sun 8:00-19:00; May and Sept Sun-Wed 9:00-19:00, Thu-Sat 9:00-21:00; Oct-April daily 9:00-19:00; Petőfi tér 2, tel. 36/510-558, www.egertermal.hu.

Getting There: It's easy to reach and within a 10-minute walk of most hotels. From Dobó Square, follow the stream four blocks south (look for signs for *Strand*), then into a park; halfway through the park, look for the bath's entrance on your left, over a bridge.

Entry Procedure: After you pay, show your wristband to an attendant to get a key to a locker (1,000-Ft deposit per key; private changing cabins available in the locker room for no extra charge). Change, stow your stuff, and join the fun.

Taking the Waters: There's a sprawling array of different pools, each one thoughtfully described in English and labeled with its depth and temperature. The best part is the green-domed, indoor-outdoor adventure bath, right at the side entrance. Its cascades, jets, bubbles, geysers, and powerful current pool will make you feel like a kid again. Exploring the complex, you'll also find big and small warm pools, a very hot sulfur pool (where Egerites sit peacefully, ignore the slight stink, and supposedly feel their arthritis ebb away), a kids' pool with splashy slide fun, and a lap pool (some of these are closed off-season).

Turkish Bath: Eger's recently refurbished Turkish-style bath is closer to the main entrance (to the left as you face the main gate; you can't enter directly from the main part of the bath). It costs 1,300 Ft in combination with the main bath, or 2,200 Ft by itself (Mon-Tue 16:30-21:00, Wed-Thu 15:00-21:00, Fri 13:00-21:00, Sat-Sun 9:00-21:00).

Baths near Eger, in Egerszálok

Two more thermal baths—Salt Hill and Demjén—sit in the countryside outside of Eger, flanking a rocky hill between the villages of Egerszálok and Demjén. While these baths lack the old-fashioned class of the Budapest options, they more than compensate with soggy fun.

Getting There: Both baths are about a mile outside the village of Egerszalók, which is itself about three miles from Eger. You can take a public **bus** from Eger's bus station to the baths (take bus going toward Demjén; for Salt Hill, get off at the *Egerszalók Gyógyfürdő* stop—tell the bus driver "EH-gehr-sah-lohk FEWR-dur"—just after leaving the town of Egerszalók; for the Demjén Baths, get off at the entrance to Demjén village and walk back to the baths; bus runs 9/day Mon-Sat, only 4/day Sun, 20-minute trip, 400 Ft). Check the return bus information carefully (especially on weekends, when frequency plummets). Or you can take a **taxi** from Eger (about 3,000 Ft; tel. 36/555-555 for a return taxi from Egerszalók). Here's a fun and very hedonistic afternoon plan: Take the bus or taxi to the spa, taxi back to Eger's Sirens' Valley for some wine-cave hopping, then taxi back to your Eger hotel.

Nearby Wineries: The village of Egerszalók has several fine wineries, including the excellent **St. Andrea**—fun to combine with your bath visit. For details, see page 703.

▲▲Salt Hill Thermal Spa

For decades Egerites would come to this "salt hill" (a natural terraced formation caused by mineral-rich spring water running

down the hillside) in the middle of nowhere and cram together to baste in pools of hot water. Then the developers arrived. Today, a giant new hotel and spa complex has been built nearby. With 12 indoor pools and five outdoor ones—many cleverly overlapping one another on several levels— these cutting-edge baths are worth the trip outside of Eger. Take some time to explore the sprawling complex. Everything is labeled in English, and each pool is clearly marked with the depth and temperature. This complex uses the same system as at Eger's thermal baths: Press your wristband against a computer screen to be assigned a locker, change in the private cabin, then have fun.

Cost and Hours: In Sept-June, 4,500 Ft for all day, 2,100 Ft

for 3 hours or less, 1,500 Ft after 17:00; all prices 1,000 Ft more in July-Aug. You'll pay 1,500 Ft extra to access "sauna world," with five different saunas. Towel rental is 1,000 Ft; massages and other treatments also available. Open June-Aug daily 10:00-20:00, likely less off-season— call ahead to check; tel. 36/688-500, www.egerszalokfurdo.hu.

Demjén Thermal Baths (Demjéni Termál Völgy)

Just over the hill from Salt Hill Thermal Spa, Demjén Baths is a less glitzy complex of nicely rustic wooden buildings and pools that are similarly nestled in hills (minus the terrace formations). Thanks to its low prices and long hours, these baths attract more locals. It also offers fewer amusements: Jets, fountains, and other "adventure bath"-type features are rare; the goal here is simply stewing in pools of warm water. (The aquapark section—open only in summer—does have waterslides and a diving pool, for an extra charge.) You'll pay, change in a cabin in the shared locker rooms, ask the attendant to assign you a locker (she'll tell you to remember your number, which you'll need to tell her when you're ready for her to unlock it for you), then go soak.

Cost and Hours: 1,400 Ft, plus 1,200 Ft for a "wellness" ticket that adds more saunas and spas, daily 9:00-24:00; aquapark costs 1,900 Ft extra and open summers only until 20:00; mobile 0630-853-7419, www.demjengyogytermal.hu.

EGER WINE

Eger is at the heart of one of Hungary's best-known wine regions, internationally famous for its **Bull's Blood** (Egri Bikavér). You'll likely hear various stories as to how Bull's Blood got its name during the Ottoman siege of Eger. My favorite version: The Ottomans were amazed at the ferocity displayed by the Egerites, and wondered what they were drinking that boiled their blood and stained their beards so red...it must be potent stuff. Local merchants, knowing that the Ottomans were Muslim and couldn't drink alcohol, told them it was bull's blood. The merchants made a buck, and the name stuck.

Creative as these stories are, they're all bunk—the term dates only from 1851. Egri Bikavér is a blend (everyone has his or her own recipe), so you generally won't find it at small producers. Cabernet sauvignon, merlot, *kékfrankos,* and *kékoportó* are the most commonly used grapes.

But Bull's Blood is just the beginning of what the Eger wine region offers. Although Eger is better known for its reds, 42 of the 62 regional varieties are white. (For details, see "Hungarian Wines" on page 538.)

Tasting Local Wine: Although it would be enjoyable to drive around the Hungarian countryside visiting wineries (and I've recommended one great choice, **St. Andrea,** later), the most accessible way to get a quick taste of local wine is at a wine shop in town. I like the Kenyeres family's **Bikavér Borház,** right on Little Dobó Square (across from Senator Ház Hotel). In addition to a well-stocked (if slightly overpriced) wine shop, they have a wine bar with indoor and outdoor seating (six tastings and two cheeses for less than 2,000 Ft, wine also sold by the glass, some English spoken, menu lists basic English description for each wine, daily 10:00-22:00, possibly later in busy times, Kis-Dobó tér 10, tel. 36/413-262).

Sirens' Valley (Szépasszony-völgy)

When the Ottoman invaders first occupied Eger, residents moved in to the valley next door, living in caves dug into the hillside. Eventually the Ottomans were driven out, the Egerites moved back to town, and the caves became wine cellars. (Most Eger families who can afford it have at least a modest vineyard in the countryside.) There are more than 300 such caves in the valley to the southwest of Eger, several of which are open for visitors.

The best selection of these caves (about 50) is in the Sirens' Valley (sometimes also translated as "Valley of the Beautiful Women"—or, on local directional signs, the less poetic "Nice Woman Valley"). While the valley can feel vacant and dead (even sometimes in the summer), if you visit when it's busy it can be a fun scene—locals showing off their latest vintage, with picnic tables and tipsy tourists spilling out into the street. At some places, you'll be offered free samples; others have a menu for tastes or glasses of wine. While you're not expected to buy a bottle, it's a nice gesture to buy one if you've spent a while at one cave (and it's usually very cheap). Most caves offer something light to eat with the wine, and you'll also see lots of non-cave, full-service restaurants. Some of the caves are fancy and finished, staffed by multilingual waiters in period costume. Others feel like a dank basement, with grandpa leaning on his moped out front and a monolingual granny pouring the wine inside. (The really local places—where the decor is cement, bottles don't have labels, and food consists of potato chips and buttered Wonder bread—can be the most fun.)

This experience is a strange mix of touristy and local, but not entirely accessible to non-Hungarian-speakers—it works best with a bunch of friends and an easygoing, social attitude. Hopping from cave to musky cave can make for an enjoyable evening, but be sure to wander around a bit to see the options before you dive in (cellars generally open 10:00-21:00 in summer, best June-Aug in the late afternoon and early evening, plus good-weather weekends in the shoulder season; it's sleepy and not worth a visit off-season, when only a handful of cellars remain open for shorter hours).

Getting to the Sirens' Valley: The valley is on the southwest outskirts of Eger. Figure no more than 1,000 Ft for a **taxi** between your hotel and the caves. During the summer, you can take an 800-Ft **tourist train** from Eger's main square to the caves (see "Helpful Hints" on page 690), then catch a later one back.

You can **walk** there in about 25 minutes: Leave the pedestrian zone on the street next to the cathedral (Törvényház utca), with the cathedral on your right-hand side. Take the first left just after the back end of the cathedral (onto Trinitárius utca), go one long block, then take the first right (onto Király utca). At the fork, bear to the left. You'll stay straight on this road—crossing busy Koháry István utca—for several blocks, passing through some nondescript residential areas (on Szépasszony-völgy utca). When you crest the hill and emerge from the houses, you'll see the caves (and tour buses) below you on the left—go left (downhill) at the fork to get there. First you'll come to a stretch of touristy non-cave restaurants; keep going past these, and eventually you'll see a big loop of caves on your left.

Wineries near the Baths in Egerszalók

The village of Egerszalók, near the Salt Hill and Demjén thermal baths (described earlier), has a variety of fun wineries. The most interesting, and well worth a visit for wine lovers, is **St. Andrea**. This slick, modern, Napa Valley-esque facility offers cellar tours and tastings of their excellent wines, which show up on fine restaurant menus across Hungary. They're evangelical both about their spirituality (hence the name) and their wine, and enjoy explaining everything in English. They make generous use of pinot noir grapes and produce some good, pungent whites with volcanic qualities. While it may be possible to simply drop in for a tasting, it's better to call ahead and let them know you're coming (3,500 Ft/person, bottles for 2,500-5,500 Ft, Mon-Sat 10:00-18:00, closed Sun, Ady Endre út 88 in Egerszalók, mobile 0630-692-5860, www.standrea.hu). It's most practical with a car (or by taxi), but you can also walk there from the bus stop in Egerszalók's town center (about a half mile; head down Ady Endre út, toward the baths).

Nightlife in Eger

Things quiet down pretty early in this sedate town. Youthful student bars and hangouts cluster along the main "walking street," Széchenyi utca (especially Fri and Sat nights). Older travelers feel more at home on Little Dobó Square, with schmaltzy live music until 21:00 or 22:00 in summer; the Bikavér Borház wine bar (described earlier) is the lively hub of activity here, and stays open later.

Sleeping in Eger

Eger is a good overnight stop, and a couple of quaint, well-located hotels in particular—Senator Ház and Offi Ház—are well worth booking in advance. The TI can help you find a room; if you're stumped, the area behind the castle has a sprinkling of cheap guesthouses *(vendégház)*. Elevators are rare—expect to climb one or two flights of stairs to reach your room. A tax of 400 Ft per person will be added to your bill (not included in the prices listed here). Most of these hotels are in pedestrian zones, so get detailed driving and parking instructions from your hotel; many offer free or cheap parking, but it's often a block or two away.

$$$ Imola Udvarház rents six spacious apartments—with kitchen, living room, bedroom, and bathroom—all decorated in modern Ikea style. They're pricey for this small town, but roomy and well-maintained, with a great location near the castle entrance. Their free on-site parking garage makes this a good choice for drivers (Sb-19,000 Ft, Db-23,000 Ft, 1,000 Ft more July-Aug, 3,000 Ft less in winter, extra person-3,000 Ft, air-con, Wi-Fi, Tírodi Sebestyén tér 4, tel. 36/516-180, www.imolaudvarhaz.hu, info@imolaudvarhaz.hu).

EGER

Sleep Code

Abbreviations (225 Ft = about $1, country code: 36, area code: 36)
S = Single, **D** = Double/Twin, **T** = Triple, **Q** = Quad, **b** = bathroom.

Price Rankings

$$$ Higher Priced—Most rooms 20,000 Ft or more.

$$ Moderately Priced—Most rooms between 15,000-20,000 Ft.

$ Lower Priced—Most rooms 15,000 Ft or less.

Unless otherwise noted, credit cards are accepted, breakfast is included, Wi-Fi is generally free, and English is spoken. Prices change; verify current rates online or by email. For the best prices, always book directly with the hotel.

Phone Tip: Remember that, if calling Eger internationally, you'll have to dial 36 twice (once for the country code, again for the area code).

$$ Senator Ház Hotel is one of my favorite small, family-run hotels in Eastern Europe. Though the 11 rooms are a bit worn, this place is cozy and well-run by András Cseh and his right-hand man, Viktor. With oodles of character, all the right quirks, and a picture-perfect location just under the castle on Little Dobó Square, it's a winner (Sb-13,200 Ft, Db-18,000 Ft, extra bed-6,000 Ft, 1,000 Ft more in July-Aug, less in winter, András offers 10 percent

cash discount for Rick Steves readers who book direct and mention this book, air-con, Wi-Fi, Dobó István tér 11, tel. 36/411-711, www.senatorhaz.hu, info@senatorhaz.hu). The Cseh family also runs **Pátria Vendégház**—two doubles (same prices as main hotel) and four luxurious apartments (Db-20,000 Ft, Tb-27,000 Ft).

$$ Offi Ház Hotel shares Little Dobó Square with Senator Ház. Its five rooms are classy and romantic, but a bit tight, with slanted ceilings. Communication can be tricky (German helps), but the location is worth the hassle (Sb-14,000 Ft, Db-17,500 Ft, Db suite-19,500 Ft, Tb suite-23,000 Ft, extra bed-5,000 Ft, 15 percent cheaper Nov-March, non-smoking, air-con, Wi-Fi, Dobó István tér 5, tel. 36/518-210, www.offihaz.hu, offihaz@t-online.hu, Offenbächer family).

$$ Szent János Hotel, less charming and more businesslike than the Senator Ház and Offi Ház, offers a good but less atmospheric location, 13 straitlaced rooms, and a pleasant winter garden to relax in. Choose between the newly renovated rooms, which face a busy pedestrian street and can be noisy on weekend nights, or the still-good older rooms, which face the quieter back side—both for the same price (Sb-15,000 Ft, Db-18,000 Ft, extra bed-6,000 Ft, cheaper Nov-April, non-smoking, air-con, Wi-Fi, a long block off Dobó Square at Szent János utca 3, tel. 36/510-350, www.hotelszentjanos.hu, hotelszentjanos@hotelszentjanos.hu).

$ **Dobó Vendégház,** run by warm Marianna Kleszo, has seven basic but colorful rooms just off Dobó Square. Marianna speaks nothing but Hungarian, but gets simple reservation emails translated by a friend (Sb-10,500 Ft, Db-15,900 Ft, extra bed-4,500 Ft, cash only, air-con in some upstairs rooms, Wi-Fi, Dobó utca 19, tel. 36/421-407, www.dobovendeghaz.hu, info@dobovendeghaz.hu).

$ **Imola Hostel,** a big, modern, and comfy hostel, is basically a college dormitory that welcomes travelers of any age into its dorm rooms in summer (July-Aug only). As there are 400 beds, finding a place should be easy (bunk in 2-3-bed room-3,300 Ft, includes sheets but no breakfast; a short hike up behind the castle or a 5-minute walk from the Old Town at Leányka utca 2; tel. 36/520-430, www.imolanet.hu/imolahostel, hostel@imolanet.hu).

Eating in Eger

HBH Restaurant (named for the Hofbräuhaus beer on tap) is doing its best to be classy in this small town. They offer traditional Hungarian dishes (including chalkboard specials) in an upscale environment (2,000-3,100-Ft main dishes, good wine list, daily 11:30-23:00, outdoor tables in summer, right at the bottom of Dobó Square at Bajcsy-Zsilinszky utca 19, tel. 36/515-516).

Palacsintavár ("Pancake Castle"), near the ramp leading up to the castle, isn't your hometown IHOP. This cellar bar (which also has pleasant sidewalk seating) serves up inventive, artfully presented crêpe-wrapped main courses to a mostly student clientele. It's decorated with old cigarette boxes, and cutting-edge rock music plays on the soundtrack (meal-sized 2,000-2,500-Ft pancake dishes, daily 12:00-23:00, Dobó utca 9, tel. 36/413-980).

Restaurant Senator Ház, on Little Dobó Square, offers the best setting for al fresco dining in town, with good Hungarian and international food (1,200-1,800-Ft light meals, 1,700-3,200-Ft main dishes). Sure, you're paying a bit extra for the setting—but it's worth it for the postcard-perfect outdoor seating from which you can survey the Little Dobó Square action (open daily 10:00-22:00, cheesy live music on summer evenings). Neighboring restaurants (such as Offi Ház) offer the same ambience.

Szantofer Vendéglő serves traditional Hungarian food at

local prices to both Egerites and tourists. The good, unpretentious, fill-the-tank grub is designed for the neighborhood gang (1,800-2,500 Ft main dishes, daily 11:30-22:00, Bródy Sándor utca 3, tel. 36/517-298).

Elefanto, above the market hall, has a pleasant tree-house ambience. As it's outside of the cute zone, it attracts more locals than tourists. Sit indoors or enjoy covered terrace seating that's delightful in warm weather. The menu is mostly Italian, with pastas (1,300-1,600 Ft), pizzas (2,500 Ft), and main dishes (2,000-3,300 Ft), plus a few Hungarian standbys thrown in (daily 12:00-22:00, Katona István tér 2, tel. 36/412-452).

Dessert: Cukrászda (pastry shops) line the streets of Eger. For deluxe, super-decadent pastries of every kind imaginable, drop by **Dobós Cukrászda** (Mon-Sat 9:30-20:00, Sun 9:00-19:00, point to what you want inside and they'll bring it out to your table, Széchenyi utca 6, tel. 36/413-335). For a more local scene, find the tiny **Sárvári Cukrászda,** a block behind the Lyceum. Their pastries are good, but Egerites line up here for homemade gelato (Mon-Fri 7:00-18:00, Sat-Sun 10:00-18:00, Kossuth utca 1, between Jókai utca and Fellner utca). You'll spot several ice-cream parlors in this town, where every other pedestrian seems to be licking a cone. Another good option is the *kürtőskalács* **window** on Szent János utca, where you can step up and grab a piping-hot "pastry horn" that's slow-cooked on a rotisserie, then rolled in toppings (daily 9:00-19:30, Szent János utca 10).

Eger Connections

BY TRAIN

The only major destination you'll get to directly from Eger's train station is **Budapest** (every 2 hours direct to Budapest's Keleti/Eastern Station, 2 hours; more frequent and faster with a change in Füzesabony—see next). For other destinations, you'll connect through Füzesabony or Budapest.

Eger is connected to the nearby junction town of **Füzesabony** (FOO-zesh-ah-boyn) by frequent trains (13/day, 17 minutes). The very rustic Füzesabony station does not have lockers or an ATM; to find an ATM, exit straight from the station, walk about two blocks, and you'll find one on your right (just past the *Napcentrum*).

In Füzesabony you can transfer to Budapest on either a slower milk-run train or a speedier InterCity train (a little pricier, as it requires an extra supplement, but get you to Budapest in just under 2 hours total).

BY BUS

Eger's bus station (unlike its train station) is right in town, a five-minute uphill walk behind Eger's cathedral and the Archbishop's Palace: Go behind the cathedral and through the park, and look for the modern, green, circular building. Blue electronic boards in the center of the station show upcoming departures.

From Eger to Budapest: The direct Eger-Budapest bus service is about the same price as the train, and can be a bit faster (3,000 Ft, 2/hour, tickets generally available just before departure). Express buses depart Eger at :15 after each hour and make the trip in one hour and 50 minutes; slower regular buses leave at :45 after each hour and take 20 minutes longer. Although Eger's bus station is closer to the town center than its train station, this bus takes you to a less central point in Budapest (near Budapest's Stadionok bus station, on the M2/red Metró line).

To the Thermal Baths near Egerszalók: Buses from the same station also connect Eger to the thermal baths near Egerszalók (Salt Hill and Demjén; see "Getting There" on page 701). However, buses marked for *Egerszalók* do not actually go to the spa; instead, you need a bus going *beyond* Egerszalók, marked for *Demjén*.

EGER

SLOVENIA
Slovenija

SLOVENIA

Tiny, overlooked Slovenia is one of Europe's most unexpectedly charming destinations. At the intersection of the Slavic, German, and Italian worlds, Slovenia is an exciting mix of the best of each culture. Though it's just a quick trip away from the tourist throngs in Venice, Munich, Salzburg, and Vienna, Slovenia has stayed off the tourist track—making it a handy detour for in-the-know Back Door travelers. Be warned: Everyone I've met who has visited Slovenia wishes they'd allotted more time for this delightful, underrated land.

Today, it seems strange to think that Slovenia was ever part of Yugoslavia. Both in the personality of its people and in its landscape, Slovenia feels more like Austria. Slovenes are more industrious, organized, and punctual than their fellow for- mer Yugoslavs...yet still friendly, relaxed, and Mediterranean. Locals like the balance. Visitors expecting minefields and rust- ing Yugo factories are pleas-  antly surprised to find Slovenia's rolling countryside dotted instead with quaint alpine villages and the spires of miniature Baroque churches, with breathtaking, snowcapped peaks in the distance.

Only half as big as Switzerland, Slovenia is remarkably diverse for its size. Travelers can hike on alpine trails in the morn- ing and explore some of the world's best caves in the afternoon, before relaxing with a glass of local wine and a seafood dinner while watching the sun set on the Adriatic.

Though not unaffected by the recent economic crisis, Slovenia enjoys a prosperity unusual for a formerly communist country. The Austro-Hungarian Empire left it with a strong work ethic and an impressive industrial infrastructure, which the Yugoslav gov- ernment expanded. By 1980, 60 percent of all Yugoslav industry was in little Slovenia (which had only 8 percent of Yugoslavia's population and 8 percent of its territory). Of the 13 new nations

Slovenia

AUSTRIA

HUNGARY

Murska Sobota

Klagenfurt

Drava

Maribor

Ptuj

Villach

Jesenice

Solčava

Velenje

Varaždin

Mt. Triglav

Bled

LOGARSKA DOLINA

Bovec

JULIAN ALPS

Lake Bled

Kranj

Celje

CROATIA

Kobarid

Lake Bohinj

Kamnik

Škofja Loka

Sava

⊛ **Ljubljana**

Soča R.

Idrija

SLOVENIA

River

Zagreb ⊛

ITALY

Nova Gorica

PREDJAMA CASTLE

Novo Mesto

Samobor

LIPICA STUD FARM

POSTOJNA CAVES

KARST

Trieste

ŠKOCJAN CAVES

Crnomelj

50 Kilometers

Piran

Koper

CROATIA

50 Miles

Adriatic Sea

ISTRIA

Opatija

Rijeka

that have joined the European Union since 2004, Slovenia was the only one rich enough to be a net donor (with a higher per-capita income than the average), and the first one to join the euro currency zone (it adopted the euro in January of 2007). Thanks to its long-standing ties to the West and can-do spirit, Slovenia already feels more "Western" than any other destination in this book.

The country has a funny way of making people fall in love with it. Slovenes are laid-back, easygoing, stylish, and fun. They won't win any world wars (they're too well-adjusted to even try)... but they're exactly the type of people you'd love to chat with over a cup of coffee.

The Slovenian language is as mellow as the people. While Slovenes use Serb, German, and English curses in abundance, the worst they can say in their native tongue is, "May you be kicked by a horse." For "Darn it!" they say, "Three hundred hairy bears!" In bad traffic, they might utter under their breath, "The street is white!"

Coming from such a small country, locals are proud of the few things that are distinctly Slovenian, such as the roofed hayrack. Foreigners think that Slovenes' fascination with these hayracks is strange...until they visit and see them absolutely everywhere (especially in the northwest). Because of

Slovenia Almanac

Official Name: Republika Slovenija, or simply Slovenija.

Snapshot History: After being dominated by Germans for centuries, Slovenian culture proudly emerged in the 19th century. In the aftermath of World War I, Slovenia merged with its neighbors to become Yugoslavia, then broke away and achieved independence for the first time in 1991.

Population: Slovenia's two million people (a count similar to Nevada's) are 83 percent ethnic Slovenes who speak Slovene, plus a smattering of Serbs, Croats, and Muslim Bosniaks. Almost 60 percent of the country is Catholic.

Latitude and Longitude: 46° N and 14° E (latitude similar to Lyon, France; Montreal, Canada; or Bismarck, North Dakota).

Area: At 7,800 square miles, it's about the size of New Jersey, but with one-fourth the population.

Geography: Tiny Slovenia has four extremely different terrains and climates: the warm Mediterranean coastline (just 29 miles long—about one inch per inhabitant); the snow-capped, forested alpine mountains in the northwest (including 9,400-foot Mount Triglav); the moderate-climate, central limestone plateau that includes Ljubljana and the cave-filled Karst region; and to the east, a corner of the Great Hungarian Plain (the Prekmurje region, near Maribor and Ptuj). If you look at a map of Slovenia and squint your eyes a bit, it looks like a chicken running toward the east.

Biggest Cities: Nearly one in five Slovenes lives in the two biggest cities: Ljubljana (the capital, pop. 270,000) and Maribor (in the east, pop. 158,000). Half of the population lives in rural villages.

Economy: Slovenia has a Gross Domestic Product of $59 billion and a GDP per capita of $28,700. Slovenia's economy is based largely on manufactured metal products (trucks and machinery), which are traded with a diverse group of partners.

Currency: Slovenia uses the euro: €1 = about $1.40.

Government: The country is led by the prime minister (currently Miro Cerar), who heads the leading vote-getting party in legislative elections. He governs along with the figurehead president (currently Borut Pahor). Slovenia's relatively peaceful secession is credited largely to former President Milan Kučan, who remains a popular figure. The National Assembly consists of about 90 elected legislators; there's also a second house of parliament, which has much less power. Despite the country's small size, it is divided into some 200 municipalities—creating a lot of bureaucracy that locals enjoy complaining about.

Flag: Three horizontal bands of white (top), blue, and red. A shield in the upper left shows Mount Triglav, with a wavy-line sea below and three stars above.

The Average Slovene: The average Slovene skis, in this largely alpine country, and is an avid fan of team handball (yes, handball). He or she lives in a 250-square-foot apartment, earns $1,400 a month, watches 16 hours of TV a week (much of it in English with Slovene subtitles), and enjoys a drink-and-a-half of alcohol every day.

Notable Slovenes: A pair of prominent Ohio politicians—perennial presidential candidate **Dennis Kucinich** and former Senator **George Voinovich,** both from the Cleveland area—are each half-Slovene. (In 1910, Cleveland had the biggest Slovenian population of any city in the world—just ahead of Trieste and Ljubljana.) Classical musicians might know composers **Giuseppe Tartini** and **Hugo Wolf.** Even if you haven't heard of architect **Jože Plečnik** yet, you'll hear his name a hundred times while you're in Slovenia—especially in Ljubljana (see page 762). Perhaps most famous of all is the illustrious **Melania Knauss**—a GQ cover girl who's also the current Mrs. Donald Trump.

Sporty Slovenes: If you follow alpine sports or team handball, you'll surely know some world-class athletes from Slovenia. NBA fans might recognize basketball players **Primož Brezec** and **Bostjan Nachbar,** as well as some other lesser players. Slovenian hockey player **Anže Kopitar** plays in the NHL. The athletic Slovenes—perhaps trying to compensate for the minuscule size of their country—have accomplished astonishing feats: **Davo Karničar** has skied down from the "seven summits" (the highest points in each of the seven continents—that means the peaks of Everest, Kilimanjaro, McKinley, and so on). **Benka Pulko** became the first person ever to drive a motorcycle around the world (that is, all seven continents, including Antarctica; total trip: 111,856 miles in 2,000 days—also the longest solo motorcycle journey by a woman; www.benkapulko.com). **Dušan Mravlje** ran across all the continents. And ultra-marathon swimmer **Martin Strel** has swum the entire length of several major rivers, including the Danube (1,775 miles), the Mississippi (2,415 miles), the Yangtze (3,915 miles), and the Amazon (3,393 miles; for more, see www. martinstrel.com).

the frequent rainfall, the hayracks are covered by a roof that allows the hay to dry thoroughly. The most traditional kind is the *toplar*, consisting of two hayracks connected by one big roof. It looks like a skinny barn with open, fenced sides. Hay hangs on the sides to dry; firewood, carts, tractors, and other farm implements sit on the ground inside; and dried hay is stored in the loft above. But these wooden *toplarji* are firetraps, and a stray bolt of lightning can burn one down in a flash. So in recent years, more farmers are moving to single hayracks *(enojni);* these are still roofed, but have posts made of concrete, rather than wood. You'll find postcards and miniature wooden models of both kinds of hayracks (a fun souvenir).

Another good (and uniquely Slovenian) memento is a creatively decorated front panel from a beehive *(panjske končnice)*. Slovenia

has a strong beekeeping tradition, and beekeepers believe that painting the fronts of the hives makes it easier for bees to find their way home. Replicas of these panels are available at gift shops all over the country. (For more on the panels and Slovenia's beekeeping heritage, see page 818.)

Slovenia is also the land of polka. Slovenes claim that polka music was invented here, and singer/accordionist Slavko Avsenik—from the village of Begunje near Bled—cranks out popular oom-pah songs that make him bigger than the Beatles (and therefore, presumably, Jesus) in Germany. You'll see the Avsenik ensemble and other oompah bands on Slovenian TV, where hokey Lawrence Welk-style shows are a local institution.

To really stretch your euros, try one of Slovenia's more than 400 farmhouse B&Bs, called "tourist farms" *(turistične kmetije)*. These are actual, working farms (often organic) that sell meals and/or rent rooms to tourists to help make ends meet. You can use a tourist farm as a home base to explore the entire country—remember, the farthest reaches of Slovenia are only a day trip away. A comfortable, hotelesque double with a private bathroom—plus a traditional Slovenian dinner and a hearty breakfast—costs as little as €50. Request a listing from the Slovenian Tourist Board (see page 1295), or find information at www.slovenia.info.

Most visitors to Slovenia are, in my experience, completely charmed by the place. With all it has going for it, it's hard to believe that Slovenia is not already overrun with tourists. Somehow, this little country continues to glide beneath the radar. Exploring its mountain trails, savoring its colorful capital, and meeting its friendly locals, you'll feel like you're in on a secret.

HELPFUL HINTS

Sunday Closures: Slovenia can be extremely sleepy on Sundays, even in the larger towns and cities, where virtually all shops are closed. Plan ahead. Fortunately, many restaurants remain open, plus a select few grocery stores.

Smoking Ban: Smoking is prohibited in public places, unless it's a specially designated (and well-ventilated) smoking room. Larger hotels still have some smoking rooms, but smoking isn't allowed in public areas. Outdoors, all bets are off.

Telephones: Slovenian phone numbers beginning with 080 are toll-free; 090 and 089 denote expensive toll lines. Most mobile phone numbers begin with 03, 04, 05, or 07. For more details on how to dial to, from, and within Slovenia, see page 1318.

Toll Sticker: To drive on Slovenia's expressways *(avtocesta)*, you'll need to display a toll sticker *(vinjeta,* veen-YEH-tah; €15/week, €30/month). If renting your car in Slovenia, it probably comes with a toll sticker (but ask just to be sure); if you're driving in from elsewhere, such as Croatia, you can buy one at a gas station, post office, or some newsstands (watch for *vinjeta* signs at gas stations as you approach the border). **Be warned:** This rule is taken very seriously. If you're found driving on expressways without the sticker, you'll immediately be fined €150.

SLOVENIAN HISTORY

Slovenia has a long and unexciting history as part of various larger empires. After Illyrian, Celtic, and Roman settlements came and went, this region became populated by Slavs—the ancestors of today's Slovenes—in the late sixth century. But Charlemagne's Franks conquered the tiny land in the eighth century, and, ever since, Slovenia has been a backwater of the Germanic world—first as a holding of the Holy Roman Empire and later, the Habsburg Empire. Slovenia seems as much German as Slavic. But even as the capital, Ljubljana, was populated by Austrians (and called Laibach by its German-speaking residents), the Slovenian language and cultural traditions survived in the countryside.

Through the Middle Ages, much of Slovenia was ruled by the Counts of Celje (highly placed vassals of the Habsburgs). In this era before modern nations—when shifting allegiances and strategic marriages dictated the dynamics of power—the Counts of Celje rose to a position of significant influence in Central and Eastern Europe. Celje daughters intermarried with some of the most powerful dynasties in the region—the Polish Piasts, the Hungarian Anjous, and the Czech Přemysls. Before long, the Counts of Celje had emerged as the Habsburgs' main rival.

In the 15th century, Count Ulrich II of Celje married into Serbia's ruling family and managed to wrest control of Hungary's massive holdings. Had he not been assassinated in 1456, this obscure Slovenian line—rather than an obscure Austrian one—may have emerged as the dominant power in the eastern half of Europe. (Instead, the Habsburgs consolidated their vanquished foe's fiefdoms into their ever-growing empire.) In homage, the three yellow stars of the Counts of Celje's seal still adorn Slovenia's coat of arms.

Soon after, with Slovenia firmly entrenched in the Counter-Reformation holdings of the Habsburg Empire, the local Reformer Primož Trubar (1508-1586) strove both to put the Word of God into the people's hands, and to legitimize Slovene as a written language. This Slovenian answer to Martin Luther secretly translated the Bible into Slovene in Reformation-friendly Germany, then smuggled copies back into his homeland.

Over the next several centuries, much of Slovenia was wracked by Habsburg-Ottoman wars, as the Ottomans attempted to push north through this territory to reach Vienna. Slovenia also found itself at the crossroads between Austria and Venice; many of their violent clashes took place here. Seemingly exhausted by all of this warfare—and by their own sporadic, halfhearted, and unsuccessful uprisings against Habsburg rule—Slovenia languished as a sleepy backwater.

When the port city of Trieste (in Slovenian territory) was granted free status in 1718, it boosted the economy of Slovenian lands. The Enlightenment spurred a renewed interest in the Slovenian culture and language, which further flourished when Napoleon named Ljubljana the capital of his "Illyrian Provinces"—Slovenia's own mini-empire, stretching from Austria's Tirol to Croatia's Dalmatian Coast. During this brief period (1809-1813), the long-suppressed Slovene language was used for the first time in schools and the government. This kicked off a full-throated national revival movement (as in so many other Central and Eastern European countries at the time)—asserting the worthiness of the Slovenian language and culture compared to the dominant Germanic worldview of the time. Inspired by the patriotic poetry of France Prešeren (1800-1849), Slovenian pride surged.

The last century saw the most interesting chapter of Slovenian history. Some of World War I's fiercest fighting occurred at the Soča (Isonzo) Front in northwest Slovenia—witnessed by young Ernest Hemingway, who drove an ambulance (see sidebars on pages 833 and 848). During World War II, Slovenia was divided among Nazi allies Austria, Italy, and Hungary—and an estimated 20,000 to 25,000 Slovenes perished in Nazi- and Italian-operated concentration camps.

Slo-what?-ia

The only thing I know about Slovakia is what I learned firsthand from your foreign minister, who came to Texas.
　　—George W. Bush, to a Slovak journalist
　　　(Bush had actually met with Dr. Janez Drnovšek,
　　　who was then Slovenia's prime minister)

Maybe it's understandable that many Americans confuse Slovenia with Slovakia. Both are small, mountainous countries that not too long ago were parts of bigger, better known, now defunct nations. But anyone who has visited Slovenia and Slovakia will set you straight—they feel worlds apart.

Slovenia, wedged between the Alps and the Adriatic, is a tidy, prosperous country. Until 1991, Slovenia was one of the six republics that made up Yugoslavia. Historically, Slovenia has had very strong ties with Germanic culture—so it feels like its neighbor to the north, Austria.

Slovakia—two countries away, to the northeast—is slightly bigger. Much of its territory is covered by the Carpathian Mountains, most notably the dramatic, jagged peaks of the High Tatras. In 1993, the Czechs and Slovaks peacefully chose to go their separate ways, so the nation of Czechoslovakia dissolved into the Czech Republic and the Slovak Republic (a.k.a. Slovakia).

To make things even more confusing, there's also **Slavonia**. This is the thick, inland "panhandle" that makes up the northeast half of Croatia, along Slovenia's southeast border. Much of the warfare in Croatia's 1991-1995 war took place in Slavonia.

I won't tell on you if you mix them up. But if you want to feel smarter than a former president, do a little homework and get it right.

As Yugoslavia entered its Golden Age under war hero Marshal Tito, Slovenia's prime location where Yugoslavia meets Western Europe (a short drive from Austria or Italy)—and the diligent national character of the Slovenian people—made it a prime candidate for industrialization.

After Tito's death in 1980, the various Yugoslav republics struggled to redefine their role in the union. While many factions reverted to age-old, pre-Tito nationalistic fervor, the Slovenes grew increasingly focused on their own future...and began to press for real reforms of the communist system. Slovenia had always been Yugoslavia's smallest, northernmost, most prosperous republic. Now Slovenes realized that Yugoslavia needed Slovenia much more than Slovenia needed Yugoslavia.

In 1988, the iconoclastic Slovenian magazine *Mladina* pressed the boundaries of Yugoslavia's nominally "free" press, publishing articles critical of the Yugoslav People's Army. Four young reporters (including Janez Janša, who would later become Slovenia's prime minister) were tried, convicted, and imprisoned, spurring outrage among Slovenes. A few months later, the Slovenian delegation defiantly walked out of the Yugoslav League of Communists Congress. The first-ever free elections in Slovenia on April 8, 1990, ended communist rule and swept reformer Milan Kučan into the presidency. Kučan attempted to pursue a Swiss-style confederated relationship with his fellow Yugoslav republics, but met with resistance from his counterparts who were more focused on their own ethnic self-interests. Later that year, in a nationwide referendum, 88 percent of Slovenes voted for independence from Yugoslavia.

And so, concerned about Serbian strongman Slobodan Milošević's nationalistic politics, and seeking the opportunity for true democracy and capitalism, Slovenia seceded. Because more than 90 percent of the people here were ethnic Slovenes—and because Slovenia was careful to respect the rights of its minority populations—the break with Yugoslavia was less dramatic than in some other countries.

After months of stockpiling weapons, Slovenia closed its borders and declared independence from Yugoslavia on June 25, 1991. Belgrade sent in the Yugoslav People's Army to take control of Slovenia's borders with Italy and Austria, figuring that whoever controlled the borders had a legitimate claim on sovereignty. Fighting broke out around these borders. Because the Yugoslav People's Army was made up of soldiers from all republics, many Slovenian troops found themselves fighting their own countrymen. (The army had cut off communication between these conscripts and the home front, so they didn't know what was going on—and often didn't realize they were fighting their friends and neighbors until they were close enough to see them.)

Slovenian civilians bravely entered the fray, blockading the Yugoslav barracks with their own cars and trucks. Most of the Yugoslav soldiers—now trapped—were young and inexperienced, and were terrified of the improvised (but relentless) Slovenian militia, even though their own resources were far superior.

After 10 days of fighting and fewer than a hundred deaths, Belgrade relented. The Slovenes stepped aside and allowed the Yugoslav People's Army to leave with their weapons and to destroy all remaining military installations as they went. When the Yugoslav People's Army cleared out, they left the Slovenes with their freedom.

After centuries of looking to the West, in May of 2004 Slovenia became the first of the former Yugoslav republics to join the European Union. The Slovenes have been practical about this move, realizing it's essential for their survival as a tiny nation in a modern world. But there are trade-offs, and "Euroskeptics" are down on EU bureaucracy. As borders disappear, Slovenes are experiencing more crime. Traditional farms are grappling with strict EU standards. Slovenian businesses are having difficulty competing with big German and other Western European firms. Before EU membership, only Slovenes could own Slovenian land. But now wealthy foreigners are buying property, driving up the cost of real estate. Still, overall, most Slovenes feel that EU membership was the right choice.

After independence, Slovenia impressed its European neighbors with its powerhouse economy and steady growth. However, the global financial crisis revealed that some of the country's affluence was deceptive; it turned out that many of Slovenia's biggest companies had been financing their operations by running up huge debts (not unlike individuals committing to a mortgage they'd never be able to afford). As all of Europe's bubble burst in 2008, those corporate debts were assumed by Slovenia's big banks—devastating the economy and sparking even more financial worries here than in many other countries.

After visionary Ljubljana mayor Zoran Janković (see page 746) failed to create a ruling coalition in the 2011 parliamentary elections, his rival Janez Janša became prime minister. Then, in the winter of 2012-2013, a massive wave of protests swept the country. Slovenes were outraged at the austerity measures proposed by the same government officials whose alleged corruption had worsened their economic straits. Economists began to speculate that Slovenia might need to ask for a Greece-style bailout from the EU to rescue its flagging economy. Janša was forced from office. A government commission ultimately alleged corruption on the part of both Janša and Janković, effectively ending their aspirations on the national political stage. Protests have died down and the economy has righted itself without international intervention, but Slovenes still feel stung and remain deeply suspicious of their politicians.

While the worldwide economic crisis has taken its toll, business here is brisk. As throughout their history, the Slovenes are adjusting to the 21st century with their characteristic sense of humor and easygoing attitude.

SLOVENIAN FOOD

Slovenian cuisine offers more variety and better quality than Croatian fare. Slovenes brag that their cuisine melds the best of Italian and German cooking—but they also embrace other international influences, especially French. Like Croatian food, Slovenian cuisine also features some pan-Balkan elements: The savory phyllo-dough pastry *burek* is the favorite fast food here, and when Slovenes host a backyard barbecue, they grill up *čevapčiči* and *ražnjići*, topped off with the eggplant-and-red-bell-pepper condiment *ajvar* (see the "Balkan Flavors" sidebar on page 1140). Slovenia enjoys Italian-style  fare, with a pizza or pasta restaurant on seemingly every corner. Hungarian food simmers in the northeast corner of the country (where many Magyars reside). And in most of the country, traditional Slovenian food has a distinctly Germanic vibe—including the "four S's": sausages, schnitzels, strudels, and sauerkraut.

Traditional Slovenian dishes are prepared with groats—a grainy mush made with buckwheat, barley, or corn. Buckwheat, which thrives in this climate, often appears on Slovenian menus. You'll also see plenty of *štruklji* (a dumpling-like savory layer cake), which can be stuffed with cheese, meat, or vegetables. *Repa* is turnip prepared like sauerkraut. Among the hearty soups in Slovenia is *jota*—a staple for Karst peasants, made from *repa*, beans, and vegetables.

In Slovenia and Croatia, *pršut* (purr-SHOOT) is one of the essential food groups. This air-cured ham (like Italian prosciutto) is soaked in salt and sometimes also smoked. Then it hangs in open-ended barns for up to a year and a half, to be dried and seasoned by the howling Bora wind. Each region produces a slightly different *pršut*. In Dalmatia, a layer of fat keeps the ham moist; in Istria, the fat is trimmed, and the *pršut* is dryer.

Since Slovenia joined the European Union, strict new standards have swept the land. Separate  rooms must be used for the slaughter, preparation, and curing of the ham. While this seems fair enough for large producers, small family farms that want to produce just enough *pršut* for their own use—and maybe sell one or two ham hocks to neighbors—find they have to invest thousands of euros to be compliant.

The cuisine of Slovenia's Karst region (the arid limestone plain south of Ljubljana) is notable. The small farms and wineries of this region have been inspired by Italy's Slow Food movement—their owners believe that cuisine is meant to be gradually appreciated, not rushed—making the Karst a destination for

Slovenian Wines

While many visitors wouldn't expect Slovenia to produce good *vino* (wine), it should come as no surprise, since this little country abuts well-respected wine-growing neighbors Italy and Hungary. In fact, Slovenia's winemaking tradition originated with its pre-Roman Illyrian and Celtic inhabitants, meaning that wine has been grown much longer here than in most other European countries. As in Croatia, Slovenian wine standards plummeted with Yugoslav-era collectivization, but in recent years ambitious vintner families are determined to bring quality back to their wines—with impressive results.

Slovenia's three main wine-growing regions are Primorska, Posavje, and Podravje.

The best-known is the **Primorska** region, in the southwest. With a Mediterranean climate (hence its name: "by the sea"), Primorska is best known for its reds. Primorska's Goriška Brda ("Hillsides of Gorica") shares the terroir of Italy's Friuli/Venezia Giulia region (and its much-vaunted, DOC-classified Collio Goriziano wines). Not surprisingly, this area produces some of Slovenia's most respected wines, made mostly with internationally known grapes such as merlot and cabernet sauvignon. Goriška Brda also produces a good white using the *rebula* grape (perhaps better known by its Italian name, *ribolla gialla*). A bit farther south (and still within Primorska), the Karst grows lots of *refošk* (*refosco*) grapes, which thrive in iron-rich red soil *(terra rossa)*. The top product is the extremely full-bodied, "big" *teran*—infused with a high lactic acid content that supposedly gives the wine healing properties. Nearby coastal areas (around Koper) also grow *refošk*, along with the white *malvazija* grape that's also widely used in Croatian Istria.

To the northeast, near Hungary, is the **Podravje** region (the Drava River Valley), dominated by white grapes—especially *laški riesling* (known internationally as Welsh riesling) and *renski riesling* (what we'd call simply riesling). The steeper right bank of the Drava River is known as Haloze, while the left bank produces Slovenske Gorice ("Slovenian Hills"). If you're visiting Ptuj or Maribor, these are the wines you'll see on local menus.

And finally, a bit to the south of Podravje is the **Posavje** region (the Lower Sava River Valley, bordering Croatia). This area—which is still focused on quantity over quality—produces both white and red wines; it's known mostly for the light, russet-colored *cviček* wine (a blend of red and white grapes).

With any type of Slovenian wine, *vrhunsko* (premium) is a mark of quality, while *kakovostno* is a notch down, and *namizno* is a table wine. Other key terms are similar to Croatian: *suho* (dry), *sladko* (sweet), and *pol-* (half).

gourmet tours. Karstic cuisine is similar to France's nouvelle cuisine—several courses in small portions, with a focus on unusual combinations and preparations—but with a Tuscan flair. The Karst's tasty air-dried ham *(pršut)*, available throughout the country, is worth seeking out (see description on page 722). Istria (the peninsula just to the south of the Karst, in southern Slovenia and Croatia) produces truffles that, locals boast, are as good as those from Italy's Piedmont (see page 1048).

Voda is water, and *kava* is coffee. Radenska, in the bottle with the three little hearts, is Slovenia's best-known brand of mineral water—good enough that the word *Radenska* is synonymous with bottled water all over Slovenia and throughout the former Yugoslavia. It's not common to ask for (or receive) tap water, but you can try requesting *voda iz pipe*.

Adventurous teetotalers should forego the Coke and sample Cockta, a Slovenian cola with an unusual flavor (which supposedly comes from berry, lemon, orange, and 11 herbs). Originally called "Cockta-Cockta," the drink was introduced during the communist period, as an alternative to the difficult-to-get Coca-Cola. This local variation developed a loyal following...until the Iron Curtain fell, and the real Coke became readily available. Cockta sales plummeted. But in recent years—prodded by the slogan "The Taste of Your Youth"— nostalgic Slovenes are drinking Cockta once more.

The premier Slovenian brand of *pivo* (beer) is Union (OO-nee-ohn), but you'll also see a lot of Laško (LASH-koh), whose mascot is the Zlatorog (or "Golden Horn," a mythical chamois-like animal). For the full story on Slovenian wines, see the sidebar.

Regardless of what you're drinking, to toast, say, *"Na ZDROW-yeh!"*—if you can't remember it, think of "Nice driving!"

Slovenia's national dessert is *potica,* a rolled pastry with walnuts and sometimes also raisins. While traditionally eaten at Christmas, it's available year-round. Slovenes eat it from the hard outer crust in, saving the nutty center for last. For more tasty treats, see the "Bled Desserts" sidebar on page 810. Locals claim that Ljubljana has the finest gelato outside of Italy—which, after all, is just an hour down the road.

SLOVENIAN LANGUAGE

Slovene is surprisingly different from languages spoken in the other former Yugoslav republics. While Serbian and Croatian are mutually intelligible, Slovene is gibberish to Serbs and Croats.

Most Slovenes, on the other hand, know Serbo-Croatian because, a generation ago, everybody in Yugoslavia had to learn it.

Linguists have identified some 46 official dialects of Slovene, and there are probably another 100 or so unofficial ones. Locals can instantly tell which city—or sometimes even which remote mountain valley—someone comes from by their accent.

The tiny country of Slovenia borders Italy and Austria, with important historical and linguistic ties to both. For self-preservation, Slovenes have always been forced to function in many different languages. All of these factors make them excellent linguists. Most young Slovenes speak effortless, flawless English—then admit that they've never set foot in the United States or Britain, but love watching American movies and TV shows (which are always subtitled, never dubbed).

Slovene pronunciation is very similar to Croatian (see page 876). Remember, *c* is pronounced "ts" (as in "cats"). The letter *j* is pronounced as "y"—making "Ljubljana" easier to say than it looks (lyoob-lyee-AH-nah). Slovene only has one diacritical mark: the *strešica*, or "little roof." This makes *č* sound like "ch," *š* sound like "sh," and *ž* sound like "zh" (as in "measure"). The letter *v* is pronounced like "u"—so the Slovenian word *avto* sounds like "auto," and the mountain Triglav is pronounced "TREE glau" (rhymes with "cow").

The only trick: As in English, which syllable gets the emphasis is unpredictable. Slovenes use many of the same words as Croatians, but put the stress on an entirely different place.

Learn some key Slovenian phrases (see the Slovenian survival phrases on the following pages). You'll make more friends and your trip will go more smoothly.

A few key words are helpful for navigation: *trg* (pronounced "turg," square), *ulica* (OO-leet-sah, road), *cesta* (TSEH-stah, avenue), *avtocesta* (OW-toh-tseh-stah, expressway), and *most* (mohst, bridge).

Slovenian Survival Phrases

In the phonetics, ī sounds like the long i in "light," and bolded syllables are stressed. The vowel "eh" sometimes sounds closer to "ay" (depending on the speaker).

English	Slovenian	Pronunciation
Hello. (formal)	Dober dan.	**doh**-behr dahn
Hi. / Bye. (informal)	Živjo.	**zheev**-yoh
Do you speak English?	Ali govorite angleško?	**ah**-lee goh-voh-**ree**-teh ahn-**glehsh**-koh
Yes. / No.	Ja. / Ne.	yah / neh
I (don't) understand.	(Ne) razumem.	(neh) rah-**zoo**-mehm
Please. / You're welcome.	Prosim.	**proh**-seem
Thank you (very much).	Hvala (lepa).	**hvah**-lah (**leh**-pah)
Excuse me. / I'm sorry.	Oprostite.	oh-proh-**stee**-teh
problem	problem	proh-**blehm**
No problem.	Ni problema.	nee proh-**bleh**-mah
Good.	Dobro.	**doh**-broh
Goodbye.	Na svidenje.	nah **svee**-dehn-yeh
one / two	ena / dve	**eh**-nah / dveh
three / four	tri / štiri	tree / **shtee**-ree
five / six	pet / šest	peht / shehst
seven / eight	sedem / osem	**seh**-dehm / **oh**-sehm
nine / ten	devet / deset	deh-**veht** / deh-**seht**
hundred / thousand	sto / tisoč	stoh / **tee**-sohch
How much?	Koliko?	**koh**-lee-koh
local currency	euro	**ee**-oo-roh
Write it?	Napišite?	nah-**peesh**-ee-teh
Is it free?	Ali je brezplačno?	**ah**-lee yeh brehz-**plahch**-noh
Is it included?	Ali je vključeno?	**ah**-lee yeh vuk-**lyoo**-cheh-noh
Where can I find / buy...?	Kje lahko najdem / kupim...?	kyeh **lah**-koh nī-dehm / **koo**-peem
I'd / We'd like...	Želel / Želeli bi...	zheh-**lehl** / zheh-**leh**-lee bee
...a room.	...sobo.	**soh**-boh
...a ticket to ___.	...vozovnico do ___.	voh-**zohv**-neet-soh doh ___
Is it possible?	Ali je možno?	**ah**-lee yeh **mohzh**-noh
Where is...?	Kje je...?	kyeh yeh
...the train station	...železniška postaja	zheh-**lehz**-neesh-kah pohs-**tī**-yah
...the bus station	...avtobusna postaja	**ow**-toh-boos-nah pohs-**tī**-yah
...the tourist information office	...turistično informacijski center	too-**rees**-teech-noh een-for-maht-**see**-skee **tsehn**-tehr
...the toilet	...vece (WC)	**veht**-seh
men / women	moški / ženski	**mohsh**-kee / **zhehn**-skee
left / right / straight	levo / desno / naravnost	**leh**-voh / **dehs**-noh / nah-**rahv**-nohst
At what time...?	Ob kateri uri...?	ohb kah-**teh**-ree **oo**-ree
...does this open / close	...se odpre / zapre	seh ohd-**preh** / zah-**preh**
(Just) a moment.	(Samo) trenutek.	(sah-**moh**) treh-**noo**-tehk
now / soon / later	zdaj / kmalu / pozneje	zuh-**dī** / kuh-**mah**-loo / pohz-**neh**-yeh
today / tomorrow	danes / jutri	**dah**-nehs / **yoo**-tree

In a Slovenian Restaurant

English	Slovenian	Pronunciation
I'd like to reserve...	*Rezerviral bi...*	reh-zehr-**vee**-rahl bee
We'd like to reserve...	*Rezervirali bi...*	reh-zehr-**vee**-rah-lee bee
...a table for one / two.	*...mizo za enega / dva.*	**mee**-zoh zah **eh**-neh-gah / dvah
Is this table free?	*Ali je ta miza prosta?*	ah-lee yeh tah **mee**-zah **proh**-stah
Can I help you?	*Izvolite?*	eez-**voh**-lee-teh
The menu (in English), please.	*Jedilni list (v angleščini), prosim.*	yeh-**deel**-nee leest (vuh ahn-**glehsh**-chee-nee) **proh**-seem
service (not) included	*postrežba (ni) vključena*	post-**rehzh**-bah (nee) vuk-**lyoo**-cheh-nah
cover charge	*pogrinjek*	poh-**green**-yehk
"to go"	*za s sabo*	zah **sah**-boh
with / without	*z / brez*	zuh / brehz
and / or	*in / ali*	een / **ah**-lee
fixed-price meal (of the day)	*(dnevni) meni*	(duh-**new**-nee) meh-**nee**
specialty of the house	*specialiteta hiše*	speht-see-ah-lee-**teh**-tah **hee**-sheh
half portion	*polovična porcija*	poh-loh-**veech**-nah **port**-see-yah
daily special	*dnevna ponudba*	duh-**new**-nah poh-**nood**-bah
fixed-price meal for tourists	*turistični meni*	too-**rees**-teech-nee meh-**nee**
appetizers	*predjedi*	prehd-yeh-**dee**
bread	*kruh*	krooh
cheese	*sir*	seer
sandwich	*sendvič*	**send**-veech
soup	*juha*	**yoo**-hah
salad	*solata*	soh-**lah**-tah
meat / poultry	*meso / perutnina*	meh-**soh** / peh-root-**nee**-nah
fish / seafood	*riba / morska hrana*	**ree**-bah / **mor**-skah **hrah**-nah
fruit	*sadje*	**sahd**-yeh
vegetables	*zelenjava*	zeh-lehn-**yah**-vah
dessert	*sladica*	slah-**deet**-sah
(tap) water	*voda (iz pipe)*	**voh**-dah (eez **pee**-peh)
mineral water	*mineralna voda*	mee-neh-**rahl**-nah **voh**-dah
milk	*mleko*	**mleh**-koh
(orange) juice	*(pomarančni) sok*	(poh-mah-**rahnch**-nee) sohk
coffee	*kava*	**kah**-vah
tea	*čaj*	chī
wine	*vino*	**vee**-noh
red / white	*rdeče / belo*	ahr-**deh**-cheh / **beh**-loh
sweet / dry / semi-dry	*sladko / suho / polsuho*	**slahd**-koh / **soo**-hoh / **pohl**-soo-hoh
glass / bottle	*kozarec / steklenica*	koh-**zah**-rehts / stehk-leh-**neet**-sah
beer	*pivo*	**pee**-voh
Cheers!	*Na zdravje!*	nah **zdrow**-yeh
More. / Another.	*Še. / Še eno.*	sheh / sheh **eh**-noh
The same.	*Isto.*	**ees**-toh
Bill, please.	*Račun, prosim.*	rah-**choon proh**-seem
tip	*napitnina*	nah-peet-**nee**-nah
Delicious!	*Odlično!*	ohd-**leech**-noh

LJUBLJANA

Slovenia's capital, Ljubljana (lyoob-lyee-AH-nah), with a lazy Old Town clustered around a castle-topped mountain, is often likened to Salzburg. It's an apt comparison—but only if you inject a healthy dose of breezy Adriatic culture, add a Slavic accent, and replace favorite son Mozart with local architect Jože Plečnik.

Ljubljana feels smaller than its population of 270,000. The castle perched on the hill over town, and several clusters of good museums that try hard but have only so much to say, do their best to please sightseers. But ultimately, this town is all about ambience. The cobbled core of Ljubljana is an idyllic place that sometimes feels too good to be true. The cityscape is slathered with one-of-a-kind architecture, festivals fill the summer, and people enjoy a Sunday stroll any day of the week. Fashion boutiques and al fresco cafés jockey for control of the Old Town, while the leafy riverside promenade crawls with stylishly dressed students sipping *kava* and polishing their near-perfect English. Laid-back Ljubljana is the kind of place where graffiti and crumbling buildings seem elegantly atmospheric instead of shoddy. But more and more of those buildings have been getting a face-lift recently, as a spunky mayor has been spiffing up the place and creating gleaming traffic-free zones left and right—making what was already an exceptionally livable city into a true pedestrians' paradise.

Batted around by history, Ljubljana has seen cultural influences from all sides—most notably Prague, Vienna, and Venice. This has left the city a happy hodgepodge of cultures. Being the midpoint between the Slavic, Germanic, and Italian worlds gives Ljubljana a special spice. People often ask me: What's the "next

The Story of Ljubljana

In ancient times, Ljubljana was on the trade route connecting the Mediterranean (just 60 miles away) to the Black Sea (toss a bottle off the bridge here, and it can float to the Danube and, eventually, all the way to Russia). Legend has it that Jason and his Argonauts founded Ljubljana when they stopped here for the winter on their way home with the Golden Fleece. Some stories say Jason slayed a dragon here, while according to others, it was St. George; either way, the dragon remains the city mascot to this day.

Some of the area's earliest known inhabitants during the Neolithic and Bronze ages lived in rustic houses on tall wooden piles within the marshy lands surrounding today's city center, and poled around the shallow lagoons in dugout canoes. Sometimes called "crannoch dwellers" (after similar homes in the Scottish Highlands), these earliest Ljubljanans left behind precious few bits of evidence that they ever existed, save for half of a wooden wheel and axle that's some 5,200 years old (and now belongs to the City Museum).

The area was later populated by the Illyrians and Celts, and was eventually Romanized (and called Emona) before being overrun by Huns, only to be resettled by Slavs—the ancestors of today's Slovenes.

In 1335, Ljubljana fell under the jurisdiction of the Habsburg emperors, who called it Laibach and steered its development for the next six centuries. Slovenian language and culture were considered backward peasant traditions, as most of Laibach's inhabitants spoke German and lived essentially Austrian lifestyles. Even today, Ljubljana still feels Austrian—especially thanks to its abundant Austrian Baroque and Viennese Art Nouveau architecture—but it has a Mediterranean flair.

Napoleon put Ljubljana on the map when he made it the capital of his Illyrian Provinces, a realm that stretched from the Danube to Dubrovnik, and from Austria to Albania (for just four short years, 1809-1813). For the first time, the Slovene language was taught in schools, awakening a newfound pride in Slovenian

Prague"? And I have to answer Kraków. But Ljubljana is the *next* "next Prague."

PLANNING YOUR TIME

Ljubljana deserves at least a full day. Rather than checking off a list of museums, spend most of your time strolling the pleasant town center, exploring the many interesting squares and architectural gems, shopping at the boutiques, and sipping coffee at sidewalk cafés along the river.

Here's the best plan for a low-impact sightseeing day: Begin on Prešeren Square, the heart of the city. Cross the Triple Bridge cultural heritage. People still look back fondly on this very brief era, which was the first (and probably only) time when Ljubljana rose to prominence on the world stage. After more than 600 years of being part of the Habsburg Empire, Ljubljana has no "Habsburg Square"...but they do have a "French Revolution Square."

In the mid-19th century, the railway connecting Vienna to the Adriatic (Trieste) was built through town—and Ljubljana boomed. An earthquake hit the city in 1895, damaging many buildings. Locals cleverly exaggerated the impact (propping up buildings that were structurally sound, and even tearing down unwanted old houses that had been unharmed) in preparation for the visit of Emperor Franz Josef—who took pity on the city and invested generously in its reconstruction. Ljubljana was made over in the Art Nouveau style so popular in Vienna, its capital at the time. A generation later, architect Jože Plečnik bathed the city in his distinctive, artsy-but-sensible, classical-meets-modern style.

In World War II, Slovenia was occupied first by the Italians, then by the Nazis. Ljubljana had a thriving resistance movement that the Nazis couldn't suppress—so they simply fenced off the entire city and made it a giant prison for three years, allowing only shipments of basic food supplies to get in. But the Slovenes—who knew their land far better than their oppressors did—continued to slip in and out of town undetected, allowing them to agitate through the end of the war.

In 1991, Ljubljana became the capital of one of Europe's youngest nations. Today the city is filled with university students, making it feel very youthful. Ljubljana has always felt free to be creative, and recent years—with unprecedented freedoms—have been no exception. This city is on the cutting edge when it comes to architecture, public art, fashion, and trendy pubs—a tendency embodied by its larger-than-life mayor, Zoran Janković (see page 746). And yet, Ljubljana's scintillating avant-garde culture has soft edges—hip, but also nonthreatening and user-friendly.

and wander through the riverside produce market before joining the town walking tour at 10:00 (at 11:00 in Oct-March). If the Jože Plečnik House is open (likely closed through fall of 2015—confirm first), wander south along the Ljubljanica River and through the Krakovo gardens to tour it. In the afternoon, commit some quality time to people-watching at a riverside café, window-shop at some colorful boutiques (perhaps following my self-guided shopping walk in the Old Town), or do more sightseeing (good options include the City History Museum, near several Jože Plečnik landmarks downtown; the Serbian Orthodox Church and Tivoli Park, with the Contemporary History Museum, west of downtown; or the Slovenian Ethnographic Museum and other sights in Metelkova, north of downtown).

Ljubljana is sleepy on Sundays (virtually all shops are closed and the produce market is quiet, but museums—except for the Jože Plečnik House—are generally open, a modest flea market stretches along the riverfront, and the TI's walking tour still runs). The city is also relatively quiet in August, when the students are on break and many locals head to beach resorts. They say that in August, even homeless people go to the coast.

Orientation to Ljubljana

Ljubljana—with narrow lanes, architecture that mingles the Old World and contemporary Europe, and cobbles upon cobbles of wonderful distractions—can be disorienting for a first-timer. But the charming central zone is compact, and with a little wandering, you'll quickly get the hang of it.

The Ljubljanica River—lined with cafés, restaurants, and a buzzing outdoor market—bisects the city, making a 90-degree turn around the base of a castle-topped mountain. Most sights are either along or just a short walk from the river. Visitors enjoy the distinctive bridges that span the Ljubljanica, including the landmark Triple Bridge (Tromostovje) and pillared Cobblers' Bridge (Čevljarski Most)—both designed by Jože Plečnik. Between these two is a very plain wooden bridge (with great views) dubbed the "Ugly Duckling." The center of Ljubljana is Prešeren Square, watched over by a big statue of Slovenia's national poet, France Prešeren.

I've organized the sights in this chapter based on which side of the river they're on: the east (castle) side of the river, where Ljubljana began, with more medieval charm; and the west (Prešeren Square) side of the river, which has a more Baroque/Art Nouveau feel and most of the urban sprawl. At the northern edge of the tourist's Ljubljana is the train station and Metelkova museum and nightlife zone; at the southern edge are the garden district of Krakovo and the Jože Plečnik House; and at the western edge is Tivoli Park.

Ljubljana's Two Big Ps: You'll hear the following two easy-to-confuse names constantly during your visit. Mind your Ps, and your visit to Ljubljana becomes more meaningful:

Jože Plečnik (YOH-zheh PLAYCH-neek, 1872-1957) is the architect who shaped Ljubljana, designing virtually all of the city's most important landmarks. For more information, see page 762.

France Prešeren (FRAHN-tseh preh-SHAY-rehn, 1800-1849) is Slovenia's greatest poet and the namesake of Ljubljana's main square.

TOURIST INFORMATION

Ljubljana's helpful, businesslike TI has a useful website (www.visitljubljana.com) and two branches: at the **Triple Bridge,** across from Prešeren Square (daily June-Sept 8:00-21:00, Oct-May 8:00-19:00, Stritarjeva 1, tel. 01/306-1215); and at the upper corner of the **market** (with pay Internet access, bike rental, and information about the rest of Slovenia; June-Sept daily 8:00-21:00; Oct-May Mon-Fri 8:00-19:00, Sat-Sun 9:00-17:00; Krekov trg 10, tel. 01/306-4575).

At either TI, pick up a pile of free resources: the big city map, the *Tourist Guide,* the monthly events guide, and a wide range of informative brochures. The TI also offers a free room-finding service.

The **Ljubljana Tourist Card,** which includes access to public transportation and covers entry to many city museums as well as the TI's walking tours and boat trips, could save busy sightseers some money (€23/24 hours, €30/48 hours, €35/72 hours).

ARRIVAL IN LJUBLJANA

By Train: Ljubljana's modern, user-friendly train station (Železniška Postaja) is at the northern edge of the city center. Emerging from the passage up to track 1a, turn right and walk under the long canopy along the train tracks to find the yellow arrivals hall. Everything is well-signed in English, including the handy train-information office (with useful handouts outlining trips to several domestic and international destinations, daily 5:30-21:30), lockers, and—near the front of the station—a big **ticket office** with clearly marked ticket windows and an **ATM** (office open daily 5:00-22:00). Arrivals are *prihodi,* departures are *odhodi,* and track is *tir.*

The main square is an easy 10-minute **walk** from the station; you can walk to any of my recommended hotels within about 20 minutes (often less). To reach Prešeren Square at the city's center, leave the arrivals hall to the right and walk a long block along the busy Trg Osvobodilne Fronte (or "Trg O.F." for short, with the bus station in the middle). After passing all of the bus stalls, turn left across Trg O.F. and go down Miklošičeva, at the building with the round red-brick columns. This takes you past some of Ljubljana's most appealing architecture to Prešeren Square.

Unscrupulous **taxis** crouch in front of the station, waiting to spring on unsuspecting tourists. The fair metered rate to any of my recommended hotels is around €3 (maybe up to €4-5 in heavy

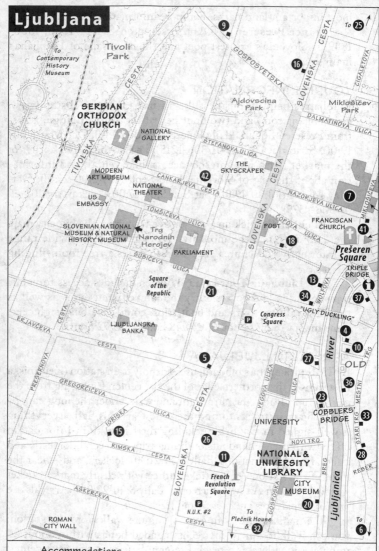

Ljubljana

LJUBLJANA

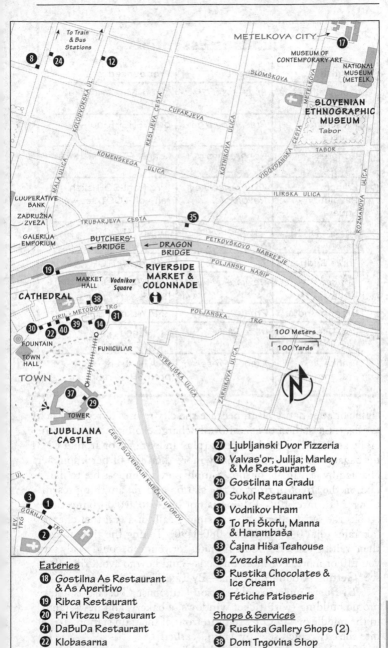

Eateries

18 Gostilna As Restaurant & As Aperitivo

19 Ribca Restaurant

20 Pri Vitezu Restaurant

21 DaBuDa Restaurant

22 Klobasarna

23 Paninoteka

24 Nobel Burek

25 To Olimpija Burek

26 Pizzeria Foculus

27 Ljubljanski Dvor Pizzeria

28 Valvas'or; Julija; Marley & Me Restaurants

29 Gostilna na Gradu

30 Sokol Restaurant

31 Vodnikov Hram

32 To Pri Škofu, Manna & Harambaša

33 Čajna Hiša Teahouse

34 Zvezda Kavarna

35 Rustika Chocolates & Ice Cream

36 Fétiche Patisserie

Shops & Services

37 Rustika Gallery Shops (2)

38 Dom Trgovina Shop

39 Kraševka Shop

40 Trgovina Ika Shop

41 Šnopc o'tecca Shop

42 Full-Service Laundry

Ljubljana Essentials

English	Slovene	Pronounced
Ljubljana Castle	*Ljubljanski Grad*	lyoob-lyee-AHN-skee grahd
Prešeren Square	*Prešernov trg*	preh-SHEHR-nohv turg
Congress Square	*Kongresni trg*	kohn-GREHS-nee turg
French Revolution Square	*Trg Francoske Revolucije*	turg frant-SOH-skeh reh-voh-LOOT-see-yeh
Square of the Republic	*Trg Republike*	turg reh-POOB lee-keh
Triple Bridge	*Tromostovje*	troh-moh-STOHV-yeh
Cobblers' Bridge	*Čevljarski Most*	chehv-LAR-skee mohst
Dragon Bridge	*Zmajski Most*	ZMAY-skee mohst
Jože Plečnik (architect)	*Jože Plečnik*	YOH-zheh PLAYCH-neek
France Prešeren (poet)	*France Prešeren*	FRAHN-tseh preh-SHAY-rehn

traffic or after hours). But, because the city refuses to regulate taxi tariffs, train-station taxis uniformly charge exorbitant rates—generally around €3-5 per kilometer (plus an extra fee of around €2-3 for bags), which is exponentially more than the €1 per kilometer charged by legitimate outfits. Simply put, it's impossible to hail a taxi on the street in front of the station and get anything resembling a fair fare. But all hope is not lost—to avoid giving these crooks the satisfaction, you can simply call for a taxi that charges fair rates (dial 041-731-831 or 080-1190). Taking the time to call, then waiting just a few more minutes for your cab, could easily save you €10 or more. For more on taxis—and how to avoid rip-offs—see "Getting Around Ljubljana—By Taxi," later.

By Bus: Ljubljana's bus station (Autobusna Postaja) is a low-profile building (with ticket windows, a bakery, and newsstands) in the middle of Trg O.F., right in front of the train station. To get into the city center, see "By Train," earlier.

By Car: As you approach Ljubljana on the expressway, the toll road ends. Once you're on the ring road, simply follow signs for *Center*. Once you get into the city center, you'll begin to see directional signs to individual hotels.

Ljubljana is not a car-friendly city; much of the central zone along the river is entirely traffic-free. Even several blocks of the main thoroughfare through the center of town, Slovenska cesta—between Šubičeva ulica and Gosposvetska cesta, north of Congress Square—is closed to all traffic except buses. So, for example, to reach the southern part of the city when entering downtown from the north, you need to circumnavigate the core by looping east along Resljeva cesta, over the Dragon Bridge by the market, and through the tunnel beneath the castle to reach Karlovška cesta, which cuts back west over the river to the southern stretch of Slovenska cesta.

Ask your hotel about parking—most have some available, usually for a price. Side-trippers will find various parking garages around the downtown core; two particularly central (and expensive) lots are the one beneath **Congress Square** (€1.20/hour for first 3 hours, then €2.40/hour, or €1.80/hour overnight) and the one called **N.U.K. #2,** near the National and University Library (€1.20/hour 7:00-19:00, €1.80/hour overnight). Both lots are accessible on Slovenska cesta only from the south—if coming from the north, see directions above. Legal, paid parking downtown is marked by blue lines (look for meters); these spaces are free Saturdays after 13:00 and all day Sunday.

If you need to gas up your rental car before returning it here, you'll find a huge gas station on Tivolska cesta (just west of the train station, near the big Union brewery).

By Plane: See "Ljubljana Connections," at the end of this chapter.

HELPFUL HINTS

Pedestrian Safety: Many Ljubljana residents commute by bike. As a pedestrian, I've had many close calls with bikes whizzing by. Keep your eyes open and stay out of the designated bike lanes on the sidewalks (often marked in red).

Closed Days: Most Ljubljana museums (except the castle and a few less-important museums) are closed on Mondays. The recommended Jože Plečnik House is closed entirely through the fall of 2015; when it reopens, it will likely be closed on Sundays, Mondays, and Fridays.

Markets: In addition to the regular **market** that sprawls along the riverfront (described under "Sights in Ljubljana"), a colorful **flea market** hops along the Ljubljanica River's Breg embankment (across the river from the castle) every Sun 8:00-14:00. On summer Saturdays, there's also a lively and colorful **arts and handicrafts market** in the same place (Sat 8:00-14:00).

Internet Access: Most hotels offer free Wi-Fi and/or a computer for their guests. The **TI** at the upper end of the market has several terminals (€1/30 minutes, see "Tourist Information," earlier). The city's **WiFree** program—with Wi-Fi hotspots near Prešeren Square and along the river—lets you get online free for up to an hour. Pick up the brochure at the TI (you'll be texted a code to enter).

Post Office: The main post office *(pošta)* is in a beautiful yellow Art Nouveau building a block up Čopova from Prešeren Square, at the intersection with Slovenska cesta (Mon-Fri 8:00-19:00, Sat 8:00-12:00, closed Sun).

Architecture Guidebooks: Ljubljana is a turn-on for architecture buffs. If you want to learn more about this city's quirky buildings, look for the excellent *Let's See the City: Ljubljana* architecture guidebook, or one of many books about Jože Plečnik's work (sold at local bookstores).

Laundry: The handiest option is **Emonec Launderette**, with self-service machines across the courtyard from the couldn't-be-more-central Hotel Emonec (described on page 773); with plenty to see and do within a few minutes' walk, this is a convenient spot to tumble-dry your undies while exploring (€5/load wash and dry, daily 11:00-20:00—if it's closed during these hours ask hotel reception to open it, Wolfova 12, tel. 01/200-1520). **Hostel Celica** also has self-service laundry—but it has only one machine, and hostel guests have priority (€8/load, not very central at Metelkova 8). For pricey full service, try **Tekstilexpress,** between the city center and Tivoli Park (€4.80/kilo, figure about €20-25 for a full load, takes 24 hours, Mon-Fri 7:00-19:00, Sat 9:00-13:00, closed Sun, Cankarjeva 10B, tel. 01/252-7354).

Car Rental: Allow about €60 per day, including tax and insurance (no extra charge for drop-off elsewhere in Slovenia). Handy options include **Hertz** (Trdinova 9, tel. 01/434-0147, www.hertz.si), **Europcar** (in City Hotel at Dalmatinova 15, mobile 031-382-052, www.europcar.si), **Avis** and **Budget** (both in Grand Hotel Union at Miklošičeva 3; Avis—tel. 01/241-7340, www.avis.si; Budget—tel. 01/421-7340, www.budget.si), and **Sixt** (at the train station, tel. 01/234-4650).

Best Views: The Skyscraper's observation deck offers the best views in town (see page 759). Views from the castle are nearly as good. At street level, my favorite views are from the wooden bridge called the "Ugly Duckling" (between the Triple and Cobblers' bridges), especially at night. On sunny, blue-sky days, the colorful architecture on and near Prešeren Square pops, and you'll take photos like crazy along the river promenade.

Updates to This Book: For updates to this book, check www.ricksteves.com/update.

GETTING AROUND LJUBLJANA

By Bus: Virtually all of Ljubljana's sights are easily accessible by foot—I haven't taken a bus here in years. And public transit is a bit of a headache: To ride a bus, you first have to buy a plastic "Urbana" card for €2, which you then load with credit to pay for rides (you can't pay the driver). A ride costs €1.20 (valid for up to 90 minutes, card shareable by up to three people). While you can buy the Urbana card at newsstands and other places around town, if you buy it at the TI, they'll let you return it to reclaim your €2 at the end of your trip. Transit info: www.lpp.si.

By Taxi: Always call for a cab, or you'll get ripped off. Because cabbies can legally charge whatever they want, even if they use the meter you'll still pay way too much. Legitimate taxis usually start at about €1.50, and then charge €1 per kilometer. But because city leaders refuse to regulate taxi tariffs, many unscrupulous cabbies (including all of those who wait at the train station) legally charge far more, and tack on bogus additional "surcharges." Crooked cabbies are a big problem in Ljubljana, but you can avoid this headache entirely by always calling a reputable taxi company instead of hailing one on the street. If you do this, Ljubljana is a fantastic taxi town with very affordable rates—a ride within the city center (such as from the station to a hotel) should run only a few euros, generally less than €5. Good companies include **Yellow Taxi** (mobile 041-731-831) and **Metro Taxi** (tel. 080-1190). Don't be intimidated—dispatchers speak English, and your hotel, restaurant, or maybe the TI (if they're not too busy) can call a cab for you.

By Bike: Ljubljana is a cyclist's delight, with lots of well-marked bike lanes. A few hotels have rental or loaner bikes, or you can rent bikes at the market square TI (€2/2 hours, €8/day; see "Tourist Information," earlier). Like many European cities, Ljubljana has a subsidized borrow-a-bike program (called BicikeLJ) with 30 locations around the city center. Once you register online with a credit card (€1 fee for a weekly subscription), rides are free or very cheap (free for the first hour, €1 for the second, €2 for the third, and so on). If you're planning on doing lots of biking, it's worth the hassle to sign up (for details, see http://en.bicikelj.si).

By Shuttle Bus: After Ljubljana pedestrianized much of its downtown core a few years back, the natives began to squawk about the hassle of getting around town without a car. To mollify critics, the city subsidizes a network of green electric carts, called **Kavalir**, which anyone (even tourists) can flag down or call to take them anywhere within the pedestrian zone...for free. Just wave one down and tell them where you want to go (or phone them—April-Oct call 031 666-331 or 031-666-332; Nov-March call 031-666-299).

Tours in Ljubljana

To help you appreciate Ljubljana, taking a walking tour—either through the TI or by hiring your own local guide—is worth ▲▲.

Walking Tour

The TI organizes excellent two-hour guided town walks of Ljubljana in English, led by knowledgeable guides. In summer, the walk also includes either a trip up to the castle (by funicular or tourist train) or a 30-minute boat ride on the river. From April through September, there are three tours daily: at 10:00, 14:00, and 17:00. From October through March, the walking tour goes daily at 11:00 (€10, or €9 if you pay at TI, meet at Town Hall around corner from Triple Bridge TI).

Local Guides

Having an expert show you around his or her hometown for two hours for €70 has to be the best value in town. Ljubljana's hard-working guides lead tours on a wide variety of topics and can tailor their tour to your interests (figure €70/2 hours, 50 percent more for same-day booking, contact TI for details, arrange at least 24 hours before). **Marijan Krišković,** who leads tours for me throughout Europe, is an outstanding guide (mobile 040-222-739, kriskovic@yahoo.com). **Barbara Jakopič,** thoughtful and extremely knowl-edgeable, also leads my tours (mobile 040-530-870, b_lucky2@yahoo.com). **Minka Kahrič,** who's traveled to the North Pole, also leads tours closer to home—including walks around Ljubljana and excursions into the countryside (€70/2-hour walking tour; driv-ing: €100/up to 4 hours, €140/up to 8 hours; mobile 041-805-962, polarnimedo@yahoo.com).

Boat Cruise

Because Ljubljana is a small town that's easily seen by foot, a boat trip on the Ljubljanica River is more romantic than informative. You have two options for your one-hour cruise (weather permit-ting): with English commentary from a live guide (€10, 2/day in summer, departs from near the Triple Bridge—about one block along the embankment away from the market), or unguided (€8, hourly in summer 10:00-20:00, operated by various companies and from various docks). For details, check with the TI.

Excursions from Ljubljana

Slovenia is a tiny country with many worthwhile sights that are near Ljubljana but tricky to reach by public transportation. To hit several efficiently in one day, you could join an excursion. Tour companies tend to come and go here—drop by any TI to ask about the latest options and which companies have the best reputa-tions. You'll find fliers everywhere. Two relatively well-established outfits are **Roundabout** (their one-day "Karst and Coast Mystery" tour takes you to Predjama Castle, Škocjan Caves, Lipica, and Piran for €45 plus admission to the caves; www.roundabout.si) and **Slovenia Explorer** (their ambitious "Slovenia in 1 Day" trip visits Lake Bled, Lake Bohinj, and Postojna Caves for €115; www.slovenia-explorer.com).

Prešeren Square Spin-Tour

The heart of Ljubljana is lively Prešeren Square (Prešernov trg, rated ▲▲), which is described in this self-guided spin tour. It's always been bustling, but now it's more people-friendly than ever, since the mayor recently outlawed buses and taxis here.

The city's meeting point is the large **statue of France Prešeren,** Slovenia's greatest poet, whose works include the lyrics to the Slovenian national anthem (and whose silhouette adorns Slovenia's €2 coin). The statue shows Prešeren, an important catalyst of 19th-century Slovenian nationalism, being inspired from above by a Muse. This statue provoked a scandal and outraged the bishop when it went up a century ago—a naked woman sharing the square with a church! To ensure that nobody could be confused about the woman's intentions, she's conspicuously depicted with typical Muse accessories: a laurel branch and a cloak. Even so, for the first few years citizens covered the scandalous statue with a tarp each night. And the model who posed for the Muse was so disgraced that no one in Slovenia would hire her—so she emigrated to South America and never returned.

Stand at the base of the statue to get oriented. The bridge crossing the Ljubljanica River is one of Ljubljana's most impor-

tant landmarks, Jože Plečnik's **Triple Bridge** (Tromostovje). The middle (widest) part of this bridge already existed, but Plečnik added the two side spans to more efficiently funnel the six streets of traffic on this side of the bridge to the one street on the other side. The bridge's Venetian vibe is intentional: Plečnik recognized that Ljubljana, located midway between Venice and then-capital Vienna, is itself a bridge between the Italian and

LJUBLJANA

Ljubljana at a Glance

▲▲▲People-Watching Ljubljana's single best activity is sitting at an outdoor café along the river and watching the stylish Slovenes strut their stuff. **Hours:** 24/7. See page 779.

▲▲Riverside Market Lively market area in the Old Town with produce, clothing, and souvenirs. **Hours:** Best in the morning, especially Sat; market hall open Mon-Fri 7:00-16:00, Sat 7:00-14:00, closed Sun. See page 745.

▲▲Serbian Orthodox Church of Sts. Cyril and Methodius Beautifully decorated house of worship giving insight into the Orthodox faith. **Hours:** Daily 8:00-19:00. See page 756.

▲▲National and University Library Jože Plečnik's pièce de résistance, with an intriguing facade and a bright reading room. **Hours:** Main staircase open Mon-Fri 8:00-20:00, Sat 9:00-14:00, closed Sun; student reading room open to the public only mid-July-mid-Aug Mon-Sat 14:00-18:00. See page 761.

▲▲Jože Plečnik House Closed through fall of 2015; final digs of the famed hometown architect who shaped so much of Ljubljana, explained by an enthusiastic guide. **Hours:** When open, English tours likely begin at the top of each hour Tue-Thu 10:00-18:00, Sat 9:00-15:00—but check online or call first to confirm, last tour departs one hour before closing, likely closed Sun-Mon and Fri. See page 764.

Germanic worlds. Across the bridge are the TI, WCs, ATMs, market and cathedral (to the left), and the Town Hall (straight ahead).

Now turn 90 degrees to the right, and look down the first street after the riverbank. Find the pale woman in the picture frame on the second floor of the first yellow house. This is **Julija,** the unrequited love of Prešeren's life. Tour guides spin romantic tales about how the couple met. But the truth is far less exciting: He was a teacher in her father's house when he was in his 30s and she was 4. Later in life, she inspired him from afar— as she does now, from across the square—but they never got together. She may have been his muse, but when it came to marriage, she opted for wealth and status.

When Ljubljana was hit by

▲▲Slovenian Ethnographic Museum Engaging, well-presented collection celebrating Slovenian culture. **Hours:** Tue-Sun 10:00-18:00, closed Mon. See page 765.

▲Cathedral Italian Baroque interior and highly symbolic, intricately designed bronze doors. **Hours:** Open long hours daily but closed 12:00-15:00. See page 749.

▲Dragon Bridge Distinctive Art Nouveau bridge adorned with the city's mascot. **Hours:** Always roaring. See page 749.

▲Ljubljana Castle Tower with good views and so-so 3-D film. **Hours:** Grounds open daily April-Sept 9:00-23:00, Oct-March 10:00-21:00; castle open daily April-Sept 9:00-21:00, Oct-March 10:00-18:00, film plays all day on the half-hour. See page 751.

▲Contemporary History Museum Baroque mansion in Tivoli Park, with exhibit highlighting Slovenia's last 100 years. **Hours:** Tue-Sun 10:00-18:00, closed Mon. See page 757.

▲City Museum of Ljubljana Modern, high-tech exhibit on the city's history. **Hours:** Tue-Sun 10:00-18:00, Thu until 21:00, closed Mon. See page 759.

▲Cobblers' Bridge Columned bridge that epitomizes Plečnik's distinctive architecture. **Hours:** Always open. See page 760.

an earthquake in 1895, locals took the opportunity (and an ample rebuilding fund from the Austro-Hungarian Empire) to remake their city in style. Today Ljubljana—especially the streets around this square—is an architecture-lover's paradise. The **Hauptmann House,** to the right of Julija, was the only building on the square to survive the quake. A few years later, the owner redecorated it in the then-trendy Viennese Art Nouveau style you see today, using bright colors (since his family sold dyes). All that remains of the original structure is the little Baroque balcony above the entrance.

Just to the right of the Hauptmann House is a car-sized **model** of the city center—helpful for orientation. The street next to it (with the McDonald's) is **Čopova,** once the route of Ljubljana's Sunday promenade. A century ago, locals would put on their Sunday best and stroll from here to Tivoli Park, listening to musicians and dropping into cafés along the way. Plečnik called it the "lifeline of the city," connecting the green lungs of the park to this urban center. Through the 20th century, this route became less pedestrian-friendly, as Slovenska cesta and railroad tracks were

LJUBLJANA

both laid across it. Things are getting better with the closure of Slovenska to all traffic except buses, but Ljubljana's best evening *paseo* thrives along the river from the Triple Bridge all the way up the river.

Continue looking to the right, past the big, pink landmark Franciscan Church of St. Mary. The characteristic glass awning marks

Galerija Emporium—the first big post-quake department store, today government-protected. At the top of the building is Mercury, god of commerce, watching over the square that has been Ljubljana's commercial heart since the city began. (If you look carefully, you can see the musta-

chioed face of the building's owner hiding in the folds of cloth by Mercury's left foot.) Since this area was across the river from medieval Ljubljana (beyond the town's limits...and the long arm of its tax collector), it was the best place to buy and sell goods. Today this sumptuously restored building houses a top-end fashion mall, making it the heart of Ljubljana's boutique culture. Step inside for a glimpse at the grand staircase.

The street between Galerija Emporium and the pink church is **Miklošičeva cesta,** which connects Prešeren Square to the train station. When Ljubljana was rebuilding after the 1895 earthquake, town architects and designers envisioned this street as a showcase of its new, Vienna-inspired Art Nouveau image.

Up Miklošičeva cesta and on the left is the prominent **Grand Hotel Union,** with a stately domed spire on the corner. When these buildings were designed, Prague was the cultural capital of the Slavic world. The new look of Ljubljana paid homage to "the golden city of a hundred spires" (and copied Prague's romantic image). The city actually had a law for several years that new corner buildings had to have these spires. Even the trees you'll see around town were part of the vision. When the architect Plečnik designed the Ljubljanica River embankments a generation later, he planted tall, pointy poplar trees and squat, rounded willows—imi-

tating the spires and domes of Prague.

Detour a block up Miklošičeva cesta to see two more architectural gems of that era (across from the Grand Hotel Union): First is a Secessionist building—marked **Zadružna Zveza**—with classic red, blue, and white colors (for the Slovenian flag). Next is the noisy, pink, zigzagged **Cooperative Bank.** The bank was designed by Ivan Vurnik, an ambitious Slovenian architect who wanted to invent a distinctive national style after World War I, when the Habsburg Empire broke up and Eastern Europe's nations were proudly emerging for the first time.

Prešeren Square is the perfect springboard to explore the rest of Ljubljana. Now that you're oriented, visit some of the areas listed next.

Sights in Ljubljana

Ljubljana is bursting with new, well-presented, we-try-harder museums celebrating Slovenian history and culture. These include the Slovenian History Exhibition at the castle, the City Museum of Ljubljana, and the Contemporary History Museum in Tivoli Park. Those of us who've fallen in love with this city and country find each of these museums fascinating in its own right, but—since they're similar and largely overlapping—some visitors might find them redundant and dull. If you get museumed out easily, just visit the one that's handiest to your sightseeing plan.

EAST OF THE RIVER, UNDER THE CASTLE: THE MARKET AND OLD TOWN

The castle side of the river is the city's most colorful and historic quarter, packed with Old World ambience.

▲▲Riverside Market (Tržnice)

In Ljubljana's thriving Old Town market, big-city Slovenes enjoy buying directly from the producer. Prices go down as the day gets late and as the week goes on. The market, worth an amble anytime, is best on Saturday mornings, when the townspeople take their time wandering the stalls. In this tiny capital of a tiny country, you may even see the president searching for the perfect melon.

→ **Self-Guided Walk:** Begin your walk through the market at the Triple Bridge (and TI). The riverside **colonnade,** which echoes the long-gone medieval city wall, was designed by (who else?) Jože Plečnik. This first stretch—nearest the Triple Bridge—is good for souvenirs: woodcarvings, replica painted frontboards from beehives, honey products (including honey brandy), and lots of colorful

Zoran Janković

The latest chapter in Ljubljana's story has been written by its mayor, Zoran Janković. Sort of the Michael Bloomberg of Slovenia, this successful businessman transformed himself into a broadly supported mayor who is unafraid to pursue an ambitious civic agenda.

As chairman of the huge Mercator supermarket chain, Janković was famous for prowling around the front lines of his stores, micromanaging all the day-to-day business. After corporate political shuffling forced him out, Janković turned his attention to the municipal realm—and, in 2006, was elected mayor of Ljubljana in a landslide.

The people of this city, who had grown accustomed to well-intentioned but ineffectual leaders who proposed, then canceled, ambitious projects, were stunned by Janković's corporate-minded, no-nonsense follow-through. Project after project materialized, on time and under budget: the funicular to the castle, several new bridges (including the Butchers' Bridge at the market), the creation of quaintly cobbled traffic-free zones throughout almost the entire town center, and the pedestrianization of miles of riverfront embankment. The sweeping changes have had their critics, among them elderly people who can no longer easily drive to their homes in the now-traffic-free center. Janković has attempted to assuage them with free shuttle buses. Ultimately, most Ljubljanans are thrilled with the transformation of their city. It's a good example of how a progressive electorate can trust a capable leader to wisely invest public funds in urban-beautification projects that benefit the common good.

After winning re-election to the mayor's office in another landslide in 2010, Janković turned his sights to the national arena. In the parliamentary elections of December, 2011, the party he formed—Positive Slovenia—eked out a nationwide victory. However, some last-minute political wrangling among members of his coalition cost him the prime ministership. Then, after the elections, the country slipped into the second downturn of a double-dip reception; reports of corruption and an unpopular agenda of austerity reforms sparked a wave of protests nationwide. A government commission investigated and accused both Janković and his opponents of corruption.

It seems that Janković's national political aspirations have ended—at least, for now—but he handily won re-election as Ljubljana mayor in 2012. For the time being, Janković will continue to focus on improving the city he calls home; his latest initiative was to close down a several-block stretch of one of Ljubljana's most heavily used downtown streets, Slovenska cesta, to all but public buses.

candles (bubbly Marta will gladly paint a special message on your candle for no extra charge). (For lots more shopping tips—here and nearby—see "Shopping in Ljubljana," later.)

Farther in, the market is almost all local, and the colonnade is populated by butchers, bakers, fishermen, and lazy cafés. Peek down at the actual river and see how the architect wanted the town and river to connect. The lower arcade (which you can access directly from the Triple Bridge, or by going down the spiral staircase by the beehive panels) is a people zone, with public WCs, inviting cafés, and a stinky fish market *(riharnica)* offering a wide variety. The recommended restaurant just below, **Ribca,** serves fun fishy plates, beer, and coffee with great riverside seating.

Across from the stairs that lead down into the fish market, about where the souvenir stands end, you reach the first small market square. On your right, notice the 10-foot-tall concrete **cone.** Plečnik wanted to make Ljubljana the "Athens of the North" and imagined a huge hilltop cone crowning the center of a national acropolis—a complex for government, museums, and culture. This ambitious plan didn't make it off the drawing board, but part of Plečnik's Greek idea came true: this marketplace, based on an ancient Greek *agora.* Plečnik's cone still captures the Slovenes' imaginations...and adorns Slovenia's €0.10 coin.

At the top of this square, you'll find the 18th-century **cathedral** standing on the site of a 13th-century Romanesque church (check out its finely decorated doors—and, if they're open, go inside; for a complete description, see later).

The building at the end of the first market square is the seminary palace. In the basement is a **market hall** *(pokrita tržnica),* with vendors selling cheeses, meats, baked goods, dried fruits, nuts, and other goodies (Mon-Fri 7:00-16:00, Sat 7:00-14:00, closed Sun). This place is worth a graze—walk all the way through. Most merchants are happy to give you a free sample (point to what you want, and say *probat, prosim*—"a taste, please").

Leaving the market hall at the opposite end, notice where the colonnade ends at a modern bridge. Jože Plečnik designed a huge, roofed **Butchers' Bridge** to be built here, but—like so many of his designs—the plans were scuttled. Decades later, aware of Plečnik's newfound touristic currency, some town politicians dusted off the old plans and proposed building the bridge. The project stalled for years until the arrival of Mayor Zoran Janković, who swiftly constructed this modern version of the bridge. While it looks nothing like Plečnik's original plans, the bridge kept the old name and has been embraced by the community (there's a handy public WC down below on the lower level). The sculptures on the bridge, by local artist Jakov Brdar, were originally intended to be temporary—but people loved them, so they stayed. (The wild-eyed,

LJUBLJANA

wild-bearded Brdar often hangs out near the bridge, asking pass-ersby how they like his creations.) Notice the mournful pose of the Adam and Eve statues (being evicted from the Garden of Eden) at the market end of the bridge. And don't miss the bizarre smaller sculptures along the railing—such as the ones that look like mischievous lizards breaking out of their eggs. Almost as soon as it was built, the bridge's railings were covered with padlocks—part of the recent Europe-wide craze for young couples to commemorate their love by locking a padlock to a bridge railing. But all those locks put too much strain on the railing—they are regularly cut off, soon to be replaced by new ones.

Sprawling up from the bridge is the **main market square,** packed with produce and clothing stands. (The colorful flower market hides behind the market hall.) The vendors in the row nearest the colonnade sell fruit from all over, but the ones located deeper in the market sell only locally grown produce. These producers go out of their way to be old-fashioned—a few of them still follow the tradition of push-

ing their veggies on wooden carts (called *cizas*) to the market from their garden patches in the suburbs. Once at the market, they simply display their goods on top of their cart, turning it into a sales kiosk. Tell the vendor what you want—it's considered rude for customers to touch the fruits and vegetables before they're bought. Over time, shoppers develop friendships with their favorite producers. On busy days, you'll see a long line at one stand, while the other merchants stand bored. Your choice is simple: Get in line, or eat subpar produce.

Near the market hall, look for the little **scales** in the wooden kiosks marked *Kontrolna Tehtnica*—allowing buyers to immediately check whether the producer cheated them (not a common problem, but just in case). The Habsburg days left locals with the old German saying, "Trust is good; control is better." Nearby, look for the innovative "Nonstop Mlekomat" stand, a vending machine that lets you buy a plastic bottle, then fill it with a liter of raw, unskimmed, farm-fresh milk for €1.

At the far end of the market—close to the Dragon Bridge—you may see a few **food trucks,** selling roasted chicken and deep-fried seafood.

Two more sights are immersed in the market action (both described next); the cathedral sits at the top of the market area, near the Triple Bridge, while the Dragon Bridge spans the river just beyond the end of the market colonnade.

▲Cathedral (Stolnica)

Ljubljana's cathedral is dedicated to St. Nicholas, protector against floods and patron saint of the fishermen and boatmen who have long come to sell their catch at the market. While the interior is worth a peek (free, open long hours daily but closed 12:00-15:00), the intricately decorated doors—created for Pope John Paul II's visit here in 1996—are even more interesting.

Go under the high arch, then take a close look at the remarkable side **door** on the left. Buried deeply in the fecund soil of their ancient and pagan history, the nation's linden tree of life sprouts with the story of the Slovenes. The ceramic pots represent the original Roman settlement here. Just to the left, above the tree, are the Byzantine missionaries Cyril and Methodius, who came here to convert the Slavs to Christianity in the ninth century. Just above, Crusaders and Ottomans do battle. Near the top, see the Slovenes going into the cave—entering the dark 20th century (World War I, World War II, and communism). At the top is Pope John Paul II (the first Slavic pontiff, who also oversaw the fall of communism). Below him are two men who are on track to becoming Slovenia's first saints; the one on the right is Frederic Baraga, a 19th-century bishop who became a missionary in Michigan and codified Chippewa grammar (notice the Native American relief on the book he's holding). In the upper right-hand corner is a sun, which has been shining since Slovenia gained its independence in 1991. Around back of the cathedral is a similar door, carved with images of the six 20th-century bishops of Ljubljana.

The cathedral's **interior** is stunning Italian Baroque. The transept is surrounded by sculptures of four bishops of Roman Ljubljana (when it was called Emona, or Aemon). Left of the main altar, notice the distinctive chair. This was designed by the very religious Jože Plečnik, whose brother was a priest here. Look up over the nave to enjoy the recently restored, gorgeous ceiling fresco.

▲Dragon Bridge (Zmajski Most)

The dragon has been the symbol of Ljubljana for centuries, ever since Jason (of Argonauts and Golden Fleece fame) supposedly slew one in a nearby swamp. This is one of the few notable bits of Ljubljana architecture not by Plečnik (but by Jurij Zaninović, a fellow student of Vienna architect Otto Wagner). While the dragon is the star of this very photogenic Art Nouveau bridge, the bridge itself was officially dedicated to the 40th anniversary of Habsburg

Emperor Franz Josef's reign (see the dates on the side: 1848-1888). Tapping into the emp's vanity got new projects funded—vital as the city rebuilt after the 1895 earthquake. But the Franz Josef name never stuck; those dragons are just too darn memorable.

From the Dragon Bridge, it's an easy funicular ride or steep hike up to Ljubljana Castle (described later). Or you can head back through the market to reach the Town Square and Old Town (see next), where I've narrated a self-guided shopping tour.

▲Town Square (Mestni Trg) and the Old Town

Ljubljana's Town Square, just across the Triple Bridge and up the street from Prešeren Square, is home to the **Town Hall** (Rotovž), highlighted by its clock tower and pillared loggia. Step inside the Renaissance courtyard to see paintings, artifacts, and a map of late 17th-century Ljubljana. Studying this map, notice how the river, hill, and wall worked together to fortify the town. Courtyards like this (but humbler) are hidden throughout the city. As rent in these old places is cheap, many such courtyards host funky and characteristic little businesses. Be sure to get off the main drag and poke into Ljubljana's nooks and crannies.

In the square between the Town Hall and the cathedral is a recent replica of the **Fountain of Three Carniolian Rivers,**

inspired in style and theme by Rome's many fountains. The figures with vases represent this region's three main rivers: Ljubljanica, Sava, and Krka. This is one of many works in town by Francesco Robba, an Italian who came to Ljubljana for a job, fell in love with a Slovene, and stayed here the rest of his life—decorating the city's churches with beautiful Baroque altars. At the nearby corner, check out the wild interior of the Nova KBM Bank, which looks more like a cutting-edge nightclub.

Just to the right as you face Town Hall, peek into #4, where **Čupterija Bar** has one of the most creative interiors in this very creative town.

Now turn with your back to the fountain. You're staring down the single street that constitutes Ljubljana's Old Town. In the early 19th century, Ljubljana consisted mainly of this solitary main drag, running along the base of Castle Hill (plus a small "New Town" across the river). Stretching south from here are two other "squares"—Stari trg (Old Square) and Gornji trg (Upper Square)—which have long since grown together into one big, atmospheric promenade lined with quaint boutiques, great restaurants, and cafés. Virtually every house along this drag has a story to tell of a famous resident or infamous incident. As you walk, keep your eyes open for Ljubljana's mascot dragon—it's everywhere.

For a self-guided shopping stroll that runs the length of this delightful street—and highlights several fine shops en route—see "Shopping in Ljubljana," later.

▲Ljubljana Castle (Ljubljanski Grad)

The castle above town offers enjoyable views of Ljubljana and the surrounding countryside. There has probably been a settlement

on this site since prehistoric times, though the first true fortress here was Roman. The 12th-century version was gradually added on to over the centuries, until it fell into disrepair in the 17th century. Today's castle—rebuilt in the 1940s and renovated in the 1970s—is a cut-rate, hollow-feeling modern replica, completely lacking any sense of real history. However, in recent years they've filled this dull shell with some worthwhile attractions, including a well-presented history exhibit and film, and some respectable restaurants. The main reason to come up here is the same reason it was built here: for the view, looking out over Ljubljana's rooftops and to the Alps on the horizon. The castle is also home to the Ljubljana Festival, with concerts throughout the summer (tel. 01/306-4293, www.ljubljanafestival.si).

Cost and Hours: You can hike up to the castle and wander the grounds for free (daily April-Sept 9:00-23:00, Oct-March 10:00-21:00). But if you want to enter the three sights at the castle (history exhibition, film, and castle tower), you'll pay €6 (€8 combo-ticket also includes funicular; €12 combo-ticket includes sights, funicular, and guided tour; sights open daily April-Sept 9:00-21:00, Oct-March 10:00-18:00, tel. 01/232-9994, www.ljubljanskigrad.si).

Tours: Guided tours of the castle in Slovene and English leave from the castle information center a few times daily from June through September (check online or call to ask times; €8, or included in €12 combo-ticket with castle sights and funicular; tour lasts 1-1.5 hours; winter tours possible to arrange upon request—call a day ahead).

Getting to the Castle: A slick **funicular** whisks visitors to the top in a jiff (€2.20 one-way, €4 round-trip, also included in combo-tickets described above, runs every 10 minutes, 1-minute ride, daily April-Sept 9:00-23:00, Oct-March 10:00-21:00, catch it at Krekov trg—across the street from the market square TI). From the top, you'll find free WCs and a few easy flights of stairs up into the heart of the castle complex (or take the elevator). Another sweat-free route to the top is via the **tourist train** that leaves at the top of each hour (or more frequently with demand) from the street in front of the Town Hall (€4 round-trip, daily in summer 9:00-21:00, shorter hours off-season, doesn't run in snow or other bad weather). There are also two handy **trails** to the castle. The steeper-but-faster route begins near the Dragon Bridge: Find Študentovska lane, just past the statue of Vodnik in the market. This lane dead-ends at a gravel path, which you'll follow up to a fork. Turn left to zigzag up the steepest and fastest route, which deposits you just below the castle wall; from here, turn left again and curl around the wall to reach the main drawbridge. Slower but a bit less steep is Reber, just off Stari trg, a few blocks south of the Town Hall: Walk up to the top of Reber, and, at the dead end, turn right and start climbing up the stairs. From here on out, keep bearing left, then go right when you're just under the castle (follow *Grad* signs).

Visiting the Castle: The castle's information office is on the courtyard above the top of the funicular. Across the way are the well-stocked Rustika gift shop and three eateries (the fancy Strelec; Gradska Kavana, the "town café"; and the recommended Gostilna na Gradu, with traditional Slovenian cuisine). The upper floors house two wedding halls—Ljubljana's most popular places to get married (free for locals).

Most of the sights worth seeing at the castle are in the opposite wing, clustered around the base of the tallest tower. As you face the tower, the entrance to the history museum is to the left, while the "Virtual Castle" film and tower climb itself are to the right.

The **Slovenian History Exhibition** offers a concise but engaging overview of this little country's story. As you enter, ask to borrow the free audioguide, then head downstairs and work your way up. Dark display cases light up when you approach, revealing actual artifacts, video clips, and touchscreens with more information. A unique feature of the museum is that you're invited to touch replicas of important historic items (in many cases, the originals are in other Ljubljana museums). Don't miss the top floor of the exhibit (go up the glassed-in staircase), which is the most interesting—covering the tumultuous 20th century. You'll learn about topics ranging from the battlefields of World War I, to the creation of the first Yugoslavia, to the fascist occupation and harrowing Italian-run concentration camps of World War II, to the cult of personality around Partisan war hero-turned-Yugoslav president Tito, to Slovenia's bid for independence.

Entering the door to the right of the tower, you'll first find the small **penitentiary** exhibit, recalling the post-Napoleonic era, when the castle was converted to a prison. It saw the most action during World War I, when it housed political prisoners (including the beloved Slovenian writer Ivan Cankar) and POWs. Modest exhibits inside actual, former cells describe the history and list the names of past inmates.

If you head downstairs from the entrance, you'll find a Gothic **chapel** with Baroque paintings of St. George (Ljubljana's patron saint, the dragon-slayer) and coats of arms of the various aristocratic families that have called this castle home.

Heading up the stairs, you'll find the informative, entertaining, and nicely animated **"Virtual Castle" film,** in which Ljubljana's mascot dragon describes this hill's layers of history (12 minutes, plays all day on the half-hour; often in English, but otherwise borrow English headset).

Finally, climb the 92 spiral steps up to the **castle tower,** with one of the best views in town.

Eating: Combine your visit to the castle with a meal at the recommended **Gostilna na Gradu,** with the best traditional Slovenian food in town (in the castle courtyard; described later, under "Eating in Ljubljana"). **Strelec** restaurant is pricey and pretentious, with an overly complicated theme and menu (a hard-to-pin-down muddle of traditional Slovenian, ancient Roman, and contemporary international); unless you're trying to impress someone, I'd stick with Gostilna na Gradu.

WEST OF THE RIVER, BEYOND PREŠEREN SQUARE: THE MUSEUM ZONE AND TIVOLI PARK

The Prešeren Square (west) side of the river is the heart of modern Ljubljana, and home to several prominent squares and fine museums. These sights are listed roughly in order from Prešeren Square and can be linked to make an interesting walk.

• *Leave Prešeren Square in the direction the poet is looking, bear to your left (up Wolfova, by the picture of Julija), and walk a block to...*

Congress Square (Kongresni Trg)

This grassy, tree-lined square hosts big town events. It's ringed by some of Ljubljana's most important buildings: the University headquarters, the Baroque Ursuline Church of the Holy Trinity,

LJUBLJANA

a classical mansion called the Kazina, and the Philharmonic Hall. Once clogged with traffic, the area around the square was recently pedestrianized, including the broad strip along the far side. The green belt at the heart of the square, called Park Zvezda ("Star Park") for its radiating paths, is fronted by several inviting cafés and restaurants; the aptly named and recommended **Zvezda** is a top spot for its local cakes.

At the top end of the square, by the entry to a pedestrian underpass, a Roman sarcophagus sits under a gilded statue of a **Roman citizen**—a replica of a Roman tomb sculpture from 1,700 years ago, when this town was called Emona. The busy street above you has been the site of the main trading route through town since ancient Roman times. Take a few steps into the underpass, and look left to find the Chopin Passage (Chopinov Prehod), which displays exposed parts of the original Roman-era road (along with a model of Emona in ancient times, and projections of Romans walking on the road).

• *Continue the rest of the way through the underpass beneath Slovenska cesta, then walk straight through the gap in the Maxi shopping mall into the...*

▲Square of the Republic (Trg Republike)

This unusual square is essentially a parking lot ringed by an odd collection of buildings. While hardly quaint, the Square of the Republic gives you a good taste of a modern corner of Ljubljana. And it's historic—this is where Slovenia declared its independence in 1991.

The **twin office towers** (with the world's biggest digital watch, flashing the date, time, and temperature) were designed by Plečnik's protégé, Edvard Ravnikar. As harrowing as these structures seem, imagine if the builders had followed the original plans—the towers would be twice as tall as they are now, and connected by a bridge, representing the gateway to Ljubljana. These buildings were originally designed as the Slovenian parliament, but they were scaled back when Tito didn't approve (since it would have made Slovenia's parliament bigger than the Yugoslav parliament in Belgrade). Instead, the **Slovenian Parliament** is across the square, in the strangely low-profile office building with the sculpted entryway. The carvings are in the Socialist Realist style, celebrating the noble Slovenian people conforming to communist ideals for the good of the entire society. Completing the square are a huge conference center (Cankarjev Dom, the white building behind the skyscrapers), a shopping mall, and some public art.

• *Just a block north, across the street and through the grassy park (Trg Narodni Herojev), you'll find the...*

Slovenian National Museum (Narodni Muzej Slovenije) and Slovenian Museum of Natural History (Prirodoslovni Muzej Slovenije)

These two museums share a single historic building facing a park behind the Parliament. While neither collection is particularly good, they're both worth considering if you have a special interest or if it's a rainy day.

The **National Museum** occupies the ground floor, featuring a lapidarium with carved-stone Roman monuments and exhibits on Egyptian mummies. (Temporary exhibits are also on this level.) Upstairs and to the right are more exhibits of the National Museum, with archaeological findings ranging from old armor and pottery to the museum's two prized possessions: a fragment of a 45,000-year-old Neanderthal flute fashioned from a cave bear's femur, supposedly the world's oldest musical instrument; and the "figural situla," a beautifully decorated hammered-bronze bucket from the fifth century B.C. Embossed with scenes of everyday Iron Age life, this object has been a gold mine of information for archaeologists.

Upstairs and to the left is the **Natural History** exhibit, featuring the flora and fauna of Slovenia. You'll see partial skeletons of a mammoth and a cave bear, plenty of stuffed reptiles, fish, and birds, and an exhibit on "human fish" (*Proteus anguinus*—long, skinny, pale-pink, sightless salamanders unique to caves in this part of Europe).

Cost and Hours: €3 for each museum, or €5 for both, some English descriptions, free audioguide for Natural History Museum, both open daily 10:00-18:00, Thu until 20:00, Prešernova 20, tel. 01/241-4400, www.nms.si and www.pms-lj.si.

• *At the far end of the building is a glassed-in annex displaying Roman stone monuments (free). Turning left around the museum building and walking one block, you'll see the...*

US Embassy

This pretty yellow chalet (with brown trim and a red roof, at Prešernova cesta 31) wins my vote for quaintest embassy building in the world. Resist the urge to snap a photo...those guards are all business.

• *Just up Prešernova cesta from the embassy are two decent but skippable art museums.*

National Gallery (Narodna Galerija)

This museum has three parts: European artists (in the new building), Slovenian artists (in the old building), and temporary exhibits. Find the work of Ivana Kobilca, a late 19th-century Slovenian Impressionist. Art-lovers enjoy her self-portrait in *Summer*. If you're going to Bled, you can get a sneak preview with Marko Pernhart's huge panorama of the Julian Alps.

Cost and Hours: €5, special exhibits typically cost extra, permanent collection free first Sun of the month, open Tue-Sun 10:00-18:00, closed Mon; if main entrance at Cankarjeva 20 is closed for renovation, use the other entrance at the big glass box between two older buildings at Prešernova 24; tel. 01/241-5418, www.ng-slo.si.

Museum of Modern Art (Moderna Galerija Ljubljana)

Newly renovated, this museum has a permanent collection of modern and contemporary Slovenian artists, as well as temporary exhibits by both Slovenes and international artists. To explore the "Continuities and Ruptures" permanent collection (aptly named for a place with such a fractured, up-and-down recent history), borrow the English floor plan and take a chronological spin through the 20th century. Unusual for a "modern" art museum is the room with Partisan art, with stiff, improvised, communist-style posters from the days when Tito and his crew were just a rag-tag militia movement.

Cost and Hours: €5, ask about combo-ticket with contemporary branch at Metelkova—see page 766, Tue-Sun 10:00-18:00, closed Mon, Tomšičeva 14, tel. 01/241-6800, www.mg-lj.si.

• *By the busy road near the art museums, look for the distinctive Neo-Byzantine design (tall domes with narrow slits) of the...*

▲▲Serbian Orthodox Church of Sts. Cyril and Methodius

Ljubljana's most striking church interior isn't Catholic, but Orthodox. This church was built in 1936, soon after the Slovenes joined a political union with the Serbs. Wealthy Slovenia attracted its poorer neighbors from the south—so it built this church for that community. Since 1991, the Serb population continues to grow, as people from the struggling corners of the former Yugoslavia flock to prosperous Slovenia. Its gorgeous interior—which feels closer to Moscow than to Rome—offers visitors a taste of this important faith.

Cost and Hours: Free, daily 8:00-19:00; services at 8:30,

10:00, 17:00, and 18:00; Prešernova cesta 35, www.spc-ljubljana.si.

Visiting the Church: Step inside for the best glimpse of the Orthodox faith this side of Dubrovnik. The church is colorfully decorated without a hint of the 21st century, mirroring a very conservative religion. Many of the church's colorful frescoes are copies of famous frescoes that decorate medieval Serbian Orthodox monasteries throughout the Balkans. On the balcony (at the back of the nave), you'll see Cyrillic script that explains the history of the church. Notice that there are no pews, because worshippers stand throughout the service. On the left, find the little room with tubs of water, where the faithful light tall, skinny beeswax candles (purchased at the little window in the back corner). The painted screen, or iconostasis, is believed to separate our material world from the spiritual realm behind it. Ponder the fact that several centuries ago, before the Catholic Church began to adapt to a changing world, all Christians worshipped this way. For more on the Orthodox faith, see the sidebar on page 922.

• *On the other side of the busy street is...*

Tivoli Park (Park Tivoli)

This huge park, just west of the center, is where Slovenes relax on summer weekends. The easiest access is through the graffiti-

covered underpass from Cankarjeva cesta (between the Serbian Orthodox Church and the Museum of Modern Art). As you emerge, the Neoclassical pillars leading down the promenade clue you in that this part of the park was designed by Jože Plečnik. Along this "main boulevard" of the park, various changing photographic exhibitions are displayed.

• *Aside from taking a leisurely stroll, the best thing to do in the park is visit the...*

▲Contemporary History Museum (Muzej Novejše Zgodovine)

In a Baroque mansion (Cekinov Grad) in Tivoli Park, a well-done exhibit called "Slovenians in the 20th Century" traces the last hundred years of Slovenia—essentially from the end of World War I to independence in 1991. Out front is a T-55 Yugoslav tank that was commandeered by the Slovenes during their war for independence. Inside, the ground floor displays temporary exhibits, and upstairs you'll find several rooms using models, dioramas, light-and-sound effects, and English explanations to creatively tell the story of one of Europe's youngest nations. While it's a little difficult to fully appreciate, the creativity and the spunky spirit of the place are truly enjoyable.

Cost and Hours: €3.50, permanent exhibit free first Sun of the month, guidebook-€5, open Tue-Sun 10:00-18:00, closed Mon, in Tivoli Park at Celovška cesta 23, tel. 01/300-9610, www. muzej-nz.si.

Getting There: The museum is a 20-minute walk from the center, best combined with a wander through Tivoli Park. The fastest approach: As you emerge from the Cankarjeva cesta underpass into the park, climb up the stairs, then turn right and go straight ahead for five minutes. You'll continue straight up the ramp, then turn left after the tennis courts and look for the big pink-and-white mansion on the hill.

Visiting the Museum: The exhibit begins at the dawn of the 20th century, during Slovenia's waning days as part of the Austro-Hungarian Empire. You'll walk through a simulated trench from the Soča Front, then learn about the creation of the post-World War I Kingdom of Serbs, Croats, and Slovenes (or, as this exhibit pointedly puts it, "Kingdom of Slovenes, Croats, and Serbs").

Your footfalls echo loudly as you enter the room describing Slovenia's WWII experience (ask them to start the 12-minute "multivision" wrap-around slideshow, with music and sound effects). You'll learn how during that war, Slovenia was divided between neighboring fascist powers Germany, Italy, and Hungary. Each one tried (but failed) to exert linguistic and cultural control over the people, hoping to eradicate the Slovenian national identity. Video screens show subtitled interviews with people who lived through those war years.

Passing through the ballroom, you reach the "Slovenia 1945-1960" exhibit, outlining both the good (modernization) and the bad (prison camps and secret police) of the early Tito years. Despite his ruthless early rule, Tito remains popular here; under his stern bust, page through the photo album of Tito's visits to Slovenia. Find the display of the country's former currencies. Examining the Yugoslav dinar, notice that the figureheads on that communist currency were generic, idealized workers, farmers, and other members of the proletariat...except for a few notable individuals (including Tito). Meanwhile, Slovenia's short-lived post-Yugoslav currency, the *tolar* (1991-2006), featured artists and scientists rather than heads of state and generals.

The most evocative room has artifacts from the Slovenes' brave declaration of independence from a hostile Yugoslavia in 1991. The well-organized Slovenes had only to weather a 10-day skirmish to gain their freedom. It's chilling to think that at one point bombers were en route to level this gorgeous city. The planes were called back at the last minute, by a Yugoslav People's Army officer with allegiances to Slovenia.

• *Hungry? Straight ahead and down the stairs from the museum, look for the* **"Hot Horse" food kiosk**, *selling €4 horseburgers (no joke). A local institution, this is a popular place to get together with friends and neigh-bors. The giant, modern, blocky, light-blue building across the busy road is the* **Pivovarna Union**—*the brewery for Ljubljana's favorite brew.*

On your way back to the center, you could stop by...

▲The Skyscraper (Nebotičnik)

This 1933 Art Deco building was the first skyscraper in Slovenia, for a time the tallest building in Central Europe, and one of the earliest European buildings that was clearly influenced by American architecture. The Skyscraper's top floor, which hosts a pricey restaurant, café, and observation deck, offers the best view of Ljubljana's skyline. Zip up in the elevator just to take a peek, or stay for a drink or meal.

There are three levels: The best is floor #12, where you can sit outside (or, in bad weather, head up the spiral stairs to the glassed-in terrace) and enjoy a drink with unobstructed views over the city and castle (€3 beer/wine/coffee, €5-8 cocktails, €5-9 light food). One floor below (#11) is the indoor club/lounge, with a similar menu. And on the next floor down (#10) is the restaurant, with pricey food (€7-9 starters, €8-17 main courses) and less-impressive views. I'd skip the restaurant and the club, and just grab a drink or snack up on the terrace.

Cost and Hours: Free to ride the elevator up for a peek, but you should buy at least a drink if you want to stick around; terrace and club open daily 9:00-very late; restaurant open Mon-Sat 12:00-21:00, closed Sun; 2 blocks from Prešeren Square at Štefanova 1, tel. 040-601-787, www.neboticnik.si.

• *A few blocks south, near several Jože Plečnik sights (see next section) at the river end of French Revolution Square, you'll find the...*

▲City Museum of Ljubljana (Mestni Muzej Ljubljana)

This thoughtfully presented museum, located in the recently restored Auersperg Palace, offers a high-tech, in-depth look at the story of this city. Though everything is well-described in English (and touchscreens provide even more information), a student on the museum's staff might be able to show you around if it's not too busy—ask.

Cost and Hours: €7—but may vary depending on temporary exhibits, Tue-Sun 10:00-18:00, Thu until 21:00, closed Mon, kid-friendly, Gosposka 15, tel. 01/241-2500, www.mestnimuzej.si.

Visiting the Museum: You'll begin your visit in the cellar, with Roman ruins (including remains of the original Roman road and sewer system, found right here) and layers of medieval artifacts. A model of the modern city—sitting upon footprints of the Roman (red) and medieval (blue) settlements—illustrates Ljubljana's many layers of history. If it's not traveling to other museums (as it often is), you may see the world's oldest wooden wheel on an axle, dating from around 3200 B.C. and discovered in the Ljubljana marshlands. Upstairs are the mayor's room (with a few exhibits) and the ever-evolving permanent collection, called Faces of Ljubljana. Exhibits on economy and trade include communist-era advertisements, while another section explains how Ljubljana has belonged to 10 different states over the last 200 years, ranging from the genteel Habsburg Empire to the oppressive Nazi regime to membership in the benevolent EU. You'll also see an actual Fiat Zastava 750 car—the classic "Fičko" car that everyone owned—or wanted to own—in communist Yugoslavia (sort of a proto-Yugo). Rounding out the collection is a range of temporary exhibits.

Nearby: Included in your ticket is an audio/videoguide that leads you on a walking tour to two nearby archaeological sites.

• *If visiting the museum, don't miss the nearby National and University Library and French Revolution Square—both described in the next section.*

SOUTH OF PREŠEREN SQUARE: JOŽE PLEČNIK'S ARCHITECTURE

Jože Plečnik is to Ljubljana what Antoni Gaudí is to Barcelona: a homegrown and amazingly prolific genius who shaped his town with a uniquely beautiful vision. And, as in Barcelona, Ljubljana has a way of turning people who couldn't care less about architecture into Plečnik fans. There's plenty to see. In addition to the Triple Bridge, the riverside market, and the sights listed here, Plečnik designed the embankments along the Ljubljanica and Gradaščica rivers in the Trnovo neighborhood; the rebuilt Roman wall along Mirje street, south of the center; the Church of St. Francis, with its classicist bell tower; St. Michael's Church on the Marsh; Orel Stadium; Žale Cemetery; and many more buildings throughout Slovenia.

Some of the best Plečnik sights are near the river, just south of Congress and Prešeren squares. I've linked them up in the order of a short self-guided walk.

• *From Prešeren Square, stroll south along the river. After the plain wooden bridge called the "Ugly Duckling," you'll come to the...*

▲Cobblers' Bridge (Čevljarski Most)

Named for the actual cobblers (shoemakers) who set up shop along the river in olden times, the bridge encapsulates Plečnik's style perhaps better than any other structure: simple, clean lines adorned with classical columns. Ideal for people-watching (with the castle hovering scenically overhead), this is one of Ljubljana's

most appealing spots.

• *Continue past Cobblers' Bridge on the right side of the river, past the fountain. After about a block, turn right up the parked-up street called Novi trg. At the top of this street, on the left, is a red-brick building embedded with gray granite blocks in an irregular checkerboard pattern. This is the...*

▲▲National and University Library
(Narodna in Univerzitetna Knjižnica, or NUK)

Widely regarded as Plečnik's masterpiece, this building is a bit underwhelming...until an understanding of its symbolism brings it to life.

Cost and Hours: Free, staircase open Mon-Fri 8:00-20:00, Sat 9:00-14:00, closed Sun. The quiet main reading room is officially open for visitors only during very limited hours (mid-July–mid-Aug Mon-Sat 14:00-18:00).

Visiting the Library: Begin by standing outside and surveying the **exterior**. On the surface, the red-and-gray color scheme evokes the red soil and chunks of granite of the Karst region, south of Ljubljana. But on a deeper level, the library's design conveys the message of overcoming obstacles to attain knowledge. The odd-sized and -shaped blocks in the facade represent a complex numerological pattern that suggests barriers on

the path to enlightenment. The sculpture on the river side is Moses—known for leading his people through 40 years of hardship to the Promised Land. On the right side of the building, find the horse-head doorknobs—representing the winged horse Pegasus (grab hold, and he'll whisk you away to new levels of enlightenment).

Step **inside**. The main staircase is dark and gloomy—modeled after an Egyptian tomb. But at the top, through the door marked *Velika Čitalnica,* is the bright, airy main reading room: the ultimate goal, a place

Jože Plečnik (1872–1957)

There is probably no other single architect who has shaped one city as Jože Plečnik (YOH-zheh PLAYCH-neek) shaped Ljubljana. From libraries, office buildings, cemeteries, and stadiums to landscaping, riverside embankments, and market halls, Plečnik left his mark everywhere. While he may not yet register very high on the international Richter scale of important architects, the Slovenes' pride in this man's work is understandable.

Plečnik was born in Ljubljana and trained as a furniture designer before his interest turned to architecture. He studied in Vienna under the Secessionist architect Otto Wagner. His first commissions, done around the turn of the 20th century in Vienna, were pretty standard Art Nouveau stuff. Then Tomáš Masaryk, president of the new nation of Czechoslovakia, decided that the dull Habsburg design of Prague Castle could use a new look to go with its new independence. But he didn't want an Austrian architect; it had to be a Slav. In 1921, Masaryk chose Jože Plečnik, who sprinkled the castle grounds with his distinctive touches. By now, Plečnik had perfected his simple, eye-pleasing style, which mixes modern and classical influences, with lots of columns and pyramids—simultaneously austere and playful.

of learning. The top-floor windows are shaped roughly like open books. Sadly, except for one month a year when the students are on summer break, you can't actually enter the reading room; you'll just have to imagine young Ljubljanans hunched studiously over their books, surrounded by Plečnik's bookshelves, railings, and high windows.

Aside from being a great work of architecture, the building also houses the most important library in Slovenia, with more than two million books (about one per Slovene). The library is supposed to receive a copy of each new book printed in the country. In a freaky bit of bad luck, this was the only building in town damaged in World War II, when a plane crashed into it. But the people didn't want to see their books go up in flames—so hundreds of locals formed a human chain, risking life and limb to save the books from the burning building.

• Directly behind the library is a mellow square with an obelisk in the middle. This is...

By the time Plečnik finished in Prague, he had made a name for himself. His prime years were spent creating for the Kingdom of Yugoslavia (before the ideology-driven era of Tito). Plečnik returned home to Ljubljana and set to work redesigning the city,  both as an architect and as an urban planner. He lived in a humble house behind the Trnovo Church (now a tourable and recommended museum), and on his walk to work every day, he pondered ways to make the city even more livable. Wandering through town, notice how thoughtfully he incorporated people, nature, the Slovenian heritage, town vistas, and symbolism into his works—it's feng shui on a grand urban scale.

For all of Plečnik's ideas that became reality, even more did not. After World War II, the very religious Plečnik fell out of favor with the new communist government and found it more difficult to get his projects completed. (It's fun to imagine how this city might look if Plečnik had always gotten his way.) After his death in 1957, Plečnik was virtually forgotten by Slovenes and scholars alike. His many works in Ljubljana were taken for granted.

But in 1986, an exposition about Plečnik at Paris' Pompidou Center jump-started interest in the architect. Within a few years, Plečnik was back in vogue. Today, scholars laud him as a genius who was ahead of his time...while locals and tourists enjoy the elegant simplicity of his works.

French Revolution Square (Trg Francoske Revolucije)

Plečnik designed the **obelisk** in the middle of the square to commemorate Napoleon's short-lived decision to make Ljubljana the capital of his Illyrian Provinces. It's rare to find anything honoring Napoleon outside of Paris, but he was good to Ljubljana. Under his rule, Slovenian culture flourished, the Slovene language became widely recognized and respected for the first time, schools were established, and roads and infrastructure were improved. The monument contains ashes of the unknown French soldiers who died in 1813, when the region went from French to Austrian control.

The Teutonic Knights of the Cross established the nearby **monastery** (Križanke, ivy-capped wall and gate, free entry) in 1230. The adaptation of these monastery buildings into the Ljubljana Summer Theatre was Plečnik's last major work (1950-1956).

• *From here, it's a scenic 10-minute walk to the next sight. From the*

*obelisk, walk down Emonska toward the twin-spired church. You'll pass
(on the left) the delightful Krakovo district—a patch of green countryside in downtown Ljubljana. Many of the veggies you see in the riverside market come from these carefully tended gardens. When you reach
the Gradaščica stream, head over the bridge (also designed by Plečnik)
and go around the left side of the church to find the house.*

▲▲Jože Plečnik House (Plečnikova Zbirka)

One of Ljubljana's most interesting sights is the house of the architect who redesigned much of the city. Unfortunately, the house is
closed for renovation, likely until the fall of 2015; ask the TI or
check online. If it's open, it's well worth a visit.

Cost and Hours: When open, likely €4, Tue-Thu 10:00-
18:00, Sat 9:00-15:00, 45-minute English tours begin at the top of
each hour, last tour departs one hour before closing, closed Sun-
Mon and Fri, Karunova 4, tel. 01/280-1600, www.mgml.si, info@
mgml.si. It's well-run by Ana and Natalija, who sometimes lead
the tours.

Getting There: It's directly behind the twin steeples of the
Trnovo Church. The 15-minute stroll from the center—the same

one Plečnik took to work each
day—is nearly as enjoyable as the
house itself. You can either walk
south along the river, then turn
right onto Gradaška and stroll
along the stream to the church;
or, from French Revolution
Square, head south on Emonska.
Either way, you'll pass through

the garden-patch district of Krakovo, where pea patches and characteristic Old World buildings gracefully cohabitate. On the way
to or from the museum, it's enjoyable to get a meal in Krakovo
(three restaurants—Pri Škofu, Manna, and Harambaša—are
described later, under "Eating in Ljubljana").

Visiting the House: Ljubljana's favorite son lived here from
1921 until his death in 1957. He added on to an existing house,
building a circular bedroom for himself and filling the place with
bric-a-brac he designed, as well as artifacts, photos, and gifts from
around the world that inspired him as he shaped Ljubljana. Living
a simple, almost monastic lifestyle, Plečnik knew what he liked,
and these tastes are mirrored in his house.

Today the house is decorated exactly as it was the day Plečnik
died, containing much of his equipment, models, and plans. The
house can be toured only with a guide, whose enthusiasm brings
the place to life. There are very few barriers, so you are in direct
contact with the world of the architect. Still furnished with

unique, Plečnik-designed furniture, one-of-a-kind inventions, and favorite souvenirs from his travels, the house paints an unusually intimate portrait of an artist.

While the house initially underwhelms some visitors, it's a ▲▲▲ pilgrimage for those who get caught up in Ljubljana's idiosyncratic sense of style. As you tour the place, be patient. Listen to its stories. Appreciate the subtle details. Notice how reverently your guide (and other Slovenes) speak of this man. Contrast the humbleness of Plečnik's home with the dynamic impact he had on the cityscape of Ljubljana and the cultural heritage of Slovenia. Wandering Plečnik's hallways, it's hard not to be tickled by this man's sheer creativity and by the unique world he forged for himself to live in. As a visitor to his home, you're in good company. He invited only his closest friends here—except during World War II, when Ljubljana was occupied by Nazis and the university was closed, Plečnik allowed his students to work with him here.

IN METELKOVA, NORTHEAST OF PREŠEREN SQUARE

Three museums face each other on a slick modern plaza next to the park called Tabor, about a 15-minute walk northeast of Prešeren Square in the dull but up-and-coming district of Metelkova. Nearby, you can explore the funky squatters' colony of Metelkova City (with Ljubljana's famous prison-turned-youth hostel).

▲▲Slovenian Ethnographic Museum (Slovenski Etnografski Muzej)

Housed in a state-of-the-art facility, this delightful museum is Ljubljana's most underrated attraction. With both permanent and temporary exhibits, the museum strives to explain what it is to be Slovene, with well-presented and well-described cultural artifacts from around the country. If you've caught the Slovenian folk culture itch, this is the place to scratch it.

Cost and Hours: €4.50, free first Sun of month, Tue-Sun 10:00-18:00, closed Mon, great café, Metelkova 2, tel. 01/300-8745, www.etno-muzej.si.

Visiting the Museum: The ground and first floors have good temporary exhibits, while upstairs you'll find two permanent exhibits.

The best exhibit, filling the third floor, is called **"Between Nature and Culture."** As you exit the elevator, turn left and find the shrunken head, which comes with a surprisingly frank exhibit that acknowledges the shortsighted tendency for museum curators—including at this museum—to emphasize things that are foreign or different. Continue through collections of "Reflections of Distant Worlds" (non-European cultures) to reach the core of the collection, which focuses on Slovenia. A good but slow-moving film visits the country's four major regions. Another exhibit ponders how people half a world away—in Slovenia and in North America—simultaneously invented a similar solution (snowshoes) for a common problem. One display deconstructs Slovenian clichés (including this country's odd fascination with its traditional hayracks). The arrangement of the collection emphasizes the evolution of an increasingly complicated civilization, from basic farming tools to ceramics to modern technology. You'll see exhibits on traditional Slovenian beekeeping, blacksmithing, weaving, shoemaking, costumes and customs, pottery, furniture, and religious objects. The children's "Ethnoalphabet" area features an A-to-Ž array of engaging, hands-on activities.

The other permanent exhibit, on the second floor (from the elevator, turn left to find the entrance), is called **"I, We, and Others."** A bit too conceptual for its own good, this heady exhibit ponders the notion of belonging. Designed for Slovenes more than foreigners (with very limited posted English information—borrow the free English audioguide from the ticket desk before heading up), it explores various aspects of how people define who they are, from individual and family to community and nation. Videos and sounds enhance the exhibits, and the curators neatly juxtapose well-known icons from different cultures (such as various national parliament buildings) in thought-provoking ways. While it's easy to get lost amid the navel-gazing, there is something particularly poignant about this topic here in the identity-obsessed Balkans.

Slovenian National Museum-Metelkova (Narodni Muzej Slovenije)

Next door to the Ethnographic Museum is this facility, where items from the Slovenian National Museum that were formerly tucked away in storage are now displayed on two floors. The very pretty historical bric-a-brac is neatly presented without much context—it's just an excuse to get a bunch of interesting stuff out into public view. Each room has a different collection: furniture, pottery and ceramics, church vestments, weapons and armor, and more. The painting gallery is nicely organized by century and style. The museum also features temporary exhibits. Everything's labeled in English, and a guide can show you around, if they're not too busy.

Cost and Hours: €3, Tue-Sun 10:00-18:00, closed Mon, Maistrova 1, tel. 01/230-7032.

Museum of Contemporary Art-Metelkova (Muzej Sodobne Umetnosti Metelkova, MSUM)

This cutting-edge branch of the Museum of Modern Art opened in 2012 to showcase changing exhibitions of present-day, mostly

Slovenian and Eastern European artists. In addition to temporary installations, it populates its permanent "The Present and Presence" exhibit with a variety of pieces from its collection. The modern space is at once sleek and playful, making this museum worth a visit for art lovers who appreciate works from the 1960s to the present.

Cost and Hours: €5, ask about combo-ticket with Museum of Modern Art, Tue-Sun 10:00-18:00, closed Mon, Maistrova 3, tel. 01/241-6825, www.mg-lj.si.

Metelkova City (Metelkova Mesto)

The heart of Slovenia's counterculture, this former military installation is now a colorful, funky, graffiti-and-wild-art-slathered squatter's colony, billed as an "autonomous cultural center." Built by the Habsburgs in the 1880s, the complex—with barracks, warehouses, and a prison—was used by a laundry list of later occupiers, from Italian fascists to Nazis to the Yugoslav People's Army. After Yugoslavia pulled its troops out of Slovenia (following the Ten-Day War), the cluster of buildings sat derelict and abandoned. In 1993, transient artists moved into the sprawling complex and set up galleries, theaters, bars, and nightclubs. While controversial at first, Meltelkova City has gradually become accepted by most Ljubljanans, and the city (which owns the property) not only tolerates but, in subtle ways, encourages this hotbed of youthful artistic expression. While edgy, this place is fascinating to explore—it's sleepy by day and lively by night (www.metelkovamesto.org).

Anchoring the area is **Hostel Celica,** one of Europe's most unusual youth hostels, which fills a former prison building. Twenty artists were invited to decorate cells that have been turned into accommodations, and the ground floor features vibrant public spaces, a good and affordable restaurant (a nice place for a €4-7 lunch or a light dinner), and a shoes-off "Oriental café." The message: Thoughtful art and architecture can transcend an ugly history. You can drop by to see the building anytime, and ask to borrow a flashlight to explore the dank and gloomy basement solitary confinement cells, with a small but interesting exhibition on the history of the building (and the various prisoners who have called it home—including Janez Janša, who did time here during communism and later became Slovenia's prime minister). But if you're interested in this place, make a point to visit at 14:00 for a free guided tour of the entire complex (tours run daily; you can also try calling to arrange a tour at other times, tel. 01/230-9700, www.hostelcelica.com).

LJUBLJANA

Shopping in Ljubljana

Ljubljana, with its easygoing ambience and countless boutiques, is made to order for whiling away an afternoon shopping. It's also a fun place to stock up on souvenirs and gifts for the folks back home. Popular items include wood carvings and models (especially of the characteristic hayracks that dot the countryside), different flavors of schnapps (the kind with a whole pear inside—cultivated to actually grow right into the bottle—is a particularly classy gift), honey mead brandy (*medica*—sweet and smooth), bars of soap wrapped in wool (good for exfoliating), and those adorable painted panels from beehives (described on page 818). Rounding out the list of traditional Slovenian items are wrought-iron products from Kropa, crystal from Rogaska, lace from Idrija, salt from Piran, and Peko shoes (similar to high-fashion Italian models, but cheaper; the name is an abbreviation of its founder's name: Peter Kozina).

There are two convenient areas in the city center that offer abundant shopping opportunities: at **Ciril-Metodov trg and near the market**; and, beginning a few steps away, the **Old Town** pedestrian lane that cuts through the downtown core. I've described options in both places below. (A third street worth exploring—with a bit more funky student style—is **Trubarjeva,** a block up from the river and easy to find from Prešeren Square.)

AT CIRIL-METODOV TRG AND NEAR THE MARKET

The most atmospheric trinket-shopping is in the first stretch of the **market colonnade,** along the riverfront next to the Triple Bridge (described earlier, under "Sights in Ljubljana").

If you're looking for serious handicrafts rather than trinkets, drop by the **Rustika** gallery, just over the Triple Bridge (on the castle side). In addition to beehive panels, they also have lace, painted chests and boxes, and other tasteful local-style mementos (Mon-Sat 9:00-20:00, Sun 10:00-20:00, Stritarjeva 9, mobile 031-459-509). There's another Rustika location up at the castle courtyard. A somewhat more downscale souvenir shop with a wide variety is **Dom Trgovina,** across from the TI on the main market square (Mon-Sat 8:00-20:00, Sun 10:00-18:00, Ciril-Metodov trg 5).

Kraševka sells high-quality artisanal products (mostly foods) from the Karst region, and also acts as a sort of information office for that area (Mon-Fri 9:00-19:00, Sat 9:00-15:00, closed Sun, Ciril-Metodov trg 10, tel. 01/232-1445).

Trgovina Ika, a small artisan boutique with its own hip and idiosyncratic sense of style, is a delightful place to browse for truly authentic Slovenian stuff that goes beyond souvenirs. Its unique items by local designers—jewelry, hats, scarves, shoes, and so on—are modern and fashionable (Mon-Fri 10:00-19:30, Sat 9:00-18:00,

Sun 10:00-14:00, Ciril-Metodov trg 13, tel. 01/123-21743).

Šnopc o'tecca is the place to sample (and buy) more than 80 types of Slovenian *šnops*—that means firewater, brandies, and liqueurs. They offer free tastes, and sell little gift bottles as well as full bottles ranging from €16 to €100 (Mon-Sat 10:00-21:00, Sun 10:00-12:30 & 15:00-19:00, Miklošičeva 2, mobile 040-533-585).

IN THE OLD TOWN

Ljubljana's main Old Town street—which changes names from Mestni trg to Stari trg, then Gornji trg—is also lined with several characteristic shops. It's a very central and touristy zone, so don't expect bargains. But it's extremely convenient to get a representative glimpse at just a few of the unique gift items produced in this proud little country. Here's a lightly narrated tour of this inviting street, from start to finish.

⊙ Self-Guided Shopping Stroll: Begin in front of the Town Hall. Before you start the walk, take the opportunity to browse the shops noted above (all of which are within a five-minute walk of here). When you're ready, head down the street.

First, on the right at #9, **Gujžina** highlights food, wines, and other products from the Hungarian-influenced region of Slovenia called Prekmurje (also called Pannonia). While the restaurant (on the left) is hit-or-miss, their wine bar (on the right) is a good place to learn more about the products of one of Slovenia's top wine-growing regions. If you want a dessert, this is a fine place to try the cake called *gibanica*—originating in Prekmurje, and beloved throughout Slovenia (€10-15 meals, daily 8:00-24:00, Mestni trg 19, mobile 083-806-406).

Sandwiched between the two entrances to Gujžina, **Piranske Soline** sells products from the giant salt pans that sit just south of Piran on Slovenia's tiny coastline, butting up against Croatia. You can pick up some locally harvested sea salt, or peruse their salt-based beauty products (bath salts, body milk, and other exfoliants; Mon-Fri 9:00-20:00, Sat 9:00-15:00, Sun 10:00-15:00, Mestni trg 19, tel. 01/425-0190, www.soline.si).

Back across the street, on the left at #7, **Honey House** sells products harvested by beekeeper Luka (Mon-Fri 9:00-20:00, Sat 10:00-18:00, closed Sun, Mestni trg 7, mobile 040-477-473). For tips on browsing your honey options, see page 819.

Also on the left, at #8, **La Chocolate** is the first of two artisanal *čokoladnice* (chocolate shops) along this strip (€4/100 grams—about 3-4 pieces, Mon-Sat 9:00-21:00, Sun 10:30-17:00, Mestni trg 8, mobile 041-463-019, www.lachocolate.si).

Farther along, on the right (at #17), **Galerija Idrijske Čipke** shows off handmade lace from the town of Idrija (Mon-Fri 10:00-19:00, Sat 10:00-14:00, closed Sun, Mestni trg 17, tel. 01/425-0051, www.idrija-lace.com).

Continuing past various clothes boutiques, look for (on the left, at #11) another chocolate shop, **Čokoladnica Cukrček**. A bit pricier than La Chocolate (€5.20/100 grams), this shop is best known for its foil-wrapped "Prešeren Balls" chocolates—a clever and civic-minded takeoff on Salzburg's "Mozart Balls," replacing the composer with Slovenia's greatest poet (Mon-Fri 9:00-22:00, Sat 9:00-20:00, Sun 10:00-19:00, Mestni trg 11, tel. 01/421-0453, www.cukrcek.si).

Continue along the street (which here changes names from Mestni trg to Stari trg), passing more clothes shops. On the left, at #3, look for **Cha** tea shop, which sells over 100 varieties of tea, plus porcelain teapots and cups from all over (Mon-Fri 9:00-20:00, Sat 9:00-15:00, Sun 10:00-14:00, Stari trg 3). It's attached to the recommended Čajna Hiša teahouse.

A few steps down on the left (at #5), **Cafetino** is the best place in town for coffee. They have more than 20 types, available espresso or Turkish-style, plus beans to take home (Mon-Fri 7:30-19:00, Sat 8:00-14:00, Sun 9:00-14:00, Stari trg 5, tel. 01/422-2950).

Next door, follow the passage to reach **Za Popen't Pivoteka**, a "bottle shop" selling 200 kinds of beer in individual bottles. While they stock a few Slovenian beers, they focus on international microbrews—including several American brands. Even if it's not authentically Slovenian, this shop is a fun browse for beer lovers. The name is a play on words, loosely meaning "foamy goodness" (Mon-Sat 11:00-20:00, closed Sun, Stari trg 5, mobile 051-266-063, www.zapopent.si).

Now you'll wade through a stretch of enticing restaurants with wonderful outdoor tables (for my recommendations here, see page 777). Notice Julija and Romeo, facing each other wistfully across the street. From here, you'll pass a few more funky shops, but mostly restaurants and cafés until the cobbled charm culminates at **Gornji trg**. Look uphill and notice the village charms of some of the oldest buildings in town: four medieval houses with rooflines slanted at the ends, different from the others on this street.

Sleeping in Ljubljana

Ljubljana has a good range of accommodations in all price ranges. I've focused my listings in or within easy walking distance of the city center. To get the best value, book ahead. The most expensive hotels raise their prices even more during conventions (Sept-Oct, and sometimes also June). To locate the following accommodations, see the map on page 734.

$$$ *Boutique Hotels in the Old Town:* Three similar (but unrelated), expensive boutique hotels cluster idyllically on a cobbled

Sleep Code

Abbreviations (€1 = about $1.40, country code: 386, area code: 01)
S = Single, **D** = Double/Twin, **T** = Triple, **Q** = Quad, **b** =
bathroom.
Price Rankings
  $$$ **Higher Priced**—Most rooms €110 or more.
   $$ **Moderately Priced**—Most rooms between €70-110.
    $ **Lower Priced**—Most rooms €70 or less.
Unless otherwise noted, Wi-Fi is generally free, credit cards
are accepted, and breakfast is included, but the modest tourist tax (about €1 per person, per night) is not. Everyone listed
here speaks English. Prices can change without notice; verify
current rates online or by email. For the best prices, always
book directly with the hotel.

square in Ljubljana's Old Town. While a bit overpriced (catering
to deep-pocketed business travelers), they offer Old World charm
with upscale touches. All of these are in old buildings with period
touches; expect lots of stairs and no elevators (the rates listed are
for May-mid-June and Sept-Oct, followed by mid-June-Aug, then
Nov-April). **Hotel Angel,** part of the Lesar group, is the slickest
and most chain-feeling of the bunch. Its 12-plus rooms have crisp
white decor (Db-€165/€120/€110, pricier suites, air-con, Wi-Fi,
parking-€5, Gornji trg 7, tel. 01/425-5089, www.angelhotel.si,
info@angelhotel.si). **Allegro Hotel** has a musical theme and 17
rooms with hardwood floors around a checkerboard-tiled garden
courtyard (Sb-€100/€80/€65, "economy" D with private bathroom
across the hall-€105/€85/€70, classic Db-€140/€130/€100, superior Db-€170/€150/€120, air-con, free guest computer and Wi-Fi,
prebook for €10 parking, Gornji trg 6, tel. 059/119-620, www.
allegrohotel.si, info@allegrohotel.si). The family-run **Antiq Hotel**
is a bit older, with less polish and 16 idiosyncratically decorated
rooms sprawling through two buildings with lots of stairs and a
mazelike floor plan (small S-€75, Sb-€95, small D-€90, Db-€110-
165, price depends on size, look for deals on their website, air-
con, guest computer and Wi-Fi, some rooms have low beams and
doors, Gornji trg 3, tel. 01/421-3560, www.antiqhotel.eu, info@
antiqhotel.eu).

  $$$ Vander Urbani Resort is a unique concept: Nestled cen-
tral as can be just off the in-love-with-life riverfront embankment,
it really does feel like an intensely hip resort in the city center—
right down to the minuscule rooftop swimming pool and sundeck.
The resort prides itself on the cutting-edge urban design of its 16
rooms, and tries to use Slovenian and organic products wherever
possible (small "zen" Db with hardwood floors-€145, standard

Db-€155, larger Db-€175, pricier suites, cheaper Nov-March, air-con, elevator, Wi-Fi, café and restaurant, Krojaška ulica 6-8, tel. 01/200-9000, www.vanderhotel.com, info@vanderhotel.com).

$$$ Cubo Hotel is a jolt of trendy minimalism on Ljubljana's hotel scene. Its 26 rooms are the best place in town for sleek, mod elegance. Choose between streetside rooms, which enjoy castle views but get some traffic noise, or quieter courtyard rooms (very flexible rates but generally Sb-€135, Db-€140-180, palatial suite-€200-250, cheaper off-season, non-smoking, air-con, elevator, Wi-Fi, Slovenska cesta 15, tel. 01/425-6000, www.hotelcubo.com, reception@hotelcubo.com).

$$$ Adora Hotel, on the other side of the church from the three boutique hotels described earlier, is a bit less charming, but also cheaper and very comfortable. Its 10 rooms have a restrained rustic style (Db-€119/€105/€80, €30 more for a bigger superior room, air-con, elevator, Wi-Fi, free loaner bikes, reserve ahead for parking-€10, Rožna ulica 7, tel. 082-057-240, www.adorahotel.si, info@adorahotel.si).

$$$ Grand Hotel Union is Ljubljana's top address, as much an Art Nouveau landmark as a hotel. You'll pay dearly for its Old World elegance, hundred years of history, professional staff, big pool, and perfect location (right on Prešeren Square). While their rack rates are outrageously high, you can often snare a great deal in the summer (July-Aug), winter, and on many weekends. The 194 plush "Executive" rooms are in the main building (official rates: Sb-€194, Db-€224; in slow times maybe as low as Sb-€110, Db-€120; non-smoking floors, air-con, elevator, Wi-Fi, Miklošičeva cesta 1, tel. 01/308-1877, www.gh-union.si, hotel.union@gh-union.si). Its 133 "Business" rooms next door are not as luxurious, almost as expensive, and a lesser value (official rates: Sb-€178, Db-€208; same potential deals as "Executive" rooms, non-smoking floors, air-con, elevator, free cable Internet, Miklošičeva cesta 3, tel. 01/308-1170, www.gh-union.si, hotel.business@gh-union.si). Both branches have access to parking (€17/day), as well as a pool and sauna on the top floor of the Business branch, and a free guest computer in the Executive branch. They also have 74 additional rooms in their annex, **Central Hotel**, two blocks up the street (official rates: Sb-€139, Db-€167; much lower prices likely July-Aug, in winter, and on weekends—maybe as low as Sb-€75, Db-€90; extra bed-€27, non-smoking rooms, air-con, elevator, guest computer and Wi-Fi, free sauna, parking garage-€19/day, Miklošičeva cesta 9, tel. 01/308-4300, www.centralhotel.si, central.hotel@gh-union.si).

$$ Slamič B&B has 17 modern rooms with hardwood floors, tasteful decor, and absentee management. Over an upscale café in a nondescript but central neighborhood, this is a fine spot for affordable elegance (Sb-€65-75, Db-€95-99; bigger and slightly nicer "deluxe" Sb-€85, Db-€99-110; Sb suite-€135, Db suite-€165; price ranges depend on size; air-con, Wi-Fi, free parking, reception open daily 7:00-23:00, Kersnikova 1, tel. 01/433-8233,www.slamic.si, info@slamic.si).

$$ Meščanka ("City Woman") rents seven rooms and apartments in a fantastic location right along the bustling riverfront promenade. The decor is mod, funky, and colorful, and the good windows work hard to provide silence (Db-€70, apartment-€90, bigger apartment-€120, cheaper Oct-March, extra bed-€20, no breakfast, air-con, guest computer and Wi-Fi, reception open 10:00-12:00 & 14:00-19:00—let them know if you're coming outside that time, Ključavničarska 4, mobile 051-880-044, www.mescanka.si, info@mescanka.si, Saša).

$$ Hotel Pri Mraku has 35 comfortable but overpriced rooms in a pleasant neighborhood near French Revolution Square. While it's a bit rough around the edges and not without its quirks, this trusty old place is my sentimental favorite in Ljubljana (Sb-€73, Db-€106, ground-floor and top-floor rooms have air-con and cost €4-5 extra, 8 percent discount for Rick Steves readers if you reserve ahead, extra bed-€23, cheaper mid-Oct-April, non-smoking floor, elevator, guest computer and Wi-Fi, restaurant with terrace under an old vine, Rimska 4, tel. 01/421-9650, www.daj-dam.si, hotelmrak@daj-dam.si).

$$ Stari Tišler ("Old Carpenter") has eight basic, simply appointed, but nice rooms—with splashes of color—above a restaurant in a characteristically old, time-warp house immersed in a nondescript commercial zone a 10-minute walk from Prešeren Square (Db-€82/€72, Tb-€120/€105, higher price is for Aug and other busy times, air-con, Wi-Fi, Kolodvorska 8, tel. 01/430-3370, www.stari-tisler.com, info@stari-tisler.com, Betty).

$$ Hotel Emonec (eh-MOH-nets), with some of the most centrally located cheap beds in Ljubljana, hides just off Wolfova lane between Prešeren and Congress squares. Its 41 minimalist rooms—in two buildings across a courtyard from each other—feel institutional, characterless, and a bit faded, with tight bathrooms and a shoestring staff, but the price and ideal location make it worth considering (Sb-€64, small Db-€67, bigger "standard" Db-€77, Tb-€90-96, Qb-€105-111, price depends on demand, cheaper Nov-April, pay guest computer, Wi-Fi, parking garage-€7, free loaner bikes for guests, they also run a handy self-service launderette—see page 738, Wolfova 12, tel. 01/200-1520, www.hotel-emonec.com, hotelemonec@siol.net).

$ B&B Petra Varl offers comfortable, affordable, nicely appointed rooms on a courtyard across from the bustling riverside market. Petra, who's an artist and speaks good English, will help you feel at home. As this place is Ljubljana's top budget option, book early (Db-€60, extra bed-€10, book direct by email for best price, includes kitchenette with basic do-it-yourself breakfast, cash only, air-con, Wi-Fi, go into courtyard at Vodnikov trg 5 and look for *B&B* sign at 5A, mobile 041-389-470, bb@varl.si).

$ Penzion Pod Lipo has 10 rooms above a restaurant in a mostly residential area about a 12-minute walk from Prešeren Square. While the rooms are old and simple, it's thoughtfully run by Marjan (Db-€65, Tb-€75, Qb-€100, breakfast in restaurant-€3.50 extra, cash only, reception open 8:00-22:00, non-smoking, guest computer, cable Internet, guest kitchen, putting green on terrace, tel. 01/251-1683, mobile 031-809-893, www.penzion-podlipo.com, info@penzion-podlipo.com).

$ Hotel Center (not to be confused with "Central Hotel," listed earlier) is a good value. Marko's 18 small, modern rooms deliver on his promise of "three-star furnishings at two-star prices." While the location, just across Slovenska cesta from the main part of town, is convenient, this place suffers from noise—from the busy road on one side, and from a nearby nightclub on the other...bring earplugs. The rooms on the upper floor, with newer windows, are more soundproof (Db-€60-69 depending on season, breakfast-€4.80, guest computer and Wi-Fi, down the passage at Slovenska cesta 51 and around back, mobile 041-263-347, www.hotelcenter.si, info@hotelcenter.si).

$ Hostel Celica, a proud, innovative, and lively place, is owned by the city and run by a nonprofit student organization. This former military prison's 20 cells *(celica)* have been converted into hostel rooms—each one unique, decorated by a different designer (free tours of the hostel daily at 14:00). The top floor features more typical hostel rooms (each with its own bathroom, for 4-12 people). The building also houses an art gallery, tourist

information, guest computer and Wi-Fi, self-service laundry (€8/load), and a variety of eateries. For more on the history of this site, see page 767 (all prices listed are per person—cell rooms: S-€53-61, D-€28-32, T-€25-30; bed in top-floor rooms with bathrooms: 3- to 5-bed room-€24-30, 7-bed dorm-€23-27, 12-bed dorm-€19-25; price depends on demand—most expensive on June-Sept weekends, cheaper Nov-March; includes breakfast, sheets, towels, and tax; no curfew, non-smoking, free Wi-Fi in public areas, pay Wi-Fi in rooms, bike and car rental, active excursions around Slovenia, Metelkova 8, a dull 15-minute walk to Prešeren Square,

8 minutes to the train station, tel. 01/230-9700, www.hostelcelica. com, info@hostelcelica.com). Light sleepers take note: The hostel hosts live music events about two nights per week until around 24:00, but otherwise maintains "quiet time" after 23:00. However, the surrounding neighborhood—a bit run-down and remote, but safe—is a happening nightlife zone, which can make for noisy weekends.

Eating in Ljubljana

At this crossroads of cultures (and cuisines), Italian and French flavors are just as "local" as meat-and-starch Slovenian food.

This cosmopolitan city also dabbles in other cuisines; you'll find Thai, Indian, Chinese, Mexican, and more. Most places seem to offer a similar menu of Slovenian/ Mediterranean fare with international flourishes. To locate these restaurants, see the map on page 734.

Lunch Deals: Ljubljana has many of the best restaurants in this book. However, quite a few of them are very expensive. To stretch your budget, make a point to have your main meal at lunch, when most of Ljubljana's top eateries serve a high-quality three-course meal (starter, main, dessert) at a very affordable price—usually €9-10, typically not including drinks. You won't have much choice (they may only have one or two options each day; some places don't offer this deal on weekends, so check before you sit down), but the quality is high and the value is outstanding. After a big lunch, you can have a light dinner—picnic, *burek*, pizza, sandwich...or just gelato. Places I recommend that offer these lunch deals include Pri Vitezu, DaBuDa, Valvas'or, Julija, Marley & Me, Pri Škofu, and Manna.

IN THE CITY CENTER

Gostilna As ("Ace"), tucked into a courtyard just off Prešeren Square, offers fish-lovers the best blowout in town. It's dressy, pricey, and pretentious (the service is deliberate, and waiters ignore the menu and recommend what's fresh). Everything is specially prepared each day and beautifully presented. It's loosely based on the Slow Food model: Servings are small, and you're expected to take your time and order two or three courses. The dining room is old-fashioned and a bit stuffy, but in good weather, their rooftop terrace is gorgeous (mostly fish and Italian, €8-18 starters, €20-25 main courses, daily 12:00-24:00, reservations smart, Čopova 5A, or enter courtyard with *As* sign near image of Julija on Wolfova, tel. 01/425-8822, www.gostilnaas.si). For cheaper food and drinks from the same kitchen, eat at the attached **As Aperitivo,** a much livelier, more casual spot. You'll sit in the leafy courtyard or the winter garden, with big windows that stay open in the summer (€10-15 salads and sandwiches, €7-11 pastas, €11-22 main courses, food served daily 12:00-24:00, longer hours for drinks). The courtyard also has a couple of other fun eateries—and, in the summer only, live music and a much-loved gelato stand.

Ribca ("Fish") hides under the first stretch of market colonnade near the Triple Bridge. This is your best bet for a relatively quick and cheap riverside lunch. Choose between the two straightforward menus: grilled fillets or fried small fish. With the fragrant fish market right next door, you know it's fresh. If you just want to enjoy sitting along the river below the bustling market, this is also a fine spot for a coffee or beer (€6-7 salads, €4 seafood salads, €4-8 main courses, €7.50 lunches, Mon 8:00-16:00, Tue-Sat 8:00-21:00, Sun 11:00-18:00, tel. 01/425-1544).

Pri Vitezu is well-respected for its seasonal menu of classic Mediterranean dishes. It sits along the newly spiffed-up Breg embankment, just beyond Cobblers' Bridge; sit out on the pedestrian mall, or in the Old World-elegant interior. Although overpriced at dinner, this place is especially worthwhile for its good-value €9 lunch special, which includes soup, salad bar, a main dish, and a dessert (otherwise €9-13 starters, €18-24 main dishes, Mon-Sat 11:00-23:00—except closed Sat Oct-April, closed Sun year-round, Breg 18-20, tel. 01/426-6058).

Asian Fusion: **DaBuDa** is the best spot in Ljubljana for Asian cuisine, featuring a well-described menu of good Thai dishes (salads, curries, wok meals, and noodles) in a very mod, dark-wood, split-level setting frequented by hip young professionals (good-value €6-7 lunch specials, €8-14 main courses at dinner, Mon-Fri 11:00-23:00, Sat-Sun 12:00-23:00, also a few outdoor tables, between Congress Square and Square of the Republic at Šubičeva 1A, tel. 01/425-3060).

Fast and Cheap: **Klobasarna** does one thing and does it well: *kranjska klobasa*—traditional Carniolan sausage, from the Slovenian uplands. The menu is simple—one wiener for €3.50, two for €5.90, extra for *jota* (hearty turnip stew)—but delicious (Mon-Sat 10:00-23:00, Sun 10:00-15:00, Ciril Metodov trg 15, mobile 051-605-017). **Paninoteka,** with wonderful outdoor seating overlooking Cobblers' Bridge, has affordable and tasty €3-4 sandwiches, as well as a full menu (€8-12 pastas and salads, €8-21 main dishes, also fine interior seating, Mon-Thu 9:00-22:30, Fri-Sat 9:00-23:00, Sun 9:00-22:00, Jurčičev trg 3, mobile 040-349-329). *Burek*, the typical Balkan phyllo-dough snack (see the

"Balkan Flavors" sidebar on page 1140), can be picked up at street stands around town. Most are open 24 hours and charge about €2-3 for a hearty portion. An easy choice is **Nobel Burek,** next to Miklošičeva cesta 30; but many locals prefer **Olimpija Burek,** around the corner at Pražakova 14 (across from the post office).

Pizzerias: Ljubljana has lots of great sit-down pizza places. Expect to pay €5-10 for an average-sized pie (wide variety of toppings). **Pizzeria Foculus,** tucked in a boring alleyway a few blocks up from the river, has a loyal local following, a happening atmosphere, an innovative leafy interior, a few outdoor tables, and Ljubljana's best pizza (over 50 types for €6-10, €6-8 salads, daily 11:00-24:00, just off French Revolution Square across the street from Plečnik's National and University Library at Gregorčičeva 3, tel. 01/251-5643). **Ljubljanski Dvor** enjoys the most convenient and scenic location of any pizzeria in town. On a sunny summer day, the outdoor riverside terrace is unbeatable. The interior has a simple pizza parlor downstairs (€5-15 pizzas and pastas), with a more refined dining room upstairs (selling the same pizzas and pastas, plus €12-20 Italian main courses; pizza parlor open Mon-Sat 10:00-24:00, Sun 12:00-24:00, upstairs restaurant opens at 12:00, just 50 yards from Cobblers' Bridge at Dvorni trg 1, tel. 01/251 6555). Ljubljanski Dvor also has a handy, cheap pizza **take-out window** (go around back to the walk-up window on Congress Square). Enjoy a €2 slice at one of their outdoor tables facing Congress Square, or get it to go and munch it along the river (Mon-Fri 8:00-24:00, Sat 9:00-24:00, Sun 12:00-24:00).

In the Old Town

The main drag through the Old Town (which starts at the Town Hall and changes names as it goes: Mestni trg, then Stari trg, then Gornji trg) is lined with inviting eateries. Tables spill into the cobbled pedestrian street, filled with happy diners. If you're at a loss for where to eat in town, stroll here to survey your options, then pick your favorite menu and ambience. As many restaurants along here are uniformly good, no one place really has the edge.

Several popular options cluster in one particularly atmospheric stretch; all except Romeo offer a similar menu of Mediterranean-Slovenian cuisine and wonderful outdoor seating: **Valvas'or,** the upscale option, has a dressy dining room and a posh gold color scheme (€10 weekday lunch deal, €10-15 starters, €14-22 main dishes, €40 degustation menu, Mon-Sat 12:00-22:00, closed Sun, Stari trg 7, tel. 01/425-0455). **Julija** features homey country-Slovenian decor inside (€9 lunch deals, €9-12 starters, €12-19 main dishes, daily 12:00-22:00, Stari trg 9, tel. 01/425-6463). **Romeo,** across the street, is a lowbrow bar serving unexceptional Mexican food...but the name sure is clever (get it? "Romeo and Julija"). And

Marley & Me comes with a warm welcome from Matej (€7-9 weekday lunch specials, €9-14 pastas, €12-22 main dishes, daily 11:00-23:00, Stari Trg 9, tel. 08/380-6610). I've also enjoyed a great salad lunch at the nearby **Čajna Hiša** teahouse (described later, under "Coffee, Tea, and Treats.")

Traditional Slovenian Food

Because Slovenes head into the countryside when they want traditional fare, Ljubljana isn't the best place to find authentic Slovenian grub. And, frankly, most visitors prefer the Mediterranean/international restaurants that are more common in the capital anyway. But you do have some good options in the city center.

Gostilna na Gradu, in the castle courtyard high above town, is your single best option for true Slovenian food in Ljubljana—if you don't mind going up to the castle to get it (the handy funicular costs €4 round-trip). Run by a well-respected chef, it serves up a seasonal menu of traditional flavors with modern flair. The portions are small, but the prices are surprisingly affordable. Choose between the dull vaulted interior, the glassed-in arcade, or the outdoor tables. Reservations are recommended before you make the trip up here (€7-12 starters, €8-15 main dishes, €30 four-course meal lets you sample several flavors, Mon-Sat 9:00-24:00—food served until 21:00, Sun 9:00-18:00—food served until 16:00, Grajska Planota 1, mobile 031-301-777, www.nagradu.si).

Touristy but Acceptable Options: Two places near the market are easy and popular options for Slovenian dishes. Both of these places cater mostly to tourists—so don't expect top quality or a great value. **Sokol,** with brisk, traditionally clad waiters, fills a fun, sprawling Slovenian-village interior with jaunty polkas on the soundtrack and a very central location. It's in all the guidebooks and deluged by tourists, so don't expect an authentic experience (€8-20 main courses, a few veggie options, Mon-Sat 7:00-23:00, Sun 10:00-23:00, on castle side of Triple Bridge at Ciril-Metodov trg 18, tel. 01/439-6855). A few blocks away, across from the main market square, **Vodnikov Hram** has an Old World interior under brick vaults and outdoor tables overlooking a parking lot. While a variation on the same theme as Sokol, it's marginally less touristy, and has slightly lower prices (€7-9 pastas, €18-19 main courses, Mon-Sat 8:00-23:00, Sun 10:00-20:00—until 17:00 in winter, Vodnikov trg 2, tel. 01/234-5260).

IN KRAKOVO

The Krakovo district—just south of the city center, where garden patches nearly outnumber simple homes—is a pleasant area to wander. It's also home to a trio of tasty restaurants. If the nearby Jože Plečnik House is open during your visit, you could combine your visit there with a meal at one of these options.

Pri Škofu ("By the Bishop") is a laid-back, informal place with appealing outdoor seating, a nondescript modern interior, and a focus on freshness, serving international cuisine with a Slovenian flair. This hidden gem is deliciously memorable; reserve ahead (creative €3 soups, €8 lunches, €9-11 pastas, €15-22 main courses at dinner, homemade €4 desserts, Mon-Fri 10:00-24:00, Sat-Sun 12:00-24:00, Rečna 8, tel. 01/426-4508).

Manna, with artfully presented, seasonal Slovenian-Mediterranean fusion cuisine, sits along the pleasant Gradaščica canal. The interior is pure Secession—the Gustav Klimt-era, early 20th-century, gold-accented Viennese style that was so influential in Ljubljana. I prefer the more artistic, café-like downstairs to the stuffy upstairs dining room, but the seating out front is hard to beat on a nice day (€11 lunch special, otherwise €9 starters, €18-24 main dishes, Mon-Fri 8:00-24:00, Sat 11:00-24:00, Sun 11:00-18:00, Eipprova 1A, tel. 05/992-2308).

Harambaša is the closest thing to a ticket to Sarajevo. Serving Balkan grilled meats, this popular-with-students eatery has Bosnian-flavored decor, old pictures, and cuisine reminiscent of the Bosnian capital. For a refresher on the meat dishes, see "Balkan Flavors" on page 1140. The menu is limited, which makes ordering easy. Their handy €7 *pola-pola* combo-plate—with lotsa meat combined with chopped onions, *kajmak* (a soft cheese spread), and *lepinja* (pita bread)—makes for a simple but filling lunch. For dessert, sample the Bosnian coffee (a high-octane brew with "mud" at the bottom) and baklava. Vegetarians need not apply (€5-7 main courses, Mon-Fri 10:00-22:00, Sat 12:00-22:00, Sun 12:00-20:00, Vrtna 8, mobile 041-843-106).

COFFEE, TEA, AND TREATS

Riverfront Cafés: Enjoying a coffee, beer, or ice-cream cone along the Ljubljanica River embankment (between the Triple and

Cobblers' bridges) is Ljubljana's single best experience—worth ▲▲▲. Tables spill into the street, and some of the best-dressed, best-looking students on the planet happily fill them day and night. (A common question from first-time visitors to Ljubljana: "Doesn't anybody here have a job?") This is some of the top people-watching in Europe. Rather than recommend a particular place (they're all about the same), I'll leave you to explore and find the spot with the breezy ambience you like best. When ordering, the easiest choice is a *bela*

kava—"white coffee," basically a caffè latte.

Teahouse: If coffee's not your cup of tea, go a block inland to the teahouse **Čajna Hiša.** They serve about 50 different types of tea, light food (including great salads), and desserts (€2-4 cakes and sandwiches, €7-9 salads, Mon-Fri 8:00-22:00, Sat 8:00-15:00, Sun 10:00-14:00, on the atmospheric main drag in the Old Town a few steps from Cobblers' Bridge at Stari trg 3, tel. 01/421-2444). They also have an attached tea shop, Cha (described on page 770).

Cakes: **Zvezda Kavarna,** a trendy, central place at the bottom of Congress Square, is a local favorite for cakes, pastries, and ice cream. A nostalgic favorite here—once popular in communist times, and recently reintroduced to great acclaim—is the *emona kocka* (Emona cube), a layer cake with nuts, cake, and chocolate (€3-5 cakes, Mon-Sat 7:00-23:00, Sun 10:00-20:00, a block up from Prešeren Square at Wolfova 14, tel. 01/421-9090). Their **Deli,** one door toward Prešeren Square, has takeaway coffee and smoothies, a wide variety of cakes to go, and some of the most decadent ice cream in town (same hours). And their **Bistro,** around the corner facing Congress Square, has a full menu.

Chocolates and Ice Cream: **Rustika** is a local chain that sells tasty homemade chocolates, cookies (including one kind with four different types of chocolate), and a wide variety of unusual and delicious artisan ice cream flavors. The menu changes from day to day, but highlights can include balsamic vinegar with vanilla or strawberry, very dark chocolate, Kanada (with maple syrup and walnuts), and Greek yogurt with honey and nuts. The handiest location is about an eight-minute walk from Prešeren Square, and comes with a delightful stroll along colorful Trubarjeva street (ice cream available summer only, Mon-Fri 8:00-19:00, Sat 9:00-13:00, closed Sun, Trubarjeva 44, mobile 059-935-730). Don't confuse this sweet shop with the Rustika gift shop.

More Ice Cream: Ljubljana is known for its Italian gelato-style ice cream. You'll see fine options all along the Ljubljanica River embankment, but many places serve ice cream only in summer. Favorites include **Rustika,** the courtyard garden at **Gostilna As** (summer only), and **Zvezda Kavarna** (all described earlier). **Fétiche Patisserie,** along the riverfront café embankment, is another good choice, with some unusual, powerful, Asian-themed flavors.

Ljubljana Connections

As Slovenia's transportation hub, Ljubljana is well-connected to both domestic and international destinations. When checking schedules, be aware of name variations: In Slovene, Vienna is "Dunaj" and Budapest is "Budimpešta."

GETTING TO CROATIA

To reach **Istria** by public transportation, you have two relatively straightforward options: In summer, two direct buses depart Ljubljana for Rovinj each day (at 9:30 in July-Sept, and at 13:45 in late June-mid-Sept, details below). From mid-July through August, there's also a train connection to Pula (Thu-Sun only, 4.75 hours, transfer in Hrpelje-Kozina); once in Pula, you can connect by bus to other Istrian destinations. On off-season weekends, you might have to get creative (try connecting through Rijeka).

If connecting directly to Croatia's **Dalmatian Coast,** you have two good options: Train to Zagreb (2.5 hours), where you can spend a little time sightseeing the city and then—when you're ready—catch a cheap Croatia Air flight or a bus down to Split or all the way to Dubrovnik (see "Zagreb Connections" on page 1087); or take the long, once-daily train connection from Ljubljana to Split (9 hours, requires a change in Zagreb).

BY TRAIN

From Ljubljana by Train to: Lesce-Bled (roughly hourly, 40-60 minutes—but bus is better because it goes right to Bled town center), **Postojna** (nearly hourly, 1 hour), **Divača** (close to Škocjan Caves and Lipica, nearly hourly, 1.75 hours), **Sežana** (close to Lipica, nearly hourly, 2 hours), **Piran** (direct bus is better—see below; otherwise allow 4 hours, train to Koper, 4/day, 2.5 hours; then bus to Piran, 7/day, 30 minutes), **Maribor** (8/day direct, 2-3 hours, more with a transfer in Zidani Most), **Ptuj** (1/day direct Mon-Fri, none Sat-Sun, 2.5 hours, more with transfer in Pragersko), **Zagreb** (4/day direct, 2.5 hours), **Rijeka** (2/day direct, 3 hours), **Pula** (1/day mid-July-Aug Thu-Sun only, 5 hours, transfer in Hrpelje-Kozina), **Split** (1/day, 9 hours, transfer in Zagreb), **Vienna** (that's *Dunaj* in Slovene, 1/day direct, 6 hours; otherwise 3/day with transfer in Villach or Maribor, 6-6.25 hours), **Budapest** (that's *Budimpešta* in Slovene; 1/day via Zagreb, 9 hours, other connections possible with 1-2 changes but complicated, no convenient night train), **Venice** (called *Benétke* in Slovene; fastest by bus—see below; otherwise 1/day with a change to a bus in Villach, 6.75 hours), **Salzburg** (2/day direct, 4-5 hours, more with transfer in Villach), **Munich** (2/day direct, 6 hours, including 1 night train; otherwise transfer in Salzburg). Train info: toll tel. 1999 (€0.90/call), www.slo-zeleznice.si.

BY BUS

The bus station is a low-profile building in front of the train station. Buses depart from the numbered stalls in the middle of the street. For any bus, you have to buy tickets at the bus station ticket windows or at the automated e-kart kiosk (pay with credit card or cash), not from the driver. For bus information, pick up one of the blue phones inside the station to be connected to a helpful English-speaking operator. Bus info: www.ap-ljubljana.si, toll tel. 1991 (€1.50/call), from the US call +386-1-234-4600.

By Bus to: Bled (Mon-Sat hourly—usually at the top of each hour, fewer on Sun, 1.25 hours), Postojna (at least hourly, 1 hour), Divača (close to Škocjan Caves and Lipica, about every 2-3 hours, 1.5 hours), Piran (5/day Mon-Fri, 2/day Sat, 4/day Sun, 2.5 hours), over the Vršič Pass to Bovec (2/day July-Aug at 6:30 and 15:00, June and Sept Sat-Sun only at 6:30, 4.25 hours to Bovec, none Oct-May), Kobarid (1/day in July-Aug over Vršič Pass, 5 hours; otherwise faster but less scenic via Idrija, 3.5 hours), Rijeka (1/day in summer, none off-season, 2.5 hours), Zagreb (1/day Mon-Fri only). to reach Croatia's Istria—specifically Rovinj—the bus is your best option (2/day in summer—faster connection departs at 9:30 and reaches Rovinj in 4 hours before continuing to Pula, July-Sept only; slower connection departs 13:45 and terminates in Rovinj in 5.5 hours, late June-Aug only; both connections also stop in Piran and Poreč; off-season: 2/week to Poreč or Pula and change there to Rovinj, generally Mon and Fri, departs 16:30). DRD runs a handy direct bus from Ljubljana to the Venice-Mestre train station (on the mainland, with easy and frequent train connections to the island; 1/day each way, 3.75 hours).

BY SHARED SHUTTLE SERVICE

If bus and train schedules don't quite get you where you need to go, GoOpti—a company with an innovative business model for shared minibus transfers—can be a convenient and inexpensive option for somewhat flexible travelers. First, go to www.goopti.com and select your destination, date, and preferred time of arrival or departure (for each route, they let you know the maximum amount of time you'd have to wait). Then, 24 hours before departure, you'll get an update of the specific pickup time, based on the needs of other passengers. Prices can flex dramatically, but it's quite affordable (for example, an advance nonrefundable purchase from Ljubljana could be €13 to Piran, or €23 to Venice; for the best price, book two months ahead). For a few euros extra, they can pick you up at your hotel rather than the train or bus station. To lock in a specific time, you can pay extra for a "VIP" transfer ("VIP flex" is similar, but refundable).

GoOpti reaches destinations in Slovenia (at least 15 places, including Ljubljana, the airport, Lake Bled, Lake Bohinj, Bovec in the Julian Alps, towns in the Karst such as Postojna and Sežana, and Piran and other Slovenian coastal destinations), but it's also handy for farther-flung international destinations—such as Venice or its airport, Trieste, various Austrian cities (Vienna, Salzburg, Klagenfurt, etc.), and Croatian cities such as Zagreb and Pula.

BY PLANE

Slovenia's only **airport** (airport code: LJU) is 14 miles north of Ljubljana, about halfway to Bled. Confusingly, the airport goes by three names: Ljubljana Airport (the international version); Brnik (for the town that it's near); and Jože Pučnik Airport (a politician for whom it was controversially renamed in 2007). Most flights are operated by Slovenia's national airline, Adria Airways (www. adria-airways.com), but additional flights are run by easyJet (www. easyjet.com), Wizz Air (www.wizzair.com), and various national carriers (Air France, Turkish Airlines, Finnair, and so on). The airport is small and manageable. Morning flights tend to cluster around the same time frame (between 6:45 and 7:30); as the airport doesn't open until 5:00, there's no need to show up before then. If you need to kill time here, follow signs (around to the left as you exit the terminal) to *Razgledna Terasa* and *Terasa Avionček* and ride the elevator up to the rooftop terrace with a café (daily 9:00-19:00). Here you can sip a coffee while you watch planes land and take off. Airport info: tel. 04/206-1000, www.lju-airport.si.

Getting Between Downtown Ljubljana and the Airport: Two kinds of buses connect the airport with Ljubljana's bus station: **public bus** #28 (to the right as you exit the airport; Mon-Fri hourly until 20:00, only 7/day Sat-Sun, 45 minutes, €4.10), and a **minibus** (to the left as you exit the airport, scheduled to depart after various arriving flights—look for schedule posted near bus stop). Two different companies run the minibus transfers, which take about 30 minutes and cost €9 to downtown: Markun (mobile 041-792-865, www.prevozi-markun.com) and Marko Nowotny (mobile 040-771-771, www.mnj.si). I'd take whichever one is departing first. For a transfer *to* the airport, your hotel or any TI can make arrangements with one of these companies a day or so in advance (same price). Unfortunately, certain evening arrivals don't coordinate well with either the bus or the minibus, so you might have to wait a while or take a pricey **taxi** (figure €25-35 to the airport if you call a reputable company, but more like €42 *from* the airport—since you have to use the pricey taxi stand out front).

To Lake Bled: For tips on going from the airport directly to Lake Bled, see page 812.

The Austrian Alternative: Since Ljubljana's airport is the only one in the country (and thus charges extremely high taxes and airport fees), many Slovenes prefer to fly out of Austria. The airport in **Klagenfurt** (airport code: KLU, also known as "Alpe-Adria Airport"), just over the Austrian border to the north, is subsidized by the local government to keep prices low and compete with Ljubljana's airport. Especially if you're connecting to Bled, it's somewhat handy to reach (from Ljubljana or Bled, take the train to Villach, then to Klagenfurt's Annabichl station, which is a 5-minute walk from the airport; total trip 3 hours from Ljubljana, or 2 hours from Bled; www.klagenfurt-airport.com). A taxi transfer to Bled runs a hefty €120 and takes about an hour (see "By Taxi" on page 739). Austrian Airlines (www.austrian.com) flies from Klagenfurt, as do low-cost carriers such as Ryanair (www.ryanair.com), TUIfly (www.tuifly.com), and Germanwings (www.germanwings.com).

LAKE BLED

Lake Bled—Slovenia's leading mountain resort—comes complete with a sweeping alpine panorama, a fairy-tale island, a cliff-hanging medieval castle, a lazy lakeside promenade, and the country's most sought-after desserts. And the glorious mountain vistas and traditional folk-life charms only crescendo as you explore the surrounding areas. Taken together, there are few more enjoyable places to simply be on vacation.

Since the Habsburg days, Lake Bled (locals pronounce it "blayd") has been *the* place where Slovenes wow visiting diplomats. In the late 19th century, the gentle hillsides surrounding the tight tangle of humble village houses sprouted a smattering of classy villas, built by aristocrats who knew how to find a fine mountain escape. Tito also had one of his vacation homes here (today's Hotel Vila Bled), and more recent visitors have included Prince Charles, Madeleine Albright, and Laura Bush. But above all, Lake Bled feels like a place that Slovenes enjoy alongside their visitors.

Lake Bled offers plenty of ways to idle away an afternoon. While the lake's main town, also called Bled, is more functional than quaint, it offers postcard views of the lake and handy access to the region. Hike up to Bled Castle for intoxicating vistas. Make a wish and ring the bell at the island church. Wander or bike the dreamy path around the lake. Sit on a dock, dip your feet in the water, and feed some of the lake's resident swans. Then dive into some of Bled's famous cakes while you take in the view of Triglav, Slovenia's favorite mountain (see "Mount Triglav" sidebar on page 828). Bled quiets down at night—there's no nightlife beyond a handful of pubs—giving hikers and other holiday makers a chance to recharge.

Bled is also a great jumping-off point for a car trip through the Julian Alps (see next chapter), and a wide variety of other worthwhile side-trips are right at its doorstep. These include the less developed lake named Bohinj, even deeper in the mountains; a spectacular (yet easy) hike in the nearby mountain gorge of Vintgar; and the pleasant Old Town of Radovljica, with its fascinating little beekeeping museum.

PLANNING YOUR TIME

Bled and its neighboring mountains deserve at least two days. With one day, spend it in and around Bled (or, to rush things, spend the morning in Bled and the afternoon day-tripping). With a second day and a car, drive through the Julian Alps using the self-guided tour in the next chapter. The circular route takes you up and over the stunning Vršič Pass, then down the scenic and historic Soča River Valley. Without a car, skip the second day, or spend it doing nearby day trips: Bus or bike to Radovljica and its bee museum, hike to Vintgar Gorge, or visit Lake Bohinj (all described under "Near Lake Bled," at the end of this chapter).

Orientation to Lake Bled

The town of Bled is on the east end of 1.5-mile-long Lake Bled. The lakefront is lined with cafés and resort hotels. A 3.5-mile path meanders around the lake. As no motorized boats are allowed, Lake Bled is particularly peaceful.

The tourists' center of Bled is a cluster of big resort hotels, dominated by the giant, red Hotel Park (dubbed the "red can"). The busy street called **Ljubljanska cesta** leads out of Bled town toward Ljubljana and most other destinations. Just up from the lakefront, across Ljubljanska cesta from Hotel Park, is the modern **commercial center** (Trgovski Center Bled), with a supermarket, travel agency, ATM, shops, and a smattering of lively cafés. Nicknamed "Gaddafi," the commercial center was designed for a city in Libya, but the deal fell through—so the frugal Slovenes built it here instead.

Bled's less-touristy Old Town, under the castle, has a web of tight streets and big but humble old houses surrounding the pointy spire of St. Martin's Church. There you'll find the bus station, some good restaurants, a few hostels, and more locals than tourists.

The mountains poking above the ridge at the far end of the

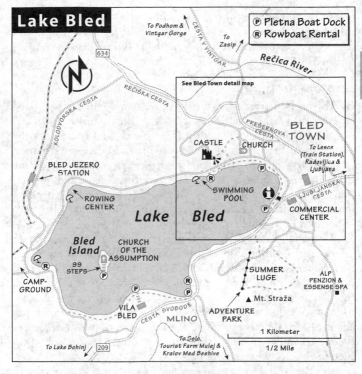

Lake Bled

Ⓟ Pletna Boat Dock
Ⓡ Rowboat Rental

To Podhom & Vintgar Gorge
To Zasip
Rečica River
634
RSAKOLODVORSKA CESTA
REČIŠKA CESTA
CESTA V VINTGAR
See Bled Town detail map
PREŠERNOVA CESTA
BLED TOWN
CASTLE
CHURCH
To Lesce (Train Station), Radovljica & Ljubljana
BLED JEZERO STATION
ROWING CENTER
Ⓡ
SWIMMING POOL
Ⓟ
ℹ
LJUBLJANSKA CESTA
COMMERCIAL CENTER
Ⓟ
Lake Bled
Bled Island
99 STEPS
Ⓟ
CHURCH OF THE ASSUMPTION
Ⓡ
CAMP-GROUND
Ⓡ
SUMMER LUGE
ALP PENZION & ESSENSE SPA
▲ Mt. Straža
VILA BLED
Ⓟ
Ⓟ
MLINO
CESTA SVOBODE
ADVENTURE PARK
1 Kilometer
1/2 Mile
To Lake Bohinj
209
To Selo, Tourist Farm Mulej & Kralov Med Beehive

lake are the Julian Alps, crowned by the three peaks of Mount Triglav. The big mountain behind the town of Bled is Stol ("Chair"), part of the Karavanke range that defines the Austrian border.

TOURIST INFORMATION

Bled's most central TI is in the long, lakefront casino building across the street from the big, red Hotel Park (as you face the lake, the TI is hiding around the front at the far left end, overlooking the lake). Pick up the good map (with the lake on one side and the whole region on the other) and the free Bled information booklet, with up-to-date details on local attractions and transportation options. Get advice on hikes and day trips, confirm transit schedules, and if you're doing any serious hiking, spring for a good regional map (July-Aug Mon-Sat 8:00-21:00, Sun 10:00-18:00; May-June and Sept-Oct Mon-Sat 8:00-19:00, Sun 11:00-17:00; Nov-April Mon-Sat 8:00-18:00, Sun 8:00-13:00; Cesta Svobode 10, tel. 04/574-1122, www.bled.si).

The TI's main branch is harder to reach for non-drivers—on the main road out of town—but it conveniently shares an office with the **Triglav National Park Information Center**, which offers lots of helpful advice for those heading into the mountains (free information, maps and guidebooks for sale; mid-April-mid-Oct daily 8:00-18:00; off-season daily 8:00-16:00; Ljubljanska cesta 27, tel. 04/578-0205, www.tnp.si).

ARRIVAL IN BLED

By Train: Two train stations have the name "Bled." The **Bled Jezero** ("Bled Lake") Station is across the lake from Bled town and is used only by infrequent, slow, tourist-oriented trains into the mountains. You're much more likely to use the **Lesce-Bled** Station in the nearby village of Lesce. The Lesce-Bled Station is on the main line and has far better connections to Ljubljana and international destinations. So if you're buying a train ticket or checking schedules, request "Lesce-Bled" rather than just "Bled." (This is so important, I'll remind you again later.)

The small **Lesce-Bled Station** is in the village of Lesce, about 2.5 miles from Bled. The nearest ATM is upstairs in the shopping center across the street (at the Gorenjska Banka on the third floor, across the parking lot from Mercator supermarket). From the station in Lesce, you can take the bus into Bled town (2/hour, 10 minutes, catch it across the street from the train station); or pay about €10 for a taxi into town. If taking the train out of Lesce-Bled, you can buy tickets at this station or on the train—nobody in Bled town sells tickets.

By Bus: Bled's main bus station is just up from the lake in the Old Town. To reach the lake, walk straight downhill on Cesta Svobode. Note that many buses also stop on the way into town, along Ljubljanska cesta; this stop is handier for walking to many of my recommended accommodations—though some bus drivers may not want to stop here (for details, see "Sleeping in Bled," later).

By Car: Coming from Ljubljana, you'll wind your way into Bled on Ljubljanska cesta, which rumbles through the middle of town before swinging left at the lake. There's a short-term parking lot just above the commercial center, but it's often full; for a longer stay, turn right at the traffic light by Gostilna Union (onto Prešernova cesta) to reach a larger lot that's not far from the lake (near the sports hall). If you're sleeping in town, ask your hotel about parking. Also see "Route Tips for Drivers" on page 812.

By Plane: For details on getting from Ljubljana's airport to Bled, see "Lake Bled Connections," later.

HELPFUL HINTS

Money: Bled town's handiest ATMs are at **SKB Banka** (upstairs in round building at commercial center) and **Gorenjska Banka** (at far end of Hotel Park; this ATM does not accept Visa cards).

Internet Access: Most hotels offer free guest computers and/or Wi-Fi. The TI also has free Wi-Fi and one free Internet terminal. In a pinch, the public library has terminals with fast access (free up to one hour per day, Mon-Fri 10:00-19:00, Sat 8:00-12:00, closed Sun, next to the post office on Ljubljanska cesta).

Post Office: If you're coming up from the lake on Ljubljanska cesta, it's just past the commercial center and library (Mon-Fri 8:00-19:00, Sat 8:00-12:00, closed Sun, slightly longer hours July-Aug, tel. 04/575-0200).

Laundry: Most hotels can do laundry for you, but it's expensive (priced by the piece). You'll get a better deal from a can-do local, **Anže Štalc.** Call Anže to arrange drop-off, and pick it up cleaned and folded 24 hours later (€15/load, €5 more for same-day express service, mobile 041-575-522).

Car Rental: The Julian Alps are ideal by car. Several companies have branches in Bled, including **Europcar** (mobile 031-382-055), **Budget** (mobile 041-644-626), **Sixt** (mobile 030-645-350), **Hertz** (tel. 04/574-5588), and the local **Avantcar** (mobile 041-400-980); as the offices tend to move around, inquire in Bled about the current locations.

Travel Agency: Kompas Bled, in the commercial center, rents bikes, sells books and maps, offers a room-booking service (including many cheap rooms in private homes—though most are away from the lake), and sells various tours around the region (May-Sept Mon-Sat 8:00-19:00, Sun 8:00-12:00 & 16:00-19:00; Oct-April Mon-Sat 8:00-19:00, closed Sun; Ljubljanska cesta 4, tel. 04/572-7500, www.kompas-bled.si, kompas.bled@siol.net).

Massage: If you're here to relax, consider a massage at the **Essense** wellness center at the recommended Alp Penzion. This modern, classy facility—hiding in the countryside about a 15-minute walk or 5-minute taxi ride above the lake—offers a wide range of spa treatments, including pedicures and Thai massage. A standard 50-minute massage will run you about €37 (call first to arrange, Cankarjeva cesta 20A, tel. 04/576-7450, www.essense.si, info@essense.si). You'll also find wellness centers with massage, saunas, and whirlpools at a few of the newer big hotels, including the recommended **Hotel Lovec,** as well as **Hotel Astoria** and **Golf Hotel** (open to non-guests for an additional charge).

GETTING AROUND LAKE BLED (LITERALLY)

By Bike: You can rent a mountain bike at the TI or at Kompas Bled travel agency (both listed earlier) for the same rates (€3.50/hour, €6/3 hours, €8/half-day, €11/day). The TI also has electric

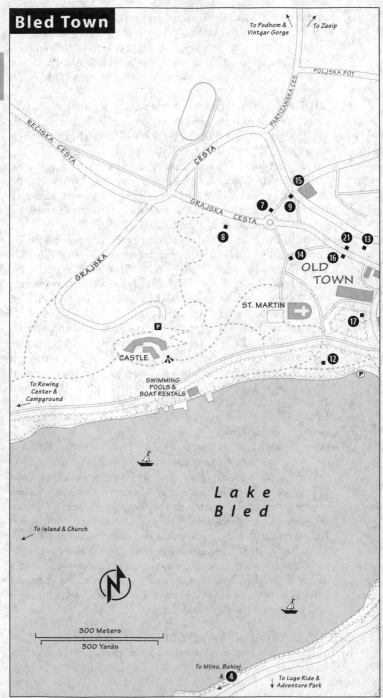

Bled Town

LAKE BLED

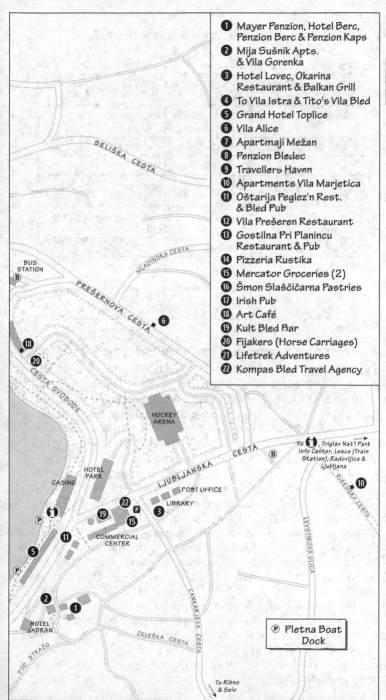

1 Mayer Penzion, Hotel Berc, Penzion Berc & Penzion Kaps
2 Mija Sušnik Apts. & Vila Gorenka
3 Hotel Lovec, Okarina Restaurant & Balkan Grill
4 To Vila Istra & Tito's Vila Bled
5 Grand Hotel Toplice
6 Vila Alice
7 Apartmaji Mežan
8 Penzion Bledec
9 Travellers Haven
10 Apartments Vila Marjetica
11 Oštarija Peglez'n Rest. & Bled Pub
12 Vila Prešeren Restaurant
13 Gostilna Pri Planincu Restaurant & Pub
14 Pizzeria Rustika
15 Mercator Groceries (2)
16 Šmon Slaščičarna Pastries
17 Irish Pub
18 Art Café
19 Kult Bled Bar
20 Fijakers (Horse Carriages)
21 Lifetrek Adventures
22 Kompas Bled Travel Agency

Ⓟ Pletna Boat Dock

Bled and the Julian Alps Essentials

English	Slovene	Pronounced
Slovenia's Biggest Mountain	*Triglav*	TREE-glau
Lake Bled	*Blejsko Jezero*	BLAY-skoh YAY-zay-roh
The Island	*Otok*	OH-tohk
Bled Castle	*Blejski Grad*	BLAY-skee grahd
Town near Bled with Train Station	*Lesce*	lest-SEH
Town with Bee Museum	*Radovljica*	rah-DOH-vleet-suh
Gorge near Bled	*Vintgar*	VEENT-gar
Rustic Lake near Bled	*Bohinj*	BOH-heen
Scenic High-Mountain Pass	*Vršič*	vur-SHEECH
Historic River Valley	*Soča*	SOH-chah

bikes, which give you a much-appreciated boost once you get them moving—well worth the small extra cost if you don't bike much (€5/1 hour, €10/4 hours, €15/8 hours). While walking around the lake is slo-mo bliss, biking it lets you fast-forward between the views of your choice. Biking is also a great way to reach Vintgar Gorge—perfect for combining a countryside pedal with a walk immersed in nature. For a longer pedal, ask for the TI's excellent biking map, with various great bike trips clearly marked and described. The bike path to the nearby town of Radovljica (and its bee museum) is about four miles one-way (get details at the TI).

By Horse and Buggy: Buggies called *fijakers* are the romantic, expensive, and easy way to get around the lake. Hire one along the lakefront between Hotel Park and the castle (see map on page 790 for location; around the lake-€40, one-way up to castle-€40, round-trip to castle with 30-minute wait time-€50, mobile 041-710-970).

By Tourist Train: A little train makes a circuit around the lake every 40 minutes in summer (€4, daily 9:00-21:00 in peak season, shorter hours off-season, weather-dependent, mobile 051-337-478).

By Tourist Bus: A handy but pricey shuttle bus passes through Bled daily in summer. It starts from the main bus station, stops at a few hotels (including Grand Hotel Toplice), then goes up to the castle and on to the Vintgar Gorge entrance (€2.30 one-way to Vintgar, €1.80 just to the castle, departs at 10:00 June-Sept and also at 9:00 July-Aug, confirm schedule at TI or bus station).

A different summertime bus is designed to reach villages to the east that are otherwise poorly served by public transportation, including Kropa (ironwork museum) and the musical village of Begunje, along with some larger towns such as Radovljica and Lesce. The bus runs only on Tuesday and Friday, and although it's billed as hop-on, hop-off, it goes just four times a day (€4/day, July-mid-Aug Tue and Fri only, ask for schedule at TI in Bled or Radovljica).

By Taxi: Your hotel can call a taxi for you. Or contact **Bled Tours,** run by friendly, English-speaking driver Sandi Demšar and his girlfriend Cvetka (€10 to the castle or to Lesce-Bled train station, €14 to Radovljica, €50 to Ljubljana airport, €120 to Klagenfurt airport in Austria, office at Ljubljanska cesta 19, mobile 031-205-611, www.bledtours.si, info@bledtours.si).

By Boat: For information on renting your own boat, see the "Boating" listing on page 801. For details on riding the characteristic *pletna* boats, see listing for "The Island" (page 796).

By Private Plane: If you have perfect weather and deep pockets, there's no more thrilling way to experience Slovenia's high-mountain scenery than from a small propeller plane soaring over the peaks. Flights depart from a grass airstrip near the village of Lesce, a 10-minute drive or taxi ride from Bled. Expensive...but unforgettable (€90 for 15-minute hop over Lake Bled only, €150 for 30-minute flight that also buzzes Lake Bohinj, €210 for deluxe 45-minute version around the summit of Triglav, arrange at least a day in advance, tel. 04/532-0100, www.alc-lesce.si, info@alc-lesce.si).

Tours at Lake Bled

Local Guides

Tina Hiti and **Sašo Golub,** an energetic young couple, are both excellent guides who enjoy sharing the town and region they love with American visitors. Hiring one of them can add immeasurably to your enjoyment and understanding of Bled and the surrounding area (€45 for 2-hour tour of Bled, arrange several days in advance, info@pg-slovenia.com, Tina's mobile 040-166-554, Sašo's mobile 040-524-774, www.pg-slovenia.com). Tina and Sašo are especially handy for side-tripping into the countryside if you don't want to drive yourself. I've spent great days with both of them and was thankful they were behind the wheel. Their most popular trip is a day in the Julian Alps (€190 round-trip from Bled, €230 to pick up or drop off in Ljubljana, extra charge for 8 or more people). They also offer many other options, including all-day shore excursions from the cruise port in Koper (€300 for a day visiting Ljubljana and Bled, up to 3 people) and trips in the Slovenian countryside to research your roots (price depends on distance). As Tina and Sašo both lead tours for me in Europe—and have two young kids—they may send you off with a well-trained substitute. Tina's father **Gorazd**, a former Yugoslav Olympian in ice hockey, brings the older generation's perspective to the trip; **Ervin** provides a younger view; and **Petra** is well-versed in mountain herbs.

Excursions

To hit several far-flung day-trip destinations in one go, consider a package tour from Bled. Destinations range from Ljubljana and the Karst region to the Austrian Lakes to Venice. For example, an all-day Julian Alps trip to the Vršič Pass and Soča Valley runs about €40 per person (sold by various agencies, including Kompas Bled). This tour is handy, but two people can rent a car for the day for about the same price and do it at their own pace using the self-guided driving tour in the next chapter.

Adventure Trips

Various Bled-based companies specialize in taking tourists on active, outdoorsy excursions into the surrounding countryside and mountains. One popular, all-day trip is white-water rafting on the Soča River (around €90/person). Other options include canyoning, river tubing, mountain biking, paragliding, rock climbing, and more. Outfits include **Lifetrek Adventures** (near the bus station at Grajska 4, mobile 040-508-853, www.lifetrek-slovenia.com) and **Amigo** (www.amigo.si). Note that these companies tend to attract a young, sometimes rowdy crowd that enjoys lubricating their adventures with alcohol.

Sights at Lake Bled

Bled doesn't have many sights, but there are plenty of rewarding and pleasant activities.

▲▲▲Walk Around the Lake

Strolling the 3.5 miles around the lake is enjoyable, peaceful, and scenic. At a leisurely pace, it takes about an hour and a half...not counting stops to snap photos of the ever-changing view. On the way, you'll pass some great villas, mostly from the beginning of the 19th century. The most significant one was a former residence of Marshal Tito—today the Hotel Vila Bled, a fine place to stop for a coffee and pretend Tito invited you over for a visit (described next). For the more adventurous, hiking paths lead up into the hills surrounding the lake (ask TI for details and maps; or hike to—and through—Vintgar Gorge, described on page 813).

▲Tito's Vila Bled

Before World War II, this villa on Lake Bled was the summer residence for the Yugoslav royal family. When Tito ran Yugoslavia, the part-Slovene communist leader took over the place and had it renovated using plans from the architect Jože Plečnik. During his heyday, Tito entertained international guests here (big shots from the communist and non-aligned world, from Indira Gandhi to Nikita Khrushchev to Kim Il Sung to Raúl Castro). Since 1984, it's been a classy hotel and restaurant, offering guests grand Lake Bled views and James Bond ambience. The garden surrounding the villa is filled with exotic trees, brought here by Tito's guests from distant lands.

The terrace has a restaurant that welcomes visitors to drop in for a meal, a piece of cake, or just a cup of coffee (reservations smart if you're dining; likely closed Nov-March). Tito fans might want to splurge for an overnight (standard Db-€195, tel. 04/575-3710, www.vila-bled.si). But even if you're not a guest here, the hotel's staff is generally tolerant of curious tourists poking around the public areas inside.

From the marbled lobby, head upstairs. This is where Tito sympathizers have a nostalgic opportunity to send an email from

his desk, sip tea in his lounge, and gawk at his **Socialist Realist wall murals.** Those murals, decorating the upper walls of a vast ballroom on the second floor, are a fascinating peek at the propaganda of the time. Follow the rousing story of the origins of postwar Yugoslavia, starting on the upper left as you enter: First you see the Nazi destruction of Belgrade in 1941, a dark moment that inspired the South Slavs to band together to fight these foreign occupiers. See Tito raising his ragtag army, then leading them into pivotal battles in Bosnia-Herzegovina (notice the minaret and the destroyed bridge over the Neretva River), followed by a winter spent enduring hardship. At the end of this long wall, Tito's victorious Partisans crush the final vestiges of the Nazis; in the upper-right corner, the spring blossoms represent a promising future for the people of Yugoslavia. The large panel at the end of the room trumpets the idealized postwar world that Tito envisioned: proud workers from all walks of life coming together for the betterment of Yugoslavia. In the shadow of a mighty factory—a symbol of heavy industry, which communists embraced as the way of the future—notice that the ironworker and the farmer are holding hands in unity. The room's focal point is the mother hoisting a young child with one arm, and the flag of the nascent Socialist Federal Republic of Yugoslavia with the other.

Getting There: The villa is a 20-minute lakeside walk from the town of Bled at Cesta Svobode 26 (it's the big, white villa with the long staircase at the southern end of the lake, just beyond the village of Mlino). You can also ask your *pletna* gondolier to drop you off here after visiting the island. Those hiking around the lake will pass the gate leading up through Tito's garden to the restaurant and lobby.

▲▲The Island (Blejski Otok)

Bled's little island—capped by a super-cute church—nudges the lake's quaintness level over the top. Locals call it simply "The Island" *(Otok)*. While it's pretty to look at from afar, it's also fun to visit.

The island has long been a sacred site with a romantic twist. On summer Saturdays, a steady procession of brides and grooms, cheered on by their entourages, heads for the island. Ninety-nine steps lead from the island's dock up to the Church of the Assumption on top. It's tradition for the groom to carry—or try to carry—his bride up these steps. About four out of five are successful (proving themselves "fit for marriage"). During the communist era, the church was closed, and weddings were outlawed here. But the tradition re-emerged—illegally—even before the regime ended, with a clandestine ceremony in 1989.

Cost and Hours: Free to visit island, church-€6, ticket includes tower climb, daily May-Sept 9:00-19:00, April and Oct 9:00-18:00, Nov-March 9:00-16:00.

Getting There: The most romantic route to the island is to cruise on one of the distinctive *pletna* boats (€12/person round-trip, includes 30-minute stay on the island; catch one at several spots around the lake—most convenient from in front of Grand Hotel Toplice or just below Hotel Park, might have to wait for more passengers to fill the boat; boats generally run from dawn, last boat leaves one hour before church closes; replaced by enclosed electric boats in winter—unless the lake freezes, in which case there are no boats; mobile 031-316-575). Other places to catch a *pletna* include the village of Mlino, partway around the lake; the bottom of the grand staircase leading up to Vila Bled (it's a shorter trip from here, but the same cost); and at the campground. For more on these characteristic little vessels, see the "*Pletna* Boats" sidebar. Note that *pletna* boatmen stick close to the 30-minute waiting time on the island—which can go very fast. For more time, you can **rent your own boat** and row to the island (see Boating listing, later). It's even possible to **swim**, especially from the end of the lake nearest the island (see "Swimming" listing, later), but you're not allowed into the church in your swimsuit. Guess you'll just have to go in naked.

Visiting the Island: At the top of the stairs, the **Potičnica café** sells *potica*, the Slovenian nut-roll cake that's traditional at Christmastime but delicious any day of the year. The attached **souvenir shop** is the best in Bled, well-stocked with a variety of high-quality Slovenian gifts, trinkets, and keepsakes.

Upstairs in the same building is the worthwhile but easy-to-miss **art gallery**, which displays changing exhibits as well as a wonderful permanent exhibit commemorating Slovenia's membership in the EU. Local sculptor Ladina Kurbor has created finely detailed clay figurines clad in the traditional national costume from each of the European Union member nations. The attached room houses figurines wearing traditional dress from various parts of Slovenia (identified on the map and explained by the posted descriptions).

The island's main attraction is the **church**. An eighth-century Slavic pagan temple dedicated to the goddess of love and fertility once stood here; the current Baroque version (with Venetian flair—the bell tower is separate from the main church) is the fifth to occupy this spot. Go inside and find the rope for the church bell, hanging in the middle of the aisle just before the altar. A local superstition claims that if you can get this bell to ring three times with one big pull of the rope, your dreams will come true. Worth a try.

If you're waiting for a herd of tourists to ring out their wishes, pass the time looking around the area in front of the altar. When the church was being renovated in the 1970s, workers dug up several medieval graves (you can see one through the glass under the bell rope). They also discovered Gothic frescoes on either side of the altar, including, above the door on the right, an unusual ecclesiastical theme: the *bris* (Jewish circumcision ritual) of Christ.

Your ticket also includes the **bell tower**. At 91 steps, it's a shorter climb than the one up from the boat dock. Up top, you'll

Pletna Boats

The *pletna* is an important symbol of Lake Bled. In addition to providing a pleasant way to reach the island, these boats also carry on a tradition dat-  ing back for generations. In the 17th century, Habsburg Empress Maria Theresa granted the villagers from Mlino—the little town along the lakefront just beyond Bled—special permission to ferry visitors to the island. (Since Mlino had very limited access to farmland, the people needed another source of income.) Mlino residents built their *pletnas* by hand, using a special design passed down from father to son for centuries—like the equally iconic gondolas of Venice. Eventually, this imperial decree and family tradition evolved into a modern union of *pletna* oarsmen, which continues to this day.

Today *pletna* boats are still hand-built according to that same centuries-old design. There's no keel, so the skilled  oarsmen work hard to steer the flat-bottomed boat with each stroke—boats piloted by an inexperienced oarsman can slide around on very windy days, especially when empty. There are 21 official *pletnas* on Lake Bled, all belonging to the same union. The gondoliers dump all of their earnings into one fund, give a cut to the tourist board, and divide the rest evenly among themselves. Occasionally a new family tries to break into the cartel, underselling his competitors with a "black market" boat that looks the same as the official ones. While some see this as a violation of a centuries-old tradition, others view it as good old capitalism. Either way, competition is fierce.

find a restored pendulum mechanism from 1890 and fine lake views that are marred by a mesh covering that makes it impossible to snap a clear picture.

To descend by a different route, walk down the trail behind the church (around the right side), then follow the path around the island's perimeter back to where your *pletna* boat awaits.

▲Bled Castle (Blejski Grad)

Bled's cliff-hanging castle, dating in one form or another from 1,000 years ago, was the seat of the Austrian Bishops of Brixen,

who controlled Bled in the Middle Ages. Today it's merely a fine tourist attraction with a little history and lots of big views. The various sights at the castle—a decent history museum, a frescoed chapel, an old-fashioned printing press, and a wine cellar—are more cute than interesting, but the real reason to come up here is to bask in the sweeping panoramas over Lake Bled and the surrounding mountainscapes.

Cost and Hours: €9, daily May-Oct 8:00-20:00, Nov-April 9:00-18:00, tel. 04/572-9782, www.blejski-grad.si.

Getting There: To really earn those views, you can **hike** up the steep hill (20-30 minutes). The handiest trails are behind big St. Martin's Church: Walk past the front door of the church with the lake at your back, and look left after the first set of houses for the *Grad* signs marking the steepest route (follow the wooden stakes all the way up the steep switchback steps); or, for a longer but less steep route, continue past the church on the same street about five minutes, bearing uphill (left) at the fork, and find the *Grad 1* sign just after the Pension Bledec hostel on the left. Once you're on this second trail, don't take the sharp-left uphill turn at the fork (instead, continue straight up, around the back of the hill). If you'd rather skip the hike, you can take the morning **tourist bus** (see "Getting Around Lake Bled," earlier), your **rental car,** a **taxi** (around €10), or—if you're wealthy and romantic—a **horse and buggy** (€40, €10 extra for driver to wait 30 minutes and bring you back down). However, all of these options take you only to the parking lot, from which it's still a steep and slippery-when-wet five-minute hike up to the castle itself.

Eating: The **restaurant** at the castle is fairly expensive, but your restaurant reservation gets you into the castle grounds for free. A well-respected local restaurateur is expected to take over here around mid-2015, which could make this an even better option—ask around locally for the latest (€12-16 pastas, €20-25 main courses, €20 fixed-price meal, daily in summer 10:00-22:00, less off-season, tel. 04/579-4424). Better yet, bring your own **picnic** to munch along the wall with million-dollar views over Lake Bled (buy sandwiches at the Mercator grocery store in the commercial center before you ascend—see page 811).

Visiting the Castle: After buying your ticket, go through the gate and huff the rest of the way up to the outer courtyard. We'll tour the castle clockwise, starting from here. As the castle is continually being spruced up, some details may be different than described.

Turning left at the entrance, you'll pass WCs, then the door to Mojster Janez's working replica of a **printing press** *(grajska tiskarna/manufaktura)* from Gutenberg's time. You can pay €2-25 for your own custom-made souvenir certificate using this very old technology. While this may seem like a tourist gimmick, there's actually some interesting history here. As in many lands, the printing press was a critical tool in the evolution of Slovenia's culture. Look above the press for a life-size mannequin of Primož Trubar (1508-1586), a Slovenian cross between Martin Luther and Johannes Gutenberg. In Trubar's time, Slovene was considered a crude peasants' language—not just unworthy of print, but actually illegal to print. So this Reformer went to Germany and, in 1550—using presses like this one—wrote and printed the two first books in the Slovene language: *Abecedarium* (an alphabet primer to teach illiterate Slovenes how to read) and *Catechismus* (a simplified version of the New Testament). Trubar smuggled his printed books back to Slovenia (hidden in barrels of playing cards) and, en route to Ljubljana, was briefly given refuge in this castle. (Trubar is still much-revered today, appearing on the Slovenian €1 coin.) Up the stairs is an exhibition in English about early printing methods and the importance of moveable type for advancing the Protestant Reformation, whose goal was to get the Word of God more easily into the hands of everyday people. You'll also see one of those first Trubar books—notice it was printed in Tübingen, Germany, an early enclave of the Reformation.

Just past the printing press is the castle's oldest tower—from the 11th century—and a **café terrace** offering pricey drinks with grand views (€2-4 coffee or beer, €6-8 cocktails).

Continue past the café and begin climbing the stairs up to grander and grander **views** over the lake. Reaching the terrace at the very top, you'll find the best vistas; the restaurant; a tiny chapel with 3-D frescoes that make it seem much bigger than it is (next to the museum entrance); a small shop selling iron items that are still forged the traditional way; and the well-presented castle **museum,** which strains to make the story of Bled, the castle, and the surrounding region of Carniola interesting. The ground floor has exhibits about geology, prehistoric artifacts, ironworking, and the seasonal life cycle of the region, while the upstairs has a cool 3-D model of the surrounding mountains, smaller models illustrating the growth of the building, more prehistory, and exhibits on the development of tourism at Lake Bled (including its many fine vacation villas). While video screens and some English information are helpful, there's only so much to say.

When you're done up here, head down the stairs between the museum and restaurant (passing WCs). Coming back down into the lower courtyard, turn left down the ramp to find the **wine** cellar *(grajska klet de Adami)*, where you can pay a hefty €14-17 to bottle and cork your own souvenir bottle of wine (you're paying for the experience more than the wine). Slovenian wines are well-explained by one of two guys (both, coincidentally, named Andrej) who dress as monks, since winemaking was a monastic responsibility in the Middle Ages. Both the printing press and the wine cellar may close earlier than the castle grounds (generally at 19:00 in summer).

Before leaving the castle, climb the stairs up to the wooden **defensive gallery** for the best views in town of the mountains east of Bled. The biggest one is called Stol ("Chair"). In the foreground, you can see the steeple marking the town of Podhom; just to the left, the folds in the hills hide the dramatic Vintgar Gorge (see page 813).

On your way out, look under the stairs to see if they've reopened the **herbal gallery** (a gift shop of traditional-meets-modern herbal brandies, cosmetics, and perfumes).

Boating

Bled is the rowing center of Slovenia. Town officials even lengthened the lake a bit so it would perfectly fit the standard two-kilometer laps, with 100 meters more for the turn (on maps, you can see the little divot taken out of the far end). Bled hosted its fourth world championship in August of 2011. The town has produced many Olympic medalists, winning gold in Sydney, silver in Athens, and bronze in London. Notice that local crew team members, whom you'll likely see running or rowing, are characters—with a tradition of wild and colorful haircuts. This dedication to rowing adds to Bled's tranquility, since no motorized boats are allowed on the lake.

If you want to get into the action, you'll find **rental rowboats** at various points around the lake (€10-15/hour). Look for them at Pension Pletna in the lakeside village of Mlino (a scenic 15-minute walk around the lake from Bled); at the swimming pool under the castle (the closest but priciest option); and in the modern building just before the campground on the far end of the lake.

Swimming

Lake Bled has several suitable spots for a swim. The swimming

pools under the castle are filled with lake water and routinely earn the "blue flag," meaning the water is top-quality (swim all day-€7, less for afternoon only, mid-June-Sept daily 8:00-19:00, closed Oct-mid-June and in bad weather, tel. 04/578-0528). Lake Bled's main beach is at the campground at the far end of the lake, though you can also swim near the village of Mlino. If you swim to the island, remember that you can't get into the church in your swimsuit.

Luge Ride (Polento Sankanje)

Bled's "summer toboggan" luge ride, atop Mount Straža overlooking the lake, allows you to scream down a steep, curvy metal rail track on a little plastic sled. A chairlift takes you to the top of the track, where you'll sit on your sled, take a deep breath, and remind yourself: Pull back on the stick to slow down, push forward on the stick to go faster. You'll drop 480 feet in altitude on the 570-yard-long track, speeding up to about 25 miles per hour as you race toward the lake.

Cost and Hours: €8/ride, cheaper for multiple rides, chairlift only–€4, weather-dependent—if it rains, you can't go; most of April daily 11:00-17:00; May-late June Sat-Sun only 11:00-18:00; late June-Aug daily 10:00-20:00; Sept daily 11:00-18:00; most of Oct Sat-Sun only 11:00-17:00; closed late Oct-early April.

Getting There: The track is high on the hillside just south of town, beyond Grand Hotel Toplice. The chairlift goes up the hill from the parking lot just past the hotel.

Adventure Park (Pustolovski Park)

Next to the luge at the top of Mount Straža, this park has a series of five high-ropes courses designed for everyone from five-year-olds to adults. You'll get rigged up in a safety harness and go through a training course, then be set loose on your choice of courses (with help from spotters on the ground). Plan on spending about two hours to do all of the courses. It's a steep hike up the hill, or you can pay €4 to ride the chairlift for the luge ride (or pay €8 to ride the chairlift up and luge back down).

Cost and Hours: €19 for adults, €15 for kids 7-14, €10 for kids under 7, late June-Aug daily 10:00-18:00, first half of Sept daily 11:00-18:00, shorter hours and Sat-Sun only rest of season, closed late Oct-early April, last entry 2 hours before closing, mobile 031-761-661, www.pustolovski-park-bled.si.

▲Kralov Med Beehive Demonstration

Tucked in Selo village, a long walk or short drive from Bled, this fascinating countryside sight is worth ▲▲▲ (or zzz) for fans of the apicultural arts. (First, read up on beekeeping on page 818.) Local beekeeper Blaž Ambrožič has built an apiary (freestanding house of beehives) and teaches visitors all about this very Slovenian form of agriculture. First you'll see the painted panels, with bees buzzing in and out. Blaž's prize possession is a gigantic Winnie-the-Pooh-style hive that he transplanted from a tree trunk. He'll demonstrate how you can hold your hand within inches of the buzzing hive without getting stung, thanks to the peaceful nature of the indigenous Carniolan bee. Inside, you can watch through a big (and safe) window as Blaž pulls out the honeycomb frames from the hive and works with his bees. You can sample (and buy) different types of honey, along with other bee-related gifts. Outside is a perennial garden that demonstrates when various plants blossom, providing much-needed pollen for the bees.

Cost and Hours: €4/person, call or email a day ahead to arrange a time, demonstrations usually last an hour or more and may even run for just two people, Selo pri Bledu 26, tel. 041-657-120, www.kralov-med.si, blazambrozic@gmail.com.

Getting There: Blaž's beehives are in the village of Selo, a five-minute drive or taxi ride or 40-minute walk from Bled town. Head out of town along the lake (past Grand Hotel Toplice), then turn left (inland) at the village of Mlino. In the next village, Selo, look for the two colorful beehive apiaries along the main road, just above the recommended Tourist Farm Mulej.

Nightlife in Bled

BLED PUB CRAWL

Bled is quiet after hours. However, the town does have a few fun bars that are lively with a young crowd (all open nightly until late). Since many young people in Bled are students at the local tourism school, they're likely to speak English...and eager to practice with a native speaker. Try a Smile, a Corona-type Slovenian lager. *Šnops* (schnapps) is a local specialty—popular flavors are plum *(slivovka)*, honey *(medica)*, blueberry *(borovničevec)*, and pear *(hruškovec)*.

Kick things off with the fun-loving local gang at **Gostilna Pri Planincu** near the bus station (described later, under "Eating in Bled"). Then head down Cesta Svobode toward the lake; just below Hotel Jelovica, you'll find the rollicking **Irish Pub** (a.k.a. "The Pub"), with Guinness and indoor or outdoor seating. For the hippest scene in town, duck across the street and wander a few more steps down toward the lake to find the **Art Café,** with a mellow ambience reminiscent of a Van Gogh painting. Around the lake near the commercial center, **Bled Pub** (a.k.a. "The Cocktail Bar" or "Troha"—for the family that owns it) is a trendy late-night spot where bartenders sling a dizzying array of mixed drinks to an appreciative, youthful crowd (between the commercial center and the lake, above the recommended Oštarija Peglez'n restaurant). If you're still standing, several other bars and cafés percolate in the commercial center, including **Kult Bled,** facing the main road. Slathered with iconic film images, it attracts a multigenerational crowd and occasionally hosts live music.

Sleeping in Bled

Bled is dominated by a few giant, gradually decaying, communist-era convention hotels. Some have been nicely renovated, while others are stale, outmoded, and overpriced. Instead, I prefer staying in smaller, pension-type accommodations in the countryside—many of them are just a short walk above the lake. These quaint little family-run pensions book up early with Germans and Brits; reserve as far ahead as possible. I've listed the high-season prices (May-Oct) unless noted. Off-season, prices are typically 10-20 percent lower. For even cheaper beds, consider one of the many *sobe* (rooms in private homes) scattered around the lake; look for signs in the neighborhood just above Prešernova cesta.

ABOVE THE LAKE

These friendly, cozy, characteristic accommodations are Bled's best values. The only catch is that they're perched on a hilltop a steep five- to ten-minute climb up from the lake (easier than it sounds). There are two ways to find them from the town center: Walk around the lake to Grand Hotel Toplice, then go up the stairs around the right side of the Hotel Jadran (on the hill across the street from Grand Hotel Toplice). Or, from the main road into town (Ljubljanska cesta), take the small service road just above the commercial center (in front of Hotel Lovec), and loop up around the big Kompas and Golf hotels. Some buses (including those to/from Ljubljana) stop at a bus stop higher up on Ljubljanska cesta, just above the traffic light; this stop is handier to these hotels than the main bus station (though bus drivers don't always want to stop since it's a hassle to open the luggage compartment here—try asking nicely). From the bus stop, you can walk down Ljubljanska cesta and take the road just above the post office, which leads up to this area. If you're sleeping up here, Mayer Penzion's restaurant is the easiest choice for dinner (described later, under "Eating in Bled").

$$ Mayer Penzion, thoughtfully run by the Trseglav family, comes with 13 great-value rooms, a helpful staff, a tasty restaurant, an atmospheric wine-tasting cellar, and beautifully handcrafted Slovenian woodwork inside and out. They book up fast in summer with return clients, so reserve early (Sb-€57, Db-€82, €5 less for 3 nights or more, extra bed-€20, family deals, elevator, guest computer and Wi-Fi, Želeška cesta 7, tel. 04/576-5740, www.mayer-sp.si, penzion@mayer-sp.si). They

LAKE BLED

Sleep Code

Abbreviations (€1 = about $1.40, country code: 386, area code: 04)
S = Single, **D** = Double/Twin, **T** = Triple, **Q** = Quad, **b** = bathroom.

Price Rankings
$$$ **Higher Priced**—Most rooms €100 or more.
$$ **Moderately Priced**—Most rooms between €60-100.
$ **Lower Priced**—Most rooms €60 or less.

Unless otherwise noted, Wi-Fi is generally free, credit cards are accepted and breakfast is included, but the modest tourist tax (about €1 per person, per night) typically is not. Everyone listed here speaks English. Prices can change without notice; verify the hotel's current rates online or by email. For the best prices, always book directly with the hotel.

---

also rent a cute, newly restored two-story Slovenian farm cottage next door (Db-€120, Tb/Qb-€150).

$$ Hotel Berc and **Penzion Berc** (pronounced "berts"), run by the Berc brothers, are next door to Mayer Penzion. Both have cozy public spaces, balconies off every room, guest computer and Wi-Fi, and free loaner bikes, and are worth reserving ahead (both cash only). The newer hotel building has 15 rooms with pleasantly woody decor (Sb-€40-50, Db-€70-80—price depends on size, season, and length of stay; Pod Stražo 13, tel. 04/576-5658, www. berc-sp.si, hotel@berc-sp.si, run by Luka). The older, adjacent *penzion* offers 11 cheaper, older, but nearly-as-nice rooms (Sb-€35-45, Db-€65-75, closed Nov-Christmas and sporadically off-season, Želeška cesta 15, tel. 04/574-1838, www.berc-sp.si, penzion@ berc-sp.si; run by Miha, who also offers local excursions).

$$ Penzion Kaps, owned by Peter (whose father, Anton, is a great craftsman), has 11 rooms with balconies, modern bathrooms, and classic old wood carvings. The inviting breakfast room clusters around a giant ceramic stove (Sb-€55, Db-€75-80, cash only, Wi-Fi, free loaner bikes, Želeška cesta 22, mobile 059-117-746, www.penzion-kaps.si, info@penzion-kaps.si).

$ Friendly **Mija Sušnik** rents out two comfortable apartments. Modern, tidy, and equipped with kitchens, these are a good budget choice for families (Db-€57, Tb-€68, Qb-€79, 20 percent extra for fewer than 3 nights, includes tax, no breakfast, cash only, Wi-Fi, laundry service-€10, free parking, Želeška cesta 3, tel. 04/574-1731, susnik@bled-holiday.com). It's just toward the lake from the bigger pensions, with a big crucifix out front. Her sister Ivanka also rents apartments, but they're farther from the lake.

$ Vila Gorenka is your non-hostel, low-budget option. The Žerovec family's old-fashioned house has 10 basic, faded, musty rooms; three of them have their own bathrooms, while the rest share two other bathrooms. Room #10 has a grand-view balcony (S-€17-25, Sb-€30, D-€34-40, Db-€50, cash only, price depends on season, no extra charge for 1-night stays, self-service continental breakfast-€2, guest computer and Wi-Fi, closed Nov-Easter, just below the bigger pensions at Želeška cesta 9, mobile 040-958-624, freeweb.siol.net/mz2, vilagorenka@gmail.com, Janez).

ON OR NEAR THE LAKE

You'll pay a premium to be closer to the lake—but it's hard to argue with the convenience.

$$$ **Hotel Lovec** (LOH-vets), a Best Western Premier, sits in a convenient (but non-lakefront) location just above the commercial center. Gorgeously renovated inside and out, and run by a helpful and friendly staff, it's a welcoming and cheery alternative to Bled's many old, dreary communist hotels. Its 60 plush rooms come with all the comforts (Sb-€128, Db-€151, €20 more for a lake-view balcony, very soft rates fluctuate with demand—email to ask for best price, cheaper Nov-Feb, family and "executive" suites available, delicious breakfast, elevator, guest computer and Wi-Fi, indoor pool, free parking, Ljubljanska cesta 6, tel. 04/620-4100, www.lovechotel.com, reservations@kompas-lovec.com).

$$$ **Vila Istra** is your elegant lakeside splurge, housed inside a prominent and gorgeously restored Art Nouveau villa from 1887. The remarkably spacious rooms include one double and five sprawling suites. Room furnishings gild the lily a bit, but respect the history of the building. It's a scenic 10-minute walk outside of the town center, halfway to the village of Mlino (Db-€110-130, suite-€190-250, price based on demand, air-con, Wi-Fi, Cesta Svobode 35, mobile 059-080-808, www.vila-istra.info, booking@bled.net).

$$$ **Grand Hotel Toplice** (TOHP-leet-seh) is the grande dame of Bled, with 87 high-ceilinged rooms, parquet floors, a genteel lakeview café/lounge, posh decor, all the amenities, and a long list of high-profile guests—from Madeleine Albright to Jordan's King Hussein to Slovene-by-marriage Donald Trump (ask to see their "wall of fame"). Once elegant, this place is a bit faded these days, but it's still a classic. Rooms in the back are cheaper, but have no lake views and overlook a noisy street—try to get one as high up as possible (I've listed the official rates followed by what you'll likely pay in slower times—non-view: Sb-€150/€110, Db-€170/€140; lake view: Sb-€180/€160, Db-€230/€200; suites with lake views-€280; 15-20 percent less Nov-April, very flexible rates—check online, air-con, elevator, guest computer and Wi-Fi, free one-hour boat rental for guests, free parking, Cesta

Svobode 12, tel. 04/579-1000, www.hotel-toplice.com, ghtoplice@ hotelibled.com). The hotel's name—*toplice*—means "spa"; guests are free to use the hotel's swanky, natural-spring-fed indoor swimming pool (a chilly 72 degrees Fahrenheit). This hotel also runs two smaller, far less luxurious hotels nearby with very dated and faded rooms and lower rates (Hotel Trst and Hotel Jadran, details at Toplice's website).

NEAR THE OLD TOWN

These places are convenient to the Old Town and several recommended eateries.

$$$ Vila Alice, a beautifully appointed option in the sleepy upper part of town, offers seven rooms in a picturesque villa with a private garden and sauna (standard Db-€120, superior Db-€155, deluxe Db-€178, pricier suites, air-con in some rooms, Wi-Fi, free parking, reception open daily 7:00-22:00, convenient for drivers at Prešernova cesta 26, tel. 04/574-3050, mobile 040-231-303, www. vila-alice.com, info@vila-alice.com).

$ Apartmaji Mežan, run by young couple Janez and Saša, has three apartments in a modern home buried in the middle of town, just uphill from the church. As it's next to an old barn, it's technically a tourist farm (Db-€50, cash only, no breakfast, guest computer and Wi-Fi, Riklijeva 6, mobile 041-210-290 or 041-516-688, www.apartmaji-mezan.si, sasa.mezan@gmail.com).

$ Penzion Bledec (BLED-ets), a family-run, official IYHF hostel, is just below the castle at the top of the Old Town. Each of the 12 rooms has its own bathroom. They have dorms (bed in 4- to 7-bed dorm-€22-24 depending on number of bunks) as well as rooms that can be rented as doubles (though "doubles" are actually underutilized triples and quads, with separate beds pushed together—so they might not be reservable July-Aug or at other busy times, Db-€54, Tb-€72; cheaper Nov-April, members pay 10 percent less, includes sheets and breakfast, great family rooms, guest computer and Wi-Fi, full-service laundry for guests-€9/ load, restaurant, Grajska 17, tel. 04/574-5250, www.youth-hostel-bledec.si, bledec@mlino.si).

$ Travellers Haven is a low-key hostel run by Mirjam. The 35 beds fill eight rooms in a nicely renovated hundred-year-old villa in the Old Town. The lodgings are well-maintained and the hangout areas are inviting, though the tight bathrooms offer little privacy (€21 for a bunk in a 4- to 6-bed room, D-€48, cheaper off-season, no breakfast but guest kitchen, reception open 8:00-13:00 & 16:00-23:00; guest computer and Wi-Fi, laundry machines, and loaner bikes; Riklijeva cesta 1, mobile 041-396-545, www. travellers-haven.si, travellers-haven@t-2.net).

OUTSIDE OF TOWN

The following listings are a bit farther out; Vila Marjetica is easily walkable to the lake, the walk to Alp Penzion is farther and steeper but still doable, and the tourist farm is best for drivers.

$$ Alp Penzion is in a tranquil countryside setting amid hayfields, within a 20-minute, partly uphill walk of the lake (better for drivers or for those who don't mind the walk). With 12 rooms (some with balconies), this place is enthusiastically run by the Sršen family, who offer lots of fun extras, including a summer barbecue grill/outdoor pub (June-Sept: Sb-€60, Db-€75-85—higher price is for rooms with balcony; Oct-May: Sb-€45, Db-€70; extra bed-€15, 3 percent cheaper if you pay cash, prices can be flexible—based on demand, family rooms, dinner possible in summer—ask when you book, air-con, guest computer and Wi-Fi, free loaner bikes, Cankarjeva cesta 20A, for location, see the map on page 787, tel. 04/574-1614, www.alp-penzion.com, bled@alp-penzion.com). Just next door is the relaxing Essense spa (described earlier, under "Helpful Hints").

$$ Apartments Vila Marjetica ("Daffodil") offers four very spacious, bright, fresh-feeling apartments in a finely restored old villa that's a 15-minute walk up from the lake along the busy main road. Each one has its own kitchen, balcony or terrace, and separate bedroom (Db-€80, Tb-€100, Qb-€120, no breakfast, Wi-Fi, free parking, Ribenska cesta 1, tel. 04/574-1165, mobile 051-308-352, vila.marjetica@gmail.com).

$ Tourist Farm Mulej, possible for hardy walkers but much better for drivers, is a new but traditional farmhouse in a tranquil valley about a half-mile from the lake (1.5 miles from Bled town). Damjana and Jože, who run this working farm (with 70 milk cows), also rent out eight modern rooms and four apartments—all with balconies—and serve breakfasts and dinners made with food they produce. Be sure to see the udderly fascinating, fully automated cow-milking machine called Lely, who's practically a member of the family (Db-€60, or €80 with dinner; €30 per extra person in apartments, or €40 with dinner; 20 percent extra for 1- or 2-night stays in June-Aug, cash only, family rooms, air-con, Wi-Fi, free loaner bikes, horseback riding free for experienced guests, Selo pri Bledu 42a, tel. 04/574-4617, www.mulej-bled.com, info.mulej@gmail.com). It's in the farm village of Selo—drive along the lakeside road south from Bled, then turn off in Mlino toward Selo, and look for the signs (to the right) once in the village. For the location, see the map on page 787.

Eating in Bled

Bled has several good restaurants, but most everything is quite similar. For variety, wait for Ljubljana.

Okarina, run by charming, well-traveled Leo Ličof, serves a diverse array of cuisines, all of them well-executed: international fare, traditional Slovenian specialties (with an emphasis on game), and Indian (Himalayan) dishes. Leo has a respect for salads and vegetables and a passion for fish. Creative cooking, fine presentation, friendly service, and an atmosphere as tastefully eclectic as the food make this place a great splurge (€9-14 pastas, €11-24 main courses, plus a few pricier splurges, Mon-Fri 12:00-15:00 & 18:00-23:00, Sat-Sun 12:00-23:00, next to recommended Hotel Lovec at Ljubljanska cesta 8, tel. 04/574-1458). In the back of the menu, look for the copy of the guest book page with Paul McCartney's visit from May 2005. Around the left side of the building is **Balkan Grill**, Leo's smaller pavilion restaurant, serving up Balkan-style grilled meats at lower prices (€5-10 grilled meats—for description see "Balkan Flavors" on page 1140, daily 18:00-23:00 and maybe also for lunch, June-Sept only, closed off-season and in bad weather).

Oštarija Peglez'n ("The Old Iron"), conveniently located on the main road between the commercial center and the lake, cooks up tasty Slovenian and Mediterranean meals, with an emphasis on fish and fun, family-style shareable plates. Choose between the delightful Slovenian cottage interior or the shady streetside terrace. Reservations are smart in summer (€8-10 salads and pastas, €12-20 main courses, daily 12:00-23:00, Cesta Svobode 19A, tel. 04/574-4218).

Vila Prešeren is the best choice for lakeside dining, featuring mod decor, good international cuisine (as well as some traditional Slovenian dishes), and a giant terrace reaching all the way down to the lakefront path. Despite the overworked waitstaff, this is a great spot to linger over a meal, a drink, or a classic Lake Bled dessert (€10-12 salads, €9-14 pastas, €12-22 main courses, daily 7:00-23:00, Veslaška promenada 14, tel. 04/575-2510). They also rent eight overpriced but well-located rooms upstairs (Db-€150, www.vilapreseren.si).

Mayer Penzion, just up the hill from the lakefront, has a dressy restaurant with good traditional cooking that's worth the short hike. This is where a Babel of international tourists come to swap hiking tips and day-trip tales. As this is the only real restaurant in the pension neighborhood, it can be very busy—reserve ahead (€8-21 main courses, Tue-Sun 18:00-24:00, closed Mon, indoor or outdoor seating, above Hotel Jadran at Želeška cesta 7, tel. 04/576-5740). The neighboring **Hotel/Penzion**

Bled Desserts

While you're in Bled, be sure to enjoy the town's specialty, a cream cake called **kremna rezina** (KRAYM-nah ray-ZEE-nah; often referred to by its German-derived name, **kremšnita,** KRAYM-shnee-tah). It's a layer of cream and a thick layer of vanilla custard artfully sandwiched between sheets of delicate, crispy crust. Heavenly. Slovenes travel from all over the country to sample this famous dessert. You may also see some newfangled strawberry and chocolate **kremšnita** variations, but purists swear by the original.

Slightly less renowned—but just as tasty—is **grmada** (gur-MAH-dah, "bonfire"). This dessert was developed by Hotel Jelovica as a way to get rid of their day-old leftovers. They take yesterday's cake, add rum, milk, custard, and raisins, and top it off with whipped cream and chocolate syrup.

There's also *prekmurska gibanica*—or just **gibanica** (gee-bah-NEET-seh) for short. Originating in the Hungarian corner of the country, *gibanica* is an earthy pastry filled with poppy seeds, walnuts, apples, and cheese, and drizzled with rum.

Yet another dessert is the very traditional **potica** (poh-TEET-seh), a walnut roll that's usually eaten at Christmastime. While it's rare to find this in bakeries, the café on the island in the lake sells several varieties.

Desserts are typically enjoyed with a lake-and-mountains view—the best spots are the terrace at Vila Prešeren, the Panorama restaurant by Grand Hotel Toplice, and the terrace across from Hotel Park (figure around €5 for cake and coffee at any of these places). For a more local (but non-lake view) setting, consider Šmon Slaščičarna (only slightly cheaper; see next page).

Berc—recommended earlier under "Sleeping in Lake Bled"—operates a restaurant in the summer (May-Sept daily 17:00-23:00).

Gostilna Pri Planincu ("By the Mountaineers") is a homey, informal bar coated with license plates and packed with fun-loving and sometimes rowdy natives. A larger dining area sprawls behind the small, local-feeling pub, and there's outdoor seating out front and on the side patio. The menu features huge portions of stick-to-your-ribs Slovenian pub grub, plus Balkan grilled-meat specialties (€10-20 main courses). Look for their €6-9 daily specials—huge, home-style traditional dishes. Upstairs is a timbered pizzeria selling €6-10 wood-fired pies (daily 9:00-23:00, pizzeria open from 11:00, Grajska cesta 8, tel. 04/574-1613). The playful cartoon mural along the outside of the restaurant shows different types of mountaineers (from left to right): thief, normal, mooch ("gopher"), climber, and naked (...well, almost).

Pizzeria Rustika, in the Old Town, offers wood-fired pizzas and salads. Its upstairs terrace is relaxing on a balmy evening (€6-10 pizzas, daily 12:00-23:00, service can be slow when it's busy, Riklijeva cesta 13, tel. 04/576-8900).

Supermarket: The **Mercator** grocery store, in the commercial center, has the makings for a bang-up picnic. They sell pre-made sandwiches for about €3, or will make you one to order (point to what you want). This is a great option for hikers and budget travelers (Mon-Fri 7:00-19:00, Sat 7:00-15:00, Sun 8:00-12:00). There's another location closer to the Old Town and castle (Mon-Sat 7:00-20:00, Sun 8:00-16:00).

Dessert: While tourists generally gulp down their cream cakes on a hotel restaurant's lakefront terrace, local residents favor the desserts at **Šmon Slaščičarna** (a.k.a. the "Brown Bear," for the bear on the sign). It's nicely untouristy, but lacks the atmosphere of the lakeside spots (€2-3 cakes, daily 7:30-21:00, near bus station at Grajska cesta 3, tel. 04/574-1616).

Splurge Restaurant Near Bled

Vila Podvin, in the village of Mošnje (about a 15-minute drive from Lake Bled, just past Radovljica), has gained a big culinary reputation in recent years. The talented celebrity chef, Uroš (who has hosted some popular Slovenian cooking shows), prides himself on melding traditional Slovenian recipes with modern techniques and flavors. The dressy but inviting interior and fine garden are equally enjoyable places to dine. Their €15 three-course lunch special—available until 15:00—is a nice way to affordably sample their menu. Reservations are smart (fixed-price meals-€35/4 courses, €55/6 courses; otherwise €10-15 starters, €20 main dishes; €2 cover, Tue-Sat 12:00-22:00, Sun 12:00-17:00, closed Mon, Mošnje 1, tel. 08/384-3470, www.vilapodvin.si). They also rent rooms and offer cooking classes (explained on their website).

Lake Bled Connections

The most convenient train connections to Bled leave from the Lesce-Bled Station, about 2.5 miles away (see details under "Arrival in Bled," earlier). Remember, when buying a train ticket to Lake Bled, make it clear that you want to go to the Lesce-Bled Station (not the Bled Jezero Station, which is poorly connected to the main line). No one in the town of Bled sells train tickets; buy them at the station just before your train departs (open Mon-Fri 5:30-21:00, Sat 7:00-15:00, Sun 14:30-19:30). If the ticket window there is closed, buy your ticket on board from the conductor (who will likely waive the €2.50 additional fee).

Note that if you're going to **Ljubljana,** the bus (which leaves from Bled town itself) is better than the train (which leaves from the Lesce-Bled train station).

From Lesce-Bled by Train to: Ljubljana (roughly hourly, 40-60 minutes), **Salzburg** (3/day, 4 hours, some change in Villach, Austria), **Munich** (3/day, 5.5 hours, some change in Villach), **Vienna** (that's *Dunaj* in Slovene, 3/day, 5.25-6 hours, transfer in Villach), **Venice** (2/day with transfers in Villach and Klagenfurt—likely partway by bus, 6.5 hours; instead consider a GoOpti mini-bus—described on page 782), **Zagreb** (4/day direct, 3-3.5 hours).

By Bus to: Ljubljana (Mon-Sat hourly—usually at :30 past the hour, fewer on Sun, 1.25 hours), **Radovljica** (Mon-Fri at least 2/hour, Sat hourly, Sun almost hourly, 15 minutes), **Lesce-Bled train station** (2/hour, 10 minutes), **Lake Bohinj** (hourly, 40 minutes to Bohinj Jezero stop, 50 minutes to Bohinj Vogel or Bohinj Zlatorog stop, 3/day in summer continue all the way to Savica Waterfall trailhead), **Podhom** (15-minute hike away from Vintgar Gorge, Mon-Fri 5/day in the morning, 1/day Sat, none Sun, 15 minutes), **Spodnje Gorje** (also 15-minute hike from Vintgar Gorge, take bus in direction of Krnica, hourly, 15 minutes). Confirm times at the TI or by using the schedules posted at the unstaffed Bled bus station. Buy tickets on the bus.

By Plane: Ljubljana Airport (airport code: LJU) is between Lake Bled and Ljubljana, about a 45-minute drive from Bled. Connecting by taxi costs around €40-50 (set price up front—since it's outside of town, they don't use the meter; be sure to use a Bled-based taxi, rather than a Ljubljana-based taxi, which will likely be more expensive). The Zup Prevozi shuttle bus is a more affordable option at €13, but it runs only two to four times each day (generally coordinated to meet easyJet flights). However, at other times you can arrange for a shuttle from Zup Prevozi for a bit less than a taxi (€36/1 person, €37/2 people, €38/3 people, €39/4 people, mobile 031-304-141, www.zup-prevozi.eu). The bus connection from Bled to the airport is cheap (total cost: about €6) but complicated and time-consuming: First, go to Kranj (Mon-Fri 12/day, Sat-Sun 8/day, 35 minutes), then transfer to a Brnik-bound bus (at least hourly, 20 minutes). Many Bled residents prefer to fly from Klagenfurt, Austria. For details on both the Ljubljana and Klagenfurt airports, see page 783.

Route Tips for Drivers: Bled is less than an hour north of Ljubljana on the slick A-2 expressway. The exit is marked for *Lesce,* but you'll also see signs for *Bled,* which will lead you directly to the lake (where the road becomes Ljubljanska cesta).

To reach Radovljica (bee museum) or Lesce (train station),

drive out of Bled on Ljubljanska cesta toward the expressway. Watch for the turnoff to *Lesce* on the right. They're on the same road: Lesce first (to reach train station, divert right when entering town), then Radovljica. (Signs to *Radovljica* will divert you out to the main road that parallels the expressway, then back down into Radovljica; instead, you could follow signs to Lesce, and drive through that town for the more direct route.)

Near Lake Bled

The countryside around Bled offers several day trips that can be done easily without a car (bus connection information is described in each section). The four trips listed here are the best (two small-town/museum experiences, two hiking/back-to-nature options). They're more convenient than can't-miss, but each is worthwhile on a longer visit, and all give a good taste of the Julian Alps. For a self-guided driving tour through farther-flung (and even more striking) parts of the Julian Alps, see the next chapter.

Vintgar Gorge

Ideal for those seeking an easy yet spectacular walk, Vintgar (VEENT-gar), worth ▲▲, is one of my favorite low-impact hikes

in Slovenia or Croatia. Just north of Bled, the river Radovna has carved this mile-long, picturesque gorge into the mountainside. Boardwalks and bridges put you right in the middle of the magic in this "poor man's Plitvice." Shaded and relatively cool, this is a refreshing place for a walk on a hot day.

The gorge—easily reachable from Bled by bus or foot—works well for those who are itching for a hike but don't have a car. From the entrance, allow about 1.5 hours for a round-trip hike, including time for photos (and there will be photos).

Cost and Hours: €4 to enter gorge, open daily April-Oct 8:00-19:00 or until dusk, June-Aug maybe until 20:00, closed Nov-March, tel. 04/572-5266.

Getting to Vintgar Gorge: The gorge is 2.5 miles north of Bled. To reach the gorge entrance, you can walk (takes at least one hour one-way), pedal a rental bike (about 30 minutes, easiest with an electric bike rented at the TI), take a bus (15-minute ride plus 15-minute walk, or 30-minute ride on summer tourist bus), or

LAKE BLED

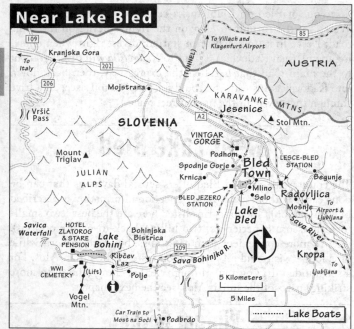

Near Lake Bled

drive (less than 10 minutes).

Walkers and **cyclists** leave Bled on the road between the castle and St. Martin's Church and take the uphill (left) road at the fork. Just after the little yellow chapel, turn right on the road with the big tree, then immediately left at the Mercator grocery store. When the road swings left, continue straight onto Partizanska (marked for *Podhom* and a walking sign for *Vintgar;* ignore the bus sign for *Vintgar* pointing left). At the fork just after the little bridge, go left for Podhom, then simply follow signs for *Vintgar*.

In summer, the easy **tourist bus** takes you right to the gorge entrance (only runs in the morning; see "Getting Around Lake Bled," page 792). Otherwise, you can take a **local bus** to one of two stops: Podhom (Mon-Fri 5/day in the morning, 1/day Sat, none Sun, 15 minutes) or Spodnje Gorje (take bus in direction of Krnica, hourly, 15 minutes). From either the Podhom or the Spodnje Gorje bus stop, it's a 15-minute walk to the gorge (follow signs for *Vintgar*).

Drivers follow signs to *Podhom*, then *Vintgar* (see walking/cycling instructions), and park for free right at the gorge entrance.

Gorge Hike: After buying your ticket, you'll hit the boardwalk trail (sometimes a bit slippery) and crisscross over the most dramatic and narrow stretch, tiptoeing over several waterfalls and marveling at the clarity of the water. Then the gorge—and the trail—flattens out and passes under a high stone footbridge and over a scenic dam. Finally, at the end of the gorge, you'll reach a footbridge over a plunging waterfall (next to a snack stand and WCs). For more views, continue on five minutes downhill (following the *Pod Slap* signs), then circle over the river again to reach a knoll, peering up at the waterfall and bridge you just crossed.

When finished, you can simply go back the way you came, or take a prettier return to Bled (described next).

Scenic Hike Back to Bled: If you still have energy once you reach the end of the gorge, consider this longer hike back with panoramic views. Behind the snack stand deep in the gorge, find the trail marked *Pod Katarina*. You'll go uphill for 25 strenuous minutes (following the red-and-white circles and arrows) before cresting the hill and enjoying beautiful views over Bled town and the region. Continue straight down the road 15 minutes to the typical, narrow, old village of Zasip, then walk (about 30 minutes) or take the bus back to Bled.

Radovljica

The town of Radovljica (rah-DOH-vleet-suh, "Radol'ca" for short), perched on a plateau above the Sava River, has the charming

Old Town that Bled lacks (and, refreshingly, lacks much of Bled's summer crowds). The traffic-free core of the town, once hemmed in by a stout wall (still faintly visible in some areas), is jammed with historic buildings that surround the long, skinny main square called Linhartov trg. While Radovljica's Old Town is a pleasant place to stroll or nurse a coffee, you can see it all in a few minutes. The main reason to visit here is to tour its small but strangely fascinating beekeeping museum—despite only having a few rooms, it still ranks as one of Europe's biggest on the apiarian arts. Skip the town on Mondays, when the museum is closed (and be aware that the museum closes for a lengthy lunch break off-season).

Tourist Information: The enthusiastic TI loves to help visitors appreciate the town of "Radol'ca" (May-Sept daily 9:00-19:00; Oct-April Mon-Fri 9:00-16:00, Sat-Sun 9:00-18:00; Linhartov trg 1, tel. 04/531-5112, www.radolca.si).

GETTING TO RADOVLJICA

Buses to Radovljica generally leave Bled every half-hour (fewer on weekends, buy ticket from driver, trip takes about 15 minutes). To reach the town center and the bee museum from the bus station, leave the station going straight ahead, cross the bus parking lot and the next street, then turn left down the far street (following brown sign for *Staro Mesto*). In five minutes, you'll reach the start of the pedestrianized Linhartov trg (with the TI—on the right—and the start of the Old Town, a few short blocks from the bee museum).

Drivers leave Bled on Ljubljanska cesta and follow the directions under "Route Tips for Drivers" on page 812. The road deadends at Radovljica's pedestrian zone, where you'll find a parking lot (by the rustic garage), the TI, and the start of my "Old Town Stroll."

A handy **bike** path scenically and peacefully connects Bled with Radovljica (about 4 miles, get details at TI).

Sights in Radovljica

▲▲Apicultural Museum (Čebelarski Muzej)

This museum celebrates Slovenia's long and very proud beekeeping heritage. While the exhibits about the history of beekeeping are oddly fascinating, the highlight is the extensive collection of colorfully painted frontboard panels (used on the front of hives)—one of Slovenia's most cherished folk arts. Replicas of these panels are sold in souvenir shops nationwide, but these are the real deal.

Cost and Hours: €3, good English descriptions, €1.60 English guidebook is a nice souvenir; May-Oct Tue-Sun 10:00-18:00, closed Mon; March-April and Nov-Dec Wed and Sat-Sun 10:00-12:00 & 15:00-17:00, Tue and Thu-Fri 8:00-15:00, closed Mon; Jan-Feb Tue-Fri 8:00-15:00, closed Sat-Mon; upstairs at Linhartov trg 1, tel. 04/532-0520, www.muzeji-radovljica.si.

Visiting the Museum: Everything is well-described in English, but this commentary will help you locate the highlights.

The **first room** of the museum traces the history of beekeeping, from the time when bees were kept in hollowed-out trees to the present day. The bust celebrates beekeeper extraordinaire Anton Janša. On the nearby wall, you'll see excerpts from his first-ever textbook on beekeeping, as well as documents from other VIBs (very important beekeepers).

In the **second room** are old-fashioned tools. When a new queen bee is born, the old queen takes half the hive's bees to a new location. Experienced beekeepers used the long, skinny instrument (a beehive stethoscope) to figure out when the swarm was working up a steady buzz, indicating they were ready to fly the coop. Then, once the bees had moved to a nearby tree, the beekeeper used the big spoons to retrieve the queen—surrounded by an angry ball of her subjects—from her new home before she could get settled in. The beekeeper transferred the furious gang into a manmade hive designed for easier, more sanitary collection of honey. You can also see the tools beekeepers used to create smoke, which makes bees less aggressive. Even today, some of Slovenia's old-fashioned bee-keepers simply light up a cigarette and blow smoke on any bees that get ornery. The life-size model of a man carrying a box on his back illustrates how dedicated beekeepers would trudge uphill with their hives to help them reach higher and higher blossoms as the summer wore on. You'll also see a variety of old beehives (and a press used to squeeze every last drop of honey out of that comb), as well as photos of apiaries—large, freestanding build-ings that house multiple hives. The map on the wall shows how the Carniolan bee—favored by beekeepers for its relatively mellow personality and fast growth in springtime—has been exported far and wide throughout the world, thanks to its adaptability to new climates.

The **third room** features the museum's highlight: whimsically painted beehive frontboards (called *panjske končnice*). Beekeepers, believing these paintings would help the bees find their way home, developed a tradition of decorating their hives with religious, his-torical, and satirical folk themes. The oldest panel dates from 1758, but the practice really took off in the 19th century. Take your time perusing these delightful illustrations. The depiction of a hunter's funeral shows all the animals happy...except his dog. In another panel, animals shave the hunter—evoking an old Slovenian saying about "shaving the fool." Panels also reveal professional stereo-types of the time: One popular panel shows two farmers fight-ing over a cow, while a lawyer milks it. Another features a giant snail running over very slow-moving tailors (who were consid-ered extremely lethargic in sewing new clothes). Historical pan-els include a bloody beheading during a local battle and several scenes of troublesome Turks. There's everything from portraits of Habsburg emperors, to a "true crime" sequence of a man mur-dering his family as they sleep, to proto-"Lockhorns" cartoons of marital strife, to awkward depictions of foreign lands (based on likely incomplete or faulty descriptions of the day), to 18th-century erotica (one with a woman showing some leg and another with a flip-up, peek-a-boo panel). A few panels blur the line between humorous and misogynistic: Look for the devil sharpening a wom-an's tongue on a wheel; the mill where old women are put in and young women are pulled out; or the man carrying a cross—and his wife—on his back. (Equal-opportunity offenders, beekeepers also painted scenes of drunk men being yanked out of bars and away

LAKE BLED

Slovenian Beekeeping

Slovenia seems to do small things in a big way—and when it comes to agriculture, what form of livestock could be smaller than a bee?

Since the days before Europeans had sugar, Slovenia has been a big honey producer. Slovenian farmer Anton Janša (1734-1773) is considered the father of modern beekeeping. Habsburg Empress Maria Theresa brought him to Vienna to become Europe's first official teacher of this art. And even today, beekeeping is considered a crucial part of Slovenian culture. The area around Lake Bled (Carniola) has about 6,000 inhabitants, including 65 beekeepers who manage 5,000 hives—the most bees per capita of any place in Europe.

Most Slovenian beekeepers maintain large buildings (called apiaries) that hold banks of smaller hives (as opposed to bee-

keepers in North America, who tend to have a few separate large hives). This innovation—one of many by Janša—allows beekeepers to maximize efficiency. Each hive has its own front panel, and each of those is painted in bright colors, often depicting creative folk scenes. This is designed to help both the bees and the beekeepers (who were, traditionally, often illiterate) distinguish the hives from each other. While bees may not be able to tell a painting of a bear from one of a flower, they can distinguish enough patterns and colors to keep themselves from accidentally going to the wrong hive—in which case they'd be attacked as an outsider.

Replicas of those characteristic **beehive panels** are available at shops in Bled and Ljubljana and make for appealing souvenirs. Basic reproductions of the beehive panels cost around €12-15, while better-quality, hand-painted ones run €20-30 or

from card games by their wives.) The life-size wooden statues were used to "guard" the beehives—and designed to look like fearsome Ottoman and Napoleonic soldiers.

The **fourth room** examines the biology of bees. In the summer only, look for the actual, functioning beehive. Try to find the queen—she's usually marked with a dot on her back. The surround-sound hive nearby lets you step inside to hear the noise of a buzzing queen. You'll also see bee-related products, including more. When perusing your options, it helps to know the stories behind each one (see page 817 for a run-down on some of the designs).

The other apian souvenir is **honey.** In 2013, Slovenian honey was designated as a unique product by the European Union—a certification that means only honey produced in a certain place and way can carry that name. Taste can differ tremendously from hive to hive, as the specific flowers and blossoms that bees gather pollen from largely determine the flavor of the honey. Ideally find a shop that will let you sample several. In general, honeys made from mixed flowers and linden blossoms (which tend to be cloudy from a natural crystallization process) have the sweetest, mildest flavor; those made from chestnut or pine trees can have a bitter aftertaste. The honeys that appear creamy are infused with flavors and are most often eaten on bread or pancakes; plain honey is more versatile.

Besides honey, beekeepers also make money by raising new queen bees. Each hive has one, and they can't be bred—one of the larvae is simply fed special "royal jelly" that encourages her to become a leader. In the springtime, when bees are born, the beekeeper keeps a close eye on the hive to figure out whether there are any potential queens about to emerge, then moves the old queen, who brings half the hive with her, to a new home (before she can find one on her own).

Slovenes still reserve an importance and affection for bees that's rare in modern times. For example, the Slovene language has two different words for "to give birth" and "to die": One they use exclusively for humans and bees, and a different one for all other animals. If a beekeeper dies, it's believed (with some pretty incontrovertible evidence) that the new beekeeper must formally "introduce" himself to the hive by going there and explaining to the bees what has happened; otherwise, they become confused and agitated, and often die themselves.

To learn more about Slovenian beekeeping, visit the insightful Apicultural Museum in Radovljica. For an even more vivid, practical experience, call Blaž at Kralov Med near Bled for a demonstration (see page 802). At either place, you'll get a sense for just how proud Slovenes are of their bees.

wax items, ornaments, and pastries. Another exhibit shows how bees—so respected here in Slovenia, and around the world—are a popular decorative motif, adorning everything from coins to buildings (in many cultures, diligent bees, who store their honey, are symbolic of banks).

The **final room** features a modern beekeeper's house, special exhibits, and a good but dry, detailed 14-minute film about the Carniolan bee.

Back at the entrance, the ticket desk sells a few choice souvenirs, including hand-painted replicas of frontboards, honey brandy, candles, ornaments, and other bee products.

Nearby: Sharing a ticket desk with the bee museum, the **Linhart Museum** celebrates one of Slovenia's leading Enlightenment thinkers. Radovljica-born Anton Linhart was an 18th-century playwright, politician, pedagogue, and historian who wrote some of the first plays in the Slovenian language and set the stage for France Prešeren. While he's important to Slovenes, it's hard to drum up much excitement for this earnest two-room museum devoted to a man who is not that interesting to outsiders (€5 combo-ticket with Apicultural Museum, same hours).

Eating in Radovljica

Several Radovljica restaurants near the bee museum have view terraces overlooking the surrounding mountains and valleys.

Lectar offers pricey, hearty Slovenian fare in a rural-feeling setting with a user-friendly, super-traditional menu. Its several heavily decorated rooms are often filled with tour groups, but in good weather, don't miss the terrace out back. Come here if you want to linger over rustic Slovenian specialties—not if you're in a hurry. The restaurant is known for its heart-shaped gingerbread cookies (called *lect*), inscribed with messages of love. In the cellar is a €1.50 "living museum" where you can watch costumed bakers make and decorate these hearts according to the traditional recipe (€6-11 starters, €9-13 main courses, Wed-Mon 12:00-22:00, closed Tue, family-friendly, Linhartov trg 2, tel. 04/537-4800).

Gostilna Avguštin, across the street, is the simpler local alternative for unpretentious, stick-to-your-ribs Slovenian fare. Their terrace in back enjoys an even better view than Lectar's (€6-9 starters, €11-20 main dishes, daily 11:00-24:00, Linhartov trg 15, tel. 04/531-4163).

Lake Bohinj

The pristine alpine Lake Bohinj (BOH-heen), 16 miles southwest of Bled, enjoys a quieter scene and (in clear weather) even better vistas of Triglav and the surrounding mountains. This is a real back-to-nature experience, with just a smattering of hotels and campgrounds, rather than the well-oiled resort machine of Bled. Some people adore Bohinj; others are bored by it. While spectacular in clear, sunny weather, it's disappointing in the clouds (and, because of its position deep in the mountains, it can be socked in here even when it's clear in Bled). But if the weather is great and you're finding Bled too touristy to allow you to really enjoy nature, go to Bohinj.

GETTING TO LAKE BOHINJ

From Bled, hourly **buses** head for Bohinj, stopping at three different destinations: Bohinj Jezero (the village of Ribčev Laz, 40

minutes), then Bohinj Vogel (a 10-minute walk from the base of the Vogel Mountain cable car, 50 minutes), and finally a few hundred yards more to Bohinj Zlatorog (Hotel Zlatorog and the one-hour hike to the Savica waterfall trailhead, 50 minutes). In summer, a few buses continue all the way to the Savica Waterfall trailhead (see details under "Savica Waterfall," later). Off-season, there are fewer buses—confirm times before you depart.

Drivers leave Bled going south along the lakefront road, Cesta Svobode; in the village of Mlino, you'll peel off from the lake and follow signs to *Boh Bistrica* (a midsize town near Lake Bohinj). Once in the town of Bohinjska Bistrica, turn right, following *Boh Jezero* signs. The road takes you to the village of Ribčev Laz and along the lakefront road with all the attractions—the drive from Bled to the lake takes about 30 minutes. You can follow this road all the way to the Vogel cable-car parking lot; at the Vogel turn-off, you can continue straight ahead to reach the Savica Waterfall trailhead, or turn right and cross the bridge to curl around the far end of the lake and see the pristine river that feeds the lake (which flows out of the pool at the base of the Savica Waterfall).

Sights at Lake Bohinj

A visit to Bohinj has three parts: a village (offering boat trips on the lake), a cable car (and nearby cemetery), and a waterfall hike. I've listed them as you'll reach them along the main road from Bled, which runs along the south side of the lake. If you plan to do everything (boat trip, cable car, waterfall hike), ask at the TI in Ribčev Laz about a combo-ticket to save some money.

Ribčev Laz Village

Coming from Bled, your first views of Bohinj will be from the little village called Ribčev Laz (loosely translated as "Good Fishin' Hole") at the southeast corner of the lake. Here you'll find a TI, a handful of hotels and ice-cream stands, and the Bohinj Jezero bus stop.

On the way into town, on a small hill to the right, is a **monument** to the four Bohinj-area mountaineers who first summited Mount Triglav on August 26, 1778.

The town's main landmark is its picturesque lakefront church, **St. John the Baptist** (to your right as you face the lake, past the stone bridge; not open to visitors).

A five-minute stroll down the main lakefront road is a dock where you can catch an electric **tourist boat** to make a silent circuit around the lake (€10 round-trip, €7 one-way, daily 10:00-18:00, runs hourly, less off-season). The boat stops at the far end of the lake, at Camp Zlatorog—a 10-minute walk from the Vogel cable car (see below).

Across from the Ribčev Laz dock is a fun concrete 3-D model of Triglav. Finally, a few more steps down the road, just beyond a boat rental dock, is a statue of **Zlatorog**, the "Golden Horn"—a mythical chamois-like creature native to the Julian Alps. Young tourists (perhaps unaware how foolish they look—and how deeply the Slovenes respect the legend of Zlatorog) enjoy climbing up on the magic beast for a photo op.

▲Vogel Mountain Cable Car

For a mountain perch without the sweat, take the cable car up to the top of Vogel Mountain, offering impressive panoramic views

of Mount Triglav and the Julian Alps. On a clear day, this is the best mountain panorama you can get without wings (the light is best in the morning).

Cost and Hours: €13.50 round-trip, Dec-Oct daily 8:00-18:00, runs every 30 minutes in summer and continuously in winter, closed Nov, www.vogel.si.

Getting There: To reach the cable-car station, drivers follow signs to *Vogel* (to the left off the main lakefront road, marked *1915* and *1917*); by bus, get off at the Bohinj Vogel stop (request this stop from driver) and hike about 10 minutes up the steep road on the left (away from the lake).

Visiting the Summit: After you arrive at the top, linger at the metal platform where you exit the cable car. These are the best views, so savor them before continuing on. (But be careful looking down.) Walking up through the cable-car station (past the Viharnik snack bar, with basic food and far-from-basic views), you'll pop out at the summit, a ski-in-winter, hike-in-summer area with a pasture filled with grazing cows (summer only) and smaller chairlifts to various recreation areas.

The first, short chairlift is designed for skiers and doesn't run in summer, but if you hike down into the little valley, you can take the second chairlift up the adjacent summit (Orlove Glave) for views into another valley on the other side. Then, from Orlove Glave, you can hike or ride the chairlift back to where you started. With plenty of time and very strong knees, you could even hike from Orlove Glave all the way back down to Lake Bohinj.

If you need a break near the cable-car station, the alpine hut Merjasec ("Wild Boar") offers tasty strudel and a wide variety of local brandies (including the notorious "Boar's Blood"—a concoction of several different flavors guaranteed to get you snorting).

World War I Cemetery

Back down below the cable car, on the main road just beyond the cable-car station and Bohinj Vogel bus stop, look for the metal gate on the left marking a World War I cemetery—the final resting place for some Soča Front soldiers (see sidebar on page 848). While no fighting occurred here (it was mostly on the other side of these mountains), injured soldiers were brought to a nearby hospital, and those who didn't recover ended up here. Notice that many of the names are not Slovenian, but Hungarian, Polish, Czech, and so on—a reminder that the entire multiethnic Austro-Hungarian Empire was involved in the fighting. If you're walking down from the cable-car station, the cemetery makes for a poignant detour on your way to the main road (look for it through the trees).

Savica Waterfall (Slap Savica)

Up the valley beyond the end of the lake is Bohinj's final treat, a waterfall called Slap Savica (sah-VEET-seh). Hardy hikers enjoy

following the moderate-to-strenuous uphill trail (including 553 stairs) to see the cascade, which dumps into a remarkably pure pool of aquamarine snowmelt.

Cost and Hours: €2.50, daily in summer from 8:00 until dusk, allow up to 1.5 hours for the round-trip hike.

Getting There: Drivers follow the lakefront road to where it ends, right at the trailhead. Without a car, getting to the trailhead is a hassle. Boats on the lake, as well as most public buses from Bled, take you only as far as the Bohinj Zlatorog stop—the end of the line, and still a one-hour hike from the trail-head (from the bus stop, follow signs to *Slap Savica*). However, during the summer (Mon-Sat July-Sept only, none Sun or off-season), three buses a day run from Bled all the way to the Savica trailhead (likely departing Bled at 10:00, 14:20, and 16:20, about an hour to the trailhead, returning at 15:20 and 18:20—but confirm times locally before making the trip). Frankly, if the connections don't fit your itinerary, it's not worth worrying about.

Sleeping at Lake Bohinj

If you'd like to get away from it all and settle in at Bohinj, consider **$$ Stare Pension** (STAH-reh). Well-run by mild-mannered Jože, it has 10 older, rustic, but well-maintained rooms (five of them with balconies) in a pristine setting at the far end of the lake (Db-€80 July-Aug, €70 May-June and Sept, €60 Oct-April, €5 less without balcony, half-board-€10 per person, guest computer and Wi-Fi, Ukanc 128, mobile 040-558-669, www.impel-bohinj. si, info@impel-bohinj.si). They also rent an eight-person villa for longer stays (info@rent-villa-slovenia.com).

THE JULIAN ALPS

Vršič Pass • Soča River Valley • Bovec • Kobarid

The countryside around Lake Bled is plenty spectacular. But to top off your Slovenian mountain experience, head for the hills. The northwestern corner of Slovenia—within yodeling distance of Austria and Italy—is crowned by the Julian Alps (named for Julius Caesar). Here, mountain culture has a Slavic flavor.

The Slovenian mountainsides are laced with hiking paths, blanketed in deep forests, and speckled with ski resorts and vacation chalets. Beyond every ridge is a peaceful alpine village nestled around a quaint Baroque steeple. And in the center of it all is Mount Triglav—ol' "Three Heads"—Slovenia's national symbol and tallest mountain.

The single best day in the Julian Alps is spent driving up and over the 50 hairpin turns of breathtaking Vršič Pass (vur-SHEECH, open May-Oct) and back down via the Soča (SOH-chah) River Valley, lined with offbeat nooks and Hemingway-haunted crannies. As you curl on twisty roads between the cut-glass peaks, you'll enjoy stunning high-mountain scenery, whitewater rivers with superb fishing, rustic rest stops, thought-provoking WWI sights, and charming hamlets.

A pair of Soča Valley towns holds watch over the region. Centrally situated Bovec is all about good times (it's the whitewater adventure-sports hub), while Kobarid has Old World charm and better restaurants, and attends to more serious matters (WWI history). Though neither is a destination in itself, both Bovec and Kobarid are pleasant, functional, and convenient home bases for exploring this gloriously beautiful region.

PLANNING YOUR TIME

Most visitors do this area as a surgical strike on a full-day side-trip from Lake Bled or Ljubljana—and even that quick glimpse is very satisfying. But I find that there's enough here to make it worth slowing down and spending a night (or possibly more). If you'd like to take advantage of the Soča Valley's many adventure sports (especially whitewater rafting on the Soča River), give yourself more time.

GETTING AROUND THE JULIAN ALPS

The Julian Alps are best by **car.** Even if you're doing the rest of your trip by train, consider renting a car here for maximum mountain day-trip flexibility. I've included a self-guided driving tour that incorporates the best of the Julian Alps (Vršič Pass and Soča Valley).

If you're without your own wheels, hiring a **local guide with a car** can be a great value, maximizing not only what you see, but what you learn. Cheaper but less personalized, you could join a day-trip **excursion** from Bled. (Both options are explained under "Tours at Lake Bled," page 793.)

In the summer, a public **bus** follows more or less the driving-tour route over the Vršič Pass described below (departs Ljubljana daily July-Aug at 6:30 and 15:00, June and Sept Sat-Sun only at 6:30, 4.25 hours to Bovec, afternoon bus also continues to Kobarid in 5 hours total, road closed Oct-May). Additional Vršič Pass buses leave from Kranjska Gora at the foot of the mountains, which is also connected by bus to Ljubljana and Bled. (Yet another option is to take a direct bus from Ljubljana to Bovec that uses the somewhat less scenic southerly route via Idrija—but then you'd miss going over the Vršič Pass.) To check or confirm schedules, see www.ap-ljubljana.si.

If you lack the time or transport to reach the Vršič Pass and Soča Valley, you could stay closer to Bled, and get a taste of the Julian Alps with a more convenient day-trip to the Vintgar Gorge or Lake Bohinj (reachable with easy and frequent bus connections; see "Near Lake Bled" in the previous chapter).

Julian Alps Driving Tour

This all-day, self-guided driving tour—rated ▲▲▲—takes you over the highest mountain pass in Slovenia, with stunning scenery and a few quirky sights along the way. From waterfalls to hiking trails, WWI history to queasy suspension bridges, this trip has it all.

Orientation to the Julian Alps

Most of the Julian Alps are encompassed by Triglav National Park (Triglavski Narodni Park). This drive is divided into two parts: the Vršič Pass and the Soča River Valley. While not for stick-shift novices, all but the most timid drivers will agree that the scenery is worth the many hairpin turns. Frequent pull-outs offer plenty of opportunities to relax, stretch your legs, and enjoy the vistas.

Planning Your Time: This drive can be done in a day, but consider spending the night along the way for a more leisurely pace. You can start and end in Bled or Ljubljana. You can return to your starting point, or do this trip one-way as a very scenic detour between these two destinations.

Length of This Tour: These rough estimates do not include stops: Bled to the top of Vršič Pass—1 hour; Vršič Pass to Trenta (start of Soča Valley)—30 minutes; Trenta to Bovec—30 minutes; Bovec to Kobarid—30 minutes; Kobarid to Ljubljana or Bled—2 hours (remember, it's an hour between Ljubljana and Bled). In other words, if you started and ended in Bled and drove the entire route without stopping, you'd make it home in less than five hours...but you'd miss so much. It takes at least a full day to really do the region justice.

Tourist Information: The best sources of information are the Bled TI (see page 787), the Triglav National Park Information Centers in Trenta (page 834) and Bled (page 787), and the TIs in Bovec and Kobarid (both listed in this chapter).

Maps: Pick up a good map before you begin (available at local TIs, travel agencies, and gas stations). The all-Slovenia *Autokarta Slovenija* or the TI's *Next Exit: Goldenhorn Route* map both include all the essential roads, but several more detailed options are also available. The 1:50,000 Kod & Kam *Posoče* map covers the entire Vršič Pass and Soča Valley (but doesn't include the parts of the drive near Bled and Ljubljana).

OK...let's ride.

Mount Triglav

Mount Triglav ("Three Heads") stands watch over the Julian Alps, and all of Slovenia. Slovenes say that its three peaks are the guardians of the water, air, and earth. This mountain defines Slovenes, even adorning the nation's flag: You'll often see the national seal, with three peaks (the two squiggly lines under it represent the Adriatic). Or take a look at one of Slovenia's €0.50 coins.

From the town of Bled, you'll see Triglav peeking up over the ridge on a clear day. (You'll get an even better view from nearby Lake Bohinj.)

It's said that you're not a true Slovene until you've climbed Triglav. One native took these words very seriously and climbed the mountain 853 times...in one year. Climbing to the summit—at 9,396 feet—is an attainable goal for any hiker in decent shape. If you're here for a while and want to become an honorary Slovene, befriend a local and ask if he or she will take you to the top.

If mountain climbing isn't your style, relax at an outdoor café with a piece of cream cake and a view of Triglav. It won't make you a Slovene...but it's close enough on a quick visit.

PART 1: VRŠIČ PASS

From Bled or Ljubljana, take the A-2 expressway north, enjoying views of Mount Triglav on the left as you drive. About 10 minutes past Bled, you'll approach the industrial city of **Jesenice,** whose iron- and steelworks once filled this valley with multicolored smoke. The city, which was known as the "Detroit of Yugoslavia," plans to convert these old factories (most of which closed in the 1980s) into a sort of theme park.

Just after the giant smokestack with the billboards, the little gaggle of colorful houses on the right (just next to the freeway) is **Kurja Vas** ("Chicken Village"). This unassuming place is locally famous for producing hockey players: 18 of the 20 players on the 1971 Yugoslav hockey team—which went to the World Championships—were from this tiny hamlet.

As you zip past Jesenice, keep your eye out for the exit marked *Jesenice-zahod, Trbiž/Tarvisio, Kr.*

Gora, and *Hrušica* (it's after the gas station, just before the tunnel to Austria). When you exit, turn left toward *Trbiž/Tarvisio* and *Kranjska Gora* (yellow sign).

Just after the exit, the big, blue building surrounded by tall lights was the former border station (the overpass you'll go under leads into Austria). Locals have fond memories of visiting Austria during the Yugoslav days, when they smuggled back forbidden Western goods. Some items weren't available at home (VCRs, Coca-Cola, designer clothes), while other goods were simply better in Austria (chocolate, coffee, dishwasher soap).

Slovenes brag that their country—"with 56 percent of the land covered in forest"—is Europe's second-greenest. As you drive toward Kranjska Gora, take in all this greenery...and the characteristic Slovenian hayracks (recognized as part of the national heritage and now preserved; see page 713). The Vrata Valley (on the left) is a popular starting point for climbing Mount Triglav. Paralleling the road on the left is a "rails-to-trails" bike path—converted from an old railway bed—that loops from here through Italy and Austria, allowing bikers to connect three countries in one day. On the right, watch for the statue of Jakob Aljaž, who actually bought Triglav, back when such a thing was possible (he's pointing at his purchase). Ten minutes later, in Gozd Martuljek, you'll cross a bridge and enjoy a great head-on view of Špik Mountain.

Kranjska Gora was once Yugoslavia's leading winter resort, and remains popular with Croatian skiers. As every Slovene and Croatian wants a ski bungalow here, it has some of the highest property values in the country. Entering Kranjska Gora, you'll see a turnoff to the left marked for *Bovec* and *Vršič.* This leads up to the pass, but winter sports fanatics may first want to take a 15-minute detour to see the biggest ski jump in the world, a few miles ahead (stay straight through Kranjska Gora, then turn left at signs for **Planica,** the last stop before the Italian border; you'll likely pay €5 to drive in and see it, or you can park before the payment booth and walk in).

Every few years, tens of thousands of sports fans flock here to watch the ski-flying world championships. This is where a local boy was the first human to fly more than 100 meters on skis. Today's competitors routinely set new world records (currently 784 feet—that's 17 seconds in the air). Nearby, you may see a newly built Nordic center, used as a home base for a wide range of winter sports. From the ski jump, you're a few minutes' walk from Italy or Austria. This region—spanning three nations—lobbied unsuccessfully under the name Senza Confini (Italian for "without borders") to host the 2006 Winter Olympics. This philosophy is in tune with the European Union's vision for a Europe of regions, rather than nations.

Back in Kranjska Gora, follow the signs for *Vršič.* Before long,

The Julian Alps & Northwest Slovenia

Self-Guided Driving Route

you'll officially enter **Triglav National Park** and come to the first of this road's 50 hairpin turns (24 up, then 26 down)—each one numbered and labeled with the altitude in meters. Notice that the turns are cobbled to provide better traction. If the drive seems daunting, remember that 50-seat tour buses routinely conquer this pass...if they can do it, so can you. Better yet, imagine the bicyclists who regularly pedal to the top. The best can do it in less than 30 minutes—faster than driving.

After switchback #8, with the cute waterfall, park your car on the right and hike up the stairs on the left to the little **Russian**

To Klagenfurt

See detail maps

85

N

5 Kilometers

5 Miles

(TUNNEL)

101

Mojstrana

HRUŠICA
EXIT

Jesenice

Begunje

A2

**Bled
Town**

Lesce

*Lake
Bled*

Radovljica

➊	Pristava Lepena
➋	Boka Pension
➌	Tourist Farm Pri Plajerju
➍	Tourist Farm Kranjc
➎	Hiša Franko

Bohinjska
Bistrica

209

FINAL CAR
TRAIN STATION

(TUNNEL)

Podbrdo

403

Kranj

Brnik

SLOVENIA

Škofja Loka

A2

210

Gorenja
Vas

Želin

408

407

River

*To Idrija
& Ljubljana*

To Idrija

Ljubljana

THE JULIAN ALPS

chapel. This road was built during World War I by at least 10,000 Russian POWs of the Austro-Hungarian Empire to supply the Soča Front. The POWs lived and worked in terrible conditions, and several hundred died of illness and exposure. On March 8, 1916, an avalanche thundered down the mountains, killing hundreds more workers. This chapel was built where the final casualty

was found. Take a minute to pay your respects to the men who built the road you're enjoying today. It's a Russian Orthodox chapel—notice that the crosses topping the steeples have three crossbars. (For more on the Orthodox faith, see page 922.)

Back on the road, after #17, look as high as you can on the cliff face to see sunlight streaming through a "**window**" in the rock. This natural formation, a popular destination for intrepid hikers, is big enough for the Statue of Liberty to crawl through.

After #22, at the pullout for Erjavčeva Koča restaurant, you may see tour-bus groups making a fuss about the mountain vista. They're looking for a ghostly face in the cliff wall, supposedly belonging to the mythical figure **Ajda.** This village girl was cursed by the townspeople after correctly predicting the death of the Zlatorog (Golden Horn), a magical, beloved, chamois-like animal. Her tiny image (with a Picasso nose) is just above the tree line, a little to the right—try to get someone to point her out to you (you can see her best if you stand at the signpost near the road).

After #24, you reach the **summit** (5,285 feet). Consider getting out of the car to enjoy the views (in peak season, you'll pay an attendant a €3.50 "ecological tax" to park here). Hike up to the hut for a snack or drink on the grand view terrace. On the right, a long gravel chute gives hikers a thrilling glissade. (From the pullout just beyond #26, it's easy to view hikers "skiing" down.) If you have time and energy to burn, from the summit consider hiking about 20 minutes uphill to the Poštarski  Dom ("Fifth Hut"). Along the way, you'll see the ruins of a telpher cable-car line, which was used to run supplies between here and the valley floor during World War I. You'll also enjoy some of the best possible views of the Ajda face.

As you begin the descent, keep an eye out for old WWI debris. A lonely guard tunnel stands after #28, followed by a tunnel marked *1916* (on the left) that was part of the road's original path. Just after, watch for the turnoff at the right, at a little gravel parking lot with a picnic table. From the platform viewpoint, you can see mountain valleys formed in two different ways: To the left, the jagged V-shaped Soča Valley, carved by a raging river; and on the right, the gentle U-shaped Trenta Valley, gouged by a glacier.

Continuing down, you'll see abandoned checkpoints from when this was the border between Italy and the Austro-Hungarian Empire. At #48 is a statue of **Julius Kugy,** an Italian botanist who wrote books about alpine flora.

At #49, the road to the right (marked *Izvir Soče*) leads to the

Hemingway in the Julian Alps

It was against the scenic backdrop of the Slovenian Alps that a young man from Oak Park, Illinois, first came to Europe—the continent with which he would forever be identified. After graduating from high school in 1917 and working briefly as a newspaper reporter, young Ernest Hemingway wanted to join the war effort in Europe. Bad vision kept him out of the army, but he craved combat experience—so he joined the Red Cross Ambulance Corps instead.

After a short detour through Paris, Hemingway was sent to the Italian Front. On his first day, he was given the job of retrieving human remains—gruesomely disfigured body parts—after the explosion of a munitions factory. Later he came to the Lower Piave Valley, not far from the Soča Front. In July of 1918, his ambulance was hit by a mortar shell. Despite his injuries, he saved an Italian soldier who was also wounded. According to legend, Hemingway packed his own wound with cigarette butts to stop the flow of blood.

Sent to Milan to recuperate, Hemingway fell in love with a nurse, but she later left him for an Italian military officer. A decade later, Hemingway wrote about Kobarid (using its Italian name, Caporetto), the war, and his case of youthful heartbreak in the novel *A Farewell to Arms*.

source of the Soča River. If you feel like stretching your legs after all that shifting, drive about five minutes down this road to a restaurant parking lot. From here, you can take a challenging 20-minute uphill hike (which includes some stretches where you'll cling to guide wires) to the Soča source. This is also the starting point for the well-explained, 12-mile Soča Trail (Soška Pot), which leads all the way to the town of Bovec, mostly following the road we're driving on today.

Nearing the end of the switchbacks, follow signs for *Bovec*. Crossing the Soča River, you begin the second half of this trip.

PART 2: SOČA RIVER VALLEY

During World War I, the terrain between here and the Adriatic made up the Soča (Isonzo) Front. As you follow the Soča River south, down what's nicknamed the "Valley of the Cemeteries," the scenic mountainsides around you tell the tale of this terrible warfare. Imagine a young Ernest Hemingway driving his ambulance through these same hills (see sidebar).

But it's not all so gloomy. There are plenty of other diversions—interesting villages and churches, waterfalls and suspension bridges, and lots more. Perhaps most impressive is the remarkable clarity and milky-blue color of the Soča itself, which Slovenes proudly call their "emerald river."

After switchback #49, you'll cross a bridge, then pass a church and a botanical garden of alpine plants (Alpinum Juliana). Across the street from the garden (on the right) is the parking lot for the Mlinarica Gorge. While the gorge is interesting, the bridge leading to it was damaged in a severe storm and hasn't yet been rebuilt—so it's best left to hardy hikers.

The last Vršič switchback (#50) sends you into the village of **Trenta.** As you get to the cluster of buildings in Trenta's "downtown," look on the left for the **Triglav National Park Information Center,** which also serves as a regional TI (daily July-Aug 8:00-20:00, May-June and Sept-Oct 10:00-18:00, Dec-April 10:00-14:00, closed Nov, tel. 05/388-9330, www.tnp.si). The €5 museum here provides a look (with English explanations) at the park's flora, fauna, traditional culture, and mountaineering history. An AV

show celebrates the region's forests, and a poetic 15-minute slideshow explains the wonders and fragility of the park (included in museum entry, ask for English version as you enter).

After Trenta, you'll pass through a tunnel; then, on the left, look for a classic **suspension bridge.** Pull over to walk out for a bounce, enjoying the river's crystal-clear water and the spectacular mountain panorama.

About five miles beyond Trenta, in the town of Soča, is the **Church of St. Joseph** (with red onion dome, tucked behind the big tree on the right). Step inside to see some fascinating art. During World War II, an artist hiding out in the mountains filled this church with patriotic sym-

bolism. The interior is bathed in Yugoslav red, white, and blue— a brave statement made when such nationalistic sentiments were dangerous. On the ceiling is St. Michael (clad in Yugoslav colors) with Yugoslavia's three WWII enemies at his feet: the eagle (Germany), the wolf (Italy),

and the serpent (Japan). The tops of the walls along the nave are lined with saints, but these are Slavic, not Catholic. Finally, look carefully at the Stations of the Cross and find the faces of hated Yugoslav enemies: a lederhosen-clad Hitler (pulling a rope to upright the cross; fourth from altar on left) and Mussolini (seated, as Herod; first from altar on right). Behind the church, the stylized cross on the hill marks a **WWI cemetery**—the final resting place of some 600 Austro-Hungarian soldiers who were killed in action.

For another good example of how the Soča River cuts like God's band saw into the land, stop about two minutes past the church at the small gravel lot (on the left) marked *Velika Korita Soče* (**"Grand Canyon of Soča"**). While the entire Soča Valley is dramatic, this half-mile, 30- to 50-foot deep stretch is considered the most impressive. Venture out onto the suspension bridge over the gorge...and bounce if you dare. If the water's high, notice the many side steams pouring into the churning river in a series of mini-waterfalls. For more views, cross over the bridge and hike down along the treacherously uneven and narrow, rocky path downstream to another bridge.

Just beyond the suspension bridge is the turnoff (on the left) to the Lepena Valley, home of the recommended Pristava Lepena ranch, with accommodations and Lipizzaner horses (described later, under "Sleeping in Bovec"). If you head up this valley, you'll find a big, gravel pullout on the right (marked *Velika Korita*) that lets you cross another springy bridge over a particularly wide stretch of the river. This is a popular place for those who enjoy hiking up alongside the "Grand Canyon" we passed earlier (about 5 miles round-trip, uneven terrain).

Soon after the Lepena Valley turn-off, watch on the left for the large **barn** (marked *Žičnica Golobar*). Pull over here if you'd like a close look at one of the stations for a primitive, industrial telpher cable-car line, which was used mostly for logging.

Roughly five miles after the town of Soča, you exit the national park, pass a WWI graveyard (on the left), and come to a fork in the road. The main route leads to the left, through Bovec.

But first, take a two-mile detour to the right (marked *Trbiž/ Tarvisio* and *Predel/Kluže*), where the WWI **Kluže Fort** keeps a close watch over the narrowest part of a valley leading to Italy (€3; July-Aug daily 9:00-20:00; June and Sept Sun-Fri 9:00-17:00, Sat 9:00-18:00; May and Oct Sat-Sun 10:00-17:00, closed Mon-Fri; closed Nov-April; www.kluze. net). In the 15th century, the Italians had a fort here to defend against the Ottomans. Half a millennium later, during World War I, it was used by Austrians to keep Italians out of their territory. Notice the ladder rungs fixed to the cliff face across the road from the fort—allowing soldiers to quickly get up to the mountaintop.

Back on the main road, immediately after the Kluže turnoff, watch for the gravel pullout on the left with the little wooden hut (look for the green sign with old photos). If you'd like to see some original **WWI-era fortifications**, pull over here and hike on the gravel path 10 minutes through the woods to reach the Ravelnik Outdoor Museum. Here you can see trenches dug into the dirt and rocks, abandoned pillboxes, rusty sheds, and other features of an evocative wartime landscape. While not entirely typical of Soča Front embattlements (remember, those were mostly high on the mountaintops and remain challenging to reach), Ravelnik offers a taste of those times.

Continue following the main road to **Bovec.** This town, which saw some of the most vicious fighting of the Soča Front, was hit hard by earthquakes in 1994 and 1998 (and by another tremor in 2004). Today, it's been rebuilt and remains the adventure-sports capital of the Soča River Valley—also known as the "Adrenaline Valley," famous for its whitewater activities. (Since the water comes from high-mountain runoff, the temperature of the Soča never goes above 68 degrees Fahrenheit.) For a good lunch stop in Bovec, turn right at the roundabout as you first reach the town; you'll pass Martinov Hram's inviting restaurant terrace on the right, and soon after, the Letni Vrt pizzeria (for details on both, see "Eating in Bovec," later). But if you're not eating or spending the night in Bovec, you could skip the town entirely and not miss much (continue along the main road to bypass the town center).

About three miles past Bovec, as you cross the bridge (with the yellow *Boka* sign), look carefully high up on the rock wall in the gorge to your right to spot the **Boka waterfall,** which carves a deep gouge into the cliff as it tumbles into the valley. (Hardy hikers can climb up for a better view of this fall—the trailhead is just after the bridge on the right—but it's an extremely strenuous hike.)

Head south along the river, with water somehow both perfectly clear and spectacularly turquoise. When you pass the intersection at the humble village of **Žaga,** you're just four miles from Italy. Continuing south, you'll pass a pullout (just before Srpenica) that is a popular put-in point for kayaking trips along the river. Keep an eye out for happy kayakers. Soon after, on the left, you'll pass the giant TKK factory (which makes caulk and other building materials).

Soon you'll see signs for **Kobarid,** home to a sleepy main square and some fascinating WWI sights. Don't blink or you'll miss the Kobarid turnoff on the right—it lets you skirt into town past the highly recommended Kobarid Museum, which tells the tale of the WWI-era Soča Front. Farther along, you'll reach the tidy main square. Driving up to the Italian mausoleum hovering over the town is a must. (These sights are described later, under "Sights in Kobarid.")

Leaving Kobarid, continue south along the Soča to **Tolmin.**

Before you reach Tolmin, decide on your preferred route back to civilization...

FINISHING THE DRIVE

While you could go back over the pass the way you came, there are various ways to make your trip a loop by circling through some more varied scenery. Which way you go depends on your final destination: Ljubljana or Bled.

To Ljubljana (or Southern Slovenia/Croatia)

From Tolmin, you have two possible driving routes to the capital. Either option brings you back to the A-1 expressway south of Ljubljana, and will get you to the city in about two hours (though the second route has fewer miles).

Nova Gorica Route: The option you'll encounter first (turnoff to the right before Tolmin) is the smoother, longer route southwest to Nova Gorica. Along this road, you'll pass a hydroelectric dam and go under a 1906 rail viaduct that once connected this area to the port of Trieste (now in Italy). In the charming town of Kanal, you'll cross over the Soča on a picturesque bridge that's faintly reminiscent of Mostar's (as in that city, young people stage a competition for jumping off this bridge into the raging river below). Father along, the striking Solkan Bridge (another link in the Trieste rail line) is the longest single-span stone arch bridge in the world. Soon after, you arrive in Nova Gorica. This fairly dull city is divided in half by the Italian border (the Italian side is called "Gorizia"). Because Italians aren't allowed to gamble in their home towns, Nova Gorica is packed with casinos catering to Italian gamblers. In fact, it's home to Europe's biggest casino. Rocks spell out the name "TITO" on a hillside above town—a strange relic of an earlier age. From Nova Gorica, you can hop on the H-4 expressway, which links easily to the main A-1 expressway.

Idrija Route: For a more off-the-beaten-path, ruggedly scenic approach, take this rural option: Continue through Tolmin, then head southeast through the hills back toward Ljubljana. Along the way, you could stop for a bite and some sightseeing at the town of Idrija (EE-dree-yah), known to all Slovenes for three things: its tourable mercury mine, fine delicate lace, and tasty *žlikrofi* (like ravioli). Back at the expressway (at Logatec), head north to Ljubljana.

To Bled

To reach Bled, you could follow either of the Ljubljana-bound routes outlined above, then carry on northward for another hour to Bled (allow about 3 hours total). But the following options are more direct.

Car Train: The fastest option is to load your car onto a "Car Train" (Autovlak) that cuts directly through the mountains. The train departs at 18:31 from Most na Soči (just south of Tolmin, along the Idrija route described above) and arrives at Bohinjska Bistrica, near Lake Bohinj, at 19:14 (€12 for the car; afternoon departure May-Sept only, also departs year-round at 7:34 and 10:27, confirm schedule at the Bled TI before making the trip). No reservations are necessary, but arrive at the train station about 30 minutes before the scheduled departure to allow time to load the car. Note: This is a very old train that can be quite jerky and bumpy. You'll stay inside your car the entire time. If you're claustrophobic, prone to motion sickness, or both, consider giving this train a miss.

To get to the car train, drive though Tolmin, then Most na Soči (turning left for *Ljubljana*). About a mile out of Most na Soči, watch on the right for the big bridge over the river, marked for *Čepovan* and *železniška postaja* (train station). Crossing the bridge, turn right to find the train station; once there, go around the far-left side of the long station building and drive up the ramp to wait your turn to load. You'll buy your ticket, make a sharp turn to pull onto the train car, creep up until they tell you to stop, kill the engine, pull your hand brake, and put the car in gear. Then you'll stay in the car and enjoy the scenery. Taking off, you'll cross a scenic viaduct, then twist through the mountains, going through multiple tunnels including a final 10-minute passage from Podbrdo beneath the mountains to Bohinjska Bistrica, where you'll unload your car. From Bohinjska Bistrica, it's just a half-hour drive back to Bled, or a 10-minute drive (in the opposite direction) to Lake Bohinj.

Through Italy via Predel Pass: Although this route requires some backtracking, it also includes a detour through Italy. From Kobarid, drive back the way you came (through Bovec), then turn off for the Kluže Fort (described on page 835), marked for *Predel* and Italy. In a few miles, after passing the fort, the road curves up through two small villages (first Log pod Mangartom, then Strmec na Predelu directly above it). Continue past the ruined fortress and cross the Italian border (there's no need to stop). Then curl down a few hairpin turns past the end of tranquil, scenic Lake Predel, and continue straight through the ghost city of Cave del Predil (a heavily industrialized former lead-mining town; overhead are the five rounded peaks of the Cinque Punte formation) and along the valley road, following signs for Slovenia. Approaching Tarvisio, turn right (continuing to follow signs for *Kranjska Gora* and Slovenia); from here, it's about a half-hour (10 miles) back across the Slovenian border to Kranjska Gora. This is where you first began your ascent of the Vršič Pass—just retrace your steps back to Bled.

Other Driving Routes: The fastest route (about 2 hours) essentially follows the car train route, but goes over rather than through the mountains. This route is partially on a twisty, rough, very poor-quality road (go through Tolmin, turn off at Bača pri Modreju to Podbrdo, then from Petrovo Brdo take a very curvy road through the mountains into Bohinjska Bistrica and on to Bled). For timid drivers, it's more sane and not too much longer to start out on the Idrija route toward Ljubljana (described above), but turn off in Želin (before Idrija) toward Skofja Loka and Kranj, then continue on to Bled.

Bovec

The biggest town in the area, Bovec (BOH-vets) has a happening main square and all the tourist amenities. It's best known as a hub for whitewater adventure sports. While not exactly quaint, Bovec is charming enough to qualify as a good lunch stop or overnight home base. If nothing else, it's a nice jolt of civilization wedged between the alpine cliffs.

Orientation to Bovec

TOURIST INFORMATION
The helpful TI on the main square offers a town map and brochure, fliers on mountain biking and water sports, and hiking and rafting maps (June-Sept daily 8:30-20:30, Oct-May daily 9:00-12:00 & 14:00-17:00 except closed Sat-Sun in Nov-April, Trg Golobarskih Žrtev 8, tel. 05/384-1919, www.bovec.si).

ARRIVAL IN BOVEC
The main road skirts Bovec, but you can turn off (watch for signs on the right) to take the road that goes through the heart of town, then rejoins the main road farther along. As you approach the city center, you can't miss the main square, Trg Golobarskih Žrtev, with the TI and a good restaurant (described later, under "Eating in Bovec"). You'll find a big, free parking lot behind the Mercator supermarket (on the left on the way into town, just before the main square), and a few pay parking spaces on or near the square itself.

Activities in Bovec

As the de facto capital of Slovenia's "Adrenaline Valley," there are many opportunities to enjoy the nature all around Bovec.

Adventure Sports

The main activity in the Soča Valley is getting out on the rushing, crystal-clear waters of the river. The main options are rafting, kayaking, and hydrospeeding (a masochistic variation on boogie boarding—sitting face-down on a short surfboard, and shooting head-first toward the rapids). The official season is March 15 until October 31, but outside of summer, the frigid water is less appealing and fewer companies operate. From an adrenaline perspective, these activities are best in spring—when the water is highest—and tamer in summer. By fall, water levels are even lower.

When conditions are ideal, most **rafting** companies put in near the Boka waterfall (just downriver from Bovec), and pick up at the village of Trnovo ob Soči. (When water levels are low, companies put in near Sprenica instead.) Most rafting trips last about 2.5-3 hours, with about 1.5 hours actually on the river, and extra time to swim.

Kayaking is available at various points along the river, which vary dramatically in difficulty; the TI's free *Water-Adventure-Sport* map outlines your options, and notes areas that are unsafe. To get a glimpse of kayakers, hang out at Napoleon Bridge just outside of Kobarid.

The most popular place for **canyoning**—a risky activity that involves wading and rappelling in rushing rivers—is in Canyon Sušec, about halfway between Bovec and Kobarid.

Other popular options include skydiving and paragliding; biking (Bovec Šport Center rents electric mountain bikes); ziplines (there's a course above Bovec, and another high in the Učja Valley); and even—gasp!—golf (Bovec has a 9-hole course, www.golfbovec.si). Of course, all of these activities come with some degree of risk (except, perhaps, golf); use common sense and investigate the safety record of any company that offers trips. The Bovec TI is a good source of information about any of these, and an ever-changing roster of local adventure travel companies run a variety of tours. Well-established outfits include Bovec Šport Center (www.bovec-sc.si) and Soča Rafting (www.socarafting.si).

Sightseeing Flights

Aero Taxi runs scenic sightseeing flights from Bovec's little airport (€40/8-minute flight to Boka waterfall and back, €90/20-minute flight to Mount Krn, €140/35-minute flight over Mount Triglav, prices are for up to 3 people, mobile 041-262-726, www.janezlet.si).

Fly Fishing

The Soča River is a popular spot for fishing, predominantly for the endemic marble trout. Only fly fishing is allowed; some areas are catch-and-release, and all areas require a permit. **Soča Fly** offers information, fly-fishing gear, and tours (www.socafly.com).

Sleeping in Bovec

Dobra Vila, Hotel Sanje ob Soči, and Hotel Mangart are all situated near the turnoff from the main road into central Bovec (about a 10-minute walk into town). Martinov Hram and Stari Kovač are closer to the main square, in the town center.

$$$ Dobra Vila, run with class by brothers Juri and Matjaš, has 11 plush, boldly stylish, yet classic rooms in a gorgeously restored former telephone office that feels like an enticing whisper of ages past (Db-€120-145 depending on size and amenities, cheaper off-season, air-con, Wi-Fi, Mala vas 112, tel. 05/389-6400, www.dobra-vila-bovec.si, welcome@dobra-vila-bovec.si). They also have the most elegant restaurant in town (€30 dinner for guests; see "Eating in Bovec," later).

$$$ Hotel Sanje ob Soči means "Dreams by the Soča"—which describes both what you'll do here, and the vision that entrepreneurial owners Boštjan and Valentina have for their sleek, modern, spa-like lodgings. The 10 rooms (Db-€98-124, includes breakfast) and nine apartments (€110-180, include kitchenettes, optional breakfast-€8 extra) fill a pine-clad, Scandinavian-feeling shell on the edge of Bovec. The rooms—all with terraces, and each one named for the mountain that dominates its view—are fairly simple and Ikea-furnished (price depends on size, 20 percent cheaper in spring and fall, air-con, Wi-Fi, children's play area, Mala vas 105a, tel. 05/389-6000, mobile 031-331-690, www.sanjeobsoci.com, info@sanjeobsoci.com).

$$$ Hotel Mangart is a big, modern, somewhat overpriced chalet-style hotel with 36 rooms on the edge of Bovec (toward the Vršič Pass). All of the rooms have balconies, except the cheaper bunk-bed hostel rooms (Db-€100 in July-Aug, €90 in May-June and Sept, €80 in Oct-May, bigger superior rooms have bathtubs and nicer decor—not worth the extra €20; hostel rooms are a great value-€25/person in a small 2-, 4-, or 6-bed room with a tight bathroom; elevator, Wi-Fi, sauna and massage for an extra fee, sprawling basement pub, Mala vas 107, tel. 05/388-4250, www. hotel-mangart.com, booking@hotel-mangart.com).

$$ Martinov Hram has 12 nice, modern rooms over a popular restaurant a few steps from Bovec's main square. While the rooms are an afterthought to the busy restaurant (reception at the bar), they're comfortable (very flexible rates, in peak season figure Sb-€40, Db-€70, a few euros less off-season, no extra charge for 1-night stays, rooms on sunny side have air-con, Wi-Fi, Trg Golobarskih Žrtev 27, tel. 05/388-6214, www.martinov-hram.si, sara.berginc@gmail.com).

$ Stari Kovač B&B is your basic budget option, with eight rooms in an old-feeling guest house a steep block downhill from the main square (Db-€48, cheaper off-season and for 3 nights or more, kitchens in each room or pay €6/person for breakfast, cash only, Wi-Fi, Rupa 3, tel. 05/388-6699, mobile 041-646-427, www. starikovac.com, info@starikovac.com).

NEAR BOVEC

$$$ Pristava Lepena is a relaxing oasis hiding out in the Lepena Valley just north of Bovec. Well-run by Milan and Silvia Dolenc, this place is its own little village, with a series of rustic-looking cabins, a restaurant, a small exercise room, a kids' play area, a tennis court, an outdoor swimming pool, and a sauna/whirlpool. Milan and Silvia organize regular events for their guests (such as musical performances, a barbecue night, and activities for kids). Hiding behind the humble split-wood shingle exteriors is surprising comfort: 13 cozy rooms (with wood-burning stoves, TV, telephone, Wi-Fi, and all the amenities) that make you feel like relaxing. This place whispers "second honeymoon" (Db-€138 in July-Aug, €122 in May-June and Sept, €106 in early Oct and late April, more for larger apartments, closed in winter except mid-Dec-early Jan, multinight stays preferred, single-night stays may be possible for 20 percent extra, dinner-€23, lunch and dinner-€35, nonrefundable 30 percent advance payment when you reserve; just south of the village of Soča, turn left off the main road toward Lepena, and follow the white horses to Lepena 2; tel. 05/388-9900, mobile 041-671-981, www.pristava-lepena.com, pristava. lepena@siol.net). The Dolences also have three Welsh ponies and five purebred Lipizzaner horses (two mares, three geldings) that guests can ride (experienced riders-€20/hour, riding lesson-€24; non-guests may be able to ride for a few euros more—call ahead and ask). Kids love their mascot mountain goats.

$$ Boka Pension fills a big modern-but-tasteful building squeezed between the road and the Soča, near the big Boka waterfall. The 20 rooms are simple but have nice woody touches (Db-€86 in mid-July-Aug, €74 in May-mid-July and Sept, cheaper off-season, €10 more for bigger suite with balcony, some road noise, air-con, elevator, cable Internet in rooms, Wi-Fi in lobby, Žaga 156a, tel. 05/384-5512, www.boka-bovec.si, penzion@boka-bovec.si).

$ Tourist Farm Pri Plajerju is on a picturesque plateau at the edge of Trenta (the first town at the bottom of the Vršič Pass road). Run by the Pretner family (gregarious Marko is a park ranger, shy Stanka is "the boss"), this organic farm raises sheep and rents five apartments in three buildings separate from the main house. As the Soča Valley doesn't have many tourist farms, this is one of your best options if you want to stay at one. However, its location deeper in the mountains makes it a bit less convenient for side-tripping—it's 30 minutes to Bovec, and an hour to Kobarid (July-Aug: Db-€45-55, Tb-€55-65, Qb-€68-78; Sept-June: Db-€40-50, Tb-€50-60, Qb-€63-70; price depends on size, breakfast-€7, dinner-€11—available some but not all nights; watch for signs to the left after coming over the pass and going through the village of Trenta, Trenta 16a; tel. 05/388-9209, mobile 041-600-590, www.eko-plajer.com, info@eko-plajer.com).

Eating in Bovec

Inexplicably, little Bovec's restaurants tend to charge a cover of €1-1.50—a greedy practice otherwise rare in Slovenia, but perhaps influenced by the town's proximity to Italy.

Martinov Hram, run by the Berginc family, has an inviting outdoor terrace under a grape trellis. Inside, the nicely traditional decor goes well with regional specialties with a focus on sheep (good homemade bread, €7-12 pastas, €8-20 main courses, daily 10:00-23:00 except closed Mon in Oct-May; on the main road through Bovec, just before the main square on the right at Trg Golobarskih Žrtev 27; tel. 05/388-6214).

Letni Vrt is big, with an outdoor terrace facing Bovec's main intersection, and sprawling indoor dining rooms—including a nice winter garden that's inviting on cold days. The menu is, likewise, almost comically lengthy—I'd stick with the good and affordable pizzas (€7-11 pizzas and pastas, €9-20 main dishes, daily 11:00-23:00, Fri-Sun only in winter, Trg Golobarskih Žrtev 1, tel. 05/389-6383).

Dobra Vila, also a recommended hotel, is the only place in town for an elegant, upscale meal of thoughtfully presented international cuisine with local flair. It's smart to call ahead (€36 fixed-price dinner for non-guests, daily 19:00-22:00, see contact information earlier).

Bovec Connections

From Bovec by Bus to: Kobarid (4-6 day, 30 minutes), **Ljubljana** (direct over scenic Vršič Pass: 2/day July-Aug, 1/day Sat-Sun only June and Sept, none off-season, 4.25 hours; some additional buses may go over Vršič Pass to Kranjska Gora, where you can change to other destinations; otherwise less scenic via Idrija).

Kobarid

Kobarid (KOH-bah-reed) feels older, and therefore a bit more appealing, than its big brother Bovec. This humble settlement was immortalized by a literary giant, Ernest Hemingway, who drove an ambulance in these mountains during World War I. He described Kobarid as "a little white town with a campanile in a valley. It was a clean little town and there was a fine fountain in the square." Sounds about right. Even though Kobarid loves to tout its Hemingway connection, historians believe that Papa did not actually visit Kobarid until he came back after the war to research his book.

Aside from its brush with literary greatness, Kobarid is known as a hub of information about the Soča Front (with an excellent WWI museum, a hilltop Italian mausoleum, and walks that connect to surrounding sites). You won't find the fountain Hemingway wrote about—it's since been covered up by houses (though the town government hopes to excavate it as a tourist attraction). You will find a modern statue of Simon Gregorčič (overlooking the main intersection), the beloved Slovenian priest-slash-poet who came from and wrote about the Soča Valley.

Orientation to Kobarid

The main road cuts right through the heart of little Kobarid, bisecting its main square (Trg Svobode). The Kobarid Museum is along this road, on the left before the square. To reach the museum from the main square, simply walk five minutes back toward Bovec.

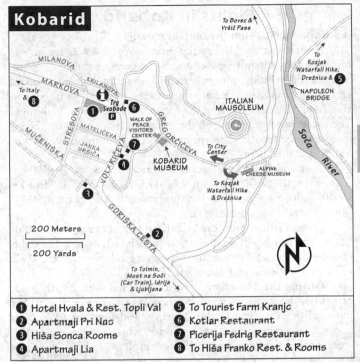

Kobarid

To Bovec &
Vršič Pass

To
Kozjak
Waterfall Hike,
Drežnica & ⑤

MILANOVA

MARKOVA

KRILANOVA

NAPOLEON
BRIDGE

To Italy
& ⑧

Trg
Svobode

ITALIAN
MAUSOLEUM

STRESOVA

MATELIČEVA

WALK
OF PEACE
VISITORS
CENTER

GREGORČIČEVA

Soča
River

MUČENIŠKA

JANKA
URSIČA

VOLARIČEVA

To City
Center

KOBARID
MUSEUM

ALPINE
CHEESE MUSEUM

To Kozjak
Waterfall Hike
& Drežnica

GORIŠKA CESTA

200 Meters

200 Yards

N

To Tolmin,
Most na Soči
(Car Train), Idrija
& Ljubljana

THE JULIAN ALPS

① Hotel Hvala & Rest. Topli Val
② Apartmaji Pri Nas
③ Hiša Sonca Rooms
④ Apartmaji Lia
⑤ To Tourist Farm Kranjc
⑥ Kotlar Restaurant
⑦ Picerija Fedrig Restaurant
⑧ To Hiša Franko Rest. & Rooms

TOURIST INFORMATION

The TI has good information on the area, and free Internet access and Wi-Fi (May-June Mon-Fri 9:00-13:00 & 14:00-18:00, Sat-Sun 10:00-14:00; July-Sept daily 9:00-19:00, until 20:00 in Aug; Oct-April Mon-Fri 9:00-13:00 & 14:00-16:00, Sat 10:00-14:00, closed Sun; on the main square at Trg Svobode 16—follow the white footprints behind the statue of Gregorčič, tel. 05/380-0490, www.dolina-soce.com).

ARRIVAL IN KOBARID

Driving into town from Bovec, watch carefully on the right for the poorly marked first turnoff into Kobarid (they want you to stay on the main road bypass around town; if you miss the turnoff, just continue on this, then turn right later to reach the main square). Turning into town, you could make a sharp left turn to reach the cheese factory (marked by the big, modern tower), or continue straight ahead to pass the Kobarid Museum, then the main square. You'll find parking on the main square (free for up to 2 hours), from which it's an easy five-minute stroll to the museum.

Sights in Kobarid

▲▲Kobarid Museum (Kobariški Muzej)

This modest but world-class museum—worth ▲▲▲ for history buffs—offers a haunting look at the tragedy of the Soča Front. The tasteful exhibits, with fine English descriptions and a pacifist tone, take an even-handed approach to the fighting—without getting hung up on identifying the "good guys" and the "bad guys." The museum's focus is not on the guns and heroes, but on the big picture of the front and on the stories of the common people who fought and died here.

Cost and Hours: €6, good selection of books; April-Sept Mon-Fri 9:00-18:00, Sat-Sun 9:00-19:00; Oct-March Mon-Fri 10:00-17:00, Sat-Sun 9:00-18:00; Gregorčičeva 10, tel. 05/389-0000, www.kobariski-muzej.si.

Tours: History buffs can call ahead to arrange a private guide to lead them through the collection (€20/hour), or tour the sights outside (€25/hour). You can also arrange a guide through the Walk of Peace Visitors Center, listed later.

Visiting the Museum: The entry is lined with hastily made cement and barbed-wire gravestones, flags representing all the nationalities involved in the fighting, and pictures of soldiers and nurses from diverse backgrounds who were brought together here (for example, the men wearing fezzes were from Bosnia-Herzegovina, which was annexed by the Austro-Hungarian Empire shortly before the war). The rooms in this front part of the museum show off typically good temporary exhibits about the war.

Buy your ticket and ask to watch the English version of the 19-minute film on the history of the Soča Front (informative but dry, plays on top floor).

The first floor up is divided into several rooms, which you'll tour counterclockwise. The White Room, filled with rusty crampons, wire-cutters, pickaxes, and shovels, explains wintertime conditions at the front. What looks like a bear trap was actually used to trap enemy soldiers. The Room of the Rear shows the day-to-day activities away from the front line, from supplying troops to more mundane activities (milking cows, washing clothes, getting a shave, lifting weights, playing with a dog). The Black Room is the museum's most somber, commemorating the more than one million casualties of the Soča Front. These heartbreaking exhibits honor the common people whose bodies fertilized the battlefields of Europe. Horrific images of war injuries are juxtaposed with a display of medals earned—prompting the question, was it worth it? The little altar was purchased by schoolchildren, who sent it to the front to offer the troops some solace.

Through the door marked *The Krn Range Room* (also on the first floor up), pass the small model of the mountaintop war zone and find your way to the Kobarid Rooms, which trace the history of this region from antiquity to today. High on the wall, look for the timelines explaining the area's turbulent history. The one in the second room shows wave after wave of invaders (including Ottomans, Habsburgs, and Napoleon). In the next room, above a display case with military uniforms, another timeline shows the many flags that flew over Kobarid's main square during the 20th century alone.

On the top floor, across from the room where the film plays (described above), you'll see a giant model of the surrounding mountains, painstakingly tracing the successful Austrian-German *Blitzkrieg* attack during the Battle of Kobarid. Crawl into the small cave and press the button to hear a patriotic song about a soldier, who reads a letter he's written to his family about the conditions here.

▲▲Italian Mausoleum (Kostnica)

The 55 miles between here and the Adriatic are dotted with more than 75 cemeteries, reminders of the countless casualties of the Soča Front. One of the most dra-

matic is this mausoleum, overlooking Kobarid. The access road, across Kobarid's main square from the side of the church, is marked by stone gate towers (with the word *Kostnica*—one tower is topped with a cross and the other with a star for the Italian army).

Take the road up Gradič Hill—passing Stations of the Cross—to the mausoleum. Built in 1938 (when this was still part of Italy) around the existing Church of St. Anthony, this octagonal pyramid holds the remains of 7,014 Italian soldiers. The stark, cold, Neoclassical architecture is pure Mussolini. Names are listed alphabetically, along with mass graves for more than 1,700 unknown soldiers *(militi ignoti)*.

Walk behind the church and enjoy the **view**. Scan the WWI battlements high on the mountain's rock face. Incredibly, the fighting was done on these treacherous ridges; civilians in the valleys only heard the distant battles. Looking up and down the valley, notice the "signal churches" evenly spaced on hilltops, each barely within view of the next—an ancient method for quickly spreading

The Soča (Isonzo) Front

The valley in Slovenia's northwest corner—called Soča in Slovene and Isonzo in Italian—saw some of World War I's fiercest fighting. While the Western Front gets more press, this eastern border between the Central Powers and the Allies was just as significant. In a series of 12 battles involving 22 different nationalities along a 60-mile-long front, 300,000 soldiers died, 700,000 were wounded, and 100,000 were declared MIA. In addition, tens of thousands of civilians died. A young Ernest Hemingway, who drove an ambulance for the Italian army in nearby fighting, would later write the novel *A Farewell to Arms* about the battles here (see "Hemingway in the Julian Alps" sidebar on page 833).

On April 26, 1915, Italy joined the Allies. A month later, it declared war on the Austro-Hungarian Empire (which included Slovenia). Italy unexpectedly invaded the Soča Valley, quickly taking the tiny town of Kobarid, which it planned to use as a home base for attacks deeper into Austro-Hungarian territory. For the next 29 months, Italy launched 10 more offensives against the Austro-Hungarian army, which was encamped on higher ground on the mountaintops. All of these Italian offensives were unsuccessful, even though the Italians outnumbered their opponents three to one. This

was unimaginably difficult warfare—Italy had to attack uphill, waging war high in the mountains, in the harshest of conditions. Trenches had to be carved into rock instead of mud. The fighting coincided with one of the most brutal winters in centuries; many unprepared conscripts—brought here from faraway lands and unaccustomed to the harsh winter conditions atop the Alps—froze to death. Some 60,000 soldiers were killed by avalanches.

Visitors take a look at this tight valley, hemmed in by seemingly impassible mountains, and wonder: Why would people fight so fiercely over such inhospitable terrain? At the time, Slovenia was the natural route from Italy to the Austro-Hungarian capitals at Vienna and Budapest. The Italians believed that if they could

messages or warnings across long distances.

If the **church** is open, go inside and look above the door to see a brave soldier standing over the body of a fallen comrade, fending off enemies with nothing but rocks.

When Mussolini came to dedicate the mausoleum, local revolutionaries plotted an assassination attempt that they believed couldn't fail. A young man planned to suicide-bomb Mussolini as the leader came back into town from this hilltop. But as Mussolini's car drove past, the would-be assassin looked at his hold this valley and push over the mountains, Vienna—and victory—would be theirs. Once committed, they couldn't turn back, and the war devolved into one of attrition—who would fall first?

In the fall of 1917, Austro-Hungarian Emperor Karl appealed to his ally Germany, and the Germans agreed to assemble an army for a new attack to retake Kobarid and the Soča Valley. In an incredible logistical accomplishment, they spent just six weeks building and supplying this new army by transporting troops and equipment high across the mountaintops under cover of darkness...above the heads of their oblivious Italian foes dozing in the valley below.

On October 24, Austria-Hungary and Germany launched an attack that sent 600,000 soldiers down into the town of Kobarid. This crucial 12th battle of the Soča Front, better known as the Battle of Kobarid, was the turning point—and saw the introduction of battlefield innovations that are commonplace in the military today. German field commanders were empowered to act independently on the battlefield, reacting immediately to developments rather than waiting for approval. Also, for the first time ever, the Austrian-German army used elements of a new surprise-attack technique called *Blitzkrieg*. (One German officer, Erwin Rommel, made great strides in the fighting here, and later climbed the ranks to become famous as Hitler's "Desert Fox" in North Africa.)

The attack caught the Italian forces off-guard, quickly breaking through three lines of defense. Within three days, the Italians were forced to retreat. (Because the Italian military worked from the top down, the soldiers were sitting ducks once they were cut off from their commanders.) The Austrians called their victory the "Miracle at Kobarid." But Italy felt differently. The Italians see the battle of Caporetto (the Italian name for Kobarid) as their Alamo. To this day, when an Italian finds himself in a mess, he might say, "At least it's not a *Caporetto*."

A year later, Italy came back—this time with the aid of British, French, and US forces—and easily retook this area. On November 4, 1918, Austria-Hungary conceded defeat. After more than a million casualties, the fighting at Soča was finally over.

fellow townspeople around him, realized the innocent blood he would also spill, and had a last-minute change of heart. Mussolini's trip was uneventful, and fascism continued to thrive in Italy.

▲Walk of Peace (Pot Miru)

This walking route—which, as of a 2012 expansion, extends more than 140 miles from these mountains all the way to the Adriatic—is designed to link museums, cemeteries, churches, and other sites related to the warfare of the Soča Front. But it also has a secondary purpose of celebrating and introducing visitors to all aspects of regional culture and natural sites. In addition to the excellent museum here in Kobarid, several other "outdoor museums" in the area let you get close to the places where the fighting actually occurred. Some are reachable by car, while others require a challenging mountain hike.

To learn more about all of these options, visit the **Walk of Peace Foundation Visitors Center,** across the street from the Kobarid Museum. They hand out good, free maps and booklets about these sites, and sell a fine €10 guidebook to WWI sights in the area. Tour their engaging, state-of-the-art exhibition. To commemorate the centennial of the fighting here (2015-2017), they plan to host a range of rotating exhibits about the war (free, July-Aug Mon-Fri 9:00-13:00 & 14:00-19:00, Sat-Sun 10:00-13:00 & 14:00-19:00, April-June and Sept-Oct slightly shorter hours, closed Nov-March—but you can try knocking on weekdays, Gregorčičeva 8, tel. 05/389-0167, www.potmiru.si).

They also arrange **guides** to join you for part of the walk (€25/hour for up to 4 hours, €20/hour for longer tours), and in the summer, they offer excursions to related sights nearby (for example, to the open-air museum in Kolovrat, €15, 3-person minimum). Contact them at least one day ahead to check their schedule and/or arrange a tour.

Kobarid Historical Walk

This shorter walk to WWI sights around Kobarid is well-explained by the free brochure available at the TI, museum, and information center (3 miles, mostly uphill, allow 3-5 hours; or you can just do a shorter, easier stretch along the river, 1-2 hours).

Alpine Cheese Museum

This humble exhibit, at the big Planika ("Edelweiss") dairy at the edge of town, examines the history of cheesemaking in this area since ancient times.

Cost and Hours: €2.50, April-Sept Mon-Sat 10:00-12:00 & 17:00-19:00; Oct Mon-Fri 9:00-12:00, Sat 10:00-12:00 & 16:00-18:00; closed Sun and Nov-March; Gregorčičeva 32, tel. 05/384-1013, www.mlekarna-planika.si/muzej. To get here, turn right into Kobarid, then take the sharp left turn that leads you down beneath the underpass to the cheese factory (marked by the tall modern tower).

Great Kozjak Waterfall (Veliki Kozjak) Hike

If you have time to kill in Kobarid and want to go for a sturdy hike, consider trekking to the Great Kozjak Waterfall—a dramatic cascade that flows through an extremely narrow gorge and plunges 50 feet into a beautiful pool. While local signs clock the hike at 30 minutes from the town center, plan on closer to 45 minutes each way. The trailhead is at the Bovec end of Kobarid: As you approach the town from Bovec, turn right into the town, then take an immediate and sharp left to go back under the main road, passing the cheese factory and following signs for *Kamp Koren*. Wind down to cross the Napoleon Bridge over the Soča (watch for kayakers), then turn left and head up the hill (you'll pass Kamp Koren). You can park in the big gravel lot across the street from the camp, or, to get closer to the trailhead, turn left just after Kamp Koren at the *Slap Kozjak* sign and follow the gravel road (park your car at the pullout after the multicolored beehives). Continue walking along the gravel path down into the ravine, passing views of a smaller waterfall. Go right at the fork, continue into the gorge, and take the high, narrow bridge over the stream (which has no railing—a little nerve-wracking for those afraid of heights). Finally, follow the boardwalk as it curls around a cliff for great views of the falls. A different, longer trail follows the Soča River Valley, eventually looping up and around to Kozjak.

Sleeping in Kobarid

My first listing is right on the main square. The other two hide on side streets about a block off the main road through town, between the museum and the main square (about a 3-minute walk to either).

$$$ Hotel Hvala is the only real hotel in town. Run by the Hvala family, its 32 contemporary rooms are comfortable, and the location can't be beat. The mural on the wall in the elevator shaft tells the story of the Soča Valley as you go up toward the top floor (Sb-€76, Db-€112, €4 less/person off-season; cheaper third-floor "mansard" Sb-€45, Db-€70; pricier superior Db with air-con and sleek new decor-€135/€160/€200 depending on size; hotel closed parts of Feb and Nov, elevator, guest computer and Wi-Fi, Trg Svobode 1, tel. 05/389-9300, www.hotelhvala.net, topli.val@siol.net).

$$ Apartmaji Pri Nas ("Our Place") has six very stylish apartments in a pleasant suburban home along the main road that skirts the town center of Kobarid (Db-€70/€50-60, 2-night minimum, no breakfast but kitchens in each unit, air-con, Wi-Fi, Goriška cesta 5, mobile 031-377-585, www.pri-nas.si, prinas.kobarid@gmail.com).

$ Hiša Sonca ("House of the Sun"), in a cheery, yellow family home along the main road, has two comfortable rooms (Db-€48, breakfast-€7, cash only, Wi-Fi, 2 blocks from main square at Mučeniška 1, mobile 031-664-253, www.apartma-hisasonca.com, hisasonca@gmail.com).

$ Apartmaji Lia, run by sweet Alenka Likar, has four tidy apartments in two buildings in the town center (Db-€40,

1-night stay-€10 extra, extra adult-€20, kids under 15-€10, cash only, no breakfast, some rooms have air-con, Wi-Fi, main house at Volaričeva 9, mobile 041-953-366, www.apartmaji-lia.si, apartmajilia@gmail.com).

IN THE MOUNTAINS HIGH ABOVE KOBARID

One of my favorite Soča Valley accommodations hides in a tiny village a twisty 10-minute drive up into the mountains above Kobarid's main square. **$$ Tourist Farm Kranjc** is a remote but scenic, well-run working sheep farm with eight comfortable rooms and a huge, shared view terrace. While this farm—which feels traditional, but with modern style—is a bit less convenient to the sights, it's ideal if you want to really feel like you're huddled high in the mountains (Db-€56, bigger "superior" Db-€62, includes breakfast, €10-12 extra per person for dinner, 20 percent more for 1-night stays, 10 percent extra for 2-night stays, air-con in attic rooms only, Wi-Fi, Koseč 9, tel. 05/3848562, mobile 041-946-088, www.turizem-kranjc.si, info@turizem-kranjc.si, Urška and the Kranjc family). It's in the village of Koseč, above Kobarid. From Kobarid, leave town by crossing the Napoleon Bridge (toward Kamp Koren and Kozjak waterfall—see directions on page 850). Just after that bridge, turn left and twist up to Drežnica, where you'll turn right to reach Koseč; once in the village, look for signs directing you up the steep road up to the left.

Eating in Kobarid

Kobarid prides itself on its restaurants, hosting a few of the best-regarded eateries in the region. (And arguably the best of them all is Hiša Franko, just outside of town and described in the next section.) Kotlar and Topli Val serve up elegant, borderline-pretentious, overpriced, but generally good meals that are worth the splurge. Pizerija Fedrig is your budget alternative.

Kotlar Restaurant, on the main square, has a classy interior that sprawls around the prow of a faux sailboat. The emphasis is on seafood and locally sourced meats (€10-13 pastas, €12-25 main dishes, Mon 18:00-23:00, Thu-Sun 12:00-15:00 & 18:00-22:00, closed Tue-Wed, Trg Svobode 11, tel. 05/389-1110, www.kotlar.si). Kotlar also rents rooms if you're in a pinch (Db-€70).

Topli Val ("Heat Wave"), Hotel Hvala's restaurant, is pricey but good, with a menu that emphasizes fish (€8-13 pastas, €9-22 main courses, lengthy list of Slovenian wines, daily 12:00-23:00, Trg Svobode 1, tel. 05/389-9300).

Picerija Fedrig serves up good €5-7 pizzas (Mon-Tue 17:00-22:00, Wed-Sun 12:00-22:00; off-season Thu-Fri 17:00-22:00,

Sat-Sun 12:00-21:30, closed Mon-Wed; a block south of the main square at Volaričeva 11, tel. 05/389-0115).

Sleeping and Eating near Kobarid

$$$ Hiša Franko is a gourmet restaurant that also rents 13 rooms less than a five-minute drive outside of Kobarid. The modern-style rooms in the main building are upscale and comfortable, while the three rooms in the adjacent yellow house are much simpler, dated, and affordable (main-building Db-€135-148 depending on size and amenities, yellow-house Db €90, includes breakfast, Wi-Fi, bike rental-€7, Staro Selo 1, tel. 05/389-4120, www.hisafranko.com, info@hisafranko.com).

What brings most people here is the upscale **restaurant,** which combines Slovenian cuisine and ingredients with modern international influences to create a memorable, if pricey, meal (three courses-€38, five courses-€53, nine courses-€75, no à la carte). The dining room is spiffy but casual and unpretentious, and the service is attentive and welcoming. Reserve ahead, especially in summer (Tue-Fri 19:00-23:00, Sat 12:00-15:00 & 19:00-23:00, Sun 12:00-15:00, closed Mon).

Getting There: To reach Hiša Franko, leave Kobarid following signs for *Italija* and *Robič* on the pleasant tree-lined road, and look for the restaurant's sign on the right.

Kobarid Connections

From Kobarid by Bus to: Bovec (4-6/day, 30 minutes), **Ljubljana** (1/day in July-Aug over Vršič Pass, 5 hours; otherwise faster but less scenic via Idrija, 3.5 hours).

CROATIA
Hrvatska

CROATIA

Sunny beaches, succulent seafood, and a taste of *la dolce vita*...in Eastern Europe?

With thousands of miles of seafront and more than a thousand islands, Croatia's coastline is Eastern Europe's Riviera. Holidaymakers love its pebbly beaches, predictably balmy summer weather, and dramatic mountains. Croatia is also historic. From ruined Roman arenas and Byzantine mosaics to Venetian bell towers, Habsburg villas, and even communist concrete, past rulers have left their mark.

Croatia feels more Mediterranean than "Eastern European." Historically, Croatia has more in common with Venice and Rome than Vienna or Budapest; especially on the coast, it's sometimes difficult to distinguish this lively place from Italy. If you've become accustomed to the Germanic efficiency of Slovenia or Hungary, Croatia's relaxed and unpredictable style can come as a shock.

Aside from its fun-in-the-sun status, Croatia is also known as one of the sites, just over a decade and a half ago, of the most violent European war in generations. Locals call it "The Homeland War" or, more casually, "The Last War" (though it's ambiguous whether they mean "final" or "most recent"). Thankfully, the bloodshed is in the past. While a trip to Croatia offers thoughtful travelers the opportunity to understand a complicated chapter of recent history, most visitors focus instead on its substantial natural wonders: mountains, waterfalls, sun, sand, and sea.

Croatia's 3,600 miles of coastline—its main draw for tourists—is loosely divided into three regions. Most people flock to the Dalmatian Coast, in the south—where dramatic limestone cliffs rise from the deep and islands are scattered just offshore (Korčula and Hvar are the most appealing). Here you'll find Croatia's top tourist town, Dubrovnik, and the big city of Split,

with its impressive Roman ruins. Way up at the northern corner of the country is the wedge-shaped peninsula called Istria, which has less dramatic scenery but arguably even more romantic towns—including my favorite, the Venetian-flavored Rovinj.

Enjoy the coast, but don't ignore the interior. The bustling capital of Zagreb is urban, engaging, and full of great museums. And Croatia's single best natural wonder (in this country that's so full of them) are the stunning waterfalls at Plitvice Lakes National Park.

It's possible to blow a lot of money here. Croatian hotels, especially on the coast, are a terrible value, and there are plenty of touristy restaurants happy to overcharge you. But if you know where to look, you can find some wonderful budget alternatives—foremost among them *sobe* (rooms in private homes). *Sobe* are a comfortable compromise: fresh, hotelesque doubles with a private bathroom,

CROATIA

Croatia Almanac

Official Name: Republika Hrvatska, or just Hrvatska for short.

Snapshot History: After losing their independence to Hungary in 1102, the Croats watched as most of their coastline became Venetian and their interior was conquered by Ottomans. Croatia was "rescued" by the Habsburgs, but after World War I it became part of Yugoslavia—a decision many Croats regretted until they finally gained independence in 1991 through a bitter war with their Serb neighbors.

Population: Of the country's 4.5 million people, 90 percent are ethnic Croats (Catholic) and 4.5 percent are Serbs (Orthodox). (The Serb population was more than double that before the ethnic cleansing of the 1991-1995 war.) About 1.3 percent of Croatians are Bosniak (Muslim). "Croatians" are citizens of Croatia; "Croats" are a distinct ethnic group made up of Catholic South Slavs. So Orthodox Serbs living in Croatia are Croatians (specifically "Croatian Serbs"), but they aren't Croats.

Latitude and Longitude: 45°N and 15°E (similar latitude to Venice, Italy or Portland, Oregon).

Area: 22,000 square miles, similar to West Virginia.

Geography: This boomerang-shaped country has two terrains: Stretching north to south is the long, rugged Mediterranean coastline (3,600 miles of beach, including more than 1,100 off-shore islands), which is warm and dry. Rising up from the sea are the rocky Dinaric Mountains. To the northeast, beginning at about Zagreb, Croatia's flat, inland "panhandle" (called Slavonia) is an extension of the Great Hungarian Plain, with hot summers and cold winters.

Biggest Cities: The capital, Zagreb (in the northern interior), has 790,000 people; Split (along the Dalmatian Coast) has 178,000; and Rijeka (on the northern coast) has 129,000.

Economy: Much of the country's wealth ($80 billion GDP, $18,000 GDP per capita) comes from tourism, banking, and trade with Italy. Unemployment is a stiff 19 percent.

Currency: 1 kuna (kn, or HRK) = about 17 cents, and 6 kunas = about $1. One kuna is broken down into 100 lipas. *Kuna* is Croatian for "marten" (a foxlike animal), recalling a time when fur pelts were used as currency. A *lipa* is a linden tree.

air-conditioning, and TV, for a fraction of the cost of an anonymous room in an overpriced resort hotel just down the beach (for details, see "Croatian Accommodation," later).

Europeans are reverent sun-worshippers, and on clear days, virtually every square inch of coastal Croatia is occupied by a sunbather on a beach towel. Nude beaches are a big deal, especially for vacationing Germans and Austrians. If you want to work on an all-around tan, seek out a beach marked *FKK* (from the German

Government: The single-house assembly (Sabor) of 153 legislators is elected by popular vote. The country's prime minister (the head of the majority party in parliament, the center-left Social Democratic party) is currently Zoran Milanović; the directly elected (but more figurehead) president is Kolinda Grabar-Kitarović.

Flag: The flag has three horizontal bands (red on top, white, and blue) with a traditional red-and-white checkerboard shield in the center.

The Average Croatian: The average Croatian will live to age 76 and have 1.4 children. One in four uses the Internet. The average Croatian absolutely adores the soccer team Dinamo Zagreb and absolutely despises Hajduk Split...or vice versa.

Notable Croatians: A pair of big-league historical figures were born in Croatia: Roman Emperor **Diocletian** (A.D. 245-313) and—supposedly—explorer **Marco Polo** (1254?-1324). More recently, many Americans whose names end in "-ich" have Croatian roots, including actor **John Malkovich** and Ohio politicians **Dennis Kucinich** and **John Kasich,** not to mention baseball legend **Roger** Marich...I mean, **Maris.** More Croatian athletes abound: tennis star **Goran Ivanišević** is internationally known; NBA fans might recognize **Toni Kukoč** or **Gordan Giricek;** and at the 2002 and 2006 Winter Olympic Games, the women's downhill skiing events were dominated by **Janica Kostelić** (her brother **Ivica Kostelić** medaled in 2006 and 2010). Actor **Goran Višnjić** (from TV's *ER*) was born and raised in Croatia, and served in the army as a paratrooper. You've likely never heard of the beloved Croatian sculptor **Ivan Meštrović,** but you'll see his expressive works all over the country (see page 976). Inventor **Nikola Tesla** (1856-1943)—who, as a rival of Thomas Edison's, invented alternating current (AC)—was a Croatian-born Serb. And a band of well-dressed 17th-century Croatian soldiers stationed in France gave the Western world a new fashion accessory—the cravat, or necktie (for the full story, see page 971).

Freikörper Kultur, or "free body culture"). First-timers get comfortable in a hurry, finding they're not the only pink novices on the rocks. But don't get too excited—these beaches are most beloved by people you'd rather see with their clothes on.

Every Croatian coastal town has two parts: The time-warp old town, and the obnoxious resort sprawl. Main drags are clogged with gift shops selling shell sculptures and tasteless T-shirts. While many European visitors enjoy this tacky-trinket tourism,

Americans are generally more interested in Old World charm. Fortunately, it's relatively easy to ignore the touristy scene and instead poke your way into twisty old medieval lanes, draped with drying laundry and populated by gossiping neighbors, humble fishermen's taverns, and soccer-playing kids.

Strolling those lanes, listen for the hauntingly beautiful *klapa* music—men's voices harmonizing a cappella, like a barbershop quartet with a soothing Adriatic flavor. Typically the leader begins the song, and the rest of the group (usually 3 to 12 singers) follows behind him with a slight delay. You'll see mariachi-style *klapa* groups performing in touristy areas; a CD of one of these performances (or of a professional group—Cambi is great) is a fun souvenir.

Now fully recovered from its war in the 1990s, Croatia is becoming one of Europe's top holiday destinations. Even so, the standards for service (at restaurants, hotels, and so on) may be lower than you might expect. Service can be relaxed...*too* relaxed by American standards, thanks to the local philosophy of *malo po malo*, "little by little"—the easygoing, no-worries, *mañana* Dalmatian lifestyle. While you'll meet plenty of wonderfully big-hearted Croatians, many of my readers characterize the Croatian waiters or hotel receptionists they've encountered as "gruff" or even "rude." Be prepared for what I call the "Croatian Shrug"—a simple gesture meaning, "Don't know, don't care." It helps me to make an attitude adjustment when I cross into Croatia. I'm used to thinking, "I should be waited upon." But Croatians think, "This is our world, and you're visiting it...so you can just wait."

Today's Croatia is crawling with a Babel of international guests speaking German, French, Italian, every accent of English... and a smattering of Croatian. And yet, despite the tourists, this place remains distinctly and stubbornly Croatian. You'd have to search pretty hard to find a McDonald's.

HELPFUL HINTS

Seasonality: Croatia is the most seasonal destination in this book. In a little coastal resort village (such as Rovinj), a few weeks can mean the difference between being a ghost town or being deluged with crowds. Peak season is July and August, though late June and most of September are nearly as popular. During these busy times, accommodations, boats, and beaches are jam-packed. Shoulder season—the most appealing time to travel here—is late May through mid-June, and late September through early October. During the off-season (mid-October-mid-May), many small towns close down entirely, with only one hotel and one restaurant remaining open during the lean winter months.

Hotel Prices: Because hotel rates fluctuate wildly by season, in this book's Croatian destinations, I've given two or three prices for each room, depending on the time of year (as explained in each town's "Sleep Code"). In high season, stays of fewer than three nights may come with a 20-50 percent surcharge. I've listed rates in euros for ease of comparison—though most hotels expect payment in the local currency, kunas (8 kunas = about €1).

Telephones: Mobile phone numbers begin with 09; numbers beginning with 060 are pricey toll lines. For more details on how to dial to, from, and within Croatia, see page 1318.

Addresses: Addresses listed with a street name and followed by "b.b." have no street number. In most small towns, locals ignore not only street numbers but also street names—navigate with a map or by asking for directions.

Buses: While Croatia has a few trains, buses are the primary means of transportation—and can even be convenient for connecting to islands (via ferry, of course). For example, if heading from the island of Korčula to Dubrovnik, the bus connection runs much more frequently than the comparable boat connection. A variety of different companies can operate the same route; for all of your options, check www.autobusni-kolodvor.com. For popular routes during peak season, drop by the station to buy your ticket a few hours in advance—or even the day before—to ensure getting a seat (ask the bus station ticket office or the local TI how far ahead you should arrive). Buses have some overhead bag storage on board, but you'll likely check your big bag under the bus (for the extra cost of about $2 per bag). If you're headed south along the coast, sitting on the right side comes with substantially better scenery (sit on the left for northbound buses). When choosing a seat, also take the direction of the sun into consideration.

Boats: Plodding car ferries and speedy catamarans inexpensively shuttle tourists between coastal destinations. Boat rides are cheap for deck passengers. A short hop, such as from Split to the islands of Hvar or Korčula, costs around $5-10; for a longer trip, such as from Split to Dubrovnik, figure $20. Most vessels are run by the national ferry company, Jadrolinija; a few smaller, private companies also run fast catamarans (including *Krilo* and *Nona Ana*). While passengers can always walk onto car ferries, seats do sell out on the fast catamarans—it's essential to buy your tickets for these as early as possible (I've suggested strategies for where and when to buy tickets for each destination). Then, to get a good seat on board, it's wise to show up 30–60 minutes before departure time. The boat schedule information in this book changes every year, without fail. It's essential to confirm before you make your plans. Jadrolinija's website (www.jadrolinija.hr) is useful, but they don't post future schedules very far in advance. Local TIs are the single best source of information for how their town is connected to the rest of the coast.

Slick Pavement: Old towns, with their well-polished pavement stones and many slick stairs, can be quite treacherous, especially after a rainstorm. (On a recent trip, one of your co-authors almost broke his arm slipping down a flight of stairs.) Tread with care.

Beaches: Croatia is known for its glimmering beaches. However, most are pebbly or rocky rather than sandy—and spiny sea urchins are not uncommon. In addition to your swimsuit, you may want to pack (or buy in Europe) a pair of water shoes for wading, as well as a beach towel (many of my recommended accommodations don't provide these). Good sunscreen, a sun hat, and bug spray can also be handy. And if you'll be hiking on Croatia's many scenic coastal trails, which can be rugged, pack sturdy shoes.

Siesta: Croatians eat their big meal at lunch, then take a traditional Mediterranean siesta. This means that many stores, museums, and churches are closed in the mid-afternoon.

Business Closures on Sundays: During the busier tourist months, from June through December, stores are allowed to be open on Sundays. Off-season, from January through May, most shops are legally required to close.

Landmine Warning: Certain parts of the Croatian interior were once full of landmines. Most of these mines have been removed, and fields that may still be dangerous are usually clearly marked. As a precaution, if you're in a former war zone, stay on roads and paths, and don't go wandering through overgrown fields and deserted villages.

CROATIAN ACCOMMODATION

Your accommodations options in Croatia are a bit different than in the rest of Eastern Europe. In the coastal destinations, I try to avoid hotels, which tend to be upgraded remnants of the old

Yugoslav aesthetic of mass tourism: Huge, impersonal resorts on a distant beach, connected to the romantic Old Town you came to see by a long walk or bus ride. Instead, consider giving hotels a miss and look for what locals call "private accommodations," which offer travelers a characteristic and money-saving alternative for a fraction of the price. You have two options: *sobe* (rooms) or *apartmani* (apartments). Often, a house renting both types is called a *vila* or *villa*—which is usually a sort of small guest house or pension.

Often run by empty-nesters, private accommodations are similar to British bed-and-breakfasts...minus the breakfast (ask your host about the best nearby breakfast spot). Generally the more you pay, the more privacy and amenities you get: private bathroom, TV, air-conditioning, kitchenette, and so on. The simplest *sobe* allow you to experience Croatia on the cheap, at nearly youth-hostel prices, while giving you a great opportunity to connect with a local family. The fanciest *sobe* are downright swanky and offer near-hotel anonymity. Apartments are bigger and cost slightly more than *sobe*, but they're still far cheaper than hotels. At most places, the only real difference between a *soba* and an apartment is that the apartment comes with a kitchenette.

Since the best-value *sobe* deservedly book up early, reservations are highly recommended. It's important to **book direct.** That means sending an email to your host rather than booking through a third-party website such as TripAdvisor.com or Booking.com, which take a hefty commission—and negate any special prices or discounts I've negotiated for readers of this book. Making your reservation directly with the host also gives you the opportunity to ask any questions you have about the accommodations, and to start to get to know the person you're staying with.

After you've reserved, keep in mind that your host loses money if you don't show up. For this reason, some hosts may request your credit-card number to secure the reservation. (They'll generally ask for payment in cash when you're there; your credit card won't be charged.)

If you like to travel spontaneously, during most of the year you'll have

no problem finding *sobe* as you go (late July and August are the exceptions). Locals hawking rooms meet each arriving boat, bus, and train. The quality can be hit or miss, but many of these are good options. Be sure you understand exactly where it's located (i.e., within easy walking distance of the attractions) before you accept. You can also keep an eye out for rooms as you walk or drive through town—you'll see blue *sobe* and *apartmani* signs everywhere. As a last resort, you can enlist the help of a travel agency on the ground to find you a room—but you'll pay 10-30 percent extra.

Window screens are rare in this area, so in warm weather be prepared to share your room with mosquitoes and other bugs.

If there seems to be no hot water, try flipping the switch with a picture of a water tank, usually next to the light switch. (Ideally, discover this switch long before you need to shower, and keep it on—otherwise you'll have to wait 20-30 minutes for the water to heat up.) In many *sobe*, the hot-water tank is tiny—barely big enough for one American-length shower. So two people traveling together may want to practice the "navy shower" method (douse yourself, turn off water, soap up, then turn water back on for a quick rinse)...or the second person may be in for a chilly surprise.

In private accommodations and some hotels, towels aren't replaced, so hang them up to reuse. The cord that dangles over the tub or shower in big resort hotels is not a clothesline—you pull it if you've fallen and can't get up.

CROATIAN HISTORY

For nearly a millennium, bits and pieces of what we today call "Croatia" were batted back and forth between foreign powers: Hungarians, Venetians, Ottomans, Habsburgs, and Yugoslavs. Only in 1991 did Croatia (violently) regain its independence.

Early History

Croatia's first inhabitants were the mysterious Illyrians. While they left behind a few scant artifacts, little is known about this group (except that they were likely the ancestors of today's Albanians).

During antiquity, the Greeks and Romans both sailed ships up and down the strategic Dalmatian Coast, founding many towns that still exist today, introducing winemaking and other agriculture, and littering the Adriatic seabed with shipwrecks. Romans built larger settlements on the Dalmatian Coast as early as 229 B.C., and in the fourth century A.D., Emperor Diocletian—who was born in what's now Croatia, and rose through the military ranks to become the most powerful man on earth—built his retirement palace in the coastal town of Split.

As Rome fell in the fifth century, Slavs (the ancestors of today's Croatians) and other barbarians flooded Europe. They moved into deserted Roman settlements (including Diocletian's now-abandoned palace) and made them their own. The northern part of Croatia's coast fell briefly under the Byzantines, who slathered churches with shimmering mosaics (the best are in the Euphrasian Basilica in Poreč, Istria).

Beginning in the seventh century, Slavic Croats began to control most of the land that is today's Croatia. In A.D. 925, the Dalmatian Duke Tomislav united the disparate Croat tribes into a single kingdom. By consolidating and extending Croat-held territory and centralizing power, Tomislav created what many consider to be the first "Croatia."

Loss of Independence

By the early 12th century, the Croatian kings had died out, and neighboring powers (Hungary, Venice, and Byzantium) threatened the Croats. For the sake of self-preservation, Croatia entered an alliance with the Hungarians in 1102, and for the next 900 years, the Croats were ruled by foreign states. The Hungarians gradually took more and more power from the Croats, exerting control over the majority of inland Croatia. Meanwhile, the Venetian Republic conquered most of the coast and peppered the Croatian Adriatic with bell towers and statues of St. Mark's winged lion. Through it all, the tiny Republic of Dubrovnik flourished—paying off whomever necessary to maintain its independence and becoming one of Europe's most important shipbuilding and maritime powers...a plucky rival to powerful Venice.

The Ottomans conquered most of inland Croatia by the 15th century and challenged the Venetians—unsuccessfully—for control of the coastline. Most of the stout walls, fortresses, and other fortifications you'll see all along the Croatian coast date from this time, built by the Venetians to defend against potential Ottoman attack. In the 17th century, the Habsburgs forced the Ottomans out of inland Croatia. Then, after Venice and Dubrovnik fell to Napoleon in the early 19th century, the coast also went to the Habsburgs—beginning a long tradition of Austrians basking on Croatian beaches.

The Yugoslav Era, World War II, and the Ustaše

When the Austro-Hungarian Empire broke up at the end of World War I, the Croats banded together with the Serbs, Slovenes, and Bosnians in the union that would become Yugoslavia. But virtually as soon as the Kingdom of Yugoslavia was formed, many Croats began to fear that the Serbs would steer Yugoslavia to their own purposes.

The parliamentarian Stjepan Radić spoke out passionately for Croat rights within the kingdom—until he was assassinated by a Serb on the morning of June 20, 1928, during a parliamentary session. This outbreak of violence alarmed Yugoslavia's Serb king, Alexander Karađorđević, who abolished the parliament and declared himself absolute ruler of the kingdom—squelching the Croats' fervently desired autonomy.

It was in this political climate, during the 1930s, that the Ustaše ("Uprisers")—a nationalistic, fascist movement bent on creating an ethnically pure "Greater Croatia"—gained popularity among a small but dangerous fringe of Croats who were chafing under Yugoslav rule. On September 9, 1934, Ustaše operatives assassinated King Alexander during a diplomatic visit to Marseilles, France.

On April 6, 1941, Hitler's Luftwaffe began aerial bombardment of Belgrade; less than two weeks later, Nazi Germany controlled Yugoslavia. Hitler divvied up the territory among his Italian, Hungarian, and Bulgarian allies, and created the misnamed "Independent State of Croatia"—encompassing much of today's Croatia and Bosnia-Herzegovina, and parts of Serbia—to be led by Ante Pavelić and the Croatian Ustaše Party. Under the watchful eye of the Nazis, the Ustaše operated one of the most brutal Nazi puppet states during World War II. Ustaše concentration camps—including the notorious Jasenovac extermination camp—were used to murder tens of thousands of Jews and Roma (Gypsies), as well as hundreds of thousands of Serbs.

Catholic Church leader Cardinal Alojzije Stepinac was one Croat who made the mistake of backing the Ustaše. By most accounts, Stepinac was a mild-mannered, extremely devout man who didn't agree with the extremism of the Ustaše...but also did little to fight it. Following the war, Stepinac was arrested, tried, and imprisoned, dying under house arrest in 1960. In the years since, Stepinac has become a martyr for Catholics and Croat nationalists.

At the end of World War II, the Ustaše (and the Nazis) were forced out by Yugoslavia's homegrown Partisan Army, led by a charismatic war hero named Josip Broz, who went by his nickname, "Tito." Tito became "president for life," and Croatia once again became part of a united Yugoslavia. The union would hold together for more than 40 years, until it broke apart in the 1990s.

Independence Regained

In April of 1990, a retired general and historian named Franjo Tuđman—and his highly nationalistic, right-wing party, the HDZ (Croatian Democratic Union)—won Croatia's first free elections (for more on Tuđman, see the sidebar). But Tuđman alarmed the large Serb minority of the new state of Croatia when he invoked the spirit of the Ustaše, who had ruthlessly run

Croatia's puppet government under the Nazis. He reintroduced symbols that had been embraced by the Ustaše, including the red-and-white checkerboard flag and the kuna currency. (While many of these symbols predated the Ustaše by centuries, they had become irrevocably tainted by their association with the Ustaše.) The 600,000 Serbs living in Croatia, mindful that their grandparents had been massacred by the Ustaše, saw the writing on the wall and began to rise up.

The first conflicts were in the Serb-dominated Croatian city of Knin. Tuđman had decreed that Croatia's policemen must wear a new uniform, which was strikingly similar to Nazi era Ustaše garb. Infuriated by this slap in the face, and prodded by Slobodan Milošević's rhetoric, Serb police officers in Knin refused. Over the next few months, tense negotiations ensued. Serbs from Knin and elsewhere began the so-called "tree trunk revolution"—blocking important Croatian tourist roads to the coast with logs and other barriers. Meanwhile, the Croatian government—after being denied support from the United States—illegally purchased truckloads of guns from Hungary. Croatian policemen and Serb irregulars from Knin fired the first shots of the conflict on Easter Sunday 1991 at Plitvice Lakes National Park.

By the time Croatia declared its independence on June 25, 1991, it was already embroiled in the beginnings of a bloody war. Croatia's Serb residents immediately declared their own independence from Croatia. The Yugoslav People's Army (now dominated by Serbs, as many Croats and Slovenes had defected) swept in, ostensibly to put down the Croat rebellion and keep the nation together. The ill-prepared Croatian resistance, made up mostly of policemen and a few soldiers who defected from the People's Army, were quickly overwhelmed. The Serbs gained control over the parts of inland Croatia where they were in the majority: a large swath around the Bosnian border (including Plitvice) and part of Croatia's inland panhandle (the region of Slavonia). They called this territory—about a quarter of Croatia—the **Republic of Serbian Krajina** (*krajina* means "border"). This new "country" (hardly recognized by any other nations) minted its own money and raised its own army, much to the consternation of Croatia—which was now worried about the safety of Croats living in Krajina.

As the Serbs advanced, hundreds of thousands of Croats fled to the coast and lived as refugees in resort hotels. The Serbs began a campaign of ethnic cleansing, systematically removing Croats from contested territory—often by murdering them. The bloodiest siege was at the town of **Vukovar,** which the Yugoslav People's Army surrounded and shelled relentlessly for three months. By the end of the siege, thousands of Croat soldiers and civilians

Franjo Tuđman (1922-1999)

Independent Croatia's first president was the controversial Franjo Tuđman (FRAHN-yoh TOOJ-mahn). Tuđman began his career fighting for Tito on the left, but later had a dramatic ideological swing to the far right. His anticommunist, highly nationalistic HDZ party was the driving force for Croatian statehood, making him the young nation's first poster boy. But even as he fought for independence from Yugoslavia, his own ruling style grew more and more authoritarian. Today, years after his death, Tuđman remains a polemical figure.

Before entering politics, Tuđman was a military officer. He fought for Tito's Partisans in World War II, and was the youngest general in the Yugoslav People's Army. But later in life, Tuđman— now a professional historian—became a Croatian nationalist who revered the Ustaše, Croatia's Nazi-affiliated government during World War II. Because the Ustaše governed the first "independent" Croatian state since the 12th century, Tuđman considered them Croatian "freedom fighters." But that same state had murdered hundreds of thousands of Serbs in its concentration camps. (In a history book he authored, Tuđman controversially deflated this estimate to between 30,000 and 60,000—a figure no legitimate historian accepts.)

In the 1980s—following Tito's death, and as Yugoslavia began to unravel—Tuđman gained support for his nationalistic, anticommunist political party, the Croatian Democratic Union (*Hrvatska Demokratska Zajednica*, HDZ). In 1990, Croatia's first free elections of the post-Tito era, voters decisively supported Tuđman and the HDZ—effectively voting out the communists. In 1992, Tuđman was formally elected president.

As Tuđman took power, he wasted no time in reintroducing many Ustaše symbols, including their currency (the kuna, still used today). These provocative actions raised eyebrows worldwide, and raised alarms in Croatia's Serb communities.

Tuđman espoused many of the same single-minded attitudes about ethnic divisions as the ruthless Serbian leader Slobodan Milošević. Croat forces—which may or may not have been acting under Tuđman's orders—carried out wide-scale

had disappeared. Many were later discovered in mass graves; hundreds remain missing, and bodies are still being found. In a surprise move, Yugoslav forces also attacked the tourist resort of **Dubrovnik**—which resisted and eventually repelled the invaders (see page 904). By early 1992, both Croatia and the Republic of Serbian Krajina had established their borders, and a tense ceasefire fell over the region.

The standoff lasted until 1995, when the now well-equipped Croatian army retook the Serb-occupied areas in a series of two offensives—**"Lightning"** *(Blijesak)*, in the northern part of the ethnic cleansing, targeting Serb and Muslim minorities. Tuđman and Milošević had secret, Hitler-and-Stalin-esque negotiations even as they were ripping into each other rhetorically. According to some reports, at one meeting they drew a map of Bosnia-Herzegovina on a cocktail napkin, then drew lines divvying up the country between themselves. Their so-called "Karađorđevo Agreement" completely left out the Bosniaks, who constituted the largest ethnic group within the nation whose fate was being decided. When Tuđman's successor moved into the president's office, he discovered reams of secret missives between Tuđman and Milošević.

To ensure that he stayed in power, Tuđman played fast and loose with his new nation's laws. He was notorious for changing the constitution as it suited him. By the late 1990s, when his popularity was slipping, Tuđman extended Croatian citizenship to anyone in the world who had Croatian heritage—a ploy aimed at getting votes from Croats living in Bosnia-Herzegovina, who were sure to line up with him on the far right.

Tuđman kept a tight grip on the media, making it illegal to report anything that would disturb the public—even if true. When Croatians turned on their TV sets and saw the flag flapping in the breeze to the strains of the national anthem, they knew something was up...and switched to CNN to get the real story. In this oppressive environment, many bright, young Croatians fled the country, causing a "brain drain" that hampered the postwar recovery.

Tuđman died of cancer at the end of 1999. While history will probably judge him harshly, the opinion in today's Croatia is qualified. Most agree that Tuđman was an important and even admirable figure in the struggle for Croatian statehood, but he ultimately went too far and got too greedy. Tuđman's HDZ party is still active, frequently naming streets, squares, and bridges for this embodiment of Croatian nationalism. The most elaborate tomb in Zagreb's national cemetery (Mirogoj) honors this "Croatian founding father." And yet, prosecutors at the International Criminal Tribunal in The Hague have said that if Tuđman were alive, he would be standing trial for war crimes.

country, and **"Storm"** *(Oluja),* farther south. Some Croats retaliated for earlier ethnic cleansing by doing much of the same to Serbs—torturing and murdering them, and dynamiting their homes. Croatia quickly established the borders that exist today, and the Erdut Agreement brought peace to the region. But most of the 600,000 Serbs who had once lived in Croatia/Krajina were forced into Serbia or were killed. While Serbs have long since been legally invited back to their ancestral Croatian homes, relatively few have returned—afraid of the "welcome" they might receive from the Croat neighbors who killed their relatives or blew up their houses just two decades ago.

As the war raged on, Croatians seized their hard-earned freedom with a nationalist fervor that bordered on fascism. It was a heady and absurd time, which today's Croatians recall with disbelief, sadness...and maybe a tinge of nostalgia. In the Croatia of the early 1990s, even the most bizarre notions seemed possible. Croatia's first post-Yugoslav president, the extreme nationalist Franjo Tuđman (see sidebar), proposed implausible directives for the new nation—such as privatizing all of the nation's resources and handing them over to 200 super-elite oligarchs. While this never quite happened, privatization relied heavily on nepotism, as Tuđman's highly placed allies enjoyed a windfall. The government began calling the language "Croatian" rather than "Serbo-Croatian" and created new words from specifically Croat roots. Some outside-the-box thinkers even briefly considered replacing the Roman alphabet with the ninth-century Glagolitic script to invoke Croat culture and further differentiate Croatian from Serbia's Cyrillic alphabet. Fortunately for tourists, this plan didn't take off.

After Tuđman's death in 1999, Croatia began the new millennium with a more truly democratic leader, Stipe Mesić. The popular Mesić, who was once aligned with Tuđman, had split off and formed his own political party when Tuđman's politics grew too extreme. Tuđman spent years tampering with the constitution to give himself more and more power, but when Mesić took over, he reversed those changes and handed more authority back to the parliament.

After a successful decade as president, the term-limited Stipe Mesić stepped down in 2010. Ivo Josipović, running on a strong anti-corruption platform, won by a landslide. Josipović served a largely effective five-year term, but was unseated in 2015 by Kolinda Grabar-Kitarović, the leader of Tuđman's right-wing HDZ party (and Croatia's first female president).

Croatia Today

In 2013, Croatia joined the European Union—a benchmark of the progress the nation has made since Tuđman. But the road to EU membership has been a rocky one, and several thorny issues face contemporary Croatians.

The legacy of the 1991-1995 war has yet to fully resolve itself in Croatia. The then-popular president, Franjo Tuđman, is now viewed with regret and suspicion by a significant segment of Croatian society (see sidebar). Others feel shame about reports that have emerged about Croatian soldiers' ethnic-cleansing activities during the war. Several Croatian officers were indicted for war crimes by the International Criminal Tribunal for the

Former Yugoslavia (ICTY) in The Hague, Netherlands. The highest-profile of these—Lieutenant General Ante Gotovina—was discovered hiding in Spain in 2005, arrested, extradited, tried, convicted...and then acquitted on appeal in 2012. Yet to this day, many Croatians feel that the soldiers branded as "war criminals" by The Hague are instead heroes of their war of independence.

Croatia's relations with its neighbors—many of whom were involved in the wars of the 1990s—are also sometimes problematic. While Croatia and Slovenia had a shared goal during those wars (namely, separating from Yugoslavia), many Croatians resent Slovenia's lack of military support. Decades later, tensions still persist. Slovenia briefly blocked Croatia's EU membership bid in an effort to resolve a longstanding border dispute. On recent trips to this region, when I show people the cover of my *Croatia & Slovenia* book, people in both countries express displeasure about being grouped together. Ironically, even many Croatians who were vehemently opposed to EU membership were outraged that Slovenia tried to prevent it.

Another vexing issue in today's Croatia is government corruption—perhaps best embodied by the country's previous prime minister, Ivo Sanader, who abruptly resigned in 2009, and soon after was arrested and convicted to a 10-year sentence.

Croatians—and especially expats living here—report that the country is excessively bureaucratic, and can be a tough place to do business. Laws tend to be implemented, then quickly overturned. In the last few years, a ban on shops being open on Sundays, a smoking ban, and a zero blood-alcohol limit for drivers have all come and gone.

In 2012, two-thirds of Croatians voted in favor of EU membership. But when it went into effect on July 1, 2013, some were caught off guard by the stringent new lifestyle that came with it. As if eager to prove they were upstanding citizens, Croatian government officials ratcheted up enforcement of often-ignored laws and regulations. Undercover tax inspectors were deployed throughout the country, ensuring that businesses small and large were properly issuing receipts and reporting their earnings. A strange paranoia swept over small-business owners during the summer of 2013, as rumors spread like wildfire about shops and restaurants being shut down for days at a time because of just a few kunas' discrepancy in their books. Given the nation's recent corruption woes, some pragmatists argue that these heightened regulations—while troublesome for a few legitimate businesspeople—may be a necessary evil.

Now firmly ensconced in the EU, continuing to emerge as a red-hot destination for holiday-makers, and with some of the growing pains of new nationhood behind it, Croatia seems poised for an ever-brighter future.

CROATIAN FOOD

Most Croatians eat to live, rather than the other way around. While the local cuisine ranges from decent to delicious, it tends to be fairly expensive and unimagi- native—and, all too often, comes with less than cheerful service. The country's tourist board has gone to great lengths to promote its cuisine and wines as major components of any trip—inflat- ing the culinary dreams of some visitors, only to leave them disap- pointed by the reality of Croatian

restaurants. Adjust your expectations and you'll eat well here—it ain't Tuscany, but it ain't bad, either.

Like its people, the food in Croatia's different regions has been shaped by various influences—predominantly Italian, Turkish, and Hungarian. And yet, the cuisine here is surprisingly uniform: Small towns in particular stick stubbornly to a very similar menu of seafood, pasta, and pizza. Because it's so easy to get into a culi- nary rut here, I've tried to recommend a few more exotic alterna- tives, where they exist.

Two staples of Croatian food, as in most Mediterranean lands, are wine and olive oil. You'll see vineyards and olive groves blanketing the Croatian countryside and islandscapes. Croatians joke that grapes are like a new bride—they demand a lot of atten- tion, while olives are like a mother—low-maintenance. Another major part of the local diet is the air-dried ham called *pršut* (a.k.a. prosciutto).

While you'll find places called *restaurant*, you'll more often see the name *konoba*—which means an unpretentious traditional restaurant, like an inn. To request a menu, say, *"Meni, molim"* (MEH-nee, MOH-leem; "Menu, please"). To get the attention of your waiter, say *"Konobar"* (KOH-noh-bahr; "Waiter"). When he's ready to take your order, he'll say, *"Izvolite."* When he brings your food, he'll likely say, *"Dobar tek!"* ("Enjoy your meal!"). When you're ready for the bill, ask for the *račun* (RAH-choon).

Main Dishes

On the coast, seafood is a specialty, and the Italian influence is obvious. According to Dalmatians, "Eating meat is food; eating fish is pleasure." They also say that a fish should swim three times: first in the sea, then in olive oil, and finally in wine—when you eat it. If you see something described as "Dalmatian-style," it usually means with lots of olive oil, parsley, and garlic.

You can get all kinds of seafood: fish, scampi, mussels, squid, octopus, you name it. Prices for many fish and seafood dishes are listed either by the kilogram (1,000 grams) or by the 100-gram unit (figure about a half-kilo, or 500 grams—that's about one pound—for a large portion). While this is a land of fisherfolk, frozen fish is not unheard of—if you want something fresh from the market, ask. When ordering, be prepared for surprises. For example, *škampi* (shrimp) often come still in their shells (sometimes with crayfish-like claws), which can be messy and time-consuming to eat. Before you order shrimp, ask if it's shelled. The menu item called "small fried fish" is generally a plate of deep-fried minnows. If you're not clear on exactly what something is, feel free to ask for clarification (though some waiters are more forthcoming than others).

Sometimes it's a pleasant surprise. Many menu items that don't sound appetizing can be delicious. Jump at the chance to sample a good, fresh anchovy—which, when done right, has a pleasant flavor and a melt-in-your-mouth texture that's a world away from the salty, withered little fish you might find topping a pizza back home. Those not accustomed to eating octopus might want to try octopus salad—a flavorful mix of octopus, tomatoes, onions, capers, and spices. In the interior, trout is popular.

If you're not a seafood-eater, there are plenty of meat options. A delicious Dalmatian specialty is *pašticada*—braised beef in a slightly sweet wine-and-herb sauce, usually served with gnocchi. Dalmatia is also known for its mutton. Since the lambs graze on salty seaside herbs, the meat—often served on a spit—has a distinctive flavor. Throughout Croatia, look for the spicy, flavorful stewed pork-and-vegetables dish called *mućkalica*. The most widely available meat dish is the "mixed grill"—a combination of various Balkan grilled meats, best accompanied by the eggplant-and-red-pepper condiment *ajvar* (see the "Balkan Flavors" sidebar on page 1140).

The best meat dish in Croatia is veal or lamb prepared under a *peka*—a metal baking lid that's covered with red-hot coals, to allow the meat to gradually cook to tender perfection. (*Ispod peka* means "under the bell.") Available only in traditional

Croatian Wine

For gourmands, one of the most pleasant surprises about a trip to Croatia is the quality of the wines. While much of the industry was state-run and focused on mass pro-duction during communist times, today vintner families are returning to their roots—literally—and making Croatian wines something to be truly proud of. Thanks partly to the interest and invest-ment of American vintners, Croatian wines are gaining respect worldwide. Because very few Croatian wines are exported, a visit here is a good chance to sample some new tastes.

The northern part of the coun-try primarily produces whites (*bijelo vino*, bee-YEH-loh VEE-noh), usu-ally dry (*suho*, SOO-hoh) but sometimes semi-dry (*polusuho*, POHL-soo-hoh) or sweet (*slatko*, SLAHT-koh). The sunny moun-tains just north of Zagreb are covered with vineyards producing whites. From Slavonia (Croatia's inland panhandle), you'll find *graševina*—crisp, dry, and acidic (like Welsh Riesling). Well-respected brands include Krauthaker and Enjingi (whose prizewinning Venje wine is a blend of five whites). The Istrian Peninsula corks up some good whites, including *malvazija*, a very popular, light, mid-range wine (Muscat is also popular). Top pro-ducers here include Degrassi (try their Terre Bianche white and red blends), Kabola, Kozlović, Fakin, and Matošević.

As you move south, along the Dalmatian Coast, the wines turn red—which Croatians call "black wine" (*crno vino*, TSUR-noh VEE-noh). The most common grape here is *plavac mali* ("lit-tle blue")—a distant relative of Californian zinfandel and Italian *primitivo* grapes. Generally speaking, the best coastal reds are produced on the long Pelješac Peninsula, across from Korčula (the most well-respected regions are Dingač and Postup). But each island also produces its own good wines. Korčula (espe-cially near the villages of Čara and Smokvica) makes excellent white wine from *pošip* grapes (which are high alcohol and low acidity), as well as *grk* ("Greek" grapes that grow only around Lumbarda) and *korčulanka*. Hvar's wines tend to be fruitier and

restaurants, this dish typically must be ordered in advance and for multiple people. You'll also find a break from seafood in the north (Zagreb) and east (Slavonia), where the food has more of a Hungarian flavor—heavy on meat served with cabbage, noodles, or potatoes.

Budget-conscious tourists reserve meat and fish for splurge dinners and mostly dine on cheaper and faster pastas and pizzas. You'll see familiar dishes, such as spaghetti Bolognese (with meat less tannic; they specialize in *pošip*, as well as *bogdanuša* ("from the gods")—which has low alcohol and high acidity.

Other wines to look for include the heavenly, sweet dessert wine called *prošek* (similar to port wine or Italian *vin santo*). While rosés aren't a big business here, some producers make them to keep up with winemaking trends; you may see them called Opolo (*pol* means "half").

When looking at wine labels, watch for these three official classifications: *stolno* ("table," the lowest grade), *kvalitetno* ("quality"—actually mid-range), and *vrhunsko* (top-quality). In general, if only the grape is listed (e.g., *mali plavac*), the quality isn't as good as when the region is prominently noted (e.g., Dingač or Postup)—though there are some exceptions (Miljenko Grgić, described next, produces a top-tier red, with mostly Dingač grapes, that he markets as simply *plavac mali*). You may also see the words *vinogorje* (vineyard), *položaj* (location), and *barrique* (barrel-aged).

The big name in Croatian wines is Miljenko Grgić. Born in Croatia in 1923, Grgić emigrated from communist Yugoslavia to the US and—as "Mike Grgich"—worked at the Chateau Montelena in Napa Valley. In the famous so-called "Judgment of Paris" in 1976, Grgić's 1973 chardonnay beat out several well-respected French wines in a blind taste test. Considered a turning point in the winemaking world, this event brought new respect to American winemakers and put Napa on the *mapa*.

Having revolutionized American winemaking, Grgić turned his sights on his Croatian homeland. He imported know-how (not to mention equipment) from California to the slopes of the Pelješac Peninsula, where he set about to making some of Croatia's first truly well-respected wines. Grgić grows his red *plavac mali* on the Pelješac Peninsula (at Dingač and nearby, at Trstanik), and his white *pošip* wine on Korčula Island. The prices for Grgić's wines match his reputation; for producers that are comparable but a bit more affordable, look for these red-wine alternatives: Madirazza (they make a great Postup), Frano Miloš (try the full-bodied Stagnum), and Matuško and Skaramuća (good Dingač). Philipp, by a famously meticulous Swiss-Croatian vintner, produces a good Postup, as well as a fine summer white that blends *rukatac* and chardonnay.

sauce) and spaghetti carbonara (with a sauce of egg, parmesan, and bacon), gnocchi (*njoki*, potato dumplings), and lasagna. Risotto (*rižoto*, a rice dish) is popular here; most common is "black risotto," mixed with squid ink and various kinds of seafood.

Side Dishes

There are many good local varieties of cheese made with sheep's or goat's milk. Pag, an island in the Kvarner Gulf, produces a famous, very salty, fairly dry sheep's-milk cheese *(paški sir)*, which is said to be flavored by the herbs the sheep eat.

A common side dish is boiled potatoes and mangold *(blitva)*; sometimes identified as "Dalmatian chard," this green is similar to Swiss chard. When ordering salad, choose between mixed (julienned cabbage, carrots and turnips, often with some tomatoes or beets, and occasionally with a bit of lettuce) or green (mostly lettuce). Throughout Croatia, salad is typically served with the main dish unless you request that it be brought beforehand.

Dessert and Beverages

For dessert, look no further than the mountains of delicious, homemade ice cream *(sladoled)* that line every street in coastal

Croatia. While most *sladoled* isn't quite gourmet (don't expect the *artigianale* brilliance of Italian *gelaterias*), I've worked hard to sample and recommend the best ice-cream parlors in each town. (Poor me.) Dalmatia's typical dessert is a flan-like, crème caramel custard, called *rozata. Prošek* is a sweet dessert wine.

Water is *voda*, and mineral water is *mineralna voda*. Jamnica is the main Croatian brand of bottled water, but you'll also see Bistra and Studenac. Many restaurants—especially fancier ones—might not want to bring you a glass of tap water, but you can try asking for *voda iz slavine*. For coffee *(kava)*, the easiest choice is *bijela kava* (BEE-yeh-lah KAH-vah)—"white coffee," or espresso with lots of milk (similar to a *caffè latte*). To get it black, ask for *crna kava* (TSUR-nah KAH-vah).

The most popular Croatian beers *(pivo)* are Ožujsko and Karlovačko, but you'll also see the Slovenian brand Laško (which is also brewed here in Croatia). Fans of dark beer *(crno pivo)* enjoy Tomislav. Most places also serve nonalcoholic beers *(bezalkoholno pivo)*; most common are Ožujsko Cool and Stella Artois NA.

Even more beloved in Croatia is wine *(vino;* see "Croatian Wine" sidebar, earlier). Along the coast, locals find it refreshing to drink wine mixed with mineral water (called, as in English, *špricer)*. When toasting with some new Croatian friends, raise your glass with a hearty *"Živjeli!"* (ZHEE-vyeh-lee).

CROATIAN LANGUAGE

Croatian was once known as "Serbo-Croatian," the official language of Yugoslavia. Most Yugoslav republics—including Croatia,

Serbia, and Bosnia-Herzegovina—spoke this same language (though Slovene is quite different). And while each of these countries has tried to distance its language from that of its neighbors since the war, the languages spoken in all of these places are still very similar. The biggest difference is in the writing: Croatians and Bosniaks use our Roman alphabet, while Serbs use Cyrillic letters.

In recent years, Croatia has attempted to artificially make its vocabulary different from Serbian. A decade ago, you'd catch a plane at the *aerodrom.* Today, you'll catch that same flight at the *zračna luka*—a new coinage that combines the old Croatian words for "air" and "port." These new words, once created, are actively injected into the lexicon. Croatians watching their favorite TV show will suddenly hear a character use a word they've never heard before...and think, "Oh, we have another new word." In this way, Croatian really is becoming quite different from Serbian (in much the same way Norwegian evolved apart from Swedish a century ago).

Here are some tips for Croatian pronunciation:

J / j sounds like "y" as in "yellow"

C / c sounds like "ts" as in "bats"

Č / č and **Ć / ć** sound like "ch" as in "chicken"

Š / š sounds like "sh" as in "shrimp"

Ž / ž sounds like "zh" as in "leisure"

Đ / đ is like the "dj" sound in "jeans"

Croatian is notorious for its seemingly unpronounceable consonant combinations. Most difficult are hv (as in *hvala,* "thank you") and nj (as in Rovinj). Foreigners are notorious for overpronouncing these combinations. In the combination hv, the h is nearly silent; if you struggle with it, simply leave off the h, or turn the hv into an f (for *hvala,* just say "FAH-lah"). When you see nj, the j is mostly silent, with a very slight "y" sound that can be omitted: for Rovinj, just say ROH-veen. Listen to locals and imitate.

When attempting to pronounce an unfamiliar word, remember that the accent is usually on the first syllable (and never on the last). Confusingly, Croatian pronunciation—even of the same word—can vary in different parts of the country. This is because modern Croatian has three distinct dialects, called Kajkavian, Shtokavian, and Chakavian—based on how you say "what?" (*kaj?, što?,* and *ča?,* respectively). That's a lot of variety for a language with only five million speakers.

Attentive travelers will frequently hear two Croatian phrases that are used as an enthusiastic affirmative, like "sure" or "OK": *može* (MOH-zheh; can do) and *ajde* (EYE-deh; let's go).

For a smoother trip, take some time to learn a few key Croatian phrases (see the Croatian survival phrases on the following pages).

CROATIA

As you navigate through Croatia, these words might help: *trg* (pronounced "turg," square), *ulica* (OO-leet-sah, road), *cesta* (TSEH-stah, avenue), *autocesta* (OW-toh-tseh-stah, expressway), *most* (mohst, bridge), *otok* (OH-tohk, island), *trajekt* (TRAH-yehkt, ferry), and *Jadran* (YAH-drahs, Adriatic).

Croatian Survival Phrases

In the phonetics, ī sounds like the long i in "light," and bolded
syllables are stressed.

English	Croatian	Pronunciation
Hello. (formal)	*Dobar dan.*	**doh**-bahr dahn
Hi. / Bye. (informal)	*Bok.*	bohk
Do you speak English?	*Govorite li engleski?*	goh-**voh**-ree-teh lee **ehn**-glehs-kee
Yes. / No.	*Da. / Ne.*	dah / neh
I (don't) understand.	*(Ne) razumijem.*	(neh) rah-**zoo**-mee-yehm
Please. / You're welcome.	*Molim.*	**moh**-leem
Thank you (very much).	*Hvala (ljepa).*	**hvah**-lah (**lyeh**-pah)
Excuse me. / I'm sorry.	*Oprostite.*	oh-proh-**stee**-teh
problem	*problem*	proh-**blehm**
No problem.	*Nema problema.*	**neh**-mah proh-**bleh**-mah
Good.	*Dobro.*	**doh**-broh
Goodbye.	*Do viđenija.*	doh veed-**jay**-neeah
one / two	*jedan / dva*	**yeh**-dahn / dvah
three / four	*tri / četiri*	tree / **cheh**-teh-ree
five / six	*pet / šest*	peht / shehst
seven / eight	*sedam / osam*	**seh**-dahm / **oh**-sahm
nine / ten	*devet / deset*	**deh**-veht / **deh**-seht
hundred / thousand	*sto / tisuća*	stoh / **tee**-soo-chah
How much?	*Koliko?*	**koh**-lee-koh
local currency	*kuna*	**koo**-nah
Write it?	*Napišite?*	nah-**peesh**-ee-teh
Is it free?	*Da li je besplatno?*	dah lee yeh beh-**splaht**-noh
Is it included?	*Da li je uključeno?*	dah leh yeh **ook**-lyoo-cheh-noh
Where can I find / buy...?	*Gdje mogu pronaći / kupiti...?*	guh-**dyeh** moh-goo **proh**-nah-chee / **koo**-pee-tee
I'd like / We'd like...	*Želio bih / Željeli bismo...*	**zheh**-lee-oh bee / **zheh**-lyeh-lee **bees**-moh
...a room.	*...sobu.*	**soh**-boo
...a ticket to ___.	*...kartu do ___.*	**kar**-too doh ___
Is it possible?	*Da li je moguće?*	dah lee yeh **moh**-goo-cheh
Where is...?	*Gdje je...?*	guh-**dyeh** yeh
...the train station	*...kolodvor*	**koh**-loh-dvor
...the bus station	*...autobusni kolodvor*	**ow**-toh-boos-nee **koh**-loh-dvor
...the tourist information office	*...turističko informativni centar*	**too**-ree-steech-koh **een**-for-mah-teev-nee **tsehn**-tahr
...the toilet	*...vece (WC)*	**veht**-seh
men / women	*muški / ženski*	**moosh**-kee / **zhehn**-skee
left / right / straight	*lijevo / desno / ravno*	**lee**-yeh-voh / **dehs**-noh / **rahv**-noh
At what time...?	*U koliko sati...?*	oo **koh**-lee-koh **sah**-tee
...does this open / close	*...otvara / zatvara*	**oht**-vah-rah / **zaht**-vah-rah
(Just) a moment.	*(Samo) trenutak.*	(**sah**-moh) treh-**noo**-tahk
now / soon / later	*sada / uskoro / kasnije*	**sah**-dah / **oos**-koh-roh / **kahs**-nee-yeh
today / tomorrow	*danas / sutra*	**dah**-nahs / **soo**-trah

In a Croatian Restaurant

English	Croatian	Pronunciation
I'd like to reserve...	Rezervirao bih...	reh-zehr-**veer**-ow bee
We'd like to reserve...	Rezervirali bismo...	reh-zehr-**vee**-rah-lee bees-moh
...a table for one / two.	...stol za jednog / dva.	stohl zah **yehd**-nog / dvah
Is this table free?	Da li je ovaj stol slobodan?	dah lee yeh **oh**-vī stohl **sloh**-boh-dahn
Can I help you?	Izvolite?	**eez**-voh-lee-teh
The menu (in English), please.	Jelovnik (na engleskom), molim.	yeh-**lohv**-neek (nah **ehn**-glehs-kohm) **moh**-leem
service (not) included	posluga (nije) uključena	**poh**-sloo-gah (**nee**-yeh) **ook**-lyoo-cheh-nah
cover charge	couvert	**koo**-vehr
"to go"	za ponjeti	zah **pohn**-yeh-tee
with / without	sa / bez	sah / behz
and / or	i / ili	ee / **ee**-lee
fixed-price meal (of the day)	(dnevni) meni	(duh-**nehv**-nee) **meh**-nee
specialty of the house	specijalitet kuće	speht-see-yah-**lee**-teht **koo**-cheh
half portion	pola porcije	**poh**-lah **port**-see-yeh
daily special	jelo dana	**yeh**-loh **dah**-nah
fixed-price meal for tourists	turistički meni	**too**-ree-steech-kee **meh**-nee
appetizers	predjela	**prehd**-yeh-lah
bread	kruh	kroo
cheese	sir	seer
sandwich	sendvič	**send**-veech
soup	juha	**yoo**-hah
salad	salata	sah-**lah**-tah
meat / poultry	meso / perad	**may**-soh / **peh**-rahd
fish / seafood	riba / morska hrana	**ree**-bah **mor**-skah **hrah**-nah
fruit	voće	**voh**-cheh
vegetables	povrće	**poh**-vur-cheh
dessert	desert	deh-**sayrt**
(tap) water	voda (od slavine)	**voh**-dah (ohd **slah**-vee-neh)
mineral water	mineralna voda	**mee**-neh-rahl-nah **voh**-dah
milk	mlijeko	mlee-**yeh**-koh
(orange) juice	sok (od naranče)	sohk (ohd **nah**-rahn-cheh)
coffee	kava	**kah**-vah
tea	čaj	chī
wine	vino	**vee**-noh
red / white	crno / bijelo	**tsehr**-noh / bee-**yeh**-loh
sweet / dry / semi-dry	slatko / suho / polusuho	**slaht**-koh / **soo**-hoh / **poh**-loo-soo-hoh
glass / bottle	čaša / boca	**chah**-shah / **boht**-sah
beer	pivo	**pee**-voh
Cheers!	Živjeli!	**zhee**-vyeh-lee
More. / Another.	Još. / Još jedno.	yohsh / yohsh **yehd**-noh
The same.	Isto.	**ees**-toh
Bill, please.	Račun, molim.	**rah**-choon **moh**-leem
tip	napojnica	**nah**-poy-neet-sah
Delicious!	Izvrsno!	**eez**-vur-snoh

DUBROVNIK

Dubrovnik is a living fairy tale that shouldn't be missed. It feels like a small town today, but 500 years ago, Dubrovnik was a major maritime power, with the third-biggest navy in the Mediterranean. Still jutting confidently into the sea and ringed by thick medieval walls, Dubrovnik deserves its nickname: the Pearl of the Adriatic. Within the ramparts, the traffic-free Old Town is a fun jumble of quiet, cobbled back lanes; low-impact museums; narrow, steep alleys; and kid-friendly squares. After all these centuries, the buildings still hint at old-time wealth, and the central promenade (Stradun) remains the place to see and be seen. If I had to pick just one place to visit in Croatia, this would be it.

The city's charm is the sleepy result of its no-nonsense past. Busy merchants, the salt trade, and shipbuilding made Dubrovnik rich. But the city's most valued commodity was always its freedom—even today, you'll see the proud motto *Libertas* displayed all over town (see *"Libertas"* sidebar).

Dubrovnik flourished in the 15th and 16th centuries, but an earthquake (and ensuing fire) destroyed nearly everything in 1667. Most of today's buildings in the Old Town are post-quake Baroque, although a few palaces, monasteries, and convents displaying a rich Gothic-Renaissance mix survive from Dubrovnik's earlier Golden Age. Dubrovnik remained a big tourist draw through the Tito years, bringing in much-needed hard currency from Western visitors. Consequently, the city never acquired the hard socialist patina of other Yugoslav cities (such as the nearby Montenegrin capital Podgorica, then known as "Titograd").

As Croatia violently separated from Yugoslavia in 1991, Dubrovnik became the only coastal city to be pulled into the

DUBROVNIK

Libertas

Libertas—liberty—has always been close to the heart of every Dubrovnik citizen. Dubrovnik was a proudly independent republic for centuries, even as most of Croatia became Venetian and then Hungarian.

In the Middle Ages, the city-state of Dubrovnik (then called Ragusa) bought its independence from whichever power was strongest—Byzantium, Venice, Hungary, the Ottomans, the Vatican—sometimes paying off more than one at a time. Dubrovnik's ships flew whichever flags were necessary to stay free, earning the derisive nickname "Town of Seven Flags." It was sort of a Hong Kong or Singapore of the Middle Ages—a spunky, trading-oriented statelet that maintained its sovereignty while being completely surrounded by an often-hostile mega-state (in Dubrovnik's case, the Ottoman Empire). Dubrovnik persevered partly because of the inherently corrupt nature of the Ottomans; always susceptible to bribery (or "tribute"), the sultans were more than happy to let Dubrovnik thrive...provided they got their cut.

As time went on, Dubrovnik's status grew. Europe's big-league nations were glad to have a second major seafaring power in the Adriatic to balance the Venetian threat; Dubrovnik emerged as an attractive alternative at times when Venetian ports were blockaded by the Ottomans. A free Dubrovnik was more valuable than a pillaged, plundered Dubrovnik.

In 1808, Napoleon conquered the Adriatic and abolished the Republic of Dubrovnik. After Napoleon was defeated, the fate of the continent was decided at the Congress of Vienna. But Dubrovnik's delegate was denied a seat at the table. The more powerful nations, no longer concerned about Venice and fed up after years of being sweet-talked by Dubrovnik, were afraid that the delegate would play old alliances off each other to re-establish an independent Republic of Dubrovnik. Instead, the city became a part of the Habsburg Empire and entered a long period of decline.

Libertas still hasn't died in Dubrovnik. In the surreal days of the early 1990s, when Yugoslavia was reshuffling itself, a movement for the creation of a new Republic of Dubrovnik gained some momentum (led by a judge who, in earlier times, had convicted others for the same ideas). Another movement pushed for Dalmatia to secede as its own nation. But now that the dust has settled, today's locals are content and proud to be part of an independent Republic of Croatia.

fighting (see "The Siege of Dubrovnik" sidebar on page 904). Imagine having your youthful memories of good times spent romping in the surrounding hills replaced by visions of tanks and warships shelling your hometown. The city was devastated, but Dubrovnik has been repaired with amazing speed. The only physical reminders of the war are lots of new, bright-orange roof tiles. Locals, relieved the fighting is over but forever hardened, are often willing to talk openly about the experience with visitors—offering a rare opportunity to grasp the harsh realities of war from an eyewitness perspective.

Though the war killed tourism in the 1990s, today the crowds are most decidedly back—even exceeding prewar levels. In fact, Dubrovnik's biggest downside is the overwhelming midday crush of multinational tourists who converge on the Old Town when their cruise ships dock. These days the city's economy is based almost entirely on tourism, and most locals have moved to the suburbs so they can rent their Old Town apartments to travelers. All of this can make the Old Town feel, at times, like a very pretty but soulless theme park. Dubrovnik lacks the gritty real-world vibe of Split or the charming local vitality of Ljubljana. But, like Venice, Dubrovnik rewards those who get off the beaten path and stick around beyond the normal midday cruise-ship window. Europeans set up here for a full week or two to explore the entire region, and even busy Americans might want to build some slack into their Dubrovnik time for a wide array of worthwhile side-trips.

PLANNING YOUR TIME

While Dubrovnik's museums are nothing special, the town is one of those places that you never want to leave. The real attraction here is the Old Town and its relaxing, breezy ambience. While Dubrovnik could easily be "seen" in a day, a second or third day to unwind (or even more time, for side-trips) makes the long trip here more worthwhile.

To hit all the key sights in a single day, start at the Pile Gate, just outside the Old Town. Walk around the city's walls to get your bearings (before it gets too hot and crowded), then work your way down the main drag (following my "Strolling the Stradun Walk"). As you explore, drop in at any museums or churches that appeal to you. Ride the cable car to the top of Mount Srđ for the sunset, then descend to the Old Town for dinner. With a second day, spread out these activities, hit the beach, or take a boat excursion from the Old Port (Lokrum Island, just offshore, requires the least brainpower, while the seafront town of Cavtat has some great art treasures).

Orientation to Dubrovnik

Nearly all of the sights worth seeing are in Dubrovnik's traffic-free, walled **Old Town** (Stari Grad) peninsula. The main pedestrian promenade through the middle of town is called the **Stradun;** from this artery, the Old Town climbs steeply uphill in both directions to the walls. The Old Town connects to the mainland through three gates: the **Pile Gate,** to the west; the **Ploče Gate,** to the east; and the smaller **Buža Gate,** at the top of the stepped lane called Boškovićeva. The **Old Port** (Gradska Luka), with leisure boats to nearby destinations, is at the east end of town. While greater Dubrovnik has about 50,000 people, the local population within the Old Town is just a few thousand in the winter—and even smaller in summer, when many residents move out to rent their apartments to tourists.

The **Pile** (PEE-leh) neighborhood, a pincushion of tourist services, is just outside the western end of the Old Town (through the Pile Gate). In front of the gate, you'll find the main TI, ATMs, a post office, taxis, buses (fanning out to all the outlying neighborhoods), a bus ticket kiosk, a cheap Konzum grocery store, and a DM pharmacy. This is also the starting point for my "Strolling the Stradun Walk."

A mile or two away from the Old Town are beaches peppered with expensive resort hotels. The closest area is **Boninovo Bay** (a 20-minute walk or 5-minute bus trip from the Old Town), but most cluster on the lush **Lapad Peninsula** to the west (a 15-minute bus trip from the Old Town). Across the bay from the Lapad Peninsula is **Port Gruž,** with the main bus station, ferry terminal, and cruise-ship port.

TOURIST INFORMATION

Dubrovnik's main TI is just outside the Old Town's **Pile Gate,** at the far end of the big terrace with the modern video-screens sculpture (June-Sept daily 8:00-21:00; May and Oct daily 8:00-20:00; Nov-April Mon-Sat 8:00-19:00, Sun 9:00-15:00; Brsalje 5, tel. 020/312-011, www.tzdubrovnik.hr). There are also locations at **Port Gruž,** across the street from the Jadrolinija ferry dock (same hours except closes earlier in Nov-April, Gruška obala, tel. 020/417-983); in the **Lapad** resort area, at the head of the main drag (June-Sept daily 8:00-20:00; May and Oct Mon-Fri 8:00-20:00, Sat-Sun 9:00-12:00 & 17:00-20:00; April Mon-Sat 9:00-12:00 & 17:00-20:00, closed Sun; closed Nov-March; Šetalište Kralja Zvonimira 7, tel. 020/437-460); on two of the Elaphite Islands, **Lopud** (Obala Iva Kuljevana 12, tel. 020/759-086) and **Šipan** (Luka b.b., tel. 020/758-084); and at the arrivals area of the **airport.**

Dubrovnik Essentials

English	Croatian	Pronounced
Old Town	*Stari Grad*	STAH-ree grahd
Old Port	*Stara Luka*	STAH-rah LOO-kah
Pile Gate	*Gradska Vrata Pile*	GRAHD-skah VRAH-tah PEE-leh
Ploče Gate	*Gradska Vrata Ploče*	GRAHD-skah VRAH-tah PLOH-cheh
Main Promenade	*Stradun*	STRAH-doon
Adriatic Sea	*Jadran*	YAH-drahn

All the TIs are government-run and legally can't sell you anything except a Dubrovnik Card—but they can answer questions and give you a copy of the free town map and two similar information booklets: the annual *Dubrovnik Riviera Info* and the monthly *The Best in Dubrovnik* (with a current schedule of events and performances); both contain helpful maps, bus and ferry schedules, museum hours, specifics on side-trip destinations, and more.

Sightseeing Pass: The heavily promoted **Dubrovnik Card** covers local public transportation; admission to the City Walls (one time only), Rector's Palace, Rupe Museum, Maritime Museum, and a few other minor sights; and various discounts around town. If you're here for three days and plan to do a lot of sightseeing and take the bus a few times, this may add up—figure out what you want to see, and do the math (150 kn/24 hours includes unlimited transit, 200 kn/3 days includes 10 transit rides, 220 kn/7 days includes 20 transit rides, sold at TIs and many sights and hotels; it's cheaper if you buy it online, then pick it up at the TI when you arrive).

ARRIVAL IN DUBROVNIK

As is the case throughout Croatia, you'll be met at the boat dock or bus station by locals trying to get you to rent a room *(soba)* at their house. If you've already reserved elsewhere, honor your reservation; if not, consider the offer (but be very clear on the location before you accept—many are nowhere near the Old Town).

By Bus: Dubrovnik's **main bus station** (Autobusni Kolodvor) is just beyond the ferry terminal along the Port Gruž embankment (about 2.5 miles northwest of the Old Town). It's straightforward and user-friendly, with pay toilets, baggage storage, and a helpful bus information window. To reach the Old Town's Pile Gate, walk straight ahead through the bus stalls, then bear right at the main

DUBROVNIK

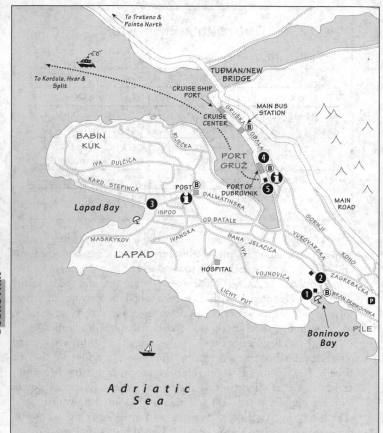

road to the city bus stop, where you can hop on a bus (#1, #1a, #1b, #1c, #3, and #8) to the Pile stop. A taxi from the main bus station to the Old Town and most accommodations runs about 75 kn.

Alternate Bus Stop for Outbound Buses: For buses that are leaving Dubrovnik toward regional destinations to the south (such as the airport or Cavtat), there's another bus stop that's much closer to the Old Town, saving you the long journey out to the main bus station. The **"cable car" bus stop** (a.k.a. "fire station" bus stop) is just uphill from the Buža Gate, overlooking the old wall, right next to the bottom station of the cable car up to Mount Srđ.

By Car Ferry or Catamaran: The big car ferries arrive at Port Gruž, two miles northwest of the Old Town. On the road in front of the ferry terminal, you'll find a bus stop (#1, #1a, #1b, #1c, #3, and #8 go to the Old Town's Pile Gate; wait on the embankment side of the street) and a taxi stand (figure 70 kn to the Old Town

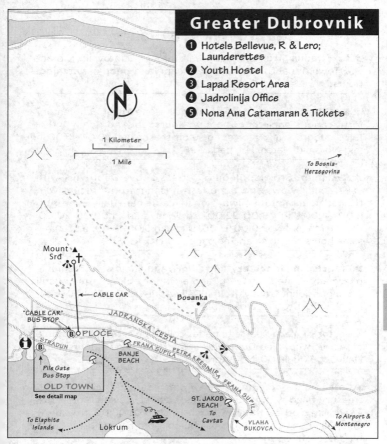

Greater Dubrovnik

1. Hotels Bellevue, R & Lero; Launderettes
2. Youth Hostel
3. Lapad Resort Area
4. Jadrolinija Office
5. Nona Ana Catamaran & Tickets

DUBROVNIK

and most accommodations). Across the street is the Jadrolinija office (with an ATM out front) and a TI. The fast *Krilo* and *Nona Ana* catamarans also arrive near this big ferry dock.

By Cruise Ship: Some ships anchor just offshore from the Old Port, then send their passengers into the Old Town on tenders. Others put in at Port Gruž, just beyond the bus station. To reach the Old Town, take a public bus or pay 80 kn for a taxi (described earlier, under "By Bus").

By Plane: Dubrovnik's small airport (Zračna Luka) is near a village called Čilipi, 13 miles south of the city. A bus meets arriving flights for most major airlines at the airport, and brings you to the Pile Gate just outside the Old Town, then continues to the main bus station (35 kn, 40 minutes). Legitimate cabbies charge around 210-250 kn for the ride between the airport and the center (though some cabbies charge as much as 300 kn; consider arranging your transfer in advance with one of the drivers

Dubrovnik at a Glance

▲▲▲**Stradun Stroll** Charming walk through Dubrovnik's vibrant Old Town, ideal for coffee, ice cream, and people-watching. **Hours:** Always open. See page 896.

▲▲▲**City Walls** Scenic mile-long walk along top of 15th-century fortifications encircling the city. **Hours:** July-Aug daily 8:00-19:30, progressively shorter hours off-season until 10:00-15:00 in mid-Nov–mid-March. See page 906.

▲▲▲**Mount Srđ** Napoleonic fortress above Dubrovnik with spectacular views and a modest museum to the recent war. **Hours:** Mountaintop—always open; cable car—daily June-Aug 9:00-24:00, Sept 9:00-22:00, April-May and Oct 9:00-20:00, Feb-March and Nov 9:00-17:00, Dec-Jan 9:00-16:00; museum—same hours as cable car. See page 923.

▲**Franciscan Monastery Museum** Tranquil cloister, medieval pharmacy-turned-museum, and a century-old pharmacy still serving residents today. **Hours:** Daily April-Oct 9:00-18:00, Nov-March 9:00-17:00. See page 912.

▲**Rector's Palace** Sparse antiques collection in the former home of rectors who ruled Dubrovnik in the Middle Ages. **Hours:** Daily May-Oct 9:00-18:00, Nov-April 9:00-16:00. See page 913.

▲**Cathedral** Eighteenth-century Roman Baroque cathedral and treasury filled with unusual relics, such as a swatch of Jesus' swaddling clothes. **Hours:** Church—daily 8:00-18:00, treasury—generally open same hours as church, both have shorter hours off-season. See page 915.

▲**Dominican Monastery Museum** Another relaxing cloister with precious paintings, altarpieces, and manuscripts. **Hours:** Daily April-Oct 9:00-18:00, Nov-March 9:00-17:00. See page 917.

listed on page 895, or through your *sobe* host; airport code: DBV, tel. 020/773-333, www.airport-dubrovnik.hr). The karstic **Đurović Cave,** which runs beneath the runway, may be open to the public; if you have extra time at the airport and want to go spelunking, ask around.

To get *to* the airport, you can take the same bus, which typically leaves from Dubrovnik's main bus station 1.5 hours before each Croatia Airlines or Austrian Airlines flight, or two hours before other airlines' international flights (the schedule is posted the day before—ask at the TI). Generally, this bus also stops at the "cable car" bus stop near the lower cable-car station just above the

▲**Synagogue Museum** Europe's second-oldest synagogue and Croatia's only Jewish museum, with 13th-century Torahs and Holocaust-era artifacts. **Hours:** May-mid-Nov daily 10:00-20:00; mid-Nov-April Mon-Fri 10:00-13:00, closed Sat-Sun. See page 920.

▲**War Photo Limited** Thought-provoking photographic look at contemporary warfare. **Hours:** June-Sept daily 10:00-22:00; May and Oct Tue-Sun 10:00-16:00, closed Mon; closed Nov-April. See page 920.

▲**Serbian Orthodox Church and Icon Museum** Active church serving Dubrovnik's Serbian Orthodox community and museum with traditional religious icons. **Hours:** Church—daily May-Sept 8:00-14:00 & 16:00-21:00 or 22:00, until 19:00 in shoulder season, until 17:00 in winter; museum—May-Oct Mon-Sat 9:00-13:00, closed Sun; Nov-April Mon-Fri 9:00-13:00, closed Sat-Sun. See page 921.

▲**Rupe Granary and Ethnographic Museum** Good folk museum with tools, jewelry, clothing, and painted eggs above immense underground grain stores. **Hours:** Wed-Mon 9:00-18:00, until 14:00 off-season, closed Tue year-round. See page 923.

Maritime Museum Contracts, maps, paintings, and models from Dubrovnik's days as a maritime power and shipbuilding center. **Hours:** Flex with demand, usually March-Oct Tue-Sun 9:00-18:00, until 16:00 in Nov-Feb, closed Mon year-round. See page 919.

Aquarium Tanks of local sea life housed in huge, shady old fort. **Hours:** Daily July-Aug 9:00-21:00, progressively shorter hours off-season until 9:00-16:00 Nov-March. See page 920.

Old Town's Buža Gate; this can save you the hassle of going to the main bus station—but confirm the schedule at the TI.

Bad-Weather Warning: If you're planning to fly into or out of Dubrovnik, be aware that the airport is located right in the blast zone of the fierce Bora winds that periodically howl along the Dalmatian Coast (especially in the late fall). It's not uncommon for flights coming into Dubrovnik to be diverted to Split instead, with passengers forced to take a dull five-hour bus journey to their intended destination. Departing flights are usually less affected (though disruptions to incoming planes could, obviously, cause delays for departures as well). Personally, I've flown out of

Dubrovnik a dozen times without incident, but it's not unheard-of for travelers to be inconvenienced by this.

By Car: Coming from the north, you'll drive over the modern Tuđman Bridge (which most locals, mindful of their former president's tarnished legacy, call simply "the New Bridge"). Immediately after crossing the bridge, you have two options: To get to the main bus station, ferry terminal (with some car-rental drop-off offices nearby), and Lapad Peninsula, take the left turn just after the bridge, wind down to the waterfront, then turn left and follow this road along the Port Gruž embankment. Or, to head for the Old Town, continue straight after the bridge. You'll pass above the Port Gruž area, then take the right turn-off marked *Dubrovnik* (with the little bull's-eye). You'll go through a tunnel, then turn left for *Grad/Old City*; individual big hotels are also signed from here.

This road passes a big parking garage (described next), then twists you around over the top of the Old Town, until you can see the lower station for the cable car. Here, you have two choices, which will determine which one-way loop you'll get stuck in: If you want to reach the Pile Gate (at the eastern end of the Old Town), make a sharp right turn just before the cable car (watch for *Grad/Old City* signs), then turn right again (passing the entrance to the "tennis court" parking lot) to curl around the back of the city wall and pop out at the Pile Gate (with another, very pricey parking lot), then back up out of town toward Boninovo Bay and Lapad. Or, if you want to head east of the Old Town, continue straight past the cable-car station for a long, scenic drive above the Viktorija area, then (after looping down again) past luxury hotels and to the Ploče Gate.

If you're sleeping in or near the Old Town, **parking** is tricky. The handiest place to park long-term is the Old Town garage, which you'll pass on the right as you head toward the Old Town (10 kn/hour, 170 kn/day, cheaper Oct-May). From here, it's about a 10-minute downhill walk to the Old Town—and a much steeper, 20-minute hike back up. If you'd like to be closer to the Old Town, you can take your chances on finding a spot—either on the street directly behind and above the City Walls (pay at meter), or in the convenient but often-crammed pay lots: "the tennis court," right up against the wall, or the lot between the wall and the cable car (all options: 10 kn/hr, 170 kn/day). If you're desperate, the priciest option is the lot just behind the DM pharmacy near the Pile Gate (a hefty 30 kn/hour or 360 kn/day). Another option is to drive to this area near the Old Town to unload your bags, then leave your car at the Old Town garage (or a cheaper, more distant one) for the duration of your visit. When in doubt, ask your *sobe* host or hotel for parking tips.

If you're sleeping at Boninovo Bay, you'll have an easier time finding parking at or near your hotel—ask.

HELPFUL HINTS

Festivals: Dubrovnik is most crowded during its Summer Festival, a month and a half of theater and musical performances held annually from July 10 to August 25 (www.dubrovnik-festival. hr). This is quickly followed by the Late Summer Festival, designed to continue the festivities into September. For other options, see "Entertainment in Dubrovnik," later.

Crowd-Beating Tips: Dubrovnik has been discovered—especially by cruise ships (nearly 800 of which visit each year, bringing a total of around 900,000 passengers—in 2013, one September day brought 16,000 passengers on six ships). Cruise-ship crowds descend on the Old Town roughly between 8:30 and 14:00 (the streets are most crowded 9:00-13:00). On busy days, try to avoid the big sights—especially walking around the wall—during these peak times, and hit the beach or take a siesta midday, when the town is hottest and most crowded.

No Euros: Dubrovnik's merchants can be stubborn about accepting only kunas—no euros. (While it's technically illegal for vendors to accept any payment other than kunas, this is rarely enforced.) Even some of the top sights—including the City Walls and the cable car to Mount Srđ—accept only kunas (or, sometimes, credit cards). Even if you're in town for just a few hours, visit an ATM to avoid hassles when it comes time to pay.

Wine Shop: For the best wine-tasting selection in a cool bar atmosphere, don't miss **D'Vino Wine Bar** (described on page 930). If you want to shop rather than taste, **Vinoteka Miličić** offers a nice variety of local wines; wry Dolores can explain your options, though she does tend to push Miličić wines (daily June-Aug 9:00-23:00, April-May and Sept-Oct 9:00-20:00, Nov-March 9:00-16:00, near the Pile end of the Stradun, tel. 020/321-777).

Internet Access: Most accommodations in Dubrovnik offer free Wi-Fi, and several cafés and bars around town provide Wi-Fi for customers. In the Old Town, the modern **Buzz Bar** has free Wi-Fi and loaner laptops with the purchase of a drink (daily 9:00-24:00, Prijeko 21, tel. 020/321-025).

English Bookstore: The **Algoritam** shop, right on the Stradun, has a wide variety of guidebooks, nonfiction books about Croatia and the former Yugoslavia, novels, and magazines—all in English (July-Aug Mon-Sat 9:00-23:00, Sun 10:00-13:00 & 18:00-22:00; June and Sept Mon-Sat 9:00-21:00, Sun 10:00-14:00; shorter hours off-season; Placa 8, tel. 020/322-044).

Laundry: Hotels charge a mint to wash your clothes; *sobe* hosts are cheaper, but often don't have the time (ask). The handy, fun, retro, self-service **Sanja and Rosie's Launderette** is just outside the Ploče Gate (cross the bridge and look left; 50-kn wash, 30-40-kn dry, clear English instructions, machines take bills, daily 8:00-22:00, put od Bosanke 2, mobile 091-896-7509, www.dubrovniklaundry.com). Two full-service launderettes are near the hotels at **Boninovo Bay**, a 20-minute uphill walk or five-minute bus trip from the Pile Gate (one at Pera Čingrije 8, the other at bana Jelačića 1, both closed Sat afternoon and all day Sun)—but unless you're staying in that area, Sanja and Rosie's is far more convenient.

Car Rental: The big international chains have offices at the airport; a few also have branches near the Port Gruž embankment where the big ships come in. In addition, the many travel agencies closer to the Old Town also have a line on rental cars. Figure €50-60 per day, including taxes, insurance, and unlimited mileage (at the bigger chains, there's usually no extra charge for drop-off elsewhere in Croatia). Be sure the agency knows if you're crossing a border (such as Bosnia-Herzegovina or Montenegro) to ensure you have the proper paperwork.

Travel Agency: You'll see travel agencies all over town. At any of them, you can buy seats on an excursion, rent a car, or book a room. The most established company is **Atlas,** just off the Stradun in the Old Town (Mon-Fri 9:00-21:00, Sat-Sun 10:00-13:00 & 16:00-20:00, Boškovićeva 5, tel. 020/442-574, www.atlas-croatia.com).

Best Views: Walking the **City Walls** late in the day, when the city is bathed in rich light, is a treat. The cable car up to **Mount Srđ** provides bird's-eye panoramas over the entire region, from the highest vantage point without wings. The **Fort of St. Lawrence,** perched above the Pile neighborhood cove, has great views over the Old Town. The **panoramic cruises** that loop around the Old Town are another fine choice. A stroll up the road east of the City Walls offers nice views back on the Old Town (best light early in the day). Better yet, if you have a car, head south of the city in the morning for gorgeously lit Old Town views over your right shoulder; various turn-offs along this road are ideal photo stops. The best one, known locally simply as **"panorama point,"** is where the road leading up and out of Dubrovnik meets the main road that passes above the town (look for the pull-out on the right, usually crowded with tour buses). Even if you're heading north, in good weather it's worth a quick detour south for this view.

Game of Thrones in Dubrovnik

Fans of the HBO television series *Game of Thrones* may feel the tingle of déjà vu during their visit to Dubrovnik. Over the last few years, part of the series has been filmed here, generally between mid-August and mid-September. Many locals have been extras, and they've become accustomed to seeing Peter Dinklage strolling down the Stradun in full costume on his way to the set, or spotting King Joffrey at the next table when dining at their favorite *konoba*.

In the show, Dubrovnik often stands in for King's Landing, while the island of Lokrum was the site of the Qarth garden party. The Fort of St. Lawrence (filmed in various battle scenes) looks over a pleasant cove that becomes Blackwater Bay for the show's purposes. Other filming locations have included Trsteno Arboretum, the rock quarry, and Gradac park (where the royal wedding took place). Filming has also taken place in other parts of Croatia, most notably the fortified town of Ston and the city of Split. Of course, the fantasy-world locations on the show don't match the real-world locations exactly; digital effects are often added to dress things up.

GoT aficionados may want to take a guided tour of filming locations; check to see if a local company offers one, or book through the international tour company, Viator.com.

The city, hardly oblivious to this potential boost in tourist popularity, may open a *Game of Thrones* exhibition with costumes and props from the show. If you're a fan, ask around town for the latest—both star sightings and sightseeing.

Updates to This Book: Check www.ricksteves.com/update for any significant changes that have occurred since this book was published.

GETTING AROUND DUBROVNIK

If you're staying in or near the Old Town, everything is easily walkable. But those sleeping on Boninovo Bay or the Lapad Peninsula will want to get comfortable using the buses. Once you understand the system, commuting to the Old Town is a breeze.

By Bus: Libertas runs Dubrovnik's public buses. Tickets, which are good for an hour, are cheaper if you buy them in advance from a newsstand or your hotel (12 kn, ask for *autobusna karta*, ow-toh-BOOS-nah KAR-tah) than if you buy them from the bus driver (15 kn). A 24-hour ticket costs 35 kn (only sold at special bus-ticket kiosks, such as the one near the Pile Gate bus stop).

When you enter the bus, validate your ticket in the machine next to the driver (insert it with the orange arrow facing out and pointing down). Because most tourists can't figure out how to validate their tickets, it can take a long time to load the bus (which means drivers are understandably grumpy, and locals aren't shy about cutting in line).

All buses stop near the Old Town, just in front of the Pile Gate (buy tickets at the newsstand). From here, they fan out to just about anywhere you'd want to go (hotels on Boninovo Bay, Lapad Peninsula, and the ferry terminal and main bus station). You'll find bus schedules and a map in the TI booklet (for more information, visit www.libertasdubrovnik.hr).

By Taxi: Taxis start at 25 kn, then charge 8 kn per kilometer. The handiest taxi stand for the Old Town is just outside the Pile Gate. The biggest operation is Radio Taxi (tel. 0800-0970).

Tours in Dubrovnik

Walking Tours

Two companies—**Dubrovnik Walking Tours** (www.dubrovnik-walking-tours.com) and **Dubrovnik Walks** (www.dubrovnik walks.com)—offer similar one-hour walking tours of the Old Town daily at 10:00 and usually also at 13:00 and 18:00 or 18:30 (90 kn). I'd skip these tours—they're pricey and brief, touching lightly on the same information explained in this chapter. However, both companies also offer themed tours, typically covering wartime Dubrovnik and the historic Jewish quarter, which may be worthwhile. Pick up their fliers locally or check online for details.

Local Guide

For an in-depth look at the city, consider hiring your own local guide. **Roberto de Lorenzo** and his mother **Marija Tiberi** are both warm people enthusiastic about telling evocative stories from medieval Dubrovnik, including some off-the-beaten-path stops tailored to your interests (500 kn/2 hours, mobile 091-541-6637, bobdel70@yahoo.com); ask about guided transfers to Bosnia-Herzegovina, Split, or beyond. **Štefica Curić Lenert** is a sharp professional guide who offers a great by-the-book tour and an insider's look at the city (550 kn/1.5 hours, other tour options explained on her website, reserve at least one day ahead, mobile 091-345-0133, www.dubrovnikprivateguide.com, stefe@ubrovnikprivateguide.com). If these guides are busy, they can refer you to another good guide for a similar price.

FROM DUBROVNIK
Package Excursions

Various travel agencies in Dubrovnik offer guided excursions (by bus and/or boat) to nearby destinations, including Mostar, Korčula, Montenegro, islands and villages near Dubrovnik, Albania, and others (figure €30-100/person, depending on the itinerary). While these excursions can be a convenient way to see otherwise difficult-to-reach destinations, the experience is generally disappointing: The buses are packed, the guides are uninspired (reading from a dull script—often in multiple languages), and quality time at the destinations is short. If you have no other way to reach a place you're dying to visit, guided excursions can still be worth considering. But I'd exhaust my other options first—consider renting a car for the day, or hiring your own driver (described next).

For pointers on excursions by boat from Dubrovnik's Old Port, see page 918.

Hire Your Own Driver

I enjoy renting my own car to see the sights around Dubrovnik. But if you're more comfortable having someone else do the driving, hire a driver. While the drivers listed here are not licensed tour guides, they speak great English and offer commentary as you roll, and can help you craft a good day-long itinerary to Mostar, Montenegro, or anywhere else near Dubrovnik (typically departing around 8:00 and returning in the early evening). They're flexible about tailoring the tour to your interests: Because there are lots of options en route to either Mostar or Montenegro, do your homework so you can tell them what you'd like to see (and not see; for example, I'd skip Međugorje to have maximum time in Mostar).

Friendly **Pepo Klaić,** a veteran of the recent war, is enjoyable to get to know and has a knack for making the experience both informative and meaningful (€250/day, €125 for half-day trip to nearer destinations, airport transfer for about €30—cheaper than a taxi, these prices for up to four people—more expensive for bigger group, mobile 098-427-301, www.dubrovnikshoretrip.com, pepoklaic@yahoo.com). **Petar Vlašić** does similar tours for similar prices, and specializes in wine tours to the Pelješac Peninsula, with stops at various wineries along the way (€30 airport transfers, €190-200 for 2-person trip to Pelješac wineries, €230 to Mostar or €250 to Montenegro including local guide, these prices for 1-3 people—more for larger groups, mobile 091-580-8721, www.dubrovnikrivieratours.com, info@dubrovnikrivieratours.com). **Pero Carević,** who runs the recommended Villa Ragusa guest house, also drives travelers on excursions (similar prices, mobile 098-765-634, villa.ragusa@du.t-com.hr).

If your destination is Mostar, likeable Bosnian driver **Ermin Elezović** will happily come pick you up for less than the Dubrovnik-based drivers (for up to 3 people: €120 for one-way transfer from Dubrovnik to Mostar with a few brief sightseeing stops en route, €240 for round-trip to Mostar with same-day return to Dubrovnik; for contact information and details, see page 1115).

Recommended local guide **Roberto de Lorenzo,** listed earlier, also offers guided transfers to Mostar, Sarajevo, Split, and beyond, peppered with historical commentary en route.

Strolling the Stradun Walk

Running through the heart of Dubrovnik's Old Town is the 300-yard-long Stradun promenade—packed with people and lined with sights. This self-guided walk (rated ▲▲▲) offers an ideal introduction to Dubrovnik's charms. It takes about a half-hour, not counting sightseeing stops.

• *Begin at the busy square in front of the west entrance to the Old Town, the Pile (PEE-leh) Gate.*

Pile Neighborhood

This bustling area is the nerve center of Dubrovnik's tourist industry—it's where the real world meets the fantasy of Dubrovnik (for

details on services offered here, see "Orientation to Dubrovnik," earlier). Behind the modern, mirrors-and-LED-screens monument (which honors the "Dubrovnik Defenders" who protected the city during the 1991-1992 siege) is a leafy café terrace. Wander over to the edge of the terrace and take in the imposing walls of the Pearl of the Adriatic. The huge, fortified peninsula just outside the City Walls is the **Fort of St. Lawrence** (Tvrđava Lovrijenac), Dubrovnik's oldest fortress. Imagine how this fort and the stout walls worked together to fortify the little harbor—and the gate just behind you. You can climb this fortress for great views over the Old Town (30 kn, or covered by same ticket as City Walls on the same day).

• *Cross over the moat (now a shady park) to the round entrance tower in the City Walls. This is the...*

Pile Gate (Gradska Vrata Pile)

Just before you enter the gate, notice the image above the entrance of **St. Blaise** (Sveti Vlaho in Croatian) cradling Dubrovnik in his arm. You'll see a lot more of Blaise, the protector of Dubrovnik, during your time here—he is to Dubrovnik what the winged lion of St. Mark is to Venice.

Inside the first part of the gate, dead ahead you'll see another

image of Blaise. Down the ramp to your left, look for the white **map** (next to the tourist map) that shows where each bomb dropped on the Old Town during the siege. Once inside town, you'll see virtually no signs of the war—demonstrating the townspeople's impressive resilience in rebuilding so well and so quickly.

Passing the rest of the way through the gate, you'll find a lively little square surrounded by landmarks. The giant, round structure in the middle of the square is **Onofrio's Big Fountain** (Velika Onofrijea Fontana). In the Middle Ages, Dubrovnik had a complicated aqueduct system that brought water from the mountains seven miles away. The water

ended up here, at the town's biggest fountain, before continuing through the city. This plentiful supply of water, large reserves of salt (a key source of Dubrovnik's wealth, from the town of Ston), and a massive granary (now the Rupe Granary and Ethnographic Museum, described later) made little, independent Dubrovnik very siege-resistant.

Tucked across the square from the church is the **Visia Dubrovnik Multimedia Museum,** showing a badly produced 3-D film about the city's history that isn't worth your 35 minutes or 75 kn (schedule posted at entry). In the evening, the theater shows first-run 3-D movies.

To the left as you come through the Pile Gate, a steep stairway leads up to the imposing **Minčeta Tower.** It's possible to enter here to begin Dubrovnik's best activity, walking around the top of the wall (described later, under "Sights in Dubrovnik")—but this walk ends near a better, less crowded entry point.

Next to the stairway is the small **Church of St. Savior** (Crkva Svetog Spasa). Appreciative locals built this votive church to thank God after Dubrovnik made it through a 1520 earthquake. When the massive 1667 quake destroyed the city, this church was one of the only buildings left intact—its Renaissance interior stands at odds against the predominantly Baroque styles in other town churches. And during the recent war, the church survived another close call when a shell exploded on the ground right in front of it (you can still see faint pockmarks from the shrapnel).

DUBROVNIK

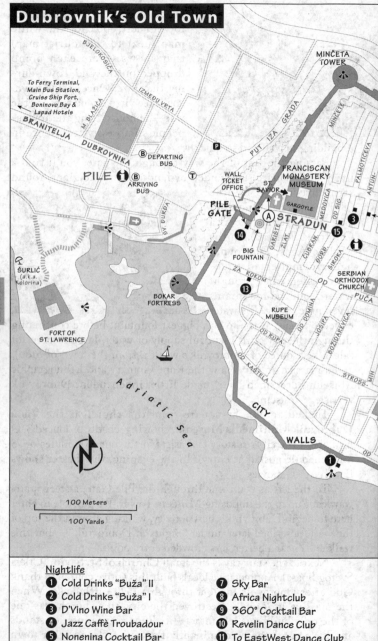

Dubrovnik's Old Town

To Ferry Terminal,
Main Bus Station,
Cruise Ship Port,
Boninovo Bay &
Lapad Hotels

BJELOKOSIĆA

IZMEĐU VRTA

MINČETA
TOWER

PUT IZA GRADA

MINČETE

M. BLAŽIĆA

BRANITELJA

DUBROVNIKA

PILE

P

B DEPARTING
BUS

B ARRIVING
BUS

SV. ĐURĐA

WALL
TICKET
OFFICE

PILE
GATE

FRANCISCAN
MONASTERY
MUSEUM

ST.
SAVIOR

A STRADUN

GARGOYLE

PALMOTIĆEVA

ANTUN

OD SIG

3

15

GARIŠTE

ZLAT

CUBRAN

MEDOVIĆA

PORB.

SIROKA

OD

PUĆA

SERBIAN
ORTHODOX
CHURCH

14

BIG
FOUNTAIN

ZA ROKOM

13

BOKAR
FORTRESS

RUPE
MUSEUM

OD DOMINA

JOSIRA

BOŽIDAREVIĆA

ŠURLIĆ
(a.k.a.
Kolorina)

FORT OF
ST. LAWRENCE

OD RUPA

STROSS-

MIH

OD KAŠTELA

A d r i a t i c   S e a

N

CITY

WALLS

OD

1

100 Meters

100 Yards

Nightlife

1 Cold Drinks "Buža" II
2 Cold Drinks "Buža" I
3 D'Vino Wine Bar
4 Jazz Caffè Troubadour
5 Nonenina Cocktail Bar
6 The Gaffe Irish Pub

7 Sky Bar
8 Africa Nightclub
9 360° Cocktail Bar
10 Revelin Dance Club
11 To EastWest Dance Club

DUBROVNIK

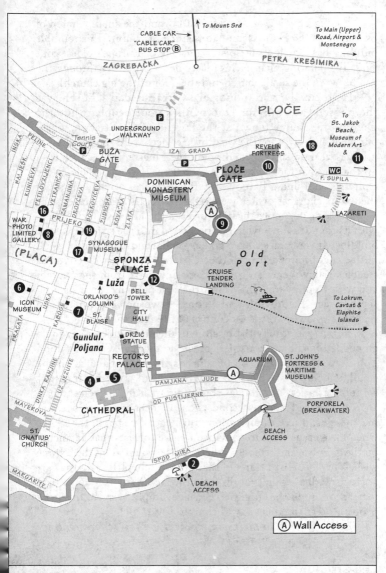

To Mount Srđ

CABLE CAR
"CABLE CAR"
BUS STOP (B)

To Main (Upper)
Road, Airport &
Montenegro

ZAGREBAČKA

PETRA KREŠIMIRA

PLOČE

To
St. Jakob
Beach,
Museum of
Modern Art
&

INSKA PELINE

"Tennis
Court"

UNDERGROUND
WALKWAY

P

BUŽA
GATE

IZA GRADA

REVELIN
FORTRESS

18

11

WC
F. SUPILA

PLOČE
GATE

10

MALJEŠK
KUNIŠEVA
PETILOVRJENCI
VETRANIĆA
ZAMANJINA
DROBROJEVA
BOŠKOVIĆEVA
ŽUDIOSKA
KOVAČKA
ZLATA

DOMINICAN
MONASTERY
MUSEUM

(A)

9

LAZARETI

WAR
PHOTO
LIMITED
GALLERY

16

PRIJEKO

19

8

17

SYNAGOGUE
MUSEUM

SPONZA
PALACE

12

Old
Port

CRUISE
TENDER
LANDING

(PLACA)

6

ICON
MUSEUM

USKA

Luža

ORLANDO'S
COLUMN

BELL
TOWER

To Lokrum,
Cavtat &
Elaphite
Islands

FRACATA
DINKA RANJINE
UZ JEZUITE
KABOGE

7

ST.
BLAISE

CITY
HALL

Gundul.
Poljana

DRŽIĆ
STATUE

RECTOR'S
PALACE

AQUARIUM

(A)

ST. JOHN'S
FORTRESS &
MARITIME
MUSEUM

MAYEROVA

4

5

DAMJANA JUDE

OD PUSTIJERNE

PORPORELA
(BREAKWATER)

CATHEDRAL

ST.
IGNATIUS'
CHURCH

MARGARITE

ISPOD MIRA

BEACH
ACCESS

2

BEACH
ACCESS

(A) Wall Access

DUBROVNIK

DUBROVNIK

The big building on the left just beyond the small Church of St. Savior is the **Franciscan Monastery Museum.** This tourable building has a delightful cloister and one of Europe's oldest continually operating pharmacies (described later; enter through the gap between the small church and the door of the big church).

Historically, the monastery's **Franciscan Church** was the house of worship for Dubrovnik's poor people, while the Dominican Church (down at the far end of the Stradun, where our walk ends) was for the wealthy. Services were staggered by 15 minutes to allow servants to drop off their masters there, then rush up the Stradun for their own service here. If you peek inside the church, you'll find a Baroque interior—typical of virtually all of the town's churches, which were rebuilt after the 1667 quake.

Looking up, notice the **bell tower** of the Franciscan Church—with its rounded top—which is integrated into the structure of the building. If your travels have taken you beyond Dubrovnik, you'll notice the difference from other Croatian towns, where church steeples follow Venetian convention: Set apart from the church, and with a pointy top. This is just the first of many contrasts we'll see between Dubrovnik and Venice—two powerful maritime republics who were rivals for control of the Adriatic.

Notice the stubby little, shin-high, mustachioed **gargoyle** embedded in the wall, just left of the Franciscan Church's door. You may see a commotion of tourists trying to balance on the small, slippery surface of the gargoyle's head. Tour guides enjoy spinning a variety of tall tales about this creature—if you can balance on one leg for three seconds, your fondest wish comes true—but these are a recent innovation. This legend began in the 1960s, when local teens tried to convince female tourists that balancing on the gargoyle and removing their blouse would grant them three wishes. (Why didn't I think of that in high school?) As for the gargoyle itself, it's simply a drain for rainwater. Why is it down here instead of up on the roofline? Perhaps simply to avoid deluging people who are on their way to church.

• *When you're finished taking in the sights on this square, continue along...*

The Stradun

Dubrovnik's main promenade—officially called the Placa, but better known as the Stradun—is alive with locals and tourists alike. This is the heartbeat of the city: an Old World shopping mall by day and sprawling cocktail party after dark, when

everybody seems to be doing the traditional evening stroll—flirting, ice-cream-licking, flaunting, and gawking. A coffee and some of Europe's best people-watching in a prime Stradun café is one of travel's great $4 bargains.

When Dubrovnik was just getting its start in the seventh century, this street was a canal. Romans fleeing from the invading Slavs lived on the island of Ragusa (on your right), and the Slavs settled on the shore. In the 11th century, the canal separating Ragusa from the mainland was filled in, the towns merged, and a unique Slavic-Roman culture and language blossomed. While originally much more higgledy-piggledy, this street was rebuilt in the current, more straightforward style after the 1667 earthquake. The ensuing fire raged for three weeks and consumed much of the city.

The distinctively shaped doors—with shop windows built right in, to provide maximum view of goods, but minimum access—indicate that this was the terrain of the merchants...and it still is.

The austerity of Dubrovnik's main drag disappoints some visitors. Rather than lavish funds on ostentatious palaces, as in Venice, Dubrovnik seems eager to downplay its wealth. For much of its history, Dubrovnik paid a hefty tribute to the sultan of the Ottoman Empire to maintain its independent status. Flaunting wealth would have raised Ottoman eyebrows...and, likely, Ottoman taxes. Unlike its rival Venice, which then as now is desperate to impress, Dubrovnik embodies a restraint that reflects the tumultuous time and place in which it thrived. Venice was surrounded by Italians, Austrians, Germans—some allies, some rivals, but all Christian. Dubrovnik sat five miles from the frontier of the Ottoman Empire; leaving the city felt like leaving the known world and the safety of what we'd today call "Western Civilization." Dubrovnik was, culturally and spiritually, an island of European Christianity surrounded on all sides by something so very different.

Today, you probably feel surrounded on all sides by hordes of international tourists. Things are worst on days when several cruise ships drop anchor—and when excursions into town feel more like incursions. But try some attitude adjustment: For much of its history, the maritime republic of Dubrovnik has been a crossroads of merchants, sailors, and other travelers from around the world. While today they may be following their tour guides' numbered paddles rather than trading exotic spices, the legions of visitors are still part of the city's tapestry of history.

If you're here in the summer (June-Sept), you'll periodically hear the rat-a-tat-tat of a drum echoing through the streets from the Stradun. This means it's time to head for this main drag to get a glimpse of the colorfully costumed **"town guards"** parading

DUBROVNIK

through (and a cavalcade of tourists running alongside them, trying to snap a clear picture). You may also see some of these characters standing guard outside the town gates. It's all part of the local tourist board's efforts to make their town even more atmospheric.

• *Branching off from this promenade are several museums and other attractions. At the end of the Stradun is a passageway leading to the Ploče Gate. Just before this passage is the lively Luža Square. Its centerpiece is the 20-foot-tall...*

Orlando's Column (Orlandov Stup)

Columns like this were typical of towns in northern Germany. Dubrovnik erected the column in 1417, soon after it had shifted allegiances from the oppressive Venetians to the Hungarians. By putting a northern European symbol in the middle of its most prominent square, Dubrovnik decisively distanced itself from Venice. Whenever a decision was made by the Republic, the town crier came to Orlando's Column and announced the news. The step he stood on indicated the importance of his message—the higher up, the more important the news. It was also used as the pillory, where people were publicly punished. The thin line on the top step in front of Orlando is exactly as long as the statue's forearm. This mark was Dubrovnik's standard measurement—not for a foot, but for an "elbow."

• *Now stand in front of Orlando's Column and orient yourself with a...*

Luža Square Spin-Tour

Orlando is looking toward the **Sponza Palace** (Sponza-Povijesni Arhiv). This building, from 1522, is the finest surviving example of Dubrovnik's Golden Age in the 15th and 16th centuries. It's a combination of Renaissance (ground-floor arches) and Venetian Gothic (upstairs windows). Houses up and down the main promenade used to look like this, but after the 1667 earthquake and fire, they were replaced with boring uniformity. This used to be the customs office *(dogana)*, but now it's an exhaustive archive of the city's history, with temporary art exhibits and a war memorial. The poignant **Memorial Room of Dubrovnik Defenders** (inside and on the  left) has photos of dozens of people from Dubrovnik who were killed fighting Yugoslav forces in 1991. A TV screen and images near the ceiling show the devastation of the city. Though the English descriptions are pointedly—if unavoidably—slanted to the Croat perspective, it's compelling to look in the eyes of the brave young men who didn't start this war...but were willing to finish it (free, long hours daily in peak season, shorter hours off-season). Beyond the memorial room, the impressive **courtyard,** which generally displays temporary exhibits, is worth a peek (25 kn, generally free after-hours).

To the right of Sponza Palace is the town's **Bell Tower** (Gradski Zvonik). The original dated from 1444, but it was rebuilt when it started to lean in the 1920s. The big clock may be an octopus, but only one of its hands tells time. Below that, the golden circle shows the phase of the moon. At the bottom, the old-fashioned digital readout tells the hour (in Roman numerals) and the minutes (in five-minute increments). At the top of each hour (and again three minutes later), the time is clanged out on the bell up top by two bronze bell-ringers, Maro and Baro. (If this all seems like a copy of the very similar clock on St. Mark's Square in Venice, locals are quick to point out that this clock predates that one by several decades.) The clock still has to be wound every two days. Notice the little window between the moon phase and the "digital" readout: The clock-winder opens this window to get some light. The Krasovac family was in charge of winding the clock for generations (1877-2005). During the 1991-1992 siege, their house was destroyed—with the winding keys inside. For days, the clock bell didn't run. But then, miraculously, the keys were discovered lying in the street. The excited Dubrovnik citizens came together in this square and cheered as the clock was wound and the bell chimed, signaling to the soldiers surrounding the city that they hadn't won yet. If you have a Dubrovnik Card, you can climb up to the gallery next to the tower for a fine view of the Stradun (entrance in the passage; likely June-Sept only—as hours are in flux, check the posted information or ask the TI for details).

To the right of the Bell Tower, you'll see the entrance to the Sloboda movie theater (the rainy-day location for cultural events in the summer), and next to that, **Onofrio's Little Fountain** (Mala Onofrijea Fontana), the little brother of the one at the other end of the Stradun. The big building beyond the fountain is the **City Hall** (Vijećnica)—the only 19th-century building inside the Old Town. The terrace at the near end of City Hall is occupied by the **Gradska Kavana,** or "Town Café." This hangout—historically Dubrovnik's favorite spot for gossiping and people-watching—has pricey drinks and seating all the way through the wall to the Old Port. Just down the street from the Town Café is the Rector's Palace, and then the cathedral (for more on each, see "Sights in Dubrovnik").

Behind Orlando is **St. Blaise's Church** (Crkva Sv. Vlaha), dedicated to the patron saint of Dubrovnik. You'll see statues and paintings of St. Blaise all over town, always holding a model of the city in his left hand. According to legend, a millennium ago

DUBROVNIK

The Siege of Dubrovnik

In June 1991, Croatia declared independence from Yugoslavia. Within weeks, the nations were at war (for more on the war, see "Understanding Yugoslavia" in the Practicalities chapter). Though warfare raged in the Croatian interior, nobody expected that the bloodshed would reach Dubrovnik.

As refugees from Vukovar (in northeastern Croatia) arrived in Dubrovnik that fall, telling horrific stories of the warfare there, local residents began fearing the worst. Warplanes from the Serb-dominated Yugoslav People's Army buzzed threateningly low over the town, as if to signal an impending attack.

Then, at 6:00 in the morning on October 1, 1991, Dubrovnik residents awoke to explosions on nearby hillsides. The first attacks were focused on Mount Srđ, high above the Old Town. First the giant cross was destroyed, then a communications tower (both have been rebuilt and are visible today). This first wave of attacks cleared the way for Yugoslav land troops—mostly Serbs and Montenegrins—who surrounded the city. The ragtag, newly formed Croatian army quickly dug in at the old Napoleonic-era fortress at the top of Mount Srđ, where just 25 or 30 soldiers fended off a Yugoslav takeover of this highly strategic position.

At first, shelling targeted military positions on the outskirts of town. But soon, Yugoslav forces began bombing residential neighborhoods, then the Pearl of the Adriatic itself: Dubrovnik's Old Town. Defenseless townspeople took shelter in their cellars, and sometimes even huddled together in the city wall's 15th-

century forts. It was the first time in Dubrovnik's long history that the walls were actually used to defend against an attack.

Dubrovnik resisted the siege better than anyone expected. The Yugoslav forces were hoping that residents would flee the town, but the people of Dubrovnik stayed. Though severely outgunned and outnumbered, Dubrovnik's defenders managed to hold the fort atop Mount Srđ, while Yugoslav forces controlled the nearby mountaintops. All supplies had to be carried up to the fort by foot or by donkey. Dubrovnik wasn't prepared for war, so its citizens had to improvise their defense. Many brave young locals lost their lives when they slung old hunting rifles over their shoulders and, under cover of darkness, climbed the hills above Dubrovnik to meet Yugoslav soldiers face-to-face.

After eight months of bombing, Dubrovnik was liberated by

the Croatian army, which attacked Yugoslav positions from the north. By the end of the siege, 100 civilians were dead, as well as more than 200 Dubrovnik citizens who lost their lives actively fighting for their hometown (much revered today as "Dubrovnik Defenders"); in the greater Dubrovnik area, 420 "Defenders" were killed, and another 900 wounded. More than two-thirds of Dubrovnik's buildings had been damaged, and more than 30,000 people had to flee their homes—but the failed siege was finally over.

Why was Dubrovnik—so far from the rest of the fighting—dragged into the conflict? Yugoslavia wanted to catch the city and surrounding region off-guard, gaining a toehold on the southern Dalmatian Coast so they could push north to Split. They also hoped to ignite pro-Serb passions in the nearby Serb-dominated areas of Bosnia-Herzegovina and Montenegro. But perhaps most of all, Yugoslavia wanted to hit Croatia where it hurt—its proudest, most historic, and most beautiful city, the tourist capital of a nation dependent on tourism. It seems their plan backfired. Locals now say, "When Yugoslavia attacked Dubrovnik, they lost the war"—because images of the historic city under siege swayed international public opinion *against* Yugoslavia.

The war initially devastated the tourist industry. Now, to the casual observer, Dubrovnik seems virtually back to normal. Aside from a few pockmarks and bright, new roof tiles, there are scant reminders of what happened here more than two decades ago. But even though the city itself has been repaired, the people of Dubrovnik are forever changed. Imagine living in an idyllic paradise, a place that attracted and awed visitors from around the world...and then watching it gradually blown to bits. It's understandable if Dubrovnik's citizens are a little less in love with life than they once were.

It's clear that in the case of this siege, the Croats of Dubrovnik were the largely innocent victims of a brutal surprise attack. But keep in mind the larger context of the war: The cousins of these Croats, who were defending the glorious monument that is Dubrovnik, bombarded another glorious monument—the Old Bridge of Mostar (see page 1119). It's just another reminder that the "good guys" and "bad guys" in these wars are far from clear-cut.

Dubrovnik has several low-key attractions related to its recent war, including the museum in the ruined fortress atop Mount Srđ and the Memorial Room of Dubrovnik Defenders in the Sponza Palace on Luža Square. Another sight, War Photo Limited, expands the scope to war photography from around the world.

St. Blaise came to a local priest in a dream and warned him that the up-and-coming Venetians would soon attack the city. The priest alerted the authorities, who prepared for war. Of course, the prediction came true. St. Blaise has been a Dubrovnik symbol—and locals have resented Venice—ever since.

The church, like most churches in this city, was built following the 1667 earthquake and fire. And, while we've heard plenty on this walk about Dubrovnik's rivalry with Venice, there's no denying that the Venetians were some of Europe's top cultural trendsetters at that time. So Dubrovnik invited a Venetian architect to design the church dedicated to their favorite saint. That's why St. Blaise's looks like it would be right at home reflected in a Venetian canal...right down to its bulbous dome, which seems transplanted here from the top of St. Mark's.

• *Your tour is finished. From here, you've got plenty of sightseeing options (all described next, under "Sights in Dubrovnik"). As you face the Bell Tower, you can go up the street to the right to reach the Rector's Palace and cathedral; you can walk straight ahead through the gate to reach the Old Port; or you can head through the gate and jog left to find the Dominican Monastery Museum. Even more sights—including an old synagogue, an Orthodox church, a modern exhibit of war photography, and the medieval granary—are in the steep streets between the Stradun and the walls.*

Sights in Dubrovnik

▲▲▲CITY WALLS (GRADSKE ZIDINE)

Dubrovnik's single best attraction is strolling the scenic mile-and-a-quarter around the City Walls. As you meander along this lofty perch—with a sea of orange roofs on one side, and the actual sea on the other—you'll get your bearings, peek down into secluded gardens, and snap pictures like mad of the ever-changing views. Bring your map, which you can use to pick out landmarks and get the lay of the land.

Cost: 100 kn to enter walls, also includes the Fort of St. Lawrence outside the Pile Gate (kunas or credit cards only—no euros).

Hours: July-Aug daily 8:00-19:30, progressively shorter hours off-season until mid-Nov-mid-March 10:00-15:00. Since the hours change with the season, confirm them by checking signs posted at the entrance (essential if you want to time your wall walk to avoid the worst crowds—explained below). The posted closing time indicates when the walls shut down, *not* the last entry—ascend well before this time if you want to make it all the way around. (If you want to linger, begin at least an hour ahead; if you're speedy, you can ascend 30 minutes before closing time.) Attendants begin circling the walls at the posted closing time to lock the gates. There's talk of someday illuminating the walls at night, in which case the hours would be extended until after dark.

Entrances and Strategies: There are three entry points for the wall (see map on page 898), and wall-walkers are required to proceed counterclockwise. The best plan is to begin at the far side of the Old Town, using the entrance **near the Ploče Gate** and Dominican Monastery. This entrance is the least crowded, and you'll tackle the steepest part (and enjoy the best views) first, as you climb up to the landward side of the wall with magnificent views across the entire Old Town and the Adriatic. If you're wiped out, overheated, or fed up with crowds after that, you can bail out halfway (at the Pile Gate), having seen the best—or you can continue around the seaward side. The other two entrances are **just inside the Pile Gate** (by far the most crowded; for this location only, you must buy your tickets at the desk across the square; if you begin here, you'll reach the Minčeta Tower—with the steepest ascent and best views—last) and **near St. John's Fort** overlooking the Old Port (next to the Maritime Museum).

Crowd Control: Because this is Dubrovnik's top attraction, it's extremely crowded. Your best strategy is to avoid the walls during the times when the cruise ships are in town. On days when the walls open at 8:00, try to get started around that time. The walls are the most crowded from about 9:00 until 11:00, when the cruise ships are docked. There's generally an afternoon lull in the crowds (13:00-14:00)—but that's also the hottest time to be atop the walls. Crowds pick up again in the late afternoon (around 17:00), peaking about an hour before closing time (18:30 in high season). During busy times, your best bet is to hit the walls around 8:30, or just before 17:00 (to avoid both the worst heat and the worst crowds).

Tips: Speed demons with no cameras can walk the walls in about an hour; strollers and shutterbugs should plan on longer. Because your ticket is electronically scanned as you enter, you can't leave and re-enter the wall later; you have to do it all in one go. If you have a Dubrovnik Card—even a multiple-day one—you can only use it to ascend the walls once.

DUBROVNIK

Warning: The walls can get deliriously hot—all that white stone and seawater reflect blazing sunshine something fierce, and there's virtually no shade. It's essential to bring sunscreen, a hat, and water. Pace yourself: There are several steep stretches, and you'll be climbing up and down the whole way around. A few scant shops and cafés along the top of the wall (mostly on the sea side) sell water and other drinks, but it's safest to bring what you'll need with you. If you have trouble with the heat, save the walls for a cloudy day. In that hazy light, the red roof tiles seem more vivid, since they're not washed out by glaring sunshine.

Audioguide: You can rent an audioguide, separate from the admission fee, for a dryly narrated circular tour of the walls (look for vendors near the Pile Gate entrance—not available at other entrances). But I'd rather just enjoy the views and lazily pick out the landmarks with my map.

Background: There have been walls here almost as long as there's been a Dubrovnik. As with virtually all fortifications on the Croatian Coast, these walls were beefed up in the 15th century, when the Ottoman navy became a threat. Around the perimeter are several substantial forts, with walls rounded so that cannon-balls would glance off harmlessly. These stout forts intimidated would-be invaders during the Republic of Dubrovnik's Golden Age, and protected residents during the 1991-1992 siege.

◑ Self-Guided Tour: It's possible to just wander the walls and snap photos like crazy as you go. And trying to hew too closely to guided commentary kind of misses the point of being high above the Dubrovnik rooftops. But this brief tour will help give you bearings to what you're seeing, as you read Dubrovnik's unique and illustrious history into its street plan.

Part 1—Ploče Gate to Pile Gate: Begin by ascending near the **Ploče Gate** (go through the gate under the Bell Tower, walk along the stoutly walled passageway between the port and the Dominican Monastery, and look for the wall entrance on your right). Buy your ticket, head up, turn left, and start walking counterclockwise. Climbing stairs, you'll walk with Mount Srđ and the cable car on your right. After passing the Dominican Monastery's fine courtyard on the left, you're walking above what was the poorest part of medieval Dubrovnik, the domain of the craftsmen—with narrow, stepped lanes that had shops on the ground floor and humble dwellings up above. Standing above the Buža Gate (one of just three places where people can enter and exit the walled Old Town), you have a great view down narrow Boškovićeva street, with its many little stone tabs sticking out next to windows. (These were used to hang banners during the city's Golden Age.)

As you walk, keep an eye on the different-colored **rooftops** for an illustration of the damage Dubrovnik sustained during the 1991-1992 siege. It's easy to see that nearly two-thirds of Dubrovnik's roofs were replaced after the bombings (notice the new, bright-orange tiles—and how some buildings salvaged the old tiles, but have 20th-century ones underneath. The pristine-seeming Old Town was rebuilt using exactly the same materials and methods with which it was originally constructed.

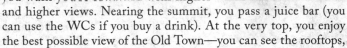

The path you're on alternates between straight stretches and stairs; as you walk you're rewarded with higher and higher views. Nearing the summit, you pass a juice bar (you can use the WCs if you buy a drink). At the very top, you enjoy the best possible view of the Old Town—you can see the rooftops, churches, and the sea. For an even better view,

if you have the energy, huff up the steep stairs to the (empty) **Minčeta Tower.** From either viewpoint, observe the valley-like shape of Dubrovnik. It's easy to imagine how it began as two towns—one where you are now, and the other on the hilly island with the church spires across the way—originally separated by a seawater canal. Notice the relatively regular, grid-like pattern of houses on this side, but the more higgledy-piggledy arrangement on the far side (a visual clue that the far side is older).

The sports court at your feet is a reminder that Dubrovnik is a living city—though it's not as vibrant as it once was. While officially 2,000 people live within these walls, most locals estimate the real number at about half that; the rest rent out their homes to tourists. And with good reason: Imagine the challenges that come with living in such a steep medieval townscape well into the 21st century. Delivery trucks rumble up and down the Stradun early each morning, and you'll see hardworking young men delivering goods on hand carts throughout the day. Looking up at the fortress atop Mount Srđ—seemingly custom-made for keeping an eye on a large swathe of coastline—the strategic position of Dubrovnik is clear. Independent Dubrovnik was not just this walled city, but an entire region.

Now continue downhill (you've earned it), noticing views on your right of the bustling Pile Gate area and the Fort of St. Lawrence (we'll reach better views of both of these soon). As the wall walk levels off, you'll pass an exit (on the left); if you're bushed and ready to head back to town, you can bail out here—but be aware that once you leave, you can't re-enter on the same ticket. Better yet, carry on straight for part 2.

Part 2—Pile Gate to Old Port: Pause to enjoy the full frontal view of the **Stradun,** barreling right at you. In the Middle

Ages, lining this drag were the merchants, and before that, this was a canal. At your feet is Onofrio's Big Fountain, which supplied water to a thirsty town. From here, you can see a wide range of church steeples representing the cosmopolitan makeup of a thriving medieval trade town (from left to right): Dominican, Franciscan (near you), the town Bell Tower, St. Blaise's (the round dome—hard to see from here), Serbian Orthodox (twin domed steeples), Cathedral, and (high on the hill) Jesuit St. Ignatius. Sit and watch the river of humanity, flowing constantly up and down one of Europe's finest main streets. Now do a 180 for a good view of the Pile Gate chaos, with a steady stream of buses lumbering up and down the hill, tethering the Old Town to Port Gruž and the Lapad resort zone.

Carry on through the guard tower and along the wall, climbing uphill again. Looking to the wall ahead of you, notice that—after we passed along a straighter, lower stretch—this wall is scampering up a mighty foundation of solid rock. We've left the canal that once separated the two parts of Dubrovnik, and now we're ascending what used to be a separate, very steep, rocky island.

On the right, across the little cove, is the **Fort of St. Lawrence,** which worked in concert with these stout walls to make Dubrovnik virtually impenetrable. (That fort is also climbable, and covered by the same ticket as the walls.) Climbing higher and looking to your left, into town, you'll see that this area is still damaged—not from the 1991-1992 siege, but from the 1667 earthquake. Notice that, unlike the extremely dense construction on the poorer far side of town, this area has more breathing space and larger gardens. Originally this was also densely populated, but after the quake, rather than rebuild, the wealthy folks who lived here decided to turn some former homes into green space. Grates cover the openings to old wells and grain stores that once supplied homes here—essential for surviving a siege.

As the walkway summits and levels out, you pass a drink stand. Farther along, at the picturesque little turret, is an artsy souvenir boutique. You'll stroll past local residents' backyards,

peering into their inviting gardens and checking the status of their drying laundry. Looking down to your right (outside the wall), you'll begin to see tables and umbrellas clinging to the rocks at the base of the wall. This is the recommended Cold Drinks "Buža" II, the best spot in town for a scenic drink. (You can't enter from atop the wall—you'll have to wait until later.) On the horizon is the isle of Lokrum and—often—cruise ships at anchor, sending their passengers to and fro on tenders. After passing Buža, look down on the left to see the neighborhood kids' makeshift soccer pitch, wedged between the walls, and a little chapel—the best they can do in this vertical town. Soon you'll see the "other" Buža (technically Buža I) ahead; just above it, notice the little statue of St. Blaise, Dubrovnik's patron, enjoying some shade under the turret.

Rounding the bend, look left to see the facade of the Jesuit St. Ignatius Church. Notice that the homes in this area are much larger. These are aristocratic palaces—VIPs wanted to live as close as possible to the Cathedral and Rector's Palace, which are just below—and this also happens to be the oldest part of town, where "Ragusa" was born on a steep offshore island.

Continue around the wall, passing two more snack bars (the second with pay WCs) and more quake-ruined houses. Eventually you'll pop out at a high plateau, where *The City Walls—Continuation* signs lead down to the next part. From here, if you're bushed, you can bail out for the exit. (In the little plant-filled square at the bottom of these stairs is a sweet cat hospice, with a donation box for feeding some homeless feline residents.) But the final stretch of our wall walk is shorter than the other two, and mostly level.

Part 3—Old Port to Ploče Gate: Continuing along the wall, you'll pass near the entrance to the skippable Maritime Museum, then walk along the top of the wall overlooking the Old Port. Imagine how this heavily fortified little harbor (facing away from Dubrovnik's historic foes, the Venetians) was busy with trade in the Middle Ages. Today it's still the economic lifeline for town—watch the steady stream of cruise-ship tenders injecting dose after dose of tourist cash into town. As you curl around the far side of the port, you'll see the outdoor tables of 360°, a cocktail bar/restaurant catering to high-rolling yachters. While it looks appealing, it's a very exclusive place that frowns on would-be visitors who dress like normal people. Gussied-up jet-set diners enjoy coming here for good but extremely expensive designer fare. (One local told me,

"The food is great—just eat a hamburger before you go.")

Just past 360°, you come to the stairs back down to where you started this wall walk. Nice work. Now head on down and reward yourself with an ice-cream cone...and some shade.

The "Other" Wall Climb: Your ticket for the City Walls also includes the Fort of St. Lawrence just outside the Old Town (valid same day only; fort described on page 896). If you've already bought a 30-kn ticket there, show it when buying your main wall ticket and you'll pay only the difference.

NEAR THE PILE GATE

This museum is just inside the Pile Gate.

▲Franciscan Monastery Museum (Franjevački Samostan-Muzej)

In the Middle Ages, Dubrovnik's monasteries flourished. And, as a part of their charity work, the monks at this monastery took on the responsibility of serving as pharmacists for the community. Visiting here today, you'll stroll through a delightful cloister and walk through a one-room museum in the old pharmacy.

Cost and Hours: 30 kn, daily April-Oct 9:00-18:00, Nov-March 9:00-17:00, Placa 2, tel. 020/321-410.

Visiting the Museum: Enter through the gap between the small church and the big monastery. Just inside the door (before the ticket-seller), a century-old **pharmacy** still serves residents. Notice the antique jars, advertisements (including one of the first known Aspirin ads), and other vintage pharmacist gear. By keeping this pharmacy open, the monastery maintains one of the world's oldest continually operating pharmacies.

Explore the peaceful, sun-dappled **cloister.** Examine the capitals at the tops of the 60 Romanesque-Gothic double pillars. Each one is different. Notice that some parts of the portals inside the courtyard are made with a lighter-colored stone—these had to be repaired after being hit during the 1991-1992 siege. The damaged 19th-century frescoes along the tops of the walls depict the life of St. Francis, who sup-

posedly visited Dubrovnik in the early 13th century. If you look closely, in a few panels you may see two layers of (different) scenes; beneath the 19th-century frescoes, restorers have found even more precious fragments of some early 18th-century paintings; where possible, these are also being resurrected.

In the far corner stands the monastery's original medieval

pharmacy. The Franciscans opened this pharmacy in 1317, and it's been in continual operation ever since. On display are jars, pots, and other medieval pharmacists' tools. Notice the row of old pharmacists' books from the 16th, 17th, and 18th centuries—expertise imported from as far away as Venice, Frankfurt, Amsterdam, and Bologna. The sick would come to get their medicine at the little window (on the left side), which limited contact with the pharmacist and reduced the risk of passing on disease. On the right side, look for the glass case marked *venena*—where poisons were locked away and carefully doled out, with a record of who had what (if only modern gun dealers were so cautiously regulated).

Around the room, you'll also find some relics, old manuscripts, and a detailed painting of early 17th-century Dubrovnik. In the painting, notice that at the top of Mount Srđ—the highly strategic locale where Napoleon built a fortress that was key during the 1991 siege (see page 923)—is a chapel. Though Dubrovnik was always heavily fortified, they avoided putting a fortress on the mountaintop—fearing it might seem overly provocative to the Ottoman Empire that surrounded them, and upon whose favor they depended for their autonomy.

Leaving the museum room, turn right and walk to the end of this corridor. While you're walking upon tombs, look up to see one with privileged position, affixed high on the wall. The **Gučetić-Gozze** family donated vast sums to help rebuild the monastery after the devastating 1667 earthquake. As thanks, the Franciscans helped them get just that much closer to God when they passed on, offering them this final resting place that was elevated...in every sense.

NEAR LUŽA SQUARE

These sights are at the far end of the Stradun (nearest the Old Port). As you stand on Luža Square facing the Bell Tower, the Rector's Palace and cathedral are up the wide street called Pred Dvorom to the right, and the Dominican Monastery Museum is through the gate by the Bell Tower and to the left.

▲Rector's Palace (Knežev Dvor)

In the Middle Ages, the Republic of Dubrovnik was ruled by a rector (similar to a Venetian doge), who was elected by the nobility. To prevent any one person from becoming too powerful, the rector's term was limited to one month. Most rectors were in their 50s—near the end of the average life span and when they were less likely to shake things up. During his term, a rector lived upstairs in this palace. Because it's been plundered twice (most recently by Napoleon's forces, who stole all the furniture), this empty-feeling museum isn't as interesting as most other European palaces. What little you'll see was donated by local aristocrats to flesh out the pathetically empty complex. The palace collection, which requires a ticket and has good English explanations, is skippable, but it does offer a glimpse of Dubrovnik in its glory days. Even if you pass on the interior, the palace's exterior and courtyard are viewable at no charge.

Cost and Hours: 70 kn, ticket also includes Maritime Museum and Rupe Ethnographical Museum, daily May-Oct 9:00-18:00, Nov-April 9:00-16:00, some posted English information, 7-kn English booklet is helpful, Pred Dvorom 3, tel. 020/322-096.

Visiting the Palace: The **exterior** is decorated in the Gothic-Renaissance mix (with particularly finely carved capitals) that was so common in Dubrovnik before the 1667 earthquake. Above the entrance is the message *Obliti privatorum publica curate*—loosely translated, "Forget your personal affairs and concern yourself with the affairs of state." This was a bold statement in a feudal era before democracy, when aristocrats were preoccupied exclusively with their self-interests.

Standing at the main door, you can generally get a free look at the palace's impressive **courtyard**—a venue for the Summer Festival, hosting music groups ranging from the local symphony to the Vienna Boys' Choir. During Dubrovnik's Golden Age, this courtyard was open to the public. People would wander in and out—gossiping, washing their laundry in the fountain, and bringing food to family members imprisoned in the cells. In the courtyard (and also visible from the door) is the only secular statue created during the centuries-long Republic. Dubrovnik republicans, mindful of the dangers of hero-worship, didn't believe that any one citizen should be singled out. They made only one exception—for Miho Pracat (a.k.a. Michaeli Prazatto), a rich citizen who donated vast sums to charity and willed a fleet of ships to the city. But notice that Pracat's statue is displayed in here, behind closed doors, not out in public.

If you pay to go **inside,** you'll start on the ground floor, where you'll see dull paintings, the green-stucco courtroom (with explanations of the Republic's unique governmental system), and one of the palace's highlights, the original bronze bell-ringers from the town Bell Tower (named Maro and Baro). Like antique robots (from the Renaissance, 1477-1478), these eerily lifelike sculptures could pivot at the waist to ring the bell. Then you'll see stonework that used to decorate city buildings. Iron chests (including a few with elaborate locking mechanisms) are displayed inside some poorly restored old prison cells, which supposedly were placed within earshot of the rector's quarters, so he would hear the moans of the prisoners...and stay honest. Leaving the prison, you'll enter the courtyard described earlier, where you can get a better look at the Pracat statue.

On the mezzanine level (stairs near the main entrance, above the prison—notice the "hand" rails), you'll find a decent display of furniture, a wimpy gun exhibit, votive offerings (mostly silver), a ho-hum coin collection, and an interesting painting of "Ragusa" in the early 17th century—back when its stout walls were surrounded by a moat.

Head back down to the courtyard and ascend the grand stairway to the upper floor (using the staircase across from mezzanine stairs, near the Pracat statue—with more "hand" rails). Upstairs, you'll explore old apartments that serve as a painting gallery. The only vaguely authentic room is the red room in the corner, decorated more or less as it was in 1500, when it was the rector's office. Mihajlo Hamzić's exquisite *Baptism of Christ* painting, inspired by Italian painter Andrea Mantegna, is an early Renaissance work from the "Dubrovnik School" (see "Dominican Monastery Museum" listing, later). This area also often displays temporary exhibits.

Back in the courtyard, you can go up the smaller stairs to the Domus Christi collection of old pharmacist tools and pots.

Handy WCs are just off the courtyard next to the shop, through which you'll exit.

Nearby: Just to the left as you face the entrance of the Rector's Palace, notice the statue of Dubrovnik poet **Marin Držić** (1508-1567). This beloved bard's most famous work concerns "Uncle Maro," an aristocrat who's as stingy as he is wealthy. His son cleans out his savings account and goes on a bender in Rome... until his father gets wind of it and comes calling. The shiny lap and bright nose of this statue, erected in 2008, might lead you to believe it's good luck to rub his schnozz—and, sure enough, you'll see a steady stream of tourists doing just that. But the truth is that when the statue went up, local kids were drawn to his prominent proboscis, and couldn't resist climbing up on his lap and grabbing it. Tourists saw the shine and assumed they were supposed to do it, too. A legend was born.

▲Cathedral (Katedrala)
Dubrovnik's original 12th-century cathedral was funded largely by the English King Richard the Lionheart. On his way back from the Third Crusade, Richard was shipwrecked nearby. He promised God that if he survived, he'd build a church on the spot where

he landed—which happened to be on Lokrum Island, just offshore. At Dubrovnik's request, Richard agreed to build his token of thanks inside the city instead. It was the finest Romanesque church on the Adriatic... before it was destroyed by the 1667 earthquake. This version is 18th-century Roman Baroque.

Cost and Hours: Church—free, open daily 8:00 until Mass begins at 18:00; treasury—15 kn, generally open same hours as church; both have shorter hours off-season.

Visiting the Cathedral: Inside, you'll find a painting from the school of Titian *(Assumption of the Virgin)* over the stark contemporary altar, and a quirky treasury *(riznica)* packed with 187 relics. Examining the treasury collection, notice that there are three locks on the treasury door—the stuff in here was so valuable, three different VIPs (the rector, the bishop, and a local aristocrat) had to agree before it could be opened. On the table near the door are several of St. Blaise's body parts (pieces of his arm, skull, and leg—all encased in gold and silver). In the middle of the wall directly opposite the door, look for the crucifix with a piece of the True Cross. On a dig in Jerusalem, St. Helen (Emperor Constantine's mother) discovered what she believed to be the cross that Jesus was crucified on. It was brought to Constantinople, and the Byzantine czars doled out pieces of it to Balkan kings. Note the folding three-paneled altar painting (underneath the cross). Dubrovnik ambassadors packed this on road trips (such as their annual trip to pay off the Ottomans) so they could worship wherever they traveled.

On the right side of the room, the silver casket supposedly holds the actual swaddling clothes of the Baby Jesus (or, as some locals call it somewhat less reverently, "Jesus' nappy"). Dubrovnik bishops secretly passed these clothes down from generation to generation...until a nun got wind of it and told the whole town. Pieces of the cloth were cut off to miraculously heal the sick, especially new mothers recovering from a difficult birth. No matter how often it was cut, the cloth always went back to its original form. Then someone tried to use it on the wife of a Bosnian king. Since she was Muslim, it couldn't help her, and it never worked again. True or not, this legend hints at the prickly relationships between faiths (not to mention the male chauvinism) here in the Balkans.

▲Dominican Monastery Museum (Dominikanski Samostan-Muzej)

You'll find many of Dubrovnik's art treasures—paintings, altar-pieces, and manuscripts—gathered around the peaceful Dominican Monastery cloister inside the Ploče Gate. As you climb the stairs up to the monastery, notice that the spindles supporting the railing are solid up until about two feet above the ground. This was to provide a modicum of modesty to ladies on their way to church—and to prevent creeps down below from looking up their skirts.

Cost and Hours: 30 kn, art buffs enjoy the 50-kn English book, daily April-Oct 9:00-18:00, Nov-March 9:00-17:00.

Visiting the Museum: Turn left from the entry and work your way clockwise around the cloister. The room in the far corner contains paintings from the **"Dubrovnik School,"** the Republic's circa-1500 answer to the art boom in Florence and Venice. Though the 1667 earthquake destroyed most of these paintings, about a dozen survive, and five of those are in this room. Don't miss the triptych by Nikola Božidarović with St. Blaise holding a detailed model of 16th-century Dubrovnik (left panel)—the most famous depiction of Dubrovnik's favorite saint. You'll also see reliquaries shaped like the hands and feet that they hold.

Continuing around the courtyard, duck into the next room. Here you'll see a painting by **Titian** depicting St. Blaise, Mary Magdalene, and the donor who financed this work.

At the next corner of the courtyard is the entrance to the striking **church** at the heart of this still-active monastery. Step inside. The interior is decorated with modern stained glass, a fine 13th-

century stone pulpit that survived the earthquake (reminding visitors of the intellectual approach to scripture that characterized the Dominicans), and a precious 14th-century Paolo Veneziano crucifix hanging above the high altar. Behind the altar, find the Vukovar Cross, embedded with panels painted by different artists from the Croatian school of Naive Art—offering an enticing taste of this unique and fascinating style (for more on Naive Art, see page 1068). Perhaps the finest piece of art in the church is the *Miracle of St. Dominic,* showing the founder of the order bringing a child back to life (over the altar to the right, as you enter; see image on previous page). It was painted in the Realist style (late 19th century) by Vlaho Bukovac.

Museum of Modern Art (Umjetnička Galerija)

While salty old Dubrovnik and modern art don't quite seem to go together, the city has a fine modern art gallery a 10-minute walk outside the Ploče Gate. You'll see a permanent collection with 20th-century Croatian art (including some paintings by local artist Vlaho Bukovac—whose home in Cavtat offers a more intimate look at his life and works), as well as changing exhibits.

Cost and Hours: 40 kn, Tue-Sun 9:00-20:00, closed Mon, put Frana Supila 23, tel. 020/426-590, www.ugdubrovnik.hr.

NEAR THE OLD PORT (STARA LUKA)

The picturesque Old Port, carefully nestled behind St. John's Fort, faces away from what was Dubrovnik's biggest threat, the Venetians. At the port, you can haggle with captains selling excursions to nearby towns and islands and watch cruise-ship passengers coming and going on their tenders. The long seaside building across the bay on the left is the Lazareti, once the medieval quarantine house. In those  days, all visitors were locked in here for 40 days before entering town. (Today it hosts folk-dancing shows—described later, under "Entertainment in Dubrovnik.") A bench-lined harborside walk leads around the fort to a breakwater, providing a peaceful perch. From the breakwater, rocky beaches curl around the outside of the wall.

Excursions

Various excursions boats depart from the Old Port. The basic option is a 50-minute **"panorama cruise"** out into the water and back again, most popular at sunset (75 kn, departures every hour; look for the old-fashioned 1878 cargo boat called *St. Ivan*, which offers a 20 percent discount to Rick Steves readers). Other popular trips are to **Lokrum Island,** just offshore, which offers the chance to hike through forests and swim at one of many rocky beaches (60 kn round-trip, 2/hour, 15-minute crossing, runs April-Oct 9:00-18:00, mid-June-Aug until 20:00, none Nov-March); and to the archipelago called the **Elaphite Islands,** with visits to three different islands (about 250 kn with lunch, several boats depart daily around 10:30-11:00, return around 15:45-19:30; so they can be sure to buy enough food, companies prefer you to reserve and pay a 50-kn deposit the day before). You generally spend two to three hours on Lopud and about an hour each on Koločep and Šipan, with about 2.5 hours on the boat.

For sightseeing rather than sunning and lazing, consider a cruise to the nearby resort town of **Cavtat** (TSAV-taht). Cavtat is set within an idyllic, horseshoe-shaped harbor hemmed in by a pair of peninsulas. Even those suffering from beach-resort fatigue will enjoy a side-trip to Cavtat, if they appreciate local art. Capping the hill just above town is a breathtaking mausoleum by the great Croatian sculptor **Ivan Meštrović** (Račić Family Mausoleum, 10 kn, Mon-Sat 10:00-17:00, closed Sun and mid-Oct-mid-April; for more on Meštrović, see page 976). Right along the main drag, a half-block up a side street, is the former home-turned-museum of the Cavtat-born, early-20th-century painter **Vlaho Bukovac** (Kuća Bukovac, 20 kn, good 40-kn guidebook; May-Oct Tue-Sat 9:00-13:00 & 16:00-20:00, Sun 16:00-20:00, closed Mon; Nov-April Tue-Sat 9:00-13:00 & 14:00-17:00, Sun 14:00-17:00, closed Mon; Bukovčeva 5, tel. 020/478-646, www.kuca-bukovac.hr). Boats to Cavtat leave about hourly from Dubrovnik's Old Port (80 kn round-trip, 50 kn one-way, about 45 minutes each way, hourly return boats from Cavtat). Note that a round-trip ticket is cheaper, but you'll have to return with the same company (rather than on whichever boat is leaving next). You can also reach Cavtat by public bus #10 (departs from Dubrovnik's main bus station and also stops at the "cable car" bus stop above the Old Town, 1-2/hour, 30–40 minutes, 20 kn).

Maritime Museum (Pomorski Muzej)

In the 15th century, when Venice's nautical dominance was peaking, Dubrovnik emerged as another maritime power and the Mediterranean's leading shipbuilding center. The Dubrovnik-built "argosy" boat (from "Ragusa," an early name for the city) was the Cadillac of ships, even mentioned by Shakespeare. This small museum traces the history of Dubrovnik's most important industry with contracts, maps, paintings, and models—all well-described in English. The main floor takes you through the 18th century, and the easy-to-miss upstairs covers the 19th and 20th centuries. Boaters will find the museum particularly interesting.

Cost and Hours: Covered by 70-kn combo-ticket with Rector's Palace and Rupe Ethnographic Museum, 7-kn English booklet, hours flex on demand—usually March-Oct Tue-Sun 9:00-18:00, until 16:00 in Nov-Feb, closed Mon year-round, upstairs in St. John's Fort, at far/south end of Old Port, tel. 020/323-904.

DUBROVNIK

Aquarium (Akvarij)

Dubrovnik's aquarium, housed in the cavernous St. John's Fort, is an old-school place, with 31 tanks on one floor. A visit here allows you a close look at the local marine life and provides a cool refuge from the midday heat.

Cost and Hours: 40 kn, kids-15 kn, English descriptions, daily July-Aug 9:00-21:00, progressively shorter hours off-season until 9:00-16:00 Nov-March, ground floor of St. John's Fort, enter from Old Port, tel. 020/323-978.

BETWEEN THE STRADUN AND THE MAINLAND

These two museums are a few steps off the main promenade toward the mainland.

▲Synagogue Museum (Sinagoga-Muzej)

When the Jews were forced out of Spain in 1492, a steady stream of them passed through here en route to today's Turkey. Finding Dubrovnik to be a flourishing and relatively tolerant city, many stayed. Žudioska ulica ("Jewish Street"), just inside the Ploče Gate, became the ghetto in 1546. It was walled at one end and had a gate (which would be locked at night) at the other end. Today, the same street is home to the second-oldest continuously functioning synagogue in Europe (after Prague's), which contains Croatia's only Jewish museum. The top floor houses the synagogue itself. Notice the lattice windows that separated the women from the men (in accordance with Orthodox Jewish tradition). Below that, a small museum with good English descriptions gives meaning to the various Torahs (including a 14th-century one from Spain) and other items—such as the written orders *(naredba)* from Nazi-era Yugoslavia, stating that Jews were to identify their shops as Jewish-owned and wear armbands. (The Ustaše—the Nazi puppet government in Croatia—interned and executed not only Jews and Roma (Gypsies), but also Serbs and other people they considered undesirable; see page 865.) Of Croatia's 24,000 Jews, only 4,000 survived the Holocaust. Today Croatia has about 2,000 Jews, including a dozen Jewish families who call Dubrovnik home.

Cost and Hours: 25 kn, 10-kn English booklet; May-mid-Nov daily 10:00-20:00; mid-Nov-April Mon-Fri 10:00-13:00, closed Sat-Sun; Žudioska ulica 5, tel. 020/321-204.

▲War Photo Limited

If the tragic story of wartime Dubrovnik has you in a pensive mood, drop by this gallery with images of warfare from around the world. The brainchild of Kiwi-turned-Croatian photojournalist Wade Goddard, this thought-provoking museum attempts to show the ugly reality of war through raw, often disturbing photographs taken in the field. You'll find well-displayed exhibits on two floors; a small permanent exhibit (on the top floor) captures the wars in the former Yugoslavia through photography and video footage. Each summer, the gallery also houses various temporary exhibits. Note that the focus is not solely on Dubrovnik, but on war anywhere and everywhere.

Cost and Hours: 40 kn; June-Sept daily 10:00-22:00; May and Oct Tue-Sun 10:00-16:00, closed Mon; closed Nov-April; Antuninska 6, tel. 020/322-166, www.warphotoltd.com.

BETWEEN THE STRADUN AND THE SEA
▲Serbian Orthodox Church and Icon Museum (Srpska Pravoslavna Crkva i Muzej Ikona)

Round out your look at Dubrovnik's major faiths (Catholic, Jewish, and Orthodox) with a visit to this house of worship—one of the most convenient places in Croatia to learn about Orthodox Christianity. Remember that people from the former Yugoslavia who follow the Orthodox faith are, by definition, ethnic Serbs. With all the hard feelings about the recent war, this church serves as an important reminder that all Serbs aren't bloodthirsty killers.

Dubrovnik never had a very large Serb population (an Orthodox church wasn't even allowed inside the town walls until the mid-19th century). During the recent war, most Serbs fled, created new lives for themselves elsewhere, and saw little reason to return. But some old-timers remain, and Dubrovnik's dwindling, aging Orthodox population is still served by this **church.** The candles stuck in the sand (to prevent fire outbreaks) represent prayers: The ones at knee level are for the deceased, while the ones higher up are for the living. The gentleman selling candles encourages you to buy and light one, regardless of your faith, so long as you do so with the proper intentions and reverence.

A few doors down, you'll find the **Icon Museum.** This small collection features 78 different icons (stylized paintings of saints, generally on a golden background—a common feature of Orthodox churches) from the 15th through the 19th centuries, all identified in English. In the library—crammed with old shelves holding some 12,000 books—look for the astonishingly detailed calendar, with portraits of hundreds of saints. The gallery on the ground floor, run by Michael, sells original icons and reproductions (open longer hours than museum).

Cost and Hours: Church—free but donations accepted, good 20-kn English book explains church and museum; daily May-Sept

The Serbian Orthodox Church

While the former Yugoslav destinations covered in this book are either Catholic (Slovenia and Croatia) or Muslim (Mostar), don't overlook the rich diversity of faiths in this region. Dubrovnik's Serbian Orthodox church—as well as Orthodox church in Ljubljana, Slovenia (page 756)—offer invaluable opportunities to learn about a faith that's often unfamiliar to American visitors.

As you explore an Orthodox church, keep in mind that these churches carry on the earliest traditions of the Christian faith. Orthodox and Catholic Christianity came from the same roots, so the oldest surviving early-Christian churches (such as the stave churches of Norway) have many of the same features as today's Orthodox churches.

Notice that there are no pews. Worshippers stand through the service, as a sign of respect (though some older parishioners sit on the seats along the walls). Women stand on the left side, men on the right (equal distance from the altar—to represent that all are equal before God). The Orthodox Church uses essentially the same Bible as Catholics, but it's written in the Cyrillic alphabet, which you'll see displayed around any Orthodox church. Following Old Testament Judeo-Christian tradition, the Bible is kept on the altar behind the iconostasis, the big screen in the middle of the room covered with curtains and icons (golden paintings of saints), which separates the material world from the spiritual one. At certain times during the service, the curtains or doors are opened so the congregation can see the Holy Book.

Unlike the decorations in many Catholic churches, Orthodox icons are not intended to be lifelike. Packed with intricate symbolism, and cast against a shimmering golden background, they're meant to remind viewers of the metaphysical nature of Jesus and the saints rather than of their physical form, which is considered irrelevant. You'll almost never see a statue, which is thought to overemphasize the physical world...and, to Orthodox people, feels a little too close to violating the commandment, "Thou shalt not worship graven images." Orthodox services generally involve chanting (a dialogue that goes back and forth between the priest and the congregation), and the church is filled with the evocative aroma of incense.

The incense, chanting, icons, and standing up are all intended to heighten the experience of worship. While many Catholic and Protestant services tend to be more of a theoretical and rote consideration of religious issues (come on—don't tell me you've never dozed through the sermon), Orthodox services are about creating a religious experience. Each of these elements does its part to help the worshipper transcend the physical world and join in communion with the spiritual one.

8:00-14:00 & 16:00-21:00 or 22:00, until 19:00 in shoulder season, until 17:00 in winter; short services daily at 8:30 and 19:00, longer liturgy Sun 10:00-11:00; museum—10 kn; May-Oct Mon-Sat 9:00-13:00 or possibly later, closed Sun; Nov-April Mon-Fri 9:00-13:00, closed Sat-Sun, Od Puča 8, tel. 020/323-283.

▲Rupe Granary and Ethnographic Museum (Etnografski Muzej Rupe)

This huge, 16th-century building was Dubrovnik's biggest granary, and today houses the best folk museum I've seen in Croatia. *Rupe* means "holes"—and it's worth the price of entry just to peer down into these 15 cavernous underground grain stores, designed to maintain the perfect temperature to preserve the seeds (63 degrees Fahrenheit). When the grain had to be dried, it was moved upstairs—where today you'll find a surprisingly well-presented Ethnographic Museum, with tools, jewelry, clothing, instruments, painted eggs, and other folk artifacts from Dubrovnik's colorful history. Borrow the free English information guide at the entry. The museum hides several blocks uphill from the main promenade, toward the sea (climb up Široka—the widest side street from the Stradun—which becomes Od Domina on the way to the museum).

Cost and Hours: Covered by 70-kn combo-ticket with Rector's Palace and Maritime Museum, Wed-Mon 9:00-18:00—or until 14:00 off-season, closed Tue year-round, od Rupa 3, tel. 020/323-013.

ABOVE DUBROVNIK
▲▲▲Mount Srđ

After adding Dubrovnik to his holdings, Napoleon built a fortress atop the hill behind the Old Town to keep an eye on his new sub-

jects (in 1810). During the city's 20th-century tourism heyday, a cable car was built to effortlessly whisk visitors to the top so they could enjoy the fine views from the fortress and the giant cross nearby. Then, when war broke out in the 1990s, Mount Srđ (pronounced like "surge") became a crucial link in the defense of Dubrovnik—the only high land that locals were able to hold. The fortress was shelled and damaged, and the cross and cable car were destroyed. Minefields and unexploded ordnance left the hilltop a dangerous no-man's land. But more recently, the mountain's fortunes have reversed. The landmines have been removed, and in 2010, the cable car was rebuilt

DUBROVNIK

to once again connect Dubrovnik's Old Town to its mountaintop. Visitors head to the top both for the spectacular sweeping views and to ponder the exhibits in a ragtag museum about the war.

Warning: While this area has officially been cleared of land-mines, nervous locals remind visitors that this was once a war zone. Be sure to stay on clearly defined paths and roads.

Getting There: The **cable car** is easily the best option for reaching the summit of Mount Srđ (100 kn round-trip, 60 kn one-way, kunas or credit cards only—no euros; at least 2/hour—gener-ally departing at :00 and :30 past each hour, more frequent with demand, 3-minute ride; daily from 9:00, June-Aug until 24:00, Sept until 22:00, April-May and Oct until 20:00, Feb-March and Nov until 17:00, Dec-Jan until 16:00; doesn't run in Bora wind or heavy rain, last ascent 30 minutes before closing, tel. 020/325-393, www.dubrovnikcablecar.com). The lower station is just above the Buža Gate at the top of the Old Town (from the main drag, huff all the way to the top of Boškovićeva, exit through gate, and climb uphill one block, then look right). You may see travel agencies sell-ing tickets elsewhere in town, but there's no advantage to buying them anywhere but here. The line you may see at the cable-car sta-tion is not to buy tickets, but to actually ride up. For tips on avoid-ing a long wait, see below.

If you have a **car,** you can drive up. From the high road above the Old Town, watch for the turnoff to *Bosanka*, which leads you to that village, then up to the fortress and cross—follow signs for *Srđ* (it's twisty but not far—figure a 20-minute drive from the Old Town area). If you're coming south from the Old Town, once you reach the main road above, you'll have to turn left and backtrack a bit to reach the Bosanka turnoff. For **hikers,** a switchback trail (used to supply the fortress during the siege) connects the Old Town to the mountaintop—but it's very steep and provides mini-mal shade. (If you're in great shape and it's not too hot, you could ride the cable car up, then hike down.)

Crowd-Beating Tips: The cable car has a limited capacity, and lines can get long when several cruise ships are in town. It tends to be most crowded in the morning, shortly after the cruises arrive (peaking around 11:00). If you come during this peak time, you may have to wait your turn while watching several cable cars fill and ascend. But as the day goes on, the lines tend to get shorter. I'd aim to visit later in the day—particularly if you can do it at sunset.

Mountaintop: From the top cable-car station, head up the stairs to the panoramic terrace. The bird's-eye **view** is truly spectac-ular, looking straight down to the street plan of Dubrovnik's Old Town. From this lofty perch, you can see north to the Dalmatian islands (the Elaphite archipelago, Mljet, Korčula, and beyond);

south to Montenegro; and east into Bosnia-Herzegovina. Gazing upon those looming mountains that define the border with Bosnia-Herzegovina—which, centuries ago, was also the frontier of the huge and powerful Ottoman Empire—you can appreciate how impressive it was that stubborn little Dubrovnik managed to remain independent for so much of its history.

The **cross** was always an important symbol in this very Catholic town. After it was destroyed, a temporary wooden one

was erected to encourage the townspeople who were waiting out the siege below. During a visit in 2003, Pope John Paul II blessed the rubble from the old cross; those fragments are now being used in the foundations of the city's newest churches. Nearby stands a huge red, white, and blue flagpole—the colors of the Croatian flag.

To reach the museum in the old fortress, walk behind the cable-car station along the rocky red soil.

Fort and Museum: The Napoleonic-era Fort Imperial (Trđava Imperijal) houses the **Dubrovnik During the Homeland War (1991-1995) Museum** (30 kn, various books for sale, same hours as cable car). As you enter, temporary exhibits are on the right, and the permanent exhibit is to the left. Photos, documents, and artifacts tell the story (with English descriptions) of the overarching war with Yugoslavia and how the people defended this fortress. The descriptions are too dense and tactical for casual visitors, but you'll see lots of photos and some actual items used in the fighting: primitive, rusty rifles (some dating from World War II) that the Croatians used for their improvised defense, and piles of spent mortar shells and other projectiles that Yugoslav forces hurled at the fortress and the city. Look for the wire-guided Russian rockets. After being launched at their target, the rockets would burrow into a wall, waiting to be detonated once their operators saw the opportunity for maximum destruction. The tattered Croatian flag seems soaked in local patriotism. A video screen shows breathless international news reports from the front line during the bombing. You'll also learn how a squadron of armed supply ships became besieged Dubrovnik's only tether to the outside world.

While the devastation of Dubrovnik was disturbing, this

museum could do a far better job of fostering at least an illusion of impartiality. Instead, descriptions rant one-sidedly against "Serbian and Montenegrin aggression" and the "Serbian imperialist war," and the exhibits self-righteously depict Croats exclusively as victims (which was essentially true here in Dubrovnik, but ignores Croat atrocities elsewhere). All of this serves only to trivialize and distract from the human tragedy of this war.

After seeing the exhibit, climb up a few flights of stairs to the **rooftop** for the view. The giant communications tower overhead flew the Croatian flag during the war, to inspire the besieged residents below. You might see some charred trees around here—these were claimed not by the war, but more recently, by forest fires. (Fear of landmines and other explosives prevented locals from fighting the wildfires as aggressively as they might otherwise, making these fires more dangerous than ever.)

Eating: Boasting undoubtedly the best view in Dubrovnik, **Restaurant/Snack Bar Panorama** has reasonable prices and drop-dead, astonishing views over the rooftops of the Old Town and to the most beautiful parts of three different countries. While there's glassed-in seating inside, in good weather I'd exit the building to find the outdoor terrace—the Old Town floats just under your nose (25-35-kn drinks, 55-75-kn cocktails, 80-90-kn pastas, 100-160-kn main dishes, open same hours as cable car).

Activities in Dubrovnik

Swimming and Sunbathing

If the weather's good and you've had enough of museums, spend a sunny afternoon at the beach. There are no sandy beaches on the mainland near Dubrovnik, but there are lots of suitable pebbly options, plus several concrete perches.

The easiest and most atmospheric place to take a dip is right off the **Old Town**. From the Old Port and its breakwater, uneven steps clinging to the outside of the wall lead to a series of great sunbathing and swimming coves (and even a showerhead sticking out of the town wall). Another delightful rocky beach hangs onto the outside of the Old Town's wall (at the bar called Cold Drinks "Buža" I; for more on this bar, and how to find it, see page 929).

A more convenient public beach is **Banje**, just outside the Ploče Gate, east of Old Town. While this is dominated by the EastWest nightclub, by day it's a public beach with an inviting swath of sand/

pebbles, ideal for sunbathing and wading with a spectacular backdrop of Dubrovnik's Old Town. To reach the beach, leave the Old Town through the Ploče Gate, walk about five minutes gradually uphill on the main road, then watch for the two staircases marked *EastWest* and climb down. (While the stairs nearer the Old Town passes through the EastWest café/bar, it is public access.) The café/bar itself is slick and swanky (in keeping with its nightclub's exclusive vibe), serving pricey food and drink. You can also rent a very expensive sun bed (100-200 kn, depending on level of luxury), but it's much more affordable to bring your own towel and find a comfy patch of sand. Pay showers are nearby.

My favorite hidden beach—**St. Jakob**—takes a lot longer to reach, but if you're up for the hike, it's worth it to escape the

crowds. Figure about a 25-minute walk (each way) from the Old Town. Go through the Ploče Gate at the east end of the Old Town, and walk along the street called Frana Supila as it climbs uphill above the waterfront. At Hotel Argentina, take the right (downhill) fork and keep going on Vlaha Bukovca. Eventually you'll reach the small church of St. Jakob. You'll see the beach—in a cozy protected cove—far below. Curl around behind the church and keep an eye out for stairs going down on the right. Unfortunately, these stairs are effectively unmarked, so it might take some trial and error to find the right ones. (If you reach the rusted-white gateway of the old communist-era open-air theater, you've gone too far.) Hike down the very steep stairs to the gentle cove, which has rentable chairs and a small restaurant for drinks (and a WC). Enjoy the pebbly beach and faraway views of Dubrovnik's Old Town.

Other, even more distant beaches are worth considering. If you're staying at—or visiting—the resorty zone of **Lapad Bay**, you'll find a fine beach there (near Hotel Kompas).

Locals prefer to swim on **Lokrum Island,** because there are (relatively) fewer tourists there. While there are no sandy or even pebbly beaches, there are several rocky ones, with ladders to lower yourself gingerly into the water. As the rocks here can be particularly jagged, you'll want to wear good water shoes, and beware of uneven footing (both underwater, and on your way to the ladders). For details on taking a boat to Lokrum, see page 918.

Sea Kayaking

Paddling a sleek kayak around the outside of Dubrovnik's imposing walls is a memorable experience. Several outfits in town offer half-day tours (most options 250-350 kn); popular itineraries include loops along the City Walls, to secluded beaches, and around Lokrum Island; many include a break for snorkeling, and some are timed to catch the sunset while bobbing just offshore from the City Walls. As this scene is continually evolving, look for fliers locally.

Shopping in Dubrovnik

Most souvenirs sold in Dubrovnik—from lavender sachets to plaster models of the Old Town—are pretty tacky. Whatever you buy, prices are much higher along the Stradun than on the side streets.

A classy alternative to the knickknacks is a type of local jewelry called *Konavoske puce* ("Konavle buttons"). Sold as earrings, pendants, and rings, these distinctive and fashionable filigree-style pieces consist of a sphere with several small posts. Though they're sold around town, it's least expensive to buy them on Od Puča street, which runs parallel to the Stradun two blocks toward the sea (near the Serbian Orthodox Church). The high concentration of jewelers along this lane keeps prices reasonable. You'll find the "buttons" in various sizes, in both silver (affordable) and gold (pricey).

You'll also see lots of jewelry made from red coral, which can only be legally gathered in small amounts from two small islands in northern Dalmatia. If you see a particularly large chunk of coral, it's likely imported. To know what you're getting, shop at an actual jeweler instead of a souvenir shop.

Gift-Shop Chains: Several pleasant gift shops in Dubrovnik (with additional branches throughout Dalmatia) hawk fun, if sometimes made-in-China, items. Look for these chains, which are a bit classier than the many no-name shops around town: **Aqua** sells pleasant nautical-themed gifts, blue-and-white-striped sailor shirts, and other gear. **Bonbonnière Kraš** is Croatia's leading chocolatier, selling a wide array of tasty candies. **Uje** has artisan olive oils and other boutiquey edibles.

Entertainment in Dubrovnik

MUSICAL EVENTS

Dubrovnik annually hosts a full schedule of events for its Summer Festival (July 10-Aug 25, www.dubrovnik-festival.hr), which is quickly followed by its Late Summer Festival. But the town also works hard to offer traditional music outside of festival time.

Spirited **Linđo folk-music** concerts are performed for tourists twice weekly (in good weather, likely at the Jadran summer cinema or possibly at the newly renovated Lazareti—old quarantine building—just outside the Old Town's Ploče Gate; rainy-day location is Sloboda movie theater below the Bell Tower; 100 kn, usually at 21:30, www.lindjo.hr).

The **Dubrovnik Symphony Orchestra** perform crowd-pleasing classics twice weekly in summer (and once weekly through winter)—usually at the Rector's Palace in good weather, or the Dominican Monastery in bad weather (100-250 kn, typically at 21:00, www.dso.hr).

Since Dubrovnik is trying to become a year-round destination, the city also offers tourist-oriented musical events most nights throughout the winter (often at a hotel). For the latest on any of these festivals and concerts, check the events listings in the *Best in Dubrovnik* brochure, or ask the TI.

NIGHTLIFE

Dubrovnik's Old Town is one big, romantic parade of relaxed and happy people out strolling. The main drag is brightly lit and packed

with shops, cafés, and bars, all open late. This is a fun scene. And if you walk away from the crowds or out on the port, you'll be alone with the magic of the Pearl of the Adriatic. Everything feels—and is—very safe after dark.

If you're looking for a memorable bar after dark, consider these:

▲▲▲Drinks with a View

Cold Drinks "Buža" offers, without a doubt, the most scenic spot for a drink. Perched on a cliff above the sea, clinging like a barnacle to the outside of the City Walls, this is a peaceful, shaded getaway from the bustle of the Old Town...the perfect place to watch cruise ships disappear into the horizon. *Buža* means "hole in the wall"—and that's exactly what you'll have to go through to get to this place. There are two different Bužas. My favorite is Buža II, the older and bigger of the pair. Filled with mellow tourists and bartenders

pouring wine from tiny screw-top bottles into plastic cups, Buža II comes with castaway views and Frank Sinatra ambience. This is supposedly where Bill Gates hangs out when he visits Dubrovnik. When the seats fill up—as often happens around sunset—you can order a drink at the bar and walk down the stairs to enjoy it "on the rocks"...literally (26-45-kn drinks, summer daily 9:00-into the wee hours, closed mid-Nov-Jan). Buža I, with a different owner, is more casual, plays hip rather than romantic music, and has concrete stairs leading down to a beach on the rocks below. While lacking a bit of Buža II's panache—and its shade—Buža I is often a bit less crowded, making it a viable alternative (18-45-kn drinks).

Getting There: Both Bužas are high above the bustle of the main drag, along the seaward wall. To reach them from the cathedral area, hike up the grand staircase to St. Ignatius' Church, then go left to find the lane that runs along the inside of the wall. To find the classic Buža II, head right along the lane and look for the *Cold Drinks* sign pointing to a literal hole in the wall. For the hipper Buža I, go left along the same lane, and locate the hole in the wall with the *No Toples No Nudist* graffiti.

Wine Bar

D'Vino Wine Bar, just a few steps off the main drag, has a relaxed atmosphere and a knowledgeable but unpretentious approach—making it the handiest place in Dalmatia to sample and learn about Croatian wines. Run by gregarious Aussie-Croat Sasha and his capable staff (including Anita), this cozy bar sells more than 60 wines by the glass and lots more by the bottle. The emphasis is on Croatian wines by small-production wineries, but they also have a few international vintages. Each wine is well-described on the menu, and the staff is happy to guide you through your options—just tell them what you like. Sit in the tight interior or linger at the sidewalk tables (20-80-kn glasses—most around 25-35 kn, 50-kn wine flights; light food—70-kn 2-person cheese plate, 90-kn antipasti plate; daily 10:30-late, Palmotićeva 4a, tel. 020/321-130, www.dvino.net). Sasha takes wine-lovers on all-day wine tours to the Pelješac Peninsula (for details and prices, email him at sasha@dvino.net); also ask about the organized tastings and other events in his adjacent tasting room.

Cocktails and People-Watching

The no-name square tucked behind the cathedral is jammed with tables from a half-dozen different cafés, which fill with tourists and locals each evening. Live jazz is provided nightly by **Jazz Caffè Troubadour,** but as their drink prices are outlandish (80-100-kn cocktails), most people prefer to sit at a nearby place where you can hear the music nearly as well.

Nonenina, a few steps from the cathedral on Pred Dvorom, is an outdoor lounge with big, overstuffed chairs at a fine vantage point for people-watching. They brag that they serve 180 different types of cocktails (60-80 kn, also 35-45-kn beers, daily 9:00-2:00 in the morning, shorter hours off-season, across from Rector's Palace).

The Gaffe Irish Pub, with a nice pubby interior and a small courtyard, is a rollicking spot to drain a pint and watch some rugby (Miha Pracata 4, mobile 098-196-2149, see full listing under "Eating in Dubrovnik," later).

Nightclubs

Dubrovnik has a variety of nightclubs. The streets branching off from the Stradun are lined with several options with drinks and pumping music, including **Sky Bar** (toward the water on Marojice Kaboge) and **Africa** (toward the mountain at Vetranićeva 3). Just follow the beat.

More places are near or just beyond the Ploče Gate at the east end of town. Head under the Bell Tower, then up the street past the Dominican Monastery. You'll pass the hole-in-the-wall entrance (right) for the snobby, upscale **360°** cocktail bar (www.360dubrovnik.com). Then, after crossing the bridge, look (on the left) for the entrance to **Revelin**—a dance club that fills one of the city wall's fortress towers (www.revelinclub-dubrovnik.com). Then head out and up the street until you reach Banje Beach, half of which is occupied by the **EastWest** dance club (www.ew-dubrovnik.com). Note that some of these are more exclusive and may charge admission on weekends.

MOVIES

The Old Town has a pair of movie theaters showing American blockbusters (usually in English with Croatian subtitles, unless the film's animated or for kids). The **Sloboda** cinema, right under the Bell Tower on Luža Square, has comfortable seating and a high-school auditorium vibe—nothing special. But in good weather, head for the fun outdoor **Jadran** cinema, where you can lick ice cream (B.Y.O.) while you watch a movie with a Dubrovnik-mountaintop backdrop. This is a cheap, casual, and very Croatian scene, where people smoke and chat, and the neighbors sit in their windowsills to watch the movie (most nights in summer only, shows begin shortly after sundown; in the Old Town near the Pile Gate).

DUBROVNIK

Sleeping in Dubrovnik

You basically have two options in Dubrovnik: a centrally located room in a private home *(soba)*; or a resort hotel on a distant beach, a bus ride away from the Old Town. Since Dubrovnik hotels are generally a poor value, I highly recommend giving the *sobe* a careful look. For locations, see the map on page 934.

Be warned that the Old Town is home to many popular discos. My listings are quieter than the norm, but if you're finding a place on your own, you may discover you have a late-night soundtrack—particularly if you're staying near the Stradun.

No matter where you stay, prices are much higher mid-June through mid-September, and highest in July and August. Reserve ahead for these peak times. Most accommodations prefer to list their rates in euros (and I've followed suit), but you'll pay in kunas.

SOBE (PRIVATE ROOMS): A DUBROVNIK SPECIALTY

In Dubrovnik, you'll almost always do better with a *soba* than with a hotel. Before you choose, carefully read the information on page 862. All of my favorite *sobe* are run by friendly English-speaking Croatians and are inside or within easy walking distance of the Old Town. There's a range of places, from simple and cheap rooms where you'll share a bathroom, to downright fancy places with private facilities, air-conditioning, kitchenettes, and satellite TV, where you can be as anonymous as you like. Most *sobe* don't include breakfast, so I've listed some suggestions later, under "Eating in Dubrovnik."

To search from home, you can use the regular booking sites (such as TripAdvisor.com or Booking.com)—but if you want to book one of the places I've listed here, **please book direct** (by sending them an email), which saves both you and your host money. There's no point booking through a third party, which only adds a middleman to the process. Another good place to search is www.dubrovnikapartmentsource. com, run by an American couple and offering a range of carefully selected, well-described accommodations.

In the Old Town, Above the Stradun Promenade

These are some of my favorite accommodations in Dubrovnik. All are located at the top of town, high above the Stradun, and all are good values. The first four are within a few steps of each other, along a little block dubbed

Sleep Code

Abbreviations

(6 kn = about $1, €1 = about $1.40, country code: 385, area code: 020)
S = Single, **D** = Double/Twin, **T** = Triple, **Q** = Quad, **b** =
bathroom.

Price Rankings

$$$ **Higher Priced**—Most rooms €95 or more.

  $$ **Moderately Priced**—Most rooms between €55-95.

   $ **Lower Priced**—Most rooms €55 or less.

If I've listed two sets of rates for an accommodation, I've
noted when the second rate applies (generally off-season,
Oct-May); if I've listed three sets of rates, separated by
slashes, the first is for peak season (July-Aug), the second is
for shoulder season (May-June and Sept-Oct), and the third is
for off-season (Nov-April). The dates for seasonal rates vary
by hotel.

    The modest tourist tax (about 7 kn per person, per
night) is not included in these rates. Hotels generally accept
credit cards and include breakfast in their rates, while most
sobe accept only cash and don't offer breakfast. While rates
are listed in euros, you'll pay in kunas. Everyone listed here
speaks English, and Wi-Fi is generally free. Prices can change
without notice; verify current rates online or by email. For the
best prices, always book directly with the hotel.

by some "Rickova ulica." If you don't mind the very steep hike up,
you'll find this to be a wonderful enclave of hospitality. When one
of these places is full, they work together to find space for you.
The last two listings are a few blocks over, and nearly as nice (and
equally steep). Because all of these hosts live off-site, be sure to let
them know when you'll arrive so they can let you in.

    $$ Villa Ragusa offers my favorite rooms for the price in the
Old Town. Pero and Valerija Carević have renovated a 600-year-
old house at the top of town that was damaged during the war.
The five comfortable, modern rooms come with atmospheric
old wooden beams, antique furniture, and thoughtful touches.
There are three doubles with bathrooms (including a top-floor
room with breathtaking Old Town views for no extra charge—
request when you reserve) and two singles that share a bathroom
(S-€40/€35/€25, Db-€80/€70/€50, €8 breakfast can be eaten here
or more scenically at nearby Stradun café, cash only, air-con, lots
of stairs with no elevator, Wi-Fi, Žudioska ulica 15, mobile 098-
765-634, www.villaragusadubrovnik.com, villa.ragusa@du.t-com.
hr). Pero offers his guests airport transfers for a reasonable €30,
and can drive you on an all-day excursion (such as to Montenegro
or Mostar) for €250—if you can split this cost with other guests,

Old Town Hotels & Restaurants

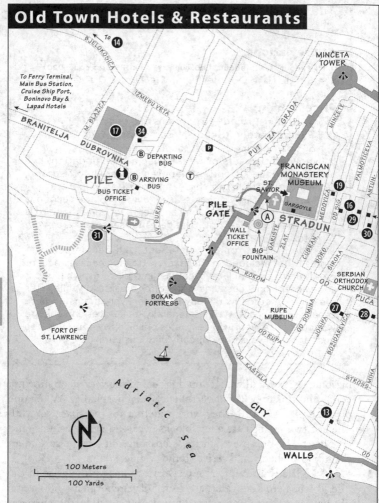

Accommodations

1. Villa Ragusa & Apts. Paviša
2. Apartments Martecchini
3. Raič Apartments
4. Apartments Kovač
5. Plaza Apartments
6. Minerva Apartments
7. Fresh Sheets B&B
8. Apartments Amoret (4)
9. Old Town Garden Cottage & Studio
10. Karmen Apartments
11. Apartments Placa
12. Renata Zijadić Rooms
13. Fresh Sheets Hostel
14. To Benussi Rooms
15. Villa Adriatica
16. Hotel Stari Grad
17. Hilton Imperial Dubrovnik
18. To Viktorija Apartments, Hotel Excelsior & Grand Villa Argentina

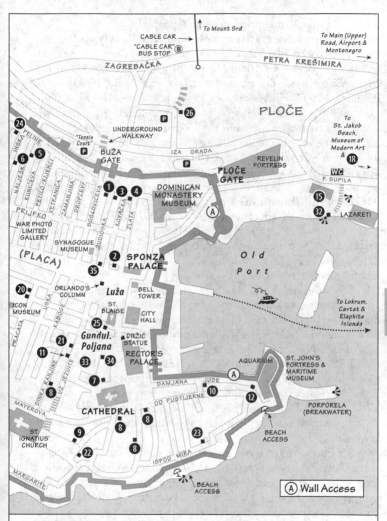

Eateries

19 Nishta Restaurant
20 Dalmatino & The Gaffe Irish Pub
21 Konoba Kamenice
22 Kopun Restaurant
23 Azur Restaurant
24 Lady Pi-Pi
25 Oliva Pizzeria
26 Tabasco Pizzeria

27 Spaghetteria Toni
28 Taj Mahal Restaurant
29 Buffet Škola
30 Dolce Vita Ice Cream
31 Orhan Restaurant
32 Komarda Restaurant
33 Produce Market
34 Konzum Groceries (2)
35 Dubrava Bistro

it's a good value (same price for up to 6 people).

$$$ Apartments Paviša, next door to Villa Ragusa and run by Pero and Davorka Paviša, has three good, older-feeling rooms at the top of the Old Town (Db-€100/€70-80/€50, book direct by email for these prices, no breakfast, cash only, air-con, lots of stairs, Wi-Fi, Žudioska ulica 19, mobile 098-427-399 or 098-175-2342, www.apartmentspavisa.com, pero.pavisa@gmail.com). They have two more rooms in the **Viktorija** neighborhood, about a 20-minute mostly uphill walk east of the Old Town. While it's a long-but-scenic walk into town, the views from these apartments are spectacular (same prices as in-town rooms, Frana Supila 59, bus stop nearby). Pero and Davorka also manage **Apartments Martecchini,** three units a bit closer to the main drag in the Old Town (small apartment-€100/€70-80/€50, bigger apartment-€120/€80-90/€60, biggest apartment-€130/€90-100/€60, prices depend on size and views, book direct by email for these prices, no breakfast, cash only, air-con, free Wi-Fi, www.apartmentsmartecchini.com).

$$ Ivana and Anita Raič are sisters renting three apartments with kitchenettes and modern, stylish flourishes (Db-€90/€70-80/€50, no breakfast, cash only, air-con, Wi-Fi, Žudioska ulica 16, Ivana's mobile 098-996-0858, Anita's mobile 099-592-1568, www.apartments-raic.com, ivanaraic@gmail.com).

$$$ Apartments Kovač, a lesser value but decent, has two simple, older apartments just inside the upper wall (Db-€100/€90/€70, extra person-€10, no breakfast, cash only, air-con, Wi-Fi, Peline 1, mobile 098-975-4284, www.apartmentskovac-dubrovnik.com, info@apartmentskovac-dubrovnik.com, Ana and Zvonko).

$$ Plaza Apartments, run by Lidija and Maro Matić, rents three clean, well-appointed, modern apartments on a plant-filled lane—the steepest and most appealing stretch of stairs leading up from the Stradun. Lidija's sweet personality is reflected in the cheerful rooms, which are a fine value if you don't mind the hike (Db-€90/€80/€70, big two-story seaview apartment-€110/€85/€75, cheaper Nov-April, these prices for Rick Steves readers, no breakfast, cash only, air-con, Wi-Fi, all apartments have kitchenettes and laundry machines, climb the stairs past Dolce Vita gelato shop to Nalješkovićeva 22, tel. 020/321-493, mobile 091-517-7048, www.apartmentsplaza.com.hr, lidydu@yahoo.com).

$$ Minerva Apartments has two cozy ground-floor units near the top of a similar lane, in the home of Dubravka Vidosavljević-Vučić (Db-€80/€75/€65, cheaper Nov-April, cash only, no breakfast, air-con, Wi-Fi, laundry machine, Antuninska 14, mobile 091-252-9677, duvivu@gmail.com).

In the Old Town, near the Cathedral and St. John's Fort

The following places are south of the Stradun, mostly clustering around the cathedral and St. John's Fort, at the end of the Old Port. To find the Karmen and Zijadić apartments from the cathedral, walk toward the big fort tower along the inside of the wall (follow signs for *akvarji*); for the Old Town Garden Cottage and Studio, climb up the grand staircase to the Jesuit St. Ignatius Church.

$$$ Fresh Sheets B&B, well-run by Canadian-Croatian couple Jon and Sanja, rents six bright, stylish, modern rooms in an ideally located building—next door to the cathedral and squeezed between two of Dubrovnik's most happening squares. Three of the rooms have shared bathrooms, and all have views over interesting squares and landmarks in the heart of the Old Town. While pricey, the hospitality, well-appointed rooms, and great location could make it worthwhile (D-€138-168, Db-€148-198, family suite-€308-338, price depends on season, for best prices book direct by email, air-con, Wi-Fi, Bunićeva Poljana 6, tel. 091-896-7509, www.freshsheetsbedandbreakfast.com, beds@igotfresh.com).

$$$ Apartments Amoret, run by Branka Dabrović and her husband Ivica, are in all the guidebooks. The spendy but comfortable apartments, with furnishings that are a step up from the norm, are in four different buildings: two over Amoret Restaurant in front of the cathedral (at Restičeva 2); nine more sharing an inviting terrace on a quiet, untouristy lane a few blocks east (at Dinka Ranjine 5); and four more nearby (at Ilije Sarake 4 and Gradičeva 1). All four classes of apartments are comparably good; in every case, the furnishings are a tasteful mix of traditional and modern. Since Branka and Ivica don't live on-site, arrange a meeting time and place when you reserve ("regular" apartments-€100/€90/€80; "standard" apartments-€120/€110/€100; "superb" apartments-€140/€130/€110; "royal" apartments for up to 4-€160/€140/€120, extra person-€20; cheaper Nov-April, 30 percent more for 1-night stays, 20 percent more for 2-night stays, 10 percent more for 3-night stays, no breakfast, cash only, air-con, Wi-Fi, mobile 091-530-4910, tel. 020/324-005, www.dubrovnik-amoret.com, amoret-dubrovnik@hotmail.com).

$$ Old Town Garden Cottage and Studio, conscientiously run by Roberto and his mother Marija (also recommended tour guides—see page 894), is unique and a top value. Hiding off of the big square in front of the Jesuit St. Ignatius Church is a very rare private garden—a peaceful oasis smack-dab in the heart of the bustling city. Here you'll find two options: A cozy freestanding cottage that sleeps up to four (Db-€90/€80/€70, extra bed-€10);

and an elegant, bright, spacious artistically appointed studio apartment (€10 more). Each comes with its own outdoor space, where you're welcome to sit and relax, and even order food from the neighboring restaurant (the recommended Kopun)...very cool, particularly in a city with virtually no green space (€20 more for 1-night stay, cash only, air-con, kitchenette, Wi-Fi, mobile 091-541-6637, bobdel70@yahoo.com). Robert and Marija also plan to renovate a roomy two-bedroom apartment (sans private garden)—ask them for details.

$$$ **Karmen Apartments** are well-run by a Brit named Marc and his Croatian wife Silva, who offer four welcoming apartments just inside the big fort. While a bit pricey, the apartments are big, well-equipped, and homey-feeling, each with a bathroom and kitchen. The decor is eclectic but tasteful, drawing from Marc and Silva's extensive art collection; the stairwell has a virtual mini-museum of historic Dubrovnik maps and documents (smaller apartment-€95/€75/€55, mid-sized apartment-€145/€110/€85, bigger apartment-€175/€120/€100, 5 percent discount for Rick Steves readers who book direct via email, usually 3-night minimum, no breakfast, cash only, air-con, Wi-Fi, near the aquarium at Bandureva 1, tel. 020/323-433, mobile 098-619-282, www.karmendu.com, marc.van-bloemen@du.t-com.hr).

$$$ **Apartments Placa** (PLAH-tsah; not to be confused with Plaza Apartments, described earlier) is run by Tonči (TOHN-chee). He rents three apartments with some antique furnishings and some modern, overlooking the market square in the heart of the Old Town. You might get some early-morning noise from the market set-up, but the double-paned windows help, and the location is wonderfully central. Since Tonči lives elsewhere, clearly communicate your arrival time (Db-€100/€90/€80, cheaper Nov-April, no breakfast, cash only, no extra charge for 1- or 2-night stays, several flights of stairs, air-con, Wi-Fi, Gundulićeva poljana 5, mobile 091-721-9202, www.dubrovnik-online.com/apartments_placa, tonci.korculanin@du.t-com.hr).

$$ **Renata Zijadić,** a friendly mom who speaks good English, offers three well-located rooms with slanting floors. One modern, sleek apartment enjoys grand views over the Old Port (€130/€100); a smaller, older, simpler double features an ornate old cabinet and no views (Db-€65/€55); and a top-floor apartment comes with low ceilings and fine vistas (€95/€85; second price is for June and Sept, cheaper Oct-May, no extra charge for 1- or 2-night stays, no breakfast, cash only, air-con, Wi-Fi; follow signs for wall access and walk up the steps marked *ulica Stajeva* going over the street to find Stajeva 1; tel. 020/323-623, www.dubrovnik-online.com/house_renata, renatadubrovnik@yahoo.com).

$ Fresh Sheets, a bright, stylish, and appealingly funky hostel run by fun-loving Jon and Sanja (who also run the recommended Fresh Sheets B&B), is your best hostel option in the Old Town. The 18 bunks (two 6-bed dorms, one 4-bed dorm, and a double room) sit above a tight but enjoyable common area. Located at the very top of Dubrovnik just inside the City Walls, it's a steep hike up from the main drag, but worth it if you enjoy youthful backpacker bonding (€22-36/bunk in a dorm, €28-38/person in a private room, likely closed Nov-March, free breakfast, guest computer and Wi-Fi, lockers, kitchenette, Svetog Šimuna 15, mobile 091-799-2086, www.freshsheetshostel.com, beds@igotfrcsh.com).

Outside Pile Gate, Just West of the Old Town

While the area in front of the Pile Gate is a congested tourist hub, one of my favorite Dubrovnik lodgings sits high on the hill above the chaos, offering a warm welcome to travelers hardy enough to make the hike.

$$$ Jadranka and Milan Benussi rent two apartments in a quiet, traffic-free neighborhood. Their delightful stony-chic home, complete with a leafy terrace, is a steep 10-minute hike above the Old Town—close enough to be convenient, but far enough to take you away from the bustle and into a calm residential zone. Jadranka speaks good English, enjoys visiting with her guests, and gives her place a modern Croatian class unusual for a *soba*. This is one of your most comfortable home bases in Dubrovnik, if you don't mind the walk (small apartment-€110/€105/€100, big apartment with balcony-€120/€115/€110, cheaper Nov-April, 30 percent extra for 1-night stays, no breakfast, cash only, air-con, kitchenettes, Wi-Fi, Miha Klaića 10, tel. 020/429-339, mobile 098-928-1300, www.dubrovnik-benussi.com, jadranka@dubrovnik-benussi.com). To find the Benussis, go to the big Hilton Hotel just outside the Pile Gate (across from the TI). Walk up the little stepped lane called Marijana Blažića at the upper-left corner of the Hilton cul-de-sac. When that lane dead-ends, go left up ulica Don Iva Bjelokosića (more steps) until you see a little church on the left. The Benussis' house is just before this church.

Beyond the Ploče Gate, East of the Old Town

To reach these options, you'll go through the Ploče Gate and walk along the road stretching east from the Old Town (with fine views back on the Old Port). This area is shared by giant waterfront luxury hotels and residential areas, so it has a bit less character than the Old Town listings (which I prefer).

$$$ Apartments Paviša, described on page 936, has two fine apartments in the Viktorija neighborhood about a 20-minute walk or short bus ride from town.

$$$ Villa Adriatica is overpriced, but has one of the finest views in Dubrovnik. Its four old-fashioned rooms sit above a travel agency and a family home just outside the Ploče Gate, a few steps from the Old Town. The rooms are antique-furnished, but have modern bathrooms, TVs, and air-conditioning. While impersonal and a lesser value than my other listings, it could be worth it just for the huge, shared terrace with priceless Old Port views, plus a common living room and kitchen furnished with museum-piece antiques. Teo manages the rooms; ask for him at the Perla Adriatic travel agency, just outside the Ploče Gate (Db-€110-120/€100-110/€80-90, cheaper Nov-April, price depends on size and view, no breakfast, cash only, air-con, Wi-Fi in some areas, Frana Supila 4, mobile 098-334-500, tel. 020/411-962, www.villa-adriatica.net, booking@villa-adriatica.net, Tomšić family).

HOTELS

If you must stay in a hotel, you have only a few good options. There are just two hotels inside the City Walls—and one of them charges $500 a night (Pucić Palace, www.thepucicpalace.com). Any big, resort-style hotel within walking distance of the Old Town will run you at least €200. These inflated prices drive most visitors to Boninovo Bay or the Lapad Peninsula, a bus ride west of the Old Town. In the mass-tourism tradition, many European visitors choose to take the half-board option at their hotel (i.e., dinner in the hotel restaurant). This can be convenient and a good value, but the Old Town is a much more atmospheric place to dine.

In and near the Old Town

$$$ Hotel Stari Grad knows it's the only real hotel option inside the Old Town—and charges accordingly. It has eight extremely stylish rooms a half-block off the Old Town's main drag. The rooftop terrace enjoys an amazing view over orange tiles. This place books up fast, so reserve early (Sb-€220/€160/€120, Db-€290/€230/€168, no extra charge for 1- or 2-night stays, includes breakfast, air-con, lots of stairs with no elevator, Wi-Fi, Od Sigurate 4, tel. 020/322-244, www.hotelstarigrad.com, info@hotelstarigrad.com).

$$$ Hilton Imperial Dubrovnik, sitting regally just outside the Pile Gate, is the closest big hotel to the Old Town. This grand 19th-century building was recently overhauled to create 147 plush rooms. If you want predictable Hilton comfort at outlandish prices a short walk from the Old Town, this is the place (Db-€250-300, less off-season, €60 extra for sea view, €70 extra for balcony but no view, €130 extra for balcony and view, most rates include breakfast, air-con, elevator, free Wi-Fi in lobby, pay Wi-Fi in rooms, parking-€27/night, Marijana Blažića 2, tel. 020/320-320,www.hilton.

com, sales.dubrovnik@hilton.com).

$$$ Adriatic Luxury Hotels is a chain with several plush hotels near Dubrovnik. Location-wise, the most enticing are **Hotel Excelsior** (Frana Supila 12) and **Grand Villa Argentina** (Frana Supila 14)—which are a scenic 10-minute walk outside the Ploče Gate, east of the Old Town—as well as the Hotel Bellevue (described in the next section). For top-of-the-top luxury lodgings without regard for the price tag, browse their options at www.adriaticluxuryhotels.com (figure a peak-season rack rate of Db-€500-600—but you'll rarely pay that much).

Near Boninovo Bay

Boninovo Bay (boh-NEE-noh-voh) is your best bet for an affordable and well-located hotel. Above this bay are Dubrovnik's only three-star hotels within walking distance of the Old Town (not to mention the city's only official youth hostel). These places offer slightly better prices and closer proximity to the Old Town than the farther-out Lapad Bay resorts. They're on or near the water, but don't have views of the Old Town (which is around the bend). Boninovo Bay is an uphill 20-minute walk or five-minute bus ride from the Old Town (straight up Branitelja Dubrovnika). Once you're comfortable with the buses, the location is great: Any bus that leaves the Pile Gate stops first at Boninovo Bay. You'll see the bay on your left as you climb the hill, then get off at the stop after the traffic light (or stay on bus #4, which stops even closer to the hotels). To reach the hotels from the Boninovo bus stop, go up Pera Čingrije (the busy road running along the top of the cliff overlooking the sea). There's a super little bakery, Pekarnica Klas, on the right (across the street from Hotel Bellevue).

$$$ Hotel Bellevue has a striking location, with its back against the cliff rising up from Boninovo Bay and an elevator plunging directly to its own pebbly beach. Its 91 top-notch rooms—all but two with sea views, many with balconies—offer upscale wood-grain elegance (standard Db-generally €250/€220, less Nov-April, very flexible rates, €50 more for balcony, air-con, elevator, guest computer and Wi-Fi, Pera Čingrije 7, tel. 020/330-000, www.hotel-bellevue.hr, welcome@hotel-bellevue.hr).

$$$ Hotel R, a homey enclave with just 10 rooms, feels friendlier and less greedy than all the big resort hotels. Well-run by the Rešetar family, it's a decent small-hotel value (Sb-€90/€75/€60, Db-€140/€115/€90, closed Nov-Easter, 10 percent more for balcony, half-board-€13, air-con, Wi-Fi, just beyond the big Hotel Lero at Iva Vojnovića 16, tel. 020/333-200, www.hotel-r.hr, helpdesk@hotel-r.hr).

$$$ Hotel Lero, 250 yards up the street from the bus stop, has 155 recently renovated rooms and a fine outdoor pool. Choose between so-so sea views with some road noise, or quieter back rooms (soft rates, but generally Sb-€110/€85, Db-€140/€106, cheaper mid-Oct-April; in busy times, you may be quoted more than these rates—try asking for a better deal; "executive" rooms with balcony not worth the extra €30/person, air-con, elevator, pay guest computer, Wi-Fi, half-board-€10, wellness and fitness center, Iva Vojnovića 14, tel. 020/341-333, www.hotel-lero.hr, sales@hotel-lero.hr).

$ Dubrovnik's official **Youth Hostel** is quiet, modern, and well-run by proud manager Laura. It's institutional, with 82 beds in 19 fresh, woody dorms and few extra hostel amenities (bunk in 4- to 6-bed dorm-€16-21 depending on season, €1.50 more for non-members, includes sheets, includes breakfast, air-con in restaurant and halls but not in rooms, free guest computer and Wi-Fi; reception open daily May-Oct 7:00-4:00 in the morning, Nov-April 8:00-14:00 & 18:00-20:00; 2:00 a.m. curfew in summer, none in winter; up the steps at ulica bana Jelačića 15-17 to ulica Vinka Sagrestana 3, tel. 020/423-241, www.hfhs.hr, dubrovnik@hfhs.hr). From the Boninovo bus stop, go down Pera Čingrije toward Hotel Bellevue, but take the first right uphill onto ulica bana Jelačića and look for signs up to the hostel on your left, on ulica Vinka Sagrestana. Several houses nearby rent rooms to those who prefer a double...and pick off would-be hostelers as they approach.

Eating in Dubrovnik

Dubrovnik disappoints diners with high prices, surly service, and mediocre quality. With the constant influx of deep-pocketed tour-ists corrupting greedy restau-rateurs, places here tend to go downhill faster than a game of marbles on the *Titanic*. Promising new restaurants open all the time, but most quickly fade, and what's great one year can be miserable the next. Therefore, lower your expectations, take my suggestions

with a grain of salt, and ask around locally for what's good this month. Don't bother looking for a "local" favorite anywhere near the Old Town—people who live here eat out at restaurants in the 'burbs. The good news is that it's atmospheric. Anywhere you dine, breezy outdoor seating is a no-brainer, and scrawny, adorable kit-tens beg for table scraps. In general, seafood restaurants are good only at seafood; if you want pasta, go to a pasta place.

IN THE OLD TOWN

Nishta ("Nothing"), featuring a short menu of delicious vegetarian fusion cuisine with Asian flair, offers a welcome change of pace from the Dalmatian seafood-pasta-pizza rut. Busy Swiss owner/chef Gildas cooks, while his wife Ruža and their staff cheerfully serve a steady stream of return diners. This tiny place—which has been a reliable and affordable crowd-pleaser for years—has just a few cramped indoor and outdoor tables. Even if you're not a vegetarian, it's worth a visit; reserve the day ahead in peak season (35-45-kn starters, 65-85 kn main courses, Mon-Sat 11:30-22:00, closed Sun and Jan-Feb, on the restaurant clogged Prijeko street—near the Pile Gate end of the street, tel. 020/322-088).

Dalmatino offers some of the best traditional Dalmatian cooking in the city, combined with a few modern twists. This is quality food and attentive service at prices that won't blow your budget. South African-Croatian owner Robert prides himself on cooking each dish to order; while this may take a few minutes longer, you can taste the results. While there are only a few outdoor tables tucked along the alley, there's a spacious, classy-but-not-stuffy dining room (50-160-kn pastas, 80-160-kn main dishes, daily 11:00-23:00, Miha Pracata 6, tel. 020/323-070, www.dalmatino-dubrovnik.com). Don't confuse Dalmatino's tables with its neighbors'.

On the Market Square: The square called Gundulićeva poljana, tucked two short blocks from the Stradun, is filled with outdoor tables. **Konoba Kamenice,** a no-frills fish restaurant, is a local institution offering inexpensive, fresh, and good meals on a charming market square, as central as can be in the Old Town. On the limited menu, the seafood dishes are excellent (try their octopus salad, even if you don't think you like octopus), while the few non-seafood dishes are uninspired. Some of the waitstaff are notorious for their playfully brusque service, but loyal patrons happily put up with it. Arrive early, or you'll have to wait (45-75-kn main courses, daily 8:00-23:00, until 22:00 off-season, Gundulićeva poljana 8, tel. 020/323-682).

Kopun, with picturesque seating on the big square in front of the Jesuit St. Ignatius Church, serves up regional specialties not only from Dubrovnik, but from elsewhere in Croatia—all well-explained in the menu. Several dishes make use of the restaurant's namesake, *kopun*—a rooster that's castrated young and plumps up. While a bit pricey and new to the scene, this place is off to a promising start (60-130-kn pastas and starters, 80-160-kn main courses, daily 11:00-23:00, Poljana Ruđera Boškovića 7, tel. 020/323-969, www.restaurantkopun.com).

Azur, tucked high inside the City Walls (near the two Buža cocktail bars), offers relief to travelers needing a break from the typical Croation menu. The sort-of-Asian-fusion menu might not fly in big cosmopolitan cities, but here on the Croatian coast, appreciative international diners cling to it like a sesame-oil life preserver (45-75-kn starters and snacks, 90-150-kn main dishes, daily 11:00-24:00, Pobijana 10, tel. 020/324-806).

Lady Pi-Pi, named for a comical, anatomically correct, and slightly off-putting statue out front, sits high above town just inside the wall. The food, prepared on an open grill, is just an excuse to sit out on their vine-covered terrace, with several tables overlooking the rooftops of Dubrovnik. Come early or be prepared to line up (70-75-kn pastas, 65-150-kn main dishes, daily May-Sept 9:00-24:00, closed Oct-April and in bad weather, Peline b.b., tel. 020/321-288).

Pizza: Dubrovnik seems to have a pizzeria on every corner. Little separates the various options—just look for a menu and outdoor seating option that appeals to you. **Oliva Pizzeria,** just behind St. Blaise's Church, puts out consistently good food (40-70-kn pizzas, Lučarica 5, daily 10:00-24:00, tel. 020/324-594; don't mistake this for their sister restaurant next door, Oliva Gourmet, with a pricier non-pizza menu). Around the side is a handy take-out window for a bite on the go. Close to the Old Town, but just far away to be frequented mostly by locals, **Tabasco Pizzeria** is tucked at the corner of the parking lot beneath the cable-car station. Unpretentious and affordable, this is the place to come if the pizza is more important than the setting—though the outdoor terrace does have views of the City Walls...over a sea of parked cars (40-50-kn pizzas, 70-85-kn "jumbo" pizzas, daily 9:00-23:00, Hvarska 48A, tel. 020/429-595).

Pasta: **Spaghetteria Toni** is popular with natives and tourists. While nothing fancy, it offers good pastas at reasonable prices. Choose between the cozy 10-table interior or the long alley filled with outdoor tables (50-95-kn pastas, 55-70-kn salads, daily in summer 11:00-23:00, closed Sun in winter, closed Jan, Nikole Božidarevića 14, tel. 020/323-134).

Bosnian Cuisine: For a break from Croatian fare, try the grilled meats and other tasty Bosnian dishes at the misnamed **Taj Mahal.** Though the service can be lacking, the menu offers an enticing taste of the Turkish-flavored land to the east. Choose between the tight interior, which feels like a Bosnian tea house, or tables out on the alley (50-65-kn salads, 60-145-kn main courses, daily 10:00-24:00, Nikole Gučetića 2, tel. 020/323-221). For a primer on Bosnian food, see the "Balkan Flavors" sidebar on page 1140.

Sandwiches: **Buffet Škola** is a rare bit of pre-glitz Dubrovnik just a few steps off the Stradun, serving take-away or sit-down sandwiches on homemade bread. Squeeze into the hole-in-the-wall interior, or sit at one of the outdoor tables (25-30 kn, 60-80-kn ham and cheese boards, daily 8:00-22:00 or 23:00, Antuninska 1, tel. 020/321-096).

Ice Cream: Dubrovnik has lots of great *sladoled*, but locals swear by the stuff at **Dolce Vita.** In addition to good ice cream, they have tasty crêpes (daily 9:00-24:00, a half-block off the Stradun at Nalješkovićeva 1A, tel. 020/321-666).

The Old Town's "Restaurant Row," Prijeko Street: The street called Prijeko, a block toward the mainland from the Stradun promenade, is lined with outdoor, tourist-oriented eateries—each one with a huckster out front trying to lure in diners. (Many of them aggressively try to snare passersby down on the Stradun, as well.) Don't be sucked into this vortex of bad food at outlandish prices. The only place worth seeking out here is Nishta (described earlier); the rest are virtually guaranteed to disappoint. Still, it can be fun to take a stroll along here—the atmosphere is lively, and the sales pitches are entertainingly desperate.

JUST OUTSIDE THE OLD TOWN, WITH A VIEW

Orhan Restaurant, overlooking the tranquil cove at the Pile neighborhood outside the Old Town, feels just beyond the tourist crush. It features disinterested service and unremarkable food, but great views on a large terrace (reserve a seat here in advance). Watch the people walk the Old Town walls across the cove. This is a handy spot for a scenic breakfast (70-115-kn pastas, 95-160-kn main courses, daily 8:00-23:00, cash only, Od Tabakarije 1, tel. 020/414-183, www.restaurant-orhan.com).

Komarda serves up forgettable food on a memorably romantic terrace, with views of Dubrovnik's walls and Old Port. Tables are scattered around a tranquil garden just above the sea and a concrete beach. As there's no point eating here unless you have a good view, consider dropping by early in the day to pick out and reserve the table of your choice for dinner (75-90-kn pastas, 90-150-kn main courses, daily 7:00-2:00 in the morning, reservations essential in summer, mobile 098-428-239, www.komarda.hr). To find it, exit the Old Town through the Ploče Gate (east). After walking through the final fortification, you'll reach a block of travel agencies. Once you pass these, look for the stairs down to Komarda, on the right.

PICNIC TIPS

Dubrovnik's lack of great restaurant options makes it a perfect place to picnic. You can shop for fresh fruits and veggies at the open-air produce market (each morning near the cathedral, on the square called Gundulićeva Poljana). Supplement your picnic with grub from the cheap **Konzum grocery store** (one location on the market square near the produce-vendors: Mon-Sat 7:00-20:00,

Sun 7:00-13:00; another near the bus stop just outside Pile Gate: Mon-Sat 7:00-20:00, Sun 8:00-13:00). Good picnic spots include the shaded benches overlooking the Old Port; the Porporela breakwater (beyond the Old Port and fort—comes with a swimming area, sunny no-shade benches, and views of Lokrum Island); and the green, welcoming park in what was the moat just under the Pile Gate entry to the Old Town.

BREAKFAST

If you're sleeping in a *soba*, you'll likely be on your own for breakfast. Fortunately, you have plenty of cafés and pastry shops to choose from, and your host probably has a favorite she can recommend. In the Old Town, **Dubrava Bistro**—which locals call "Snack Bar"—has great views and fine outdoor seating at the most colorful end of the Stradun. While the ham resembles Spam and the continental breakfast is paltry, you can't beat the real estate. Locals who hang out here—catching up with their friends as they stroll by—call this their low-tech version of "Facebook" (basic 38-46-kn egg dishes, 23-kn caffè lattes; you'll pay 25 percent less if you sit inside—but then there's no point eating here; daily 8:00-24:00, Placa 6, tel. 020/321-229). For better food in a less atmospheric setting, **The Gaffe Irish Pub** has a good menu of breakfast options (36-45 kn, served daily 9:00-11:00, Miha Pracata 4, tel. 020/640-152). In the Pile neighborhood, I like **Restaurant Orhan,** right on the cove (described earlier; 50 kn for omelet or continental breakfast, served daily 8:00-11:00). Some of the other restaurants listed in this section (including **Konoba Kamenice**) also serve breakfast. Not many places serve before 9:00 or 10:00; if you'll be departing early, stock up on groceries the night before.

Dubrovnik Connections

While ferries and catamarans have traditionally used Dubrovnik's Port Gruž (a bus ride away from the Old Town), a planned redevelopment could relocate some or all boats to the far end of the port, under the big bridge. Ask locally for the latest.

By Catamaran: Two handy, speedy catamarans connect Dubrovnik to points north. Schedule specifics and the procedure for buying tickets have been notoriously changeable in recent years—confirm all details online, or ask at the TI. Of the two options, the *Krilo* catamaran—which typically leaves Dubrovnik in the late afternoon—offers more departures (daily June-Sept, 3-4/week May and Oct) and more destinations: It stops at Mljet National Park (1.25 hours), Korčula (2 hours), Hvar (3 hours), and Split (4 hours). You can buy *Krilo* tickets at www.krilo.hr; book a few days ahead, if possible. A different catamaran, called *Nona Ana*, has a shorter season (June-Sept) and doesn't go as far north. Every day, *Nona Ana* stops at two ports on Mljet Island, near the national park: Sobra (1 hour) and Polače (1.5 hours). In the peak months of July and August, it sometimes continues to Korčula (4/week, 2.5 hours). In the winter (Oct-May), the boat goes only to Šipan (one of the Elaphite Islands near Dubrovnik) and Sobra (on Mljet). Tickets for the *Nona Ana*—which can sell out, especially in peak season—are sold at the kiosk next to the boat at Port Gruž. Try to be at the ticket window when it opens, one hour before departure, or even earlier in peak season. Confirm schedules at www.gv-line.hr.

By Bus to: Split (at least hourly, typically at the top of the hour, less off-season, 3.5-5 hours), **Korčula** (summer: 2/day at 9:00 and 15:00; off-season: Mon-Sat 1/day at 15:00, Sun 2/day at 15:00 and 18:00; 3.5 hours; also consider the shuttle-bus service described next), **Rijeka** (4/day, 12.5-13 hours), **Zagreb** (10/day including some overnight options, 10 hours), **Kotor** in Montenegro (3/day in summer, 2/day in winter, 2.5 hours), **Mostar** (3/day, 4-5 hours), **Sarajevo** (4/day in summer, 2/day in winter, 5-6.5 hours; includes a night bus in summer only at 22:30), **Pula** and **Rovinj** (1/day overnight departing at 15:30, 15 hours to Pula, 16 hours to Rovinj). As usual, schedules are subject to change—confirm locally before making the trip to the bus station. For bus information, check www.libertasdubrovnik.com or call 060-305-070 (a pricey toll line, but worth it).

By Shuttle Bus to Korčula: Korčula-based Korkyra Info Travel Agency runs a handy door-to-door shuttle service from your Dubrovnik accommodations to Korčula; reserve ahead (typically departs at 14:00 and at 17:00, daily May-Sept, by request only off-season, may stop briefly in Ston if you want, 2 hours, 150 kn one-way, mobile 091-571-4355, www.korkyra.info, info@korkyra.info). Korkyra Info can also arrange for a private transfer, including stops (such as wine-tastings and a quick visit to Ston; €140 for up to 8 people).

By Plane: To quickly connect remote Dubrovnik with the rest of your trip, consider a cheap flight. For information on Dubrovnik's airport, see "Arrival in Dubrovnik—By Plane," earlier.

Can I Get to Greece from Dubrovnik? Your best bet is to fly (though there are no direct flights, aside from the occasional charter flight from Dubrovnik to Athens—you'll generally have to transfer elsewhere in Europe). Even though Croatia and Greece are nearly neighbors, no direct boats connect them, and the overland connection is extremely long and rugged.

DUBROVNIK

What About Italy? Flying is the easiest option, though there are only a few direct flights (on Croatia Airlines to Rome or Venice; or on easyJet to Rome or Milan). You can take a direct night boat from Dubrovnik to Bari, or head to Split for more boat connections (for more on all of these boats, see page 992). The overland connection is overly long (figure 5 hours to Split, then 5 hours to Zagreb, then 7 hours to Venice).

DUBROVNIK

SPLIT

Dubrovnik is the darling of the Dalmatian Coast, but Split (pronounced as it's spelled) is Croatia's "second city" (after Zagreb), bustling with 178,000 people. If you've been hopping along the coast, landing in urban Split feels like a return to civilization. While most Dalmatian coastal towns seem made for tourists, Split is real and vibrant—a shipbuilding city with ugly sprawl surrounding an atmospheric Old Town, which teems with Croatians living life to the fullest.

Though today's Split throbs to a modern, youthful beat, its history goes way back—all the way to the Roman Empire. Along with all the trappings of a modern city, Split has some of the best Roman ruins this side of Italy. In the fourth century A.D., the Roman Emperor Diocletian (245-313) wanted to retire in his native Dalmatia, so he built a huge palace here. Eventually, the palace was abandoned. Then locals, fleeing seventh-century Slavic invaders, moved in and made themselves at home, and a medieval town sprouted from the rubble of the old palace. In the 15th century, the Venetians took over the Dalmatian Coast. They developed and fortified Split, slathering the city with a new layer of Gothic-Renaissance architecture.

But even as Split grew, the nucleus remained the ruins of Diocletian's Palace. To this day, 2,000 people live or work inside the former palace walls. A maze of narrow alleys is home to fashionable boutiques and galleries, wonderfully atmospheric cafés, and Roman artifacts around every corner.

Today's Split has a split personality, as it struggles to decide how it fits into Croatia's tourist-mecca image: Is it a no-nonsense, metropolitan transit point; an impressive destination in its own

Split Essentials

English	Croatian	Pronounced
Old Town	*Stari Grad*	STAH-ree grahd
City Harbor	*Gradska Luka*	GRAHD-skah LOO-kah
Harborfront promenade	*Riva*	REE-vah
Peristyle (old Roman square)	*Peristil*	PEH-ree-steel
Soccer team	*Hajduk*	HIGH-dook
Local sculptor	*Ivan Meštrović*	EE-vahn MESH-troh-veech
Adriatic Sea	*Jadran*	YAH-drahn

right, with sights to rival Dubrovnik's—or both? While largely lacking Dubrovnik's over-the-top romance, Split settles for being nobody's "second-best." It is its own city—an antidote to all that's quaint and cutesy in Dalmatia.

PLANNING YOUR TIME

Split is southern Croatia's hub for bus, boat, train, and flight connections to other destinations in the country and abroad. This means that many visitors stop in Split only long enough to change boats. But the city is the perfect real-life contrast to the lazy, prettified Dalmatian beach resorts—it deserves at least a full day. Begin by strolling Diocletian's Palace, then take a coffee break along the Riva promenade or have lunch in the Old Town. After lunch, browse the shops or visit a couple of Split's museums (the Meštrović Gallery, which is a long walk or short bus or taxi ride from the Old Town, is tops). Promenading along the Riva with the natives is *the* evening activity, while nursing a drink at an atmospheric open-air café is a close second.

Orientation to Split

Split sprawls, but almost everything of interest to travelers is around the City Harbor (Gradska Luka). At the top of this harbor is the Old Town (Stari Grad). Between the Old Town and the sea is the Riva, a waterfront pedestrian promenade lined with cafés and shaded by palm trees. The main ferry terminal (Trajektni Terminal) juts into the harbor from the east side. Along the harborfront embankment between the ferry terminal and the Old

Split Overview

To Airport & Trogir

HRVATSKE MORNARICE

To Bene Beach

SUBURBAN BUS STATION

KAŠTELANSKA

ARCHAEOLOGICAL MUSEUM

ZRINSKO FRANKOPANSKA

DOMOVINSKOG RATA

LOVREBEK

MATOŠEVA

MAZURANIĆEVO ŠET.

MANDALINSKA PUT

VUKOVARSKA

See detail maps

MARJAN PENINSULA

(TUNNEL)

MATEJUŠKA (FISHERMEN'S PORT)

VAROŠ

OLD TOWN

MARMONT

DIOCLETIAN'S PALACE

KRIŽEVA

ZOO

SENJSKA

LUČAC

ZVONIMIRA

MARASOVIĆEVA

KIVA

MEŠTROVIĆ GALLERY

MIHANOVIĆEVA

JADROLINIJA CATAMARAN

TRAIN STATION

MUSEUM OF CROATIAN ARCH. MONUMENTS

City Harbor

KRILO CATAMARAN

BUS STATION

ŠET. IVANA MEŠTROVIĆA

OBALA BRANIMIRA

DOMOVINSKOG

B Bus to/from Airport

JEŽINAC BEACH

MAIN FERRY TERMINAL

BAČVICE BEACH

To Kaštelet Chapel

500 Meters

500 Yards

Adriatic Sea

To Zadar & Rijeka

To Hvar, Korčula & Dubrovnik

Town are the long-distance bus station (Autobusni Kolodvor) and the forlorn little train station (Željeznička Stanica). West of the Old Town, poking into the Adriatic, is the lush and hilly Marjan peninsula.

Split's domino-shaped Old Town is made up of two square sections. The east half was once Diocletian's Palace, and the west half is the medieval town that sprang up next door. The shell of Diocletian's ruined palace provides a checkerboard street plan, with a gate at each end. But the streets built since are anything but straight, making the Old Town a delightfully convoluted maze (double-decker in some places). At the center of the former palace is a square called the Peristyle (Peristil), where you'll find the TI, cathedral, and highest concentration of Roman ruins.

TOURIST INFORMATION

Split has two TI locations: One is in the little chapel on the square called the Peristyle, in the very center of Diocletian's Palace, and the other is on the Riva at #9, facing the harbor (same hours for both: May-Sept Mon-Sat 8:00-21:00, Sun 8:00-13:00—longer if there's a cruise ship in town; April and Oct Mon-Sat 8:00-20:00, Sun 8:00-13:00; Nov-March Mon-Fri 9:00-16:00, Sat 9:00-13:00, closed Sun; Peristyle tel. 021/345-606, Riva tel. 021/360-066, www.visitsplit.com). The TIs hand out a stack of free info: a good town map, the *Discover Split* newspaper (with an even more detailed map), *Split in Your Pocket* mini-guidebooks and maps, and piles of brochures.

Sightseeing Pass: If you're staying in town at least three nights, bring your hotel reservation to the TI to claim your **Splitcard,** which covers free admission to several sights (including the City Museum, Ethnographic Museum, and cathedral) and offers a 50 percent discount at other sights (including the Meštrović Gallery, Archaeological Museum, and Gallery of Fine Arts), plus minor discounts at other attractions, shops, and restaurants around town. Busy sightseers staying less than three nights may find the card worth paying for; you can buy one a few doors down from the Riva TI at Turistički Biro, at #12 on the Riva (35 kn/72 hours).

ARRIVAL IN SPLIT

By Boat, Bus, or Train: Split's ferry terminal (Trajektni Terminal), main bus station (Autobusni Kolodvor), and train station

(Željeznička Stanica) all share a busy and practical strip of land called Obala Kneza Domagoja, on the east side of the City Harbor. From any of them, you can see the Old Town and Riva; just **walk** around the harbor toward the big bell tower (about a 10-minute walk). Along the way, you'll pass travel agencies, baggage-storage offices, people trying to rent rooms, a post office, Internet cafés, shops, and cafés. Arriving or leaving from this central location, you never need to deal with the concrete, exhaust-stained sprawl of outer Split.

Boats arrive at various piers. The **Jadrolinija passenger catamaran** to and from Hvar and Korčula usually docks at the Obala Lazareta embankment, right in front of the Old Town. The *Krilo* **passenger catamaran** to those destinations—and, sometimes, the Jadrolinija catamaran as well—uses pier #11, partway along the harbor. Bigger **car ferries** use various docks along the harbor. The main terminal, at the far end, has ATMs, WCs, a grocery store, and the large Jadrolinija ticket and information office, which is open long hours daily and generally has a helpful English-speaking staff.

By Cruise Ship: In recent years—as packed-to-the-gills Dubrovnik has had to turn away cruise ships—Split has become a popular port of call for Mediterranean cruises. Dubrovnik's loss is Split's gain—and passengers' gain too, as the city is particularly easy to see in a quick visit. Cruise ships either dock along the main harbor in front of the Old Town, or anchor in the harbor and send tenders into the harbor (for directions on the short walk to the Old Town, see above).

By Plane: Split's airport (Zračna Luka Split-Kaštela) is across the big bay, 15 miles northwest of the center, near the town of Trogir (airport code: SPU, tel. 021/203-506, www.split-airport. hr). Buses operated by three different companies (Croatia Airlines, Promet, and Žele) connect the airport to the main bus station along Split's harbor (see arrival instructions earlier). While each bus has its own schedule, at least one departs every 30 minutes or so, and they cost about the same (30-35 kn); just take whichever bus is leaving next (at Split's bus station, all companies use stall #5). Another option is to take public bus #37, which stops along the main road in front of the airport (21 kn, 3/hour Mon-Fri, 2/hour Sat-Sun, 45 minutes); the catch is that bus #37 uses Split's suburban bus station, which is a dreary 10-minute walk north of downtown. The most expensive option is a taxi, which costs a hefty 250 kn between the airport and downtown Split.

By Car: Driving around the city center can be tricky—Split is split by its Old Town, which is welded to the harbor by the pedestrian-only Riva promenade. This means drivers needing to get 300 yards from one side of the Old Town to the other must drive about 15 minutes entirely around the center, which can be miserably clogged with traffic. A semicircular ring road and a tunnel under the Marjan peninsula help relieve the situation a bit.

Drivers are treated to the ugly side of Split as they approach town (don't worry—it gets better). From the expressway, you'll pass through an industrial zone, then curl through a few tunnels as you twist your way down into Split's striking, bowl-like setting. While you're still quite a distance from downtown, you'll come to a fork where you'll have to make a decision about which side of town you want to drive to (east or west); ask your hotel in advance for directions, and be ready for your turn. (While many hotels are individually signposted at the fork, it's a long list and hard to read quickly as you zip past.)

At the main fork, turning to the right (marked with *Centar* signs) takes you to the **west end** of the Old Town, including the Varoš neighborhood. Or, if you continue straight (marked

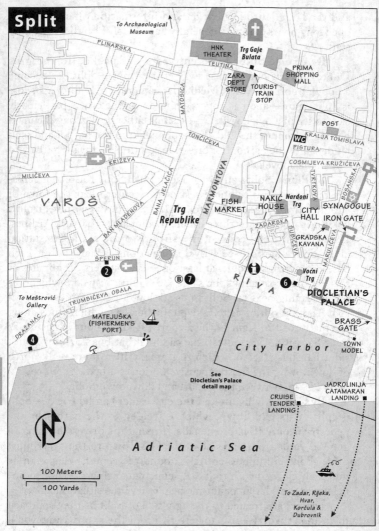

Split

To Archaeological Museum

FLINARSKA

HNK THEATER

Trg Gaje Bulata

TEUTINA

PRIMA SHOPPING MALL

ZARA DEP'T STORE

TOURIST TRAIN STOP

POST

KRALJA TOMISLAVA

WC

PISTURA

MATOŠIĆA

TONČIĆEVA

COSMIJEVA KRUŽIĆEVA

TVRTKOVA

BOSANSKA

KRIŽEVA

BANA JELAČIĆA

MARMONTOVA

FISH MARKET

NAKIĆ HOUSE

Nardoni Trg

SYNAGOGUE

MILIČEVA

VAROŠ

BAN MLADENOVA

Trg Republike

CITY HALL

IRON GATE

ZADARSKA

SUBIĆEVA

GRADSKA KAVANA

MARULIĆEVA

ŠPERUN

②

B ⑦

ⓘ

Voćni Trg

⑥

RIVA

DIOCLETIAN'S PALACE

To Meštrović Gallery

TRUMBIĆEVA OBALA

DRAŽANAC

④

MATEJUŠKA (FISHERMEN'S PORT)

BRASS GATE

TOWN MODEL

City Harbor

See Diocletian's Palace detail map

JADROLINIJA CATAMARAN LANDING

CRUISE TENDER LANDING

N

Adriatic Sea

100 Meters

100 Yards

To Zadar, Rijeka, Hvar, Korčula & Dubrovnik

SPLIT

Trajekt—"ferry"), you'll eventually reach other *Centar* signs and the **east end** of the Old Town, with the ferry terminal, the bus and train stations, and the Lučac neighborhood. You'll pop out right at the southeast corner of Diocletian's Palace (by the Green Market). For handy (but expensive) parking, when the road swings left to the ferry terminal, continue straight, and then turn right into a parking lot just outside the palace walls (10 kn/hour).

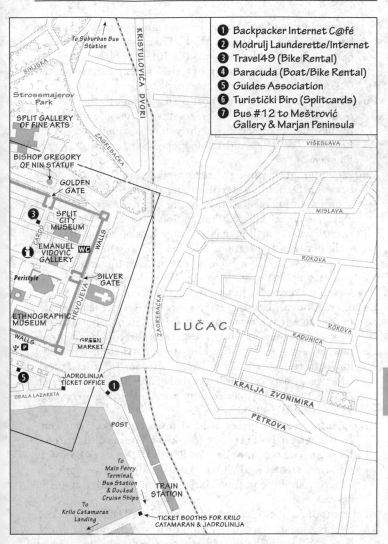

1. Backpacker Internet C@fé
2. Modrulj Launderette/Internet
3. Travel49 (Bike Rental)
4. Baracuda (Boat/Bike Rental)
5. Guides Association
6. Turistički Biro (Splitcards)
7. Bus #12 to Meštrović Gallery & Marjan Peninsula

HELPFUL HINTS

Festivals: For one week in late August, Split celebrates Diocletian Days, when 50 actors from Rome walk the streets in ancient garb. A boat brings "Diocletian" to the Riva, people wearing togas attend dinner in the palace cellars, and the Diocletian Games are staged along the Riva.

Internet Access: Internet cafés are plentiful in the Old Town; look for signs, especially around the Peristyle, or try **Modrulj Launderette** (described later). Closer to the stations and ferry terminal, **Backpacker C@fé** has Internet access, coffee and drinks with outdoor seating, luggage storage, and used paperbacks for sale (30 kn/hour, Wi-Fi-15 kn/hour, daily July-Aug 6:30-21:00, shoulder season 7:00-20:30, shorter hours off-season, near the beginning of Obala Kneza Domagoja, tel. 021/338-548). For locations, see map above.

Post Office: A modern little post office is next to the bus station. They sell empty boxes, so this is a good opportunity to mail home any dead weight you've accumulated (Mon-Fri 7:00-20:00, Sat 7:00-13:00, closed Sun, on Obala Kneza Domagoja).

Luggage Storage: Seemingly custom-made for a quick stopover between Dalmatian destinations, this transit hub has no shortage of luggage-storage options. The train station has lockers, and the adjacent bus station has a left-luggage desk *(garderoba)*. A small luggage-storage kiosk is along the sidewalk between the stations and the Old Town. All of these options cost 15 kn for the day; anyone charging more is ripping you off. Just west of the Old Town, Modrulj Launderette (described next) also has a left-luggage service.

Laundry: Modrulj Launderette, a rare self-service launderette, is conveniently located in the Varoš neighborhood at the west end of the Old Town, near several recommended restaurants—handy if multitasking is your style (self-service-50 kn/load, full-service-75 kn/load, air-con, Internet access, left-luggage service; April-Oct daily 8:00-20:00; Nov-March Mon-Sat 9:00-17:00, closed Sun; Šperun 1—see map on page 954, tel. 021/315-888).

Bike Rental: Several places around town rent bikes; one central location is **Travel49** (60 kn/4 hours, 100 kn/day, Dioklecijanova 5, mobile 098-858-141). Another option is Baracuda (listed next). One good—if strenuous—option is a loop around the nearby Marjan peninsula, with a stop at a beach.

Boat Rental: As the transportation hub of the Dalmatian Coast, Split is a handy place to rent your own boat. **Baracuda**, which faces the Matejuška fishermen's port, rents a wide range of boats (one day costs €160-1,600, depending on the boat; you can pay €80 extra to hire a skipper). They also offer transfers to the islands (e.g., €370 to Hvar, €710 to Korčula), scuba diving (€50/1.5 hours for beginners, €95/5 hours for licensed divers), fishing trips (€100/person for 1-2 people, €65/person for 3 or more, about 5 hours), and bike rental (20 kn/hour, 60 kn/4 hours; daily 8:00-20:00, closed Sun in winter, Trumbićeva Obala 13, tel. 021/362-462, mobile 091-566-5741, www. baracuda.hr, baracuda@st.t-com.hr).

Who's Hajduk?: You'll see the word *Hajduk* (high-dook), and a distinctive red-and-white checkerboard circle design (or red-and-blue stripes), all over town and throughout northern Dalmatia. Hajduk Split is the fervently supported soccer team, named for a band of highwaymen bandits who rebelled against Ottoman rule in the 17th-19th centuries. Most locals adore Hajduk as much as they loathe their bitter rivals, Dinamo Zagreb.

G'day, *Gospod*: You may notice a surprising concentration of Australians in Split. Many of them are actually Australian-born Croats, returning to the cosmopolitan capital city of their parents' Dalmatian homeland.

GETTING AROUND SPLIT

Most of what you'll want to see is within walking distance, but some sights (such as the Meštrović Gallery) are more easily reached by bus or taxi.

By Bus: Local buses, run by Promet, cost 11 kn per ride (or 10 kn if you buy a ticket at a newsstand or Promet kiosk, ask for a *putna karta*; zone I is fine for any ride within Split). For a round-trip within the city, buy a 17-kn transfer ticket, which works like two individual tickets (must buy at kiosk). Validate your ticket in the machine or with the driver as you board the bus. Bus information: www.promet-split.hr.

By Taxi: Taxis start at 20 kn, then cost around 8 kn per kilometer. Figure 50 kn for most rides within the city (for example, from the ferry terminal to most hotels)—but if going from one end of the Old Town to the other, it can be faster to walk. To call for a taxi, try Radio Taxi (tel. 021/1777).

By Tourist Train: An hourly tourist train leaves from the square at the top of Marmontova and does a loop around the Marjan peninsula with a stop at Bene Beach (20 kn one-way, departs on the hour 9:00-20:00, mobile 095-530-6962).

Tours in Split

Walking Tours

Split's Old Town, with fragments of Diocletian's Palace, is made to order for a walking tour, and it seems that Split has hundreds of tour guides leading cruise-ship excursions around the town. My self-guided walk (described later) covers basically the same information you'll get from a guide. But if you'd like to hear it live, join a tour. This is a constantly changing scene, but on my last visit, two fiercely competitive companies were offering dueling 1.25-hour walks, leaving about every 60 to 90 minutes throughout the day and into the evening. The red **Sirena tours** cost 100 kn and have a

SPLIT

more purely historical focus (these generally meet outside the south gate of the Old Town, on the Riva); the blue **Split Walking Tour** costs 90 kn and is more overtly commercial, cross-promoting the company's other offerings (these typically meet at the north gate to the Old Town, the Golden Gate). Various companies have also offered "free" tours (joining the tour is "free," but guides expect a healthy tip), but these have been shut down—at least temporarily—by city authorities. Regardless, I'd pay a bit extra for a more serious operation, but you can chat with the umbrella-toting touts to find out what your options are. Yet another choice: The local **guides association** offers tours three times daily in summer (100 kn, May-Sept Mon-Sat at 10:00, 11:30, and 13:00); while these guides are usually more polished and professional, the starting point—at their office on the Riva (see map on page 954)—is a little less convenient.

Local Guides

You can hire an insider to show you around. **Maja Benzon** is a smart and savvy local guide; she leads good walking tours through the Old Town (500 kn/up to 2 hours, 600 kn/3 hours, mobile 098-852-869, maja.benzon@gmail.com). You can also hire a guide through the **guides association,** which has an office on the Riva (525 kn/1.5-2 hours; May-Sept Mon-Fri 8:30-17:30, Sat 9:00-15:00, closed Sun; off-season generally open weekday mornings only; Obala Lazareta 3, tel. 021/360-058 or 021/346-267, mobile 098-361-936, www.guides.hr, info@guides.hr).

FROM SPLIT

A staggering variety of pop-up travel agencies sell tickets for bus or boat excursions to nearby destinations. There's no shortage of enticing side-trips: the town of Trogir; the Roman ruins of Solin (ancient Salona); whitewater rafting on the Cetina River; the islands of Brač, Hvar, and Šolta (either separately or together; the "Blue Cave" on Vis is another favorite); the pilgrimage site at Međugorje; Dubrovnik; and the waterfalls at Krka National Park or Plitvice Lakes National Park. Because new companies come and go every year, I can't recommend any outfit in particular. If you're interested in a side-trip, comparison-shop for a tour that suits your interests.

Various tour boats line up along the Riva each morning and evening, hawking trips to nearby islands. Popular itineraries include a combination cruise to Hvar and the "Green Cave" and "Blue Cave" on Vis, all in one day. Aside from the standard side-trips, there are a few more interesting or adventurous alternatives. For example, the **Summer Blues** catamaran does party-oriented "sail 'n swim" cruises with swimming stops, dancing, food, and lots of drinks (www.summer-blues.com). Various companies also offer kayaking tours from Split.

Split Walk

▲▲▲DIOCLETIAN'S PALACE (DIOKLECIJANOVA PALAČA)

Split's top activity is visiting the remains of Roman Emperor Diocletian's enormous retirement palace, sitting on the harbor in the heart of the city. This monstrous complex was two impressive structures in one: luxurious villa and fortified Roman town. My self-guided walk takes you through Diocletian's back door; down into the labyrinth of cellars that supported the palace; up to the Peristyle (the center of the palace); into Diocletian's mausoleum—now the town's cathedral, with a crypt, treasury/museum, and climbable tower; over to Jupiter's Temple (later converted into a baptistery); down the main artery of the palace; and finally to what was once the palace's front entrance. The ruins themselves are now integrated with the city's street plan, so exploring them is free—except for the cellars and the cathedral sights/temple, which you'll pay to enter. In peak season, the cellars are open late (on most days until 20:00 or 21:00), and the cathedral sights generally close at 19:00. If visiting off-season, do this walk as early as possible, because the cathedral sights close at noon. For exact hours, see the individual sight listings.

Fragments of the palace are poorly marked, and there are no good guidebooks or audioguides for understanding the remains. For most visitors, this walk provides enough details; for more in-depth information, you could join a walking tour or hire a guide (see "Tours in Split," earlier).

Background

Diocletian grew up just inland from Split, in the town of Salona (Solin in Croatian), which was then the capital of the Roman province of Dalmatia. He worked his way up the Roman hierarchy and ruled as emperor for the unusually long tenure of 20 years (A.D. 284-305). Despite all of his achievements, Diocletian is best remembered for two questionable legacies: dividing the huge empire among four emperors (which helped administer it more efficiently, but began a splintering effect that arguably led to the empire's decline); and torturing and executing Christians, including thousands right here

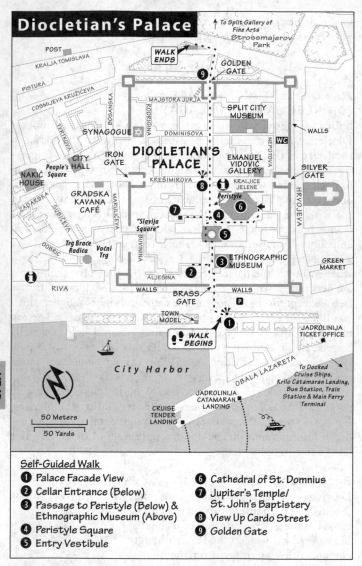

Diocletian's Palace

POST
KRALJA TOMISLAVA

PISTURA

COSMIJEVA KRUŽIĆEVA

TVRTKOVA

ZADARSKA

SUBIĆEVA

DOBRIĆ

NAKIĆ
HOUSE

People's
Square

CITY
HALL

IRON
GATE

BOSANSKA

RODRIGINA

MARULIĆEVA

BUVININA

SYNAGOGUE

MAJSTORA JURJA

DOMINISOVA

**DIOCLETIAN'S
PALACE**

KREŠIMIROVA

GRADSKA
KAVANA
CAFÉ

"Slavija
Square"

Trg Braće
Radića

Voćni
Trg

ALJEŠINA

**WALK
ENDS**

9 GOLDEN
GATE

SPLIT CITY
MUSEUM

NEPOTOVA

WC

EMANUEL
VIDOVIĆ
GALLERY

Kraljice
Jelene

8

Peristyle

7

4

5

3 ETHNOGRAPHIC
MUSEUM

2

6

HRVOJEVA

WALLS

SILVER
GATE

GREEN
MARKET

RIVA

WALLS

BRASS
GATE

WALLS

P

TOWN
MODEL

**WALK
BEGINS**

1

JADROLINIJA
TICKET OFFICE

City Harbor

OBALA LAZARETA

To Docked
Cruise Ships,
Krilo Catamaran Landing,
Bus Station, Train
Station & Main Ferry
Terminal

50 Meters

50 Yards

CRUISE
TENDER
LANDING

JADROLINIJA
CATAMARAN
LANDING

To Split Gallery of
Fine Arts
Strossmajerov
Park

Self-Guided Walk

1 Palace Façade View
2 Cellar Entrance (Below)
3 Passage to Peristyle (Below) &
Ethnographic Museum (Above)
4 Peristyle Square
5 Entry Vestibule

6 Cathedral of St. Domnius
7 Jupiter's Temple/
St. John's Baptistery
8 View Up Cardo Street
9 Golden Gate

on the Dalmatian Coast. Soon after the end of Diocletian's reign, his successor, Constantine, not only legalized Christianity, but made it the official religion of the empire—effectively making Diocletian's purges some of the last in Roman history.

As Diocletian grew older, he decided to return to his homeland for retirement. Since he was in poor health, the medicinal sulfur spring here was another plus. His massive palace took only 11 years to build—and this fast pace required a big push (more than

2,000 slaves died during construction). Huge sections of his palace still exist, modified by medieval and modern developers alike.

• *Start in front of the palace, at the east end of the Riva. To get a sense of the original palace, check out the big illustration posted across from the palace entry. Across the street at the end of the Riva, notice the big car-size model of today's Old Town, which is helpful for orientation. (Both the sign and the model are usually crowded with tour groups.) Now study the...*

Palace Facade

The "front" of today's Split—facing the harbor—was actually the back door of Diocletian's Palace. There was no embankment in front of the palace back then, so the water came right up to this door—sort of an emergency exit by boat. Looking out to the water, appreciate the palace's strategic location: It's easy to fortify, and to spot enemies approaching either by land or by sea.

Visually trace the outline of the gigantic palace, which was more than 600 feet long on each side. On the corner to the right stands a big, rectangular guard tower (one of the original 16). To the left, the tower is gone and the corner is harder to pick out (look for the beginning of the newer-looking buildings). Mentally erase the ramshackle two-story buildings added 200 years ago, which obscure the grandeur of the palace wall.

Halfway up the facade, notice the row of 42 arched window frames (mostly filled in today). Diocletian and his family lived in the seaside half of the palace. Imagine him strolling back and forth along this fine arcade, enjoying the views of his Adriatic homeland. The inland, non-view half of the palace was home to 700 servants, bodyguards, and soldiers.

• *Go through the door in the middle of the palace (known as the "Brass Gate," located under* The Substructure of Diocletian's Palace *banner). Just inside the door and to the left is the entrance to...*

Diocletian's Cellars (Podromi)

Since the palace was constructed on land that sloped down to the sea, these chambers were built to level out a foundation for the massive structure above (like a modern "daylight basement").

These cellars were filled with water from three different sources: a freshwater spring, a sulfur spring, and the sea. Later, medieval residents used them as a dump. Rediscovered only in the last century, the cellars enabled archaeologists to derive the floor plan of some of the palace's long-gone upper sections. These underground chambers now house art exhibits and a little strip of souvenir stands. One particularly well-preserved stretch can be toured, offering the best look in town at Roman engineering.

Cost and Hours: 40 kn, some posters inside explain the site; June-Sept daily 9:00-21:00; April-May and Oct Mon-Sat 9:00-20:00, Sun 9:00-18:00 except in April, when it closes Sun at 14:00; Nov-March Mon-Sat 9:00-18:00, Sun 9:00-14:00.

Visiting the Cellars: Use the free map you get at the entry to navigate this labyrinthine complex of cellars. First visit the **western cellars** (to the left as you enter). Near the ticket-seller, notice the big **topographical map** of the Split area, clearly showing the city's easily defensible location—with a natural harbor sheltered by tall mountains. You'll see the former Roman city of Salona, Diocletian's birthplace, just inland.

This network of cellars is quite a maze, so follow these instructions carefully: Head into the main part of the cellars by going through the door on the right, just past the ticket-seller. This takes you into the complex's vast, vaulted **main hall**—the biggest space in the cellars, with stout pillars to support everything upstairs. When those first villagers took refuge in the abandoned palace from the rampaging Slavs in 641, the elite lived upstairs, grabbing what was once the emperor's wing. They carved the rough holes you see in the ceiling to dump their garbage and sewage. Over the generations, the basement (where you're standing) filled up with layers of pungent waste that solidified, ultimately becoming a precious bonanza for 19th- and 20th-century archaeologists. Today this hall is used for everything from flower and book shows to fashion catwalks. (And, in 2013, it was used to film scenes for HBO's *Game of Thrones*.)

Exit the main hall through either of the doors on the left, cross through the narrow corridor, and enter the long room. Look just overhead—the holes you see once held beams to support floorboards, making this a two-story cellar. Face the giant replica of a golden Diocletian coin at the far end, and turn left, then immediately right into a small circular room, which has a headless, pawless black granite sphinx—one of 13 that Diocletian brought home from Egypt (only four survive, including a mostly intact one we'll see soon on the Peristyle). Look up to admire the circular brickwork. Then continue straight into another small room, which adjoins one that displays a stone olive-oil press.

Backtrack through the round room and into a room that displays two petrified beams, like the ones that once filled the double-decker holes we saw earlier. At the far (right) end of this room is an unexcavated wing—a compost pile of ancient lifestyles, awaiting the tiny shovels and toothbrushes of future archaeologists.

Facing the mound of ancient garbage, turn left into another round room, featuring a bust of Diocletian (or is it Sean Connery?). From here, turn left and go through another room (passing WCs on the right) to return to the long room you were in earlier, then turn right and exit out the bottom of this hall. On your right, look for original Roman sewer pipes—square outside and round inside—designed to fit into each other to create long pipes.

From here, head back out to the exit. If you'd like to see more cellars—mostly with their ceilings missing, so they're open to the air—cross over into the **eastern cellars** (same ticket). This section is less interesting than the western part, but worth a quick visit.

• *When you're finished, head back to the main gallery. Ignore the tacky made-in-Malaysia trinket shops as you head down the passage and up the chunky stairs into the...*

Peristyle (Peristil)

This square was the centerpiece of Diocletian's Palace. As you

walk up the stairs, the entry vestibule into the residence is above your head, Diocletian's mausoleum (today's Cathedral of St. Domnius) is to your right, and the street to Jupiter's Temple (supported by wooden beams) is on your left. The TI is in the small chapel, at the end of the square on the right. Straight ahead, beyond the TI/chapel, is the narrow street that leads to the palace's former main entrance, the Golden Gate.

Go to the middle of the square and take it all in. The red granite pillars—which you'll see all over Diocletian's Palace—are from Egypt, where Diocletian spent many of his pre-retirement years. Imagine the pillars defining fine arcades—now obscured by medieval houses. The black sphinx is the only one of Diocletian's collection of 13 that's still (mostly) intact.

"Roman soldiers" pose for tips (daily 9:00-17:00), and every day at noon in summer (mid-June–mid-Sept), an actor playing Diocletian appears at the top of the stairs to address the crowd in Latin.

Without realizing it, you're standing in the middle of one of Split's most inviting bars, Luxor. The red cushions on the steps ringing the square belong to the bar; if you want to sit on one, you have to buy a drink (especially worthwhile in the evening, when the Peristyle is less crowded and there's often live music).

• *Climb the stairs (above where you came in) into the domed, open-ceilinged...*

Entry Vestibule

Impressed? That's the idea. This was the grand entry to Diocletian's living quarters, meant to wow visitors. Emperors were believed

to be gods. Diocletian called himself "Jovius"—the son of Jupiter, the most powerful of all gods. Four times a year (at the changing of the seasons), Diocletian would stand here and over-look the Peristyle. His subjects would lie on the ground in worship, praising his name and kissing his scarlet robe. Notice the four big niches at floor level, which once held statues of the four tetrarchs who ruled the unwieldy empire after Diocletian retired. The empty hole in the ceiling was once capped by a dome (long since collapsed), and the ceiling itself was covered with frescoes and mosaics.

In this grand space, you'll likely run into an all-male band of *klapa* singers, performing traditional a cappella harmonies. Just stand and enjoy a few glorious tunes—you'll rarely find a better group or acoustics. A 100-kn *klapa* CD is the perfect souvenir.

Wander out back to the harborside through medieval build-ings (some with seventh-century foundations), which evoke the way local villagers came in and took over the once-spacious and elegant palace. Back in this area, you'll find the beautifully restored home of the **Ethnographic Museum** (described later, under "Sights in Split").

• *Now go back into the Peristyle and turn right, climbing the steps to the...*

Cathedral of St. Domnius (Katedrala Sv. Duje)

The original octagonal structure was Diocletian's elaborate mau-soleum, built in the fourth century. But after the fall of Rome, it was converted into the town's cathedral. Construction of the bell tower began in the 13th century and took 300 years to complete. Before you go inside, notice the sarcophagi ringing the cathedral. In the late Middle Ages, this was prime post-mortem real estate, since being buried closer to a cathedral improved your chances of getting to heaven.

Cost and Hours: Several sights associ-ated with the cathedral require tickets: the cathedral interior, the unimpressive treasury/

museum, the crypt, the tower climb, and—a block away—Jupiter's Temple (described later). While ticketing options always seem in flux, you'll likely have an option to pay 25 kn for the cathedral, crypt, and baptistery (the three most worthwhile parts); a 45-kn ticket adds the skippable treasury/museum and steep-but-scenic bell tower. (You can also pay 15 kn just for the tower climb—buy ticket at tower door.) All of the sights are open similar hours, but the cathedral can close unexpectedly for services. In general, hours are summer Mon-Sat 8:00-19:00, Sun 12:30-18:30, cathedral often closed Sat afternoons for weddings; winter daily 7:00-12:00, maybe later on request; Kraj Sv. Duje 5, tel. 021/345-602.

Visiting the Cathedral: To get inside in peak season (April-Oct), you must loop around the outside of the cathedral. Facing the main door at the bottom of the stairs, circle around the right side—passing the crypt (included in the cathedral ticket and described later)—to find the door in the building behind. Buy your ticket here and climb up the stairs. (In winter, you can usually enter the cathedral through the main door.) Once inside, the first flight of stairs leads to the cathedral interior (described below), but if you bought the 45-kn ticket and want to see the **treasury/museum** first, head up one more flight. The single-room museum contains dusty display cases of vestments, giant psalter books, icon-like paintings, reliquaries, chalices, monstrances, and other church art, with very sparse English descriptions. After visiting, head back down to the cathedral.

Step into the church **interior.** You'll enter into the apse; head around the side of the altar to reach the main (though still tiny) part of the church. This is the oldest—and likely smallest—building used as a cathedral anywhere in Christendom. Imagine the place in pre-Christian times, with Diocletian's tomb in the center. The only surviving pieces of decor from those days are the granite columns and the relief circling the base of the dome (about 50 feet up)—a ring

of carvings heralding the greatness of the emperor. The small red-marble pillars around the top of the pulpit (near the main door) were scavenged from Diocletian's sarcophagus. These pillars are all that remain of Diocletian's remains.

Diocletian brutally persecuted his Christian subjects. Just before he moved to the Dalmatian Coast, he had Bishop Domnius of Salona killed, along with several thousand Christians. When Diocletian died, there were riots of happiness. In the seventh century, his mausoleum became a cathedral dedicated to the martyred bishop. The apse (behind the altar) was added in the ninth century. The sarcophagus of St. Domnius (to the right of the altar, with early-Christian carvings) was once the cathedral's high altar. To the left of today's main altar is the impressively detailed, Renaissance-era altar of St. Anastasius, who is lying on a millstone that is tied to his neck. On Diocletian's orders, this Christian martyr was drowned in A.D. 302. To the left of St. Anastasius' altar is the "new" altar of St. Domnius; his relics lie in the 18th-century Baroque silver

reliquary, above a stone relief showing him about to be beheaded. Posthumous poetic justice: Now Christian saints are entombed in Diocletian's mausoleum...and Diocletian is nowhere to be found. As you exit through the 13th-century main doors, notice the 14 panels on each of the two wings—showing 28 scenes from the life of Christ.

Exiting the church, you'll see the entrance to the **bell tower** on your right. Climbing the 183 steep steps to the top of the 200-foot-tall bell tower rewards you with sweeping views of Split, but it's not for claustrophobes or those scared of heights.

To visit the **crypt** *(kripta)*, also included with your ticket, exit the main door of the cathedral, go down the stairs, and loop left to find its low-profile entrance. This musty, domed cellar (with eerie acoustics) was originally used to level the foundation of Diocletian's mausoleum. Later, Christians turned it into another chapel, dedicated to the Italian Saint Lucia, who was martyred by Diocletian. (The legend you'll likely hear about Diocletian torturing and murdering Christians in this very crypt, which began about the same time this became a church, is probably false.) Lucia stands above a small altar where the faithful have left scraps of paper scrawled with their prayers and their thanks. Ponder the contrast of this dark and gloomy space with Santa Lucia, whose name means "light." Notice the freshwater well in the middle of the room. Because this water was believed to have healing properties, the faithful would wash their eyes with it (particularly appropriate, since Santa Lucia is also the patron saint of eyesight).

• *Return to the middle of the Peristyle square. Remember that Diocletian believed himself to be Jovius (Jupiter, Jr.). As worshippers exited the mausoleum of Jovius, they would look straight ahead to the temple of Jupiter. (Back then, there were none of these medieval buildings cluttering up the view.) Make your way through the narrow alley (directly across from the cathedral entry), past another headless, pawless sphinx, to explore the small...*

Jupiter's Temple/St. John's Baptistery

About the time the mausoleum became a cathedral, this temple was converted into a baptistery (same ticket and hours as cathe-

dral; off-season, if it's locked, go ask the person at the cathedral to let you in). Inside, the big 12th-century baptismal font—large enough to immerse someone (as was the tradition in those days)—is decorated with the intricate, traditional woven-rope *pleter* design. Observant travelers will see examples of this motif all over the country. On the font, notice the engraving: a bishop (on the left) and the king on his throne (on the right). At their feet (literally under the feet of the bishop) is a submissive commoner—neatly summing up the social structure of the Middle Ages. Standing above the font is a statue of St. John the Baptist counting to four, done by the great Croatian sculptor Ivan Meštrović (see page 976). The half-barrel vaulted ceiling, completed later, is considered the best-preserved of its kind anywhere. Every face and each patterned box is different.

• *Back at the Peristyle, stand in front of the little chapel with your back to the square. The small street just beyond the chapel (going left to right) connects the east and west gates. If you've had enough Roman history, head right (east) to go through the Silver Gate and find Split's busy, open-air Green Market. Or, head to the left (west), which takes you to the Iron Gate and People's Square (see "Sights in Split," later) and, beyond that, the fresh-and-smelly fish market. But if you want to see one last bit of Roman history, continue straight ahead up the...*

Cardo

A traditional Roman street plan has two roads: Cardo (the north-south axis) and Decumanus (the east-west axis). Split's Cardo street was the most important in Diocletian's Palace, connecting the main entry with the heart of the complex. As you walk, you'll pass several noteworthy sights: in the first building on the right, a bank with modern computer gear all around its exposed Roman ruins (look through window); at the first gate on the left, the courtyard of a Venetian merchant's palace (a reminder that Split was dominated by Venice from the 15th century on); farther along on the right, an alley to the **City Museum** (described later, under "Sights in Split"); and, beyond that on the right, **Nadalina,** an artisan chocolatier selling mostly dark chocolate creations with some innovative Dalmatian flavors—such as dried fig and prosecco (32 kn/100 grams, chocolate bars, Mon-Fri 8:30-20:30, Sat 9:00-14:00, closed Sun, mobile 091-210-8889).

At the end of the street, just before the Golden Gate, detour a few steps to the left along covered **Majstora Jurja** street—lined with some of the most appealing outdoor cafés in town, lively both day and night (described later, under "Nightlife in Split"). Near the start of this street, just after its initial jog, stairs climb to the miniscule **St. Martin's Chapel,** burrowed into the city wall. Dating from the fifth century, this is one of the earliest Christian chapels anywhere. St. Martin is the patron saint of soldiers, and the chapel was built for the troops who guarded this gate (free, sporadic hours—just climb the stairs to see if it's open).

• *Backtrack to the main drag and go inside the huge...*

Golden Gate (Zlatna Vrata)

This great gate was the main entry of Diocletian's Palace. Its name wasn't literal—rather, the "gold" suggests the importance of this gateway to Salona, the Roman provincial capital at the time. Standing inside the gate itself, you can appreciate the double-door design that kept the palace safe. Also notice how this ancient building is now being used in very different ways from its original purpose. Above, on the outer wall, you can see the bricked-in windows that contain part of a Dominican convent. At the top of the inner wall is somebody's garden terrace.

Go outside the gate and look back at the recently restored fortification—with all its structural elements gleaming. This mostly uncluttered facade gives you the best opportunity in town to visualize how the palace looked before so many other buildings were grafted on. Straight ahead as you exit this gate is Salona (Solin), which was a major city of 60,000 (and Diocletian's hometown) before there was a Split. The big statue by Ivan Meštrović is **Bishop Gregory of Nin,** a 10th-century Croatian priest who tried to convince the Vatican to allow sermons during Mass to be said in Croatian, rather than Latin. People rub his toe for good luck (though only nonmaterial wishes are given serious consideration).

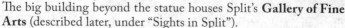

The big building beyond the statue houses Split's **Gallery of Fine Arts** (described later, under "Sights in Split").

• *Your tour is finished. Now enjoy the rest of Split.*

Sights in Split

IN OR NEAR THE OLD TOWN

In addition to the palace, cellars, and cathedral described on my self-guided walk, you can also enjoy these attractions.

Public Spaces

My self-guided walk (described earlier) takes you through the main artery of town, but just a few steps away are some delightful squares and other public zones that are worth exploring.

▲▲▲The Riva

The official name for this seaside pedestrian drag is the "Croatian National Revival Embankment" (Obala Hrvatskog Narodnog

Preporoda), but locals just call it "Riva" (Italian for "harbor"). This is the town's promenade, an integral part of Mediterranean culture. After dinner, Split residents collect their families and friends for a stroll on the Riva. It offers some of the best people-watching in Croatia; make it a point to be here for an hour or two after dinner. The stinky smell that sometimes accompanies the stroll (especially at the west end) isn't from a sewer. It's sulfur—a reminder that the town's medicinal sulfur spas have attracted people here since the days of Diocletian.

The Riva is a broad, sleek, carefully landscaped people zone. A clean, synchronized line of modern white lampposts and sun screens sashays down the promenade. Some think that the starkly modern strip is at odds with the rest of the higgledy-piggledy Old Town, while others see this as simply the early-21st century's contribution to the architectural hodgepodge that is Split.

At the west end of the Riva, the people-parade of Croatian culture turns right and heads away from the water, up **Marmontova.** Although it lacks the seafront cachet, this drag is equally enjoyable and feels more local. As you walk up Marmontova, on the left is the plain-Jane outer facade of the arcade that defines Trg Republike, a grand and genteel Napoleonic-era square. Duck through the passage across from the fish market to bask in its "poor man's St. Mark's Square" ambience, and maybe to linger over a drink at the recommended Bajamonti café. A bit farther up Marmontova, on the right, look for the whimsical fountain nicknamed "The Teacup," with a hand squirting water across the sidewalk into a funnel. At the top of Marmontova are some department stores, a lively café square, and the Croatian National Theater (Hrvatsko Narodno Kazalište, HNK).

▲People's Square (Narodni Trg)

Locals call this lively square at the center of the Old Town *Pjaca*, pronounced the same as the Italian *piazza* (PYAH-tsah). Stand in the center and enjoy the bustle. Look around for a quick lesson in Dalmatian history. When Diocletian lived in his palace,

a Roman village popped up here, just outside the wall. Face the former wall of Diocletian's Palace (behind and to the right of the 24-hour clock tower). This was the western entrance, or so-called "Iron Gate." By the 14th century, a medieval town had developed, making this the main square of Split.

On the wall just to the right of the lane leading to the Peristyle, look for the life-size relief of **St. Anthony.** Notice the creepy "mini-me" clutching the saint's left leg—depicting the sculptor's donor, who didn't want his gift to be forgotten. Above this strange statue, notice the smaller, faded relief of a man and a woman arguing.

Turn around and face the square. On your left is the city's grand old café, **Gradska Kavana,** which has been the Old Town's venerable meeting point for generations. Today it's both a café and a restaurant with disappointing food but the best outdoor ambience in town.

Across the square, the white building jutting into the square was once the **City Hall,** and now houses temporary exhibitions. The loggia is all that remains of the original Gothic building.

At the far end of the square is the out-of-place **Nakić House,** built in the early 20th-century Viennese Secession style—a reminder that Dalmatia was part of the Habsburg Empire, and ruled by Vienna, from Napoleon's downfall through World War I.

The lane on the right side of the Nakić House leads to Split's **fish market** (Ribarnica), where you can see piles of the still-wriggling catch of the day. No flies? It's thanks to the sulfur spring in the nearby spa building (with the gray statues, on the corner). Just beyond the fish market is the pedestrian boulevard Marmontova (described earlier).

Radić Brothers Square (Trg Braće Radića)

This little piazza is just off the Riva between the two halves of the Old Town. Overhead is a **Venetian citadel.** After Split became part of the Venetian Republic, there was a serious danger of attack by the Ottomans, so octagonal towers like this were built all along the coast. But this imposing tower had a second purpose: to encourage citizens of Split to forget about any plans of rebellion. At its base is an inviting juice bar, invoking the more popular nickname of the square—Voćni Trg ("Fruit Square"), for the produce that was once sold here.

In the middle of the square is a studious sculpture by Ivan

Meštrović of the 16th-century poet **Marko Marulić,** who is considered the father of the Croatian language. Marulić was the first to write literature in the Croatian vernacular, which before then had generally been considered a backward peasants' tongue.

On the downhill (harbor) side of the square is **Croata,** a necktie boutique that loves to explain how Croatian soldiers who fought with the French in the Thirty Years' War (1618-1648) had a distinctive way of tying their scarves. The French found it stylish, adopted it, and called it *à la Croate*—or eventually, *cravate*—thus creating the modern necktie that many people wear to work every day throughout the world. Croata's selection includes ties with traditional Croatian motifs, such as the checkerboard pattern from the flag or writing in the ninth-century Glagolitic alphabet. Though pricey, these ties make nice souvenirs. Basic ties run about 500 kn, while handmade ones with 24-carat gold accents can run 2,800-3,800 kn. The shop also sells women's scarves (Mon-Fri 8:00-20:00, Sat 8:00-13:00, closed Sun, Mihovilova Širina 7, tel. 021/346-336). Croata has a bigger, second location on the Peristyle.

Green Market

This lively open-air market bustles at the east end of Diocletian's Palace. Residents shop for produce and clothes here, and there are plenty of tourist souvenirs as well. Browse the wide selection of T-shirts, and ignore the sleazy black-market tobacco salesmen who mutter at you: *"Cigaretta?"*

Matejuška Fishermen's Port

While Split's harborfront Riva is where the beautiful people stroll, the city's fishermen roots still thrive just to the west. The neighbor-

hood called Matejuška—at the little harbor where the Varoš district hits the water (a five-minute walk beyond the end of the Riva, with the water on your left)—has long been Split's working fishermen's harbor. While the area has received a facelift to match the one along the Riva, it still retains its striped-collar character. The enclosed harbor area is filled with working fishing boats and colorful dinghies that bob in unison. Along the breakwater, notice the new fishermen's lockers, where people who earn their living from the Adriatic still keep their supplies. You'll see the most fisherman action here in the mornings.

The far side of the breakwater—all glitzy white marble—is another world, with a pebbly beach, attractive plaza, and some of the best views looking back on the Riva. After its recent renovation, this jetty has become a popular open-air, after-hours hangout

SPLIT

for young people. Like Split itself, these two worlds—the grizzled fishermen mending their nets, and the teenagers laughing and flirting—coexist more smoothly than anyone might have guessed.

Beyond Matejuška, the harborfront embankment (which runs toward the Marjan peninsula) has also been rejuvenated and is now spiffed up with cafés facing moored sailboats, creating a relaxing, scenic, largely tourist-free zone.

Museums and Sights
Ethnographic Museum (Etnografski Muzej)

This museum shows off the culture, costumes, furniture, tools, jewelry, weapons, and paintings of Dalmatia. The modest but vibrant collection, with a confusing treehouse floor plan, is displayed in a gorgeously renovated early-medieval palace (parts of which once formed the private residential halls of Diocletian). You'll find it in the upper level of the Old Town, behind Diocletian's entry vestibule. Check out the artsy "golden fleece" entry door. The ground floor sports the remains of a seventh-century church, and the exhibits usually include a good look at traditional folk dress. Your ticket also includes access to the roof of the vestibule (find the stairs at the far end of the museum); while it's not high enough to be thrilling, and you can't actually see down into the vestibule, it provides a nice view over the rooftops of Split.

Cost and Hours: 15 kn, good English explanations; June-Sept Mon-Sat 9:30-19:00, Sun 10:00-13:00; Oct-May Mon-Fri 9:00-16:00, Sat 9:00-13:00, closed Sun; Severova 7, tel. 021/344-164, www.etnografski-muzej-split.hr.

Split City Museum (Muzej Grada Splita)

This museum traces how the city grew over the centuries. It's a bit dull, but it can help you appreciate a little better the layers of history you're seeing in the streets. The ground floor displays Roman fragments (including coins from the days of Diocletian), temporary exhibits, a model of the Peristyle during Diocletian's time, and the museum's highlight: a semicircular marble table (called a "mensa") used by the Romans. As depicted in Hollywood movies, the Romans ate lying down (multiple people would lounge and feast, while servants dished things up from the straight side). This table has been painstakingly reconstructed from shards and splinters discovered in the cellars. The upstairs focuses on the Middle Ages (find the terrace displaying carved stone monuments), and the top floor covers the 16th century to the present.

The 15th-century Papalić Palace, which houses the City Museum, is a sight all its own. At the end of the palace, near Cardo street, look up to see several typical Venetian-style Gothic-Renaissance windows. The stone posts sticking out of the wall next to them were used to hang curtains.

Cost and Hours: 20 kn, some English descriptions, 40-kn guidebook is overkill; April-Oct Tue-Fri 9:00-21:00, Sat-Mon 9:00-16:00; Nov-March generally Tue-Fri 9:00-17:00, Sat-Sun 10:00-13:00, closed Mon; Papalićeva 1, tel. 021/360-171, www.mgst.net.

Emanuel Vidović Gallery

This small but intriguing museum celebrates the work of Split native Emanuel Vidović (1870-1953), who gained fame as a Post-Impressionist painter. On the first floor is a reconstruction of his cluttered studio; notice the creepy dolls' heads. Elsewhere on the first floor—and upstairs—hang many of his works: hazy, Turner-esque landscapes; church interiors; shimmering street and village scenes from Split and around Dalmatia; and paintings of those bizarre dolls. Located just a few steps off the Peristyle, it's an easy opportunity to get to know an unfamiliar but locally respected artist.

Cost and Hours: 20 kn; May-Oct Tue-Fri 9:00-21:00, Sat-Mon 9:00-16:00; Nov-April Tue-Fri 9:00-17:00, Sat 9:00-13:00, Sun 10:00-13:00, closed Mon; Poljana Kraljice Jelene bb, tel. 021/360-155, www.galerija-vidovic.com.

Split Synagogue

The tiny, modest synagogue of Split is hidden down a tiny side-street, not coincidentally located just outside the walls of Diocletian's Palace. Ring the bell and climb the stairs to step into the unassuming, lived-in religious home of Split's Jewish community, which numbered around 300 before the Holocaust (and about a hundred today). You'll see a replica of a little, clay menorah lamp that was discovered in the ruins of ancient Salona, indicating that the Jewish presence here goes back to Roman times. This is the third-oldest practicing synagogue in Europe (after Prague and Dubrovnik); a rabbi comes from Zagreb a few times each year.

Cost and Hours: Free but donations requested, loaner yarmulkes, Mon-Fri 10:00-14:00, closed Sat-Sun, Židovski Prolaz 1, tel. 021/345-672, www.zost.hr.

Split Gallery of Fine Arts (Galerija Umjetnina Split)

This collection, beautifully displayed in a finely restored old hospital just behind Diocletian's Palace, features mostly Croatian artwork from the 14th to the 21st century. It's basically a hodgepodge with few highlights—best reserved for art lovers. Cross through the courtyard, climb up the stairs, and follow the one-way route through the chronologically displayed collection, which is heavy on the 20th century.

Cost and Hours: 20 kn; May-Sept Mon 11:00-16:00, Tue-Fri 11:00-19:00, Sat 11:00-15:00, closed Sun; Oct-April Mon

9:00-14:00, Tue-Fri 9:00-17:00, Sat 9:00-13:00, closed Sun; mod café, go straight out the Golden Gate and a bit to the left—behind the statue of Gregory of Nin—to Kralja Tomislava 15, tel. 021/350-110, www.galum.hr.

Archaeological Museum (Arheološki Muzej)

If you're intrigued by all the "big stuff" from Split's past (buildings and ruins), consider paying a visit to this collection of its "little stuff." A good exhibit of artifacts (mostly everyday domestic items) traces this region's history chronologically, from its Illyrian beginnings through its notable Roman period (items from Split and Salona) to the Middle Ages. About a 10-minute walk north of the Old Town, it's worth the trip for archaeology fans. Don't confuse this with the less-interesting Museum of Croatian Archaeological Monuments, on the way to the Ivan Meštrović Gallery.

Cost and Hours: 20 kn; June-Sept Mon-Sat 9:00-14:00 & 16:00-20:00, closed Sun; Oct-May Mon-Fri 9:00-14:00 & 16:00-20:00, Sat 9:00-14:00, closed Sun; Zrinsko Frankopanska 25, tel. 021/329-340, www.mdc.hr/split-arheoloski.

IVAN MEŠTROVIĆ SIGHTS, WEST OF THE OLD TOWN

The excellent Meštrović Gallery and nearby Kaštelet Chapel are just outside the Old Town. Both sights are covered by the same ticket and have the same hours.

Cost and Hours: 30 kn, covers both the gallery and the chapel; May-Sept Tue-Sun 9:00-19:00, closed Mon; Oct-April Tue-Sat 9:00-16:00, Sun 10:00-15:00, closed Mon; gallery tel. 021/340-800, chapel tel. 021/358-185, www.mdc.hr.

Getting There: Both sights are located along Šetalište Ivana Meštrovića. You can take **bus** #12 from the little cul-de-sac at the west end of the Riva (departs hourly, likely at :50 past the hour—but check the schedule; get off at the stop in front of the gallery, just after your bus passes a museum prominently marked *Muzej Hrvatskih Arheoloških Spomenika*). You can also **walk** (about 30 minutes): Follow the harbor west of town toward the big marina, swing right with the road, and follow the park until you see the gallery on your right (at #46). A **taxi** from the west end of the Old Town to the gallery costs about 50 kn (much more from the east end of the Old Town). To reach the chapel, it's a five-minute walk past the gallery down Šetalište Ivana Meštrovića to #39 (on the left, in an olive grove).

Cuisine Art: Café Galerija is just above the ticket office.

▲▲Meštrović Gallery (Galerija Meštrović)

Split's best art museum is dedicated to the sculptor Ivan Meštrović, the most important of all Croatian artists. Many of Meštrović's

finest works are housed in this palace, designed by the sculptor himself to serve as his residence, studio, and exhibition space. If you have time, it's worth the trek.

⊃ Self-Guided Tour: Each work is labeled, but there's very little description otherwise (and the 80-kn guidebook is overkill for most visitors). This tour will help you navigate the highlights. Before you begin, read the sidebar (see page 976) for background on Meštrović's life; while the collection is presented thematically rather than chronologically, knowing the artist's journey helps to make sense of what you'll see.

After buying your ticket (and confirming the time for your return bus to the Old Town—likely at :10 past the hour), climb the stairs toward Meštrović's house, pausing in the **garden** to admire a smattering of sculptures. On the right, see Persephone reaching skyward for freedom—an idea that came to Meštrović while he was imprisoned by the Ustaše in World War II. Beyond her, you'll see Cyclops struggling to hurl a giant shot put—in keeping with Meštrović's theme of the struggles of great men. Tucked behind the trees nearby is an eagle, which was a study for a mountaintop monument honoring one great man in particular, the Montenegrin King Petar II Petrović-Njegoš. To the left as you face the building is a statue of a woman playing a lute, and reliefs of women playing a lute and harp flank the door of the villa. Much as he enjoyed depicting the travails of men, Meštrović also often sculpted women serenely engaging in music.

Go up another set of stairs to reach the **Entrance Hall.** The sculptures here evoke some of Michelangelo's nudes and were fittingly carved from that great sculptor's favorite medium: Carrara marble. The head of a woman glancing pensively out a window is Meštrović's second wife, Olga, who was one of his favorite models. Notice the smaller black sculptures by the two staircases: on the left, representing birth, and on the right, representing death—Meštrović strove to capture the full range of human experience in his work.

Go to the left to find a maternal pyramid of love called *Madonna and Children.* While the woman is clearly garbed in the head scarf of the Virgin Mary, she cradles not one, but two children; these are Olga and Meštrović's first two kids.

Now enter the **Dining Room** at the end of the main floor. This is the most intimate space in the villa—the only room that still feels even a little bit lived in—and is decorated with more

Ivan Meštrović (1883-1962)

Ivan Meštrović (EE-vahn MESH-troh-veech), who achieved international fame for his talents as a sculptor, was Croatia's answer

to Rodin. You'll see Meštrović's works everywhere, in the streets, squares, and museums of Croatia.

Meštrović came from humble beginnings. He grew up in a family of poor, nomadic farm workers just inland from Split. At an early age, his drawings and wooden carvings showed promise, and a rich family took him in and made sure he was properly trained. He eventually went off to school in Vienna, where he fell in with the Secession movement and found fame and fortune. He lived in Prague, Paris, and Switzerland, fully engaged in the flourishing European artistic culture at the turn of the 20th century (he counted Rodin among his friends). After World War I, Meštrović moved back to Croatia and established an atelier, or workshop, in Zagreb (now a museum).

Later in life—like Diocletian before him—Meštrović returned to Split and built a huge seaside mansion (today's Meštrović Gallery). The years between the World Wars were Meštrović's happiest and most productive. It was during this time that he sculpted his most internationally famous works, a pair of giant Native American warriors on horseback in Chicago's Grant Park. But when World War II broke out, Meštrović—an outspoken supporter of the ideals of a united Yugoslavia—was briefly imprisoned by the anti-Yugoslav Ustaše (Croatia's Nazi puppet government). After his release, Meštrović fled to Italy, then to the US, where he lectured at prominent universities such as Notre Dame and Syracuse. (President Eisenhower literally handed Meštrović his new US passport in 1954.) After the war, the Yugoslav dictator Tito invited Meštrović to return, but the very religious artist refused to cooperate with an atheist regime. (Meštrović was friends with the Archbishop Alojzije Stepinac, who was imprisoned by Tito.) Meštrović died in South Bend, Indiana.

sculptures of Meštrović and his family. Entering, go straight ahead to the windows and do a clockwise loop around the room. First look for the self-portrait bust of Meštrović and the bust of a woman in a traditional Dalmatian head scarf—this is Meštrović's mother, another one of his favorite models. Notice that the two giant caryatids carved from Dalmatian stone (embedded with fragments of seashells) are also clad in this traditional garb. On the wall to the right of the fireplace, you'll see two painted

Viewing Meštrović's works, his abundant talent is evident. He worked in wood, plaster, marble, and bronze, and dabbled in painting. Meštrović's figures typically have long, angular fingers, arms, and legs. Whether whimsical or emotional, Meštrović's expressive, elongated faces—often with prominent noses—powerfully connect with the viewer.

Here are a few themes you'll see recurring in Meštrović's works as you tour his museum:

Religion: Meštrović was a devout Catholic.

Dalmatian Traditions: Meštrović felt a poignant nostalgia for the simple lifestyles and customs of his home region of Drniš, and he used his art to elevate them to be on par with religious and mythological themes. This is most evident in the angular scarves many of his female subjects wear around their heads.

Yugoslav Symbolism: Meštrović was a strong supporter of the first (pre-WWII) incarnation of Yugoslavia. He created sculptures not only in Croatia, but throughout Yugoslavia, many of them honoring heroes of Yugoslav tradition.

The Secession: Living and studying in Vienna in the early 20th century, Meštrović was exposed to the slinky cultural milieu of the likes of Gustav Klimt.

Struggling Men, Serene Women: While Meštrović frequently sculpted both male and female nudes, they often carry starkly different tones: Meštrović's ripped men tend to be toiling against an insurmountable challenge; his smooth and supple women are celebrating life, often through the medium of music (dancing, singing, playing instruments, and so on).

Tumult: Meštrović's life coincided with a time of great turmoil in Europe. He lived through World War I, the creation of the first Yugoslavia, World War II, the postwar/communist Yugoslavia, and the dawn of the Atomic Age in the United States. This early 20th-century angst—particularly surrounding his arrest and exile during World War II—comes through in his work.

Meštrović's works can be found throughout Split, Croatia, and the former Yugoslavia. In Split, in addition to the Meštrović Gallery and Kaštelet Chapel, you'll find his statues of Marko Marulić (see page 971), Gregory of Nin (page 968), and John the Baptist (page 967). Zagreb has another fine atelier/museum of Meštrović's works (see page 1071).

portraits of Meštrović—one as a young man (painted by his contemporary, Vlaho Bukovac), and another shortly before his death. Other busts in the room depict Meštrović's children. A painting of the *Last Supper* hangs in virtually every Dalmatian dining room, and Meštrović's is no exception—he painted this version himself, on wood. He also designed the furniture in this room.

Now climb the stairs. On the **landing**, look for a large bronze relief panel called *My People's Artist*. The old man and the young boy are linked by the *gusle*, a traditional Balkan stringed instrument. Here, Meštrović uses the *gusle* to represent the oral transmission of history (and specifically, the story of the pivotal Battle of Kosovo in 1389, a date etched into the minds of all Yugoslavs, particularly Serbs). Much as Meštrović dresses his women in traditional peasant clothes, he deeply believes in the regeneration of culture and customs over time. Meštrović's detailed drawings in this room—including some inspired by Dante's *Divine Comedy*—are worth a look.

Next, turn right into the **Secession Room.** Two of the finest works in this room—*Little Girl Singing* and *The Katunarić Family*—show the influence of Meštrović's contemporary, Rodin: smoothed rather than angular features, which make the final product less strictly lifelike, but also more expressive and visually pleasing. Other pieces in this room include several small studies for larger statues, some of which were never completed.

Pass through the room of drawings into the **Long Hall,** lined with life-size figures and a view terrace. The *Vestal Virgin*, sitting with her knees apart and feet together, is demonstrating a favorite pose of Meštrović's. And, once again, we see women finding solace and joy in music: dancing (while playfully tossing her hair), playing a lute, and so on. For contrast, look at the facing wall to see sketches of male nudes struggling. Step out onto the terrace to enjoy the Dalmatian views that inspired the artist.

At the end of the hall—past another small landing with drawings—is the **Study Room,** filled with miniature sculptures Meštrović created to prepare for larger-scale works: *Moses*, *Prometheus* (the figure tied to a rock, to be eaten by birds for eternity), and *Cyclops* (a large version of which we saw outside). Notice the small study of *Job*, then go into the small side-room to see the much larger final version.

One of Meštrović's most powerful works, **Job**—howling with an agony verging on insanity—was carved by the artist in exile, as his country was turned upside-down by World War II. Like Picasso's *Guernica*, it's a silent scream against the inanity of war. The curator has intentionally placed it in a separate room to emphasize the feeling of alienation. Meštrović sketched his inspiration for this piece (displayed on the wall) while he was imprisoned by the Ustaše.

Head down the stairs and make a U-turn left into the **Sacral Room.** Meštrović was very religious, and here you can see some of his many works depicting biblical figures. The giant, wood-carved *Adam* and *Eve* dominate the room. Also notice the woodcarved relief panels of *Merry Angels* and *Grieving Angels*. (These are similar to the panels you'll see at the Kaštelet Chapel down the road.) Smaller statues around the room include four evangelists

(Matthew, John, and two Lukes—but no Mark), Moses, a *pietà*, and both bronze and wooden heads of Christ.

The smaller side-room displays another of the gallery's highlights: the quietly poignant **Roman Pietà**. Meštrović follows the classical pyramid form, with Joseph of Arimathea (top), Mary (left), and Mary Magdalene (right) surrounding the limp body of Christ. But the harmony is broken by the painful angles of the mourning faces. Also notice how Jesus' oversized, ruined body drags down those trying to support his dead weight; if he stood up, he'd be towering over all of them. For Meštrović, Christ's suffering was personal: the women wear those traditional Dalmatian head scarves, the features of Joseph are a self-portrait, and Mary Magdalene is modeled after Meštrović's daughter Marija. This sculpture is plaster; there's a bronze version at the Vatican and a marble one on the campus of The University of Notre Dame in the US.

To reach the last part of the Meštrović experience, head down the stairs to the road, cross the street, turn right, and walk about five minutes. You'll see the low-profile entrance to the chapel on the left, through a doorway marked *39*, in an olive grove.

▲▲Kaštelet Chapel

If you enjoy the gallery, don't miss the nearby Kaštelet Chapel ("Chapel of the Holy Cross"). Meštrović bought this 16th-century

fortified palace to display his 28 wood reliefs of Jesus' life. You can see how Meštrović's style changed over time, as he carved these over a nearly 30-year span, completing the last 12 when he was in the US. (However, note that he didn't carve the reliefs in chronological order; the ticket office sells a booklet identifying the topic and year for each one.) While the earlier pieces are well-composed and powerful, the later ones seem more hastily done, as Meštrović rushed to complete his opus. Work clockwise around the room, tracing the life of Christ. Notice that some of the Passion scenes are out of order (a side-effect of Meštrović's nonlinear schedule). The beautiful *pietà* back near the entrance still shows some of the original surface of the wood, demonstrating the skill required to create depth and emotion in just a few inches of medium. Dominating the chapel is an extremely powerful wooden crucifix, with Christ's arms, legs, fingers, and toes bent at unnatural angles—a typically expressionistic flair Meštrović used to exaggerate suffering.

Activities in Split

Hitting the Beach

Since it's more of a big city than a resort, Split's beaches aren't as scenic (and the water not as clear) as small towns elsewhere along the coast. Save your Split time for big-city sights and culture, and hit the beach in smaller towns. However, if the weather's great and you want to go for a dip, here are a few ideas.

The beach that's most popular—and crowded—is **Bačvice,** in a pebbly cove just a short walk east of the main ferry terminal. As it's very shallow, it's especially popular with kids. This means it can be unpleasantly crowded when the weather's good. After dark, it becomes a hopping meat-market nightlife zone for older "kids."

You'll find less crowded beaches just to the east of Bačvice. Each cove has its own little swimming zone; the fourth cove over, called **Trstenik**, is perhaps the most inviting. A pebbly beach—with free access—flanks the big deck in front of the Radisson Hotel, where you can rent a chair (100 kn), buy a drink at the bar, and use the free showers.

Or head in the other direction to Marjan, the peninsular city park, which is ringed with several sunbathing beaches. Along the southern edge of Marjan, just below the Meštrović Gallery, is a rocky but more local-feeling and less crowded beach called **Ježinac** (Croatian for "sea urchin"...be sure to wear water shoes). **Bene Beach** is along the northern edge of Marjan—so it offers more shade. You can get to Bene Beach by bus #12 (the same one that goes to the Meštrović Gallery), tourist train (described earlier, under "Getting Around Split"), bike, or foot (about a 45-minute walk from the Old Town).

Nightlife in Split

The Riva

Every night, the sea of Croatian humanity laps at the walls of Diocletian's Palace along the town's pedestrian promenade. Choose a bench and watch life go by, or enjoy a drink at one of the many outdoor cafés. Live music (funded by the tourist board) enlivens the Riva nightly through the summer (June-mid-Sept).

Old Town Bars

The labyrinthine lanes of the Old Town are packed with mostly interchangeable bars and cafés featuring pleasant tables crammed between ancient stone buildings under a starry Croatian sky. Even if you're not interested in drinking, make a point to wander some of these areas after dark just to people-watch and take in the hubbub in these otherwise hidden zones. If you're staying in the Old Town, you'll hear bar-goers late into the night. If you can't beat 'em, join 'em. One way is to simply lose yourself in the twisty lanes by following the music and the sound of socializing Croatians to the spot you like best. Or, if you prefer a little direction to your ramblings, explore the following neighborhoods. Note that, while each of the bars listed here has an interior, there's little reason to sit anywhere but under the open sky. Prices and menus are similar at most places (beer, wine, cocktails, coffee drinks); ordering something simply gives you an excuse to sit in a gorgeous outdoor space, nurse a drink, and focus on your travel partner. The action at these places really gets rolling around 22:00 and peaks around 23:00 or 24:00. Bars are supposed to close their outdoor seating areas at 2:00 in the morning.

On the Peristyle: The obvious choice is right on the main square of the Old Town, Diocletian's former entry hall. All day long, the Peristyle steps serve as makeshift café tables for the bar called **Luxor,** with red cushions and small tables scattered along the steps. If you sit on a cushion, you're expected to order a drink (but you can sit or stand elsewhere for free). In the evening—as twilight encroaches and floodlights transform the square into one of the most atmospheric public spaces in Europe—live music breaks out (generally starting between 20:00 and 21:00 and continuing until around midnight). The smooth marble tiles of the Peristyle—worn to a slippery sheen by two millennia of visitors—becomes a dance floor, as people salsa, foxtrot, or pop-and-lock their way around the majestic space. Where else can you cut a rug in the grand entry hall of a Roman palace?

Majstora Jurja: This street, which runs along the north edge of Diocletian's Palace (just inside the wall), is lined with a mellow gaggle of low-key hangouts. Some mood music plays, but the soundtrack here is mostly chatting, laughing, and flirting. West of the Golden Gate, the lineup of café/bars includes the nondescript **Kala** and **Mosquito.** Two better options are nearby: Up the side street at Dominisova 9, **Galerija** has the classiest atmosphere, with an upscale-feeling (but not stuffy), gallery-like ambience and a display case of cakes. A bit farther along Majstora Jurja is **Teak,** with a namesake woody interior that feels almost distinguished. East of the Golden Gate is a tamer zone, with the soccer-themed **Mali Flek** and then the **Red Room,** filling a large square with tables.

"Slavija Square": This is my own nickname for the tight, stepped area that's squeezed in front of Hotel Slavija, near Radić Brothers Square (Trg Braće Radića; from the square's statue of Marulić, enter the Old Town and bear right, following the beat). This area is more youthful and rowdy, with throbbing techno music and cocktails that flow freely. Clambering up the steps are several bars, including the mellow **Figa** and the hip **Fluid,** with predictable thumpa-thumpa atmosphere. Near the top of the stairs, the engagingly scruffy **Split Circus** boasts magic-marker walls and several varieties of *rakija*, the ubiquitous Balkan firewater. A few steps beyond, through the enclosed courtyard on the right, **Ghetto** has a mellower sailors' bordello-theme interior, with heart-shaped chairs, red velvet, and vivid graffiti.

Behind the Loggia: For the youngest, trendiest scene in the Old Town, head for the zone locals call *Iza Lođa* ("Behind the Loggia"). From the grand People's Square, follow the beat behind the former City Hall loggia to discover a well-dressed meat market populated by sleazy young men and tipsy American girls determined to make bad decisions. The main magnet here is the standing-room-only **Gaga,** with a pounding dance beat, indoor and outdoor bar areas, and a laser-light show on the ancient stones above. At the far end of the little square, like a mellow grandparent observing the rowdy younger generation, is **La Linea** (which locals call simply "taverna")—an old sailors' pub decorated with nautical flags.

Other Areas: The large square at the top of Marmontova, just before the **Zara** store, is crammed with tables belonging to a half-dozen, identical-feeling cafés. And with the arrival of the recommended Bajamonti café, **Trg Republike** (the grand Napoleonic square just west of the Riva) could also become a happening nightlife option.

Clubbing at Bačvice Beach

This family-friendly beach by day becomes a throbbing party area for young locals late at night. Since all Old Town bars have to close by 2:00 in the morning, night owls hike on over to the Bačvice crescent of clubs. The three-floor club complex is a cacophony of music, with the beat of one club melting into the next—all with breezy terraces overlooking the harbor.

Sleeping in Split

Split has more and more sleeping options every year, as little guest houses frequently pop up. But even with the abundance of beds, prices can be high in this big city. Split also suffers from perhaps the worst nighttime noise of any destination in this book—bring

Sleep Code

Abbreviations

(6 kn = about $1, €1 = about $1.40, country code: 385, area code: 021)
S = Single, **D** = Double/Twin, **T** = Triple, **Q** = Quad, **b** = bathroom.

Price Rankings

$$$ **Higher Priced**—Most rooms €125 or more.

$$ **Moderately Priced**—Most rooms between €70-125.

$ **Lower Priced**—Most rooms €70 or less.

If I've listed two sets of rates for an accommodation, I've noted when the second rate applies (generally off-season, Oct-May); if I've listed three sets of rates, separated by slashes, the first is for peak season (July-Sept), the second is shoulder season (May-June and Oct), and the third is off-season (Nov-April). The dates for seasonal rates vary by hotel.

The modest tourist tax (about 7 kn per person, per night) is not included in these rates. Hotels generally accept credit cards and include breakfast in their rates, while most *sobe* accept only cash and don't offer breakfast. While rates are listed in euros, you'll pay in kunas. Everyone listed here speaks English, and Wi-Fi is generally free. Prices change; verify current rates online or by email. For the best prices, always book directly with the hotel.

SPLIT

earplugs, and always ask for a quiet room (if possible). If you're on your own for breakfast, see my suggestions on page 991.

OUTSIDE THE OLD TOWN

These good values are within a five-minute walk of the Old Town. They're nearly as convenient as the Old Town options, but cheaper. Of these places, only Hotel Luxe has a full-time reception desk; for the others, call ahead to arrange your arrival time.

In the Lučac Neighborhood, East of the Old Town

The Lučac neighborhood—which lines up along the busy street called Kralja Zvonimira—feels urban and a bit gritty, but it's handy to the Old Town. You'll find more Old World atmosphere on Petrova street, a block below the main road.

$$$ Hotel Luxe, a sleek, minimalist hotel with 30 upscale-mod rooms, is a comfy splurge that combines a fine location (near the Old Town) with sea views—rare in this city. While it fronts a dreary, busy urban street, all of its rooms face the quieter back side, and most have views over the harbor (non-view "classic" Db-€165/€115/€85, partial-view Db-€195/€140/€100, bigger "comfort" Db with view and small balcony-€245/€165/€115, "superior" Db with view and big balcony-€315/€195/€135, Sb

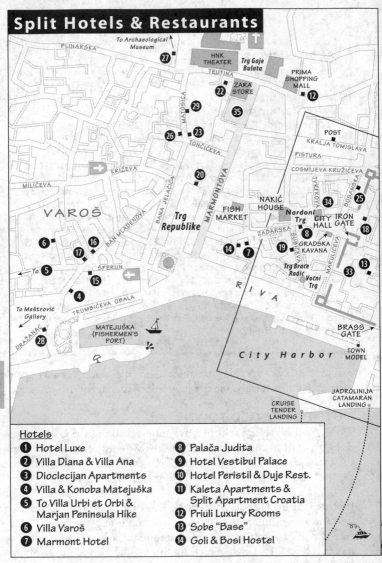

Split Hotels & Restaurants

Hotels

1. Hotel Luxe
2. Villa Diana & Villa Ana
3. Dioclecijan Apartments
4. Villa & Konoba Matejuška
5. To Villa Urbi et Orbi & Marjan Peninsula Hike
6. Villa Varoš
7. Marmont Hotel
8. Palača Judita
9. Hotel Vestibul Palace
10. Hotel Peristil & Duje Rest.
11. Kaleta Apartments & Split Apartment Croatia
12. Priuli Luxury Rooms
13. Sobe "Base"
14. Goli & Bosi Hostel

in any category is €15 less, cheaper Nov-Feb, air-con, elevator, Wi-Fi, spa with small gym and Jacuzzi, free parking behind hotel, Kralja Zvonimira 6, tel. 021/314-444, www.hotelluxesplit.com, hotelluxe@hotelluxesplit.com).

$$$ Villa Diana has six pleasant, though pricey and small, rooms in a stone house over a restaurant (Sb-€109/€90/€66, Db-€149/€116/€80, Tb-€170/€129/€93, rates vary with demand—email them directly for better rates, pricier apartment also available,

Restaurants & Nightlife
- ⑮ Šperun Restaurant & Bistrot Šperun Deva
- ⑯ Konoba Varoš Restaurant
- ⑰ Tonik Juice Bar
- ⑱ Trattoria Bajamont
- ⑲ Apetit Restaurant
- ⑳ Bajamonti Restaurant
- ㉑ Uje Oilbar
- ㉒ Maslina Restaurant
- ㉓ Ristorante Pizzeria Galija
- ㉔ Zlatna Vrata Pizza & Pasta
- ㉕ Fast Food None
- ㉖ Kantun Paulina
- ㉗ Paradox Wine & Cheese Bar
- ㉘ Leut Restaurant
- ㉙ Hajduk Ice Cream
- ㉚ Nadalina Chocolate Shop
- ㉛ Luxor Bar
- ㉜ Majstora Jurja Nightlife
- ㉝ "Slavija Square" Nightlife
- ㉞ "Behind the Loggia" Nightlife
- ㉟ Marmontova Nightlife
- ㊱ To Bačvice Beach

SPLIT

cheaper Nov-March, air-con, Wi-Fi, free parking, next door to Villa Ana at Kuzmanića 3—see directions in next listing, tel. 021/482-460, www.villadiana.hr, info@villadiana.hr).

$$ Villa Ana, my sentimental favorite in Split, has five modern, comfortable rooms in a smart little freestanding stone house (Sb-€80, Db-€100, Tb-€115, can be cheaper at last minute in shoulder season, roughly €20 less Nov-March, includes breakfast, air-con, Wi-Fi, reception open sporadically 7:00-22:00, may be closed mid-Dec-mid-Jan, a few tight free parking spots out front; 2 long blocks east of Old Town up busy Kralja Zvonimira, follow the driveway-like lane opposite the lonely skyscraper to Vrh Lučac 16; if using GPS, enter the address Kralja Zvonimira 14 to get close; tel. 021/482-715, www.villaana-split.hr, info@villaana-split.hr, Danijel Bilobrk and helpful Branka).

$ Dioclecijan Apartments, run by Tomislav Skalić and his wife Ivana, has two small rooms and one apartment in a pleasant local neighborhood. The decor is a tasteful mix of new and traditional. As the owners live off-site, carefully arrange a meeting time in advance (Db-€55/€40, apartment-€80/€65, lower price is for Oct-March, 1-night stays cost €5 more in rooms or €10 more in apartment, prices soft, cash only, no breakfast, air-con, Wi-Fi, Petrova 19, Tomislav's mobile 091-537-1826, Ivana's mobile 091-536-7486, tskalic1976@gmail.com).

In the Varoš Neighborhood, West of the Old Town

In addition to hosting the following accommodations, the atmospheric Varoš neighborhood—with twisty lanes climbing up toward the forested peak of the Marjan peninsula—is also home to several recommended eateries and the self-service Modrulj Launderette.

$$ Villa Matejuška, run by kind Andreja, has six apartments with old-fashioned beams and stone walls on a tight lane just up from the fishermen's port (Db-€110-135/€80-105/€60-85, price depends on size, cash only, no extra charge for 1-night stays, no breakfast, air-con, Wi-Fi, Tomića Stine 3, mobile 098-222-822, www.villamatejuska.hr, villamatejuska93@gmail.com). A second branch, **$$ Villa Urbi et Orbi,** has six cheaper units a steep five-minute hike up the street (Db-€100-110/€70-80/€50-60, price depends on size, 4-person apartment-€170/€140/€120, same amenities as Villa Matejuška; from Villa Matejuška, continue up Senjska, head straight up the stairs, then turn right on Šenoina to #2; mobile 099-734-2777, www.villaurbietorbi.hr, villaurbietorbi97@gmail.com).

$$ Villa Varoš, run with class by Croatian-American Joanne Đonlić and her son Jure, has eight rooms and an apartment (with its own terrace) on a residential lane just beyond the restaurant-lined Šperun street. Thin walls and echoey halls can make for a noisy night (Db-€80/€65, Tb-€85/€70, apartment-€120/€90, lower prices are for Oct-March, rates include tax, no breakfast, air-con, stairs with no elevator, Wi-Fi, Miljenka Smoje 1, tel. 021/483-469, Joanne's mobile 098-469-681, Jure's mobile 098-229-408, www.villavaros.hr, joanne.d.o.o@st.t-com.hr).

INSIDE THE OLD TOWN

While the Old Town is convenient and atmospheric, it's also a happening nightlife zone, so you're likely to encounter some noise (especially on weekends). Old Town bars can stay open until 2:00 in the morning...earplugs are essential.

$$$ Marmont Hotel is an enjoyable oasis offering four-star comfort, with 21 classy rooms in a quiet corner of the Old Town. The slight aroma you may notice is from the fish market, just around the corner (standard Sb-€195/€150/€120, superior Sb-€245/€190/€155, Db-€220/€180/€140, superior Db-€270/€220/€180, pricier "deluxe" rooms also available, air-con, elevator, Wi-Fi, sun terrace, Zadarska 13, tel. 021/308-060, www.marmonthotel.com, booking@marmonthotel.com).

$$$ Palača Judita is a splurge, designed for people who are willing to pay extra for good service and serenity in a cozy B&B atmosphere (rather than a traditional hotel). Its eight rooms are beautifully located in a 16th-century Renaissance palace on the appealing "People's Square," with solid windows to help block out the after-hours ruckus (Db-€269-319/€169-229/€99-139; price varies dramatically depending on size, amenities, and when you book; includes breakfast, air-con, Wi-Fi, free parking and porter service, Narodni Trg 4, tel. 021/420-220, www.juditapalace.com, booking@juditapalace.com).

$$$ Hotel Vestibul Palace is the swankiest spot in Split's Old Town, with modern decor in an old shell. Tucked in a corner just behind the entry vestibule on the upper level of Diocletian's Palace, this plush place offers seven rooms with maximum style and service for maximum prices. Throughout the day, you'll hear the harmonious voices of the *klapa* singers echoing up from the vestibule below; they take their breaks at the hotel's outdoor tables. Sleep here only if you value location, comfort, and service without regard for the price tag (Sb-€355/€255/€140, small "standard" Db-€375/€275/€160, superior Db-€475/€380/€200, pricier suites also available, air-con, no elevator, guest computer and Wi-Fi, valet parking, Iza Vestibula 4, tel. 021/329-329, www.vestibulpalace.com, info@vestibulpalace.com). They also have four more rooms in a nearby annex, called Villa Vestibul, and plan even more in a new property just outside the Old Town.

$$$ Hotel Peristil has 12 classy rooms over a restaurant just steps from the couldn't-be-more-central square of the same name. Run by the Caktaš family, it's homey and convenient, if pricey (Sb-€135/€110/€95, Db-€160/€135/€120, extra bed-€35, air-con, stairs with no elevator, Wi-Fi, some noise from nearby bars, just behind TI and inside the Silver Gate at Poljana Kraljice Jelene 5, tel. 021/329-070, www.hotelperistil.com, booking@hotelperistil.com).

$$ Kaleta Apartments, run by the Raić family, consists of several tastefully decorated apartments spread across two buildings. Two stylish, modern apartments are squeezed between cafés along a tight alley in a lively area at the back of the Old Town (the good windows do a heroic job of keeping noise to a minimum). Their other three units, including a larger one with a couch and eat-in space, share a common lounge in a quieter building a few blocks away, near the People's Square (Db-€75-90, €60-80 in Oct-May, price depends on size of room, cash only, air-con, guest computer and Wi-Fi, Majstora Jurja 4, mobile 099-509-4299, www.kaletaapartments.com, kaletaapartments@email.t-com.hr).

$$ Split Apartment Croatia, run by go-getter Nikša, is an agency with a line on apartments around Split. Nikša rents three of his own rooms, near the People's Square (Db-€75/€55/€40, no breakfast, air-con, free Wi-Fi). He can also arrange a room for you elsewhere for similar prices (you pay him 20 percent, then the rest to the owner, cash only; his office at Majstora Jurja 4 serves as a sort of reception desk, offering free coffee and guest computer; mobile 091-390-9416, www.split-apartment.com, info@split-apartment.com). Nikša also has five elegant, nicely equipped rooms just north of the Old Town in a building called **Priuli Luxury Rooms** (Db-€110/€85/€50, Sinjska 1, tel. 021/341-083, www.priulisplit.com).

$ Sobe "Base" has three good rooms in the Old Town. Tina and her dad, retired ship's captain Ivo, offer many amenities unusual for this price range, including free Wi-Fi and Internet terminals in each room. You can't be more central: All of the colorful rooms—located over a gift shop—overlook the front steps of the cute little Jupiter's Temple. Although it's in the midst of some bustling bar action, the double-paned windows do their darnedest to provide reasonable peace; earplugs help, too (Db-€80/€70, lower price is for Sept-June, cash only, no extra charge for 1- or 2-night stays, no breakfast, clearly communicate your arrival time, air-con, Kraj Svetog Ivana 3, tel. 021/317-375, mobile 098-361-387, www.base-rooms.com, mail@base-rooms.com).

$ Goli & Bosi Hostel ("Nude and Barefoot") is a design hostel filling an old shopping mall in a hidden square in Split's Old Town, just off of Marmontova. It's big (135 beds in 25 rooms), industrial-strength, and unabashedly stylish. The neon-yellow halls (inspired by the sulfur springs that lured Diocletian here)—scrawled with important dates from Croatian history—give way to white, minimalist rooms. It's expensive (the private rooms are downright overpriced), but it's stylish and offers lots of fun amenities, including shared view balconies, an "auditorium" for watching movies, a restaurant out front, and lots of parties (bunk in 4- to 8-bed dorm-€32/€28/€25, small Sb-€90/€72/€60, small Db-€105/€90/€82, larger "premium" Db-€150/€130, cheaper

SPLIT

mid-Oct–mid-April, private rooms include breakfast but dorm dwellers pay €5 extra, elevator, air-con, Wi-Fi, tries to be sound-proof in sleeping areas, Morpurgova Poljana 2, tel. 021/510-999, www.golibosi.com, info@golibosi.com).

Eating in Split

I've concentrated my listings inside Split's Old Town and within the adjacent Varoš district, just a couple of blocks west, which has several characteristic *konoba*s (traditional restaurants). Reservations are wise, especially for dinner.

IN VAROŠ, WEST OF THE OLD TOWN

Šperun Restaurant has a classy, cozy Old World ambience and a passion for good Dalmatian food. Owner Damir Banović (with the

help of his animated dad, Zdravko) serves a mix of Croatian and "eclectic Mediterranean," specializing in seafood. A "buffet" table of *antipasti* (starters) in the lower dining room shows you what you're getting, so you can select your ideal meal (not self-service—order from the waiter). This place distinguishes itself by offering a warm welcome and good food for reasonable prices (40-90-kn pastas, 60-130-kn meat and seafood dishes, daily 9:00-23:00— but likely closed Sun Nov-March, air-con, a few sidewalk tables, reservations wise in summer, Šperun 3, tel. 021/346-999). Their annex across the street, **Bistrot Šperun Deva,** has a simpler and cheaper menu, lots of outdoor seating, and a handy à la carte breakfast for *sobe*-dwellers (20-50-kn salads, 60-75-kn main courses, daily 8:00-23:00—except closed 13:00-18:00 Mon-Tue, closed off-season, Šperun 2).

Konoba Matejuška offers charm, good food, and fair prices in a cozy, mellow, five-table cellar. This place is tiny and justifi-ably popular, so reserve at least a day before (60-80-kn starters, 50-150-kn main courses, daily 12:00-23:00, Tomića Stine 3, tel. 021/355-152).

Konoba Varoš, though old-school, bigger, and more imper-sonal than others listed here, is beloved by natives and tour-ists alike for its great food. Serious waiters serve a wide range of Croatian cooking (including pastas, seafood, and meat dishes) under droopy fishnets in a slightly gloomy throwback interior (55-85-kn pastas, 60-130-kn main courses, daily 9:00-24:00, lots of groups, reservations smart, Ban Mladenova 7, tel. 021/396-138).

Smoothies and Fruit Juices: For a healthier energy boost, head for **Tonik Juice Bar**, run by Croat-Aussie Stefanie. Select from the diverse menu of smoothies and juice combos (20-40 kn). In summer, they also serve light meals (35-kn sandwiches, 30-kn muesli for breakfast, June-Sept daily 7:00-22:00, shoulder season daily 8:00-21:00, closed Nov-March, near the launderette and Šperun street restaurants at Ban Mladenova 5, mobile 098-641-376).

IN AND NEAR THE OLD TOWN

Trattoria Bajamont, not to be confused with Bajamonti (listed below), is buried on a narrow lane deep in the Old Town. They offer unpretentious, affordable Dalmatian home cooking with an emphasis on fish. The handwritten menu informs you of the day's options—all fresh from the market. In this tight, casual, and cozy eatery, the busy kitchen and seven tables are all crammed into a single room (with more tables on the alley outside). Because the place can be crowded, you may have to share your table—and be prepared for the service to be chaotic and a bit quirky (90-120-kn pastas, 90-150-kn fish dishes, cash only, daily 8:00-24:00—but closed Sun outside peak season, Bajamontijeva 3, tel. 021/355-356).

Apetit serves up traditional Dalmatian cuisine in an appealingly modern, second-floor dining room. As there's no outdoor seating, this is a good bad-weather option (60-85-kn pastas, 60-125-kn main courses; 90-kn daily special includes soup, salad, and main dish; lots of groups, daily 10:00-24:00, Šubićeva 5, tel. 021/332-549).

Bajamonti sits regally at the top of Split's beautiful, arcaded square, Trg Republike, just off the west end of the Riva. This place brings a certain grand-café elegance to Split's otherwise rustic-*konoba*-heavy dining scene. The interior is classy, with checkerboard-tiled, split-level elegance, but the best seating is on the grand square out front, facing the sea. The food is pricey, with an emphasis on fish (90-120-kn pastas, 120-170-kn main courses, 75-95-kn lunches, daily 7:30-24:00, Trg Republike 1, tel. 021/341-033).

Uje Oilbar is the flagship restaurant of Croatia's popular chain of upscale olive-oil boutiques. Tucked away in a hidden corner of the Old Town, it serves simple plates and boards of Dalmatian *pršut* (prosciutto), cheeses, olives, and, of course, olive oils—50 different types. The menu is short, and it feels more like a big snack than a hearty meal; to assemble a filling meal, you'll run up quite a bill. But the rustic-mod interior, pleasant (if cramped) outdoor seating, and refreshingly good-quality local flavors can make a light meal here worthwhile (35-65-kn olive-oil tastings, 70-100-kn small plates and taster boards, daily 12:00-24:00, Dominisova 3, mobile 095-200-8008).

Maslina ("Olive"), an unpretentious family-run spot filled with locals, hides behind a shopping mall on the busy Marmontova pedestrian street. They serve a wide range of 45-70-kn pizzas and pastas, plus 70-120-kn meat and fish dishes (Tue-Sat 11:00-24:00, Sun-Mon 12:00-24:00, Teutina 1A, tel. 021/314-988, Pezo family). It's virtually impossible to find on your own, so follow these directions carefully: Approaching the top of Marmontova from the harbor, look for the low-profile archway on the left beyond the café tables (just before the big Zara store). Walk along the skinny path between the building and the old wall to reach the restaurant.

Pizzerias: **Ristorante Pizzeria Galija,** at the west end of the Old Town, has a boisterous local following and good wood-fired pizza, pasta, and salads. They have a cozy interior and a terrace (40-75 kn, Mon-Sat 9:00-24:00, Sun 12:00-24:00, air-con, just a block off of Marmontova at Tončićeva 12, tel. 021/347-932; the recommended Hajduk ice-cream shop is nearby). **Zlatna Vrata** ("Golden Gate"), right in the Old Town, offers wood-fired pizzas and pasta dishes. The food and interior are nothing special, but there's wonderful outdoor seating in a tingle-worthy Gothic courtyard with pointy arches and lots of pillars. They plan to start serving a more extensive and expensive menu in the near future, so prices may increase (50-75 kn, Mon-Sat 7:00-24:00, closed Sun, just inside the Golden Gate and—as you face outside—up the skinny alley to the left, on Majstora Jurja, tel. 021/345-015).

Take-Away: **Fast Food None** ("Grandma's") is a stand-up or take-away pizza joint handy for a quick bite in the Old Town. In addition to pizzas and bruschettas with various toppings, they serve up a pair of traditional pizza-like specialties (with crust on bottom and top, like a filled pizza): *viška pogača,* with tomatoes, onion, and anchovy; and *soparnik,* with a thin layer of spinach, onion, and olive oil. They can also make you a grilled sandwich— just point to what you want (10-30 kn, Mon-Sat 7:00-23:00, closed Sun, just outside Diocletian's Palace on the skinny street that runs along the wall at Bosanska 4, tel. 021/347-252). **Kantun Paulina** ("Paulina's Corner") is a local favorite for take-away *ćevapčići*— Balkan grilled meats (17-20 kn, Mon-Sat 8:30-24:00, Sun 10:00-24:00, Matošića 1). For descriptions of your options, see the "Balkan Flavors" sidebar on page 1140.

Wine Bar: **Paradox Wine & Cheese Bar,** in an unassuming urban zone behind the National Theater, offers an inviting opportunity to sample some local wines. Their well-structured menu lists 120 wines, 50 of which are available by the glass (20-120-kn glasses, 100-800-kn bottles). Sit either in the cozy old-meets-modern interior or out on the terrace (also 25-40-kn light bites, including cheese and prosciutto, daily 9:00-24:00, Dubrovačka 18, mobile 099-817-0711).

Breakfast: The budget choice is to simply buy some pastries at a bakery and eat them on a harborfront bench. **Hotel Peristil** serves an all-you-can-eat breakfast—including eggs—to non-guests for 60 kn (daily 7:00-11:00); the adjacent **Duje Restaurant,** just behind the cathedral, has a similar deal. For a cheap alternative, head over to the Matejuška fishermen's port, where **Leut** restaurant serves a 30-45-kn breakfast on their terrace (from 9:30). Several of my recommended restaurants also offer breakfast.

Gelato: Split has several spots for delicious ice cream *(sladoled).* Most ice-cream parlors *(kuća sladoleda)* are open daily 8:00-24:00. Natives recommend **Hajduk,** named for Split's soccer team; ask them to dip your cone in milk chocolate for no extra charge (a block off the main Marmontova pedestrian drag, around the corner from Pizzeria Galija at Matošićeva 4).

Split Connections

BY BOAT

As the transport hub for the Dalmatian Coast, Split has good boat connections to nearly anywhere you want to go. The fast passenger catamarans dock close to the Old Town: the *Krilo* catamaran uses dock #11 (a.k.a. Gat Sv. Petra), which is along the pier halfway between the main ferry terminal and the Old Town; and the Jadrolinija catamaran usually arrives and departs at the handy Obala Lazareta embankment just in front of the Old Town

(although it may sometimes use dock #11 instead—ask when you buy your ticket). Big car ferries can arrive or depart from all along the harbor (electronic boards display which dock each boat leaves from). Note that these locations sometimes change according to boat traffic.

Note: The following boat information is subject to change—always confirm before you make your plans. To check Jadrolinija schedules, see www.jadrolinija.hr; for *Krilo* catamaran schedules, see www.krilo.hr. Or drop by Split's helpful Jadrolinija boat ticket office, in the main ferry terminal (open 24/7 in summer, daily 5:30-24:00 off-season, tel. 021/338-333).

Buying Tickets

If you want to take a fast passenger **catamaran** (either *Krilo* or Jadrolinija), buy your tickets in advance.

Krilo tickets can be bought anytime; in peak season, it's smart to buy yours at least the day before your scheduled departure. You may be able to buy *Krilo* tickets online; check www.krilo.hr.

Otherwise, find the *sales* kiosk marked *Kapetan Luka* at the departure dock.

Jadrolinija catamaran tickets are not sold until 6:00 in the morning on the day of departure. As these boats can sell out quickly in peak season, buy your tickets in the morning. Catamaran tickets—even for afternoon departures—can sell out by 8:30; to play it safe, line up by 8:00. Off-season, you can usually wait until 9:00 for morning departures, or until noon (or later) for afternoon departures. If your trip hinges on a specific boat, ask at the ticket desk the day before what time you should show up. For Jadrolinija catamarans, you can buy tickets at three locations: the kiosk on the parking island right in front of the Old Town; next to the *Krilo* kiosk alongside the harbor; and in the main terminal (if the kiosk near the Old Town has a long line, you could walk five minutes to the next one, where the wait is probably shorter).

If tickets do sell out, you're not entirely out of luck. Each route is also operated by slower car ferries with unlimited room for walk-on passengers. The downside is that car ferries take longer and drop you off at ports that are not convenient to the main town on each island (Stari Grad on Hvar, Vela Luka on Korčula), requiring an additional bus trip to your final destination. The ticket-seller can advise you of alternatives.

If you're a passenger walking onto a Jadrolinija **car ferry**, there's no need to buy tickets in advance. (Tickets are sold at the same three locations noted above.) However, if you're driving onto a car ferry, it's smart to buy your tickets from one of the Jadrolinija kiosks mentioned above and line up early—ask locally for advice on your particular boat.

While I haven't listed specific fares below, walk-on passage for both catamarans and ferries is quite affordable. The passenger fare on a trip from Split to Hvar or Korčula costs only around 35-60 kn, depending on the type of boat and season. Taking a car on the slow ferry that follows a similar route costs 265-530 kn.

Weather Disruptions: Catamarans are the quickest way to the islands, but they're also the most susceptible to inclement weather. In very rough or windy weather, cancellations are possible (decisions are made a couple of hours before departure—ask at the ticket booth what time you should come back to check). In poor weather, the *Krilo* is more stable (and provides a more comfortable ride) than Jadrolinija's catamaran; if you have an option, go with *Krilo*. If the catamarans aren't running, look into taking the slower car ferries instead (which typically go in any weather).

Getting from Split to the Dalmatian Islands

To Hvar Island: Ideally catch a boat heading to Hvar town, the most interesting part of the island. Two companies run speedy

SPLIT

Sailing Between Croatia and Italy

Many travelers are tempted to splice a little bit of Croatia into their Italian itinerary, or vice versa. But zipping across the Adriatic isn't as effortless as it seems. Most sea crossings involve an overnight on the boat, and the Italian towns best connected to Croatia—Ancona, Pescara, and Bari—are far from Italy's top sights. Plan thoughtfully. For example, if you're in northern Italy and want to sample Croatia, it's much easier to dip into Istria than it is to get all the way down to Croatia's Dalmatian Coast.

If you decide to set sail, you have several options, run by various companies. Split is the primary hub, but you can also go from other cities (usually Dubrovnik or Zadar; some international ferries also call at the small Dalmatian islands). Almost all boats go to Ancona, Italy, which is about two-thirds of the way up the Italian coast (on the calf of Italy's "boot"). Others go to Pescara, about 100 miles south of Ancona; and to Bari, near the southern tip of Italy (the "heel"). Most trips are overnight and last 8-10 hours, but there are faster daytime catamarans. Note that these connections are highly subject to change from year to year; do an Internet search to be confident you know all of your options.

Slow Night Boats: Figure about €45-60 per person for one-way deck passage (about 10-20 percent more in peak season, roughly July-Aug; sometimes even more on weekends). Onboard accommodation costs extra (about €20 per person for a couchette in a 4-berth compartment, €60-75 per person in 2-bed compartment with private shower and WC). These companies operate night boats to Italy:

catamarans (50-60 minutes) from Split to Hvar town: **Jadrolinija** (July-Aug 5/day, June and Sept 4/day, Oct-May 2/day) and *Krilo* (generally 1-2/day depending on season; an additional catamaran, bound for Vis, stops at Hvar only on Tue and Fri; as schedules have been in flux, confirm at www.krilo.hr). You can also reach Hvar Island on the **local car ferries** from Split (7/day in summer, 3/day in winter, 1.75 hours); these are frequent but take longer and are less convenient, since they take you to the town of Stari Grad, across the island and a 20-minute bus trip from Hvar town. On the other hand, these are a good backup plan in case the relatively rare morning catamaran departures sell out, or if the catamarans stop running due to bad weather.

To Korčula Island and Dubrovnik: Ideally, look for a boat heading to "Korčula" (that is, Korčula town) rather than "Vela Luka" (at the opposite end of the island, a 1-hour bus ride away). The most convenient options to Korčula town are direct catamarans, which take about 2.5 hours: *Krilo* runs in the early morning (daily June-Sept, 3-4/week May and Oct, none Nov-April),

Jadrolinija goes from Split to Ancona, from Zadar to Ancona, and from Dubrovnik to Bari (tel. 051/211-444 or 021/338-333, www.jadrolinija.hr).

SNAV connects Split to Ancona, including the only non-overnight option, on a fast, 4.5-hour daytime catamaran (Croatian tel. 021/322-252, Italian tel. 081-428-5555, www.snav.it).

Blue Line sails from Split to Ancona; in summer, some crossings stop en route at Stari Grad on Hvar Island (can book at Split Tours travel agency in Split, tel. 021/352-533, www.blueline-ferries.com).

Other companies serving these routes come and go each year—ask the Split TI or poke around Split's main terminal building to discover the latest.

Trains Within Italy: From **Ancona,** you can catch a train to Venice (almost hourly, 4.25-5.25 hours, most transfer in Bologna), Florence (almost hourly, 3-4.25 hours, most transfer in Bologna), or Rome (8/day direct, 3-4.5 hours). From **Pescara,** trains head to Rome (6/day direct, 3.75-4.25 hours) and Florence (almost hourly, 4.5-5.25 hours, transfer in Bologna). From **Bari,** you can hop a train to Naples (6/day, 3.75-6 hours, most transfer in Caserta), Rome (3/day direct, 4.75 hours), or Florence (8/day, 6.75-8.5 hours, transfer in Rome or Bologna). For timetables, check www.ferroviedellostato.it or www.bahn.com (Germany's excellent all-Europe website).

Note that in Italian, Split is called "Spalato" (which is also the sound you hear if seasickness gets the best of you).

SPLIT

while **Jadrolinija's** catamaran goes year-round in the late afternoon. The *Krilo* catamaran also continues to Dubrovnik (4 hours). If the catamarans don't work for you, you could go instead to Vela Luka—either on a different Jadrolinija catamaran (generally 1/day, 2 hours) or on Jadrolinija's slower **local car ferries** (1-2/day, 2-3 hours)—then take the bus from there.

BY BUS

Each of the following routes is served by multiple companies, which charge slightly different rates. Always ask about the fastest option—which can save hours of bus time. It's smart to arrive about 30 minutes before your bus departs to buy tickets (better yet, during peak season, come to the station to buy them earlier in the day). The generally English-speaking staff at Split's bus station gives out handy little schedules for popular journeys. Bus info: www.ak-split.hr, toll tel. 060-327-777.

By Bus to: Zagreb (at least hourly, 5-8 hours depending on route), **Dubrovnik** (at least hourly, less off-season, 3.5-5 hours),

Korčula (1 night bus leaves at 24:45 and arrives around 6:00), **Trogir** (1-2/hour, 30 minutes), **Zadar** (at least hourly, 3 hours), **Mostar** (7/day, 4-4.5 hours), **Međugorje** (4/day, 3.5 hours), **Sarajevo** (6/day in summer, 4/day in winter, 7.5-8 hours), **Rijeka** (7-10/day including some night buses, 6-8 hours). Zagreb-bound buses sometimes also stop at **Plitvice** (confirm with driver and ask him to stop at the national park entrance; about 7-8/day in summer—the best are the direct connections with Prijevoz Knežević, described on page 1103; 4/day in winter, 4-6 hours).

BY TRAIN

From Split, trains go to **Zagreb** (2/day, 6.5 hours; 1 direct night train, 9 hours); in Zagreb, you can transfer to **Ljubljana** (4/day, 9 hours total). Train info: tel. 021/338-525 or toll tel. 060-333-444, www.hznet.hr.

Near Split: The Dalmatian Islands

Rovinj in Istria (see the next chapter) is my favorite small seaside town in Croatia... but many would disagree with me. In fact, every traveler seems to have their own favorite town or island, many of which speckle the Dalmatian Coast between Split and Dubrovnik. I favor two in particular: Hvar and Korčula. While I've offered a quick introduction to each, for full coverage—as well as some nearby destinations—pick up the latest edition of my *Rick Steves Croatia & Slovenia* guidebook. For boat connections, see the "Split Connections" section above; for more tips on getting around by boat or bus, see page 861.

HVAR

Hvar's hip cachet, upscale-ritzy "Croatian Riviera" buzz, and easy proximity to Split have quickly turned this tidy little Dalmatian fishing village into one of the most popular (and most expensive) destinations in Croatia. The island desperately wants to be thought of as Croatia's answer to Mykonos or St-Tropez...and it's getting there. Yachts and sailboats tie up five deep in the harbor, bringing ashore a steady stream of über-wealthy yuppies dressing up for a night on the town. Although some travelers may find all of the glitz and high prices off-putting, Hvar has real history and authentic charm, and the setting is undeniably gorgeous.

The island's main town—also called Hvar—surrounds its tidy **harbor**, shared by those fancy yachts, a humble fishing fleet, and tourist boats. The harbor is dominated by the looming Arsenal building (housing the **TI,** www.tzhvar.hr), where ships were

repaired and resupplied during the town's seafaring heyday. Ticket booths for the two main boat companies—Jadrolinija and Krilo—face each other across the harbor.

Running perpendicular to the harbor is Hvar's cozy main piazza, **St. Stephen's Square** (Trg Svetog Stjepana), which sits in a rare patch of flat land between hills. The square is ringed by scenic cafés and restaurants, and dominated by the town's cathedral, with a modern, ornately sculpted bronze entrance door. The bus station, a taxi stand, a supermarket, and other tourist services cluster in a busy zone just behind the cathedral.

From St. Stephen's Square, steep, stepped lanes branch up into the residential lanes of the Old Town. In those streets, you'll find the **Benedictine Convent,** where cloistered sisters make delicate lace using fibers from the *agava* (a cactus-like plant with broad, flat, tapered, spiny leaves). The convent's endearing little lace museum is open to visitors for brief periods in the summer.

The highest hill overlooking the harbor is capped by a stout 14th-century **fortress,** whose crenellated walls reach down to corral the red rooftops of town in a protective embrace. It's a stiff 20- to 30-minute hike up to the top, and—while there's little to see inside the fortress—the views are spectacular.

From the harbor, a seafront promenade curls in both directions. East of town, it passes a **Franciscan Monastery,** with an offbeat museum containing the island's most famous painting (a 17th-century depiction of the Last Supper, loaded with symbolism) and oldest tree (a gnarled cypress whose branches are held up by big crutches). West of town, the promenade curls back around some renovated communist-era hotels to a more rugged landscape. In either direction, you'll spot several concrete pads and ladders trying to seduce you into the cool blue.

To escape the crowds, ask the TI for tips about walking or taking a bus out to farther-flung beaches or smaller towns on the island. Or chat up the captains at the harbor to see if they can sell you on an excursion to the remote coves and beaches of the Pakleni Islands, just offshore (where nude and clothed beaches abound).

Sleeping on Hvar: In keeping with its posh reputation, Hvar is pricey. Accommodations are limited inside the Old Town; you could splurge at **Villa Nora** (www.villanora.eu) or sleep on a

SPLIT

budget at **Ivana and Paško Ukić**'s rooms (www.hvar-apartments-center.com). You'll have far more options—and spend less—if you're willing to walk 10 or 20 minutes into the "suburbs." A good choice is Marica's **Apartments Mare** (www.apartments-mare-hvar.com), or her sister/neighbor, **Ana Dujmović** (www.hvar-croatia.com/dujmovic).

Eating in Hvar: For traditional Croatian "tapas," find **Konoba Menego,** high up along the main stepped street between the main square and the fortress. **Alviž**, near the bus station, has unpretentious, affordable, stick-to-your-ribs meals. And **Gariful** ("Carnation"), sitting on the harbor just past all of the yachts, is a scenic seafood splurge.

KORČULA

The island town of Korčula (KOHR-choo-lah, on the island of the same name) boasts an atmospheric Old Town, a smattering of surprisingly engaging museums, and a dramatic, fjord-like mountain backdrop. Humbler and harder to reach than its glitzy big sister Hvar, Korčula—while certainly on the tourist trail—is much sleepier and has an appealing (if occasionally frustrating) backwater charm. At its heart, Korčula is a traditional, blue-collar, salt-of-the-earth shipbuilding and fishing town with a dim patina of tourism.

Korčula—with a formerly walled Old Town filling a peninsula that juts out into the water—has a "mini-Dubrovnik" vibe. That's intentional: Venice would have liked to claim the *real* Dubrovnik, but when that failed, instead they fortified Korčula—which sits at the southern frontier of their empire. Most of the wall has long since been dismantled, but a few mighty towers still stand.

Boats to and from nearby islands dock on either side of the Old Town peninsula, depending on the direction the wind is blowing. (Car ferries tether Korčula to the outside world via a crossing from Dominče, about a 5-minute drive from Korčula town, to Orebić, across the channel on the Pelješac Peninsula.) Where the Old Town meets  the mainland, you'll find a cluster of tourist services—travel agencies, cafés, and the Jadrolinija ticket office; tickets for other boat companies are sold by various travel agencies around town. The **TI** is just around the corner, facing the ferry dock on the west side of the Old Town (www.visitkorcula.eu).

Every Croatian island has a claim to fame. Korčula has two: Its medieval folk dance, the *Moreška* (moh-REHSH-kah)—in which the forces of the good king and the bad king do battle for the honor of a fair princess—is performed every Thursday night (as well as Mondays in the summer). And Korčula is supposedly the birthplace of Marco Polo, who is honored at gift shops around town—and at a touristy but surprisingly enjoyable museum, facing the harbor where the Old Town meets the mainland.

While rocky beaches stretch in both directions from the town center, almost all of Korčula's sights are on the Old Town peninsula. You'll enter town by ascending the Great Land Gate's grand staircase, which puts you at the start of the narrow **main drag,** called Ulica Korčulanskog Statuta 1214. This street is Korčula's backbone, in more ways than one: While most medieval towns slowly evolved with twisty, mazelike lanes, Korčula was carefully planned to resemble a fish skeleton. The streets to the west (left) of this one are straight, to allow the refreshing northwesterly Maestral winds into town. To the east (right), they're curved (notice you can't see the sea) to keep out the bad-vibe southeasterly Jugo winds.

At the crest of town, the main drag opens up into **St. Mark's Square** (Trg Sv. Marka), which is ringed by a smattering of modest but endearing sights. St. Mark's Cathedral has a humble interior with a Tintoretto painting and antique weapons that were used in pivotal battles near strategically located Korčula. The adjoining Church Museum is an eclectic, strangely fascinating collection of ecclesiastical brick-a-brack and oddities. And across the square, the Town Museum features exhibits on town history; the top floor has a traditionally furnished townhouse, demonstrating how people have lived in these tight quarters for centuries.

Continuing to the tip of the Old Town, you'll find a surviving city wall tower. At the very top of the tower—up a rickety, ladder-like staircase—is an evening and late-night cocktail bar called **Buffet "Massimo,"** offering a scenic way to unwind. As you face the water from the tower, you could turn right and loop around the east side of the wall, following the seawall past several restaurants (some better than others) with grand views.

Sleeping in Korčula: As throughout Croatia, Korčula's hotels are typically overpriced, but affordable and welcoming *sobe* and apartments fill both the Old Town and the surrounding neighborhoods. **Apartments Lenni,** run by Lenni and Pero Modrinić, has cozy, well-priced apartments nestled right in the heart of the Old Town (www.ikorcula.net/lenni). On the mainland, but immediately adjacent to the Old Town, Zvonko and Marija's **Royal Apartments** offer hotelesque comfort for *sobe* prices (www. korcularoyalapartments.com). Farther along the waterfront, but still an easy and scenic 10-minute stroll into the Old Town, **Rezi and Andro Depolo**'s rooms are a good budget choice (rezi.

depolo@gmail.com). If you want a hotel splurge, snazzy but unpretentious **Hotel Korsal** sits in a tacky but convenient hotel zone a 10-minute walk from the Old Town (www.hotel-korsal.com).

Eating in Korčula: Sitting right along the main drag in the middle of the Old Town, **Pizzeria Amfora** is a reliable choice for stick-to-your-ribs pastas and pizzas. The eastern seawall of the Old Town is lined with tourist-focused eateries that face gorgeous views; **Pizzeria Tedeschi** is a good budget choice, while **Filippi** is a foodie splurge. On the opposite side of the Old Town, a charming little square just up a flight of stone steps from the TI has a cluster of more youthful, hipster-style eateries: **Maje i Tonke** has Dalmatian small plates, while **Nonno** has handmade pastas.

ROVINJ AND ISTRIA

Rising dramatically from the Adriatic as though being pulled up to heaven by its grand bell tower, Rovinj (roh-VEEN; in Italian: Rovigno/roh-VEEN-yoh) is a welcoming Old World oasis in a sea of tourist kitsch. Among the villages of Croatia's coast, there's something particularly romantic about Rovinj—the most Italian town in Croatia's most Italian region, Istria. Rovinj's streets are delightfully twisty, its ancient houses are characteristically crumbling, and its harbor—lively with real-life fishermen—is as salty as they come. Like a little Venice on a hill, Rovinj is the stage set for your Croatian seaside dreams.

Rovinj was prosperous and well-fortified in the Middle Ages. It boomed in the 16th and 17th centuries, when it was flooded with refugees fleeing both the Ottoman invasions and the plague. Because the town was part of the Republic of Venice for five centuries (13th to 18th centuries), its architecture, culture, and even language are strongly Venetian. The local folk groups sing in a dialect actually considered more Venetian than what the Venetians themselves speak these days. (You can even see Venice from Rovinj's church bell tower on a very clear day.)

After Napoleon seized the region, then was defeated, Rovinj became part of Austria. The Venetians had neglected Istria, but the Austrians invested in it, bringing the railroad, gas lights, and a huge Ronhill tobacco factory. (This factory—recently replaced by an enormous, state-of-the-art facility you'll pass on the highway farther inland—is one of the town's most elegant structures, and is slated for extensive renovation in the coming years.) The Habsburgs tapped Pula and Trieste to be the empire's major ports—cursing those cities with pollution and sprawl, while allowing Rovinj to

Istria

Rovinj is just one of many worthwhile attractions on the peninsula called Istria, where pungent truffles, Roman ruins, striking hill towns, quaint coastal villages, carefully cultivated food and wine, and breezy Italian culture all compete for your attention.

While you could spend days exploring Istria, two destinations outside Rovinj are especially worthwhile (each one deserves a half-day side-trip). Down at the tip of Istria is big, industrial Pula, offering a bustling urban contrast to the rest of the time-passed coastline, plus some remarkable Roman ruins (including an amphitheater so intact, you'll marvel that you haven't heard of it before). The charming hill town of Motovun—with sweeping views over the surrounding terrain, including a truffle-packed forest—is one of the country's most appealing reasons to head inland.

Getting Around Istria

Istria is a cinch for **drivers,** who find distances short and roads and attractions well-marked (though summer traffic can be miserable, especially on weekends). Istria is neatly connected by a speedy highway nicknamed the *ipsilon* (the Croatian word for the letter Y, which is what the highway is shaped like). One branch of the "Y" (A-9) runs roughly parallel to

the coast from Slovenia to Pula, about six miles inland; the other branch (A-8) cuts diagonally northeast to the Učka Tunnel (leading to Rijeka). You'll periodically come to toll booths, where you'll pay a modest fee for using the *ipsilon*. Following road signs here is easy (navigate by town names), but if you'll be driving a lot, pick up a good map to more easily navigate the back roads.

If you're relying on **public transportation,** Istria can be frustrating: The towns that are easiest to reach (Poreč and Pula) are less appealing than Istria's highlights (Rovinj and Motovun). Linking up the coastal towns by bus is doable if you're patient and check schedules carefully, but the hill towns probably aren't worth the hassle. Even if you're doing the rest of your trip by public transportation, consider renting a car for a day or two in Istria.

By Boat to Venice, Piran, or Trieste: Various companies connect Venice daily in summer with Rovinj, Poreč, and Pula

Istria

To Venice
ITALY
Trieste
A-3
To Ljubljana
Pivka
Divača
A-1
SLOVENIA
Ilirska
Bistrica
Piran
Izola
Koper
SALT
FIELDS
Portorož
CROATIA
A-7
Umag
Buje
Grožnjan
Buzet
44
Roč
Brtonigla
Oprtalj
Završje
Livade
Lupoglav
Opatija
Motovun
Mirna
River
Hum
Rijeka
Valley
UČKA
To
Zagreb
Novigrad
A-8
TUNNEL
A-9
Poreč
Pazin
ISTRIA
Vrsar
Matošević
Žminj
Brestova
Limski
Porozina
Canal
RONHILL
Labin
FACTORY
Rovinj
Cres
Bale
A-9
N
Vodnjan
10 Kilometers
Fažana
10 Miles
Brijuni
Islands
Pula
Adriatic Sea
"Ipsilon" Highway
Expressway
Other Roads
Medulin
Rail Line
Boat Route

ROVINJ AND ISTRIA

(about three hours). While designed for day-trippers from Istria to Venice, these services can be used for one-way travel. As the companies and specific routes change from year to year, check each of these websites to see what might work for your itinerary: **Venezia Lines** (www.venezialines.com), **Adriatic Lines** (www.adriatic-lines.com), and **Commodore Cruises** (www.commodore-cruises.hr). **Trieste Lines** (www.triestelines.it) connects Rovinj and Poreč to Piran (Slovenia), then Trieste (Italy).

linger in its trapped-in-the-past quaintness.

Before long, Austrians discovered Istria as a handy escape for a beach holiday. Tourism came to Rovinj in the late 1890s, when a powerful Austrian baron bought one of the remote, barren islands offshore and brought it back to life with gardens and a grand villa. Before long, another baron bought another island...and a tourist boom was under way. In more recent times, Rovinj has become a top destination for nudists. The resort of Valalta, just to the north, is a popular spot for those seeking "southern exposure"... as a very revealing brochure at the TI illustrates (www.valalta.hr). Whether you want to find PNBs (pudgy nude bodies), or avoid them, remember that the German phrase *FKK* (*Freikörper Kultur,* or "free body culture") is international shorthand for nudism.

Rovinj is the star attraction of Croatia's wedge-shaped Istrian Peninsula. With more time in Istria  (EE-stree-ah; "Istra" in Croatian), visit the striking Roman ruins in urban Pula and the laid-back hill town of Motovun (both described later in this chapter).

Rovinj is the most atmospheric of all of Croatia's small coastal towns. Maybe that's because it's always been a real town, where poor people lived. You'll find no fancy old palaces here—just narrow streets lined with skinny houses that have given shelter to humble families for generations. While it's becoming known on the tourist circuit, Rovinj retains the soul of a fishermen's village; notice that the harbor is still filled not with glitzy yachts, but with a busy fishing fleet.

PLANNING YOUR TIME

While you can reach Rovinj by bus (see "Rovinj Connections," later), it's most worthwhile by car (which allows you to easily visit nearby destinations, such as Pula and Motovun). For drivers, Rovinj fits neatly between Slovenia and Croatia (for example, on a Ljubljana-Lake Bled-Julian Alps-Rovinj-Plitvice-Split itinerary).

Rovinj is hardly packed with diversions. You can get the gist of the town in a one-hour wander. The rest of your time is for enjoying the ambience, savoring a slow meal, or pedaling a rental bike to a nearby beach. With a second day, side-trip to Pula and Motovun; to fill a lazy afternoon on a single day, choose just one of these attractions. Be aware that much of Rovinj (like other small Croatian coastal towns) closes down from mid-October through Easter.

Orientation to Rovinj

Rovinj, once an island, is now a peninsula. The Old Town is divided in two parts: a particularly charismatic chunk on the oval-shaped peninsula, and the rest on the mainland (with similarly time-worn buildings, but without the commercial cuteness that comes with lots of tourist money). Where the mainland meets the peninsula is a broad, bustling public space called Tito Square (Trg Maršala Tita). The Old Town peninsula—traffic-free except for the occasional moped—is topped by the massive bell tower of the Church of St. Euphemia. At the very tip of the peninsula is a small park.

TOURIST INFORMATION

Rovinj's TI, facing the harbor, has several handy, free materials, including a town map and an info booklet (June-Sept daily 7:00-22:00; Oct and May daily 8:00-21:00; Nov-April Mon-Fri 8:00-15:00, Sat 8:00-13:00, closed Sun; along the embankment at Obala Pina Budičina 12, tel. 052/811-566, www.tzgrovinj.hr).

ARRIVAL IN ROVINJ

By Car: Only local cars are allowed to enter the Old Town area (though if you're overnighting in this area, they may let you drive in just long enough to drop off your bags—ask your host for details). To get as close as possible—whether you're staying in the Old Town, or just visiting for the day—use the big water-front Valdibora parking lots just north of the Old Town, which come with the classic Rovinj view (July-Aug: 6.5 kn/hour, April-June and Sept: 5 kn/hour, Oct-March: 2 kn/hour). As you drive in from the highway through the outskirts of Rovinj, the road forks, sending most hotel traffic to the left (turn off here if you're staying outside the Old Town); but if you want to reach the Old Town, go right instead, then follow *Centar* signs, which eventually lead you directly to the two Valdibora lots: "Valdibora 1" (a.k.a. "Big Valdibora," farther from the Old Town), then "Valdibora 2" (a.k.a. "Little Valdibora," closer to the Old Town). During busy times, the slightly closer Valdibora 2 is reserved for residents; in this case, signs will divert you into Valdibora 1.

If both Valdibora lots are full, you'll be pushed to another pay lot farther out, along the bay northwest of the Old Town (a scenic 15-minute walk from town; summer: 5-6 kn/hour, free 23:00-6:00; winter: 2 kn/hour, free 20:00-6:00 and on Sun). Even if the Valdibora lots are available, budget-oriented drivers may prefer this somewhat cheaper outer lot—the cost adds up fast if you're parking over several nights. Accommodations outside of the Old Town generally have on-site (or nearby streetside) parking, often

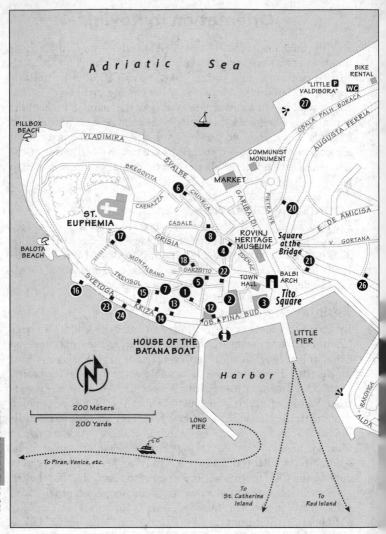

free; a few places in the Old Town have parking available outside of town.

By Bus: The bus station is on the south side of the Old Town, close to the harbor. Leave the station to the left, then walk on busy Carera street directly into the center of town. Note that there are plans to move the bus station to the other side of the Old Town, just above the long waterfront parking lots. If your bus stops here instead, simply head down to the main road and walk along the parking lots into town.

By Boat: The few boats connecting Rovinj to Venice, Piran,

Rovinj

1. Villa Markiz
2. Porta Antica Apartments
3. Hotel Adriatic
4. Villa Cissa
5. Casa Garzotto (Reception & Apts.)
6. Casa Garzotto (Rooms)
7. Trevisol Apartments
8. B&B Casale
9. Residence Dream
10. To Villa Baron Gautsch; Hotel Vila Lili; Vila Kristina; Hotels Monte Mulini, Lone & Eden
11. To Elda Markulin Apts., Apartmani Tomo, Hotel Park & Restaurant Maestral
12. Scuba Restaurant
13. Veli Jože Restaurant
14. Santa Croce Restaurant
15. Lampo Restaurant
16. La Puntuleina Restaurant
17. Monte Restaurant
18. Krčma Ulika Restaurant
19. Sidro Restaurant
20. Gostionica/Trattoria Toni
21. Bacchus Wine Bar
22. Piassa Granda Wine Bar
23. Valentino Champagne & Cocktail Bar
24. Monte Carlo Bar
25. Launderette
26. Internet Café
27. Start of Self-Guided Walk

ROVINJ AND ISTRIA

Trieste, and other Istrian towns dock at the long pier protruding from the Old Town peninsula. Just walk up the pier, and you're in the heart of town.

HELPFUL HINTS

Internet Access: In public areas (such as the harborfront square), check for a free (if slow) Wi-Fi signal called "Hotspot Croatia." **A-Mar Internet Club** has pay Wi-Fi, several terminals, and long hours (36 kn/hour at a terminal, 10 kn/hour for Wi-Fi, daily 9:00-22:00, shorter hours off-season, on the main drag in the mainland part of the Old Town, Carera 26, tel. 052/841-211).

Laundry: The full-service **Galax** launderette hides up the street beyond the bus station. You can usually pick up your laundry after 24 hours, though same-day service might be possible if you drop it off early enough in the morning (90 kn/load wash and dry; Easter-Sept daily 6:00-20:00, until later in summer; Oct-Easter Mon-Fri 7:00-19:00, Sat 9:00-15:00, closed Sun; up Benussia street past the bus station, on the left after the post office, tel. 052/816-130).

Local Guide: Vukica Palčić is a very capable guide who knows her town intimately and loves to share it with visitors (€50 for a 1.5-hour tour, mobile 098-794-003, vukica.palcic@pu.t-com.hr).

Best Views: The town is full of breathtaking views. Photography buffs will be busy in the magic hours of early morning and evening, and even by moonlight. The postcard view of Rovinj is from the parking lot embankment at the north end of the Old Town (at the start of the "Rovinj Ramble," next). For a different perspective on the Old Town, head for the far side of the harbor on the opposite (south) end of town. The church bell tower provides a virtual aerial view of the town and a grand vista of the outlying islands.

Rovinj Ramble

This self-guided walk, rated ▲▲▲, introduces you to Rovinj in about an hour. Begin at the parking lot just north of the Old Town.

Old Town View

Many places offer fine views of Rovinj's Old Town, but this is the most striking. Boats bob in the harbor, and behind them Venetian-looking homes seem to rise from the deep. (For an aerial perspective, notice the big billboard overhead and to the left.)

The Old Town is topped by the church, whose bell tower is capped by a weathervane in the shape of Rovinj's patron saint, Euphemia. Local fishermen look to this saintly weathervane for direction: When Euphemia is looking out to sea, it means the stiff, fresh Bora wind is blowing, bringing dry air from the interior...a sailor's delight. But if she's facing the land, the humid Jugo wind will soon bring bad weather from the sea. After a day or so, even a tourist learns to look to St. Euphemia for the weather forecast.

As you soak in this scene, ponder how the town's history created its current shape. In the Middle Ages, Rovinj was an island, rather than a peninsula, and it was surrounded by a double wall—a protective inner wall and an outer seawall. Because it was so well-defended against pirates and other marauders (and carefully quarantined from the plague), it was extremely desirable real estate. And yet, it was easy to reach from the mainland, allowing it to thrive as a trading town. With more than 10,000 residents at its peak, Rovinj became immensely crowded, which explains today's pleasantly claustrophobic Old Town.

Over the centuries—as demand for living space trumped security concerns—the town walls were converted into houses, with windows grafted on to their imposing frame. Gaps in the wall, with steps that seem to end at the water, are where fishermen would pull in to unload their catch directly into the warehouses on the bottom level of the houses. (Later you can explore some of these lanes from inside the town.) Today, if you live in one of these houses, the Adriatic is your backyard.

• *Now head into town. In the little park near the sea, just beyond the end of the parking lot, look for the big, blocky...*

Communist-Era Monument

Dating from the time of Tito, this celebrates the Partisan Army's victory over the Nazis in World War II and commemorates the

victims of fascism. The minimalist reliefs on the ceremonial tomb show a slow prisoners' parade, the victims prodded by a gun in the back from a figure with a Nazi-style helmet. Notice that one side of the monument is in Croatian, and the other is in Italian. With typical Yugoslav grace and subtlety, this jarring block shatters the otherwise harmonious time-warp vibe of Rovinj. Fortunately, it's the only modern structure anywhere near the Old Town.

• *Now walk a few more steps toward town and past the playground, stopping to explore the covered...*

Market

The front part of the market, near the water, is for souvenirs. But natives delve deeper in, to the produce stands. Separating the gifty stuff from the nitty-gritty produce is a line of merchants aggressively pushing free samples. Everything is local and mostly homemade. Consider this snack-time tactic: Loiter around, joking with

Italo-Croatia

Apart from its tangible attractions, one of Istria's hallmarks is its biculturalism: It's an engaging hybrid of Croatia and Italy. Like most of the Croatian Coast, Istria has variously been controlled by Illyrians, Romans, Byzantines, Slavs, Venetians, and Austrians. After the Habsburgs lost World War I, most of today's Croatia joined Yugoslavia—but Istria became part of Italy. During this time, the Croatian vernacular was suppressed, while the Italian language and culture flourished. But this extra chapter of Italian rule was short-lived. After World War II, Istria joined Yugoslavia, and Croatian culture and language returned. What followed was a so-called "Italian exodus," during which many Istrian Italians chose to relocate to Italy—leaving behind hill towns, valley villages, and farm estates that are abandoned even to this day.

The Istrians who stayed behind were saddled with an identity crisis. Many people here found it difficult to abandon their ties to Italy, and continued to speak the language and embrace the culture. Today, depending on who you ask, Istria is the most Italian part of Croatia...or the most Croatian part of Italy. Istria pops up on Italian weather reports. A few years ago, Italy's then-Prime Minister Silvio Berlusconi declared that he still considered Istria part of Italy—and he wanted it back. When I wrote an article about Istria for a newspaper, some Italian readers complained that I made it sound "too Croatian," while some Croatians claimed my depiction was "too Italian."

People who actually live here typically don't worry about the distinction. Locals insist that they're not Croatians and not Italians—they're Istrians. They don't mind straddling two cultures. Both languages are official (and often taught side-by-side in schools), street signs are bilingual, and most Istrians dabble in each tongue—often seeming to foreign ears as though they're mixing the two at once.

As a result of their tangled history, Istrians have learned how to be mellow and take things as they come. They're gregarious, open-minded, and sometimes seem to thrive on chaos. A twentysomething local told me, "My ancestors lived in Venice. My great-grandfather lived in Austria. My grandfather lived in Italy. My father lived in Yugoslavia. I live in Croatia. My son will live in the European Union. And we've all lived in the same town."

the farmers while sampling their various tasty walnuts, figs, cherries, grapes, olive oils, honey, *rakija* (the powerful schnapps popular throughout the Balkans), and more. If the sample is good, buy some more for a picnic. In the center of the market, a delightful and practical fountain from 1908 reminds locals of the infrastructure brought in by their Habsburg rulers a century ago. The hall labeled *Ribarnica/Pescheria* at the back of the market is where you'll find fresh, practically wriggling fish. This is where locals gather ingredients for their favorite dish, *brodet*—a stew of various kinds of seafood mixed with olive oil and wine...all of Istria's best bits rolled into one dish. It's slowly simmered and generally served with polenta (unfortunately, it's rare in restaurants).

• *Continue up the broad street, named for* **Giuseppe Garibaldi**—*one of the major players in late 19th-century Italian unification. Imagine: Even though you're in Croatia, Italian patriots are celebrated in this very Italian-feeling town (see the "Italo-Croatia" sidebar). After one long block, on your left, you'll come to the wide cross-street called...*

Square at the Bridge (Trg na Mostu)

This marks the site of the medieval bridge that once connected the fortified island of Rovinj to the mainland (as illustrated in the small painting above the door of the Kavana al Ponto—"Bridge Café"). Back then, the island was populated mostly by Italians, while the mainland was the territory of Slavic farmers. But as Rovinj's strategic importance waned, and its trading status rose, the need for easy access became more important than the canal's protective purpose—so in 1763, it was filled in. The two populations integrated, creating the bicultural mix that survives today.

Notice the breeze? Via Garibaldi is nicknamed Val di Bora ("Valley of the Bora Wind") for the constant cooling wind that blows here. On the island side of Trg na Mostu is the Rovinj Heritage Museum (described later, under "Sights in Rovinj"). Next door, the town's cultural center posts lovingly hand-lettered signs in Croatian and Italian announcing upcoming musical events (generally free, designed for locals, and worth noting and enjoying).

Nearby (just past Kavana al Ponto, on the left), the Viecia Batana Café—named for Rovinj's unique, flat-bottomed little fishing boats—has a retro interior with a circa-1960 fishermen's mural that evokes an earlier age. The café is popular for its chocolate cake and "Batana" ice cream.

• *Now proceed (passing handwritten signs in Croatian and Italian listing upcoming events) to the little fountain in the middle of the square, facing the harbor.*

Tito Square (Trg Maršala Tita)

This wide-open square at the entrance to the Old Town is the crossroads of Rovinj. The **fountain,** with a little boy holding a water-spouting fish, celebrates the government-funded water system that finally brought running water to the Old Town in 1959. Walk around the fountain, with your eyes on the relief, to see a successful socialist society at the inauguration of this new water system. Despite the happy occasion, the figures are pretty stiff—conformity trumped most other virtues in Tito's world.

Now walk out to the end of the concrete pier, called the **Mali Molo ("Little Pier").** From here, you're surrounded by Rovinj's crowded harbor, with fishing vessels and excursion boats that shuttle tourists out to the offshore islands. If the weather's good, a **boat trip** can be a fun way to get out on the water for a different angle on Rovinj (see "Activities in Rovinj," later, for details).

Scan the **harbor.** On the left is the MMC, the local meeting and concert hall (described later, under "Nightlife in Rovinj"). Above and behind the MMC, the highest bell tower inland marks the Franciscan monastery, which was the only building on the mainland before the island town was connected to shore. Along the waterfront to the right of the MMC is the multicolored Hotel Park, a typical monstrosity from the communist era, now tastefully renovated inside. A recommended bike path starts just past this hotel, leading into a nature preserve and the best nearby beaches (which you can see in the distance; for more on bike rental, see "Activities in Rovinj," later).

Now head back to the base of the pier. If you were to walk down the **embankment** between the harbor and the Old Town

(past Hotel Adriatic), you'd find the TI, the recommended House of the Batana Boat museum, and a delightful "restaurant row" with several tempting places for a drink or a meal. Many fishermen pull their boats into this harbor, then simply carry their catch across the street to a waiting restaurateur. (This self-guided walk finishes with a stroll down this lane.)

Backtrack 20 paces past the fountain and face the Old Town entrance gate, called the **Balbi Arch.** The winged lion on top is a reminder that this was Venetian territory for centuries.

• *Head through the gate into the Old Town. Inside and on the left is the red...*

Town Hall

On the old Town Hall, notice another Venetian lion, as well as other historic crests embedded in the wall. The Town Hall actually sports an Italian flag (along with ones for Rovinj, Croatia, and the EU) and faces a square named for Giacomo Matteotti, a much-revered Italian patriot.

Continue a few more steps into town. Gostionica/Trattoria Cisterna faces another little square, which once functioned as a cistern (collecting rainwater, which was pulled from a subterranean reservoir through the well you see today). The building on your left is the Italian Union—yet another reminder of how Istria has an important bond with Italy.

• *Now begin walking up the street to the left of Gostionica/Trattoria Cisterna. Passing the recommended Piassa Granda wine bar on your left, veer right up...*

Grisia Street

The main "street" (actually a tight lane) leading through the middle of the island is choked with tourists during the midday rush

and lined with art galleries. This inspiring town has attracted many artists, some of whom display their works along this colorful stretch. Notice the rusty little nails speckling the walls—each year in August, an art festival invites locals to hang their best art on this street. With paintings lining the lane, the entire community comes out to enjoy each other's creations.

As you walk, keep your camera ready, as you can find delightful scenes down every side lane. Remember that, as crowded as it is today, little Rovinj was even more packed in the Middle Ages. Keep an eye out for arches that span narrow lanes (such as on the right, at Arsenale street)—the only way a walled city could grow was up. Many of these additions created hidden little courtyards, nooks, and crannies that make it easy to get away from the crowds and claim a corner of the town for yourself. Another sign of Rovinj's overcrowding are the distinctive chimneys poking up above the rooftops. These chimneys, added long after the buildings were first constructed, made it possible to heat previously underutilized rooms...and squeeze in even more people.

• *Continue up to the top of Grisia. Capping the town is the can't-miss-it...*

▲Church of St. Euphemia (Sv. Eufemija)

Rovinj's landmark Baroque church dates from 1754. It's watched over by an enormous 190-foot-tall campanile, a replica of the famous bell tower on St. Mark's Square in Venice. The tower is topped by a copper weather-vane with the weather-predicting St. Euphemia, the church's namesake.

Cost and Hours: Free, generally open May-Sept daily 10:00-18:00, Easter-April and Oct-Nov open only for Mass and with demand, generally closed Dec-Easter.

Visiting the Church: The vast, somewhat gloomy interior boasts some fine altars of Carrara marble (a favorite medium of Michelangelo's). Services here are celebrated using a combination of Croatian and Italian, suiting the town's mixed population.

To the right of the main altar is the church's highlight: the chapel containing the relics of St. Euphemia. Before stepping into the chapel, notice the altar featuring Euphemia—depicted, as she usually is, with her wheel (a reminder of her torture) and a palm frond (symbolic of her martyrdom), and holding the fortified town of Rovinj, of which she is the protector.

Now head into the little chapel behind the altar. In the center is a gigantic tomb, and on the walls above are large paintings that illustrate two significant events from the life of this important local figure. St. Euphemia was the virtuous daughter of a prosperous early fourth-century family in Chalcedon (near today's Istanbul). Euphemia used her family's considerable wealth to help the poor. Unfortunately, her pious philanthropy happened to coincide with anti-Christian purges by the Roman Emperor Diocletian. When she was 15 years old, Euphemia was arrested for refusing to worship the local pagan idol. She was brutally tortured, her bones broken on a wheel. Finally she was thrown to the lions as a public spectacle. But, the story goes, the lions miraculously refused to attack her. You can see this moment depicted in one of the paintings above—as a bored-looking lion tenderly nibbles at her right bicep.

Flash forward to the year 800, when a gigantic marble sarcophagus containing St. Euphemia's relics somehow found its way into the Adriatic and floated all the way up to Istria, where Rovinj fishermen discovered it bobbing in the sea. They tugged it back to town, where a crowd gathered. The townspeople realized what it was and wanted to take it up to the hilltop church. But nobody could move it...until a young boy with two young calves showed up. He said he'd had a dream of St. Euphemia—and, sure enough, he succeeded in dragging her relics to where they still lie. In the painting above, see the burly fishermen looking astonished as the boy succeeds in moving the giant sarcophagus). Note the depiction of Rovinj fortified by a double crenellated wall—looking more like a castle than like the creaky fishing village of today. At the top of the hill is an earlier version of today's church.

Now turn your attention to Euphemia's famous sarcophagus. The front panel (with the painting of Euphemia) is opened with much fanfare every September 16, St. Euphemia's feast day, to display the small, withered, waxen face of Rovinj's favorite saint.
• *If you have time and energy, consider climbing the...*

Bell Tower

Scaling the church bell tower's creaky wooden stairway requires an enduring faith in the reliability of wood. It rewards those who

brave its 192 stairs with a commanding view of the town and surrounding islands. The climb doubles your altitude, and from this perch you can also look down—taking advantage of the quirky little round hole in the floor to photograph the memorable staircase you just climbed.

Cost and Hours: 15 kn, same hours as church, enter from inside church—to the left of the main altar.
• *Leave the church through the main door. A peaceful café on a park terrace (once a cemetery) is just ahead and below you. Just to the right, a winding, cobbled lane leads past the café entrance and down toward the water, then forks. A left turn here zigzags you past a WWII pillbox and leads along the "restaurant row," where you can survey your options for a drink or a meal (see "Eating in Rovinj," later). A right turn curls you down along the quieter northern side of the Old Town peninsula. Either way, Rovinj is yours to enjoy.*

Sights in Rovinj

▲House of the Batana Boat (Kuća o Batani)

Rovinj has a long, noble shipbuilding tradition, and this tiny but interesting museum gives you the story of the town's distinctive *batana* boats. Locals say this museum puts you in touch with the soul of this town.

The flat-bottomed vessels are favored by local fishermen for their ability to reach rocky areas close to shore that are rich with certain shellfish. The museum explains how the boats are built, with the help of an entertaining elapsed-time video showing a boat built from scratch in five minutes. You'll also meet some of the

ROVINJ AND ISTRIA

salty old sailors who use these vessels (find the placemat with wine stains, and put the glass in different red circles to hear various seamen talk in the Rovinj dialect). Another movie shows the boats at work. Upstairs is a wall of photos of *batana* boats still in active use, a tiny library (peruse photos of the town from a century ago), and a video screen displaying *bitinada* music—local music with harmonizing voices that imitate instruments. Sit down and listen to several (there's a button for skipping ahead). The museum has no posted English information, so pick up the comprehensive English flyer as you enter.

Cost and Hours: 10 kn; June-Sept daily 10:00-14:00 & 19:00-23:00; Oct-Dec and March-May Tue-Sun 10:00-13:00 & generally also 16:00-18:00, closed Mon; closed Jan-Feb; Obala Pina Budicina 2, tel. 052/812-593, mobile 091-154-6598, www.batana.org, Ornela.

Activities: The museum, which serves as a sort of cultural heritage center for the town, also presents a variety of engaging *batana*-related activities. On

some summer evenings, you can take a boat trip on a *batana* from the pier near the museum. The trip, which is accompanied by traditional music, circles around the end of the Old Town peninsula and docks on the far side, where a traditional wine cellar has a fresh fish dinner ready, with local wine and more live music (June-mid-Sept, generally Tue and Thu at 20:30, boat trip-60 kn, dinner-160 kn extra, visit or call the museum the day before to reserve). Also on some summer evenings, you can enjoy an outdoor food market with traditional Rovinj foods and live *bitinada* music. The centerpiece is a *batana* boat being refurbished before your eyes (in front of museum, 20-30-kn light food, mid-June-early Sept generally Tue and Sat 20:00-23:00). Even if you're here off-season, ask at the museum if anything special is planned.

Rovinj Heritage Museum (Zavičajni Muzej Grada Rovinja)

This ho-hum museum combines art old (obscure classic painters) and new (obscure contemporary painters from Rovinj) in an old mansion. Rounding out the collection are some model ships, a small archaeological exhibit, and temporary exhibits.

Cost and Hours: 15 kn; mid-June-mid-Sept Tue-Fri 10:00-14:00 & 18:00-22:00, Sat-Sun 10:00-14:00 & 19:00-22:00, closed Mon; off-season Tue-Sat 10:00-13:00, closed Sun-Mon; Trg Maršala Tita 11, tel. 052/816-720, www.muzej-rovinj.com.

Aquarium (Akvarij)

This century-old collection of local sea life is one of Europe's oldest aquariums. Unfortunately, it's also tiny (with three sparse rooms holding a few tanks of what you'd see if you snorkeled here), disappointing, and overpriced.

Cost and Hours: 30 kn, daily June-Aug 9:00-21:00, Sept 9:00-20:00, Oct-May 10:00-16:00 or longer depending on demand, across the street from the end of the waterfront parking lot at Obala G. Paliage 5, tel. 052/804-712.

Activities in Rovinj

Boat Trips

For a different view on Rovinj, consider a boat trip. The scenery is pleasant rather than thrilling, but the craggy and tree-lined coastline and offshore islets are a lovely backdrop for an hour or two at sea. You'll see captains hawking boat excursions at little shacks all along Rovinj's harbor. The most common option is a 1.5-hour loop around the "Golden Cape" (Zlatni Rt) and through Rovinj's own little **archipelago** for about 75 kn; this is most popular at sunset. For a longer cruise, consider the four-hour, 150-kn sail north along the coast and into the underwhelming **Limski Canal** (a.k.a. "Limski Fjord"), where you'll have one to two hours of free time. Dolphin sightings are not unusual, and some outfits throw in a "fish picnic" en route for extra. I'd just stroll the harbor and comparison-shop to find the option that suits your interest.

You can also take a boat to one of the larger offshore islands. This lets you get away from the crowds and explore some relatively untrampled beaches. These boats—run by the big hotel chain with branches on those islands—depart about hourly from the end of the concrete pier in the Old Town known as the Mali Molo ("Little Pier"). The two choices are **St. Catherine** (Sv. Katarina—the lush, green island just across the harbor, about a 5-minute trip, 25 kn) and **Red Island** (Crveni Otok—farther out, about a 15-minute trip, boats may be marked "Hotel Istra," 40 kn).

▲Swimming and Sunbathing

Rovinj doesn't have any sandy beaches—just rocky ones. (The nearest thing to a sandy beach is the small, finely pebbled beach on Red Island/Crveni Otok.) The most central spot to swim or sunbathe is at **Balota Beach,** on the rocks along the embankment on the south side of the Old Town peninsula, just past La Puntuleina

ROVINJ AND ISTRIA

restaurant (no showers, but scenic and central). On nice days, Balota can get crowded; if you continue around Rovinj's peninsula to the tip, just before the old WWII pillbox you'll find the more secluded **"Pillbox Beach,"** where steps lead steeply down to a cluster of more secluded rocks. For bigger beaches, go to the wooded **Golden Cape** (Zlatni Rt) south of the harbor (past the big, waterfront Hotel Park). This cape is lined with walking paths and beaches, and shaded by a wide variety of trees and plants. For a scenic sunbathing spot, choose a perch facing Rovinj on the north side of the Golden Cape. Another beach, called **Kuvi,** is beyond the Golden Cape. To get away from it all, take a boat to an island on Rovinj's little archipelago (see previous listing).

▲Bike Rides

The TI's free, handy biking map suggests a variety of short and long bike rides. The easiest and most scenic is a quick loop around the Golden Cape (Zlatni Rt, described above). You can do this circuit and return to the Old Town in about an hour (without stops). Start by biking south around the harbor and past the waterfront Hotel Park, where you leave the cars and enter the wooded Golden Cape. Peaceful miniature beaches abound. The lane climbs to a quarry (much of Venice was paved with Istrian stone), where you're likely to see beginning rock climbers inching their way up and down. Cycling downhill from the quarry and circling the peninsula, you hit

the Lovor Grill (open daily in summer 10:00-16:00 for drinks and light meals)—a cute little restaurant housed in the former stables of the Austrian countess who planted what today is called "Wood Park." From there, you can continue farther along the coast or return to town (backtrack two minutes and take the right fork through the woods back to the waterfront path).

For a more ambitious, inland pedal, pick up the TI's free *Basìlica* bike map, narrating a 12-mile loop that connects several old churches.

Bike Rental: Bikes are rented at subsidized prices from the city parking lot kiosk (5 kn/hour, open 24 hours daily except no rentals in winter, fast and easy process; choose a bike with enough air in its tires or have them pumped up, as the path is rocky and gravelly). Various travel agencies around town rent bikes for much more (around 20 kn/hour); look for signs—especially near the bus station—or ask around.

ROVINJ AND ISTRIA

Nightlife in Rovinj

ROVINJ AFTER DARK

Rovinj is a delight after dark. Views that are great by day become magical in the moonlight and floodlight. The streets of the Old Town are particularly inviting when empty and starlit.

Concerts

Lots of low-key, small-time music events take place right in town (ask at the TI, check the events calendar at www.tzgrovinj.hr, and look for handwritten signs in Croatian and Italian on Garibaldi Street near the Square at the Bridge). Groups perform at various venues around town: right along the harborfront (you'll see the bandstand set up); in the town's churches (especially St. Euphemia and the Franciscan church); in the old cinema/theater by the market; at the pier in front of the House of the Batana Boat (described earlier, under "Sights in Rovinj"); and at the Multi-Media Center (a.k.a. the "MMC," which locals call "Cinema Belgrade"—its former name), in a cute little hall above a bank across the harbor from the Old Town.

Wine Bars

Rovinj has two good places to sample Istrian and Croatian wines, along with light, basic food—such as prosciutto-like *pršut*, truffles, and olive oil. Remember, two popular local wines worth trying are *malvazija* (a light white) and *teran* (a heavy red). At **Bacchus Wine Bar,** owner Paolo serves about 80 percent Istrian wines, with the rest from elsewhere in Croatia and international vintners (15-60 kn/deciliter, most around 20-30 kn, 65-250-kn bottles, daily 7:00-1:00 in the morning, shorter hours off-season, Carera 5, tel. 052/812-154). **Piassa Granda,** on a charming little square right in the heart of the Old Town, has a classy, cozy interior and more than 100 types of wine (25-35-kn glasses, 40-70-kn Istrian small plates, more food than Bacchus, daily 10:00-16:00 & 18:00-24:00, Veli trg 1, mobile 098-824-322, Helena).

Lounging

Valentino Champagne and Cocktail Bar is a romantic, justifiably pretentious place for an expensive late-night waterfront drink. Fish, attracted by its underwater lights, swim by from all over the bay...to the enjoyment of those nursing a

ROVINJ AND ISTRIA

cocktail on the rocks (literally—you'll be given a small seat cushion and plunk down in your own seaside niche). Or you can choose to sit on one of the terraces. Classy candelabras twinkle in the twilight, as couples cozy up to each other and the view. While the drinks are extremely pricey, this place is unforgettably cool (60-75-kn cocktails, 60-kn non-alcoholic drinks, daily April-May 12:00-24:00, June-Sept 18:00-24:00, closed Oct-March, Via Santa Croce 28, tel. 052/830-683, Patricia).

If Valentino is too pricey, too chichi, or too crowded for your tastes, a couple of alternatives are nearby. The **Monte Carlo** bar, along the same drag but a bit closer to the harbor, is fun-loving and serves much cheaper drinks (25-30 kn), but lacks the atmospheric "on the rocks" setting of Valentino (daily 8:00-late, closed Oct-Easter, mobile 091-579-1813). Or consider **La Puntuleina,** beyond Valentino, with a similarly rocky ambience but lower prices (20-40-kn drinks) and a bit less panache (listed later, under "Eating in Rovinj"). I'd scout all three and pick the ambience you prefer.

Batana Boat Activities

In summer, the House of the Batana Boat often hosts special events such as a boat trip and traditional dinner, and an outdoor food court. For details, see the listing earlier, under "Sights in Rovinj."

Sleeping in Rovinj

As throughout Croatia, most Rovinj accommodations (both hotels and *sobe*) prefer multi-night stays—especially in peak season (July-Aug). While a few places levy surcharges for shorter stays, many are fine with even one-night stays (I've noted this in each listing). Don't show up here without a room in August: Popular Rovinj is packed during that peak month.

IN THE OLD TOWN

All of these accommodations (with one exception) are on the Old Town peninsula, rather than the mainland section of the Old Town. Residence Dream is just around the atmospheric harbor, an easy five-minute walk away. Rovinj has no real hostel, but *sobe* are a good budget option.

$$$ **Villa Markiz,** run by Andrej with the help of eager-to-please Ivana, has four extremely mod, stylish apartments in an old shell in the heart of the Old Town. You'll climb a steep and narrow staircase to reach the apartments, each of which has a small terrace (Db-€130/€80-100/€60). Only the gorgeous top-floor, two-story penthouse apartment has sea views (€250/€150-180/€140; no breakfast, air-con, free Wi-Fi, Pod Lukovima 1, tel.

Sleep Code

Abbreviations (6 kn = about $1, €1 = about $1.40, country code: 385)
S = Single, **D** = Double/Twin, **T** = Triple, **Q** = Quad,
b = bathroom.

Price Rankings

$$$ Higher Priced—Most rooms €110 or more.

$$ Moderately Priced—Most rooms between €70-110.

$ Lower Priced—Most rooms €70 or less.

If I've listed three sets of rates, separated by slashes, the first is for peak season (typically mid-July through late Aug), the second is for shoulder season (roughly June-mid-July and late Aug-Sept), and the third is for off-season (Oct-May). If I've listed only two rates, the first is for peak season and the second for shoulder/off-season. The dates for seasonal rates vary by hotel.

The modest tourist tax (about 7 kn per person, per night) is not included in these rates. Hotels generally accept credit cards and include breakfast in their rates, while most *sobe* accept only cash and don't offer breakfast. While rates are listed in euros, you'll pay in kunas. Unless I note otherwise, everyone listed here speaks English (or has a relative or neighbor who can help translate), and Wi-Fi is generally free. Prices can change without notice; verify current rates online or by email. For the best prices, always book directly with the hotel.

052/841-380, Ivana mobile 099-652-7660, Andrej mobile 098-934-0321, dani7cro@msn.com).

$$$ Porta Antica rents 16 comfortable, nicely decorated apartments in five different buildings around the Old Town (all except La Carera are on the peninsula). Review your options on their website and be specific in your request (Db-€110-200/€90-170/€80-120, price depends on size and views, extra person-€25, no extra charge for 1-night stays, no breakfast, air-con, non-smoking, Wi-Fi, reception and main building next door to TI on Obala Pina Budičina, mobile 099-680-1101, www.portaantica.com, portaantica@yahoo.it, Claudia).

$$$ Hotel Adriatic, a lightly renovated holdover from the communist days, features 27 rooms overlooking the main square, where the Old Town peninsula meets the mainland. The quality of the drab, worn rooms doesn't justify the outrageously high prices...but the location might. Of the big chain of Maistra hotels (described on page 1024), this is the only one in the Old Town (rates flex with demand, in top season figure Sb-€150, Db-€225; these prices are per night for 1- or 2-night stays—cheaper for 3 nights or more, all Sb are non-view, most Db have views—otherwise €20 less, no elevator, air-con, pay Wi-Fi, some nighttime noise—especially on weekends, Trg Maršala Tita, tel. 052/803-510, www.maistra.hr, adriatic@maistra.hr).

$$ Villa Cissa, run by Zagreb transplant Veljko Despot, has three apartments with tastefully modern, artistic decor above an art gallery in the Old Town. Kind, welcoming Veljko—who looks a bit like Robin Williams—is a fascinating guy who had an illustrious career as a rock-and-roll journalist (he was the only Eastern Bloc reporter to interview the Beatles) and record-company executive. Now his sophisticated, artistic style is reflected in these comfortable apartments. Because the place is designed for longer stays, you'll pay a premium for a short visit (50 percent extra for 2-night stays, prices double for 1-night stays), and it comes with some one-time fees, such as for cleaning. But it's worth the added expense. Veljko lives off-site, so be sure to clearly communicate your arrival time (smaller apartment-€108/€98/€88 plus €30 one-time cleaning fee, bigger apartment-€110 more plus €50 one-time cleaning fee, extra person-20 percent more, cash only, air-con, Wi-Fi, lively café across the street, Zdenac 14, tel. 052/813-080, www.villacissa.com, info@villacissa.com).

$$ Casa Garzotto is an appealing mid-range option, with four apartments, four rooms, and one large family apartment in three different Old Town buildings. These classy and classic lodgings have modern facilities but old-fashioned charm, with antique furniture and historic family portraits on the walls. Thoughtfully run by a friendly staff, it's a winner (rooms—Sb-€80/€80/€70, Db-€120/€105/€90; apartments—Db-€165/€140/€120; 2-bedroom family apartment—Db-€175/€150/€120, extra person-€25-30; includes breakfast, off-site parking, loaner bikes, and other thoughtful extras; 30 percent extra for 1-night stays, air-con, lots of stairs, Wi-Fi in main building, reception and most apartments are at Garzotto 8, others are a short walk away, tel. 052/811-884, mobile 099-800-7338, www.casa-garzotto.com, casagarzotto@gmail.com).

$$ Trevisol Apartments has four new, modern units on a sleepy Old Town street, plus a few others around town. Check your options on their website, reserve your apartment, and arrange a time to meet (Db-€90/€75/€50; bigger seaview Db-€110/€80/€60; extra charge for 1-night stays: 50 percent in peak season, 30 percent off-season; no breakfast, air-con, Wi-Fi, Trevisol 40, main office at Sv. Križa 33, mobile 098-177-7404, www.lvi.hr, Adriano).

$$ B&B Casale has three simple but affordable and nicely appointed rooms atmospherically located in a tight lane in the heart of the Old Town. As there's no air-conditioning, thin windows, and lots of outdoor cafés nearby, it can be noisy at night (Db-€80/€55/€46, breakfast-€9/person, cash only, Wi-Fi, Casale 2, tel. 052/814-828, mobile 099-888-5947, adr.cer@gmail.com, Adriano).

$$ Residence Dream, tucked in a tight warren of lanes in the touristy restaurant ghetto just around the harbor from the Old Town peninsula, has three modern, pleasantly furnished rooms above a busy restaurant. While you're not right in the heart of the Old Town, it's close enough, and it's worth considering if other mid-range places are full (Db-€85/€75/€60, extra bed-€15, breakfast-60 kn, air-con, Wi-Fi, good windows but may have some restaurant noise, Rakovca 18, tel. 052/830-613, mobile 091-579-9239, www.dream.hr, dream@dream.hr).

ON THE MAINLAND, SOUTHEAST OF THE OLD TOWN

To escape the high prices of Rovinj's Old Town, consider the resort neighborhood just south of the harbor. These are a 10- to 20-minute walk from the Old Town (in most cases, at least partly uphill), but most of that walk is along the very scenic harbor-front—hardly an unpleasant commute. While the big Maistra hotels are an option, I prefer cheaper alternatives in the same area. Given the cost and inconvenience of parking if you're sleeping in the Old Town (see "Arrival in Rovinj," earlier, for details), accommodations in this area are handy for drivers. The big hotels are signposted as you approach town (follow signs for *hoteli*, then your specific hotel). Once you're on the road to Hotels Eden and Park, the smaller ones are easy to reach: Villa Baron Gautsch is right on the road to Hotel Park; Hotel Vila Lili and Vila Kristina are a little farther on the main road toward Eden (to the left just after turnoff for Hotel Park, look for signs).

Guest Houses and Small Hotels

These are a bit closer to the Old Town than the Maistra hotels, and offer much lower rates and more personality. The first three are hotelesque and sit up on the hill behind the big resort hotels, while the last two choices lack personality but are a great budget option relatively close to the Old Town (an easy and scenic 10-minute walk).

$$ Villa Baron Gautsch, named for a shipwreck, is a German-owned pension with 17 bright, crisp, comfortable rooms and an inviting, shared view terrace (Db-€80/€70/€60, €10 more for balcony, they also have two Sb for half the Db price, no extra charge for 1-night stays, closed late Oct-Easter, cash only, air-con, no elevator, Wi-Fi, free street parking, Ronjgova 7, tel. 052/840-538, www.baron-gautsch.com, baron.gautsch@gmx.net, Sanja).

$$ Hotel Vila Lili is a family-run hotel with 20 nicely deco-rated but slightly faded rooms above a restaurant on a quiet lane. While the rooms are pricey, the extra cost buys you more hotel amenities than the cheaper guest houses listed here (Sb-€65/€55,

Db-€110/€100, pricier suites also available, no extra charge for 1-night stays, includes breakfast, elevator, air-con, Wi-Fi, parking-35 kn/day, Mohorovičića 16, tel. 052/840-940, www. hotel-vilalili.hr, info@hotel-vilalili.hr, Petričević family).

$$ Vila Kristina, run by Kristina Kiš and her family, has 10 rooms and five apartments along a busy road. All but one of the units has a balcony. I'd skip the overpriced apartments (Db-€95/€85, apartment Db-€140/€120, no extra charge for 1-night stays, includes breakfast, air-con, no elevator, Wi-Fi, Luje Adamovića 16, tel. 052/815-537, www.kis-rovinj.com, kristinakis@ mail.inet.hr).

$ Elda Markulin, whose son runs the Baccus Wine Bar, rents three rooms and four apartments in a new, modern house a short walk up from the main harborfront road (Db-€50/€45/€40, apartment-€75/€60/€50, cash only, air-con, Wi-Fi, Mate Balote 12, tel. 052/811-018, mobile 095-900-8654, markulin@hi.t-com. hr). To reach it from the Old Town, walk along the waterfront; after you pass the recommended Maestral restaurant and the rag-tag boatyard on your right, turn left onto the uphill Mate Balote (just before the park).

$ Apartmani Tomo, next door to Elda (see directions above), is run with Albanian pride by Tomo Lleshdedaj, who rents seven rooms and nine studio apartments. While the lodg-ings are basic and communication can be a bit challenging, it's a handy location for a budget last resort (Db-€50/€40/€35, Db with kitchen-€70/€60/€50, smaller studio Db-€75/€65/€55, bigger stu-dio Db-€85/€75/€65, extra person-€10, cash only, air-con, Wi-Fi, Mate Balote 10, tel. 052/813-457, mobile 091-578-1518, no email— reserve by phone).

Maistra Hotels

The local hotel conglomerate, Maistra, has several hotels in the lush parklands just south of the Old Town. As all of the hotels were recently either completely renovated or built from scratch, these are a very expensive option; most of my readers—looking for proximity to the Old Town rather than hanging out at a fancy hotel—will prefer to save money and stay at one of my other list-ings. However, the Maistra hotels are worth considering if you can get a deal. These hotels have extremely slippery pricing, based on the type of room, the season, and how far ahead you book. (I've listed the starting rate for a 1- or 2-night stay in July-Aug; you'll pay less if you stay longer or visit off-season. Complete rates are explained on the website, www.maistra.hr.) I've listed the hotels in the order you'll reach them as you approach from the Old Town. All hotels have air-conditioning, elevators, free parking, and pay

Wi-Fi, and include breakfast in their rates. The Maistra chain also has several other properties (including the Old Town's Hotel Adriatic, described earlier; Hotel Katarina, a cheaper option with basic rooms picturesquely set on the small island facing the Old Town; and other more distant, cheaper options). Most Maistra hotels close during the winter.

$$$ Hotel Park is the humblest of the pack, with just three stars. It has 202 renovated but dull rooms in a colorized communist-era hull, and a seaside swimming pool with sweeping views to the Old Town. This is the handiest for walking into the Old Town—it's a 10-minute stroll, entirely along the stunning harborfront promenade (Sb-€144, Db-€180, about €50 more for sea view, tel. 052/808-000, park@maistra.hr).

$$$ Hotel Monte Mulini is the fanciest of the bunch, with five stars, 99 rooms and 14 suites (all with seaview balconies), a beautiful atrium with a huge glass wall overlooking the cove, an infinity pool, and over-the-top prices (Db-€585, tel. 052/636-000, www.montemulinihotel.com, montemulini@maistra.hr).

$$$ Hotel Lone (LOH-neh), named for the cove it over-looks, is the newest and by far the most striking in the collection—the soaring atrium of this "design hotel" feels like a modern art museum. Also extremely expensive, its 248 rooms come wrapped in a vivid package (Db-€350, tel. 052/632-000, www.lonehotel.com, lone@maistra.hr).

$$$ Hotel Eden offers four stars and 325 upscale, imaginatively updated rooms with oodles of contemporary style behind a brooding communist facade (rates about €30 more than Hotel Park, tel. 052/800-400, eden@maistra.hr).

Eating in Rovinj

It's expensive to dine in Rovinj, but the food is generally good, with a few truffle dishes on most menus (see "Istrian Food and Wine" sidebar). Interchangeable restaurants cluster where Rovinj's Old Town peninsula meets the mainland, and all around the harbor. Be warned that most eateries—like much of Rovinj—close for the winter (roughly mid-Oct to Easter). If you're day-tripping into the Istrian interior, consider dining at one of the excellent restaurants in or near Motovun (see page 1047), then returning to Rovinj after dark.

ALONG ROVINJ'S "RESTAURANT ROW"

The easiest dining option is to stroll the Old Town embankment overlooking the harbor (Obala Pina Budičina), which changes its name to Svetoga Križa and cuts behind the buildings after a few blocks. Window-shop the pricey but scenic eateries along here, each of which has its own personality (all open long hours daily). Some have sea views, others are set back on charming squares, and still others have atmospheric interiors. I've listed these in the order you'll reach them. You'll pay top dollar, but the ambience is memorable.

Scuba, at the start of the row, is closest to the harbor—so, they claim, they get first pick of the daily catch from arriving fishing boats. They serve both seafood and tasty Italian dishes, in a contemporary interior or at outdoor tables with harbor views (70-80-kn pastas, 60-150-kn main dishes, daily 11:00-24:00, Obala Pina Budičina 6, mobile 098-219-446).

Veli Jože, with a smattering of outdoor tables (no real views) and a rollicking, folksy interior decorated to the hilt, is in all the guidebooks but still delivers on its tasty, traditional Istrian cuisine (50-80-kn pastas, 45-55-kn basic grill dishes, 110-160-kn main courses, daily 11:00-24:00, Sv. Križa 1, tel. 052/816-337).

Santa Croce, with tables scenically scattered along a terraced incline that looks like a stage set, is well-respected for its seafood and pastas. Classy and sedate, and with attentive service, it attracts a slightly older clientele (45-60-kn pastas, 70-150-kn main courses, no sea views, daily 18:00-23:00, Sv. Križa 11, tel. 052/842-240).

Lampo is simpler, with a basic menu of salads, pizzas, and pastas. The only reason to come here is for the fine waterfront seating at a reasonable price (45-65-kn pastas, 60-120-kn main courses, daily 11:00-24:00, Sv. Križa 22, tel. 052/811-186).

La Puntuleina, at the end of the row, is the most scenic (and most expensive) option. This upscale restaurant/wine bar features Istrian, Italian, and Mediterranean cuisine served in the contemporary dining room, or outside—either on one of the many terraces, or at tables scattered along the rocks overlooking a swimming hole. The menu is short, and Miriam and Giovanni occasionally add seasonal specials. As the outdoor seating is deservedly popular, reserve ahead (10-kn cover charge, 80-110-kn pastas, 120-180-kn main courses, daily 12:00-23:00, closed Nov-Easter, on the Old Town embankment past the harbor at Sv. Križa 38, tel. 052/813-186). You can also order just a drink to sip while sitting down on the rocks.

Just before La Puntuleina, don't miss the inviting **Valentino Champagne and Cocktail Bar**—with no food but similar "drinks on the rocks" ambience (described earlier, under "Nightlife in Rovinj"). If you're on a tight budget, dine cheaply elsewhere, then come here for an after-dinner finale.

Istrian Food and Wine

Foodies consider Istria the best part of Croatia. Though much of the country is arid and barren, Istria is noticeably greener—

its fertile soil bursts with a cornucopia of delicious ingredients. Like the Istrian people, Istrian cuisine is a mix of various cultural influences, including Italian-style elements, farmer fare, game, and seafood. Truffles are used liberally, and are a big hit with the many tourists who come here for their pungent flavor (see sidebar on page 1048).

Istrian menus come with an enticing list of pastas. You'll see familiar dishes such as gnocchi and risotto, but Istria also adds some unique noodles to the mix. *Fuži* are little pasta squares that are rolled up to create hollow noodles, roughly shaped like penne; *pljukanci* are short, thick, nearly transparent twists (similar to Italian *trofie*).

Pršut is the air-cured ham that is Istria's answer to prosciutto. You'll often find game on the menu, as well as *boškarin*—the meat of an indigenous Istrian longhorn cattle. *Ombolo* is pork loin—a locally beloved dish.

Istria is also a major wine growing region. About 80 percent of Istrian wines are white, and much of that uses the grape called *malvazija* (mahl-VAH-zee-yah; better known to English-speakers as malvasia)—producing a light white wine that can be either sweet *(slatko)* or dry *(suho)*. *Malvazija* comes in several forms: "fresh" (table wine, aged in stainless steel) or aged in barrels (often in French oak or in local Istrian acacia; look for *barrique* on the label). White blends (usually including some *malvazija*) are also common.

When it comes to red wine, you'll see plenty of the heavy, very "big" *teran*, from *refošk* grapes. Because *teran* is full-bodied, it's often blended with merlot or other grapes to soften its flavor. *Teran* pairs well with *pršut*.

INTERNATIONAL FARE ON THE OLD TOWN PENINSULA

Offering upscale, international (rather than strictly Croatian) food and presentation, these options are expensive but creative.

Monte Restaurant is your upscale, white-tablecloth splurge—made to order for a fine dinner out. With tables strewn around a covered terrace just under the town bell tower, this atmospheric place features inventive cuisine that melds Istrian products with international techniques. Come here only if you value a fine dining experience, polished service, and the chance to learn about local food and wines without regard for price (plan to spend

350-700 kn per person for dinner, daily 12:00-14:30 & 18:30-23:00, reserve ahead in peak season, Montalbano 75, tel. 052/830-203, Đekić family).

Krčma Ulika, a classy hole-in-the-wall run by Inja Tucman, has a mellow, cozy, art-strewn interior. Inja enjoys surprising diners with unexpected flavor combinations. The food is a bit over-priced and can be hit-or-miss, but the experience feels like an innovative break from traditional Croatian fare. As portions are small (Inja encourages diners to order two courses), the price can add up (15-kn cover, 80-100-kn starters and pastas, 180-200-kn main courses, daily 13:00-15:00 & 19:00-24:00—except closed for lunch in Aug, closed mid-Oct-April, cash only, Porečka 6, tel. 052/818-089, mobile 098-929-7541).

AFFORDABLE ALTERNATIVES ON THE MAINLAND

These options are a bit less expensive than most of those described above. I've listed them in the order you'll reach them as you walk around Rovinj's harbor.

Maestral combines affordable, straightforward pizzas and seafood with Rovinj's best view. If you want an outdoor table overlooking bobbing boats and the Old Town's skyline—without breaking the bank—this is the place. It fills a big building surrounded by workaday shipyards about a 10-minute walk from the Old Town, around the harbor toward Hotel Park (35-45-kn sandwiches, 45-60-kn pizzas and pastas, 50-100-kn fish and meat dishes, daily 9:00-24:00, closed Oct-March, obala N. Nazora b.b., look for *Bavaria* beer sign, tel. 052/830-565).

Sidro, around the harbor with views back on the Old Town, has a typical menu of pasta, pizza, and fish. But it's particularly well-respected for its Balkan meat dishes such as *ćevapčići* (see the "Balkan Flavors" sidebar on page 1140) and a spicy pork-and-onion stew called *mućkalica*. With unusually polite service and a long tradition (run by three generations of the Paoletti family since 1966), it's a popular local hangout (45-75-kn pastas, 55-90-kn grilled meat dishes, 110-140-kn steaks and fish, daily 11:00-23:00, closed Nov-Feb, harborfront at Rismondo 14, tel. 052/813-471).

Gostionica/Trattoria Toni is a hole-in-the-wall serving up small portions of good Istrian and Venetian fare. Choose between the cozy interior (tucked down a tight lane), or the terrace on a bus-tling, mostly pedestrian street (40-95-kn pastas, 40-140-kn main courses, daily 12:00-15:00 & 18:00-22:30, just up ulica Driovier on the right, tel. 052/815-303).

BREAKFAST

Most rental apartments come with a kitchenette handy for break-fasts (stock up at a neighborhood grocery shop). Cafés and bars along the waterfront serve little more than an expensive croissant with coffee. The best budget breakfast (and a fun experience) is a picnic. Within a block of the market, you have all the necessary stops: the Brionka bakery (fresh-baked cheese or apple strudel); mini-grocery stores (juice, milk, drinkable yogurt, and so on); market stalls (cherries, strawberries, walnuts, and more, as well as an elegant fountain for washing); an Albanian-run bread kiosk, Pekarna Laste, between the market and the water...plus benches with birds chirping, children playing, and fine Old Town views along the water. For a no-fuss alternative, you can shell out 60 kn for the buffet breakfast at Hotel Adriatic (daily 7:00-10:00, until 11:00 July-Aug; described earlier, under "Sleeping in Rovinj").

Rovinj Connections

BY BUS

Rovinj's bus station is open daily 6:30-9:15 & 9:45-16:30 & 17:00-21:30. As always, confirm the following times before planning your trip. Bus schedules are dramatically reduced on Saturdays and especially on Sundays, as well as (in some cases) off-season. Bus information: Tel. 060-333-111 or 052/811-453, www.autobusni-kolodvor.com.

From Rovinj by Bus to: Pula (about hourly, 45 minutes), **Poreč** (3-6/day, 1 hour), **Rijeka** (4-5/day, 2-3.5 hours), **Zagreb** (6-9/day, 3-6 hours), **Venice** (1/day Mon-Sat departing very early in the morning—likely at 5:40, arriving Venice at 10:00, none Sun).

To Slovenia: In the summer, two daily buses connect Rovinj to Slovenia (**Piran** and **Ljubljana**): a slow one departing at 8:00 (3 hours to Piran, 5.5 hours to Ljubljana, late June-Aug only) or an express one departing at around 16:35 (2 hours to Piran, 4 hours to Ljubljana, July-Sept only); as this connection changes from year to year, confirm schedules at www.ap-ljubljana.si. Twice weekly off-season (generally Mon and Fri), an early morning bus begins in Pula, then heads to Poreč, Portorož (with an easy transfer to Piran), and Ljubljana. You can also reach Piran (and other Slovenian destinations) with transfers in Umag and Portorož.

To the Dalmatian Coast: A bus departs Rovinj every evening at 19:00 for the Dalmatian Coast, arriving in **Split** at 6:00 and **Dubrovnik** at 11:00. (If this direct bus isn't running, you can take an earlier bus to Pula, from where this night bus leaves at 20:00; also note that Pula has two daytime connections to Split.)

ROVINJ AND ISTRIA

Pula

Pula (POO-lah, Pola in Italian) isn't quaint. Istria's biggest city is an industrial port town with traffic, smog, and sprawl...but it

has the soul of a Roman poet. Between the shipyards, you'll discover some of the top Roman ruins in Croatia, including a stately amphitheater—a fully intact mini-Colosseum that marks the entry to a seedy Old Town with ancient temples, arches, and columns.

Strategically situated at the southern tip of the Istrian Peninsula, Pula has long been a center of industry, trade, and military might. In 177 B.C., the city became an important outpost of the Roman Empire. It was destroyed during the wars following Julius Caesar's death and rebuilt by Emperor Augustus. Many of Pula's most important Roman features—including its amphitheater—date from this time (early first century A.D.). But as Rome fell, so did Pula's fortunes. The town changed hands repeatedly, caught in the crossfire of wars between greater powers—Byzantines, Venetians, and Habsburgs. After being devastated by Venice's enemy Genoa in the 14th century, Pula gathered dust as a ghost town...still of strategic military importance, but otherwise abandoned.

In the mid-19th century, Italian unification forced the Austrian Habsburgs—whose navy had been based in Venice—to look for a new home for their fleet. In 1856, they chose Pula, and over the next 60 years, the population grew thirtyfold. (Despite the many Roman and Venetian artifacts littering the Old Town, most of modern Pula is essentially Austrian.) By the dawn of the 20th century, Pula's harbor bristled with Austro-Hungarian warships, and it had become the crucial link in a formidable line of imperial defense that stretched from here to Montenegro. As one of the most important port cities of the Austro-Hungarian Empire, Pula attracted naval officers, royalty...and a young Irishman named James Joyce who was on the verge of revolutionizing the literary world.

Today's Pula, while no longer quite so important, remains a vibrant port town and the de facto capital of Istria. It offers an enjoyably urban antidote to the rest of this stuck-in-the-past peninsula.

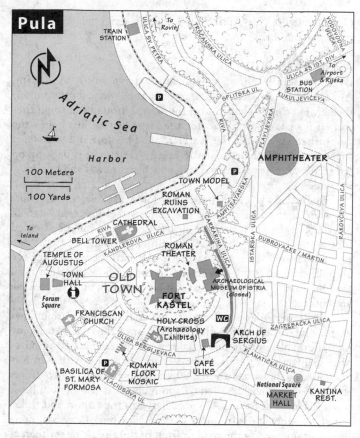

Map labels: Pula; N; TRAIN STATION; To Rovinj; ULICA SV. PETRA; TRSCANSKA ULICA; VODNJANSKA ULICA; SPLITSKA UL.; BUS STATION; To Airport & Rijeka; KUKULJEVIĆEVA; Adriatic Sea; RIVA; FLAVIJEVSKA; AMPHITEATER; Harbor; 100 Meters; 100 Yards; TOWN MODEL; ROMAN RUINS EXCAVATION; AMFITEATARSKA; CARARINA ULICA; ISTARSKA ULICA; DUBROVAČKE / MARTIN; RAKOVČEVA ULICA; To Island; RIVA; CATHEDRAL; BELL TOWER; KANDLEROVA ULICA; ROMAN THEATER; TEMPLE OF AUGUSTUS; TOWN HALL; OLD TOWN; i; Forum Square; FORT KAŠTEL; ARCHAEOLOGICAL MUSEUM OF ISTRIA (closed); FRANCISCAN CHURCH; HOLY CROSS (Archaeology Exhibits); WC; ZAGREBAČKA ULICA; ULICA SERGIJEVACA; ARCH OF SERGIUS; FLANATIČKA ULICA; BASILICA OF ST. MARY FORMOSA; FLACIUSOVA UL.; ROMAN FLOOR MOSAIC; CAFÉ ULIKS; National Square; MARKET HALL; KANTINA REST.

PLANNING YOUR TIME

Pula's sights, while top-notch, are quickly exhausted. Two or three hours should do it: Visit the amphitheater, stroll the circular Old Town, and maybe see a museum or two. As it's less than an hour from Rovinj, there's no reason to spend the night.

Orientation to Pula

Although it's a big city, the tourist's Pula is compact: the amphitheater and, beside it, the ring-shaped Old Town circling the base of an old hilltop fortress. The Old Town's main square, the Forum, dates back to Roman times.

TOURIST INFORMATION

Pula's TI overlooks the Old Town's main square, the Forum. It offers a free map and information on the town and all of Istria (daily June-Sept 8:00-21:00—or until 22:00 in July-Aug, May and

Oct 8:00-18:00, Nov-April 9:00-16:00, Forum 3, tel. 052/219-197, www.pulainfo.hr).

ARRIVAL IN PULA

By Car: Pula is about a 45-minute drive south of Rovinj. Approaching town, follow *Centar* signs, then watch for the amphitheater. Parking is plentiful on the streets around the amphitheater; if it's parked up, head for the large pay lot just below the amphitheater, toward the waterfront. This lot, and any street spaces marked in blue, cost the same (4 kn/hour; if parking on street, pay at meter or buy parking voucher at newsstand to display in window).

By Bus: As you exit the bus station, walk toward the yellow mansion, then turn left onto the major street (ulica 43 Istarske Divizije); at the roundabout, bear left again, and you'll be headed for the amphitheater (about a 10-minute walk total).

By Train: The train station is a 15-minute walk from the amphitheater, near the waterfront (in the opposite direction from the Old Town). Walk with the coast on your right until you see the amphitheater.

By Plane: Pula's small airport, which is served by various low-cost airlines, is about 3.5 miles northeast of the center. A handy and affordable **shuttle bus** is coordinated to depart 20 minutes after many budget flights arrive—check for details with your airline (30 kn to downtown Pula, 90 kn to Rovinj, run by two different companies—check schedule and prebook at www.brioni.hr or www.fils.hr). **Public bus #23** goes between the airport and Pula's bus station, but it's infrequent (10/day Mon-Fri, 4/day Sat, none Sun) and stops along the road in front of the airport rather than at the airport itself (coming from town to the airport, watch for buses to Valtura). The fair rate for a **taxi** into downtown Pula is about 80 kn, but most manage to charge more like 100 kn (don't pay more than that). Airport info: Tel. 052/530-105, www.airport-pula.com.

HELPFUL HINTS

Car Rental: All of the big rental companies have their offices at the airport (see airport info above); the TI has a list of a few local outfits with offices downtown.

Local Guide: If you'd like a guide to help you uncover the story of Pula, **Mariam Abdelghani** leads great tours of the major sites (€80 for a 2-hour city tour, €160 for an all-day tour of Istria, mobile 098-419-560, mariam.abdelghani@gmail.com).

ROVINJ AND ISTRIA

Pula Walk

This self-guided walk is divided between Pula's two most interesting attractions: the Roman amphitheater and the circular Old Town. About an hour for each is plenty. More time can be spent sipping coffee al fresco or dipping into museums.
• *Begin at Pula's main landmark, its...*

Amphitheater (Amfiteatar)

Of the dozens of amphitheaters left around Europe and North Africa by Roman engineers, Pula's is the sixth-largest (435 feet

long and 345 feet wide) and one of the best-preserved anywhere. This is the top place in Croatia to resurrect the age of the gladiators.

Cost and Hours: 40 kn, daily May-Sept 8:00-21:00—often later in July-Aug and for special events, April 8:00-20:00, Oct 9:00-19:00, Nov-March 9:00-17:00. The 30-kn audioguide, available at the kiosk inside, narrates 20 stops with 30 minutes of flat, basic data on the structure.

Gladiator Shows: About once each week in the summer, costumed gladiators re-enact the glory days of the amphitheater in a show called *Spectacvla Antiqva* (60 kn, 1/week late June-mid-Sept, details at www.pulainfo.hr).

➲ **Self-Guided Tour:** Go inside and explore the interior, climbing up the seats as you like. An "amphi-theater" is literally a "double theater"—imagine two theaters, without the back wall behind the stage, stuck together to maximize seating. Pula's amphitheater was built over several decades (first century A.D.) under the reign of three of Rome's top-tier emperors: Augustus, Claudius, and Vespasian. It was completed around A.D. 80, about

the same time as the Colosseum in Rome. It remained in active use until the beginning of the fifth century, when gladiator battles were outlawed. The location is unusual but sensible: It was built just outside town (too big for tiny Pula, with just 5,000 people) and near the sea (so its giant limestone blocks could be transported here more easily from the quarry six miles away).

Notice that the amphitheater is built into the gentle incline of a hill. This economical plan, unusual for Roman amphitheaters, saved on the amount of stone needed, and provided

ROVINJ AND ISTRIA

a natural foundation for some of the seats (notice how the upper seats incorporate the slope). It may seem like the architects were cutting corners, but they actually had to raise the ground level at the lower end of the amphitheater to give it a level foundation. The four rectangular towers anchoring the amphitheater's facade are also unique (two of them are mostly gone). These once held wooden staircases for loading and unloading the amphitheater more quickly—like the massive corkscrew ramps in many modern stadiums. At the top of each tower was a water reservoir, used for powering fountains that sprayed refreshing scents over the crowd to mask the stench of blood.

And there was plenty of blood. Imagine this scene in the days of the gladiators. More than 25,000 cheering fans from all social classes filled the seats. The Romans made these spectacles cheap or even free—distracting commoners with a steady diet of mind-less entertainment prevented discontent and rebellion. (Hmm... *The Voice*, anyone?) Canvas awnings rigged around the top of the amphitheater shaded many seats. The fans surrounded the "slaying field," which was covered with sand to absorb blood spilled by man and beast, making it easier to clean up after the fight. This sand *(harena)* gave the amphitheater its nickname...arena.

The amphitheater's "entertainers" were gladiators (named for the *gladius,* a short sword that was tucked into a fighter's boot). Some gladiators were criminals, but most were prisoners of war from lands conquered by Rome, who dressed and used weapons according to their country of origin. A colorful parade kicked off the spectacle, followed by simulated fights with fake weapons. Then the real battles began. Often the fights represented stories from mythology or Greek or Roman history. Most ended in death for the loser. Sometimes gladiators fought exotic animals—gath-ered at great expense from far corners of the empire—which would enter the arena from the two far ends (through the biggest arches). There were female gladiators, as well, but they always fought other women.

While the life of a gladiator seems difficult, consider that it wasn't such a bad gig—compared to, say, being a soldier. Gladiators were often better paid than soldiers, enjoyed terrific celebrity (both in life and in death), and only had to fight a few times each year.

Ignore the modern seating, and imagine when the arena (sandy oval area in the center) was ringed with two levels of stone seating and a top level of wooden bleachers. Notice that the outline of the arena is marked by a small moat (now covered with wooden slats)—just wide enough to keep the animals off the laps of those with the best seats, but close enough so that blood still sprayed their togas.

After the fall of Rome, builders looking for ready-cut stone

picked apart structures like this one—scraping it as clean as a neat slice of cantaloupe. Sometimes the scavengers were seeking the iron hooks that were used to connect the stone; in those oh-so "Dark Ages," the method for smelting iron from ore was lost. Most of this amphitheater's interior structures—such as steps and seats—are now in the foundations and walls of Pula's buildings...not to mention palaces in Venice, across the Adriatic. In fact, in the late 16th century, the Venetians planned to take this entire amphitheater apart, stone by stone, and reassemble it on the island of Lido on the Venetian lagoon. A heroic Venetian senator—still revered in Pula—convinced them to leave it where it is.

Despite these and other threats, the amphitheater's exterior has been left gloriously intact. The 1999 film *Titus* (with Anthony Hopkins and Jessica Lange) was filmed here, and today the amphitheater is still used to stage spectacles—from Placido Domingo to Elton John—with seating for about 5,000 fans. Recently, the loudest concerts were banned, because the vibrations were damaging the old structure.

Before leaving, don't miss the museum exhibit (in the "subterranean hall"—follow *exhibition* signs down the chute marked #17). This takes you to the lower level of the amphitheater, where gladiators and animals were kept between fights. When the fight began, gladiators would charge up a chute and burst into the arena, like football players being introduced at the Super Bowl. As you go down the passage, you'll walk on a grate over an even lower tunnel. Pula is honeycombed with tunnels like these, originally used for sewers and as a last-ditch place of refuge in case of attack. Inside, the exhibit—strangely dedicated to "olive oil and wine production in Istria" instead of, you know, gladiators—is surprisingly interesting. Browse the impressive collection of amphorae (old clay jugs), find your location on the replica of a fourth-century A.D. Roman map (oriented with east on top), and ogle the gigantic grape press and two olive-oil mills.

On your way out, check the corridor across from the ticket booth to see if there are any temporary exhibits.

• *From the amphitheater, it's a few minutes' walk to Pula's Old Town, where more Roman sights await. Exit the amphitheater, cross the street, turn left, and walk one long block along the small wall up the busy road (Amfiteatarska ulica). When you reach the big park on your right, look for the little, car-sized...*

Town Model

Use this handy model of Pula to get oriented. Next to the amphitheater, the little water cannon spouting into the air marks the pale-blue house nearby, the site of a freshwater spring (which makes this location even more strategic). The big star-shaped fortress on the hill is Fort Kaštel, designed by a French architect during the Venetian era (1630). Read the street plan of the Roman town into this model: At the center (on the hill) was the *castrum*, or military base. At the base of the hill (the far side from the amphitheater) was the forum, or town square. During Pula's Roman glory days, the hillsides around the *castrum* were blanketed with the villas of rich merchants. The Old Town, which clusters around the base of the fortress-topped hill, still features many fragments of the Roman period, as well as Pula's later occupiers. We'll take a counterclockwise stroll around the fortified old hill through this ancient zone.

The huge anchor across the street from the model celebrates Pula's number-one employer—its shipyards.

• *Continue along the street. At the fork, bear right (on Kandlerova ulica—level, not uphill). Notice the* **Roman ruins** *on your right. Just about any time someone wants to put up a new building, they find ruins like these. Work screeches to a halt while the valuable remains are excavated. In this case, they've discovered three Roman houses, two churches, and 2,117 amphorae—the largest stash found anywhere in the world. (The harbor is just behind, which suggests this might have been a storehouse for off-loaded amphorae.) I guess the new parking garage has to wait.*

After about three more blocks strolling through gritty, slice-of-life Pula, on your right-hand side, you'll see Pula's...

Cathedral (Katedrala)

This church combines elements of the two big Italian influences on Pula: Roman and Venetian. Dating from the fifth century A.D., the Romanesque core of the church (notice the skinny, slit-like windows) marks the site of an early-Christian seafront settlement in Pula. The Venetian Baroque facade and bell tower are much more recent (early 18th century). Typical of the Venetian style, notice how far away the austere bell tower is from the body of the church. The bell tower's foundation is made of stones that were scavenged from the amphitheater. The church's sparsely decorated interior features a classic Roman-style basilica floor plan, with a single grand hall—the side naves were added in the 15th

century, after a fire.

Cost and Hours: Free, generally open daily 10:00-18:00 in summer, less off-season.

• *Keep walking through the main pedestrian zone, past all the tacky souvenir shops and Albanian-run fast-food and ice-cream joints. After a few more blocks, you emerge into the...*

Forum

Every Roman town had a forum, or main square. Twenty centuries later, Pula's Forum not only serves the same function but has kept the old Roman name.

Two important buildings front the north end of the square, where you enter. The smaller build-

ing (on the left, with the columns) is the first-century A.D. Roman **Temple of Augustus** (Augustov Hram). Built during the reign of, and dedicated to, Augustus Caesar, this temple took a direct hit from an Allied bomb in World War II. After the war, the Allied occupiers rebuilt it as a sort of mea culpa—notice the patchwork repair job. It's the only one remaining of three such temples that once lined this side of the square. Inside the temple is a single room with fragments of ancient sculptures (10 kn, May-Sept Mon-Sat 9:00-20:00, Sun 10:00-15:00, often closed Oct-April, sparse English labels). The surviving torso from a statue of Augustus, which likely stood on or near this spot, dates from the time of Christ. Other evocative chips and bits of Roman Pula include the feet of a powerful commander with a pathetic little vanquished barbarian obediently at his knee (perhaps one of the Histri—the indigenous Istrians that the Romans conquered in 177 B.C.).

Head back out on to the square. As Rome fell, its long-subjugated subjects in Pula had little respect for the former empire's symbols, and many temples didn't survive. Others were put to new use: Part of an adjacent temple (likely dedicated to Diana) was incorporated into the bigger building on the right, Pula's medieval **Town Hall** (Gradska Palača). If you circle around behind this building, you can still see Roman fragments embedded in the back. The Town Hall encapsulates many centuries of Pula architecture: Romanesque core, Gothic reliefs, Renaissance porch, Baroque windows...and a few Roman bits and pieces. Notice the interesting combination of flags above the door: Pula, Croatia, Istria (with its mascot goat), Italy (for the large ethnic minority

ROVINJ AND ISTRIA

here), and the European Union (which Croatia joined in 2013).

• *Consider dropping by the TI on this square before continuing our circular stroll down the main drag, Sergijevaca. You'll pass by a small park on your right, then a block of modern shops. Halfway along the second building on the right—after the Calzedonia shop—watch for the poorly marked doorway with a green* Roman mosaic *plaque next to it. Go through the door and down the corridor (often occupied by vendors), and pop out the back door. Emerging on the other side, turn left, walk to the metal grill, and look down to see the…*

Roman Floor Mosaic (Rimski Mozaik)

This hidden mosaic is a great example of the Roman treasures that lie below the old center of Pula. Uncovered by locals who were cleaning up from World War II bombs, this third-century floor was carefully excavated and cleaned up for display right where it was laid nearly two millennia ago. (Notice that the Roman floor level was about six feet below today's.) The centerpiece of the mosaic depicts the punishment of Dirce. According to the ancient Greek legend, King Lykos of Thebes was bewitched by Dirce and abandoned his pregnant queen. The queen gave birth to twin boys (depicted in this mosaic), who grew up to kill their deadbeat dad and tie Dirce to the horns of a bull to be bashed against a mountain. This same story is famously depicted in the twisty *Toro Farnese* sculpture partly carved by Michelangelo (on display in Naples' Archaeological Museum).

• *For an optional detour to Byzantine times, walk into the parking lot just beyond the mosaic. Near the end of the lot, on the left-hand side, is a fenced-off grassy field. At the far end of the field is the small…*

Basilica of St. Mary Formosa (Kapela Marije Formoze)

We've seen plenty of Roman and Venetian bric-a-brac, but this chapel survives from the time of another Istrian occupier: Byzantium. For about 170 years after Rome fell (the sixth and seventh centuries A.D.), this region came under the control of the Byzantine Empire and was ruled from Ravenna (now in Italy, across the Adriatic, south of Venice). Much of this field was once occupied by a vast, richly decorated basilica. This lonely chapel is all that's left, but it still gives a feel for the architecture of that era—including the Greek cross floor plan (with four equal arms) and heavy brick vaulting.

• *Back on the main drag (Sergijevaca), continue through Pula's most colorful and most touristy neighborhood. After a block, the stepped lane on the left leads up to the deconsecrated Church of the Holy Cross, which is now a state-of-the-art museum space housing temporary exhibits from the Archaeological Museum (explained on page 1040).*

Continuing along Sergijevaca, in a few short blocks you'll arrive at the...

Arch of Sergius (Slavoluk Sergijevaca)

This triumphal arch, from the first century B.C., was Michelangelo's favorite Roman artifact in Pula. Marking the edge of the original

Roman town, it was built to honor Lucius Sergius Lepidus. He fought on the side of Augustus in the civil wars that swept the empire after Julius Caesar's assassination. The proto-feminist inscription proudly explains, "Silvia of the Sergius family paid for this with her own money." Statues of Silvia's husband, Lucius, plus her son and her brother-in-law, once stood on the three blocks at the top of the arch. (Squint to see the *Sergivs* name on each block.) On the underside of the arch is a relief of an eagle (the symbol of Rome) clutching an evil snake in its talons.

• *Before going under the arch, look to your left to see a famous Irishman appreciating the view from the terrace of...*

Café Uliks

In October 1904, a young writer named James Joyce moved from Dublin to Pula with his girlfriend, Nora Barnacle. By day, he taught English to Austro-Hungarian naval officers at the Berlitz language school (in the yellow building nearby). By night, he imagined strolling through his hometown as he penned short stories that would eventually become the collection *Dubliners*. But James and Nora quickly grew bored with little Pula and moved to Trieste in March 1905. Even so, Pula remains proud of its literary connections.

• *Now pass through the arch, into a square next to remains of the town wall. Continue straight ahead (up two bustling blocks, along the in-love-with-life Flanatička street) to...*

National Square (Narodni Trg) and Market Hall

Pula's market hall was an iron-and-glass marvel when inaugurated in the 19th century. This structure is yet another reminder of the way the Austro-Hungarian Empire modernized Pula with grace and gentility. You'll find meats, cheeses, and smelly fish on the ground floor (Mon-Sat 7:00-13:30, Sun 7:00-12:00), and an inviting food circus upstairs (Mon-Fri 7:00-15:00, Sat 7:00-14:00, Sun 7:00-12:00). All around is a busy and colorful farmers market that bustles until about 13:00, when things quiet down.

• *Our tour is finished. If you're ready for lunch, consider one of the cheap options inside or near the market hall, or walk one block to Kantina (see "Eating in Pula," later).*

When you're done here, backtrack to the town wall. As you face the Arch of Sergius, take a right and walk under the leafy canopy next to the wall. Keep an eye out (mostly on your left, along the wall) for more Roman remains. Among these are the **Twin Gates** (Porta Gemina), marking the entrance to a garden that's home to the **Archaeological Museum of Istria** (described next). You'll also see entrances to the Austro-Hungarian-era **tunnels** that burrow under the hill; called Zerostrasse, this space often hosts special exhibits. With more time, you can also consider a trip to the hilltop fortress, **Fort Kaštel**. Otherwise, we've completed our circular tour—the amphitheater is just around the corner.

Sights in Pula

Archaeological Museum of Istria (Arheološki Muzej Istre) in the Church of the Holy Cross (Sv. Srca)

Pula's century-old archaeological museum (at Carrarina 3) is closed for renovation for several years. When open, it shows off some of what you've seen in the streets, plus lots more—stone monuments, classical statues, ancient pottery...you name it. While it's closed, temporary exhibits drawing from the collection's highlights are displayed a few blocks away, inside the Church of the Holy Cross. Beautifully restored and repurposed as a modern exhibition space, and with good English descriptions, it's arguably a more satisfying home for the collection. Historians will want to check out the latest exhibits.

Cost and Hours: 20 kn—but can change depending on exhibits, daily 9:00-23:00, until 21:00 off-season, www.ami-pula. hr.

Roman Theater (Rimsko Kazalište)

The remains of an ancient theater are free to visit, on the hill behind the (currently closed) Archaeological Museum. Part of the stage is still intact, along with the semicircle of stone seats (some of which are still engraved with the names of the wealthy theatergoers who once sat in them). To find it, go up the hill around the right side of the museum. This was the smaller of the two theaters in Roman Pula; the second was south of the center (and is no longer intact).

Fort Kaštel

For a bird's-eye view over the town, head up to its centerpiece fortress. This deserted-feeling place, hosting the Historical Museum of Istria, is worth visiting only for the chance to wander the ramparts. While neither the museum nor the fortress is worth the hike up here, it's a good way to kill some extra time in Pula and sample the views over the town and amphitheater (various trails lead up from the streets below).

Eating in Pula

The best lunch options are in and near the town's **market hall** (which is also where my self-guided walk ends). The top floor of the market is a food circus with a number of cheap and tempting eateries with both indoor and terrace seating. Back outside, around the right side of the market hall, you'll find a pair of fiercely competitive bakeries serving fresh batches of cheap and delicious *burek*, the savory phyllo-dough pastry. One no-name bakery is built into the market hall itself, and Pekarna Corona faces it from across the market square.

 Kantina Restaurant, a block away, serves good lunches (including veggie options) and hearty, creative 35-kn salads both in an elegant vaulted cellar and on a lazy shady terrace. The service can be slow—if you're in a rush, eat at the market hall instead (60-85-kn pastas, 90-150-kn meat dishes, daily 12:00-23:00, closed Sun off-season, at the end of the pedestrian zone at Flanatička 16, tel. 052/214-054).

Pula Connections

By Bus from Pula to: Rovinj (about hourly, 45 minutes), **Poreč** (9/day, 1.5 hours), **Opatija** (12-14 day, 2 hours), **Rijeka** (nearly hourly, 2-2.5 hours), **Zagreb** (almost hourly, 4-6 hours), **Split** (2/day, 10 hours, plus 1 night bus—described next), **Venice** (1/day departing at 5:00, arrives Venice 10:15). A night bus departs Pula at 20:00, going to **Split** (arrives 6:00), where you can connect to **Dubrovnik** (arrives 11:00). To reach destinations in **Slovenia** (including Piran and Ljubljana), most connections require a change in Umag. In the summer (July-Sept only), a handy, express, direct bus departs at 16:00 and heads for **Rovinj** (30 min), then **Piran** (3 hours) and **Ljubljana** (5 hours). Or you can take the 8:00 bus from Rovinj (late June-Aug only, described on page 1029). Year-round, two days a week you can take a very early bus from Pula to Portorož (with a connection to Piran) and then on to Ljubljana (departs Pula at 5:30). Slovenia connections are run by Fils Pula (confirm schedules at www.fils.hr). In the summer, be aware that bus connections are more frequent on weekdays (fewer departures Sat-Sun). Bus info: Toll tel. 060-304-090.

By Train to: Zagreb (3/day, 6 hours, transfer in Rijeka), **Ljubljana** (1/day mid-July-Aug Thu-Sun only, 5 hours, transfer in Hrpelje-Kozina).

Motovun

Most tourists in Croatia focus on the coast. For a dash of variety, head inland. Some of the best bits of the Croatian interior lie just a short drive from Rovinj. Dotted with picturesque hill towns, speckled with wineries and olive-oil farms, embedded with precious truffles, and grooved by meandering rural roads, the Istrian interior is worth a visit.

Dramatically situated a thousand feet above vineyards and a truffle-filled forest, Motovun (moh-toh-VOON, Montona in Italian, pop. 531) is the best-known and most-touristed of the Istrian hill towns. And for good reason: Its hilltop Old Town is particularly evocative, with a colorful old church and a rampart walk with the best spine-tingling vistas in the Istrian interior. It's hard to believe that race-car driver Mario Andretti  was born in such a tranquil little traffic-free hamlet. Today Motovun's quiet lanes are shared by locals, tourists, and artists—who began settling here a generation ago, when it was nearly deserted.

Orientation to Motovun

Motovun is steep. Most everything of interest to tourists is huddled around its tippy-top. The main, upper entrance gate into town deposits you at the main square, with the church on your left and Hotel Kaštel on the right. From there, you're just about two blocks in every direction from a sheer drop-off. This hilltop zone is circled by an old rampart that today offers Motovun's most scenic stroll.

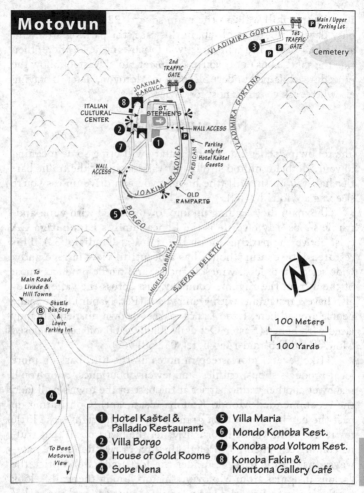

Motovun

1. Hotel Kaštel & Palladio Restaurant
2. Villa Borgo
3. House of Gold Rooms
4. Sobe Nena
5. Villa Maria
6. Mondo Konoba Rest.
7. Konoba pod Voltom Rest.
8. Konoba Fakin & Montona Gallery Café

TOURIST INFORMATION

Motovun's TI comes and goes (tel. 052/681-726, www.tz-motovun. hr). Fortunately, the reception desk at Hotel Kaštel kindly dispenses tourist information. Ask for the free map of Motovun and surroundings, which lists restaurants, shops, wineries, and accommodations.

ARRIVAL IN MOTOVUN

Motovun's striking hilltop setting comes with a catch: Visitors usually have to hike up part of the way. A steep, twisty road connects the base of the hill with the Old Town up top. If it's not too crowded, drive as far up this road as possible until you're directed to park in the lot partway up (near the lower church, a steep

10-minute uphill walk to the main square, 22 kn/day). On very busy days, this lot can fill up; in this case, the parking attendant at the foot of the hill will direct you to park in the lot there, then ride the shuttle bus up. If you're staying at Hotel Kaštel, follow the procedure explained under "Sleeping in Motovun," later. If staying elsewhere, ask your *sobe* host for advice.

Motovun Walk

The following self-guided commentary will bring some meaning to your Motovun hilltop stroll. The walk begins at the traffic barrier halfway up the hill (the highest you can drive unless you're sleeping at Hotel Kaštel).

The main drag leading up into town is lined with wine-and-truffle shops. My favorite is the Lanča family's **Etnobutiga ČA** (just above the parking lot on the right, at Gradiziol 33). This restored 17th-century house has a beautiful view terrace and a wide selection of local wines, brandies, and truffle products (most of them from the Zigante company, just across the valley); they also have a restaurant with grand views (Pod Napun). Like many people around here, Livio Lanča makes his own mistletoe brandy laced with honey (Easter-Oct daily 10:00-22:00, off-season closed Mon, closed Feb-mid-March, tel. 052/681-767).

Hike several more steep minutes up the hill, passing more local-products shops, truffles, and jewelry boutiques. Soon you'll reach yet another traffic barrier at the base of the town's wall (and the recommended Mondo Konoba restaurant). Continuing up past the barrier, you'll earn grand views on the right—the little town across the valley floor is Livade, the heart of all that truffle commerce—then go through the first of two **defensive gateways.** Inside this passage (under the fortified gate), notice the various insignias from Motovun's history lining the walls—look for the Venetian lion, the Latin family tombstone, and the seal of Motovun (with a pyramid of five towers being watched over by an angel). The area above the gate was a storehouse for weapons in the 15th century, when Motovun first flourished.

Emerging from the gateway, you're greeted by more sweeping views of the valley below on your right-hand side. (A coffee or light meal with this view is unforgettable; the town's lone ATM is to your left.) Just up and to the left, you'll find another defensive gateway, which is the main entrance into the heart of the **Old Town.** (Inside this gateway, notice the recommended Konoba pod Voltom restaurant.)

To your left as you come through the main gate is the yellow town church, **St. Stephen's.** The crenellated tower is a reminder of a time when this hilltop town needed to be defended. While unassuming from the outside, this austere house of worship has an impressive pedigree: It's based on designs by the famous Venetian architect Andrea Palladio (1508-1580), who greatly influenced the Neoclassical architecture of Washington, DC. The interior is a little gloomy but refreshingly lived-in—used more by locals than by tourists. On the left, notice a painting of the heart of Jesus, its eyes following you around the church (free, generally open daily 10:00-18:00 and during frequent services).

As you stand on the square in front of the church, imagine Motovun during its annual **film festival,** when it's filled with 20,000 movie lovers from throughout the region and around the world—often including a minor celebrity or two. This square fills to capacity, and films are projected on a giant screen at the far end (generally late July or early Aug, www.motovunfilmfestival.com).

Facing the church is the **Italian Cultural Center,** which plays an important role in this very Italian corner of Croatia. While the building is not open to the public, if your timing is right you'll enjoy beautiful music spilling out from its windows and filling the square. The local *klapa* music troupe—with men's voices harmonizing a cappella—practices here twice weekly (usually Mon and Fri evenings, at 21:00 in summer and 20:00 in winter, www.klapamotovun.com). If you hear them, find a bench and enjoy the show.

At the other end of the square is a leafy little piazza dominated by the big, pink **Hotel Kaštel**—the main industry in town. This is also where bigwigs in town for the local film festival call home—ask the staff about recent sightings of B-, C-, and D-list celebrities. (For example, if you're staying here, you may be showering in the same bathroom once graced by Jason Biggs, star of *American Pie.* Lucky you.)

Between the church and Hotel Kaštel, follow the lane to the

ramparts. Take the five-minute stroll around the Old Town on these fortifications. While most of Croatia is overrun by stray cats, Motovun seems populated by dog lovers. If you see or hear dogs in people's backyards, it's a safe bet that they are trained to hunt for truffles in the surrounding forest.

As you breathe in the

ROVINJ AND ISTRIA

stunning panorama, notice that well-defended Motovun has been fortified three times—two layers of wall up top, and a third down below.

Sleeping in Motovun

Because it's not on the coast, Motovun's accommodations don't charge extra for one- or two-night stays. In fact, if you're staying for three or more nights, try to score a discount. Except for the big hotel, all of the places here keep the same rates all year long. Most Motovun accommodations lack air-conditioning; thick old walls and a nice breeze generally keep things cool.

$$ Hotel Kaštel, dominating Motovun's hilltop (and its tourist industry), is can-do, ideally located, and the only real hotel in this little burg. Most of the 33 colorful rooms have views. True to its name, the building used to be a castle, so the floor plan can be confusing (Sb-€65/€61/€57, standard Db-€110/€103/€96, Db suite or "superior" Db with air-con-€134/€126/€116, "exclusive" Db with air-con and balcony-€165/€154/€142; 10 percent discount with this book if you book direct, elevator, air-con only in some rooms, laundry service, Wi-Fi, Trg Andrea Antico 7, tel. 052/681-607, www.hotel-kastel-motovun.hr, info@hotel-kastel-motovun.hr). Guests have free access to part of the spa facilities, with a beautiful indoor pool and a spa offering a wide range of massages (starting at 150 kn/30 min, 10 percent discount with this book). Guests with cars should tell the attendant at the traffic barrier that you have a reservation here; if there's room on top, he'll let you drive up. Otherwise he'll tell you where to park and call the hotel, which will send down a free car to shuttle you up (runs until about 18:00); either way, call ahead to the hotel to figure out your options.

$ Villa Borgo, beautifully located next to the loggia just below Motovun's uppermost gate, has 11 simple but stylish rooms with a nice budget flair. There are several types of rooms: with grand views (Db-€71/€58), with no views (Db-€61/€52), top-floor rooms that share a bathroom (D-€42), and a big apartment (Db-€82/€62, extra bed-€16). All rooms share a spectacular view terrace (lower prices are for Nov-May, includes breakfast, no air-con but fans, Wi-Fi, April-Oct staffed until 20:00, off-season call first, Borgo 4, mobile 098-434-797, tel. 052/681-708, www.villaborgo.com, info@villaborgo.com).

$ House of Gold is an injection of creativity in creaky old Motovun, filling a historic house on the road up into town with modern, minimalist, artsy decor. Youthful but still respectable—and just the right kind of funky—the three rooms share a common room with a big-screen TV, wood stove, and kitchen (non-view Sb-€35, bigger view Db-€65, huge attic Db-€75, includes breakfast, 2-night minimum, cash only, Wi-Fi, just above the middle parking lot at Gradziol 46, mobile 098-353-968, www.motovunaccommodation.com, brankarusnov@gmail.com, Branka). It's on the main road just above the parking lot halfway up into town—a steep 10- to 15-minute walk to the main square. Enter through the back alley: Head up the main street to the first parking lot on the left (marked *ulica Fossal*); hook right at the end of the parking lot, and walk along the path until you see the golden dwarf.

$ **Sobe Nena,** run by Nevija and Ricardo, is a good budget option in a tidy house at the very bottom of Motovun's hill. The two rooms are old-fashioned and basic, sharing a bathroom, but there's a fine garden to relax in. Ricardo speaks only a little English (Nevija speaks none), but they can call their daughter Doris to translate if necessary. It's a steep hike up into town, but you can catch the shuttle bus from the lower parking lot (if it's running), or—if you have a car—drive up to the parking lot partway up the hill (S-€20, D-€40, cash only, across from the gas station at Kanal 32, tel. 052/681-719, mobile 099-609-0883, sobe.nena@gmail.com).

$ **Villa Maria** is a good value, offering two fine rooms with view terraces, plus a third non-view room, in the Sviličić family home on a quiet back lane just below the main part of town (Db-€50, breakfast-€5, cash only, air-con, Wi-Fi, facing the defensive gate turn right and go down and around to Borgo 32, tel. 052/681-559, lorenasvilicic@gmail.com).

Eating in and near Motovun

IN MOTOVUN

Considering this is a small hill town with just a few real restaurants, all of them are impressively good; the first two listings are particularly notable. Every menu is topped by pricey (but tasty) truffle dishes—but keep in mind that these are a better investment when truffles are in season and the flavors are pungent (see sidebar, next page); otherwise you'll get older, blander truffles.

Mondo Konoba, run by a Croatian-Italian hybrid family and located just below the lower town gate (on the left, at the base of the wall), serves up Sicilian-Istrian fusion cuisine that ranks with any restaurant in the region. Most diners skip the unpretentious, pastel-blue dining room in favor of the inviting little outdoor terrace, with more tables across the street at the base of the town wall. The Mondo family's pack of five truffle-hunting dogs occasionally pays a visit (60-100-kn pastas, 95-185-kn main courses, June-Sept daily 12:00-15:30 & 18:00-22:00, closed Tue Oct-May and all of

Truffle Mania

A mysterious fungus with a pungent, unmistakable flavor is all the rage in Istria. Called *tartufi* in both Croatian and Italian, these precious tubers have been gathered here since Roman times and were favored by the region's Venetian and Austrian rulers. More recently, local peasants ate them as a substitute for meat (often mixed with polenta) during the lean days after World War II.

In 1999, local entrepreneur Giancarlo Zigante discovered a nearly three-pound white truffle. In addition to making Giancarlo Zigante a very wealthy man (see below), this giant truffle legitimized Istria on the world truffle scene. Today, Istria is giving France's Provence and Italy's Piedmont a run for their money in truffle production. Most of Istria's truffles are concentrated in the Motovun Forest, the damp, oak-tree-filled terrain surrounding Motovun, Livade, and Buzet.

A truffle is a tuber that grows entirely underground, usually at a depth of eight inches, near the roots of oak trees. Since no part of the plant grows aboveground, they're particularly difficult to find...and, therefore, valuable. Traditionally, Istrian truffle-gatherers use specially trained dogs to find truffles. This is most productive at night, when the darkness forces the dog to rely more on its sense of smell rather than sight.

Jan, Barbakan 1, tel. 052/681-791).

Konoba pod Voltom is actually inside the town's upper, main gate (on the right, with the *Taberna* sign above the door). Motovun's most traditional eatery serves excellent, well-presented Istrian food in a cozy dining room. In good weather (June–Sept only), it's hard to beat their view loggia, just below and outside the gate (45-60-kn pastas, 60-110-kn main courses, 80-260-kn truffle splurges, daily 12:00-22:00, closed Jan, tel. 052/681-923).

Other Scenic Eateries: Two other, simpler places also have seating along the wall, with these same mammoth views. **Konoba Fakin,** run by the winemaking family of the same name, offers a short menu of Istrian dishes (45-90-kn pastas, 50-145-kn main dishes, daily 10:00-24:00, tel. 052/681-598). The **Montona Gallery** café, with tables along the rampart between the two gates, serves drinks, ice cream, snacks, and 30- to 60-kn pizzas (daily 9:00-24:00, tel. 052/681-754).

On the Main Square: Hotel Kaštel's **Palladio Restaurant** has ambitiously executed food and delightful seating right on the leafy main square—but I'd skip the dull interior (50-80-kn pastas,

There are two general types of truffles: white (more valuable and with a deeper and more pungent flavor—*Tuber magnatum*, known as the "Queen of the Truffles") and black. Each type of truffle has a "season"—a specific time of year when its scent is released, making it easier to find (May-Nov for black, mid-Sept-Jan for white). Once dug up, they look pretty unassuming—like a tough, dirty pinecone.

Truffles can be eaten in a variety of ways. Thanks to their powerful and distinctive kick, they're often used sparingly for flavor—grated like parmesan cheese, or as truffle oil sprinkled over a dish. But you'll also find them in cheese, salami, olive oil, tapenade, pâté, and even ice cream. Truffle is commonly served with pasta—sometimes in a rich cream sauce, and other times more simply, just with olive oil. Truffle soufflé and truffle frittata (scrambled eggs) are also popular.

Some people find that the pungent, musty aftertaste follows them around all day...and all night, when its supposed aphrodisiac qualities kick in. Because they're so rare and difficult to find, truffles are incredibly expensive—but many people are more than happy to pay royally for that inimitable flavor. Long overshadowed by other famous truffle regions, Istria is becoming more well-known for this precious local product.

If you're a truffle nut, you'll find yourself in heaven here; if not, you may still appreciate the chance to sample a little taste of truffle. While you do that, ponder how one giant tuber changed the economy of an entire region.

70-165-kn main dishes, 10 percent discount with this book, daily 7:00-22:00; also listed under "Sleeping in Motovun," earlier).

NEAR MOTOVUN

While Motovun's eateries, listed above, are excellent, several other places are nearby. If good food is your priority, consider driving about 10 minutes down to Livade (in the valley below Motovun), or about 30 minutes to Brtonigla (between Motovun and the coast).

In Livade

The flat little crossroads village of Livade, sitting in the valley facing the back of Motovun's hill, is home to the first and last name in Istrian truffles. In 1999, Giancarlo Zigante unearthed the biggest white truffle the world had ever seen—2.9 pounds, as verified by *The Guinness Book of World Records*. (In 2007, the record was broken by a 3.3-pound Tuscan truffle.) Zigante's hunk of fungus—now revered as if a religious relic—kicked off a truffle craze that continues in Istria today (see sidebar). Today Zigante has a virtual monopoly on Istria's truffle industry, producing a wide range of truffle goodies. If you're a connoisseur, or just curious, make a pilgrimage to this truffle mecca.

Zigante's large facility here is divided into two parts: The **Zigante Tartufi shop** offers shelves upon shelves of both fresh and packaged truffle products (plus local wines, olive oils, brandies, and more). There's also a little tasting table where you can sample the earthy goods, and a brain-sized replica of that famously massive chunk of white truffle. A small jar of preserved truffles will run you 85-270 kn, depending on the size, type of truffle, and preparation. You can even pick up a recipe sheet telling you what to do with the precious stuff once you get it home (daily 9:00-21:00, off-season 10:00-20:00, Livade 7, tel. 052/664-030, www.zigantetartufi.com). The adjacent **Restaurant Zigante,** one of Istria's fanciest (and most expensive), dishes up all manner of truffle specialties. The decor—inside or out on the terrace—is whitetablecloth classy, the service is deliberate but friendly, and the truffles, as if on a cooking game show, are prepared in a dizzying variety of ways. If you want the full dose of this local delicacy from a place that knows its truffles, this is a worthwhile splurge (85-160-kn starters, 190-300-kn main dishes, 400-600-kn fixed-price meals—even more during white truffle season, daily 12:00-23:00, until 22:00 in winter, Livade 7, tel. 052/664-302).

Eating near Livade, in Gradinje: A five-minute drive east of Livade, in the hamlet of Gradinje, is a rustic, unpretentious eatery serving up the most affordable truffle dishes around. **Konoba Dolina** ("Valley Inn") has a nondescript interior and a pleasant terrace out front. Because it's just beyond the tourist trail, the prices are reasonable and the ambience is more authentic (45-95-kn meals, truffle splurges up to 120 kn, Wed-Mon 12:00-22:00, closed Tue, tel. 052/664-091). First make your way to Gradinje (go into Livade and turn right at the main roundabout, then drive through the countryside for a few minutes). Once in Gradinje, go all the way through town, then look for signs on the left.

In Brtonigla, Between Motovun and Rovinj

Brtonigla (bur-toh-NEEG-lah, Verteneglio in Italian, literally "black soil") is a tiny wine village surrounded by vineyards. It's a bit closer to the sea than Motovun, and sits above gentle slopes rather than a dramatic hilltop. Once in town, you'll find just a handful of haphazard streets, and this fine restaurant.

Konoba Astarea, a restaurant down the street and around the corner (on the main road toward Buje), is a local favorite for traditional, take-your-time Istrian cuisine with a focus on fish and lamb. While this isn't gourmet cooking and truffles are an afterthought, it's rustic food done very, very well. Anton and Alma

Kernjus cultivate a convivial atmosphere; compared with some of the region's stuffy eateries, this feels like a well-worn neighborhood hangout. Anton ignores the long menu; he'd rather pull up a chair to explain your options. This is a good place to try black risotto (with squid ink). Choose between the warmly cluttered, borderline-kitschy dining room huddled around the blazing open fire, where Alma does a lot of the cooking; the cool and welcoming terrace with faraway sea views; or the relaxing back garden. It's smart to reserve ahead (figure 200-300 kn per person for a full-blown multicourse meal, or order à la carte: 45-80-kn pastas, 60-180-kn main courses, daily 11:00-23:00, closed Nov, tel. 052/774-384).

ZAGREB

Surprise: The landlocked Croatian capital is, quite possibly, the country's most underrated destination. In this land of time-passed coastal villages, Zagreb (ZAH-grehb) offers a welcome jolt of big-city sophistication. You can't get a complete picture of modern Croatia without a visit here—away from the touristy resorts, in the lively and livable city that is home to one out of every six Croatians (pop. 790,000).

In Zagreb, you'll find historic neighborhoods, a thriving café culture, an appealing variety of restaurants, my favorite urban people-watching in Croatia, and virtually no tourists. The city is also Croatia's best destination for museum-going, with wonderful collections highlighting distinctively Croatian artists (the Naive Art movement and sculptor Ivan Meštrović), a quirky exhibit telling the tales of fractured relationships, and a smattering of other fine options (modern art, city history, arts and crafts, and much more). Get your fill here before heading to smaller cities and towns, where worthwhile museums are in short supply.

Zagreb began as two walled medieval towns, Gradec and Kaptol, separated by a river. As Croatia fell under the control of various foreign powers—Budapest, Vienna, Berlin, and Belgrade—the two hill towns that would become Zagreb gradually took on more religious and civic importance. Kaptol became a bishopric in 1094, and it's still home to Croatia's most important church. In the 16th century, the Ban (Croatia's governor) and the Sabor (parliament) called Gradec home. The two towns officially merged in 1850, and soon after, the railroad connecting Budapest with the Adriatic port city of Rijeka was built through the city. Zagreb prospered. After centuries of being the de facto religious, cultural, and political center of Croatia, Zagreb officially became a European capital when the country declared its independence in 1991. Today, while tourism is on the rise, Zagreb may be the only destination in this book that still feels undiscovered. The city richly rewards those who choose to visit.

PLANNING YOUR TIME

Many visitors just pass through Zagreb, but the city is worth a look. Throw your bag in a locker at the station and zip into the center for a quick visit—or, better yet, spend a night or two. If you enjoy urban bustle and good museums, you won't regret spending a full day (or more) here.

If you're very tight on time, you can get a decent sense of Zagreb in just a few hours. Make a beeline for Jelačić Square to visit the TI and get oriented. Take the funicular up to Gradec, visit the excellent Croatian Museum of Naive Art and/or the Museum of Broken Relationships, and stroll St. Mark's Square. Then wander down through the Stone Gate to the lively Tkalčićeva scene (good for a drink or meal), through the market (closes at 14:00), and on to Kaptol and the cathedral. Depending on how much you linger, this loop can take anywhere from three hours to a full day.

With additional time, visit more of Zagreb's museums (the Meštrović Atelier and City Museum, both in the compact Gradec zone, are well worthwhile), wander the series of parks called the "Green Horseshoe" (with even more museums), or pay a visit to the beautiful Mirogoj Cemetery (one of Europe's finest final resting places).

If you're moving on from Zagreb to Plitvice Lakes National Park (described in the next chapter), be warned that the last bus leaves in midafternoon (usually 16:00); confirm your bus departure carefully to ensure that you don't get stranded in Zagreb.

Orientation to Zagreb

Zagreb, just 30 minutes from the Slovenian border, stretches from the foothills of Medvednica ("Bear Mountain") to the Sava River. In the middle of the sprawl, you'll find the modern **Lower Town** (Donji Grad, centered on **Jelačić Square**) and the historic **Upper Town** (Gornji Grad, comprising the original hill towns of **Gradec** and **Kaptol**). To the south is a U-shaped belt of parks, squares, and museums that make up the **"Green Horseshoe."** The east side of the

Zagreb Essentials

English	Croatian	Pronounced
Jelačić Square	*Trg bana Jelačića*	turg BAH-nah YEH-lah-chee-chah
Gradec (original civic hill town)	*Gradec*	GRAH-dehts
Kaptol (original religious hill town)	*Kaptol*	KAHP-tohl
Café street between Gradec and Kaptol	*Tkalčićeva ("Tkalči" for short)*	tuh-KAHL-chee- chay-vah (tuh-KAHL-chee)
Main train station	*Glavni Kolodvor*	GLAHV-nee KOH-loh-dvor
Bus station	*Autobusni Kolodvor*	OW-toh-boos-nee KOH-loh-dvor

U is a series of three parks, with the train station at the bottom (south) and Jelačić Square at the top (north).

Zagrebians have devised a brilliant scheme for confusing tourists: Street names can be given several different ways. For example, the street that is signed as ulica Kralja Držislava ("King Držislav Street") is often called simply Držislavova ("Držislav's") by locals. So if you're looking for a street, don't search for an exact match—be willing to settle for something that just has a lot of the same letters.

TOURIST INFORMATION

Zagreb has Croatia's best-organized TI, right on Jelačić Square (June-Sept Mon-Fri 8:30-21:00, Sat-Sun 9:00-18:00; Oct-May Mon-Fri 8:30-20:00, Sat 9:00-18:00, Sun 10:00-16:00; Trg bana Jelačića 11, tel. 01/481-4051, www.zagreb-touristinfo.hr). More TIs are in the train station, bus station, and airport (all open Mon-Fri 9:00-21:00, Sat-Sun 10:00-17:00), as well as a branch in the Burglars' Tower at the top of the funicular in Gradec (daily 9:00-21:00 in summer, fewer hours off-season).

All TIs offer piles of free, well-produced tourist brochures; highlights include the one-page city map (with handy transit map and regional map on back), the monthly events guide, and the great *Step By Step* brochure (with a couple of good self-guided walking tours). I'd skip the Zagreb Card (free transportation and discounts at most Zagreb museums, 60 kn/24 hours, 90 kn/72 hours, sold at kiosk inside main TI).

ARRIVAL IN ZAGREB

By Train: Zagreb's main train station (Glavni Kolodvor) is a few long blocks south of Jelačić Square, at the base of the Green Horseshoe. The straightforward arrivals hall has a train information desk, ticket windows, luggage lockers (lining the hallway to the left as you exit the platform, 15 kn/day), ATMs, pay WCs, Konzum grocery store, and newsstands. To reach the city center, go straight out the front door. You'll run into a taxi stand, and then the tracks for **tram** #6 (direction: Črnomerec zips you to Jelačić Square; direction: Sopot takes you to the bus station—the third stop, just after you turn right and go under the big overpass). You can also take tram #13 to Jelačić Square (direction: Žitnjak). For either tram, buy a 10-kn ticket from the kiosk, and validate it when you board the tram. If you **walk** straight ahead through the long, lush park, you'll wind up at the bottom of Jelačić Square in 10 minutes.

By Bus: The user-friendly but inconveniently located bus station (Autobusni Kolodvor) is a few long blocks southeast of the main train station. The station has all the essentials—ATMs, post office, mini-grocery store, left-luggage counter...everything from a smut store to a chapel. Upstairs, you'll find ticket windows and access to the buses (follow signs to *izlaz na perone;* wave ticket in front of turnstile to open gate). Tram #6 (direction: Črnomerec) takes you to the main train station, then on to Jelačić Square. Walking from the bus station to Jelačić Square takes about 25 minutes.

By Plane: Zagreb's small airport is 10 miles south of the center (airport code: ZAG, tel. 01/626-5222, www.zagreb-airport.hr). If you have time to kill, head up the stairs (near the main security checkpoint) to the rooftop café view terrace, where you can enjoy a drink while watching planes take off and land, with the Zagreb skyline on the distant horizon. A shuttle bus connects the airport to the bus station (2/hour, 30 minutes, 30 kn); from there, you can walk outside and hop on a tram into town (see "By Bus," above). It can be worth the convenience to pay for a taxi right to your hotel (30 minutes; the fair metered rate is around 180-200 kn, but some crooked cabbies might try to charge you more). It's cheaper to take a taxi from the city to the airport—figure 100-150 kn.

GETTING AROUND ZAGREB

The main mode of public transportation is the **tram,** operated by ZET (Zagreb Electrical

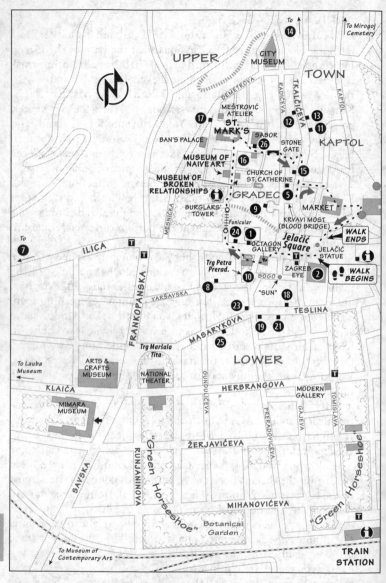

Transport). A single ticket costs 10 kn (good for 1.5 hours in one direction, including transfers). You can buy tickets from a kiosk near the tram stop (ask for *ZET karta*—zeht KAR-tah), or from the driver. When you board, punch your ticket in the yellow box nearest the front of the tram. A day ticket *(dnevna karta)* costs 30 kn. The most useful tram for tourists is #6, connecting Jelačić Square with the train and bus stations.

Zagreb

1. Jägerhorn Hotel
2. Hotel Dubrovnik
3. Hotel Astoria
4. To Studio Kairos
5. Sobe Zagreb 17
6. Hotel Central
7. To Hotel Ilica
8. Shappy Hostel & Jazz.ba
9. Fulir Backpackers Inn
10. Trg Petra Preradovića Eateries
11. Pivnica Medvedgrad Pub
12. Restaurant Agava
13. Rocket Burger
14. To Takenoko
15. The Cookie Factory
16. Trilogija Wine Bar & Old Pharmacy
17. Konoba Didov San
18. Vinodol Restaurant
19. Ribice i Tri Točkice
20. Chooso Bar
21. Sandwich Bar Pingvin
22. Mimice Restaurant
23. Zagreb Slastičarnica Ice Cream
24. Slastičarnica Vincek Ice Cream
25. Nishta Vegetarian Rest.
26. Lav Caffe Galerija Coffee House

ZAGREB

Taxis start at 10-15 kn, then run 5-7 kn per kilometer (exact rate depends on company, 3 kn extra for each piece of baggage). To avoid getting overcharged, call one of the main companies: Radio Taxi (tel. 01/661-0200 or 060-800-800), Cammeo (tel. 060-7100), or Ecotaxi (tel. 060-7777). If you hail a cab on the street, beware of corrupt cabbies; ask for an estimate up front. A typical ride within the city center shouldn't run more than about 30 kn, and the trip to the airport should cost no more than 150 kn—or 200 kn from the airport (agree on a price first).

HELPFUL HINTS

Schedule Quirks: Virtually all of Zagreb's museums are closed on Sunday afternoon and all day Monday; most also close early Saturday afternoon. Some museums stay open late one night a week in summer (usually Thu). On Sunday morning, the city is thriving—but by afternoon, it's extremely quiet.

Changing of the Guard: Zagreb's "Changing of the Guard" ceremony (a very recent innovation) enlivens the city center on summer weekends. The 17th-century-costumed guards wear jaunty red scarves (an homage to the tale of how Croat soldiers "invented" the necktie) as they proceed through the center of town—passing landmarks such as St. Mark's Square, Tkalčićeva street, Jelačić Square, and the statue of Mary in front of the cathedral (mid-April-Sept only, generally Sat-Sun, begins at 12:00 on St. Mark's Square, ask for complete schedule at TI). While little more than a photo op, this ceremony is one of the many ways Zagreb is working hard to please visitors.

Updates to This Book: For updates to this book, check www.ricksteves.com/update.

Tours in Zagreb

Local Guides

While I've covered the basics in my self-guided walk, Zagreb gets even more interesting with a good tour guide. I recommend two knowledgeable guides who know their city well and enjoy sharing its charms with visitors: **Darija Gotić** (550 kn/2-3-hour tour, mobile 098-186-7719, info@assistere.biz) or **Dijana Bebek Miletić** (630 kn/3-hour tour, mobile 091-303-3979, dijana.bebek.miletic@ live.com).

Secrets of Grič Tour

This after-hours walking tour of Gradec (nicknamed "Grič") brings that historic quarter to life with a costumed guide imparting local legends (150 kn, May-Sept Sat only at 21:00, one hour, reservations required, mobile 091-461-5672 or 091-461-5677, www. tajnegrica.hr).

Segway Tour

Already popular in many other cities, Segway tours have come to Zagreb, offering a low-impact, narrated zip around town on a stand-up motorized scooter (basic 75-minute "leisure" tour-300 kn/person, longer and pricier options available by request—contact them to arrange a tour, tel. 01/301-0390, mobile 095-903-4227, www.segway.hr, zagreb@segway.hr).

Hop-On, Hop-Off Bus Tour

The local transit company runs two hop-on, hop-off routes through the city, a handy way to get to Zagreb's many outlying sights. Unfortunately, the frequency is sparse—only five per day on one route, and two per day on the other (70 kn, May-Sept only, daily 12:00-18:00, details at TI).

Bike Tours

Blue Bike runs a variety of different bike-tour routes through the city, starting on Jelačić Square (175 kn, daily at 10:00 and 17:00— or at 14:00 off-season, reservations required, mobile 098-188-3344, www.zagrebbybike.com). They also rent bikes (100 kn/day).

Bus-plus-Walking Tours

The IBUS tour, which combines a two-hour town walk with a one-hour bus tour, can help you get your bearings (165 kn, April-Oct daily at 10:00, www.ibus.hr).

Zagreb Walk

The following self-guided orientation walk, rated ▲▲, begins and ends at Jelačić Square, linking almost everything that's worth seeing in this city, including the two hilltop towns that merged in 1850 to become Zagreb: Gradec and Kaptol. If you don't enter any of the sights, the entire circular route takes about 1.5 hours. But if you take your time, you can use it as a framework for a full day of sightseeing. If you want to explore the market—which is near the end of this walk—keep in mind that it gets quiet after about 14:00. To avoid feeling rushed, you may want to tour the market first (just a block away from our starting point), then embark on this walk.

▲▲Jelačić Square (Trg bana Jelačića)

The "Times Square" of Zagreb bustles with life. Watching the crowds pile in and out of trams and seeing the city buzz with

activity, you feel the energy of an on-the-rise capital of a vibrant new nation. This is also a popular place for any kind of special event in town—from concerts and sporting events, to folk festivals, to protests and rallies. The city's busy pedestrian scene, sense of style, and utter lack of tourists make it arguably Croatia's best

ZAGREB

people-watching destination.

It's hard to believe that this frenetic Donji Grad ("lower town") once held the townspeople's farm fields. Our walk takes you from here up to two towns—Gradec and Kaptol—that merged in 1850 to become the city of Zagreb. At that time, it was a small settlement of about 16,000 people. But under the auspices of the Austro-Hungarian Empire, the newly united Zagreb began to industrialize and grow like mad. These former fields sprouted aristocratic villas as well as low-rent housing for factory workers.

Today, the square features a prominent equestrian statue of national hero **Josip Jelačić** (YOH-seep YEH-lah-cheech, 1801-1859), a 19th-century governor who extended citizens' rights and did much to unite the Croats within the Habsburg Empire. In Jelačić's time, the Hungarians were exerting extensive control over Croatia, even trying to make Hungarian the official language. Meanwhile, Budapesters revolted against Habsburg rule in 1848. Jelačić, ever mindful of the need to protect Croatian cultural autonomy, knew that he'd have a better shot at getting his way from Austria than from Hungary. Jelačić chose the lesser of two evils  and fought alongside the Habsburgs to put down the Hungarian uprising. A century later, in the Yugoslav era, Jelačić was considered a dangerously nationalistic symbol, and this statue was dismantled and stored away. But when Croatia broke away in 1991, Croatian patriotism was in the air, and Jelačić returned. Though Jelačić originally faced his Hungarian foes to the north, today he's staring down the Serbs to the south.

Get oriented. As you face Jelačić's statue, down a long block to your left is a funicular that takes you up to one of Zagreb's original villages, Gradec. To the right, look for the TI. If you exit the square ahead and to the right, you'll reach the city's other original village, Kaptol, and the cathedral (you can't miss its huge, pointy, Neo-Gothic spires—visible from virtually everywhere in Zagreb). And if you just need a break, several fine cafés ring the square. For the best view in town, you can pay 20 kn to ascend to the **"Zagreb Eye"** viewing platform at the top of the tallest glass skyscraper at the bottom of the square (ride elevator to 16th floor, daily 10:00-23:00, restaurant and café, www.zagrebeye.hr).

Taking the small street behind Jelačić and then going a little to the left would lead you to the market (best in the morning—depending on the time, consider visiting the market now, using the tips on page 1074, before continuing on the walk) and the enticing café-and-restaurant street, Tkalčićeva (lively any time of day or night; we'll circle back here later on the walk). On the left side of this small street (still on the square), pause at the modern building with an arcade of blocky pillars to take in a creative bit of public art. Look closely at the first pillar and find the small silver plaque with a little ball labeled *Venus* (about eight feet up, facing the building). This is one piece of the 10-part work called **"Zagreb's Solar System."** Its center lies a short walk away, two blocks in front of Jelačić (on Bogovićeva street): a large spherical sculpture called *The Grounded Sun*, made in 1971. Decades later, a different artist decided to piggyback on that idea, and created nine new sculptures, together titled *Nine Views*. Scattered around the city are each of the nine planets—completely to scale (both the size of each planet—from the size of a marble to the size of a basketball—and each one's distance from the "sun"). The artist, Davor Preis, did the project in secret, so Zagrebians had to seek out each of the nine planets on their own, in a kind of citywide scavenger hunt.

But for now, head up to the hill called Gradec.

Walk from Jelačić Square to Gradec

Go a long block down busy Ilica street (to the left as you face Jelačić), then enter the big **"Octagon" shopping gallery** on the left (at #5, enter under *Privedna Banka Zagreb* sign). This was the ultimate in iron-and-glass shopping elegance a century ago, and still features a few of the city's top shops (including Croata, the tie store that loves to explain how Croatians invented the necktie; for the whole story, see page 971).

Walk all the way through the gallery, exiting into the inviting café-lined square called **Trg Petra Preradovića.** It hosts a flower market all day, and inviting al fresco cafés throughout the day and into the night. Survey your options for a coffee break, then turn right and head back out to Ilica street, then turn left and continue the way you were headed.

After another block, cross the tram tracks and turn right up Tomića, where you'll see a small **funicular** (ZET Uspinjača) crawling up the hill. Dating from the late 19th century, this funicular is looked upon fondly by Zagrebians—both as a bit of nostalgia and as a way to avoid some steps. You can walk up if you want, but the ride is more fun and takes only 55 seconds. Locals claim this is the "shortest funicular in the world" (4 kn, validate ticket in yellow box before you board, leaves every 10 minutes daily 6:30-22:00).

Gradec

From the top of the funicular, you'll enjoy a fine panorama over Zagreb. The tall tower on the left as you exit is one of

Gradec's original watchtow-
ers, the **Burglars' Tower** (Kula
Lotrščak). After the Tatars ransacked Central Europe in the
early 13th century, King Béla IV
decreed that towns be fortified—
so Gradec built a wall and guard
towers (just like Kraków and
Budapest did). Look for the little
cannon in the top-floor window. Every day at noon, this cannon
fires a shot, supposedly to commemorate a 15th-century victory
over the besieging Ottomans.

The **Strossmayer Promenade** runs along the top of the hill,
overlooking the city. The fenced section next to the funicular station is dubbed Strossmartre (a pun on "Montmartre"), which, in
good summer weather, hosts a fun little outdoor café, and often
features works by local artists and live music. This fine promenade
is just the start; along the outside of Gradec is a forested green belt
that—while just a few minutes' walk away—feels miles from the
city. It's a favorite place for locals to go for an urban hike, walk
their dogs, or get away from the asphalt heat of summer.

Head up the street to the right of the tower, entering Gradec
(often called "Grič" for short). Although this is one of the oldest parts of Zagreb, it lacks the cutesy cobbled charm you might
expect. That's because little remains of medieval Gradec. When
the Ottomans overran Europe, they never managed to take
Zagreb, but the threat was enough to scare the nobility into the
countryside. When the Ottomans left, the nobles came back, and
they replaced the medieval buildings here with Baroque mansions.

At the first square, to the right, you'll see the Jesuit **Church
of St. Catherine.** It's not much to look at from the outside, but the
interior is intricately decorated—bubbly pink-and-white Baroque,
dripping with stucco (only open to visitors during Mass). The
same applies to several mansions on Gradec. This simple-outside,
ornate-inside style is known as "Zagreb Baroque."

As you continue up the street, notice the old-timey **street
signs,** holdovers from the Austro-Hungarian era: in both Croatian
(Gospodzka ulicza) and German (Herren Gasse).

From here, you're a few steps from Zagreb's two most
interesting museums: On the right is the **Museum of Broken
Relationships,** and a few steps down on the left is the **Croatian
Museum of Naive Art** (both listed later, under "Sights in
Zagreb"). Now's the time to visit these, before continuing on our
walk.

In the next block, on the left, is the yellow **"city parliament"**
building (basically the town hall, and a popular place for weddings

on summer Saturdays). To the left of the door, look for the plaque honoring **Nikola Tesla** (1856-1943), the prominent scientist who championed alternating current (AC) as a better electrical system than Thomas Edison's direct current (DC). Although Tesla was an ethnic Serb (his father was an Orthodox priest), he was born in a remote village in central Croatia, so both Serbs and Croats claim him. (Today, Tesla is a rare figure who is revered both in Zagreb and in Belgrade.) This plaque proudly trumpets that on May 24, 1892, Tesla came to this building and suggested that Zagreb become the first city in the world to build an AC power station. But the plaque fails to mention that the city parliament rejected this suggestion...so Tesla went to the US, where he successfully pitched the same idea to Buffalo, New York.

While Zagreb eventually did adopt AC, this part of town still clings to a much, much older form of lighting. Flanking the doors of the city parliament are two of the 217 old-fashioned **gaslights** that still illuminate Gradec. These are lit and extinguished each day by two city employees. Notice that each lamp is numbered.

At the end of the block, you'll come to **St. Mark's Square** (Markov trg), centered on the **Church of St. Mark.** The origi-

nal church here was from the 13th century, but only a few fragments remain. The present church's colorful tile roof, from 1880, depicts two coats of arms. On the left, the red-and-white checkerboard symbolizes north-central Croatia, the three lions' heads stand for the Dalmatian Coast, and the marten (*kuna*, like the money) running between the two rivers (Sava and Drava) represents Slavonia—Croatia's northern, inland panhandle. On the right is the seal of Zagreb, featuring a walled city.

In the years since these tiles were laid, the **city seal** has changed in two ways (as you can see by comparing it to the city flag that flies from the city parliament building). First, while the castle doors are closed on the roof, today's seal shows wide-open doors—to demonstrate that Zagreb is strong, but still welcoming to visitors. Second, the city color has been changed from red to blue. If you pay attention around town, you'll notice the liberal use of Zagreb's distinctive hue of blue—for example, on city buses and trams. And devoted fans of the immensely popular local soccer team, Dinamo Zagreb, are called the "Bad Blue Boys."

While it would be nice to see the inside of St. Mark's Church, the priest doesn't appreciate tourists, so it's closed except during services. (If you manage to slip in, you'll see frescoes with Bible scenes, and sculptures by the talented 20th-century sculptor Ivan Meštrović: the crucifix over the main altar, a *pietà* on the left, and on the right, Madonna and Child sitting cross-legged, in a typical Meštrović pose. If you can't get in, you can still enjoy some Meštrović works at his nearby museum, described later.)

As you face the church, the long building on the right is the **Sabor,** or parliament. From the 12th century, Croatian noblemen would gather here to make important decisions regarding their territories. This gradually evolved into today's modern parliament. While this square used to be a congested parking lot, Zagreb's mayor declared it a traffic-free zone; now members of parliament either have to be bussed in from off-site parking lots (watch for the cute little blue bus that comes and goes periodically), or have their drivers sit tight nearby (look for unmarked black cars patiently waiting on the street in front of the city parliament).

Across the square from the Sabor (to your left as you face the church) is **Ban's Palace** (Banski Dvori), today the offices for the prime minister. This was one of the few buildings in central Zagreb damaged in the war following Croatia's independence. In October of 1991, Yugoslav People's Army pilots targeted this building in an airstrike. (Notice the different-colored tiles where the roof had to be patched.) They landed a direct hit on the room where Croatian President Franjo Tuđman and his right-hand man, Stipe Mesić (who would later succeed him as president), were scheduled to be meeting. But coincidentally, the meeting had been moved to another location at the last minute—so Croatia's first two presidents survived. (It's eerie to think what might have become of this fledgling nation if its leadership had been wiped out at this early stage.)

Before moving on, consider visiting two more excellent museums, which sit just a short walk away (both described in detail later, under "Sights in Zagreb"). The talented 20th-century sculptor **Ivan Meštrović's former home and studio** is now a museum of his works. It's about a block away: Go down the street behind the church on the left-hand side, and you'll see the museum on the right. And the extensive, well-presented **Zagreb City Museum** explains the story of this town from prehistoric times to the modern day. To reach it, walk along the front of the Sabor and continue straight ahead two blocks, watching for the museum on your right.

Walk from Gradec to Kaptol

For an interesting stroll from St. Mark's Square to the cathedral, head down the street (Kamenita ulica) to the right of the parliament building. Near the end of the street, on the right, you'll see the oldest **pharmacy** in town—recently restored and gleaming (c. 1355, marked *gradska ljekarna*). Across the street is **Lav Caffe**

Galerija, a fun, relaxing coffee house and art gallery; this is just one of many inviting coffee-break opportunities you'll see between here and the end of this walk.

Just beyond, you'll reach Gradec's only surviving town gate, the **Stone Gate** (Kamenita Vrata). Inside is an evocative chapel.

The focal point is a painting of Mary that miraculously survived a major fire in the house up above in 1731. When this medieval gate was reconstructed in the Baroque style, they decided to turn it into a makeshift chapel. The candles (purchased in the little shop and lit in the big metal bin) represent Zagrebians' prayers. Notice the soot-blackened ceiling over the forest fire of blazing candles in the bin. The stone plaques on the wall give thanks *(hvala)* for prayers that were answered. You may notice people making the sign of the cross as they walk through here, and often a crowd of worshippers gathers, gazing intently at the painting. Mary was made the official patron saint of Zagreb in 1990.

As you leave the Stone Gate and come to **Radićeva,** turn right and begin walking downhill. Looking down to the bottom of Radićeva, you'll see where this street is becoming a popular shopping zone, with local boutiques popping up all the time—a fun area to browse later.

But for now, head just a few steps down Radićeva, then watch for the orange building at **#30** on your left. Go through the big, arched entryway (noticing the old-fashioned sign above the garbage cans, threatening a fine of one crown if this area is not left tidy) and bear right down the wooden steps. At the bottom of these stairs, you'll come to a little row of evocative **old-time houses.** In times past, this was one of the most popular areas in town...as home of the red light district. While prostitution is illegal now, it was once allowed and carefully regulated, with routine medical examinations for the working girls. Legally, only a woman (over age 30) could own and operate a brothel. Locals note, with some irony, that the balconies on the opposite side of these houses of ill repute—which we'll see in a moment—face the stern spires of the cathedral.

Turn left, walking along the row of old houses (and noticing the remains of the old Gradec town wall on your left), then turn right down the stairs. You've just dropped down into the middle of Zagreb's most appealing street, **Tkalčićeva.** Do a slow spin to savor this in-love-with-life drag. This traffic-free street combines some of the most atmospheric old homes of Zagreb with some of its most enticing eateries and people-watching. (For starters, you're literally surrounded by tables for the recommended Pivnica Medvedgrad brewpub.)

If you need a break from sightseeing, Tkalčićeva is just the ticket: Nurse a coffee, beer, or meal anywhere along this street (I've listed several recommendations under "Eating in Zagreb," later).

If you stood here 200 years ago, you'd be washed away by a rushing river that separated Gradec (behind you) and Kaptol (in front of you). In the Middle Ages, the two towns were at odds and sometimes fought. ("Downriver" from here is a cross-street that's still called Krvavi Most—"Blood Bridge.") But in 1850, after the towns had long since set aside their differences, they merged to become Zagreb. The polluted, stinky river had become a nuisance, so they diverted its flow and covered over the valley to create Tkalčićeva.

Turn right and enjoy a stroll down Tkalčićeva (toward the onion-domed church tower of Holy Mary Church). You'll pass (on the right) the balconies of the brothels we saw earlier, then a fine park on the right with a genteel lady prepared for rain. Just beyond the park, next to the door for the recommended Cookie Factory, is the *Mars* plaque for the solar system sculpture. Directly across the street, walk up the hill toward the cathedral towers (on Skalinska, passing outdoor restaurant tables).

Kaptol

As you walk uphill, you're entering Kaptol, the second of medieval Zagreb's twin towns.

At the top of the street, turn right and go down the stairs to find Zagreb's lively-in-the-morning **market** *(dolac)*. If you're here at prime time, browse the market's double-decker delights (noticing that the meat and cheese halls are below your feet—use the stairs or elevator in the blocky white building to get there). For pointers on what to see at the market, see "Sights in Zagreb," later.

When you're done at the market, go through the gap between the buildings toward the **cathedral** spires. Crossing the square, you can enter Croatia's most important house of worship (described later, under "Sights in Zagreb"). From here, you can head downhill one block to Jelačić Square—where our walk began.

Sights in Zagreb

Zagreb has more than its share of museums, and many of them are excellent—making up for the lack of great Croatian museums outside of the capital. It would take you days to see all of the city's museums; I've selected the most worthwhile (still enough to fill a couple of days—choose the ones that interest you the most).

▲▲▲Croatian Museum of Naive Art (Hrvatski Muzej Naivne Umjetnosti)

This remarkable spot, founded in 1952 as the "Peasant Art Gallery," is one of the most enjoyable little museums in Croatia. It features expressionistic paintings by untrained peasant artists. On one easy floor, the museum displays 80 paintings made mostly by Croatians from the 1930s to the 1980s.

Cost and Hours: 20 kn, pick up the English explanations as you enter, Tue-Fri 10:00-18:00, Sat-Sun 10:00-13:00, closed Mon, ulica Sv. Ćirila i Metoda 3, tel. 01/485-1911, www.hmnu.org.

This museum presents an easily digestible sampling of the top names from the naive art movement. Viewing these evocative works, it's important to remember that this isn't considered "folk art" or "amateur art"—but top-quality works by great artists who were, by fluke or fate, never formally trained.

❍ Self-Guided Tour: Buy your ticket and follow the one-way route through the six numbered rooms, which you'll circle counter-clockwise.

Room 1: Immediately to the right as you enter is the first of many paintings by **Ivan Generalić** (1914-1992), the founder and star of Croatian naive art (his self-portrait, with a blue background, dominates the room). Generalić was discovered in the 1930s by a Paris-trained Croatian artist. The first few paintings show his evolution as an artist (and the evolution of Croatian naive art in general): While his early works come with a social or political agenda (such as

The Requisition, where two policemen repo a cow from an impoverished couple), he eventually mellows his focus to show simple, typical village scenes that gradually become more and more fantastical *(Harvesters)*, and eventually strips away people entirely to focus on the land (on the opposite wall, see 1938's *Cows in the Forest* and 1959's *The Flood*). In 1953, Generalić—still relatively unknown outside his homeland—did a show in Paris, sold everything, and came home rich. This put Croatian naive art on the international map and kick-started a new vigor in the movement.

Woodcutters, from 1959, shows the next phase, as Generalić's works became even more rich with fantasy—the peacock, the men clinging to tree tops, and the trademark "coral

Origins of Naive Art

Starting in the late 19th century, the art world began to broaden its definition of great art, seeking out worthy art orig-inating outside the esteemed academies and salons of the day. Their goal: to demon-strate that art was not simply a trained skill, but an inborn talent. Intellectuals began to embrace an "anti-intellectual" approach to art. Interest grew in the indigenous art of Africa,

Mesoamerica, and Polynesia (Picasso went through an African mask phase, and Gauguin went to live in Tahiti); com-poser Béla Bartok collected traditional folk melodies from the Hungarian countryside; the "art brut" movement preserved artwork by people deemed "insane" by mainstream soci-ety; the autodidactic (self-taught) painter Grandma Moses became well-known in the US and Europe; and art by children gained acclaim.

Here in Croatia in the 1930s, the focus was on art by untrained peasants. At that time, as in much of rural Europe, 85 percent of Croatians lived virtually medieval lifestyles—with no electricity or other modern conveniences—and a majority were illiterate and uneducated. These artists cap-tured this humble reality, creating figurative works in an increasingly abstract age. By the 1950s and 1960s, Croatian naive art had emerged at the forefront of a Europe-wide phenomenon.

trees." Instead of showing, Generalić is evoking; naive art strove to capture the spirit and emotion of peasant life. Paintings such as this one inspired Generalić's followers (called the "Hlebine School," for the village where Generalić lived). In the adjacent painting, *Solar Eclipse* (1961), villagers cower and roosters crow as the sun is mysteriously gobbled up by a black disc. People respond in different ways: some by staging impromptu religious proces-sionals, other by clutching their belongings close and fleeing.

Flanking the door to the next room are works by the next generation of naive art—two big-name follow-ers who were inspired (if not trained) by Generalić: on the left, the gruesome *Evangelists on Calvary* crucifix, by **Ivan**

Večenaj, who focused on religious scenes; and on the right, *Winter Landscape with Woman,* by **Mijo Kovačić,** who specialized in peasant landscapes.

Room 2: The next room features more works by Večenaj and Kovačić. Studying Kovačić's many landscapes, notice how he took a style of painting pioneered by Generalić and brought it to the next level. Winter scenes were most common, because the peasant artists were busy working the fields the rest of the year. (Early on, such artists were sometimes called "Sunday painters," because they had to work their "real" jobs from Monday to Saturday.) Kovačić also enjoyed winter scenes for the evocative black-and-white contrast they allowed. Like Dalí, Magritte, and other surrealists, Kovačić juxtaposed super-realism (look at each individual hair on the swine in his painting *Swineherd,* pictured below) with fantastical, almost otherworldly settings. Also in this room are some landscapes and portraits by **Dragan Gaži,** a friend and neighbor of Generalić's. His *The Wind in Winter* (1973) is an intoxicating landscape.

You may notice that these supposedly "untrained" artists seem to borrow from other painters—most notably, the countryside

peasant scenes often feel ripped from a Pieter Bruegel canvas. While not formally schooled, there's no doubt that these artists were aware of, and often inspired by, their artistic forebears.

Also notice that naive artists in Croatia frequently painted on glass. It was cheaper and more readily available in rural areas than art canvases, and—because it required no special technique—was an easier medium for the untrained naive artists to work on.

Room 3: On the right, find the portraits of Roma (Gypsy) people by **Martin Mehkek.** For the one depicting his cross-eyed neighbor Steve, Mehkek mostly painted with his fingers, using brushes only for fine details (such as the Hitler-style moustache). On the other side of the room is *Guiana '78*—by **Josip Generalić,** the founder's less-talented son—showing the gruesome aftermath of the Jim Jones mass suicide, with a pair of monkeys surveying the smiling corpses. (While vivid, this painting doesn't reflect the Croatian peasant experience, and the curator admits it's not the best representative of naive art.) Filling out the room are more of those distinctively spiny, bonsai-like trees that pervade naive works, these by **Ivan Lacković Croata.** Notice that Croata's fine works focus on different seasons.

But this room's highlight is Večenaj's *Moses and the Red Sea*

(1973), an expressionistic retelling of the familiar biblical story. Moses, glowing against an inky black sky and with feet muddy from having just crossed the seabed, watches the sea—literally red with Egyptian blood—washing away his pursuers. The footprints emerging from the sea (at the bottom) suggest that the Israelites' exodus has been a successful one. On the left, see the pyramids (Egypt), and on the right, the cozy village (the Promised Land). Flying around Moses are 10 birds (representing the Commandments); he's equipped with some of his typical symbols, including the horn around his neck, the ram, and the snake (which, as the story goes, he had conjured from a staff to convince the pharaoh to allow the Israelites leave Egypt).

Room 4: This room shows off two big names from the latter part of the movement. On the left are lyrical landscapes by **Ivan Rabuzin,** arguably the movement's second most important artist, after Ivan Generalić. Like a visual haiku, Rabuzin's dreamlike world of hills, trees, and clouds is reminiscent of Marc Chagall. Rabuzin's works are especially popular among the museum's many Japanese visitors. On the right are **Emerik Feješ**'s colorful scenes of famous monuments from around Europe—Paris, Venice, Vienna, and Milan. Feješ never traveled to any of these places—his paintings are based on romantic black-and-white postcards of the era, which Feješ "colorized" in his unique style.

Room 5: On the left, see **Matija Skurjeni**'s almost crayon-like *Animal World* (1961). While it looks like the roll call for Noah's ark, it's loaded with symbolism. The dinosaur is Skurjeni's self-portrait, the other large animals are his friends and artistic colleagues, the butterflies fluttering around represent spirituality (a new spin on the white dove of the Holy Spirit)...and the devil in the base of the tree, with wings and a crown, is one of Skurjeni's harshest critics—who also happened to be the curator of this museum at the time. On the other side of the door, **Drago Jurak**'s *Luxury Boat* (1974) looks like a Bollywood *Titanic*. On the right are works by naive artists from other countries (Russia, Japan, France, and Poland).

Room 6: Here you'll see pencil sketches used by naive artists to create their works (including one for Generalić's *Solar Eclipse*).

After the sketch was complete, the artist would put it against a pane of glass to paint the scene—small details first, gradually filling in more and more of the background. Then the glass painting would literally be flipped over to be viewed. All of the works on glass you've seen in this collection were actually painted backward.

▲▲Museum of Broken Relationships

Opened in 2010 by a couple who had recently broken up, this extremely clever museum lives up to all the attention it's received in the international press. The museum's mission is simple: collect true stories of failed couples from around the world, tell their story in their own words, and display the tale alongside an actual item that embodies the relationship. The items and stories provide insights into a shared human experience—we can all relate to the anger, sadness, and relief expressed in these poignant, at times hilarious, displays. In addition to the predictable "he cheated on me so I broke his favorite fill-in-the-blank" items, the ever-changing  collection delves into other types of fractured connections: an unrequited childhood crush, the slow fade of lovers who gradually grew apart, disappointment in a politician who failed to live up to lofty expectations, the premature end of a love cut short by death, and so on. You'll see discarded wedding albums, sex toys with stories about unreasonable requests for kinky acts, films that attempt to capture the essence of a relationship, children's playthings representing the innocence of young love (and, perhaps, the universality of stuffed animals), and plenty of items broken with vengeful wrath. The museum is small—just a few rooms—but rewards those who take the time to read each story. The collection has been such a hit, they've taken it on the road, garnering fans in cities worldwide.

Cost and Hours: 25 kn, daily June-Sept 9:00-22:30, Oct-May 9:00-21:00, café, 230-kn catalog tells all the stories with photos, Sv. Ćirila i Metoda 2, tel. 01/485-1021, www.brokenships.com.

▲Ivan Meštrović Atelier

Ivan Meštrović—Croatia's most famous artist—lived here from 1922 until 1942 (before he fled to the US after World War II). The house, carefully decorated by Meštrović himself, has been converted into a delightful gallery of the artist's works, displayed in two parts: residence and studio. Split's Meštrović Gallery (described on page 974) is the definitive museum of this 20th-century Croatian sculptor, but if you're not going there, Zagreb's gallery is a convenient place to gain an appreciation for this pro-lific, thoughtful artist. For more on Meštrović, see page 976.

Cost and Hours: 30 kn, 20-kn English catalog, Tue-Fri 10:00-18:00, Sat-Sun 10:00-14:00, closed Mon, behind St. Mark's Square at Mletačka 8, tel. 01/485-1123, www.mestrovic.hr.

❷ Self-Guided Tour: When you buy your ticket, be sure to pick up the large floor plan—it's the only way to identify the pieces on display here (they're marked only by number; I've noted the number for important works in this tour). Then enter the high-ceilinged dining room of Meštrović's **home.** He designed the cru-cifix on the wall (#83, Christ being supported by an angel), the wood-carved chandeliers, and the furniture, right down to the carvings on the backs of the chairs. Overlooking the table is a sculpture of his mother (#59), wearing the traditional headdress of her Dalmatian village homeland, legs crossed, hands clasped in intent prayer—a favorite pose of Meštrović's. At the other end of the table is a self-portrait bust of Meštrović, head cocked quiz-zically (#76). In the alcove at the bottom of the stairs, see the *Madonna and Baby*, tenderly kissing (#38).

Head **upstairs** to see sketches and plaster casts Meštrović did in preparation for some of his larger works. The rooms on this floor are filled with busts and small, characteristically elongated statues, all of them expressive. In the far room, appreciate his fine ceiling frescoes; in the adjoining room, find Meštrović's powerful sculp-ture depicting his mentor and friend, Auguste Rodin, furiously at work (#26).

Continue up to the **top floor,** where you'll find several evoca-tive pieces: Meštrović's wife breastfeeding their son (#54); a por-trait of Michelangelo, Meštrović's artistic ancestor, holding a chisel and hammer, and portrayed with his trademark high fore-head and smashed nose (#56); and a copy of the powerful *pietà* from St. Mark's Church (#89). The next room holds a cowering *Job* (#88), the head of an archangel (#97), a tender portrait of a mother teaching her child to pray (#55), and a small model of one of Meštrović's biggest and best-known works, *Bishop Gregory of Nin* (#61, in Split, described on page 968). In the small, final room is a woman with a beehive 'do praying (#33).

Back downstairs, you'll cross through the **garden** to reach the studio. Outside are several more fine pieces, including another one of the museum's top works: *The History of the Croats* (#90), with a woman sitting cross-legged (remember this pose?) with a book resting on her lap. The top of the book has a unique Croatian spiral design, and along the front of it are the letters of Croatia's Glagolitic alphabet. Back against the wall, *John the Evangelist* stu-diously takes notes, looking up for divine inspiration (#71). And the small *Prince Marko on Šarac* (#16)—while clearly a Croatian theme—evokes two of Meštrović's most famous works, the giant Native Americans on horseback that stand in Chicago's Grant Park. Those towering sculptures were created in this very studio, and later transported (in pieces) to the United States. Originally, those sculptures were commissioned to be a cowboy and an Indian...but Meštrović said, "How about *two* Native Americans...?"

Go into Meštrović's **studio.** Next to the door to the inner courtyard is a skinny, Modigliani-esque sculpture of Meštrović's first wife, Ruža (#70); in the middle of the room are two sculptures modeled after his second wife, Olga: The unfinished, walnut-carved *Mother and Child* (#100), and the exquisite, white-marble *Woman Beside the Sea* (#58, one of the collection's highlights). Nearby is a sculpture of the *Evangelist Luke* (#72)— the twin of John out in the garden. Upstairs around the gallery are smaller pieces, including a study for the spiny-fingered hand of Split's *Bishop Gregory of Nin* (#62).

On your way out, take a moment to linger in the **courtyard**—with the large *Woman in Agony* (#67) in the center, and less-agonized women all around.

▲Zagreb City Museum (Muzej Grada Zagreba)

This collection, with a modern, well-presented exhibit that sprawls over two floors of an old convent, traces the history of the city through town models, paintings, furniture, clothing, and lots of fascinating artifacts.

Cost and Hours: 30 kn, 20-kn audioguide nicely supplements the posted descriptions, Tue-Fri 10:00-18:00, Sat 11:00-19:00, Sun 10:00-14:00, closed Mon, at north end of Gradec at Opatička 20, tel. 01/485 1361, www.mgz.hr.

Visiting the Museum: After buying your ticket, head through the door and turn left, then work your way up through the ages. Each display has a fine English description. On the largely skip-pable ground floor, you'll loop through the prehistoric and Roman periods, and the medieval growth of the twin towns of Gradec and Kaptol. You'll see city symbols and flags, a town model from 1795, statues from the main portal of the cathedral (17th-century Baroque) and other religious art, and a small collection of cleverly decorated 18th-century weathervanes.

Upstairs, the exhibit lingers on Zagreb's boom time in the 19th century, when it was an increasingly spruced-up and genteel outpost of the Austro-Hungarian Empire. The exhibits consider various facets of society during that era. You'll see more religious art, furniture, aristocratic portraits, another town model (from the 1860s), a life-size portrait of national hero Josip Jelačić (and his actual uniform), and colorfully painted shooting targets. One room has a giant city map on the floor, punctuated with models of key buildings. You'll also find models of old storefronts, theater costumes, and exhibits on public utilities and social life.

The coverage of the tumultuous 20th century is perhaps most engaging, evincing an understandably bad attitude about the Serb-dominated first Yugoslav period. Propaganda posters cheer on the communist period, while all of this historical heaviness is balanced by a lighthearted exhibit about Zagreb's popular cartoon industry. The finale is a room dedicated to the creation of independent Croatia, including an exhibit on damage sustained during the war and a film with clips from various landmarks in Croatian independence: a violent riot at a heated 1990 soccer match between Dinamo Zagreb and Belgrade's Crvena Zvezda ("Red Star") team; the election and arrival in parliament of pro-independence Franjo Tuđman; and the return of the statue of Jelačić to his namesake square.

▲▲Market (Dolac)

In 1930, Zagreb tore down much of Kaptol's rickety old medieval Old Town to build this as-central-as-possible market. Today, it's jammed with producers from the surrounding countryside—and all over Croatia—selling all manner of fruits, vegetables, meats, cheeses, fish, and other foodstuffs. A stroll through the market offers insight into the colorful local culture, and the chance to pick up a few picnic items.

Cost and Hours: Free, open Mon-Fri 7:00-15:00, Sat 7:00-14:00, Sun 7:00-13:00. To reach the market easily from Jelačić Square, walk one block up the street to the left of the Jelačić statue, and climb up the stairs.

Visiting the Market: The market has two sections—indoor (with meat and cheese) and outdoor (produce, just above). Begin by exploring the outdoor section, then head inside. At the top of the stairs coming up from Jelačić Square, notice the statue of the *kumica*—a villager wearing a traditional dress (with a head scarf) and balancing a basket of produce on her head.

Outside is the **produce market,** with vendors from all around selling what's fresh. What you'll see changes with the season (for instance, in fall, look for nuts and mushrooms), but a few things are mainstays. The honey *(med)* is a reminder that the mountain behind Zagreb is called Medvednica. In Croatian, a bear is poetically called a *medved*—literally "honey-seer." So *Medvednica* means "place of the honey-seer." The big red umbrellas over some stalls evoke the parasols that are part of the traditional costume for the region around Zagreb. The stalls behind the boxy white building (which is the entrance to the lower, indoor market) sell various components of that same costume (such as embroidered scarves); while tourists can buy them, most customers are locals. Nearby, the few "souvenir" stands (at the top part of the market, near the cathedral) show off colorful, traditional wooden toys, still made the way they have been for centuries (men do the carving, women do the painting); the wooden birds on sticks—which flap their wings when you roll them along the floor—are a favorite.

As you face the top of the market, to the left you'll see the fragrant **fish market** *(ribarnica)*. While Zagreb is far from the sea, the freshest catch is trucked in daily.

To get to the indoor market *(tržnica)*, enter the boxy white building and descend using the stairs or elevator. You'll pop out in the **meat market.** Stroll the stalls, noticing—in addition to the typical array of sausages, salamis, and *pršut* (cured ham)—the local affection for horsemeat (from a young horse—*ždrebetina,* or an adult—*konjetina).* Also watch for piles of a local delicacy called *čvartci.* Vaguely similar to pork rinds, these were created as a way to use up otherwise unused bits and pieces of pork; they'd press all of the fat out of them, creating a crispy snack. While this used to be simple peasant food, these days meat production is streamlined to process pork leftovers in other ways—and so *čvartci* are considered a rare, and expensive, delicacy (*prešani čvartci* are even more pressed—and more expensive).

From the meat market, look for the **dairy** section (marked *mlijenči proizvodi).* Most cheese here is cow cheese *(kravlji),* typically very fresh and soft, and sometimes with flavorings (such as paprika or chives) mixed in. Goat cheese *(kozji)* is more rare. In this area, you'll also see some local starches. The extremely skinny noodles called *rezanci* are used in soups; the big, flat squares that look like tortillas *(mlinci)* are served with poultry—they soak up drippings to become soft and delicious.

▲▲Cathedral (Katedrala)

The most important church in a very devoutly Catholic country, Zagreb's cathedral is worth a visit. The full name is the Cathedral of the Assumption of the Blessed Virgin Mary and the Saintly Kings Stephen and Ladislav (whew!)—but most locals just call it "the cathedral." Inside, you'll see monuments to many late, great Croatians, and get a taste of the

faith that pervades in this country.

Cost and Hours: Free, Mon-Sat 10:00-17:00, Sun 13:00-17:00.

Visiting the Cathedral: Before entering, stand in the square in front of the cathedral (near the gilded Madonna on a pillar—sculpted by the same artist who did the Jelačić statue on the main square) to ponder the history of this site. In 1094, when a diocese was established at Kaptol, this church quickly became a major center of high-ranking church officials. In the mid-13th century, the original cathedral was destroyed by invading Tatars, who used it as a stable. It was rebuilt and surrounded by a stout medieval wall—practically turning it into a castle to defend against potential Ottoman invasion. You can still see the pointy tops of the round guard towers on either side of the church; until a century ago, this wall ran along the road behind you, completely enclosing the building. (The St. Mary pillar stands upon the round footprint of another one of the towers.) The church was severely damaged again, this time by an earthquake in 1880. The current version is Neo-Gothic (completed in 1902), incorporating a few original Gothic elements. Much of the wall was torn down to allow the town to grow.

Walking closer to the main door, look to the left to see the **two spires** displayed inside the wall. The one on the left, eroded down to a pathetic nub, demonstrates what happens when you use abundant—but porous—limestone to build a church in a climate with cold, freezing winters. (They can get away with using limestone on the coast, but in chilly Zagreb, it's just not the right material.) Some part of the church will certainly be covered by scaffolding during your visit—as it has been for decades, as restorers have gradually been replacing worn elements with new ones... this time, using a more durable stone.

Just before entering the church, appreciate the modern tympanum (carved semicircular section over the door). Then step inside and wander down the nave, taking in the opulence of the church. When it was completed, Zagreb was a small city of about 70,000 people; affording a church this finely decorated hints at the wealth of the city during its boom time. (In later times, that money dried up; the big chandeliers hanging in the nave were reportedly imported from Las Vegas—the best source for affordable glitz—in the 1970s.)

First, head to the **main altar** and look closely at the silver relief: a whimsical scene of the Holy Family doing chores around the house (Mary sewing, Joseph and Jesus building a fence...and angels helping out).

From the altar, turn left, then head to the front of the church. In the front-left corner (on the wall, between the confessionals), find **Ivan Meštrović's monument to Alojzije Stepinac.** We'll learn more about Stepinac in a moment, but for now pay attention to this beautifully carved piece of sculpture. Meštrović, the talented Croatian sculptor, worked in the early 20th century before fleeing communist Yugoslavia. Notice that this work was carved in "Detroit, Mich, USA," where Meštrović lived out his days in a self-imposed exile. Meštrović was a close friend of Stepinac, and carved this monument from half a world away.

Facing the nearby altar, on the right look for the monument to **Josip Jelačić,** the statesman whose statue adorns Zagreb's main square. Remember that Jelačić gained fame fighting against the Hungarians during the Habsburg era; the monument explains that his efforts allowed Zagreb to become an archbishopric, increasing its independence. But the large altar next to him celebrates three early Hungarian sainted kings, who (back when Croatia was part of Hungary, centuries before Jelačić) founded this church. And so, in an almost too-on-the-nose illustration of the complex layers of history in this part of the world, an "anti-Hungarian" monument stands side-by-side with a "pro-Hungarian" one. (You can imagine a Croat viewing this and thinking, "Those wonderful Hungarians, to whom we owe this church—thank God we defeated them.")

Walk up the steps to the area behind the main altar. Here you'll find a glass case containing a waxy, eerily lifelike sculpture of **Alojzije Stepinac.** (His actual remains are below.) Stepinac was the Archbishop of Zagreb during World War II, when he shortsightedly supported the Ustaše (Nazi puppet government in Croatia)—thinking, like many Croatians, that this was the ticket to greater independence from Serbia. When Tito came to power, he put Stepinac on trial and sent him to jail for five years, before he was banished to live out his life in the remote, poor village where he had been born. But Stepinac never lost his faith, and many Croatian Catholics consider him something of a martyr—and arguably the most inspirational figure of their faith. He's also respected in the US, where some Catholic schools bear his name. But many Serbs today consider Stepinac a villain who cooperated with the brutal Ustaše.

Before leaving, pull up a pew and ponder the role of faith in contemporary Croatian life. By definition, Croats are Catholics. And, although religion was not encouraged in communist Yugoslavia, it was also not prohibited (as it was in most Warsaw Pact countries). Politicians, military officers, and civil servants (such as teachers) couldn't publicly profess their faith, but many were privately devout. And with the breakup of Yugoslavia and the ensuing wars, Catholicism has seen a huge boost. In this part of the world where ethnicity is tied to faith, nationalism (which is also on the rise) hews closely to religion—too closely, many impartial observers fear. The increasing influence of the Catholic Church on Croatian politics will be a hot potato here for years to come.

As you leave the cathedral, look high on the wall to the left of the door. This strange script is the **Glagolitic alphabet** *(glagoljca),* invented by Byzantine missionaries Cyril and Methodius in the ninth century to translate the Bible into Slavic languages. Though these missionaries worked mostly in Moravia (today's eastern Czech Republic), their alphabet caught on only here, in Croatia. (Glagolitic was later adapted in Bulgaria to become the Cyrillic alphabet—still used in Serbia, Russia, and other parts east.) In 1991, when Croatia became its own country and nationalism surged, some Croats flirted with the idea of making this the official alphabet.

MUSEUMS IN AND NEAR THE GREEN HORSESHOE

With extra time, stroll around the Green Horseshoe (the U-shaped belt of parks and museums in the city center). The museums on and near this park aren't nearly as interesting as those on Gradec, but may be worth a peek on a rainy day. The Modern Gallery, described later, is also in this area.

Mimara Museum (Muzej Mimara)

This grand, empty-feeling building displays the eclectic art collection of a wealthy Dalmatian, ranging from ancient artifacts to paintings by European masters. After buying your ticket, head up to the top floor (2) and tour the fine painting gallery. While the names are major—Rubens, Rembrandt, Velázquez, Renoir, Manet—the paintings themselves are minor (I wouldn't prioritize these over the works of Croatian artists on display elsewhere in Zagreb, especially those at the Naive Art Museum or the Meštrović Atelier). The first floor displays sculpture and applied arts, while the ground floor has vases, carpets, and objects from the Far East.

Cost and Hours: 40 kn, 90-kn English guidebook, free and excellent smartphone audio tour available for download on their Wi-Fi network; July-Sept Tue-Fri 10:00-19:00, Sat 10:00-17:00, Sun 10:00-14:00, closed Mon; Oct-June Tue-Sat 10:00-17:00, Thu until 19:00, Sun 10:00-14:00, closed Mon; Rooseveltov trg 5, tel. 01/482-8100, www.mimara.hr.

Arts and Crafts Museum (Muzej za Umjetnost i Obrt)

This decorative arts collection of furniture, ceramics, and clothes is well-displayed. From the entry, go upstairs, then work your way clockwise and up to the top floor—passing through each artistic style, from Gothic to the present. It's mostly furniture, with a few paintings and other items thrown in. The ground floor features temporary exhibits.

Cost and Hours: 30 kn, some rooms have laminated English descriptions to borrow, otherwise very limited English, Tue-Sat 10:00-19:00, Sun 10:00-14:00—sometimes later depending on special exhibits, closed Mon, Trg Maršala Tita 10, tel. 01/488-2125, www.muo.hr.

Botanical Garden (Botanički Vrt)

For a back-to-nature change of pace from the urban cityscape, wander through this relaxing garden, run by the University of Zagreb.

Cost and Hours: Free, April-Oct Mon-Tue 9:00-14:30, Wed-Sun 9:00-18:00—until 19:00 in summer, closed Nov-March, at southwest corner of the Green 'Shoe, Marulicev trg 9A, tel. 01/489-8060.

ELSEWHERE IN ZAGREB

▲Mirogoj Cemetery (Groblje Mirogoj)

Of Europe's many evocative cemeteries, Mirogoj (MEE-roh-goy) is one of the finest, studded with great architecture and beautifully

designed tombs. This peaceful spot, a short bus ride from the city center, memorializes many of the greats who built the Croatian nation. Anyone can enjoy a quiet walk here, but to provide context to your stroll, stop by the TI first for their free, thorough booklet of maps and descriptions identifying the most significant graves.

The cemetery was designed by Herman Bollé, an Austrian architect who lived and worked for most of his career in Zagreb, leaving his mark all over the city before becoming a permanent resident in this cemetery. From the stately domed main mausoleum, a long arcade (with VIP tombs) stretches along the road in both directions, punctuated by smaller domes. Entering

ZAGREB

through the main gate, circle behind the mausoleum to find the biggest tomb here: of Franjo Tuđman, the leader who spearheaded the creation of independent Croatia but left behind a questionable legacy (for more on Tuđman, see page 868). Continuing straight past Tuđman's grave, you'll reach the Central Cross, which usually has a field of flowers around it, and beyond that, a monument to the dead of World War I. In every direction, as far as the eye can see, are the final resting places of great Croatians.

Cost and Hours: Free, daily April-Sept 6:00-20:00, Oct-March 7:30-18:00.

Getting There: Catch bus #106 from in front of the Cathedral (3/hour) and ride six stops, or about 10 minutes, to the stop called simply "Mirogoj" (the one *after* the stop called "Mirogoj Arkada"). The return bus leaves from across the street.

Art Museums

In addition to the art gallery at the Mimara Museum (described earlier), art lovers may want to visit a trio of other Zagreb art museums. Three different collections cover works from the 20th century through today: The **Modern Gallery** features art from the early 20th century (a few blocks south of Jelačić Square at Andrije Hebranga 1, www.moderna-galerija.hr); the **Museum of Contemporary Art** focuses on mid-century art (south of the river and not as convenient to visit, avenija Dubrovnik 17, www.msu.hr); and the innovative **Lauba,** with more cutting-edge works from the past few years (Baruna Filipovića 23A, www.lauba.hr). For details on any of these, check their websites or ask at the TI.

Sleeping in Zagreb

As this is a convention and business town, rates at business-oriented hotels are highest on weekdays mid-February through mid-July, then again from September through November. At other times of year, and weekends year-round, you'll generally enjoy lower rates. I've listed the average rates—they may be slightly higher or lower with demand. If I've listed two sets of rates separated by slashes, the first is for high season and the second is for low season.

$$$ Jägerhorn Hotel is the top choice in Zagreb for afford-able elegance in an excellent location (one long block from Jelačić Square, along the busy Ilica boulevard but tucked back on a qui-eter courtyard). Its 18 rooms are small but well-appointed, and a fine downtown refuge (Sb-€95/€85, Db-€110/€100, higher price is for June-Sept, air-con, guest computer and Wi-Fi, free parking, Ilica 14, tel. 01/483-3877, www.hotel-jagerhorn.hr, info@hotel-jagerhorn.hr).

Sleep Code

Abbreviations
(6 kn = about $1, €1 = about $1.40, country code: 385, area code: 01)
S = Single, **D** = Double/Twin, **T** = Triple, **Q** = Quad,
b = bathroom.

Price Rankings
$$$ Higher Priced—Most rooms €100 or more.
$$ Moderately Priced—Most rooms between €60-100.
$ Lower Priced—Most rooms €60 or less.

Unless otherwise noted, credit cards are accepted, Wi-Fi is generally free, and breakfast is included, but the modest tourist tax (about 7 kn per person, per night) is not. While rates are listed in euros, you'll pay in kunas. Everyone listed here speaks English. Prices can change without notice; verify the hotel's current rates online or by email. For the best prices, always book directly with the hotel.

$$$ Hotel Dubrovnik is a professional-feeling, business-class hotel with 245 rooms. While lacking personality, it's comfortable and ideally located at the bottom of Jelačić Square (small Sb-€95, bigger Sb-€110, Db-€135, bigger and nicer "deluxe" Db-€175, suite-€200-220, extra bed-€35, rooms overlooking the square don't cost extra but can come with some noise, often cheaper on weekends, prices can flex up or down with demand, air-con, non-smoking floors, elevator, guest computer and Wi-Fi, Gajeva 1, tel. 01/486-3555, www.hotel-dubrovnik.hr, reservations@hotel-dubrovnik.hr).

$$$ Hotel Astoria, a Best Western, offers 100 smallish but plush, recently renovated rooms and a high-class lobby. It's on a somewhat grimy street that's handy to the train station (about a 10-minute walk from Jelačić Square). If you can get a good price, it's worth considering (Sb-€89/€79, Db-€103/€93, rates flex up and down with demand, various discounts offered—including military, fancier suites also available, air-con, elevator, non-smoking rooms, guest computer and Wi-Fi, free parking, Petrinjska 71, tel. 01/480-8900, www.hotelastoria.hr, recepcija@hotelastoria.hr).

$$ Studio Kairos has affordable prices, classy comfort, a warm welcome, and four creatively decorated rooms—all with different themes. It's a bit less conveniently located than my other listings, on a pleasant shopping street about a 15-minute walk from Jelačić Square (Sb-€58-69, Db-€75-87, price depends on room size, cash only, shared kitchen, air-con, Wi-Fi, self-service pay laundry, Vlaška 92, tel. 01/464-0680, mobile 091-464-0690, danijela@studio-kairos.com, www.studio-kairos.com, Danijela).

$$ Sobe Zagreb 17, run by mom-and-daughter team Rumica and Irena, rents seven stylish rooms with colorful and cute decor

ZAGREB

in a grubby but wonderfully located building, just a few minutes' walk from Gradec, the Tkalčićeva restaurant street, and Jelačić Square (Db-€60-100 depending on size and demand, Qb apartment-€120, no breakfast, cash only, air-con, Wi-Fi, Radićeva 22, mobile 091-170-0000, www.sobezagreb17.com, info@sobezagreb17.com).

$$ InZagreb, run by Ivana and Ksandro Kovačić, rents 10 mostly one-bedroom apartments in various buildings around the city. While locations vary, most are in untouristy urban zones within a 10- to 20-minute walk of the main square. The units are nicely equipped and come with several welcoming, creative touches. Visit their website, find the apartment that appeals to you, and make a reservation. Clearly communicate your arrival time, and they'll pick you up at the train or bus station (no extra charge) or at the airport (150 kn extra) and take you to your home-away-from-home in Zagreb (Db-€65-89 depending on apartment and location, no 1-night stays, no breakfast, kitchenettes, air-con, Wi-Fi, laundry machine, mobile 091-652-3201, www.inzagreb.com, info@inzagreb.com). Ivana, a licensed guide, also offers a variety of custom tours around town.

$$ Hotel Central has a communist-holdover vibe, disinterested staff, and 76 overpriced, overly perfumed, but reasonably modern rooms. I'd consider this only if you value its proximity to the train station, which sits just across the street (Sb-€70, larger Sb-€75, Db with one big bed-€95, twin Db-€105, Tb-€135, rates can flex with demand, air-con, elevator, guest computer and Wi-Fi, Branimirova 3, tel. 01/484-1122, www.hotel-central.hr, info@hotel-central.hr).

$ Hotel Ilica is a 15-minute walk or short tram ride from Jelačić Square. The hotel's idiosyncratic sense of style—with faux chandeliers and Roman busts that Liberace would find gaudy—helps compensate for its dull urban neighborhood. It's set back on its own courtyard with a garden behind it, making it an oasis of quiet in the heart of the city. With 24 rooms, four apartments, and a staff that prides itself on its personal service, this quirky place is an excellent value if you don't mind commuting to your sightseeing by tram (Sb-€46, Db-€59, larger twin Db-€79, big apartment-€119, 10 percent discount for Rick Steves readers who book direct, air-con, guest computer and Wi-Fi, off-street courtyard parking-39 kn/€5 per day, Ilica 102, two tram stops from Jelačić Square at Britanski trg stop, tel. 1/377-7522, www.hotel-ilica.hr, info@hotel-ilica.hr).

$ Shappy Hostel—slick, shabby-chic, and modern—is the most appealing of Zagreb's many new design hostels. Surrounding a courtyard in a very central, urban-feeling area, it has 41 beds in 13 rooms, including 9 private, hotelesque doubles that are worth considering even for non-hostelers. The hip and funky bar in the courtyard is also open to non-guests (bunk in 4- to 10-bed dorm-€17-25 depending on size and season, Db-€60/€55, no breakfast, air-con, Wi-Fi, free parking, lockers, Varšavska 8, tel. 01/483-0483, mobile 091-511-5341, www.hostel-shappy.com, info@hostel-shappy.com).

$ Fulir Backpackers Inn, a funky slumbermill named for a legendary Zagrebian bon vivant, is loosely run by Leo, a can-do Croat who once lived in Ohio. It's colorful, friendly, and youthful, with a big 10-bunk dorm (€14/€12), two six-bed rooms (€16/€14), and a quad (€18/€16). Located in an old house just a few steps from Jelačić Square, this hostel puts you in the heart of Zagreb (includes sheets, no breakfast, free lockers, guest computer and Wi-Fi, self-service laundry, upstairs at the end of the courtyard at Radićeva 3a, tel. 01/483-0882, mobile 099-483-0882, www.fulir-hostel.com, fulir@fulir-hostel.com).

Eating in Zagreb

As a cosmopolitan European capital, Zagreb enjoys a refreshingly varied restaurant scene. It's also a good value; while most of the touristy towns in this book have inflated-for-tourists prices, most diners here are natives, and competition to lure value-conscious local foodies keeps things affordable. Traditional Zagreb-area cuisine is hearty peasant grub—sausage, sauerkraut, potatoes, *sarma* (cabbage rolls)—that seems more "Eastern European" than the seafood, pizza, and pastas of the coast. But consider skipping traditional Croatian food altogether here in Zagreb—the city provides some desperately needed diversity (non-Croatian options are limited almost everywhere else in the country). Look beyond restaurants, too: Several enticing sandwich shops, chichi bakeries, and gourmet coffee bars are scattered around the center, catering to businesspeople on their lunch breaks.

PEOPLE-WATCHING AND COFFEE-SIPPING

One of my favorite Zagreb pastimes is lingering over a drink or meal along its thriving people zones, watching an endless parade of fashionable locals saunter past, and wondering why they don't create such an inviting space in my hometown. The best place is on **Tkalčićeva street,** Zagreb's main café street and urban promenade rolled into one. It's a parade of fashionable locals and *the* place to see and be seen (starts a block behind Jelačić Square, next to the market). I've listed my favorite Tkalčićeva eateries next. Honorable mention goes to **Trg Petra Preradovića,** an inviting square just a short walk from Jelačić Square (up Ilica street) that bustles with appealing outdoor cafés and bars.

Downtown Zagreb abounds with boutique bakeries and dessert shops. If you'd like a sweet treat with your coffee, it's generally fine to buy a pastry elsewhere, then eat it with coffee ordered at an outdoor café—provided that café doesn't serve food of its own.

EATING ON OR NEAR TKALČIĆEVA STREET

Tkalčićeva has the highest concentration of inviting restaurants in town. Strolling its entire length (about a 10-minute walk), you'll pass plenty of drinks-only cafés, but also pizzerias, Turkish eateries, *ćevapi* (grilled meat) joints, cake and dessert shops (including some specializing in doughnuts), and the restaurants listed below.

Pivnica Medvedgrad ("Bear Town"—a fortress near Zagreb) is a rollicking brewpub serving five different in-house beers (each one well-described in the menu) and heavy, stick-to-your-ribs pub grub that feels closer to Prague than to Dubrovnik. The food offers a welcome break from the pizzas-pastas-and-seafood rut you'll encounter on the coast, and the outdoor seating right on Tkalčićeva's most colorful stretch will seduce you into staying for another beer—if you can score a table. The pubby interior is convivial, but less enticing (30-60-kn meals, daily 10:00-24:00, food served until 22:00, Tkalčićeva 36, tel. 01/492-9613).

Restaurant Agava holds court above the very middle of Tkalčićeva, with terraces climbing up the hill and an interior that feels like an old-time Zagreb home. It's dressy yet affordable, and serves international cuisine (60-80-kn pastas and starters, 65-130-kn main dishes, reservations smart, daily 9:00-24:00, Tkalčićeva 39, tel. 01/482-9826, www.restaurant-agava.hr).

Rocket Burger, an unpretentious American-style diner, dishes up decent 25-40-kn burgers at outdoor tables with prime Tkalčićeva views (also 30-35-kn American-style breakfasts, Mon-Thu 11:00-23:00, Fri-Sun 9:00-24:00, Tkalčićeva 44).

Takenoko, in the glitzy modern shopping mall at the very top end of Tkalčićeva, is a good chance for high-quality pan-Asian (mostly Japanese) cuisine with a pinch of Mediterranean fusion. The classy atmosphere and stiff service make it feel like a splurge. Choose between their sushi menu (105-185-kn combos) and their Asian fusion menu (105-130-kn dishes). Reservations are advised (Mon-Sat 12:00-24:00, Sat 12:00-18:00, in Centar Kaptol at Nova Ves 17, tel. 01/486-0530, www.takenoko.hr).

At the Market (Dolac): Zagreb's busy market offers plenty of options (Mon-Fri 7:00-15:00, Sat 7:00-14:00, Sun 7:00-13:00).

Assemble a fresh picnic direct from the producers; for pointers on local ingredients to look for, see page 1074. Or, for something already prepared, duck into one of the many cheap restaurants and cafés on the streets around the market. The middle level of the market, facing Jelačić Square, is home to a line of places with cheap food and indoor or outdoor seating.

Dessert: **The Cookie Factory** has a wide array of delicious American-style cookies, brownies, smoothies, and other goodies. Pull up a table for a brownie à la mode, or get a cookie sandwich to go. They have outdoor tables along a delightful stretch of Tkalčićeva. Sometimes when you're traveling, something oh-so-American just hits the spot... (10-20-kn treats, Sun-Thu 9:00-22:00, Fri-Sat 9:00-23:00, Tkalčićeva 21, mobile 099-494-9400).

IN THE UPPER TOWN (GRADEC)

Trilogija, just above the Stone Gate, is a casual wine bar serving up delicious, well-presented, and affordable international dishes made with local ingredients. There's no printed menu because they cook what they find at the market—your server can explain the chalkboard menu. As this place is deservedly popular, reservations are smart (35-75-kn small dishes, 90-120-kn large dishes, Mon-Sat 11:00-24:00, Sun 11:00-16:00—except closed Sun Nov-April, Kamenita 5, tel. 01/485-1394).

Konoba Didov San ("Grandfather's Dream") serves up traditional food from the Dalmatian hinterland (specifically the Neretva River Delta, near Metković). You'll find the normal Dalmatian specialties, plus eel, frogs, and snails. Choose between the homey, traditional interior and the outdoor tables. Reservations are smart on weekends (25-65-kn starters, 60-120-kn main courses, daily 10:00-24:00, a few steps up from the Ivan Meštrović Atelier at Mletačka 11, tel. 01/485-1154).

IN THE LOWER TOWN, NEAR JELAČIĆ SQUARE

These places are all within a level five-minute walk of Jelačić Square.

Vinodol is a sprawling, white-tablecloth-classy dinner spot, with a peaceful covered terrace and a smartly appointed dining room under an impressive vaulted ceiling. The good, reasonably priced cuisine includes lamb or veal prepared *peka*-style, under a baking lid covered with hot coals (*peka* portion costs 90 kn, served only at certain times—generally at 13:00 and 19:00; 50-120-kn main courses, open daily 10:00-24:00, Teslina 10, tel. 01/481-1427).

Nishta, the highly recommended vegetarian restaurant in Dubrovnik (see page 943), recently opened a larger location near Zagreb's main bus station, with an eclectic menu of international meatless cuisine and an extensive salad bar (20-30-kn starters, 50-70-kn main dishes, Mon-Sat 11:00-22:00, closed Sun, Masarykova 11, tel. 01/889-7444).

Ribice i Tri Točkice ("Fish and...") serves up fish, seafood, and...whatever else they feel like. Enjoy the casual, colorful upstairs dining room and the affordably priced fish, bought daily at the market. Or sit at the outdoor tables, on an urban street. Restaurants on the coast offer ample opportunity to sample Croatian fish, but this is a good opportunity to have some in the big city (30-90-kn dishes, order sides separately, daily 10:00-23:00, Petra Preradovića 7/1, tel. 01/563-5479).

Cheese Bar offers an easy opportunity to sample Croatian wines (45 bottles available by the glass, most 20-30 kn) accompanied by a plate of local cheeses with olives (65 kn). While the cheese isn't quite the gourmet experience you'd hope for (most taste about the same, with different spices), the stay-a-while ambience is pleasant, and the location—a block from Jelačić Square or the cathedral—couldn't be more central (daily 8:00-23:00, Cesarčeva 4, mobile 091-888-8628).

Fast and Cheap: **Sandwich Bar Pingvin,** busy with locals dropping by for take-away, is a favorite for quick, cheap, tasty sandwiches with chicken, turkey, steak, or fish (plus some pasta dishes). They'll wrap it all in a piece of grilled bread and top it with your choice of veggies and sauces to go—or, to eat here, sit at one of the few tiny tables or stools (17-33 kn, Mon-Sat 10:00-late, Sun 18:00-late, about a block below Jelačić Square at Teslina 7). For *ćevapčići*—the classic Balkan grilled-meat dish (described on page 1140)—drop by the Sarajevan-owned **Jazz.ba,** hiding in a very central, nondescript neighborhood (15-20-kn small plates, 35-50-kn big plates, daily 10:00-23:00, Varšavska 8, mobile 091-955-5001).

Fried and Fishy: **Mimice** is a local institution and an old-habits-die-hard favorite of the older generation. Although it's quite tired and dreary, I like it as a cheap and memorable time-warp serving up simple fish dishes (16-31 kn, order starches and sauces separately). Choose what you want from the limited menu (if confused, survey the room for a plate that looks good and ask what it is), pay, and take your receipt to the next counter to claim your food. Order the smelt to get a plate of tiny deep-fried fish (Mon-Sat 7:00-21:00, closed Sun, Jurišićeva 21). As Zagreb is a Catholic town, you'll have to wait in line if you're here on a Friday.

Dessert: Several inviting places in the center offer good *sladoled* (Italian gelato-style ice cream). Two central locations are **Zagreb Slastičarnica,** which usually features some creative and unusual flavors (daily 8:00-23:00, hiding behind the statue of Tesla just past the bottom of the Trg Petra Preradovića café square at Masarykova 4, tel. 01/481-0955); and **Slastičarnica Vincek,** whose specialty is the chocolate-and-walnuts Vincek flavor (Mon-Sat 8:30-23:00, closed Sun, two blocks west of Jelačić Square on the busy tram-lined Ilica street at #18).

Zagreb Connections

From Zagreb by Train to: Rijeka (3/day direct, 4-5 hours), **Pula** (3/day, 6 hours, transfer in Rijeka), **Split** (2/day, 6.5 hours, plus 1 direct night train, 9 hours), **Sarajevo** (1/day, 9 hours), **Mostar** (1/day, 11.5 hours, bus is faster), **Ptuj** (3/day, 3.5-4.25 hours, usually requires 2 transfers) **Ljubljana** (4/day direct, 2.5 hours), **Vienna** (2/day with change in Budapest or Sevnica, 8-10 hours, more with multiple changes), **Budapest** (2/day direct, 6-7 hours), **Lake Bled** (via Lesce-Bled, 4/day direct, 3-3.5 hours), **Munich** (2/day direct, including a night train, 9 hours). Train info: Tel. 060-333-444.

By Bus to: Samobor (about 2-3/hour, 30-50 minutes), **Plitvice Lakes National Park** (about hourly until around 16:00, 2-2.5 hours; the best choice is the express bus operated by Prijevoz Knežević—see page 1103), **Rijeka** (hourly, 2-3.5 hours), **Rovinj** (6-9/day, 3-6 hours), **Pula** (almost hourly, 4-6 hours), **Split** (at least hourly, 5-8 hours), **Mostar** (4/day, 9 hours, includes a night bus), **Sarajevo** (4/day, 8 hours, includes night bus), **Dubrovnik** (10/day including some overnight options, 10 hours), **Korčula** (1/day, 9-13.5 hours depending on route), **Kotor** (1/night, 14.5 hours).

Bus schedules can be sporadic (for example, several departures clustered around the same time, then nothing for hours)—confirm your plans carefully (inquire locally, or use the good online schedules at www.akz.hr). The TI is very helpful with providing bus information. Popular buses, such as the afternoon express to Split, can fill up quickly in peak season. Unfortunately, it's impossible to buy bus tickets anywhere in the center, so to guarantee a seat, you'll have to get to the station early (locals suggest even two hours in advance). Better yet, call the central number for the bus station to check schedules and reserve the bus you want, ideally at least 24 hours ahead: Tel. 060-313-333 (from abroad, dial +385-1-611-2789). If you can't get an English-speaker on the line, and the TI isn't too busy, they might be willing to call for you.

ZAGREB

PLITVICE LAKES NATIONAL PARK

Nacionalni Park Plitvička Jezera

Plitvice (PLEET-veet-seh) is one of Europe's most spectacular natural wonders. Imagine Niagara Falls diced and sprinkled over a heavily forested Grand Canyon. There's nothing like this lush valley of 16 terraced lakes, laced together by waterfalls, boat rides, and miles of pleasant plank walks. Countless cascades and water that's both strangely clear and full of vibrant colors make this park a misty natural wonderland. Decades ago, after eight or nine visits, I thought I really knew Europe. Then I discovered Plitvice and realized you can never exhaust Europe's surprises.

While Plitvice never fails to blow visitors away, a trip here brings you through one of the poorest, remotest areas of inland Croatia. This part of the country is still war-torn (bombed-out churches and homes you'll see in many villages here most likely belonged to local Serbs who fled after the war), and the national park represents the only real industry for miles around. I find that many of the people in this region can be insular, a bit cranky, and greedy to catch their share of the passing tourist dollar. Public transportation is workable but far from slick, making this region best by car. Pack along a bit of patience; any hassles you encounter are well worth the spray you'll feel on your face from those waterfalls.

PLANNING YOUR TIME

You can see all of the best scenery at Plitvice in just a three- to four-hour hike. While you can give yourself longer here, it's not necessary. Other trails pale in comparison to this convenient main route.

Since it takes some time to get here (about two hours by car

or bus from Zagreb), the most sensible plan is to spend the night in the area (either at one of the park's hotels, or at a guest house nearby). If you're coming from the north (e.g., Ljubljana), you can take the train to Zagreb in the morning, spend a few hours seeing the Croatian capital, then take the bus (generally no buses after about 16:00) or pick up a rental car and drive to Plitvice in the late afternoon. To avoid crowds, get up early and hit the trails (ideally by 8:30); by early afternoon, you'll be ready to move on (south to the coast, or north to Zagreb). Two nights and a full day at Plitvice is probably overkill for all but the most avid hikers.

Crowd-Beating Tips: Plitvice is swamped with international tour groups, many of whom aren't shy about elbowing into position for the best photos. While it's impossible to avoid crowds entirely, you'll get at least some of the park to yourself if you hike early or late. The park's trails are most crowded between 10:00 and 15:00. I try to hit the trails by 8:30 and begin with the Lower Lakes; that way, the crowds are moving in just as I'm finishing up. If arriving in the afternoon, starting the hike after 15:00 also works well (though off-season, be careful to check when buses and boats stop running). The Upper Lakes are often less crowded later in the day, especially in the afternoon.

GETTING TO PLITVICE

Plitvice Lakes National Park, a few miles from the Bosnian border, is located on the old highway between Zagreb and Split. While driving is the easiest option, it's also reachable by bus.

If taking a bus to Plitvice, confirm schedules locally or online, and also confirm that your bus will actually stop at Plitvice. The park's official bus stop is along the main road, about a 5- to 10-minute walk from the hotels.

From Zagreb

By **car**, Plitvice is two hours south of Zagreb on the old highway #1 (a.k.a. D-1). Leaving Zagreb, take the A-1 expressway south for about an hour, exiting at Karlovac (marked for *1* and *Plitvice*). From here, D-1 takes you directly south about another hour to the park (see "En Route," later). If you're staying at the park hotels, you can park for free at the hotel lot; to park at the lots at Entrance 1 or Entrance 2, you'll have to pay. For information about driving onward from Plitvice, see "Route Tips for Drivers" at the end of this chapter.

Buses leave from Zagreb's main bus station in the direction of Plitvice (trip takes 2-2.5 hours). Various bus companies handle the route; the best option is an **express bus** that runs daily in summer, operated by a local company, Prijevoz Knežević (departs Zagreb 8:15, arrives Plitvice 10:20, late June-early Sept only, confirm schedule at www.prijevoz-knezevic.hr; also see page 1103). If they won't sell you a ticket for the Prijevoz Knežević express at the main ticket window, ask at the window for "Croatia Zovko Bus." If the express doesn't suit your schedule, you can just go to any ticket window and ask for the next departure. Non-express buses run from Zagreb about hourly until about 16:00; avoid the sporadic late-night buses, which don't get you to the park until after midnight (for schedules, see www.autobusni-kolodvor.com or www.akz.hr; look for "Plitvička Jezera").

En Route: By car or bus, you'll see some thought-provoking terrain between Zagreb and Plitvice. Exiting the expressway at Karlovac, then heading south on D-1, you'll pass through the village of **Turanj**—part of the war zone from two decades ago. Notice the military museum (on the right as you drive through), with tanks, heavy-artillery cannons, and other war machines that actually saw action. The destroyed, derelict houses belonged to Serbs who have not come back to reclaim and repair them. Farther along, about 25 miles before Plitvice, you'll pass through the striking village of **Slunj,** perched picturesquely on travertine formations (like Plitvice's) and surrounded by sparkling streams and waterfalls. The most traditional part of the town, perched just above the water, is called **Rastoke**, which has a memorable restaurant (see page 1102). If you're driving, this is worth a photo stop. This town, too, looks very different from how it did before the war—when it was 30 percent Serb. As in countless other villages in the Croatian interior, the Orthodox church has been destroyed...and locals still seethe when they describe how the Serbs "defiled" the town's delicate beauty.

From Split

Drivers head north on the A-1 expressway, exiting at Gornja Ploča; from here, you'll follow road D-1 about an hour north (passing Udbina and Korenica) to the park.

Two daily **express buses** run from Split to Plitvice in summer (departing 15:30 late June-late Sept, with additional departure at 10:15 July-Aug, 4-4.5 hours, operated by Prijevoz Knežević, www.prijevoz-knezevic.hr; also see schedule on page 1104). Many other non-express options run a similar route (about 7-8/day in summer, 4/day in winter, 4-6 hours).

Orientation to Plitvice

Plitvice's 16 lakes are divided into the Upper Lakes (Gornja Jezera) and the Lower Lakes (Donja Jezera). The park officially has two entrances *(ulaz)*, each with ticket windows and snack and gift shops. Entrance 1 overlooks the bottom of the Lower Lakes. Entrance 2 is about 1.5 miles south, near the cluster of Plitvice's three hotels (Jezero, Plitvice, and Bellevue; see "Sleeping in and near Plitvice," later). There is no town at Plitvice. The nearest village, Mukinje, is a residential community mostly for park workers.

Cost: The price to enter the park varies by season: 180 kn July-Aug, 110 kn April-June and Sept-Oct, and 55 kn Nov-March. This price covers park entry, boat, and shuttle bus. Park hotel guests pay the entry fee only once for their entire stay; if you're staying off-site and want to visit the park on several days, you'll have to buy separate tickets each day.

Hours: The park is open every day, but the hours vary by season. In summer, it's generally open 7:00-20:00; in spring and fall, 8:00-18:00; and in winter, 8:00-16:00. The last boats and shuttle buses depart earlier (generally 30-60 minutes before the park closes—if hiking late in the day, ask about this before you head out). The short boat hop between P-1 (below the hotels) and P-2 (at the Upper Lakes) runs later. Again, for fewer tour-group crowds, visit early or late in the day.

Services: While you'll find WCs at both entrances, once you're on the trails, they're quite rare: The only convenient one is near the P-3 boat dock (the Kozjak Lake boat dock for the Lower Lakes). There is no WC at the P-2 boat dock—the only WC at the Upper Lakes is at the ST-3 bus stop, far at the top of these lakes. Plan accordingly.

TOURIST INFORMATION

A handy map of the trails is on the back of your ticket, and big maps are posted all over the park. Unless you're planning a more ambitious hike than the usual circuit I describe, I'd skip the big map and the various English-language guidebooks (both sold at entrances, hotels, and shops throughout the park). The park has a good website: www.np-plitvicka-jezera.hr.

GETTING AROUND PLITVICE

Plitvice is designed for hikers. But the park has a few ways (included in entry cost) to help you connect the best parts.

By Shuttle Bus: Remember, buses connect the hotels at Entrance 2 (stop ST-2, below Hotel Jezero) with the top of the Upper Lakes (stop ST-3) and roughly the bottom of the Lower Lakes (stop ST-1, a 10-minute walk from Entrance 1). Buses

Park Signs and Symbols

While spectacular, Plitvice—long poorly run by government bureaucrats—is not as user-friendly for individuals as it could be. The trails can be confusingly marked. Here's a decoder for the symbols you'll see on signs:

Boat icons point you to one of the park's three boat docks:

P-1 is the dock that's a steep hike below the park's three hotels.

P-2, a short crossing across the water from the P-1 dock, is at the bottom of the Upper Lakes.

P-3 is all the way across the biggest lake, at the top of the Lower Lakes.

Train icons direct you to one of the three stops for the shuttle buses (not actual trains) that move visitors around the park:

ST-1 is a 10-minute walk below Entrance 1, just above the Lower Lakes.

ST-2 is below Entrance 2 and the park's three hotels (and above the P-1 boat dock).

ST-3 is at the top of the Upper Lakes.

Letters denote various recommended hiking routes. These are largely nonsensical; while I mention these letters occasionally to help you find your way, don't get too hung up on them.

start running early and continue until late afternoon (frequency depends on demand—generally 3-4/hour; buses run from March until the first snow—often Dec). Note that the park refers to its buses as "trains," which confuses some visitors. Also note that no local buses take you along the major road (D-1) that connects the entrances. The only way to get between them without a car is by shuttle bus (inside the park) or by foot (about a 40-minute walk).

By Boat: Low-impact electric boats ply the waters of the biggest lake, Kozjak, with three stops: a steep hike below Entrance 2 and the park hotels (stop P-1), at the bottom of the Upper Lakes (P-2), and at the far end of Kozjak, at the top of the Lower Lakes (P-3). From Hotel Jezero to the Upper Lakes, it's a quick five-minute ride; the boat goes back and forth continuously. The trip from the Upper Lakes to the Lower Lakes takes closer to 20 minutes, and the boat goes about twice per hour—

often at the top and bottom of every hour. (With up to 10,000 people a day visiting the park, you might have to wait for a seat on this boat.)

Sights in Plitvice

Plitvice is a refreshing playground of 16 terraced lakes, separated by natural travertine dams and connected by countless waterfalls. Over time, the water has simultaneously carved out, and, with the help of mineral deposits, built up this fluid landscape.

Plitvice became Croatia's first national park in 1949, and was a popular destination during the Yugoslav period. On Easter Sunday in 1991, the first shots of Croatia's war with Yugoslavia were fired right here—in fact, the war's first casualty was a park policeman, Josip Jović. The Serbs held Plitvice until 1995, and most of the Croatians you'll meet here were evacuated and lived near the coast as refugees. During those five years, the park saw virtually no tourists, and was allowed to grow wild—allowing the ecosystem to recover from the impact of so many visitors. Today, the war is a fading memory, and the park is again a popular tourist destination, with nearly a million visitors each year (though relatively few are from the US).

▲▲▲HIKING THE LAKES

Plitvice's system of trails and boardwalks makes it possible for visitors to get immersed in the park's beauty. In some places, the path leads literally right up the middle of a waterfall. The official park map and signage recommend a variety of hikes, but there's no need to adhere strictly to these suggestions if you want to create your own route.

Planning Your Time: Most visitors stick to the main paths and choose between two basic plans: uphill or downhill. Each one has pros and cons. Park officials generally recommend hiking uphill, from the Lower Lakes to the Upper Lakes, which offers slightly better head-on views of the best scenery (this is the route described next). It also saves the most scenic stretch of lakes and falls—the Upper Lakes—for last. If you get an early start, going in this direction helps keep you in front of the crowds. Hiking downhill, from Upper to Lower, is easier (though you'll have to hike steeply up out of the canyon at the end), and since most groups go

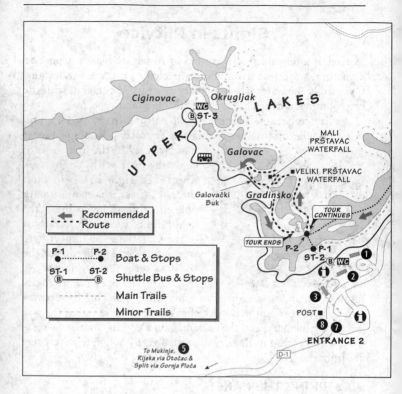

the opposite way, you'll be passing—but not stuck behind—the crowds. (Regardless of where and when you go, you won't be able to avoid the crowds entirely.)

Walking briskly and with a few brief photo stops, figure at least an hour for the Lower Lakes, about an hour for the Upper Lakes, and a half-hour to connect them by boat—though it can take longer than this when the park is crowded, which it often is.

Lower Lakes (Donja Jezera)

The lower half of Plitvice's lakes are accessible from Entrance 1. If you start here, the route marked *B* leads you along the boardwalks to Kozjak, the big lake that connects the Lower and the Upper Lakes (described later).

From the entrance, you'll descend a steep path with lots of **switchbacks,** as well as thrilling postcard views over the canyon of the Lower Lakes. As you reach the lakes and begin to follow the boardwalks, you'll have great up-close views of the travertine formations that make up Plitvice's many waterfalls. Count the trout. If you're tempted to throw in a line, don't. Fishing is strictly forbidden.

After you cross the path over the first lake, an optional

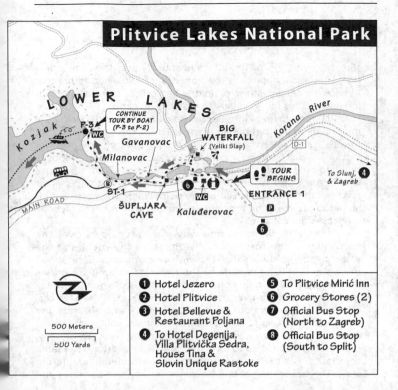

Plitvice Lakes National Park

1 Hotel Jezero
2 Hotel Plitvice
3 Hotel Bellevue & Restaurant Poljana
4 To Hotel Degenija, Villa Plitvička Sedra, House Tina & Slovin Unique Rastoke
5 To Plitvice Mirić Inn
6 Grocery Stores (2)
7 Official Bus Stop (North to Zagreb)
8 Official Bus Stop (South to Split)

10-minute detour (to the right) takes you down to the **Big Waterfall** (Veliki Slap). It's the biggest of Plitvice's waterfalls, where the Plitvica River plunges 250 feet over a cliff into the valley below. Depending on recent rainfall, the force of the Big Waterfall varies from a light mist to a thundering deluge.

If you're a hardy hiker, consider climbing the steep steps from the Big Waterfall up to a **viewpoint** at the top of the canyon (marked *Sightseeing Point/ Vidikovac*; it's a strenuous 10-minute hike to the top). Take the stairs up, bearing to the right at the top (near the shelter) to find a nice viewpoint overlooking the Big Waterfall. From here, you can carry on along the road that actually goes up over the top of the Big Waterfall, offering more views over the park. (Go as far as you like, then return the way you came.) The giant mill perched at the top of the Big Waterfall was used to grind grains; this very poor part of Croatia was traditionally inhabited by farmers.

PLITVICE LAKES

The Science of Plitvice

Virtually every visitor to Plitvice eventually asks the same question: How did it happen? A geologist once explained to me that Plitvice is a perfect storm of unique geological, climatic, and biological features found in very few places on earth.

Plitvice's magic ingredient is calcium carbonate ($CaCO_3$), a mineral deposit from the limestone. This is the same thing that makes "hard water" hard. If you have hard water, you may get calcium deposits on your cold-water faucet. But these deposits build up only at the faucet, not inside the pipes. That's because when hard water is motionless (as it usually is in the pipes), it holds on to the calcium. But at the point where the water is subjected to pressure and movement—as it pours out of the faucet—it releases the calcium.

Plitvice works the same way. As water flows over the park's limestone formations, it dissolves the rock, and the water becomes supersaturated with calcium carbonate. When the water is still, it holds on to the mineral—which helps create the beautiful deep-blue color of the pools. But when the water speeds up and spills over the edges of the lakes, it releases carbon dioxide gas. Without the support of the carbon dioxide, the water can't hold on to the calcium carbonate, so it gets deposited on the lake bed and at the edges of the lakes. Eventually, these deposits build up to form a rock called travertine (the same composition as the original limestone, but formed in a different way). The travertine coating becomes thicker, and barriers—and

When you're done at the Big Waterfall, backtrack up to the main trail and continue on the boardwalks. You'll skirt the rim of Kaluđerovac Lake; then, after you pass another bank of waterfalls, a smaller trail branches off (on the left) toward **Šupljara ("Bottomless") Cave.** You can actually climb through this slippery cave all the way up to the trail overlooking the Lower Lakes (though it's not recommended). This unassuming cavern is a big draw. In the 1960s, several German and Italian "Spaghetti Westerns" were filmed at Plitvice and in other parts of Croatia (which, to European eyes, has terrain similar to the American West). The most famous, *Der Schatz im Silbersee (The Treasure in Silver Lake)*, was filmed here at Plitvice, and the treasure was hidden in this cave. The movie—complete with *Deutsch*-speaking "Native Americans"—is still a favorite in Germany, and popular theme tours bring German tourists to movie locations here in Croatia. (If you drive the roads near Plitvice, keep an eye out for strange, Native American-sounding names such as Winnetou—fictional characters from these beloved stories of the Old West, by the German writer Karl May.)

After Šupljara Cave, you'll stick to the east side of Gavanovac eventually dams and new waterfalls—are formed. The moss and grass serve as a natural foundation for the calcification. In other words, the stone hangs down like the foliage because the foliage guides the growth of the stone. Because of this ongoing process, Plitvice's landscape is always changing.

And why is the water so clear? For one thing, it comes directly from high-mountain runoff, giving it little opportunity to become polluted or muddy. And because the water calcifies everything it touches, it prevents the creation of mud—so the bottoms of the lakes are entirely stone. Also, a different mineral in the water, magnesium carbonate, both gives the water its special color (which, park rangers brag, changes with the direction of the sunshine) and makes it highly basic, preventing the growth of plant life (such as certain algae) that could cloud the water.

The park contains nearly 1,300 different species of plants. Wildlife found in the park include deer, wolves, wildcats, lynx, wild boar, voles, otters, 350 species of butterflies, 42 types of dragonflies, 21 species of bats, and more than 160 species of birds (including eagles, herons, owls, grouse, and storks). The lakes (and local menus) are full of trout, and you'll also see smaller, red-finned fish called *klen* ("chub" in English). Perhaps most importantly, Plitvice is home to about 40 or 50 brown bears—a species now extremely endangered in Europe. You'll see bears, the park's mascot, plastered all over the tourist literature (and one scary representative in the lobby of Hotel Jezero).

Lake, pass some picturesque terraces, then walk along the shore of Milanovac Lake, before crossing over one more time to the west, where you'll cut through a comparatively dull forest. You'll head up the paved road, branching off to the left (following the boat icon) to emerge at a pit-stop-perfect clearing with WCs, picnic tables, a souvenir shop, and a self-service restaurant. Here you can catch the shuttle boat across Lake Kozjak to the bottom of the Upper Lakes (usually every 30 minutes).

Lake Kozjak (Jezero Kozjak)

The park's biggest lake, Kozjak, connects the Lower and Upper Lakes. The 20-minute boat ride between Plitvice's two halves offers a great chance for a breather. You can hike between the lakes along the west side of Kozjak, but the scenery's not nearly as good as in the rest of the park.

Upper Lakes (Gornja Jezera)

Focus on the lower half of the Upper Lakes, where nearly all the exotic beauty is (between P-2 and Lake Galovac). You'll soon experience some of the most striking waterfalls in the whole park.

Enjoy the stroll, taking your time…and lots of photos.

Climbing up steeply on stepped boardwalks from the boat dock (following signs for *C*), you'll pass deep pools with fallen trees stretching along the bottom, illustrating just how magnificently clear the water here is. Soon you'll curl along the waterline of Gradinsko Lake. At the end of the lake, you'll come to the park's finest cascades, which tumble dramatically from Galovac into Gradinsko. You'll hear the waterfalls, then you'll see them, and finally you'll feel them, as the spray pelts you while you stroll the boardwalks (careful—cover your camera). First you'll pass by thundering **Veliki ("Big") Prštavac,** then hook up a tight-and-steep uphill bend—literally walking in the middle of a waterfall—to the nearly as spectacular **Mali ("Small") Prštavac.** Then you'll stroll along a whole wall of other waterfalls. Continuing up, you'll weave through another grand set of pools and falls, including views down on the pond of **Galovački Buk.** Walk along here, enjoying more ponds and cascades. Eventually you'll emerge at a fork in the path. Here, you have two options:

1. Make your hike a loop by turning left (following signs for the boat icon, *P-2,* and *E, H,* and *K*). This is the easiest and most enjoyable choice for most hikers. First, you'll walk down a stepped boardwalk with gurgling water underfoot. Then you'll circle back around the far (south) side of Gradinsko Lake and through a forest. Finally you'll pass a small picnic shelter, then walk down past one last set of falls to the P-2 boat dock, where you can take the boat back over to the hotels (P-1 stop).

2. Turn right (following the icon for the shuttle bus and *C*) to continue hiking up to the top of the Upper Lakes. I'd choose this option only if you have energy and time to burn. This route leads you somewhat pointlessly along the top of the best waterfalls (heard, but not seen), then loops you the long way around the Galovac Lake and eventually to the ST-3 bus stop. From here on up, the scenery is less stunning, and the waterfalls are fewer and farther between. At the top, you'll finish at shuttle bus stop ST-3 (with food stalls and a WC), where the bus zips you back to the entrances and hotels.

Nice work!

Sleeping in and near Plitvice

AT THE PARK

The most convenient way to sleep at Plitvice is to stay at the park's lodges, which are run by the same office (reservation tel. 053/751-015, www.np-plitvicka-jezera.hr, info@np-plitvicka-jezera.hr; reception numbers for each hotel listed below). Warning: Because of high volume in peak season, the booking office sometimes doesn't

Sleep Code

Abbreviations

(6 kn = about $1, €1 = about $1.40, country code: 385, area code: 053)
S = Single, **D** = Double/Twin, **T** = Triple, **Q** = Quad,
b = bathroom.

Price Rankings

$$$ **Higher Priced**—Most rooms €100 or more.

$$ **Moderately Priced**—Most rooms between €60-100.

$ **Lower Priced**—Most rooms €60 or less.

If I've listed three sets of rates, separated by slashes, the first
is for peak season (July-Aug), the second is for shoulder season (May-June and Sept-Oct), and the third is for off-season
(Nov-April). The dates for seasonal rates vary by hotel.

Unless otherwise noted, credit cards are accepted, Wi-Fi
is free, and breakfast is included, but the tourist tax (about 7
kn per person, per day) is not. While rates are listed in euros,
you'll pay in kunas. Everyone listed here speaks English (or
has a relative or neighbor who can help translate). Prices can
change without notice; verify the hotel's current rates online
or by email. For the best prices, always book directly with the
hotel.

respond to emails. Instead, to make a reservation, use the park's
website to book your room (look for the "Online booking" box).
In a pinch, try calling the booking office or the hotel directly (they
speak English). Note that none of these hotels has air-conditioning
(which is rarely needed in this climate), and all of them include
breakfast in their rates and have free Wi-Fi in the lobby.

$$$ Hotel Jezero is big and modern, with all the comfort—
and charm—of a Holiday Inn. It's well-situated right at the park
entrance and offers 200 rooms that feel newish, but generally have
at least one thing that's broken. Rooms facing the park have big
glass doors and balconies (Sb-€83/€76/€61, Db-€118/€108/€86;
elevator, reception tel. 053/751-400).

$$ Hotel Plitvice, a better value than Jezero, offers 57
rooms and mod, wide-open public spaces on two floors with no
elevator. For rooms, choose from economy (fine, older-feeling;
Sb-€72/€65/€50, Db-€96/€82/€70), standard (just a teeny bit bigger; Sb-€77/€70/€55, Db-€106/€96/€74), or superior (bigger still,
with a sitting area; Sb-€82/€75/€60, Db-€116/€106/€84, reception
tel. 053/751-100).

$$ Hotel Bellevue, dated and faded, feels like a Tito-era
leftover, with a musty orange-and-dark-brown color scheme in its
77 rooms. While not up to the standards of the other park hotels,
it's cheap (Sb-€55/€50/€40, Db-€74/€68/€54, no elevator, closed
Nov-March, reception tel. 053/751-700).

OUTSIDE THE PARK

While the park's lodges are the easiest choice for non-drivers, those with a car should consider sleeping at one of the many other options near the park. Prices here are likewise high, but the accommodations recommended below at least offer a bit more personality.

North of Plitvice

Dozens of mid-size hotels and small *sobe* line the highway for about 10 miles north of the national park. Options are so abundant here that spontaneous travelers could simply show up without reservations and take their pick. I've listed some favorites below. To reach Plitvička Sedra and Tina, turn left off the main road toward *Bihać*, after entering the town of Rakovica. The Degenija is right along the main road, a bit closer to Plitvice.

$$$ Hotel Degenija is a bit too pricey, but offers all of the big hotel comforts in a homier package than the park lodges. Its 20 modern, stylish rooms are in a building behind the bustling roadside restaurant (economy Db-€93/€84/€78, comfort Db-€110/€92/€85, superior Db-€115/€97/€90, bigger suites also available, air-con, elevator, Wi-Fi, Selište Drežničko 57a, tel. 047/782-143, www.hotel-degenija.com, rezervacije.degenija@email.t-com.hr). The busy restaurant is justifiably popular with tour groups (30-50-kn pastas and pizzas, 65-90-kn main courses, daily 7:00-23:00).

$$ Villa Plitvička Sedra may be the best value around. It's a homey yet modern-feeling, stone-and-wood complex that sits in a pleasant parklike setting, with tennis courts and a billiards pavilion, just off the main road. The 22 rooms have all the comforts you'll need for an overnight near the park (standard Db-€55/€40, larger superior Db with balcony-€70/€65, air-con, guest computer and Wi-Fi, Irinovac 149, tel. 047/784-401, www.restoran-sedra.hr, info@restoran-sedra.hr). The restaurant is also inviting (35-80-kn meals, open long hours daily).

$ House Tina is a neon-yellow farmhouse surrounded by fields (and a dozen other B&Bs) just off the main road. They have 11 rooms, including two nicely woody bungalows that sleep four each (Db-€60/€50/€45, bungalow-€96/€88/€80, studio apartment-€120/€100/€90, some with air-con, Wi-Fi, Grabovac 175, Rakovica, tel. 04/778-4197, mobile 098-963-4048, www.housetina.com, ljubica.vukovic@ka.t-com.hr).

In Rastoke: **$ Slovin Uniq Rastoke**—described later, under "Eating in and near Plitvice"—also rents two rooms above the restaurant (Db-€40-50/€30-40/€30-35, price depends on size), along with a cozy, primitive bungalow with modern features, such as air-conditioning, TV, and Wi-Fi (Db-€65/€50/€45).

South of Plitvice

$$$ Plitvice Mirić Inn, on the road just south of Plitvice's hotels and the village of Mukinje, offers the friendliest welcome in the region. The Mirić family (daughter Lili speaks great English) has 13 tidy, modern rooms. While a bit pricey, it comes with lots of good travel advice (Db-€105/€80, optional dinner-€20, air-con, Wi-Fi, Jezerce 18/1, mobile 099-214-2250 or 098-930-6508, www. plitvice-croatia.com, info@plitvice-croatia.com).

In Mukinje Village: Just south of the park is the village of Mukinje, which feels like a holdover from communist times: It's basically a planned workers' town, where crumbling concrete apartment blocks mingle with newer chalet-style homes renting rooms to travelers. Unfortunately, attitudes here seem trapped in communist times, too; most of the *sobe* I've inspected here are run by locals who are grouchy and indifferent, and the prices are too high. While you could drive into town and check a few options, you'll find a warmer welcome at some of the places listed earlier.

Eating in and near Plitvice

Local cuisine is hearty countryside grub, offering a nice, land-locked change of pace from the seafood-heavy and Italian-flavored menus of most of Croatia's tourist towns. You'll see mushroom soups, soft spreadable cheeses, and grilled trout pulled fresh from the lakes. Restaurants here are functional—don't expect high cuisine.

AT THE PARK

The park runs a variety of equally uninspired restaurants, with institutional food and ambience. If you're staying at the hotels, you

have the option of paying for half-board with your room (lunch or dinner, 90 kn each). The half-board option is worth doing if you're here for dinner, but don't lock yourself in for lunch—you'll want more flexibility as you explore Plitvice (excellent picnic spots and decent food stands abound inside the park). Most people opting for half-board dine at the restaurants inside **Hotel Jezero** and **Hotel Plitvice,** but you can also use the voucher at other park eateries (you'll pay the difference if the bill is more). **Restaurant Poljana,** behind Hotel Bellevue, has the same park-lodge atmosphere in both of its sections: cheap, self-service cafeteria (30-45-kn meals) and sit-down "national restaurant" with open wood-fired grill (65-110-kn meals);

both parts have dreary communist decor. All of these eateries are open long hours daily.

For **picnic** fixings, there's a small grocery store at Entrance 1 and another one with a larger selection across road D-1 (use the pedestrian overpass). At the P-3 boat dock, you can buy grilled meat and drinks. Friendly old ladies sell homemade goodies (such as strudel and hunks of cheese) throughout the park, including at Entrance 1.

OUTSIDE THE PARK

Many truck stop-type restaurants, mostly catering to tour buses (and their drivers, who dine like kings in exchange for bringing in so much business) line the highway for miles in both directions from Plitvice. Most are unexciting, but two good options are at the recommended **Hotel Degenija** and **Villa Plitvička Sedra** (for details, see "Sleeping in and near Plitvice," earlier). Many country-side accommodations also have a half-board option; ask about this when you book.

Eating in Bosnia: Adventurous drivers may want to make a short drive across the border, to the town of Bihać (BEE-hahch), Bosnia-Herzegovina, for a bite. This small Bosnian city is about a 30-minute drive from the national park (be sure to bring your passport and the "green card" to take your rental car over the border). If this is your only chance to dip into Bosnia, and you have an evening to kill, it can be a fun option. For more on Bosnian food, see page 1140.

A MEMORABLE MEAL SURROUNDED BY WATERFALLS 30 MINUTES NORTH OF PLITVICE

On the main highway between Zagreb and Plitvice, about 30 minutes before the national park, you'll pass above, then through, the striking town of Slunj (pronounced "sloon"), which is surrounded by its own little "mini-Plitvice" ecosystem of waterfalls. This can be an enjoyable pit stop, whether or not you eat here. The lower part of the town—buried deep amid all those cascades—is the village of Rastoke (meaning roughly "beautiful water"), which has its share of touristy restaurants. The most elaborate is the complex of **Slovin Unique Rastoke,** where you can explore a series of canals, waterfalls, canyons, and viewpoints. The grounds also have an old mill, a small "ethno collection" (traditional local furniture, tools, and so on), and a trail down to the Korona River canyon. While you can pay 25 kn to explore (they'll give you a map), it's free for those who dine at their restaurant, **Pod Rastočkim Krovom** ("Under Rastoke's Roof"). They specialize in trout—you can see their ponds out back—and also have a wide range of other local dishes, including some prepared with grains ground by traditional mills (20-35-kn soups and pastas, 60-80-kn main courses, open long hours daily, Rastoke 25B, mobile 099-215-0907, www.slunj-rastoke.com). Even though the whole complex feels a bit hokey and tour group-oriented (just like everything around Plitvice), it comes with a chance to see some pretty waterfalls.

Getting There: Approaching the town of Slunj from the north, you'll see Rastoke filling the valley below. After crossing the first bridge, turn right at the *Rastoke* sign, then park next to—and walk over—the dilapidated old concrete bridge; finally, you turn right and walk down the hill to Slovin Unique Rastoke.

Plitvice Connections

To reach the park, see "Getting to Plitvice," earlier in this chapter. Moving on from Plitvice is trickier. **Buses** pass by the park in each direction—northbound (to **Zagreb**, 2-2.5 hours) and southbound (to coastal destinations such as **Split**, 4-6 hours).

The park lodge reception desk should have a printout of the specific bus schedule, or you can check at www.autobusni-kolodvor.com (look for "Plitvička Jezera").

In summer, the best choice is the **Prijevoz Knežević express bus** (see the sidebar); these buses are designed to zip Plitvice hikers to major destinations, including Zagreb, Zadar, and Split. (In contrast, the regular buses take longer, make several stops en route, and can fill up before even reaching the park.) You can buy tickets for express buses only at the little sales kiosks next to the bus stops at both Plitvice entrances (daily 8:00-17:00, mobile 098-650-757, www.prijevoz-knezevic.hr); for other buses, buy your ticket on board.

There is no bus station at the park—just a low-profile *Plitvice Centar* bus stop shelter. To reach it from the park, go out to the main road from either Hotel Jezero or Hotel Plitvice, then turn right; the bus stops are just after the pedestrian overpass. The one on the hotel side of the road is for buses headed for the coast (southbound); the stop on the opposite side is for Zagreb (northbound). Try to carefully confirm the bus schedule with the park or hotel staff, then head out to the bus stop and wave down the bus. (It's easy to confuse public buses with private tour buses, so don't panic if a bus doesn't stop for you—look for a bus with your final destination marked in the windshield.)

But here's the catch: If the bus is full, they won't stop at Plitvice to pick you up. This is most common on days when the buses are jammed with people headed to or from the coast. For example, on Fridays—when everyone is going from Zagreb to

Daily Express Buses in Peak Season

These buses—operated by a local company, Prijevoz Knežević (www.prijevoz-knezevic.hr), help travelers easily connect Plitvice with major Croatian destinations: Zagreb, Split, Skradin, and Zadar. As this is the 2014 schedule, use it only as a guideline; be sure to confirm times locally or online. Additional buses may be added in the future.

Zagreb to Plitvice		Plitvice to Zagreb	
Depart Zagreb	8:15*	Depart Plitvice	16:15**
Arrive Plitvice	10:20	Arrive Zagreb	18:20
*Runs late June through early Sept		**Runs late June through mid-Oct	

Split to Plitvice			Plitvice to Split		
Depart Split	10:15*	15:30**	Depart Plitvice	9:30*	16:30**
Skradin (Krka National Park)	11:35	17:00	Zadar	11:15	18:45
Zadar	13:00	18:00	Skradin (Krka National Park)	12:20	19:20
Arrive Plitvice	14:45	19:45	Arrive Split	13:50	20:50
*July and Aug only			*Late June through late Sept		
**Late June through late Sept			**July and Aug only		

Split—you're unlikely to have any luck catching a southbound bus at Plitvice after 12:00, as they tend to be full. Similarly, on Sunday afternoons, northbound buses are often full. In general, don't plan on taking the last bus of the day. One advantage of the Prijevoz Knežević express buses, mentioned above, is that they originate at Plitvice, so they don't arrive full.

While there's a chance you'll miss a bus and have to wait for the next one, bus travel from Plitvice usually works fine...if you're patient.

ROUTE TIPS FOR DRIVERS

Plitvice's biggest disadvantage is that it's an hour away from the handy A-1 expressway that connects northern Croatia to the Dalmatian Coast. You have three ways to access this expressway from Plitvice, depending on which direction you're heading.

Going North: If you're heading north (to Zagreb or Slovenia), get on the expressway at **Karlovac:** From Plitvice, drive about one hour north on D-1 to the town of Karlovac, where you can access A-1 northbound. Alternatively, you can take A-1 southbound to A-6, which leads west to Rijeka, Opatija, and Istria (though this route is more boring and only slightly faster than the route via Otočac, next).

Going to Central Croatia: If you're going to central destinations on the coast, such as Istria (Rovinj or Pula), get on the expressway at **Otočac.** From Plitvice, go south on D-1, then turn west on road #52 to the town of Otočac (about an hour through the mountains from Plitvice to Otočac). After Otočac, you can get on A-1 (north to Zagreb, south to the Dalmatian Coast); or continue west and twist down the mountain road to the seaside town of Senj, on the main coastal road of the Kvarner Gulf. From Senj, it's about an hour north along the coast to Rijeka, then on to Istria.

During the recent war, the front line between the Croats and Serbs ran just east of **Otočac** (OH-toh-chawts), and a few bullet holes still mar the town's facades. (Watch for minefield warning signs just east of Otočac, but don't let them make you too nervous: It's safe to drive here, but not necessarily safe to get out of your car and wander through the fields.) Today Otočac is putting itself back together, and it's a fine place to drop into a café for a coffee, or pick up some produce at the outdoor market. The Catholic church in the center of town, destroyed in the war but now rebuilt, displays its damaged church bells in a memorial out back. The crucifix nearby is made of old artillery shells.

Also in the churchyard are big white blocks, each one honoring a Croatian hero; notice that the top of each one is carved a character from Glagolitic script (the ancient Croatian alphabet). Just up the main street, you'll come to a fine, manicured park, dominated by a huge monument honoring the lives lost in the fight to create a free Croatian nation. It reads: "In order to make real the vision of a Croatian homeland, they laid upon the altar their dreams, their hopes, and their lives." Noticing the giant block splintering into four pieces, it's easy to imagine how this might illustrate the splitting up of the Yugoslav state...and to wonder how local Serbs feel about this relatively new monument.

At the far end of the park is the Orthodox church. Otočac used to be about one-third Serbian, but the Serbs were forced out during the war, and this church fell into disrepair. But, as Otočac and Croatia show signs of healing, about two dozen Serbs have returned to town and reopened their church (for more on the Serbian Orthodox Church, see page 922).

Going South: If you're heading south (to Split and the rest of Dalmatia) from Plitvice, catch the expressway at **Gornja Ploča.** Drive south from Plitvice on D-1, through Korenica, Pećane, and Udbina, then follow signs for the A-1 expressway (and *Lovinac*) via Kurjak to the Gornja Ploča on-ramp. Once on A-1, you'll twist south through the giant Sveti Rok tunnel to Dalmatia.

BOSNIA-HERZEGOVINA

Bosna i Hercegovina

MOSTAR

The mid-1990s weren't kind to Bosnia-Herzegovina: War. Destruction. Genocide. But apart from the tragic way it separated from Yugoslavia, the country has long been—and remains—a remarkable place, with ruggedly beautiful terrain, a unique mix of cultures and faiths, kind and welcoming people who pride themselves on their hospitality, and some of the most captivating sightseeing in southeastern Europe.

There's so much to see in this country. But for the scope of this book, I've selected just one destination: Mostar (MOH-star). Safe, stable, and within easy reach of the Dalmatian Coast, Mostar is worth considering as a detour—both geographical and cultural—from the Croatian mainstream. In Mostar's cobbled Old Town, you can poke into several mosques, tour old-fashioned Turkish-style houses, shop your way through a bazaar of souvenir stands, and hear the call to prayer echoing across the rooftops. For me, it's the single best side-trip from Dubrovnik.

Mostar encapsulates the best and the worst of the former Yugoslavia. During the Tito years, its residents enjoyed an idyllic mingling of cultures—Catholic Croats, Orthodox Serbs, and Muslim Bosniaks living together in harmony, their differences spanned by an Old Bridge that epitomized an optimistic vision of a Yugoslavia where ethnicity didn't matter. But then, as the country unraveled in the early 1990s, Mostar was gripped by a

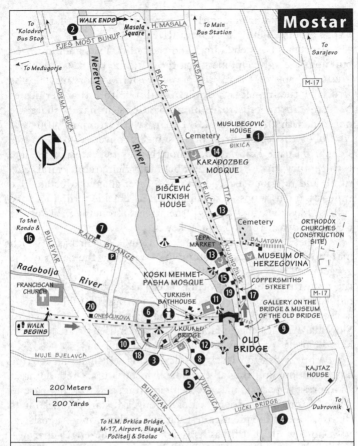

1 Muslibegović House
2 Hotel Bristol
3 Hotel Kriva Ćuprija
4 Hotel Kriva Ćuprija II
5 Villa Anri
6 Motel Emen
7 Villa Fortuna
8 Pansion Čardak & Pansion Nur
9 B&B Shangri La
10 Villa Botticelli
11 Bridge View Eateries

12 Restoran Hindin Han
13 Nacionalni Restoran Aščinica Balkan (2)
14 Saray Restaurant
15 Urban Grill
16 To Pivnica Štefanijino Šetalište Brewpub
17 Ali Baba Nightclub
18 Oscar Nightclub
19 Fortuna Tours
20 Future Synagogue Site

gory three-way war among those same peoples...and that famous bridge crumbled into the Neretva River.

Mostar is still rebuilding, and the bullet holes and destroyed buildings are ugly reminders that the last time you saw this place, it was probably on the nightly news. Western visitors may also be struck by the immediacy of the Muslim culture that permeates Mostar—at this crossroads of civilizations, minarets share the horizon with church steeples. During the Ottomans' 400-year control of this region, many Slavic subjects converted to Islam (see sidebar on page 1126). And, although they retreated in the late 19th century, the Ottomans left behind a rich architectural, cultural, and religious legacy that has forever shaped Mostar. Five times each day, loudspeakers on minarets crackle to life, and the call to prayer warbles through the streets. In many parts of the city, you'd swear you were in Turkey.

If these images intrigue you, read on—Mostar has so much more to offer. Its setting is stunning: straddling the banks of the gorgeous Neretva River, with tributaries and waterfalls carving their way through the rocky landscape. The sightseeing—mosques, old Turkish-style houses, and that spine-tingling Old Bridge—is more engaging than much of what you'll find in Croatia or Slovenia. And it's cheap: Hotels, food, and museums are less than half the prices you'll pay in Dubrovnik or Ljubljana.

While a visit to Mostar was depressing not that long ago, the city gets more uplifting all the time: Mostarians are rebuilding at an impressive pace, tentatively re-integrating, and working hard to make Mostar tourist-friendly. Before long, Mostar will reclaim its status as one of the premier destinations in the former Yugoslavia. Visit now, while it still has its rough-around-the-edges charm—you'll have seen it before it really took off.

PLANNING YOUR TIME

Because of its cultural hairiness, a detour into Bosnia-Herzegovina feels like a real departure from a Dalmatian vacation. And yet Mostar is easier to reach from Dubrovnik or Split than many popular Dalmatian islands (it's within a three-hour drive or bus ride from either city).

The vast majority of tourists in Mostar are day-trippers from the coast, which means the Old Town is packed at midday, but empty in the morning and evening. You can get a good feel for Mostar in just a few hours, but a full day—and, ideally, an overnight—gives you time to linger and ponder. My self-guided walk provides a framework for a visit of any duration. With extra time, be sure to venture to the western part of the city, which most tourists miss.

You have three basic options for getting here: take a package tour from Dalmatia; rent a car for a one-day side-trip into Mostar; or (my favorite) spend the night here en route between Croatian destinations. To work a Mostar overnight into your itinerary, consider a round-trip plan that takes you south along the coast, then back north via Bosnia-Herzegovina (for example, Split-Korčula-Dubrovnik-Mostar-back to Split).

GETTING TO MOSTAR

By Car: Coming with your own car gives you maximum flexibility (for detailed route information, see "Route Tips for Drivers" on page 1143). If you do plan to drive here, let your car-rental company know in advance, to ensure you have the appropriate paperwork for crossing the border. If you're not up for driving yourself, consider splurging on a **driver** to bring you here (for drivers based in Dubrovnik, see page 895; for a Mostar-based driver, see page 1115). Drivers may suggest several detours en route. Do your homework to know which ones interest you (for example, Međugorje isn't worth the extra time for most visitors), and don't hesitate to say you want to just max out on time in Mostar itself.

By Bus: Especially if you're spending the night in Mostar, public buses work well to connect Mostar with destinations on the Dalmatian Coast (particularly Split and Dubrovnik). For details, see "Mostar Connections" on page 1142.

By Package Tour: Taking a package excursion from a Dalmatian resort town seems like an efficient way to visit Mostar. Unfortunately, in reality it can be less rewarding than doing it on your own—count on lots of hours on a crowded bus, listening to a lackluster, multilingual tour guide reading from a script, and relatively little time in the destinations themselves. But if you just want a quick one-day look at these places, an excursion can be a necessary evil. These all-day tours are sold from Split, Hvar, Korčula, Dubrovnik, and other Croatian coastal destinations for about €50-60. The best tours focus almost entirely on Mostar (it still won't be enough time); avoid tours that include a pointless boat trip on the Neretva River or time in Međugorje. Those that add a quick visit to the worthwhile town of Počitelj are a better deal. Ask for details at any travel agency in Dalmatia.

Orientation to Mostar

Mostar—a mid-sized city with around 130,000 people—is situated in a basin surrounded by mountains and split down the middle by the emerald-green Neretva River. Bosniaks live mostly on the east side of the river (plus a strip on the west bank), Croats in the modern sprawl to the west. The populations are beginning to mix again, albeit with tentative baby steps. Most of the

Bosnia-Herzegovina Almanac

Official Name: Bosna i Hercegovina (abbreviated "BiH"); the *i* means "and"—Bosnia and Herzegovina (the country's two regions). For simplicity, I generally call the whole country "Bosnia" in this book. "Bosna" (literally "running water") is the name of a major river here, while the tongue-twisting name "Herzegovina" (hert-seh-GOH-vee-nah) comes from the German word for "dukedom" (Herzog means "duke").

Snapshot History: Bosnia-Herzegovina's early history is similar to the rest of the region: Illyrians, Romans, and Slavs (oh, my!). In the late 15th century, Turkish rulers from the Ottoman Empire began a 400-year domination of the country. Many of the Ottomans' subjects converted to Islam, and their descendants remain Muslims today. Bosnia-Herzegovina became part of the Austro-Hungarian Empire in 1878, then Yugoslavia after World War I, until it declared independence in the spring of 1992. The bloody war that ensued came to an end in 1995. (For details, see "Understanding Yugoslavia" on page 1347.)

Population: About 3.9 million. (There were about 100,000 identified casualties of the recent war, but many estimates of total casualties are double that number.) Someone who lives in Bosnia-Herzegovina, regardless of ethnicity, is called a "Bosnian." A southern Slav who practices Islam is called a "Bosniak." Today, about half of all Bosnians are Bosniaks (Muslims), a little more than a third are Orthodox Serbs, and about 15 percent are Catholic Croats.

Political Divisions: As a part of the Dayton Peace Accords that ended the conflict here in 1995, the nation is divided into three separate regions: the Federation of Bosnia and Herzegovina (FBiH, shared by Bosniaks and Croats, very roughly in the western and central parts of the country), the Republika Srpska (RS, dominated by Serbs, generally to the north and east), and the Brčko District (BD, a tiny corner of the country, with a mix of the ethnicities). For the most part, each of the three native ethnic groups stay in "their" part of this divided country, but tourists can move freely between them.

Language: Technically, Bosnia-Herzegovina has three languages—Bosnian, Serbian, and Croatian. But all three are mutually intelligible dialects of what was until recently considered a single language: Serbo-Croatian. Bosniaks and Croats use basically the same Roman alphabet we do, while Serbs generally use the Cyrillic alphabet. You'll see both alphabets on currency and other official documents. Many people also speak English.

Area: 19,741 square miles (about the size of West Virginia). In both size and population, Bosnia is comparable to Croatia.

Geography: Bosnia and Herzegovina are two distinct regions that share the same mountainous country. Bosnia constitutes the majority of the country (in the north, with a continental climate), while Herzegovina is the southern tip (about a fifth of the total area, with a hotter Mediterranean climate). The nation's capital, Sarajevo, has an estimated 310,000 people, Mostar is Herzegovina's biggest city (with approximately 130,000 people) and unofficial capital.

Red Tape: To enter Bosnia-Herzegovina, Americans and Canadians need only a passport (no visa required).

Economy: The country's economy has struggled since the war—the per capita GDP is just $8,400, and the official unemployment rate is around 43 percent.

Currency: The official currency is the Convertible Mark (Konvertibilna Marka, abbreviated KM locally, BAM internationally). The official exchange rate is $1 = about 1.50 KM. But merchants are usually willing to take euros, and they'll often accept Croatian kunas, roughly converting prices with a simple formula: **2 KM = €1 = 8 kn**

Telephones: Bosnia-Herzegovina's country code is 387. If calling from another country, first dial the international access code (00 in Europe, 011 in the US), then 387, then the area code (minus the initial zero), then the number.

Flag: The flag of Bosnia-Herzegovina is a blue field with a yellow triangle along the top edge. The three points of the triangle represent Bosnia-Herzegovina's three peoples (Bosniaks, Croats, Serbs), and the triangle itself resembles the physical shape of the country. A row of white stars underscores the longest side of the triangle. These stars—and the yellow-and-blue color scheme—echo the flag of the European Union (a nod to the EU's efforts to bring peace to the region). Though this compromise flag sounds like a nice idea, almost no Bosnian embraces it as his or her own; each group has its own unofficial but highly prized symbols and flags (such as the fleur-de-lis for the Bosniaks, the red-and-white checkerboard shield for the Croats, and the cross with the four C's for the Serbs)—many of which offend the other groups.

sights are in the Bosniak zone, but visitors move freely through-out the city, and most don't even notice the division. The cobbled, Turkish-feeling Old Town (called the "Stari Grad" or—borrowing a Turkish term—the "Stara Čaršija") surrounds the town's center-piece, the Old Bridge.

The skyline is pierced by the minarets of various mosques, but none is as big as the two major Catholic (Croat) symbols in town, both erected since the recent war: the giant white cross on the hilltop (marking the place from where Croat forces shelled the Bosniak side of the river, including the Old Bridge); and the enor-mous (almost 100-foot-tall) bell tower of the Franciscan Church of Sts. Peter and Paul. A monumental Orthodox cathedral on the hillside across the river was destroyed in the war, but is now being rebuilt.

A note about safety: Mostar is as safe as any city its size, but it doesn't always *feel* safe. You'll see bombed-out buildings every-where, even in the core of the city. Some are marked with *Warning! Dangerous Ruin* signs, but for safety's sake, never wander into any building that appears damaged or deserted. In terms of petty theft, the Old Town has as many pickpockets as any tourist zone in Europe: Watch your valuables, especially on the Old Bridge.

TOURIST INFORMATION

The practically worthless TI shares a building with a tour office, but it does give out a free town map and a few other brochures on Mostar and Herzegovina (sporadic hours, generally May-Oct daily 9:00-12:00, maybe later in busy times, likely closed Nov-April, a block from the Old Bridge at Rade Bitange 5, tel. 036/580-275, www.turizam.mostar.ba).

ARRIVAL IN MOSTAR

By Bus or Train: The **main bus station** (where most buses arrive in town) sits next to the giant but mostly deserted **train station,** north of the Old Town on the east side of the river. At the bus sta-tion, you'll find ticket windows and a left-luggage counter (2 KM/bag) in the Autoprevoz lobby facing the bus stalls. You can check schedules and buy tickets in this office for most buses *except* the many connections operated by Globtour, whose office is nearby (exit Autoprevoz, turn left, and walk to the end of the bus-station area). Because these two companies don't cooperate well, you may have to check with both to get the complete schedule. To find your way to the town center, walk through the bus stalls and parking lot and turn left at the big road, which leads you to the Old Town area in about 15 minutes. A taxi into town costs about 7-10 KM.

If you're arriving by bus, it's possible (though unlikely) that you'll arrive at Mostar's makeshift secondary bus station, called

"Kolodvor," on the west/Croat side of town. From here, it's a dreary 20-minute walk into town: Turn right out of the bus station area, turn left down the busy Dubrovačka street, and head straight to the river (which you can follow south into the Old Town).

For details on both stations, see "Mostar Connections," later.

By Car: For tips on driving to Mostar from the Dalmatian Coast, see page 1143.

HELPFUL HINTS

Local Cash: Need Convertible Marks? The most convenient ATM in town is to the left of Fortuna Tours' door, right at the top of Coppersmiths' Street (but on a short visit, you can generally skip a trip to the ATM, as most vendors here also accept Croatian kunas and euros).

Travel Agency: The handy **Fortuna Tours** travel agency, right in the heart of the Old Town (at the top of Coppersmiths' Street), sells all the tourist stuff, can book a local guide or arrange a transfer, and answers basic questions (long hours daily, Kujundžiluk 2, tel. 036/551-887, main office tel. 036/552-197, www.fortuna.ba, headoffice@fortuna.ba).

Local Guides: Hiring a guide is an excellent investment to help you understand Mostar. I've enjoyed working with **Alma Elezović,** a warm-hearted Bosniak who loves sharing her city and her wartime stories with visitors (€20/person, up to €70/group for 2-3-hour tour, mobile 061-467-699, http://almasguidedtours.blogspot.com, aelezovic@gmail.com). If Alma is busy, she may send you with her son **Jaz** (pronounced "yahz"), a well-trained guide who speaks perfect English and offers a younger generation's perspective. Other companies around town can arrange for a local guide at extremely reasonable prices (2-hour tour—€30/2 people, €40/4 people, includes entry to mosque and/or Turkish house); try **Fortuna Tours,** listed previously.

Local Driver: Ermin Elezović, husband of local guide Alma (see above), is a gregarious, English-speaking driver who enjoys taking visitors on day trips from Mostar. You can also hire him for a transfer between Mostar and destinations anywhere in Croatia (prices for a van for up to 6 people: €120 for one-way transfer to Sarajevo, Split, or Dubrovnik with a few brief sightseeing stops on the way; €240 for an all-day round-trip from Mostar to Sarajevo, Split, or Dubrovnik; also available for longer trips—contact Ermin and Alma for help planning out a multiday itinerary; mobile 061-908-597, elezovicermin@gmail.com).

Updates to This Book: For updates to this book, check www.ricksteves.com/update.

Sights in Mostar

CENTRAL MOSTAR

Mostar's major sights line up along a handy L-shaped axis. I've laced them together as an enjoyable orientation walk: From the Franciscan Church, you'll walk straight until you cross the Old Bridge. Then you'll turn left and walk basically straight (with a couple of detours) to the big square at the far end of town. This walk is designed to help you see both the main tourist zones and the parts of workaday Mostar that many visitors miss.

• *Begin at the...*

▲Franciscan Church of Sts. Peter and Paul

In a town of competing religious architectural exclamation points, this spire is the tallest. The church, which adjoins a working Franciscan monastery, was built in 1997, after the fighting subsided (the same year the big cross on the hill was erected). The tower, which looks at first glance like a minaret on steroids, is actually modeled after typical Croatian/Venetian campanile bell towers. Step inside to see the cavernous interior, still not fully decorated. (Sunday Mass here is an inspiration.)

• *The church fronts the busy boulevard called...*

▲Bulevar

"The Boulevard" was once the modern main drag of Mostar. In the early 1990s, this city of Bosniaks, Croats, and Serbs began to

fracture under the pressure of politicians' propaganda. In October of 1991, Bosnia-Herzegovina—following Croatia's and Slovenia's example, but without the blessing of its large Serb minority—began a process of splitting from Yugoslavia. Soon after, the Serb-dominated Yugoslav People's Army invaded. Mostar's Bosniaks and Croats joined forces to battle the Serbs and succeeded in claiming the city as their own, forcing out the Serb residents.

But even as they fended off the final, distant bombardments of Serb forces, Mostar's Bosniaks (Muslims) and Croats (Catholics) began to squabble. Neighbors, friends, and even relatives took up arms against one another. As fighting raged between the Croat and Bosniak forces, this street became the front line—and virtually all of its buildings were destroyed. Then as now, the area to the east of here (toward the river) was held by Bosniaks, while the western part of town was Croat territory.

While many of the buildings along here have been rebuilt, some damage is still evident. Stroll a bit, imagining the hell of a split community at war. Mortar craters in the asphalt leave poignant scars. During those dark war years, the Croats on the hill above laid siege to the Bosniaks on the other side, cutting off electricity, blocking roads, and blaring Croatian rabble-rousing pop music and Tokyo Rose-type propaganda speeches from loudspeakers. Through '93 and '94, when the Bosniaks dared to go out, they sprinted past exposed places, for fear of being picked off by a sniper. Local Bosniaks explain, "Night was time to live" (in black clothes). When people were killed along this street, their corpses were sometimes left here for months, because it wasn't safe to retrieve the bodies. Tens of thousands fled. Scandinavian countries were the first to open their doors, but many Bosnians ended up elsewhere in Europe, the US, and Canada.

The stories are shocking, and it's difficult to see the war impartially. But looking back on this complicated war, I try not to broadly cast one side as the "aggressors" and another as the "victims." Bosniaks were victimized in Mostar, just as Croats were victimized during the siege of Dubrovnik (explained on page 904). And, as the remains of a destroyed Orthodox cathedral on the hillside above Mostar (not quite visible from here) attest, Serbs also took their turn as victims. Every conflict has many sides, and it's the civilians who often pay the highest toll—no matter their affiliation.

Cross the boulevard and head down Onešćukova street. A few steps down on the left, the vacant lot with the menorah-ornamented metal fence will someday be the **Mostar Synagogue**. While the town's Jewish population has dwindled to a handful of families since World War II, many Jews courageously served as aid workers and intermediaries when Croats and Bosniaks were killing each other. In recognition of their loving help, the community of Mostar gave them this land for a new synagogue.

• *Continue past the synagogue site, entering the Old Town and following the canyon of the...*

Radobolja River Valley

Cross the small river called Radobolja, which winds over waterfalls and several mills on its way to join the Neretva, and enter the city's cobbled historic core (keeping the river on your right). As you step upon the smooth, ankle-twisting river stones, you suddenly become immersed in the Turkish heritage of Mostar. Around you are several fine examples of Mostar's traditional heavy limestone-shingled roofs. From the arrival of the Ottomans all the way through the end of World War II, Mostar had fewer than 15,000 residents—this compact central zone was pretty much all there was to the city. It wasn't until the Tito years that it became industrialized and grew like crazy. As you explore, survey the atmospheric eateries clinging to the walls of the canyon—and choose one for a meal or drink later in the day (I've noted a couple under "Eating in Mostar," later).

Walk straight ahead until you reach a square viewpoint platform on your right. It's across from a charming little mosque and above the stream (you may have to squeeze between souvenir stands to get there). The mosque is one of 10 in town. Before the recent war, there were 36, and before World War II, there were even more (many of those damaged or destroyed in World War II were never repaired or replaced, since Tito's communist Yugoslavia discouraged religion). But the recent war inspired Muslims to finally rebuild. Each of the town's reconstructed mosques was financed by a Muslim nation or organization (this one was a gift from an international association for the protection of Islamic heritage). Some critics (read: Croats) allege that these foreign Muslim influences—which generally interpret their faith more strictly than the typically progressive and laid-back Bosniaks—are threatening to flood the country with a rising tide of Islamic fundamentalism.

• *Look upriver. Spanning the river below the mosque (partly obscured by trees) is the...*

▲Crooked Bridge (Kriva Ćuprija)

This miniature Old Bridge was built nearly a decade before its more famous sibling, supposedly to practice for the real deal. Damaged—but not destroyed—during the war, the original bridge was swept away several years later by floods. The bridge you see today is a reconstruction.

• *Continue on the same street deeper into the city center. After a few steps, a street to the left (worth a short detour) leads to the TI, then to a copper-domed hammam (Turkish bathhouse), which was destroyed in World War II and only recently rebuilt. A happening nightlife and restaurant scene tumbles downhill toward the river from here, offering spectacular views of the Old Bridge.*

Back on the main drag, continue along the shopping zone, past several market stalls, to the focal point of town, the...

▲▲▲Old Bridge (Stari Most)

One of the most evocative sights in the former Yugoslavia, this iconic bridge confidently spanned the Neretva River for more

than four centuries. Mostarians of all faiths love the bridge and speak of "him" as an old friend. Traditionally considered the point where East meets West, the Old Bridge is as symbolic as it is beautiful. Dramatically arched and flanked by two boxy towers, the bridge is stirring—even if you don't know its history.

Before the Old Bridge, the Neretva was spanned only by a rickety suspension bridge, guarded by *mostari* ("watchers of the bridge"), who gave the city its name. Commissioned in 1557 by the Ottoman Sultan Süleyman the Magnificent, and completed just nine years later, the Old Bridge was a technological marvel for its time..."the longest single-span stone arch on the planet." (In other words, it's the granddaddy of the Rialto Bridge in Venice.) Because of its graceful keystone design—and the fact that there are empty spaces inside the structure—it's much lighter than it appears. And yet, nearly 400 years after it was built, the bridge was still sturdy enough to support the weight of the Nazi tanks that rolled in to occupy Mostar. Over the centuries, it became the symbol of the town and region—a metaphor in stone for the way the diverse faiths and cultures here were able to bridge the gaps that divided them.

All of that drastically changed in the early 1990s. Beginning in May of 1993, as the city became engulfed in war, the Old Bridge frequently got caught in the crossfire. Old tires were slung over its sides to absorb some of the impact from nearby artillery and shrapnel. In November of 1993, Croats began shelling the bridge from the top of the mountain (where the cross is now—you can just see its tip peeking over the hill from the top of the bridge). The bridge took several direct hits on November 8; on November 9, another shell caused the venerable Old Bridge to lurch, then tumble in pieces into the river. The mortar inside, which contained pink bauxite, turned the water red as it fell in. Locals said that their old friend was bleeding.

The decision to destroy the bridge was partly strategic—to cut off a Bosniak-controlled strip on the west bank from Bosniak forces on the east. (News footage from the time shows Bosniak soldiers scurrying back and forth over the bridge.) But there can be no doubt that, like the Yugoslav Army's siege of Dubrovnik, the attack was also partly symbolic: the destruction of a bridge representing the city's Muslim legacy.

The War in Bosnia-Herzegovina

As Yugoslavia began to break apart, during the summer of 1991, Bosnia-Herzegovina was suspiciously quiet. Even optimists knew it couldn't last. Bosnia-Herzegovina was the most ethnically diverse place in the Balkans, a microcosm of Yugoslavia's warring groups: Muslim Bosniaks (43 percent of the population), Serbs (31 percent), and Croats (17 percent).

Bosnia-Herzegovina's president, Alija Izetbegović, began to pursue independence in the fall of 1991. While most Bosnian Croats and virtually all Bosniaks supported this move, Bosnia's substantial Serb minority resisted it. The Serbs within Bosnia-Herzegovina created their own "state," called the Republic of the Serb People of Bosnia-Herzegovina. Its president, Radovan Karadžić, enjoyed the semisecret military support of Slobodan Milošević and the Yugoslav People's Army. The stage was set for a bloody secession.

In the spring of 1992, as a referendum on Bosnian independence loomed, the Serbs began a campaign of ethnic cleansing against Bosniaks and Croats residing in eastern Bosnia. The well-orchestrated Karadžić forces secretly notified Serb residents to evacuate before they invaded each mixed-ethnicity town, then encircled the remaining Bosniaks and Croats with heavy artillery and sniper fire in an almost medieval-style siege. Many people were executed on the spot, while others were arrested and taken to concentration camps. Survivors were forced to leave the towns their families had lived in for centuries.

It was during this initial wave of Bosnian Serb ethnic cleansing—orchestrated by Radovan Karadžić and his generals—that the world began to hear tales as horrifying as anything you can imagine. Militia units would enter a town and indiscriminately kill anyone they saw: civilian men, women, and children. Soldiers rounded up families, then forced parents to watch as they slit the throats of their children—and then the parents were killed, too. Perhaps most despicable was the establishment of so-called "rape camps": concentration camps where mostly Bosniak women were imprisoned and systematically raped by Serb soldiers. Most of these atrocities were not militarily strategic, but intentionally gruesome and violent. The Bosnian Serb leadership sought not only to remove people from "their" land, but to do so in such a heinous way to ensure that the various groups could never again tolerate living together. These are the stories that turned "Balkans" into a dirty word.

Bosnia-Herzegovina was torn apart. Even the many mixed families were forced to choose sides. If you had a Serb mother and a Croat father, you were expected to pick one ethnicity or the other—and your brother might choose the opposite. The majority of people, who did not want this war and couldn't comprehend why it was happening, now faced the excruciating realization that their neighbors and friends were responsible for looting and burning their houses, or worse.

Even as the Serbs and Croats fought brutally in the streets, their leaders—Slobodan Milošević and Franjo Tuđman, respectively—were secretly meeting to carve up Bosnia into Serb and Croat sectors, at the Bosniaks' expense (the so-called Karađorđevo Agreement). Bosniak President Alija Izetbegović, completely left out of the conversation, desperately pleaded with the international community to support the peaceful secession of a free Bosnian state.

At first, the Bosniaks and Croats teamed up to fend off the Serbs. But even before the first wave of fighting had subsided, Croats and Bosniaks turned their guns on each other. The Croats split off their own mini-state, the Croatian Republic of Herzeg-Bosnia. A bloody war raged for years among the three groups: the Serbs (with support from Serbia proper), the Croats (with support from Croatia proper), and—squeezed between them—the internationally recognized Bosniak government, with little support from anybody.

The United Nations Protection Force (UNPROFOR) exercised their very limited authority to provide humanitarian aid. The UN tried to designate "safe areas" where civilians were protected, but because the UNPROFOR troops were not allowed to use force, even in self-defense, they became helpless witnesses to atrocities.

For three and a half years, the capital of Sarajevo was surrounded by Karadžić's Bosnian Serb army. Other Bosniak cities were also besieged, most notoriously Srebrenica in July of 1995. While a Dutch unit of UNPROFOR troops sat impotently by, General Ratko Mladić invaded Srebrenica and oversaw the murder of at least 8,000 of its residents, mostly men. Additionally, 35,000 to 40,000 Bosniak women and children were forcibly removed from the city; many of them (including babies) died en route.

After four long years, in the late summer of 1995, NATO began bombing Bosnian Serb positions, forcing them to relax their siege and come to the negotiating table. The Dayton Peace Accords—brokered by US diplomats at Wright-Patterson Air Force Base near Dayton, Ohio—finally brought an end to the wars of Yugoslav succession.

The Dayton Peace Accords carefully divided Bosnia-Herzegovina into three different units: the Federation of Bosnia and Herzegovina (Bosniaks and Croats), the Serb-dominated Republika Srpska, and the mixed-ethnicity Brčko District. While this compromise helped bring the war to an end, it also created a nation with four independent and redundant governments—further crippling this war-torn and impoverished region.

After the war, city leaders decided to rebuild the Old Bridge. Chunks of the original bridge were dredged up from the river. But the limestone had been compromised by soaking in the water for so long, so it couldn't be used (you can still see these pieces of the old Old Bridge on the riverbank below). Having pledged to rebuild the bridge authentically, restorers cut new stone from the original quarry, and each block was hand-carved. Then they assembled the

stones with the same technology used by the Ottomans 450 years ago: Workers erected wooden scaffolding and fastened the blocks together with iron hooks cast in lead. The project was overseen by UNESCO and cost over $13 million, funded largely by international donors.

It took longer to rebuild the bridge in the 21st century than it did to build it in the 16th century. But on July 23, 2004, the new Old Bridge was inaugurated with much fanfare and was immediately embraced by both the city and the world as a sign of reconciliation.

Since its restoration, another piece of bridge history has fully returned, as young men once again jump from the bridge 75 feet down into the Neretva (which remains icy cold even in summer). Done both for the sake of tradition and to impress girls, this custom was carried on even during the time when the destroyed bridge was temporarily replaced by a wooden one. Now the tower on the west side of the bridge houses the office of the local "Divers Club," a loosely run organization that carries on this long-standing ritual. On hot summer days, you'll see divers making a ruckus and collecting donations at the top of the bridge. They tease and tease, standing up on the railing and pretending they're about to jump... then getting down and asking for more money. (If he's wearing trunks rather than Speedos, he's not a diver—just a teaser.) Once they collect about €30, one of them will take the plunge.

Before moving on, see how many of the town's 10 mosques you can spot from the top of the bridge (I counted seven minarets).

Inside the Halebija Tower at the near end of the bridge, up the stairs (above the Divers Club), the **"War Photo" exhibition** displays 50 somber, poignant wartime images taken by photojournalist Wade Goddard. Though small, the collection of black-and-white images puts a human face on the suffering by focusing not on the conflict itself, but on the everyday people whose lives were ripped apart by the war (6 KM, daily mid-July-mid-Oct 9:00-21:00; April-mid-July and mid-Oct-Nov 11:00-18:00, closed

Dec-March, mobile 062-345-789).

• *If you'd like to see one of the best* **views** *in town—looking up at the Old Bridge from the riverbank below—backtrack the way you came into the shopping zone, take your first left (at the Šadrvan restaurant, a good place to try the powerful "Bosnian coffee"), then find the steps down to the river on the left.*

When you're ready to continue, hike back up to the Old Bridge and cross to the other side. After the bridge on the right are two different exhibits worth a quick visit.

Gallery on the Bridge

This excellent bookstore—operated by the local Islamic cultural center—has a good, free photo exhibition of powerful images of war-torn Mostar, displayed inside a former mosque for soldiers who guarded the bridge. They play a montage of videos and photos of the bridge—before, during, and after the war—that's nearly as good as the similar film shown at the Museum of Herzegovina (described later). The shop also sells an impressively wide range of books about the former Yugoslavia and its troubled breakup.

Cost and Hours: Free, daily 7:00-24:00.

• *Just beyond the bookstore, tucked into the corner on the right, look for the stairs leading up to the...*

Museum of the Old Bridge (Muzej Stari Most)

Located within one of the Old Bridge's towers, this museum features a film and photos about the reconstruction of the bridge, archaeological findings, and a few other paltry exhibits about the history of the town and bridge, all in English. First climb up the stairs just after the bridge and buy your ticket, before hiking the rest of the way up to the top of the tower, where you can enjoy fine views through grubby windows. Then go around below to the archaeological exhibit. The museum offers more detail than most casual visitors need; consider just dropping into the smaller, free photo exhibition described previously, then moving along.

Cost and Hours: 5 KM, daily April-Aug 8:00-18:00, Feb-March and Sept-Nov 8:00-16:00, closed Dec-Jan, lots of stairs, Bajatova 4, tel. 036/551-6021.

• *After the Old Bridge, the street swings left and leads you along...*

▲▲Coppersmiths' Street (Kujundžiluk)

This lively strip, with the flavor of a Turkish bazaar, offers some of the most colorful shopping this side of Istanbul. You'll see Mostar's characteristic bridge depicted in every possible way, along with blue-and-white "evil eyes" (believed in the Turkish culture to keep bad spirits at bay), old Yugoslav Army kitsch (including spent bullet and shell casings engraved with images of Mostar), and hammered-copper decorations (continuing the long tradition that gave the street its name). Partway up, the homes with the colorfully painted facades double as galleries for local artists. The artists live and work upstairs, then sell their work right on this street. Pop into the *atelier d'art* ("Đul Emina") on the right to meet Sead Vladović and enjoy his impressive iconographic work (daily 9:00-20:00). This is the most touristy street in all of Bosnia-Herzegovina, so don't expect any bargains. Still, it's fun. As you stroll, check out the fine views of the Old Bridge.

• *Continue uphill. After the street levels out, about halfway along the street on the left-hand side, look for the entrance to the...*

▲Koski Mehmet-Pasha Mosque (Koski Mehmet-Paša Džamija)

Mostar's Bosniak community includes many practicing Muslims. Step into this courtyard for a look at one of Mostar's many mosques. This mosque, dating from the early 17th century, is notable for its cliff-hanging riverside location—and because it's particularly accessible for tourists. But Mostar's other mosques share many of its characteristics—much of the following information applies to them as well.

Cost and Hours: 4 KM to enter mosque, 4 KM more to climb minaret, daily April-Oct 9:00-18:00, until 19:00 at busy times, Nov-March 9:00-15:00; if it seems crowded with tour groups, you can enter a very similar mosque later on this walk instead.

Visiting the Mosque: The **fountain** *(šadrvan)* in the courtyard allows worshippers to wash before entering the mosque, as directed by Islamic law. This practice, called ablution, is both a literal and a spiritual cleansing in preparation for being in the presence of Allah. It's also refreshing in this hot climate, and the sound of running water helps worshippers concentrate.

The **minaret**—the slender needle jutting up next to the dome—is the Islamic equivalent of the Christian bell tower, used to call people to prayer. In the old days, the *muezzin* (prayer leader) would climb the tower five times a day and chant, "There is only one God, and Muhammad is his prophet." In modern times, loudspeakers are used instead. Climbing the minaret's 89 claustrophobic, spiral stairs is a memorable experience, rewarding you at the top with the best views over Mostar—and the Old Bridge—that you can get without wings (entrance to the right of mosque entry).

Because this mosque is accustomed to tourists, you don't need to take off your shoes to enter (but stay on the green carpet), women don't need to wear scarves, and it's fine to take photos inside. Near the front of the mosque, you may see some of the small, overlapping rugs that are beneath this covering (reserved for shoes-off worshippers).

Once **inside,** notice the traditional elements of the mosque. The niche *(mihrab)* across from the entry is oriented toward Mecca (the holy city in today's Saudi Arabia)— the direction all Muslims face to pray. The small stairway *(mimber)* that seems to go nowhere is symbolic of the growth of Islam—Muhammad had to stand higher and higher to talk to his growing following. This serves as a kind of pulpit, where the cleric gives a speech, similar to a sermon or homily in Christian church services. No priest ever stands on the top stair, which is symbolically reserved for Muhammad.

The balcony just inside the door is traditionally where women worship. For the same reason I find it hard to concentrate on God at yoga classes, Muslim men decided prayer would go better without the enjoyable but problematic distraction of bent-over women between them and Mecca. These days, women can also pray on the main floor with the men, but they must avoid physical contact.

Muslims believe that capturing a living creature in a painting or a sculpture is inappropriate. (In fact, depictions of Allah and the prophet Muhammad are strictly forbidden.) Instead, mosques are filled with ornate patterns and Arabic calligraphy (of the name "Muhammad" and important prayers and sayings from the Quran). You'll also see some floral and plant designs, which you'd never see in a more conservative, Middle Eastern mosque.

Before leaving, ponder how progressive the majority of Mostar's Muslims are. Most of them drink alcohol, wear modern European clothing (you'll see very few women wearing head scarves or men with beards—and those you do see are likely tourists from the Middle East), and almost never visit a mosque to pray. In so many ways, these people don't fit our preconceived notions of Islam...and yet, they consider themselves Muslims all the same.

The mosque's **courtyard** is shared by several merchants. When you're done haggling, head to the terrace behind the mosque for the best view in town of the Old Bridge.

• *Just beyond this mosque, the traffic-free cobbles of the Old Town end. Take a right and leave the cutesy tourists' world. Walk up one block to the big...*

The Muslims of Bosnia

While Muslim immigrants have only recently become a fixture in many European cities, Bosnia-Herzegovina is one place where Muslims have continuously been an integral part of the cultural tapestry for centuries.

During the more than 400 years that Bosnia was part of the Ottoman Empire, the Muslim Turks did not forcibly convert their subjects (unlike some Catholic despots at the time). However, it was advantageous for non-Turks to adopt Islam (for lower taxes and better business opportunities), so many Slavs living here became Muslims. In fact, within 150 years of the start of Ottoman rule, half of the population of Bosnia-Herzegovina was Muslim.

The Ottomans became increasingly intolerant of other faiths as time went on, and uprisings by Catholics and Orthodox Christians eventually led to the end of Ottoman domination in the late 19th century. But even after the Ottomans left, many people in this region continued practicing Islam, as their families had been doing for centuries. These people constitute an ethnic group called "Bosniaks," and many of them are still practicing Muslims today (following the Sunni branch of the Muslim faith). Most Bosniaks are Slavs—of the same ethnic stock as Croats and Serbs—and look pretty much the same as their neighbors; however, some Bosniaks have ancestors who married into Turkish families, and they may have some Turkish features.

The actions of a small but attention-grabbing faction of Muslim extremists have burdened Islam with a bad reputation in the Western world. But judging Islam based on Osama bin Laden and al-Qaeda is a bit like judging Christianity based on the Oslo gunman and the Ku Klux Klan. Visiting Mostar is a unique opportunity to get a taste of a fully Muslim society, made a bit less intimidating because it wears a more-familiar European face.

▲▲New Muslim Cemetery

In this cemetery, which was a park before the war, every tomb is dated 1993, 1994, or 1995. As the war raged, more exposed cemeteries were unusable. But this tree-covered piece of land was relatively safe from Croat snipers. As the casualties mounted, locals buried their loved ones here under cover of darkness. Many of these people were soldiers, but some were civilians. Strict Muslim graves don't display  images of people, but here you'll see photos of war dead who were young, less-traditional members of the Muslim community. The

Here's an admittedly basic and simplistic outline (written by a non-Muslim) designed to help travelers from the Christian West understand a very rich but often misunderstood culture that's worthy of respect:

Muslims, like Christians and Jews, are monotheistic. They call God "Allah." The most important person in the Islamic faith is Muhammad, Allah's most important prophet, who lived in the sixth and seventh centuries A.D.

The "five pillars" of Islam are the same among Muslims in Bosnia-Herzegovina, Turkey, Iraq, Indonesia, the US, and everywhere else. Followers of Islam should:

1. Say and believe, "There is only one God, and Muhammad is his prophet."

2. Pray five times a day, while facing Mecca. Modern Muslims explain that it's important for this ritual to include several elements: washing, exercising, stretching, and thinking of God.

3. Give to the poor (one-fortieth of your wealth, if you are not in debt).

4. Fast during daylight hours through the month of Ramadan. Fasting is a great social equalizer and helps everyone to feel the hunger of the poor.

5. Visit Mecca. This is interpreted by some Muslims as a command to travel. Muhammad said, "Don't tell me how educated you are, tell me how much you've traveled."

Good advice for anyone, no matter what—or if—you call a higher power.

fleur-de-lis shape of many of the tombstones is a patriotic symbol for the nation of Bosnia. The Arabic squiggles are the equivalent of an American having Latin on his or her tombstone—old-fashioned and formal.

• *Go up the wide stairs to the right of the cemetery (near the mosque). At #4 (on the right, just before and across from the bombed-out tower), you'll find the...*

Museum of Herzegovina (Muzej Hercegovine)

This humble little museum is made worthwhile by a deeply moving **film** that traces the history of the town through its Old Bridge: fun circa-1957 footage of the diving contests; harrowing scenes of the bridge being pummeled, and finally toppled, by artillery; and a stirring sequence showing the bridge's reconstruction and grand reopening on that day in 2004—with high-fives, Beethoven's *Ode to Joy*, fireworks, and more divers. (This includes much of the same footage as the similar film at the Gallery on the Bridge, described earlier, but doesn't focus solely on the wartime damage.)

The museum itself displays fragments of this region's rich history, including historic photos and several items from its Ottoman period. There are sparse English descriptions, but without a tour guide the exhibits are a bit difficult to appreciate. Topics include the Turkish period, Herzegovina under the Austro-Hungarian Empire, village life, and (in the basement) local archaeology. One small room commemorates the house's former owner, Dzemal Bijedić, who was Tito's second-in-command during the Yugoslav period until he was killed in a mysterious plane crash in 1977. (If Bijedić had lived, many wonder whether he might have succeeded Tito...and succeeded in keeping Yugoslavia together.)

Cost and Hours: 5-KM museum entry includes 12-minute film, no narration—works in any language, ask about "film?" as you enter; Mon-Fri 9:00-16:00, Sat 10:00-15:00, closed Sun; often closed in winter—call first; Bajatova 4—walking up these stairs, it's the second door that's marked for the museum, under the overhanging balcony, tel. 036/551-602, www.muzejhercegovine.com.

• *Backtrack to where you left the Old Town. Notice the **Tepa Market**, with locals buying clothing and produce, in the area just beyond the pedestrian zone. Now walk (with the market on your left) along the lively street called **Braće Fejića**. (There's no sign, but the street is level and busy with cafés.) You're in the "new town," where locals sit out in front of boisterous cafés sipping coffee while listening to the thumping beat of distinctly Eastern-sounding music.*

Stroll down this street for a few blocks. At the palm trees (about 50 yards before the minaret—look for sign to Ottoman House*), you can side-trip a block to the left to reach the...*

▲Bišćević Turkish House (Bišćevića Ćošak)

Mostar has three traditional Turkish-style homes that are open for tourists to visit. The Bišćević House is the oldest, most interesting, and most convenient for a quick visit, but two others are described at the end of this listing. Dating from 1635, the Bišćević House is typical of old houses in Mostar, which mix Oriental style with Mediterranean features.

Cost and Hours: 4 KM, March-Nov Mon-Fri 8:00-19:00, Sat-Sun 9:00-18:00, generally closed Dec-Feb—but you can arrange a visit by calling ahead to Fortuna Tours, tel. 036/552-197, Bišćevića 13.

Visiting the House: First you'll step through the outer (or animals') garden, then into the inner (or family's) garden. This inner zone is surrounded by a high wall—protection from the

sun's rays, from thieves...and from prying eyes, allowing women to take off the veil they were required to wear in public. Enjoy the geometrical patters of the smooth river stones in the floor (for example, the five-sided star), and keep an eye out for the house's pet turtles. It's no coincidence that the traditional fountain *(šadrvan)* resembles those at the entrance to a mosque—a reminder of the importance of running water in Muslim culture. The little white building is a kitchen—cleverly located apart from the house so that the heat and smells of cooking didn't permeate the upstairs living area.

Buy your ticket and take off your shoes before you climb up the wooden staircase. Imagine how a stairway like this one could be pulled up for extra protection in case of danger (notice that this one has a "trap door" to cover it). The cool, shady, and airy living room is open to the east—from where the wind rarely blows. The overhanging roof also prevented the hot sun from reaching this area. The loom in the corner was the women's workplace—the carpets you're standing on would have been woven there. The big chests against the wall were used to bring the dowry when the homeowner took a new wife. Study the fine wood carving that decorates the space.

Continue back into the main gathering room *(divanhan)*. This space—whose name comes from the word "talk"—is designed in a circle so people could face each other, cross-legged, for a good conversation while they enjoyed a dramatic view overlooking the Neretva. The room comes with a box of traditional costumes—great for photo fun. Put on a pair of baggy pants and a fez and really lounge.

Other Turkish Houses: If you're intrigued by this house, consider dropping by Mostar's two other Turkish houses. The **Muslibegović House** (Muslibegovića Kuća) feels newer because it dates from 1871, just a few years before the Ottomans left town. This homey house—which also rents out rooms to visitors (see "Sleeping in Mostar," later)—has many of the same features as the Bišćević House. If they're not too busy, Sanela or Gabriela can give you an English tour (4 KM, mid-April–mid-Oct daily 10:00-18:00, closed to visitors off-season, just two blocks uphill from the Karađozbeg Mosque at Osman Đikića 41, tel. 036/551-379, www.muslibegovichouse.com). To find it, go up the street between the Karađozbeg Mosque and the cemetery, cross the busy street, and continue a long block uphill on the alley. The wall with the slate roof on the left marks the house.

The **Kajtaz House** (Kajtazova Kuća), hiding up a very residential-feeling alley a few blocks from the Old Bridge, feels lived-in because it still is (in the opposite direction from most of the other sights, at Gaše Ilića 21).

• *Go back to the main café street and continue to the...*

▲Karađozbeg Mosque (Karađozbegova Džamija)

The city's main mosque was completed in 1557, the same year work began on the Old Bridge. This mosque, which welcomes visitors, feels less touristy than the one back in the Old Town. Before entering the gate into the complex, look for the picture showing the recent war damage sustained here. You'll see that this mosque has most of the same elements as the Koski Mehmet-Pasha Mosque (described earlier), but some of these decorations are original. Across the street is another cemetery with tombstones from that terrible year, 1993.

Cost and Hours: 4 KM to enter mosque (free for Muslims), 4 KM more to climb minaret, daily May-Sept 9:00-19:30, Oct-April 10:00-15:00. Inside the mosque, either stay on the designated area or remove your shoes. Women can choose whether to cover their heads, but women wearing shorts will be asked to cover their legs with a loaner scarf.

• *Now leave the tourists' Mostar and continue into modern, urban Mostar along the street in front of the Karađozbeg Mosque. This grimy, mostly traffic-free street is called...*

▲Braće Fejića

Walking along the modern town's main café strip, enjoy the opportunity to observe this workaday Bosniak town. You'll see the humble offices of the ragtag B&H Airlines; a state-run gambling office (Lutrija BIH) taxing its less-educated people with a state lottery; and lots of cafés that serve drinks but no food. People generally eat at home before going out to nurse an affordable drink. (Café ABC has good cakes and ice cream; the upstairs is a popular pizza hangout for students and families.)

At the small mosque on the left, obituary announcements are tacked to the tree, listing the bios and funeral times for locals who have recently died. A fig tree grows out of the mosque's minaret, just an accident of nature illustrating how that plant can thrive with almost no soil (somehow, the Bosniaks can relate). Walking farther, look back and up to see a few ruins—still ugly nearly two decades after the war. There's a messy confusion about who owns what in Mostar. Surviving companies have no money. Yugo Bank, which held the mortgages, is defunct. No one will invest until clear ownership is established. Until then, the people of Mostar sip their coffee in the shadow of these jagged reminders of the warfare that wracked this town a couple of decades ago.

Near the end of the pedestrian zone, through the parking lot on the right, look for the building with communist-era reliefs of 12th-century Bogomil tomb decor—remembering the indigenous culture that existed here even before the arrival of the Ottomans.

When you finally hit the big street (with car traffic), head left one block to the big **Masala Square** (literally, "Place for Prayer"). Historically this was where pilgrims gathered before setting off for Mecca on their hajj. This is a great scene on balmy evenings, when it's a rendezvous point for the community. The two busts near the fountain provide perfect goal posts for budding soccer stars.

• *For a finale, you can continue one block more out onto the bridge to survey the town you just explored. From here, you can backtrack to linger in the places you found most inviting. Or you can venture into...*

WESTERN (CROAT) MOSTAR

Most tourists stay on the Bosniak side of town. But for a complete look at this divided city, it's well worth strolling to the west side. While there's not much in the way of sightseeing here, and much of this urban zone isn't particularly pretty, it does provide an interesting contrast to the Muslim side of town. As this is the location of some of Mostar's new shopping malls, this area feels more vital each year, and a few of the tree-lined streets seem downright elegant.

As you cross the river and the Bulevar, the scarred husks of destroyed buildings begin to fade away, and within a block you're immersed in concrete apartment buildings—making it clear that, when the city became divided, the Muslims holed up in the original Ottoman Old Town, while the Croats claimed the modern Tito-era sprawl. The relative lack of war damage (aside from a few stray bullet holes) emphasizes that it was the Croats laying siege to the Muslims of Mostar. You'll also notice some glitzy new shopping centers and more pizza and pasta restaurants than *ćevapčići* joints (in other words, even the food over here is more Croatian than Bosnian).

Looking at a map, you'll notice that many streets on this side of town are named for Croatian cities (Dubrovačka, Splitska, Vukovarska) or historical figures (Kneza Branimira, Kralja Tomislava, and Kralja Petra Krešimira—for the dukes who first united the Croats in the ninth and tenth centuries). This side of town also has several remnants of Mostar's brief period of Habsburg rule (1878-1918). During this time, the empire quickly expanded what had been a sleepy Ottoman backwater, laying out grand boulevards and erecting genteel buildings that look like they'd be at home in Vienna.

All streets converge at the big roundabout (about a 15-minute walk from the Old Town) called the **Rondo,** which is a good place to get oriented to this neighborhood. Overlooking this lively intersection is the stately Hrvatski Dom ("Croatia House") cultural center. In this part of town, notice how even the street signs are politically charged: *Centar* signs pointedly direct traffic *away* from the (Bosniak) Old Town, and many road signs point toward Široki Brijeg—a Croat stronghold in western Herzegovina.

The adjacent **Park Zrinjevac** is a pleasant place to stroll, and was the site of an infamously ill-fated attempt at reconciliation. In the early 2000s, idealistic young Mostarians formed the Urban Movement of Mostar, which searched for a way to connect the still-feuding Catholic and Muslim communities. As a symbol of their goals, they chose Bruce Lee, the deceased kung-fu movie star, beloved by both Croats and Bosniaks for his characters' honorable struggle against injustice. A life-size bronze statue of Lee was unveiled with fanfare in this park in November of 2005—but was almost immediately vandalized. The statue was repaired, and may or may not have been returned to its pedestal (which you'll still find in the park).

Several interesting sights lie close to this roundabout. A block toward the Old Town from the Rondo (on Kralja Višeslava Humskog), look for the big **Muslim cemetery** with tombstones from the early 1990s. These are the graves of those killed during the first round of fighting, when the Croats and Bosniaks teamed up to fight the Serbs.

If you head from the Rondo down Kneza Branimira (across from the park), you'll enjoy an inviting boulevard shaded by plane trees. When first built, this street was called **Štefanijino Šetalište**—"Stéphanie's Promenade," after the Belgian princess who married Austria's Archduke Rudolf (the heir apparent of the Habsburg Empire until he died in a mysterious murder-suicide pact with his mistress). Partway down the street on the left is the recommended Pivnica Štefanijino Šetalište, a good place for a microbrew or a meal.

If you head up Kralja Petra Krešimira IV from the Rondo, after two long blocks on the left you'll see an abandoned, derelict park leading to a gigantic **Partisan**

Cemetery and Monument. This socialist-style monument spreads all the way up the hill. It oozes with symbolism trumpeting the pivotal WWII Battle of the Neretva, when Tito and his Partisan Army turned the tables on Nazi forces (just 30 miles north of here). It was designed by Bogdan Bogdanović, who created many such monuments and memorials throughout Yugoslavia, and was dedicated by Tito himself in 1965. From the terrace at the top, scattered with symbolic gravestones for those who gave their lives to free Yugoslavia from the Nazis, small streams once trickled down to the large enclosure at the bottom, ultimately flowing beneath a stylized broken bridge representing the Bridge at the Neretva. Today the monument is overgrown and ignored—a tragic symbol of post-Tito ethnic discord. Local Croats—who have little nostalgia for the Yugoslav period, which they now view as a time of oppression—seem to intentionally neglect the place. This formerly hallowed ground is a mess of broken concrete and a popular place for drunken benders, garbage dumping, and drug deals (be careful if you decide to explore, and avoid it after dark). A pensive stroll here comes with a poignant reflection on how one generation's honored war dead can become the next generation's unwanted burden.

NEAR MOSTAR

While Mostar has its share of attractions, there's also plenty to see within a short drive. Ideally try to splice one or two of these stops into your trip between Mostar and the coast (see my "Route Tips for Drivers," later, for tips on linking them up).

Blagaj

Blagaj (BLAH-gai, rhymes with "pie") was the historical capital of this region until the arrival of the Ottomans. Deep in Blagaj is an

impressive cliff face with a scenic house marking the source of the Buna River. The building, called the **Tekija,** is a former monastery for Turkish dervishes (an order that emphasizes poverty and humility, famous for the way they whirl in a worshipful trance). Built in the 15th century and recently restored, the house is surrounded by a modern visitors center complex with a café, gift shop, and coin-op WCs. It's free to enter and look around the Tekija, which feels similar to the tourable Turkish houses in Mostar (for a description, see page 1128). You'll take your shoes off and tiptoe across a patchwork of small rugs from room to room. Gazing out the windows at the towering cliff stretching to heaven, and hearing the constant, steady flow of water, it's easy to imagine how this could be considered a very spiritual place.

Blagaj is easiest to see on the way to or from Mostar—just turn off from the main road and follow the Buna River, following *tekija* signs to the big parking lot.

Počitelj

Počitelj (POTCH-ee-tell) is an artists' colony filled with a compelling mix of Christian and Muslim architecture. Ideally situated right along the main Mostar-to-Croatia road, it's one of the most popular rest stops for passing tour buses, so it's hardly undiscovered. But it's still worth a stop for its dramatically vertical townscape and beautifully restored Ottoman architecture. Hike up steeply through town to the mosque (free entry—women must cover their heads), then continue up to the fortress for panoramic views over the countryside to appreciate Počitelj's strategic position.

Međugorje

Međugorje is an unassuming little village "between the hills" (as its name implies) that ranks with Lourdes, Fátima, and Santiago

de Compostela as one of the most important pilgrimage sites in all of Christendom. To the cynical non-Catholic, it's just a strip of crassly commercial hotels, restaurants, and rosary shops leading up to a dull church, all tied together by a silly legend about a hilltop apparition. But if you look into the tear-filled eyes of the pilgrims who've journeyed here, it's clear that to some, this place offers much more than what you see on the surface. For true believers, Međugorje represents a once-in-a-lifetime opportunity to tread on sacred soil: a place where, over the past three-plus decades, the Virgin Mary has appeared to six local people. More than 30 million pilgrims have visited Međugorje since the sightings began—summer and winter, war (which didn't touch Međugorje) and peace, rain and shine.

The center of pilgrim activity is **St. James' Church** (Crkva Sv. Jakova), which was built before the apparitions. As you face the church, you'll see two trails leading up to the hills. Behind and to the left of the church is **Apparition Hill** (at Podbrdo), where the sightings occurred (a one-mile hike, topped by a statue of

MOSTAR

Mary). Directly behind the church is the **Great Hill** (Križevac, or "Cross Mountain"), where a giant hilltop cross, which predates the visions, has become a secondary site of pilgrimage (1.5-mile hike). Pilgrims often do one or both of these hikes barefoot, as a sign of penitence. Near the church is a giant statue of the **Resurrected Savior** (Uskrsli Spasitelj), also known as the "Weeping Knee." While the elongated, expressionistic sculpture—exemplifying Christ's suffering—is inherently striking, the eternal dampness of its right knee attracts the most attention from pilgrims. Miraculously (or not), it's always wet—go ahead and touch the spot that's been highly polished by worshippers and skeptics alike.

Believers and nonbelievers alike appreciate the parade of kitsch that lines the **main street** leading up to the church. While rosaries are clearly the big item, you can get basically anything you want stamped with Catholic imagery (Mary is particularly popular, for obvious reasons).

Nightlife in Mostar

Be sure to enjoy the local scene after dark in Mostar. Though the town is touristy, it's also a real urban center with a young popula-

tion riding a wave of raging hormones. The meat market in the courtyard next to the old Turkish bathhouse near the TI is fun to observe. The Old Bridge is a popular meeting place for locals as well as tourists (and pick-

pockets). A stroll from the Old Bridge down the café-lined Braće Fejića boulevard, to the modern Masala Square at the far end of town (described earlier), gives you a great peek at Mostarians socializing away from the tourists. Wherever you wind up, order a cocktail or try a Turkish-style hubbly-bubbly (šiša, SHEE-shah). Ask to have one of these big water pipes fired up for you and choose your flavored tobacco: apple, cappuccino, banana, or lemon.

Ali Baba is an actual cave featuring a fun, atmospheric, and

youthful party scene. While this place has gone in and out of business over the past few years, it's worth checking to see if its open to enjoy a drink in a unique and very cool space (look for low-profile entrance along Coppersmiths' Street, just

down from the Old Bridge—watch for signs tucked down a rocky alley).

Oscar Nightclub is a caravanserai for lounge lizards—an exotic world mixing babbling streams, terraces, lounge chairs, and big sofas where young and old enjoy cocktails and *šiša* (June-Aug open "nonstop," closed Sept-May, up from the Old Bridge on Onešćukova street, near the Crooked Bridge at the end of the pedestrian zone).

Sleeping in Mostar

Most of my listings are small, friendly, accessible, affordable guest houses in or very near the Old Town. Many hotels and pensions in town promise "parking," but it's often street parking out front—private lots are rare. Mostar's Old Town can be very noisy on weekends, with nightclubs and outdoor restaurants rollicking into the wee hours. If you're a light sleeper, consider Villa Fortuna, the Muslibegović House, or Shangri La, which are quieter than the norm.

$$$ The **Muslibegović House,** a Bosnian national monument that also invites tourists in to visit during the day, is in an

actual Turkish home dating from 1871. The complex houses 10 homey rooms and two suites, all of which combine classic Turkish style (elegant and comfortable old beds, creaky wooden floors with colorful carpets, lounging sofas; guests remove shoes at the outer door) with modern comforts (air-con, Wi-Fi, flatscreen TVs). Situated on a quiet residential lane just above the bustle of Mostar's main pedestrian drag and Old Town zone, this is a memorable experience (Sb-€60, Db-€90/€75, "pasha suite"-€105, includes a tour of the house, closed Nov-Feb, 2 blocks uphill from the Karađozbeg Mosque at Osman Đikića 41, tel. 036/551-379, www.muslibegovichouse.com, muslibegovichouse@gmail.com; Taž, Sanela, and Gabriela).

$$$ Hotel Bristol is the only business-class place near central Mostar. Its 47 rooms don't quite live up to their four stars, but the location is handy, overlooking the river a 10-minute walk from the heart of the Old Town (Sb-€51, Db-€82, apartment-€90, extra bed-€15, air-con, elevator, guest computer and Wi-Fi, some street noise, limited parking, Mostarskog Bataljona, tel. 036/500-100, www.bristol.ba, info@bristol.ba).

$$ Hotel Kriva Ćuprija ("Crooked Bridge"), by the bridge of the same name, is tucked between waterfalls in a picturesque

Sleep Code

Abbreviations

($1 = about 1.50 KM, €1 = about $1.40, country code: 387, area code: 036)
S = Single, **D** = Double/Twin, **T** = Triple, **Q** = Quad,
b = bathroom.

Price Rankings

  $$$ **Higher Priced**—Most rooms €80 or more.
  $$ **Moderately Priced**—Most rooms between €60-80.
   $ **Lower Priced**—Most rooms €60 or less.

If I've listed three sets of rates, separated by slashes, the first
is for peak season (typically mid-July through late Aug), the
second is for shoulder season (roughly June-mid-July and
late Aug-Sept), and the third is for off-season (Oct-May). If
I've listed only two rates, the first is for peak season and the
second for shoulder/off-season. The dates for seasonal rates
vary by hotel. Unless otherwise noted, prices include breakfast and Wi-Fi is generally free. Prices can change without
notice; verify current rates online or by email. For the best
prices, always book directly with the hotel.

valley a few steps from the Old Bridge. It's an appealing oasis with
10 stylish rooms and a restaurant with atmospheric outdoor seating (Sb-€39, Db-€65, apartment-€75, extra bed-€18, 10 percent
discount on rooms and food with this book, can be noisy, air-con,
Wi-Fi, free parking, call to reconfirm if arriving after 19:00, enter
at Onešćukova 23 or Kriva Ćuprija 2, tel. 036/360-360, mobile
061-135-286, www.motel-mostar.ba, info@motel-mostar.ba,
Sami). Their second location—**Hotel Kriva Ćuprija II**—offers 10
modern rooms in a restored Habsburg-style building on a dreary
urban street, about 200 yards to the south. As it's a less convenient location and lacks soul, I prefer the original (same prices,
discount, amenities, and contact information as main hotel; some
traffic noise, Maršala Tita 186, next to the Lučki Bridge, reception
tel. 036/554-125).

$$ Villa Anri, a bit more hotelesque than other pensions
in Mostar, sits a block farther from the bustle near the Bulevar.
The stony facade hides eight rooms (six with balconies) com-
bining old Herzegovinian style and bright colors. The big draw
is the rooftop terrace, shared by two rooms, which offers grand
views over the Old Bridge area (Db-€70/€60/€55, Db with grand
terrace-€95/€80/€60, Tb-€95/€80/€60, Tb with grand ter-
race-€115/€90/€70, cash only, air-con, Wi-Fi, free parking, Braće
Đukića 4, tel. 036/578-477, www.villa-anri-mostar.ba, villa.anri@
gmail.com).

$$ Motel Emen has six modern, sleek rooms overlooking a
busy café street a few cobbled blocks from the Old Bridge (Sb-€50,

Db-€70, bigger Db with balcony-€80, all rooms €10 less Oct-May, air-con, guest computer and Wi-Fi, free parking, Onešćukova 32, tel. 036/581-120, www.motel-emen.com, info@motel-emen.com).

$ Villa Fortuna is an exceptional value, located in a nondescript urban neighborhood a few minutes' walk farther away from the Old Bridge. Owners Nela and Mili Bijavica rent eight tasteful, modern rooms above the main office of Fortuna Tours. The courtyard in front offers free, secure parking, and in back there's a pleasant garden with a traditional Herzegovinian garden cottage (Sb-€30, Db-€40, apartment-€80, these prices if you book direct by email, breakfast-€5, non-smoking, air-con, Wi-Fi, Rade Bitange 34, tel. 036/580-625, mobile 063-315-017 or 063-299-189, www.villafortuna.ba, villa_fortuna@bih.net.ba). Fortuna Tours can also put you in touch with locals renting rooms and apartments.

$ Pansion Čardak, run by Suzana and Nedžad Kasumović, has five straightforward rooms sharing a kitchen and Internet nook in a stone house set just back from the bustling Crooked Bridge area (Db-€50-60/€45, higher price is for bigger room or room with terrace, Tb-€75/€60, Qb-€90/€70, cash only, breakfast at nearby restaurant-€3-4, air-con, Wi-Fi, free parking, Jusovina 3, tel. 036/578-249, mobile 061-385-988, www.pansion-cardak.com, info@pansion-cardak.com).

$ Pansion Nur, run by Feđa, a relative of Suzana and Nedžad (above), has four simpler but cheaper rooms and a shared kitchen (twin Db-€40/€35, Db-€50/€40, Tb-€60/€50, suite-€70/€60, cash only, no breakfast, air-con, Wi-Fi, free parking, Jusovina 8b, tel. 036/580-296, mobile 062-160-872, www.pansion-nur.com, info@pansion-nur.com).

$ B&B Shangri La fills a gorgeously restored Austro-Hungarian building on a hill above the Old Town, squeezed between war ruins. The eight rooms come in all different sizes, but all of them are modern and nicely appointed (Db-€41-58 depending on size and amenities, breakfast-€6, air-con, Wi-Fi, free parking, Kalhanska 10, mobile 061-169-362, www.shangrila.com.ba, info@shangrila.com.ba, Nijaz).

$ Villa Botticelli, overlooking a charming waterfall garden just up the valley from the Crooked Bridge, has five colorful rooms at affordable prices (Sb-€30, Db-€40, breakfast-€3, air-con, Wi-Fi, Muje Bjelavca 6, enter around back along the alley, mobile 063-319-057, www.villabotticelli.com, info@villabotticelli.com, Snježana and Zoran).

Eating in Mostar

Most of Mostar's tourist-friendly restaurants are conveniently concentrated in the Old Town. If you walk anywhere that's cobbled,  you'll stumble onto dozens of tempting restaurants charging the same reasonable prices and serving rustic, traditional Bosnian food. In my experience, the menus at most places are nearly identical—though quality and ambience can vary greatly. As eateries tend to come and go quickly here, and little distinguishes these places anyway, don't be too focused on a particular spot. Grilled meats are especially popular—read the "Balkan Flavors" sidebar before you dine. As for local wines, most are made with one of two indigenous grapes: *blatina* (literally "muddy"; a thick, heavy, earthy red) and *žilavka* (literally "root"; a bright, fairly acidic white).

ON THE EMBANKMENT, WITH OLD BRIDGE VIEWS

For the best atmosphere, find your way into the several levels of restaurants that clamber up the riverbank and offer perfect views of the Old Bridge. In terms of the setting, this is the most memorable place to dine in Mostar—but be warned that the quality of the food along here is uniformly low, and prices are relatively high (figure 8-18 KM for a meal). If you want a good perch, it's fun and smart to drop by earlier in the day and personally reserve the table of your choice.

To reach two of the most scenic eateries, go over the Old Bridge to the west side of the river, and bear right on the cobbles until you get to the old Turkish bathhouse (with the copper domes on the roof). To the right of the bathhouse is the entrance to a lively courtyard surrounded with cafés. Crossing straight through the courtyard, you'll find stairs leading down to several riverfront terraces belonging to two different restaurants: **Babilon** (my choice for better food) and **Teatar.** Poke around to find your favorite bridge panorama before settling in for a drink or a meal.

Two other places (including a pizzeria) are a bit closer to the bridge—to reach these, look for the alley on the left just before the bridge tower.

NEAR THE OLD BRIDGE

While they lack the Old Bridge views, these places are just as central as those listed above, and they serve food that's generally a step up. The first three places are in the atmospheric Old Town, while

Balkan Flavors

All of the countries of the Balkan Peninsula—basically from Slovenia to Greece—have several foods in common: The Ottomans from today's Turkey, who controlled much of this territory for centuries, imported some goodies that remained standard fare here long after they left town. Whether you're in Mostar, Croatia, or Slovenia, it's worth seeking out some of these local tastes.

A popular, cheap fast food you'll see everywhere is **burek** (BOO-rehk)—phyllo dough filled with meat, cheese, spinach, or apples. *Burek* rivals pizza-by-the-slice as the most popular take-away snack food in the former Yugoslavia.

Grilled meats are a staple of Balkan cuisine. You'll most often see **ćevapčići** (cheh-VAHP-chee-chee), or simply **ćevapi** (cheh-VAH-pee)—minced meat (typically a mix of lamb and beef) formed into a sausage-link shape, then grilled. It's similar—and similarly named—to a kebab. *Ćevapi* enthusiasts (a group that includes pretty much everyone in the Balkans) distinguish between different variations. For example, Sarajevo-style *(sarajevski ćevapi)* is typically eaten with grilled onions and stuffed into a pita-like flatbread called *somun*; Banja Luka-style *(banjalučki ćevapi)* is one long, continuous *ćevap* with hot peppers on the side.

Ražnjići (RAZH-nyee-chee) is small pieces of steak on a skewer, like a shish kebab. **Pljeskavica** (plehs-kah-VEET-suh) is similar to **ćevapčići,** except the meat is in the form of a hamburger-like patty. **Pileći** is chicken, and **piščančje** is grilled chicken breast. **Sudžukice** are sausages, and **ćufte** are meatballs.

You just can't eat any of this stuff without the ever-present condiment **ajvar** (EYE-var). Made from red bell pepper and eggplant, *ajvar* is like ketchup with a kick. Many Americans pack a jar of this distinctive sauce to remember the flavors of the Balkans when they get back home. (You may even be able to find it at specialty grocery stores in the US—look for "eggplant/red pepper spread.")

Particularly in Bosnia, another side-dish you'll see is the soft, spreadable—and tasty—cheese called **kajmak. Lepinje** is a pita-like grilled bread, which is often wrapped around *ćevapčići* or *pljeskavica* to make a sandwich. **Uštipci** is a fry bread that's especially popular throughout Bosnia-Herzegovina.

Ajvar, kajmak, lepinje, and diced raw onions are the perfect complement to a **"mixed grill"** of various meats on a big platter—the quintessence of Balkan cuisine on one plate.

the last one is in the modern part of town.

Restoran Hindin Han is pleasantly situated on a woody terrace over a rushing stream. It's respected locally for its good cooking and fair prices (big 12-16-KM salads, 7-15-KM grilled dishes, 12-20-KM fish and other main dishes, Sarajevsko beer on tap, daily 11:00-24:00, Jusovina 10, tel. 036/581-054). To find it, walk west from the Old Bridge, bear left at the Šadrvan restaurant, cross the bridge, and you'll see it on the left.

Nacionalni Restoran Aščinica Balkan ("Balkan National Restaurant/Cafeteria") is a convenient cafeteria-style eatery with two handy locations. They serve up tasty, home-cooked Bosnian specialties; you can order from the menu, but it's more fun to order a "mix" *(mješanac)* plate from the display case—the small 10-KM plate is plenty for a light meal (16-KM "medium" and 20-KM "large" plates also available, 3-KM salads, Bosnian coffee, tempting dessert display case, daily 10:00-22:00, one location right at the end of the Old Town cobbles before the market, the other a couple of blocks away on the new town's main drag at Braće Fejića 57, tel. 036/551-868).

Saray is an untouristy, nondescript little eatery just uphill from the Karađozbeg Mosque in the modern part of town. They have a basic menu of cheap and very tasty grilled meats— spe cializing in the classic *ćevapčići* (little sausage-shaped meat patties)—and outdoor seating overlooking a playground that offers good people- and kid-watching while you eat (4-10-KM grilled meat dishes, big 7-KM salads, daily 7:00-23:00, Karađozbegova 3, mobile 062-062-301).

Urban Grill's food is nothing special—it has basically the same menu as other places in town—but its terrace offers one of Mostar's best unobstructed views of the Old Bridge (8-17-KM grilled meat and other meals, 10-12-KM pastas and salads, Bosnian coffee, daily 8:00-22:00, enter along the main cobbled Old Town drag at Mala Tepa 26, tel. 036/552-235).

IN THE WEST (CROAT) SIDE OF TOWN

While less charming and romantic, a stroll to the west side of town (still inhabited primarily by Croats) offers an interesting contrast to the cutesy Old Town—and a completely different array of restaurants. Here you'll find more pizza and pasta places than grilled meats, as well as shiny new shopping centers with modern food courts. For more on this neighborhood, see page 1131.

Pivnica Štefanijino Šetalište ("Stéphanie's Promenade Brewpub"), named for the onetime Austro-Hungarian crown princess, mingles modern Croat class with Habsburg grandeur. It fills a stylish cellar and an inviting outdoor terrace with happy diners, sipping beers and digging into international fare. It sits along its gorgeous, tree-lined namesake boulevard (9-15-KM main dishes, Mon-Fri 8:00-23:00, Sat-Sun 15:00-23:00, Kneza Branimira 11, tel. 036/319-319, www.stefanija.info).

Mostar Connections

BY BUS

Not surprisingly for a divided city, Mostar has two different, autonomous bus terminals, each served by different companies. Mostar's **main bus station** (called "Autobusna Stanica") is on the east/Bosniak side of the river, about a 15-minute walk north of the Old Town (for details, see "Arrival in Mostar," earlier). Most buses you're likely to take use this station; for information on the other station (on the west/Croat side of town), see the end of this section.

Schedules and Tickets: At the main station, two primary companies (one Bosniak, one Croat) operate independent offices, providing schedule information and tickets only for their own buses. Because the companies are reluctant to cooperate, there's no single information or ticket office for all Mostar buses—visit both companies to know your options before buying tickets. As you face the bus station, near the left end is the Bosniak company **Autoprevoz** (tel. 036/551-900, www.autoprevoz-bus.ba); they also sell tickets for a few other companies (including Eurolines and Bogdan Bus). Near the right end is the Croat-owned **Globtour** (look for *Mediteran Tours* sign, tel. 036/550-065, www.globtour. com), which sells tickets only for its own buses. Local and regional connections (not listed below) are operated by Mostar Bus, whose buses depart from across the street from the main bus station (www.mostarbus.ba).

Tracking down reliable **schedule** information in Mostar is tricky, but you can start by checking the websites listed above, then calling or visiting both companies at the station to confirm your options and buy tickets. Note that buses to seasonal destinations (such as along the Dalmatian Coast) run more frequently in peak season, roughly June through mid-September.

From Mostar's Main Bus Station: Both Autoprevoz and Globtour operate buses to **Sarajevo** (6/day on Autoprevoz, 4/day on Globtour, 2.5 hours). Globtour exclusively handles buses to **Medugorje** (6-7/day, 40 minutes), **Zagreb** (4/day, 9 hours, includes a night bus), **Split** (5/day, 4-4.5 hours; additional departures by Eurolines in summer), and **Dubrovnik** (3/day, 4-5 hours). That important Dubrovnik connection is tricky: Most days, all Dubrovnik buses depart early in the day, making an afternoon return from Mostar to Dubrovnik impossible. However, in summer (June-Aug), Eurolines adds two more departures each day—including a handy 17:30 departure, which makes day-tripping from Dubrovnik workable (tickets sold at Autoprevoz office). Globtour also runs a handy bus to Montenegro's **Bay of Kotor** (departs Mostar at 7:00, arrives at Kotor at 12:30 and Budva at 13:30, then returns the same day); a second bus runs on a similar schedule, via Croatia.

From Mostar's West/Croat Bus Station: A few additional buses, mostly to Croatian destinations and to Croat areas of Bosnia-Herzegovina, depart from the west side of town. These use a makeshift "station" (actually a gravel lot behind a gas station) on Vukovarska street, called "Kolodvor." It's about a 15-minute walk due west of the main bus station. Most buses using the Kolodvor station are operated by the Euroherc company. In addition to one daily bus apiece to **Zagreb, Split,** and **Sarajevo,** this station has several departures to **Metković** (at the Croatian border, with additional connections to Croatian destinations; 8/day) and to **Međugorje** (7/day Mon-Fri, 3/day Sat, none Sun). Additionally, some Croat buses leave from a bus stop near the Franciscan Church. But because the connections are sparse, the location is inconvenient, and the "station" is dreary, I'd stick with the main bus station and ignore this option unless you're desperate.

BY TRAIN

Mostar is on the train line that runs from Ploče (on the Croatian coast between Split and Dubrovnik) to Zagreb, via Mostar and Sarajevo. But I'd avoid the train, which tends to be cramped and slow; buses are typically much more efficient and comfortable. The train schedule changes frequently, but it's usually possible to go by train to **Ploče** (with good bus connections to elsewhere in Dalmatia; 2 hours) and **Sarajevo** (2.5 hours). Some trains continue from Sarajevo all the way to **Zagreb** (11.5 hours from Mostar; bus is faster). Train info: Tel. 036/550-608.

ROUTE TIPS FOR DRIVERS:
FROM DUBROVNIK TO MOSTAR

While there are a variety of ways to connect Dubrovnik (and the rest of the Dalmatian Coast) to Mostar, the vast majority of traffic follows the coastal road north, then cuts east into Bosnia. Because this is one of the most direct routes, it can be crowded (allow about 2.5 hours).

Begin by driving north of Dubrovnik, passing some of the places mentioned in the Near Dubrovnik chapter: **Trsteno** (with its arboretum) and **Ston** and **Mali Ston** (with a mighty wall and waterfront restaurants, respectively). After passing the Ston turn-off, you'll see the long, mountainous, vineyard-draped **Pelješac Peninsula** across the bay on your left.

Soon you'll come to a surprise border crossing, at **Neum.**
Here you'll cross into Bosnia-Herzegovina—then, six miles later,
cross back out again.

You won't be back in Croatia for long. Just north of Neum, the
main coastal road jogs away from the coast and around the striking **Neretva River Delta**—the extremely fertile "garden patch of
Croatia," which produces a significant portion of Croatia's fruits
and vegetables. The Neretva is the same river that flows under
Mostar's Old Bridge upstream—but in Metković, it spreads out
into 12 branches as it enters the Adriatic, flooding a vast plain and
creating a bursting cornucopia in the middle of an otherwise rocky
and arid region. Enjoying some of the most plentiful sunshine on
the Croatian coast, as well as a steady supply of water for irriga-
tion, the Neretva Delta is as productive as it is beautiful.

At the Neretva Delta, turn off for the town of **Metković;**
at the far end of that town, you'll cross the border into **Bosnia-
Herzegovina,** then continue straight on the main road (M-17)
directly into Mostar. As you drive, you'll see destroyed buildings
and occasional roadside memorials bearing the likenesses of fresh-
faced soldiers who died in the recent war.

Along the way are a few interesting detours: In Čapljina,
you can turn off to the left to reach **Međugorje** (see page 1134).
If you stay on the main road, keep your eyes peeled soon after
the Čapljina turnoff for a mountaintop castle tower (on the right
side of the road), which marks the medieval town of **Počitelj** (see
page 1134). With extra time, just before Mostar (in Buna), you
can detour a few miles along the Buna River into **Blagaj** (see
page 1133).

Approaching **Mostar** on M-17, you'll pass the airport, then
carry on straight toward *Sarajevo* (ignoring the first turn-off to
the left for *Centar*). As you skirt the city, take the left turn for
Centar and *Posušje.* When you come to the traffic light, you can
turn right to reach the east side of the river (for the Muslibegović
House or Hotel Kriva Ćuprija II); or continue straight to reach the
west side of the river (for my other accommodations). If you continue straight, you'll bear right onto Bulevar street and continue
on that main artery for several blocks (passing several destroyed
buildings). At the street called Rade Bitange (just after the giant
church bell tower), turn right to find the public parking lot (2 KM/
hour, 10 KM/8 hours)—less than a 10-minute walk from the Old
Bridge. Be warned that signage is poor; if you get lost, try asking
for directions to "Stari Most" (STAH-ree most)—the Old Bridge.

AUSTRIA
Österreich

VIENNA

Wien

Vienna is the capital of Austria, the cradle of classical music, the home of the rich Habsburg heritage, and one of Europe's most livable cities. The city center is skyscraper-free, pedestrian-friendly, dotted with quiet parks, and traversed by electric trams. Many buildings still reflect 18th- and 19th-century elegance, when the city was at the forefront of the arts and sciences. Compared with most modern European urban centers, the pace of life is slow.

Vienna (*Wien* in German—pronounced "veen") has always been considered the easternmost city of the West. For 640 years, Vienna was the capital of the enormous Austrian Empire (a.k.a. the Austro-Hungarian Empire, a.k.a. the Habsburg Empire). Stretching from the Alps of northern Italy to the rugged Carpathians of Romania, and from the banks of the Danube to sunny Dubrovnik, this multiethnic empire was arguably the most powerful European entity since Rome. And yet, Vienna was a kind of Eastern European melting pot—of its 50 million people, only six million were Austrian. Today, the truly Viennese person is not Austrian, but a second-generation Habsburg cocktail, with grandparents from the distant corners of the old empire—Hungary, the Czech Republic, Slovakia, Poland, Slovenia, Croatia, Bosnia-Herzegovina, Serbia, Romania, and Italy.

Vienna reached its peak in the 19th century, when it was on a par with London and Paris in size and importance. It became one

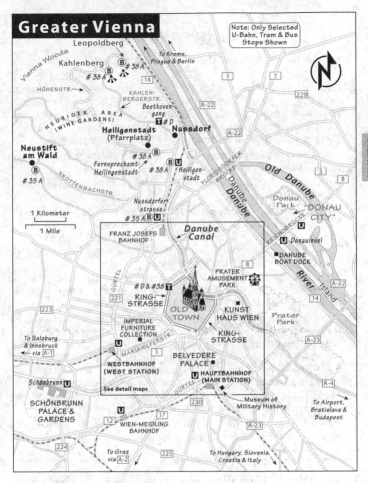

of Europe's cultural capitals, home to groundbreaking composers (Beethoven, Mozart, Brahms, Strauss), scientists (Doppler, Boltzmann), philosophers (Freud, Husserl, Schlick, Gödel, Steiner), architects (Wagner, Loos), and painters (Klimt, Schiele, Kokoschka). By the turn of the 20th century, Vienna was one of the world's most populous cities and sat on the cusp between stuffy Old World monarchism and subversive modern trends.

However, after starting and losing World War I, the Habsburgs lost their far-flung holdings. Then came World War II: While Vienna's old walls had long held out would-be invaders—Germanic barbarians (in Roman times), marauding Magyars (today's Hungarians, 10th century), Mongol hordes (13th century), Ottoman Turks (the sieges of 1529 and 1683)—they were no match for WWII bombs, which destroyed nearly a quarter of the city's

Austria Almanac

Official Name: Republik Österreich ("Eastern Empire"), or simply Österreich.

Population: Of Austria's 8.3 million people, 91 percent are ethnic Austrians; 4 percent are from the former Yugoslavia. Three out of four Austrians are Catholic; about one in twenty is Muslim. German is the dominant language (though there are a few Slovene- and Hungarian-speaking villages in border areas).

Latitude and Longitude: 47°N and 13°E. The latitude is the same as Minnesota or Washington state.

Area: With 32,400 square miles, Austria is similar in size to South Carolina or Maine.

Geography: The northeast is flat and well-populated; the less-populated southwest is mountainous, with the Alps rising up to the 12,450-foot Grossglockner peak. The 1,770-mile-long Danube River meanders west-to-east through the upper part of the country, passing through Vienna.

Biggest Cities: One in five Austrians lives in the capital of Vienna (1.7 million in the city; 2.4 million in the greater metropolitan area). Graz has 265,000 people; Linz has 191,000.

Economy: Austria borders eight other European countries and is well-integrated into the EU economy. The Gross Domestic Product is $350 billion (similar to that of Massachusetts). Its per-capita GDP of $40,000 is among Europe's highest. One of its biggest moneymakers is tourism. Austria produces wood, paper products (nearly half the land is forested)...and Red Bull Energy Drink. The country's aging population increasingly collects social security—a situation that will strain the national budget in years to come.

Government: Austria has been officially neutral since 1955, and its citizens take a dim view of European unity. Although

buildings. In the Cold War, neutral Austria took a big bite out of the USSR's Warsaw Pact buffer zone—and Vienna became, for a time, a den of spies.

Today Vienna has settled down into a somewhat sleepy, pleasant place where culture is still king. Classical music is everywhere. People nurse a pastry and coffee over the daily paper at small cafés. It's a city of world-class museums, big and small. Anyone with an interest in painting, music, architecture, beautiful objects, or Sacher-Torte with whipped cream will feel right at home.

From a practical standpoint, Vienna serves as a prime "gateway" city. The location is central and convenient to most major Eastern European destinations. Actually farther east than Prague, Ljubljana, and Zagreb, and just upstream on the Danube from Budapest and Bratislava, Vienna is an ideal launchpad for a journey into the East.

VIENNA

right-leaning parties made substantial gains in recent elections, the government continues to be a center-left coalition, currently headed by Federal President Heinz Fischer and Chancellor Werner Faymann (both Social Democrats). Austria is the only EU nation that lets 16- and 17-year-olds vote.

Flag: Three horizontal bands of red, white, and red.

Cuisine: Austrian treats include Wiener schnitzel (breaded veal cutlet); *Knödel* (dumplings); *Apfelstrudel* (apple strudel); *Kaiserschmarr'n* (fluffy, caramelized pancake strips); and fancy desserts like the Sacher-Torte, Vienna's famous chocolate cake.

Language: Austria's official language is German. It's important to greet people in the breakfast room and those you pass on the streets or meet in shops. The Austrian version of "Hi" is a cheerful *"Grüss Gott."* You'll get the correct pronunciation after the first volley—listen and copy. For German survival phrases, see the charts at the end of this chapter.

Gemütlichkeit: The Austrians are not Germans—and they cherish their distinct cultural and historical traditions. Austria is mellow and relaxed compared with Deutschland. *Gemütlichkeit* is the word most often used to describe this special Austrian cozy-and-easy approach to life. On the other hand, Austria feels relatively stiff and formal compared with most of Eastern Europe (except maybe Hungary).

The Average Austrian: A typical Austrian is 43 years old, has 1.41 children, and will live to be 79. He or she inhabits a 900-square-foot home and spends leisure time with a circle of a few close friends. Chances are high that someone in that closely knit circle is a smoker—Austrians smoke more cigarettes per day than any other Europeans.

PLANNING YOUR TIME

For a big city, Vienna is pleasant and laid-back. Packed with sights, it's worth two days and two nights on even the speediest trip. To be grand-tour efficient, you could sleep on the train on your way in and out—Berlin, Prague, Kraków, Venice, Rome, and the Rhine Valley are each handy night trains away. Daytime trains connect Vienna to many Eastern European destinations, including Budapest, Zagreb, Ljubljana, and Prague.

Palace Choices: The Hofburg and Schönbrunn are both world-class palaces, but seeing both is redundant—with limited time or money, I'd choose just one. The Hofburg comes with the popular Sisi Museum and is right in the town center, making for an easy visit. With more time, a visit to Schönbrunn—set outside town amid a grand and regal garden—is also a great experience. (For efficient sightseeing, drivers should note that

Schönbrunn Palace is conveniently on the way out of town toward Salzburg.)

Vienna in One to Four Days

Below is a suggested itinerary for how to spend your time. I've left the **evenings** open for your choice of activities. The best options are taking in a concert, opera, or other musical event; enjoying a leisurely dinner (and people-watching) in the stately old town or atmospheric Spittelberg Quarter; heading out to the *Heuriger* wine pubs in the foothills of the Vienna Woods; or touring the Haus der Musik interactive music museum (open nightly until 22:00). Plan your evenings based on the schedule of musical events while you're in town. If you've downloaded my audio tours (see "Rick Steves Audio Europe" sidebar on page 13), the Vienna City Walk works wonderfully in the evening. Whenever you need a break, linger in a classic Viennese café.

Day 1

9:00   Take the 1.5-hour Red Bus City Tour, or circle the Ringstrasse by tram, to get your bearings.

10:30 Drop by the TI for planning and ticket needs.

11:00 Take the Opera tour (schedule varies, confirm at TI).

14:00 Follow my Vienna City Walk, including visits to the Kaisergruft and St. Stephen's Cathedral (nave closes at 16:30, or 17:30 June-Aug).

Day 2

9:00   Browse the colorful Naschmarkt.

11:00 Tour the Kunsthistorisches Museum.

14:00 Tour the Hofburg Palace Imperial Apartments and Treasury.

Day 3

10:00 Visit Belvedere Palace, with its fine collection of Viennese art and great city views.

15:00 Tour Schönbrunn Palace to enjoy the royal apartments and grounds.

Day 4

10:00 Enjoy (depending on your interest) the engaging Karlsplatz sights (Karlskirche, Wien Museum, Academy of Fine Arts, and The Secession).

12:00 Tour the Albertina Museum.

15:00 Shoppers can stroll Mariahilfer Strasse. Nonshoppers can rent a bike and head out to the modern Donau City "downtown" sector, Danube Island (for fun people-watching), and the Prater amusement park.

Orientation to Vienna

Vienna sits between the Vienna Woods (Wienerwald) and the Danube (Donau). To the southeast is industrial sprawl. The Alps,  which arc across Europe from Marseille, end at Vienna's wooded hills, providing a popular playground for walking and sipping new wine. This greenery's momentum carries on into the city. More than half of Vienna is parkland, filled with ponds, gardens, trees, and statue-maker memories of Austria's glory days.

Think of the city map as a target with concentric sections: The bull's-eye is St. Stephen's Cathedral, the towering cathedral south of the Danube. Surrounding that is the old town, bound tightly by the circular road known as the Ringstrasse, marking what used to be the city wall. The Gürtel, a broader, later ring road, contains the rest of downtown. Outside the Gürtel lies the uninteresting sprawl of modern Vienna.

Addresses start with the *Bezirk* (district) number, followed by the street and building number. The Ringstrasse (a.k.a. the Ring) circles the first district. Any address higher than the ninth *Bezirk* is beyond the Gürtel, far from the center.

Much of Vienna's sightseeing—and most of my recommended restaurants—are located in the Old Town (the first district, inside the Ringstrasse). Walking across this circular area takes about 30 minutes. St. Stephen's Cathedral sits in the center, at the intersection of the two main (pedestrian-only) streets: Kärntner Strasse and the Graben.

Several sights sit along, or just beyond, the Ringstrasse: To the southwest are the Hofburg and related Habsburg sights and the Kunsthistorisches Museum; to the south is a cluster of intriguing sights near Karlsplatz; to the southeast is Belvedere Palace. A branch of the Danube River (*Donau* in German, DOH-now) borders the Ring to the north.

As a tourist, concern yourself only with this compact old center. When you do, sprawling Vienna suddenly becomes manageable.

TOURIST INFORMATION

Vienna's main TI is a block behind the Opera at Albertinaplatz (daily 9:00-19:00, free Wi-Fi, theater box office, tel. 01/211-140, www.vienna.info). There's also an airport TI (daily 7:00-22:00, run by a private company). At either TI, confirm your sightseeing plans, and pick up two copies of the free and essential city map with a list of museums and hours (also available at most hotels). Rip up one copy of the Vienna map—reducing it down to just the city-center inset—and keep it in your pocket for ready reference. (Stuff the other copy in your backpack in case you need it.) Also look for the monthly program of concerts (called *Wien-Programm*) and the *Vienna from A to Z* booklet (both described below), and the annual city guide (called *Vienna Journal*). Ask about their program of guided walks (€14 each). While hotel and ticket-booking agencies at the train station and airport can answer questions and give out maps and brochures, I'd rely on the official TI.

Wien-Programm: This monthly entertainment guide is particularly important, listing all sorts of events, including music, theater, walks, expositions, and museum exhibits. Note the key for abbreviations on the inside cover, which helps make this dense booklet useful even for non-German speakers.

Vienna from A to Z: Consider this handy booklet, sold by the main TI for €3.60. Every major building in Vienna sports a numbered flag banner that keys into this booklet and into the TI's city map—handy for finding your way if you get turned around.

Sightseeing Passes and Combo-Tickets

The much-promoted €22 **Vienna Card** (www.wienkarte.at) is not worth the mental overhead for most travelers. It gives you a 72-hour transit pass (worth €16.50) and minor discounts (usually 10-25 percent) at the city's museums. It might save the busy sightseer a few euros (though seniors and students will do better with their own discounts). The 48-hour version (€19) is an even worse deal.

Some sights offer **combo-tickets** that cover several venues at a single price. If you're seeing those sights anyway, a combo-ticket can save you money and let you skip ticket-buying lines at your next sight. Buy these combo-tickets at any of the participating sights.

Sisi Ticket: This €25.50 ticket covers the Hofburg Imperial Apartments (with its Sisi Museum and Porcelain Collection) as well as Schönbrunn Palace's Grand Tour and the Imperial Furniture Collection. When used at Schönbrunn, the ticket lets you enter the palace immediately, without a reserved entry time. The ticket saves €0.50 off the combined cost of the Hofburg Apartments and Schönbrunn, making the good Imperial Furniture Collection effectively free.

Hofburg Treasury and Kunsthistorisches Museum/New Palace: If you're seeing the Hofburg Treasury (royal regalia and crown jewels) and the Kunsthistorisches Museum (world-class art collection), this €20 combo-ticket is well worth it (and you get the New Palace as a bonus).

Haus der Musik and Mozarthaus: The Haus der Musik (mod museum with interactive exhibits) has a combo deal with Mozarthaus Vienna (exhibits and artifacts about the great composer) for €17—a €5 savings for music lovers.

ARRIVAL IN VIENNA
By Train

Vienna has just finished building an impressive new Hauptbahnhof (main train station, in the location of the former Südbahnhof) and is part way through the process of consolidating most—but not all—train departures there. Confirm carefully which station your train uses. Some trains headed west (to Salzburg and Munich) may continue to leave from the Westbahnhof, and regional trains to Krems will probably continue to leave from the Franz-Josefs-Bahnhof. From most of Vienna's stations, the handiest connection to the center is the U-Bahn (subway) system; line numbers and stop names are noted below. For some stations, there's also a handy tram connection. (See the "Vienna's Public Transportation" map on page 1158.)

Wien Hauptbahnhof

Vienna's new central station (to the south of downtown) opened in early 2014 and is gradually coming online, with twelve pass-through tracks, shopping, and all the services you may need. The city hopes that, besides bringing most of Vienna's train connections under a single roof, the station will inject life into a neighborhood that's been mildly run-down. But with just one U-Bahn line linking to the station, it's often better to reach it by tram or bus.

Getting into Vienna: To reach the city center, ride the U-1 for 2-3 stops (direction: Leopoldau) to Karlsplatz or Stephansplatz, or take tram #D (which runs along the Ring). To reach Mariahilfer Strasse, hop on bus #13A. Tram #O runs from the station to Landstrasse and the Wien-Mitte station (for airport trains).

Westbahnhof (West Station)

This station (at the west end of Mariahilfer Strasse, on the U-3 and U-6 lines) has a modern, user-friendly mall of services, shops, and eateries (including the recommended Buffet Trześniewski—near track 9—with €1.20 finger sandwiches). You can't help but admire how nicely the station's drab, functionalist 1950s shell has been spruced up. From here trains run to/from many points to the west (including **Melk, Hallstatt, Salzburg, Innsbruck,** and **Munich**), though some of these trains may shift to the Hauptbahnhof. You'll find travel agencies, grocery stores, ATMs, change offices, a post office, luggage lockers (€2-4.50, on the ground floor by the WC).

The private **Westbahn** service also leaves from here. It connects Vienna and Salzburg hourly and offers an alternative to the state-run ÖBB trains, including free Wi-Fi and the option to buy your ticket on board for no extra charge (www.westbahn.at). Westbahn's regular fares are half those of ÖBB, but Westbahn doesn't offer the range of money-saving passes that ÖBB does. Eventually Westbahn may move its service to the Hauptbahnhof—check when booking.

Getting into Vienna: For the city center, follow orange signs to the U-3 (direction: Simmering). If your hotel is along Mariahilfer Strasse, your stop is on this line, but it may be simpler to walk.

Franz-Josefs-Bahnhof

This small station in the northern part of the city serves **Krems** and other points on the **north bank of the Danube.** Connections from **Český Krumlov** in the Czech Republic sometimes arrive here too.

Getting into Vienna: Although the station doesn't have a U-Bahn stop, convenient tram #D connects it to the city center. Also note that trains coming into town from this direction stop at the Spittelau station (on the U-4 and U-6 lines), one stop before they end at the Franz-Josefs-Bahnhof; consider hopping off your train at Spittelau for a handy connection to other points in Vienna. (Similarly, if you're headed out of town and you're not near the tram #D route, take the U-Bahn to Spittelau and catch your train there.)

Wien-Mitte Bahnhof

This smaller station, just west of the Ring, is the terminus for S-Bahn and CAT trains to the airport. Be aware that its U-Bahn station is called "Landstrasse." From here, take the U-3 to hotels near Stephansplatz or Mariahilfer Strasse, and the U-4 to hotels that are closer to the airport. It's also connected directly to the Hauptbahnhof by tram #O.

By Plane

Vienna International Airport, 12 miles from the center, is easy to reach from downtown (airport code: VIE, airport tel. 01/700-722-233, www.viennaairport.com). It's freshly renovated, with a striking, black-and-white, "less-is-more" color scheme. The arrivals hall has an array of services: TI (run by a private company called Ruefa), shops, ATMs, eateries, and a handy supermarket. Ramps lead down to the lower-level train station.

Connecting the Airport and Central Vienna

By Train: Trains connect the airport with the Wien-Mitte Bahnhof, on the east side of the Ring (described earlier). Choose between two ways of getting to Wien-Mitte: the regular S-7 **S-Bahn train** (€4.40, 24 minutes), and the express **CAT train**

(€12, 16 minutes). Both run twice an hour on the same tracks. The airport tries to steer tourists into taking the CAT train, but it's hard to justify spending almost €8 to save eight minutes of time. I'd take the S-7, unless the CAT is departing first and you're in a big hurry. Trains from downtown start running about 5:00, while the last train from the airport leaves about 23:30.

The **S-Bahn** works just fine and is plenty fast. From the arrivals hall, go down either of the big ramps, follow the red ÖBB signs, then buy a regular two-zone public transport ticket from the multilingual red "Fahrkarten" machines. The €4.40 price includes any transfers to other trams, city buses, S and U-Bahn lines (see www.wienerlinien.at). Trains to downtown are marked *Floridsdorf*. If you'll be using public transportation in Vienna a lot, consider buying a transit pass from the machines instead of a single ticket (see page 1157). As these passes are only valid in Vienna's central zone, you'll need to also buy a €2.10 single ticket to cover the stretch between the airport and the limits of the inner zone.

To take the fast **CAT** (which stands for City Airport Train), follow the green signage down the ramp to your right as you come out into the arrivals hall and buy a ticket from the green machines (one-way-€12, or €14 to also cover the connecting link from Wien-Mitte to your final destination by public transit; round-trip ticket valid 30 days-€19, 4 tickets-€38; usually departs both airport and downtown at :06 and :36 past the hour, www.cityairporttrain. com).

By Bus: Convenient express airport buses go to various points in Vienna: Morzinplatz/Schwedenplatz U-Bahn station (for city-center hotels, 20 minutes), Westbahnhof (for Mariahilfer Strasse hotels, 45 minutes), and Wien-Meidling Bahnhof (30 minutes). Double check your destination as you board (€8, round-trip-€13, 2/hour, buy ticket from driver, tel. 0810-222-333 for timetable info, www.viennaairportlines.at or www.postbus.at).

By Taxi: The 30-minute ride into town costs a fixed €35 from the several companies with desks in the arrivals hall. You can also take a taxi from the taxi rank outside; you'll pay the metered rate (plus a trivial baggage surcharge), which should come out about the same. Save by riding the cheap train/bus downtown, then taking a taxi to your destination.

Connecting the Airport and Other Cities

There are direct bus connections (from platforms 7, 8, and 9) to **Bratislava** and its airport (1-3/hour, 45-60 minutes, two different companies: Blaguss (www.eurolines.at) and Slovak Lines/Post Bus www.slovaklines.sk or www.postbus.at); **Budapest** (5/day, 3-3.5 hours, operated by Blaguss, www.eurolines.at); and **Prague** (8/day, 5.5 hours, www.studentagency.eu, also stops in **Brno**).

VIENNA

Bratislava Airport

The airport in nearby Bratislava, Slovakia—a hub for some low-cost flights—is just an hour away from Vienna (see page 1292 in the Bratislava chapter).

HELPFUL HINTS

Teens Sightsee Free: Those under 19 get in free to state-run museums and sights.

Music Sightseeing Priorities: Be wary of Vienna's various music sights. Many "homes of composers" are pretty disappointing. My advice to music lovers is to concentrate on these activities: Take in a concert, tour the Opera house, snare cheap standing-room tickets to see an opera there (even just part of a performance), enjoy the Haus der Musik, and scour the wonderful Collection of Ancient Musical Instruments in the Hofburg's New Palace. If in town on a Sunday, don't miss the glorious music at the Augustinian Church Mass (see page 1199).

Skip This: The highly advertised experience called Time Travel Vienna (just off the Graben on Habsburgergasse) promises "history, fun, and action." In reality, it's €18 and 45 minutes wasted in a tacky succession of amusement-park history vignettes with much of the information in German only.

Internet Access: You'll find free Wi-Fi hotspots around town, including at the TI, Westbahnhof, Stephansplatz, Naschmarkt, City Hall Park, Prater Park, and Donauinsel. If you need a computer, **Netcafe** is inside a Persian restaurant at the Hotel Capricorno, near the Danube Canal (€4/hour or free with drink, daily 11:00-21:00, Schwedenplatz 3). **Netcafe-Refill** is at Mariahilfer Strasse 103, close to many recommended hotels (€4.50/hour, Mon-Fri 9:00-21:00, Sat 10:00-20:00, closed Sun, tel. 01/595-5558).

Post Offices: The main post office is near Schwedenplatz at Fleischmarkt 19 (Mon-Fri 7:00-22:00, Sat-Sun 9:00-22:00). Convenient branch offices are at the Westbahnhof (Mon-Fri 7:00-21:00, Sat 9:00-18:00, Sun 9:00-14:00) and near the Opera (Mon-Fri 7:00-19:00, closed Sat-Sun, Krugerstrasse 13).

English Bookstore: Stop by the woody and cool **Shakespeare & Co.**, in the historic and atmospheric Ruprechtsviertel district near the Danube Canal (Mon-Fri 9:00-21:00, Sat 9:00-20:00, closed Sun, north of Hoher Markt at Sterngasse 2, tel. 01/535-5053, www.shakespeare.co.at). See the map on page 1181.

Keeping Up with the News: Don't buy newspapers. Read them for free in Vienna's marvelous coffeehouses. It's much classier.

Laundry: **Schnell & Sauber Waschcenter** is big, open long hours, close to Mariahilfer Strasse accommodations, and easily reached from downtown by U-Bahn (self-serve-€9/load, free Wi-Fi; daily 6:00-24:00, Westbahnstrasse 60, U-6: Burggasse/Stadthalle, or take tram #49 to Urban-Loritz-Platz, see map on page 1241, mobile 0660-760-4546, www.schnellundsauber.at).

Travel Agency: Conveniently located on Stephansplatz, **Ruefa** sells tickets for flights, trains, and boats to Bratislava. They'll waive the €8 service charge for train and boat tickets for my readers (Mon-Fri 9:00-18:00, closed Sat-Sun, Stephansplatz 10, tel. 01/513-4000, Gertrude and Sandra speak English).

Toll Sticker: Austria requires cars on its expressways to display a toll sticker (*Vignette*, €8.70/10 days, €25.30/2 months, www.asfinag.at). If your car doesn't have one, buy one at a gas station when you cross the border.

Drinking Water: The Viennese are proud of their perfectly drinkable tap water from Alpine springs. You'll spot locals refilling their little bottles at fountains all over town. In response to—and anticipation of—global warming, the city has installed shiny public water fountains with signs reminding people to stay hydrated (one is on the Graben at the corner of Spiegelgasse). Some restaurants even serve *Leitungswasser* (tap water), though they'll often charge a nominal fee (about €0.40) for the service.

GETTING AROUND VIENNA
By Public Transportation

Take full advantage of Vienna's efficient transit system, which includes trams (a.k.a. streetcars), buses, U-Bahn (subway), and

S-Bahn (faster suburban) trains. It's fast, clean, and easy to navigate. The free Vienna city map, available at TIs and hotels, includes a small schematic transit map.

I generally stick to the tram to zip around the Ring (trams #1, #2, and #D) and take the U-Bahn to outlying sights, hotels, and Vienna's train stations (see map on next page). There are five color-coded U-Bahn lines: U-1 red, U-2 purple, U-3 orange, U-4 green, and U-6 brown. Two useful trams (#D and #O) have letters instead of numbers (a relic from long ago). If you see a bus number that starts with *N* (such as #N38), it's a night bus, which operates after other public transit stops running. Transit info: tel. 01/790-9100, www.wienerlinien.at.

Tickets and Passes: Trams, buses, the U-Bahn, and the

VIENNA

Vienna's Public Transportation

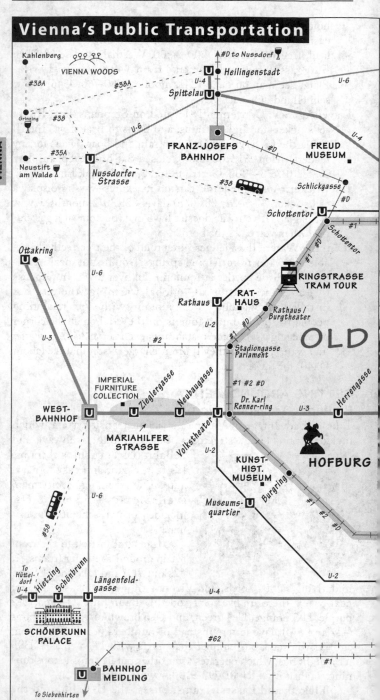

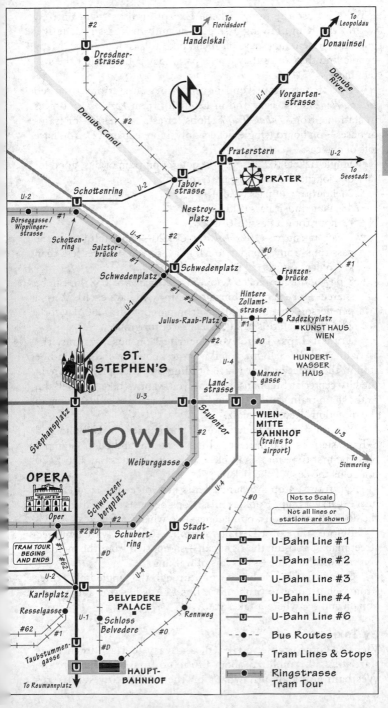

VIENNA

To Floridsdorf

To Leopoldau

Handelskai

Donauinsel

Dresdner-
strasse

Danube River

U-1

Vorgarten-
strasse

Danube Canal

#2

N

Praterstern

U-2

To Seestadt

Schottenring

U-2

Tabor-
strasse

PRATER

Börsegasse /
Wipplinger-
strasse

#1

Schotten-
ring

Nestroy-
platz

U-4

Salztor-
brücke

#1

U-1

#2

Schwedenplatz

Schwedenplatz

#0

Franzen-
brücke

#1

U-1

#1 #2

Hintere
Zollamt-
strasse

Julius-Raab-Platz

#1

Radezkyplatz

#2

KUNST HAUS
WIEN

ST.
STEPHEN'S

#0

U-4

HUNDERT-
WASSER
HAUS

Land-
strasse

Marxer-
gasse

Stephansplatz

U-3

Stubentor

WIEN-
MITTE
BAHNHOF
(trains to
airport)

U-3

To Simmering

TOWN

#2

U-4

Weiburggasse

Not to Scale

Not all lines or
stations are shown

OPERA

#0

Schwartzen-
bergplatz

Stadt-
park

Oper

#2 #D

Schubert-
ring

#2

TRAM TOUR
BEGINS
AND ENDS

#1
#62

#D

U-2

U-4

	U-Bahn Line #1
	U-Bahn Line #2
	U-Bahn Line #3
	U-Bahn Line #4
	U-Bahn Line #6

Karlsplatz

Resselgasse

BELVEDERE
PALACE

Rennweg

Bus Routes

#62

#1

Schloss
Belvedere

U-1

#0

Tram Lines & Stops

Taubstummen-
gasse

#D

Ringstrasse
Tram Tour

To Reumannplatz

HAUPT-
BAHNHOF

S-Bahn all use the same tickets. Except on days spent entirely within the Ring, buying a single- or multiday pass is usually a good investment (and pays off if you take at least four trips). Many people find that, once they have a pass, they end up using the system more.

Buy tickets from vending machines in stations (marked *Fahrkarten/Ticket*, easy and in English), from *Vorverkauf* offices in stations, from *Tabak-Trafik* shops, or as a last resort for trams or buses—on board (single tickets only, more expensive). You have lots of choices:

- Single tickets (€2.20, €2.30 if bought on tram or bus, good for one journey with necessary transfers)
- 24-hour transit pass (€7.60)
- 48-hour transit pass (€13.30)
- 72-hour transit pass (€16.50)
- 7-day transit pass (*Wochenkarte*, €16.20—the catch is that the pass runs from Monday to Monday, so you may get less than seven days of use)
- 8-day "Climate Ticket" *(Acht-Tage-Klimakarte*, €38.40, can be shared—for example, four people for two days each). With a per-person cost of €4.80/day (compared with €7.60/day for a 24-hour pass), this can be a real saver for groups.

Transit Tips: To get your bearings on buses, trams, the U-Bahn, and the S-Bahn, you'll want to know the end-of-the-line stop in the direction that you're heading. For example, if you're in the city center at Stephansplatz and you want to take the U-Bahn to the main train station (Hauptbahnhof), you'd take U-1 going in the direction "Reumannplatz."

You must stamp your ticket at the barriers in U-Bahn and S-Bahn stations, and in the machines on trams and buses (stamp it only the first time for a multiple-use pass). Cheaters pay a stiff €70 fine, plus the cost of the ticket.

On trams, stop announcements are voice-only and easy to miss—carry a map. Rookies miss stops because they fail to open the door. Push buttons, pull latches—do whatever it takes.

Before you exit a U-Bahn station, study the wall-mounted street map. Choosing the right exit—signposted from the moment you step off the train—saves lots of walking.

Cute little electric buses wind through the tangled old center (from Schottentor to Stubentor). Bus #1A is best for a joyride—hop on and see where it takes you.

By Taxi

Vienna's comfortable, civilized, and easy-to-flag-down **taxis** start at €2.50. You'll pay about €10 to go from the Opera to the Westbahnhof. Pay only what's on the meter—any surcharges (other than the €2 fee for calling a cab or €11 fee for the airport) are just crude cabbie rip-offs. Rates are legitimately higher at night.

Consider the luxury of having your own **car and driver.** Johann (a.k.a. John) Lichtl is a gentle, honest, English-speaking cabbie who can take up to four passengers in his car (€27/1 hour, €25/hour for 2 hours or more, €27 to or from airport, mobile 0676-670-6750). Consider a custom-tailored city driving tour (2 hours), a day trip to the Danube Valley (€160), or a visit to the Mauthausen concentration camp memorial with a little Danube sightseeing en route (€200).

By Bike

With more than 600 miles of bike lanes (and a powerful Green Party), Vienna is a great city on two wheels. Bikes ride the U-Bahn for free (but they aren't allowed during weekday rush hours).

The bike path along the Ring is wonderfully entertaining—you'll enjoy the shady park-like ambience of the boulevard while rolling by many of the city's top sights. Besides the Ring, your best sightseeing by bike is through Stadtpark (City Park), across Danube Island, and out to the modern Donau City business district. These routes are easy to follow on the free tourist city map available from the TI. Pedestrians should stay out of red-colored pavement (the usual marking for bike lanes), but also watch out for bike lanes just marked with white lines.

Borrowing a Free/Cheap Bike: Citybike Wien lets you borrow bikes from public racks all over town (toll tel. 0810-500-500, www. citybikewien.at).

The three-speed bikes are heavy and clunky—and come with a basket, built-in lock, and ads on the side—but they're perfect for a short, practical joyride in the center (such as around the Ringstrasse).

While bike programs in many other European cities are difficult for tourists to take advantage of, Vienna's system is easy to use. Bikes are locked into more than 100 stalls scattered through the city center. To borrow a bike, use the computer terminal at any rack: Press the credit card button, insert and pull out your card, register your name and address, and select a username and password for future rentals (you can also register online at www.citybikewien.at). Then, unlock the bike you want by punching in its number. First-time registration is €1, and they'll place a refundable €20 hold on your card while you're using the bike (only one bike per credit card—couples must use two different cards). Since the bikes are designed for short-term use, it costs more per hour the longer you keep it (first hour-free, second hour-€1, third hour-€2, €4/hour after that). When you're done, drop off your bike at any stall, and make sure it's fully locked into the rack to avoid being charged for more time.

Renting a Higher-Quality Bike: If you want to ride beyond the town center—or you simply want a better set of wheels—check out **Pedal Power,** with a handy central location near the Opera house. The local authority on bike touring in town and to points along the Danube, Pedal Power rents bikes and provides good biking info (€5/hour, €17/4 hours, €27/24 hours, daily May-Sept 8:30-18:00, Elisabethstrasse 13—see map on page 1181, tel. 01/729-7234, www.pedalpower.at). For a better selection and better gear, it's smart to use their main office by Prater Park. Though less central, it's very easy to get to (U-1 or U-2: Praterstern, then walk 100 yards to Ausstellungsstrasse 3). They can also deliver a bike to your hotel and pick it up when you're done (€32/day including delivery, service available year-round), and they organize bike tours (described later). Pedal Power offers a Rick Steves discount to anyone with this book.

Tours in Vienna

To sightsee on your own, download my series of free audio tours that illuminate some of Vienna's top sights and neighborhoods (see sidebar on page 13).

Walking Tours

The *Walks in Vienna* brochure (available at the TI) and the TI website describe many guided walks. A basic 1.5-hour "Vienna at First Glance" introductory walk is offered daily throughout the summer (€14, leaves at 14:00 from in front of the main TI, just behind the Opera, in both English and German, just show up, tel. 01/774-8901, mobile 0664-260-4388, www.wienguide.at).

Bike Tours

Pedal Power runs a three-hour tour twice daily from May to September, covering the central district. The morning tour is English-only, while the afternoon tour is bilingual (€29/tour includes bike, €10 extra to keep bike for the day, departs at 10:00 and 14:30 from the statue in Schillerplatz in front of the Academy of Fine Arts, across the Ring from the Opera, tel. 01/729-7234, www.pedalpower.at). They also rent bikes and offer Segway tours daily in summer (www.segway-vienna.at).

For a private bike tour, contact guide **Wolfgang Höfler** (€150/3 hours, bike not included, mobile 0676-304-4940, www.vienna-aktivtours.com, office@vienna-aktivtours.com; also leads walking tours—see listing, later, under "Local Guides").

Bus Tours

Red Bus City Tours' convertible buses do a 1.5-hour loop, hitting the highlights of the city with a 20-minute shopping break in the middle. They cover the main first-district attractions as well as a big bus can, along with the entire Ringstrasse. But the most interesting part of the tour is outside the center—zipping through Prater Park, over the Danube for a glimpse of the city's Danube Island playground, and into the "Donau City" skyscraper zone. If the weather's good, the bus goes topless and offers great opportunities for photos. Tours start one block behind the Opera at the main TI—see the map on page 1181 for the location (€14 ticket from driver, ask about discount with this book if purchased from "office" in the souvenir shop at Operngasse 2—right by where the tour begins; departs hourly April-Oct 10:00-18:00, Nov-March at 11:00, 13:00, and 15:00; pretty good recorded narration in any language, your own earbuds are better than the beat-up headphones they provide, tel. 01/512-4030, www.redbuscitytours.at, Gabriel).

Vienna Sightseeing offers a three-hour city tour, including a tour of Schönbrunn Palace (€39, 3/day April-Oct, 2/day Nov-March). They also run hop-on, hop-off bus tours with recorded commentary. The schedule is posted curbside (three different one-hour routes, €13/1 route, €16/2 routes, €20/all day, departs from the Opera 4/hour July-Aug 10:00-20:00, runs less frequently and stops earlier off-season, tel. 01/7124-6830, www.viennasightseeing.at). Given the city's excellent public transportation and mostly walkable sights, I'd skip this tour; if you just want a quick guided city tour, take the Red Bus tours recommended above.

Ring Tram Tour

One of Europe's great streets, the Ringstrasse is lined with many of the city's top sights. Take a tram ride around the ring with my free audio tour (see page 13), which gives you a fun orientation and a ridiculously quick glimpse of some major sights as you glide by. Neither tram #1 nor #2 makes the entire loop around the Ring, but you can see it all by making one transfer between them (at the Schwedenplatz stop). You can use a single transit ticket to cover the whole route, including the transfer (though you're not allowed to interrupt your trip, except to transfer). For more on riding Vienna's trams, see page 1157.

The **Vienna Ring Tram,** a yellow made-for-tourists streetcar, is an easier though pricier option, running clockwise along the entire Ringstrasse (€8 for 30-minute loop, 2/hour 10:00-17:30, recorded narration, includes a good set of earbuds you can keep and reuse, www.wienerlinien.at). The 25-minute tour starts every half-hour at Schwedenplatz. At each stop you'll see an ad for this

Vienna at a Glance

▲▲▲**Opera** Dazzling, world-famous opera house. **Hours:** By guided tour only, July-Aug generally Mon-Sat at the top of each hour 10:00-16:00; fewer tours Sept-June and Sun. See page 1178.

▲▲▲**St**. **Stephen's Cathedral** Enormous, historic Gothic cathedral in the center of Vienna. **Hours:** Foyer—Mon-Sat 6:00-22:00, Sun 7:00-22:00; main nave—Mon-Sat 9:00-11:30 & 13:00-16:30, Sun 13:00-16:30, until 17:30 June-Aug. See page 1184.

▲▲▲**Hofburg Imperial Apartments** Lavish main residence of the Habsburgs. **Hours:** Daily July-Aug 9:00-18:00, Sept-June 9:00-17:30. See page 1189.

▲▲▲**Hofburg Treasury** The Habsburgs' collection of jewels, crowns, and other valuables—the best on the Continent. **Hours:** Wed-Mon 9:00-17:30, closed Tue. See page 1195.

▲▲▲**Kunsthistorisches Museum** World-class exhibit of the Habsburgs' art collection, including works by Raphael, Titian, Caravaggio, Rembrandt, and Bruegel. **Hours:** June-Aug daily 10:00-18:00; Sept-May Tue-Sun 10:00-18:00, closed Mon; Thu until 21:00 year-round. See page 1204.

▲▲▲**Schönbrunn Palace** Spectacular summer residence of the Habsburgs, rivaling the grandeur of Versailles. **Hours:** Daily July-Aug 8:30-18:30, April-June and Sept-Oct 8:30-17:30, Nov-March 8:30-17:00. See page 1223.

▲▲**Haus der Musik** Modern museum with interactive exhibits on Vienna's favorite pastime. **Hours:** Daily 10:00-22:00. See page 1179.

▲▲**Hofburg New Palace Museums** Uncrowded collection of armor, musical instruments, and ancient Greek statues, in the elegant halls of a Habsburg palace. **Hours:** Wed-Sun 10:00-18:00, closed Mon-Tue. See page 1197.

▲▲**Albertina Museum** Habsburg residence with decent apartments and world-class temporary exhibits. **Hours:** Daily 10:00-18:00, Wed until 21:00. See page 1200.

▲▲**Kaisergruft** Crypt for the Habsburg royalty. **Hours:** Daily 10:00-18:00. See page 1202.

▲▲**Belvedere Palace** Elegant palace of Prince Eugene of Savoy, with a collection of 19th- and 20th-century Austrian art (including Klimt). **Hours:** Daily 10:00-18:00, Lower Palace only until 21:00 on Wed. See page 1215.

▲St. **Peter's Church** Beautiful Baroque church in the old center. **Hours:** Mon-Fri 7:00-20:00, Sat-Sun 9:00-21:00. See page 1182.

▲**Spanish Riding School** Prancing white Lipizzaner stallions. **Hours:** Spring (Feb-June) and fall (mid-Aug-Dec) only, performances usually Sat-Sun at 11:00, plus less-impressive training sessions generally Tue-Fri 10:00-12:00. See page 1197.

▲St. **Michael's Church Crypt** Final resting place of about 100 wealthy 18th-century Viennese. **Hours:** By tour Mon-Fri at 11:00 and 13:00, no tours Sat-Sun. See page 1203.

▲**Natural History Museum** Big building facing the Kunsthistorisches, featuring the ancient *Venus of Willendorf*. **Hours:** Wed-Mon 9:00-18:30, Wed until 21:00, closed Tue. See page 1209.

▲**Karlskirche** Baroque church offering the unique (and temporary) chance to ride an elevator up into the dome. **Hours:** Mon-Sat 9:00-18:00, Sun 13:00-19:00. See page 1211.

▲**Academy of Fine Arts** Small but exciting collection by 15th- to 18th-century masters. **Hours:** Tue-Sun 10:00-18:00, closed Mon. See page 1212.

▲**The Secession** Art Nouveau exterior and Klimt paintings *in situ*. **Hours:** Tue-Sun 10:00-18:00, closed Mon. See page 1213.

▲**Naschmarkt** Sprawling, lively outdoor market. **Hours:** Mon-Fri 6:00-18:30, Sat 6:00-17:00, closed Sun, closes earlier in winter. See page 1214.

▲**Museum of Military History** Huge collection of artifacts tracing the military history of the Habsburg Empire. **Hours:** Daily 9:00-17:00. See page 1220.

▲**Kunst Haus Wien Museum** Modern art museum dedicated to zany local artist/environmentalist Hundertwasser. **Hours:** Daily 10:00-19:00. See page 1220.

▲**Imperial Furniture Collection** Eclectic collection of Habsburg furniture. **Hours:** Tue-Sun 10:00-18:00, closed Mon. See page 1222.

tram tour (look for *VRT Ring-Rund Sightseeing*). The schedule clearly notes the next departure time.

Horse-and-Buggy Tour

These traditional horse-and-buggies, called *Fiakers,* take rich romantics on clip-clop tours lasting 20 minutes (Old Town-€55), 40 minutes (Old Town and the Ring-€80), or one hour (all the above, but more thorough-€110). You can share the ride and cost with up to five people. Because it's a kind of guided tour, talk to a few drivers before choosing a carriage, and pick someone who's fun and speaks English (tel. 01/401-060).

Local Guides

You'll pay about €140-150 for two hours. Get a group of six or more together and call it a party. The tourist board's website (www.vienna.info) has a long list of local guides with their specialties and contact information.

My favorite private Vienna guides are: **Lisa Zeiler** (€150/2 hours, mobile 0699-1203-7550, lisa.zeiler@gmx.at); **Wolfgang Höfler** (a generalist with a knack for having psychoanalytical fun with history, enjoys the big changes of the 19th and 20th centuries, €150/2 hours, mobile 0676-304-4940, www.vienna-aktivtours.com, office@vienna-aktivtours.com, also leads bike tours—described earlier); **Adrienn Bartek-Rhomberg** (€150/half-day, see website for tour topics, mobile 0650-826-6965, www.experience-vienna.at, office@experience-vienna.at); and **Gerhard Strassgschwandtner** (who runs the Third Man Museum—see page 1233—and is passionate about history in all its marvelous complexity, €140/2 hours, mobile 0676-475-7818, www.special-vienna.com, gerhard@special-vienna.com). If these folks are booked, any of them can set you up with another good guide.

Vienna City Walk

This self-guided walk connects the top three sights in Vienna's old center: the Opera, St. Stephen's Cathedral, and Hofburg Palace. These and many of the other sights you'll see along this walk are covered in more detail elsewhere in this chapter (to find the full descriptions, flip to "Sights in Vienna," later) and offer an overview of Vienna's past and present. Allow one hour, and more time if you plan to step into any of the major sights along the way. You can download a free Rick Steves **audio tour** of this walk; see page 13.

• *Begin at the square outside Vienna's landmark Opera house. (The*

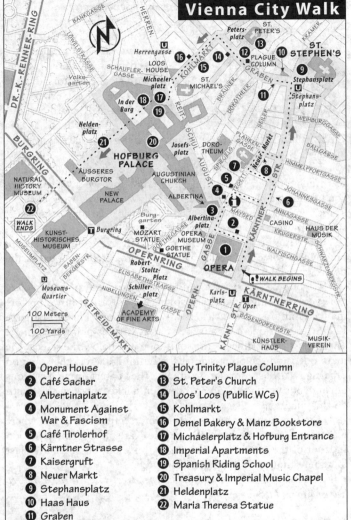

Vienna City Walk

1. Opera House
2. Café Sacher
3. Albertinaplatz
4. Monument Against War & Fascism
5. Café Tirolerhof
6. Kärntner Strasse
7. Kaisergruft
8. Neuer Markt
9. Stephansplatz
10. Haas Haus
11. Graben
12. Holy Trinity Plague Column
13. St. Peter's Church
14. Loos' Loos (Public WCs)
15. Kohlmarkt
16. Demel Bakery & Manz Bookstore
17. Michaelerplatz & Hofburg Entrance
18. Imperial Apartments
19. Spanish Riding School
20. Treasury & Imperial Music Chapel
21. Heldenplatz
22. Maria Theresa Statue

entrance faces the Ringstrasse; we're starting at the busy pedestrian square that's to the right of the entrance as you're facing it.)

❶ Opera House

If Vienna is the world capital of classical music, this building is its throne room, one of the planet's premier houses of music. It's typical of Vienna's 19th-century buildings in that it features a revival style—Neo-Renaissance—with arched windows, half-columns, and the sloping, copper mansard roof typical of French

Renaissance *châteaux*.

Since the structure was built in 1869, almost all of the opera world's luminaries have passed through here. Its former musical directors include Gustav Mahler, Herbert von Karajan, and Richard Strauss. Luciano Pavarotti, Maria Callas, Placido Domingo, and many other greats have sung from its stage.

In the pavement along the side of the Opera (and all along Kärntner Strasse, the bustling shopping street we'll visit shortly), you'll find star plaques forming a Hollywood-style walk of fame. These represent the stars of classical music—famous composers, singers, musicians, and conductors.

Looking up at the Opera, notice the giant outdoor screen onto which some live performances are projected (as noted in the posted schedules).

If you're a fan, take a guided tour of the Opera. If you're not, you still might consider springing for an evening performance (standing-room tickets are surprisingly cheap; see page 1229). Regular opera tickets are sold at various points near here: The closest ticket office is the small one just below the screen; the main one is on the other side of the building, across the street on Operngasse. For information about other entertainment options during your visit, check in at the Wien Ticket kiosk in the booth on this square.

The Opera house marks a busy intersection in Vienna, where Kärntner Strasse meets the Ring. The Karlsplatz U-Bahn station in front of the Opera is an underground shopping mall with fast food, newsstands, and lots of pickpockets.

• *Walk behind the Opera and across the street toward the dark-red awning to find the famous...*

❷ Café Sacher

This is the home of the world's classiest chocolate cake, the Sacher-Torte: two layers of cake separated by apricot jam and covered in dark-chocolate icing, usually served with whipped cream. It was invented in a fit of improvisation in 1832 by Franz Sacher, dessert chef to Prince Metternich (the mastermind diplomat who redrew the map of post-Napoleonic Europe). The cake became world famous when the inventor's

son served it next door at his hotel (you may have noticed the fancy doormen). Many locals complain that the cakes here have gone downhill, and many tourists are surprised by how dry they are— you really need that dollop of *Schlagobers*. Still, coffee and a slice of cake here can be €8 well invested for the historic ambience alone (daily 8:00-24:00). While the café itself is grotesquely touristy, the adjacent Sacher Stube has ambience and natives to spare (same prices, daily 10:00-24:00). For maximum elegance, sit inside.

• *Continue past Hotel Sacher. At the end of the street is a small, triangular, cobbled square adorned with modern sculptures.*

❸ Albertinaplatz

As you approach the square, to the right you'll find the **TI.** On your left, the tan-and-white Neoclassical building with the statue

alcoves marks the tip of the Hofburg Palace—the sprawling complex of buildings that was long the seat of Habsburg power (we'll end this walk at the palace's center). The balustraded terrace up top was originally part of Vienna's defensive rampart. Later, it was the balcony of Empress Maria Theresa's daughter Maria Christina, who lived at this end of the palace. Today, her home houses the **Albertina Museum,** topped by a sleek, controversial titanium canopy (called the "diving board" by critics). The museum's plush, 19th-century staterooms are hung with facsimiles from its choice collection of prints, watercolors, and drawings (the originals are too light-sensitive to be displayed continuously), and a modern addition is dedicated to classical modern art, covering each artistic stage from Impressionism to the present day.

Albertinaplatz itself is filled with sculptures that make up the powerful, thought-provoking ❹ **Monument Against War and Fascism,** which commemorates the dark years when Austria came under Nazi rule (1938-1945).

The memorial has four parts. The split white monument, *The Gates of Violence,* remembers victims of all wars and violence. Standing directly in front of it, you're at the gates of a concentration camp. Then, as you explore the statues, you step into a montage of wartime images: clubs and WWI gas masks, a dying woman birthing a future soldier, and chained slave laborers sitting on a pedestal of granite cut from the infamous quarry at Mauthausen concentration camp (located not far up the Danube from here). The hunched-over figure on the ground behind is a Jew forced to scrub anti-Nazi graffiti off a street with a toothbrush. Of

Vienna's 200,000 Jews, more than 65,000 died in Nazi concentration camps. The sculpture with its head buried in the stone is Orpheus entering the underworld, meant to remind Austrians (and the rest of us) of the victims of Nazism...and the consequences of not keeping our governments on track. Behind that, the 1945 declaration that established Austria's second republic—and enshrined human rights—is cut into the stone.

Viewing this monument gains even more emotional impact when you realize what happened on this spot: During a WWII bombing attack, several hundred people were buried alive when the cellar they were using as shelter was demolished.

Austria was led into World War II by Germany, which annexed the country in 1938, saying Austrians were wannabe Germans anyway. But Austrians are not Germans—never were, never will be. They're quick to proudly tell you that Austria was founded in the 10th century, whereas Germany wasn't born until 1870. For seven years just before and during World War II (1938-1945), there was no Austria. In 1955, after 10 years of joint occupation by the victorious Allies, Austria regained total independence on the condition that it would be forever neutral (and never join NATO or the Warsaw Pact). To this day, Austria is outside of NATO (and Germany).

Behind the monument is ❺ **Café Tirolerhof,** a classic Viennese café full of things that time has passed by: chandeliers, marble tables, upholstered booths, waiters in tuxes, and newspapers. For more on Vienna's cafés, see page 1254.

Often parked nearby are the Red Bus City Tour buses, offering a handy way to get a quick overview of the city (see "Tours in Vienna," earlier).

• *From the café, turn right on Führichsgasse, passing the cafeteria-style Rosenberger Markt Restaurant. Walk one block until you hit...*

❻ Kärntner Strasse

This grand, traffic-free street is the people-watching delight of this in-love-with-life city. Today's Kärntner Strasse (KAYRNT-ner SHTRAH-seh) is mostly a crass commercial pedestrian mall—its famed elegant shops are long gone. But locals know it's the same road Crusaders marched down as they headed off from St. Stephen's Cathedral for the Holy Land in the 12th century. Its name indicates that it leads south, toward the region of Kärnten (Carinthia, a province divided between Austria and Slovenia). Today it's full of shoppers and street musicians.

Where Führichsgasse meets Kärntner Strasse, note the city **Casino** (across the street and a half-block to your right, at #41)—once venerable, now tacky, it exemplifies the worst of the street's evolution. Turn left to head up Kärntner Strasse, going away from the Opera. As you walk along, be sure to look up, above the modern storefronts, for glimpses of the street's former glory. Near the end of the block, on the left at #26, **J & L Lobmeyr Crystal** ("Founded in 1823") still has its impressive brown storefront with gold trim, statues, and the Habsburg double-eagle. In the market for some $400 napkin rings? Lobmeyr's your place. Inside, breathe in the classic Old World ambience as you climb up to the glass museum (free entry, Mon-Fri 10:00-19:00, Sat 10:00-18:00, closed Sun).

• At the end of the block, turn left on Marco d'Aviano Gasse (passing the fragrant flower stall) to make a short detour to the square called Neuer Markt. Straight ahead is an orange-ish church with a triangular roof and cross, the Capuchin Church. In its basement is the...

❼ Kaisergruft

Under the church sits the Imperial Crypt, filled with what's left of Austria's emperors, empresses, and other Habsburg royalty. For centuries, Vienna was the heart of a vast empire ruled by the Habsburg family, and here is where they lie buried in their fancy pewter coffins. You'll find all the Habsburg greats, including Maria Theresa, her son Josef II (Mozart's patron), Franz Josef, and Empress Sisi. Before moving on, consider paying your respects here.

• Stretching north from the Kaisergruft is the square called...

❽ Neuer Markt

A block farther down, in the center of Neuer Markt, is the **four rivers fountain** showing Lady Providence surrounded by figures symbolizing the rivers that flow into the Danube. The sexy statues offended Empress Maria Theresa, who actually organized "Chastity Commissions" to defend her capital city's moral standards. The modern buildings around you were rebuilt after World War II. Half of the city's inner center was intentionally destroyed by Churchill

to demoralize the Viennese, who were disconcertingly enthusiastic about the Nazis.

• *Lady Providence's one bare breast points back to Kärntner Strasse (50 yards away). Before you head back to the busy shopping street, you could stop for a sweet treat at the heavenly, recommended Kurkonditorei Oberlaa (to get there, disobey the McDonald's arrows—it's at the far-left corner of the square).*

Leave the square and return to Kärntner Strasse. Turn left and continue down Kärntner Strasse. As you approach the cathedral, you're likely to first see it as a reflection in the round-glass windows of the post-modern Haas Haus. Pass the U-Bahn station (which has WCs) where the street spills into Vienna's main square...

❾ Stephansplatz

The cathedral's frilly spire looms overhead, worshippers and tour-ists pour inside the church, and shoppers and top-notch street entertainers buzz around the outside. You're at the center of Vienna.

The Gothic **St. Stephen's Cathedral** (c. 1300-1450) is known for its 450-foot south tower, its colorful roof, and its place in Viennese history. When it was built, it was a huge church for what was then a tiny town, and it helped put the fledgling city on the map. At this point, you may want to take a break from the walk to tour the church (see my self-guided tour on page 1185).

Where Kärntner Strasse hits Stephansplatz, the grand, soot-covered building with red columns is the **Equitable Building** (filled with lawyers, bankers, and insurance brokers). It's a fine example of Neoclassicism from the turn of the 20th century—look up and imagine how slick Vienna must have felt in 1900.

Facing St. Stephen's is the sleek concrete-and-glass ❿ **Haas Haus,** a postmodern building by noted Austrian architect Hans Hollein (finished in 1990). The curved facade is supposed to echo the Roman fortress of Vindobona (its ruins were found near here). Although the Viennese initially protested having this stark mod-ern tower right next to their beloved cathedral, it's since become a fixture of Vienna's main square. Notice how the smooth, rounded glass reflects St. Stephen's pointy architecture, providing a great photo opportunity—especially at twilight.

• *Exit the square with your back to the cathedral. Walk past the Haas Haus and bear right down the street called...*

⓫ Graben

This was once a *Graben,* or ditch—originally the moat for the Roman military camp. Back during Vienna's 19th-century heyday, there were nearly 200,000 people packed into the city's inner center (inside the Ringstrasse), walking through dirt streets. Today this area houses 20,000. Graben was a busy street with three lanes of traffic until the 1970s, when it was turned into one of Europe's first pedestrian-only zones. Take a moment to absorb the scene—you're standing in an area surrounded by history, postwar rebuilding, grand architecture, fine cafés, and people enjoying life...for me, quintessential Europe.

As you stroll down the Graben from Stephansplatz, after about 50 yards you'll reach a modern water dispenser. Vienna has suffered fiercely hot summers lately, leading the city government to install watering stations and shady benches for its citizens and visitors.

In another fifty yards, you reach Dorotheergasse, on your left, which leads (after two more long blocks) to the **Dorotheum** auction house. Consider poking your nose in here later for some fancy window-shopping. Also along this street are two recommended eateries: the sandwich shop Buffet Trześniewski—one of my favorite places for lunch—and the classic Café Hawelka (both described later).

In the middle of the Graben pedestrian zone is the extravagantly blobby ⓬ **Holy Trinity plague column** *(Pestsäule).* The

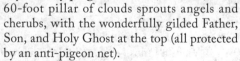

60-foot pillar of clouds sprouts angels and cherubs, with the wonderfully gilded Father, Son, and Holy Ghost at the top (all protected by an anti-pigeon net).

In 1679, Vienna was hit by a massive epidemic of bubonic plague. Around 75,000 Viennese died—about a third of the city. Emperor Leopold I dropped to his knees (something emperors never did in public) and begged God to save the city. (Find Leopold about a quarter of the way up the monument, just above the brown banner. Hint: The typical inbreeding of royal families left him with a gaping under bite.) His prayer was heard by Lady Faith (the statue below Leopold, carrying a cross). With the help of a heartless little cupid, she tosses an old naked woman—symbolizing the plague—into the abyss and saves the city. In gratitude, Leopold vowed to erect this monument, which became a model for other cities ravaged by the same plague.

• *Thirty yards past the plague monument, look down the short street to the right, which frames a Baroque church with a stately green dome.*

⑬ St. Peter's Church

Leopold I ordered this church to be built as a thank-you for surviving the 1679 plague. The church stands on the site of a much older church that may have been Vienna's first (or second) Christian church. Inside, St. Peter's shows Vienna at its Baroque best. Note that the church offers free organ concerts (Mon-Fri at 15:00, Sat-Sun at 20:00).

• *Continue west on Graben, where you'll immediately find some stairs leading underground to...*

⑭ Loos' Loos

In about 1900, a local chemical-maker needed a publicity stunt to prove that his chemicals really got things clean. He purchased two wine cellars under Graben and had them turned into classy WCs in the Modernist style (designed by Adolf Loos—Vienna's answer to Frank Lloyd Wright), complete with chandeliers and finely crafted mahogany. While the chandeliers are gone, the restrooms remain a relatively appealing place to do your business—in fact, they're so inviting that they're used for poetry readings. Locals and tourists happily pay €0.50 for a quick visit.

• *Graben dead-ends at the aristocratic supermarket Julius Meinl am Graben. From here, turn left. In the distance is the big green-and-gold dome of the Hofburg, where we'll head soon. The street leading up to the Hofburg is...*

⑮ Kohlmarkt

This is Vienna's most elegant and unaffordable shopping street, lined with Cartier, Armani, Gucci, Tiffany, and the emperor's

palace at the end. Strolling Kohlmarkt, daydream about the edible window displays at ⑯ **Demel,** the ultimate Viennese chocolate shop (#14, daily 9:00-19:00, www.demel.com). The room is filled with Art Nouveau boxes of Empress Sisi's choco-dreams come true: *Kandierte Veilchen* (candied violet petals), *Katzenzungen* (cats' tongues), and so on. The cakes here are moist (compared to the dry Sacher-Tortes). The enticing window displays change monthly, reflecting current happenings in Vienna. Wander inside. There's an impressive cancan of Vienna's most beloved cakes—displayed to tempt visitors into springing for the €10 cake-and-coffee deal (point to the cake you want).

Farther in, you can see the bakery in action. Sit inside, with a view of the cake-making, or outside, with the street action (upstairs is less crowded). Shops like this boast "K.u.K."—signifying that during the Habsburgs' heyday, it was patronized by the *König und Kaiser* (king and emperor—same guy). If you happen to be looking through Demel's window at exactly 19:01, just after closing, you can witness one of the great tragedies of modern Europe: the daily dumping of its unsold cakes.

Next to Demel, the **Manz Bookstore** has a Loos-designed facade. By the way, across the street (and back a few steps) is a fine travel book and map shop (Freytag & Berndt, which carries most of my guidebooks).

• *Kohlmarkt ends at the square called...*

⑰ Michaelerplatz

This square is dominated by the **Hofburg Palace.** Study the grand Neo-Baroque facade, dating from about 1900. The four heroic giants illustrate Hercules wrestling with his great challenges (Emperor Franz Josef, who commissioned the gate, felt he could relate).

In the center of this square, a scant bit of **Roman Vienna** lies exposed just beneath street level.

Spin Tour: Do a slow, clockwise pan to get your bearings, starting (over your left shoulder as you face the Hofburg) with **St. Michael's Church,** which offers fascinating tours of its crypt. To the right of that is the fancy **Loden-Plankl shop,** with traditional Austrian formalwear, including dirndls. Farther to the right, across Augustinerstrasse, is the wing of the palace that houses the **Spanish Riding School** and its famous white Lipizzaner stallions. Farther down this street lies **Josefsplatz,** with the Augustinian Church, and the Dorotheum auction house. At the end of the street are Albertinaplatz and the Opera (where we started this walk).

Continue your spin: Two buildings over from the Hofburg (to the right), the modern **Loos House** (now a bank) has a facade featuring a perfectly geometrical grid of square columns and windows. Compared to the Neo-Rococo facade of the Hofburg, the stern Modernism of the Loos House appears to be from an entirely different age. And yet, both of these—as well as the Eiffel Tower and Mad Ludwig's fairy-tale Neuschwanstein Castle—were built in the same generation, roughly around 1900. In many ways, this jarring juxtaposition exemplifies the architectural turmoil of the turn of the 20th century, and represents the passing of the torch from Europe's age of divine monarchs to the modern era.

• *Let's take a look at where Austria's glorious history began—at the...*

Hofburg Palace

This is the complex of palaces where the Habsburg emperors lived (except in summer, when they lived out at Schönbrunn Palace).  Enter the Hofburg through the gate, where you immediately find yourself beneath a big rotunda (the netting is there to keep birds from perching). The doorway on the right is the entrance to the ⓲ **Imperial Apartments,** where the Habsburg emperors once lived in chandeliered elegance. Today you can tour its lavish rooms, as well as a museum about Empress Sisi, and a porcelain and silver collection. To the left is the ticket office for the ⓳ **Spanish Riding School.**

Continuing on, you emerge from the rotunda into the main courtyard of the Hofburg, called **In der Burg.** The Caesar-like statue is of Habsburg Emperor Franz II (1768-1835), grandson of Maria Theresa, grandfather of Franz Josef, and father-in-law of Napoleon. Behind him is a tower with three kinds of clocks (the yellow disc shows the phase of the moon tonight). To the right of Franz are the Imperial Apartments, and to the left are the offices of Austria's mostly ceremonial president (the more powerful chancellor lives in a building just behind this courtyard).

Franz Josef faces the oldest part of the palace. The colorful red, black, and gold gateway (behind you), which used to have a drawbridge, leads over the moat and into the 13th-century Swiss Court (Schweizerhof), named for the Swiss mercenary guards once stationed there. Study the gate. Imagine the drawbridge and the chain. Notice the Habsburg coat of arms with the imperial eagle above and the Renaissance painting on the ceiling of the passageway.

As you enter the Gothic courtyard, you're passing into the historic core of the palace, the site of the first fortress, and, historically, the place of last refuge. Here you'll find the ⓴ **Treasury** (Schatzkammer) and the **Imperial Music Chapel** (Hofmusikkapelle), where the Boys' Choir sings Mass. Ever since Joseph Hayden and Franz Schubert were choirboys here, visitors have gathered like groupies on Sundays to hear the famed choir sing.

Returning to the bigger In der Burg courtyard, face Franz and turn left, passing through the **tunnel,** with a few tourist shops and restaurants, to spill out into spacious ㉑ **Heldenplatz** (Heroes' Square). On the left is the impressive curved facade of the **New Palace** (Neue Burg). This vast wing was built in the early 1900s to be the new Habsburg living quarters (and was meant to have a matching building facing it). But in 1914, the heir to the throne, Archduke Franz Ferdinand—while waiting politely for his long-lived uncle, Emperor Franz Josef, to die—was assassinated in Sarajevo. The archduke's death sparked World War I and the eventual end of eight centuries of Habsburg rule.

Today the building houses the **New Palace museums,** an eclectic collection of weaponry, suits of armor, musical instruments, and ancient Greek statues. The two equestrian statues depict Prince Eugene of Savoy (1663-1736), who battled the Ottoman Turks, and Archduke Charles (1771-1847), who battled Napoleon. Eugene gazes toward the far distance at the prickly spires of Vienna's City Hall.

Spin Tour: Make a slow 360-degree turn, and imagine this huge square filled with people.

In 1938, 300,000 Viennese gathered here, entirely filling vast Heroes' Square, to welcome Adolf Hitler and celebrate their annexation with Germany—the *"Anschluss."* The Nazi tyrant stood on the balcony of the New Palace and declared, "Before the face of German history, I declare my former homeland now a part of the Third Reich. One of the pearls of the Third Reich will be Vienna." He never said "Austria," a word that was now forbidden.

When pondering why the Austrians—eyes teary with joy and vigorously waving their Nazi flags—so willingly accepted Hitler's rule, it's important to remember that Austria was already a fascist nation. Austrian Chancellor Engelbert Dollfuss, though pro-Catholic, pro-Habsburg, and anti-Hitler, was a fascist dictator who silenced any left-wing opposition. Also, memories of the grand Habsburg Empire were still fresh in the collective psyche. The once vast and mighty empire of 50 million at its 19th-century peak came out of World War I a tiny landlocked land of six million that now suffered terrible unemployment. The opportunistic Hitler promised jobs along with a return to greatness—and the Austrian people gobbled it up.

Standing here, it's fascinating to consider Austrian aspirations for grandeur. In fact, the Habsburgs envisioned an Imperial Forum stretching from here across the Ringstrasse.

• *Walk on through the Greek-columned passageway (the Äusseres Burgtor), cross the Ringstrasse, and stand between the giant Kunsthistorisches and Natural History Museums, purpose-built in the 1880s to house the private art and history collections of the empire and to celebrate its culture and power. The emperor planned to tie these grand buildings and the palace together with two mighty triumphal arches spanning the Ringstrasse, connecting them into an awe-inspiring ensemble. And today, while the emperor's vision died with his empire, a huge statue of perhaps the greatest of the Habsburgs, Maria Theresa, stands in the center of it all.*

㉒ Maria Theresa Monument

Vienna's biggest monument shows the empress holding a scroll from her father granting the right of a woman to inherit his throne. The statues and reliefs surrounding her speak volumes about her reign: Her four top generals sit on horseback while her four top advisors stand. Behind them, reliefs celebrate cultural leaders of her day, including little Wolfie Mozart with mentor "Papa" Joseph Haydn (with his hand on Mozart's shoulder, facing the Natural History Museum). The moral of this propaganda: a strong military and a wise ruler are prerequisites for a thriving culture—attributes that characterized the 40-year rule of the woman who was perhaps Austria's greatest monarch.

• *Our walk is finished. You're in the heart of Viennese sightseeing. Surrounding this square are some of the city's top museums. And the Hofburg Palace itself contains many of Vienna's best sights and museums. From the Opera to the Hofburg, from chocolate to churches, from St. Stephen's to Sacher-Tortes—Vienna waits for you.*

Sights in Vienna

IN THE OLD TOWN, WITHIN THE RING

These sights are listed roughly from south to north. For a self-guided walk connecting many of central Vienna's top sights—including some of the ones listed here—see my "Vienna City Walk," earlier.

▲▲▲Opera (Wiener Staatsoper)

The Opera house, facing the Ring and near the TI, is a central point for any visitor. Vienna remains one of the world's great cities for classical music, and this building still belts out some of the finest opera, both classic and cutting-edge. Although the critical reception of the building 130 years ago led the architect to commit suicide, and though it's been rebuilt since its destruction by WWII bombs, it's still a sumptuous place. The interior has a chandeliered lobby and carpeted staircases perfect for making the scene. The theater itself features five wraparound balconies, gold-and-red decor, and a bracelet-like chandelier.

Depending on your level of tolerance for opera, there are several different ways to experience the Opera house. You can simply admire the Neo-Renaissance building from the outside (and maybe slip inside the lobby for a peek when the evening box office opens around 17:00). You could take a guided tour of the lavish interior (see below), or visit the nearby Opera Museum to learn about the company's history. Best of all, attend a performance of Vienna's opera company, which can be surprisingly easy and cheap to do—and doesn't have to take up a whole evening (get details on page 1229).

Opera House Tours

The only way to see the Opera house interior (besides attending a performance) is with a guided 45-minute tour in English. You'll see the chandeliered halls where opera-goers gather at intermission, enjoying elaborate spaces with coffered ceilings, gold trim, and iron-work lamps. You'll learn about the opera's history (see the Opera Museum description, next), and to compare the old parts of the building (such as Emperor Franz Josef's ornate reception room) with the post-war reconstruction. The highlight is the 2,000-seat theater itself—where the main floor is ringed by box seating, under a huge sugar-doughnut chandelier. You may see workers on the stage erecting sets for that evening's performance and learn the ingenious ways they load and unload the elaborate equipment so quickly. Certain tours (marked with an asterisk on the tour schedule) take you onto the wings of the stage itself.

To take a tour, just show up at the tour entrance, located at the southwest corner of the building. Be there 20 minutes before your tour starts and buy a ticket. No reservations are taken, and they don't sell out.

Cost and Hours: €6.50, includes modest Opera Museum. Tours generally run several times a day at the top of each hour between 10:00 and 16:00, but the schedule is different every day, as it's determined by rehearsals and performances. There are lots of tours in July and August (when there are no performances), and fewer tours September through June and on Sundays year-round. Find the monthly schedule online, in the Opera's monthly *Prolog* magazine, or posted at the tour entrance; tel. 01/514-442-606, www.wiener-staatsoper.at.

Opera Museum (Staatsopernmuseum)

This exhibit traces the illustrious history of the Vienna State Opera (not opera in general), highlighting its most famous singers, directors, and performances. You'll peruse old posters and photos, costumes, models of set designs, a musical score by Wagner, and one of Margot Fonteyn's ballet slippers. It's all in a single room, with lots of English information and a soundtrack of choice arias.

Cost and Hours: €3, included in Opera tour ticket; Tue-Sun 10:00-18:00, closed Mon; a block west of the Opera (near the Albertina Museum), tucked down a courtyard at Hanuschgasse 3, tel. 01/514-442-100).

▲▲Haus der Musik

Vienna's "House of Music" is a high-tech experience that celebrates this hometown specialty. The museum, spread over five floors and well-described in English, is unique for its effective use of interactive touch-screen computers and headphones to explore the physics of sound. One floor is dedicated to the heavyweight Viennese

VIENNA

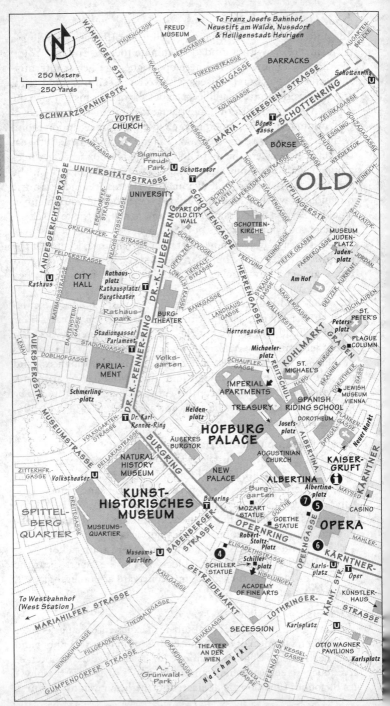

VIENNA

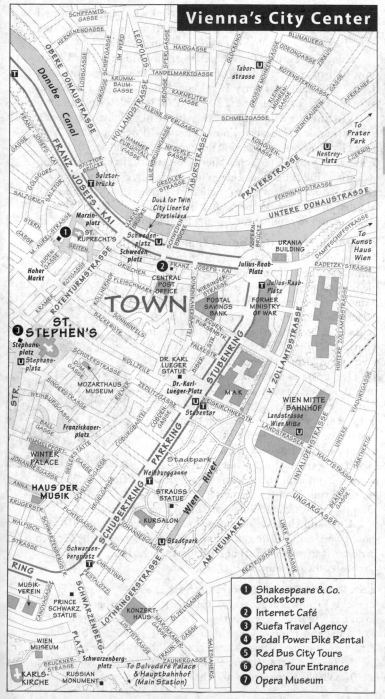

Vienna's City Center

SCHIFFAMTS-
GASSE
HERMINENGASSE
IM WERD
LEOPOLDS-
GASSE
SPERLGASSE
HAIDGASSE
BLUMAUERG.
ODEONGASSE
ZIRKUSG.

FLOSSGASSE
SCHIFFGASSE
KRUMM-
BAUMGASSE
TANDELMARKTGASSE
GROSSE
SPERLGASSE
GLOCKENG.
GROSSE MOHRENGASSE
ROTENSTERNGASSE
GASSE
AFRIKANER-

Tabor-
strasse U

FRANZ-JOSEFS-KAI
GÖLLNER
SALZTOR
SALZGRIES

HOLLANDSTRASSE
KARMELITER-
GASSE
KLEINE SPERLGASSE
KLEINE
MOHREN-
GASSE
SCHMELZGASSE

To
Prater
Park

LILIENBRUNNGASSE
NEGERLE-
GASSE
KLEINE PFARRG.
KARMELITER-

ROMÖDIEN-
GASSE
FERDINANDSTRASSE
Nestroy-
plata U

Obere Donaustrasse

Danube Canal

HOLLANDSTRASSE
HAMMER-
FUSSGALL-
GASSE
GREDLER-
STRASSE

TABORSTRASSE
PRATERSTRASSE

UNTERE DONAUSTRASSE

CZERNIN

To
Kunst
Haus
Wien

Salztor-
brücke

Dock for Twin
City Liner to
Bratislava

MARIEN-
BRÜCKE
SCHWEDEN-
BRÜCKE
ASPERN-
BRÜCKE

DAMPFSCHIFFSTRASSE
RADETZKYSTRASSE

STERN GASSE
M. AUREL STR.
JUDEN-GASSE

① Morzin-
platz
ST. RUPRECHT'S
SEITEN.

ROTENTURMSTRASSE

Schweden-
platz U
Schweden-
platz

GRIECHEN.

FLEISCHMARKT

Julius-Raab-
Platz

URANIA
BUILDING

Hoher
Markt
KRAMER

ROTGASSE

GONZAGA-
② FRANZ-JOSEFS-KAI

WIESINGER-

DOMINIKANERBASTEI

Julius-Raab-
Platz U

FORMER
MINISTRY
OF WAR

HINTERE ZOLLAMTSSTRASSE

STR.

③ ST.
STEPHEN'S

Stephans-
platz U
Stephans-
platz

SONNENFELS

FLEISCHMARK

BÄCKERSTR.

TOWN
CENTRAL
POST
OFFICE

POSTAL
SAVINGS
BANK

ROCHEN-

FALKESTR.

STUBENRING

MAK

V. ZOLLAMTSSTRASSE

WIEN MITTE
BAHNHOF

Landstrasse
Wien Mitte U
Landstrasser

INVALIDENSTRASSE

VIADUKTGASSE

SCHULERSTRASSE
DOM-
GASSE

MOZARTHAUS
MUSEUM
RIEMER
ZEDLITZGASSE

DR. KARL
LUEGER
STATUE

Dr.-Karl-
Lueger-Platz
Stubentor U

WEISKIRCHNERSTR.

UNTERE

WEIHBURGGASSE
SINGERSTRASSE
BALL-
GASSE
Franziskaner-
platz
GRÜNANGERG.
BALLGASSE
COBURGBASTEI
COBDEN-
GASSE
PARKRING

Stadtpark

LANDSTRASSE

HAUPTSTRASSE

ZARTNERG.

HIMMELPFORT-
GASSE
JOHANNESGASSE
SEILER-
STÄTTE

WINTER
PALACE
Weihburggasse T

Wien River

UNGARGASSE

BEATRIX-
GASSE

ANNA
KRUGERSTR.
HAUS DER
MUSIK
SEILERSTÄTTE
SCHELLINGGASSE
STRAUSS
STATUE

STRASSE
WALFISCH-
GASSE
SCHWARZENBERGSTR.
FICHTEGASSE
JOHANNESGASSE

SCHUBERTRING

Kursalon

AM HEUMARKT

LINKE BAHNGASSE

RING
Schwarzen-
bergplatz
CHRISTINEN.
FICHTE
Stadtpark U

BEATRIXGASSE

MUSIK-
VEREIN
PESTALOZZI.
CANOVAGASSE

PRINCE
SCHWARZ.
STATUE

LOTHRINGERSTRASSE

KONZERT-
HAUS

LISZTSTRASSE

MARROKKANER-
GASSE

ÖLZELTGASSE

SALESIANERG.

WIEN
MUSEUM
BRUCKNER-
STRASSE
Schwarzenberg-
platz T

KARLS-
KIRCHE

SCHWARZENBERG-
PLATZ

RUSSIAN
MONUMENT

TRAUN.G.
ZAUNERGASSE

To Belvedere Palace
& Hauptbahnhof
(Main Station)

① Shakespeare & Co.
Bookstore
② Internet Café
③ Ruefa Travel Agency
④ Pedal Power Bike Rental
⑤ Red Bus City Tours
⑥ Opera Tour Entrance
⑦ Opera Museum

composers (Mozart, Beethoven, and so on) who virtually created classical music as we know it. Really experiencing the place takes time. It's open late and makes a good evening activity.

Cost and Hours: €12, includes audioguide for third floor only, half-price after 20:00, €17 combo-ticket with Mozarthaus, daily 10:00-22:00, last entry 30 minutes before closing, two blocks from the Opera at Seilerstätte 30, tel. 01/513-4850, www.hdm.at.

Visiting the Museum: The first floor highlights the Vienna Philharmonic Orchestra, known the world over for their New Year's Eve concerts. The second floor explores the physics of sound. Wander through the "sonosphere" and marvel at the amazing acoustics. The third floor celebrates the famous hometown boys: Haydn, Mozart, Beethoven, Schubert, Strauss (father and son), Mahler, Schönberg, Webern, and Berg. Before leaving, pick up a virtual baton to conduct the Vienna Philharmonic.

▲Dorotheum Auction House (Palais Dorotheum)

For an aristocrat's flea market, drop by Austria's answer to Sotheby's. The ground floor has shops, an info desk with a schedule of upcoming auctions, and a few auction items. Some pieces are available for immediate sale (marked *VKP,* for *Verkaufpreis*— "sales price"), while others are up for auction (marked *DIFF. RUF*). Labels on each item predict the auction value.

The upstairs floors have antique furniture and fancy knickknacks (some for immediate sale, others for auction), many brought in by people who've inherited old things and don't have room for them. The top floor has a fancy antique gallery with fixed prices. Wandering through here, you feel like you're touring a museum with exhibits you can buy. Afterward, you can continue your hunt for the perfect curio on the streets around the Dorotheum, which are lined with many fine antique shops.

Cost and Hours: Free, Mon-Fri 10:00-18:00, Sat 9:00-17:00, closed Sun, classy little café on second floor, between the Graben pedestrian street and Hofburg at Dorotheergasse 17, tel. 01/51560, www.dorotheum.com.

▲St. Peter's Church (Peterskirche)

Baroque Vienna is at its best in this gem, tucked away a few steps from the Graben.

Cost and Hours: Free, Mon-Fri 7:00-20:00, Sat-Sun 9:00-21:00; free organ concerts Mon-Fri at 15:00, Sat-Sun at 20:00; just off the Graben between the Plague Monument and Kohlmarkt, tel. 01/533-6433, www.peterskirche.at.

Visiting the Church: Admire the rose-and-gold, oval-shaped Baroque interior, topped with a ceiling fresco of Mary kneeling to be crowned by Jesus and the Father, while the dove of the Holy Spirit floats way up in the lantern. Taken together, the church's elements—especially the organ, altar painting, pulpit, and coat of arms (in the base of the dome) of church founder Leopold I—make St. Peter's one of the city's most beautiful and ornate churches.

To the right of the altar, a dramatic golden statue shows the martyrdom of St. John Nepomuk (c. 1340-1393). The Czech saint defied the heretical King Wenceslas, so he was tossed to his death off the Charles Bridge in Prague (for the story, see page 72). In true Baroque style, we see the dramatic peak of his fall, when John has just passed the point of no return. The Virgin Mary floats overhead in a silver cloud.

The present church (from 1733) stands atop earlier churches dating back 1,600 years. On either side of the nave are glass cases containing skeletons of Christian martyrs from Roman times. Above the relic on the left is a painting of the modern saint Josemaría Escrivá, founder of the conservative Catholic organization Opus Dei, of *Da Vinci Code* notoriety.

Mozarthaus Vienna Museum

In September of 1784, 27-year-old Wolfgang Amadeus Mozart moved into this spacious apartment with his wife, Constanze, and their week-old son Karl. For the next three years, this was the epicenter of Viennese high life. It was here that Mozart wrote *Marriage of Figaro* and *Don Giovanni* and established himself as the toast of Vienna. Today, the actual apartments are pretty boring (mostly bare rooms), but the museum does flesh out Mozart's Vienna years with paintings, videos, and a few period pieces.

Cost and Hours: €10, includes audioguide, €17 combo-ticket with Haus der Musik, daily 10:00-19:00, last entry 30 minutes before closing, a block behind the cathedral, go through arcade at #5a and walk 50 yards to Domgasse 5, tel. 01/512-1791, www.mozarthausvienna.at.

Jewish Museum Vienna (Jüdisches Museum Wien)

The museum operates two buildings a 10-minute walk apart; the main museum is on Dorotheergasse (near the Hofburg), and a smaller, more archeological exhibit is at Judenplatz (near Am Hof). The **Jewish Museum Dorotheergasse** fills a four-story downtown building with exhibits, a bookstore, and a small, reasonably priced café serving Middle Eastern fare. It documents Vienna's Jewish community from earliest times to the present. The smaller, less interesting **Museum Judenplatz** was built around the scant remains of a medieval synagogue. The classy square above the ruins, called Judenplatz, is now dominated by a blocky **memorial** to the 65,000 Viennese Jews killed by the Nazis.

Cost and Hours: €10 ticket includes both museums; Dorotheergasse location, at #11—Sun-Fri 10:00-18:00, closed Sat; Judenplatz location, at #8—Sun-Thu 10:00-18:00, Fri 10:00-14:00, closed Sat; tel. 01/535-0431, www.jmw.at.

Winter Palace of Prince Eugene of Savoy

In the early 1700s, the diplomat-soldier Prince Eugene of Savoy lived in this "winter" mansion in the center of town, while spending his summers in the airy Belvedere Palace on the outskirts (see page 1215). Today, it mostly houses temporary exhibits, plus a room of giant paintings showing the layout of major early 18th-century Habsburg army battles (helpful for military strategists like Eugene). The grand building's ornate, gilded rooms are nice (with chandeliers, ceiling frescoes, and damask walls), but there are better palaces in town, and it's probably not worth your time and money unless you have a special interest in whatever temporary exhibit is showing.

Cost and Hours: €9, €25 Prinz Eugen Ticket includes Belvedere Palace, daily 10:00-18:00, Himmelpfortgasse 8, www.belvedere.at.

▲▲▲St. Stephen's Cathedral (Stephansdom)

This massive church is the Gothic needle around which Vienna spins. According to the medieval vision of its creators, it stands like a giant jeweled reliquary, offering praise to God from the center of the city. The church and its towers, especially the 450-foot south tower, give the city its most iconic image. (Check your pockets for €0.10 coins; those minted in Austria feature the south tower on the back.) The cathedral has survived Vienna's many wars and today symbolizes the city's spirit and love of freedom.

Cost: It's free to enter the foyer and north aisle of the church, but it costs €4 to get into the main nave, where most of the interesting items are located (more for special exhibits). Going up the towers costs €4 (by stairs, south tower) or €5 (by elevator, north tower). You'll pay €5 to visit the catacombs and €4 to see the treasury (for more on the towers, catacombs, and treasury, see the end of this tour). The €16 combo-ticket—covering entry, both towers, catacombs, treasury, and audioguide—is overkill for most visitors.

Hours: The church doors are open daily 6:00-22:00 (Sunday opens at 7:00), but the main nave is open for tourists Mon-Sat 9:00-11:30 & 13:00-16:30, Sun 13:00-16:30, until 17:30 June-Aug. During services, you can't enter the main nave (unless you're attending Mass) or access the north tower elevator or catacombs, but you can go into the back of the church.

Information: Tel. 01/515-523-526, www.stephanskirche.at.

Tours: The €4.50 tours in English are entertaining (daily at

15:45, check information board inside entry to confirm schedule; price includes main nave entry). The €1 audioguide is helpful. You can download a free Rick Steves **audio tour** of St. Stephen's; see page 13.

○ **Self-Guided Tour:** This tour will give you a good look at the cathedral, inside and out.

Cathedral Exterior: Before we go inside, let's circle around the cathedral for a look at its impressive exterior. We'll stop at several points along the way to take it all in.

• *As you face the church's main entry, go to the right across the little square, and find the old-time photos next to the door marked* 3a *Stephansplatz (see map). From here, you can take in the sheer magnitude of this massive church, with its skyscraping spire.*

The church we see today is the third one on this spot. It dates mainly from 1300 to 1450, when builders expanded on an earlier structure and added two huge towers at the end of each transept.

The impressive 450-foot **south tower**—capped with a golden orb and cross—took two generations (65 years) to build and was finished in 1433. The tower is a rarity among medieval churches in that it was completed before the Gothic style—and the age of faith—petered out. The half-size **north tower** (223 feet), around the other side of the church, was meant to be a matching steeple. But around 1500, it was abandoned in midconstruction, when the money was needed to defend the country against the Ottomans rather than to build church towers.

The cathedral was heavily damaged at the end of World War II. Near where you are standing are **old photos** showing the destruction. In 1945, Vienna was caught in the chaos between the occupying Nazis and the approaching Soviets. Allied bombs sparked fires in nearby buildings, and the embers leapt to the cathedral rooftop. The original timbered Gothic roof burned, the cathedral's huge bell crashed to the ground, and the fire raged for two days. Civic pride prompted a financial outpouring, and the roof was rebuilt to its original splendor by 1952—doubly impressive considering the bombed-out state of the country at that time.

• *Circle the church exterior counterclockwise, passing the* **entrance to the south tower.** *If you're up for climbing the 343 stairs to the top, you could do it now, but it's better to wait until the end of this tour (tower climb described later).*

As you hook around behind the church, look for the cathedral bookshop (Dombuchhandlung) at the end of the block. Pause in front of that shop and look toward the cathedral.

Just above street level, notice the marble **pulpit** under the golden starburst. The priest would stand here, stoking public opinion against the Ottomans, in front of crowds far bigger than could fit into the church. Above the pulpit (in a scene from around 1700), a saint stands victoriously atop a vanquished Turk.

The Romanesque-style main entrance is the oldest part of the church (c. 1240—part of a church that stood here before). Right behind you is the site of Vindobona, a Roman garrison town. Before the Romans converted to Christianity, there was a pagan temple here, and this entrance pays homage to that ancient heritage. Roman-era statues are embedded in the facade, and the two **octagonal towers** flanking the main doorway are dubbed the "heathen towers" because they're built with a few recycled Roman stones (flipped over to hide the pagan inscriptions and expose the smooth sides).

• *Enter the church.*

Cathedral Interior: Find a spot to peer through the gate down the immense nave—more than a football field long and nine

stories tall. It's lined with clusters of slender pillars that soar upward to support the ribbed crisscross arches of the ceiling. Stylistically, the nave is Gothic with a Baroque overlay. It's a spacious, glorious venue that's often used for high-profile concerts (there's a ticket office outside the church, to the right as you face the main doorway).

To the right as you enter, in a gold-and-silver sunburst frame, is a crude Byzantine-style **Maria Pócs Icon** (Pötscher Madonna), brought here from a humble Hungarian village church. The picture of Mary and Child is said to have wept real tears in 1697, as Central Europe was once again being threatened by the Turks. Along the left wall is the **gift shop.** Step in to marvel at the 14th-century statuary decorating its wall—some of the finest carvings in the church.

To the left of the gift shop is the gated entrance to the **Chapel of Prince Eugene of Savoy.** Prince Eugene (1663-1736), a teenage seminary student from France, arrived in Vienna in 1683 as the city was about to be overrun by the Ottoman Turks. He volunteered for the army and helped save the city, launching a brilliant career as a military man for the Habsburgs. His specialty was conquering the Ottomans. When he died, the grateful Austrians buried him here, under this chapel, marked by a tomb hatch in the floor.

• *Nearby is the entrance to the main nave. Buy a ticket and start down the nave toward the altar. At the second pillar on the left is the pulpit.*

This Gothic sandstone **pulpit** (c. 1500) is a masterpiece carved from three separate blocks (see if you can find the seams). A spiral stairway winds up to the lectern, surrounded and supported by

the four church "fathers," whose writings influenced early Catholic dogma. The pulpit is as crammed with religious meaning as it is with beautifully realistic carvings. The top of the stairway's railing swarms with lizards (animals of light) and toads (animals of darkness). The "Dog of the Lord" stands at the top, making sure none of those toads pollutes the sermon. Below the toads, wheels with three parts (the Trinity) roll up, while wheels with four spokes (the four seasons and four cardinal directions, symbolizing mortal life on earth) roll down.

Find the guy peeking out from under the stairs. This may be a **self-portrait** of the sculptor. In medieval times, art was done for the glory of God, and artists worked anonymously. But this pulpit was carved as humanist Renaissance ideals were creeping in from Italy—and individual artists were becoming famous. So the artist included what may be a rare self-portrait bust in his work. He leans out from a window, sculptor's compass in hand, to observe the world and his work.

• *Continue up. When you reach the gate that cuts off the front of the nave, turn right and enter the south transept. Go all the way to the doors.*

Look to the left to find a **plaque** commemorating Wolfgang Amadeus Mozart (1756-1791), who spent most of his adult life in Vienna. He attended Mass and was married in St. Stephen's, and two of his children were baptized here. He set up house in a lavish apartment a block east of the church (this house is now the lackluster Mozarthaus museum, described earlier). Mozart lived at the heart of Viennese society— among musicians, actors, and aristocrats. He played in a string quartet with Joseph Haydn. At church, he would have heard Beethoven's teacher playing the organ. (Mozart may have met the star-struck young Beethoven in Vienna—or maybe not; accounts vary.)

After his early success, Mozart fell on hard times. When he died at age 35 (in 1791), he was not buried at St. Stephen's, because the cemetery that once surrounded the church had been cleared out a decade earlier as an anti-plague measure. Instead, his remains (along with most Viennese of his day) were dumped into a mass grave outside of town. But he was honored with a funeral service in St. Stephen's—held in the Prince Eugene of Savoy Chapel, where they played his famous (unfinished) *Requiem*.

• *Now head to the chapel at the front-right corner of the church.*

This imposing, red-marble **tomb of Frederick III** is like a big king-size-bed coffin with an effigy of Frederick lying on top (not visible—but there's a photo of the effigy on the left). The top of the tomb is decorated with his coats of arms, representing the many territories he ruled over. Frederick III (1415-1493) is considered the "father" of Vienna for turning the small village into a royal town with a cosmopolitan feel.

• Walk to the middle of the church.

The tall, ornate, black marble **high altar** (1641, by Tobias and Johann Pock) is topped with a statue of Mary that barely fits under the towering vaults of the ceiling. It frames a large painting of the stoning of St. Stephen, painted on copper. Stephen (at the bottom), having refused to stop professing his faith, is pelted with rocks by angry pagans. As he kneels, ready to die, he gazes up to see a vision of Christ, the cross, and the angels of heaven.

During World War II, many of the city's top art treasures were stowed safely in cellars and salt mines—hidden by both the Nazi occupiers (to protect against war damage) and by citizens (to protect against Nazi looters). The **stained-glass windows** behind the high altar were meticulously dismantled and packed away. The pulpit was encased in a shell of brick. As the war was drawing to a close, it appeared St. Stephen's would escape major damage. But as the Nazis were fleeing, the bitter Nazi commander in charge of the city ordered that the church be destroyed. Fortunately, his underlings disobeyed. Unfortunately, the church accidentally caught fire during Allied bombing shortly thereafter, and the wooden roof collapsed onto the stone vaults of the ceiling. The Tupperware-colored glass on either side of the nave dates from the 1950s. Before the fire, the church was lit mostly with clear Baroque-era windows.

• After exploring the nave, consider touring the catacombs or the treasury, or ascending either one of the two towers.

Catacombs (Katakomben): The catacombs (viewable by guided tour only) hold the bodies—or at least the innards—of 72 Habsburgs, including that of Rudolf IV, the man who began building the south tower. This is where Austria's rulers were buried before the Kaisergruft was built (see page 1202), and where later Habsburgs' entrails were entombed. The copper urns preserve the imperial organs in alcohol. I touched Maria Theresa's urn and it wobbled (€5, daily 10:00-11:30 & 13:30-16:30, tours generally depart on the half-hour and are in German and English). Just be at the stairs in the left/north transept to meet the guide.

Treasury: Tucked away in a loft in the oldest part of the church, the treasury offers precious relics, dazzling church art, a portrait of Rudolf IV (considered the earliest German portrait), and wonderful views down on the nave (€4 admission includes audioguide, daily 10:00-18:00, look for elevator just inside the cathedral's entry).

Ascending the North Tower: This tower, reached from inside the church (look for the *Aufzug zur Pummerin* sign), holds the famous "Pummerin" bell. Cast from captured Ottoman cannons, this bell rings in the New Year. This tower is easier to ascend than the south tower (described next), but it's much shorter and not as exciting, with lesser views (€5, daily 9:00-17:30 & 19:00-21:30, entrance inside the church on the left/north side of the nave; you can access this elevator without buying a ticket for the main nave).

Climbing the South Tower: The iconic south tower offers a far better view than the north tower, but you'll earn it by hiking 343 tightly wound steps up the spiral staircase (€4, daily 9:00-17:30; this hike burns about one Sacher-Torte of calories). To reach the entrance, exit the church and make a U-turn to the left. This tower, once key to the city's defense as a lookout point, is still dear to Viennese hearts. (It's long been affectionately nicknamed "Steffl," Viennese for "Stevie.") No church spire in (what was) the Austro-Hungarian Empire is taller—by Habsburg decree. While at the top, use your city map to locate the famous sights.

HOFBURG PALACE

The complex, confusing, and imposing Imperial Palace, with 640 years of architecture, demands your attention. This first Habsburg residence grew with the family empire from the 13th century until 1913, when the last "new wing" opened. The winter residence of the Habsburg rulers until 1918, it's still home to the Austrian president's office, 5,000 government workers, and several important museums. For an overview of the palace layout, see map on page 1191.

Planning Your Time: Don't get confused by the Hofburg's myriad courtyards and many museums. Focus on three sights: the Imperial Apartments, the Treasury, and the museums at the New Palace (Neue Burg). With more time, consider the Hofburg's many other sights, covering virtually all facets of the imperial lifestyle.

Eating at the Hofburg: Down the tunnel to Heldenplatz is a tiny but handy sandwich bar called **Hofburg Stüberl.** It's ideal for a cool, quiet sit and a drink or snack (same €3 sandwich price whether you sit or go, Mon-Fri 7:00-18:00, Sat-Sun 10:00-16:00). The recommended **Soho Kantine,** off the Burggarten near the butterfly house, is a cheap-but-not-cheery option (described on page 1250).

▲▲▲Hofburg Imperial Apartments (Kaiserappartements)

These lavish, Versailles-type, "wish-I-were-God" royal rooms are the downtown version of the grander Schönbrunn Palace. If you're rushed and have time for only one palace, make it this one. Palace visits are a one-way romp through three sections: a porcelain and silver collection, a museum dedicated to the enigmatic and troubled Empress Sisi, and the luxurious apartments themselves.

The Imperial Apartments are a mix of Old World luxury and modern 19th-century conveniences. This is where Emperor Franz Josef I lived and worked along with his wife, Elisabeth, known as Sisi. The Sisi Museum traces the development of her legend, analyzing how her fabulous but tragic life created a 19th-century Princess Diana. You'll read bits of her poetic writing, see exact copies of her now-lost jewelry, and learn about her escapes, dieting mania, and chocolate bills.

Cost and Hours: €11.50, includes well-done audioguide; €25.50 Sisi Ticket also covers Schönbrunn Palace (where you can skip the line) and Imperial Furniture Collection; daily July-Aug 9:00-18:00, Sept-June 9:00-17:30, last entry one hour before closing; enter from under the rotunda just off Michaelerplatz, through the Michaelertor gate; tel. 01/533-7570, www.hofburg-wien.at.

Information: With the included audioguide and the self-guided tour below, you won't need the €9 *Imperial Apartments/Sisi Museum/Silver Collection* guidebook. If you listen to the entire audioguide, allow 40 minutes for the silver collection, 30 minutes for the Sisi Museum, and 40 minutes for the apartments.

Your ticket grants you admission to three separate exhibits, which you'll visit on a pretty straightforward one-way route. The first floor holds a collection of precious porcelain and silver knickknacks *(Silberkammer)*. You then go upstairs to the Sisi Museum, which has displays about her life. This leads into the 20-odd rooms of Imperial Apartments *(Kaiserappartements)*, starting in Franz Josef's rooms, then heading into the dozen rooms where his wife Sisi lived.

➲ **Self-Guided Tour:** Your visit (and the excellent audioguide) starts on the ground floor.

Imperial Porcelain and Silver Collection: Here you'll see the Habsburg court's vast tableware collection, which the audioguide actually manages to make fairly interesting. Browse the collection to gawk at the opulence and to take in some colorful Habsburg trivia. (Who'd have thunk that the court had an official way to fold a napkin—and that the technique remains a closely guarded secret?) Still, I wouldn't bog down here, as there's much more to see upstairs.

Once you're through all those rooms of dishes, climb the stairs—the same staircase used by the emperors and empresses who lived here. At the top is a timeline of Sisi's life. Swipe your ticket to pass through the turnstile, consider the (rare) WC, and enter the room with the **model of the Hofburg.** Circle to the far side to find where you're standing right now, near the smallest of

Vienna's Hofburg Palace

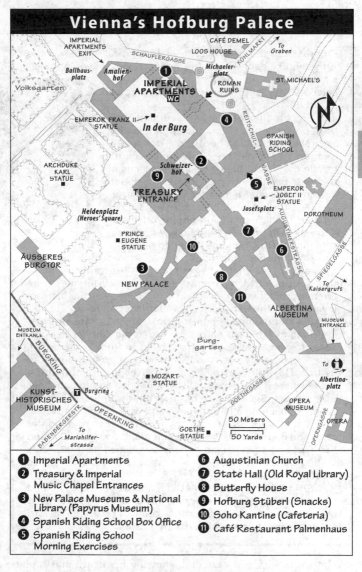

1. Imperial Apartments
2. Treasury & Imperial Music Chapel Entrances
3. New Palace Museums & National Library (Papyrus Museum)
4. Spanish Riding School Box Office
5. Spanish Riding School Morning Exercises
6. Augustinian Church
7. State Hall (Old Royal Library)
8. Butterfly House
9. Hofburg Stüberl (Snacks)
10. Soho Kantine (Cafeteria)
11. Café Restaurant Palmenhaus

the Hofburg's three domes. That small dome tops the entrance to the Hofburg from Michaelerplatz.

To the left of the dome (as you face the facade) is the steeple of the Augustinian Church. It was there, in 1854, that Franz Josef married 16-year-old Elisabeth of Bavaria, and their story began.

Sisi Museum: Empress Elisabeth (1837-1898)—a.k.a. "Sisi" (SEE-see)—was Franz Josef's mysterious, beautiful, and narcissistic wife. This museum traces her fabulous but tragic life. The

Sisi (1837-1898)

Empress Elisabeth—Franz Josef's beautiful wife—was the 19th-century equivalent of Princess Diana. Known as "Sisi" since childhood, she became an instant celebrity when she married Franz Josef at the age of 16.

Sisi's main goals in life seem to have been preserving her reputation as a beautiful empress, maintaining her Barbie-doll figure, and tending to her fairy-tale, ankle-length hair. In the 1860s, she was considered one of the most beautiful women in the world. But, in spite of severe dieting and fanatical exercise, age took its toll. After turning 30, she refused to allow photographs or portraits, and was generally seen in public with a delicate fan covering her face (and bad teeth).

Complex and influential, Sisi was adored by Franz Josef, whom she respected. Although Franz Josef was supposed to have married her sister Helene (in an arranged diplomatic marriage), he fell in love with Sisi instead. It was one of the Habsburgs' few marriages for love.

Sisi's personal mission and political cause was promoting Hungary's bid for autonomy within the empire. Her personal tragedy was the death of her son Rudolf, the crown prince, in an apparent suicide (an incident often dramatized as the "Mayerling Affair," named after the royal hunting lodge where it happened). Disliking Vienna and the confines of the court, Sisi traveled more and more frequently. (She spent so much time in Budapest, and with Hungarian statesman Count Andrássy, that many believe her third daughter to be the count's.) As the years passed, the restless Sisi and her hardworking husband became estranged. In 1898, while visiting Geneva, Switzerland, she was murdered by an Italian anarchist.

Sisi's beauty, bittersweet life, and tragic death helped create her larger-than-life legacy. However, her importance is often inflated by melodramatic accounts of her life. The Sisi Museum seeks to tell a more accurate story.

exhibit starts with Sisi's sad end, showing her **death mask,** photos of her **funeral procession** (by the Hercules statues facing Michaelerplatz), and an **engraving** of a grieving Franz Josef. It was at her death that the obscure, private empress' legend began to grow.

Sisi was nearly 5'8" (a head taller than her husband), had a 20-inch waist (she wore very tight corsets), and weighed only about 100 pounds. (Her waistline eventually grew...to 21 inches. That was at age 50, after giving birth to four children.) The statue, a copy of one of 30 statues that were erected in her honor in European cities, shows her holding one of her trademark fans. It doesn't show off her magnificent hair, however, which reached down to her ankles.

Imperial Apartments: After the Sisi Museum, a one-way route takes you through a series of royal rooms. The first room—as if to make clear that there was more to the Habsburgs than Sisi—shows a family tree tracing the Habsburgs from 1273 (Rudolf I at upper left) to their messy WWI demise (Karl I, lower right). From here, enter the private apartments of the royal family (Franz Josef's first, then Sisi's).

Franz Josef's apartments illustrate the lifestyle of the last great Habsburg ruler. In these rooms, he presided over defeats and liberal inroads as the world was changing and the monarchy becoming obsolete. Here he met with advisors and welcomed foreign dignitaries, hosted lavish, white-gloved balls and stuffy formal dinners, and raised three children. He slept (alone) on his austere bed while his beloved wife, Sisi, retreated to her own rooms. He suffered through the execution of his brother, the suicide of his son and heir, the murder of his wife, and the assassination of his nephew, Archduke Ferdinand, which sparked World War I and spelled the end of the Habsburg monarchy.

Among the rooms you'll see is the **audience room** where Franz Josef received commoners from around the empire. Imagine you've traveled for days to have your say before the emperor. You're wearing your new fancy suit—Franz Josef required that men coming before him wear a tailcoat, women a black gown with a train. You've rehearsed what you want to say. You hope your hair looks good.

Suddenly, you're face-to-face with the emp himself. (The **portrait** on the easel shows Franz Josef in 1915, when he was more than 80 years old.) Despite your efforts, you probably weren't in this room long. He'd stand at the **lectern** (far left) as the visiting commoners had their say. (Standing kept things moving.) You'd hear a brief response from him (quite likely the same he'd given all day), and then you'd back out of the room while bowing (also required). On the lectern is a partial **list** of 56 appointments he had on January 3, 1910 (three columns: family name, meeting topic, and *Anmerkung*—the emperor's "action log").

Franz Josef's **bedroom** shows off his spartan lifestyle. Notice his no-frills **iron bed.** He typically rose at 3:30 and started his day in prayer, kneeling at the **prayer stool** against the far wall. While he had a typical emperor's share of mistresses, his dresser was always well-stocked with **photos** of Sisi.

Sisi's Rooms: In Sisi's **bedroom,** refurbished in the Neo-Rococo style in 1854, there's a red carpet covered with oriental rugs. There were always lots of fresh flowers. She not only slept

VIENNA

Emperor Franz Josef (1830-1916)

Franz Josef I—who ruled for 68 years (1848-1916)—was the embodiment of the Habsburg Empire as it finished its six-century-long ride. Born in 1830, Franz Josef had a stern upbringing that instilled in him a powerful sense of duty and—like so many men of power—a love of all things military.

His uncle, Ferdinand I, suffered from profound epilepsy, which prevented him from being an effective ruler. As the revolutions of 1848 rattled royal families throughout Europe, the Habsburgs forced Ferdinand to abdicate and put 18-year-old Franz Josef on the throne. Ironically, as one of his first acts as emperor, Franz Josef—whose wife would later become closely identified with Hungarian independence—put down the 1848 revolt in Hungary with bloody harshness. He spent the first part of his long reign understandably paranoid, as social discontent continued to simmer.

Franz Josef was very conservative. But worse, he wrongly believed that he was a talented military tactician, leading Austria into catastrophic battles against Italy (which was fighting for its unification and independence) in the 1860s. As his army endured severe, avoidable casualties, it became clear: Franz Josef was a disaster as a general.

Wearing his uniform to the end, Franz Josef never saw what a dinosaur his monarchy was becoming, and never thought it strange that the majority of his subjects didn't even speak German. Franz Josef had no interest in democracy and pointedly never set foot in Austria's parliament building. But, like his contemporary Queen Victoria, he was a microcosm of his empire—old-fashioned but sacrosanct. His passion for low-grade paperwork earned him the nickname "Joe Bureaucrat." Mired in these petty details, he missed the big picture. In 1914, he helped start a Great War that ultimately ended the age of monarchs. The year 1918 marked the end of Europe's big royal families: Hohenzollerns (Prussia), Romanovs (Russia), and Habsburgs (Austria).

here, but also lived here—the bed was rolled in and out daily—until her death in 1898. The desk is where she sat and wrote her letters and poems. In her **dressing/exercise room,** servants worked three hours a day on Sisi's famous hair. She'd exercise on the wooden structure and on the rings suspended from the doorway to the left. Afterward, she'd get a massage on the red-covered bed.

In the **main bathroom,** you'll see her huge copper tub (with the original wall coverings behind it), where servants washed her hair. Sisi was the first Habsburg to have running water in her bathroom (notice the hot and cold faucets).

In the **small salon,** the portrait is of Crown Prince Rudolf, Franz Josef's and Sisi's only son. On the morning of January 30,

1889, the 30-year-old Rudolf and a beautiful baroness were found shot dead in an apparent murder-suicide in his hunting lodge in Mayerling. The scandal shocked the empire and tainted the Habsburgs; Sisi retreated further into her fantasy world, and Franz Josef carried on stoically with a broken heart.

The tour ends in the **dining room**. It's dinnertime, and Franz Josef has called his extended family together. The settings are modest...just silver. Gold was saved for formal state dinners. Next to each name card was a menu listing the chef responsible for each dish. (Talk about pressure.) Franz Josef enforced strict protocol at mealtime: No one could speak without being spoken to by the emperor, and no one could eat after he was done. While the rest of Europe was growing democracy and expanding personal freedoms, the Habsburgs preserved their ossified worldview to the bitter end.

In 1918, World War I ended, Austria was created as a modern nation-state, the Habsburgs were tossed out...and Hofburg Palace was destined to become a museum.

▲▲▲Hofburg Treasury (Weltliche und Geistliche Schatzkammer)

One of the world's most stunning collections of royal regalia, the Hofburg Treasury shows off sparkling crowns, jewels, gowns, and assorted Habsburg bling in 21 darkened rooms. The treasures, well-explained by an audioguide, include the crown of the Holy Roman Emperor, Charlemagne's saber, a unicorn horn, and more precious gems than you can shake a scepter at.

Cost and Hours: €12, €20 combo-ticket with Kunsthistorisches Museum and New Palace museums, Wed-Mon 9:00-17:30, closed Tue, last entry 30 minutes before closing, audioguide-€4; from the Hofburg's central courtyard pass through the black, red, and gold gate, then follow *Schatzkammer* signs to the Schweizerhof; tel. 01/525-240, www.kaiserliche-schatzkammer.at.

○ **Self-Guided Tour:** Here's a rundown of the highlights (the audioguide is much more complete).

Room 2: The personal **crown of Rudolf II** (1602) occupies the center of the room along with its accompanying scepter and orb; a bust of Rudolf II (1552-1612) sits nearby. The crown's design symbolically merges a bishop's miter ("Holy"), the arch across the top of a Roman emperor's helmet ("Roman"), and the typical medieval king's crown ("Emperor").

Two centuries later (1806), this crown and scepter became the official regalia of Austria's rulers, as seen in the large **portrait of Franz I** (the open-legged guy behind you). Napoleon Bonaparte had just conquered Austria and dissolved the Holy Roman Empire. Franz (ruled 1792-1835) was allowed to remain in power, but he had to downgrade his title from "Franz II, Holy Roman Emperor" to "Franz I, Emperor of Austria."

Rooms 3 and 4: These rooms contain some of the **coronation vestments and regalia** needed for the new Austrian (not Holy Roman) Emperor. There was a different one for each of the emperor's subsidiary titles—e.g., King of Hungary or King of Lombardy. So many crowns and kingdoms in the Habsburgs' vast empire!

Room 5: Ponder the **Cradle of the King of Rome,** once occupied by Napoleon's son, who was born in 1811 and made King of Rome. While pledging allegiance to democracy, Napoleon in fact crowned himself Emperor of France and hobnobbed with Europe's royalty. When his wife Josephine could not bear him a male heir, Napoleon divorced her and married into the Habsburg family.

Room 6: For Divine Right kings, even child-rearing was a sacred ritual that needed elaborate regalia for public ceremonies. The 23-pound **gold basin and pitcher** were used to baptize noble children, who were dressed in the **baptismal dresses** displayed nearby.

Room 7: These jewels are the true "treasures," a cabinet of wonders used by Habsburgs to impress their relatives (or to hock when funds got low).

Room 8: The eight-foot-tall, 500-year-old **"unicorn horn"** (actually a narwhal tusk), was considered to have magical healing powers bestowed from on high. This one was owned by the Holy Roman Emperor—clearly a divine monarch.

Religious Rooms: The next several rooms of **religious objects**—crucifixes, chalices, mini-altarpieces, reliquaries, and bishops' vestments. Habsburg rulers mixed the institutions of church and state, so these precious religious accoutrements were also part of their display of secular power. The big red-silk and gold-thread **mantle,** nearly 900 years old, was worn by Holy Roman Emperors at their coronations.

Room 11: The collection's highlight is the 10th-century **crown of the Holy Roman Emperor.** It was probably made for Otto I (c. 960), the first king to call himself Holy Roman Emperor. The

Imperial Crown swirls with symbolism "proving" that the emperor was both holy and Roman: The cross on top says the HRE ruled as Christ's representative on earth, and the jeweled arch over the top is reminiscent of the parade helmet of ancient Romans. The jewels themselves allude to the wearer's kinghood in the here and now. Imagine the impression this priceless, glittering crown must have made on the emperor's medieval subjects.

Nearby is the 11th-century **Imperial Cross** that preceded the emperor in ceremonies. Encrusted with jewels, it had a hollow compartment (its core is wood) that carried substantial chunks thought to be from *the* **cross** on which Jesus was crucified and *the* **Holy Lance** used to pierce his side (both pieces are displayed in the same glass case). Holy Roman Emperors actually carried the lance into battle in the 10th century. Look behind the cross to see how it was a box that could be clipped open and shut, used for holding holy relics. You can see bits of the "true cross" anywhere, but this is a prime piece—with the actual nail hole.

Room 12: Now picture all this regalia used together. The **painting** shows the coronation of Maria Theresa's son Josef II as Holy Roman Emperor in 1764. Set in a church in Frankfurt (filled with the bigwigs—literally—of the day), Josef is wearing the same crown and royal garb that you've just seen.

More Hofburg Sights
▲▲Hofburg New Palace Museums: Armor, Music, and Ancient Greek Statues

The New Palace (Neue Burg) houses three separate collections— an armory (with a killer collection of medieval weapons), historical musical instruments, and classical statuary from ancient Ephesus. The included audioguide brings the exhibits to life and lets you hear the collection's fascinating old instruments being played. An added bonus is the chance to wander alone among the royal Habsburg halls, stairways, and painted ceilings.

Cost and Hours: €14 ticket covers all three collections and the Kunsthistorisches Museum across the Ring, €20 combo-ticket adds the Hofburg Treasury, Wed-Sun 10:00-18:00, closed Mon-Tue, last entry 30 minutes before closing, almost no tourists, tel. 01/525-240, www.khm.at.

▲Spanish Riding School (Spanische Hofreitschule)

This stately 300-year-old Baroque hall at the Hofburg Palace is the home of the renowned Lipizzaner stallions. The magnificent building was an impressive expanse in its day. Built without central pillars, it offers clear views of the prancing horses under lavish chandeliers, with a grand statue of Emperor Charles VI on horseback at the head of the hall.

Lipizzaner stallions were a creation of horse-loving Habsburg Archduke Charles, who wanted to breed the perfect animal. He imported Andalusian horses from his homeland of Spain, then mated them with a local line to produce an extremely intelligent and easily trainable breed. Italian and Arabian bloodlines were later added to tweak various characteristics. The name "Lipizzaner"

VIENNA

comes from Lipica in Slovenia, where the stud farm was located until 1920 (when Slovenia became part of Yugoslavia and the horses were moved to the Austrian city of Graz). Lipizzaner stallions are known for their noble gait and Baroque profile. These regal horses have changed shape with the tenor of the times: They were bred strong and stout during wars, and frilly and slender in more cultured eras. But they're always born black, fade to gray, and turn a distinctive white in adulthood.

The school offers three ways to see the horses: performances, morning exercises, and guided tours of the stables. To see what the options are during your visit, go to www.srs.at and enter your dates under "Event Search," or call 01/533-9031. Photos are not allowed, nor are children under age 3.

At any time of day and at no cost, you can just walk by the stables (there's a big window from the covered passageway along Reitschulgasse) and usually see the horses poking their heads out of their stalls.

Performances: The Lipizzaner stallions put on great 80-minute performances in spring and fall. The pricey seats book up months in advance, but standing room is usually available the same day, and there's not a bad view in the house (seats-about €50-160, standing room-about €25, prices can vary depending on the show; Feb-late June and mid-Aug-Dec usually Sat-Sun at 11:00, no shows in Jan or late June-mid-Aug; box office opens at 9:00 and is located inside the Hofburg—go through the main Hofburg entryway from Michaelerplatz, then turn left into the first passage; tel. 01/533-9031, www.srs.at). If buying tickets online, look for the tiny English flag at the top of the page when you're redirected to the ticket purchase site.

Morning Exercises: For a less expensive, more casual experience, morning exercises with music take place on weekday mornings in the same hall and are open to the public. Don't have high expectations, as the horses often do little more than trot and warm up. Tourists line up early at Josefsplatz (the large courtyard between Michaelerplatz and Albertinaplatz), at the door marked *Spanische Hofreitschule*. But there's no need to show up when the doors open at 10:00, since tickets never really "sell out." Only the horses stay for the full two hours. As people leave, new tickets are printed, so you can just prance in with no wait at all. You can also buy tickets for the training sessions at the box office (€14 at the door, family discounts, generally March-late June and early-Aug-Dec Tue-Fri 10:00-12:00, occasionally also on Mon).

Guided Tours: One-hour guided tours are given almost every afternoon year-round. You'll see the Winter Riding School with its grand Baroque architecture, the Summer Riding School in a shady courtyard, and the stables (€16; tours usually daily at 14:00,

15:00, and 16:00; in English and German, purchase tickets online or at the box office).

▲Augustinian Church (Augustinerkirche)

Built into the Hofburg, this is the Gothic and Neo-Gothic church where the Habsburgs got latched (weddings took place here), then later dispatched (the royal hearts are in the vault).

Cost and Hours: Church—free, open long hours daily; vault—€2.50 suggested donation, usually open to the public immediately after 11:00 Sun Mass only; Augustinerstrasse 3—facing Josefsplatz, with its statue of the great reform emperor Josef II and the royal library next door.

Visiting the Church: In the front, notice the windows above on the right, from which royals witnessed the Mass in private. Don't miss the exquisite, pyramid-shaped memorial (by the Italian sculptor Antonio Canova) to Maria Theresa's favorite daughter. The church's 11:00 Sunday Mass is a hit with music lovers—both a Mass and a concert, often with an orchestra accompanying the choir (acoustics are best in front). Pay by contributing to the offering plate and buying a CD afterwards. Check posters by the entry, or www.hochamt.at (click on "Programm"), to see what's on—typically you'll hear one of Mozart or Haydn's many short Masses. The hearts of 54 Habsburg nobles are in urns in a vault off the church's Loreto Chapel (on the right beyond the Maria Christina memorial).

State Hall (Prunksaal) and
Austrian National Library Museums

The National Library (Österreichische Nationalbibliothek) runs four museums in different parts of the Hofburg complex. The

most worthwhile is the **State Hall** (Prunksaal), a postcard-perfect Baroque library entered from Josefplatz, next to the Augustinian Church (see map on page 1191). In this former royal library, with a statue of Charles VI in the center, you'll find yourself whispering. The setting takes you back to 1730 and gives you the sense that, in imperial times, knowledge of the world was for the elite—and with that knowledge, the elite had power. More than 200,000 old books line the walls, but patrons go elsewhere to read them—the hall is just for show these days.

The entrance to the National Library's main, modern reading area— with crowds of students at exam times—is on Heldenplatz. The public isn't really allowed in, except to walk through to visit the **Papyrus Museum** in the basement. This little collection tells the story of writing in Egypt from 3000 B.C. to A.D. 1000, with scant English descriptions.

A couple blocks north of the Hofburg, in the building at Herrengasse 9 (across from the Herrengasse U-Bahn station), the library also runs the **Globe Museum** (the world's largest, with 250 terrestrial and celestial spheres) and a modest two-room museum on **Esperanto** and other artificial languages.

Cost and Hours: €7 for State Hall; €4 combo-ticket for Papyrus, Globe, and Esperanto museums; daily 10:00-18:00, Thu until 21:00; tel. 01/53410, www.onb.ac.at.

Burggarten (Palace Garden) and Butterfly House

This greenbelt, once the backyard of the Hofburg and now a people's park, welcomes visitors to loiter on the grass. On nice days, it's lively with office workers enjoying a break. The statue of Mozart facing the Ringstrasse is popular. The iron-and-glass pavilion (c. 1910 with playful Art Nouveau touches) now houses the recommended Café Restaurant Palmenhaus and a small but fluttery butterfly exhibit.

Cost and Hours: €6; April-Oct daily 10:00-16:45, Sat-Sun until 18:15; Nov-March daily 10:00-15:45.

▲▲Albertina Museum

This charming museum has three highlights: impressive state rooms of the former palace, a permanent collection of art from Impressionist to modern, and excellent temporary exhibits. The building, at the southern tip of the Hofburg complex (near the Opera), was the residence of Maria Theresa's favorite daughter, Maria Christina, who was the only one allowed to marry for love rather than political strategy. Her many sisters were jealous. (Marie-Antoinette had to marry the French king...and lost her head over it.) Maria Christina's husband, Albert of Saxony, was a great collector of original drawings and amassed an enormous assortment of works by Dürer, Rembrandt, Rubens, Schiele, and others. As it's Albert and Christina's gallery, it's cleverly called the "Albertina."

Cost and Hours: €12, daily 10:00-18:00, Wed until 21:00, helpful audioguide-€4, overlooking Albertinaplatz across from the TI and Opera, tel. 01/534-830, www.albertina.at.

Visiting the Museum: Begin on the first floor with the State Rooms and Batliner Collection.

State Rooms *(Prunkräume):* Wander freely under chandeliers and across parquet floors through a couple dozen rooms of imperial splendor, unconstrained by velvet ropes. It's a kaleidoscope of colors, as each room's damask walls and curtains are a different rich shade of red, yellow, or green. You'll see the billiard room,

Empress Maria Theresa (1717-1780) and Her Son, Emperor Josef II (1741-1790)

Maria Theresa was the only woman to officially rule the Habsburg Empire in that family's 640-year reign. She was a strong and effective empress (r. 1740-1780). People are quick to remember Maria Theresa as the mother of 16 children (10 survived into adulthood). Ponder the fact that the most powerful woman in Europe either was pregnant or had a newborn for most of her reign. Maria Theresa ruled after the Austrian defeat of the Ottomans, when Europe recognized Austria as a great power. (Her rival, the Prussian king, said, "When at last the Habsburgs get a great man, it's a woman.")

The last of the Baroque imperial rulers, and the first of the modern rulers of the Age of Enlightenment, Maria Theresa marked the end of the feudal system and the beginning of the era of the grand state. She was a great social reformer. During her reign, she avoided wars and expanded her empire by skillfully marrying her children into the right families. For instance, after daughter Marie-Antoinette's marriage into the French Bourbon family (to Louis XVI), a country that had been an enemy became an ally. (Unfortunately for Marie-Antoinette, Maria Theresa's timing was off.)

To stay in power during an era of revolution, Maria Theresa had to be in tune with her age. She taxed the Church and the nobility, provided six years of obligatory education to all children, and granted free health care to all in her realm. Maria Theresa also welcomed the boy genius Mozart into her court.

The empress' legacy lived on in her son, Josef II, who ruled as emperor himself for a decade (1780-1790). He was an even more avid reformer, building on his mother's accomplishments. An enlightened monarch, Josef mothballed the too-extravagant Schönbrunn Palace, secularized the monasteries, established religious tolerance within his realm, freed the serfs, made possible the founding of Austria's first general hospital, and promoted relatively enlightened treatment of the mentally ill. Josef was a model of practicality (for example, reusable coffins à la *Amadeus*, and no more than six candles at funerals)—and very unpopular with other royals. But his policies succeeded in preempting the revolutionary anger of the age, largely enabling Austria to avoid the turmoil that shook so much of the rest of Europe.

the tea salon, the bedrooms, and the tiny Goldkabinett, with walls plated in 23-carat gold.

Batliner Collection: This manageable collection sweeps you quickly through modern art history, featuring minor works by major artists. Start with a room of classic Impressionism: Monet's water lilies, Degas' dancers, and Renoir's cute little girls. By 1900, the modern world was approaching, as seen in Munch's moody landscapes and (Vienna's own) Gustav Klimt, with his eerie femme fatales. The next few rooms illustrate how art transitioned from Impressionist to abstract. The subject matter becomes increasingly flat and two-dimensional, eventually dissolving into a pattern of paint that would become purely abstract art.

Temporary Exhibits: A highlight of the museum is their special exhibitions, which often feature works from the Albertina's world-renowned collection of drawings and paintings.

CHURCH CRYPTS NEAR THE HOFBURG

Two churches near the Hofburg offer starkly different looks at dearly departed Viennese: the Habsburg coffins in the Kaisergruft, and the commoners' graves in St. Michael's Church.

▲▲Kaisergruft (Imperial Crypt)

Visiting the imperial remains of the Habsburg family is not as easy as you might imagine. These original organ donors left their bodies—about 150 in all—in the unassuming Kaisergruft, their hearts in the Augustinian Church (viewable Sun after Mass—see page 1199), and their entrails in the crypt below St. Stephen's Cathedral (described on page 1188). Don't tripe.

Cost and Hours: €5.50, daily 10:00-18:00, last entry 20 minutes before closing, €0.50 map includes Habsburg family tree and a chart locating each coffin, crypt is in the Capuchin Church at Tegetthoffstrasse 2 at Neuer Markt; tel. 01/512-6853, www.kaisergruft.at.

Visiting the Kaisergruft: Descend into a low-ceilinged crypt full of gray metal tombs. Start up the path, through tombs ranging from simple caskets to increasingly big monuments with elaborate metalwork ornamentation.

You soon reach the massive pewter tomb under the dome of **Maria Theresa.** The only female Habsburg monarch, she had to be granted special dispensation to rule. Her 40-year reign was enlightened and progressive. She and her husband, **Franz I,** recline Etruscan-style atop their fancy coffin, gazing into each other's eyes as a cherub crowns them with glory. They were famously in love (though Franz was less than faithful), and their numerous children were married off to Europe's royal houses. Maria Theresa outlived her husband by 15 years, which she spent in mourning. Old and fat, she installed a special lift to transport herself down into the Kaisergruft to visit her dear, departed Franz. At the four corners of the tomb are the Habsburgs' four crowns: the Holy Roman Empire, Hungary, Bohemia, and Jerusalem. At his parents' feet lies **Josef II,** the patron of Mozart and Beethoven. Compare the Rococo splendor of Maria Theresa's tomb with the simple coffin of Josef, who was known for his down-to-earth ruling style during the Age of Enlightenment.

Down three steps, the next room illustrates the Habsburgs' fading 19th-century glory. There's the appropriately austere military tomb of the long-reigning **Franz Josef** (see sidebar on page 1194). Alongside is his wife, **Elisabeth**—a.k.a. "Sisi" (see page 1192)—who always wins the "Most Flowers" award. Their son was Crown Prince **Rudolf**. Rudolf and his teenage mistress supposedly committed suicide together in 1889 at Mayerling hunting lodge...or was it murder? It took considerable legal hair-splitting to win Rudolf this hallowed burial spot: After examining his brain, it was determined that he was mentally disabled and therefore incapable of knowingly killing himself and his girl.

In the final room (with humbler copper tombs), you reach the final Habsburgs. **Karl I** (see his bust, not a tomb) was the last of the Habsburg rulers, and was deposed in 1918. His son was Crown Prince **Otto,** who is buried near his mother, **Zita.** When Otto was laid to rest here in 2011, it was probably the last great Old Regime event in European history. The monarchy died hard in Austria. Today there are about 700 living Habsburg royals, mostly living in exile. When they die, they will be buried in their countries of exile, not here.

Body parts and ornate tombs aside, the real legacy of the Habsburgs is the magnificence of this city. Step outside. Pan up. Watch the clouds glide by the ornate gables of Vienna.

▲St. Michael's Church Crypt (Michaelerkirche)

St. Michael's Church, which faces the Hofburg on Michaelerplatz, offers a striking contrast to the imperial crypt. Regular tours take visitors underground to see a typical church crypt—filled with the rotting wooden coffins of well-to-do commoners.

Cost and Hours: €7 for 45-minute tour, Mon-Fri at 11:00 and 13:00, no tours Sat-Sun, mostly in German but with enough English, wait at the sign that advertises the tour at the church entrance and pay the guide directly, mobile 0650-533-8003, www.michaelerkirche.at.

Visiting the Crypt: Climbing below the church, you'll see about a hundred 18th-century coffins and stand on three feet of debris, surrounded by niches filled with stacked lumber from decayed coffins and countless bones. You'll meet a 1769 mummy in lederhosen and a wig, along with a woman who is clutching a cross and has flowers painted on her high heels. You'll learn about death in those times—from how the wealthy didn't want to end up in standard shallow graves, instead paying to be laid to rest beneath the church, to how, in 1780, the enlightened emperor Josef II ended the practice of cemetery burials in cities but allowed the rich to become the stinking rich in crypts under churches. You'll also discover why many were buried with their chin strapped shut (because when the muscles rot, your jaw falls open and you get that ghostly skeleton look that nobody wants).

KUNSTHISTORISCHES MUSEUM AND NEARBY

In the 19th century, the Habsburgs planned to link their palace and museum buildings with a series of arches across the Ringstrasse. Although that dream was never fully realized, the awe-inspiring museums still face off across Maria-Theresien-Platz, with a monument to Maria Theresa at its center (for more on this monument, see page 1178).

▲▲▲Kunsthistorisches Museum

This exciting museum, across the Ring from the Hofburg Palace, showcases the grandeur and opulence of the Habsburgs' collected

artwork in a grand building (built in 1888 to display these works). While there's little Viennese art here, you will find world-class European masterpieces galore (including canvases by Raphael, Caravaggio, Velázquez, Dürer, Rubens, Vermeer, Rembrandt, and a particularly exquisite roomful of Bruegels), all well-displayed on one glorious floor, plus a fine display of Egyptian, classical, and applied arts.

Cost and Hours: €14 (free for kids under 19), ticket also covers New Palace museums across the Ring, €20 combo-ticket also includes the Hofburg Treasury; June-Aug daily 10:00-18:00; Sept-May Tue-Sun 10:00-18:00, closed Mon; Thu until 21:00 year-round, last entry 30 minutes before closing, audioguide-€4, on the Ringstrasse at Maria-Theresien-Platz, U-2 or U-3: Volkstheater/ Museumsplatz (exit toward *Burgring*),
tel. 01/525-240, www.khm.at.

❷ Self-Guided Tour: The Kunsthistorwhateveritis Museum—let's just say "Koonst"—houses the family collection of Austria's luxury-loving Habsburg rulers. Their joie de vivre is reflected in this collection—some of the most beautiful, sexy, and fun art from two centuries (c. 1450-1650). At their peak of power in the 1500s, the Habsburgs ruled Austria, Germany, northern Italy, the Netherlands, and Spain—and you'll see a wide variety of art from all these places and beyond.

Of the museum's many exhibits, we'll tour only the Painting Gallery (Gemäldegalerie) on the first floor. Italian-Spanish-French art is in one half of the building, and Northern European art in the other. On our tour, we'll get a sampling of each. The museum seems to constantly move paintings from room to room, so be flexible. Use the map to guide your route through the first floor, looking for the following paintings and artists.

Titian—*Danae* and *Ecce Homo:* In the long career of Titian the Venetian (it rhymes), he painted portraits, Christian Madonnas, and sexy Venuses with equal ease. Here, Titian captured Danae—a luscious nude reclining in bed—as she's about to be seduced. Zeus, the king of the gods, descends as a shower of gold to consort with her—you can almost see the human form of Zeus within the cloud. Danae is helpless with rapture, opening her legs to receive him, while her servant tries to catch the heavenly spurt with a golden dish. How could ultra-conservative Catholic emperors have tolerated such a downright pagan and erotic painting? Apparently, without a problem.

In the large canvas *Ecce Homo,* a crowd mills about, when suddenly there's a commotion. They nudge each other and start to point. Follow their gaze diagonally up the stairs to a battered figure entering way up in the corner. "Ecce Homo!" says Pilate. "Behold the man." And he presents Jesus to the mob. For us, as for the unsympathetic crowd, the humiliated Son of God is not the center of the scene, but almost an afterthought.

Raphael—*Madonna of the Meadow:* Young Raphael epitomized the spirit of the High Renaissance, combining symmetry, grace, beauty, and emotion. This Madonna is a mountain of motherly love—Mary's head is the summit and her flowing robe is the base—enfolding Baby Jesus and John the Baptist. The geometric perfection, serene landscape, and Mary's adoring face make this a masterpiece of sheer grace—but then you get smacked by an ironic fist: The cross the little tykes play with foreshadows their gruesome deaths.

Correggio and Parmigianino: The Kunst displays excellent small canvases in the smaller side rooms. For example, in a room near Raphael, you may find Correggio's *Jupiter and Io,* showing Zeus seducing another female, this time disguised as a cloud. Parmigianino's *Self-Portrait in a Convex Mirror* depicts the artist gazing into a convex mirror and perfectly reproducing the curved reflection on a convex piece of wood. Amazing.

Arcimboldo—Portraits of the Seasons: These four cleverly deceptive portraits by the Habsburg court painter depict the four

VIENNA

Kunsthistorisches Museum—First Floor

ROOM 17 — VERMEER

ROOM 16

ROOM 15

ROOM 14

SAAL — TEMPORARY

WC

STAIRS TO SECOND FLOOR

ROOM 18

SAAL XI

SAAL X — BRUEGEL

SAAL IX

THESEUS STATUE

ROOM 19

SAAL XII

NORTHERN EUROPEAN ART

STAIRS FROM GROUND FLOOR

ROOM 20

SAAL XIII

SAAL XIV — RUBENS

SAAL XV — DÜRER

ROOM 21 — REMBRANDT

TOUR ENDS

ROOM 22

ROOM 23

ROOM 24

MAIN

To Ringstrasse

Maria-Theresien

seasons (and elements) as people. For example, take *Summer*—a.k.a. "Fruit Face." With a pickle nose, pear chin, and corn-husk ears, this guy literally is what he eats. Its grotesque weirdness makes it typical of Mannerist art.

Caravaggio—*Madonna of the Rosary* and *David with the Head of Goliath:* Caravaggio shocked the art world with brutally honest reality. Compared with Raphael's super-sweet *Madonna of the Meadow*, Caravaggio's *Madonna of the Rosary* (the biggest canvas in the room) looks perfectly ordinary, and the saints kneeling around her have dirty feet.

In *David with the Head of Goliath*, Caravaggio turns a third-degree-interrogation light on a familiar Bible story. David shoves the dripping head of the slain giant right in our noses. The painting, bled of color, is virtually a black-and-white crime-scene

photo—slightly overexposed. Out of the deep darkness shine only a few crucial details. This David is not a heroic Renaissance man like Michelangelo's famous statue, but a homeless teen that Caravaggio paid to portray God's servant. And the severed head of Goliath is none other than Caravaggio himself, an in-your-face self-portrait.

Velázquez—Habsburg Family Portraits: When the Habsburgs ruled both Austria and Spain, cousins kept in touch through portraits of themselves and their kids. Diego Velázquez was the greatest of Spain's "photojournalist" painters—heavily influenced by Caravaggio's realism, capturing his subjects without passing judgment, flattering, or glorifying them.

For example, watch little Margarita Habsburg grow up in three different portraits, from age two to age nine. Margarita was destined from birth to marry her Austrian cousin, the future Emperor Leopold I. Pictures like these, sent from Spain every few years, let her pen pal/fiancé get to know her.

Also see a portrait of Margarita's little brother, *Philip Prosper*, wearing a dress. Sadly, Philip was a sickly boy who would only live two years longer. The amulets he's wearing were intended to fend off illness. His hand rests limply on the back of the chair—above an adorable puppy who seems to be asking, "But who will play with me?"

Canaletto: Before leaving this wing, find paintings of the Habsburg summer palace, Schloss Schönbrunn, by Canaletto, one of which also shows the Viennese skyline in the distance. Then cross the stairwell and enter the part of the museum dedicated to Northern Art.

Dürer—Landauer Altarpiece: Albrecht Dürer combined meticulous Northern detail with Renaissance symmetry. So this altarpiece may initially look like a complex hog pile of saints and angels, but it's perfectly geometrical. The crucified Christ forms a triangle in the center, framed by triangular clouds and flanked by three-sided crowds of people—appropriate for a painting about the Trinity. Dürer practically invented the self-portrait as an art form, and he included himself, the lone earthling in this heavenly vision (bottom right), with a plaque announcing that he, Albrecht Dürer, painted this in 1511.

Peter Paul Rubens: Stand in front of Rubens' *Self-Portrait* and admire the darling of Catholic-dominated Flanders (northern Belgium) in his prime: famous, wealthy, well-traveled, the friend of kings and princes, an artist, diplomat, man about town, and—obviously—confident. Rubens' work runs the gamut, from realistic portraits to lounging nudes, Greek myths to altarpieces, from pious devotion to violent sex. But, can we be sure it's Baroque? Ah yes, I'm sure you'll find a pudgy, winged baby somewhere.

How could Rubens paint all these enormous canvases in one lifetime? He didn't. He kept a workshop of assistants busy painting backgrounds and minor figures, working from his own small sketches. Then the master stepped in to add the finishing touches. For example, the giant canvas *The Miracles of St. Ignatius of Loyola* was painted partly by assistants, guided by Rubens' sketches (displayed nearby).

Rembrandt van Rijn: Rembrandt became wealthy by painting portraits of Holland's upwardly mobile businessmen, but his greatest subject was himself. In the *Large Self-Portrait* we see the

VIENNA

hands-on-hips, defiant, open-stance determination of a man who will do what he wants, and if people don't like it, tough. In typical Rembrandt style, most of the canvas is a dark, smudgy brown, with only the side of his face glowing from the darkness. (Remember Caravaggio? Rembrandt did.) Unfortunately, the year this was painted, Rembrandt's fortunes changed.

Looking at the *Small Self-Portrait* from 1657, consider Rembrandt's last years. His wife died, his children died young, and commissions for paintings dried up as his style veered from the common path. He had to auction off paintings to pay his debts, and he died a poor man.

Jan Vermeer: In his small canvases, Dutch painter Jan Vermeer quiets the world down to where we can hear our own heartbeat, letting us appreciate the beauty in common things.

The curtain opens, and we see *The Art of Painting*, a behind-the-scenes look at Vermeer at work. He's painting a model dressed in blue, starting with her laurel-leaf headdress. The studio is its own little dollhouse world framed by a chair in the foreground and the wall in back. Then Vermeer fills this space with the few gems he wants us to focus on—the chandelier, the map, the painter's costume. Everything is lit by a crystal-clear light, letting us see these everyday items with fresh eyes.

Pieter Bruegel the Elder: The undisputed master of the slice-of-life village scene was Pieter Bruegel the Elder (c. 1525-1569)—think of him as the Norman Rockwell of the 16th century. He celebrated their simple life, but he also skewered their weaknesses—not to single them out as hicks, but as universal examples of human folly.

The Peasant Wedding, Bruegel's most famous work, is less about the wedding than the food. It's a farmers' feeding frenzy, as the barnful of wedding guests scrambles to get their share of free eats. Two men bring in the next course, a tray of fresh pudding. The bagpiper pauses to check it out. A guy grabs bowls and passes them down the table, taking our attention with them. Everyone's going at it, including a kid in an oversized red cap who licks the bowl with his fingers. In the middle of it all, look who's been completely forgotten—the demure bride sitting in front of the blue-green cloth. According to Flemish tradition, the bride was not allowed to speak or eat at the party, and the groom was not in attendance at all. (One thing: The guy carrying the front end of the food tray—is he stepping forward with his right leg, or with his left, or with...all three?)

▲Natural History Museum (Naturhistorisches Museum)

In the twin building facing the Kunsthistorisches Museum, you'll find moon rocks, dinosaur stuff, and the fist-sized *Venus of*

Willendorf—at 25,000 years old, the world's oldest sex symbol. The four-inch-tall, chubby stone statuette, found in the Danube Valley, is a generic female (no face or feet) resting her hands on her ample breasts. The statue's purpose is unknown, but she may have been a symbol of fertility for our mammoth-hunting ancestors. Even though the museum is not glitzy or high-tech, it's a hit with children and scientifically curious grown-ups. Of the museum's 20 million objects, you're sure to find something interesting. The collection's presentation is almost charming in its old school-ness.

Cost and Hours: €10, Wed-Mon 9:00-18:30, Wed until 21:00, closed Tue, on the Ringstrasse at Maria-Theresien-Platz, U-2 or U-3: Volkstheater/Museumsplatz, tel. 01/521-770, www.nhm-wien.ac.at.

MuseumsQuartier

The vast grounds of the former imperial stables now corral a cutting-edge cultural center for contemporary arts and design,

including several impressive museums. The **Leopold Museum** features several temporary exhibits of modern Austrian art; the top floor holds the largest collection of works by Egon Schiele (1890-1918). The **Museum of Modern Art** (Museum Moderner Kunst, a.k.a.

"MUMOK") is Austria's leading gallery for international modern and contemporary art. For many, the MuseumsQuartier is most enjoyable not for its galleries but as a youthful gathering spot in the evening for light, fun meals and cocktails.

Cost and Hours: Leopold Museum—€12; June-Aug daily 10:00-18:00; Sept-May Wed-Mon 10:00-18:00, closed Tue; Thu until 21:00 year-round, last entry 30 minutes before closing; audioguide-€3.50 but worth it only for enthusiasts, tel. 01/525-700, www.leopoldmuseum.org; **Museum of Modern Art**—€10, Mon 14:00-19:00, Tue-Sun 10:00-19:00, Thu until 21:00, good audioguide-€3, tel. 01/52500, www.mumok.at.

Information: At the visitors center, various combo-tickets are available for those interested in more than just the Leopold and Modern Art museums. You can also rent a €4 audioguide that explains the complex (behind Kunsthistorisches Museum, U-2 or U-3: Volkstheater/Museumsplatz, tel. 01/525-5881, www.mqw.at).

KARLSPLATZ AND NEARBY

These sights cluster around Karlsplatz, just southeast of the Ringstrasse (U-1, U-2, or U-4: Karlsplatz). If you're walking there from central Vienna, use the U-Bahn station's passageway (at the Opera) to avoid crossing busy boulevards. Once at Karlsplatz, allow about 30 minutes walking time to connect the various sights: the Karlskirche, Secession, and Naschmarkt.

Karlsplatz

This picnic-friendly square, with its Henry Moore sculpture in the pond, is ringed with sights. The massive, domed Karlskirche and its twin spiral columns dominates the square. The small green, white, and gold pavilions that line the street across the square from the church are from the late-19th-century municipal train system *(Stadtbahn)*. One of Europe's first subway systems, this precursor to today's U-Bahn was built with a military purpose in mind: to move troops quickly in time of civil unrest—specifically, out to Schönbrunn Palace. With curvy iron frames, decorative marble slabs, and painted gold trim, these are pioneering works in the *Jugendstil* style, designed by Otto Wagner, who influenced Klimt and the Secessionists. One of the pavilions has a sweet little exhibit on **Otto Wagner** that illustrates the Art Nouveau lifestyle around 1900. It also shows models for his never-built dreams and the grand expansion of Vienna (€4, described in English, April-Oct Tue-Sun 10:00-18:00, closed Mon and Nov-March, near the Ringstrasse, tel. 01/5058-7478-5177, www.wienmuseum.at).

▲Karlskirche (St. Charles' Church)

Charles Borromeo, a 16th-century bishop from Milan, inspired his parishioners during plague times. This "votive church" was dedicated to him in 1713, when an epidemic spared Vienna. The church offers the best Baroque in the city, with a unique combination

of columns (showing scenes from the life of Charles Borromeo, à la Trajan's Column in Rome), a classic pediment, and an elliptical dome.

Cost and Hours: €8, ticket covers church interior, elevator ride, and skippable one-room museum; Mon-Sat 9:00-18:00, Sun 13:00-19:00, last entry 30 minutes before closing; elevator runs until 17:30, last ascent at 17:00; audioguide-€2; www.karlskirche.at. The entry fee may seem steep, but remember that it helps to fund the restoration. There are often classical music concerts performed here on period instruments (usually Thu-Sat; ask about Rick Steves discount, see www.concert-vienna.info).

Visiting the Church: The dome's colorful 13,500-square-foot fresco—painted in the 1730s by Johann Michael Rottmayr—shows Signor Borromeo (in red-and-white bishops' robes) gazing up into heaven, spreading his arms wide, and pleading with Christ to spare Vienna from the plague.

The church is especially worthwhile for the chance to ride an **elevator** (installed for renovation work) up into the cupola. The industrial lift takes you to a platform at the base of the 235-foot dome (if you're even slightly afraid of heights, skip this trip). Consider that the church was built and decorated with a scaffolding system essentially the same as this one. Once up top, you'll climb stairs to the steamy lantern at the extreme top of the church.

Wien Museum Karlsplatz

This underappreciated city history museum, worth ▲ for those intrigued by Vienna's illustrious past, walks you through the story of Vienna with well-presented artifacts.

Cost and Hours: €8, free first Sun of the month, open Tue-Sun 10:00-18:00, closed Mon, Karlsplatz 8, tel. 01/505-8747, www.wienmuseum.at.

▲Academy of Fine Arts (Akademie der Bildenden Künste)

Few tourists make their way to Vienna's art academy to see its small but impressive collection of paintings, starring Botticelli, Guardi, Rubens, Van Dyck, and other great masters. The highlight is a triptych by the master of medieval surrealism, Hieronymus Bosch. The collection's location in a working art academy gives it a certain sense of realness.

Cost and Hours: €8 includes permanent collection and special exhibits, Tue-Sun 10:00-18:00, closed Mon; audioguide-€2, photography fee-€5; 3 blocks from the Opera at Schillerplatz 3, tel. 01/588-162-222, www.akbild.ac.at.

Visiting the Museum: The *Gemäldegalerie* is upstairs, on the school's first floor. The first room, dedicated to the Academy itself, is dominated by a portrait of the school's founder, Empress Maria Theresa, in an aqua-blue dress.

The next section of 18th-century Italian works includes a series of "postcard" scenes of Venice by **Francesco Guardi** in his proto-Impressionistic style.

In the long hall, among the still lifes and landscapes, find **Rembrandt's** *Portrait of a Young Woman,* wearing a ruff collar that was all the rage (c. 1632). See **Peter Paul Rubens'** typical fleshy nudes, such as his voluptuous *Three Graces.* The small sketchy cartoons were used to create giant canvases for a church in Belgium;

it later burned down, leaving only these rare sketches. Nearby, Rubens' talented protégé, **Anthony van Dyck,** shows his prowess in a small-but-famous self-portrait painted at the age of 15.

The Italian Renaissance is represented by Titian and—one of the museum's prize pieces—a round **Botticelli** canvas. Recently cleaned to show off its vivid reds and blues, it depicts the Madonna tenderly embracing the Baby Jesus while angels look on.

The last room holds the captivating, harrowing *Last Judgment* triptych by **Hieronymus Bosch** (c. 1482, with some details added by Lucas Cranach). In the left panel, at the bottom, God pulls Eve from Adam's rib in the Garden of Eden. Just above that, we see a female (representing the serpent) hold out the forbidden fruit to tempt Eve. Above that, Adam and Eve are being shooed away by an angel. At the top of this panel, God sits on his cloud, evicting the fallen angels (who turn into insect-like monsters). In the middle panel, Christ holds court over the living and the dead. These disturbing images crescendo in the final (right) panel, showing an unspeakably horrific vision of hell that few artists have managed to top in the more than half-millennium since Bosch.

On your way out of the academy, ponder how history might have been different had the school accepted a student who applied to study here twice but was rejected both times—Adolf Hitler.

▲The Secession

This little building, strategically located behind the Academy of Fine Arts, was created by the Vienna Secession movement, a group

of nonconformist artists led by Gustav Klimt, Otto Wagner, and friends.

The young trees carved into the walls and the building's bushy "golden cabbage" rooftop are symbolic of a renewal cycle. Today, the Secession continues to showcase cutting-edge art, as well as one of Gustav Klimt's most famous works, the *Beethoven Frieze.*

● Self-Guided Tour: Start in the basement, home to the museum's highlight: Gustav Klimt's classic *Beethoven Frieze.* One of the masterpieces of Viennese Art Nouveau, this 105-foot-long fresco (now somewhat cracked and faded) was the multimedia centerpiece of a 1902 exhibition honoring Ludwig van Beethoven. Klimt's still-powerful work was inspired by Beethoven's *Ninth Symphony.* Klimt embellished the work with painted-on gold (aided by his brother, a goldsmith) and by gluing on reflective glass and mother-of-pearl for the ladies' dresses and jewelry. Working clockwise around the room, follow Klimt's story:

Left Wall: Floating female figures drift and weave and search—like we all do—for happiness. Unfortunately, their aspirations are dashed and brought to earth, leaving them kneeling and humble. They plead for help from heroes stronger than themselves—represented by the firm knight in gold, who revives their hopes and helps them carry on.

Center Wall: The women encounter many obstacles in their pursuit of happiness—the three dangerous Gorgons (naked ladies with snake hair), the gorilla-faced monster of fear, and the three seductive women of temptation. These obstacles can leave us bent over with grief (like the woman on the right) while our hopes pass by overhead.

Right Wall: But we can still find happiness through art, thanks to Lady Poetry (with the lyre) and the great hero of the arts: Beethoven. In the original 1902 exhibition, a statue of Beethoven appeared at this crucial turning point in the narrative, where the blank space is today.

Beethoven's presence inspires the yearning souls to carry on. Swept up in a column of fire, they finally reach true happiness. At the climax of the frieze, a heavenly choir serenades a naked couple embracing in ecstasy, singing the "Ode to Joy"—Friedrich Schiller's poem incorporated into the Ninth Symphony: "Joy, you beautiful spark of the gods...under thy gentle wings, all men shall become brothers."

The Rest of the Secession: There's a small exhibit of scale models and photos about the construction of the influential Secession building. Finally, don't overlook the interesting temporary exhibits (included in your ticket).

▲Naschmarkt

In 1898, the city decided to cover up its Vienna River. The long, wide square they created was filled with a lively produce market that still bustles most days (closed Sun). It's long been known as *the* place to get exotic faraway foods. In fact, locals say, "From here start the Balkans."

Hours and Location: Mon-Fri 6:00-18:30, Sat 6:00-17:00, closed Sun, closes earlier in winter; between Linke Wienzeile and Rechte Wienzeile, U-1, U-2, or U-4: Karlsplatz.

Visiting the Naschmarkt: From near the Opera, the Naschmarkt (roughly, "Nibble Market") stretches along Wienzeile street. This "Belly of Vienna" comes with two parallel lanes—one lined with fun and

reasonable eateries, the other featuring the town's top-end produce and gourmet goodies. This is where top chefs like to get their ingredients. At the gourmet vinegar stall, you can sample the vinegar as you would perfume—with a drop on your wrist. Farther from the center, the Naschmarkt becomes likably seedy and surrounded by sausage stands, Turkish *Döner Kebab* stalls, cafés, and theaters. At the market's far end is a line of buildings with fine Art Nouveau facades. Each Saturday, the Naschmarkt is infested by a huge flea market where, in olden days, locals would come to hire a monkey to pick little critters out of their hair (flea market sets up west of the Kettenbrückengasse U-Bahn station).

Mariahilfer Strasse

While there are more stately and elegant streets in the central district, the best opportunity to simply feel the pulse of workaday Viennese life is a little farther out, along Mariahilfer Strasse. An easy plan is to ride the U-3 to the Zieglergasse stop, then stroll and browse your way downhill to the MuseumsQuartier U-Bahn station. If you're interested in how Austria handles its people's appetite for marijuana, search out two interesting stores along the way: Bushplanet Headshop (at Esterhazygasse 32, near the Neubaugasse U-Bahn stop) and Bushplanet Growshop (set back in a courtyard off Mariahilfer Strasse at #115, both locations Mon-Fri 10:00-19:00, Sat 10:00-18:00, closed Sun, www.bushplanet.at; see map on page 1241).

MORE SIGHTS BEYOND THE RING

The following museums are located outside the Ringstrasse but inside the Gürtel, or outer ring road.

South of the Ring
▲▲Belvedere Palace (Schloss Belvedere)

This is the elegant palace of Prince Eugene of Savoy (1663-1736), the still-much-appreciated conqueror of the Ottomans. Today you can tour Eugene's lavish palace, see sweeping views of the gardens and the Vienna skyline, and enjoy world-class art starring Gustav

Klimt, French Impressionism, and a grab bag of other 19th- and early-20th-century artists. Whereas Vienna's other art collections show off works by masters from around Europe, this has the city's best collection of home-grown artists.

Cost and Hours: €12.50 for Upper Belvedere Palace only, €19

Vienna

To Neustift am Wald,
Nussdorf &
Heiligenstadt Heurigen

WÄHRING

FRANZ
JOSEFS
BAHNHOF

Friedens-
brücke

FLAKTURM

Danube Canal

SPITTELAUER LÄNDE
BRIGITTENAUER LÄNDE
ROSSAUER LÄNDE

Währinger Strasse-
Volksoper

Palais
Liechtenstein
Park

ALSERGRUND

Michelbeuren
AKH

FREUD
MUSEUM

BARRACKS

OBERE

FRANZ

Schottentor-
Universität

Schotten-
ring

Alser
Strasse

BÖRSE

OLD

WÄHRINGER STR.

MARIA THERESIEN-STRASSE

SCHOTTENRING

Josefstädter
Strasse

UNIVERSITÄTSSTR.

UNIVERSITY

SCHOTTEN

HERRENG.

SCHOTTENKIRCHE

Am Hof

Herren-
gasse

Juden-
platz

Hoher
Markt

ST.
STEPHEN'S

KINDERSPITAL   ALSER STRASSE

HERNALSER GÜRTEL

UNFELDER

LERCHE GÜRTEL

Thaliastrasse

Rathaus
CITY
HALL

LANDES GERICHTSSTR.

Burg-
theater

Michaeler-
platz

GRABEN

ROTEN

MARKT

WÄHRINGER GÜRTEL

JOSEFSTADT

PARLIAMENT

Volks-
garten

Helden-
platz

HOFBURG
PALACE

Stephans-
platz

KAISER-
GRUFT

Burggasse-
Stadthalle

REICHSRATSTR.

DR. KARL

RENNER RING LUEGER-RING

MUSEUMSTR.

Volkstheater

BURGRING

KÄRNTNER STR.

ALBERTINA

OPERA

HAUS
DER
MUSIK

KUNSTHISTORISCHES
MUSEUM

SPITTELBERG

Museums-
Quartier

ACADEMY
OF FINE ARTS

GETREIDEMARKT

OPERNRING

KÄRNTNERRING

GAUERMANNG.

GAUDENZDORFER GÜRTEL

Karlsplz.

LOTHRINGER-
STRASSE

NEUBAU GÜRTEL

IMPERIAL
FURNITURE
COLLECTION

MARIAHILFER

Neubaugasse

THEATER
AN DER
WIEN

Karlsplatz

Karlsplatz

KARLS-
KIRCHE

WESTBAHNHOF
(WEST STATION)

MARIAHILFER STR.

Esterházy
Park

A.-
Grünwald-
Park

Naschmarkt

SCHLEIFMÜHLG.

GUSSHAUSSTR.

Westbahnhof

Zieglergasse

WIENZEILE

Europa-
platz

To Schönbrunn Palace
& Wien-Meidling
Bahnhof

MARIAHILFER GÜRTEL

WIENZEILE

Ketten-
brücken-
gasse

THIRD MAN
MUSEUM

Gumpendorfer
Strasse

Pilgramgasse

RECHTE

See detail map

Taubstumm-
mengasse

Margareten-
gürtel

LINKE   Wien   River

Schütte
Linotz
Park

FAVORITENSTR.

SCHÖN-

BRUNNERSTR.

MARGARETEN GÜRTEL

GAUDENZDORFER GÜRTEL

WIEDNER HAUPTSTRASSE

Alois-
Drasche-
Park

SCHELLINGG.

WIEDNER GÜRTEL

Südtirole
Platz

To Wien-Meidling
Bahnhof

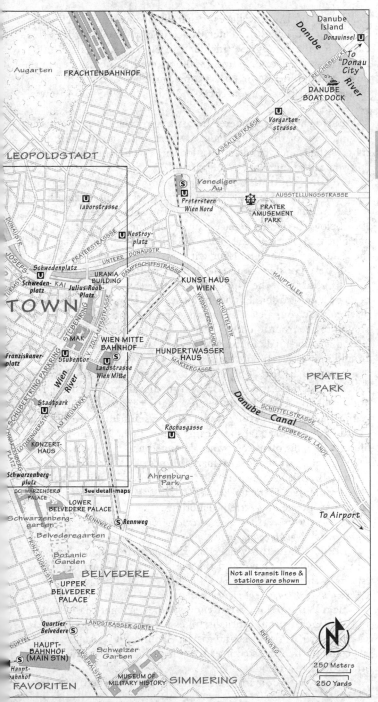

for Upper and Lower Palaces (generally not worth it), €25 Prinz Eugen Ticket includes Winter Palace in city center, gardens free except for the Orangerie (included in big tickets); daily 10:00-18:00, Lower Palace only until 21:00 on Wed, grounds open until dusk; audioguide-€4 or €6/2 people, no photos allowed inside; entrance at Prinz-Eugen-Strasse 27, tel. 01/7955-7134, www.belvedere.at.

Eating at the Belvedere: There's a charming little café on the ground floor of the Upper Palace, where you can dine with portraits of the emperor and empress looking down upon you; in summer you can sit outdoors in the garden.

Getting There: The palace is a 15-minute walk south of the Ring. To get there from the center, catch tram #D at the Opera (direction: Hauptbahnhof). Get off at the Schloss Belvedere stop (just below the Upper Palace gate), cross the street, walk uphill one block, go through the gate (on left), and look immediately to the right for the small building with the ticket office.

○ **Self-Guided Tour:** The Belvedere Palace is actually two grand buildings—the Upper Palace and Lower Palace—separated by a fine garden. For our purposes, the **Upper Palace** is what matters. Buy your ticket at the office behind the palace, then go around to the front to enter. Once inside, the palace's eclectic collection is tailor-made for browsing. There are two grand floors, set around impressive middle halls.

Ground Floor: The main floor displays a collection of Austrian Baroque (on the left) and medieval art (on the right). The Baroque section includes a fascinating room of grotesquely grimacing heads by **Franz Xaver Messerschmidt** (1736-1783), a quirky 18th-century Habsburg court sculptor who left the imperial life to follow his own, somewhat deranged muse. After his promising career was cut short by mental illness, Messerschmidt relocated to Bratislava and spent the rest of his days sculpting a series of eerily lifelike "character heads" *(Kopfstücke)*. Their most unusual faces are contorted by extreme emotions.

• *From the entrance, climb the staircase to the **first floor** and enter the grand red-and-gold, chandeliered...*

Marble Hall: This was Prince Eugene's party room. *Belvedere* means "beautiful view," and the **view from the Marble Hall** is especially spectacular.

• *Facing the garden, to the right is the...*

East Wing: Alongside Renoir's ladies, Monet's landscapes, and Van Gogh's rough brushstrokes are similar works by their lesser-known Austrian counterparts. Around 1900, Austrian artists come to the fore, soaking up Symbolism, Expressionism, and other Modernist trends.

In the two rooms full of sumptuous paintings by **Gustav**

Klimt, you can get caught up in his fascination with the beauty and danger he saw in women. To Klimt, all art was erotic art. He painted during the turn of the century, when Vienna was a splendid laboratory of hedonism.

The famous painting of *Judith I* (1901) shows no biblical heroine—Klimt paints her as a high-society Vienna woman with an ostentatious dog-collar necklace. With half-closed eyes and slightly parted lips, she's dismissive...yet mysterious and bewitching. Holding the head of her biblical victim, she's the modern femme fatale.

In what is perhaps Klimt's best-known painting, *The Kiss,* two

lovers are wrapped up in the colorful gold-and-jeweled cloak of bliss. Klimt's woman is no longer dominating, but submissive, abandoning herself to her man in a fertile field and a vast universe. In a glow emanating from a radiance of desire, the body she presses against is a self-portrait of the artist himself.

Klimt nurtured the next generation of artists, especially **Egon Schiele.** While Klimt's works are mystical and otherworldly, Schiele's tend to be darker and more introspective. One of Schiele's most recognizable works, *The Embrace,* shows a couple engaged in an erotically charged, rippling moment of passion. Striking a darker tone is *The Family,* which depicts a crouching couple. This family portrait from 1918 is especially poignant because his wife died while he was still working on it.

The Rest of the Upper Palace: The Belvedere's collection goes through the whole range of 19th- and 20th-century art: Historicism, Romanticism, Impressionism, Realism, tired tourism, Expressionism, Art Nouveau, and early Modernism.

Grounds and Gardens: The delightfully manicured grounds are free and fun to explore. The only area with an entry fee is the **Orangerie garden,** along the west side of the Lower Palace (and accessed through that palace).

East of the Ring
Museum of Applied Arts (Museum für Angewandte Kunst)
Facing the Old Town from across the Ring, the MAK, as it's called, is a design museum best known for its collection of furniture and decorative art from Vienna's artistic golden age (around 1900). The permanent "Vienna 1900" exhibit on the top floor is usually most visitors' main destination, and the MAK Design Lab (MAK Design Labor in German) in the basement is also worth seeing.

Cost and Hours: €8, free Tue after 18:00; open Wed-Sun 10:00-18:00, Tue 10:00-22:00, closed Mon; Stubenring 5, U-3: Stubentor, tel. 01/711-360, www.mak.at.

Austrian Postal Savings Bank
(Die Österreichische Postsparkasse)

Built between 1904 and 1912, the Postal Savings Bank was one of the key buildings in the development of modern architecture. Secessionist architect Otto Wagner believed "necessity is the master of art," and he declared that "what is impractical can never be beautiful." This is a textbook example of form following function, and the form is beautiful. Today it's a pilgrimage site for architects from all over the world (for whom it's a ▲▲▲ sight). It's still a bank (though private now). You can enter the atrium for free, and visit a pleasant, small museum that tells the building's story in both German and English.

Cost and Hours: Foyer and atrium—free, museum—€6 (get tickets from counter 14 in the atrium); open Mon-Fri 10:00-17:00, closed Sat-Sun; just inside the Ringstrasse at Georg-Coch-Platz 2, tel. 059-9053-3825, www.ottowagner.com.

▲Museum of Military History
(Heeresgeschichtliches Museum)

While much of the Habsburg Empire was built on strategic marriages rather than the spoils of war, a big part of Habsburg history is military. And this huge place, built around 1860 as an arsenal by Franz Josef, tells the story well with a thoughtful motto (apparently learned from the school of hard knocks): "War belongs to museums."

Cost and Hours: €6, includes good audioguide, free first Sun of the month, open daily 9:00-17:00, on Arsenalstrasse, tel. 01/795-610, www.hgm.or.at. It's a 5-minute walk from the Hauptbahnhof, or a 10-minute walk behind the Belvedere Palace.

Visiting the Museum: You'll wander the wings of this vast museum nearly all alone. Its two floors hold a rich collection of artifacts and historic treasures from the times of Maria Theresa to Prince Eugene to Franz Josef. The particularly interesting 20th-century section includes exhibits devoted to Sarajevo in 1914 (with the car Franz Ferdinand rode in and the uniform he wore when he was assassinated), Chancellor Dolfuss and the pre-Hitler Austrian Fascist party, the *Anschluss*, and World War II.

▲Kunst Haus Wien Museum and Hundertwasserhaus

This "make yourself at home" museum and nearby apartment complex are a hit with lovers of modern art, mixing the work and philosophy of local painter/environmentalist Friedensreich Hundertwasser (1928-2000), a.k.a. "100H2O."

Cost and Hours: €10 for museum, €12 combo-ticket includes special exhibitions, half-price on Mon, open daily 10:00-19:00, extremely fragrant and colorful garden café, tel. 01/712-0491, www.kunsthauswien.com.

Getting There: It's located at Untere Weissgerberstrasse 13, near the Radetzkyplatz stop on trams #O and #1 (signs point the way). By U-Bahn, take U-3 or U-4 to Landstrasse and either walk 10 minutes downhill (north) along Untere Viaduktgasse (a block east of the station), or transfer to tram #O (direction: Praterstern) and ride three stops to Radetzkyplatz.

Visiting the Museum and Apartments: Stand in front of the colorful checkerboard building that houses the **Kunst Haus Wien Museum.** Consider Hundertwasser's style. He was against "window racism": Neighboring houses allow only one kind of window, but 100H2O's windows are each different—and he encouraged residents in the Hundertwasserhaus (a 5-10 minute walk away, described later) to personalize them. He recognized "tree tenants" as well as human tenants. His buildings are spritzed with a forest and topped with dirt and grassy little parks—close to nature and good for the soul.

Floors and sidewalks are irregular—to "stimulate the brain" (although current residents complain it just causes wobbly furniture and sprained ankles). Thus 100H2O waged a one-man fight—during the 1950s and 1960s, when concrete and glass ruled—to save the human soul from the city. (Hundertwasser claimed that "straight lines are godless.")

Inside the museum, start with his interesting biography.

His fun paintings are half psychedelic *Jugendstil* and half just kids' stuff. Notice the photographs from his 1950s days as part of Vienna's bohemian scene. Throughout the museum, keep an eye out for the fun philosophical quotes from an artist who believed, "If man is creative, he comes nearer to his creator."

The Kunst Haus Wien provides by far the best look at Hundertwasser, but for an actual lived-in apartment complex by the green master, walk 5-10 minutes to the one-with-nature **Hundertwasserhaus** (at

Löwengasse and Kegelgasse). This complex of 50 apartments, subsidized by the government to provide affordable housing, was built in the 1980s as a breath of architectural fresh air in a city of boring, blocky apartment complexes. Though not open to visitors, it's worth visiting for its fun and colorful patchwork exterior and the Hundertwasser festival of shops across the street. Don't miss the view from Kegelgasse to see the "tree tenants" and the internal winter garden that residents enjoy.

North of the Ring
Sigmund Freud Museum

Freud enthusiasts (and detractors) enjoy seeing the apartment and home office of the man who fundamentally changed our understanding of the human psyche. Dr. Sigmund Freud (1856-1939), a graduate of Vienna University, established his practice here in 1891. For the next 47 years, he received troubled patients who hoped to find peace by telling him their dreams, life traumas, and secret urges. It was here that he wrote his influential works, including the landmark *Interpretation of Dreams* (1899). The museum is narrowly focused on Freud's life. If you're looking for a critical appraisal of whether he was a cocaine-addicted charlatan or a sincere doctor groping toward an understanding of human nature, you won't find it here.

Cost and Hours: €9, includes audioguide, daily 10:00-18:00, tiny bookshop, half a block from the Schlickgasse stop on tram #D, Berggasse 19, tel. 01/319-1596, www.freud-museum.at.

West of the Ring, on Mariahilfer Strasse
▲Imperial Furniture Collection (Hofmobiliendepot)

Bizarre, sensuous, eccentric, or precious, this collection (on four fascinating floors) is your peek at the Habsburgs' furniture—from the empress's wheelchair ("to increase her fertility she was put on a rich diet and became corpulent") to the emperor's spittoon—all thoughtfully described in English. Evocative paintings help bring the furniture to life. The Habsburgs had many palaces, but only the Hofburg was permanently furnished. The rest were done on the fly—set up and taken down by a gang of royal roadies called the "Depot of Court Movables" (Hofmobiliendepot). When the monarchy was dissolved in 1918, the state of Austria took possession of the Hofmobiliendepot's inventory—165,000 items. Now this royal storehouse is open to the public in a fine, sprawling museum.

Cost and Hours: €8.50, covered by Sisi Ticket (see page 1152), Tue-Sun 10:00-18:00, closed Mon, Mariahilfer Strasse 88, main entrance around the corner at Andreasgasse 7, U-3: Zieglergasse, tel. 01/5243-3570, www.hofmobiliendepot.at.

▲▲▲SCHÖNBRUNN PALACE
(SCHLOSS SCHÖNBRUNN)

Among Europe's palaces, only Schönbrunn rivals Versailles. This former summer residence of the Habsburgs is big, with 1,441 rooms. But don't worry—only 40 rooms are shown to the public.

Of the plethora of sights at the vast complex, the highlight is a tour of the palace's Royal Apartments— the chandeliered rooms where the Habsburg nobles lived. You can also stroll the gardens, tour the coach museum, and visit a handful of lesser sights nearby.

Schönbrunn is sprawling and can be mobbed with tourists. Here's how I'd plan my time for an efficient visit: First, see the Royal Apartments with the "Grand Tour" ticket, reserved in advance to avoid crowds (details below). After the Royal Apartments, wander the gardens, which are free. With more time and energy, pick and choose among the other sightseeing options and buy tickets as you go. Allow at least three hours (including transit time) for your excursion to Schönbrunn.

Getting There: While on the outskirts of Vienna, Schönbrunn is an easy 10-minute subway ride from downtown. Take U-4 (which conveniently leaves from Karlsplatz) to Schönbrunn (direction: Hütteldorf) and follow signs for *Schloss Schönbrunn*. Exit bearing right, then cross the busy road and continue to the right, to the far, far end of the long yellow building. There you'll find the visitors center, where tickets are sold.

Hours: Royal Apartments—daily July-Aug 8:30-18:30, April-June and Sept-Oct 8:30-17:30, Nov-March 8:30-17:00, last entry 30 minutes before closing; gardens—generally open 6:30-20:00.

Cost: The Royal Apartments offer two tour options: The best is the 40-room **Grand Tour** (€14.50, 50 minutes, includes audioguide), which covers both the rooms of Franz Josef and Sisi, as well as the (more-impressive) Rococo rooms of Maria Theresa. The **Imperial Tour** (€11.50, 35 minutes, includes audioguide) covers only the less-interesting first 22 rooms.

If venturing beyond the apartments, consider a combo-ticket: The **Classic Pass** includes the Grand Tour, as well as other sights on the grounds—the Gloriette viewing terrace, maze, and privy garden (€18.50, available April-Oct only). The **Classic Pass Plus** adds an *Apfelstrudel* demo and tasting (€21.50, available April-Oct only). Note that the **Sisi Ticket** (€25.50; see page 1152) gives you the Schönbrunn Grand Tour (with no waiting in line), plus the Hofburg Imperial Apartments (in town) and the Imperial Furniture Collection.

Reservations: In summer and good-weather weekends, definitely make a reservation. Otherwise, you'll likely have to wait in line at the ticket desk, and then wait again until your assigned entry time—which could be hours later. Book your ticket at www. schoenbrunn.at, where you reserve an entry time, then print your ticket (or ask your hotel to print it for you). Tickets can also be reserved by phone and picked up at the visitors center (tel. 01/8111-3239). Those with a Sisi Ticket can enter without a reserved entry time.

Other Crowd-Beating Tips: Even with a reserved entry time, the palace can be a jam-packed sauna of shoulder-to-shoulder mobs shuffling through. It's busiest from 9:30 to 11:30. Crowds start to subside after 14:00. Without a reservation, come late in the day. If you have time to kill before your entry time, spend it exploring the gardens or Coach Museum.

Information: Tel. 01/8111-3239, www.schoenbrunn.at. No photos in the Royal Apartments.

▲▲▲Royal Apartments

In the 1500s, the Habsburgs built a small hunting lodge near a beautiful spring (*schön-brunn*), and for the next three centuries, they made it their summer getaway from stuffy Vienna. The palace's exterior (late-1600s) is Baroque, but the interior was finished under Maria Theresa (mid-1700s) in let-them-eat-cake Rococo.

⊙ Self-Guided Tour: Your tour of the apartments, accompanied by an audioguide, follows a clearly signed one-way route. Think of the following mini-tour as a series of bread crumbs, leading you along while the audioguide fills in the details.

Begin in the **Guards' Room,** where jauntily dressed mannequins of Franz Josef's bodyguards introduce you to his luxurious world. Continue through the Billiard Room to the **Walnut Room.** Wow. Rococo-style wood paneling and gilding decorate this room where Franz Josef—a hard-working modern monarch—received official visitors. Nearby is the **Study**—Franz Josef (see his mustachioed portrait) worked at this desk, sometimes joined by his beautiful, brown-haired wife Sisi (see her portrait). In the **Bedroom** there are a praying stool, iron bed, and little toilet, which attest to Franz Josef's spartan lifestyle.

Empress Sisi's Study and Dressing Room: See her portrait in a black dress, as well as (a reconstruction of) the spiral staircase that once led down to her apartments. The long-haired mannequin and makeup jars in the dressing room indicate how obsessive Sisi was about her looks.

Franz Josef's and Sisi's Bedroom: The huge wood-carved double bed suggests marital bliss, but the bed is not authentic—and as for the bliss, history suggests otherwise. Nearby is **Sisi's**

Salon. Though this was Sisi's reception room, the pastel paintings show her husband's distinguished ancestors—the many children of Maria Theresa (including Marie-Antoinette, immediately to the left as you enter).

Follow along to the **Dining Room.** The whole family ate here at the huge table; today it's set with dinnerware owned by Maria Theresa and Sisi. Next is the **Children's Room,** with portraits of Maria Theresa (on the easel) and some of her 11 (similar-looking) daughters. The bathroom was installed for the last Habsburg empress, Zita.

Hall of Mirrors: In this room, six-year-old Mozart performed for the family (1762). He amazed them by playing without being able to see the keys, he jumped playfully into Maria Theresa's lap, and he even asked six-year-old Marie-Antoinette to marry him.

Great Gallery: Imagine the parties they had here: waltzers spinning across the floor, lit by chandeliers reflecting off the mirrors, beneath stunning ceiling frescoes, while enjoying views of the gardens and a decorative monument called the Gloriette. When WWII bombs rained on Vienna, the palace was largely spared. It took only one direct hit—crashing through this ballroom—but, thankfully, that bomb was a dud.

Blue Chinese Salon: It was here, in 1918, that the last Habsburg emperor made the decision to relinquish power. The nearby black-lacquer **Vieux-Laque Room** may convince you the Grand Tour ticket was worth it. Continue to the **Napoleon Room.** When Napoleon conquered Austria, he took over Schönbrunn and made this his bedroom. He dumped Josephine and took a Habsburg princess as his bride, and they had a son (cutely pictured holding a wreath of flowers).

Rich Room: This darkened room has what may have been Maria Theresa's wedding bed, where she and her husband Franz produced 16 children. Then comes the **Study,** with a fitting end to this palace tour—a painting showing the happy couple who left their mark all over Schönbrunn.

▲▲Palace Gardens and Nearby Sights

The large, manicured grounds fill the palace's backyard, dominated by a hill-topping monument called the Gloriette. Unlike the gardens of Versailles, meant to shut out the real world, Schönbrunn's park was opened to the public in 1779 while the monarchy was in full swing. It was part of Maria Theresa's reform policy, making the garden a celebration of the evolution of civilization from autocracy into real democracy.

Today it's a delightful, sprawling place to wander—especially on a sunny day. You can spend hours here, enjoying the views and the people-watching. And most of the park is free, as it has been for more than two centuries (open daily sunrise to dusk, entrance on either side of the palace).

Getting Around the Gardens: A **tourist train** makes the rounds all day, connecting Schönbrunn's many attractions (€6, 2/hour in peak season, none Nov-mid-March, one-hour circuit). Unfortunately, there's no bike rental nearby.

Visiting the Gardens: The gardens are laid out on angled, tree-lined axes that gradually incline, offering dramatic views back to the palace. The small side gardens flanking the palace are the most elaborate: to the left of the palace is the **Privy Garden/ Crown Prince Garden** (*Kronprinzengarten*, €3); to the right are the free **Sisi Gardens.** Better yet, just explore, using a map (such as the one in this book, or pick one up at the palace). Highlights include several whimsical **fountains,** such as the faux "Roman ruins," the obelisk, and the Neptune Fountain (straight back from the palace). Next to the Neptune Fountain is a kid-friendly **maze** *(Irrgarten)* and playground area (€4.50).

The **Gloriette** is a purely decorative monument celebrating an obscure Austrian military victory. You can pay for a pricey drink in the café, shell out €3 to hike up to the viewing terrace, or skip the whole thing, as views are about as good from the lawn in front (included in Schönbrunn passes described earlier, daily April-Sept 9:00-18:00, July-Aug until 19:00, Oct 9:00-17:00, closed Nov-March).

Nearby Sights: To the right of the palace is a large zoo complex and several affiliated sights. Europe's oldest **zoo** *(Tiergarten)* was built by Maria Theresa's husband for the entertainment and education of the court in 1752 (€16.50, daily April-Sept 9:00-18:30, closes earlier off-season, tel. 01/877-9294, www.zoovienna.at). Nearby are two skippable sights. The **palm house** *(Palmenhaus*; €4, daily May-Sept 9:30-18:00, Oct-April 9:30-17:00, last entry 30 minutes before closing) and the **Desert Experience House** *(Wüstenhaus;* €4, same hours as palm house).

▲Coach Museum Wagenburg

The Schönbrunn coach museum is a 19th-century traffic jam of 50 impressive royal carriages and sleighs. Highlights include silly sedan chairs, the death-black hearse carriage (used for Franz Josef in 1916, and for Empress Zita in 1989), and an extravagantly gilded imperial carriage pulled by eight Cinderella horses. This was rarely used other than for the coronation of Holy Roman Emperors, when it was disassembled and taken to Frankfurt for the big event. You'll also get a look at one of Sisi's impossibly narrow-waisted gowns, and (upstairs) Sisi's "Riding Chapel," with portraits of her 25 favorite horses.

Cost and Hours: €6, daily May-Oct 9:00-18:00, Nov-April 10:00-16:00, audioguide-€2, 200 yards from palace, walk through right arch as you face palace, tel. 01/525-243-470.

EAST OF THE DANUBE CANAL
▲Prater Park (Wiener Prater)
This place has been Vienna's playground since the 1780s, when the reformist Emperor Josef II gave his hunting grounds to the people of Vienna as a public park. For the tourist, the "Prater" is the sugary-smelling, tired, and sprawling amusement park (Wurstelprater). The park still tempts visitors with its huge 220-foot-tall, famous, and lazy Ferris wheel *(Riesenrad)*, roller coaster, bumper cars, Lilliputian railroad, and endless eateries. Especially if you're traveling with kids, this is a fun, goofy place to share the evening with thousands of Viennese.

Cost and Hours: Rides cost €1.50-€5 and run May-Sept 9:00-24:00—but quiet after 22:00, March-April and Oct 10:00-22:00, Nov-Dec 10:00-20:00, grounds always open, U-1: Praterstern, www.prater.at.

Entertainment in Vienna

Vienna—the birthplace of what we call classical music—still thrives as Europe's music capital. On any given evening, you'll have your choice of opera, Strauss waltzes, Mozart chamber concerts, and lighthearted musicals. The Vienna Boys' Choir lives up to its worldwide reputation.

Besides music, you can spend an evening enjoying art, watching a classic film, or sipping Viennese wine in a village wine garden. Save some energy for Vienna after dark.

MUSIC
In Vienna, it's music *con brio* from October through June, reaching a symphonic climax during the Vienna Festival each May and June. Sadly, in summer (generally July and August), the Boys' Choir, Opera, and many other serious music companies are—like you—on vacation. But Vienna hums year-round with live classical music; touristy, crowd-pleasing shows are always available.

For music lovers, Vienna is also an opportunity to make pilgrimages to the homes (now mostly small museums) of favorite composers. If you're a fan of Schubert, Brahms, Haydn, Beethoven, or Mozart, there's a sight for you. But I find these homes inconveniently located and generally underwhelming. The centrally located Haus der Musik (see page 1179) is my favorite setting for celebrating the great musicians and composers who called Vienna home.

Venues: Vienna remains the music capital of Europe, with 10,000 seats in various venues around town mostly booked with classical performances. The best-known entertainment venues are the Staatsoper (a.k.a., "the Opera"), the Volksoper (for musicals and operettas), the Theater an der Wien (opera and other performances), the Wiener Musikverein (home of the Vienna Philharmonic Orchestra), and the Wiener Konzerthaus (various events). Schedules for these venues are listed in the monthly *Wien-Programm* (available at TI). You can also check event listings at www.viennaconcerts.com.

Buying Tickets: Most tickets run from €45 to €60 (plus a stiff booking fee when purchased in advance by phone or online, or through a box office like the one at the TI). A few venues charge as little as €30; look around if you're not set on any particular concert. While it's easy to book tickets online long in advance, spontaneity is also workable, as there are invariably people selling their extra tickets at face value or less outside the door before concert time. If you call a concert hall directly, they can advise you on the availability of (cheaper) tickets at the door. Vienna takes care of its starving artists (and tourists) by offering cheap standing-room tickets to top-notch music and opera (generally an hour before each performance).

Vienna Boys' Choir (Wiener Sängerknaben)

The boys sing (from a high balcony, heard but not seen) at the 9:15 Sunday Mass from mid-September through June in the Hofburg's **Imperial Music Chapel** (Hofmusikkapelle). The entrance is at Schweizerhof; you can get there from In der Burg square or go through the tunnel from Josefsplatz.

Reserved seats must be booked in advance (€5-29; reserve by fax, email, or mail: fax from the US 011-431-533-992-775, send email to office@hofburgkapelle.at, or write Wiener Hofmusikkapelle, Hofburg-Schweizerhof, 1010 Wien; call 01/533-9927 for information only—they can't book tickets at this number; www.hofburgkapelle.at).

Much easier, standing room inside is free and open to the first 60 who line up. Even better, rather than line up early, you can simply swing by and stand in the narthex just outside, where you can hear the boys and see the Mass on a TV monitor.

The Boys' Choir also performs at the new concert hall, **MuTh,** on Fridays at 17:30 in September and October (€39-89, Am Augartenspitz 1 in Augarten park, U-2: Taborstrasse, tel.

01/347-8080, www.muth.at, tickets@muth.at).

They're talented kids, but, for my taste, not worth all the commotion. Remember, many churches have great music during Sunday Mass. Just 200 yards from the Hofburg's Boys' Choir chapel, the Augustinian Church has a glorious 11:00 service each Sunday (see page 1199).

OPERA
Vienna State Opera (Staatsoper)

The Vienna State Opera puts on 300 performances a year, featuring the "Orchestra of the Opera" in the pit. (Any musician aspiring to join the Vienna Philharmonic Orchestra must put in three years here before even being considered.) In July and August the singers rest their voices (or go on tour). Since there are different operas nearly nightly, you'll see big trucks out back and constant action backstage—all the sets need to be switched each day. Even though the expensive seats normally sell out long in advance, the opera is perpetually in the red and subsidized by the state, so affordable seats are often available. The excellent "electronic libretto" translation screens help make the experience worthwhile for opera newbies. (Press the button to turn yours on; press again for English.)

Opera Tickets: Main-floor seats go for €80-100; bargain-hunters get limited-view seats for €20-30. You can book tickets in advance by phone (tel. 01/513-1513, phone answered daily 10:00-21:00) or online (www.wiener-staatsoper.at). In person, you can head to one of the Opera's two box offices: on the west side of the building (across Operngasse and facing the Opera), or the smaller one just under the big screen on the east side of the Opera (facing Kärntner Strasse; both offices open Mon-Fri 9:00 until two hours before each performance, Sat 9:00-12:00, closed Sun).

Unless Placido Domingo is in town, it's easy to get one of 567 **standing-room tickets** (*Stehplätze*, €3 up top or €4 downstairs, can purchase one ticket/person, tickets sold until 20 minutes after curtain time). While the front doors open one hour before the show starts, a side door (middle of building, on the Operngasse side) opens 80 minutes before curtain time, giving those in the know an early grab at standing-room tickets. Just walk straight in, then head right until you see the ticket booth marked *Stehplätze*. If fewer than 567 people are in line, there's no need to line up early. If you're one of the first 160 in line, try for the "Parterre" section and you'll end up dead-center at stage level, directly under the Emperor's Box (otherwise, you can choose between the third floor—*Balkon*, or the fourth floor—*Galerie*). Dress is casual (but do your best) at the standing-room bar. Locals save their spot along the rail by tying a scarf to it.

Rick's Crude Tips: For me, three hours is a lot of opera.

But just to see and hear the Opera in action for half an hour is a treat. And if you go, you'll get the added entertainment of seeing Vienna all dressed up. I'd buy a standing-room ticket and plan to just watch the first part of the show. Unfortunately if you buy a ticket but show up after the performance has started, you may be forced to watch it on a closed-circuit TV instead. While most will not want to stand through the entire performance, there are some spots that offer a wall for leaning. Regulars prefer the *Balkon* or *Galerie* sections because each ticket holder gets a section of railing along with a "subtitle" digital screen to read the libretto—and the acoustics are better. Once you've saved your spot with your scarf, you can leave to check your belongings. Even those with standing-room tickets are considered "ticket holders," and are welcome to explore the building. As you leave, wander around the first floor (fun if skipping out early, when halls are empty) to enjoy the sumptuous halls (with prints of famous stage sets and performers) and the grand entry staircase. The last resort (and worst option) is to drop in to the Café Oper Vienna and watch the performance live on TV screens (inside the Opera, reasonable menu and drinks).

"**Live Opera on the Square**": Demonstrating its commitment to bringing opera to the masses, each spring and fall the Vienna Opera projects several performances live on a huge screen on its building, puts out chairs for the public to enjoy...and it's all free. (These projected performances are noted as *Oper live am Platz* in the official Opera schedule—posted all around the Opera building; they are also listed in the *Wien-Programm* brochure.)

Vienna Volksoper

For less serious operettas and musicals, try Vienna's other opera house, located along the Gürtel, west of the city center (see *Wien-Programm* brochure or ask at TI for schedule, Währinger Strasse 78, tel. 01/5144-43670, www.volksoper.at).

Theater an der Wien

Considered the oldest theater in Vienna, this venue was designed in 1801 for Mozart operas—intimate, with just a thousand seats. It treats Vienna's music lovers to a different opera every month—generally Mozart with a contemporary setting and modern interpretation. Although Vienna now supports three opera companies, this is the only company playing through the summer (facing the Naschmarkt at Linke Wienzeile 6, tel. 01/58885, www.theater-wien.at).

Touristy Mozart and Strauss Concerts

If the music comes to you, it's touristy—designed for flash-in-the-pan Mozart fans. Powdered-wig orchestra performances are given almost nightly in grand traditional settings (€25-50). Pesky wigged-and-powdered Mozarts peddle tickets in the streets. They rave about the quality of the musicians, but you'll get second-rate chamber orchestras, clad in historic costumes, performing the greatest hits of Mozart and Strauss. (The musicians are usually quite good—often Hungarians, Poles, and Russians working a season here to fund music studies back home—but often haven't performed much

together, so they aren't "tight".) These are casual, easygoing concerts with lots of tour groups. While there's usually not a Viennese person in the audience, the tourists generally enjoy the evening.

To sort through your options, check with the ticket office in the TI (same price as on the street, but with all venues to choose from). Savvy locals suggest getting the cheapest tickets, as no one seems to care if cheapskates move up to fill unsold pricier seats.

Of the many fine venues in Vienna, the **Sala Terrena at Mozarthaus** might be my favorite.

Intimate chamber-music concerts take place in a small room richly decorated in Venetian Renaissance style (€43-49, Thu-Fri and Sun at 19:30, Sat at 18:00, near St. Stephen's Cathedral at Singerstrasse 7, tel. 01/512-3457, www.viennaconcerts. com/mozarthaus.php). Don't confuse this with the Mozarthaus Vienna Museum on Domgasse, which also holds concerts.

Strauss and Mozart Concerts in the Kursalon

For years, Strauss and Mozart concerts have been held in the Kursalon, the hall where the "Waltz King" himself directed wildly popular concerts 100 years ago (€40-62, concerts generally nightly at 20:15, Johannesgasse 33 at corner of Parkring, tram #2: Weihburggasse or U-4: Stadtpark, tel. 01/512-5790 to check on availability—generally no problem to reserve—or buy online at www.soundofvienna.at). Shows last two hours and are a mix of ballet, waltzes, and a 15-piece orchestra. It's touristy—tour guides holding up banners with group numbers wait out front after the show. Even so, the performance is playful, visually fun, fine quality for most, and with a tried-and-tested, crowd-pleasing format. The conductor welcomes the crowd in German (with a wink) and English; after that...it's English only.

OTHER MUSIC

Musicals

The Wien Ticket pavilion next to the Opera (near Kärntner Strasse) sells tickets to contemporary American and British musicals performed in German (€10-109). Same-day tickets are available at a 24 percent discount from 14:00 until 18:00 (ticket pavilion open daily 10:00-19:00). Or you can reserve (full-price) tickets for the musicals by phone or online (Wien Ticket, tel. 01/58885, www. wein-ticket.at).

Films of Concerts

To see free films of great concerts in a lively, outdoor setting near City Hall, see "Nightlife in Vienna," next.

Organ Concerts

St. Peter's Church puts on free organ concerts weekdays at 15:00 and weekends at 20:00 (see page 1182).

Classical Music to Go

To bring home Beethoven, Strauss, or the Wiener Philharmonic on a top-quality CD, shop at Gramola on the Graben or EMI on Kärntner Strasse. The Arcadia shop at the Opera is also good.

Nightlife in Vienna

If powdered wigs and opera singers in Viking helmets aren't your thing, Vienna has plenty of alternatives.

The Evening Scene

More than ever, Vienna has become a great place to just be out and about on a balmy evening. While tourists are attracted to the historic central district and its charming, floodlit corners, locals go elsewhere. Depending on your mood and taste, you can join them. Survey and then enjoy lively scenes with bars, cafés, trendy restaurants, and theaters in these areas: **Donaukanal** (the Danube Canal, especially popular in the summer for its imported  beaches); **Naschmarkt** (after the produce stalls close up, the bars and eateries bring new life to the place through the evening; see page 1214); **MuseumsQuartier** (surrounded by far-out museums, a young scene of bars with local students filling the courtyard; see page 1210); and **City Hall** (on the park-like Rathausplatz, where in summer free concerts and a food circus of eateries attract huge local crowds—described next).

City Hall Open-Air Classical-Music Cinema and Food Circus

A thriving people scene erupts each evening in summer (July-Aug) at the park in front of City Hall (Rathaus, on the Ringstrasse). Thousands of people keep a food circus of 24 simple stalls busy. There's not a plastic cup anywhere, just real plates and glasses—Vienna wants the quality of eating to be as high as the music that's about to begin. About 2,000 folding chairs face a 60-foot-wide screen up against the City Hall's Neo-Gothic facade. When darkness falls, an announcer explains the program, and then the music starts. The program is different every night— mostly movies of opera and classical concerts, with some films. Ask at the TI or check www.filmfestival-rathausplatz.at for the schedule (programs generally last about 2 hours, starting when it's dark—between 21:30 in July and 20:30 in Aug).

Since 1991, the city has paid for 60 of these summer event nights each year. Why? To promote culture. Officials know that the City Hall Music Festival is mostly a "meat market" where young people come to hook up. But they believe many of these people will develop a little appreciation of classical music and high culture on the side.

English Cinema

Several great theaters offer three or four screens of English movies nightly (€6-9): **Burg Kino,** a block from the Opera, facing the Ring (see below), tapes its weekly schedule to the door—box office opens 30 minutes before each showing; **English Cinema Haydn,** near my recommended hotels on Mariahilfer Strasse (Mariahilfer Strasse 57, tel. 01/587-2262, www.haydnkino.at); and **Artis International Cinema,** right in the town center a few minutes from the cathedral (Schultergasse 5, tel. 01/535-6570).

The Third Man at Burg Kino

This movie is set in 1949 Vienna—when it was divided, like Berlin, between the four victorious Allies. Reliving the cinematic tale of a divided city about to fall under Soviet rule and rife with smuggling is an enjoyable two-hour experience while in Vienna (€7-9, in English; about 2 showings weekly—usually Sun afternoon and Tue early evening; Opernring 19, tel. 01/587-8406, www.burgkino.at).

Fans of the movie will enjoy a visit to the **Third Man Museum** (Dritte Mann Museum), the life's work of two enthusiasts who have lovingly collected a vast collection of artifacts about the film, postwar Vienna, and the movie's popularity around the world. (€7.50, Sat only 14:00-18:00, or by appointment for *Third Man* nuts; also some guided tours on summer Wed at 14:00—confirm on website; private showings for groups, U4: Kettenbrückengasse, a long block south of the Naschmarkt at Pressgasse 25, tel. 01/586-4872, www.3mpc.net).

Sleeping in Vienna

Accommodations in Vienna are cheap and plentiful—a €100 double here might go for €150 in Munich and €200 in Milan. Within the Ring, you'll need to shell out over €100 for a double room with bath. But around Mariahilfer Strasse, two people can stay comfortably for €70. The prices I've listed are for high season—generally April through June and September, October, and December. Expect them to spike higher for conventions (most frequent in Sept-Oct), dip in July and August, and drop in November and from January to March.

Many of the smaller places I've listed occupy a single upper floor of a traditional apartment building, with a shared entryway that is often dingier and darker than the pension itself. Don't let this give you the wrong impression—most pensions can't afford to maintain the entrance without their not-always-cooperative neighbors chipping in.

While few accommodations in Vienna are air-conditioned, you can generally get fans on request. Viennese elevators can be confusing: In most of Europe, 0 is the ground floor, and 1 is the first floor up (our "second floor"). But in Vienna, elevators can also have floors like P, U, M, and A before getting to 1—so floor 1 can actually be what we'd call the fourth or fifth floor.

For more tips on accommodations, see the "Sleeping" section in the Practicalities chapter.

WITHIN THE RING, IN THE OLD CITY CENTER

You'll pay extra to sleep in the atmospheric old center, but if you can afford it, staying here gives you the classiest Vienna experience and enables you to walk to most sights.

$$$ Hotel Schweizerhof is classy, with 55 big rooms, all the comforts, shiny public spaces, and a formal ambience. It's centrally located midway between St. Stephen's Cathedral and the Danube Canal (Sb-€86-103, Db-€120-160, Tb-€143-188, fourth bed-€35, ask about discount with this book if you pay cash, grand breakfast, fans on request, elevator, Wi-Fi, Bauernmarkt 22, U-1 or U-3: Stephansplatz, tel. 01/533-1931, www.schweizerhof.at, office@schweizerhof.at).

$$$ Pension Aviano is a peaceful, family-run place and is the best value among my pricier listings. It has 17 rooms, all comfortable and some beautiful, with flowery carpets and other Baroque frills. It's high above the old-center action on the third and fourth floors of a typical downtown building (Sb-€112, Db-€155-177

Sleep Code

Abbreviations (€1 = about $1.40, country code: 43, area code: 01)
S = Single, **D** = Double/Twin, **T** = Triple, **Q** = Quad,
b = bathroom, **s** = shower only, **t** = toilet only.

Price Rankings

  $$$ **Higher Priced**—Most rooms €130 or more.

  $$ **Moderately Priced**—Most rooms between €75-130.

   $ **Lower Priced**—Most rooms €75 or less.

English is spoken at each place. Unless otherwise noted,
credit cards are accepted, rooms have no air-conditioning,
breakfast is included, and Wi-Fi is generally free. Prices
change; verify current rates online or by email. For the best
prices, always book directly with the hotel.

depending on size, extra bed-€25-33, ask about discount if you
book directly with the hotel and mention Rick Steves, non-smoking, fans, elevator, guest computer, Wi-Fi, between Neuer Markt
and Kärntner Strasse at Marco d'Avianogasse 1, tel. 01/512-8330,
www.secrethomes.at, aviano@secrethomes.at, Frau Kavka).

$$$ Hotel am Stephansplatz is a four-star business hotel
with 56 rooms. It's plush but not over-the-top, and reasonably
priced for its sleek comfort and incredible location facing the
cathedral. Every detail is modern and quality, and breakfast is
superb, with a view of the city waking up around the cathedral
(Sb-€159-209, Db-€179-299, also has pricier suites that can be
triples, prices vary with demand and room size, air-con, elevator,
guest computer, Wi-Fi, gym and sauna, Stephansplatz 9, U-1 or
U-3: Stephansplatz, tel. 01/534-050, www.hotelamstephansplatz.
at, office@hotelamstephansplatz.at).

$$$ Hotel Pertschy, circling an old courtyard, is big and
hotelesque. Its 56 huge rooms are elegantly creaky, with chandeliers and Baroque touches. Those on the courtyard are quietest (Sb-€90-130, Db-€140-200 depending on size, extra
bed-€36, non-smoking rooms, elevator, guest computer, Wi-Fi,
Habsburgergasse 5, U-1 or U-3: Stephansplatz, tel. 01/534-490,
www.pertschy.com, info@pertschy.com).

$$$ Hotel zur Wiener Staatsoper, run by the same family
as the Schweizerhof, is quiet, with a more traditional elegance.
Its 22 tidy rooms come with high ceilings, chandeliers, and fancy
carpets on parquet floors (tiny Sb-€98, Db-€150, extra bed-
€25, fans on request, elevator, Wi-Fi, a block from the Opera at
Krugerstrasse 11; U-1, U-2, or U-4: Karlsplatz; tel. 01/513-1274,
www.zurwienerstaatsoper.at, office@zurwienerstaatsoper.at, manager Claudia).

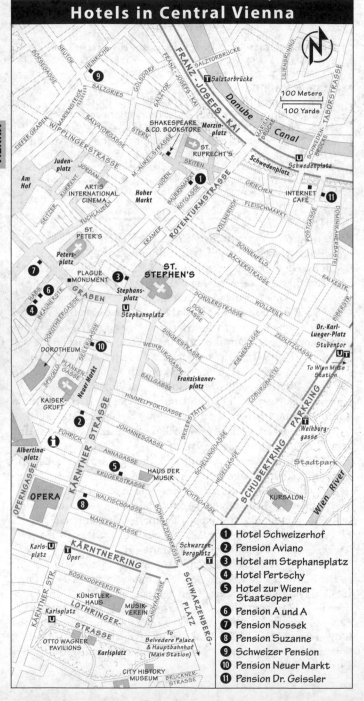

Hotels in Central Vienna

1. Hotel Schweizerhof
2. Pension Aviano
3. Hotel am Stephansplatz
4. Hotel Pertschy
5. Hotel zur Wiener Staatsoper
6. Pension A und A
7. Pension Nossek
8. Pension Suzanne
9. Schweizer Pension
10. Pension Neuer Markt
11. Pension Dr. Geissler

$$ Pension A und A, a friendly nine-room B&B run by Andreas and Andrea, offers a sleek, mod break from crusty old Vienna. This place, wonderfully located just off the Graben, has a nice entryway and period elevator—but open the door and you'll find white minimalist hallways and contemporary style in the rooms (Db-€120-150 depending on size, air-con, Wi-Fi, Habsburgergasse 3, tel. 01/890-5128, www.aunda.at, office@aunda.at).

$$ At **Pension Nossek,** an elevator takes you above any street noise into Frau Bernad and Frau Gundolf's world, tastefully decorated with lace and flowers, and with a small guest sitting room. With 32 rooms right on the wonderful Graben, this is a particularly good value (S-€60-67, Ss-€70, Sb-€90, Db-€130, Db suite-€165, extra bed-€37, air-con, elevator, guest computer, Wi-Fi, Graben 17, U-1 or U-3: Stephansplatz, tel. 01/5337-0410, www.pension-nossek.at, reservation@pension-nossek.at).

$$ Pension Suzanne, as Baroque and doily as you'll find in this price range, is wonderfully located a few yards from the Opera. It's small, but run with the class of a bigger hotel. The 26 rooms are packed with properly Viennese antique furnishings and paintings (Sb-€90, Db-€118-139 depending on size, ask about small discount with this book if you pay cash, extra bed-€25, spacious apartment for up to 6 also available, fans on request, elevator, guest computer, Wi-Fi, Walfischgasse 4; U-1, U-2, or U-4: Karlsplatz and follow signs for Opera exit; tel. 01/513-2507, www.pension-suzanne.at, info@pension-suzanne.at, delightfully run by manager Michael).

$$ Schweizer Pension has been family-owned for four generations. Anita and her son Gerald offer lots of tourist info and 11 homey rooms (four with shared facilities) for a great price, with parquet floors. It does feel kind of Swiss—tidy and well-run (S-€56, big Sb-€82, D-€79, Db-€99, Tb-€125, cash only, entirely non-smoking, elevator, Wi-Fi, full-service laundry-€18/load, Heinrichsgasse 2, U-2 or U-4: Schottenring, tel. 01/533-8156, www.schweizerpension.com, schweizer.pension@chello.at). They also rent a quad with bath (€139—too small for 4 adults but great for a family of 2 adults/2 kids under age 15).

$$ Pension Neuer Markt is family-run and perfectly central, with 37 comfy but faded rooms, and hallways with a cruise-ship ambience (Ss-€70-80, Sb-€90-100, Db-€120, prices vary with season and room size, extra bed-€20, in hot weather request a quiet courtyard-side room when you reserve, fans, elevator, guest computer, Wi-Fi, Seilergasse 9, tel. 01/512-2316, www.hotelpension.at, neuermarkt@hotelpension.at, Wolfgang).

$$ Pension Dr. Geissler, a respectable budget option, has 23 plain-but-comfortable rooms on the eighth floor of a modern, nondescript apartment building just off Schwedenplatz, about 10 blocks northeast of St. Stephen's near the Bratislava ferry terminal

(S-€48, Ss-€68, Sb-€76, D-€65, Ds-€77, Db-€95, elevator, Wi-Fi in most rooms, Postgasse 14, U-1 or U-4: Schwedenplatz—Postgasse is to the left as you face Hotel Capricorno, tel. 01/533-2803, www.hotelpension.at, dr.geissler@hotelpension.at).

ON OR NEAR MARIAHILFER STRASSE

Lively Mariahilfer Strasse connects the Westbahnhof (West Station) and the city center. The U-3 subway line runs underneath the street on its way between the Westbahnhof and St. Stephen's Cathedral. This vibrant, inexpensive area is filled with stores, cafés, and even a small shopping mall. It's a great neighborhood to stay in, and a glut of hotel rooms keeps prices low and competition keen. Its smaller hotels and pensions are generally immigrant-run, often by well-established Hungarian families. Most of these listings are within a five-minute walk of a U-Bahn stop. If you're driving, your hotel may provide discounted parking at a local garage for €13-19 per day. As you'd expect, the far end of Mariahilfer Strasse (around and past the Westbahnhof) is rougher around the edges, whereas the section near downtown is more gentrified.

Closer to Downtown

$$$ NH Atterseehaus Suites, part of a Spanish chain, is a stern, stylish-but-passionless business hotel on Mariahilfer Strasse. It rents 73 "suites" that are ideal for families, each with a living room, two TVs, bathroom, desk, and kitchenette (rack rate: Db-€99-200, but going rate usually closer to €110-125, extra bed-€35, 1 kid under age 12 stays free, breakfast-€17/person, non-smoking rooms, air-con, elevator, Wi-Fi, parking-€19/day, Mariahilfer Strasse 78, U-3: Zieglergasse, tel. 01/524-5600, www.nh-hotels.com, nhatterseehaus@nh-hotels.com).

$$ Hotel Pension Corvinus is bright, modern, and proudly and warmly run by a Hungarian family: parents Miklós and Judit and sons Anthony and Zoltán. Its 15 comfortable rooms are spacious, and some are downright sumptuous (Sb-€69-79, Db-€99-109, Tb-€119-129, ask about prices for Rick Steves readers who book by email or phone, 2 percent discount if you pay cash, extra bed-€26, ask about family rooms and apartments with kitchens, air-con, elevator, guest computer, Wi-Fi, parking-€15/day, on the third floor at Mariahilfer Strasse 57, U-3: Neubaugasse, tel. 01/587-7239, www.corvinus.at, hotel@corvinus.at).

$$ Hotel Kugel is run with pride and attitude by the gentlemanly, hands-on owner, Johannes Roller. Its 25 fine rooms have Old World charm and are a good value, especially for families (Db-€90, nicer Db with canopy bed-€100, family Qb-€150, Quint/b available, these prices if you book directly with the hotel, guest computer, Wi-Fi, free minibar, some tram noise, Siebensterngasse

43, at corner with Neubaugasse, U-3: Neubaugasse, tel. 01/523-3355, www.hotelkugel.at, office@hotelkugel.at).

$$ Hotel Pension Mariahilf's 12 rooms are clean, well-priced, and good-sized (if a bit outmoded), with a slight Art Deco flair (Sb-€66, twin Db-€80, Db-€90, Tb-€105, 5-person apartment with kitchen-€159, these prices if you book directly with the hotel and mention Rick Steves, elevator, Wi-Fi, parking-€18/day, Mariahilfer Strasse 49, U-3: Neubaugasse, tel. 01/586-1781, www.mariahilf-hotel.at, info@mariahilf-hotel.at, Babak).

$$ K&T Boardinghouse rents five modern, spacious rooms on the first floor of a quiet building a block off Mariahilfer Strasse (Db-€79, Tb-€99, Qb-€119, 2-night minimum, no breakfast, air-con-€8/day, cash or PayPal only but reserve with credit card, coffee in rooms, guest computer, Wi-Fi; Chwallagasse 2, U-3: Neubaugasse; tel. 01/523-2989, mobile 0676-553-6063, www.ktboardinghouse.at, kt2@chello.at, run by Tina, who also guides day-trips to Hungary and Slovakia). From Mariahilfer Strasse, turn left at Café Ritter and walk down Schadekgasse one short block; tiny Chwallagasse is the first right.

$$ Haydn Hotel is a formal-feeling business hotel one floor below Hotel Corvinus, with 21 bland, spacious, modern rooms (Sb-€90, Db €120, extra bed-€30, suites and family apartments, ask about Rick Steves discount off these prices if you pay cash, all rooms non-smoking, air-con, elevator, guest computer, Wi-Fi, parking-€17/day, Mariahilfer Strasse 57, U-3: Neubaugasse, tel. 01/5874-4140, www.haydn-hotel.at, info@haydn-hotel.at, Nouri).

$$ Pension Kraml is a charming, 17-room place tucked away on a small street between Mariahilfer Strasse and the Naschmarkt. It's family-run and feels classic, with breakfast served in the perfectly preserved family restaurant (no longer in operation) that the owner's grandmother ran in the 1950s. The rooms are big and quiet, with a homey, Old World ambiance (S-€45, D-€58, Ds or Dt-€68, Db-€78, T-€78, Tb-€99, Qb-€120, Quint/b-€135, family apartment available, these prices for guests who book directly with the hotel, guest computer, Wi-Fi, lots of stairs and no elevator, Brauergasse 5, midway between U-3: Zieglergasse and U-4: Pilgramgasse, tel. 01/587-8588, www.pensionkraml.at, pension.kraml@chello.at, Stephan Kraml).

$ Pension Hargita rents 24 bright and attractive rooms (mostly twins) with woody Hungarian-village decor. While the pension is directly on bustling Mariahilfer Strasse, its windows block noise well. Don't let the dark entryway put you off—this spick-and-span, well-located place is a great value (S-€40, Ss-€47, Sb-€57, D-€54, Ds-€60, tiny Db-€65, Db-€68, Ts-€75, Tb-€82, Qb-€114, cash preferred, extra bed-€10, breakfast-€5, completely non-smoking, lots of stairs and no elevator, air-con in common

VIENNA

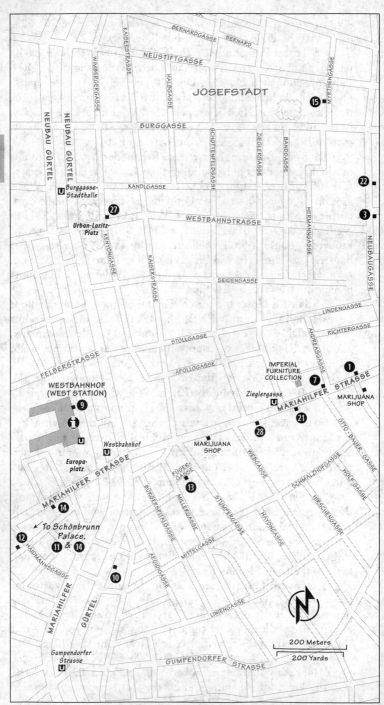

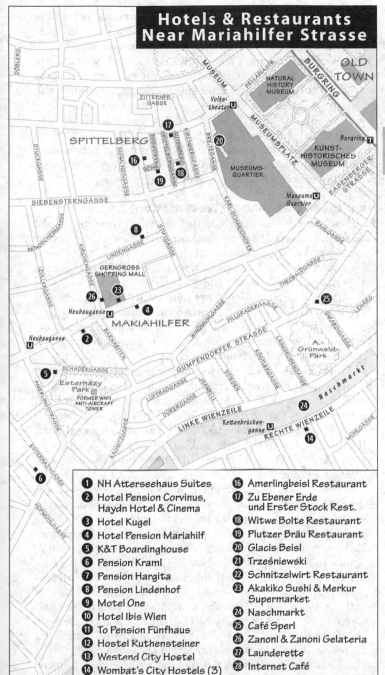

Hotels & Restaurants Near Mariahilfer Strasse

1. NH Atterseehaus Suites
2. Hotel Pension Corvinus, Haydn Hotel & Cinema
3. Hotel Kugel
4. Hotel Pension Mariahilf
5. K&T Boardinghouse
6. Pension Kraml
7. Pension Hargita
8. Pension Lindenhof
9. Motel One
10. Hotel Ibis Wien
11. To Pension Fünfhaus
12. Hostel Ruthensteiner
13. Westend City Hostel
14. Wombat's City Hostels (3)
15. Hostel Wien
16. Amerlingbeisl Restaurant
17. Zu Ebener Erde und Erster Stock Rest.
18. Witwe Bolte Restaurant
19. Plutzer Bräu Restaurant
20. Glacis Beisl
21. Trześniewski
22. Schnitzelwirt Restaurant
23. Akakiko Sushi & Merkur Supermarket
24. Naschmarkt
25. Café Sperl
26. Zanonl & Zanoni Gelateria
27. Launderette
28. Internet Café

VIENNA

areas, guest computer, Wi-Fi, bike parking, corner of Mariahilfer Strasse at Andreasgasse 1, right at U-3: Zieglergasse, tel. 01/526-1928, www.hargita.at, pension@hargita.at, Erika and Tibor).

$ Pension Lindenhof rents 19 very basic, very worn but clean and very inexpensive rooms. It's a dark and mysteriously dated time warp filled with plants (and a fun guest-generated postcard wall); the stark rooms have outrageously high ceilings and teeny bathrooms (S-€30, Sb-€37, D-€40, Db-€54, T-€60, Tb-€81, Q-€80, Qb-€108, hall shower-€2, breakfast-€3, cash only, elevator, no Internet access, next door to a harmless strip bar at Lindengasse 4, U-3: Neubaugasse, tel. 01/523-0498, www.pensionlindenhof.at, pensionlindenhof@yahoo.com, run by Gebrael family).

Near the Westbahnhof (West Station)

$$ Motel One, a German chain that seems ready to take on the hotel world, surveyed business customers and offers only what they want to pay for. The result is what the chain calls a "low-budget design hotel": 441 sleek and modern rooms, built cruise-ship tight with quality materials but no frills, a 24-hour reception but minimal service, and refreshingly straightforward pricing (Sb-€71, Db-€86, no triples but you can slip in a child under age 16 for free, breakfast-€7.50, Wi-Fi, air-con, parking-€13/day, attached to the Westbahnhof at Europaplatz 3, tel. 01/359-350, www.motel-one.com, wein-westbahnhof@motel-one.com).

$$ Hotel Ibis Wien, a modern high-rise hotel with American charm, is ideal for anyone tired of quaint old Europe. Its 341 cookie-cutter rooms are bright, comfortable, and modern, with all the conveniences (Sb-€69-75, Db-€87-93, Tb-€106, breakfast-€11, air-con, elevator, guest computer, Wi-Fi, parking garage-€13/day; exit Westbahnhof to the right and walk 400 yards, Mariahilfer Gürtel 22, U-3: Westbahnhof; tel. 01/59998, www.ibishotel.com, h0796@accor.com).

$ Pension Fünfhaus is plain, clean, and bare-bones—almost institutional—with tile floors and 47 rooms. The neighborhood is, well...improving (you might see a few ladies loitering late at night), but really not that bad, and this "pension" does the job if you want rock-bottom prices and few services—but try Hargita, Kraml, or Lindenhof first (S-€35, Sb-€44, D-€51, Db-€62, Tb-€87-95, 4-person apartment-€106, cash only, includes very basic breakfast, Wi-Fi in breakfast room, closed mid-Nov-Feb, Sperrgasse 12, U-3: Westbahnhof, tel. 01/892-3545, www.pension5haus.at, vienna@pension5haus.at, Frau Susi Tersch). Half the rooms are in the main building and half are in the annex at Grandgasse 8, which has good rooms, but its location near the train tracks is a bit sketchy at night. From the station, walk five minutes on Mariahilfer Strasse to #160, then turn right on Sperrgasse.

CHEAP DORMS AND HOSTELS NEAR MARIAHILFER STRASSE AND THE WESTBAHNHOF

$ Hostel Ruthensteiner is your smallest and coziest option, with 100 beds in four- to eight-bed dorms and lots of little touches (€17 dorm beds, D-€48, Db-€70, includes lockers and sheets, includes towels in private rooms, towel rental in dorms-€1, breakfast-€3-4, non-smoking, guest computer, Wi-Fi, kitchen, laundry-€6/load, comfy common areas with piano and guitars, bike rental; Robert-Hamerling-Gasse 24; tel. 01/893-4202, www.hostelruthensteiner. com, info@hostelruthensteiner.com). From the Westbahnhof, follow Mariahilfer Strasse away from the center to #149, and turn left on Haidmannsgasse. Go one block, then turn right.

$ Westend City Hostel, just a block from the Westbahnhof and Mariahilfer Strasse, is well-run and well-located in a residential neighborhood, so it's quiet after 20:00. It has a small lounge, high-ceilinged rooms, a tiny back courtyard, and 180 beds in 4- to 12-bed dorms, each with its own bath (€19-28/person depending on day of week and how many in the room, Db-€70-92, cheaper Nov-mid-March—except around New Year's; includes sheets and locker, towel purchase-€4, breakfast included when you book directly with the hostel, cash only, elevator, pay guest computer, Wi-Fi, laundry-€7/load, Fügergasse 3, tel. 01/597-6729, www. westendhostel.at, info@westendhostel.at).

$ Wombat's City Hostel has three well-run locations—each with about 250 beds and four to six beds per room (€18-22 dorm beds, D-€60-70, lockers, bar, Wi-Fi, generous public spaces; near tracks behind the Westbahnhof at Grangasse 6, even closer to the station at Mariahilfer Strasse 137, and near the Naschmarkt at Rechte Wienzeile 35; tel. 01/897-2336, www.wombats-hostels. com, office@wombats-vienna.at).

$ Hostel Wien is your classic, huge, and well-run official youth hostel, with 260 beds (€19-22/person in 2- to 6-bed rooms, price depends on season, includes sheets and breakfast, towel purchase-€3, nonmembers pay €3.50 extra, pay guest computer, Wi-Fi in lobby, always open, no curfew, lockers and lots of facilities, coin-op laundry, Myrthengasse 7, take bus #48A from Westbahnhof, tel. 01/523-6316, hostel@chello.at, www.1070vienna.at).

Eating in Vienna

The Viennese appreciate the fine points of life, and right up there with waltzing is eating. The city has many atmospheric restaurants. As you ponder the Hungarian and Bohemian influence on many menus, remember that Vienna's diverse empire may be no more, but its flavors linger. In addition to restaurants, this section covers two uniquely Viennese institutions: the city's classic café

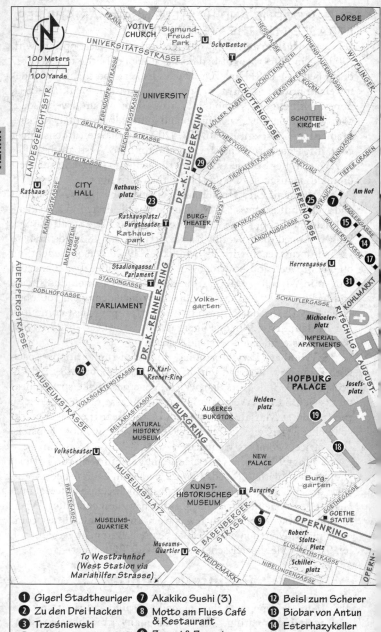

VIENNA

1 Gigerl Stadtheuriger
2 Zu den Drei Hacken
3 Trześniewski
4 Reinthaler's Beisl & Café Hawelka
5 Cantinetta La Norma
6 Gyros

7 Akakiko Sushi (3)
8 Motto am Fluss Café & Restaurant
9 Zanoni & Zanoni Gelateria (2)
10 Rest. Ofenloch
11 Brezel-Gwölb

12 Beisl zum Scherer
13 Biobar von Antun
14 Esterhazykeller
15 Hopferl Bierhof
16 Zum Schwarzen Kameel Rest. & Wine Bar

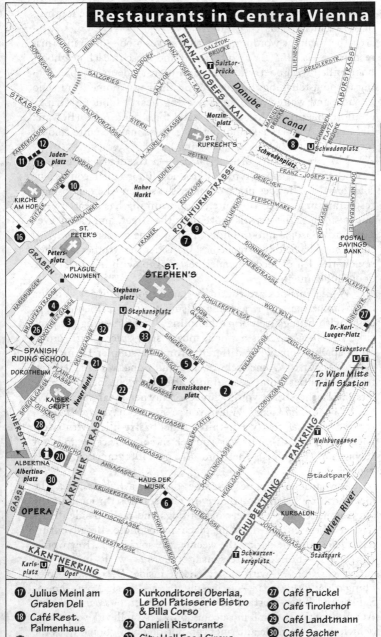

Restaurants in Central Vienna

VIENNA

17 Julius Meinl am Graben Deli

18 Café Rest. Palmenhaus

19 Soho Kantine

20 Rosenberger Markt Rest.

21 Kurkonditorei Oberlaa, Le Bol Patisserie Bistro & Billa Corso

22 Danieli Ristorante

23 City Hall Food Circus

24 Justizcafe

25 Café Central

26 Café Bräunerhof

27 Café Pruckel

28 Café Tirolerhof

29 Café Landtmann

30 Café Sacher

31 Demel

32 American Bar

33 Billa Supermarket

culture, and its unique *Heuriger* wine pubs nestled in the foothills of the Vienna Woods.

The Viennese word for a pub that serves food—or an informal restaurant—is *Beisl* (BYE-zul). You'll find these in each neighborhood, filled with poetry teachers and their students, couples loving without touching, housewives on their way home from cello lessons, and waiters who enjoy serving hearty food and drinks at affordable prices. Ask at your hotel for a good *Beisl*. (Beware: Because of Austria's lax smoking laws, pubs may be quite smoky; fortunately, most have outdoor seating.)

Most restaurants offer a "*menu*"—a fixed-price meal—at lunchtime on weekdays (typically around €10 for a main course plus soup or salad). Besides price, consider the season when choosing a restaurant in Vienna. In winter, indoor dining has great appeal, but in summer the crowds move onto the street, and balmy evenings drive people into the hills to enjoy wine gardens *(Heurigen)* surrounded by fields of grapevines. Consider the weather and then review this list of recommended restaurants with indoor or outdoor dining in mind.

While cuisines are routinely named for countries, Vienna claims to be the only *city* with a cuisine of its own: Vienna soups come with fillings (semolina dumpling, liver dumpling, or pancake slices). *Gulasch* is a thick, meaty stew spiced with onion and paprika, somewhat different from the soupier Hungarian dish. Of course, Wiener schnitzel is traditionally a breaded and fried veal cutlet (some restaurants offer only cheaper pork cutlets, and others give you a choice). Another meat specialty is boiled beef *(Tafelspitz)*. While you're sure to have *Apfelstrudel,* try *Topfenstrudel,* too (wafer-thin strudel pastry filled with sweet cheese and raisins). The *dag* you see in some prices stands for "decigram" (10 grams). Therefore, *10 dag* is 100 grams, or about a quarter-pound.

For hardcore Viennese cuisine, drop by a *Würstelstand*. The local hot-dog stand is a fixture on city squares throughout the old center, serving a variety of hot dogs and pickled side dishes with a warm corner-meeting-place atmosphere. Be adventurous: Generally, the darker the weenie, the spicier it is. Key words: *Weisswurst*—boiled white sausage; *Bosna*—with onions and curry; *Käsekrainer*—with melted cheese inside; *Debreziner*—spicy Hungarian; *Frankfurter*—our weenie; *frische*—fresh; *Kren*—horseradish; and *Senf*—mustard (ask for *süss*—sweet, or *scharf*—sharp). At sausage stands, you'll most commonly get a roll with your wurst (which won't resemble an American hot-dog bun). Sometimes the sausage is inside the roll; sometimes you get it on a plate with a fork and the roll to the side.

NEAR ST. STEPHEN'S CATHEDRAL

Each of these eateries is within about a five-minute walk of the cathedral (U-1 or U-3: Stephansplatz).

Gigerl Stadtheuriger offers a fun, near-*Heuriger* wine-cellar experience without leaving the city center. Just point to what looks good. As in other *Heurigen* (see page 1258), food is sold by the piece or weight; 100 grams *(10 dag)* is about a quarter-pound (cheese and cold meats cost about €4 per 100 grams, salads are about €2 per 100 grams; price sheet posted on wall to right of buffet line). The *Karree* pork with herbs is particularly tasty and tender. They also have entrées, spinach strudel, quiche, *Apfelstrudel*, and, of course, casks of new and local wines (sold by the *Achtel*, about 4 oz). Meals run €8-12 (daily 15:00-24:00, indoor/outdoor seating, behind cathedral, a block off Kärntner Strasse, a few cobbles off Rauhensteingasse on Blumenstock, tel. 01/513-4431).

Zu den Drei Hacken, a fun and typical *Weinstube* (wine pub), is famous for its local specialties (€13-19 main courses, €9-13 weekday lunches, Mon-Sat 11:00-23:00, closed Sun, indoor/outdoor seating, Singerstrasse 28, tel. 01/512-5895).

Trześniewski is an institution—justly famous for its elegant open-face finger sandwiches (€1.20) and small beers (€1 each). Three different sandwiches and a *kleines Bier (Pfiff)* make a fun, light lunch. Point to whichever delights look tasty (or grab the English translation sheet and take time to study your 22 sandwich options). The classic favorites are *Geflügelleber* (chicken liver), *Matjes mit Zwiebel* (herring with onions), and *Speck mit Ei* (bacon and eggs). Pay for your sandwiches and a drink. Take your drink tokens to the lady on the right. Sit on the bench and scoot over to a tiny table when a spot opens up. In the fall, try their fancy grape juices—*Most* or *Traubenmost*. Started by a Polish cook who moved to Vienna, Trześniewski (chesh-NEFF-ski) has been a Vienna favorite for more than a century...and many of its regulars seem to have been here for the grand opening. You can grab an early, quick dinner here, but the selection can get paltry by the end of the day, and filling up here isn't cheap (Mon-Fri 8:30-19:30, Sat 9:00-17:00, closed Sun; 50 yards off the Graben, nearly across from brooding Café Hawelka, Dorotheergasse 2; tel. 01/512-3291). Their other locations serve the same sandwiches with the same menu but without the historic ambience: at Mariahilfer Strasse 95 (near many recommended hotels, Mon-Fri 8:30-19:00, Sat 9:00-18:00, closed Sun, U-3: Zieglergasse, tel. 01/596-4291) and in the Westbahnhof train station (near track 9, Mon-Fri 7:00-23:00, Sat-Sun 8:00-23:00, U-3: Westbahnhof, tel. 01/982-2975).

Reinthaler's Beisl is a time warp that serves simple, traditional fare all day. It's handy for its location (a block off the Graben, across the street from Trześniewski) and because it's a rare restaurant in the center that's open on Sunday. Its fun, classic interior winds way back, and it also has a few tables on the quiet street outside (use the handwritten daily menu rather than the printed English one, €8-13 main courses, daily 11:00-22:30, at Dorotheergasse 4, tel. 01/513-1249).

Cantinetta La Norma, a short walk from the cathedral, serves fresh, excellent Italian dishes amid a cozy, yet energetic ambience. Even on weeknights the small dining area is abuzz with friendly chatter among its multinational, loyal regulars (€8-11 pizzas and pastas, €14-20 main courses, weekday lunch specials, daily 11:00-24:00, outdoor seating, Franziskaner Platz 3, tel. 01/512-8665, run by friendly Paco and Hany).

Gyros is a humble little Greek/Turkish joint (more sit-down than takeout) run by Yilmaz, a fun-loving Turk from Izmir. He simply loves to feed people—the food is great, the prices are decent, and you almost feel like you took a quick trip to Istanbul (€9-13 plates, Mon-Sat 11:00-23:00, closed Sun, a long block off Kärntner Strasse at corner of Fichtegasse and Seilerstätte, mobile 0699-1016-3726).

Akakiko Sushi is a local chain of pan-Asian restaurants with a Japanese emphasis. They serve sushi, of course, but also €9-11 noodle soups, rice dishes, and more. The €10-13 bento box meals are a decent value. There are several convenient locations: Singerstrasse 4 (a block off Kärntner Strasse near the cathedral), Rotenturmstrasse 6 (also near the cathedral), Heidenschuss 3 (near other recommended eateries just off Am Hof, U-3: Herrengasse), and Mariahilfer Strasse 42 (fifth floor of Kaufhaus Gerngross, near many recommended hotels, U-3: Neubaugasse). Though they lack charm, these are fast, modern, air-conditioned, and reasonable (all open daily 10:30-23:30).

Motto am Fluss Café and Restaurant, on the upper floors of the Bratislava riverboat terminal, is good for a bite or drink overlooking the Danube Canal. The classy café, on the top floor, has indoor and outdoor tables (€10-13 main courses, €9-10 weekday lunch specials, daily 8:00-24:00, tel. 01/252-5511); the pricey and elegant restaurant is one floor down and serves modern cuisine (indoor seating only but with great canal-perch tables, €18-26 main courses, extensive wine-by-the-glass list, €21 three-course lunches, daily 11:30-14:30 & 18:00-24:00, tel. 01/252-5510).

Ice Cream!: **Zanoni & Zanoni** is a *gelateria* run by an Italian family, with several branches around town. They're mobbed by happy Viennese hungry for their €2 two-scoop cones to go. The downtown branch has a fun outdoor area where you can people-watch while licking your gelato (daily 7:00-24:00, 2 blocks up Rotenturmstrasse from cathedral at Lugeck 7, tel. 01/512-7979). There's another location behind the Kunsthistorisches Museum, facing the Ring (at Burgring 1, U-2 or U-3: Volkstheater/ Museumsplatz) and another along the side of the Gerngross mall (at Kirchengasse 1, off Mariahilfer Strasse).

NEAR AM HOF SQUARE

The streets around the square called Am Hof (U-3: Herrengasse) hide atmospheric medieval lanes with both indoor and outdoor eating action. The following eateries are all within a block or two of the square.

Restaurant Ofenloch serves good, old-fashioned Viennese cuisine with formal service, both indoors and out. This 300-year-old eatery, with great traditional ambience, is dressy (with white tablecloths) but intimate and woodsy (€13-16 lunch specials, €16-20 main courses, €3 cover charge, Mon-Sat 11:00-23:00, closed Sun, Kurrentgasse 8, tel. 01/533-8844).

Brezel-Gwölb, a Tolkienesque nook with tight indoor tables and outdoor dining on a quiet little square, serves fine but forgettable food in an unforgettable atmosphere. It's ideal for a romantic late-night glass of wine (€9-16 main courses, €11 three-course weekday lunches, daily 11:30-24:00; leave Am Hof on Drahtgasse, then take first left to Ledererhof 9; tel. 01/533-8811).

Beisl zum Scherer, around the corner, is untouristy and serves traditional main dishes for €9-16. Outside tables face a stern Holocaust memorial on a pretty square. Inside seating comes with a soothing woody atmosphere and intriguing decor. It's named for a pre-WWI satirical newspaper that was published here. In the evening, let friendly Sakis explain the daily specials—which don't show up on the English menu (Mon-Sat 11:30-24:00, closed Sun, Judenplatz 7, tel. 01/533-5164).

Biobar von Antun is an earthy little place that serves three-course vegan meals (soup, salad, and main course) for €9-12 weekdays at lunch, and €13-15 at other times. They also have hearty €10-11 salads and fancy juices (Mon-Fri 11:30-14:30 & 17:30-22:30, Sat-Sun 12:00-22:30, on Judenplatz at Drahtgasse 3, tel. 01/968-9351, Antun Peskovic).

Esterhazykeller, both ancient and popular, has traditional fare in two serving areas. For a cheap and sloppy buffet, descend to the subbasement, a wine cellar that dates back to 1683. While the food is self-serve from the deli counter (a meal-sized plate costs around €10), you'll order drinks at your table (Mon-Fri 16:00-23:00, Sat-Sun 11:00-23:00). For table service from an only slightly pricier menu on a pleasant square, sit upstairs or outside (€10-12 main courses, €7 weekday lunches, daily 11:00-23:00, may close for lunch in Aug-Sept and/or in bad weather, just below Am Hof at Haarhof 1, tel. 01/533-3482).

The outdoor seating at **Hopferl Bierhof** on the same square might be a better option if it's hot and you're in the mood for a beer. It has a large, meaty menu and nice ambience, with Ottakringer beer on tap (€10-20 main courses, daily 11:30-24:00, Naglergasse 13, tel. 01/533-4428).

Zum Schwarzen Kameel Wine Bar ("The Black Camel") is filled with a professional local crowd enjoying small plates from the same kitchen as their fancy restaurant, but at a better price. This is *the* place for horseradish and thin-sliced ham (*Beinschinken mit Kren*, €10/plate, *Achtung*—the horseradish is *hot*). Stand, grab a stool, find a table on the street, or sit anywhere you can—it's customary to share tables in the wine-bar section. Fine Austrian wines are sold by the *Achtel* (eighth-liter glass) and listed on the board. They also have a buffet of tiny €1.25 open-face finger sandwiches. Prices are the same inside or at their street-side outdoor tables (daily 8:00-24:00, Bognergasse 5, tel. 01/533-8125).

For a splurge, the adjacent **Zum Schwarzen Kameel Restaurant** is a tiny, elegant alternative. The dark-wood, 12-table, Art Nouveau restaurant serves fine gourmet Viennese cuisine (€23-36 main courses, €68 and €86 five-course set-price meals, pricey wine, €3 cover charge, daily 12:00-24:00, tel. 01/533-8125).

Gourmet Supermarket: **Julius Meinl am Graben,** a posh supermarket with two floors of temptations right on the Graben, has been famous since 1862 as a top-end delicatessen with all the gourmet fancies. Assemble a meal from the picnic fixings on the shelves. There's also a café, with light meals and great outdoor seating; a stuffy and pricey restaurant upstairs; and a take-out counter with good benches for people-watching while you munch (shop open Mon-Fri 8:00-19:30, Sat 9:00-18:00, closed Sun; restaurant open Mon-Sat until 24:00, closed Sun; Am Graben 19, tel. 01/532-3334).

NEAR THE OPERA

These eateries are within easy walking distance of the Opera (U-1, U-2, or U-4: Karlsplatz).

Café Restaurant Palmenhaus overlooks the Palace Garden (Burggarten—see page 1200). Tucked away in a green and peaceful corner two blocks behind the Opera in the Hofburg's backyard, this is a world apart. If you want to eat modern Austrian cuisine surrounded by palm trees rather than tourists, this is the place. And, since it's at the edge of a huge park, it's great for families. They specialize in fresh fish with generous vegetables—options are listed on the chalkboard (€10 weekday lunches, €18-26 main courses; daily 10:00-24:00, Sun until 23:00; Nov-Feb daily from 11:00 except Jan-Feb closed Mon-Tue; extensive fine-wine list, indoors in greenhouse or outdoors, Burggarten 1, tel. 01/533-1033).

Soho Kantine is a cave-like, government-subsidized cantina, serving the National Library staff but open to all, and offering unexciting, institutional sit-down lunches in the Hofburg. Pay for your meal—your choice of bland meat or bland vegetarian—and a drink at the bar, take your token to the kitchen, and then sit down and eat with the locals. Wednesday is schnitzel day and Friday is fish day (€6.50-7 two-course lunch, Mon-Fri 11:30-15:00, closed Sat-Sun and Aug, hard to find—just past the butterfly house in a forlorn little square, look for *Soho* sign in entry corridor, Burggarten, mobile 0676-309-5161).

Rosenberger Markt Restaurant is mobbed with tour groups. Still, if you're OK with a freeway-cafeteria ambience in the center of the German-speaking world's classiest city, this self-service catery is fast and easy. It's just a block toward the cathedral from the Opera. The best cheap meal here is a small salad or antipasto plate stacked high (daily 11:00-22:00, lots of fruits, veggies, fresh-squeezed juices, addictive banana milk, ride the glass elevator downstairs, Maysedergasse 2, tel. 01/512-3458).

Kurkonditorei Oberlaa may not have the royal and plush fame of Demel (see page 1174), but this is where Viennese connoisseurs serious about the quality of their pastries go to get fat. With outdoor seating on Neuer Markt, it's particularly nice on a hot summer day. Upstairs has more temptations and good seating (€12 three-course weekday lunches—€15 Sat-Sun, great selection of cakes, daily 8:00-20:00, Neuer Markt 16, other locations about town, including the Naschmarkt, tel. 01/5132-9360).

Le Bol Patisserie Bistro (next to Oberlaa) satisfies your need for something French. The staff speaks to you in French, serving fine €10-14 salads, baguette sandwiches, and fresh croissants (Mon-Sat 8:00-22:00, Sun 10:00-20:00, Neuer Markt 14).

Danieli Ristorante is your best classy Italian bet in the old town. White-tablecloth dressy, but not stuffy, it has reasonable prices. Dine in their elegant back room or on the street (€11-19 pastas, €9-15 pizzas, €17-26 main courses, daily 12:00-24:00, 30 yards off Kärntner Strasse opposite Neuer Markt at Himmelpfortgasse 3, tel. 01/513-7913).

Supermarkets: **Billa Corso** is a top-end version of the Billa supermarket chain and sells hot, gourmet, ready-made meals (by weight). You're welcome to sit and enjoy whatever you've purchased in either eating area: inside (air-conditioned) and out on the square. They also have a great deli selection of salads, soups, and picnic items (warm food-€2/100 grams, WC on ground floor, Mon-Fri 8:00-20:00, Sat 8:00-19:00, closed Sun, Neuer Markt 17, on the corner where Seilergasse hits Neuer Markt, tel. 01/961-2133). A non-gourmet **Billa** is on a side street around the corner from St. Stephen's Church (Mon-Fri 7:15-19:30, Sat 7:15-18:00, closed Sun, Singerstrasse 6).

CITY HALL FOOD CIRCUS

During the summer, scores of outdoor food stands and hundreds of picnic tables are set up in the park in front of the City Hall (Rathausplatz). Local mobs enjoy mostly ethnic meals for decent-but-not-cheap prices and classical entertainment on a big screen. The fun thing here is the energy of the crowd and a feeling that you're truly eating as the Viennese do...not schnitzel and quaint traditions, but trendy "world food" with young people out having fun in a nice Vienna park setting (July-Aug daily from 11:00 until late, in front of City Hall on the Ringstrasse, U-2: Rathaus).

JUST WEST OF THE RING

Justizcafe, the cafeteria serving Austria's Supreme Court of Justice, offers a fine view, great prices, and a memorable breakfast or lunchtime experience—even if the food is somewhat bland. Your goal is the black boxy structure on the top of the Palace of Justice. To reach it, enter the building through its grand front door, pass through tight security (no guns; Swiss Army knives OK but better to leave them in your room), say "wow" to the eye-popping Historicist courtyard, head to the very back of the building and ride the elevator to the fifth floor, then walk back to the front past rows of judges' chambers. You can sit behind the windows inside or dine outside on the roof, enjoying one of the best views of Vienna while surrounded by legal beagles—go early or late to miss the crush (€6.50 breakfasts, €8-12 two- and three-course lunches, Mon-Fri 7:00-10:00 & 11:00-14:30, closed Sat-Sun, Schmerlingplatz 10, U-2 or U-3: Volkstheater/Museumsplatz, mobile 0676-755-6100).

SPITTELBERG

This charming cobbled grid of traffic-free lanes is a favorite dining neighborhood for the Viennese. It's handy, set between the MuseumsQuartier and Mariahilfer Strasse (near many recommended hotels, or wander over here after you close down the Kunsthistorisches Museum; U-2 or U-3: Volkstheater/Museumsplatz). Tables tumble down sidewalks and into breezy courtyards; the charming buildings here date mostly from the early 1800s, before the Mariahilfer neighborhood was built. It's only worth a special trip on a balmy summer evening, as it's dead in bad weather. Stroll Spittelberggasse, Schrankgasse, and Gutenberggasse, then pick your favorite. Don't miss the vine-strewn wine garden at Schrankgasse 1. To locate these restaurants, see the map on page 1241.

Amerlingbeisl, with a charming, casual atmosphere both on the cobbled street and in its vine-covered courtyard, is a great value, serving a mix of traditional Austrian and international dishes (check the board with daily specials—some vegetarian—for €7-10, €14 main courses, daily 9:00-2:00 in the morning, Stiftgasse 8, tel. 01/526-1660).

Zu Ebener Erde und Erster Stock (loosely translated as "Downstairs, Upstairs") is a charming little restaurant with a mostly traditional Austrian menu. Filling a cute 1750 building, it's true to its name, with two dining rooms: casual and woody downstairs (traditionally for the poor); and a fancy Biedermeier-style dining room with red-velvet chairs and violet tablecloths upstairs (where the wealthy convened). There are also a few al fresco tables along the quiet side street. Reservations are smart (€10-18 main courses, €29 traditional three-course fixed-price meal, seasonal specials, €3 cover charge, Mon-Fri 7:30-21:30, last seating at 20:00, closed Sat-Sun, Burggasse 13, tel. 01/523-6254, www. zu-ebener-erde-und-erster-stock.at).

Witwe Bolte is classy. The interior is tight, but its tiny square has a wonderful leafy ambience (€12-20 main courses, €2 cover charge, daily 11:45-23:30 except closed 15:00-17:30 mid-Jan-mid-March, Gutenberggasse 13, tel. 01/523-1450).

Plutzer Bräu, next door to Amerlingbeisl, feels a bit more commercial. It's a big, sprawling, impersonal brewpub serving stick-to-your-ribs pub grub (€8-9 meatless dishes, €10-20 main courses, ribs, burgers, traditional dishes, Tirolean beer from the keg, also brew their own, daily 11:00-2:00 in the morning, food until 23:00—22:00 on Sun, Schrankgasse 4, tel. 01/526-1215).

Glacis Beisl, at the top edge of the MuseumsQuartier just before Spittelberg, is popular with locals. A gravelly wine garden tucked next to a city fortification, its outdoor tables and breezy ambience are particularly appealing on a balmy evening (€10-19 main courses, €10 weekday lunch specials, daily 11:00-24:00, Breitegasse 4, tel. 01/526-5660).

MARIAHILFER STRASSE AND THE NASCHMARKT

Mariahilfer Strasse (see map on page 1241) is filled with reasonable cafés serving all types of cuisine. For a quick yet traditional bite, consider the venerable **Trześniewski** sandwich bar's branch at Mariahilfer Strasse 95, or its imitators (one is at #91).

Schnitzelwirt is an old classic with a 1950s patina and a mixed local and tourist clientele. In this smoky, working-class place, no one finishes their schnitzel (notice the self-serve butcher paper and plastic bags for leftovers). Walk to the no-smoking section in the back, passing the kitchen piled high with breaded cutlets waiting for the deep fryer. The €9-11 schnitzels are served with a starch or salad; if you order the €6 version, you may want to add a €3 side. They also serve Austrian standards including *Szegediner Gulasch.* You'll find no tourists, just cheap schnitzel meals (Mon-Sat

10:00-23:00, closed Sun, Neubaugasse 52, U-3: Neubaugasse, tel. 01/523-3771).

Supermarket: Merkur, in the basement of the Gerngross shopping mall at Mariahilfer Strasse 42, is big and open fairly late (Mon-Wed 8:00-20:00, Thu-Fri 8:00-21:00, Sat 8:00-18:00, closed Sun, U-3: Neubaugasse).

Naschmarkt: For a picnic or a trendy dinner, try the **Naschmarkt,** Vienna's sprawling produce market. This thriving Old World scene comes with plenty of fresh produce, cheap local-style eateries, cafés, kebab and sausage stands, and the best-value sushi in town (Mon-Fri 6:00-18:30, Sat 6:00-17:00, closed Sun, closes earlier in winter; U-1, U-2, or U-4: Karlsplatz, follow *Karlsplatz* signs out of the station). Picnickers can buy supplies at the market and eat on nearby Karlsplatz (plenty of chairs facing the Karlskirche) or pop in to the Burggarten behind the famous Mozart statue.

In recent years, the Naschmarkt has become fashionable for dinner (or cocktails), with an amazing variety of local and ethnic eateries to choose from. Prices are great, the produce is certainly fresh, and the dinners are as local as can be. The best plan: Stroll through the entire market to survey the many options, and then pick the place that appeals. For more on the Naschmarkt, see page 1214.

Vienna's Café Culture

In Vienna, the living room is down the street at the neighborhood coffeehouse. This tradition is just another example of the Viennese expertise in good living. Each of Vienna's many long-established (and sometimes even legendary) coffeehouses has its individual character (and characters). These classic cafés can be a bit tired, with a shabby patina and famously grumpy waiters who treat you like an uninvited guest invading their living room. Yet these spaces somehow also feel welcoming, offering newspapers, pastries, sofas, quick and light workers' lunches, elegant ambience, and "take all the time you want" charm for the price of a cup of coffee. Rather than buy the *International New York Times* ahead of time, spend the money on a cup of coffee and read the paper for free, Vienna-style, in a café.

VIENNESE COFFEE TERMS

As in Italy and France, Viennese coffee drinks are espresso-based. Obviously, *Kaffee* means coffee and *Milch* is milk; *Obers* is cream, and *Schlagobers* is whipped cream. Beyond those basics, here are some uniquely Viennese coffee terms (use them elsewhere, and you'll probably get a funny look):

- *Schwarzer, Mokka:* straight, black espresso; order it *kleiner* (small) or *grosser* (big)
- *Verlängeter* ("lengthened"): espresso with water, like an Americano
- *Brauner:* with a little milk
- *Schale Gold* ("golden cup"): with a little cream
- *Melange:* like a cappuccino
- *Franziskaner:* a *melange* with whipped cream rather than foamed milk, often topped with chocolate flakes
- *Kapuziner:* strong coffee with a dollop of sweetened cream (oddly, not a cappuccino, which derives its name from the same word)
- *Verkehrt* ("incorrect"), *Milchkaffee:* with lots and lots of milk — similar to a *caffè latte*
- *Einspänner* ("buggy"): with lots and lots of whipped cream, served in a glass with a handle (as it was the drink of horse-and-buggy drivers, who only had one hand free)
- *Fiaker* ("horse-and-buggy driver"): black, with kirsch liqueur or rum, served with a cherry
- *(Wiener) Eiskaffee:* coffee with ice cream
- *Maria Theresia:* coffee with orange liqueur

Americans who ask for a "latte" are mistaken for Italians and given a cup of hot milk.

CAFÉS

These are some of my favorite Viennese cafés. All of them, except for Café Sperl, are located inside the Ring (see map on page 1245).

Café Central, while a bit touristy, remains a classic place, lavish under Neo-Gothic columns and celebrated by 19th-century Austrian writers. They serve fancy coffees (€4-7), breakfasts (€7-17), two-course weekday lunch specials (€10), and traditional main dishes (€13-19), and entertain guests with live piano—schmaltzy tunes on a fine, Vienna-made Bösendorfer each evening from 17:00-22:00 (Mon-Sat 7:30-22:00, Sun 10:00-22:00, free Wi-Fi, corner of Herrengasse and Strauchgasse, U-3: Herrengasse, tel. 01/533-3764).

Café Sperl dates from 1880 and is still furnished identically to the day it opened—from the coat tree to the chairs (Mon-Sat 7:00-23:00, Sun 11:00-20:00 except closed Sun July-Aug, just off Naschmarkt near Mariahilfer Strasse, Gumpendorfer 11, U-2: MuseumsQuartier, tel. 01/586-4158; see map on page 1241).

Café Bräunerhof, between the Hofburg and the Graben, offers classic ambience with few tourists and live music on weekends (light classics, no cover, Sat-Sun 15:15-18:00), along with €7 lunches on weekdays (Mon-Fri 8:00-20:00, Sat-Sun 8:00-18:30, no hot food after 15:00, Stallburggasse 2, U-1 or U-3: Stephansplatz, tel. 01/512-3893).

Café Hawelka has a dark, "brooding Trotsky" atmosphere, paintings by struggling artists who couldn't pay for coffee, a saloon-wood flavor, chalkboard menu, smoked velvet couches, an international selection of newspapers, and a phone that rings for regulars. Frau Hawelka died just a couple weeks after Pope John Paul II did. Locals suspect the pontiff wanted her much-loved *Buchteln* (marmalade-filled doughnuts) in heaven. The café, which doesn't serve hot food, remains family-run (daily 8:00-24:00, just off the Graben, Dorotheergasse 6, U-1 or U-3: Stephansplatz, tel. 01/512-8230).

Other Classics in the Old Center: All of these places are open long hours daily: **Café Pruckel** (at Dr.-Karl-Lueger-Platz, across from Stadtpark at Stubenring 24); **Café Tirolerhof** (2 blocks from the Opera, behind the TI on Tegetthoffstrasse, at Führichgasse 8); and **Café Landtmann** (directly across from the City Hall on the Ringstrasse at Dr.-Karl-Lueger-Ring 4). The Landtmann is unique, as it's the only grand café built along the Ring with all the other grand buildings. **Café Sacher** and **Demel** (see page 1174) are famous for their cakes, but they also serve good coffee drinks.

Wein in Wien: Vienna's Wine Gardens

The *Heuriger* (HOY-rih-gur), a uniquely Viennese institution, dates back to the 1780s, when Emperor Josef II decreed that vintners needed no special license to serve their own wines and juices to the public in their own homes. Many families grabbed this opportunity and opened *Heurigen* (HOY-rih-gehn)—wine-garden restaurants. (The name comes from the fact that they served *heurig*—new—wine from the most recent vintage.)

A tradition was born. Today, *Heurigen* are licensed, but they do their best to maintain the old-village atmosphere, serving each fall's vintage until November 11 of the following year, when a new vintage year begins. To go with your wine, a *Heuriger* serves a variety of prepared foods that you choose from a deli counter. This is the most intimidating part of the *Heurigen* experience for tourists, but it's easily conquerable—see the sidebar for tips. Some *Heurigen* compromise by offering a regular menu that you can order from. At many establishments, strolling musicians entertain—and ask for tips.

Most *Heurigen* are decorated with enormous antique presses from their vineyards. Some places even have play zones for kids. The experience is best in good weather, but you can eat indoors too. Many places are open irregularly, closing in winter or during the grape-picking season, so call or check websites before heading out.

I've listed three good *Heuriger* neighborhoods, all on the northern outskirts of town. To get here from downtown Vienna, it's best to use public transit (cheap, 30 minutes, runs late in the evening, directions given per listing below), or take a 15-minute taxi ride from the Ring (about €15-20). Keep in mind that there are more than 1,700 acres of vineyards within Vienna's city limits and countless *Heuriger* taverns. Every Viennese has their favorite and will be only too glad to tell you about it.

Choose a neighborhood rather than a particular place. The ambience at any single *Heuriger* can change depending on that evening's clientele (locals, tour groups, workplace parties, birthdays). Each neighborhood I've described is a square or hub with two or three recommended spots and many other wine gardens worth considering. Wander around, then choose the *Heuriger* with the best atmosphere. (And for a near-*Heuriger* experience without leaving downtown Vienna, drop by Gigerl Stadtheuriger—see page 1247—which has the same deli-counter system as a *Heuriger*, but not the semirural atmosphere.)

NEUSTIFT AM WALDE

This district is farthest from the city but is still easy to reach by public transit. It feels a little less touristy than other places, and is the only one of the neighborhoods I list where you'll actually see the vineyards.

Fuhrgassl Huber, which brags it's the biggest *Heuriger* in Vienna, can accommodate 1,000 people inside and just as many outside. You can lose yourself in its sprawling backyard, with vineyards streaking up the hill from terraced tables. Musicians stroll most nights after 19:00 (open Mon-Sat 14:00-24:00, Sun 12:00-24:00, Neustift am Walde 68, tel. 01/440-1405, family Huber).

Das Schreiberhaus Heurigen-Restaurant is a popular, family-owned place right at the bus stop. Its creaky, old-time dining rooms are papered with celebrity photos. There are 600 spaces inside and another 600 outside, music nightly after 19:00 unless it's slow, and a cobbled backyard that climbs in steps up to the vineyards. Alone among my listings, this place offers a €9 all-you-can-eat lunch buffet on weekdays until 15:00 (open daily 11:00-24:00, Rathstrasse 54, tel. 01/440-3844).

Weinhof Zimmermann, a 10-minute uphill walk from the bus stop, is my favorite. It's a sprawling farmhouse where the green tables on patios echo the terraced fields all around. While dining, you'll feel like you're actually right in the vineyard. The idyllic setting comes with rabbits in petting cages, great food, no city views but lovely hillside vistas, and wonderful peace (Tue-Sat 15:00-24:00, Sun 13:00-24:00, closed Mon, tel. 01/440-1207, www.weinhof-zimmermann.at). Get off bus #35A at the Agnesgasse

The *Heuriger* Experience

To understand how a *Heuriger* works, think of a full-service pre-pared-foods counter at an American supermarket, and imagine a seating section with tables nearby.

You choose from the array of deli items and hot dishes at the counter, and the staff arranges them nicely on a plate and brings it to your table. Then a waiter appears and takes your drink order. You'll pay at the counter for your food, and pay your waiter for your drinks.

Food is generally sold by weight, often in *"10 dag"* units (that's 100 grams, or about a quarter-pound). The buffet has several sections: The core of your meal is a warm dish, generally meat (such as ham, roast beef, roast chicken, roulade, or meat loaf) carved off a big hunk. There are also warm sides *(Beilagen)*, such as casseroles and sauerkraut, and a wide variety of cold sides—various salads and spreads. Rounding out the menu are bread and cheese (they'll slice it off for you).

Unfortunately, only one of the *Heuriger* I've listed (Schübel-Auer) labels its dishes (and only in German). But many *Heuriger* staff speak English, and pointing also works. Here's a menu decoder of items to look for...or to avoid:

Aufstrich	spread
Backhühner	roasted chicken
Blunzen	black pudding (sausage made from blood)
Bohnen	big white beans
Bratlfett	gelatinous jelly made from fat drippings
Fleckerl	noodles
FleischlaberIn	fried ground-meat patties

stop (at the corner of Rathstrasse and Agnesgasse—one stop before the Neustift am Walde stop), then hike a block uphill on Agnesgasse and turn left on Mitterwurzergasse to #20.

Getting to the Neustift am Walde Heurigen: Ride bus #35A to the Neustift am Walde stop. To pick up the bus, either take tram D to Liechtenwerder Platz, or the U-6 subway to Nussdorfer Strasse.

NUSSDORF

An untouristy district, characteristic and popular with the Viennese, Nussdorf has plenty of *Heuriger* ambience. This area feels very real, with a working-class vibe, streets lined with local shops, and characteristic *Heurigen* that feel a little bit rougher around the edges.

Kartoffel	potato
Kernöl	vegetable oil
Knoblauch	garlic
Knödl	dumpling
Kornspitz	whole-meal bread roll
Krapfen	donut
Kräuter	herbs
Kren	horseradish
Kummelbraten	crispy roast pork with caraway
Lauch	leek
Leberkäse	meat loaf
Liptauer	spicy cheese spread
Presskopf	jellied brains and innards
Roastbeef	roast beef
Schinken	ham
Schinkenfleckerln	pasta with cheese and ham
Schmalz	a spread made with pig fat
Spanferkel	suckling pig
Speck	fatty bacon
Specklinsen	lentils with bacon
Stelze	grilled knuckle of pork
Sulz	gelatinous brick of meaty goo
Waldbauernflade	rustic bread
Zwiebel	onion

Pay for your food at the buffet, then find a table. Once seated, order your wine (or other drinks) from a server. A quarter-liter (*Viertel*, FEER-tehl, 8 oz) glass of new wine costs about €2-3. *Most* (mohst) is lightly alcoholic grape juice—wine in its earliest stages. Once it gets a little more oomph, it's called *Sturm* (shtoorm). Teetotalers can order *Traubenmost* (TROW-behn-mohst), grape juice.

Schübel-Auer Heuriger is my favorite here—the back entrance is right at the tram stop, and it offers a big and user-friendly buffet (most dishes are labeled, and the patient staff speaks English). Its rustic ambience can be enjoyed indoors or out (Tue-Sat 16:00-24:00, closed Sun-Mon, closed mid-Dec-mid-Feb, Kahlenberger Strasse 22, tel. 01/370-2222).

Heuriger Kierlinger, next door, is also good, with a particularly rollicking, woody room around its buffet (Mon-Sat 15:30-24:00, Sun 15:30-23:00, Kahlenberger Strasse 20, tel. 01/370-2264).

Bamkraxler ("Tree-Climber") is not a *Heuriger,* but rather a *Biergarten* with a regular menu and table service—which some prefer to the *Heuriger* cafeteria line. It's a fun-loving, family-oriented place with fine keg beer (tapped daily at 17:00) and a big kids' playground (€10-15 main courses, €7-10 wurst plates, Tue-Sat 16:00-24:00, Sun 11:00-24:00, closed Mon, open all year, Kahlenberger Strasse 17, tel. 01/318-8800). To get here from the tram, walk all the way through either of the other listings, pop out on Kahlenberger Strasse, and walk 20 yards uphill.

Getting to the Nussdorf Heurigen: Take tram #D from the Ringstrasse (stops include the Opera, Hofburg/Kunsthistorisches Museum, and City Hall) to its endpoint, the Beethovengang stop (despite what it says on the front of the tram, the Nussdorf stop isn't the end—stay on for one more stop). Exit the tram, cross the tracks, go uphill 40 yards, and look for Schübel-Auer and Kierlinger on your left.

HEILIGENSTADT (PFARRPLATZ)

A 5- to 10-minute walk from Nussdorf is Pfarrplatz, a tiny village square watched over by a church. Beethoven lived—and began work on his Ninth Symphony—here in 1817; he'd previously written his Sixth Symphony *(Pastorale)* while staying in this then-rural district. He hoped the local spa would cure his worsening deafness. (Confusingly, though Pfarrplatz is the historic center of Heiligenstadt, today the name "Heiligenstadt" is more often associated with a big train and U-Bahn station some blocks away, near the river. If you're lost, ask for Pfarrplatz.)

Mayer am Pfarrplatz (a.k.a. Beethovenhaus), right next to the church, is famous and touristy. It feels more polished compared with the other *Heurigen* I list, which is not necessarily a good thing. The inner courtyard, under cozy vines, has a California vibe and often an accordion player, and the sprawling backyard has a big children's play zone. You can order €12-18 main courses from the menu (daily 16:00-24:00 except April-Oct Sat-Sun from 12:00, Pfarrplatz 2, tel. 01/370-1287).

Weingut and Heuriger Werner Welser is a block uphill (go up Probusgasse). It's traditional, with dirndled waitresses and lederhosened waiters. It feels a bit crank-'em-out, but it's still lots of fun, with music nightly from 19:00 (open daily 15:30-24:00, Probusgasse 12, tel. 01/318-9797).

Getting to the Heiligenstadt Heurigen: Take the U-4 line to its last station, Heiligenstadt, then transfer to bus #38A. Get off at Fernsprechamt/Heiligenstadt, walk uphill for a minute or two, and take the first right onto Nestelbachgasse, which leads you to Pfarrplatz and the Beethovenhaus. You can also walk from the Nussdorf *Heuriger* (at the end station of tram #D); bring one of the free city maps to guide you.

Vienna Connections

BY TRAIN

For schedules, check Germany's excellent all-Europe timetable at www.bahn.com. Austria's own timetable at www.oebb.at includes prices, but it's not as user-friendly as the German site—and it doesn't always remind you about discounts or special passes. For general train information in Austria, call 051-717 (to get an operator, dial 2, then 2).

From Vienna by Train to: **Bratislava** (2/hour, 1 hour, alternating between Bratislava's main station and Petržalka station, or try going by bus or boat), **Salzburg** (3/hour, 2.5-3 hours), **Hallstatt** (hourly, 3.5-4 hours, last connection leaves around 15:00, change in Attnang-Puchheim), **Budapest** (every 2 hours direct on express Railjet, 3 hours, more with transfers; may be cheaper by Orange Ways bus: 2-3/day, 3 hours, www.orangeways.com), **Prague** (6/day direct, 4.75 hours; more with 1 change, 5-6 hours; 1 night train, 6 hours), **Český Krumlov** (7/day with at least one change, 4-6 hours), **Munich** (6/day direct, 4.25 hours; otherwise about hourly, 5-5.75 hours, transfer in Salzburg or Plattling), **Zürich** (nearly hourly, 9-10 hours, 1 with changes in Innsbruck and Feldkirch, night train), **Ljubljana** (1 convenient early-morning train, 6 hours; otherwise 7/day with change in Villach, Maribor, or Graz, 6-7 hours), **Zagreb** (3/day with change in Budapest or Villach, 8-9 hours, more with multiple changes), **Kraków** (3/day, 7-9 hours with 1-2 changes, plus a direct night train, 8 hours), **Warsaw** (2/day direct, plus 1 night train, 7-8.75 hours), **Rome** (3/day, 12-13 hours, plus several overnight options), **Venice** (3/day, 8-9.5 hours with changes—some may involve bus connection; plus 1 direct night train, 12 hours), **Frankfurt** (6/day direct, 7 hours; plus 1 direct night train, 10 hours), and **Paris** (7/day, 12-13 hours, 1-3 changes).

BY BOAT

High-speed boats connect Vienna to the nearby capitals of Bratislava (Slovakia) and Budapest (Hungary). While it's generally cheaper and faster to take the train—and the boat is less scenic and romantic than you might imagine—some travelers enjoy the Danube riverboat experience.

To Bratislava: The **Twin City Liner** runs 3-5 times daily from the terminal at Vienna's Schwedenplatz, where Vienna's town center hits the canal (€30-35 one-way, 1.25-hour trip downstream; U-1 or U-4: Schwedenplatz, mid-April-Oct only, can fill up—reservations smart, Austrian tel. 01/58880, www.twincityliner.com). Their main competitor, **LOD,** is a bit cheaper, but runs only twice a day at most and is less convenient—since it uses Vienna's Reichsbrücke dock on the main river, farther from the city center (€23 one-way, €38 round-trip, 1.5-hour trip downstream; Handelskai 265, U-1: Vorgartenstrasse, tel. from Austria 00-421-2-5293-2226, www.lod. sk).

To Budapest: In the summer, the Budapest-based Mahart line runs daily high-speed hydrofoils down the Danube to Budapest (€109 one-way, €125 round-trip, runs Wed, Fri, and Sun, June-Sept only). The boat leaves Vienna at 9:00 and arrives in Budapest at 14:30 (Budapest to Vienna: 9:00-15:30). In Vienna, you board at the DDSG Blue Danube dock at the Reichsbrücke (Handelskai 265, U-1: Vorgartenstrasse). To confirm times and prices, and to buy tickets, contact DDSG Blue Danube in Vienna (Austrian tel. 01/58880, www.ddsg-blue-danube.at) or Mahart in Budapest (Hungarian tel. 1/484-4013 or 1/484-4010, www. mahartpassnave.hu).

German Survival Phrases for Austria

When using the phonetics, pronounce Ī sounds like the long i in "light."

English	German	Pronunciation
Good day.	Grüss Gott.	**grews** gote
Do you speak English?	Sprechen Sie Englisch?	**shprehkh**-ehn zee **ehgn**-lish
Yes. / No.	Ja. / Nein.	yah / nīn
I (don't) understand.	Ich verstehe (nicht).	ikh fehr-**shtay**-heh (nikht)
Please.	Bitte.	**bit**-teh
Thank you.	Danke.	**dahng**-keh
I'm sorry.	Es tut mir leid.	ehs toot meer līt
Excuse me.	Entschuldigung.	ehnt-**shool**-dig-oong
(No) problem.	(Kein) Problem.	(kīn) proh-**blaym**
(Very) good.	(Sehr) gut.	(zehr) goot
Goodbye.	Auf Wiedersehen.	owf **vee**-der-zayn
one / two	eins / zwei	īns / tsvī
three / four	drei / vier	drī / feer
five / six	fünf / sechs	fewnf / zehkhs
seven / eight	sieben / acht	**zee**-behn / ahkht
nine / ten	neun / zehn	noyn / tsayn
How much is it?	Wieviel kostet das?	**vee**-feel **kohs**-teht dahs
Write it?	Schreiben?	**shrī**-behn
Is it free?	Ist es umsonst?	ist ehs oom-**zohnst**
Included?	Inklusive?	in-kloo-**zee**-veh
Where can I buy / find...?	Wo kann ich kaufen / finden...?	voh kahn ikh **kow**-fehn / **fin**-dehn
I'd like / We'd like...	Ich hätte gern / Wir hätten gern...	ikh **heh**-teh gehrn / veer **heh**-tehn gehrn
...a room.	...ein Zimmer.	īn **tsim**-mer
...a ticket to ___.	...eine Fahrkarte nach ___.	ī-neh **far**-kar-teh nahkh
Is it possible?	Ist es möglich?	ist ehs **mur**-glikh
Where is...?	Wo ist...?	voh ist
...the train station	...der Bahnhof	dehr **bahn**-hohf
...the bus station	...der Busbahnhof	dehr **boos**-bahn-hohf
...the tourist information office	...das Touristen- informations- büro	dahs too-**ris**-tehn- in-for-maht-see-**ohns**- **bew**-roh
...the toilet	...die Toilette	dee toh-**leh**-teh
men	Herren	**hehr**-rehn
women	Damen	**dah**-mehn
left / right	links / rechts	links / **rehkhts**
straight	geradeaus	geh-**rah**-deh-ows
What time does this open / close?	Um wieviel Uhr wird hier geöffnet / geschlossen?	oom **vee**-feel oor veerd heer geh-**urf**-neht / geh-**shloh**-sehn
At what time?	Um wieviel Uhr?	oom **vee**-feel oor
Just a moment.	Moment.	moh-**mehnt**
now / soon / later	jetzt / bald / später	yehtst / bahld / **shpay**-ter
today / tomorrow	heute / morgen	**hoy**-teh / **mor**-gehn

In a German / Austrian Restaurant

English	German	Pronunciation
I'd like / We'd like...	Ich hätte gern / Wir hätten gern...	ikh **heh**-teh gehrn / veer **heh**-tehn gehrn
...a reservation for...	...eine Reservierung für...	ī-neh reh-zer-**feer**-oong fewr
...a table for one / two.	...einen Tisch für eine Person / zwei Personen.	ī-nehn tish fewr ī-neh pehr- zohn / tsvī pehr-zohnehn
Non-smoking.	Nichtraucher.	**nikht**-rowkh-er
Is this seat free?	Ist hier frei?	ist heer frī
Menu (in English), please.	Speisekarte (auf Englisch), bitte.	**shpī**-zeh-kar-teh (owf **ehng**-lish) **bit**-teh
service (not) included	Trinkgeld (nicht) inklusive	**trink**-gehlt (nikht) in-kloo-**zee**-veh
cover charge	Eintritt	**īn**-trit
to go	zum Mitnehmen	tsoom **mit**-nay-mehn
with / without	mit / ohne	mit / **oh**-neh
and / or	und / oder	oont / **oh**-der
menu (of the day)	(Tages-) Karte	(**tah**-gehs-) **kar**-teh
set meal for tourists	Touristenmenü	too-**ris**-tehn-meh-**new**
specialty of the house	Spezialität des Hauses	shpayt-see-ah-lee-**tayt** dehs **how**-zehs
appetizers	Vorspeise	**for**-shpī-zeh
bread / cheese	Brot / Käse	broht / **kay**-zeh
sandwich	Sandwich	**zahnd**-vich
soup	Suppe	**zup**-peh
salad	Salat	zah-**laht**
meat	Fleisch	flīsh
poultry	Geflügel	geh-**flew**-gehl
fish	Fisch	fish
seafood	Meeresfrüchte	**meh**-rehs-**frewkh**-teh
fruit	Obst	ohpst
vegetables	Gemüse	geh-**mew**-zeh
dessert	Nachspeise	**nahkh**-shpī-zeh
mineral water	Mineralwasser	min-eh-**rahl**-vah-ser
tap water	Leitungswasser	**lī**-toongs-vah-ser
milk	Milch	milkh
(orange) juice	(Orangen-) Saft	(oh-**rahn**-zhehn-) zahft
coffee / tea	Kaffee / Tee	kah-**fay** / tay
wine	Wein	vīn
red / white	rot / weiß	roht / vīs
glass / bottle	Glas / Flasche	glahs / **flah**-sheh
beer	Bier	beer
Cheers!	Prost!	prohst
More. / Another.	Mehr. / Noch eins.	mehr / nohkh īns
The same.	Das gleiche.	dahs **glīkh**-eh
Bill, please.	Rechnung, bitte.	**rehkh**-noong **bit**-teh
tip	Trinkgeld	**trink**-gehlt
Delicious!	Lecker!	**lehk**-er

For more user-friendly German phrases, check out *Rick Steves' German Phrase Book and Dictionary* or *Rick Steves' French, Italian & German Phrase Book*.

SLOVAKIA
Slovensko

BRATISLAVA

The Slovak capital, Bratislava (brah-tee-SLAH-vah), long a drab lesson in the failings of the communist system, has become downright charming. Its old town bursts with colorfully restored facades, lively outdoor cafés, swanky boutiques, in-love-with-life locals, and (on sunny days) an almost Mediterranean ambience. The rejuvenation doesn't end in the old town. The ramshackle quarter to the east is gradually being flattened and redeveloped into a new forest of skyscrapers. The hilltop castle is getting a face-lift. And even the glum commie suburb of Petržalka is undergoing a Technicolor makeover. Bratislava and Vienna have forged a new twin-city alliance for trade and commerce, bridging Eastern and Western Europe.

You sometimes get the feeling that workaday Bratislavans—who strike some visitors as gruff—are being pulled to the cutting edge of the 21st century kicking and screaming. But many Slovaks embrace the changes and fancy themselves as the yang to Vienna's yin: If Vienna is a staid, elderly aristocrat sipping coffee, then Bratislava is a vivacious young professional jet-setting around Europe. Bratislava at night is a lively place; its very youthful center thrives. And though it has tens of thousands of university students, there are no campuses as such—so the old town is the place where students go to play.

Bratislava's priceless location—on the Danube (and the tourist circuit) smack-dab between Budapest and Vienna—makes it a very worthwhile "on the way" destination. Frankly, Bratislava used to leave me cold. But all the changes are positively inspiring.

PLANNING YOUR TIME

A few hours are plenty to get the gist of Bratislava. Head straight to the old town and follow my self-guided walk, finishing with a stroll along the Danube riverbank to the thriving, modern Eurovea development. With more time, take advantage of one or more of the city's fine viewpoints: Ascend to the "UFO" observation deck atop the funky bridge, ride the elevator up to the Sky Bar for a peek (and maybe a drink), or hike up to the castle for the views (but skip the ho-hum museum inside). If you spend the evening in Bratislava, you'll find it lively with students, busy cafés, and nightlife.

Note that all museums and galleries are closed on Monday.

Day-Tripping Tip: Bratislava can be done as a long side-trip from Budapest (or a short one from Vienna), but it's most convenient as a stopover to break up the journey between Budapest and Vienna. But pay careful attention to train schedules, as the Vienna connection alternates between Bratislava's two train stations (Hlavná Stanica and Petržalka). If checking your bag at the station, be sure that your return or onward connection will depart from there.

Orientation to Bratislava

Bratislava, with 430,000 residents, is Slovakia's capital and biggest city. It has a small, colorful old town *(staré mesto),* with the castle on the hill above. This small area is surrounded by a vast construction zone of new buildings, rotting residential districts desperately in need of beautification, and some colorized communist suburbs (including Petržalka, across the river). The northern and western parts of the city are hilly and cool (these "Little Carpathians" are draped with vineyards), while the southern and eastern areas are flat and warmer.

TOURIST INFORMATION

The helpful TI is at Klobučnícka 2, on Primate's Square behind the Old Town Hall (daily May-Sept 9:00-19:00, Oct-April 9:00-18:00, tel. 02/16186, www.visitbratislava.eu). Pick up the free *Bratislava Guide* (with map) and browse their brochures; they can help you find a room in town for a small fee. They also have a branch at the airport.

Discount Card: The TI sells the €10 Bratislava City Card, which includes free transit and sightseeing discounts for a full day—but it's worthwhile only if you're doing the old town walking tour (€14 without the card—see "Tours in Bratislava," later; also available for €12/2 days, €15/3 days).

Slovakia Almanac

Official Name: Slovenská Republika, though locals call it Slovensko. The nation is the eastern half of the former Czechoslovakia (split peaceably in 1993).

Population: 5.5 million people. The majority are native Slovaks who are Roman Catholic and speak Slovak. But one in ten has Hungarian roots ("stranded" here when Hungary lost this land after WWI), and an estimated one in ten is Roma (Gypsy). Slovakia has struggled to incorporate both of these large and often-mistreated minority groups.

Latitude and Longitude: 48°N and 19°E (similar latitude to Paris or Vancouver, BC).

Area: 19,000 square miles (the size of Massachusetts and New Hampshire combined).

Geography: The northeastern half of Slovakia features the beautiful rolling hills and spiky, jagged peaks of the Carpathian Mountains. The southwestern half is quite flat—a continuation of the Great Hungarian Plain. The climate is generally cool and cloudy.

Biggest Cities: Only two cities have more than 100,000 inhabitants: Bratislava in the west (the capital, 430,000) and Košice in the east (235,000).

Economy: The Gross Domestic Product is about $96 billion, and the GDP per capita is about $17,700 (roughly half that of the average German).

Currency: Slovakia uses the euro (€1=about $1.40). You'll find ATMs at the train stations and airport.

Government: Slovakia's mostly figurehead president, Andrej Kiska, heads a government that isn't dominated by any single political party. Slovakia also has a 150-seat National Council (like a parliament), the leader of which is the prime minister, Robert Fico.

Flag: Horizontal bands of white, blue, and red with a shield bearing a "patriarchal cross" (with two crossbars instead of one)

ARRIVAL IN BRATISLAVA
By Train

If you're choosing which of Bratislava's two train stations to use, consider this: Hlavná Stanica is far from welcoming, but it's walkable to some accommodations and the old town; Petržalka (in a suburban shopping area) is small, clean, and modern, but you'll have to take a bus into town. Frequent bus #93 connects the two stations (5-12/hour, 10 minutes; take bus #N93 after about 23:00). For public transit info and maps, see http://imhd.zoznam.sk.

Hlavná Stanica (Main Train Station): This decrepit and demoralizing station is about a half-mile north of the old town. It was still standing on my last visit...but barely. The city hopes to tear it down and start from scratch. If those plans go forward,

atop three humps. The three humps represent three historic mountain ranges of Slovakia: Mátra (now in northern Hungary, near Eger), Fatra, and Tatra. The double-barred cross represents St. Stephen (István) of Hungary, commemorating the many centuries that Slovakia was part of Hungary.

Cuisine: Today's Slovak cooking shows some Hungarian and Austrian influences, but it's closer to Czech—lots of starches and gravy, and plenty of pork, cabbage, potatoes, and dumplings. Keep an eye out for Slovakia's national dish, *bryndzové halušky* (small potato dumplings with sheep's cheese and bits of bacon).

Language: The official language is Slovak, which is closely related to Czech and Polish—although many Bratislavans also speak English. The local word used informally for both "hi" and "bye" is easy to remember: *ahoj* (pronounced "AH-hoy," like a pirate). "Please" is *prosím* (PROH-seem), "thank you" is *ďakujem* (DYAH-koo-yehm), "good" is *dobrý* (DOH-bree), and "Cheers!" is *Na zdravie!* (nah ZDRAH-vyeh).

Slovaks You May Recognize: Andy Warhol (American Pop artist who gained more than his 15 minutes of fame, born to Slovak immigrants), **Martina Hingis** (Swiss tennis player born in Slovakia), film director **Ivan Reitman** (*Ghostbusters*, *Stripes*; born in Slovakia to Jewish Holocaust survivors), actor **Paul Newman** (whose mother was born in Slovakia), **Tomáš Garrigue Masaryk** (founder of Czechoslovakia, whose father was Slovak), **Alexander Dubček** (leader of the 1968 Prague Spring uprising), and **Štefan Banič** (emigrated to America and invented the parachute).

these arrival instructions could also become obsolete.

As you emerge from the tracks, the left-luggage desk is to your right (€2-2.50, depending on weight; look for *úschovňa batožín*; reconfirm open hours at the desk so you'll be able to get your bags when you need them). There are also a few €2 lockers along track 1.

Getting from the Station to Downtown: It's a 15-minute **walk** to the town center. Walk out the station's front door and follow the covered walkway next to the looped bus drive; it will bend right and lead to a double pedestrian overpass. Cross the near arch and head downhill on the busy main drag, Štefánikova (named for politician Milan Štefánik, who worked for the post-WWI creation

Welcome to Slovakia

In many ways, Slovakia is the "West Virginia of Europe"—relatively poor and undeveloped, but spectacularly beautiful in its own rustic way. Sitting quietly in the very center of Central Europe, wedged between bigger and stronger nations (Hungary, Austria, the Czech Republic, and Poland), Slovakia was brutally disfigured by the communists, then overshadowed by the Czechs. But in recent years, this fledgling republic has found its wings.

Recent economic reforms have caused two very different Slovakias to emerge: the modern, industrialized, flat, affluent west, centered on the capital of Bratislava; and the remote, poorer, mountainous, "backward" east, with high unemployment and traditional lifestyles.

Slovakia has spent most of its history as someone else's backyard. For centuries, Slovakia was ruled from Budapest and known as "Upper Hungary." At other times, it was an important chunk of the Habsburg Empire, ruled from neighboring Vienna. But most people think first of another era: the 75 years that Slovakia was joined with the Czech Republic as the country of "Czechoslovakia." From its start in the aftermath of World War I, this union of the Czechs and Slovaks was troubled; some Slovaks chafed at being ruled from Prague, while many Czechs resented the financial burden of their poorer neighbors to the east.

After they gained their freedom from the communists during 1989's peaceful "Velvet Revolution," the Czechs and Slovaks began to think of the future. The Slovaks wanted to rename the country Czecho-Slovakia, and to redistribute power to give themselves more autonomy within the union. The Czechs balked, relations gradually deteriorated, and the Slovak nationalist candidate Vladimír Mečiar fared surprisingly well in the 1992 elections. Taking it as a sign that the two peoples wanted to part ways, politicians pushed through (in just three months) the

of Czechoslovakia). This once-elegant old boulevard is lined with Habsburg-era facades—some renovated, some rotting. In a few minutes, you'll pass the nicely manicured presidential gardens on your left. Next comes the Grassalkovich Palace, Slovakia's "White House" (with soldiers at guard out front), which faces the busy intersection called Hodžovo Námestie. The old town is just a long block ahead of you now. You can cross the intersection at street level or find the stairs and escalators down to the underground passageway *(podchod)*. Head for the green steeple with an onion-shaped midsection. This is St. Michael's Gate, at the start of the old town (and the beginning of my self-guided walk, described later).

To shave a few minutes off the trip, go part of the way by **bus** #93 or #X13 (after 23:00, use bus #N93). Walk out the station's front door to the line of bus stops to the right. Buy a 15-minute peaceful separation of the now-independent Czech and Slovak Republics. (The people in both countries never actually voted on the change, and most opposed it.) The "Velvet Divorce" became official on January 1, 1993.

At first the Slovaks struggled. Communist rule had been particularly unkind to them, and their economy was in a shambles. Visionary leaders set forth bold solutions, including the 2003 implementation of a flat tax (19 percent), followed by EU membership in 2004. Before long, major international corporations began to notice the same thing the communists had: This is a great place to build stuff, thanks to a strategic location (300 million consumers live within a day's truck drive), low labor costs, and a well-trained workforce. Not surprisingly, multiple foreign automakers have plants here. Today Slovakia produces one million cars a year, making the country the world's biggest car producer (per capita) and leading the *New York Times* to dub Slovakia "the European Detroit."

The flat tax and other aggressively pro-business policies have not been without their critics—especially in the very impoverished eastern half of the country, where poor people feel they're becoming even poorer. With the rollback of social services and the proverbial cracks widening, many seem to have been left behind by Slovakia's bold new economy.

Even so, particularly if you zoom in on its success story around Bratislava, the evidence is impressive. Bratislava has only 3 percent unemployment. The standard of living (as it relates to local costs) puts Bratislava in 10th place among European cities. Slovakia joined the EU in 2004; in 2009, it adopted the euro currency. While most of Europe is struggling through difficult economic times, much of Slovakia seems poised for its brightest future yet.

ticket from the machines for €0.70 (select *základný lístok—platí 15 minút*, then insert coins—change given). Ride two stops to Hodžovo Námestie, across from Grassalkovich Palace, then walk straight ahead toward the green steeple, passing a pink-and-white church.

Tram #13 is another option from the station, if it's running again (the tracks have been closed for construction). Trams *(električky)* use the same tickets as buses; ride to the Poštová stop, then walk straight down Obchodná street toward St. Michael's Gate.

Petržalka Train Station (ŽST Petržalka): Half of the trains from Vienna arrive at this small, quiet train station, across the river in the modern suburb of Petržalka (PET-ur-ZHAL-kuh). From this station, ride bus #93 (direction: Hlavná Stanica) or #94 (direction: STU) four stops to Zochova (the first stop after the bridge, near St. Michael's Gate); after 23:00, use bus #N93. Buy a €0.70/15-minute *základný lístok* ticket (described earlier).

By Bus, Boat, or Plane

For information on Bratislava's buses, riverboats, and airport, see "Bratislava Connections," at the end of this chapter.

HELPFUL HINTS

Internet Access: Free Wi-Fi hotspots are at the three major old town squares (Main Square, Primate's Square, and Hviezdoslav Square). You'll see signs advertising computer terminals around the old town.

Local Guidebook: For in-depth suggestions on Bratislava sightseeing, dining, and more, look for the excellent and eye-pleasing *Bratislava Active* guidebook by Martin Sloboda (see "Tours in Bratislava," next; around €10, sold at every postcard rack).

Toll Sticker: Slovakia requires cars on its expressways to display a toll sticker (*úhrada*, €10/10 days, €14/month, www.dialnicnenalepky.sk). If your car doesn't have one, buy one at a gas station when you cross the border.

Tours in Bratislava

Walking Tours

The TI offers a one-hour old town walking tour in English every day in the summer at 14:00 (€14, free with €10 Bratislava City Card; book and pay at least two hours in advance). Those arriving by boat will be accosted by guides selling their own 1.5-hour tours (half on foot and half in a little tourist train, €10, in German and English).

Local Guide

MS Agency, run by **Martin Sloboda** (a can-do entrepreneur and tireless Bratislava booster, and author of the great local guidebook described earlier), can set you up with a good guide (€130/3 hours, €150/4 hours); he can also help you track down your Slovak roots. Martin, who helped me put this chapter together, is part of the generation that came of age as communism fell and whose energy and leadership are reshaping the city (mobile 0905-627-265, www.msagency.sk, sloboda@msagency.sk).

Bratislava Old Town Walk

This self-guided orientation walk passes through the heart of delightfully traffic-free old Bratislava and then down to its riverside commercial zone (figure 1.5 hours, not including stops, for this walk). If you're coming from the station, make your way toward the green steeple of St. Michael's Gate (explained in "Arrival in Bratislava," earlier). Before going through the passage into the old town, peek over the railing on your left to the inviting garden below—once part of the city moat.

BRATISLAVA

• *Step through the first, smaller gate, walk along the passageway, and pause as you come through the green-steepled...*

St. Michael's Gate (Michalská Brána)

This is the last surviving tower of the city wall. Just below the gate, notice the "kilometer zero" plaque in the ground, marking the point from which distances in Slovakia are measured.

• *You're at the head of...*

Michalská Street

Pretty as it is now, the old center was a decrepit ghost town during the communist era, partly because WWII bombing left Bratislava a damaged husk. The communist regime believed that Bratislavans of the future would live in large, efficient apartment buildings. They saw the old town as a useless relic of the bad old days of poor plumbing, cramped living spaces, social injustice, and German domination—a view that left no room to respect the town's heritage. In the 1950s, they actually sold Bratislava's original medieval cobbles to cute German towns that were rebuilding themselves with elegant Old World character. Locals avoided this desolate corner of the city, preferring to spend time in the Petržalka suburb across the river.

With the fall of communism in 1989, the new government began a nearly decade-long process of restitution—sorting out who had the rights to the buildings, and returning them to their original owners. During this time, little repair or development took place (since there was no point investing in a property until ownership was clearly established). By 1998, most of these property issues had been sorted out, and the old town was made traffic-free. The city replaced all the street cobbles, spruced up the public

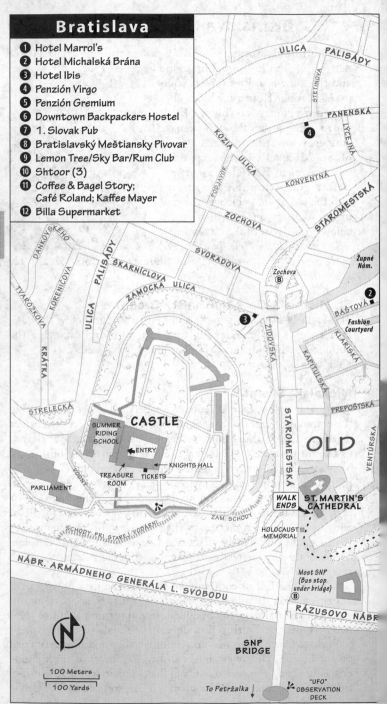

Bratislava

1. Hotel Marrol's
2. Hotel Michalská Brána
3. Hotel Ibis
4. Penzión Virgo
5. Penzión Gremium
6. Downtown Backpackers Hostel
7. 1. Slovak Pub
8. Bratislavský Meštiansky Pivovar
9. Lemon Tree/Sky Bar/Rum Club
10. Shtoor (3)
11. Coffee & Bagel Story;
    Café Roland; Kaffee Mayer
12. Billa Supermarket

BRATISLAVA

ULICA PALISÁDY

ŠTETINOVA

PANENSKÁ

LYCEJNÁ

KOZIA ULICA

PODJAVOR

KONVENTNÁ

STAROMESTSKÁ

DANKOVSKÉHO

KORENICOVA

ULICA PALISÁDY

ŠKARNICLOVA

ZÁMOCKÁ ULICA

ZOCHOVA

SVORADOVA

Župné Nám.

Zochova
B

Fashion
Courtyard

BAŠTOVÁ

KLARISKÁ

KAPITULSKÁ

PREPOŠTSKÁ

TVARÓŽKOVA

KRÁTKA

STRELECKÁ

ŽIDOVSKÁ

STAROMESTSKÁ

VENTÚRSKA

CASTLE

SUMMER
RIDING
SCHOOL

ENTRY

KNIGHTS HALL

TREASURE
ROOM

TICKETS

OLD

VODNÝ

PARLIAMENT

WALK
ENDS

ST. MARTIN'S
CATHEDRAL

HOLOCAUST
MEMORIAL

ZAM. SCHODY

SCHODY PRI STAREJ VODÁRNI

NÁBR. ARMÁDNEHO GENERÁLA L. SVOBODU

Most SNP
(Bus stop
under bridge)

RÁZUSOVO NÁBR.

100 Meters

100 Yards

SNP
BRIDGE

To Petržalka

"UFO"
OBSERVATION
DECK

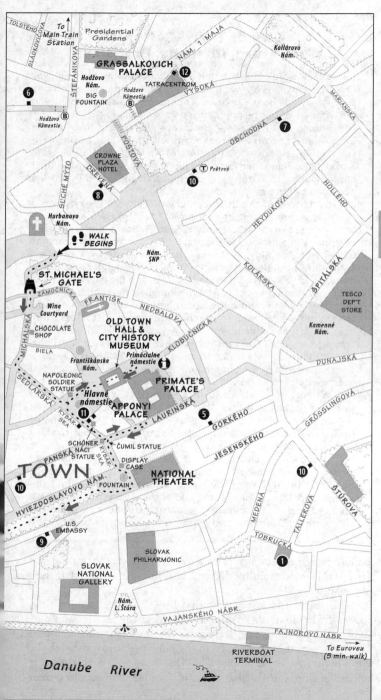

City of Three Cultures:
Pressburg, Pozsony, Bratislava

Historically more of an Austrian and Hungarian city than a Slovak one, Bratislava has always been a Central European melting pot. Everyone from Hans Christian Andersen to Casanova has sung the wonders of this bustling burg on the Danube.

For most of its history, Bratislava was part of the Austrian Empire and known as Pressburg, with a primarily German-speaking population. (Only the surrounding rural areas were Slovak.) The Hungarians used Pozsony (as they called it) as their capital during the century and a half that Buda and Pest were occupied by Ottoman invaders.

By its turn-of-the-20th-century glory days, the city was a rich intersection of cultures—about 40 percent German, 40 percent Hungarian, and 20 percent Slovak. Shop clerks greeted customers in all three languages. It was said that the mornings belonged to the Slovaks (farmers who came into the city to sell their wares at market), the afternoons to the Hungarians (diplomats and office workers filling the cafés), and the evenings to the Austrians (wine producers who ran convivial neighborhood wine pubs where all three groups would gather). In those wine pubs, the vintner would listen to which language his customers used, then bring them a glass with the serving size expected in their home country: 0.3 liters for Hungarians, 0.25 liters for Austrians, and 0.2 liters for Slovaks (a distinction that still exists today). Jews (one-tenth of the population), and Roma (Gypsies) rounded out the city's ethnic brew.

When the new nation of Czechoslovakia was formed from the rubble of World War I, the city shed its German and Hungarian names and took the newly created Slavic name of Bratislava. The Slovak population was on the rise, but the city remained tricultural.

World War II changed all of that. With the dissolution of Czechoslovakia, Slovakia became an "independent" country under the thumb of the Nazis—who all but wiped out the Jewish population. Then, at the end of the war, a Czechoslovakia reunited under the Soviet Russian thumb rudely expelled the city's ethnic Germans and Hungarians in retribution for the

buildings, and encouraged private owners to restore their property. (If you see any remaining decrepit buildings, it's likely that their ownership is still in dispute.)

The cafés and restaurants that line this street are inviting, especially in summer. Poke around behind the facades and outdoor tables to experience Bratislava's charm. Courtyards and passageways—most of them open to the public—burrow through the city's buildings. For example, a half-block down Michalská street on the left, the courtyard at #12 was once home to vintners; their misdeeds of Hitler and Horthy (Hungary's wartime leader).

Bratislava's urban heritage suffered terribly under the communists. The historic city's multilayered charm and delicate cultural fabric were ripped apart, then shrouded in gray. The communists were prouder of their ultramodern SNP Bridge than of the city's historic Jewish quarter—which they razed to make way for the bridge. Now the bridge and its highway slice through the center of the old town, and the heavy traffic rattles the stained glass windows of St. Martin's Cathedral. Similarly, the city's Germanic heritage was deliberately obscured.

But Bratislava's most recent chapter is one of great success. Since the fall of communism, the city has gone from gloomy victim to thriving economic center and social hub. With a healthy market economy, it now has the chance to re-create itself as Slovakia's national capital. Its population of about 430,000 includes some 60,000 students (at the city's six universities), creating an atmosphere of youthful energy and optimism. Its remarkable position on the Danube, a short commute from Vienna, is prompting its redevelopment as one of Europe's up-and-coming cities.

Bratislava and Vienna have realized that it's mutually beneficial to work together to bring the Slovak capital up to snuff. They're cooperating in a new "twin city" commerce superzone. In the coming years, foreign investors talk of erecting a Bratislavan skyline of 600-foot-tall skyscrapers and a clutch of glittering megamalls. Bratislavans also have high hopes for revitalizing the city's transport infrastructure: The highway that barrels between the old town and the castle will be diverted underground (through a tunnel beneath the Danube); a bullet train will swoosh to a stop at a slick modern train station; a new six-station subway line will lace the city together; and the entire riverfront will be transformed into a people-friendly park.

As the city pulls funding together, expect lots of construction during your visit. You'd never have guessed it a few years ago, but today calling Bratislava "the next Berlin on a smaller scale" is only a bit of a stretch.

BRATISLAVA

former cellars are now coffee shops, massage parlors, crafts boutiques, and cigar shops. Across the street, on the right, the dead-end passage at #5 has an antique shop and small café, while #7 is home to a fashion design shop.

On the left (at #6), the **Cukráreň na Korze** chocolate shop is highly regarded among locals for its delicious hot chocolate and creamy truffles (Mon-Thu 9:00-21:00, Fri-Sat 9:00-22:00, Sun 10:00-21:00, tel. 02/5443-3945).

Above the shop's entrance, the **cannonball** embedded in the wall recalls Napoleon's two sieges of Bratislava (the 1809 siege was 42 days long), which caused massive suffering—even worse than during World War II. Keep an eye out for these cannonballs all over town...somber reminders of one of Bratislava's darkest times.

• *Two blocks down from St. Michael's Gate, where the street jogs slightly right (and its name changes to Ventúrska), detour left along Sedlárska street and head to the...*

Main Square (Hlavné Námestie)

A modest town hall square that feels too petite for a national capital, this is the centerpiece of Old World Bratislava. Cute little kiosks, with old-time cityscape engravings on their roofs, sell local handicrafts and knickknacks (Easter through October). Similar stalls fill the square from mid-November until December 23, when the Christmas market here is a big draw (www.vianocnetrhy. sk).

Virtually every building around this square dates from a different architectural period, from Gothic (the yellow tower) to Art Nouveau (the fancy facade facing it from across the square).

Cafés line the square. You can't go wrong here. Choose the ambience you like best (indoors or out) and sip a drink with Slovakia's best urban view. The Art Nouveau **Café Roland,** once a bank, is known for its 1904 Klimt-style mosaics and historic photos of the days when the city was known as Pressburg (Austrian times) or Pozsony (Hungarian times). The barista stands where a different kind of bean counter once did, guarding a vault that now holds coffee (Hlavné Námestie 5; the café may have a new name by the time you visit). The classic choice is the kitty-corner **Kaffee Mayer.** This venerable café, an institution here, has

been selling coffee and cakes to a genteel clientele since 1873. You can enjoy your pick-me-up in the swanky old interior or out on the square (€3-3.50 cakes, small selection of expensive-for-Bratislava hot meals, daily 9:30-22:00, Fri-Sat until 23:00, Hlavné Námestie 4, tel. 02/5441-1741).

Peering over one of the benches on the square is a cartoonish statue of a **Napoleonic officer** (notice the French flag marking the embassy right behind him). With bare feet and a hat pulled over his eyes, it's hardly a flattering portrait—you could call it the locals' revenge for Napoleon's sieges. Across the square, another soldier from that period stands at attention.

At the top of the Main Square is the impressive **Old Town Hall** (Stará Radnica), with its bold yellow tower. Near the bottom of the tower (to the left of the window), notice another cannonball embedded in the facade—yet another reminder of Napoleon's impact on Bratislava. Over time, the Old Town Hall grew, annexing the buildings next to it and creating a mishmash of architectural styles along this side of the square. (A few steps down the street to the right are the historic apartments and wine museum at the **Apponyi House**—described later, under "Sights in Bratislava.")

Step through the passageway into the Old Town Hall's gorgeously restored **courtyard,** with its Renaissance arcades. (The **City History Museum**'s entrance is here—described later.)

Then, to see another fine old square, continue through the other end of the courtyard into **Primate's Square** (Primaciálne Námestie). The pink mansion on the right is the **Primate's Palace,** with a fine interior decorated with six English tapestries (described later). At the far end of this square is the **TI.**

• *Backtrack to the Main Square. With your back to the Old Town Hall, go to the end of the square and follow the street to the left (Rybárska Brána). On your way you'll pass a pair of...*

Whimsical Statues

Playful statues (such as the Napoleonic officer we met earlier) dot Bratislava's old town. Most date from the late 1990s, when city leaders wanted to entice locals back into the newly prettied-up center.

Just at the beginning of the street, as you exit the main square,

you'll come to a jovial chap doffing his top hat. This is a statue of **Schöner Náci,** who lived in Bratislava until the 1960s. This eccentric old man, a poor carpet cleaner, would dress up in his one black suit and top hat, and go strolling through the city, offering gifts to the women he fancied. (He'd often whisper *"schön"*—German for "pretty," which is how he got his nickname.) Schöner Náci now gets to spend eternity greeting visitors outside his favorite café, Kaffee Mayer. Once he lost an arm when a bunch of drunks broke it off. (It was replaced.) As Prague gets more expensive, Bratislava has become one of the cheaper alternatives for weekend "stag parties," popular with Brits lured here by cheap flights and cheap beer.

• *Continue down Rybárska.*

At the end of this block, at the intersection with Panská, watch out on the right for **Čumil** ("the Peeper"), grinning at passersby from a manhole. This was the first, and is still the favorite, of Bratislava's statues. There's no story behind this one—the artist simply wanted to create a fun icon and let the townspeople make up their own tales. Čumil has survived being driven over by a truck—twice—and he's still grinning.

• *Keep along Rybárska to reach the long, skinny square called...*

Hviezdoslav Square (Hviezdoslavovo Námestie)

The landscaping in the center of this square makes it particularly inviting. At the near end is the impressive, silver-topped

Slovak National Theater (Slovenské Národné Divadlo). Beyond that, the opulent yellow Neo-Baroque building is the Slovak Philharmonic (Slovenská Filharmónia). When the theater opened in the 1880s, half the shows were in German and half in Hungarian. Today, it's a proud Slovak institution—typical of the ethnic changes that have marked this city's life.

Right in front of the theater (by the McDonald's), look down into the glass **display case** to see the foundation of the one-time Fishermen's Gate into the city. Surrounding the base of the gate is water. This entire square was once a tributary of the Danube, and the Carlton Hotel across the way was a series of inns on different islands. The buildings along the old town side of the square mark where the city wall once stood. Now the square is a lively zone on balmy evenings, with several good restaurants (including some splurgy steakhouses) offering al fresco tables jammed with visiting European businessmen looking for good-quality, expense-account meals.

Stroll down the long art-and-people-filled square. Each summer, as part of an arts festival, it's ornamented with entertaining modern art. After passing a statue of the square's namesake (Pavol Országh Hviezdoslav, a beloved Slovak poet), you'll come upon an ugly fence and barriers on the left, which mark the fortified US Embassy. Just past the embassy is the low-profile entrance to the **Sky Bar,** an affordable rooftop restaurant with excellent views (ride elevator to seventh floor; see "Eating in Bratislava," later). Farther along, after the giant chessboard, the glass pavilion is a popular venue for summer concerts. On the right, near the end of the park, a statue of Hans Christian Andersen is a reminder that the Danish storyteller enjoyed his visit to Bratislava, too.

• *Reaching the end of the square, you run into the barrier for a busy highway. Turn right and walk one block to find the big, black marble slab facing a modern monument—and, likely, a colorful wooden reconstruction of a synagogue.*

Holocaust Memorial

This was the site of Bratislava's original synagogue. You can see an etching of the building in the big slab.

Turn your attention to the memorial. The word "Remember" carved into the base in Hebrew and Slovak commemorates the 90,000 Slovak Jews who were deported to Nazi death camps. Nearly all were killed. The fact that the town's main synagogue and main church (to the right) were located side by side illustrates the tolerance that characterized Bratislava before Hitler. Ponder the modern statue: The two pages of an open book, faces, hands in the sky, and bullets—all under the Star of David—evoke the fate of 90 percent of the Slovak Jews.

• *Now head toward the adjacent church, up the stairs.*

St. Martin's Cathedral (Dóm Sv. Martina)

If the highway thundering a few feet in front of this historic church's door were any closer, the off-ramp would go through the

nave. Sad as it is now, the cathedral has been party to some pretty important history. While Buda and Pest were occupied by Ottomans from 1543 to 1689, Bratislava was the capital of Hungary. Nineteen Hungarian kings and queens were crowned in this church— more than have been crowned anywhere in Hungary. In fact, the last Hungarian coronation (not counting the Austrian Franz Josef) was not in Budapest, but in Bratislava. A replica of the Hungarian crown still tops the steeple.

It's worth walking up to the cathedral's entrance to observe some fragments of times past (circle around the building, along the busy road, to the opposite, uphill side). Directly across from the church door is a broken bit of the 15th-century town wall. The church was actually built into the wall, which explains its unusual north-side entry. In fact, notice the fortified watchtower (with a WC drop on its left) built into the corner of the church just above you.

BRATISLAVA

There's relatively little to see inside the cathedral—I'd skip it (€2, Mon-Sat 9:00-11:30 & 13:00-18:00, Sun 13:30-16:00). If you do duck in, you'll find a fairly gloomy interior, some fine carved-wood altarpieces (a Slovak specialty), a dank crypt, a replica of the Hungarian crown, and a treasury in the back with a whimsical wood carving of Jesus blessing Habsburg Emperor Franz Josef.

Head back around the church for a good view (looking toward the river) of the huge bridge called **Most SNP,** the communists' pride and joy (the "SNP" stands for the Slovak National Uprising of 1944 against the Nazis, a typi-cal focus of communist remem-brance). As with most Soviet-era landmarks in former communist countries, locals aren't crazy about this structure—not only for the questionable starship *Enterprise*

design, but also because of the oppressive regime it represented. However, the restaurant and observation deck up top have been renovated into a posh eatery called (appropriately enough) "UFO." You can visit it for the views, a drink, or a full meal.

• *You could end the walk here. Two sights (both described later, under "Sights in Bratislava") are nearby. To hike up to the* **castle,** *take the underpass beneath the highway, go up the stairs on the right marked by the* Hrad/Castle *sign, then turn left up the stepped lane marked* Zámocké Schody. *Or hike over the SNP Bridge (pedestrian walkway on lower level) to ride the elevator up to the* **UFO** *viewing platform.*

*But to really round out your Bratislava visit, head for the river and stroll downstream (left) to a place where you get a dose of modern development in Bratislava—***Eurovea.*** *Walk about 10 minutes down-stream, past the old town and boat terminals, until you come to a big, slick complex with a grassy park leading down to the riverbank.*

Eurovea

Just downstream from the old town is the futuristic Eurovea, with four vibrant layers, each a quarter-mile long: a riverside park, luxury condos, a thriving modern shopping mall, and an office

park. Walking out onto the view piers jutting into the Danube and survey-ing the scene, it looks like a computer-generated urban dreamscape come true. Exploring the old town gave you a taste of where this country has been. But wandering this riverside park, enjoying a drink in one of its chic outdoor lounges, and then browsing through the thriving mall, you'll enjoy a glimpse of where Slovakia is heading.

• *Our walk is finished. If you haven't already visited them, consider circling back to some of the sights described next.*

Sights in Bratislava

If Europe had a prize for "capital city with the most underwhelming museums," I'd cast my vote for Bratislava. You can easily have a great day here without setting foot in a museum. Focus instead on Bratislava's street life and the grand views from the castle and UFO restaurant. If it's rainy or you're in a museum-going mood, the Primate's Palace (with its cheap admission and fine tapestries) ranks slightly above the rest.

ON OR NEAR THE OLD TOWN'S MAIN SQUARE

These museums are all within a few minutes' walk of one another, on or very near the Main Square.

▲Primate's Palace (Primaciálny Palác)

Bratislava's most interesting museum, this tastefully restored French-Neoclassical mansion (formerly the residence of the arch-

bishop, or "primate") dates from 1781. The religious counterpart of the castle, it filled in for Esztergom—the Hungarian religious capital—after that city was taken by the Ottomans in 1543. Even after the Ottoman defeat in the 1680s, this remained the winter residence of Hungary's archbishops.

Cost and Hours: €3, Tue-Fri 10:00-17:00, Sat-Sun 11:00-18:00, closed Mon, Primaciálne Námestie 1, tel. 02/5935-6394, www.bratislava.sk.

Visiting the Museum: The palace, which now serves as a government building, features one floor of fine exhibits. Follow signs for *Expozícia* up the grand staircase to the ticket counter. There are three main attractions: the Mirror Hall, the tapestries, and the archbishop's chapel.

The **Mirror Hall,** used for concerts, city council meetings, and other important events, is to the left as you enter and worth a glance (if it's not closed for an event).

A series of large public rooms, originally designed to impress, are now an art gallery. Distributed through several of these rooms is the museum's pride, and for many its highlight: a series of six English **tapestries,** illustrating the ancient Greek myth of the tragic love between Hero and Leander. The tapestries were woven in England by Flemish weavers for the court of King Charles I (in the 1630s). They were kept in London's Hampton Court Palace until Charles was deposed and beheaded in 1649. Cromwell sold them to France to help fund his civil war, but after 1650, they disappeared. Centuries later, in 1903, restorers broke through a false wall in this mansion and discovered the six tapestries, neatly folded and perfectly preserved. Nobody knows how they got there (perhaps they were squirreled away during the Napoleonic invasion, and whoever hid them didn't survive). The archbishop—who had just sold the palace to the city, but emptied it of furniture before he left—cried foul and tried to get the tapestries back...but the city said, "A deal's a deal."

After traipsing through the grand rooms, find the hallway that leads through the smaller rooms of the archbishop's private quarters, now decorated with minor Dutch, Flemish, German, and Italian paintings. At the end of this hall, a bay window looks down into the archbishop's own private marble **chapel.** When the archbishop became too ill to walk down to Mass, this window was built for him to take part in the service.

On your way back to the entry, pause at the head of the larger corridor to study a 1900 view of the then-much-smaller town by Gustáv Keleti. The museum's entry hall also has grand portraits of Maria Theresa and Josef II.

City History Museum (Mestské Múzeum)

Delving into the bric-a-brac of Bratislava's past, this museum includes ecclesiastical art on the ground floor and a sprawling, chronological look at local history upstairs. The displays occupy rooms once used by the town council—courthouse, council hall, chapel, and so on. Everything is described in English, and the included audioguide tries hard, but nothing quite succeeds in bringing meaning to the place. On your way upstairs, you'll have a chance to climb up into the Old Town Hall's tower, offering so-so views over the square, cathedral, and castle.

Cost and Hours: €5, includes audioguide, €6 combo-ticket with Apponyi House, Tue-Fri 10:00-17:00, Sat-Sun 11:00-18:00, closed Mon, last entry 30 minutes before closing, in the Old Town Hall—enter through courtyard, tel. 02/5920-5130, www.muzeum.bratislava.sk.

Apponyi House (Apponyiho Palác)

This nicely restored mansion of a Hungarian aristocrat is meaningless without the included audioguide (dull but informative). The museum has two parts. The cellar and ground floor feature an interesting exhibit on the vineyards of the nearby "Little Carpathian" hills, with historic presses and barrels, and a replica of an old-time wine-pub table. Upstairs are two floors of urban apartments from old Bratislava, called the Period Rooms Museum. The first floor up shows off the 18th-century Rococo-style rooms of the nobility—fine but not ostentatious, with ceramic stoves. The second floor up (with lower ceilings and simpler wall decorations) illustrates 19th-century bourgeois/middle-class lifestyles, including period clothing and some Empire-style furniture.

Cost and Hours: €4, includes audioguide, €6 combo-ticket with City History Museum, Tue-Fri 10:00-17:00, Sat-Sun 11:00-18:00, closed Mon, last entry 30 minutes before closing, Radničná 1, tel. 02/5920-5135, www.muzeum.bratislava.sk.

BEYOND THE OLD TOWN
Bratislava Castle (Bratislavský Hrad)

This imposing fortress, nicknamed the "upside-down table," is the city's most prominent landmark. The oldest surviving chunk is the 13th-century Romanesque watchtower (the one slightly taller than the other three). When Habsburg Empress Maria Theresa took a liking to Bratislava in the 18th century, she transformed the castle from a military fortress to a royal residence suitable for holding

court. She added a summer riding school (the U-shaped complex next to the castle), an enclosed winter riding school out back, and lots more. Maria Theresa's favorite daughter, Maria Christina, lived here with her husband, Albert, when they were newlyweds. Locals nicknamed the place "little Schönbrunn," in reference to the Habsburgs' summer palace on the outskirts of Vienna.

Turned into a fortress-garrison during the Napoleonic Wars, the castle burned to the ground in an 1811 fire started by careless soldiers, and was left as a ruin for 150 years before being recon-

structed in 1953. Unfortunately, the communist rebuild was drab and uninviting; the inner courtyard feels like a prison exercise yard.

A more recent renovation has done little to improve things, and the museum exhibits inside aren't really worth the cost of admission (described next). The best visit is to simply hike up (it's free to enter the grounds), enjoy the views over town, and take a close-up look at the stately old building (the big, blocky, modern building next door is the Slovak Parliament).

For details on the best walking route to the castle, see page 1282.

Castle Museum

The newly restored castle has a few sights inside, with more likely to open in the future. Two small exhibits are skippable: the mis-named **Treasure Room** (a sparse collection of items found at the castle site, including coins and fragments of Roman jugs) and the **Knights Hall** (offering a brief history lesson in the castle's construction and reconstruction). You can also enter the **palace** itself. A blinding-white staircase with gold trim leads to the Music Hall, with a prized 18th-century *Assumption* altarpiece by Anton Schmidt (first floor); a collection of historical prints depicting Bratislava and its castle (second floor); and temporary exhibits (third/top floor). From the top floor, a series of very steep, modern staircases take you up to the Crown Tower (the castle's oldest and tallest) for views over town—though the vista from the terrace in front of the castle is much easier to reach and nearly as good.

Cost and Hours: €6 all-inclusive "Road A" ticket, €2 for pointless "Road B" ticket (covers only the less interesting parts of palace—the Treasure Room and Knights Hall); Tue-Sun 10:00-18:00, closed Mon; ticket office is right of main riverfront entrance—enter exhibits from passage into central courtyard, tel. 02/2048-3110, www.snm.sk.

▲▲The SNP Bridge and UFO

Bratislava's bizarre, flying-saucer-capped bridge, completed in 1972 in heavy-handed communist style, has been reclaimed by capitalists. The flying saucer-shaped struc-ture called the UFO (at the Petržalka end of the bridge) is now a spruced-up, over-priced café/restaurant and observation deck, allowing sweeping 360-degree views of Bratislava from about 300 feet above the Danube. Think of it as the Slovak Space Needle.

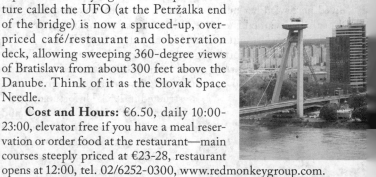

Cost and Hours: €6.50, daily 10:00-23:00, elevator free if you have a meal reser-vation or order food at the restaurant—main courses steeply priced at €23-28, restaurant opens at 12:00, tel. 02/6252-0300, www.redmonkeygroup.com.

Getting There: The elevator entrance is underneath the tower. Walk across the bridge from the old town (there are pedestrian walkways on the lower level). If you take the downstream (old-town side) walkway, you'll pass historical photos of the bridge's construction, including the demolition of the city's synagogue and other old town buildings.

◒ Self-Guided Tour: The **"elevator"** that takes you up is actually a funicular—you'll notice you're moving at an angle. At the top, walk up the stairs to the observation deck.

Begin by viewing the **castle** and **old town.** The area to the right of the old town, between and beyond the skyscrapers, is a massive construction zone. A time-lapse camera set up here over the next few years would catch skyscrapers popping up like dandelions. International investors are  throwing lots of money at Bratislava. (Imagine having so much prime, undeveloped real estate available downtown in the capital of an emerging European economic power...and just an hour down the road from Vienna, no less.) Most of the development is taking place along the banks of the Danube. In a decade, this will be a commercial center.

The huge TV tower caps a forested hill beyond the old town. Below and to the left of it, the pointy monument is **Slavín,** where more than 6,800 Soviet soldiers who fought to liberate Bratislava from the Nazis are buried. Under communist rule, a nearby church was forced to take down its steeple so as not to draw attention away from the huge Soviet soldier on top of the monument.

Now turn 180 degrees and cross the platform to face **Petržalka,** a planned communist suburb that sprouted here in the  1970s. The site was once occupied by a village, and the various districts of modern Petržalka still carry their original names (which now seem ironic): "Meadows" *(Háje),* "Woods" *(Lúky),* and "Courtyards" *(Dvory).* The ambitious communist planners envisioned a city laced with Venetian-style canals to help drain the marshy land, but the plans were abandoned after the harsh crackdown on the 1968 Prague Spring uprising. Without the incentives of private ownership, all they succeeded in creating was a grim and decaying sea of miserable concrete apartment *paneláky* ("panel buildings," so-called because they're made of huge prefab panels).

Today, one in four Bratislavans lives in Petržalka, and things are looking better. Like Dorothy opening the door to Oz, the formerly drab buildings have been splashed with bright new colors.

Far from being a slum, Petržalka is a popular neighborhood for Bratislavan yuppies who can't yet afford to build their dream houses. Locals read the Czech-language home-improvement magazine *Panel Plus* for ideas on how to give their *panelák* apartments some style (browse it yourself at www.panelplus.cz).

Petržalka is also a big suburban-style shopping zone (note the supermall down below). But there's still some history here. The **park** called Sad Janka Kráľa (originally, in German, Aupark)— just downriver from the bridge—was technically the first public park in Europe in the 1770s and is still a popular place for locals to relax and court.

Scanning the **horizon** beyond Petržalka, two things stick out: on the left, the old communist oil refinery (which has been fully updated and is now state-of-the-art); and on the right, a sea of modern windmills. These are just over the border, in Austria... and Bratislava is sure to grow in that direction quickly. Austria is about three miles that way, and Hungary is about six miles farther to the left.

Before you leave, consider a drink at the café (€3-4 coffee or beer, €7-20 cocktails). If nothing else, be sure to use the memorable WCs (guys can enjoy a classic urinal photo).

Sleeping in Bratislava

I'd rather sleep in Budapest (or in Vienna)—particularly because good-value options in central Bratislava are slim, and service tends to be surly. Business-oriented places charge more on weekdays than on weekends. Expect prices to drop slightly in winter and in the hottest summer months. Hotel Michalská Brána is right in the heart of the old town, while the others are just outside it—but still within a 5-10-minute walk.

$$$ Hotel Marrol's, on a quiet street, is the town's most enticing splurge. Although the immediate neighborhood isn't interesting, it's a five-minute walk from the old town, and its 54 rooms are luxurious and tastefully appointed Old World country-style. While pricey, the rates drop on weekends (prices flex, but generally Mon-Thu: Db-€160, Fri-Sun: Db-€120, Sb-€10 less, non-smoking, elevator, air-con, Wi-Fi, loaner laptops, free minibar, gorgeous lounge, Tobrucká 4, tel. 02/5778-4600, www.hotelmarrols.sk, rec@hotelmarrols.sk).

$$ Hotel Michalská Brána is a charming boutique hotel just inside St. Michael's Gate in the old town. The 14 rooms are sleek, mod, and classy, and the location is ideal—right in the heart of town, but on a relatively sleepy lane just away from the hubbub (Sb-€69-73, Db-€79-83, higher prices are for Mon-Thu nights, extra bed-€20, pricier suites available, non-smoking, air-con, elevator,

BRATISLAVA

Sleep Code

Abbreviations (€1 = about $1.40, country code: 421, area code: 02)
S = Single, **D** = Double/Twin, **T** = Triple, **Q** = Quad, **b** = bathroom

Price Rankings

$$$ **Higher Priced**—Most rooms €100 or more.

$$ **Moderately Priced**—Most rooms between €50-100.

$ **Lower Priced**—Most rooms €50 or less.

Unless otherwise noted, English is spoken, credit cards are accepted, rooms have no air-conditioning, breakfast is included, and Wi-Fi is generally free. Prices change; verify current rates online or by email. For the best prices, always book directly with the hotel.

Wi-Fi, Baštová 4, tel. 02/5930-7200, www.michalskabrana.sk, reception@michalskabrana.com).

$$ Hotel Ibis, part of the Europe-wide chain, offers 120 nicely appointed rooms just outside the old town, overlooking a busy tram junction—request a quieter room (Mon-Thu: Sb/Db-€85, Fri-Sun: Sb/Db-€69, rates flex with demand, you'll likely save €20 or more with advance booking on their website, breakfast-€10, elevator, air-con, guest computer and Wi-Fi, Zámocká 38, tel. 02/5929-2000, www.ibishotel.com, h3566@accor.com).

$$ Penzión Virgo sits on a quiet residential street, an eight-minute walk from the old town. The 11 boutiqueish rooms are classy and well-appointed (Sb-€61, Db-€74—but often discounted to around Sb/Db-€55, extra bed-€13, breakfast-€6, Wi-Fi, inexpensive parking, Panenská 14, tel. 02/3300-6262, www.penzionvirgo.sk, reception@penzionvirgo.sk).

$$ Penzión Gremium has six nondescript rooms and three apartments in a very central location, just a block behind the National Theater and a few steps from the old town. It's on a busy street with good windows but no air-conditioning, so it can be noisy on rowdy weekends (Sb-€60, Db-€70, Db apartment-€90, prices soft, breakfast-€7, elevator reaches some rooms, Wi-Fi, Gorkého 11, tel. 02/2070-4874, www.penziongremium.sk, recepcia@penziongremium.sk).

$ Downtown Backpackers Hostel is a funky but well-run place located in an old-fashioned townhouse. Rooms are named for famous artists and decorated with reinterpretations of their paintings (45 beds in 7 rooms, D-€54, bunk in 7-8-bed dorm-€18, bunk in 10-bed dorm-€17, breakfast-€3-5, Wi-Fi, free laundry facilities, kitchen, bike rental nearby, Panenská 31—across busy boulevard from Grassalkovich Palace, 10 minutes on foot from main station, tel. 02/5464-1191, mobile 0905/259-714, www.backpackers.sk, info@backpackers.sk).

Eating in Bratislava

Bratislava is packed with inviting new eateries. In addition to places serving the heavy Slovak staples, you'll find trendy new bars  and bistros, and a smattering of ethnic offerings. For a fun drink and snack that locals love, try a Vinea grape soda and a sweet *Pressburger* bagel in any bar or café.

Like the Czechs, the Slovaks produce excellent beer (*pivo*, PEE-voh). One of the top brands is Zlatý Bažant ("Golden Pheasant"). Bratislava's beer halls are good places to sample Slovak and Czech beers, and to get a hearty, affordable meal of stick-to-your-ribs pub grub. Long a wine-producing area, the Bratislava region makes the same wines that Vienna is famous for. But, as nearly all is consumed locally, most people don't think of Slovakia as wine country.

The best plan may be to stroll the old town and keep your eyes open for the setting and cuisine that appeals to you most. Or consider one of these options.

1. Slovak Pub ("1." as in "the first") attracts a student crowd. Enter from Obchodná, the bustling shopping street just above the old town, and climb the stairs into a vast warren of rustic, old countryside-style pub rooms with uneven floors. Enjoy the lively, loud, almost chaotic ambience while dining on affordable and truly authentic Slovak fare, made with products from the pub's own farm. This is a good place to try the Slovak specialty, *bryndzové halušky* (several varieties for €4-5; €4-12 main courses, Mon 10:00-23:00, Tue-Sat 10:00-24:00, Sun 12:00-24:00, Obchodná 62, tel. 02/5292-6367, www.slovakpub.sk).

Bratislavský Meštiansky Pivovar ("Bratislava Town Brew-pub"), just above the old town behind the big Crowne Plaza hotel, brews its own beer and also sells a variety of others. Seating stretches over several levels in the new-meets-old interior (€7-15 main courses, Mon-Sat 11:00-24:00, Sun 11:00-23:00, Drevená 8, mobile 0944-512-265, www.mestianskypivovar.sk).

Lemon Tree/Sky Bar/Rum Club, a three-in-one place just past the fenced-in US Embassy on the trendy Hviezdoslavovo Námestie, features the same Thai-meets-Mediterranean menu throughout (€8-12 pasta and noodle dishes, €16-19 main courses). But the real reason to come here is for the seventh-floor Sky

Bar, with fantastic views of the old town and the SNP Bridge. It's smart to reserve a view table in advance if you want to dine here—or just drop by for a pricey vodka cocktail on the small terrace. You've got the best seat in town, and though prices are expensive for Bratislava, they're no more than what you'd pay for a meal in Vienna (daily 11:00-late, Sun from 12:00, Hviezdoslavovo Námestie 7, mobile 0948-109-400, www.spicy.sk).

At **Eurovea** (the recommended end to my walking tour, 10 minutes downstream from the old town), huge outdoor terraces rollicking with happy eaters line the swanky riverfront residential and shopping-mall complex. You'll pay high prices for the great atmosphere and views at international eateries—French, Italian, Brazilian—and a branch of the Czech beer-hall chain Kolkovna. Or you can head to the food court in the shopping mall, where you'll eat well for €4.

Shtoor is a hip, rustic-chic café (named for a revered 19th-century champion of Slovak culture, Ľudovít Štúr) with coffee drinks and €3-5 sandwiches and quiches (takeaway or table service, open long hours daily). They have three locations: in the heart of the old town at Panská 23; just east of the old town (near Eurovea) at Štúrova 8; and inside a Barnes & Noble-type bookstore, Martinus.sk, at Obchodná 26.

Coffee & Bagel Story (a chain) sells...coffee and €3 takeout bagel sandwiches. The handiest location is on the town's main square at Hlavné Námestie 8, with picnic tables right out front.

Supermarket: Try **Billa,** in the Tatracentrum complex across the street from Grassalkovich Palace (Mon-Sat 7:00-22:00, Sun 8:00-20:00).

Bratislava Connections

BY TRAIN

Bratislava has two major train stations: the main station closer to the old town (Hlavná Stanica, abbreviated "Bratislava hl. st." on schedules) and Petržalka station (sometimes called ŽST Petržalka), in the suburb across the river (for full details, see "Arrival in Bratislava," earlier). When checking schedules, pay attention to which station your train uses.

From Bratislava by Train to: Budapest (7/day direct, 2.75 hours to Keleti Station, more with transfers; also doable—and possibly cheaper—by Orange Ways bus, 1-4/day, 2.5 hours, www.orangeways.com), **Vienna** (2/hour, 1 hour; buy the €15 round-trip EU Regio day pass, which is cheaper than a one-way fare; departures alternate between the two stations—half from main station, half from Petržalka), **Sopron** (hourly, 2.5 hours, leaves from Petržalka), **Prague** (5/day direct, 4.25 hours). To reach other

Hungarian destinations (including **Eger** and **Pécs**), it's generally easiest to change in Budapest.

BY BUS

Two different companies run handy buses that connect Bratislava, **Vienna,** and the **airports** in each city: Blaguss/Eurolines (www.blaguss.sk or www.eurolines.at) and Slovak Lines/Postbus (tel. 0810-222-3336, www.postbus.at or www.slovaklines.sk). You can book ahead online, or (if arriving at the airport) just take whichever connection is leaving first. The bus schedules are handily posted at www.airportbratislava.sk (find the "Navigation—From the Airport" tab).

The buses run about hourly from Bratislava's airport to Bratislava (15 minutes, stops either at the main bus station east of the old town or at the Most SNP stop underneath the SNP Bridge), continues on to Vienna's airport (1 hour), and ends in Vienna (1.25 hours, Erdberg stop on the U-3 subway line). They then turn around and make the reverse journey (€7.50-10, depending on route).

BY BOAT

Riverboats connect Bratislava to Vienna. Conveniently, these boats dock right along the Danube in front of Bratislava's old town. While they are more expensive, less frequent, and slower than the train, some travelers enjoy getting out on the Danube. It's prudent to bring your passport if crossing over for the day (though it's unlikely anyone will ask for it).

The **Twin City Liner** offers three to five daily boat trips between a dock at the edge of Bratislava's old town, along Fajnorovo nábrežie, and Vienna's Schwedenplatz (where Vienna's town center hits the canal; €30-35 each way, 1.25-hour trip; can fill up—reservations smart, Austrian tel. 01/58880, www.twincityliner.com).

The competing Slovak **LOD** line connects the cities a little more cheaply, but just twice a day. These boats are slower, as they use Vienna's less-convenient Reichsbrücke dock on the main river, farther from the city center (€23 one-way, €38 round-trip, 1.5-hour trip, tel. 02/5293-2226, www.lod.sk).

BY PLANE

You have two options for reaching Bratislava: You can fly into its own airport, or into the very nearby Vienna Airport.

Bratislava Airport (Letisko Bratislava)

This airport (airport code: BTS, www.letiskobratislava.sk) is six miles northeast of downtown Bratislava. Budget airline Ryanair (www.ryanair.com) has many flights here. Some airlines market it as "Vienna-Bratislava," thanks to its proximity to both capitals. It's compact and manageable, with all the usual amenities (including ATMs).

From the Airport to Downtown Bratislava: The airport has easy **public bus** connections to Bratislava's main train station (Hlavná Stanica, €1.30, bus #61, 4-5/hour, 30 minutes). To reach the bus stop, exit straight out of the arrivals hall, cross the street, buy a ticket at the kiosk, and look for the bus stop on your right. For directions from the train station into the old town, see "Arrival in Bratislava," earlier. A **taxi** from the airport into central Bratislava should cost less than €20.

To Budapest: Take the bus or taxi to Bratislava's main train station (described above), then hop a train to Budapest.

To Vienna: Take either the Slovak Lines/Postbus bus, which runs to Vienna's Hauptbahnhof (every 1-2 hours, 2-hour trip, €7.70, www.slovaklines.sk or www.postbus.at) or the Blaguss/Eurolines bus to the Erdberg stop on Vienna's U-3 subway line, on which it's a straight shot to Stephansplatz or Mariahilfer Strasse (every 1-2 hours, 1.5-hour trip, €7.20, www.blaguss.sk or www.eurolines.at). A taxi from Bratislava Airport directly to Vienna costs €60-90 (depending on whether you use a cheaper Slovak or more expensive Austrian cab).

Vienna International Airport

This airport, 12 miles from downtown Vienna and 30 miles from downtown Bratislava, is well-connected to both capitals (airport code: VIE, airport tel. 01/700-722-233, www.viennaairport.com). For a full description of this airport, see page 1154.

To reach **Bratislava** from the airport, the easiest option is to take the Blaguss/Eurolines or Slovak Lines/Postbus bus described earlier (under "By Bus"). Ask the TI which bus is leaving first, then head straight out the door and hop on. After about 45 minutes, the bus drops off in downtown Bratislava, then heads to the airport. I'd skip the train connection, which takes longer and involves complicated changes (airport train to Wien-Mitte Bahnhof in downtown Vienna, S-Bahn/subway to Südbahnhof, train to Bratislava, figure 1.75 hours total).

PRACTICALITIES

Contents

This chapter covers the practical skills of European travel: how to get tourist information, pay for purchases, sightsee efficiently, find good-value accommodations, eat affordably but well, use technology wisely, and get between destinations smoothly. To study ahead and round out your knowledge, check out "Resources" for a summary of recommended books and films. If you're visiting Slovenia, Croatia, or Bosnia-Herzegovina, the "Understanding Yugoslavia" section gives you a good picture of how Yugoslavia was formed, and why it broke apart.

Tourist Information

BEFORE YOUR TRIP

National tourist offices are a wealth of information. Before your trip, get the free general information packet and request any specifics you may want (such as regional and city maps and festival schedules).

Czech Tourist Office: www.czechtourism.com
Polish Tourist Office: www.poland.travel
Hungarian Tourist Office: www.gotohungary.com
Slovenian Tourist Office: www.slovenia.info
Croatian National Tourist Office: http://us.croatia.hr
Bosnia-Herzegovina Tourist Office: www.bhtourism.ba
Austrian Tourist Office: www.austria.info
Slovakian Tourist Office: www.slovakia.travel

IN EASTERN EUROPE

Your best first stop in every town is generally the tourist information office—abbreviated **TI** in this book. You'll find local TIs are usually well-organized and always have an English-speaking staff.

TIs are good places to get a city map and information on public transit (including bus and train schedules), walking tours, special events, and nightlife. Many TIs have information on the entire country or at least the region, so try to pick up maps for destinations you'll be visiting later in your trip. If you're arriving in town after the TI closes, call ahead or pick up a map in a neighboring town.

The TIs in Eastern Europe are government-run, which means their information isn't colored by a drive for profit. They're not allowed to make money by running a room-booking service—though they can almost always give you a list of local hotels and private rooms. If they're not too busy, they can call around for you to check on availability. Better yet, consult an online booking site, which can provide a broader range of options.

Travel Tips

Emergency and Medical Help: In all of the countries in this book, dial 112 for medical or other emergencies. For police, dial 112 in Slovakia, Hungary, Poland, or Austria; dial 158 in the Czech Republic; dial 113 in Slovenia; dial 92 in Croatia; and dial 122 in Bosnia-Herzegovina. If you get sick, do as the locals do and go to a pharmacist for advice. Or ask at your hotel for help—they'll know the nearest medical and emergency services.

Theft or Loss: To replace a passport, you'll need to go in person to the appropriate embassy or consulate (see page 1355). If your credit and debit cards disappear, cancel and replace them (see "Damage Control for Lost Cards" on page 1301). File a police report, either on the spot or within a day or two; you'll need it to submit an insurance claim for lost or stolen rail passes or travel gear, and it can help with replacing your passport or credit and debit cards. For more information, see www.ricksteves.com/help. Precautionary measures can minimize the effects of loss—back up your digital photos and other files frequently.

Borders: All of the countries in this book, except Croatia and Bosnia-Herzegovina, have officially joined the open-borders Schengen Agreement. (Croatia will likely join by 2016.) That means that there are no border checks between any of these countries, or between them and Western European countries such as Germany, Austria, and Italy. You'll simply zip through the border without stopping.

Non-Schengen countries (Bosnia-Herzegovina, as well as Croatia until it joins) still have traditional border checkpoints—you'll still have to stop upon entering or exiting these countries. But whether traveling by car, train, or bus, you'll find that border crossings are generally a nonevent: Flash your passport, maybe wait a few minutes, and move on. Drivers may be asked to show proof of car insurance ("green card"), so be sure you have it when you pick up your rental car.

Even as border checkpoints fade, when you cross any international border, you must still change phone cards, postage stamps, currencies (in most cases), and underpants.

Time Zones: The countries listed in this book are generally six/nine hours ahead of the East/West Coasts of the US. The exceptions are the beginning and end of Daylight Saving Time: Europe "springs forward" the last Sunday in March (two weeks after most of North America), and "falls back" the last Sunday in October (one week before North America). For a handy online time converter, try www.timeanddate.com/worldclock.

Weekends: Saturdays are virtually weekdays, with earlier closing hours and no rush hour (though transportation connections can be less frequent than on weekdays). Sundays have the same pros and cons as they do for travelers in the US (special events, limited hours, banks and many shops generally closed, limited public-transportation options, no rush hour). Rowdy evenings are rare on Sundays.

Watt's Up? Europe's electrical system is 220 volts, instead of North America's 110 volts. Most newer electronics (such as laptops, battery chargers, and hair dryers) convert automatically, so you won't need a converter, but you will need an adapter plug with two round prongs, sold inexpensively at travel stores in the US. Avoid bringing older appliances that don't automatically convert voltage; instead, buy a cheap replacement in Europe.

Discounts: Discounts are not listed in this book. However, seniors (age 60 and over), youths under 18, and students and teachers with proper identification cards (www.isic.org) can get discounts at many sights. Always ask, though some discounts are available only for local residents or citizens of the European Union (EU).

PRACTICALITIES

Smoking: While the specifics vary by country, in almost all of the destinations in this book, smoking is generally banned indoors (though people still smoke like chimneys on terraces and other outdoor areas). The two exceptions are the Czech Republic and Austria. Czech businesses may decide whether to be smoking, non-smoking, or have a designated non-smoking section. Austrian restaurants and cafés are required to set aside at least half their space for non-smokers; smaller establishments that physically can't accommodate two viable zones can go all-smoking or entirely non-smoking. In all of these countries—as throughout Europe—there are more smokers than back home, so you'll still get a whiff of the nicotine-stained Old World. If you require a completely non-smoking eating section or hotel room, be very specific in your request, and understand that it may not be granted.

Online Translation Tip: You can use Google's Chrome browser (available free at www.google.com/chrome) to instantly translate websites. With one click, the page appears in (very rough) English translation. You can also paste the URL of the site into the translation window at www.google.com/translate.

Money

This section offers advice on how to pay for purchases on your trip (including getting cash from ATMs and paying with plastic), dealing with lost or stolen cards, VAT (sales tax) refunds, and tipping.

EXCHANGE RATES

Most of the countries in this book still use their traditional currencies. So far, only Slovenia, Austria, and Slovakia officially use the euro currency—and the others are unlikely to adopt it anytime soon. But even in countries that don't officially use the euro, many businesses (especially hotels) quote prices in euros anyway. (Even if they do, they typically prefer payment in the local currency.)

Here are the rough exchange rates for each country. I've also suggested a strategy for roughly converting prices into US dollars. Note that in some cases, I've favored easier-to-remember equations even if they offer less precise conversions. For a more precise conversion, see the latest rates at www.oanda.com...and use a calculator.

1 euro (€) = about $1.40 (used in Slovenia, Austria, and Slovakia). To convert prices in euros to dollars, add 40 percent: €20 = about $28, €50 = about $70, and so on.

20 Czech crowns (*koruna*, Kč) = about $1. To estimate prices in dollars, drop the last digit and divide in half: 150 Kč = about $8.

3 Polish złoty (zł, or PLN) = about $1. To calculate prices in dollars, divide by three: 85 zł = a little under $30.

225 Hungarian forints (Ft, or HUF) = about $1. To very roughly figure dollars, divide by two and drop the last two digits: 10,000 Ft = about $50 (actually $44).

6 Croatian kunas (kn, or HRK) = about $1. To very roughly estimate dollars, multiply by two and drop the last digit: 70 kn = about $14 (actually $11).

1.50 Bosnian convertible marks (KM, or BAM) = about $1. To convert prices into dollars, subtract one-third: 60 KM = about $40. Note that most merchants in Mostar will take euros or Croatian kunas.

So, that 20-zł Polish woodcarving is about $7, the 5,000-Ft Hungarian dinner is about $22, and the 2,000-Kč taxi ride through Prague is...uh-oh.

WHAT TO BRING

Bring both a credit card and a debit card. You'll use the debit card at cash machines (ATMs) to withdraw local cash for most purchases, and the credit card to pay for larger items. Some travelers carry a third card, in case one gets demagnetized or eaten by a temperamental machine.

For an emergency stash, bring several hundred dollars in hard cash in $20 bills. If you need to exchange the bills, go to a bank; avoid using currency-exchange booths because of their lousy rates and/or outrageous fees.

Cash

Cash is just as desirable in Europe as it is at home. Small businesses (B&Bs, mom-and-pop cafés, shops, etc.) prefer that you pay your bills with cash. Some vendors will charge you extra for using a credit card, and some won't take credit cards at all. Cash is the best—and sometimes only—way to pay for cheap food, bus fare, taxis, and local guides.

Throughout Europe, ATMs are the standard way for travelers to get cash. To withdraw money from an ATM (known as *Bankomat* in all of these countries), you'll need a debit card (ideally with a Visa or MasterCard logo for maximum usability), plus a PIN code. Know your PIN code in numbers; there are only numbers—no letters—on European keypads. For increased security, shield the keypad when entering your PIN code, and don't use an ATM if anything on the front of the machine looks loose or damaged (a sign that someone may have attached a "skimming" device to capture account

information). Try to withdraw large sums of money to reduce the number of per-transaction bank fees you'll pay.

When possible, use ATMs located outside banks—a thief is less likely to target a cash machine near surveillance cameras, and if your card is munched by a machine, you can go inside for help. Stay away from "independent" ATMs such as Travelex, Euronet, Moneybox, Cardpoint, and Cashzone, which charge huge commissions, have terrible exchange rates, and may try to trick users with "dynamic currency conversion" (described at the end of "Credit and Debit Cards," next).

Although you can use a credit card for an ATM transaction, it only makes sense in an emergency, because it's considered a cash advance (borrowed at a high interest rate) rather than a withdrawal.

While traveling, if you want to monitor your accounts online to detect any unauthorized transactions, be sure to use a secure connection (see page 1328).

Pickpockets target tourists. To safeguard your cash, wear a money belt—a pouch with a strap that you buckle around your waist like a belt and tuck under your clothes. Keep your cash, credit cards, and passport secure in your money belt, and carry only a day's spending money in your front pocket.

Credit and Debit Cards

For purchases, Visa and MasterCard are more commonly accepted than American Express. Just like at home, credit or debit cards work easily at larger hotels, restaurants, and shops. I typically use my debit card to withdraw cash to pay for most purchases. I use my credit card only in a few specific situations: to book hotel reservations by phone, to buy advance tickets for events or sights, to cover major expenses (such as car rentals, plane tickets, and long hotel stays), and to pay for things near the end of my trip (to avoid another visit to the ATM). While you could use a debit card to make most large purchases, using a credit card offers a greater degree of fraud protection (because debit cards draw funds directly from your account).

Ask Your Credit- or Debit-Card Company: Before your trip, contact the company that issued your debit or credit cards.

• Confirm your **card will work overseas,** and alert them that you'll be using it in Europe; otherwise, they may deny transactions if they perceive unusual spending patterns.

• Ask for the specifics on transaction **fees.** When you use your credit or debit card—either for purchases or ATM withdrawals—you'll typically be charged additional "international transaction" fees of up to 3 percent (1 percent is normal) plus $5 per transaction. If your card's fees seem high, consider getting a card just for your

EU Enlargement and the "New Europe"

The European Union (EU) began as a political and economic alliance of mostly Western European nations, with Germany, France, and Italy at the helm. But over the last decade or so, the geographical and political center of Europe has shifted from Brussels to Prague. Since 2004, 11 formerly communist "Eastern European" countries—including most of the ones in this book—have joined the EU. And this enlargement has been a fitful process, both for the existing members and for the new ones.

Many Eastern Europeans, concerned that EU bureaucracy could threaten their prized traditions, have a "Euroskeptic" take on things. One Polish farmer grumbled that he has to get "passports" for each of his cows. EU hygiene standards are incompatible with slow-simmering national specialties. (My Czech friend complained, "The EU has made many of our best dishes illegal.") And many are simply exhausted after generations of outside meddling. A wise Czech grandmother pointed out that in her lifetime, her country had been ruled from Vienna (Habsburgs), Berlin (Nazis), and Moscow (communists). She said, "Now that we're finally ruled from Prague, why would we want to turn our power over to Brussels?"

Longstanding EU members have had their own doubts. Wealthy nations had already spent vast fortunes to improve the floundering economies of poorer member countries (such as Portugal, Greece, and Ireland), and were reluctant to take on more "charity cases." Some Westerners fretted about the influx of cheap labor from the East (see "The Polish Plumber Syndrome" on page 1306). Others felt threatened that their political clout would be diluted. And the economic crisis in Greece during the Great Recession—which nearly caused the end of the euro currency—demonstrated that the convenience of tying economies together is fraught with pitfalls.

On the other hand, the advantages of the EU are evident everywhere. New expressways, train stations, public spaces, and museums throughout Eastern Europe were paid for, at least partly, by EU funds. New members that have adopted the euro currency (including Slovenia and Slovakia) find they match up pretty well, economically, with their Western European counterparts. And, just as intended, Western companies are finding that easier access to the affordable resources and labor of Eastern Europe—thanks partly to all of those new highways—is a boon all around.

As the "New Europe" takes shape, players on both sides will continue to define their roles and seek compromise. So far, the general consensus in the East is that joining the EU was the right move. And they appreciate having a seat at the table. In 2014, Poland's Donald Tusk took over the EU's top job, as president of the European Council—a sign of how far Europe has come in just a generation.

trip: Capital One (www.capitalone.com) and most credit unions have low-to-no international fees.

• If you plan to withdraw cash from ATMs, confirm your daily **withdrawal limit,** and if necessary, ask your bank to adjust it. Some travelers prefer a high limit that allows them to take out more cash at each ATM stop (saving on bank fees), while others prefer to set a lower limit in case their card is stolen. Note that foreign banks also set maximum withdrawal amounts for their ATMs.

• Get your bank's emergency **phone number** in the US (but not its 800 number, which isn't accessible from overseas) to call collect if you have a problem.

• Ask for your credit card's **PIN** in case you need to make an emergency cash withdrawal or encounter Europe's "chip-and-PIN" system; the bank won't tell you your PIN over the phone, so allow time for it to be mailed to you.

Chip and PIN: While much of Europe is shifting to a "chip-and-PIN" security system for credit and debit cards, Eastern Europe still uses the old magnetic-swipe technology. (European chip-and-PIN cards are embedded with an electronic security chip, and require the purchaser to punch in a PIN rather than sign a receipt.) If you happen to encounter chip and PIN, it will probably be at payment machines, such as those at toll roads or self-serve gas pumps. On the outside chance that a machine won't take your card, find a cashier who can make your card work (they can print a receipt for you to sign), or find a machine that takes cash. But don't panic. Most travelers who are carrying only magnetic-stripe cards don't run into problems. You can always use an ATM to withdraw cash with your magnetic-stripe card, even in countries where people predominantly use chip-and-PIN cards.

Dynamic Currency Conversion: If merchants offer to convert your purchase price into dollars (called dynamic currency conversion, or DCC), refuse this "service." You'll pay even more in fees for the expensive convenience of seeing your charge in dollars. Some ATMs and retailers try to confuse customers by presenting DCC in misleading terms. If an ATM offers to "lock in" or "guarantee" your conversion rate, choose "proceed without conversion." Other prompts might state, "You can be charged in dollars: Press YES for dollars, NO for euros." Always choose the local currency in these situations.

Damage Control for Lost Cards

If you lose your credit, debit, or ATM card, you can stop people from using your card by reporting the loss immediately to the respective global customer-assistance centers. Call these 24-hour US numbers collect: Visa (tel. 303/967-1096), MasterCard (tel.

636/722-7111), and American Express (tel. 336/393-1111).

To make a collect call from any phone, use these numbers: Austria tel. 800-200-288; Bosnia tel. 00-800-0010; Croatia tel. 0800-220-111; Czech Republic tel. 00-800-222-55288; Hungary tel. 06-800-011-11; Poland tel. 00-800-111-1111; Slovakia tel. 0800-000-101; Slovenia tel. 1180. Press zero or stay on the line for an English-speaking operator. European toll-free numbers (listed by country) can also be found at the websites for Visa and MasterCard.

Providing the following information will allow for a quicker cancellation of your missing card: full card number, whether you are the primary or secondary cardholder, the cardholder's name exactly as printed on the card, billing address, home phone number, circumstances of the loss or theft, and identification verification (your birth date, your mother's maiden name, or your Social Security number—memorize this, don't carry a copy). If you are the secondary cardholder, you'll also need to provide the primary cardholder's identification-verification details. You can generally receive a temporary card within two or three business days in Europe (see www.ricksteves.com/help for more).

If you report your loss within two days, you typically won't be responsible for any unauthorized transactions on your account, although many banks charge a liability fee of $50.

TIPPING

Europeans generally tip substantially less than in the US. And, while some waiters and taxi drivers in touristy cities have learned to expect Yankee-sized tips when they spot an American, you should feel free to "go local" and tip like the natives do. The proper amount depends on your resources, tipping philosophy, and the circumstances, but some general guidelines apply.

Restaurants: Tip only at restaurants that have table service. If you order your food at a counter, don't tip.

At restaurants that have a waitstaff, round up the bill 5-10 percent after a good meal. My rule of thumb is to estimate about 10 percent, then round slightly to reach a convenient total (for a 370-Kč meal, I pay 400 Kč—an 8-percent tip). I'm a little more generous in Budapest, where a minimum 10 percent tip is expected (I'll hand over 4,000 Ft for a 3,600-Ft bill—that's 11 percent). Anywhere in Eastern Europe, a 15 percent tip is overly generous, verging on extravagant. At some tourist-oriented restaurants, a 10-15 percent "service charge" may be added to your bill, in which case an additional tip is not necessary. (More commonly, menus or bills remind you that the tip is *not* included.) If you're not sure whether your bill includes the tip, just ask.

Taxis: For a typical ride, round up your fare a bit (for instance,

VAT Rates

To be eligible to get a VAT refund, you usually need to spend the listed minimum at a single store.

Country of Purchase	VAT Standard Rate*	Minimum in Local Currency	Approx. Minimum in US $
Austria	20%	€75.01	$105
Croatia	25%	740 kn	$124
Czech Republic	21%	2,001 Kč	$100
Hungary	27%	52,001 Ft	$231
Poland	23%	200 zł	$67
Slovakia	20%	€175.01	$245
Slovenia	22%	€50.01	$70

* VAT rates fluctuate based on many factors, including what kind of item you are buying. Your refund will likely be less than the rate listed above, especially if it's subject to processing fees.

PRACTICALITIES

if the fare is 71 kn, pay 75 kn). If the cabbie hauls your bags and zips you to the airport to help you catch your flight, you might want to toss in a little more. But if you feel like you're being driven in circles or otherwise ripped off, skip the tip.

Services: In general, if someone in the service industry does a super job for you, a small tip (the equivalent of a euro or two) is appropriate...but not required. If you're not sure whether (or how much) to tip for a service, ask your hotelier or the TI.

When in doubt, ask: If you're not sure whether (or how much) to tip for a service, ask your hotelier or the TI; they'll fill you in on how it's done on their turf.

GETTING A VAT REFUND

Wrapped into the purchase price of your Eastern European souvenirs is a Value-Added Tax (VAT) that varies per country. You're entitled to get most of that tax back if you make a purchase of more than a set amount at a store that participates in the VAT refund scheme. Typically, you must ring up the minimum at a single retailer—you can't add up your purchases from various shops to reach the required amount.

Getting your refund is usually straightforward and, if you buy a substantial number of souvenirs, well worth the hassle. If you're lucky, the merchant will subtract the tax when you make your purchase. (This is more likely to occur if the store ships the goods to your home.) Otherwise, you'll need to:

Get the paperwork. Have the merchant completely fill out the necessary refund document. You'll have to present your passport. Get the paperwork done before you leave the store to ensure you'll have everything you need (including your original sales receipt).

Get your stamp at the border or airport. Process your VAT document with the customs service at your last stop in the country in which you made your purchase (or, if you bought it in the European Union, at your last stop in the EU). Arrive an additional hour before you need to check in for your flight to allow time to find the local customs office—and to stand in line. It's best to keep your purchases in your carry-on. If they're too large or dangerous to carry on (such as knives), pack them in your checked bags and alert the check-in agent. You'll be sent (with your tagged bag) to a customs desk outside security, which will examine your bag, stamp your paperwork, and put your bag on the belt. You're not supposed to use your purchased goods before you leave. If you show up at customs wearing your chic Czech shirt, officials might look the other way—or deny you a refund.

Collect your refund. You'll need to return your stamped document to the retailer or its representative. Many merchants work with services, such as Global Blue or Premier Tax Free, that have offices at major airports, ports, or border crossings (either before or after security, probably strategically located near a duty-free shop). These services, which extract a 4 percent fee, can refund your money immediately in cash or credit your card (within two billing cycles). If the retailer handles VAT refunds directly, it's up to you to contact the merchant for your refund. You can mail the documents from home, or more quickly, from your point of departure (using an envelope you've prepared in advance or one that's been provided by the merchant). You'll then have to wait—it could take months.

CUSTOMS FOR AMERICAN SHOPPERS

You are allowed to take home $800 worth of items per person duty-free, once every 30 days. You can take home many processed and packaged foods: vacuum-packed cheeses, dried herbs, jams, baked goods, candy, chocolate, oil, vinegar, mustard, and honey. Fresh fruits and vegetables and most meats are not allowed, with exceptions for some canned items. As for alcohol, you can bring in one liter duty-free (it can be packed securely in your checked luggage, along with any other liquid-containing items).

To bring alcohol (or liquid-packed foods) in your carry-on bag on your flight home, buy it at a duty-free shop at the airport. You'll increase your odds of getting it onto a connecting flight if it's packaged in a "STEB"—a secure, tamper-evident bag. But stay away from liquids in opaque, ceramic, or metallic containers, which usually cannot be successfully screened (STEB or no STEB).

For details on allowable goods, customs rules, and duty rates, visit www.cbp.gov.

Sightseeing

Eastern Europe's best attractions are modern museums that chronicle the communist regime and celebrate its demise (such as Budapest's House of Terror and Memento Park, and Gdańsk's European Solidarity Center). But many museums here are dusty, old-fashioned collections of art or historical artifacts. While these don't quite rank with the Louvre or the Prado, many are surprisingly engaging if you take the time to learn more. With the right attitude, it's an exciting opportunity to be introduced to talented artists and important historical figures who are relatively unknown outside of their home country. Generally, you'll follow a confusing, one-way tour route through a maze of rooms with squeaky parquet floors, monitored by grumpy grannies who listlessly point you in the right direction. While some museums label exhibits in English, most don't post full explanations; you'll have to buy a book or borrow laminated translations. In some cases, neither option is available.

Sightseeing can be hard work. Use these tips to make your visits to Eastern Europe's finest sights meaningful, fun, efficient, and painless.

PLAN AHEAD
Set up an itinerary that allows you to fit in all your must-see sights. For a one-stop look at opening hours, see the "At a Glance" sidebars for each major city (Prague, Kraków, Warsaw, Budapest, Ljubljana, Dubrovnik, and Vienna). Most sights keep stable hours, but in some areas (especially coastal Croatia), hours tend to fluctuate from season to season. If you have your heart set on visiting particular sights, it's always smart to confirm the latest hours by checking their websites or asking at the local TI.

Don't put off visiting a must-see sight—you never know when a place will close unexpectedly for a holiday, strike, or restoration. Many museums are closed or have reduced hours at least a few days a year, especially on holidays such as Christmas, New Year's, and Labor Day (May 1). A list of holidays is on page 1357; check museums' websites for possible closures during your trip. In summer, some sights may stay open late. Off-season, many museums have shorter hours.

The Polish Plumber Syndrome

You'll likely enjoy a taste of Eastern European culture on your next trip...to London or Dublin. When eight Eastern European countries joined the European Union in 2004, Great Britain and Ireland had to welcome their new comrades to work without a visa. This sparked a wave of immigration into the British Isles. Many Poles, Czechs, and Estonians ended up in the hospitality industry.

The transplants enjoyed more money and an irreplaceable cross-cultural experience. But Eastern Europe went through a somewhat alarming "brain drain," as many of its youngest and most westward-thinking residents rushed away. In Britain and Ireland, tourists began to encounter desk clerks who didn't quite speak fluent English. More recently, the global financial crisis has tightened up the job market—making immigration less appealing both to the expat workers, and to the native job-seekers in the countries that are hosting them. Quite a few of these transplants have lost their jobs and returned home to the East.

Other Western European countries have had to open their borders, but it's controversial. One popular symbol—invented by a right-wing French politician—was an invading "Polish plumber" who'd put French plumbers out of a job. The Polish tourist board countered by putting up clever ads in France featuring an alluring Polish hunk stroking a pipe wrench, saying, "I'm staying in Poland...come visit me!"

This is just one more step in the Europe-wide process of integration. European Gen Xers have been dubbed the "Erasmus Generation"—after the Erasmus Student Network, an EU organization that fosters study-abroad opportunities within Europe. As European thirtysomethings have grown up accustomed to attending universities in other countries, it seems natural for them to identify as "Europeans" rather than as Spaniards, Slovenes, or Swedes. Multilingualism, international résumés, and cross-cultural marriages are the norm.

Going at the right time helps avoid crowds. This book offers tips on the best times to see specific sights. Try visiting popular sights very early, at lunch, or very late. Evening visits are usually peaceful, with fewer crowds.

Study up. To get the most out of the sight descriptions in this book, read them before you visit. Note: To avoid redundancy, many cultural or historical details are explained for one sight in this book and not repeated for another; to get the full picture, read the entire chapter for each destination you'll visit.

AT SIGHTS

Here's what you can typically expect:

Entering: Be warned that you may not be allowed to enter if you arrive 30 to 60 minutes before closing time. And guards start ushering people out well before the actual closing time, so don't save the best for last.

Some important sights have a security check, where you must open your bag or send it through a metal detector. Some sights require you to check daypacks and coats. (If you'd rather not check your daypack, try carrying it tucked under your arm like a purse as you enter.)

Photography: If the museum's photo policy isn't clearly posted, ask a guard. Generally, taking photos without a flash or tripod is allowed. Some sights ban photos altogether.

Temporary Exhibits: Museums may show special exhibits in addition to their permanent collection. Some exhibits are included in the entry price, while others come at an extra cost (which you may have to pay even if you don't want to see the exhibit).

Expect Changes: Artwork can be on tour, on loan, out sick, or shifted at the whim of the curator. To adapt, pick up a floor plan as you enter, and ask museum staff if you can't find a particular piece.

Audioguides: Some sights rent audioguides, which generally offer recorded descriptions in English, though they're usually dull and rarely worth the cost (about $6-8). But if you like audioguide tours, bring your own earbuds—you can enjoy better sound and avoid holding the device to your ear. To save money, bring a Y-jack and share one audioguide with your travel partner. Increasingly, museums are offering apps (often free) that you can download to your mobile device.

I've produced free downloadable audio tours of some of the sights in Prague and Vienna; see page 13.

Services: Important sights may have an on-site café or cafeteria (usually a handy place to rejuvenate during a long visit). The WCs at sights are free and generally clean.

Before Leaving: At the gift shop, scan the postcard rack or thumb through a guidebook to be sure that you haven't overlooked something that you'd like to see.

Every sight or museum offers more than what is covered in this book. Use the information in this book as an introduction—not the final word.

PRACTICALITIES

Sleeping

I favor hotels and restaurants that are handy to your sightseeing activities. Rather than list hotels scattered throughout a city, I describe two or three favorite neighborhoods and recommend the best accommodations values in each, from dorm beds to fancy doubles with all the comforts.

A major feature of this book is its extensive and opinionated listing of good-value rooms. I like places that are clean, central, relatively quiet at night, reasonably priced, friendly, English-speaking, professional-feeling but small enough to have a hands-on owner and stable staff, run with a respect for local traditions, and not listed in other guidebooks. I'm more impressed by a convenient location and a fun-loving philosophy than flat-screen TVs and a pricey laundry service. My favorites are small, family-run hotels and friendly local people who rent hotelesque private rooms without a reception desk. I've also thrown in a few hostels and other cheap options for budget travelers.

Book your accommodations well in advance, especially if you'll be traveling during busy times. See page 1357 for a list of major holidays and festivals in Eastern Europe; for tips on making reservations, see page 1312.

Some people make reservations as they travel, calling hotels a few days to a week before their arrival. If you'd rather travel without any reservations at all, you'll have greater success snaring rooms if you arrive at your destination early in the day. If you anticipate crowds (weekends are worst) on the day you want to check in, call hotels at about 9:00 or 10:00, when the receptionist knows who'll be checking out and which rooms will be available. If you encounter a language barrier, ask the fluent receptionist at your current hotel to call for you.

RATES AND DEALS

Accommodations in Eastern Europe cost about as much as comparable beds in the West. While most accommodations listed in this book cluster at about $80-120 per double, they range from $15 bunks to $500-plus splurges (maximum plumbing and more).

I've described my recommended accommodations using a Sleep Code (see the sidebar). Prices listed are for one-night stays in peak season, and assume you're booking directly with the hotel (not through an online hotel-booking engine or TI). Booking services extract a commission from the hotel, which logically closes the door on special deals. Book direct.

My recommended hotels each have a website (often with a built-in booking form) and an email address; you can expect a response in English within a day (and often sooner).

Sleep Code

To help you easily sort through these listings, I've divided the accommodations into three categories based on the highest price for a standard double room with bath during high season:

$$$ **Higher Priced**
$$ **Moderately Priced**
$ **Lower Priced**

I always rate hostels as $, whether or not they have double rooms, because they have the cheapest beds in town. Prices can change without notice; verify the hotel's current rates online or by email. For the best prices, always book directly with the hotel.

Abbreviations

To pack maximum information into minimum space, I use the following code to describe accommodations in this book. Prices listed are per room, not per person. When a price range is given for a type of room (such as double rooms listing for €80-100), it means the price fluctuates with the season, size of room, or length of stay; expect to pay the upper end for peak-season stays. In Croatia, where accommodation prices vary dramatically by season, I've separated high , mid-, and low-season rates with slashes (explained in each destination's "Sleep Code").

S = Single room (or price for one person in a double).

D = Double or twin room. "Double beds" can be two twins sheeted together and are usually big enough for nonromantic couples.

T = Triple (often a double bed with a single).

Q = Quad (usually two double beds; adding an extra child's bed to a T is usually cheaper).

b = Private bathroom with toilet and shower or tub.

s = Private shower or tub only (the toilet is down the hall).

According to this code, a couple staying at a "Db-2,700 Kč" place in Prague would pay a total of 2,700 Czech crowns (about $135) for a double room with a private bathroom. At hotels, unless otherwise noted, breakfast is included, hotel staff speak basic English, and credit cards are accepted (though private accommodations rarely provide breakfast or accept credit cards). If the city adds a room tax, it generally isn't included in the rates I list. There's almost always Wi-Fi (which may be called "WLAN") and/or a guest computer available, either free or for a fee.

Some accommodations quote their rates in euros, while others use the local currency. Occasionally I've converted a few prices to make it easier for you to compare hotel rates—so you might notice a little variation between the rates listed here and those quoted by hotels.

If you're on a budget, it's smart to email several hotels to ask for their best price. Comparison-shop and make your choice. This is especially helpful when dealing with the larger hotels that use "dynamic pricing," a computer-generated system that predicts the demand for particular days and sets prices accordingly: High-demand days will often be more than double the price of low-demand days. This makes it impossible for a guidebook to list anything more accurate than a wide range of prices. I regret this trend. While you can assume that hotels listed in this book are good, it's very difficult to say which ones are the better value unless you email to confirm the price.

As you look over the listings, you'll notice that a few accommodations promise special prices to Rick Steves readers. To get these rates, you must book direct (that is, not through a booking site like TripAdvisor or Booking.com), mention this book when you reserve, and then show the book upon arrival. Rick Steves discounts apply to readers with ebooks as well as printed books. Because we trust hotels to honor this, please let me know if you don't receive a listed discount. Note, though, that discounts understandably may not be applied to promotional rates.

In general, prices can soften if you do any of the following: offer to pay cash, stay at least three nights, or mention this book. You can also try asking for a cheaper room or a discount, or offer to skip breakfast.

TYPES OF ACCOMMODATIONS
Hotels

In Eastern Europe, you can choose from a delightful variety of stylish and charming hotels and guesthouses. Hotel prices are roughly on par with midrange Western European countries: You can find a central, basic, comfortable double for $100 just about anywhere. Plan on spending $90-130 per double in big cities, and $60-90 in smaller towns. You can uncover some bargains, but I think it's worth paying a little  more for comfort and a good location. In general, a triple room is cheaper than the cost of a double and a single. Traveling alone can be expensive: A single room can be close to the cost of a double.

The Good and Bad of Online Reviews

User-generated travel review websites—such as TripAdvisor, Booking.com, and Yelp—have quickly become a huge player in the travel industry. These sites give you access to actual reports—good and bad—from travelers who have experienced the hotel, restaurant, tour, or attraction.

My hotelier friends in Europe are in awe of these sites' influence. Small hoteliers who want to stay in business have no choice but to work with review sites—which often charge fees for good placement or photos and tack on commissions if users book through the site instead of directly with the hotel.

While these sites work hard to weed out bogus users, my hunch is that a significant percentage of reviews are posted by friends or enemies of the business being reviewed. I've even seen hotels "bribe" guests (for example, offer a free breakfast) in exchange for a positive review. Also, review sites can become an echo chamber, with one or two flashy businesses camped out atop the ratings, while better, more affordable, and more authentic alternatives sit ignored farther down the list. (For example, I find review sites' restaurant recommendations skew to very touristy, obvious options.)

Remember that a user-generated review is based on the experience of one person. That person likely stayed at one hotel and ate at a few restaurants, and doesn't have much of a basis for comparison. A guidebook is the work of a trained researcher who has exhaustively visited many alternatives to assess their relative value. I recently checked out some top-rated TripAdvisor listings in various towns; when stacked up against their competitors, some are gems, while just as many are duds.

Both types of information have their place, and in many ways, they're complementary. If a hotel or restaurant is well-reviewed in a guidebook or two, and also gets good ratings on one of these sites, it's likely a winner.

When you check in, the receptionist will normally ask for your passport and keep it for a couple of hours. Don't worry. Hotels are legally required to register each guest with the local police. Americans are notorious for making this chore more difficult than it needs to be.

Breakfast, almost always served buffet style, usually includes rolls, cold cuts, cheese, cereal, yogurt, fruit, coffee, milk, and juice; some places also provide eggs.

Hotel elevators, while becoming more common, are often very small: Pack light, or you may need to take your bags up one at a time. Most hotel rooms have a TV and telephone, and these days, most hotels offer free Wi-Fi. Pricier hotels also have

Making Hotel Reservations

Given the erratic accommodations values in Eastern Europe (and the quality of the places I've found for this book), I recommend that you reserve your rooms several weeks in advance—or as soon as you've pinned down your travel dates, particularly if you'll be traveling during peak times. Note that some national holidays jam things up and merit your making reservations far in advance (see page 1357).

Requesting a Reservation: It's usually easiest to book your room through the hotel's website. (For the best rates, always use the hotel's official site and not a booking agency's site.) If there's no reservation form, or for complicated requests, send an email (see below for a sample request). Most recommended hotels take reservations in English.

The hotelier wants to know:
- The number and type of rooms you need
- The number of nights you'll stay
- Your date of arrival (use the European style for writing dates: day/month/year)
- Your date of departure
- Any special needs (such as bathroom in the room or down the hall, cheapest room, twin beds vs. double bed, and so on)

Make sure you mention any discounts—for Rick Steves readers or otherwise—when you make the reservation.

Confirming a Reservation: Most places will request a credit-card number to hold your room. If they don't have a secure online reservation form—look for the *https*—you can email it (I do), but it's safer to share that confidential info via a phone call or two emails (splitting your number between them).

air-conditioning and minibars.

If you're arriving early in the morning, your room probably won't be ready. You can drop your bag safely at the hotel and dive right into sightseeing.

Hoteliers can be a great help and source of advice. Most know their city well, and can assist you with everything from public transit and airport connections to finding a good restaurant, the nearest launderette, or a Wi-Fi hotspot.

Even at the best places, mechanical breakdowns occur: Air-conditioning malfunctions, sinks leak, hot water turns cold, and toilets gurgle and smell. Report your concerns clearly and calmly at the front desk. For more complicated problems, don't expect instant results.

If you suspect night noise will be a problem (if, for instance, your room is over a nightclub), ask for a quieter room in the back or on an upper floor. To guard against theft in your room, keep

From:	rick@ricksteves.com
Sent:	Today
To:	info@hotelcentral.com
Subject:	Reservation request for 19-22 July

Dear Hotel Central,

I would like to reserve a room for 2 people for 3 nights, arriving 19 July and departing 22 July. If possible, I would like a quiet room with a double bed and a bathroom inside the room.

Please let me know if you have a room available and the price.

Thank you!
Rick Steves

Canceling a Reservation: If you must cancel your reservation, it's courteous—and smart—to do so with as much advance notice as possible, especially for smaller family-run places. Be warned that cancellation policies can be strict; read the fine print or ask about these before you book. Internet deals may require prepayment, with no refunds for cancellations.

Reconfirming a Reservation: Always call to reconfirm your room reservation a few days in advance. For smaller hotels and B&Bs, I call again on my day of arrival to tell my host what time I expect to get there (especially important if arriving late—after 17:00).

Phoning: For tips on how to call hotels overseas, see page 1318.

valuables out of sight. Some rooms come with a safe, and other hotels have safes at the front desk. I've never bothered using one.

Checkout can pose problems if surprise charges pop up on your bill. If you settle your bill the afternoon before you leave, you'll have time to discuss and address any points of contention (before 19:00, when the night shift usually arrives).

Above all, keep a positive attitude. Remember, you're on vacation. If your hotel is a disappointment, spend more time out enjoying the city you came to see.

Private Rooms

Private accommodations—which are particularly prevalent in Croatia—offer travelers a characteristic and money-saving alternative for a fraction of the price of a hotel. Rooms in private homes are called *sobe* in Slovenia and Croatia; the German word *Zimmer* works there, too, and throughout Eastern Europe. These places are inexpensive, at least as comfortable as a cheap hotel, and a good way to get some local insight. The boss changes the sheets, so people staying several nights are most desirable—and those who stay less than three nights are often charged a lot more (typically 20-50 percent; this surcharge is often waived outside of peak season). For more on Croatian *sobe,* see page 857.

Hostels

You'll pay about $20-30 per bed to stay at a hostel. Travelers of any age are welcome if they don't mind dorm-style accommodations and meeting other travelers. Most hostels offer kitchen facilities, guest computers, Wi-Fi, and a self-service laundry. Nowadays, concerned about bedbugs, hostels are likely to provide all bedding, including sheets. Family and private rooms may be available on request.

Independent hostels tend to be easygoing, colorful, and informal (no membership required); www.hostelworld.com is the standard way backpackers search and book hostels, but also try www.hostelz.com and www.hostels.com.

Official hostels are part of Hostelling International (HI) and share an online booking site (www.hihostels.com). HI hostels typically require that you either have a membership card or pay extra per night.

OTHER ACCOMMODATION OPTIONS

Whether you're in a city or the countryside, renting an apartment, house, or villa can be a fun and cost-effective way to go local. Websites such as HomeAway and its sister sites VRBO and GreatRentals let you correspond directly with European property owners or managers.

Airbnb and Roomorama make it reasonably easy to find a place to sleep in someone's home. Beds range from air-mattress-in-living-room basic to plush-B&B-suite posh. If you want a place to sleep that's free, Couchsurfing.org is a vagabond's alternative to Airbnb. It lists millions of outgoing members, who host fellow "surfers" in their homes.

Eating

Eastern Europe offers good food for relatively little money—especially if you steer clear of the easy-to-avoid tourist-trap restaurants. This is affordable sightseeing for your palate.

Slavic cuisine has a reputation for being heavy and hearty, with lots of pork, potatoes, and cabbage. And, to be fair, some of that reputation is well-earned. But the food here is also delicious, and there's a lot more diversity from country to country than you might

expect. For example, Hungarian cuisine is rich and spicy (think paprika), while Slovenia and Croatia have good seafood and lots of Italian-style dishes (pastas and pizzas), and Polish food is more "northern" (with lots of dill, berries, and cream—like Russian cuisine). Tune in to the regional and national specialties and customs (see each country's introduction in this book for details).

For a change of pace, seek out vegetarian, Italian, Indian, Chinese, and similar places, which are especially good in big cities such as Prague, Budapest, or Kraków (I've listed a few tasty options).

When restaurant-hunting, choose a spot filled with locals, not the place with the big neon signs boasting, "We Speak English and Accept Credit Cards." Venturing even a block or two off the main drag leads to higher-quality food for less than half the price of the tourist-oriented places. Locals eat better at lower-rent locales. Most restaurants tack a menu on to their door for browsers and have an English menu inside. If the place isn't full, you can usually just seat yourself (get a waiter's attention to be sure your preferred table is OK)—the American-style "hostess," with a carefully managed waiting list, isn't common here. Once seated, feel free to take your time. In fact, it might be difficult to dine in a hurry. Only a rude waiter will rush you. Good service is relaxed (slow to an American).

When you're in the mood for something halfway between a restaurant and a picnic meal, look for take-out food stands, bakeries (with sandwiches and savory pastries to go), shops selling pizza by the slice, or simple little eateries offering fast and easy sit-down restaurant food. In Poland, don't miss the deliriously cheap "milk bar" cafeterias (see page 234). Many grocery stores sell pre-made sandwiches, and others might be willing to make one for you from what's in the deli case.

The Czech Republic is beer country, with Europe's best and cheapest brew. Poland also has fine beer, but the national drink is *wódka*. Hungary, Slovenia, and Croatia are known for their wines. Each country has its own distinctive liqueur, most of them a variation on *slivovice* (SLEE-voh-veet-seh)—a plum brandy so highly valued that it's the de facto currency of the Carpathian Mountains (often used for bartering with farmers and other mountain folk). Menus list drink size by the tenth of a liter, or deciliter (dl). Nondrinkers will find all the standard types of Coke and Pepsi, along with some fun-to-sample local alternatives (such as Slovenia's Cockta, described on page 724).

Hurdling the Language Barrier

Many visitors are pleasantly surprised to learn that the language barrier in Eastern Europe is no bigger than in Western Europe. In fact, I find it much easier to communicate in Hungary or Croatia than in Italy or Spain. Why is that? Because the Eastern European countries are small and not politically powerful, their residents realize that it's unreasonable to expect visitors to learn Hungarian (with only 12 million speakers worldwide), Croatian (5 million), or Slovene (2 million). It's essential to find a common language with the rest of the world—so they learn English early and well. In Croatia, for example, all school-children start learning English in the third grade. (I've had surprisingly eloquent conversations with Croatian grade-schoolers.)

Of course, not everyone speaks English. In these situations, it's relatively easy to get your point across. I've often bought a train ticket simply by writing out the name of my destination (preferably with the local spelling—for example, "Praha" instead of "Prague"); the time I want to travel (using the 24-hour clock); and, if I'm not traveling on the same day I'm buying the ticket, I include the date I want to leave (day first, then the month as a Roman numeral, then the year). Here's an example of what I'd show a ticket-seller at a train station: "Warszawa, 17:30, 15.VII.16."

Eastern Europeans, realizing that their language intimidates Americans, often invent easier nicknames for themselves—so Šárka goes by "Sara," András becomes "Andrew," and Jaroslav tells you, "Call me Jerry."

The people in most of this book's destinations—the Czech Republic, Slovakia, Poland, Slovenia, Croatia, and Bosnia-Herzegovina—speak Slavic languages. These languages are closely related to one another and to Russian, and are, to varying degrees, mutually intelligible (though many spellings change—for example, Czech *hrad*, or "castle," becomes Croatian *grad*). Slavic languages have simple vocabularies but are highly inflected—that is, the meaning of a sentence depends on complicated endings that are tacked onto the ends of the words (as in Latin).

Slavic words are notorious for their seemingly unpronounceable, long strings of consonants. Slavic pronunciation can be tricky. In fact, when the first Christian missionaries, Cyril and Methodius, came to Eastern Europe a millennium ago, they invented a whole new alphabet to represent these strange Slavic sounds. A modified version of that alphabet—called Cyrillic—is still used today in the eastern Slavic countries (such as Serbia and Russia).

Fortunately, the destinations covered in this book all use the same Roman alphabet we do, but they add lots of different diacritics—little markings below and above some letters—to represent a wide range of sounds (for example, č, ą, ó, đ, ł). I explain each of these diacritics in this book's various country introductions.

Hungarian is another story altogether—it's completely unrelated to Slavic languages, German, or English. For more on the challenging Magyar tongue, see page 539.

It's easy to throw up your arms in defeat and assume you'll never pronounce these words. But unlike English, Eastern European languages are entirely phonetic—you can always sound words out with confidence, once you learn a few basic rules. My advice: Take the time to wrestle with each language, and you'll be amazed how quickly you get comfortable.

German is spoken in Vienna. As part of the same language family as English, German sounds more familiar to American ears than the Slavic languages. Throughout Eastern Europe, speaking German can come in handy, especially if you're interacting with somebody over age 40 (while few people under communism learned English, German ranked right up there with Russian as a popular second language). A few words of Italian can come in handy in Slovenia and Croatia.

There are certain universal English words all Eastern Europeans know: hello, please, thank you, super, pardon, stop, menu, problem, and no problem. Another handy word that people throughout the region will understand is *Servus* (SEHR-voos)—the old-fashioned greeting from the days of the Austro-Hungarian Empire. If you draw a blank on how to say hello in the local language, just offer a cheery *"Servus!"*

Get an ear for the local language (see the language section in each of this book's country introductions), learn the key phrases (find survival phrases for each language in the country chapters), and travel with a phrase book. Consider Lonely Planet's good *Eastern Europe Phrasebook*, which covers all the languages spoken in the destinations in this book (except German).

Don't be afraid to interact with locals. Eastern Europeans can initially seem shy or even brusque—a holdover from the closed communist society—but often a simple smile is the only icebreaker you need to make a new friend. You'll find that doors open a little more quickly when you know a few words of the language. Give it your best shot, and the natives will appreciate your efforts.

Communicating

"How can I stay connected in Europe?"—by phone and online—may be the most common question I hear from travelers. You have three basic options:

1. "Roam" with your US mobile device. This is the easiest option, but likely the most expensive. It works best for people who won't be making very many calls, and who value the convenience of sticking with what's familiar (and their own phone number). In recent years, as data roaming fees have dropped and free Wi-Fi has become easier to find, the majority of travelers are finding this to be the best all-around option.

2. Use an unlocked mobile phone with European SIM cards. This is a much more affordable option if you'll be making lots of calls, since it gives you 24/7 access to low European rates. Although remarkably cheap, this option does require a bit of shopping around for the right phone and a prepaid SIM card. Savvy travelers who routinely buy European SIM cards swear by this tactic.

3. Use public phones, and get online with your hotel's guest computer and/or at Internet cafés. These options work particularly well for travelers who simply don't want to hassle with the technology, or want to be (mostly) untethered from their home life while on the road.

Each of these options is explained in greater detail in the following pages. Mixing and matching works well. For example, I routinely bring along my smartphone for Internet chores and Skyping on Wi-Fi, but also carry an unlocked phone and buy SIM cards for affordable calls on the go.

For an even more in-depth explanation of this complicated topic, see www.ricksteves.com/phoning.

HOW TO DIAL

Many Americans are intimidated by dialing European phone numbers. You needn't be. It's simple, once you break the code.

Dialing in Eastern Europe

The following instructions apply whether you're dialing from a mobile phone or a landline (such as a pay phone or your hotel-room phone). If you're roaming with a US phone number, follow the "Dialing Internationally" directions described later.

About half of all European countries use area codes; the other half use a direct-dial system without area codes.

In countries that use area codes (such as Slovakia, Slovenia, Croatia, Bosnia, and Austria), punch in just the phone number if you're dialing locally, and add the area code (which starts with a zero) if calling long distance within the same country. For example, Dubrovnik's area code is 020, and the number of one of my recommended Dubrovnik B&Bs is 453-834. To call the B&B within Dubrovnik, just dial 453-834. To call it from Split, dial 020/453-834.

Hungary, which also uses area codes, is a special case: To call within the same city, just dial the local number. But for long distance within Hungary, add the prefix 06, followed by the area code and number. For more on the confusing Hungarian phone system, see page 522.

To make calls within a country that uses a direct-dial system (such as the Czech Republic or Poland), you dial the same number whether you're calling across the country or across the street.

Don't be surprised that, in some countries, local phone numbers have different numbers of digits within the same city, or even the same hotel (e.g., a hotel can have a 6-digit phone number, a 7-digit mobile phone number, and an 8-digit fax number).

Dialing Internationally to or from Eastern Europe

Always start with the **international access code**—011 if you're calling from the US or Canada, 00 from anywhere in Europe). If you're dialing from a mobile phone, simply insert a + instead (by holding the 0 key).

• Dial the **country code** of the country you're calling (see the European calling chart in this chapter, or 1 for the US or Canada).

• Then dial the area code (if applicable) and the local number, keeping in mind that calling many countries requires dropping the initial zero of the phone number. The European calling chart lists specifics per country.

Calling from the US to Europe: To call, for example, the Dubrovnik B&B from the US, dial 011 (US access code), 385 (Croatia's country code), 20 (Dubrovnik's area code without the initial zero), and 453-834.

Calling from any European country to the US: To call my office in Edmonds, Washington, from anywhere in Europe, I dial 00 (Europe's access code), 1 (the US country code), 425 (Edmonds' area code), and 771-8303.

More Dialing Tips

The chart on the next page shows how to dial per country. For online instructions, see www.countrycallingcodes.com or www.howtocallabroad.com.

Remember, if you're using a mobile phone, dial as if you're in that phone's country of origin. So, when roaming with your US phone number in Croatia, dial as if you're calling from the US. But if you're using a European SIM card, dial as you would from that European country.

European Calling Chart

Just smile and dial, using this key:
AC = Area Code, LN = Local Number.

European Country	Calling long distance within ...	Calling from the US or Canada to ...	Calling from a European country to ...
Austria	AC + LN	011 + 43 + AC (without initial zero) + LN	00 + 43 + AC (without initial zero) + LN
Belgium	LN	011 + 32 + LN (without initial zero)	00 + 32 + LN (without initial zero)
Bosnia-Herzegovina	AC + LN	011 + 387 + AC (without initial zero) + LN	00 + 387 + AC (without initial zero) + LN
Croatia	AC + LN	011 + 385 + AC (without initial zero) + LN	00 + 385 + AC (without initial zero) + LN
Czech Republic	LN	011 + 420 + LN	00 + 420 + LN
Denmark	LN	011 + 45 + LN	00 + 45 + LN
Estonia	LN	011 + 372 + LN	00 + 372 + LN
Finland	AC + LN	011 + 358 + AC (without initial zero) + LN	999 (or other 900 number) + 358 + AC (without initial zero) + LN
France	LN	011 + 33 + LN (without initial zero)	00 + 33 + LN (without initial zero)
Germany	AC + LN	011 + 49 + AC (without initial zero) + LN	00 + 49 + AC (without initial zero) + LN
Gibraltar	LN	011 + 350 + LN	00 + 350 + LN
Great Britain & N. Ireland	AC + LN	011 + 44 + AC (without initial zero) + LN	00 + 44 + AC (without initial zero) + LN
Greece	LN	011 + 30 + LN	00 + 30 + LN
Hungary	06 + AC + LN	011 + 36 + AC + LN	00 + 36 + AC + LN
Ireland	AC + LN	011 + 353 + AC (without initial zero) + LN	00 + 353 + AC (without initial zero) + LN
Italy	LN	011 + 39 + LN	00 + 39 + LN

European Country	Calling long distance within ...	Calling from the US or Canada to ...	Calling from a European country to ...
Latvia	LN	011 + 371 + LN	00 + 371 + LN
Montenegro	AC + LN	011 + 382 + AC (without initial zero) + LN	00 + 382 + AC (without initial zero) + LN
Morocco	LN	011 + 212 + LN (without initial zero)	00 + 212 + LN (without initial zero)
Netherlands	AC + LN	011 + 31 + AC (without initial zero) + LN	00 + 31 + AC (without initial zero) + LN
Norway	LN	011 + 47 + LN	00 + 47 + LN
Poland	LN	011 + 48 + LN	00 + 48 + LN
Portugal	LN	011 + 351 + LN	00 + 351 + LN
Russia	8 + AC + LN	011 + 7 + AC + LN	00 + 7 + AC + LN
Slovakia	AC + LN	011 + 421 + AC (without initial zero) + LN	00 + 421 + AC (without initial zero) + LN
Slovenia	AC + LN	011 + 386 + AC (without initial zero) + LN	00 + 386 + AC (without initial zero) + LN
Spain	LN	011 + 34 + LN	00 + 34 + LN
Sweden	AC + LN	011 + 46 + AC (without initial zero) + LN	00 + 46 + AC (without initial zero) + LN
Switzerland	LN	011 + 41 + LN (without initial zero)	00 + 41 + LN (without initial zero)
Turkey	AC (if there's no initial zero, add one) + LN	011 + 90 + AC (without initial zero) + LN	00 + 90 + AC (without initial zero) + LN

PRACTICALITIES

- The instructions above apply whether you're calling to or from a European landline or mobile phone.
- If calling from any mobile phone, you can replace the international access code with "+" (press and hold 0 to insert it).
- The international access code is 011 if you're calling from the US or Canada.
- To call the US or Canada from Europe, dial 00, then 1 (country code for US and Canada), then the area code and number. In short, 00 + 1 + AC + LN = Hi, Mom!

Note that calls to a European mobile phone are substantially more expensive than calls to a fixed line. Off-hour calls are generally cheaper.

For tips on communicating over the phone with someone who speaks another language, see "Hurdling the Language Barrier," earlier.

USING YOUR SMARTPHONE IN EUROPE

Even in this age of email, texting, and near-universal Internet access, smart travelers still use the telephone. I call TIs to smooth out sightseeing plans, hotels to get driving directions, museums to confirm tour schedules, restaurants to check open hours or to book a table, and so on.

Most people enjoy the convenience of bringing their own smartphone. Horror stories about sky-high roaming fees are dated and exaggerated, and major service providers work hard to avoid surprising you with an exorbitant bill. With a little planning, you can use your phone—for voice calls, messaging, and Internet access—without breaking the bank.

Start by figuring out whether your phone works in Europe. Most phones purchased through AT&T and T-Mobile (which use the same technology as Europe) work abroad, while only some phones from Verizon or Sprint do—check your operating manual (look for "tri-band," "quad-band," or "GSM"). If you're not sure, ask your service provider.

Roaming Costs

"Roaming" with your phone—that is, using it outside its home region, such as in Europe—generally comes with extra charges, whether you are making voice calls, sending texts, or reading your email. The fees listed here are for the three major American providers—Verizon, AT&T, and T-Mobile; Sprint's roaming rates tend to be much higher. But policies change fast, so get the latest details before your trip. For example, as of mid-2014, T-Mobile waived voice, texting, and data roaming fees for some plans.

Voice calls are the most expensive. Most US providers charge from $1.29 to $1.99 per minute to make or receive calls in Europe. (As you cross each border, you'll typically get a text message explaining the rates in the new country.) If you plan to make multiple calls, look into a global calling plan to lower the per-minute cost, or buy a package of minutes at a discounted price (such as 30 minutes for $30). Note that you'll be charged for incoming calls whether or not you answer them; to save money, ask your friends to stay in contact by texting, and to call you only in case of an emergency.

Text messaging costs 20 to 50 cents per text. To cut that cost, you could sign up for an international messaging plan (for example, $10 for 100 texts). Or consider apps that let you text for free (iMessage for Apple, Google Hangouts for Android, or WhatsApp for any device); however, these require you to use Wi-Fi or data roaming. Be aware that Europeans use the term "SMS" ("short message service") to describe text messaging.

Data roaming means accessing data services via a cellular network other than your home carrier's. Prices have dropped dramatically in recent years, making this an affordable way for travelers to bridge gaps between Wi-Fi hotspots. You'll pay far less if you set up an international data roaming plan. Most providers charge $25-30 for 100-120 megabytes of data. That's plenty for basic Internet tasks—100 megabytes lets you view 100 websites or send/receive 1,000 text-based emails, but you'll burn through that amount quickly by streaming videos or music. If your data use exceeds your plan amount, most providers will automatically kick in an additional 100- or 120-megabyte block for the same price. (For more, see "Using Wi-Fi and Data Roaming," later.)

Setting Up (or Disabling) International Service

With most service providers, international roaming (voice, text, and data) is disabled on your account unless you activate it. Before your trip, call your provider (or visit their website), and cover the following topics:

• Confirm that your phone will work in Europe.

• Verify global roaming rates for voice calls, text messaging, and data.

• Tell them which of those services you'd like to activate.

• Consider add-on plans to bring down the cost of international calls, texts, or data roaming.

When you get home from Europe, be sure to cancel any add-on plans that you activated for your trip.

Some people would rather use their smartphone exclusively on Wi-Fi, and not worry about either voice or data charges. If that's you, call your provider to be sure that international roaming options are deactivated on your account. To be double-sure, put your phone in "airplane mode," then turn your Wi-Fi back on.

Using Wi-Fi and Data Roaming

A good approach is to use free Wi-Fi wherever possible, and fill in the gaps with data roaming.

Wi-Fi is readily available throughout Europe. At accommodations, access is usually free, but you may have to pay a fee, especially at expensive hotels. At hotels with thick stone walls, the Wi-Fi signal from the lobby may not reach every room. If Wi-Fi is important to you, ask about it when you book—and be specific

("In the rooms?"). Get the password and network name at the front desk when you check in.

When you're out and about, your best bet for finding free Wi-Fi is often at a café. They'll usually tell you the password if you buy something. Or you can stroll down a café-lined street, smartphone in hand, checking for unsecured networks every few steps until you find one that works. Some towns have free public Wi-Fi in highly trafficked parks or piazzas. You may have to register before using it, or get a password at the TI.

Data roaming is handy when you can't find Wi-Fi. Because you'll pay by the megabyte (explained earlier), it's best to limit how much data you use. Save bandwidth-gobbling tasks like Skyping, watching videos, or downloading apps or emails with large attachments until you're on Wi-Fi. Switch your phone's email settings from "push" to "fetch." This means that you can choose to "fetch" (download) your messages when you're on Wi-Fi rather than having them continuously "pushed" to your device. And be aware of apps—such as news, weather, and sports tickers—that automatically update. Check your phone's settings to be sure that none of your apps are set to "use cellular data."

I like the safeguard of manually turning off data roaming on my phone whenever I'm not actively using it. To turn off data and voice roaming, look in your phone's settings menu—try checking under "cellular" or "network," or ask your service provider how to do it. If you need to get online but can't find Wi-Fi, simply turn on data roaming long enough for the task at hand, then turn it off again.

Figure out how to keep track of how much data you've used (in your phone's menu, look for "cellular data usage"; you may have to reset the counter at the start of your trip). Some companies automatically send you a text message warning if you approach or exceed your limit.

There's yet another option: If you're traveling with an unlocked smartphone (explained later), you can buy a SIM card that also includes data; this can be far cheaper than data roaming through your home provider.

USING EUROPEAN SIM CARDS

Although using your American phone in Europe is easy, it's not always cheap. And unreliable Wi-Fi can make keeping in touch frustrating. If you're reasonably technology-savvy, and would like to have the option of making lots of affordable calls, it's worth getting comfortable with European SIM cards.

Here's the basic idea: With an unlocked phone (which works with different carriers; see below), get a SIM card—the microchip that stores data about your phone—once you get to Europe. Slip

---

Internet Calling

To make totally free voice and video calls over the Internet, all you need are a smartphone, tablet, or laptop; a strong Wi-Fi signal; and an account with one of the major Internet calling providers: Skype (www.skype.com), FaceTime (preloaded on most Apple devices), or Google+ Hangouts (www.google. com/hangouts). If the Wi-Fi signal isn't strong enough for video, try sticking with an audio-only call. Or...wait for your next hotel. Many Internet calling programs also work for making calls from your computer to telephones worldwide for a very reasonable fee—generally just a few cents per minute (you'll have to buy some credit before you make your first call).

---

in the SIM, turn on the phone, and bingo! You've got a European phone number (and access to cheaper European rates).

Getting an Unlocked Phone

Your basic options are getting your existing phone unlocked, or buying a phone (either at home or in Europe).

Some phones are electronically "locked" so that you can't switch SIM cards (keeping you loyal to your carrier). But in some circumstances it's possible to unlock your phone—allowing you to replace the original SIM card with one that will work with a European provider. Note that some US carriers are beginning to offer phones/tablets whose SIM card can't be swapped out in the US but will accept a European SIM without any unlocking process.

You may already have an old, unused mobile phone in a drawer somewhere. Call your service provider and ask if they'll send you the unlock code. Otherwise, you can buy one: Search an online shopping site for an "unlocked quad-band phone," or buy one at a mobile-phone shop in Europe. Either way, a basic model typically costs $40 or less.

Buying and Using SIM Cards

Once you have an unlocked phone, you'll need to buy a SIM card (note that a smaller variation called "micro-SIM" or "nano-SIM"—used in most iPhones—is less widely available).

SIM cards are sold at mobile-phone shops, department-store electronics counters, and newsstands for $5–10, and usually include about that much prepaid calling credit (making the card itself virtually free). Because SIM cards are prepaid, there's no contract and no commitment; I routinely buy one even if I'm in a country for only a few days.

In most Eastern European countries, buying a SIM card is as easy as buying a pack of gum. However, an increasing number of countries—including Hungary—require you to register the SIM card with your passport (an anti-terrorism measure). This takes only a few minutes longer: The  shop clerk will ask you to fill out a form, then submit it to the service provider. Sometimes you can register your own SIM card online. Either way, an hour or two after submitting the information, you'll get a text welcoming you to that network.

When using a SIM card in its home country, it's free to receive calls and texts, and it's cheap to make calls—domestic calls average 20 cents per minute. You can also use SIM cards to call the US—sometimes very affordably: (Lebara and Lycamobile, which operate in multiple European countries, let you call a US number for less than 10 cents a minute). Rates are higher if you're roaming in another country. But if you bought the SIM card within the European Union, roaming fees are capped no matter where you travel throughout the EU (about 25 cents/minute to make calls, 7 cents/minute to receive calls, and 8 cents for a text message).

While you can buy SIM cards just about anywhere, I like to seek out a mobile-phone shop, where an English-speaking clerk can help explain my options, get my SIM card inserted and set up, and show me how to use it. When you buy your SIM card, ask about rates for domestic and international calls and texting, and about roaming fees. Also find out how to check your credit balance (usually you'll key in a few digits and hit "Send"). You can top up your credit at any newsstand, tobacco shop, mobile-phone shop, or many other businesses (look for the SIM card's logo in the window).

To insert your SIM card into the phone, locate the slot, which is usually on the side of the phone or behind the battery. Turning on the phone, you'll be prompted to enter the "SIM PIN" (a code number that came with your card).

If you have an unlocked smartphone, you can look for a European SIM card that covers both voice and data. This is often much cheaper than paying for data roaming through your home provider.

LANDLINE TELEPHONES AND INTERNET CAFÉS

If you prefer to travel without a smartphone or tablet, you can still stay in touch using landline telephones, hotel guest computers, and Internet cafés.

Types of Telephone Cards

Europe uses two different types of telephone cards. Both types are sold at post offices, newsstands, street kiosks, tobacco shops, and train stations.

Insertable Phone Cards: These cards can only be used at pay phones: Simply take the phone off the hook, insert the card, wait for a dial tone, and dial away. The phone displays your credit ticking down as you talk. Each European country has its own insertable phone card—so your Czech card won't work in a Polish phone.

International Phone Cards: These prepaid cards, which are less common in Eastern Europe than they are in Western Europe, can be used to make inexpensive calls—within Europe, or to the US, for pennies a minute—from nearly any phone, including the one in your hotel room. The cards come with a toll-free number and a scratch-to-reveal PIN code. If the voice prompts aren't in English, experiment: Dial your code, followed by the pound sign (#), then the phone number, then pound again, and so on, until it works.

Landline Telephones

Phones in your **hotel room** can be great for local calls and for calls using cheap international phone cards (described in the sidebar). Many hotels charge a fee for local and "toll-free" as well as long-distance or international calls—always ask for the rates before you dial. Since you'll never be charged for receiving calls, it can be more affordable to have someone from the US call you in your room.

While **public pay phones** are on the endangered species list, you'll still see them in post offices and train stations. Pay phones generally come with multilingual instructions. Most public phones work with insertable phone cards (described in the sidebar).

You'll see many cheap **call shops** that advertise low rates to faraway lands, often in train-station neighborhoods. While these target immigrants who want to call home cheaply, tourists can use them, too. Before making your call, be completely clear on the rates.

Internet Cafés and Public Internet Terminals

Finding public Internet terminals in Europe is no problem. Many hotels have a computer in the lobby for guests to use. Otherwise, head for an Internet café, or ask the TI or your hotelier for the nearest place to access the Internet.

European computers typically use non-American keyboards. A few letters are switched around, and command keys are labeled in the local language. Many European keyboards have an "Alt

Gr" key (for "Alternate Graphics") to the right of the space bar; press this to insert the extra symbol that appears on some keys. Europeans have different names for, and different ways to type, the @ symbol. If you can't locate a special character (such as the @ symbol), simply copy it from a Web page and paste it into your email message.

Internet Security

Whether you're accessing the Internet with your own device or at a public terminal, using a shared network or computer comes with the potential for increased security risks. Ask the hotel or café for the specific name of their Wi-Fi network, and make sure you log on to that exact one; hackers sometimes create a bogus hotspot with a similar or vague name (such as "Hotel Europa Free Wi-Fi"). It's better if a network uses a password (especially a hard-to-guess one) rather than being open to the world.

While traveling, you may want to check your online banking or credit-card statements, or to take care of other personal-finance chores, but Internet security experts advise against accessing these sites entirely while traveling. Even if you're using your own computer at a password-protected hotspot, any hacker who's logged on to the same network can see what you're up to. If you need to log on to a banking website, try to do so on a hard-wired connection (i.e., using an Ethernet cable in your hotel room), or, if that's not possible, use a secure banking app on a cellular telephone connection.

If using a credit card online, make sure that the site is secure. Most browsers display a little padlock icon, and the URL begins with *https* instead of *http*. Never send a credit-card number over a website that doesn't begin with *https*.

If you're not convinced a connection is secure, avoid accessing any sites (such as your bank's) that could be vulnerable to fraud.

MAIL

You can mail one package per day to yourself worth up to $200 duty-free from Europe to the US (mark it "personal purchases"). If you're sending a gift to someone, mark it "unsolicited gift." For details, visit www.cbp.gov and search for "Know Before You Go."

Eastern European postal services work fine, but for quick transatlantic delivery (in either direction), consider services such as DHL (www.dhl.com).

Transportation

In Eastern Europe, I travel mostly by public transportation. For long distances between big cities (such as Prague to Kraków, Warsaw to Budapest, or Vienna to Dubrovnik), I prefer to take a cheap flight or a night train. For shorter distances (like Gdańsk to Warsaw or Ljubljana to Zagreb), I take a daytime train or bus. In areas with lots of exciting day-trip possibilities, such as the Czech countryside or Slovenia's Julian Alps, I rent a car for a day or two—or hire a local with a car to drive me around (which can be cheaper than you might think; in this book, I recommend several drivers and tour guides with cars).

If you're debating between public transportation and car rental, consider these factors: Cars are best for three or more traveling together (especially families with small kids), those packing heavy, and those scouring the countryside. Trains, buses, and boats are best for solo travelers, blitz tourists, city-to-city travelers, those with an ambitious, multicountry itinerary, and those who don't want to drive in Europe. While a car gives you more freedom, trains, buses, and boats zip you effortlessly and scenically from city to city, usually dropping you in the center, often near a tourist office. Cars are great in the countryside, but an expensive headache in places like Prague, Budapest, and Dubrovnik.

Throughout this book, I suggest whether trains, buses, or boats are better for a particular destination (in the "Connections" section at the end of each chapter).

TRAINS

Trains are punctual and cover cities well, but frustrating schedules make a few out-of-the-way recommendations difficult—or impossible—to reach (usually the bus will get you there instead; see "Buses," later).

Schedules: Pick up train schedules from stations as you go, or print them out from an online source. To study ahead on the Web, check www.bahn.com, Germany's excellent all-Europe timetable. Individual countries also have their own train timetable websites:

- **Czech Republic:** www.idos.cz
- **Poland:** www.rozklad-pkp.pl
- **Hungary:** www.elvira.hu
- **Slovenia:** www.slo-zeleznice.si
- **Croatia:** www.hznet.hr
- **Austria:** www.oebb.at
- **Slovakia:** www.cp.sk

Tickets: Buy tickets at the train station (or on board, if the station is unstaffed). In many big-city train stations, it can be tricky to find the correct line (you'll see separate ticket windows

PRACTICALITIES

Public Transportation in Eastern Europe

To Copenhagen
To Rødby (Denmark)
To Ystad (Sweden)
To Ystad & Copenhagen
To Karlskrona (Sweden)

LITH.

Baltic Sea

KALININGRAD (RUSSIA)

Gdynia
Gdańsk
Sopot
To Vilnius & Riga

Lübeck
Puttgarten
Hamburg
To Amsterdam

Świnoujście
Szczecin
Tczew
Malbork

Toruń
To Brest & Moscow

Frankfurt an der Oder
Poznań
Warsaw

Berlin
Forst

To Amsterdam

GERMANY
POLAND

Leipzig
Görlitz
Wrocław
Częstochowa

Dresden
Zgor.
Opole
Schona
Lichkov
Katowice
Oświęcim (Auschwitz)
To Frankfurt
Karlovy Vary
Prague
CZECH. REP.
Kraków
Medyka

Cheb
Plzeň
Zeb.
Žil.
Zak.
Plaveč
To L'viv

Furth
Český Krumlov
České Bud.
Brno
SLOVAKIA
UKR.
Nürnberg
Sum.
Břeclav
Levoča
Košice

To Frankfurt
Passau
Gmünd
Spišská Nova Ves
Cana

Munich
Linz
Vienna
Bratislava
Eger
Miskolc
Füzesabony

Salzburg
Heg.
Győr
Budapest

Innsbruck
Graz
Sopron

To Zürich
AUSTRIA
Klagen-furt
Siófok
Curtici

Villach
Spiel.
HUNGARY
To Bucharest

Tarvisio
Jes.
Mar.
Hodos

ITALY
Bled
Kop.
Pécs

To Milan
Gor.
O.N.G.
Ljubljana
SLOVENIA
Subotica

Verona
Mon.
Zagreb
ROMANIA

Venice
Sež.
Rijeka
Koper
CROATIA
Šid

Piran
Zadar
Plitvice
Belgrade

Bologna
Rovinj
Pula
BOSNIA-HERZ.
SERBIA
BULG.

ITALY
Split
Sarajevo
Niš
Kalotina

Florence
Ploče
Mostar

Ancona
Korčula
MONT.
Pres.
To Sofia & Istanbul

N
Not to Scale
Dubrovnik
KOS.
MACE-DONIA

Rome
Kotor
Bar
Skopje

To Naples
Bari
ALB.
To Athens

Adriatic Sea

--- - - - --- Bus Route   ·········· Ferry Route

——— Railway   ══o══ Border Station

for domestic trips, international journeys, immediate departures, and other concerns). Before getting in line, confirm with fellow travelers that you've chosen the right one. Many ticket-sellers speak limited English—be prepared to write out your destination and time. Bigger cities have train-ticket offices, either downtown (such as in Budapest) or in the station (such as in Warsaw and Ljubljana), where you can take a number to wait for an English-speaking clerk to sort through your options; I've listed these in this book. Especially if you have a complicated request (such as reserving a night-train berth a few days ahead), these offices can save you some frustration, and—in some cases—a needless trip to the station. While most short-haul journeys do not require a reservation, you are required to reserve on some high-speed trains (such as the Warsaw-Kraków express). It's also smart to reserve a sleeping berth if you're taking a night train.

Night Trains: To cover the long distances between the major destinations in this book, consider using night trains. Each night on the train saves a day for sightseeing. However, Eastern European night trains aren't as new, plush, or comfy as those in Western Europe (such as Germany's slick CityNightLine). Expect a bumpy, noisy ride and gross WCs. In general, if a higher degree of comfort is important to you, look for an affordable flight (see "Flights," later), hire a driver to take you door-to-door (perhaps with some sightseeing stops en route), or take a day train. Thefts on night trains do occur, so lock the door and secure your belongings (to make it difficult—or at least noisy—for thieves to rip you off). When sleeping on a night train, I wear my money belt.

Rail Passes: Rail passes are rarely the best option for travel in Eastern Europe for two reasons: Point-to-point tickets are cheap and simple here, and most rail passes don't conveniently combine these countries. One handy option may be the European East Pass, covering the Czech Republic, Hungary, Slovakia, and Austria (but not Poland, Slovenia, Croatia, or Bosnia). Another option is the Global Pass, which covers all the countries in this book but is usually too expensive to be a good value. Each country except Slovakia and Bosnia has its own individual rail pass, valid for trips only within that country. Various pre-selected two- and three-country options are also available. Again, none of these passes is likely to save you much money, but if a pass matches your itinerary, give it a look and crunch the numbers.

For more detailed advice on figuring out the smartest rail pass options for your train trip, visit the Trains & Rail Passes section of my website at www.ricksteves.com/rail.

BUSES

While the train can get you most places faster than a bus can, this book covers a few areas where buses are worth considering. For example, Ljubljana and Lake Bled are connected by both train and bus—but the bus station is right in the town center of Bled, while the train station is a few miles away. And a few destinations, including Croatia's Plitvice Lakes National Park and Rovinj, are accessible only by bus. In general, trains are best in Poland and Hungary; buses are often better in Slovakia and Croatia; and it's a toss-up in the Czech Republic and Slovenia. When in doubt, ask at the local TI for advice.

BOATS

Boats can be your best option along the Croatian coast. For details, see "Boats" on page 861.

RENTING A CAR

If you're renting a car in Eastern Europe, bring your US driver's license. In Austria, Bosnia-Herzegovina, Hungary, Poland, and Slovenia you're also required to have an International Driving Permit (sold at your local AAA office for $15 plus the cost of two passport-type photos; see www.aaa.com). While that's the letter of the law, I've often rented cars without having this permit. If all goes well, you'll likely never be asked to show the permit—but it's a must if you end up dealing with the police.

Most rental companies require you to be at least 21 years old and to have held your license for one year. Drivers under the age of 25 may incur a young-driver surcharge, and some rental companies do not rent to anyone 75 or older. If you're considered too young or old, look into leasing (covered later), which has less-stringent age restrictions.

Research car rentals before you go. It's cheaper to arrange most car rentals from the US. Call several companies or look online to compare rates, or arrange a rental through your home-town travel agent.

Most of the major US rental agencies (including Avis, Budget, Enterprise, Hertz, and Thrifty) have offices throughout Eastern Europe. Also consider the two major Europe-based agencies, Europcar and Sixt. It can be cheaper to use a consolidator, such as Auto Europe/Kemwel (www.autoeurope.com) or Europe by Car (www.europebycar.com), which compares rates at several companies to get you the best deal—but because you're working with a middleman, it's especially important to ask in advance about add-on fees and restrictions.

Regardless of the car-rental company you choose, read the fine print carefully for add-on charges—such as one-way drop-off

Driving in Eastern Europe

Not to Scale

GERMANY

To Gdańsk
110m
2.5h

215m
5h

Toruń

135m • 3.5h

Warsaw

Berlin

180m • 3.75h

190m • 4h

Poznań

265m
6.5h

140m • 3.5h

120m
2.25h

POLAND

210m
4h

185m • 4.5h

390m • 9.5h

Częstochowa

90m • 2h

Dresden

65m
1.5h

65m
1.75h

40m
1.25h

Kraków

Terezín

290m • 5.5h

Auschwitz

80m • 2h

100m • 2.75h

40m
1h

Prague

40m
1.25h

CZECH
REPUBLIC

Zakopane

45m
1.5h

25k • .75h

Kutná
Hora

175m • 3.5h

Poprad

Karlštejn
Castle

100m • 2.25h

130m • 2h

200m

200m • 4h

SLOVAKIA

115m
3.5h

210m • 3.5h

Brno

80m
2h

80m
1.5h

Český
Krumlov

135m • 3.25h

40m
1h

240m
5.5h

Eger

Vienna

Bratislava

80m • 2h

140m • 2.5h

200m • 3.5h

125m
2h

150m • 2.5h

Budapest

Munich

90m
1.5h

Salzburg

240m
4h

235m • 4h

290m • 4.5h

145m • 2.5h

HUNGARY

AUSTRIA

150m • 2.5h

Bled

SLOVENIA

Pécs

30m
1h

Ljubljana

90m • 2h

Zagreb

SERBIA

ITALY

60m
1.5h

140m

150m • 3.5h

CROATIA

100m • 1.75h

75m
2h

Trieste

100m • 2h

90m • 2.5h

85m • 2h

260m • 4h

260m • 6h

Venice

50m • 1.5h

Rovinj

Rijeka

BOSNIA-
HERZEGOVINA

30m • .75h

55m
1.5h

140m • 3.5h

Plitvice

Pula

Sarajevo

85m
1.75h

90m
2.5h

Mostar

Zadar

100m • 2h

65m
2h

110m • 2.5h

Ston

Adriatic Sea

35m
1h

MONT.

Split

105m • 2.5h

5h

Note: Your times may
vary based on traffic,
construction, and road
conditions.

m = miles
h = hours
--- = car ferry

Korčula

35m • 1h

3.4h

Dubrovnik

PRACTICALITIES

fees, airport surcharges, or mandatory insurance policies—that aren't included in the "total price." You may need to query rental agents pointedly to find out your actual cost.

For the best deal, rent by the week with unlimited mileage. A diesel car can help you save money on fuel. I normally rent the smallest, least-expensive model with a stick shift (generally much cheaper than an automatic). Almost all rentals are manual by default, so if you need an automatic, request one in advance; be aware that these cars are usually larger models (more expensive and not as maneuverable on narrow, winding roads).

Figure on paying roughly $300 for a one-week rental. Allow extra for supplemental insurance, fuel, tolls, and parking. For trips of three weeks or more, look into leasing; you'll save money on insurance and taxes. Be warned that one-way international trips can be very expensive (for details, see "International Drop-Off Fees," later).

As a rule, always tell your car-rental company up front exactly which countries you'll be entering. Some companies levy extra insurance fees for trips taken in certain countries with certain types of cars (such as BMWs, Mercedes, and convertibles). Double-check with your rental agent that you have all the documentation you need before you drive off (especially if you're crossing borders into non-Schengen countries, such as Bosnia-Herzegovina, where you might need to present proof of insurance).

Big companies have offices in most cities; ask whether they can pick you up at your hotel. Small local rental companies can be cheaper but aren't as flexible.

Compare pickup costs (downtown can be less expensive than the airport), and explore drop-off options. Always check the hours of the location you choose: Many rental offices close from midday Saturday until Monday morning and, in smaller towns, at lunchtime.

When selecting a location, don't trust the agency's description of "downtown" or "city center." In some cases, a "downtown" branch can be on the outskirts of the city—a long, costly taxi ride from the center. Before choosing, plug the addresses into a mapping website. You may find that the "train station" location is handier. But returning a car at a big-city train station or downtown agency can be tricky; get precise details on the car drop-off location and hours, and allow ample time to find it.

When you pick up the rental car, check it thoroughly and make sure any damage is noted on your rental agreement. Find out how your car's lights, turn signals, wipers, radio, and fuel cap function, and know what kind of fuel the car takes (diesel vs. unleaded). When you return the car, make sure the agent verifies its condition with you. Some drivers take pictures of the returned vehicle as proof of its condition.

International Drop-Off Fees

If you're planning a multicountry itinerary by car, be aware of often-astronomical international drop-off fees. There's typically no extra charge for picking up and dropping off a car in different towns within the same country, but you'll pay through the nose to drop off across the border. (For example, you can generally pick up a car in Zagreb, drive it nine hours to Dubrovnik, and turn it in there for no charge—but if you drive the same car from Zagreb just two hours to Ljubljana and drop it off, it can cost you hundreds of extra dollars.)

For some itineraries, you may just have to live with the extra expense. But in most cases, you can plan your itinerary smartly to avoid it. Some people plan a circular itinerary (for example, Prague-Kraków-Budapest-Bratislava-Vienna-Prague) to ensure they can drop the car off where they picked it up. Others connect the longer distances on their itinerary with trains or flights, then rent a car strategically for a day or two in places where it's warranted (such as the Czech or Slovenian countrysides). This is a particularly smart plan when you remember that in most big cities, a car is an expensive and worthless burden (i.e., fighting urban traffic and paying for pricey secure parking).

Navigation Options

When renting a car in Europe, you have several alternatives for your digital navigator: Use your smartphone's online mapping app, download an offline map app, or rent a GPS device with your rental car (or bring your own GPS device from home).

Online mapping apps used to be prohibitively expensive for overseas travelers—but that was before most carriers started offering affordable international data plans. Before I head out each morning, I make a point to use my hotel's Wi-Fi hotspot to download all of the maps I'll need for that day. Once you're underway, if you need to update your route, check traffic conditions, or enable turn-by-turn voice instructions, you'll have to use data roaming or find another hotspot. However, GPS information—that blinking blue dot showing where you are on that map—does not use the Internet, and works fine offline. If you're already getting a data plan for your trip, this is probably the way to go (see "Using Your Smartphone in Europe," earlier).

A number of well-designed apps allow you much of the convenience of online maps without any costly demands on your data plan. City Maps 2Go is one of the most popular; OffMaps, Google Maps, and Navfree also all offer good, zoomable offline maps for much of Europe (some are better for driving, while others are better for navigating cities).

Some drivers prefer using a dedicated GPS unit—not only to

avoid the data-roaming fees, but because a stand-alone GPS can be easier to operate (important if you're driving solo). The major downside: It's expensive—around $10-30 per day. Your car's GPS unit may only come loaded with maps for its home country—if you need additional maps, ask. Make sure your device's language is set to English before you drive off. If you have a portable GPS device at home, you can take that instead. Many American GPS devices come loaded with US maps only—you'll need to buy and download European maps before your trip. This option is far less expensive than renting.

Car Insurance Options

When you rent a car, you are liable for a very high deductible, sometimes equal to the entire value of the car. Limit your financial risk with one of these options: Buy Collision Damage Waiver (CDW) coverage from the car-rental company, get coverage through your credit card (free if your card automatically includes zero-deductible coverage), or get collision insurance as part of a larger travel-insurance policy.

CDW includes a very high deductible (typically $1,000-1,500). Though each rental company has its own variation, basic CDW costs $10-30 a day (figure roughly 30 percent extra) and reduces your liability, but does not eliminate it. When you pick up the car, you'll be offered the chance to "buy down" the basic deductible to zero (for an additional $10-30/day; this is sometimes called "super CDW" or "zero-deductible coverage").

If you opt for **credit-card coverage,** there's a catch. You'll technically have to decline all coverage offered by the car-rental company, which means they can place a hold on your card (which can be up to the full value of the car). In case of damage, it can be time-consuming to resolve the charges with your credit-card company. Before you decide on this option, quiz your credit-card company about how it works.

If you're already purchasing a **travel-insurance policy** for your trip, adding collision coverage is an option. For example, Travel Guard (www.travelguard.com) sells affordable renter's collision insurance as an add-on to its other policies; it's valid everywhere in Europe except the Republic of Ireland, and some Italian car-rental companies refuse to honor it, as it doesn't cover you in case of theft.

For more on car-rental insurance, see www.ricksteves.com/cdw.

Leasing

For trips of three weeks or more, consider leasing (which automatically includes zero-deductible collision and theft insurance). By technically buying and then selling back the car, you save lots of money on tax and insurance. Leasing provides you a brand-new car with unlimited mileage and a 24-hour emergency assistance program. However, leases aren't generally available in Eastern Europe—you'll have to pick up and drop off the car elsewhere in Europe (such as Germany or Italy). You can lease for as little as 21 days to as long as five and a half months. Car leases must be arranged from the US. One of many companies offering affordable lease packages is Europe by Car (US tel. 800-223-1516, www.europebycarblog.com/lease).

DRIVING

Road Rules: Be aware of typical European road rules; for example, many countries—including most of the ones in this book—

AND LEARN THESE ROAD SIGNS

Speed Limit (km/hr) — Yield — No Passing — End of No Passing Zone

One Way — Intersection — Main Road — Freeway

Danger — No Entry — No Entry for cars — All Vehicles Prohibited

Parking — No Parking — Customs — Peace

require headlights to be turned on at all times, and it's generally illegal to drive while using your mobile phone without a hands-free headset. In Europe, you're not allowed to turn right on a red light, unless there is a sign or signal specifically authorizing it, and on expressways it's illegal to pass drivers on the right. Ask your car-rental company about these rules, or check the US State Department website (www.travel.state.gov, search for your country in the "Learn about your destination" box, then click on "Travel and Transportation").

Fuel: Gas is expensive—often about $6-8 per gallon. Diesel cars are more common in Europe than back home, so be sure you know what type of fuel your car takes before you fill up. Fuel pumps are color-coded for unleaded (green) or diesel (black).

Road Conditions: Eastern Europe is nearing the end of an impressive binge of superhighway construction. It's not unusual to discover that a much faster road has been built between major destinations since your five-year-old map was published. (This is another good reason to travel with the most up-to-date maps available and study them before each drive.) Over the last several years, superhighways have opened between Dresden and Prague (A-17); between Warsaw and Berlin (A-2); and from Budapest all the way

south to Ploče, Croatia (via Zagreb and Split). As soon as a long-enough section is completed, the roads are opened to the public.

Occasionally backcountry roads are the only option (especially in Poland). These can be bumpy and slow, but they're almost always paved (or, at least, they once were). In Poland, where the network of new expressways is far from complete, locals travel long distances on two-lane country roads. Since each lane is about a lane and a half wide, passing is commonplace. Slower drivers should keep to the far-right of their lane, and not be surprised when faster cars zip past them. Especially in Croatia and Slovenia, keep a close eye out for bikers—you'll see scads of them on mountain roads, struggling to earn a thrilling downhill run.

Tolls: In many countries, driving on highways requires a toll sticker (generally available at the border, post offices, gas stations, and sometimes car-rental agencies). You'll need a sticker in the **Czech Republic** (*dálniční známka*, 310 Kč/10 days, 440 Kč/1 month, www.sfdi.cz); **Slovakia** (*úhrada*, €10/10 days, €14/month, www.dialnicnenalepky.sk); **Hungary** (*autópálya matrica*, 2,975 Ft/week, 4,780 Ft/month, www.motorway.hu); **Slovenia** (*vinjeta*, €15/week, €30/month, www.dars.si); and **Austria** (*Vignette*, €8.70/10 days, €25.30/2 months, www.asfinag.at). Fines for not having a toll sticker can be stiff. Your rental car may already come with the necessary sticker—ask. In **Croatia,** you'll take a toll ticket as you enter the expressway, then pay when you get off, based on how far you've traveled. In **Poland,** drivers also pay tolls to use completed expressway segments.

Parking: Parking is a costly headache in big cities. You'll pay about $10-25 a day to park safely. Rental-car theft can be a problem in cities (especially Prague), so ask at your hotel for advice.

FLIGHTS

The best comparison search engine for both international and intra-European flights is www.kayak.com. For inexpensive flights within Europe, try www.skyscanner.com or www.hipmunk.com; for inexpensive international flights, try www.vayama.com.

Flying to Europe: Start looking for international flights four to five months before your trip, especially for peak-season travel. Off-season tickets can be purchased a month or so in advance. Depending on your itinerary, it can be efficient to fly into one city and out of another. If your flight requires a connection in Europe, see our hints on navigating Europe's top hub airports at www.

r)cksteves.com/hub-airports.

Flying Within Europe: If you're considering a train ride that's more than five hours long, a flight may save you both time and money. When comparing your options, factor in the time it takes to get to the airport and how early you'll need to arrive to check in.

Low-cost airlines allow you to cheaply connect many of the destinations in this book. Two well-established budget airlines  are based in Eastern Europe: **Wizz Air** (www.wizzair.com, with hubs in Budapest, Prague, Warsaw, Gdańsk, and Katowice, near Kraków) and **Smart Wings** (www.smartwings.net, based in Prague). Well-known cheapo airlines that fly to Eastern European destinations include **easyJet** (www.easyjet.com), **Ryanair** (www.ryanair.com), **Air Berlin** (www.airberlin.com), and **Norwegian Air** (www.norwegian.no).

Now that the established airlines in Eastern Europe face more competition, they've been forced to adapt. Many national carriers charge reasonable fares for short-distance trips. For example, check out Croatia Airlines (www.croatiaairlines.com) and Poland's LOT Airlines (www.lot.com). On recent trips, I've flown affordably on LOT between Kraków and Ljubljana, and between Kraków and Budapest, avoiding lengthy overland journeys.

Be aware of the potential drawbacks of flying on the cheap: nonrefundable and nonchangeable tickets, minimal or nonexistent customer service, and stingy baggage allowances with steep overage fees. If you're traveling with lots of luggage, a cheap flight can quickly become a bad deal. To avoid unpleasant surprises, read the small print before you book. Also be aware that you may fly out of less convenient, secondary airports. For example, some of Wizz Air's flights from "Kraków" actually depart from Katowice, 50 miles away.

Resources

RESOURCES FROM RICK STEVES

Books: *Rick Steves Eastern Europe* is one of many books in my series on European travel, which includes country guidebooks (such as *Croatia & Slovenia*), city and regional guidebooks (including *Budapest*; *Prague & the Czech Republic*; and *Vienna, Salzburg & Tirol*), Snapshot guides (excerpted chapters from my country guides), Pocket Guides (full-color little books on big cities, including Vienna), and my budget-travel skills handbook, *Rick Steves*

PRACTICALITIES

Europe Through the Back Door. Most of my titles are available as ebooks. My phrase books—for German, French, Italian, Spanish, and Portuguese—are practical and budget-oriented. My other books include *Europe 101* (a crash course on art and history designed for travelers); *Mediterranean Cruise Ports* and *Northern European Cruise Ports* (how to make the most of your time in port); and *Travel as a Political Act* (a travelogue sprinkled with tips for bringing home a global perspective). A more complete list of my titles appears near the end of this book.

Video: My public television series, *Rick Steves' Europe,* covers European destinations in 100 shows, including several episodes that explore Eastern Europe. To watch full episodes online for free, see www.ricksteves.com/tv. Or raise your travel I.Q. with video versions of our popular classes, including one talk on Croatia and Slovenia, and another on the Czech Republic, Poland, and Hungary (see www.ricksteves.com/travel-talks).

Audio: My weekly public radio show, *Travel with Rick Steves,* features interviews with travel experts from around the world. All of this audio content is available for free at Rick Steves' Audio Europe, an extensive online library organized by destination. Choose whatever interests you, and download it via the Rick Steves Audio Europe smartphone app, www.ricksteves.com/audioeurope, iTunes, or Google Play.

MAPS

The black-and-white maps in this book are concise and simple, designed to help you locate recommended places and get to local TIs, where you can pick up more in-depth maps of towns or regions (usually free). For navigation—whether by car or on foot—I rely on electronic maps on my smartphone or tablet. Google or Apple mapping apps work just like back home. But, because they work with the Internet, you'll either have to download the maps and route instructions you need while on Wi-Fi, or incur data roaming charges. Or consider an offline mapping app (such as CityMaps2Go), which lets you download searchable, detailed maps that don't require access to the Internet. For more on digital navigation options, see page 1335.

Begin Your Trip at
www.RickSteves.com

My **website** is *the* place to explore Europe. You'll find thousands of fun articles, videos, photos, and radio interviews on European destinations; money-saving tips for planning your dream trip; monthly travel news; my travel talks and travel blog; my latest guidebook updates (www.ricksteves.com/update); and my free Rick Steves Audio Europe app. You can also follow me on Facebook and Twitter.

Our **Travel Forum** is an immense, yet well groomed collection of message boards, where our travel-savvy community answers questions and shares their personal travel experiences (www.ricksteves.com/forums).

Our **online Travel Store** offers travel bags and accessories that I've designed specifically to help you travel smarter and lighter. These include my popular bags (rolling carry-on and backpack versions), money belts, totes, toiletries kits, adapters, other accessories, and a wide selection of guidebooks, planning maps, and DVDs.

Choosing the right **rail pass** for your trip—amid hundreds of options—can drive you nutty. Our website will help you find the perfect fit for your itinerary and your budget. We offer easy, one-stop shopping for rail passes, seat reservations, and point-to-point tickets.

Want to travel with greater efficiency and less stress? We organize **tours** with more than three dozen itineraries and more than 800 departures reaching the best destinations in this book...and beyond. Our 16-day Eastern Europe tour visits the Czech Republic, Poland, Hungary, Croatia, and Slovenia; our 14-day Adriatic tour focuses on Slovenia, Croatia, and a bit of Bosnia-Herzegovina. We also offer an 8-day tour of Prague and Budapest, and a 12-day tour of Berlin, Prague, and Vienna. You'll enjoy great guides, a fun bunch of travel partners (with small groups of 24 to 28 travelers), and plenty of room to spread out in a big, comfy bus when touring between towns. You'll find European adventures to fit every vacation length. For all the details, and to get our Tour Catalog and a free Rick Steves Tour Experience DVD (filmed on location during an actual tour), visit www.ricksteves.com or call us at 425/608-4217.

If you prefer paper maps and are driving, you'll want to pick up a good, detailed map in Europe. I'd recommend a 1:200,000- or 1:300,000-scale map for each country. In Croatia and Slovenia, my favorite maps of the region are by the Slovenian cartographer Kod & Kam (sold all over). If you'll be hiking, you'll find no shortage of excellent, very detailed maps locally.

Tour Packages for Students

Andy Steves (Rick's son) runs **WSA Europe**, offering three-day and longer guided and unguided packages—including accommodations, sightseeing, and unique local experiences—for budget travelers across 11 top European cities, including Budapest, Kraków, and Prague (from €99; see www.wsa europe.com for details).

RECOMMENDED BOOKS AND MOVIES

To learn about Eastern Europe past and present, check out a few of these books and films.

Nonfiction

Lonnie Johnson's *Central Europe: Enemies, Neighbors, Friends* is the best historical overview of the countries in this book. Timothy Garton Ash has written several good "eyewitness account" books analyzing the fall of communism in Eastern Europe, including *History of the Present* and *The Magic Lantern*. Michael Meyer's *The Year that Changed the World* intimately chronicles the exciting events of 1989, culminating in the fall of the Berlin Wall. Anne Applebaum's *Iron Curtain: The Crushing of Eastern Europe 1944–1956* is a readable account of how the Soviets exerted their influence on the nations they had just liberated from the Nazis; her *Gulag: A History* delves into one particularly odious mechanism they used to intimidate their subjects. Tina Rosenberg's dense but thought-provoking *The Haunted Land* asks how those who actively supported communism in Eastern Europe should be treated in the post-communist age. For a good background on Croatia, read Benjamin Curtis' *A Traveller's History of Croatia*. And Benjamin Curtis' *The Habsburgs: The History of a Dynasty* is an illuminating portrait of the Austrian imperial family that shaped so much of Eastern European history.

Patrick Leigh Fermor's *Between the Woods and the Water* is the vivid memoir of a young man who traveled by foot and on horseback across the Balkan Peninsula (including Hungary) in 1933. Rebecca West's classic, bricklike *Black Lamb and Grey Falcon* is the definitive travelogue of the Yugoslav lands (written during a journey between the two World Wars). For a more recent take, Croatian journalist Slavenka Drakulić has written a quartet of insightful essay collections from a woman's perspective: *Café Europa: Life After Communism; The Balkan Express; How We Survived Communism and Even Laughed;* and *A Guided Tour Through the Museum of Communism.*

Drakulić's *They Would Never Hurt a Fly* profiles Yugoslav

war criminals. Dominika Dery's memoir, *The Twelve Little Cakes*, traces her experience growing up in communist Czechoslovakia in the 1970s. For a thorough explanation of how and why Yugoslavia broke apart, read *Yugoslavia: Death of a Nation* (by Laura Silber and Allan Little).

For information on Eastern European Roma (Gypsies), consider the textbook-style *We Are the Romani People* by Ian Hancock, and the more literary *Bury Me Standing* by Isabel Fonseca.

Fiction

The most prominent works of Eastern European fiction have come from the Czechs. These include *I Served the King of England* (Bohumil Hrabal), *The Unbearable Lightness of Being* (Milan Kundera), and *The Good Soldier Švejk* (Jaroslav Hašek). Czech existentialist writer Franz Kafka wrote many well-known novels, including *The Trial* and *The Metamorphosis*. Bruce Chatwin's *Utz* is set in communist Prague.

James Michener's *Poland* is a hefty look into the history of the Poles. *Zlateh the Goat* (Isaac Bashevis Singer) includes seven folktales of Jewish Eastern Europe. Joseph Roth's *The Radetzky March* details the decline of an aristocratic Slovenian family in the Austro-Hungarian Empire.

Imre Kertész, a Hungarian-Jewish Auschwitz survivor who won the Nobel Prize for Literature in 2002, is best known for his semi-autobiographical novel *Fatelessness (Sorstalanság)*, which chronicles the experience of a young concentration-camp prisoner. Márai Sándor's reflective *Embers* paints a rich picture of cobblestoned, gaslit Vienna just before the empire's glory began to fade.

Joe Sacco's powerful graphic novel *Safe Area Goražde* describes the author's experience living in a mostly Muslim town in Bosnia-Herzegovina while it was surrounded by Serb forces during the wars of the 1990s. Sacco's follow-up, *The Fixer and Other Stories*, focuses on real-life characters he met in siege-time Sarajevo.

Arthur Phillips' confusingly titled 2002 novel *Prague* tells the story of American expats negotiating young-adult life in post-communist Budapest, where they often feel one-upped by their compatriots doing the same in the Czech capital (hence the title).

Films

Each of these countries has produced fine films. Below are a few highlights.

Czech Republic

The Czech film industry is one of the strongest in Eastern Europe; even under communism its films were seen and honored worldwide. Before he directed *One Flew Over the Cuckoo's Nest* and

Amadeus, Miloš Forman directed *Loves of a Blonde* (1965), about the relationship between a rural Czech woman and a jazz pianist from Prague; and *The Firemen's Ball* (1967), a satirical look at small-town Czechoslovakia under communism. Another Czech New Wave film, *Intimate Lighting* (1965), finds two musicians reuniting in the 1960s.

In *Alice* (1988), Czech artist Jan Švankmajer adapts Lewis Carroll's *Alice's Adventures in Wonderland* in stop-motion animation combined with live action. The comedy *Czech Dream* (2004) features two film students who document the opening of a fake hypermarket in a hilarious, disturbing commentary on consumerism.

Two films directed by Jirí Menzel cover everyday life during World War II. The Oscar-winning *Closely Watched Trains* (1966) follows a young Czech man working at a German-occupied train station. *I Served the King of England* (2006), an adaptation of Bohumil Hrabal's novel, finds a man reminiscing about his past as an ambitious waiter who suffers the consequences of World War II.

Other great Czech films about World War II include *Divided We Fall* (2000), where a Czech couple hides a Jewish friend during Nazi occupation; *Protektor* (2009), whose main character must reconcile his job at a Nazi-propaganda radio station and his relationship with his Jewish wife; and *All My Loved Ones* (1999), the story of a Jewish family whose son is sent to England in the "Kindertransports" organized by Nicholas Winton (the British humanitarian who saved almost 700 Czech Jewish children).

Recent Czech films also cover life under communism and the Velvet Revolution. *The Elementary School* (1991), set in the late 1940s, looks at a rowdy classroom in suburban Prague that faces reform under the strict guidance of a war-hero teacher. The mystery *In the Shadow* (2012) tracks a burglary in 1950s Czechoslovakia that sets off a political investigation of Jewish immigrants. *Larks on a String* (1990) covers bourgeois Czechs who are forced into communist labor camps and struggle to maintain their humanity. The TV miniseries *Burning Bush* (2013) details the communist occupation of Czechoslovakia and the Prague Spring, focusing on Jan Palach, the Czech student who set himself on fire and died in protest against the Soviet occupation. In the Oscar-winning *Kolya* (1996), a concert-cellist in Soviet-controlled Czechoslovakia must care for an abandoned Russian boy just before the Velvet Revolution breaks out.

The Czechs also have a wonderful animation tradition that successfully competes with Walt Disney in Eastern Europe and China. The most popular character is Krtek (or Krteček, "Little Mole"), who gets in and out of trouble. You'll see plush black-and-white Krtek figures everywhere. Křemílek and Vochomůrka are brothers who live in the woods, Maxipes Fík is a clever dog, and the duo Pat and Mat are builders who can't seem to get anything right.

Poland

Several Polish films have won Oscars and major awards at Cannes. In *Katyń* (2007), acclaimed, Oscar-winning director Andrzej Wajda re-creates the Soviet Army's massacre of around 22,000 Polish officers, enlisted men, and civilians during World War II. Some of Wajda's earlier works include *Ashes and Diamonds* (1958), *The Promised Land* (1979), and the two-part series *Man of Marble* (1977) and *Man of Iron* (1981).

Polish filmmaker Krzysztof Kieslowski made several masterpieces, including *The Decalogue* (1989), consisting of 10 short films inspired by the Ten Commandments. Kieslowski also filmed the multilingual Three Colors Trilogy: *Red* (1994), *White* (1994), and *Blue* (1993).

Among other recent films, one Polish favorite is *Karol: A Man Who Became Pope* (2005), a Polish-Italian biopic made in English about the humble beginnings of St. John Paul II. Another fascinating religious tale is *Ida* (2014), the story of a young novitiate nun in 1960s Poland, who—just before taking her vows—discovers a terrible family secret.

Hungary

The surreal dark comedy *Kontroll* (2003) is about ticket inspectors on the Budapest Metró whose lives are turned upside down by a serial killer lurking in the shadows. *Fateless*, the 2005 adaptation of Imre Kertész's Nobel Prize-winning novel about a young man in a concentration camp, was scripted by Kertész himself. *The Witness* (a.k.a. *Without a Trace*, 1969), a cult classic about a simple man who mysteriously wins the favor of communist bigwigs, is a biting satire of the darkest days of Soviet rule. *Time Stands Still* (1981), a hit at the 1982 Cannes Film Festival, tells the story of young Hungarians in the 1960s. *Children of Glory* (2006) dramatizes the true story of the Hungarian water polo team that defiantly trounced the Soviets at the Olympics just after the 1956 Uprising.

Croatia and Slovenia

To grasp the wars that shook this region in the early 1990s, there's no better film than the Slovene-produced *No Man's Land*, which won the 2002 Oscar for Best Foreign Film. Angelina Jolie wrote and directed (but did not appear in) 2011's wrenching, difficult-to-watch *In the Land of Blood and Honey*, a love story set against the grotesque backdrop of the war in Bosnia.

On a lighter note, a classic from Tito-era Yugoslavia, *The Battle of Neretva* (1969), imported Hollywood talent in the form of Yul Brynner and Orson Welles to tell the story of a pivotal and inspiring battle in the fight against the Nazis. More recent Croatian films worth watching include *Border Post* (2006), about various Yugoslav soldiers working together just before the war broke out; and *When Father Was Away on Business* (1985), about a prisoner on the Tito-era gulag island of Goli Otok, near Rab. Other local movies include *Armin* (2007), *How the War Started on My Island* (1996), *Underground* (1995), and *Tito and Me* (1992).

Documentaries

Documentaries about this region are also worth looking for. The BBC produced a remarkable six-hour documentary series called *The Death of Yugoslavia*, featuring interviews with all of the key players (it's difficult to find on DVD, but try searching for "Death of Yugoslavia" on YouTube; the book *Yugoslavia: Death of a Nation*, noted earlier, was a companion piece to this film). The BBC also produced a harrowing documentary about the infamous Bosnian massacre, *Srebrenica: A Cry from the Grave* (also available on YouTube). The 1998 Oscar-winning documentary *The Last Days* recounts the fate of Jews when the Nazis took over Hungary in 1944.

Hollywood Meets Eastern Europe

Several award-winning films have covered key moments in Eastern European history. *Schindler's List* (1993), Steven Spielberg's Best Picture-winner, tells the story of a compassionate German businessman in Kraków who saved his Jewish workers during the Holocaust. Roman Polanski's *The Pianist* (2002) is a biopic about the struggle for survival of Władysław Szpilman (played by Adrien Brody, in an Oscar-winning role), a Jewish concert pianist in Holocaust-era Warsaw. *The Unbearable Lightness of Being* (1988), starring a young Daniel Day-Lewis, adapts the Milan Kundera novel about a love triangle set against the backdrop of the Prague Spring uprising. And *Sunshine* (1999, starring Ralph Fiennes, directed by István Szabó) somewhat melodramatically traces three generations of an aristocratic Jewish family in Budapest, from the Golden Age, through the Holocaust, to the Cold War.

Two acclaimed German movies offer excellent insight into the surreal and paranoid days of the Soviet Bloc. The Oscar-winning *Lives of Others* (2006) chronicles the constant surveillance that the communist regime employed to keep potential dissidents in line. For a funny and nostalgic look at post-communist Europe's fitful transition to capitalism, *Good Bye Lenin!* (2003) can't be beat.

Eastern European filmmakers have always been very active in Hollywood. "Crossover" directors—who started out making films in their own countries and then turned out English-language Oscar winners—include Michael Curtiz (from Hungary; *Casablanca*,

White Christmas), Miloš Forman (from Czechoslovakia; *One Flew Over the Cuckoo's Nest, Amadeus*) and Roman Polanski (from Poland; *Chinatown, The Pianist*).

You may recognize Eastern Europe backdrops in many blockbuster Hollywood movies—particularly Prague, whose low costs and well-trained filmmaking workforce appeal to studios. In many cases, Prague stands in for another European city. Films shot at least partly in Prague include everything from *Amadeus* to *Mission: Impossible;* from *The Chronicles of Narnia* to *Wanted;* from *The Bourne Identity* to the *Hostel* films; and from *Hannibal* to *Shanghai Knights.* Elsewhere in the Czech Republic, they've filmed the James Bond reboot *Casino Royale* and *The Illusionist.* Many American studios have taken advantage of Hungary's low prices to film would-be blockbusters in Budapest, including *I Spy, A Good Day to Die Hard*, and *Mission: Impossible—Ghost Protocol.* More often, Budapest stands in for other cities—for example, as Buenos Aires in the 1996 film *Evita,* and as various European locales in Stephen Spielberg's 2005 film *Munich.* And fans of HBO's *Game of Thrones* may recognize locations in Dubrovnik and other Croatian coastal towns, where much of the series is filmed (for details, see page 893).

Understanding Yugoslavia

If you're struggling to understand the complicated breakup of Yugoslavia, read this admittedly oversimplified, as-impartial-as-possible history to get you started. (For a more complete version, see www.ricksteves.com/yugo.)

The Balkan Peninsula—between the Adriatic and the Black Sea, basically running from Hungary to Greece—has always been a crossroads of cultures, divided by a series of cultural, ethnic, and religious fault lines. The most important religious influences were **Western Christianity** (i.e., Roman Catholicism, introduced by Charlemagne and later championed by the Austrian Habsburgs), **Eastern Orthodox Christianity** (from the Byzantine Empire), and **Islam** (from the Ottomans).

Two major historical factors made the Balkans what they are today: The first was the **split of the Roman Empire** in the fourth century A.D., dividing the Balkans down the middle into Roman Catholic (west) and Byzantine Orthodox (east)—roughly along today's Bosnian-Serbian border. The second was the **invasion of the Ottomans** (from today's Turkey) in the 14th century, which kicked off five centuries of Islamic influence in Bosnia-Herzegovina and Serbia, further dividing the Balkans into Christian (north) and Muslim (south).

Because of these and other events, several distinct ethnic

Yugoslav Succession

Legend:
- Former Yugoslavia Border
- Current Borders
- Province within Serbia
- SLOVENE — Language
- "Serbian Krajina" (Serb-Controlled Croatia 1991-1995)
- Republika Srpska (Serb territory in Bosnia-Herz.)

100 Kilometers

100 Miles

PRACTICALITIES

identities emerged. The major ethnicities of Yugoslavia are all considered "South Slavs." They're all descended from the same ancestors and speak closely related languages, but are distinguished by their religious practices. Roman Catholic **Croats** and **Slovenes** are found mostly west of the Dinaric Mountains (Croats along the Adriatic coast and Slovenes farther north, in the Alps); Orthodox Christian **Serbs** live mostly east of the Dinaric range; and Muslim **Bosniaks** (whose ancestors converted to Islam under the Ottomans) live mostly in the Dinaric Mountains. The region also has several smaller ethnic groups: the Slavic **Montenegrins** and **Macedonians**, plus **Hungarians** (concentrated in the north) and **Albanians** (concentrated in Kosovo and the south). The groups overlapped a lot—which is exactly why the breakup of Yugoslavia was so contentious.

The lands of Yugoslavia were shuttled between various kingdoms and empires for much of their history, but by the late 19th century, most of the area was part of the Austro-Hungarian Empire. When that empire split apart at the end of World War I, the various mostly Slavic groups in the region formed a new country: Yugoslavia ("Land of the South Slavs"). The union was almost immediately contentious, as various groups—especially Serbs and Croats—struggled to take control. By the dawn of World War II, it was already clear that Yugoslavia was a troubled proposition.

The seeds of the 1990s interethnic conflict were planted in World War II. Yugoslavia was invaded by Nazi Germany, then chopped up into puppet states for the Axis Powers. Some groups took advantage of changing circumstances in wartime Yugoslavia to exact revenge on their former compatriots. In occupied Croatia, the puppet Ustaše party imprisoned and executed large numbers of Serbs. In the eastern mountains, a Serbian royalist paramilitary group called the Četniks were every bit as brutal against Croats and Bosniaks. A third group—the homegrown Partisan Army—fought against Nazis, Ustaše, and Četniks to secure freedom for Yugoslavia. Unlike the other "Eastern European" countries, Yugoslavia was not liberated by the Soviet Union. This unique status allowed it to determine its own path after the war.

After the short but rocky Yugoslav union between the World Wars, it seemed that no one could hold the southern Slavs together in a single nation. But one man could, and did: Partisan war hero Josip Broz, who is better known by his code name, Tito. With a Slovene for a mother, a Croat for a father, a Serb for a wife, and a home in Belgrade, Tito was a true Yugoslav. Tito had a compelling vision that this fractured union of the South Slavs could function (see the sidebar).

Tito's new incarnation of Yugoslavia aimed for a more equitable division of powers. It was made up of six republics, each dominated by one ethnic group: **Croatia, Slovenia, Serbia, Bosnia-Herzegovina, Montenegro,** and **Macedonia.** Within Serbia, Tito set up two autonomous provinces, each one an enclave for an ethnicity that was a minority in greater Yugoslavia: Albanians in **Kosovo** (to the south) and Hungarians in **Vojvodina** (to the north). By allowing these two provinces some degree of independence, Tito hoped they would balance the political clout of Serbia, preventing a single republic from dominating the union.

While each republic had a measure of self-rule, the union was carefully overseen by President-for-Life Tito. Tito respected—and even celebrated—the diversity of his union, but he placed Yugoslav unity above all. He said that the borders between the republics should be "like white lines in a marble column."

Tito's Yugoslavia was communist, but it wasn't Soviet communism. He refused to formally join either the Warsaw Pact or NATO, and ingeniously played the East and the West against each other. Economically, Tito's vision was for a "third way," somewhere between communism and capitalism. While large industries

Tito (1892-1980)

The Republic of Yugoslavia was the vision of a single man, who made it reality. Josip Broz—better known as Marshal Tito—presided over the most peaceful and prosperous era in this region's long and troubled history. Three decades after his death, Tito is beloved by many of his former subjects...and yet, he was a communist dictator who dealt brutally with his political enemies. This love-him-and-hate-him autocrat is one of the most complex figures in the history of this very complicated land.

Josip Broz was born in 1892 to a Slovenian mother and a Croatian father in the northern part of today's Croatia (then part of the Austro-Hungarian Empire). After growing up in the rural countryside, he was trained as a metalworker. He was drafted into the Austro-Hungarian army, went to fight on the Eastern Front during World War I, and was captured and sent to Russia as a prisoner of war. Freed by Bolsheviks, Broz fell in with the Communist Revolution...and never looked back.

At war's end, Broz returned home to the newly independent Yugoslavia, where he worked alongside the Soviets to build a national Communist Party. As a clandestine communist operative, he adopted the code name he kept for the rest of his life: Tito. Some believe this was a Spanish name he picked up while participating in that country's civil war, while others half-joke that the name came from Tito's authoritarian style: "*Ti, to!*" means "You, do this!" But one thing's clear: In this land where a person's name instantly identifies his ethnicity, "Tito" is ethnically neutral.

When the Nazis occupied Yugoslavia, Tito raised and commanded a homegrown, communist Partisan Army. Through guerilla tactics, Tito's clever maneuvering, and sheer determination, the Partisans liberated their country. And because they did so mostly without support from the USSR, Yugoslavia was able to set its own postwar course.

The war hero Tito quickly became the "president for life" of postwar Yugoslavia. But even as he introduced communism to his country, he retained some elements of a free-market economy—firmly declining to become a satellite of Moscow. He also pioneered the worldwide Non-Aligned Movement, joining with nations in Africa, the Middle East, Asia, and Latin America in refusing to ally with the US or USSR. Stubborn but suitably cautious, Tito expertly walked a tightrope between East and West.

There was a dark side to Tito. In the early years of his regime, Tito resorted to brutal, Stalin-esque tactics to assert his control. Immediately following World War II, the Partisan Army massacred tens of thousands of soldiers who had supported the Nazis. Then Tito systematically arrested, tried, tortured, or executed those who did not accept his new regime. Survivors whose lives were ruined during this reign of terror will never forgive Tito for what he did.

But once he gained full control, Tito moved away from

strong-arm tactics and into a warm-and-fuzzy era of Yugoslav brotherhood. Tito believed that the disparate peoples of Yugoslavia could live in harmony. For example, every Yugoslav male had to serve in the People's Army, and Tito made sure that each unit was a microcosm of the complete Yugoslavia—with equal representation from each ethnic group. Yugoslavs from diverse backgrounds were required to work together and social-ize—as a result, they became friends. He also worked toward economic diversification: Yugoslav tanks, some of the best in the world, were made of parts assembled in five different republics.

Tito's reign is a case study in the power of the cult of per-sonality. Rocks on hillsides throughout Yugoslavia were rear-ranged to spell "TITO," and his portrait hung over every family's dinner table. Each of the six republics renamed one of its cities for their dictator. The main street and square in virtually every town were renamed for Tito. Each year, young people would embark on a months-long, Olympics-style relay, from each cor-ner of Yugoslavia, to present a ceremonial baton to Tito on his official birthday (May 25). Tito also had vacation villas in all of Yugoslavia's most beautiful areas, including Lake Bled, the Brijuni Islands, and the Montenegrin coast. People sang patri-otic anthems to their Druža (Comrade) Tito: "Comrade Tito, we pledge an oath to you."

Tito died in 1980 in a Slovenian hospital. His body went on a grand tour of the Yugoslav capitals: Ljubljana, Zagreb, Sarajevo, and Belgrade, where he was buried before hundreds of thou-sands of mourners, including more heads of state than at any other funeral in history. At his request, his tomb was placed in the greenhouse where he enjoyed spending time.

The genuine outpouring of grief at Tito's death might seem unusual for a man who was, on paper, an authoritarian commu-nist dictator. But even today, many former Yugoslavs—especially Slovenes and Bosniaks—believe that his iron-fisted government was a necessary evil that kept the country strong and united. The eventual balance Tito struck between communism and cap-italism, and between the competing interests of his ethnically diverse nation, led to this region's most stable and prosperous era. In a recent poll in Slovenia, Tito had a higher approval rating than any present-day politician, and 80 percent of Slovenes said they had a positive impression of him.

And yet, the Yugoslavs' respect for their former leader was not enough to keep them together. Tito's death began a long, slow chain reaction that led to the end of Yugoslavia. As the decades pass, the old joke seems more and more appropriate: Yugoslavia had eight distinct peoples in six republics, with five languages, three religions (Orthodox Christian, Catholic, and Muslim), and two alphabets (Roman and Cyrillic), but only one Yugoslav—Tito.

PRACTICALITIES

were collectivized, small businesses were also permitted. Though Yugoslavs could not become really rich, through hard work it was possible to attain modest wealth to buy a snazzy car, a vacation home, Western imports, and other niceties. Yugoslavia was also the most free and open of the communist states. Tourists (from both East and West) flocked here for vacation, and Yugoslavs could travel to far more places abroad than could residents of the Eastern Bloc.

Tito died in 1980, and before long, the fragile union he had held together started to unravel. The breakup began in the late 1980s in the autonomous province of Kosovo, with squabbles between the Serb minority and the ethnic-Albanian majority. Serbian politician Slobodan Milošević traveled to Kosovo to rouse his Serb comrades, which alarmed some of the other republics. When Milošević-led Serbia annexed Kosovo soon after, and negotiations among the Yugoslav republics broke down, Croatia and Slovenia decided it was time to declare independence (both on June 25, 1991). Small, relatively homogenous Slovenia weathered a brief 10-day skirmish (see page 720), while Croatia—which had a large Serb minority—was pulled into a gruesome war lasting several years (see page 867). Bosnia-Herzegovina declared its independence a few months later. But, because that republic was by far Yugoslavia's most ethnically diverse (with large populations of Muslim Bosniaks, Serbs, and Croats), its separation was hotly contested—plunging Bosnia into a horrifying four years of guerrilla warfare, medieval-style sieges, systematic rape, and ethnic cleansing. (For more on the war in Bosnia, see page 1120.)

Peace accords in 1995 brought an end to most of the hostilities throughout Yugoslavia, establishing the borders of Croatia and Bosnia that still exist today. Over the next several years, Slobodan Milošević and others accused of war crimes were arrested and tried by an international tribunal at The Hague, Netherlands (though Milošević died behind bars before a verdict was handed down). Later, additional parts of the former Yugoslavia split off, leaving behind seven independent nations where once was one: Croatia, Slovenia, Bosnia-Herzegovina, Montenegro, Serbia, Macedonia, and Kosovo.

Peace has reigned in these countries for more than two decades. The physical scars of war have mostly been repaired. And, considering that hospitality has been a forte of this region since long before the age of Yugoslavia, outside visitors feel welcome and safe—and are impressed at the candor of the people they meet, who are often willing to share their own wartime experiences. But, understandably, the psychological scars will take the longest to heal. Tensions still persist between formerly warring groups.

Thoughtful visitors to the former Yugoslavia grapple with

trying to understand what happened here just a generation ago. Many find it hard to get an impartial take on the current situation, or even on historical "facts." A very wise Bosniak once told me, "Listen to all three sides—Muslim, Serb, and Croat. Then decide for yourself what you think." A Serb told me a similar local saying: "You have to look at the apple from all sides."

APPENDIX

Contents

Useful Contacts

Emergency Needs

In all of the countries in this book, dial 112 for medical or other emergencies. For police, dial 112 in Croatia, Slovakia, Hungary, Poland, or Austria; dial 158 in the Czech Republic; dial 113 in Slovenia; and dial 122 in Bosnia-Herzegovina.

US Embassies and Consulates

Austria: Boltzmanngasse 16, tel. 01/313-390; consular services at Parkring 12a, Vienna, passport services available Mon-Fri 8:00-11:30, tel. 01/313-397-535, www.usembassy.at.

Bosnia-Herzegovina: Robert C. Frasure Street 1, Sarajevo, passport services available Mon-Fri 14:00-15:30 plus Fri 8:00-10:30, tel. 033/704-000, on weekends and after hours call the same number and press 0 after the recording, http://sarajevo.usembassy. gov. There's also a branch office in Mostar (Husnije Repca 3, tel. 036/580-580).

Croatia: Ulica Thomasa Jeffersona 2, Zagreb, passport services available Mon-Thu 13:00-15:00 plus Wed 9:00-11:00, tel. 01/661-2200, after business-hours tel. 01/661-2400, passport services tel.

01/661-2345, http://croatia.usembassy.gov.

Czech Republic: Tržiště 15, Prague, emergency passport services available Mon-Fri 8:00-11:30, tel. 257-022-000, http://prague.usembassy.gov.

Hungary: Szabadság tér 12, Budapest, passport services available Mon-Fri 8:00-17:00, tel. 1/475-4400, after-hours emergency tel. 1/475-4703 or 1/475-4924, www.usembassy.hu.

Poland: Ulica Piękna 12, Warsaw, appointments required for routine services, tel. 022-504-2784, after-hours emergency tel. 022-504-2000, http://poland.usembassy.gov; also a US Consulate in Kraków at ulica Stolarska 9, appointments required for routine services, tel. 012-424-5100, krakow.usconsulate.gov.

Slovakia: Hviezdoslavovo námestie 4, Bratislava, passport services available Mon-Fri 8:00-11:45 & 14:00-15:15, tel. 02/5443-0861, http://slovakia.usembassy.gov.

Slovenia: Prešernova 31, Ljubljana, passport services available Mon-Fri 9:00-11:30 & 13:00-15:00, tel. 01/200-5595, after business hours tel. 01/200-5500, http://slovenia.usembassy.gov.

Canadian Embassies and Consulates

For after-hours emergencies, Canadian citizens can call collect to the Foreign Services Office in Ottawa at 613/996-8885.

Austria: Laurenzerberg 2, Vienna, passport services available Mon-Fri 8:30-12:30 & 13:30-15:30, tel. 01/531-383-000, www.austria.gc.ca.

Bosnia-Herzegovina: Services provided by Canadian Embassy in Budapest, Hungary (listed below).

Croatia: Prilaz Djure Deželića 4, Zagreb, passport services available Mon-Thu 10:00-12:00 & 13:00-15:00, Fri 10:00-13:00, tel. 01/488-1200, www.croatia.gc.ca.

Czech Republic: Ve Struhách 95/2, Prague, passport services Mon-Thu 9:00-12:00, Fri and afternoons by appointment, tel. 272-101-800, www.czechrepublic.gc.ca; also provides services for Slovakia.

Hungary: Ganz utca 12-14, Budapest, passport services available Mon-Thu 8:30-12:30 & 13:00-16:30, Fri 8:00-13:30, tel. 1/392-3360, www.hungary.gc.ca; also provides services for Bosnia-Herzegovina and Slovenia.

Poland: ulica Jana Matejki 1-5, Warsaw, passport services available Mon-Fri 8:30-16:30, tel. 022-584-3100, www.poland.gc.ca.

Slovakia: Mostová 2, Bratislava, passport services available Mon-Fri 8:30-12:30 & 13:30-16:30, tel. 02/5920-4031; some services provided through Canadian Embassy in Prague, Czech Republic (listed above).

Slovenia (consulate office): Linhartova cesta 49a, Ljubljana; passport services available Mon, Wed, and Fri 8:00-12:00; tel. 01/252-

4444, some services provided through Canadian Embassy in Budapest, Hungary (listed above).

Directory Assistance

Dial 1188 in the Czech Republic, 913 in Poland, 198 in Hungary, 988 in Croatia or Slovenia, 1181 in Slovakia, and 118 in Austria.

Holidays and Festivals

This list includes selected festivals in this region, plus national holidays observed throughout Eastern Europe. Many sights and banks close on national holidays—keep this in mind when planning your itinerary. Catholic holidays are celebrated in Poland, Slovakia, Croatia, and Slovenia (and to a lesser extent in Hungary and the Czech Republic). Muslims (most predominant in Bosnia) observe the month of Ramadan. Before planning a trip around a festival, verify its dates by checking the festival's website or TI sites.

Jan 1	New Year's Day
Jan 6	Epiphany, Catholic countries
Jan 19	Anniversary of Jan Palach's Death, Prague (flowers in Wenceslas Square)
Feb 8	National Day of Culture, Slovenia (celebrates Slovenian culture and national poet France Prešeren)
Early March	One World International Human Rights Film Festival, Prague (www.oneworld.cz)
March 15	National Day, Hungary (celebrates 1848 Revolution)
Late March	Ski Jumping World Cup Finals, Planica, Slovenia (www.planica.info)
Easter Sunday	April 5 in 2015, March 27 in 2016
April	Budapest Spring Festival (www.festivalcity.hu)
April 27	National Resistance Day, Slovenia
April 30	Witches' Night, Czech Republic (similar to Halloween, with bonfires)
May 1	Labor Day
May 3	Constitution Day, Poland (celebrates Europe's first constitution)
May 8	Liberation Day, Czech Republic and Slovakia

Ascension	May 14 in 2015, May 5 in 2016 (Catholic countries)
Whitsunday (Pentecost) and Whitmonday	May 24-25 in 2015, May 15-16 in 2016 (Catholic countries)
Early to Mid-May	Prague International Marathon (www.pim.cz)
Mid- to Late May	"Prague Spring" Music Festival (www.festival.cz)
Mid-May to	Vienna Festival of Arts and Music, (www.festwochen.at)
Early June	Corpus Christi June 4 in 2015, May 26 in 2016 (Catholic countries)
June-July	Prague Proms, Prague (music festival, www.pragueproms.cz)
Early June	Dance Week Festival, Zagreb, Croatia (www.danceweekfestival.com)
Mid-June	Celebration of the Rose, Český Krumlov, Czech Republic (medieval festival, music, theater, dance, knights' tournament)
Ramadan	June 18-July 17 in 2015, June 6-July 5 in 2016 (Muslim holy month)
June 22	Antifascist Struggle Day, Croatia
June 25	National Day, Slovenia; Statehood Day, Croatia
Late June	Wikiani Midsummer Festival, Kraków, Poland (wreaths on rafts in Vistula River, fireworks, music)
Late June	Jewish Culture Festival, Kraków, Poland (www.jewishfestival.pl)
Late June	Midsummer Eve celebrations, Austria
July 5	Sts. Cyril and Methodius Day, Czech Republic and Slovakia
July 6	Jan Hus Day, Czech Republic
July-Aug	Dubrovnik Summer Festival, Croatia (www.dubrovnik-festival.hr)
Early July-late Aug	Ljubljana Summer Festival, Slovenia (www.ljubljanafestival.si)
Mid-July-mid-Aug	International Music Festival, Český Krumlov, Czech Republic (www.festivalkrumlov.cz)
Late July	International Folklore Festival, Zagreb, Croatia (costumes, songs, dances from all over Croatia, www.msf.hr)

Late July	Formula 1 races, Budapest (www.hungaroinfo.com/formel1)
Late July-mid-Aug	St. Dominic's Fair, Gdańsk, Poland (3 weeks of market stalls, music, and general revelry)
Aug 5	National Thanksgiving Day, Croatia
Early Aug	Sziget Festival, Budapest (rock and pop music, www.sziget.hu)
Aug 15	Assumption of Mary, Catholic countries
Aug 20	Constitution Day and St. Stephen's Day, Hungary (fireworks, celebrations)
Aug 29	National Uprising Day, Slovakia (commemorates uprising against Nazis)
Late Aug	Diocletian Days, Split, Croatia(toga-clad celebrations)
Late Aug-early Sept	Jewish Summer Festival, Budapest (www.zsidonyarifesztival.hu)
Sept	Dvořák's Prague Music Festival, Prague (www.dvorakovapraha.cz)
Sept 1	Constitution Day, Slovakia
Sept 28	St. Wenceslas Day, Czech Republic (celebrates national patron saint and Czech statehood)
Oct	International Jazz Festival, Prague (www.agharta.cz)
Oct 8	Independence Day, Croatia
Mid-Oct	Café Budapest Festival (contemporary arts, www.cafebudapestfest.hu)
Oct 23	Republic Day, Hungary (remembrances of 1956 Uprising)
Oct 26	National Day, Austria
Oct 28	Independence Day, Czech Republic
Oct 31	Reformation Day, Slovenia
Nov 1	All Saints' Day/Remembrance Day, Catholic countries (religious festival, some closures)
Nov 11	Independence Day, Poland; St. Martin's Day (official first day of wine season), Slovenia and Croatia
Nov 17	Velvet Revolution Anniversary, Czech Republic and Slovakia
Dec 5	St. Nicholas Eve, Prague (St. Nick gives gifts to children in town square)

Dec 24-25	Christmas Eve and Christmas Day
Dec 26	Boxing Day/St. Stephen's Day; Independence and Unity Day, Slovenia
Dec 31	St. Sylvester's Day, Prague and Vienna (fireworks)

Conversions and Climate

NUMBERS AND STUMBLERS

- Europeans write a few of their numbers differently than we do. 1 = 1, 4 = 4, 7 = 7.
- In Europe, dates appear as day/month/year, so Christmas is 25/12/16. In Hungary, dates are written as year/month/day, so Christmas 2016 is 2016/12/25 (or dots can be used instead: 2016.12.25).
- Commas are decimal points and decimals are commas. A dollar and a half is $1,50, one thousand is 1.000, and there are 5.280 feet in a mile.
- Hungarians usually list their surname first (for example, Bartók Béla instead of Béla Bartók).
- When counting with fingers, start with your thumb. If you hold up your first finger to request one item, you'll probably get two.
- What Americans call the second floor of a building is the first floor in Europe.
- On escalators and moving sidewalks, Europeans keep the left "lane" open for passing. Keep to the right.

METRIC CONVERSIONS

A kilogram is 2.2 pounds, and 1 liter is about a quart, or almost 4 to a gallon. A kilometer is six-tenths of a mile. I figure kilometers to miles by cutting them in half and adding back 10 percent of the original (120 km: 60 + 12 = 72 miles, 300 km: 150 + 30 = 180 miles).

1 foot = 0.3 meter	1 square yard = 0.8 square meter
1 yard = 0.9 meter	1 square mile = 2.6 square kilometers
1 mile = 1.6 kilometers	1 ounce = 28 grams
1 centimeter = 0.4 inch	1 quart = 0.95 liter
1 meter = 39.4 inches	1 kilogram = 2.2 pounds
1 kilometer = 0.62 mile	32°F = 0°C

CLOTHING SIZES

When shopping for clothing, use these US-to-European comparisons as general guidelines (but note that no conversion is perfect).

- Women's dresses and blouses: Add 30
  (US size 10 = European size 40)
- Men's suits and jackets: Add 10
  (US size 40 regular = European size 50)
- Men's shirts: Multiply by 2 and add about 8
  (US size 15 collar = European size 38)
- Women's shoes: Add about 30
  (US size 8 = European size 38-39)
- Men's shoes: Add 32-34
  (US size 9 = European size 41; US size 11 = European size 45)

EASTERN EUROPE'S CLIMATE

First line is the average daily high; second line, average daily low; third line, average number of rainy days. For more detailed weather statistics for destinations in this book (as well as the rest of the world), check www.wunderground.com.

	J	F	M	A	M	J	J	A	S	O	N	D
AUSTRIA • Vienna												
	34°	38°	47°	58°	67°	73°	76°	75°	68°	56°	45°	37°
	25°	28°	30°	42°	50°	56°	60°	59°	53°	44°	37°	30°
	15	14	13	13	13	14	13	13	10	13	14	15
CROATIA • Dubrovnik												
	53°	55°	58°	63°	70°	78°	83°	82°	77°	69°	62°	56°
	42°	43°	57°	52°	58°	65°	69°	69°	64°	57°	51°	46°
	13	13	11	10	10	6	4	3	7	11	16	15
CZECH REPUBLIC • Prague												
	31°	34°	44°	54°	64°	70°	73°	72°	65°	53°	42°	34°
	23°	24°	30°	38°	46°	52°	55°	55°	49°	41°	33°	27°
	13	11	10	11	13	12	13	12	10	13	12	13
HUNGARY • Budapest												
	34°	39°	50°	62°	71°	78°	82°	81°	74°	61°	47°	39°
	25°	28°	35°	44°	52°	58°	62°	60°	53°	44°	38°	30°
	13	12	11	11	13	13	10	9	7	10	14	13
POLAND • Kraków												
	32°	34°	45°	55°	67°	72°	76°	73°	66°	56°	44°	37°
	22°	22°	30°	38°	48°	54°	58°	56°	49°	42°	33°	28°
	16	15	12	15	12	15	16	15	12	14	15	16
SLOVENIA • Ljubljana												
	36°	41°	50°	60°	68°	75°	80°	78°	71°	59°	47°	39°
	25°	25°	32°	40°	48°	54°	57°	57°	51°	43°	36°	30°
	13	11	11	13	16	16	12	12	10	14	15	15

APPENDIX

FAHRENHEIT AND CELSIUS CONVERSION

F°	C°
120	50
104	40
95	35
86	30
82	28 — perfect weather
68	20
50	10
32	0

For Weather

F°	C°
105	40.6
104.5	40.3
104	40
103.5	39.7
103	39.4
102.5	39.2
102	38.9
101.5	38.6
101	38.3
100.5	38.1
100	37.8
99.5	37.5
99	37.2
98.6	37 — perfect health

For Health

Europe takes its temperature using the Celsius scale, while we opt for Fahrenheit. For a rough conversion from Celsius to Fahrenheit, double the number and add 30. For weather, remember that 28°C is 82°F—perfect. For health, 37°C is just right. At a launderette, 30°C is cold, 40°C is warm (usually the default setting), 60°C is hot, and 95°C is boiling.

APPENDIX

Packing Checklist

Whether you're traveling for five days or five weeks, you won't need more than this. Pack light to enjoy the sweet freedom of true mobility.

Clothing

- ❏ 5 shirts: long- & short-sleeve
- ❏ 2 pairs pants or skirt
- ❏ 1 pair shorts or capris
- ❏ 5 pairs underwear & socks
- ❏ 1 pair walking shoes
- ❏ Sweater or fleece top
- ❏ Rainproof jacket with hood
- ❏ Tie or scarf
- ❏ Swimsuit
- ❏ Sleepwear

Money

- ❏ Debit card
- ❏ Credit card(s)
- ❏ Hard cash ($20 bills)
- ❏ Money belt or neck wallet

Documents & Travel Info

- ❏ Passport
- ❏ Airline reservations
- ❏ Rail pass/train reservations
- ❏ Car-rental voucher
- ❏ Driver's license
- ❏ Student ID, hostel card, etc.
- ❏ Photocopies of all the above
- ❏ Hotel confirmations
- ❏ Insurance details
- ❏ Guidebooks & maps
- ❏ Notepad & pen
- ❏ Journal

Toiletries Kit

- ❏ Toiletries
- ❏ Medicines & vitamins
- ❏ First-aid kit
- ❏ Glasses/contacts/sunglasses (with prescriptions)
- ❏ Earplugs
- ❏ Packet of tissues (for WC)

Miscellaneous

- ❏ Daypack
- ❏ Sealable plastic baggies
- ❏ Laundry soap
- ❏ Spot remover
- ❏ Clothesline
- ❏ Sewing kit
- ❏ Travel alarm/watch

Electronics

- ❏ Smartphone or mobile phone
- ❏ Camera & related gear
- ❏ Tablet/ereader/media player
- ❏ Laptop & flash drive
- ❏ Earbuds or headphones
- ❏ Chargers
- ❏ Plug adapters

Optional Extras

- ❏ Flipflops or slippers
- ❏ Mini-umbrella or poncho
- ❏ Travel hairdryer
- ❏ Belt
- ❏ Hat (for sun or cold)
- ❏ Picnic supplies
- ❏ Water bottle
- ❏ Fold-up tote bag
- ❏ Small flashlight
- ❏ Small binoculars
- ❏ Insect repellent
- ❏ Small towel or washcloth
- ❏ Inflatable pillow
- ❏ Some duct tape (for repairs)
- ❏ Tiny lock
- ❏ Address list (to mail postcards)
- ❏ Postcards/photos from home
- ❏ Extra passport photos
- ❏ Good book

APPENDIX

Pronouncing Eastern European Place Names

Remember that in all of these languages, j is pronounced as "y," and c is pronounced "ts." Diacritical markings over most consonants (such as č, š, ś, or ž) have the same effect as putting an h after it in English; for example, č is "ch," š or ś is "sh," ž is "zh."

Name	Pronounced
Auschwitz (Concentration Camp, Poland)	OWSH-vits
Birkenau (Concentration Camp, Poland)	BEER-keh-now
Bled (Slovenia)	bled (as it's spelled); locals say "blayd"
Bohinj (Slovenia)	BOH-heen
Bovec (Slovenia)	BOH-vets
Bratislava (Slovakia)	brah-tee-SLAH-vah
Brtonigla (Croatia)	bur-toh-NEEG-lah
Budapest (Hungary)	BOO-dah-pest in English, BOO-daw- pesht in Hungarian
Český Krumlov (Czech Republic)	CHESS-key KROOM-loff
Dubrovnik (Croatia)	doo-BROHV-nik
Eger (Hungary)	EH-gehr
Egerszalók (Hungary)	EH-gehr-sah-lohk
Esztergom (Hungary)	EHS-tehr-gohm
Füzesabony (Hungary)	FOO-zesh-ah-boyn
Gdańsk (Poland)	guh-DAYNSK
Gdynia (Poland)	guh-DIN-yah
Gödöllő (Palace, Hungary)	GER-der-ler
Herzegovina (Bosnia-Herzegovina)	hert-seh-GOH-vee-nah
Istria (Croatia)	EE-stree-ah
Jadrolinija (Croatian Ferry Company)	yah-droh-LEE-nee-yah
Kazimierz (Poland)	kah-ZHEE-mezh
Kobarid (Slovenia)	KOH-bah-reed
Konopiště (Castle, Czech Republic)	KOH-noh-peesh-tyeh
Korčula (Croatia)	KOHR-choo-lah
Kraków (Poland)	KRACK-cow in English, KROCK-oof in Polish

Name	Pronounced
Kutná Hora (Czech Republic)	KOOT-nah HO-rah
Ljubljana (Slovenia)	lyoob-lyee-AH-nah
Malbork (Castle, Poland)	MAHL-bork
Mostar (Bosnia-Herzegovina)	MOH-star
Motovun (Croatia)	moh-toh-VOON
Nowa Huta (Poland)	NOH-vah HOO-tah
Oświęcim (Poland)	ohsh-VEENCH-im
Pécs (Hungary)	paych
Plitvice (National Park, Croatia)	PLEET-veet-seh
Praha (Czech name for Prague, Czech Republic)	PRAH-hah
Pula (Croatia)	POO-lah
Radovljica (Slovenia)	rah-DOH-vleet-suh
Rijeka (Croatia)	ree-YAY-kah
Rovinj (Croatia)	roh-VEEN
Soča (River Valley, Slovenia)	SOH-chah
Sopot (Poland)	SOH-poht
Sopron (Hungary)	SHOH-prohn
Split (Croatia)	split (as it's spelled)
Szentendre (Hungary)	SEHN-tehn-dreh
Terezín (Concentration Camp, Czech Republic)	TEH-reh-zeen
Toruń (Poland)	TOH-roon
Vintgar (Gorge, Slovenia)	VEENT-gar
Visegrád (Hungary)	VEE-sheh-grahd
Vršič (Pass, Slovenia)	vur-SHEECH
Warszawa (Polish name for Warsaw, Poland)	vah-SHAH-vah
Wieliczka (Salt Mine, Poland)	veel-EECH-kah
Wien (German name for Vienna, Austria)	veen
Zagreb (Croatia)	ZAH-grehb

APPENDIX

INDEX

MAP INDEX

Explore Europe

At ricksteves.com you can browse through thousands of articles, videos, photos and radio interviews, plus find a wealth of money-saving travel tips for planning your dream trip. And with our mobile-friendly website, you can easily access all this great travel information anywhere you go.

TV Shows

Preview the places you'll visit by watching entire half-hour episodes of Rick Steves' Europe (choose from all 100 shows) on-demand, for free.

ricksteves.com

your travel dreams into affordable reality

Radio Interviews

Enjoy ready access to Rick's vast library of radio interviews covering travel

tips and cultural insights that relate specifically to your Europe travel plans.

Travel Forums

Learn, ask, share! Our online community of savvy travelers is a great resource for first-time travelers to Europe, as well as seasoned pros. You'll find forums on each country, plus travel tips and restaurant/hotel reviews. You can even ask one of our well-traveled staff to chime in with an opinion.

Travel News

Subscribe to our free Travel News e-newsletter, and get monthly updates from Rick on what's happening in Europe.

Audio Europe™

Pack Light and Right

Gear up for your next adventure at ricksteves.com

Light Luggage

Pack light and right with Rick Steves' affordable, custom-designed rolling carry-on bags, backpacks, day packs and shoulder bags.

Accessories

From packing cubes to moneybelts and beyond, Rick has personally selected the travel goodies that will help your trip go smoother.

Rick Steves has

Save time and energy

This guidebook is your independent-travel toolkit. But for all it delivers, it's still up to you to devote the time and energy it takes to manage the preparation and logistics that are essential for a happy trip. If that's a hassle, there's a solution.

Rick Steves Tours

A Rick Steves tour takes you to Europe's most interesting places with great

great tours, too!

with minimum stress

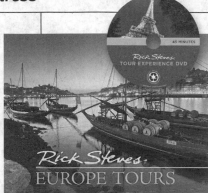

guides and small groups of 28 or less. We follow Rick's favorite itineraries, ride in comfy buses, stay in family-run hotels, and bring you intimately close to the Europe you've traveled so far to see. Most importantly, we take away the logistical headaches so you can focus on the fun.

customers—along with us on 40 different itineraries, from Ireland to Italy to Istanbul. Is a Rick Steves tour the right fit for your travel dreams? Find out at ricksteves.com, where you can also get Rick's latest tour catalog and free Tour Experience DVD.

Join the fun
This year we'll take 18,000 free-spirited travelers—nearly half of them repeat

Europe is best experienced with happy travel partners. We hope you can join us.

See our itineraries at ricksteves.com

Credits

CONTRIBUTORS

Honza Vihan

Honza, who co-authors Rick Steves Prague & the Czech Republic, grew up roaming the Czech countryside in search of the Wild West. Once the borders opened, he set off for South Dakota. His journey took him to China, Honduras, India, and Iran, where he contributed to several travel guides. Honza lives in Prague with his family, teaches Chinese, and leads Rick Steves tours through Eastern Europe.

Gene Openshaw

Gene is the co-author of a dozen Rick Steves books, specializing in Europe's art, history, and contemporary culture. For this book, he helped write sightseeing tours in Prague (Old Town Walk, Prague Castle, Jewish Quarter, etc.) and in Vienna (Vienna City Walk, St. Stephen's, Hofburg Treasury, Kunsthistorisches Museum, etc.). When not traveling, Gene enjoys composing music, recovering from his 1973 trip to Europe with Rick, and living everyday life with his daughter.

ACKNOWLEDGMENTS

The authors would like to acknowledge our friends and colleagues for their invaluable insights. Thanks to Ian Watson, Dave Hoerlein, Rick Garman, Trevor Holmes, and Ben Curtis; *Děkuji* to Honza Vihan (Czech Republic); *Dziękuję* to Katarzyna Derlicka and Agnieszka Syroka (Poland); *Köszönjük szépen* to Péter Pölczman, Andrea Makkay, Elemér Boreczky, George Farkas, Etelka Parine Berecz, István Koteczki, and Eszter Bokros (Hungary); *Hvala lepa* to Marijan Krišković, Tina Hiti, Sašo Golub, Amir Telibečirović, Bojan Kočar, Barbara Jakopić, and Gorazd Hiti (Slovenia, Croatia, and Bosnia); and *D'akujeme* to Susana Minich (Slovakia).

Avalon Travel
a member of the Perseus Books Group
1700 Fourth Street
Berkeley, CA 94710

For the latest on Rick's lectures, guidebooks, tours, public radio show, and public television
series, contact Rick Steves' Europe, 130 Fourth Avenue North, Edmonds, WA 98020,
425/771-8303, www.ricksteves.com, rick@ricksteves.com.

ISBN 978-1-63121-054-9
ISSN 1547-8505
8th edition

Rick Steves' Europe
Managing Editor: Risa Laib
Editorial & Production Manager: Jennifer Madison Davis
Editors: Glenn Eriksen, Tom Griffin, Suzanne Kotz, Cathy Lu, Carrie Shepherd
Editorial & Production Assistant: Jessica Shaw
Editorial Intern: Stacie Larsen
Maps & Graphics: David C. Hoerlein, Sandra Hundacker, Lauren Mills, Mary Rostad

Avalon Travel
Senior Editor & Series Manager: Madhu Prasher
Editor: Jamie Andrade
Associate Editor: Maggie Ryan
Copy Editor: Jennifer Malnick
Proofreader: Gayle Hart
Indexer: Stephen Callahan
Production & Typesetting: McGuire Barber Design
Cover Design: Kimberly Glyder Design
Maps & Graphics: Kat Bennett, Mike Morgenfeld

Want More Eastern Europe?
Maximize the experience with Rick Steves as your guide

Guidebooks
Prague, Budapest, and Croatia guides make side-trips smooth and affordable

Planning Maps
Use the map that's in sync with your guidebook

Rick's TV Shows
Preview where you're going with 7 shows on Eastern Europe

Free! Rick's Audio Europe™ App
Hear Eastern Europe travel tips from Rick's radio shows

Small Group Tours
Rick offers great itineraries through Eastern Europe

3 1901 05504 7692

For all the details, visit ricksteves.com